M000304974

BIOGRAPHICAL DICTIONARY OF SOCIAL AND CULTURAL ANTHROPOLOGY

BIOGRAPHICAL DICTIONARY OF SOCIAL AND CULTURAL ANTHROPOLOGY

Edited by Vered Amit

Routledge
Taylor & Francis Group

LONDON AND NEW YORK

First published 2004
First published in paperback 2009
by Routledge

2 Park Square, Milton Park, Abingdon, OX14 4RN

Simultaneously published in the USA and Canada
by Routledge

270 Madison Ave, New York, NY 10016

Routledge is an imprint of the Taylor & Francis Group, an informa business

© 2004, 2009 Routledge

Typeset in Joanna by Taylor & Francis Books
Printed and bound in Great Britain by CPI Antony Rowe,
Chippenham, Wiltshire

British Library Cataloguing in Publication Data
A catalogue record for this book is available from the British Library

Library of Congress Cataloging in Publication Data
A catalog record for this book has been requested

ISBN10 0–415–22379–2 (hbk)
ISBN10 0–415–47553–8 (pbk)
ISBN10 0–203–64459–X (ebk)

ISBN13 978–0–415–22379–9 (hbk)
ISBN13 978–0–415–47553–2 (pbk)
ISBN13 978–0–203–64459–1 (ebk)

THIS BOOK IS DEDICATED TO THE MEMORY OF ROTEM AMIT, WHO LOVED, APPRECIATED, AND DEVOURED ALL MANNER OF REFERENCE WORKS THROUGHOUT HER LIFE.

Contents

Editorial advisory committee

Contributors

Robert Ackerman
University of Cambridge, UK

Mario I. Aguilar
University of St Andrews, UK

Emily Alward
Independent scholar, USA

Vered Amit
Concordia University, Canada

Robert Anderson
Simon Fraser University, Canada

Sally Anderson
University of Copenhagen, Denmark

Eduardo Archetti
University of Oslo, Norway

Rita Astuti
London School of Economics and Political Science, UK

Florence E. Babb
University of Iowa, USA

Les Back
Goldsmiths College, UK

Stephen G. Baines
University of Brasilia, Brazil

Roger Ballard
University of Manchester, UK

Mukulika Banerjee
University College, London, UK

Marcus Banks
University of Oxford, UK

Alan Barnard
University of Edinburgh, UK

Henyo T. Barretto Filho
University of Brasilia, Brazil

Laurent Barry
École des Hautes Études en Sciences Sociales, France

Ira Bashkow
University of Virginia, USA

Luís Batalha
Pólo Universitário do Alto da Ajuda, Portugal

Joanna Bator
Polish Academy of Sciences, Poland

Gerd Baumann
University of Amsterdam, The Netherlands

Simona Bealcovschi
Université de Montréal, Canada

Jeremy Beckett
University of Sydney, Australia

Irène Bellier
CNRS, France

Nicole Belmont
École des Hautes Études en Sciences Sociales, France

Jonathan Benthall
University College, London, UK

Bernardo Bernardi
Retired scholar, Italy

Lisa Bier
Southern Connecticut State University, USA

Aletta Biersack
University of Oregon, USA

Dorothy K. Billings
Wichita State University, USA

Nancy J. Black
Metropolitan State University, USA

Hector Blackhurst
University of Manchester, UK

Aleksandar Boskovic
Rhodes University, South Africa

Daniel Boyarin
University of California, Berkeley, USA

Zoe Bray
European University Institute, Italy

Caroline B. Brettell
Southern Methodist University, USA

Kenneth Brown
CNRS, France

Susan Brownell
University of Missouri, USA

Anne Brydon
Wilfred Laurier University, Canada

John R. Campbell
University College, London, UK

Jack Campisi
Mashantucket Pequot Museum and Research Center, USA

Pat Caplan
Goldsmiths College, UK

Virginia Caputo
Carleton University, Canada

Conerly Casey
University of California, Los Angeles, USA

Arachu Castro
Harvard University, USA

John L. Caughey
University of Maryland, College Park, USA

Richard Chenhall
Menzies School of Health Research, Australia

John M. Cinnamon
Miami University, USA

Kim Clark
University of Western Ontario, Canada

Sally Cole
Concordia University, Canada

Simon Coleman
University of Durham, UK

Chantal Collard
Concordia University, Canada

Peter Collins
University of Durham, UK

David B. Coplan
University of the Witwatersrand, South Africa

Jane K. Cowan
University of Sussex, UK

Robert Crépeau
Université de Montréal, Canada

Dara Culhane
Simon Fraser University, Canada

Regna Darnell
University of Western Ontario, Canada

Michelle Day
University of Chicago, USA

Guillermo de la Peña
Centro de Investigaciones y Estudios Superiores en Antropologia Social, Mexico, Mexico

Carol Delaney
Stanford University, USA

Luis Díaz G. Viana
Consejo Superior de Investigaciones Científicas, Spain

Pascal Dibie
Université Paris, France

Leland Donald
University of Victoria, Canada

Hastings Donnan
Queen's University, Belfast, UK

Judith Doyle
Mount Allison University, Canada

Henk Driessen
University of Nijmegen, The Netherlands

Susan Drucker-Brown
Cambridge University, UK

Noel Dyck
Simon Fraser University, Canada

Jeremy Eades
Ritsumeikan Asia Pacific University, Japan

R.F. Ellen
University of Kent, Canterbury, UK

Harri Englund
University of Helsinki, Finland

Judith Ennew
Cambridge University, UK

Thomas Hylland Eriksen
University of Oslo, Norway

T.M.S. Evens
University of North Carolina, USA

Richard Fardon
School of Oriental and African Studies, UK

Allen Feldman
Institute for Humanities Studies, Slovenia

Deane Fergie
University of Adelaide, Australia

Thomas Fillitz
University of Vienna, Austria

Andrew Finlay
Trinity College, Republic of Ireland

Michael D. Fischer
University of Kent, Canterbury, UK

William H. Fisher
College of William and Mary, USA

Kim Fleet
Independent scholar, Australia

Sarah Franklin
Lancaster University, UK

Brian Freer
York University, Canada

Susan Frohlick
University of Manitoba, Canada

Katsuyoshi Fukui
Kyoto University, Japan

C.J. Fuller
London School of Economics and Political Science, UK

Christine Ward Gailey
University of California, Riverside, USA

Daniella Gandolfo
Columbia University, USA

Faye Ginsburg
New York University, USA

Stephen D. Glazier
University of Nebraska, Lincoln, USA

Frederic W. Gleach
Cornell University, USA

Harvey E. Goldberg
The Hebrew University of Jerusalem, Israel

Adolfo González Henriquez
Atlantic University, Columbia

Byron Good
Harvard University, USA

Yehuda Goodman
Tel Aviv University, Israel

Kusum Gopal
London School of Economics and Political Science, UK

Robert J. Gordon
University of Vermont, USA

Nelson H.H. Graburn
University of California, Berkeley, USA

Sarah Green
University of Manchester, UK

Alexandra Greene
St Andrews University, UK

R.D. Grillo
University of Sussex, UK

Roy Richard Grinker
University of Washington, USA

Rosana Guber
Instituto de Desarrollo Económico Social, Argentina

P.H. Gulliver
York University, Canada

Bret Gustafson
Washington University, USA

Ueli Gyr
Universität Zürich, Switzerland

Bernhard Hadolt
Universität Wien, Austria

Dieter Haller
University of Texas, Austin, USA

Mary E. Hancock
University of California, Santa Barbara, USA

Don Handelman
The Hebrew University of Jerusalem, Israel

Richard Handler
University of Virginia, USA

Marie-Élisabeth Handman
École des Hautes Études en Sciences Sociales, France

Chris Hann
Max-Planck Institut, Germany

Mark Harris
University of St Andrews, UK

Keith Hart
University of Aberdeen, UK

Robert M. Hayden
University of Pittsburgh, USA

Suzette Heald
Brunel University, UK

Joy Hendry
Oxford Brookes University, UK

David Hicks
State University of New York, USA

Jane Hill
University of Arizona, USA

Eric Hirsch
Brunel University, UK

Lawrence A. Hirschfeld
University of Michigan, USA

Janet Hoskins
University of Southern California, USA

Deborah House
Texas Tech University, USA

David Howes
Concordia University, Canada

Eugene Hunn
University of Washington, USA

Hasse Huss
Stockholm University, Sweden

Edvard Hviding
University of Bergen, Norway

Tim Ingold
University of Aberdeen, UK

Takashi Irimoto
Hokkaido University, Japan

William Irons
Northwestern University, USA

André Iteanu
CNRS, France

Jason Baird Jackson
University of Oklahoma, USA

John L. Jackson, Jr
Duke University, USA

Michael Jackson
University of Copenhagen, Denmark

Marco Jacquemet
Barnard College, USA

Allison James
University of Sheffield, UK

Ian James
University of St Andrews, UK

Stefan Jansen
University of Hull, UK

Nitish Jha
International Water Management Institute, South Africa

Jeffrey C. Johnson
East Carolina University, USA

Christine Jourdan
Concordia University, Canada

Bruce Kapferer
University of Bergen, Norway

Aneesa Kassam
University of Durham, UK

William W. Kelly
Yale University, USA

Michael G. Kenny
Simon Fraser University, Canada

Galina Khizrieva
Russian State University for the Humanities,
Russia

Paul Kockelman
Columbia University, USA

Tamara Kohn
University of Durham, UK

Andrey Korotayev
Russian State University for the Humanities,
Russia

Grazyna Kubica-Heller
Jagiellonian University, Poland

Wladyslaw Kwasniewicz
Jagellonian University, Poland

James Laidlaw
University of Cambridge, UK

Sarah Lamb
Brandeis University, USA

Michael Lambek
University of Toronto, Canada

Marie Nathalie Leblanc
Concordia University, Canada

Takie Lebra
University of Hawaii, Manoa, USA

Richard Lee
University of Toronto, Canada

Daniel Lefkowitz
University of Virginia, USA

José Sergio Leite Lopes
Museu Nacional, Brazil

Winnie Lem
Trent University, Canada

Joan Leopold
London Metropolitan University, UK

Michael D. Levin
University of Toronto, Canada

Herbert S. Lewis
University of Wisconsin, Madison, USA

I.M. Lewis
London School of Economics and
Political Science, UK

Marianne E. Lien
University of Oslo, Norway

Carlos David Londoño Sulkin
University of Regina, Canada

Norman Long
Agricultural University, The Netherlands

Alejandro Lugo
University of Illinois Urbana-Champaign, USA

Tanya Luhrmann
University of Chicago, USA

Stephen M. Lyon
University of Kent, Canterbury, UK

Irma McClaurin
Fisk University, USA

Judith Macdonald
University of Waikato, New Zealand

Carole McGranahan
University of Colorado, USA

Keith E. McNeal
University of California, San Diego, USA

Saba Mahmood
University of California, Berkeley, USA

Bill Maurer
University of California, Irvine, USA

Andrés Médina
Universidad Nacional Autónoma de México,
Mexico

Margaret Meibohm
University of Pennsylvania, USA

Marit Melhuus
University of Oslo, Norway

Marguerite Mendell
Concordia University, Canada

Charles Menzies
University of British Columbia, Canada

Milos Milenkovic
University of Belgrade, Serbia

Daniel Miller
University College, London, UK

Laura Miller
Loyola University, USA

Kay Milton
Queen's University, UK

Yukio Miyawaki
Osaka Prefecture University, Japan

Hanne O. Mogensen
University of Copenhagen, Denmark

Philip Moore
Curtin University of Technology, Australia

Roland S. Moore
Pacific Institute for Research and Evaluation,
USA

R. Christopher Morgan
University of Victoria, Canada

Anne Friederike Müller
King's College, London, UK

John Mulvaney
Australian National University, Australia

Stephen O. Murray
Instituto Obregón, USA

Fred Myers
New York University, USA

Peter Niedermueller
Humboldt University, Germany

Finn Sivert Nielsen
University of Copenhagen, Denmark

Georg W. Oesterdiekhoff
Universität Würzburg, Germany

Eugene Ogan
University of Minnesota, Minneapolis, USA

Carmen Ortiz
Consejo Superior de Investigaciones Científicas, Spain

Jimmy M. Pagan, Jr
The State University of New Jersey, USA

Richard J. Parmentier
Brandeis University, USA

Thomas C. Patterson
University of California, Riverside, USA

Norbert Peabody
University of Cambridge, UK

Deborah Pellow
Syracuse University, USA

Glenn Petersen
City University of New York, USA

James Piscatori
University of Oxford, UK

Evie Plaice
University of New Brunswick, Canada

Alice Pomponio
St Lawrence University, USA

Ines Prica
Institute of Ethnology and Folklore Research,
Zagreb, Croatia

James Quesada
San Francisco State University, USA

Naomi Quinn
Duke University, USA

Rayna Rapp
New York University, USA

Nigel Rapport
University of St Andrews, UK

Judith A. Rasson
Central European University, Hungary

Todd W. Rawls
University of Chicago, USA

Stephen P. Reyna
University of New Hampshire, USA

Bruno Riccio
University of Bologna, Italy

David Riches
University of St Andrews, UK

Bruce Rigsby
The University of Queensland, Australia

Laura Rival
University of Oxford, UK

Gaspar Rivera-Salgado
University of Southern California, USA

Richard Rottenburg
Universität Viadrina Grosse, Germany

Sandra Rouse
UK

Tom Ryan
University of Waikato, New Zealand

Fernando I. Salmerón Castro
CIESAS, Mexico

Cristina Sánchez-Carretero
Consejo Superior de Investigaciones Científicas, Spain

Alan R. Sandstrom
Indiana University-Purdue University, Fort
Wayne, USA

Paul Sant Cassia
University of Durham, UK

Vilma Santiago-Irizarry
Cornell University, USA

Nicole Sault
University of Costa Rica, Costa Rica

Werner Schiffauer
Europa-Universität Viadrina, Germany

Thomas K. Schippers
Université de Nice, France

Alexander Hugo Schulenburg
Corporation of London, UK

Mary Scoggin
Peking University, China

Robbyn Seller
McGill University, Canada

David Shankland
University of Wales – Lampeter, UK

Mutsuhiko Shima
Tohoku University, Japan

Jack Sidnell
University of Toronto, Canada

Marilyn Silverman
York University, Canada

Sydel Silverman
City University of New York, USA

Monique Skidmore
Australian National University

Jonathan Skinner
Queen's University Belfast, UK

Dan I. Slobin
University of California, Berkeley, USA

Alan Smart
University of Calgary, Canada

Josephine Smart
University of Calgary, Canada

Raymond T. Smith
University of Chicago, USA

Jacqueline S. Solway
Trent University, Canada

Trevor Stack
University of St Andrews, UK

John E. Stanton
University of Western Australia, Australia

Claudia Steiner
Universidad de los Andes, Bogota, Columbia

R.L. Stirrat
University of Sussex, UK

Paul Stoller
West Chester University, USA

Sarah Strauss
University of Wyoming, USA

Bernhard Streck
Universität Leipzig, Germany

Tanka Subba
North Eastern Hill University, India

Melissa J.F. Tantaquidgeon
USA

Michael Taylor
Ministry of Agriculture, Botswana

Gerry Tierney
Webster University, USA

Catherine Tihanyi
Western Washington University, USA

Tine Tjørnhøj-Thomsen
University of Copenhagen, Denmark

Susan R. Trencher
George Mason University, USA

Henry Trueba
University of Texas, USA

Cynthia A. Tysick
State University of New York, Buffalo, USA

Patricia Uberoi
Institute of Economic Growth, University
Enclave, India

Tatiana Uvarova
Russian Academy of Sciences, Russia

Cecilia Van Hollen
University of Notre Dame, USA

Roberto Varela
Universidad Nacional Autónoma de México,
Mexico

Kinsco Verebélyi
Eötvös Loránd Tudományegyetem, Hungary

Gerard Verschoor
Wageningen University, The Netherlands

Drew Walker
Johns Hopkins University, USA

Huon Wardle
University of St Andrews

Kay B. Warren
Harvard University, USA

James Weiner
Australian National University, Australia

Richard Werbner
University of Manchester, UK

Sarah S. Willen
Emory University, USA

Andrew Willford
Cornell University, USA

Brett Williams
American University, USA

Richard A. Wilson
University of Connecticut, USA

Thomas M. Wilson
State University of New York, Binghamton,
USA

Helena Wulff
Stockholm University, Sweden

Takako Yamada
Kyoto University, Japan

Michael Young
Australian National University, Australia

Walter P. Zenner
University of Albany, USA

Introduction and Guidelines

Why biography?

There is an inherent danger that this reference work will be viewed and read as a kind of academic 'Who's Who', thus diverting attention away from the key ideas, practices, and institutions that have shaped social and cultural anthropology to more superficial concerns of individual career status and prestige. This is a very real danger. Yet there are also some important insights that can accrue from a biographical approach that can deepen, rather than trivialise, our understanding of the dynamic contexts and processes through which the approach, discipline, and craft of anthropology have developed.

Perhaps the most difficult challenge in compiling this dictionary has been locating contributors who could undertake the various entries with relative ease. Many of the potential contributors whom we approached were very familiar with particular stages of research and/or publications by the individual scholar being included in the dictionary. They were not however equally familiar with the wider corpus of work undertaken by this figure. This recurrent circumstance highlighted a much broader tendency within the field of anthropology (and many other academic disciplines) to iconise particular published works. In the process, our very familiarity with the manuscript or the research interest attributed to a scholar can obscure both the broader contributions she or he has made as well as the shifting social, political, and temporal contexts or concerns framing these efforts. In a recent publication (2002),

Anthony P. Cohen complained that the book for which he was probably best known, *The Symbolic Construction of Community*, was the least meritorious of his four books and espoused views which he was already busy rethinking by the time it was actually published. Yet seventeen years later, he was still being asked to account for this work as if it represented his current views and research interests. By the same logic with which we have been critical of the use of the 'ethnographic present' (Fabian 1983) in many monographs for dehistoricising and therefore distorting its protagonists, we should also be wary of the tendency to displace anthropological voices and works from the intellectual trajectories through which they were developed.

There are several other temptations in reading the disciplinary history of anthropology that a biographical approach can help reorient if not entirely obviate. The first is the most obvious: ignoring the past. We have all encountered students or colleagues who didn't think anything published over five years ago was worth reading or citing. And some of us have probably been exasperated when the 'new' ideas or research projects we were reading about seemed to be retreading ground already well, perhaps better, covered in earlier work. The temptation to search for the latest fashion, that much lampooned but still sought after 'cutting edge', can lead to a tediously unimaginative reinvention of the wheel. Fortunately, there is now a growing body of scholarship within anthropology that is carefully charting the history of the discipline, including scholars such as Regna Darnell,

Richard Handler, Adam Kuper, and George Stocking, who have contributed and/or featured in entries within this dictionary. However, to the extent that attending to the history of a discipline is meant to inform and therefore link up with current practices and ideas, it would be as distorting to cut off our inventory of scholarship at some arbitrary boundary of the 'past' as to focus only on very recent accomplishments. As a result, this dictionary includes scholars whose work traverses the history of anthropology from its disciplinary beginnings in the late nineteenth century to research in the twenty-first century.

Biography can also ameliorate a temptation to stereotype intellectual careers by assigning them to broad, homogenous categories: functionalism, structuralism, post-modernism, and so on. Many of the entries in this dictionary illustrate not only shifts and reorientations over the course of individual careers but also remind us that these protagonists reflected upon, reacted to, doubted or disagreed with, criticised or nuanced successive disciplinary and academic trends. And far from monolithic 'schools' of thought, many contributors to this dictionary have sought to draw attention to the very particular interlocutors of their biographical subjects, pivotal relationships variously with teachers, mentors, colleagues, collaborators, students, spouses, or rivals that helped shape research efforts, ideas, and organisations.

As you flip through the starting pages of this dictionary, it will not be long before it becomes apparent that these anthropological networks regularly cross national borders. The editorial consultants who provided me with so much crucial advice in developing this volume hold positions in universities distributed across fifteen different countries. However, the countries in which they currently work were often not the locales in which they received some or all of their anthropological training. A number have held visiting appointments in universities situated in yet other countries. And like most of their contemporaries, they regularly attend conferences or conduct fieldwork, and correspond or collaborate with people in still other countries. However, these kind of transnational connections are hardly new. From its professional beginnings, anthropology has been framed in terms of border crossings of one kind or another. The most famous (or, in some versions, infamous) of these has involved fieldwork, 'away', far removed from the researcher's usual abode or academic institution. However, this kind of border crossing has been more common in some renderings of anthropology than others. In some locales, anthropological fieldwork was primarily oriented within the country where researchers also customarily resided and worked, while professional networks of training, collaboration, or intellectual exchange extended far beyond these national borders.

Consider the situation of many of the Mexican anthropologists featured in this dictionary. Scholars such as Guillermo Bonfil, Manuel Gamio, Alfonso Villa Rojas, Rodolfo Stavenhagen, Angel Palerm, or Guillermo de la Peña contributed at different periods to the development of a national anthropology focused on the study of Mexican populations, particularly indigenous peoples and variously disadvantaged groups. Yet many of these anthropologists received at least part of their training outside Mexico, perhaps not surprisingly in the USA but also in Britain, France, and Peru. Angel Palerm collaborated with Eric Wolf and worked in Washington for a time. Julio de la Fuente trained variously with George Murdock and Sol Tax, and collaborated with Bronislaw Malinowski on a seminal study of Oaxaca. Guillermo Bonfil was trained in, and conducted his fieldwork in, Mexico but was a co-signatory of the 'Declaracion de Barbardos' with ten other anthropologists from various countries. And similar relationships can be traced for many of their other colleagues in Mexico.

As the efforts of Mexican anthropologists to develop a critical and politically engaged anthropology aptly illustrate, anthropological projects do not operate in an academic bubble. Some entries therefore outline the ramifications of political systems and events through the lives and careers of particular anthropologists. We can see anthropologists resisting or fleeing oppressive political regimes, marginalised within their own countries or as exiles elsewhere, denied university positions, seeking to influence government policies, serving as politicians themselves, setting up anthropological projects, departments, or institutes even in the face of concerted official opposition and harassment. In many periods and countries, it has not been easy to be an anthropologist, a particular kind of scholar, an intellectual of any kind, or to be associated with certain political beliefs or social identities. Anthropologists have charted the effects of these social phenomena in the lives of others but this dictionary reminds us that not a few have also experienced these pressures in their own lives and careers.

In a sense, this dictionary tries to do for the practitioners of anthropology what they themselves have done best: the elucidation of general social and cultural processes through a focus on particular lives and situations. However, because the nature of the dictionary format only allows for thumbnail sketches, the biographies included in this volume should be viewed as introductions, inviting review of much wider bodies of work, not only of the scholars featured in them but also of the larger academic organisations and networks to which they contributed.

The boundaries of the project

In North America, anthropology has developed as the umbrella for four distinct fields of study: cultural anthropology, linguistics, archaeology, and physical or biological anthropology. When these fields are applied to one topic of study – e.g. their founding common focus on indigenous peoples – their coherence as sub-domains of one discipline appears reasonable and unforced. It is also true that many North American departments of anthropology, both large and small, continue to maintain some measure of this intradisciplinary scope, and recently the American Anthropological Association changed its administrative structure to reaffirm the inclu-

sion of all four sub-fields. Nonetheless, the gap in terms of literature, methods, and practitioners between some of these sub-fields is major and growing. In many cases, it is thus much easier to trace theoretical and empirical commonalities between social/cultural anthropology and such disciplines or programmes as sociology, cultural studies, cultural geography, or political science than with either archaeology, physical, or biological anthropology.

The four-field division of anthropology does not necessarily travel very well outside North America. In some countries, social or cultural anthropology has been allied with history or folklore studies rather than with archaeology, archaeology but not biological anthropology, physical anthropology but not archaeology, or altogether none of these. However, what has tended to recur in many countries has been the close association and overlap between the study of the social use of speech and the study of culture or social organisation. As a result, in this dictionary we have elected to limit the featured scholarship to social and cultural anthropology as well as linguistic anthropology.

Many anthropologists, however, draw on the work of scholars in other academic disciplines and this influence has often been reciprocal. As ethnographic methods and the study of culture have ramified through a wide range of fields, it has sometimes become very difficult to tell where social and cultural anthropology leaves off and other disciplines begin. This blurring of boundaries became abundantly evident in the many recommendations I received for the inclusion in the dictionary of scholars from sister disciplines. However, trying to track all these cross-influences and exchanges is a task that goes beyond the mandate of one reference source. Thus the *Biographical Dictionary of Social and Cultural Anthropology* is not intended to be an index to the contributions of all the scholars whose work has influenced anthropologists. Rather, its aim is more modestly intended as outlining key figures that at some point in their careers have directly engaged in the discipline of sociocultural anthropology.

In sketching out this engagement, I have chosen to focus on several kinds of possible contributions that have often overlapped. First, priority was given to the inclusion of persons who, through their research and/or writing, advanced anthropological knowledge or raised important debate in one or more of three major categories: theoretical, empirical (with a particular emphasis on ethnography), and epistemological. For example, Bronislaw Malinowski's seminal ethnography of the Trobriand Islanders is still read and debated today, nearly eighty years later. Beyond this specific research, Malinowski, perhaps more than any other figure, established extended ethnographic fieldwork as the hallmark of anthropological research practice. However, this kind of intellectual input occurs within and is made possible by a particular institutional context. An effort was therefore made to also take cognisance of the fuller range of practices that comprise an academic discipline including teaching and institutional development. Many of the figures included in this dictionary had their most lasting impact on the development of social and cultural anthropology through their development of institutions, departments, and programmes of research and/or through their mentorship of subsequent generations of scholars. Thus Franz Boas established the contemporary four-field division of North American anthropology, founded the journal, *American Anthropologist*, and trained numerous students who eventually exerted considerable influence in their own right on the development of Americanist anthropology, not least in terms of their control of the American Anthropological Association.

The biographies of Bronislaw Malinowski and Franz Boas exemplify some of the contradictions vested in the long-standing transnational influences upon anthropology. They were seminal figures in the establishment and development of two of the largest and most influential traditions of anthropology, British social and American cultural anthropology. Yet both were themselves expatriates from respectively Poland and Germany where they had received a considerable portion of their own education. In London, Malinowski continued to train Polish anthropologists such as Andrzej Waligórski and Joseph Obrebski amongst students from countries as far flung as Japan and Mexico. One of Boas's primary achievements during his years at the American Museum of Natural History was the Jesup North Pacific Expedition, which relied on the research efforts of Russian exiles. Nonetheless, in their influence on the international development of anthropology, the traditions that these two expatriates helped to found have probably been more often criticised for their hegemonic tendencies than lauded for an egalitarian appreciation of, and openness towards, numerous less dominant loci of anthropological production. How many anthropologists in how many countries have gnashed their teeth over the insularity of American institutions even as they prepared to make their annual pilgrimage to the American Anthropological Association meetings? Yet by going, they make the meetings of what is after all a national association, international.

This dictionary is shaped by these contradictions. First and foremost this is an English-language volume. While the contributors, editorial consultants, and scholars featured in the dictionary hail from numerous countries, our common language of communication has been English. This has undoubtedly privileged recognition of work that has either originally been published in or has been translated into English. British and especially American anthropologists dominate the list of entries. In this respect, the dictionary reflects influences that extend well beyond the particular history and circumstance of anthropology. English is the dominant international language. And if Britain no longer exercises the academic influence of its heyday, the sheer scale of the American academic sector, its extraordinarily numerous post-secondary institutions, scholars, students, presses, and readers ensures its international dominance within the much larger academic world of many disciplines. In developing this dictionary, I have therefore sought both to recognise the major output of past and currently pre-eminent anthropology centers while going beyond them to outline at least some of the work that has emanated from numerous other as yet less influential but nonetheless vigorous nexuses of anthropological production.

Organising the volume

Keeping this ambit in mind, the selection of scholars to be included in this dictionary proceeded on the basis of a fairly lengthy process of consultation with the members of the editorial advisory committee. These twenty-one editorial advisors were themselves selected to try and ensure a broad range of expertise across a number of different subjects, approaches, and regions. When combined, their initial recommendations produced a voluminous list far exceeding the capacity of this volume. Along the way, I also received numerous suggestions and advice (some solicited, some volunteered) from anthropologists who were not members of the editorial committee. Several rounds of further consultations were then held to try and prune down the list to a more manageable number. While it would simply not have been possible for me to develop the directory of scholars included in the dictionary without the advice of the editorial committee, at the end of the day, the final decision and hence responsibility for any sins of commission and especially omission can only be laid at my own doorstep. Without a doubt, many members of the committee were disappointed about at least some of the exclusions I felt it necessary to make.

However, undoubtedly the most formidable task has involved finding contributors with sufficient knowledge to write highly condensed biographies of such an extraordinarily varied range of anthropologists, many with careers that spanned decades. As suggestions led to other suggestions, I learned a great deal about the breadth and distribution of the international networks organising contemporary anthropology. And if the occasional bit of pettiness arose, I have been repeatedly impressed by the generosity with which hundreds of contributors undertook a task that commands little prestige and even more modest tangible returns. Hundreds of other people we contacted and whose names do not appear in the dictionary also generously provided us with extremely helpful advice and information. Nonetheless when the dust settled and the submission of the dictionary, already past its original deadline, could no longer be delayed, some forty-four entries we had hoped to include could not be submitted. For some of these entries, in spite of following up numerous leads, we were just not able to find contributors able and/or willing to take on the task. For others, we found contributors but they were not, in the end, able to deliver the entries they had contracted for.

All of which is to emphasise, that as for most such reference works, there are people I very much wanted to include as entries in this dictionary who for one reason or another, within the time frame and resources available, I couldn't.

Guidelines for reading the dictionary

Entries were assigned (by me) maximum word limits of respectively 300, 500, 800, or, in a few cases, 600 words, and contributors were asked as much as possible to keep within these restrictions. Each contributor was asked wherever possible, to provide specific biographical information about the scholar featured in their respective entry, specifically about birthplace and date, post-secondary education, fieldwork locales and periods, and a short list of key publications. In order to ensure that entries did not become mostly bibliographic, contributors were asked to restrict this opening list of key publications to no more than two in the case of shorter entries and four in the case of longer ones. Thus readers should keep in mind that these are very partial and select lists of publications, and are encouraged to read more widely from the much larger corpus of work published by each of the scholars featured in the dictionary. When dealing with non-English publications, wherever possible, we tried to list an English-language edition when this existed. When the publication had not been translated, we listed its non-English title with a working translation of this title provided in parentheses after it. At the end of some entries, suggestions for further reading are provided that review the work or are the biographies of the scholar in question.

References

Cohen, Anthony P. (2002) 'Epilogue', in Vered Amit (ed.) *Realizing Community: Concepts, Social Relationships and Sentiments*, London and New York: Routledge, pp. 165–70.

Fabian, Johannes (1983) *Time and the Other: How Anthropology Makes its Object*, New York: Columbia University Press.

Vered Amit

Acknowledgements

I would like to thank the many contributors whose efforts made this reference work possible. I would also like to thank the members of the editorial advisory committee, many of whom additionally served as contributors, for their valuable suggestions, advice, and support throughout the process of compiling this dictionary. Laura Shea provided exceptionally skilled and thoughtful assistance. Her diplomacy, sleuthing skills, and perseverance made my own job much easier. Dominic Shryane's reminders kept us moving ahead steadily. Finally, I would like to thank Noel Dyck for his help, advice, and good humour in treading the slipstream of my preoccupation with this project for the last four years.

Abélès, Marc

b. 1950, Paris, France

Marc Abélès advocates a political anthropology that views traditional and modern societies in the same light, with a special interest in the relation between politics and space. During the mid-1970s, Abélès conducted field research in an acephalous society, the Ochollo of southern Ethiopia. Assemblies took decisions, with dignitaries and sacrificers carrying out rituals that set the political field apart from the rest of the village territory. The spatial organisation of the village itself accentuated the assembly places. The most important meeting place occupied the highest possible spot on the summit of the rock on which Ochollo was perched, in congruence with an ideology that valued the 'high' more than the 'low'.

Abélès's next important study dealt with politics in the French *département* of Yonne in Burgundy. He combined fieldwork with archival study reaching back to the middle of the nineteenth century. In the local context, power was often transmitted by family dynasties, the family name guaranteeing eligibility by itself. Rootedness is a criterion by which politicians on all levels are judged, including the president of the French Republic. For instance, as Abélès illustrated, François Mitterand made clever use of his symbolic attachment to the French territory.

European Union politics, which Abélès investigated in the first half of the 1990s, seem to be the antithesis of French politics in several respects. There are few rituals. Officials working for the Commission are often unable to locate themselves historically. Deterritorialisation is another characteristic of European politics. The public and the private are also less ostensibly separated than in France; lobbyists can enter the buildings of the European Parliament, which is interpreted as an opening towards civil society.

By contrast, the French National Assembly, where Abélès carried out fieldwork at the end of the 1990s, appears to be a city within a city. Spatial arrangements in the National Assembly building underline the antagonistic nature of parliamentary politics, which is rightly described by the 'battle' metaphor that representatives often use. Abélès distinguished between battles of opinions, where truth is at stake, and battles of interests, which are determined by power relationships. The latter are more characteristic of the European Parliament, the former of the French National Assembly in its best moments.

In 2000, Abélès conducted research among charity foundations in the USA, revealing that, despite their philanthropic appearance, these foundations are driven by a concern with profitability. Abélès is also interested in the globalisation of environmentalist movements.

Education

École Normale Supérieure, Paris, 1968–73

Ph.D. École des Hautes Études en Sciences
Sociales, Paris, 1976

Fieldwork

Ochollo, Ethiopia, 1974–5
Yonne, France, 1982–8
European Parliament, Strasbourg, France;
  Luxemburg; Brussels, Belgium, 1990–2
European Commission, Brussels, Belgium, 1993
French National Assembly, Paris, France, 1998
Silicon Valley, USA, 2000

Key Publications

(1983) *Le Lieu du politique* (The Place of the
  Political), Paris: Société d'Ethnographie.
(1990) *Anthropologie de l'état* (Anthropology of
  the State), Paris: Armand Colin.
(1991) *Quiet Days in Burgundy: A Study of Local Politics*
  (Jours tranquilles en 1991), trans. A. McDermott,
  Cambridge, UK: Cambridge University Press.
(2000) *Un Ethnologue à l'Assemblée* (An Anthropologist at the Parliament), Paris: Odile Jacob.

ANNE FRIEDERIKE MÜLLER

Aberle, David F.

b. 1918, St Paul, Minnesota, USA

d. 23 September 2004, Vancouver Canada

David Aberle wrote his dissertation under Ruth
Benedict and became a significant figure in culture
and personality studies in the early 1950s. His
interests gradually turned to social movements
and kinship, and to more materialist explanations
of cultural and social variables. In his best-
known work, a study of Navaho peyotism, he
used relative deprivation theory to explain
why individual Navaho became peyotists. This
work includes rich ethnographic description
and analysis of Navaho peyote beliefs and
rituals, and an influential classification of
social movements. Aberle's other important
publications on the Navaho include papers on
contemporary Navaho kinship and on economic conditions on the Navaho Reservation.

In addition to a major paper on matrilineal
kinship in cross-cultural perspective, Aberle's
main effort in kinship studies was a collaboration with Isidore Dyen on the historical
reconstruction of the proto-Athapaskan kinship system. They applied the formal method
of lexical reconstruction developed by Dyen to
reconstruct proto-Athapaskan kinship terminology and then used inferences based on
cross-cultural data to reconstruct other prob-
able features of the wider proto-Athapaskan
kinship system.

Aberle's anthropology was influenced by his
social justice concerns. Examples of socially
concerned applied anthropology are his testimony before the Navaho Tribal Council about
peyotism and its Navaho followers, his involvement in studying the impact of Navaho
relocation resulting from efforts to resolve the
Hopi–Navaho land dispute, and as an advocate
for Navahos displaced by this dispute.

Education

BA Harvard University, 1940
Ph.D. Columbia University, 1950

Fieldwork

Navaho Reservation, summers 1939, 1949–54,
  1962, 1965–6, 1968, 1971, 1974–8, 1980

Key Publications

(1966) *The Peyote Religion among the Navaho*,
  Chicago: Aldine Publishing Co.
with Dyen, Isidore (1974) *Lexical Reconstruction:*
  The Case of the Proto-Athapaskan Kinship System,
  Cambridge, UK: Cambridge University Press.

LELAND DONALD

Abu-Lughod, Lila

b. 21 October 1952, Champaign, Illinois, USA

Lila Abu-Lughod is a leading ethnographer of
the Middle East, whose work has helped shape
linguistic anthropology, the anthropology of

emotion, and anthropological theories of gender. Her innovative ethnographic writing and insightful theoretical critiques helped bring emotion, verbal art, women, and the Middle East to the forefront of anthropological practice in the 1990s.

Abu-Lughod's dissertation, published in 1986 as *Veiled Sentiments*, looked at oral poetry and emotion in an Awlad 'Ali Bedouin community in Egypt. Abu-Lughod observed that Awlad 'Ali women expressed opposed sentiments in everyday conversation (strength and independence) and in performances of oral poetry (vulnerability and attachment). These opposed discourses, Abu-Lughod argued, articulated fundamental tensions of Bedouin social life. But careful attention to sociolinguistic detail – the form and function of oral poetry, the social contexts of poetic performance, and the cultural aesthetics of verbal art – allowed Abu-Lughod to show that neither discourse occupied a privileged position ontologically. *Veiled Sentiments* thus dramatically revised anthropological notions of everyday resistance, while providing rich evidence for the socially constructed nature of emotion. Her work on emotion continued with *Language and the Politics of Emotion* (edited with C. Lutz), a volume important for situating the anthropology of emotion in the study of discourse.

Abu-Lughod's work with Bedouin women led to an important critique of anthropology's culture concept. Her (1991) essay, 'Writing against culture', argued that anthropological descriptions of people and practices in terms of 'culture' are unavoidably essentialising, obscuring individual agency and erasing the historical contingency of actual lives. Her 1993 book, *Writing Women's Worlds*, is a beautifully written attempt to avoid this representational trap. Abu-Lughod skilfully weaves Bedouin women's own narratives into an insightful exploration of their lives – as traditional anthropological paradigms, such as kinship, might query them. Abu-Lughod's work on

women in the Middle East continued with *Remaking Women*, a collection of essays that explore gender as a nexus for symbolic negotiations of power that articulate discourses of tradition and modernity, secularism and religion, post-coloniality and nationhood in the Middle East.

Abu-Lughod's subsequent work has looked at the role of melodramatic television serials in constructing modern consciousness in Egypt. Integrating ethnographic study of reception with textual analysis of media messages, Abu-Lughod argues that the serials popularise new discourses of (modern) selfhood characterised by the individuated experiencing of interiorised emotion.

Education

BA Carleton College, 1974
MA Harvard University, 1978
Ph.D. Harvard University, 1984

Fieldwork

Awlad 'Ali Bedouin, Egypt, 1978–80, 1985, 1986–7, 1989
Islam, television and public culture, Egypt, 1989–90, 1993, 1996–7, 1999
Health and medicine, Egypt, 2001

Key Publications

(1986) *Veiled Sentiments: Honor and Poetry in a Bedouin Society*, Berkeley: University of California Press.
with Lutz, C. (eds) (1990) *Language and the Politics of Emotion*, Cambridge, UK: Cambridge University Press.
(1993) *Writing Women's Worlds: Bedouin Stories*, Berkeley: University of California Press.
(ed.) (1998) *Remaking Women: Feminism and Modernity in the Middle East*, Princeton: Princeton University Press.

DANIEL LEFKOWITZ

Adams, Richard N.

b. 4 August 1924, Ann Arbor, Michigan, USA

After his doctoral research in Muquiyauyo, Peru, Richard Adams chose to work in applied anthropology in Latin America. From 1950 to 1956, he collaborated in nutrition and public health programmes throughout Central America, training practitioners in beliefs and practices associated with illness in rural and Indian communities. He also worked on programmes in Guatemalan's Instituto Indigenista Nacional. During these years he undertook studies of Mayan Indian medical practices (1952) and rural political ideologies in Guatemala (1957), but the major product was a series of national surveys of rural culture in Panama, Nicaragua, Honduras, El Salvador, and Ladino society in Guatemala (1958).

In practice Adams found that 'applied anthropology' depended as much on cultural relativism and common sense as on the prevalent anthropological theories – historicism, functionalism, structuralism, and Marxism – each of which in its own way was inadequate for understanding the social dynamics of post-colonial Central America. In 1956, he accepted a professorship at Michigan State University and in 1962 moved to the University of Texas, where he developed the anthropology doctoral programme, and served in the Institute of Latin American Studies. At Texas he sought more dynamic concepts and holistic theories while carrying out research, teaching and consultation in Argentina, Brazil, Bolivia, Chile, Mexico, Peru, Paraguay, Nicaragua, Guatemala, and Australia.

From 1960 to 1985 he sought a holistic dynamic model that would serve both simple and complex societies. This led to a study of Guatemalan society from 1944 to 1966, tracing social power structure changes over an era of attempted social revolution (1970). This was followed by treatises on social power (1975, 1978), the role of energy in Victorian society (1982), and then on energy and self-organisation in social evolution (1988). This included comparisons of changing human energy use in seventy nations over the previous century. He constructed a rigorous set of concepts, univocally defining social power as the ability to influence the conduct of others through controlling energetic processes of interest to them, and analysed the structures within which individuals and social groups operated. Taking off from Leslie White's energy thesis, he argued that social complexity grew through a sequence of growth in social power, based first on identity, then integrating through co-ordination and centralisation, and expanding thorough emergent levels of social integration.

The model saw social evolution as one phase of the dynamic self-organisation common to all of nature. It examined social development in terms of the Laws of Thermodynamics, natural selection, Lotka's principle, minimum dissipation, the trigger–flow processes, and Prigogine's dissipative structures – energy/material assemblages, poised far from the thermodynamic equilibrium, whose maintenance and reproduction require the constant self-organisation of energy flows and conversions. Significant energy increases could trigger stochastic oscillations that produced new, more encompassing complex structures at higher levels of integration. At each such level of integration, the degree of centralisation depended directly on strategic controls over the energy flows. The survival of the human species and its several societies – and the maintenance of any level – depended on self-organising power structures to sustain energy flow. Failure would lead to some social disintegration.

Adams served as president of the American Anthropological Association and the Society for Applied Anthropology, as vice-president of the American Association for the Advancement of Science, and was a founder and president of the Latin American Studies Association. With the Ford Foundation, he assisted the development of anthropology in Argentina, Brazil, and Paraguay. While Adams saw his work as seeking to understand the dynamics of society, in the heightened political atmosphere of the era it was criticised as variously beholden to revolutionary and imperialist interests.

By 1990, these macro-theoretical explorations found little resonance in the field where interests were swinging to post-modernism and social concerns with more immediate problems of energy depletion and environmental degradation. In 1991 Adams retired to Guatemala with his wife who was farming there and turned his attention to local ethnic relations. He published on historical materials from the archives and co-authored a study of changing ethnic relations in Guatemala from 1944 to 2000 at the Centro de Investigaciones Regionales Mesoamericanas in 2002. This work examined the state's efforts to cope with the consolidation of the imagined community of Maya Indians.

Education

BA Michigan State University, 1947
MA Yale University, 1949
Ph.D. Yale University, 1951

Fieldwork

Peru, 1949–50; 1958
El Salvador, Honduras, Panama, Nicaragua, 1950–6, 1959
Guatemala, 1950–6, 1959, 1962–9, 1984–
Bolivia, Chile, 1958
Nicaragua, 1979

Key Publications

(1970) *Crucifixion by Power: Essays on Guatemalan National Social Structure, 1944–1966*, Austin: University of Texas Press.
(1975) *Energy and Structure: A Theory of Social Power*, Austin: University of Texas Press.
(1988) *The Eighth Day: Social Evolution as the Self-Organization of Energy*, Austin: University of Texas Press.
(1995) *Etnias en evolución social: estudios de Guatemala y Centroamérica* (Etnias on Social Evolution: Studies of Guatemala and Central America),

Mexico: Universidad Autónoma Metropolitana, Iztapalapa.

ROBERTO VARELA

Agar, Michael H.

b. 1945, Chicago, Illinois, USA

A pioneer in the anthropological study of drug use, Michael Agar is above all a staunch advocate of the utility of cognitive and linguistic ethnography for understanding social problems. Approaching drug use through observation and systematic interviews with addicts, he has been funded in numerous grants from the National Institute on Drug Abuse to carry out studies of heroin, LSD, PCP and other drug use. Agar's *Ripping and Running* (1973) argued that, through ethnography, the unstated assumptions governing the drug-procuring behaviour of male heroin addicts could be made explicit and more understandable to treatment counsellors and policymakers trying to help the men shake their habits.

His occupational ethnography of long-haul trucking represents another high point in a career devoted to practical anthropology. Agar's study of independent truckers demystified a mythologised occupation, transmitting the insider's view of how trucking works. He did so by quoting from interviews with truckers and placing those quotes in the context of his observations on truck runs – and an analysis of economic constraints ultimately structuring the profession.

Because Agar's writing style is clear and jargon-free, he has reached an audience beyond his fellow anthropologists. In a series of publications, including *The Professional Stranger* (1996), *Cognition and Ethnography* (1974), and *Speaking of Ethnography* (1985), he explained to a lay audience how ethnography and sociolinguistics can be conducted both scientifically and humanistically. Accordingly, these books have been useful for undergraduate and graduate students alike as textbooks.

A mainstream press publication, entitled *Language Shock: Understanding the Culture of Conversation* (1994), serves to translate highly technical treatises on sociolinguistics into a witty discussion about language frames, speech acts, and other linguistic features. Agar coined the term 'languaculture' to underscore how language and culture are tightly bound together. As a good anthropological story-teller/teacher should, he illustrated this close relationship using accounts of his own life experience with cultural miscommunications in different parts of the world.

Whether his writings describe research methods or analyse the lived experience of truckers or addicts, the common thread running through much of Agar's work is the principle of honest demystification.

Education

AB Stanford University, 1967
Ph.D. University of California, Berkeley, 1971

Fieldwork

The Lambardi, Karnataka, India, 1965–6
Heroin addicts in treatment, Kentucky, USA, 1968–70
Heroin addicts, New York, USA, 1973–5
Drug users, Houston, USA, 1976–7
Owner-operator truckers, Maryland, USA, 1981–7
Political language and bilingualism, Austria, 1986–7, 1989–90
A Mexican-American business, Mexico City, Mexico, 1991–3
LSD-using adolescents, suburban Washington, USA, 1992
Health professionals and drug users, Baltimore, USA, 1993, 1998–
Community residents in Roatan, Honduras, 1997

Key Publications

(1973) *Ripping and Running: A Formal Ethnographic Study of Urban Heroin Addicts*, New York: Seminar Press.

(1986) *Independents Declared: The Dilemmas of Independent Trucking*, Washington, DC: Smithsonian Institution Press.
(1994) *Language Shock: Understanding the Culture of Conversation*, New York: William Morrow.
(1996 [1980]) *The Professional Stranger: An Informal Introduction to Ethnography*, second edn, New York: Academic Press.

ROLAND S. MOORE

Aguirre-Beltran, Gonzalo

b. 7 September 1908, Tlacotalpan (Veracruz), Mexico

d. 5 February 1996, Veracruz, Mexico

Gonzalo Aguirre-Beltran explored a wide range of subjects and issues: race relations, medical anthropology, cultural change, applied linguistics, development, political anthropology, regional studies. In addition, he was one of the main organisers of the Indigenista movement in Mexico and Latin America. In his work, the indigenous and black populations of the Americas never appear simply as passive subjects of colonial and neo-colonial exploitation, but as actors of their own histories and participants in the dynamics of *mestizaje*, a complex process of biological and cultural blending.

Initially trained as a medical doctor, Aguirre-Beltran found his true vocation as an ethnohistorian and anthropologist when as director of a rural clinic in the state of Veracruz, he wrote one of the first detailed studies of agrarian rebellions in colonial Mexico. Encouraged by Manuel Gamio, he then undertook an ambitious research project on the Mexican black population, from its origins in colonial slavery to the twentieth century. In 1945–6 he became a graduate student at Northwestern University, where he worked under the guidance of Melville Herskovits and Irving Hallowell.

In 1948 he became a senior researcher in the newly created Instituto Nacional Indigenista (INI), where he constructed his theory of the regions of refuge, positing that the indigenous population has to be understood in the context of regional power relationships that subordinate Indian rural communities to a non-indigenous dominant urban sector. Accordingly, the INI should co-ordinate the actions of government development agencies in order to allow the acculturation of the indigenous people and their full participation in the benefits of the modern nation. This would not imply the obliteration of indigenous culture but its blending into a new *mestizo* national one.

In 1952 Gonzalo Aguirre-Beltran became the director of the first INI 'co-ordinating center' in Chiapas, which would provide the model for similar centers in Mexico and Latin America in general. Throughout his career he occupied the positions of sub-director and director general of INI, as well as director of the Instituto Indigenista Interamericano and vice-minister of Education. In 1975 he was the first recipient of the Malinowski Award granted by the International Society for Applied Anthropology. His ideas were harshly criticised by the new indigenous movements that emerged after 1970 and by his younger, more radical colleagues, but he never ceased to defend them on the basis of research and fresh arguments.

Education

Doctor of Medicine, National University of Mexico, 1931

Graduate Diploma (Anthropology), Northwestern University, 1946

Fieldwork

Huatusco (Veracruz), Mexico, 1932–40
Cuijla (Guerrero), Mexico, 1942–3, 1954
The Chiapas Highlands, Mexico, 1950–1
Tarascan Sierra, Mexico, 1951–2
Tarahumaran Sierra, Mexico, 1952
The Papaloapan Basin, Mexico, 1957–9
Sierra of Zongolica, Veracruz, Mexico, 1960

Key Publications

(1946) *La Población Negra de México, 1519–1810. Estudio Etnohistórico* (The Black Population of Mexico, 1519–1810. An Ethnohistorical Study), Mexico City: Fuente Cultural; second edn (enlarged), Mexico City: Fondo de Cultura Economica, 1972.

(1953) *Formas de Gobierno Indígena* (Indigenous Forms of Government), Mexico City: Imprenta Universitaria.

(1957) *El Proceso de Aculturacion* (The Process of Acculturation), Mexico City: Universidad Nacional Autónoma de México.

(1967) *Regions of Refuge (Regiones de Refugio)*, Mexico City: Instituto Indigenista Interamericano; English edn, Washington: International Society for Applied Anthropology, 1975.

GUILLERMO DE LA PEÑA

Angrosino, Michael V.

b. 1947, Brooklyn, New York, USA

Michael V. Angrosino distinguished himself in the field of applied anthropology with the publication of *Do Applied Anthropologists Apply Anthropology?* in 1976. This book introduced the term 'the new applied anthropology', which is still widely used in the literature; it also launched the course of over twenty years of exploration in the world of applied anthropology, particularly with social policy implications of advocacy at the grassroots level. His focus is in the area of qualitative research methodologies, especially life history and intensive participant observation, which he has employed over the years on a variety of applied projects, particularly in the area of medical anthropology.

Anthropology Field Projects and *Doing Cultural Anthropology* illustrate his commitment to the philosophy of learning-by-doing. They also illustrate his commitment to students by presenting them with viable projects and the methods they might use to solve social problems, always with an eye out for ethical treatment of the persons with whom they interact.

One of Angrosino's major contributions to anthropology is through his work with stigmatised individuals, particularly mentally retarded persons. Throughout his work, Angrosino seeks a humane approach towards investigating the lives of these individuals. *Opportunity House* represents a summation of nearly two decades of ethnographic research. In this book, Angrosino discloses the unique qualities of each individual in the study, and discloses the humanity of people who have been marginalised by society. He presents these individuals as persons who collaborate with him in order to present an intimate, insider's view of their daily lives. They share their feelings and insights, as well as their hopes and dreams; in so doing, they illustrate the collaborative and interactional nature of this kind of anthropological research. This approach allows us to see how these individuals view themselves, and, in so doing, Angrosino presents a glimpse of his own humanity as well as the persons who are in the study group. Few academics have presented stigmatised persons with the dignity, sensitivity, and respect they deserve, or contributed more to the understanding of this misunderstood minority group.

Education

BA City University of New York, 1968
Ph.D. University of North Carolina at Chapel Hill, 1972
Postdoctoral Fellow, Vanderbilt University Institute for Public Policy Studies, 1981
Certification in Oral History Research, Vermont College, 1989
MA Saint Mary-of-the-Woods College, 1999

Fieldwork

Trinidad, August 1970–September 1971, June–August 1973 (overseas Indian ethnic identity)
Saba, June–July 1970 (Life History collection)

Aruba, June–August 1975 (labour migration and cultural pluralism)
Tampa, Nashville, Washington, DC, USA, September 1981–June 1996 (community-based treatment for adults with mental retardation and chronic mental illness)
Indianapolis, Tampa, New York, USA, September 1996–present (cultural diversity training programmes)

Key Publications

(ed.) (1976) *Do Applied Anthropologists Apply Anthropology?*, Athens: University of Georgia.
with Crane, Julia (eds) (1984) *Anthropology Field Projects: A Student Handbook*, Prospect Heights, IL: Waveland.
(1998) *Opportunity House: Ethnographic Stories of Mental Retardation*, Walnut Creek, CA: AltaMira.
(ed.) (2002) *Doing Cultural Anthropology: Projects for Ethnographic Data Collection*, Prospect Heights, IL: Waveland.

GERRY TIERNEY

Appadurai, Arjun

b. 4 February 1949, Bombay, India

From the beginning of his academic career, Arjun Appadurai's work has been characterised by an integration of historical, ethnographic, and theoretical approaches, reflecting his training at the University of Chicago's interdisciplinary Committee on Social Thought. His dissertation research focused on the politics of a Sri Vaisnava temple in the Madras region of south India, for which he was awarded the University of Chicago's prize for the best doctoral dissertation in the social sciences in 1976. The dissertation was published first by the University of Cambridge Press under the title *Worship and Conflict under Colonial Rule: A South Indian Case* (1981), and later reprinted by Orient Longman in 1983. Subsequent articles, published through the mid-1980s, ranged from reconsideration of more traditional topics like caste and hierarchy to innovative explorations of 'gastro-politics' and 'gratitude as a social mode'. Appearing in such journals as *American Ethnologist* and *Man*, these pieces began to develop Appadurai's reputation as a social theorist.

But it was the introduction to his edited volume entitled *The Social Life of Things* that really brought Appadurai's name to the attention of scholars outside the realm of South Asian studies. Using an ethnohistorical approach, Appadurai proposed a new way of looking at commodities, or things that have value. He argues that the value created through the act of economic exchange is itself embodied in commodities, the objects that are exchanged. Rather than emphasising the forms or processes of exchange, we can learn a great deal by focusing on the commodities themselves, tracing their connections and trajectories through time, or, in other words, their 'social lives'. That work has continued to be cited internationally as a seminal contribution to the understanding of commodities in a cultural context, and was the impetus for a retrospective conference on the subject, held in the Netherlands in 1999, more than a decade after the initial publication of the volume.

With his wife, historian Carol Breckenridge, Appadurai began a working group on the study of what they termed 'Public Culture' in the mid-1980s. These explorations in globalisation and transnational cultural forms ultimately led to the development of the Center for Transnational Cultural Studies at the University of Pennsylvania, and the creation of a journal, *Public Culture*, which had its inaugural issue in the autumn of 1988, and as of 2003 was still going strong. An article first published in *Public Culture* in 1990, 'Disjuncture and difference in the global cultural economy', was subsequently refined and reprinted in several other venues, and became the cornerstone of Appadurai's book, *Modernity at Large* (1996). The key concept introduced in that article was the topographic metaphor of 'scapes': ethnoscapes, finanscapes, mediascapes, technoscapes, and ideoscapes. Together, these provide a framework for making sense of the workings of transnational cultural flows, and a way of connecting the deterritorialising forces of globalisation with the situated production of specific localities. In *Modernity at Large*, Appadurai moves beyond the necessary construction of scaffolding for intellectual engagement of the interrelations of the global and the local, presenting an argument for the central role of the imagination as a social force for the development of new forms of identity and, ultimately, for the emergence of new political forms beyond the national.

Moving in 1992 from the University of Pennsylvania back to his Alma Mater, the University of Chicago, Appadurai headed the Humanities Institute, bringing a wide variety of international scholars into dialogue on topics including diaspora and the globalisation of media. He continued in 1996 as Samuel N. Harper professor of anthropology and South Asian languages and civilizations, as well as director of the University of Chicago Globalization Project, funded principally by the Ford and MacArthur Foundations. In the late 1990s, Appadurai's research focus shifted to a complex study of ethnic relations and social crisis in his home town of Mumbai, India. With major funding from the Ford Foundation, he began a 3-year collaborative project addressing issues including poverty, housing, media, and violence in this global city, around the core theme of grassroots globalisation. He also continues to work on comparative ethnographic analyses of ethnic violence, and the emergence of transnational organisational forms.

Education

Intermediate Arts, Elphinstone College, University of Bombay, 1967
BA Brandeis University, 1970
MA University of Chicago, 1973
Ph.D. University of Chicago, 1976

Fieldwork

Madras, India, 1973–4, 1977, 1986, 1988
Rural Maharashtra State, India, 1981–2
Delhi, India, 1986, 1988 (short term)

Mumbai (Bombay), India, 1986, 1988, 1995–6, 1997, 1998, 2000–1

Key Publications

(1986) (ed.) *The Social Life of Things: Commodities in Cultural Perspective*, New York: Cambridge University Press.
(1988) 'Putting hierarchy in its place', *Cultural Anthropology* 3, 1: 37–50.
(1990) 'Disjuncture and difference in the global cultural economy', *Public Culture* 2, 2: 1–24.
(1996) *Modernity at large: cultural dimensions of globalization*, Minneapolis: University of Minnesota Press.

SARAH STRAUSS

Appell, George N.

b. 1926, York, Pennsylvania

George Appell's theoretical work is informed by years of experience and motivated by his concern for indigenous communities that have been cut loose from their sociocultural moorings because of social change imposed on them in the wake of globalisation. Based on extensive fieldwork, he has developed an analytical system that allows researchers to document resource ownership by indigenous jural units and, thereby, help prevent the unlawful capture or destruction of such resources by outsiders. Sudden change – for which these communities are unprepared – harms the physiological and psychosocial health of their members, he argues. He encourages research on threatened indigenous peoples, to enable them to understand the worth of their own cultures, and help them adapt to social change. To this end, he established the Fund for Urgent Anthropological Research and a project that aims to compile the rapidly disappearing oral literature of the peoples of Sabah. He is the president and founder of the Borneo Research Council, which supports scholarship on Bornean societies. He was the first to use the case study method for instruction on ethical issues in anthropological inquiry. He has also helped develop a theory of cognatic social structure. A prolific writer, Appell has almost 150 books, articles, and reviews to his name.

Education

BA Harvard University, 1949
MBA Harvard University, 1952
MA Harvard University, 1957
Ph.D. Australian National University, 1966

Fieldwork

Sabah, Malaysia, 1959–60, 1961–3, 1986, 1990, 1992, 1994, 1996, 1999, 2002
East Kalimantan, Indonesia, 1980–1
Northwest Territories, Canada, 1957, 1977
Maine, USA, 1971–3 (part time)
Denmark, 1971–2 (part time)

Key Publications

(ed.) (1976) *The Societies of Borneo: Explorations in the Theory of Cognatic Social Structure*, Special Publication 6, Washington, DC: American Anthropological Association.
(1978) *Dilemmas and Ethical Conflicts in Anthropological Inquiry: A Case Book*, Waltham, MA: Crossroads Press.

NITISH JHA

Apthorpe, Raymond

b. 1932, Luton, UK

Raymond Apthorpe is a distinguished anthropologist of development whose work has involved research, consultancy, and teaching in Africa, Europe, East Asia, and Australia. After a theoretically focused, library-based D.Phil. (Institute of Social Anthropology, 1957), he went to the Rhodes–Livingstone Institute, Lusaka, where he undertook fieldwork among the Nsenga, publishing papers on their history, social and political ideas, and, with John Blacking, their music. He was also responsible for organising workshops on the practical and social scientific problems of contemporary Africa. Thereafter, with posts in Nigeria and Uganda (as professor of sociology at Makerere), and in Europe (IDS Sussex, East Anglia, the Hague, and later Swansea), he increasingly focused on the problems of development, including land settlement schemes, planned social change, and the sociology of planning and planners (or 'planistrators' as he likes to call them).

In great demand for consultancies, his work is never simply 'applied', but always grounded in a wide-ranging knowledge of social theory and the current theoretical literature. His thinking has often represented a radical departure from orthodoxy. For example, during the 1960s, in noting the continuity between development planning and colonialism, Apthorpe criticised the then-prevailing paradigms of African society – the traditional and 'tribal' community models – that pervaded both. This dual orientation towards theory and practice continued to inform his later work in East Asia (Taiwan, the Philippines, and elsewhere), especially in his writing, from the mid-1980s, on the language of policy and the power of policy language, in which he made effective use of Foucault long before it became fashionable. Apthorpe's insistence that the study of discourse must be situated in an analysis of its institutional context is also apparent in his work in the 1990s focusing on aid, conflict, and development, and the evaluation of emergency aid programmes in Africa and Europe (Balkans).

As a development anthropologist his work is inevitably multidisciplinary, involving co-operation with political scientists and economists, even when he finds himself doing battle with them over their respective approaches to development. This he sees primarily as social development, with social policy needed to relieve the consequences of economics. Tending to call what he does 'sociology', but for long a member of the Association of Social Anthropologists (from 1956), Apthorpe is a critical humanist with considerable understanding of,

and commitment to, the situation of people whose societies emerged from colonial rule into the world of development; an intellectual (and witty) writer passionately concerned with the practical application of anthropology.

Education

BA Durham University, 1953
D.Phil. University of Oxford, 1957

Fieldwork

Zambia, 1957–61
Taiwan, 1970–5

Key Publications

(ed.) (1970) *People, Planning and Development Studies: Some Reflections on Social Planning*, London: Cass.
(1986) 'Development policy discourse', *Public Administration and Development* 6, 4: 377–89.
with Gasper, D. (eds) (1996) *Arguing Development Policy: Frames and Discourses*, London: Cass.
with Chiviya, E. and Kaunda, G. (1995) *Decentralization in Malawi: Local Governance and Development*, Lilongwe: UNDP/Ministry of Local Government and Rural Development.

R.D. GRILLO

Archetti, Eduardo P.

b. 1943, Santiago del Estero, Argentina

d. 6 June 2005, Oslo, Norway

Eduardo Archetti was a scholar with an exceptionally open mind and a broad range of interests. His main works covered such diverse themes as agrarian reform and issues of development, food and knowledge systems, the use and significance of texts in the anthropological endeavour, gender and the construction of masculinities, morality, and the meanings of sports and dance for understanding national identities. Nevertheless, underpinning many of his queries was a sustained interest in social transformations, modernity, and its implications for social life.

The thrust of Archetti's research was devoted to different Argentinian realities. He had the rare privilege of doing 'anthropology at home', but from a foreign vantage point. Having lived and worked in Norway since 1976, he combined insider knowledge with outsider perspectives. His first major study focused on the Italian immigrant community of northern Santa Fé. This study combined detailed ethnography of the settler community with a careful historical contextualisation. He was able to demonstrate key elements (encompassing both sentiments and economic factors) affecting a demographic transition with implications for family structure and the organisation of production.

Archetti pursued the tension between economic and cultural factors and their explanatory power in his work on the guinea pig from the highlands of Ecuador. This study represented not only a well-grounded criticism of a development project and the rational approach of planners, but it was also a unique contribution to the more general study of ritual, consumption, and indigenous knowledge. Archetti explored the complex social and cultural practices surrounding the guinea pig revealing its profound symbolic significance with respect to gender relations as well as the relation between humans and animals.

The interest in ritual and gender is further developed in Archetti's innovative studies of tango, football, and polo, serving as prisms through which Argentinian nationalism is refracted. By juxtaposing such distinct social phenomena, Archetti was able to demonstrate how the national narrative is constructed around metaphors of movement and performance, and how masculine identities are inscribed in the creation of otherness.

Education

BA University of Buenos Aires, 1964
MA University of Buenos Aires, 1967
Ph.D. École Pratique des Hautes Études, 1976

Fieldwork

Santa Fé, Argentina, February 1973–March 1974.
Pichincha, Ecuador, April 1976–May 1977
Zambia, January–July 1981
Salcedo, Chimborazo and Azuay, Ecuador, July 1983–December 1983, 1986
Buenos Aires, Argentina, July–December 1984, January–August 1988, August–December 1993, October–December 1994
Shorter fieldwork: Albertville, France, 1992; Lillehammer, Norway, 1994

Key Publications

with Stølen, Kristi Anne (1975) *Explotación familiar y acumulación de capital en el campo argentino* (Family Farms and Capital Accumulation in Rural Argentina), Buenos Aires: Siglo XXI Editores.
(1997) *Pigs, Food, Symbol and Conflict of Knowledge in Ecuador* (El mundo social y simbólico del cuy, 1992), Oxford: Berg.
(ed.) (1994) *Exploring the Written. Anthropology and the Multiplicity of Writing*, Oslo: Scandinavian University Press.
(1999) *Masculinities. Football, Polo and the Tango in Argentina*, Oxford: Berg.

MARIT MELHUUS

Ardener, Edwin W.

b. 1927, London, UK

d. 1987, Oxford, UK

Edwin Ardener's work has contributed greatly to the ethnography and historiography of West Africa, and to theoretical discourse in British social anthropology around themes of ethnicity, language, politics, gender, and history. After reading anthropology at the LSE he conducted thirty months of fieldwork with the Ibo of Mba-Ise in Nigeria, followed by eleven years in the Cameroons. His researches (often with his wife, Shirley Ardener) focused on the impacts of the plantation system on social and economic life in the Southern Cameroons and involved extensive survey work as well as fieldwork with the Bakweri and Esu. He returned to the UK and the post of lecturer in social anthropology at the University of Oxford in 1963. His lectures and writings examining 'history' and 'ethnicity' often drew from his Cameroon material as well as from examples in Europe. Other important works on the relationship between 'social anthropology and language' are partly represented in the 1971 ASA volume he edited by that title. His discussions on the 'problem of women' provided a timely and theoretically rich contribution to a burgeoning field of gender studies, particularly with his development of 'muted group theory'. Ardener acted as chair of the Institute of Social Anthropology at Oxford for many years, as chairman of the ASA, and as one of the key contributors in the establishment of the human sciences degree at Oxford.

Education

BA London School of Economics
MA University of Oxford

Fieldwork

Nigeria, 1949–52
Cameroons, 1952–63
Cameroons, 1963–9, summer months
Scottish Hebrides, UK, 1980s

Key Publications

(1989) *Edwin Ardener: The Voice of Prophecy and Other Essays*, ed. M. Chapman, Oxford: Blackwell.
(1996) *Kingdom on Mount Cameroon: Studies in the History of the Cameroon Coast, 1500–1970*, ed. S. Ardener, Oxford: Berghahn.

TAMARA KOHN

Ardener, Shirley

Shirley Ardener's anthropological career began in the 1950s and 1960s when she was based in West Africa with her husband (and fellow anthropologist), Edwin Ardener. Her fieldwork included interview- and survey-based studies of the socioeconomic, marriage, and migration patterns of tribal groups in the Southern Cameroons who laboured in the plantations. Ardener's commitment to her research in Africa continues to the present with frequent trips to Cameroon and publications that examine issues of microcredit, gender, and family as well as archival work on Cameroon studies.

It is, however, with the study of gender in British social anthropology that Shirley Ardener's name and published work are most closely associated. In 1972 she was one of a small group of women anthropologists who founded a seminar on the anthropology of women at Queen Elizabeth House, Oxford. In 1983 the seminar group was formally recognised as the Center for Cross-Cultural Research on Women (CCCRW) and Ardener became its director. Edited volumes (twenty-five so far) emanating from the seminars have made significant contributions to gender studies. In a descriptive extension of Edwin Ardener's analysis of the silence of thinking, feeling women in pre-1970s ethnographic descriptions ('muted group theory'), Shirley Ardener suggested that the 'mutedness' of one group may indeed be seen as the flip side of the dominant group's (men's? academy's?) 'deafness'. Over the years, the research output from the CCCRW has certainly attempted to address this shortcoming and books produced cover a diverse range of topics including 'women in peace and war', 'rotating savings and credit associations for women', 'bilingual women', 'the incorporated wife', etc. Ardener's own contributions to most of the volumes as either contributor, editor, or series editor may certainly be seen as the inspirational drive that has allowed for success.

Ardener has also long been a member of the sub-faculty of anthropology and geography at the University of Oxford, and since 1989 she has co-convened several successful seminar series at the Institute of Social and Cultural

Anthropology (e.g. 'Ethnicity and Identity', which has produced nine edited volumes). She has influenced generations of human sciences, anthropology, and archaeology students at Oxford who have attended her tutorials and lectures. In 1995 she retired as director of the CCCRW, but continues to be actively involved as a senior associate and continues with her writing and teaching in Oxford. For her contributions to social anthropology she was given the Wellcome Medal in 1962 and for that as well as her contributions to gender studies and the CCCRW she was awarded the OBE.

Education

B.Sc. (Econ.) London School of Economics
MA Stat. University of Oxford

Fieldwork

Nigeria, Cameroon, 1950s to present

Key Publications

(ed. and chapter 'Sexual insult and female militancy'; also in *Man* 8, 3, 1973) (1975) *Perceiving Women*, London: J.M. Dent & Sons Ltd.

(ed. and introductory essay) (1981) *Defining Females: The Nature of Women in Society*, London: Croom Helm.

(ed. and introductory essay) (1981) *Women and Space*, London: Croom Helm.

(ed. with commentaries) (2002) *Swedish Ventures in Cameroon 1883–1923*, Oxford: Berghahn Press.

TAMARA KOHN

Arensberg, Conrad Maynadier

b. 12 September 1910, Pittsburgh, Pennsylvania, USA

d. 10 February 1997, New York City, USA

Conrad Arensberg was a leader in the devel-

opment of theory, method, and applied approaches in American anthropology over most of the twentieth century. Because of his intellectual interests, interdisciplinary endeavours, and scholarly achievements, as well as his personal warmth and openness, he had an incalculable effect on the growth of the profession of anthropology in the USA in general, but more particularly in the lives of hundreds of colleagues and students over the thirty years in which he taught at Columbia University in New York City. He was also among the first American anthropologists to marry the theoretical and methodological perspectives of British structural-functionalism with a more humanistic and historical American cultural anthropology. He achieved this first in what has become one of the classic ethnographic 'community' studies in world anthropological history, in the rural west of Ireland, from 1932–4. Arensberg was arguably the most influential American ethnographer to conduct field research in Europe for over a generation; to this day students in Ireland and students of Irish society and culture in Europe and beyond still use his ethnographic studies of Clare (done in the main with Solon T. Kimball) as prime sources.

Arensberg's first ethnographic research was as part of W. Lloyd Warner's 'Yankee City' project, wherein Arensberg showed his interest in the study of class, work, ethnicity, and culture in complex societies. This research, along with that done soon after in Ireland, constitute some of the earliest studies of modern, urban, and rural industrial society, and were pioneering efforts in what some would now call 'anthropology at home'. In the course of this work Arensberg problematised the nature of community as both method and object of study, as one way in his view to keep anthropology firmly on its footing as one of the natural sciences, which was one of his lifelong interests (a number of articles that elaborated his ideas about theory and method were standard reading for a generation of anthropologists trained in the 1960s and 1970s; many of these essays are collected in *Culture and Community*, co-authored with Kimball). In Arensberg's view culture could be observed and compared through the study of repetitive interactions of individuals and groups. This was the basis of 'interaction theory', which he applied in his ethnographic research, as part of wider comparisons of complex cultural systems (an interest which led to such works as *Trade and Markets in Early Empires* (1957), co-edited with Karl Polanyi and Harry Pearson.

Arensberg's professional career kept pace with his scholarly accomplishments. After service in the US Army in the Second World War, in 1946 he began his association with Columbia University by becoming the chair of the sociology department of Barnard College. In 1952 he moved to Columbia's graduate department of anthropology, where he stayed until his retirement in 1979, after which he continued at the university in the Joint Program in Applied Anthropology at Teachers College. In 1991 he was given the Malinowski Award of the Society for Applied Anthropology, and the first Conrad M. Arensberg Award of the Society for the Anthropology of Work. In 1945–6 he served as president of the Society for Applied Anthropology, and in 1980 he was president of the American Anthropological Association.

Arensberg is justly remembered as an inspirational leader in the growth of anthropological method, theory, and teaching, whose erudition and imagination helped make both the USA and Western Europe acceptable locales for ethnographic research, thus helping to liberate anthropologists from the constraints of a past imperialist science. His research and writing influenced the development of historical, economic and applied anthropology, and he was among the first anthropologists to focus on work and ethnicity in industrial society. But perhaps his most enduring legacy is the personal model he set for his students. His generous giving of his time, advice, and expertise influenced three generations of Columbia scholars, and this generosity was extended to many people of other universities, not least to those graduate students who

sought his counsel when preparing their doctoral ethnographic field research in Ireland.

Education

BA *summa cum laude*, Harvard University, 1931
Ph.D. Harvard University, 1934

Fieldwork

Newburyport, Massachusetts, USA, 1930–2
Ennis, County Clare, Ireland, 1932–4
New England cities, various locales and intermittent research, USA, 1938–41

Key Publications

(1937) *The Irish Countryman: An Anthropological Study*, New York: The Macmillan Company.
with Kimball, Solon T. (1940) *Family and Community in Ireland*, Cambridge, MA: Harvard University Press.
with Kimball, Solon T. (1965) *Culture and Community*, New York: Harcourt, Brace & World.
(1981) 'Cultural holism through interactional systems', *American Anthropologist* 83, 3: 562–81.

THOMAS M. WILSON

Arguedas, José María

b. 1911, Andahuaylas, Peru

d. 1969, Lima, Peru

When J.M. Arguedas graduated with a degree in ethnology from the University of San Marcos in 1957, he was already a widely published writer of fiction, articles in folklore, and critical essays in language and literature. Arguedas's intellectual formation happened in the context of a burgeoning *Indigenista* movement, a loose collective of Latin American artists and intellectuals whose work called attention to the oppressive living conditions of native peoples. Arguedas was critical of *Indigenista* forms of representation, which he thought were intellectualist and detached from the realm of experience. However, because he openly shared in the nationalist and socialist impetus of the movement, vindicating of indigenous peoples and cultures, Arguedas is often classed as an *Indigenista* writer and intellectual.

Arguedas's non-fictional writings present descriptive and interpretive accounts of contemporary life, cultural practices, and beliefs among Indians and *mestizos* of the central and southern Andes. Whether as part of these works or as independent pieces, Arguedas published numerous Quechua myths, songs, and poems, such as the collection, *Canto kechwa*, which he translated into Spanish with exceptional lyricism. As is evident in the ethnohistorical essays of *Formación de una cultura nacional indoamericana*, Arguedas was greatly interested in processes of cultural transformation. While disturbed by the loss of forms of cultural and artistic expression as a result of modernisation, he mostly emphasised the marvellously creative ways in which Andean cultures had adapted and preserved themselves in the face of imposed Western influences. One of these essays, 'Puquio: a culture in process of change' (also published as an appendix to *Yawar Fiesta*), registers the transformation of the Andean town of Puquio – where Arguedas had lived as a child – as a result of the 1926 construction of a road that linked the southern Andes with the coastal, relatively modern cities of Ica and Lima. Notable for its ethnographic sensitivity, the article contains three bilingual versions of the Andean myth of Inkarri and a rendering of the local 'feast of the water', which gracefully evoke the intimate tenor of his informants' voices. Also set in Puquio, *Yawar Fiesta*, Arguedas' first novel, centers upon irreconcilable, traditionalist and progressive forces, which come into conflict over a governmental ban on a bloody, 'indigenised' form of bullfighting. By revealing the violence both of the ritual and of its repression, the novel reveals Arguedas's ambivalence towards the notion of progress prevalent in his day. Rather than a 'backward', anti-modern defense of tradition, the novel belies any fast identifica-

tion of modernity with reason and suggests that irrational forces are often integral to modernisation.

If Arguedas thought that he could 'rectify' the distorted – racist or, conversely, idealised – character of conventional representations of Indians, it was because he believed that a childhood spent in close intimacy with the Indian world had positioned him uniquely to do so. Born to white and Spanish-speaking parents in the highland town of Andahuaylas, after his mother's death Arguedas was often left to the care and company of Indian servants. He was deeply influenced by the melodious cadence of Quechua poetry and music, which in his writings he lets seep into Spanish, creating a hybrid language that he believed was better able than standard Spanish to preserve and communicate the 'essence' of his early highland life. The article, 'The novel and the problem of expression in Peru' (published as a prologue to *Yawar Fiesta*) exposes the paradox inherent in this technique, whereby highly artificial manipulations of language seem to convey more realistically the particularity of his experiences. The formal tone of some of his anthropological writings shows that Arguedas was not immune to the discipline's pressures to scientific veracity. However, his views on language and writing always carried the mark of the animated natural world of his childhood, in which words mingled with the things they represented; this can be seen at play in *Deep Rivers*. These ideas about language, which he put forth in ways more intuitive than philosophical, were the focus of intense exchanges among Peruvian intellectuals who questioned the 'sociological value' of his fiction and insisted upon the need for a neat distinction between creative and social scientific writings. Arguedas committed suicide in 1969.

Education

BA Universidad Nacional Mayor de San Marcos, Lima, 1957

Ph.D. Universidad Nacional Mayor de San Marcos, Lima, 1963

Fieldwork

Peru, scattered periods in various sites on the
  coast and south/central Andes
Spain, 1958

Key Publications

(1938) *Canto kechwa* (Kechwa Song), Lima:
  Club del Libro Peruano.
(1975) *Formación de una cultura nacional indoamericana* (Formation of a National Indoamerican
  Culture), ed. and introduction Ángel Rama,
  Mexico: Siglo Veintiuno.
(1978) *Deep Rivers* (Los ríos profundos), Austin:
  University of Texas Press (fiction).
(1985) *Yawar Fiesta* (Yawar fiesta), Austin: University of Texas Press (fiction).

DANIELLA GANDOLFO

Arizpe Schlosser, Lourdes

b. 1944, Mexico City, Mexico

The axis of Lourdes Arizpe's contributions is
an insistence on articulating ethnography and
fieldwork with theoretical statements that
consider wider social systems in all their
complexity. In this sense, she has had a wide
experience in different Mexican regions, she
has made important contributions to ethnography, and she has also offered original
theoretical insights into subjects such as kinship, rural to urban migration, gender relationships, pluralism, and culture in general. In
her researches about the Nahua from Sierra de
Puebla, she transcended the traditional tendency to treat the community and kinship
system as a field isolated from the broader
culture and instead underlined the complex
interconnection of kinship with politics,
region, and especially economics. In her work
on Indian migrations to Mexico City, she
brought numerous fundamental issues into the
discussion including the historical presence of
the Indian population among the inhabitants
of the city and the differential character of
migratory flows when criteria of family

structure, social class, and ethnic group are
taken into account. With this, she rejected old
conceptions and established the specificity of
the migratory phenomenon in Mexico and
other Latin American countries. On the other
hand, when studying Indian immigrants in the
city she included the communities of origin as
part of the same field, thus recognising
different types of migrants (seasonal, temporal, and permanent) and emphasising economic processes at local, national, and
international levels.

Later, in her focus on the study of culture
within the framework of globalisation processes, she undertook to understand the
problems a conservative society confronts in
the face of modernising forces. She conducted
a sophisticated study in a provincial city,
among a deep Catholic society known for its
authoritarian tendencies. Loyal to anthropological techniques, such as ethnography, she
probed the differences in religiousness and
authoritarianism according to social class. She
underlined the deep differences introduced by
globalisation and the late, reactionary response
by conservative sectors such as the bourgeoisie
and the peasants, as well as the pragmatism of
the new emergent classes and the radicalism of
the poorest sectors, such as agriculture day
labourers. She was thus able to provide a
remarkable portrait of the different political
and religious positions, connecting gender and
social class.

Education

MA Escuela Nacional de Antropología e
  Historia/National University of Mexico,
  UNAM, 1970
Ph.D. London School of Economics, 1975

Fieldwork

Sierra de Puebla, Mexico, 1969–70
Mazahuas, State of Mexico and Mexico City,
  Mexico, 1972–4
Zamora, Michoacan, Mexico, 1980, 1984
Punjab, Tamil Nadu, India, 1982
Dacca, Joydepure, Bangladesh, 1982

Lacandonia, Chiapas, Mexico, 1990

Key Publications

(1972) *Parentesco y economia en una sociedad nahua* (Kinship and Economy in a Nahua Society), Mexico: Instituto Nacional Indigenista.

(1978) *Migracion, etnicismo y cambio economico: un estudio de migrantes campesinos a la Ciudad de Mexico* (Migration, Ethnicity and Economic Change: A Study of Migrating Peasants in Mexico City), Mexico: El Colegio de Mexico.

(1989) *Cultura y desarrollo: una etnografia de las creencias de una comunidad mexicana* (Culture and Development: An Ethnography of the Beliefs of a Mexican Community), Mexico: El Colegio de Mexico/UNAM/M.A. Porrua.

ANDRÉS MÉDINA

Arutiunov, Sergei Aleksandrovich

b. 1932, Tbilisi, Georgia

Sergei Arutiunov's anthropological views were formed in the early 1960s. His academic career began just after the start of the Cold War. His interest in the study of concrete ethnographic facts predefined the breadth of his scholarly interests and the geographic span of his fieldwork and teaching activities (a visiting professor to the Universities of Bern, Cambridge, Pittsburgh, Arizona, Stanford, Georgetown, Fairbanks-Alaska, Hokkaido, Berkeley), and inspired him to create more than 400 works on the ethnic history of the peoples of the circumpolar, Southeast Asia, and Transcaucasus peoples. His fieldwork materials on this ethnic history prepared the ground for a shift in his scientific interest towards the sphere of ethnogenetic model studies and to investigations of methods of adaptive activity among different peoples. He was able to use his command of Eastern languages and his linguistic qualifications to collect linguistic data that were the basis of his ethnic self-identification studies and his works on a theory of ethnicity.

Sergei Arutiunov is an authority in applied anthropology and the ethnopolitics of the Caucasus region, and is the most respected specialist of ethnic conflict studies in contemporary Russia. In 1990 he was elected as a corresponding member of the Russian Academy of Science. He is an author of over fifteen books to date.

Education

MA Moscow Institute of Oriental Studies, 1953

BA Moscow Institute of Oriental Studies, 1954

Ph.D. Institute of Archaeology, Moscow, 1962

Fieldwork

Chukot peninsular, northeast Siberia, 1958, 1962, 1963, 1965, 1967, 1970, 1977, 1987

Lower Ob river basin, northwest Siberia, 1971, 1972, 1980, 1982, 1985, 1986, 1988, 1991

Armenia, 1974, 1976, 1978, 1984, 1988

India, 1975, 1979, 1983

Japan, 1960, 1963

Vietnam, 1958, 1980

Key Publications

(1969) *Drevniye kultury asiatskikh eskimosov* (Ancient Cultures of Asiatic Eskimos), Moscow: Nauka.

(1969) *Etnicheskaya istoriya naseleniya poberezhia Beringova morya* (Ethnic History of the Bering Sea Area), Moscow: Nauka.

GALINA KHIZRIEVA

Asad, Talal

Talal Asad's work is a critical exploration of the conceptual assumptions that govern the West's knowledges of the non-West. The first clear articulation of this project goes back to his

1973 publication, *Anthropology and the Colonial Encounter*, a volume that called for resituating anthropological knowledge within the context of unequal power relations between the West and the non-West. Asad has since argued that the concepts used in anthropological description should be interrogated not simply in terms of their analytical adequacy, but in their historical deployment within Western projects of social and political governance and transformation. Importantly, Asad focused his inquiries on the categories and practices by which the non-West has been conscripted into the projects of modernity. His studies, in this sense, opened up what might be called the anthropology of modern power.

Since the 1980s, Asad has turned his attention more systematically to the study of religion, not merely to the study of a religion (Islam, Christianity), but to the question of what it means for a discipline like anthropology to be engaged in the study of 'religion' at all. Asad has sought to document the genealogy of the modern idea of religion, tracing the historical articulation of this notion across a number of disciplines as a key development in the constitution of modern social and political life. He has approached this inquiry from at least three distinct angles: first, through a critical engagement with the dominant anthropological traditions in the study of religion; second, through a series of historical investigations into specific religious formations (primarily medieval Christian and contemporary Islamic), studies that have provided points of contrast from which to highlight some of the key assumptions embedded in our modern concept of religion; and last, through an examination of the concept in relation to the practices of social and individual discipline underlying modern liberal-democratic political forms. In his most recent book, *Formations of the Secular* (2003), Asad focuses on the emergence of the concept of the secular, a modern corollary of religion, one that is often assumed to be the natural ground from which the social emerges. Asad puts this assumption to test by tracing the historical shifts within law, aesthetics, literature, and subjectivity

within the modern period that secured such an understanding of the secular in the Anglo-European world and the Middle East. Asad's call in this book for an 'anthropology of the secular' is yet another important extension of his original question: how can the juxtaposition between the 'strangeness of the non-European world' and the 'familiarity of the West' (a classic anthropological trope) be productively explored so as to yield the contingent, historical, and genealogical character of the concepts through which this encounter is framed within systems of Western knowledge and power.

Education

D.Phil. University of Oxford, 1968
B.Litt. University of Oxford, 1961
MA University of Edinburgh, 1959

Fieldwork

The Sudan, 1961–6
Egypt, 1971–2; for short periods between 1975–2002.

Key Publications

(1970) *The Kababish Arabs: Power, Authority and Consent in a Nomadic Tribe*, London: Hurst Press.
(ed.) (1973) *Anthropology and the Colonial Encounter*, London: Ithaca Press.
(1993) *Genealogies of Religion: Discipline and Reasons of Power in Christianity and Islam*, Baltimore: John Hopkins University Press.
(2003) *Formations of the Secular: Christianity, Islam, Modernity*, Stanford: Stanford University Press.

SABA MAHMOOD

Augé, Marc

b. 2 September 1935, Poitiers, France

Marc Augé was first trained in literature and philosophy. He discovered anthropology – a discipline that he regards as a science of composites – while attending Georges Balandier's lectures at the École Pratique des Hautes Études. Starting off as a specialist of Africa, Marc Augé eventually helped open up French anthropology to the study of contemporary worlds, new objects, and fieldwork. Reflecting the crisis of meta-narratives, he travelled outside the main streams that marked the discipline, such as structuralism, functionalism, Marxism, or post-modernism and published more than twenty books. Since his university years, he has remained close to socialist political ideas, taking public positions without becoming a 'special adviser' to whatever power was in place at the time. He held several positions in French and international journals of anthropology as well as in publishing houses. An anthropology of encounters could well sum up his trajectory. First affiliated to ORSTOM (the French Institute of Scientific and Technological Research in Overseas Territories), Marc Augé joined the École des Hautes Études en Sciences Sociales (EHESS) in 1970, where he was elected president in 1985.

The influence of Balandier's seminal work in political anthropology is visible in Augé's monograph on the Alladians of the Ivory Coast (*Rivage Alladian*, 1969 [The Alladian Shore] and in his case study of the concept of power (*Théorie des pouvoirs et idéologie*, 1975 [Theory of Powers and Ideology]. In terms of politics, Augé has been influenced by his experience in Petit Bassam (Ivory Coast) during the 1960s and 1970s, when public discussions on the ideologies and means of development were raging and still full of hope. He interacted with French anthropologists whom he met on the Ivory Coast such as Emmanuel Terray and Jean Louis Dozon – who later on joined the EHESS – as well as Michel Agier, others he met in the course of his later career such as Françoise Héritier along with British anthropologists in Cambridge, Manchester, or Oxford (Edmund Leach, Meyer Fortes, Darryl Ford, and Jack Goody) and many international colleagues and representatives of other disciplines he met during his tenure as president of the EHESS. Augé was especially interested in relations among cultures, an intellectual perspective that is salient in *Powers of Life and Death* (1977) and *Genius of Paganism* (1982), two books that reflect his effort at intertwining Western literature with African materials and his focus on dynamic processes rather than structures. When he started writing about the world around him, as in *Traversée du Luxembourg* (1985) [Crossing Luxembourg] or *In the Metro*, (2002/1986 *Ethnologie dans le Metro*). Africa served as the comparative dimension he employed in thinking about a changing world. While the conditions of knowledge production have changed in the move from colonisation to current globalisation, Augé has argued that anthropology can remain an effective means for thinking about contemporary worlds if primary emphasis is placed on contextualising the conditions of production and reproduction of cultures.

Marc Augé's international recognition has been confirmed by his ten years as the president of a school that draws students from all over the world. Travelling extensively in Asia, East Europe, Russia, Latin America, and the USA, he interacted with colleagues for whom anthropology is an instrument of struggle as much as a profession, and he became sensitive to the changes of scale and the reflexivity of art movements (photos, images, architecture). *Non places* (1992) marks a turning point in terms of his awareness of the importance of consumerism in present societies as well as for rethinking the role of contemporary anthropology in making sense of contemporary conditions. Augé contributed to visual anthropology, making films and art books, wrote on medical anthropology, on genetics, on clones, on death, and also addressed questions of communication and translation.

Education

École Normale Supérieure Ulm, 1957–61
Agrégation de Lettres, 1960
Licence de Sociologie, Sorbonne, Paris, 1964
Ph.D. Sorbonne, Paris, 1967
Doctorat d'Etat, Sorbonne, Paris, 1973

Fieldwork

Ivory Coast, 1964–5, 1967–8, until 1970 (several periods of long-term fieldwork)
Togo, 1970–85 (several periods of short-term missions)
South America, from 1985 (short-term stays in Columbia and Venezuela)
Paris, France; Europe, from 1985.

Key Publications

(1982) *Génie du paganisme* (Genius of Paganism), Paris: Gallimard (German, Romanian, and Spanish translations).
(1995) *Non places. Introduction to an Anthropology of Supermodernity*, London and New York: Verso (*Non lieux. Introduction à une étude de la surmodernité*, 1992) (Brazilian, German, Italian, Portuguese, Spanish, and Turkish translations).
(1998) *A Sense for the Other. The Timeliness and Relevance of Anthropology*, Stanford: Stanford University Press (*Le Sens des autres. Actualité de l'anthropologie*, 1994) (Brazilian, Italian, and Spanish translations).
(1999) *An Anthropology for Contemporaneous Worlds*, Stanford: Stanford University Press (*Pour une anthropologie des mondes contemporains*, 1994).

IRÈNE BELLIER

Austin, Diane

b. 22 July 1946, Melbourne, Australia

Although Diane Austin's major publications have dealt mainly with her studies of class, education, and religion in Jamaica, a long series of papers has shown great skill in comparative analysis and a theoretical sophistication that derives partly from her early training in philosophy. Commenting widely on the work of other social scientists, such as Maurice Bloch, her analysis of the work of Clifford Geertz is among the most penetrating. To the analysis of Australian society she has brought that combination of anthropological sensitivity and sociological breadth that has characterised her work in the Caribbean. Apart from a series of essays collected into a 1984 book on Australian society and its study by sociologists, she has carried out extensive fieldwork among the Western Arrernte, supplemented by archival research. Several volumes are in preparation dealing with problems such as the conflict between kin-based and market-based society, and the process of racialisation, employing research from both Jamaica and Australia. Austin's vision of anthropology is rooted in tradition but looks to a new intellectual agenda to grasp the realities of cultural distinction and social integration in the twenty-first century; she brings to that task a deep awareness of the theoretical, historical, and philosophical issues involved.

Education

BA Australian National University, 1967
MA Australian National University, 1969
MA University of Chicago, 1970
Ph.D. University of Chicago, 1974

Fieldwork

Kingston, Jamaica, 1971, 1972, 1973, 1975–6, 1977
Kingston and Frankfield, Jamaica, 1982, 1986–7, 1990–1
Western Arrernte, Central Australia, 1989–90, 1991, 1993, 1997, 1998, 1999, 2000

Key Publications

(1984) *Urban Life in Kingston, Jamaica: The Culture and Class Ideology of Two Neighborhoods*, New York, London, Paris, Montreux, and Tokyo: Gordon & Breach.
(1997) *Jamaica Genesis: Religion and the Politics of Moral Order*, Chicago: University of Chicago Press

RAYMOND T. SMITH

B

Babcock, Barbara A.

b. 1943, Danville, Pennsylvania, USA

Barbara A. Babcock's earlier research focused on a reflexive semiotics of text and culture; her later, ongoing work, based on long-term field research in Native American Pueblos, has addressed issues of cultural constraint and individual capabilities, creativity through culture, the politics of representation, and the commodification of gender and maternity. Babcock's later thinking is especially informed by feminist theory.

Babcock's early work discussed how symbolic forms – narrativist and behavioural, ironic and parodic – contain their own negation and sense of paradox, thereby instilling reflexive perspectives through which cultures and individuals free themselves, at least momentarily, from normative constraints. This freedom is crucial to cultural self-knowing, and enables culture to speak about itself. So, for example, symbolic inversion offers alternatives to cultural codes, values, and norms.

A fulcrum in Babcock's later Pueblo research is the Cochiti potter, Helen Cordero. Cordero reinvented Pueblo figurative ceramics, and created the first 'story-teller doll', the figure of her grandfather, his mouth open and narrating, while on his body clamber and cling many children, his listeners. Through Cordero and other Pueblo women, Babcock addresses how they have become agents of change and exchange precisely because they embody a synchronic essentialism for Anglo consumers. Yet, despite their commodification, money and mobility enable these women to mediate with the outside world. Through their ceramic figures, Pueblo women tell stories about story-telling, traditionally a male domain, thereby taking on the right to represent and to interpret their worlds to the outside, displacing the dominance of Pueblo male discourse. The Pueblo female principle, one of fertility and generativity, is crucial to Pueblo ritual and religion, and traditionally is appropriated by men who dominate these domains. Through their figurative ceramics, Pueblo women reappropriate both their own symbolic power and the right of men to articulate this. The ceramic figures done by Pueblo women are powerfully reflexive. In negating male authority, these figures and their makers consciously offer alternatives, political and economic, to Pueblo women.

Babcock has applied these and other ideas of the politics of gender and representation, and of the search by women for liberty in a patriarchal world, in insightful studies of the anthropological thought of women anthropologists (especially Elsie Clews Parsons and Ruth Benedict, both highly articulate feminists) in the Southwest.

Education

BA Northwestern University, 1965

MA University of Chicago, 1967
Ph.D. University of Chicago, 1975

Fieldwork

Pueblo communities, American Southwest;
Native American galleries, tourist shops,
markets, museums throughout the USA,
1977–present.

Key Publications

(1978) (ed.) *The Reversible World: Symbolic Inversion
in Art and Society*, Ithaca: Cornell University
Press.
with Monthan, Guy and Monthan, Doris
(1986) *The Pueblo Storyteller: Development of a
Figurative Ceramic Tradition*, Tucson: University
of Arizona Press.
with Parezo, Nancy (1988) *Women Anthropologists
and the Native American Southwest, 1880–1980*,
Albuquerque: University of New Mexico
Press.
with Young, Katherine (eds) (1994) Bodylore,
Journal of American Folklore, 107, 423, special
issue.

DON HANDELMAN

Bailey, F.G.

b. 24 February 1924, Liverpool, UK

F.G. Bailey produced important contributions
to the anthropology of politics, South Asia,
and social change. He has published fifteen
books and thirty-nine articles in his distinguished career thus far. Bailey opened new
doors of inquiry within British social anthropology with his seminal, *Tribe, Caste, and Nation*,
first published in 1960. In this ethnography of
rural Orissa, eastern India, Bailey analysed the
interconnections between village politics and
wider economic and political systems. Usher-
ing in a departure from the consensus, or
holistic models formulated by the Oxford-
based luminaries, A.R. Radcliffe-Brown and E.
Evans-Pritchard, Bailey, building on Max

Gluckman's work at Manchester, employed
both Marxian and Weberian perspectives, and
thus viewed societies as inherently conflictual.
Bailey argued that the boundaries and social
salience of the categories, 'tribe', 'caste', and
'nation' interacted and were transformed
within a changing political arena, challenging
the notion that subjects within traditional
societies were constituted by collective value
systems. 'Political entrepreneurs' were a force
for social change, authoring what Bailey called
'bridge actions', which were attempts to utilise
the new opportunities provided by bureaucratic authority, inspired by nationalist ideologies, yet constrained by the local politics of
the 'moral community'. The success or failure
for such bridge actions was mediated by
differentials of power.

Tribe, Caste, and Nation, in particular, but also
other works by Bailey, proved to be influential
in the anthropology of South Asia as he
brought questions of power and the nation
to bear upon local politics. His theory of social
change through 'bridge actions' was challenged by Louis Dumont, who offered an
avowedly culturalist explanation of Hindu
hierarchy in his study, *Homo Hierarchicus*.
Dumont argued that Bailey had underesti-
mated the holistic cultural logic of hierarchy
within the caste system and its constitutive
power over social actors. Bailey, in turn,
suggested that Dumont privileged the ideology
of elites, failing to observe the fissures of
interest within it that were differentiated by
power. The debate between Dumont, his
students, and Bailey and his, animated much
South Asian anthropology during the 1970s
and 1980s.

While Dumont's structuralist version of
cultural determinism and American interpre-
tivism, as inspired by Clifford Geertz, gained
academic currency, Bailey, against this grain,
theorised abstract rules of political manœuvre.
The result was his most influential work,
Stratagems and Spoils. In it he argued that certain
principles of the political 'game' were universal. Though the work employed examples
from his fieldwork, historical examples were

also utilised in an attempt to examine the common principles of political competition. He developed an analytic 'tool kit' that influenced the development of political anthropology in the 1970s. In short, he argued that all political structures must contain rules about 'prizes', 'personnel', 'leadership', 'competition', and 'control'. Though accused by critics of offering too rationalistic an interpretation of politics, Bailey was careful to distinguish 'normative' from 'pragmatic' rules within the 'game'. Therefore, goal-oriented actions did not presuppose an instrumental rationality.

Bailey refined his theoretical formulations in such works as *Morality and Expediency* (1977), *The Tactical Uses of Passion* (1983), and *Humbuggery and Manipulation* (1988). Added to his arsenal was an interest in language and rhetoric. While continuing to examine the rules of the political 'game', Bailey also turned his analysis in the 1980s and 1990s to rhetorical moves within the social sciences at a time when postmodernism was challenging epistemological foundations. In his book, *The Prevalence of Deceit*, Bailey conceded some points to post-modernists regarding the relativity of truth claims in ethnographic writing; but, in doing so, he argued that post-modernists attempted to mask their implicit moralistic 'truths'. Bailey 'deconstructed' the logic of certain 'post-modernists' through an analysis of their writing strategies. Academia, like village politics, he suggested, followed the rules of the 'game', though this was often unrecognised.

Returning to his archive of field notes in the 1990s, Bailey published three more ethnographies about Orissa. This trilogy echoed many of the themes introduced in his earlier work, but added new insights, befitting his greater sensitivity to rhetoric. *The Witch-Hunt* (1994), in particular, was widely praised for its captivating ethnographic narrative, as well as for its contribution to studies of witchcraft and social change. In 2001, Bailey published, *Treasons, Stratagems, and Spoils*, a sequel to his theoretical treatise. In this work, over four decades of writing and thinking about politics

and culture are synthesised with his characteristic wit and artistry as a writer.

Education

MA B.Litt. University of Oxford, 1950
Ph.D. University of Manchester, 1955

Fieldwork

Orissa, India., 1952–4, 1955–6, 1959
Cuneo, Italy, 1968

Key Publications

(1960) *Tribe, Caste, and Nation: A Study of Political Activity and Political Change in Highland Orissa*, Manchester: Manchester University Press.
(1969) *Stratagems and Spoils: A Social Anthropology of Politics*, Oxford: Basil Blackwell.
(1991) *The Prevalence of Deceit*, Ithaca: Cornell University Press.
(1994) *The Witch-Hunt: Or, the Triumph of Morality*, Ithaca: Cornell University Press.

ANDREW WILLFORD

Balandier, Georges

b. 21 December 1920, Aillevillers (Haute-Saône), France

In his long and prolific career as a researcher, teacher, and writer, Georges Balandier has made critical and formative contributions to African studies, historical, political, and urban anthropology, the anthropology of colonialism and underdevelopment, the study of social change, and, more recently, the anthropology of modernity and post-modernity.

Following the Second World War, Balandier worked under Michel Leiris at the Musée de l'Homme in Paris. From 1946 to 1952, he worked for the Institut Français d'Afrique Noire in a number of France's African colonies, including in Senegal, Mauritania, Guinea (Conakry), and Congo (Brazzaville). Diverse in ethnographic as well as geographic interests, Balandier conducted research on

Senegalese fishermen, Gabonese villagers, and urban Africans in colonial Brazzaville. In a seminal 1951 article, 'La situation coloniale, approche théorique', Balandier laid out an approach to 'the colonial situation' as a complex, 'total social phenomenon' that linked colonising and colonised societies in a complex and ongoing situation of conflict, adaptation, and crisis. In his attempt to theorise social change under colonisation, Balandier departed from the then-dominant synchronic perspectives of British structural-functionalism. On the one hand, his studies of colonial Africa are very much products of the post-Second World War ethnographic present, in which Africans sought greater autonomy and access to the benefits of modernity. At the same time his focus on history, power relations, conflict, and crisis prefigures the much more recent anthropology of colonialism.

In 1952 Balandier returned to France, where he took up teaching and administrative duties at the Centre National de Recherches Scientifiques, the École des Hautes Études en Sciences Sociales, and, later, the Sorbonne. He helped to found African studies in France and trained a generation of Africanist scholars, including Claude Meillassoux, Emmanuel Terray, Marc Augé, Jean Copans, and Jean-Loup Amselle. In 1955, he published two important monographs based on his research in Central Africa, *Sociologie actuelle de l'Afrique Noire* and *Sociologie des Brazzavilles Noires*. These works draw on both sociological and ethnographic method to explore in detail the social dynamics of the colonial situation and resulting demographic, economic, and social crises in rural and urban Gabon and Congo. Balandier's most widely read book, *Ambiguous Africa* (originally published in 1957), is a memoir of his years in Africa and explores multiple intersections of tradition, modernity, social mutations, and colonial crises in societies 'in the throes of reconstruction' after 'contact with our economic, administrative, and religious imperatives'.

In the late 1950s, as African colonies moved toward independence, he turned his attention to emerging concerns of development, under-development, and the Third World. He continued to explore social dynamics, the sociology of mutations, tradition, and continuity, development, social change, dependency, colonisation and decolonisation, and the social costs of progress. In the 1960s, he applied his dynamic, processual approach to the anthropology of political systems and the interpretation of power.

Since the 1970s, while continuing to draw on the experiences, concerns, and insights that emerged during his post-war fieldwork in Africa, Balandier has turned his attention to the socioanthropology of modernity and hypermodernity. He argues for the ongoing relevance of anthropological detours in exploring modernity's unfamiliar terrains characterised by movement, uncertainty, and the consciousness of disorder. According to Balandier, 'modernity scrambles the cards', resulting in fluidity, complexity, confusion, 'blurred and incomplete maps', and precarious forms of knowledge and competency. Anthropology, with its profound analysis of social relations and cultural practices, can complement dominant technical and quantitative forms of knowledge by offering qualitative interpretations of modernity. In *Le Grande Système* [The Great System] (2001), Balandier explores the tension he sees between global economic and technological networks, on the one hand, and the impoverishment of cultural and symbolic systems, on the other.

After a half-century of active contributions to anthropology and sociology, George Balandier remains an active and relevant voice in French anthropology and sociology. Many of his early works on colonial Africa are still in print and widely read. His more recent works on modernity, disorder, the imaginary, and the contradictions of globalisation speak to central concerns in contemporary anthropology and would undoubtedly be of interest to Anglophone readers if available in translation. Scholars of colonialism and post-colonialism will no doubt continue to find much of value in this pioneering scholar's work.

Education

École Pratique des Hautes Études
Faculté des Letters et Institut d'Ethnologie de
 Paris
Docteur ès Letters, Sorbonne, Paris, 1954

Fieldwork

Senegal, Guinea, Congo (Brazzaville), Gabon,
 1946–52

Key Publications

(1966) *Ambiguous Africa: Cultures in Collision*
 (Afrique ambiguë, 1957), New York: Pantheon.
(1970) *The Sociology of Black Africa: Social Dynamics*
 in Central Africa (Sociologie actuelle de l'Afrique Noire:
 dynamique des changements sociaux en Afrique
 Centrale, 1955), New York: Praeger.
(1985) *Le détour: pouvoir et modernitê* (The Detour:
 Power and Modernity), Paris: Fayard
(2001) *Le Grand Système* (The Great System),
 Paris: Fayard.

JOHN M. CINNAMON

Balikci, Asen

b. 1929, Istanbul, Turkey

Anthropologist, prize-winning ethnographic
filmmaker with interests in human ecology
in the Canadian Arctic (Netsilik Inuit), in
Siberia, in Afghanistan (Lakenkhel Pakhtuns),
and in interethnic relations and the culture of
poverty in post-socialist Bulgaria, Balikci has
been a pivotal figure in popularising and
defining visual anthropology as an academic
discipline. Balikci has always focused on the
details of the human condition; the camera is
always an intimate observer in his films. His
multicultural trajectory (Turkey, Switzerland,
the USA, Canada, Eastern Europe) emerges as a
fascination with acculturation across cultural
or environmental frontiers (*The Netsilik Eskimo*
Series, National Film Board, Canada; *Chronicle of*
Sireniki; *Siberia through Siberian Eyes*). Later, this led
him to focus on globalisation and the symbolic

geography of local life among the Turkish,
Bulgar, and Pomak peoples of Eastern Europe.
 Balikci has always sought to involve the
people among whom he conducted his
research, which was a natural outgrowth of
his role as a professor of anthropology at the
Université de Montréal (1969–94). Balikci
later combined his research on Balkan post-
socialist culture and his teaching by holding
many seminars, which led to a recent series of
collaborative films: *Pomak Woman*, *Old Ibrahim's*
World, *Balkan Portraits*, *Roma Portraits*, *Ephtim D.*,
Portrait of a Bulgarian Pensioner.
 Balikci's long and productive career as an
educator and ethnographic film producer/
maker shows no signs of slowing down.

Education

Licence en geographie, Université de Genève,
 1952
Ph.D. Columbia University, 1962

Fieldwork

Northwest Territories, 1959–65
Yukon Territory, 1961
Afghanistan, 1973–6
Siberia, 1989–91
Pomak, Bulgaria, 1994–5

Key Publications and Films

(1970) *The Netsilik Eskimo*, Garden City, NY:
 Doubleday (Waveland Press, 1989).
with Asch, T. (1983) *The Sons of Hadji Omar*,
 Smithsonian Institute and National Film
 Board (Canada).

SIMONA BEALCOVSCHI

Banton, Michael Parker

b. 8 September 1926, UK

For the past half-century Michael Banton has
played a central role in analysing the ever more
racially and ethnically plural character of
British society as a result of the steady growth

of its non-European population. Despite having formally retired from his position as founding professor of sociology at the University of Bristol more than a decade ago, he is still one of the leading figures in the study of race and ethnic relations in the UK.

Much has changed during the course of Banton's long career, no less in the structure of the local (and global) social order than in the perspectives commonly deployed to make sense of it. Banton began his academic career as a student of economics at the London School of Economics shortly after the end of the Second World War, where he had the good fortune to be allocated Edward Shils as his tutor. Shils swiftly weaned Banton away from his initial concerns, and having convinced him that no meaningful distinction could be made between sociology and anthropology, persuaded him to take a course in ethnology taught by Edmund Leach.

These conjunctions set the stage for the development of his future career. As a postgraduate research student Banton flew in the face of then-established conventions. Despite his firm commitment to ethnographic research methods, Banton resisted the temptation to head off to some exotic destination in a faraway forest, desert, or mountain range. Instead he chose to focus on what his nominally more adventurous colleagues must then have regarded as a desperately prosaic phenomenon: the process of 'colonial immigration' (as it was then described) from Sierra Leone to Stepney.

Nevertheless Banton's choice was prescient, at least in a British context. Not only did he ignore the ever-growing divide between sociology and anthropology, but also ploughed the first furrow in a field that has since grown ever larger, so much so that it currently runs from explorations of the dynamics of racial and ethnic polarisation at one end of the spectrum to the dynamics of transnational networks at the other. Having been active in this arena since its inception, and having been an active participant in virtually all the debates that subsequently sprang up within it, Banton's œuvre is not only a monument to careful scholarship, but also provides an illuminating record

of the far-reaching changes that have occurred in the analytical perspectives deployed to make sense of these issues over the years. Banton's own terminology highlights these changes. Hence whilst his earliest publications refer to 'colonial' immigrants, those same persons are successively redesignated as 'colored' and then as 'New Commonwealth' before being swept away entirely in the mid-1960s. Instead the issue of race relations becomes the core focus of his concerns.

But although Banton swiftly became a leading light in the sociology of race relations, the arguments have since moved on, as has Banton himself. Besides arguing that history must always be taken into account (he has long been a critic of 'presentism'), he also began to insist that analyses that explore the dynamics of ethnic polarisation and hence of ethnic plurality invariably throw up much more illuminating insights than those that remain couched in a monochromatic concern with race, racism, and racial exclusion. This had major consequences. First, he was much better equipped than many to make sense of the way in which ethnic plurality, rather than 'race', gradually became the central focus of popular hostility to the minority presence from the 1980s onwards; second, he played a leading role in arguing that whilst it might make analytical sense to class all those subjected to exclusion on the grounds of their physical appearance as 'black', it was a gross mistake to assume that membership of a sociopolitical *category* would necessarily precipitate the formation of an active sociopolitical *group*. As Banton's own students went on to demonstrate, 'black' people categorised invariably continued to sustain their own diverse ethnic self-definitions, regardless of their denigrators' presuppositions.

There can be little doubt that the central key to Banton's long and distinguished career lies in his systematic rejection of the conventional divide between sociology and anthropology. In consequence he has always been prepared to pay as much attention to the capacity of social actors to devise strategies with which to resist the worst of the constraints to which they were subjected, as to the social processes through which those structures generated; and no matter how contentious the issues, he has always discussed them in an exceptionally level-headed way. In a field where discussion often becomes both politically excited and emotionally overblown, Banton's commitment to careful and rational scholarship stands out like a lighthouse.

Education

B.Sc. London School of Economics, 1950
Ph.D. London School of Economics, 1954
D.Sc. University of Edinburgh, 1964

Fieldwork

London, UK, migrant workers from West Africa, 1950–2
Freetown, Sierra Leone: rural migrants, 1952–3

Key Publications

(1955) *The Coloured Quarter: Negro Immigrants in an English City*, London: Jonathan Cape.
(1977) *The Idea of Race*, London: Tavistock; Boulder, CO: Westview Press.
(1983) *Racial and Ethnic Competition*, Cambridge, UK: Cambridge University Press.
(1987) *Racial Theories*, Cambridge, UK: Cambridge University Press (second edn, 1998).

ROGER BALLARD

Barbeau, Marius

b. 5 March 1883, Ste-Marie-de-Beauce, Quebec, Canada

d. 27 February 1969, Ottawa, Ontario, Canada

Marius Barbeau, along with Edward Sapir and Diamond Jenness, established a national professional anthropology in Canada. Barbeau, a native of Quebec with abortive career forays into the priesthood and the law, returned from his Rhodes scholarship at Oxford just in time

to join Sapir's new Division of Anthropology under the Geological Survey of Canada, established in 1910. Barbeau remained in Ottawa from 1911 until his retirement in 1949. He lectured at Laval University in Quebec City from 1942 until his first stroke in 1954.

Barbeau was a passionate fieldworker, dividing his efforts fairly evenly between Quebec folklore and British Columbia ethnology. Most of his ethnographic reports, ranging from the arts (songs, argillite carving, totem poles) to texts (historical narratives, traditional myths, contemporary stories) were published by the National Museum of Canada. Barbeau established the folklore of contemporary descendants of European settlers as a legitimate part of North American anthropology. This work appeared in French in Quebec and in English in the *American Journal of Folklore*, edited by Franz Boas. He also established a strong Quebec presence in the Canadian anthropological tradition. Many of his ethnographic materials appeared in French as well as in English.

Barbeau achieved a public face for Canadian anthropology through the media, beginning with radio documentaries in 1932. He was active in the arts and popularised the work of Canadian painter, Cornelius Krieghoff. He wrote frequently for a popular audience. Folkways Records released a documentary on his career collecting 'Canadian Indian Folklore' in 1957. The National Film Board of Canada produced documentaries of his totem pole and Quebec folklore work in 1959. In 1962, he produced eight programs for CBC-Radio. At the age of seventy-eight, Barbeau described himself in an autobiographical outline as 'ethnologist, folklorist, musician, and historian'.

Barbeau was not a theoretician; his efforts to trace migration through folklore, for example, were received poorly. His contribution resided in the documentation of oral tradition, both in Quebec and among Canadian Aboriginal peoples.

In 1966, the National Museum of Canada established a separate Folklore Division that retains Barbeau's professional papers and field notes; additional materials are held by Laval University's Folklore Archives. Barbeau is commemorated by the Salon Barbeau at the Canadian Museum of Civilisation building opened in 1989.

Education

LL.L. Laval, 1907
B.Sc. Diploma in Anthropology, University of Oxford, 1910

Fieldwork

Huron-Wyandot, Southern Ontario and Oklahoma, 1911–12
French Canada, 1914–46
Tsimshian, 1914–47
Skeena, 1920–39
Stoney and Kootenay, 1923
Nass, 1927
Haida and Tlingit, Alsaka, 1939–47
Tahltan and Kwakiutl, 1947
Iroquois, 1949–51

Key Publications

(1915) *Huron and Wyandot Mythology*, Ottawa: Geological Survey of Canada, Anthropological Series 11.
with Sapir, Edward (1925) *Folk Songs of French Canada*, New Haven: Yale University Press.
(1929) *Totem Poles of the Gitksan*, Upper Skeena River, British Columbia, Ottawa: National Museum of Canada.
(1953) *Haida Myths*, Ottawa: National Museum of Canada.

Further Reading

Nowry, Laurence (1995) *Man of Mana: Marius Barbeau*, Toronto: NC Press.

REGNA DARNELL

Barley, Nigel

b. 25 July 1947, Kingston, UK

Nigel Barley's contributions to the anthropological discipline are far-reaching quite literally because of the breadth of readership that consumes his writings. Barley's work is informative, detailed, jargon-free, and extremely entertaining. His first book (1986 below) was tremendously popular and its publication with Penguin ensured a broad-ranging audience. Some would place Barley on the margins of the anthropological discipline because of his irreverent wit, his career outside of the academy, and his commitment to publishing for a wide public. Others, however, would place Barley nearer to the center because of the way he has contributed to the popularisation of the discipline (he has been likened to Margaret Mead in this respect). Correspondingly, the use of his texts in the teaching of anthropology has been a topic of controversy. Many use his books to make their undergraduate teaching fun and easily accessible, while some avoid them because they view this humour as a sign of disrespect by making light of both the discipline and the subject/informants' views and beliefs. Most often, however, Barley's humour is directed at himself and the awkward and occasionally dangerous situations that fieldwork may present.

Barley's initial studies in anthropology at Oxford were library based and focused on the Anglo-Saxons. After completing his doctorate he embarked on two years of fieldwork with the Dowayo of Northern Cameroon. Upon his return to the UK he began his career at the Museum of Mankind where he works as Assistant Keeper in charge of Western and Central Africa in the Department of Ethnography. He carries on publishing prolifically despite the demands of this post, and finds an easy compatibility between his writing and his curating and lecturing work at the museum. The thematic foci in most of his works have been 'ritual', 'meaning', and 'diversity'. One of his books on the Dowayo of Cameroon focuses on a circumcision ceremony, while another book on travel in Sulawesi culminates in anecdotal descriptions of what happened when he brought four carvers back to London to build a traditional rice barn at the Museum of Mankind. His more recent publications have included a study of clay pots and their meanings in Africa, an anthropological study of Kalabari ancestral screens, and a biographical study on the life of Sir Stamford Raffles (the nineteenth-century colonial official and spectacular collector of Indonesian art and antiquities, whose collection is held in the British Museum). He has also written a useful comparative work focusing on death rituals, beliefs about death, and the artefacts that mark the diversity of its meanings. Barley has curated many exhibitions at the British Museum, including the permanent collection in the Sainsbury African Galleries.

Education

BA (Hons), modern and medieval languages, University of Cambridge, 1969
D.Phil., anthropology, University of Oxford, 1973

Fieldwork

Northern Cameroon, 1977–9,
Eastern Indonesia, 1986–8,
Bali, 1999
Ghana, 2000
Sarawak, 2001

Key Publications

(1986 [1983]) *The Innocent Anthropologist*, Harmondsworth: Penguin Books.
(1988) *Not a Hazardous Sport*, Harmondsworth: Penguin Books.
(1991) *The Duke of Puddle Dock: Travels in the Footsteps of Stamford Raffles*, NY: Henry Holt & Company.
(1995) *Dancing on the Grave: Encounters with Death*, London: John Murray.

TAMARA KOHN

Barnard, Alan

b. 22 February 1949, Baton Rouge, Los Angeles, USA

As a doctoral student under Adam Kuper, Alan

Barnard left for the Kalahari Desert in 1974 to undertake his fieldwork with people who had for two decades been attracting much anthropological attention; the San. Nonetheless, he bucked the trend of his predecessors by focusing his research with San who had been living in an area that had for almost a century been occupied by white farmers.

His thesis on transformations in Khoi kin categories developed the theoretical perspective of 'regional structural comparison', which he has continued to develop in later work. What earlier writers may have described merely as cultural differences, he presents as part of larger, regional structures of beliefs and practices; a structure of structures. As such, his work has developed that of his own supervisor, Adam Kuper, and Kuper's mentor, Isaac Schapera. Barnard's seminal work on the Khoisan, *Hunters and Herders of Southern Africa*, was the first such overview after Schapera's 1930 classic, *The Khoisan of Southern Africa*.

Barnard's work provided an important contribution to the 'Great Kalahari Debate', when revisionism fundamentally challenged the isolationist representations of Khoisan that had hitherto been prevalent. While in some senses Barnard's structuralist focus on kinship had given him classicist leanings, his ability to accept and integrate the revisionist challenges to Khoisan history and ethnography, while rejecting its excesses, displayed his ability to integrate theoretical developments without sacrificing the centrality of thorough ethnography to academic understanding.

Alan Barnard's endearing contributions to anthropology have arisen through his ability to capture grander patterns in ethnography and anthropological theory, and present them in an illuminating and accessible manner to a variety of audiences. His work has progressed from general patterns of kinship, to comparative ethnography of Khoisan peoples of Southern Africa, to the history and development of anthropological thought, particularly with reference to hunter-gatherers. His prolific writing has catered for specialists, students of anthropology, as well as children.

Education

BA George Washington University, 1971
MA McMaster University, 1972
Ph.D. University of London, 1976

Fieldwork

Archaeological experience in England, 1970, 1971; South Africa, 1972, 1973; and Namibia, 1973
Khoisan groups throughout Southern Africa, 1973, 1979, 1982, 1991, 1993, 1995, 1997
Gantsi Farms, Botswana, 1974–5, 1982
National traditions in anthropology, including Japan, 2002 onwards

Key Publications

with Good, Anthony (1984) *Research Practices in the Study of Kinship*, London, Academic Press.
(1992) *Hunters and Herders of Southern Africa; A Comparative Ethnography of the Khoisan Peoples*, Cambridge, UK: Cambridge University Press.
with Spencer, Jonathan (eds) (1996) *Encyclopedia of Social and Cultural Anthropology*, London: Routledge.
(2000) *History and Theory in Anthropology*, Cambridge, UK: Cambridge University Press.

MICHAEL TAYLOR

Barnes, John A.

b. 9 September 1918, Reading, UK

After an undergraduate background in mathematics and distinguished wartime service in the Royal Navy, John A. Barnes began his academic career in 1946 as a member of the research team at the Rhodes–Livingstone Institute, under the direction of Max Gluckman. His fieldwork with the Ngoni people of Nyasaland and northern Rhodesia (today Malawi and Zambia) resulted in publications on Lamba village organisation, Ngoni history, marriage, and politics, and on research and analytical methods. As was the case with many anthropologists carrying out research after the Second World War, he emphasised the phenomenon of change. His study of Ngoni political history, from the days before the British conquest, through their defeat, and until the late 1940s, dealt with both the dynamics of the spreading Ngoni polity ('the snowball state') and with the arrangements of politics under colonial rule in the 1940s.

Barnes next carried out fieldwork in Norway, extending his interests in the study of large-scale societies and the methods for studying them. He focused on class, social networks, and the organisation of collective action. He was an early contributor to the literature on social networks. From 1956 to 1969 he taught in Australia and turned his attention to the peoples of Australia and of Papua New Guinea. His *Inquest on the Murngin* (1968) took a new look at the well-worn but confused topic of the Murngin kinship system. His 'African models in the New Guinea Highlands' (1962) was a timely and important critique of the tendency to view kinship and the political systems of 'stateless peoples' as if they were just variations on the models that Fortes and Evans-Pritchard had drawn for the Tallensi and Nuer.

In 1969 Barnes was installed as the first chair of sociology at the University of Cambridge, and in his inaugural lecture he offered an explanation for why it had taken that institution so long to recognise sociology as a discipline.

A prolific writer, he deals with a wide variety of theoretical and methodological issues, drawing upon the literature of many disciplines. He is especially concerned with the nature and practice of the social sciences, the ethics of social inquiry, and ways in which the social sciences can be more successful at explaining human behaviour. 'I would very much like to know to what extent and in what ways, at what level of specificity and within what limits or probability, human affairs are orderly, predictable, and determinate' (1971: xvii). He advocates the construction of models – models of 'what actually happens' (1990: 22) – rather than a search for 'social laws'.

Education

BA University of Cambridge, 1939
D.Phil. University of Oxford, 1951

Fieldwork

Central Africa (Ngoni and Lamba), 1946–7,
   1948–9
Norway, 1952–3

Key Publications

(1954) *Politics in a Changing Society: A Political
   History of the Fort Jameson Ngoni*, Oxford: Oxford
   University Press.
(1971) *Three Styles in the Study of Kinship*, Berkeley:
   University of California.
(1990) *Models and Interpretations: Selected Essays*,
   Cambridge, UK: Cambridge University Press.
(1994) *A Pack of Lies: Towards a Sociology of Lying*,
   Cambridge, UK: Cambridge University Press.

HERBERT S. LEWIS

Barnett, Homer Garner

b. 25 April 1906, Bisbee, Arizona, USA

d. 9 May 1985, Eugene, Oregon, USA

Homer Garner Barnett was internationally
recognised for his work on cultural change
and acculturation, and was a pioneer in the
emerging field of applied anthropology. For
over twenty years he conducted ethnographic
research and 'culture element distribution
studies' (CEDs) among the Indians of the
Pacific Northwest and the Palau Islanders of
Micronesia. Barnett was a firm believer that
anthropology had much to offer in the
improvement of the human condition. As a
result his body of work has appealed to
sociologists, psychologists, business, governments, and the layperson.

Barnett's major theoretical work on cultural
change, *Innovation: The Basis of Cultural Change*,
posits innovative behaviour within all cultures
and provides a typology of individuals likely to
be acceptors of innovations. Drawing on his

fieldwork among the Indians of the Pacific
Northwest, Barnett outlined a new approach to
problems of cultural dynamics in contact
situations, stressing careful examination of
conditions surrounding the cultural process
of innovation. His later work, *Being a Palauan*,
synthesises his earlier work on cultural change
through a detailed ethnography that elucidates
the ways in which the Palauans view their
culture: specifically, how older Palauan culture
had responded to successive contact with the
Spanish, Germans, Japanese, and Americans.

In 1955 Barnett accepted the position of
adviser to Jan van Baal, governor-general of
Netherlands New Guinea. The fruit of that
labour was *Anthropology in Administration*, a survey
of the work of anthropologists in cross-cultural
contexts. Barnett recognised America's growing power on the world stage and cautioned
temperance and responsibility in our contact
with minority populations. To Barnett anthropologists offered unique talents that could be
used to assist government officials in effectively recognising the social, economic, and
educational needs of their indigenous populations. By assisting in the administering of
elections, settling disputes, and directing
resettlement plans the anthropologist would
apply his or her knowledge and skills to assure
sound policy decision-making.

In addition to being a renowned field
anthropologist Barnett was also an exceptional
teacher and mentor. In 1962 he directed a five-
year, National Science Foundation survey of ten
displaced communities in the Pacific. He administered the survey by soliciting the help of
graduate students and scholars from other institutions. As a result he attracted students from
all over the world, with many of whom he kept
in close personal contact until his death in 1985.

Education

AB Stanford University, 1927
Ph.D. University of California, Berkeley, 1938

Fieldwork

Oregon coast, summer 1934

Gulf of Georgia Salish, Vancouver, British
  Columbia, summer 1934, summer 1935,
  summer 1936
Yurok, Pacific Northwest coast, USA, 1938
Yakima, Washington, USA, 1946
Palau Islands, 1947–8
Fiji, 1952–3
Netherlands New Guinea, 1955

Key Publications

(1953) Innovation: The Basis of Cultural Change, New
  York: McGraw-Hill
(1955) The Coast Salish of British Columbia,
  Eugene, OR: University of Oregon Press.
(1956) Anthropology in Administration, Evanston,
  IL: Row, Peterson.
(1960) Being a Palauan, New York: Holt

CYNTHIA A. TYSICK

Barth, Fredrik

b. 22 December 1928, Leipzig, Germany

Fredrik Barth has maintained international
renown as fieldworker and theoretician
through five decades. Barth has published a
dozen monographs based on fieldwork in
almost as many locations, and he has remained
dedicated to comparative analysis for theory
development, often through tightly focused,
even terse, journal articles. He has given
important contributions to a diversity of
anthropological fields, such as human action,
social organisation, ecology, economy, ethnicity, knowledge, ritual, and cultural complexity.

After an international childhood (mainly in
the USA) and wartime youth in Norway, Barth
studied art before leaving for the University of
Chicago where his father had become a
professor of geology. Barth studied anthropology and palaeontology before returning to
Norway to do his first fieldwork, among
mountain peasants. This early work signalled
a key concern in Barth's later comparative
efforts: the active ecological adaptation of a
local community to opportunities and con-

straints posed by the environment. Shortly
after, Barth was on fieldwork in Iraq as
osteologist for a University of Chicago expedition, while also doing research on social
organisation in southern Kurdistan. This work
provided foundations for a leading light in
Barth's anthropology: the active role of
society's members in creating and changing
society, through interaction among persons
placed in different social positions. The
Kurdish situation where stated norms and
actual practice did not converge inspired
Barth's processual analyses, in which people
are portrayed as actors who consciously make
their own choices of behaviour from a
complex set of opportunities and constraints;
an 'aggregate' of actors' choices then generating a social form.

Barth's thinking towards 'generative' models of the unpredictable processes of social life
was further refined through studies at the
London School of Economics in 1952, and
through further fieldwork among nomads and
agriculturalists in different parts of the Middle
East. Barth's doctoral work at the University of
Cambridge (with Edmund Leach) resulted in
the classic Political Leadership among Swat Pathans
(1959). This line of work culminated in 1966
with the influential theoretical essay, 'Models
of social organization', in which Barth addressed fundamental problems in the social
sciences by suggesting a generative analysis of
social forms, general enough to encompass
most types of human action (with particular
emphasis on the actors' values and transactions), yet specific enough to accommodate
variation resulting from the peculiarities of
individual persons and situations.

Heading a very active department at the
University of Bergen in the 1960s, Barth
organised and published a number of symposia, the most influential of which was Ethnic
Groups and Boundaries (1969). This book established the view that it is the relationship
between groups, not their 'cultural stuff',
which gives them social significance and
meaning. Soon after, Barth carried out fieldwork among the Baktaman, a small group in
the mountainous interior of New Guinea. This

work departed from his consistent attention to transaction and strategy to focus on ritual, knowledge, and symbolism, and became influential in American cultural anthropology. Subsequent fieldwork (with his wife, Unni Wikan) and resulting articles and monographs have merged Barth's long-standing and more recent theoretical concerns by analysing Middle East cultural pluralism in Oman and by developing generative models of cultural variation in Bali or New Guinea.

While Barth's extraordinary fieldwork, publication record, and consistently innovative theoretical contributions are well-known foundations of his international prominence among anthropologists, he has also been active in applications of anthropology to development issues. As a professor at the universities of Bergen (1961–72) and Oslo (1973–85) Barth had a central role in the intellectual and institutional growth of Norwegian anthropology, as well as in Norwegian research policy. In 1985 Barth was appointed a research fellow under the Norwegian Ministry of Culture. He has since alternated between home in Oslo, fieldwork in various locations, and professorships in the USA (Emory University and Boston University). Barth has remained a prominent contributor to anthropological debates while continuing fieldwork in Bhutan and his comparative work in the anthropology of knowledge.

Education

MA University of Chicago, 1949
Ph.D. University of Cambridge, 1957

Fieldwork

Sollia, eastern Norway, 1950
South Kurdistan, Iraq, 1951
Travellers, eastern Norway, 1953
North West Frontier Province, Pakistan, 1954, 1960, 1978–9
Fars, Iran, 1957–8
Baluchistan, Pakistan, 1961
West and north-coast Norway, 1961–3
Darfur, Sudan, 1964, 1965–7

Upper Fly River, Papua New Guinea, 1968, 1972, 1981–2
Oman, 1974, 1975–6
Bali, Indonesia, 1983–8 (intermittent)
Bhutan, 1985, 1989, 1991, 1993–ongoing (intermittent)
Sichuan, China, 1992–ongoing (intermittent)

Key Publications

(1959) *Political Leadership among Swat Pathans*, London: Athlone Press.
(1964) *Nomads of South Persia: The Basseri Tribe of the Khamseh Confederacy*, Oslo: Universitetsforlaget/Boston: Little Brown.
(1987) *Cosmologies in the Making: A Generative Approach to Cultural Variation in Inner New Guinea*, Cambridge, UK: Cambridge University Press.
(1993) *Balinese Worlds*, Chicago: The University of Chicago Press.

EDVARD HVIDING

Bartolomé, Leopoldo J.

b. 6 December 1942, Posadas, Argentina

Following on from his early research on Chaco Indians, Bartolomé analysed the stagnant agrarian system based on *yerba-mate* production in the Argentine northeastern province of Misiones. He showed that *colonos* (farmers) of Eastern European descent, stereotyped as backwards ethnic groups, could not evolve into successful rural capitalists but rather remained peasant producers, meeting unstable economic policies with conservative strategies.

As chair of the Urban Program of Resettlement and Social Action, *Ente Binacional Yacyretá* (1979–89), in the twin cities, Posadas (Argentina) and Encarnación (Paraguay), Bartolomé showed that forced resettlement in big projects affects the survival system of the urban poor, adding uncertainty to the people's current organisation. He also advised international associations and the private sector.

Since 1974 Bartolomé has successfully combined applied and basic research with the creation of the department of social anthropology in Misiones. He also endured state terror and the persecution of intellectuals during the latest Argentine dictatorship.

Education

Graduate in Anthropological Sciences, Buenos Aires University, Argentina, 1967
MA University of Wisconsin, Madison, USA, 1971
Ph.D. University of Wisconsin, Madison, USA, 1974

Fieldwork

Presidencia Roque Sáenz Peña, Chaco, Argentina, 1968
Apóstoles, Misiones, Argentina, 1973–4
Posadas, Misiones, Argentina, 1978–81, 1985–91

Key Publications

(1991) *The Colonos of Apóstoles: Adaptive Strategy and Ethnicity in a Polish-Ukrainian Settlement in Northeast Argentina*, New York: AMS Press, Inc. (Spanish translation by Editorial Universitaria, UNAM, Argentina, 2000).
(1993) 'The Yacyretá experience with urban resettlement: some lessons and insights', in Michael M. Cernea and Scott Guggenheim (eds) *Anthropological Approaches to Resettlement Policy, Practice, and Theory*, Boulder, Colorado: Westview Press, pp. 109–32.

ROSANA GUBER

Basso, Keith

b. 1940, Asheville, North California, USA

Through long-term field research among the Western Apache in Arizona, especially the Cibecue, Keith Basso has acquired a profound understanding of their language and ways. From the very start of his research, including his dissertation on Western Apache witchcraft, he has turned to language in order to grasp Apache perceptions and knowledge of the world – in short, what it means to be Apache. His early work takes a more classically ethnoscientific approach as he examines semantic categories to understand the Apache world. Basso has engaged this theoretical framework in novel ways, for instance in the analysis of the Cibecue classificatory verb system, or in an examination of cultural adaptation as the extension of a system of classification through the displacement of referential meaning and the development of metaphor.

Basso also investigates the pragmatic aspects of language in connection with the specific discursive forms communication takes. He has examined the contexts in which silence as a mode of interaction is chosen over dialogue, concluding that uncertainty and ambiguity are common denominators of those contexts. His work on Western Apache 'portraits of the whiteman' shows how typifications of interactions with non-natives in various roles are depicted in a joking but critical way, to reflect their understandings of the 'whiteman', of the 'whiteman's' attitude – usually condescending, sometimes apologetic, and often strange – and of their expectations of themselves.

His more recent work has been concerned with Apache moral order as depicted through stories linked to places and place names. The depth of this work goes beyond the analysis of narratives, elaborating the relationship of people to their landscape by portraying how they construct it through tales of mythical or real events, and, in turn, how the landscape, as charted in names that stand as emblems of these stories, serves as a moral map to guide individual behaviour and to further wisdom.

Basso's work has revealed Western Apache ways of thinking about the world and about themselves within that world. He has done this through a sensitive, thorough, and often humorous understanding of their language and culture. His examination of language has been multifaceted, concentrating on both the constitution of semantic categories and the meaning and use of discursive forms, always revealing the intimate and complex link between language and being-in-the-world.

Education

BA Harvard University, 1962
MA Stanford University, 1963
Ph.D. Stanford University, 1967

Fieldwork

Arizona, Fort Apache Indian Reservation, USA, 1959 to present

Key Publications

(1970) *The Cibecue Apache*, New York: Holt, Rinehart, & Winston
(1979) *Portraits of 'the Whiteman': Linguistic Play and Cultural Symbols among the Western Apache*, Cambridge, New York: Cambridge University Press.
(1990) *Western Apache Language and Culture: Essays in Linguistic Anthropology*, Tucson: University of Arizona Press.
(1996) *Wisdom Sits in Places: Landscape and Language among the Western Apache*, Albuquerque: University of New Mexico Press.

ROBBYN SELLER

Bastide, Roger

b. 1 April 1898, Nîmes, France

d. 1974, Paris, France

As a young man, Bastide wrote poetry, an interest that he retained throughout his life. The turning point in his career was certainly his appointment in 1938 as professor of sociology at the University of São Paulo in Brazil, where he taught until 1953. During this 16-year period, he was able to investigate Brazilian culture in depth. He began a thorough study of African-Brazilian religions, studying the candomblé religion of Bahia in the Nordeste and becoming an initiate into Nagô (Yoruba) candomblé. He returned to France in 1954 where he taught at the École Pratique des Hautes Études and at the Sorbonne in Paris. He wrote his doctoral thesis on candomblé in 1957. When he first arrived in Brazil, Bastide had intended studying African-Brazilian religions as cases of syncretism and survivals of African religion imported to Brazil by slave ancestors, but he quickly dissociated himself from this position, dominant during this period. He realised that these cults had to be understood in the context of racial relations. He proposed analysing the 'African' logic underlying African-Brazilian religions by adopting the native point of view and taking into account the interrelationship between the sociological and the sacred dimensions of these ritual practices.

The sacred is a central concept in Bastide's sociology of religion. The sacred is the primordial and transcendent experience, external and superior to the individual. Bastide was intensely aware of the limits imposed on ethnology by Western ethnocentrism and Cartesianism. He argued for the importance of taking into account the symbolism, values, and history of non-Western societies. His sociology (or anthropology) of religion focused more on the individual than the group and aimed at situating the individuals in terms of symbolic construction and religious experience. Bastide formulated the concept of 'coupure' [fracture] to explain the permanence of African cults in Brazil, a predominantly Catholic, white, and oppressive society at the time. In that context, trance constitutes a catharsis for the oppressed individual who can avoid exposing contradictions implicit to co-existing cultures. The study of the interpenetration of civilisations and cultures constitutes a very important aspect of Bastide's work. In contrast to many of his contemporaries, he studied acculturation in a dynamic perspective. For Bastide, social change was inherent to any sociological context and he argued that it is essential to relate the field of acculturation studies to the domain of values, norms, symbols, and collective representations, as well as to the domain of structures, institutions, and social organisations. Accordingly,

Bastide distinguished between external causality, the action of the social milieu, and internal causality, which corresponds to values and collective as well as individual representations. Dual causality, Bastide argued, constitutes the two dimensions of a dialectical process central to sociological explanation of cultural mutations or social change. From this perspective, it is not the adoption of cultural traits that is important but rather the way in which these traits are modified by a new internal context. With dual causality, Bastide suggested, anthropologists are neither forced to adopt a strictly functionalist type of explanation nor to reduce everything to psychology or individual strategies. Bastide's discussion of colonial situations was always subtle and based on a comprehensive distinction between external and internal colonialism.

Bastide also wrote about psychoanalysis and social psychiatry in terms of how individuals adapt to cultural tradition and social status. His last studies were oriented towards the study of Africans, Haitians, and West Indians living in France. After his death in 1974, Bastide's work sunk into oblivion. However, during the last few years, particularly in France and Brazil, some researchers have been diffusing Bastide's work. They organised symposiums on his contribution to sociology and anthropology, and a new periodical, *Bastidiana*, has been published in France since 1993. The contemporary reader is struck by the actuality of Bastide's discussions of social change, identity quest, causality, racism, colonialism, occidental ethnocentrism, and the limits of a Cartesian ethnology, among the many topics he covered in his prolific career.

Education

Agrégé de philosophie, Sorbonne, Paris, 1924
Doctorat ès lettres, Sorbonne, Paris, 1957.

Fieldwork

Brazil, 1938–53

Key Publications

(1971) *African Civilisations in the New World* (*Les Amériques noires: Les civilisations africaines dans le Nouveau Monde*, 1967, trans. Peter Green, New York: Harper & Row Publishers.
(1972) *The Sociology of Mental Disorder* (*Sociologie des maladies mentales*, 1967), trans. Jean McNeil, New York: D. McKay Co.
(1973) *Applied Anthropology* (*Anthropologie appliquée*, 1971), trans. Alice L. Morton, London: Croom Helm.
(1978) *The African Religions of Brazil: Toward a Sociology of the Interpenetration of Civilizations* (*Les religions africaines du Brésil. Vers une sociologie des interpénétrations de civilisations*, 1960), trans. Helen Sebba, Baltimore: Johns Hopkins University Press.

ROBERT CRÉPEAU

Bateson, Gregory

b. 9 May 1904, Grantchester, Cambridgeshire, UK

d. 4 July 1980, San Francisco, California, USA

Through his efforts to elucidate a 'pervading unity' underlying all the world's phenomena, Gregory Bateson was to make incisive contributions to communication theory, family therapy, dolphin studies, and ecology. Only a non-specialist, interdisciplinary anthropology, he contended, could expect to treat the vast intricacies of social milieux.

Bateson studied anthropology at Cambridge with A.C. Haddon. He first undertook fieldwork among the Iatmul in New Guinea (where he met Margaret Mead, also fieldworking, with her then-husband, Reo Fortune). The fieldwork resulted in an unconventional ethnography, *Naven*, concerning cultural 'style' and form, village formation, initiation, and gender relations; it was also a disquisition on the perspectivalism or 'context' that underlies scientists' supposedly objective inductions. Bateson spoke of the 'ethos' (emotional tone) and 'eidos' (intellectual patterning) of Iatmul culture. He distinguished between 'centripetal' (complementary behaviour) and 'peripheral' (symmetrical behaviour) mechanisms of social organisation, and he described how 'schismogenesis' could occur if the cumulative reactions of people or groups to one another's behaviour was not counteracted.

The exponential curve of schismogenesis, and that of its opposite, 'mutual love', Bateson extrapolated, pertained not just to the Iatmul but to universal behaviours: evidenced in class war, the arms race, megalomania, and true love. The universality of feedback mechanisms, of circular or 'recursive' causal systems, in both biology and society, would be advocated by Bateson throughout his life, emphasising how informations 'continually enter into, become entangled with, and then re-enter the universe they describe' (Harries-Jones 1995: 3).

Indeed Bateson, who became one of the founders of the new science of cybernetics, advocated the universality of feedback mechanisms in both biology and society, throughout his life.

Before this, however, Bateson married Margaret Mead, in 1935, and set out with her for an ethnographic field trip to Bali. Researching into posture, gesture, painting, childhood relationships, play, and the 'schizophrenia' of trance, Bateson took some 25,000 photographs, some of which appeared in their joint publication, *Balinese Character* (1942).

Bateson and Mead separated in 1948. Bateson had by then exchanged St John's College Cambridge for the New School for Social Research, New York, and then Harvard University; now he was to make a further move, to the Langley Porter Clinic in San Francisco.

At Langley Porter, 1948–9, Bateson worked with psychiatrist Jurgen Ruesch and produced *Communication*, a book which argued that 'information' was synonymous with 'negative entropy' or order. The what and the how of reiterative communication provided the vital context within which 'behaviour' came to be learned.

Between 1949 and 1963, Bateson headed a research team at Veterans Adminstration Hospital, Palo Alto, further exploring communicative practices among dogs, otters, monkeys, and wolves, and among human alcoholics. Between 1954 and 1959, this came together in a psychotherapeutic project on schizophrenic communication that Bateson directed. Schizophrenics, it was surmised, display abnormal communicative behaviours that derive from their experiencing a repetitive pattern of paradoxical injunctions at some stage in their lives (the 'double-bind' theory).

From Palo Alto, Bateson moved to be associate director of the Communications Institute at St Thomas, the Virgin Islands, followed by an associate directorship at the Oceanic Institute, Waimanalo, Hawaii. For nine years he worked with John Lilly on various projects exploring dolphin communication. This culminated in his perhaps most influential work, *Steps to an Ecology of Mind*, a series of collected papers that span his career and work to disclose the patterns connecting different points of view in an ecological field. All living organisms contribute to the patterning within an ecosystem and its regeneration. Indeed, organism-plus-environment make a single recursive system of ongoing life, with parts and whole continuously modifying one another.

In 1976 Bateson was appointed to the Board of Regents of the University of California, a mark of the estimation in which he was now held within the American academy; but he resigned three years later in protest over the 'evil' of nuclear weapons. His final work, *Mind and Nature*, was a reflection on the patterns that connected human consciousness to much of the natural world.

In his combining of insights into culture and character formation, into the logic and paradoxes of perception and learning, into the recursive effects of messages in communicative circuits, and into the mathematics of progression and stability, Bateson was the most distinctive anthropologist.

Education

BA University of Cambridge, 1926
MA University of Cambridge, 1930

Fieldwork

New Britain and New Guinea, 1927–30
Bali, 1936–8
Langley Porter Clinic, University of California Medical School, San Francisco, 1948–9
Veterans Administration Hospital, Palo Alto, California, 1949–63
Communications Institute, St Thomas, Virgin Islands, 1963–4
Oceanic Institute, Waimanalo, Hawaii, 1965–72.

Key Publications

(1936) *Naven: A Survey of Problems Suggested by the Composite Picture of the Culture of a New Guinea Tribe Drawn from Three Points of View*, Cambridge, UK: Cambridge University Press (2nd edn Stanford University Press, 1958).

with Ruesch, Jurgen (1951) *Communication: The Social Matrix of Psychiatry*, New York: Norton.

(1972) *Steps to an Ecology of Mind: Collected Essays in Anthropology, Psychiatry, Evolution and Epistemology*, New York: Ballantine.

(1979) *Mind and Nature: A Necessary Unity*, New York: Dutton.

Further Reading

(1995) Harries-Jones, P. *A Recursive Vision*, Toronto: University of Toronto Press.

NIGEL RAPPORT

Bauman, Richard

b. 1940, New York City, USA

Richard Bauman's work is situated at the crossroads of folklore and linguistic anthropology; indeed, his theoretical contributions have aimed at bridging the two disciplines. While Bauman often investigated the more traditional objects of folklore studies, including oral narratives, he displaced the concern with oral literature from that of a 'thing', a static, decontextualised text, to an understanding of it as performance, fully integrated to the social and cultural lives of the performers and audience. In doing so, he has brought to anthropology the consideration of the poetic aspects of oral accounts rather than simply what they can reveal as cultural descriptions, and to folklore studies an integration of the oral text to the social context and relations that produce it. The notion of performance has permeated much of his work, reflecting a broader concern with the role of language in social life, and locates his work firmly within the framework of the ethnography of speaking approach. In this perspective, performance, as a form of communication, is seen as a socially recognised cultural practice, and an individual performance as a particular communicative, and thus interactive, event. Important to Bauman's theoretical insight is the link between the event being narrated and the event of narrating. The narrated event is recreated rather than repeated, and thus emerges through and within the performance, in what he has called the emergent quality of performance. In attending to the interactive aspects of performed narratives, Bauman has not ignored their formal attributes, locating them within, and linking them to, the context of performance.

While Bauman's early work considered performance as a one-time event, in his more recent work, for example research carried out in Mexico, the notion has acquired another dimension. Developing his earlier framework of the emergent quality of performance he regards theatrical production not as one final enactment but as a dynamic process that includes the way in which lines are distributed, practised, and rehearsed, as well as the interactions between those acting, directing, and observing, so that the whole production becomes a series of recontextualisations, none of which reproduces the text exactly as it was written. Rather, the text is creatively and interactively reconstituted with each new rendering. This work addresses an underlying concern, apparent in Bauman's other work, with the tension between the traditional, in this case the written text and the expectations for the performance faithfully to reproduce it, and creativity, which takes place as the enactments of the text that constantly, and contextually, transform it. Entwined with this is a notion of authority with regards to who controls the text and its output, and how the social relations that this authority involves are negotiated through performance.

Bauman's eclectic background – he has degrees in English, folklore studies, anthropology, and American civilisation – is made apparent in the richness of his theoretical approach and the diversity of his research. In addition to having carried out anthropological fieldwork in several regions, he has completed historical ethnolinguistic research on the Quakers that focused on their use of language, including rhetorical strategies and their own recorded meta-discourse about proper language use, as well as the significance of speech and silence in their relation to Quaker religious beliefs and practices. In this research, Bauman's focus goes beyond performance, but does not exclude it, situating it within the broader sociolinguistic scope of Quaker language use. Bauman's more recent theoretical work shows a concern with language ideology and authority that is nascent in this research.

Bauman has been very active in the academic community, sitting on several learned society executive committees and editorial boards. He was appointed distinguished professor at Indiana University in 1991, where he has been recognised for his teaching and mentoring.

Education

BA University of Michigan, 1961
MA Indiana University, 1962
MS University of Pennsylvania, 1968
Ph.D. University of Pennsylvania, 1968

Fieldwork

Ayrshire and Galloway, Scotland, 1962–3
Lunenburg County, Nova Scotia, 1970
East, Central, and West Texas, 1971–85
Guanajuato, Mexico, 1985–9
Historical research on the Quakers in England (1650–89) and Pennsylvania (1750–1800), and on medieval Iceland.

Key Publications

(1977) *Verbal Art as Performance*, Prospect Heights, IL: Waveland Press.
(1983) *Let Your Words Be Few: Speaking and Silence as Cultural Symbols among Seventeenth-Century Quakers*, Cambridge, UK: Cambridge University Press.
(1986) *Story, Performance, and Event: Contextual Studies of Oral Narrative*, Cambridge, UK: Cambridge University Press.
(1996) 'Transformations of the word in the production of Mexican festival drama', in Michael Silverstein and Greg Urban (eds) *Natural Histories of Discourse*, Chicago: University of Chicago Press.

ROBBYN SELLER

Baumann, Gerd

b. 1953, Aachen, Germany

Baumann's work examines cultural boundary crossings and collective cross-cultural competences. His Sudanese ethnography studied Nuba villagers engaging with the dominant Arab-Islamic culture and yet reinventing a sense of local integrity. The structuring of data in an innovative way was of ethnographic importance: in three 'tours' of village life, all domains, from economics to aesthetics, were shown in succession as Sudanese phenomena, local phenomena, and mutually translatable social realities. This translatability held the key to a successful 'local reintegration' in the face of 'national integration'.

The dialectic of self and other was explored

anew in London's multi-ethnic suburb Southall. Instead of focusing on a one-community study, Baumann analysed multiethnic Southall as a single social field. 'Ethnic' or 'cultural communities', which were apparently bounded, interacted with each other to the point of establishing a 'demotic discourse', to rival and relativise the politically dominant discourse of boundedness. The conceptions of 'culture' and 'community' were thus the pivotal points of Southall-Londoners contesting their identities and differences.

Baumann's recent work has reanalysed religious syncretisation, cross-community rituals, aesthetic crossovers, pluricultural ideas about kinship and cross-cultural convergences. His current work focuses on nation-state civil cultures and on a structuralist approach to cognitive 'grammars of alterity'.

Education

Cand.phil. University of Cologne, 1975
Ph.D. Queen's University of Belfast, 1980

Fieldwork

Nuba Moutains, Sudan, 1976, 1978–9
Southall, London, 1986–91

Key Publications

(1996) *Contesting Culture. Discourses of Identity in Multi-Ethnic London*, Cambridge, UK: Cambridge University Press.
(1999) *The Multicultural Riddle. Re-Thinking National, Ethnic and Religious Identities*, New York and London: Routledge.

WERNER SCHIFFAUER

Baxter, P.T.W.

b. 1925, Leamington Spa, UK

Two themes have dominated the work of Paul Baxter, both traceable to the impact of his first fieldwork among the Borana of northern Kenya: the first is an attempt to understand the functioning of pastoralism, in particular, East African pastoral societies; the second a fascination with the culture of the Oromo peoples of both Kenya and Ethiopia. The Borana ethnography obliged Baxter to grapple with the complexity of their generation-grading system. This was the focus of his doctoral thesis and his analysis there, and, in subsequent publications, has provided a benchmark for all later discussions of the phenomenon. He has not been content, however, to document only worlds that are on the wane. His own observations of the gradual destruction of the Borana way of life have led him to publish widely on the effects of sedentarisation and other pastoral development projects on the lives of East African pastoralists. These pieces are based on solid anthropological understanding but he uses this understanding to point out to policy-makers some of the unintended and deleterious consequences of their schemes. This commitment to the subjects of his research has also engaged Baxter in occasionally controversial support for the Oromo peoples of Ethiopia in their struggles with a series of unsympathetic and exploitative governments. Complementing this political commitment have been Baxter's sensitive interpretations of Oromo expressive culture, especially poetry and song.

Education

BA University of Cambridge, 1949
B.Litt. University of Oxford, 1951
D.Phil. University of Oxford, 1954

Fieldwork

Kenya, 1951–3
Uganda, 1954–5
Ghana, 1956–61
Ethiopia, 1968–9

Key Publications

(1978) *Age, Generation and Time*, London: C. Hurst.
(1990) *Property, Poverty, and People*, Manchester: University of Manchester International Development Centre.

HECTOR BLACKHURST

Beals, Alan R.

b. 24 January 1928, Oakland, California, USA

During his graduate studies, Alan R. Beals conducted studies of a small California agricultural settlement and an American B-29 bomber crew. His primary contributions, however, have been to the study of rural and peri-urban villages in south India. Beals went beyond the traditional study of a single village to examine similarities and differences among three different villages and how they were embedded in regional economic and political systems. One village he studied was a short distance from the city of Bangalore, and had been subject to urbanising and modernising influences for more than a century. Two other villages were, at the time of his first visits, more remote, but later became drawn into relationships with cities at a distance. Beals's repeated trips to south India allowed him to produce detailed accounts of changes in the villages produced by government policies, rural–urban migration, and economic engagement with the wider world.

One focus of his south Indian work was the development and resolution of conflict, a subject he explored more theoretically and comparatively in joint publications with Bernard J. Siegel. They argued that 'strains', or aspects of cultural systems in which uncertainties could lead to conflict, and 'stresses', or new external influences, were factors in the development of 'pervasive' or persistent factionalism. They tried to escape functionalist approaches that gave conflict a positive role in maintaining social systems, arguing that the cost or benefit of conflict had to be empirically determined in each case.

Beals also produced an analysis of the three villages based on ecology, broadly conceived as the study of interrelationships among land, agriculture, society, and culture. He did not argue for a simple determination of culture or society by the physical environment. Instead, he stressed the historical development of each village and gave 'world view', or ideas about the nature and proper functioning of the universe, the lion's share of credit for shaping south Indian civilisation.

Beals was the primary author of an undergraduate textbook, *Culture in Process*, which maintained that cultural traditions were the outcome of multiple decisions made by the members of a group. In other writing for students, he provided rich ethnographic descriptions that stressed the need for individuals to master their cultural and social settings, and wrote about the fieldwork encounter with openness, humour, and humility.

Education

BA University of California, Los Angeles, 1948
Ph.D. University of California, Berkeley, 1954

Fieldwork

Tulelake, California, 1949, 1988
Randolph Air Force Base, Texas, 1951–2
Karnataka, India, 1952–3, 1958–60, 1965–6
Chiapas, Mexico, 1981–2
Yucatan Peninsula, Mexico, 1992

Key Publications

with Siegel, Bernard J. (1966) *Divisiveness and Social Conflict: An Anthropological Approach*, Stanford: Stanford University Press.
(1974) *Village Life in South India: Cultural Design and Environmental Variation*, Chicago: Aldine.
(1979) *Culture in Process*, third edn, New York: Holt, Rinehart & Winston.
(1980) *Gopalpur: A South Indian Village*, fieldwork edn, New York: Holt, Rinehart & Winston.

MARGARET MEIBOHM

Beckett, Jeremy

b. 1931, Northwood, Middlesex, UK

Jeremy Beckett is known primarily for his ethnographic work with Torres Strait Islanders and with Aboriginal people living in far-west New South Wales. In all his work Beckett emphasises the importance of recognising political and economic relationships grounding the forms of life he has focused on while not losing sight of the importance of understanding how people make sense of their lives. In his New South Wales work he focused first on Aboriginal peoples' connections with the pastoral industry. This led to a series of important articles focusing on the accommodations that Aboriginal people made to European arrival and the encroaching pastoral industry. As well as documenting and analysing the changing social relations in this part of New South Wales, Beckett has continued to work with some of the people he first met long ago. This has resulted in the publication of several life histories and his exploration of this as a genre of Aboriginal narrative. In his later work, carried out in Torres Straits, Beckett retained his interest in exploring a local cultural scene as part of a complex bundle of relations he examined as welfare colonialism. His research here was fundamental in the Islanders' quest for legal recognition of the existence of their ownership (native title) in the Torres Strait, and subsequently the recognition of native title on the mainland of Australia. Beckett's published work is known for its clarity of theoretical insight and for the tightness of his ethnographic presentation.

Education

BA (Hons) University College London, 1954
MA Australian National University, 1958
Ph.D. Australian National University, 1964

Fieldwork

Western New South Wales, 1956 ongoing
Torres Straits, 1958 ongoing
Philippines and Pacific Islands for short periods

Key Publications

(1987) *Torres Strait Islanders*, Cambridge, UK: Cambridge University Press.
(ed.) (1988) *Past and Present*, Canberra: AIATSIS Press.

PHILIP MOORE

Beidelman, T.O.

b. 1931, USA

US- and British-trained, Thomas Owen Beidelman has contributed a unique and prolific body of work to both anthropological traditions. Often depicted as structuralist, his work engages the examination of native symbolic categories, moral ideologies, and values, and is directly rooted in classic social theory – Mauss, Hertz, Weber, Simmel, Durkheim – rather than in the abstractions of a Lévi-Straussian approach. Beidelman's work is firmly grounded in history, ethnographically rich, and theoretically complex.

T.O. Beidelman began his undergraduate career as a psychology major at the University of Illinois, where he came under the influence of Oscar Lewis, who instilled in him an interest in India that later waned. After beginning graduate work at Berkeley, Beidelman was drafted into the army. The USA was then involved in the Korean War, and military service led him to Korea and Japan, where he became further invested in pursuing the study of culture.

After discharge, Beidelman returned to Illinois. The anthropology faculty there had grown with the recruitment, among others, of Edward Winter, a Harvard-trained Africanist who had spent time at the London School of Economics and Oxford. Beidelman ('Marking time: becoming an anthropologist', 1998) has publicly acknowledged Winter's influence, since it was he who introduced the young graduate student to classical social theory, contemporary British anthropology, and sociology. This led Beidelman to consider the ties between anthropology, sociology, and history, the hallmark of his work, distancing him from a narrowly construed Boasian tradition.

Winter's influence is also evident in Beidelman's decision to leave Illinois to pursue graduate studies at Oxford, and to work in East Africa. His publications on the Kaguru are extensive, including hundreds of articles and two book-length ethnographies (1986, 1997), focusing mostly on cosmology and ritual. In 1987, *Moral Imagination in Kaguru Modes of Thought* (1986) won the prestigious Herskovitz Award from the African Studies Association. Beidelman has published significant historical works: on Robertson Smith's contributions to the sociology of religion (1974) and a Weberian analysis of missionary activity in Africa (1982). He has also worked on the anthropology of classical Greece and of New York City landmarking.

Beidelman began his teaching career at Harvard, soon moving to a tenured position at Duke. In 1965, John Middleton recruited him to the anthropology department at New York University, where he has been consistently acknowledged as an inspiring instructor.

Education

BA University of Illinois, Champaign-Urbana, 1953
M.A. University of Illinois, Champaign-Urbana, 1956
D.Phil. University of Oxford, 1961

Fieldwork

Kaguru, Ngulu, and Baraguyo peoples of Tanzania, 1957–8, 1961–3, 1966, 1967, 1975, 1976

Key Publications

(1974) *W. Robertson Smith and the Sociological Study of Religion*, Chicago: The University of Chicago Press.
(1982) *Colonial Evangelism: A Socio-Historic Study of an East African Mission at the Grassroots*, Bloomington: Indiana University Press.
(1986) *Moral Imagination in Kaguru Modes of Thought*, Bloomington: Indiana University Press.
(1997) *The Cool Knife: Metaphors of Gender, Sexuality and Moral Education in Kaguru Initiation Ritual*, Washington: Smithsonian Institution Press.

VILMA SANTIAGO-IRIZARRY

Bell, Diane

b. 11 June 1943, Melbourne, Australia

Diane Bell is a pioneering feminist ethnographer, prolific writer, public intellectual, and iconoclastic contributor to anthropology in and of Australia. Her scholarly contributions focus on issues of global significance: gender, race, religion, ethics, human rights, and social justice.

In the early 1980s Diane Bell's Warrabri ethnography opened new vistas on the cultural landscape between *jilimi* (women's camp), ceremonial grounds, and *jukurrpa* (Dreaming). Bell concluded that desert women have a central position in their society and religious responsibilities all their own. What was first received as a provocative and controversial conclusion is now accepted as a standard premise of Australian anthropology.

Bell applied her interest in indigenous rights in the first half of the 1980s. She was prominent amongst those who sought to professionalise Australian anthropology. In 1985–6 she stepped up to the challenge that was served by the 'Warumungu case' where courts' rights to anthropologists' field materials was first defined.

In 1986 Diane Bell led a team project that explored Australian society through stories about significant material objects in the lives of three and more generations of women.

In 1989 Bell published an article with her close friend and collaborator, Topsy Napurrula Nelson. They argued that speaking of rape within Aboriginal communities was 'everybody's business'. Prominent indigenous scholars vehemently disagreed. By 2002 the position that sexual violence in Aboriginal communities requires addressing was echoed by prominent Aboriginal men, women, policy-makers, and anthropologists.

Since the 1990s Bell has held senior academic positions in the USA. In 1996 she was diverted from researching her 'New Age' project to work on another 'hard' Australian issue. Ngarrindjeri women's beliefs were at the center of a controversy about whether the traditions of Aboriginal people in the 'settled south' should count at law like those in the 'outback'.

At the end of that landmark ethnography Bell called on Australians to pursue their 'race debate' openly and with courage, vision, and leadership. She called for it to include the enunciation and honouring of principles by which all Australians might live together with decency and fairness.

This is the essence of Diane Bell and her work: ethnographically founded and outspoken leadership on difficult social and cultural issues. It is why Bell will continue to be a controversial and significant figure in Australia and its anthropology, and beyond these confines a scholar and ethnographer of international significance.

Education

TPTC Frankston Teachers' College, 1961
BA (Hons) Monash University, 1975
Ph.D. Australian National University, 1981

Fieldwork

Warrabri, central Australia, 1976–80
Across the Northern Territory, 1980–8
All states of Australia, 1986–7
New Age movement, USA, 1993–4
Mescalero, New Mexico, summer 1994
South Australia, 1996–8

Key Publications

with Ditton, Pam (1984 [1980]) *Law: The Old and the New*, Canberra: Aboriginal History.
(1983) *Daughters of the Dreaming*, Melbourne: McPhee Gribble (second edn. 1993, Sydney: Allen & Unwin; third edn 2002, Melbourne: Spinifex Press).
(1987) *Generations: Grandmothers, Mothers and Daughters*, Fitzroy, Victoria: McPhee Gribble/ Penguin Books.
(1998) *Ngarrindjeri Wurruwarrin: A World That Is, Was, and Will Be*, Melbourne: Spinifex Press.

DEANE FERGIE

Benedict, Ruth

b. 5 June 1887, New York State, USA

d. 17 September 1948, New York City, USA

For Ruth Benedict, anthropology provided a solution for a childless marriage and restlessness of spirit. She had been a social worker and schoolteacher, explored feminist biography, and written poetry under the pseudonym of Anne Singleton before, in 1919, at the new School for Social Research, she discovered anthropology through Alexander Goldenweiser and Elsie Clews Parsons. Parsons introduced her to Franz Boas at Columbia, and he invited her to enter the graduate programme there. Boas, Edward Sapir, and Margaret Mead became her role models and friends.

Benedict's dissertation on the vision quest in North America compared the distribution of traits in various tribes, foreshadowing her later explication of pattern and integration according to what Sapir called the 'feeling-tone' of each culture. Although Benedict was not primarily a fieldworker, she was deeply impressed by the difference in style of the Plains and the Pueblos, enshrining this contrast as Dionysian versus Apollonian. In *Patterns of Culture* (1934), she added two additional extreme cases of integrated cultural patterns: the megalomania of the Kwakiutl as described by Boas and the paranoid schizophrenia of the Dobuans as presented by Mead's then-husband, Reo Fortune. Although Benedict borrowed these terms from abnormal psychology, she was most intrigued by the normality within a particular cultural context of patterns that would have been dysfunctional in her own society. Cultural relativism in this sense became the keynote of her anthropology and provided her with a sense of validation and personal freedom. Culture was, for her, personality writ large. The life history became a favored method of testing the working out of cultural patterns in individual lives.

Benedict's alienation from the mainstream of American society between the two world wars provided her with a standpoint for critique in terms of the documentation of alternative lifeways. Her anthropology was humanistic, more literary than that of most contemporaries (therefore accessible to a literate but non-professional American public), and psychological in the sense of its profound disquiet about the effect of cultural constraints on the development and self-fulfilment of the individual.

Anthropology was a discipline committed to solving the problems of the real world. *Race, Science, and Politics* (1940) offered a Boasian commentary on the relevance of cross-cultural perspective to the issues confronting a war-torn world emerging from a debilitating Depression. Along with other Boasians, Benedict took a strong stance against racism in response to Nazi Germany.

During the Second World War, Benedict worked for the Office of War Information on overseas intelligence. Anthropology helped to break down the characteristic isolationism of an American society under conditions of rapid social change. *The Chrysanthemum and the Sword* (1946) was written in the hope of making Japanese society intelligible to American policy-makers and the American public so that post-war policy would be humane, culturally appropriate, and respectful of the complexity and beauty of Japanese tradition. Along with Margaret Mead, Rhoda Metraux, and others, Benedict directed Columbia's post-war research programme on contemporary cultures, emphasising those of relevance to American overseas interests. Benedict argued that the anthropologist could study 'culture at a distance'. Her Japanese work involved some interviews with Japanese Americans of various generations but she never visited Japan, using records from literature and history to uncover the cultural pattern underlying contemporary behaviour. Above all, what she called 'multi-cultural awareness', the capacity to think anthropologically, provided a path through the difficult decisions of the post-war period.

Her later work, much of it remaining unpublished at the time of her death, focused on the concept of synergy, arguing that individual choice could transcend cultural determinism, allowing movement 'beyond cultural relativism' to cultural critique of the society that had produced anthropology. Benedict's cultural relativism was linked intimately to informed value judgement based on a prior understanding of opposed cultural patterns in their own terms.

Benedict spent her entire professional life at Columbia University, although she held no formal position until after her marriage disintegrated. She began teaching in 1923 but was promoted to professor only in 1948, just before her death. She was at the time president of the American Anthropological Association. Many had expected that Benedict would succeed Boas as chair of the Columbia Department in 1936, but the administration, eager to break the stranglehold of Boas's immediate circle of students and former students, appointed Ralph Linton instead. The humanistic tradition in which Benedict pioneered persisted through the positivism of the post-war period and has recently undergone a renaissance.

Education

BA Vasser College, 1909
Ph.D. Columbia University, 1923

Fieldwork

Serrano Indians, 1922
Zuni Pueblo, 1924, 1925, 1927

Cochiti Pueblo, 1927
Pima, 1927
Apache, 1931
Blackfoot, 1939

Key Publications

(1934) 'Anthropology and the abnormal', *Journal of Normal and Abnormal Psychology* 10: 59–82.
(1934) *Patterns of Culture*, Boston: Houghton Mifflin.
(1946) *The Chrysanthemum and the Sword: Patterns of Japanese Culture*, Boston: Houghton Mifflin
(1959) *An Anthropologist at Work: Writings of Ruth Benedict*, ed. Margaret Mead, Boston: Houghton Mifflin.

REGNA DARNELL

Berlin, Brent

b. 1936, Pampa, Texas, USA

Brent Berlin began his career in the Central Highlands of Chiapas, Mexico, in 1960, with a dissertation that analysed the implicit semantic logic of the Tzeltal Mayan system of numeral classifiers. This interest in ethnosemantics led directly to his next and perhaps most important research effort, a collaborative investigation of the conceptual bases of Tzeltal botany with Dennis Breedlove and Peter Raven. Their *Principles of Tzeltal Plant Classification* (1974) motivated a statement of 'general principles of folk biological classification and nomenclature', which remains today the canonical theoretical framework for the analysis of ethnobiological vocabularies, despite a variety of theoretical and empirical challenges. Berlin's *Ethnobiological Classification* (1992) reviews two decades of ethnobiological research inspired by his Tzeltal work. What seems established beyond dispute is Berlin's claim that folk biologists 'discover' real patterns in nature rather than inventing 'natures', as postmodern theorists would argue. The regularities evident in folk biological classification systems around the world, and the close correspon-

dence of 'folk generic' taxa and of the taxonomic structure of these systems to modern biosystematics, affirms the central role of evolved cognitive processes in constructing our images of the natural environment.

Curiously, Berlin is probably best known not for his ethnobiological contributions but for his collaboration with Paul Kay in *Basic Color Terms* (1969), developed as a graduate seminar project at the University of California at Berkeley, where Berlin taught from 1966–4. Berlin and Kay argued that a functionally specific core set of basic color terms are named in a strict implicational order across languages, while the referential cores of named basic color terms map response patterns in the brain.

In the 1970s Berlin joined with his wife, Elois Ann Berlin, in a decade-long field investigation of the ethnobiology and medical anthropology of the Aguaruna Jívaro in northeastern Peru, while from the mid-1980s until the present they have devoted their energies to an ambitious regional study of the ethnomedical and medicinal ethnobotanical knowledge of some twenty Tzeltal and Tzotzil communities in the Central Highlands of Chiapas.

While Berlin's work has not been without controversy, his contributions as a master fieldworker, seminal theorist, and leader in the development of truly co-operative research programmes engaging scholars and indigenous peoples has been widely recognised. He was elected to the National Academy of Sciences in 1980 and awarded the Fyssen Foundation Prize in 2000.

Education

BA University of Oklahoma, 1959
MA Stanford University, 1960
Ph.D. Stanford University, 1964

Fieldwork

Tzeltal Maya, Chiapas, Mexico, 1960s
Aguaruna Jívaro, Upper Marañon River, Peru, 1970s

Tzeltal and Tzotzil Maya, Chiapas, Mexico, 1980s–present

Key Publications

(1968) *Tzeltal Numeral Classifiers: A Study in Ethnographic Semantics*, The Hague: Janua Linguarum.

with Kay, Paul (1969) *Basic Color Terms: Their Universality and Evolution*, Berkeley: University of California Press,

with Breedlove, Dennis and Raven, Peter (1974) *Principles of Tzeltal Plant Classification; An Introduction to the Botanical Ethnography of a Mayan-Speaking People of Highland Chiapas*, New York and London: Academic Press.

(1992) *Ethnobiological Classification*, Princeton, NJ: Princeton University Press.

EUGENE HUNN

Bernard, H. Russell

b. 1940, New York, USA

H. Russell Bernard has made major contributions to cultural anthropology across a broad range of topics over an almost 40-year span. He has published widely in such areas as anthropological linguistics, technology, and social change, native ethnography, research methods in cultural anthropology, text analysis, and social network analysis. His work involves a unique blend of qualitative and quantitative approaches best exemplified by his work on native ethnographies for the former and estimates of hard-to-count populations for the latter.

In a series of articles Bernard and colleagues questioned the conventional practice of using informant's verbal reports of behaviour as a proxy for actual behaviour. This series stimulated a debate, particularly in the area of social network analysis, which led to a number of important findings in the area of the validity of retrospective data. Earlier work on social networks included studies of group dynamics in such social settings as crews on an ocean-going research vessel and social relations among prisoners, leading to important insights on the nature of human communications under stress and formal methodological developments on means for determining social groups. Yet other investigations of social networks looked into ways of estimating the size of an individual's personal network, particularly in various cross-cultural settings. Based on this earlier work on personal network size, Bernard and colleagues developed innovative methods for estimating the size of hard-to-count event populations. Such event populations included, for example, the number of HIV positive people, rapes, and homeless in the USA.

A major contribution to the field of anthropology lies in Bernard's writings on and teaching of anthropological methods. His books on anthropological and social science research methods and his editorship of several important anthropological journals, most recently *Field Methods*, have been critically important in providing undergraduates, graduate students, faculty, and practitioners alike with methodological training. Additionally, his involvement in National Science Foundation-supported institutes over the last twenty years has provided methodological training to both anthropological faculty and graduate students, further enhancing the advancement of methodological knowledge and applications in cultural anthropology.

Education

BA Queens College, 1961
MA University of Illinois, 1963
Ph.D. University of Illinois, 1968

Fieldwork

Island of Kalymnos, Greece, 1964–5; 1996; 2001
Athens, Greece, 1969–70
Island of Naxos, Greece, summers of 1975, 1976, and 1977
Crete, September–November 1990
Mezquital Valley, Mexico, summers of 1962,

1967, 1968, 1971; 2 months each in 1969 and 1974

Tarpon Springs, Florida, USA, 7 months between 1963–4

Robert F. Kennedy Correction Center, West Virginia, USA, during 1972–4

Scripps Institution of Oceanography, San Diego, USA, January–September 1972

Key Publications

(1973) 'On the social structure of an ocean-going research vessel and other important things', *Social Science Research* 2: 145–84.

(1988) *Research Methods in Cultural Anthropology*, Newbury Park: Sage Publications.

(1989) *Native Ethnography: A Mexican Indian Describes His Culture*, Newbury Park: Sage Publications.

(1989) 'Estimating the size of an average personal network and of an event population', in M. Kochen (ed.) *The Small World*, Norwood, NJ: Ablex Publishing.

JEFFREY C. JOHNSON

Berndt, Catherine Helen

b. 8 May 1918, Auckland, New Zealand

d. 12 May 1994, Perth, Western Australia

Catherine Helen Berndt's (née Webb) outstanding contribution to knowledge of Aboriginal societies in Australia spanned a career of over six decades. She was raised in Auckland, New Zealand; the eldest daughter of a family that included proudly a Maori ancestry. Catherine had long been interested in the worlds of others. Her early interest in the history of her own family was sparked by the lost knowledge of Gaelic among its members, and issues arising from Scots interaction with the English.

Completing a classics degree at Victoria College, Wellington, she was influenced by her uncle, Reo Fortune, to study in Dunedin under H.D. Skinner at the University College of Otago. Unable to offer a higher degree in anthropology in New Zealand at that time, Skinner encouraged her to travel overseas to study for her MA under A.P. Elkin at the University of Sydney. And it was there, in Elkin's study on their second day at university, that Catherine met Ronald Berndt, her future husband (see Berndt, Ronald). It is not possible to refer to the career of one without the other; throughout her professional life, she worked in very close collaboration with her husband.

Known best for her social anthropological research in Aboriginal Australia and Papua New Guinea, her writings on the changing status of Aboriginal women and within the arena of oral literature have, among other themes, contributed immensely to contemporary intellectual debate.

In the course of her shared career with Ronald, they published many books together. More particularly, though, Catherine's own list of publications is formidable. These include *Women's Changing Ceremonies in Northern Australia* (1950), 'Women and the "secret life"' (1965), 'Monsoon and honey wind' (1970), 'Digging sticks and spears' (1970), and 'Aboriginal women and the notion of the "marginal man"' (1979). Her books for children gave her particular delight; the most successful include *Pheasant and Kingfisher* (1987), *When the World Was New* (1988), *This Is Still Rainbow Snake Country* (1988), and *Humans and Other Beings* (1989).

Catherine's academic and teaching career was equally extensive. In 1950 she received the Percy Smith Medal from the University of Otago, and she and Ronald Berndt both held travel grants from the Indian University Grants Commission, and in 1968 were funded by the Wenner–Gren Foundation to participate in the International Congress of Ethnological Sciences in Japan. In 1980 she received the New South Wales Premier's Special Children's Book Award, with medal, for *Land of the Rainbow Snake* (1979). In 1982 she was only the seventh woman to be elected a fellow in the Academy of the Social Sciences in Australia.

Education

BA University of New Zealand, 1939
Certificate of Proficiency – Anthropology, University of New Zealand, 1940
Diploma of Anthropology, University of Sydney, 1943
MA University of Sydney, 1949
Ph.D. London School of Economics, 1955

Fieldwork

Ooldea, South Australia, 1939, 1940–1
Murray Bridge, South Australia, 1941–3
Birrundudu, north-central Northern Territory, Australia, 1945–6
Arnhem Land, Australia, 1946–79
Kainantu, Eastern Highlands, Papua New Guinea, 1951–3
Balgo Hills, Western Desert, Western Australia, 1957–81

Key Publications

with Berndt, R.M. (1945) *A Preliminary Report on Fieldwork in the Ooldea Region, Western South Australia*, Sydney: Australian National Research Council.
(1950) *Women's Changing Ceremonies in Northern Australia*, Paris: L'Homme.
with Berndt, R.M. (1964) *The World of the First Australians*, Sydney: Ure Smith.
with Berndt, R.M. and Stanton, J.E. (1993) *A World That Was: The Yaraldi of the Murray River and The Lakes, South Australia*, Melbourne: Melbourne University Press.

JOHN E. STANTON

Berndt, Ronald Murray

b. 14 July 1916, Adelaide, South Australia

d. 2 May 1990, Perth, Western Australia

Ronald M. Berndt's outstanding contribution to knowledge of Aboriginal societies in Australia spanned a career of six decades. Throughout his professional life, he worked in close collaboration with his wife Catherine (see Berndt, Catherine), without whom his contribution would have been undoubtedly diminished.

Although his fascination with anthropology began in childhood, it was in his first professional appointment in 1939, as a honorary ethnologist at the South Australian Museum that he had a formal linkage. Here, he met an Aboriginal man, Albert Karloan, who was to become a crucial collaborator and mentor in his first research, ultimately published as *A World That Was* (1993). His participation in a scientific expedition to Ooldea, on the Trans-Australian Line, encouraged him to obtain formal training in the discipline and, in 1940, he commenced studies at the University of Sydney under A.P. Elkin. One of his fellow students was to become his wife.

They subsequently returned to Ooldea for a year's fieldwork that yielded a rich corpus of ethnographic material on the classical Aboriginal culture of the region. Their *A Preliminary Report on Fieldwork in the Ooldea Region, Western South Australia* (1945) remains a seminal work for its treatment of contemporary adaptive strategies. Elkin was to send them, in 1944, to investigate reports of atrocious Aboriginal labour conditions on pastoral stations in the Northern Territory; their findings were later published as *End of an Era: Aboriginal Labour in the Northern Territory* (1987).

Ronald Berndt's major ethnographic focus was, however, in Arnhem Land, Northern Territory. It was here that he and his wife conducted detailed research on mythology, ritual, and song over a period of forty years. Several major monographs resulted, including *Kunapipi* (1951), *Djanggawul* (1952), *An Adjustment Movement in Arnhem Land* (1962), and *Love Songs of Arnhem Land* (1976).

The Berndts also conducted research during 1951–3 in the Eastern Highlands of Papua New Guinea, yielding a wealth of material for their respective doctoral dissertations. These were written at the London School of Economics, under the supervision of Raymond Firth, and Ronald's thesis was subsequently published as *Excess and Restraint* (1962).

After travelling to North American univer-

sities on a Carnegie Fellowship, Ronald Berndt
was offered in 1956 a senior lectureship in
anthropology at the University of Western
Australia, with the challenge of establishing
the discipline there; in 1959 he was promoted
to reader, and appointed foundation professor
of anthropology in 1963. He remained as head
of the department until shortly before his
retirement in 1981. Still active, Berndt also
oversaw the establishment of the Museum of
Anthropology to house their own unsurpassed
collections, among others.

Ronald shared his enthusiasm and passion
for anthropology, and in particular Aboriginal
anthropology, as an enlightened disciplinary
insight. He promoted an active involvement in
contemporary issues, and this was reflected in
his own capacious commitment to a public
role for anthropology. He played a crucial role
in promoting Aboriginal-initiated research and
the encouragement of Aboriginal participation
within the discipline.

Education

Dip.anthrop. University of Sydney, 1943
BA University of Sydney, 1950
MA University of Sydney, 1951
Ph.D. London School of Economics, 1955

Fieldwork

Ooldea, South Australia, 1939, 1940–1
Murray Bridge, South Australia, 1941–3
Birrundudu, north-central Northern Territory,
  Australia, 1945–6
Arnhem Land, Australia, 1946–79
Kainantu, Eastern Highlands, Papua New
  Guinea, 1951–3
Balgo Hills, Western Desert, Western Australia,
  1957–81

Key Publications

with Berndt, C.H. (1945) *A Preliminary Report on
  Fieldwork in the Ooldea Region, Western South
  Australia*, Sydney: Australian National Re-
  search Council (Oceania Bound Offprint).

(1951) *Kunapipi: A Study of an Australian Aboriginal
  Religious Cult*, Melbourne: Cheshire.
with Berndt, C.H. (1964) *The World of the First
  Australians*, Sydney: Ure Smith.
with Berndt, C.H. and Stanton, J.E. (1993) *A
  World That Was: The Yaraldi of the Murray River and
  The Lakes, South Australia*, Melbourne: Mel-
  bourne University Press.

JOHN E. STANTON

Berreman, Gerald R.

b. 1930, Oregon, USA

Gerald Berreman's interests have primarily
focused on comparative social inequality and
related subjects including human rights, environmental issues and movements, anthropological ethics, and ethnographic methods.
Using a social interactionist theoretical approach that merges aspects of symbolic
interactionism, ethnomethodology, and practice theory, Berreman focuses on the ways in
which cognition, beliefs, and values articulate
with power and behaviour. This approach and
accompanying methods have grounded his 40-
year longitudinal study of caste, gender, class,
and environment in India, starting with his
doctoral study of a Garhwal village (Sirkanda)
in the Himalayas, which produced an ethnographic study widely recognised as a classic in
the field. Berreman also pursued a broad
understanding through a comparative study
of ethnic diversity and inequality and their
impact in a more anonymous urban setting in
work conducted in a city (Dehra Dun) located
on an adjacent plain in the Himalayan foothills.

Berreman's most intensive work related to
environmental and development issues, has
been carried out in India and Nepal, where he
has studied the response to development by
local inhabitants, administrators, and other
powerful outsiders particularly where plans
have given rise to local movements, including
the well-known Chipko grassroots environmental movement.

Berreman's early field experience in a

small-scale society in an Aleutian village fostered a continuing interest in such societies, led to his interest and participation in the 'hunter-gatherer debate', and grounded his later role as an outspoken participant in the debunking of the Tasaday hoax in the 1970s–1980 where he raised central questions regarding the lifestyle, technology, and language of a group claimed as a stone age tribe found living in the Philippines.

Berreman's activist position is apparent in his work in applied anthropology, and his advocacy of the 'politics of truth' that in tandem with his research interests have consistently been combined with a commitment to positions that have an articulated ethical grounding. In 1972 he co-authored the American Anthropological Association's 'Principles of Professional Responsibility'. He has participated throughout his career in the statement and discussion of anthropological ethics and in public and professional advocacy for human rights including the rights of populations with whom anthropologists work and concomitant responsibilities of anthropologists.

Education

BA University of Oregon, 1952
MA University of Oregon, 1953
Ph.D. Cornell University, 1959

Fieldwork

Aleutian Islands, summer 1952, summer 1962
India 1957–8, 1968–9, winter 1972, December 1978–January 1979, 1981–2, December 1989–January 1990, March 1994
Nepal, January–July 1994, December 1996–January 1997
India and Nepal, December 1995–January 1996
Fiji, July–August 1991

Key Publications

(1999) 'Seeking social justice: ethnic politics in India, the United States and Japan', in Plenary Lectures: Second International Human Rights Seminar, 1998, Osaka, Japan: Kansai University

(1997) Hindus of the Himalayas: Ethnography and Change, second edn, London: Oxford University Press.

(1991) 'The Incredible Tasaday', Cultural Survival Quarterly 15, 1: 2–45.

(1991) 'Ethics versus realism in anthropology', in C. Fluehr-Lobban (ed.) Ethics and the Profession of Anthropology, Philadelphia: University of Pennsylvania Press.

SUSAN R. TRENCHER

Beteille, André

b. 1935, Calcutta, India

Until the 1950s Indian anthropology was defined mainly by colonial tribal studies. André Beteille's preoccupation with caste polity grew from a resolve to focus, instead, on Indian society, its politics, social stratification, and civic rights. In addition, there is, he observed, a dominant tendency to adopt a structural view of India as against the historical view of Western civilisation; the emphasis being on differences and contrast; the 'gaze' 'on ritual ceremony and religious thought away from technology, politics and law'.

His tutelage under M.N. Srinivas followed the orthodox British anthropological tradition of A. R. Radcliffe-Brown preferring 'structure' to 'culture'. However, Beteille's perception of social structure was mainly influenced by Emile Durkheim's concept of social morphology and collective representations, defining social structure in terms of the enduring groups in society, their arrangements, and their relationships.

He was deeply critical of Louis Dumont's thesis that India can be regarded as an archetype of hierarchy. He argued that regional political processes operate at different levels of state, institution, and locality. Thus, collective identities are important in the distribution process and caste identities did not remain the same from one political context to another, or from one territory to another. The caste system has the structural properties of segmentary systems, several levels of differentiation and styles of life. Each segment comprises certain diacritical distinctions and syncretic values that distinguish it from other segments, and syncretic unity is seen in terms of the whole, internal solidarity. The segments of different orders assume importance at different levels of the political system while the political process plays a pivotal part in bringing about changes in the nature of segmentation in the caste system. The fusion of political context is likely to affect other aspects of intercaste relations such as commensality and intermarriage.

Beteille stated that while the West is allowed to claim its history, India is regarded as the static, unchanging Vedic East. Additionally, hierarchy is a theological, Christian concept rather than a sociological notion. This led him to explore further, Western notions of *Homo equalis* in relation to ideas of equality and inequality. Referring to the destruction of aboriginal society in Australia, native Indians in the USA, the slave trade, and colonialism he noted the paradox in the theory and practice of equality.

He argued that if we are to take equality seriously we need to enlarge the concept and recognise that the different components of the concept do not harmonise with each other. Given the inequalities generated by the market and the state, the West is not as egalitarian as its ideals profess. Also, the pursuit of equality limits the attainment of other ends such as efficiency, liberty, and self-realisation of the individual. The task of social theory is to recognise the diversity of human ends and to understand and interpret each society according to its own historical circumstances. He argued that since there are contradictions in equality and inequality, the focus should be on the interplay of the two systems. He preferred another dichotomy, that of harmonic and disharmonic systems. Harmonic was defined as a natural consistency between the normative and existential orders, and disharmonic was defined as the opposite.

More recently, Beteille has focused on issues of civic rights. He is severely critical of provisions in the Indian Constitution, which, while recognising equality as a fundamental right, tolerates widespread, pernicious inequalities. He is particularly concerned with the pervasive apathy to the suffering of the Backward castes and tribes who continue to face numerous constraints on their civic rights, individual mobility, and social freedom. Although social equality and individual autonomy cannot be taken for granted, a modern society must seek to affirm these values.

Beteille argued that it is erroneous to compare caste and race. Anthropologists, he noted tend to study caste from a biological point of view, as they do race. In the Indian subcontinent, the tremendous genetic diversity of the population renders any division on the basis of race meaningless. Further, 'the efforts to disentangle tribe and caste' was introduced by the British. For millennia, tribe and caste civilisations had co-existed and were closely implicated in each other. The colonial imposition of various classifications, racial, linguistic, ecological, and religious, on tribal peoples, relied on livelihood as a means of determining their social status. Tribes with the simplest technologies were seen to be more closely integrated to primitive society than those with advanced technologies. Such essentialist understandings continue to pervade the modern Indian polity. Thus, unwittingly, Beteille has pioneered through his insights and ethnography a critique of colonial knowledge.

Education

BA Presidency College, Calcutta
Ph.D. Delhi School of Economics

Fieldwork

Kerala, Tamil Nadu, south India

Key Publications

(1965) *Caste, Class and Power; Changing Patterns in a*

Tanjore village, Berkeley: University of California Press.

(1983) *The Idea of Natural Inequality and Other Essays,* New Delhi and New York: Oxford University Press.

(1991) *Society and Politics in India, Essays in Comparative Perspective,* London and Atlantic Highlands, NJ: Athlone Press,

(2000) *Antinomies of Society: Essays on Ideologies and Institutions,* New Delhi and New York: Oxford University Press.

KUSUM GOPAL

Bibeau, Gilles

b. 1940, Tracy, Quebec, Canada

Gilles Bibeau has played a leading role in the development of medical anthropology. His areas of research include: the quest for meaning and traditional healing in Zaïre; the scientific (and not so scientific) representation of sexuality and AIDS in Africa; the popular semiology of mental health problems in Quebec rural areas; the life-experience of transience (focusing on the adaptation process of immigrants); and the culture of drug addicts and shooting galleries. As an outgrowth of his research in rural Quebec, Bibeau has been responsible (in concert with Ellen Corin) for the elaboration of an ethnographically oriented and semiologically inspired research methodology that is currently being used by national teams in eight countries (including Brazil, Mali, India, and Italy) in the context of an international comparative study of the ways people identify, explain, and handle mental health problems in their daily lives. This research initiative is a model example of the comparative method in action: local knowledges are integrated into a comprehensive paradigm and also issue in concrete proposals for health care reform. In recent years, Bibeau has made a point of taking anthropology public by intervening in debates on issues ranging from cultural pluralism to the new public health, and Quebec/Canadian identity to human rights. In the course of these debates, Bibeau has emerged as one of Quebec's most engaged and engaging public intellectuals.

Education

B.Sc. University of Montreal, 1961
Ph.D. University of Laval, 1979

Fieldwork

Ubangi and Kinshasa, Zaïre, 1966–78
Abitibi and Montreal, Quebec, 1985–
Chennai, India, 1997–
Salvador, Brazil, 1997–

Key Publications

with Corin, E. (eds) (1995) *Beyond Textuality: Asceticism and Violence in Anthropological Interpretation,* Berlin: Mouton de Gruyter.

(1997) 'Cultural psychiatry in a creolizing world', *Transcultural Psychiatry* 34, 1: 9–41.

DAVID HOWES

Bilu, Yoram

b. 1942, Tel Aviv, Israel

Bilu's research has been associated mainly with the psychocultural study of religion. While exploring various manifestations of Judaism as practised in modern Israel, he has also contributed to the understanding of their historical roots. His earlier ethnographic and historic work (late 1970s) dealt with ethnopsychiatry, particularly among Jewish immigrants from Morocco. Bilu focused on their local models of illness, diagnostic labels, and healing rituals, and pointed to the dynamics of continuity and change of traditional beliefs and practices under the immigrants' new circumstances in Israel. In the early 1980s, Bilu followed the renaissance of the folk-veneration of saints among these groups. He outlined their creative coping strategies – as embodied in their new adaptations of traditional idioms of 'the saint' – and argued that the emergence of saints' sanctuaries in the urban periphery of Israel was an expression of new and more assertive ethnic celebration by North African and Middle Eastern Jews. In the early 1990s Bilu carried out clinical work with ultra-Orthodox psychiatric patients, offering guidelines for culture-sensitive therapy. This was followed by research into the strategies by which Jewish fundamentalist communities grapple with modernity and the secularised mainstream society. Recently he has explored modes of sanctification of space, in both traditional and civil (state-based) religions, and has followed new forms of mysticism in Israel, with a special emphasis on Habad (Lubavitch) messianism.

Education

BA The Hebrew University of Jerusalem, Jerusalem, Israel, 1968
MA The Hebrew University of Jerusalem, Jerusalem, Israel, 1971
Ph.D. The Hebrew University of Jerusalem, Jerusalem, Israel, 1979

Fieldwork

Two *moshavim* (semi-collective villages) of Moroccan Jews, southwest of Jerusalem, 1974–7
Saints' sanctuaries in Israel's urban periphery, 1981–90 (intermittently)
Psychiatric clinic, northern Jerusalem, 1990–3 (intermittently)
Ultra-Orthodox schools, northern Jerusalem, 1996–7 (intermittently)

Key Publications

(1985) 'The taming of the deviants and beyond: an analysis of Dybbuk possession and exorcism in Judaism', *The Psychoanalytic Study of Society* 11: 1–32 (L. Bryce Boyer Award, 1986).
(2000) *Without Bounds: The Life and Death of Rabbi*

Ya'aqov Wazana, Detroit: Wayne State University Press.

YEHUDA GOODMAN

Blacking, John Anthony Randall

b. 1928, Guildford, Surrey, UK

d. 1990

John Blacking achieved international recognition as a major figure in the field of ethnomusicology. Trained as an anthropologist under Meyer Fortes (1950–3), and later as an ethnomusicologist with André Schaeffner (1953), Blacking played a critical role in establishing the discipline of ethnomusicology. In his prolific career, he published over a hundred books, articles, reviews, recordings, and reports on subjects including the nature of musicality and musical experience, dance, ethnography, ritual, tradition and change, identity, music education, and anthropological research in Ireland. He founded degree programmes in ethnomusicology as well as a professional association. At the time of his death in 1990, he was internationally renowned for his work examining the crucial role of music and dance in expressing the human condition.

After completing a degree in anthropology in 1953, Blacking moved to South Africa where he became involved in several field recording expeditions to Kwazulu and Mozambique. He stayed in South Africa until taking up a professorship at The Queen's University of Belfast in 1970. Between the years 1953 and 1958, Blacking conducted his now famous fieldwork among the Venda people of the Sibasa district of the Northern Transvaal (then Rhodesia). This research combined anthropological field techniques with musical research. Blacking learned to speak Tshivenda, participated in music and dance activities, and kept careful records of all aspects of Venda life. In 1967 he published the book, *Venda Children's Song*, which examined girls' initiation schools and the links between Venda musical and social systems. In providing transcriptions of the words and music of fifty-six children's songs, Blacking sought to demonstrate the relationship between Venda concepts of music, genres, and language. Blacking's 'cultural analysis of music' and the idea that musical structures and social structures are interdependent guided much of his work throughout his career.

In 1973, another of Blacking's best-known publications, How Musical is Man?, broadened the scope of ethnomusicological enquiry by exploring musical ability as a defining characteristic of being human. He argued that 'Western' society could be improved by participating in music like the Venda. This publication was followed by his only other single authored work in 1987. A number of Blacking's essays exploring aesthetic, epistemological, and ideological issues are brought together in the edited collection, Music, Culture and Experience.

Blacking's semiotic approach to analysing musical meaning, and his insistence on music as humanly organised sound that provides cues for understanding human organisation, continue to influence the field of ethnomusicology today.

Education

BA University of Cambridge, 1953
Ph.D. University of the Witwatersrand, 1965

Fieldwork

Rhodesia, 1956–8

Key Publications

(1967) Venda Children's Song. A Study in Ethnomusicological Analysis, Johannesburg: Witwatersrand University Press (reprinted 1995, University of Chicago Press).
(1973) How Musical Is Man?, Seattle: University of Washington Press.
(1987) A Common-Sense View of All Music: Reflections on Percy Grainger's Writings on Ethnomusicology and

Music Education, Cambridge, UK: Cambridge University Press.
(1995) Music, Culture and Experience: Selected Papers of John Blacking, Chicago: University of Chicago Press.

VIRGINIA CAPUTO

Bloch, Maurice E.F.

b. 21 October 1939, Caen, France

From Blessing to Violence opens with the remark that social science originates in the radical idea that society and culture are natural, not God-given, phenomena governed by general laws of an earthly character. The kind of materialism endorsed by Bloch, however, does not dismiss people's ideas and representations of the world as irrelevant to human history; rather, it requires a commitment to the notion that such ideas and representations must be the product of a complex, yet natural process taking place in history. It is to the understanding of this natural and historical process that Bloch has devoted both his ethnographic and theoretical work.

Bloch's first monograph on the Merina of Madagascar (1971) is perhaps best described as a post-colonial study, underscoring his commitment to the historical analysis of cultural phenomena. Rather than abstracting the principles of Merina 'social structure', Bloch chose to concentrate on the discrepancy between his informants' ideas of how they ought to conduct their lives in imitation of the ancestral past, and the practical arrangements they made under radically changed historical circumstances (due to colonialism, independence, conversion to Christianity, migration, schooling, etc.) In arguing that this discrepancy is ultimately resolved through ritual activities that negate historical change and human creativity, Placing the Dead set the scene for Bloch's exploration of the relationship between cognition and ideology, and of the nature of religious experience.

In a number of theoretical articles published in the late 1970s, Bloch set out to solve the paradox at the heart of any theory that postulates the social determination of people's categories of understanding (e.g. Emile Durkheim's sociology, A. R. Radcliffe-Brown's structuralism, many versions of Marxism), namely that if such categories are socially determined, there would be no way for human actors to criticise and transform the society in which they live (e.g. for Merina people to create a society radically different from that of their ancestors). Bloch solved the paradox by drawing a distinction between cognition and ideology: the former shaped by cognitive universals and developing independently of differences in social and cultural context; the latter consisting of socially determined representations created and transmitted in ritual contexts, whose content denies historical change. Bloch has subsequently engaged in the systematic exploration of these two distinct ways of hiding (ideology) and knowing (cognition) the world.

Bloch's writings in the 1980s have been largely devoted to the analysis of ritual as the context where ideology is produced and transmitted. The most significant contributions of this body of work are the ethnographic analysis of how rituals, by systematically negating everyday cognition, create an alienating representation of the world in which human creativity is denied; the detailed historical analysis of how the Merina circumcision ritual (1800–1970) was used, at times overtly, to legitimise political power; the finding that, despite significant changes in ritual practices due to changing sociopolitical circumstances, the core of the circumcision ritual remained remarkably stable; the further contention that the same minimal structure characterises all human ritual activities, ranging from sacrifices to initiations, from marriages to millenaristic movements; the conclusion that ritual activity and the ideological representations created therein are motivated by human existential needs that arise from the universal perception of the transience of human life and by the desire to transcend it.

Underlying Bloch's work on ritual is the assumption that human cognition constrains people's representations of such phenomena as birth, ageing, and death. The bulk of Bloch's writings in the 1990s, on topics such as memory, knowledge acquisition, the relationship between language and thought, domain specificity, or intuitive biology, can thus be seen as the logical development of his research on ritual and ideology. Having looked at the ways in which ideological representations are created, transmitted, and used, his attention has progressively turned to the exploration of the cognitive structures that enable and constrain human knowledge and its transmission. While Bloch has largely used psychological findings to wage a critique of anthropology (e.g. of anthropologists' naive assumption that narratives about the past equate with people's memory of the past), he has also been committed to reminding cognitive scientists of the unique contribution that anthropology can make to the interdisciplinary study of human cognition.

Education

BA London School of Economics, 1961
Ph.D. University of Cambridge, 1967

Fieldwork

Madagascar, 1964–6, 1971 (Merina); 1971, 1988–9 and shorter regular visits since (Zafimaniry)

Key Publications

(1971) *Placing the Dead. Tombs, Ancestral Villages, and Kinship Organization in Madagascar*, London: Seminar Press.

(1986) *From Blessing to Violence: History and Ideology in the Circumcision Ritual of the Merina of Madagascar*, Cambridge, UK: Cambridge University Press.

(1992) *Prey into Hunter: The Politics of Religious Experience*, Cambridge, UK: Cambridge University Press.

(1998) *How We Think They Think: Anthropological Approaches to Cognition, Memory and Literacy*, Boulder, CO: Westview Press.

RITA ASTUTI

Blok, Anton

b. 1935, Amsterdam, The Netherlands

Anton Blok's initial interests during fieldwork in a Sicilian agro-town were settlement patterns, land tenure, and agrarian reform. Only later did he turn to the development of the rural Mafia in response to larger social, political, and economic forces. Blok's widely acclaimed monograph was part of, and contributed to, a major shift in Mediterranean ethnography: a move away from the community study to the problem-oriented monograph informed by history and political economy. He became a leading exponent of historical anthropology, inspired by Eric Wolf's work on peasant societies and by Norbert Elias's *magnum opus* on state formation and the civilising process. His second major work, which is based on extensive archival research, is a standard monograph on political banditry in the hinterland of eighteenth-century Maastricht.

Anton Blok's research interests, which he himself calls 'chance encounters', revolve upon the relationships between violence, status, and reputation. The assumption underlying his collected essays is that unintended conditions and unintended consequences of intended social action make society and culture opaque. Blok goes beyond rich ethnographic and historical detail in an attempt to find family resemblances between cases and similarities across cultures. Chapters include a reconsideration of the narcissism of minor differences in the light of ethnic violence; an exploration of the meanings of 'senseless violence'; an analysis of animal symbolism in Mediterranean notions of honour; and a discussion of female rulers as social males.

Anton Blok retired from the University of Amsterdam in 2000.

Education

BA University of Amsterdam, 1960
MA University of Amsterdam, 1964
Ph.D. University of Amsterdam, 1972

Fieldwork

Sicily, 1961, 1965–7 (30 months); brief visits in 1983, 1984, and 1998

Key Publications

(1974) *The Mafia of a Sicilian Village, 1860–1960. A Study of Violent Peasant Entrepreneurs*, Oxford: Basil Blackwell.
(2001) *Honour and Violence*, Cambridge, UK: Polity Press.

HENK DRIESSEN

Boas, Franz

b. 9 July 1858, Minden, Germany

d. 21 December 1942, New York City, USA

Franz Boas was unquestionably the leading figure in the intellectual and institutional development of anthropology in North America during the twentieth century. Born to a prosperous Jewish family in Germany, Boas sought to make a career in North America where opportunities were better for a Jewish scholar. His initial fieldwork with the Eskimo of Baffin Island completed his metamorphosis from the psychophysics of his doctoral study through geography to ethnology.

Although in retrospect Boasian dominance of North American anthropology seems inevitable, Boas had great difficulty finding a permanent position and establishing his disciplinary leadership. Boas returned to the Royal Ethnological Museum in Berlin before beginning Northwest Coast fieldwork in 1885.

He worked as an editor of *Science*, as docent in psychology at Clark University, and as organiser of exhibits at the World's Columbian Exposition in Chicago in 1893, under the patronage of Frederick Ward Putnam of Harvard. His fieldwork was sponsored piecemeal by the Bureau of American Ethnology and the British Association for the Advancement of Science.

With an anonymous financial inducement provided by his uncle-by-marriage, New York physician, Abraham Jacobi, Boas obtained a position divided between the American Museum of Natural History and Columbia University; the latter became permanent in 1899. Until his resignation from the American Museum in 1905, Boas had the best of both worlds: his own research and that of his students was supported by the museum but the academic programme at Columbia enabled him to increase the professional standards of the discipline. The primary achievement of the museum years was the Jesup North Pacific Expedition, intended to resolve the question of American Indian origins. Fieldwork took place both on the Northwest Coast and in Siberia, utilising the skills of Russian scholars exiled to the area (Waldemar Bogoras [Vladimir Bogoraz-Tan], Waldemar Jochelson, and Leo Sternberg). Jesup withdrew his support when the work appeared without closure and, despite the value of the ethnographic work carried out, Boas never produced the final synthetic volume.

Boas was a key player in the 1898 reorganisation of the *American Anthropologist* as a national journal, balancing the power of the government anthropologists in Washington, DC and the archaeologists in Cambridge with that of his own revived American Ethnological Society in New York. On the founding of the American Anthropological Association (AAA) in 1902, Boas lost his battle to restrict membership to employed and professionally trained anthropologists, but succeeded in consolidating actual power within a smaller executive council. The last effective challenge to Boas's control over the discipline came in 1919 when he was censured by the AAA for

accusing colleagues working in Mexico of spying during the First World War. Thereafter, Boasians controlled the AAA and its publications, also holding most of the increasing number of academic positions in the country.

Boas has often been depicted in the history of anthropology as anti-theoretical. Although his method was often deconstructive in practice, Boas had a coherent theoretical programme. His critique of classical evolutionism was essentially completed during the 1880s. He argued that each culture had a unique history that could be reconstructed through contemporary distribution of culture traits and motifs, a position later labelled historical particularism. Change was not unilineal and could not be decided in advance. Further, each culture had its own psychological integration. Boas enjoined ethnographers to access 'the native point of view,' for example, obtaining myths and historical accounts to accompany material objects. Using the Northwest Coast as his cultural laboratory, Boas traced borrowings and migrations, documenting the historical interaction of many cultures. His own work centerd especially on the Kwakiutl where he established a long-term local collaboration with George Hunt to obtain native language texts that could be used as a database for ethnology, linguistics, and psychology. Although Boas was a self-taught linguist, he developed a pre-phonemic sense of sound patterning unique to each language and argued that grammatical categories could not be adapted from Indo-European languages but must arise from the language described. Culture, for Boas, was a symbolic form rather than a set of observable behaviours.

Boas established the four sub-disciplinary structure of Americanist anthropology, with his own work in human biology, ethnology, and linguistics providing theoretical guidance to archaeology as the history of peoples without writing. Although American anthropologists since the Second World War have worked around the globe, Boas's preoccupation with the intersection of history and psychology in particular cultures has remained a distinctive feature of the Americanist tradition, particularly in contrast to British social anthropology.

Education

Ph.D. University of Kiel, 1882

Fieldwork

Eskimo, 1882–3
Northwest Coast, twenty-six trips, beginning in 1887

Key Publications

(1911) 'Introduction', in *Handbook of American Indian Languages*, Washington, DC: Bureau of American Ethnology.
(ed.) (c.1938) *General Anthropology*, Boston, New York: D.C. Heath & Company.
(1911) *The Mind of Primitive Man*, New York: The Macmillan Company.
(1940) *Race, Language and Culture*, New York: Free Press.

REGNA DARNELL

Boddy, Janice

b. 1951, Toronto, Canada

Janice Boddy is best known for her pathbreaking interpretive ethnography of a sexually segregated riverine community of northern Sudan. *Wombs and Alien Spirits* explores the complex ways in which zar spirit possession is related to local ideas about fertility, sexual differentiation, and complementarity, and a concern for cultural integrity; to kinship and marriage ideals; and to conceptions of the self. Superseding functional and instrumental accounts of possession, Boddy illustrates how expressive forms controlled and produced by women provide the means for counter-hegemonic discourse.

Zar is associated with pharaonic circumcision and the incidence of sterility and miscarriage among village women. In the book and various essays Boddy explores the meaning of pharaonic circumcision for women as an enhancement of fertility at a cultural level while documenting the paradox that it is equally destructive of physiological fertility and women's health.

Boddy expanded her subtle investigation of Muslim women's experience with the life history of a Somali woman, producing a popular book that has been translated into some fourteen languages. Boddy has subsequently engaged in a deep archival study documenting the complex interrelationships among British colonial agents and Sudanese addressing female circumcision. Her forthcoming book, *Civilizing Women: British Crusades in Colonial Sudan*, paints a subtle picture of gendered colonialism.

Education

BA McGill University, 1972
MA University of Calgary, 1974
Ph.D. University of British Columbia, 1982

Fieldwork

Democratic Republic of Sudan, 1976–7, 1983–4
UK, archival work, 1990–1, 1994–2001
North America, 1992, 1993

Key Publications

(1989) *Wombs and Alien Spirits: Women, Men and the Zar Cult in Northern Sudan*, Madison: University of Wisconsin Press.
(1994) *Aman: The Story of a Somali Girl*, Toronto: Knopf; London: Bloomsbury; New York: Pantheon.

MICHAEL LAMBEK

Bogoraz-Tan, Vladimir G.

b. 1865, Taganrog, Russia

d. 1936, Leningrad, Russia

Vladimir Bogoraz-Tan did not have a special

background in ethnography or anthropology. He began his studies of East Siberian populations when he was exiled to the Kolimskiy district for his participation in the revolutionary movement.

In the beginning Bogoraz worked as a folklorist. He recorded the songs, tales, and stories of the local Russian population. Then the glossary of the Kolimskiy Russians followed, which included both linguistic and also ethnographic information on regional material culture. As part of his work in the Kolimskiy district, Bogoraz took part in the first population census of the Russian Empire (1897).

V. Bogoraz was invited as an ethnographer to participate in the Yakutskaya expedition organised by the East Siberian Department of the Russian Empire Geographical Society. There his research focused on the native peoples of Yakutia – Chukchee and Evens. For about three years Bogoraz studied their languages, material culture, everyday life, means of subsistence, economics and social organisation.

At the beginning of 1899, on the recommendation of the Russian Academy of Sciences, Franz Boas, a well-known American ethnologist and linguist, invited V. Bogoraz to take part in the Jesup North Pacific expedition. This American–Russian expedition aimed to investigate the ancient connections between the native populations of Northwest America and Northeast Siberia. Bogoraz focused on the language, ethnography, and anthropology of the Kamchatka and Chukotka population, mainly Chukchee. Over the course of a year (June 1900–June 1901), Bogoraz visited practically all the groups of reindeer Chukchee, villages of settled Eskimos, Koryaks, and Itelmens.

Then Bogoraz left for the USA, where his works were published first in English, and only later, after the Great October Socialist Revolution, were they translated into Russian by the author himself. His research results became the basis for detailed publications about material culture, religion, social organisation, language,

and mythology of the Chukchee people at the end of the nineteenth century. They also included about 200 Chukchee folklore texts. During the next century Bogoraz's monographs became the most complete and often the only source of ethnographic information about the Chukchee.

His linguistic studies have become the theoretical basis for subsequent research into Northern peoples' languages, a focus that especially characterised the Leningrad ethnographic school. This interest was not only of scientific but also of practical importance. In the early 1930s V. Bogoraz wrote the first Chukchee school primer.

During the Soviet period, Bogoraz worked at the Museum of Ethnography and Anthropology (1918), and taught at Leningrad University (Department of Ethnography and Geography, 1925). He was also among the founders of the Institute of the Northern Peoples (1930).

Education

1880–2, University of St Petersburg

Fieldwork

Kolimskiy district, East Siberia (political exile), 1890–8
Yakutia, East Siberia, 1895–7
Kamchatka, Chukotka, North Pacific, 1900–1

Key Publications

(1904–9) *The Chukchee. Parts I.II.III. Memoirs of the American Museum of Natural History, vol. XI, the Jesup North Pacific Expedition,* ed. F. Boaz, Leiden: E.J. Brill; New York: G.E. Stechert.

(1910) *The Chukchee Mythology. Memoirs of the American Museum of Natural History, vol. XII. the Jesup North Pacific Expedition,* ed. F. Boaz, Leiden: E.J. Brill; New York: G.E. Stechert.

TATIANA UVAROVA

Bohannan, Laura Altman Smith

b. 20 July 1922, New York City, USA

d. 18 March 2002, Chicago, USA

Laura Bohannan's work engaged important questions in the structure of non-state societies and in anthropological method and epistemology. Her fieldwork with the Tiv of east central (Middle Belt) Nigeria (with her husband at the time, P.J. Bohannan) resulted in important ethnographic and lasting literary works. Her undergraduate studies in classics at Arizona and her doctoral work at Oxford with Evans-Pritchard marked her writings. Employment for women anthropologists was difficult in the USA in the 1950s and it was only in 1962 that she secured a position at the University of Illinois, Chicago; she retired in 1990.

Her contributions on kinship and genealogy (central to Africanist preoccupations at Oxford at the time) pointed to the differences between legal and biological categories, and the adaptability of ideas and politics. With Paul Bohannan she created one of the more complete bodies of ethnography on a stateless society and its economy, institutions, rituals, and beliefs, a lasting resource for anthropologists and historians, indigenous and professional.

It is, however, for her imaginative cross-cultural experiments and fiction that she is best known in and beyond anthropology.

Her novel about her fieldwork among the Tiv, Return to Laughter, originally published in 1955 and in print almost fifty years later, continues to instruct, engage, amuse, and infuriate readers. Published under a pseudonym (E.S. Bowen) to distance it from the author's professional roles, it nevertheless attracted criticism. Despite this controversial beginning it has become a classic account of what fieldwork involves and is widely used as an introduction to fieldwork and life in an 'alien' culture, in anthropology and other fields. It retains its relevance as a subtle treatment of questions of cross-cultural morality and cultural relativism. The novel also raises, albeit indirectly, important methodological and epistemological issues. Bohannan is regarded as having 'initiated a new anthropological writing paradigm', addressing the questions about the ethnographer as actor in the fieldwork situation and about the production of anthropological knowledge.

With 'Shakespeare in the Bush' (originally broadcast on the BBC in 1952), an account of the discussion with Tiv elders of the relationships in Hamlet and their reinterpretation of the 'universal themes' of Shakespeare in Tiv terms, this novel made and sustained Laura Bohannon's international and cross-disciplinary reputation. Both are widely used in teaching in fields other than anthropology. Her work continues to have great recognition in anthropology and in many other disciplines.

Education

BA University of Arizona, 1943
MA University of Arizona, 1947
D.Phil. University of Oxford, 1951

Fieldwork

Tiv, east central Nigeria, 1949–51 (Colonial Social Science Research Fellow)
Wanga, Kenya, 1954–6

Key Publications

(1952) 'A Tiv genealogical charter', [Africa 22, 4].
(1955) Return to Laughter (as Eleanor Smith Bowen), New York. Harpers.
(1966) 'Shakespeare in the Bush', Natural History, August/September.
with Bohannan, P.J. (1968) Tiv Economy, Evanston, IL: Northwestern University Press.

MICHAEL D. LEVIN

Bohannan, Paul James

b. 5 March 1920, Lincoln, Nebraska, USA

After wartime service and completing his degree at the University of Arizona, a Rhodes

Scholarship took Paul Bohannan to Oxford where he studied with E. Evans-Pritchard. His fieldwork with his wife, Laura Bohannan, on the Tiv of east central Nigeria was a major contribution to studies of stateless societies. When he returned to the USA, first to Princeton University and then Northwestern, he turned to fieldwork among the middle-class divorced in the USA. The latter years of his career have been devoted to works on general anthropological themes addressed to the public and senior undergraduates.

The Tiv research focused on legal and political institutions, order and dispute settlement, the stability of institutions and social and cultural logic in the absence of a state, the form and dynamics of segmentary descent systems, and the problem of comparison of cultures. His 1957 *Justice and Judgement among the Tiv* initiated a friendly scholarly dispute with Max Gluckman about the use of jurisdictional vocabulary in the study of court cases: this debate centerd on the issue of whether indigenous concepts or universal concepts should have priority in writing ethnography. Bohannan argued for the use of local terms because Western-derived concepts 'falsified the legal folk culture'; Gluckman argued for the universalism of the idea of 'the reasonable man', a standard that he claimed was of great utility for comparative study of legal and juridical procedure. This debate was not settled and it has continued in anthropology in various forms of the opposition between particularism and universalism (and in other forms between appropriation and authenticity), and specifically in the debates over the writing of ethnography about the adequacy of translation and whether scholarly concepts obscure more than clarify the ideas they are intended to represent.

In African studies and legal and economic anthropology Bohannan was a collaborator with many scholars. As author of several textbooks and editor of many collections of papers intended for undergraduate use, he contributed to the diffusion of anthropological ideas in North American universities. Significant among these, the result of a symposium,

was *Markets in Africa*, co-edited with George Dalton. These papers, and his own on money and spheres of exchange, reflected his association with Karl Polanyi and the substantivist side of the substantivist–formalist debate in economic anthropology.

A notable aspect of his fieldwork in Nigeria was his collaboration with his wife, which began with the first publications on Tiv and continued after their marriage ended. Their joint publication, *Tiv Economy*, won the Melville J. Herskovits Award of the African Studies Association (USA) in 1969 for the best book published in African studies.

The second major fieldwork topic, studies of the American middle-class divorced, was directed at opening up the American concepts of the family and marriage to broader possible understandings of intimate relations. This project produced a series of works that allowed Bohannan to explore the social basis of marriage and the definition of the family comparatively yet still within American culture.

The studies of divorce were directed at modelling the events sequences and understanding the relational patterns of persons from courtship through marriage and divorce. His interviews with divorced women and men brought new information into discussions that had been primarily legal and psychological. These narratives of marriage and divorce brought out the implications of divorce for visions of the family and suggested alternative models of the family within the norms of American culture. These studies are a valuable model of the use of ethnographic methods and the comparative knowledge of cultural difference to make visible to actors – marriage partners, helping and legal professionals – perceptions of patterns of relationship outside the limits of the established terms of discourse.

The third phase of Bohannan's publications has been a series of works making the case for anthropology in the academy and in popular thinking. His views reflect his training and an American four-field approach, but are more broadly a reflection of a liberal view of education that presents information and ideas to readers and asks them to engage with the work of many authors, not just the one before them.

Bohannan's rewarding and brief memoir, 'It's been a good field trip' (1997), in addition to offering the reader his own view of his career and his opinions on the direction for anthropology at the turn of the millennium, has insightful observations on university life and culture in Britain and the USA.

Education

BA University of Arizona, 1943
B.Sc. University of Oxford
D.Phil. University of Oxford, 1951
postgraduate study, Chicago Institute of Psychoanalysis, 1967–71

Fieldwork

Tiv, Nigeria, 1949–53
Wanga, Nyanza Province, Kenya 1955
American middle-class divorced, 1964–70

Key Publications

(1968) *Justice and Judgement among the Tiv*, second edn (new Preface), London: Oxford University Press.
(1965) *Markets in Africa* (a symposium edited with George Dalton), Evanston, IL: Northwestern University Press.
with Bohannan, Laura (1968) *Tiv Economy*, Evanston, IL: Northwestern University Press.
(1995) *How Culture Works*, New York: The Free Press.

MICHAEL D. LEVIN

Boissevain, Jeremy Fergus

b. 1928, London

Jeremy Boissevain came to social anthropology after directing the CARE aid programmes in the Philippines, Japan, India, Malta, and Sicily. This early grassroots involvement may explain his lifelong interest in local-level politics and

his focus on the pragmatic choices of actual people. His two monographs on rural Malta, in which he paid systematic attention to the interactions between village life and wider society, belong to the classics in Mediterranean ethnography and cultural anthropology. In 1969 his *Hal-Farrug. A Village in Malta* was published in the influential 'Case Studies in Cultural Anthropology Series' at Holt, Rhinehart & Winston.

Following his fieldwork in Malta and Sicily, Jeremy Boissevain became involved in developing a comparative anthropology of the Mediterranean area of which he was a leading advocate in the 1970s and 1980s.

During his studies at the London School of Economics, where Lucy Mair and Raymond Firth were among his main teachers, Jeremy Boissevain developed a critical stance towards structural-functionalism that had dominated Anglo-Saxon anthropology between 1930 and 1960. Inspired by Edmund Leach's book on Highland Burma, Frederick Bailey's work on politics and social change in Orissa, and Fredrik Barth's study of political leadership among the Swat Pathans, Jeremy Boissevain became a prominent representative of an actor-oriented approach. In his influential book, *Friends of Friends*, he set forth a processual perspective on people, groups, and institutions as interlinking, multilevel networks. Being averse to grand theories, network analysis allowed him to remain near to the small politics of people in their daily interactions. Although he was well aware of the methodological limits of network analysis, he made a forceful plea to include it in the research tool kit of every ethnographic fieldworker.

Jeremy Boissevain's innovative work also includes contributions to the study of local power relations and ethnicity (an early book on the social adjustment of Italians in Montreal and a later study of small entrepreneurship among the Surinamese of Amsterdam), and of tourism (mainly with regard to its impact on Maltese society). In the late 1980s and early 1990s he revisited his early interest in ritual and social change by studying the revival of celebrations throughout Europe as a reaction to the homogenising pressure of the market, the mass media, and the Eurocrats. Jeremy Boissevain, who is emeritus professor of social anthropology at the University of Amsterdam where he worked from 1966–93, is currently working on a volume with his collected essays on Maltese society and culture.

Education

BA Haverford College, Pennsylvania, USA, 1952
Ph.D. London School of Economics, 1962

Fieldwork

Fezzan, Libya, 1959 (1 month)
Malta 1960–1 (14 months); 1967, 1968, 1969, 1973, 1974, 1986–7, 1993
Sicily 1962–3 (7 months); 1965 (2 months)
Montreal 1964–5 (13 months, part time)
Amsterdam 1983 (12 months, part time)

Key Publications

(1965) *Saints and Fireworks: Religion and Politics in Rural Malta*, London: Athlone Press.
(1974) *Friends of Friends. Networks, Manipulators and Coalitions*, Oxford: Basil Blackwell.
(ed.) (1992) *Revitalizing European Rituals*, London and New York: Routledge.

HENK DRIESSEN

Bonfil Batalla, Guillermo

b. 1935, Mexico City, Mexico

d. 1991, Mexico City, Mexico

During the 1960s Guillermo Bonfil, together with other Latino-American anthropologists, developed a critical research approach exemplified in his own pioneering study of the nutrition problems of a Yucatan Mayan community. Bonfil subsequently carried out fieldwork in several multiethnic regions, with

original contributions, as in his study of the 'graniceros' (traditional experts in meteorology) from Sierra Nevada, in the Mexican Central Plateau.

Bonfil's basic concern was for the acknowledgement of the importance of the history and culture of indigenous peoples in the configuration of national societies in Latin America in general, and in Mexico in particular. With this in mind, he critically reviewed 'Indian', pointing out its colonial roots, and proposing instead a return to the names Indian peoples attribute to themselves. Along this line, he carried out fieldwork at Cholula, an ancient religious center that has been urban since pre-Hispanic times. Bonfil sought to explain the dense Mesoamerican tradition of Cholula that he interpreted as an expression of resistance to the hegemony of the dominant national culture of Puebla City, the state capital. Later on, he extended his reflective thinking to the Indigenous peoples elsewhere in the American continent, with an orientation inspired by the so called 'Declaracion de Barbados', a political document denouncing ethnocide in the Americas that he co-signed in 1971 with ten other anthropologists (eight Latin Americans, a Swede, and an American). He also participated in diverse academic and political meetings attended by Indigenous leaders. He critically explored the different meanings of the 'ethnic group' concept, and proposed that it be replaced with the term 'profound people', inspired by African thinkers, such as Abdel Malek and Amilcar Cabral, among others. He turned his attention back to the Mexican nation, and the revision of national culture and history in accord with the point of view of the Indigenous peoples and in opposition to the official history. He argued that the Mesoamerican cultural tradition incorporated a civilising project shared by the majority of Mexicans. He named this civilising project 'Profound Mexico', which he contrasted with the 'Imaginary Mexico' project of the dominant European elites. He considered the systematic neglect of the cultural tradition of indigenous peoples as a central political and cultural problem for Mexican nation-building. With this in mind, he formulated a political forum that advocated the recognition of the diversity of Indian peoples. He developed a theoretical framework that addressed the formative cultural influences of European colonisation on Mexico and other Latin American countries. Finally, he introduced a number of concepts useful in formulating a cultural policy opposed to the powerful inertia of colonisation, which is, at the same time, both ancient and contemporary.

Education

MA National School of Anthropology and History (ENAH)/National University of Mexico (UNAM), 1961

Ph.D. National University of Mexico (UNAM), 1970

Fieldwork

Sudzal, Yucatán, 1960

Cholula, Puebla, 1965–7

Chalco, Amecameca, Estado de Mexico, 1967–70

Key Publications

(1961) *Diagnostico sobre el hambre en Sudzal, Yucatan* (Diagnosis on Hunger in Sudzal, Yucatan), Mexico: Instituto Nacional de Antropologia e Historia.

(1973) *Cholula. La ciudad sagrada en la era industrial* (Cholula. The Sacred City in the Industrial Era), Mexico: UNAM.

(1987) *Mexico profundo. Una civilizacion negada* (Profound Mexico. A Neglected Civilization), Mexico: Centro de Investigaciones y Estudios Superiores de Antropología Social, SEP.

ANDRÉS MÉDINA

Boon, James

b. 1946, Florida, USA

James Boon is an anthropologist ironist whose work is highly comparative, bridging Indonesian studies, Euro-American colonial and intellectual histories, and philosophies of synaesthesic arts and experience. Uniting Boon's *drôle* corpus is an attempt to show how these separate fields interpenetrate. Boon's formative educational roots are in French literature and cultural anthropology, interests and influences that are sustained throughout his writings. For example, whilst completing a Ph.D. based upon fieldwork in Bali (assisting Clifford Geertz), Boon published a 'structuralist' study of Lévi-Strauss's literary roots, doing to the thoughts and texts of Lévi-Strauss and the French Symbolist poets what Lévi-Strauss had been doing to the thoughts and texts of savage and civilised others.

Boon successfully, and entertainingly, grounds his literary criticism and anthropology of anthropology (meta-anthropology) in his Indonesian ethnography. Hence, Balinese culture can be understood through a Shakespearean lens: a 'social romance' of flexible values and actions, of epic and heroic struggles between traditional familial aristocracies, ruling blood lines and sacred forces, and modern colonial (Dutch/British), communist, and commercial forces. Drawing upon sixteenth–nineteenth-century Balinese narratives and contrastive histories, Boon's 'bittersweet Baliology' rereads Western Indonesianisations and Europeanisations, and counters colonialist stereotypes and the tendency to represent Indonesia as a place of spectacle and the extreme.

In his writings, Boon also alerts us to the process of anthropological transposition from fieldwork (the tribal) to textual interpretation (the scribal), a potentially confining institutional process with the power to define and reify, to deprivilege and unsettle. Boon's attention to the serio-comic, and his method of piquant cultural counterpoint, are an attempt to prevent anthropology's fascination with the extreme and the 'extra-vagant' – the culture industry – from deteriorating into a redundant academic version of the old curiosity shop.

Education

BA Princeton University, 1968
Ph.D. University of Chicago, 1973

Fieldwork

Java and Bali, 1971–2
Bali, 1982, 1992 (including Singapore)
The Netherlands, Switzerland, Australia, Hong Kong, Greece, 1972, 1976, 1984, 1987, 1990, 1999 (archival/museum work)

Key Publications

(1972) *From Symbolism to Structuralism: Lévi-Strauss in a Literary Tradition*, Oxford: Basil Blackwell; New York: Harper & Row.
(1982) *Other Tribes, Other Scribes: Symbolic Anthropology in the Comparative Study of Cultures, Histories, Religions, and Texts*, Cambridge, UK: Cambridge University Press.
(1990) *Affinities and Extremes: Crisscrossing the Bittersweet Ethnology of East Indies History, Hindu-Balinese Culture, and Indo-European Allure*, London: The University of Chicago Press.

JONATHAN SKINNER

Borneman, John

b. 3 May 1952, Wisconsin, USA

Drawing on long association with Berlin as ethnographer, research fellow, and visiting professor, John Borneman's ethnographic accounts of the transformations of the German state mark a shift in the anthropology of Europe away from the rural and marginal to the central and motor forces of contemporary European life, such as nationalism, citizenship, and governmentality. His monograph on kin and state in Berlin before and after the dramatic changes of 1989 problematises the divergent 'national' traditions of law and social policy of the two Germanys in terms of generational adaptations to the new, 'unified' state, and is perhaps the best example of a perspective in political anthropology that foregrounds the state and its dialectical relationship to even the most intimate aspects of daily life. Much more than a local study, Borneman's work functions as a critical commentary on the apparent impasse in post-modern theorising, showing how anthropologists, so long transfixed by the particular, might in their practice address the pressing concerns of cultural and historical complexity. Influenced by political theory, queer studies, and narrative theory, Borneman elaborates on these themes in *Subversions of International Order* (1998), which explores topics like love and sexuality, and their role in identity formation and embeddedness in history. Borneman has also published widely on processes of retribution and reconciliation and since 1999 has been researching these issues in Lebanon.

Education

BA University of Wisconsin-Madison, 1973
MA University of Washington, 1983
MA Harvard University, 1985
Ph.D. Harvard University, 1989

Fieldwork

Berlin, Germany, 1984–2000 (extended and shorter periods of research)
Prague, Warsaw, Budapest, Moscow, 1994 (2 months)
Beirut, Lebanon, 1999–present

Key Publications

(1992) *Belonging in the Two Berlins: Kin, State, Nation*, Cambridge, UK: Cambridge University Press.
(1997) *Settling Accounts: Violence, Justice, and Accountability in Postsocialist Europe*, Princeton: Princeton University Press.

HASTINGS DONNAN

Borofsky, Robert

b. 1944, Boston, Massachusetts, USA

Robert Borofsky has conducted ethnographic

research in Trinidad (1967) and the Cook Islands (1977–81), specifically on the island of Pukapuka. In his ethnographic investigations in Pukapuka, Borofsky reveals how understanding the Pukapukan constructions of knowledge and pasts may help anthropologists overcome the natural limitations of anthropological understanding. However, Borofsky's contribution to the field of anthropology transcends his notable fieldwork in Pukapuka. Currently, Borofsky is writing on the anthropology of anthropology, a two-volume work that will utilise anthropological perspectives to study anthropology itself. He helped coin the term 'public anthropology', which he describes as 'making anthropology a more socially-engaged discipline'. By revitalising anthropology's role in the broader society, Borofsky hopes to revitalise a discipline in its own constructions of knowledge. 'Public Anthropology' subsequently became the name of the University of California Press's Series as well as an activist perspective. Borofsky's work on Pacific ethnology, symbolism, and ritualism has earned him an impressive international reputation. He serves as the director of the Center for a Public Anthropology, is editor of the aforementioned University of California Press's Series in Public Anthropology, and webmaster of the www.publicanthropology.org website, along with his duties as professor of anthropology at Hawaii Pacific University.

Education

BA Union College, Schenectady, New York, 1966
Ph.D. University of Hawaii, Manoa, 1982

Fieldwork

Trinidad, 1967
Pukapuka, Cook Islands, 1977–81
Public anthropology, 1989–present

Key Publications

(1987) *Making History: Pukapukan and Anthropologi-*

cal Constructions of Knowledge, Cambridge, UK: Cambridge University Press.
(ed.) (1994) *Assessing Cultural Anthropology*, New York: McGraw-Hill.

JIMMY M. PAGAN, JR

Bourgois, Philippe

b. 8 December 1956, New York, USA

Perhaps in deference to his last name, Philippe Bourgois has made class struggle a primary referent in his work. His documenting power in dangerous ethnographic settings is likely the result of being raised by an Auschwitz survivor and United Nations development economist. Even before beginning doctoral fieldwork on a US multinational corporation (*Ethnicity at Work: Divided Labor on a Central American Banana Plantation*) he was almost expelled from Stanford for his eyewitness denunciation of US complicity in human rights violations in El Salvador. This was followed by several years' work on the Nicaraguan Atlantic coast during the early years of the Sandinista revolution.

Concomitant to Bourgois's commitment to the lived-experience of social injustice is an ardent adherence to ethnography he considers the *raison d'être* of cultural anthropology. Bourgois explores the relationship of macro-power structures with experiences of social suffering in settings historically shaped by inequalities and the struggle for dignity. He examines humans contending with structural forces beyond their control and prioritising those relegated to the lowest rungs of social hierarchies.

In *In Search of Respect: Selling Crack in El Barrio*, he befriended Puerto Rican youth trapped in the drug economy. He denounces 'US inner-city apartheid' by depicting the real politics of stigmatisation and how dealers and addicts confront the institutional violence of larger society in contradictorily self-destructive ways that blur moralistic distinctions between victim and victimiser. He describes how their adherence to capitalist methods would bring them success on Wall Street were they not systematically excluded from it. His work has expanded the boundaries of medical anthropology enabling him to found the Department of Anthropology, History, and Social Medicine at the University of California, San Francisco.

Education

BA Harvard University, 1978
MA Stanford University, 1980
Ph.D. Stanford University, 1985

Fieldwork

Costa Rica and Panama, 1982–3
East Harlem, 1985–91
San Francisco, 1994–2002

Key Publications

(1989) *Ethnicity at Work: Divided Labor on a Central American Banana Plantation*, Baltimore: Johns Hopkins University Press.
(1995) *In Search of Respect: Selling Crack in El Barrio*, New York: Cambridge University Press.

JAMES QUESADA

Bourguignon, Erika

b. 18 February 1924, Vienna, Austria

Erika Bourguignon was born in Vienna, Austria, in 1924. One of her childhood homes was literally around the corner from that of Sigmund Freud (then in his eighties). She and her parents left Austria as refugees in 1938, eventually settling in New York City. Bourguignon earned her BA at Queens College of the City University of New York (where she studied under Hortense Powdermaker) and her Ph.D. in anthropology from Northwestern University (where she studied under A.I. Hallowell and Melville J. Herskovits). Her Ph.D. dissertation, 'Syncretism and ambivalence: an ethnohistorical study' elaborated some of Herskovits's ideas concerning 'socialised ambivalence' in Haiti. In 1949 Bourguignon began teaching as a temporary

lecturer at the Ohio State University. She has continued to be affiliated with Ohio State for over fifty years.

Professor Bourguignon's major academic contributions are in the area of psychological anthropology; with a special focus on the relationships between trance, spirit possession, altered states of consciousness, and social change. Her many insights stem from fieldwork in Haiti as well as broadly based cross-cultural surveys utilising the Human Relations Area Files. A number of Bourguignon's students at Ohio State have gone on to make major contributions to the study of trance and spirit possession, notably Felicitas D. Goodman, Jeannette Henney, and Esther Pressel. Today, Professor Bourguignon is recognised as one of the founders of the field of anthropology of consciousness.

Bourguignon has always been a strong advocate of empirical research and has been highly critical of what she sees as shortcomings in 'experiential' approaches to culture. Nevertheless, her most recent publications delve into subjective issues of memory and the construction of meaning. For example, *Exile: A Memoir of 1939*, a life history of Bourguignon's aunt, Bronka Schneider, underscores the difficulties of combining personal and professional lives. It also raises questions about the limits of cultural relativism. For anthropologists of Bourguignon's generation, a major problem has been to reconcile their support of cultural relativism (as espoused by Herskovits) while simultaneously opposing evil movements like Nazism and fascism. *Exile: A Memoir* successfully bridges this seeming contradiction.

Education

BA Queens College, City University of New York, 1945
Ph.D. Northwestern University, 1951

Fieldwork

Lac de Flambeau Indian Reservation, Wisconsin, summer 1946

Barche, Furcy, and Port-au-Prince, Haiti, 1947–8

Bex les Bains and Zurich, Switzerland, 1938–9

United States, 1939–present

Key Publications

(ed.) (1973) *Religion, Altered States of Consciousness, and Social Change,* Columbus, OH: Ohio State University Press.

(1976) *Possession,* San Francisco: Chandler & Sharp.

(1979) *Psychological Anthropology,* New York: Holt, Rinehart & Winston.

with Schneider, Bronka and Hill Rigney, Barbara (eds) (1998) *Exile: A Memoir of 1939,* Columbus, OH: Ohio State University Press.

STEPHEN D. GLAZIER

Boyarin, Jonathan A.

b. 1956, Asbury Park, New Jersey, USA

Jonathan Boyarin's first experience of community was among the Jewish chicken farmers of Farmingdale, New Jersey. As an undergraduate at Reed College in Portland, Oregon, in the mid-1970s, two insights combined to shape his intellectual path for the following decades. First, he was attracted to anthropology as the one discipline of social analysis where the inescapable and formative presence of the observer in what he or she observes could be not only admitted, but also integrated into research and the presentation of research results. Second, finding himself for the first time in a milieu without a strong Jewish presence, he began to conceive of himself as someone already shaped in powerful ways by the fact of Jewishness, and decided that his best path towards autonomous adulthood was to acquire for himself positive and critical resources of Jewish thought and identity. This decision led to intense study of Yiddish language and culture; the Ph.D. in anthropology at the New School under the tutelage of Stanley Diamond; over a quarter century of

(continued) residence on the Lower East Side of Manhattan; fieldwork in Paris and Jerusalem, as well as on the Lower East Side; growing participation in local religious life, and study of religious texts; and several books and articles addressing both specifically Jewish themes and comparative issues in cultural theory arising out of his study of problems in Jewishness.

The major foci of his intellectual and scholarly life have been Jewish cultural studies (he was co-founder of the Jewish cultural studies discussion group of the MLA), collective memory, text and culture, and rhetorics of space and time.

Boyarin currently practises as an attorney in New York City.

Education

BA Reed College, Portland, Oregon, 1977

Uriel Weinreich Program in Yiddish Language, Literature and Culture, summer 1977, summer 1979

MA New School for Social Research, 1980

Graduate Fellow, YIVO Institute for Jewish Research, 1977–82

Ph.D. New School for Social Research, New York, 1984

School of Criticism and Theory, Dartmouth College, summer 1988

JD Yale Law School, 1998

Fieldwork

Jerusalem, 1991

On the Jewish community of the Lower East Side, New York City, 1985–7

On the Polish Jewish immigrant community in Paris, 1982–3

Key Publications

(1992) *Storm from Paradise: The Politics of Jewish Memory,* Minneapolis, MN: University of Minnesota Press.

(1994) *Remapping Memory: The Politics of Timespace,* Minneapolis, MN: University of Minnesota Press.

(1995) *Palestine and Jewish History: Criticism at the Borders of Ethnography*, Minneapolis, MN: University of Minnesota Press.

(1996) *Thinking in Jewish*, Chicago: University of Chicago Press.

DANIEL BOYARIN

Briggs, Charles L.

b. 1953, Albuquerque, New Mexico, USA

Charles L. Briggs's work has focused on the relationship between types of language use and the inhabitance of social categories.

He has maintained throughout his work a focus on genres of discourse. His doctoral research in Córdova, New Mexico, focused on the verbal art of elderly men in genres such as proverbs, scriptural allusions, and historical discourse. His subsequent research among the Warao people of the Delta Amacuro, Venezuela, focused on genres such as ritual wailing by women, shamanic recitation of myth, and dispute mediation by men. He went on to study non-Warao discourse about Warao people, focusing on the genres of public health statistics and of 'cultural reasoning'.

In theoretical terms, Briggs has distinguished between genres of discourse and the types of situation in which discourse is uttered. He has shown that the same genre can be lifted from one type of situation into another. He found, for example, that Warao shamans lifted a genre of myth from ritual contexts into conversation between themselves as well as into pedagogical discussions with their sons and sons-in-law. He has argued that people also lift genres that are usually performed in other situations by other people. He found, for example, that Warao women in their ritual wailing criticised and parodied the talk of men in dispute mediation. He also found that public health officials in the Delta Amacuro lifted the genre of 'cultural reasoning' from the writings of anthropologists. Briggs has also argued that ethnographers must take account of the types of situation in which

genres are learned and performed in each society, rather than imposing the interview as an alien type of situation.

Briggs has emphasised that the performance of discourse genres is closely linked to the inhabitance of social categories. The competence in performance of elderly Córdovan men both underwrote their authority as elders of the community and exemplified the values of community in the face of social transformations. Co-resident Warao women displayed their affective relations to each other by co-ordinating their ritual wailing, while posing a challenge to the authority of men by parodying the genres of dispute mediation. Briggs also found that public health officials reworked the genre of 'cultural reasoning' to blame Warao people for their own misfortunes, including a disastrous cholera epidemic. This enabled officials to evade their own responsibility, while defending themselves from accusations of racism.

Education

BA Colorado College, 1974
MA University of Chicago, 1978
Ph.D. University of Chicago, 1981

Fieldwork

Córdova, New Mexico, 1972–3, 1978–9, 1983
Delta Amacuro, Venezuela, 1986–2002 (various periods)

Key Publications

(1986) *Learning How To Ask: A Sociolinguistic Appraisal of the Role of the Interview in Social Science Research*, Cambridge and New York: Cambridge University Press.

(1988) *Competence in Performance: The Creativity of Tradition in Mexicano Verbal Art*, Philadelphia: University of Pennsylvania Press.

with Mantini-Briggs, Clara (2003) *Stories in the Time of Cholera: Racial Profiling during a Medical*

Nightmare, Berkeley, CA: University of California Press.

TREVOR STACK

Briggs, Jean L.

b. 29 May 1929, Washington, DC, USA

Jean Briggs's work focuses on the psychology of interpersonal relations and the socialisation of children, especially among the Inuit of the Central and Eastern Canadian Arctic.

Never in Anger is an account of her nineteen months' sojourn in a contact-traditional camp of Utkuhiksaklingmiut in the Central Canadian Arctic. It shows remarkable insight into the careful ways Inuit construct personal relationships and how they structure and express emotions. It is also a pioneer work of reflexive ethnography in which the observer is also a contextualised character, in her case a *kapluna* [white] daughter. Indeed many of Briggs's insights on Inuit life stem from her own often tension-filled relations with her hosts.

Briggs's findings, which have stood the test of time, show that Inuit self-control is based on the need for year-round small-group co-operation and the fear that anger will lead to violence. The child's first major test is when another child is born and the toddler is put aside by the mother. Inuit consider asking too many questions, making verbal generalisations, personal boasting, and attempting to predict the future to be infantile, lacking the key ingredient of *ihuma*, adult rationality.

Inuit Morality Play, based on five trips totalling twenty-three months among the Qipisamiut of Baffin Island, is a remarkable essay in the microsociality and sociolinguistics of child rearing. Briggs describes vignettes in which adults engage a 3-year-old 'Chubby Maata', like other children, in powerful play-dramas, about absence, aggression, rivalry, and so on in ways that challenge them to manage such situations before they actually face them. Thus Briggs's work demonstrates in minute detail the on-going construction of 'culture', which

is subject to variation, and, for today's Inuit, is changing rapidly.

Briggs has also delivered talks and published on many important topics including gender relations, conflict and aggression management, language and meaning, Inuit health, formal and informal education, ethnic identity and cultural change (1997), and anthropological fieldwork methods.

For *Inuit Morality Play* Briggs was awarded the Victor Turner Prize for Ethnographic Writing and the Boyer Prize for contributions to psychoanalytic anthropology by the American Anthropological Association. She was awarded an honorary doctorate by the University of Bergen (1996) and was elected Fellow of the Royal Society of Canada (2001). After teaching for thirty years at Memorial University, Newfoundland, professor emeritus Jean Briggs continues to work on an Utkuhiksalingmiutitut dictionary.

Education

BA Vassar College, 1951
MA Boston University, 1960
Ph.D. Harvard University, 1967

Fieldwork

Alaskan Inupiaq, 1960, 1961
Canadian Inuit, 1963–5, 1968, 1971, 1972–3,
   1974, 1975, 1979–80, 1992, 1993, 1997,
   1998, 1999, 2000, 2001, 2002
Israeli Bedouin, 1985
Siberian Yupik, 1993

Key Publications

(1970) *Never in Anger: Portrait of an Eskimo Family*, Cambridge, MA: Harvard University Press.
(1997) 'From trait to emblem and back: living and representing culture in everyday life', *Arctic Anthropology* 34, 1: 227–35.
(1998) *Inuit Morality Play: The Emotional Education of a Three Year Old*, New Haven: Yale University Press and St Johns, Newfoundland: Institute

of Social and Economic Research, Memorial University.

NELSON H. H. GRABURN

Bright, William

b. 1928, Oxnard, California, USA

d. 15 October 2006, Louisville, Colorado, USA

William Bright's contributions to linguistics, linguistic anthropology, and sociolinguistics encompass a protean diversity of specialties and roles. Bright's major contributions to the study of the indigenous languages of the Americas include his 1957 grammar of Karuk (earlier spelled 'Karok'), originally a dissertation written under the direction of Mary Haas. Bright's appointment at the University of California, Los Angeles (UCLA), in 1959 permitted him to expand his interests to languages in Southern California, and he published and directed research on Cahuilla, Cupeño, and Luiseño, as well as on Nahuatl, a language of central Mexico for which he identified an informant in the Los Angeles area. During the same period, Bright began work on South Asian languages under the direction of another Berkeley linguist, Murray Emeneau, and after earning his doctorate undertook a two-year Rockefeller Fellowship in India, which yielded grammatical sketches of Kannada and Tamil, the latter in collaboration with A.K. Ramanujan. In both Native American and South Asian linguistics, Bright began very early to publish not only on grammar and phonology, but also on the other major topics to which he returned throughout his career in over 400 published works: language contact, loan vocabulary, and other 'areal' phenomena; the social dimensions of language variation; historical linguistics and linguistic relationships; personal names and place names; poetry and song; and writing systems. Bright's holism was one of the factors that shaped modern linguistic anthropology, called 'sociolinguistics' in early work to which Bright contributed along with his friends and collaborators, John Gumperz and Dell H.

Hymes. Bright's edited volume of 1966, containing the proceedings of a conference he organised at UCLA on the emerging field that he labelled 'sociolinguistics', included major contributions by these authors as well as other important figures and is widely seen as a watershed volume.

In addition to published contributions that shaped and advanced the study of language in anthropology, Bright made major contributions as an editor. Between 1965 and 1987 Bright steered the journal, *Language*, the flagship publication of the Linguistic Society of America, through the treacherous seas of theoretical schism that dominated linguistics in this era. In spite of the proliferation of new journals with specialised theoretical agendas during this period, under his editorship *Language* continued to publish new work by many of the most significant figures in every theoretical camp, as well as advancing Bright's own preference for holism, theoretical eclecticism, and solid empirical foundations. In 1992, Bright became editor of the most important international English-language journal in sociolinguistics, *Language in Society*, and continued in this position until 1999, publishing contributions from leading figures across the full scope of the field. In 1997, Bright founded a new journal, *Written Language and Literacy*, now in its seventh volume. In addition to journals, Bright's editorial contributions included the *Oxford Encyclopedia of Linguistics* (1992), a major four-volume work of reference now going into a second edition under a new editor, many editions of Native American texts including texts both in the original languages and in translation (as with *A Coyote Reader* of 1993), a volume on *The World's Writing Systems* (1996), and a forthcoming volume on the Native American place names of the USA. Bright served as editorial director of the Malki Museum Press, run by the Morongo Indian Reservation at Banning, California, from 1977 until 1984, and served on many other editorial boards throughout his career.

Bright's career and contributions were been shaped not only by the many collegial relationships that he enjoyed across the globe, but also by members of his family. Early publications include co-authored work with his first wife, Elizabeth Bright, and his second wife, the late Jane Orstan Bright. Bright shared as well joint interests with the late Marcia Andersen Bright, an anthropologist, and with his fourth wife, Debra Levy, a psychologist. The psycholinguist Lisa Menn, whom Bright married in 1986, was also a scholarly inspiration as well as a life companion. Finally, Bright credited his daughter, Susan Bright, a well-known writer and lecturer on human sexuality, inspiration that permitted him to branch out into popular writing on questions such as the etymologies of Native American place names and the history of Coyote.

Education

AB University of California, Berkeley, 1949
Ph.D. University of California, Berkeley, 1955

Fieldwork

Karuk language in northwestern California, 1949–51
Fieldwork and teaching in India, 1955–7, 1967
Southern California languages, 1959–79
Yurok language in northwestern California (with Jane O. Bright), 1962–3
Cakchiquel and other languages (Guatemala), 1975–9

Key Publications

(1957) *The Karok Language*, Berkeley and Los Angeles: University of California Press.
(ed.) (1966) *Sociolinguistics*, The Hague: Mouton.
(1976) *Variation and Change in Language: Essays*, selected and introduced by Anwar S. Dil, Stanford, CA: Stanford University Press.
(1990) *Language Variation in South Asia*, New York: Oxford University Press.

JANE HILL

Brodkin, Karen

b. 1941, New York City, USA

Karen Helen Brodkin is a feminist anthropologist whose research interests include gender, work and kinship, ethnological and feminist theory, racialisation, and contemporary capitalist culture in North America. Until the mid-1990s, Brodkin published under her married name, Karen Brodkin Sacks.

Following early teaching positions at Oakland University, Fordham University, and Clark University, Brodkin moved to Duke University on a post-doctoral fellowship in 1978; she later became research director for the Business and Professional Women's Organization in Washington, DC. In 1987 she moved to the University of California, Los Angeles, as professor of anthropology and director of the Women's Studies Program; she remains active in both programmes.

One of the founding theoreticians of Marxist feminist anthropology, Brodkin established her national reputation in the mid-1970s through a series of articles on gender, race, class, and the state. Her first book, *Sisters and Wives*, examined tensions between women's marital and natal kin roles in three African societies through periods of colonisation, and class and state formation. Through the case studies she demonstrated how analysing gendered kinship is key to understanding relations of production.

In the 1980s Brodkin shifted her research to gender and labour in the USA. She and Dorothy Remy published the first anthology to bring together researchers on women and work in the contemporary USA, *My Troubles Are Going to Have Trouble with Me* (1984). *Caring by the Hour* examined a decade-long effort by Duke hospital workers to unionise. Focusing on how race and class shape leadership for women, her concept of 'centrewomen' deeply influenced later approaches to working-class women's grassroots organisational strategies.

In the late 1980s Brodkin theorised how

gender articulated with race and class to forge differential experiences of social power and oppression, on the one hand, and vehicles for organising, on the other. 'Toward a unified theory of class, race and gender' (1989) argued that theorising the intersections of gender with race and class can be keenly attentive to local variation without sacrificing the ability to note overarching patterns, a level of theorising that is crucial to organising across states and societies. The 1990s found Brodkin delving deeper into racialisation as a process that is heavily classed and gendered. *How Jews Became White Folks and What That Says about Race in America* is her pioneering effort to integrate gender fully into the analysis of race and class. Honoured in 1999 by the Society for the Anthropology of North America (SANA), Brodkin's plenary address at the SANA/Canadian Anthropology Society meetings appeared as 'Global capitalism: what's race got to do with it?' (2000). Brodkin's current project concerns working-class social movements in Los Angeles.

Education

BA Brandeis University, 1963
MA Harvard University, 1964
Ph.D. University of Michigan, 1971

Fieldwork

North Carolina (mid-1980s)
Los Angeles (1990s to present)

Key Publications

(1974) 'Engels revisited: women, the organization of production, and private property', in M. Rosaldo and L. Lamphere (eds) *Women, Culture, and Society*, Palo Alto: Stanford.
(1979) *Sisters and Wives: The Past and Future of Sexual Equality*, Westport: Greenwood.
(1988) *Caring by the Hour*, Urbana: Illinois.
(1998) *How Jews Became White Folks and What That*

Says about Race in America, New Brunswick: Rutgers.

CHRISTINE WARD GAILEY

Bromberger, Christian

b. 1946, Paris, France

Educated in France's two main anthropological traditions −Lévi-Strauss's structuralism and Leroi-Gourhan's material culture studies − Christian Bromberger's work is often an innovative synthesis of both, such as, for example, his seminal article, 'Technology and the semantic analysis of objects: towards a semio-technology' (2002 [1979]). Since the 1970s he continues to alternate fieldwork, mainly in Iran, Italy, and the south of France, with prolific writing (more than 140 publications), and lecturing, both in France and abroad. After having explored the fields of semiotics, linguistics, and vernacular architecture (in Iran and southern France) in his early writings, he has been a pioneer in the anthropology of sport (especially soccer) and the study of 'supporterism' in the 1980s. Throughout the diversity of his research, which includes such topics as social and cross-cultural attitudes towards body hair, Bromberger tries to outline − both theoretically and methodologically − an anthropology of what he qualifies as 'ordinary crazes and passions' (*les passions ordinaires*) in contemporary societies.

Education

Licence de Lettres (BA) and Certificat d'Ethnologie, Paris, 1966
Agrégation de Lettres Classiques (MA), Paris, 1968
Diploma of the Centre de Formation à la Recherche Ethnologique (CFRE), Paris, 1969
Habilitation en Ethnologie (equivalent of a Doctorate), University of Provence, Aix-en-Provence, 1990

Fieldwork

Iran (mainly the northwestern Gilân province), 1971, 1972, 1974, 1977, 1978, 1982, 1991, 1993, 1996, 1997, 1998, 2000, 2002

Italy (especially Turin and Naples), frequent short fieldwork trips during the 1980s

France (especially the Provence region), intermittent fieldwork since 1972

Key Publications

(1989) *Habitat, Architecture and Rural Society in the Gilân Plain (Northern Iran)* (*Habitat, architecture et société rurale dans la Plaine de Gilân* (*Iran septentrional*, 1986), Bonn: F.Dümmlers Verlag

(1995) *Le Match de football, ethnologie d'une passion partisane à Marseille, Naples et Turin* (The Soccer Match, Anthropology of a Partisan Passion in Marseilles, Naples and Turin), Paris: Éditions de la Maison des Sciences de l'Homme.

THOMAS K. SCHIPPERS

Bromley, Julian V.

b. 1921, Moscow, Russia

d. 1990, Moscow, Russia

J. Bromley achieved recognition through his focus on theoretical ethnology, particularly for his contribution to the development of the theory of ethnos. Bromley argued against such theoretical approaches as sociobiology that insisted that the ethnos was mainly a biological phenomenon. He regarded it first and foremost as a historical-cultural unit, closely connected with its socioeconomic base. Bromley defined these 'synthetic' formations as ethno-social organisms (ESO). The main difference between a historical-cultural unit in general and the ethnos is the construction and expression of their members' selfhood. The latter have ethnic self-consciousness and *self-ethnic-identity* (ethnicity, nationality), expressed by ethnonym, a principal element for the antithesis of 'we–they'.

Bromley connected the characteristic features of the objective existence of the ethnos with sociocultural spheres. The unique make-up of each ethnos was created not by some individual specific feature, but by a combination of elements, unique to each given ethnos. The units proposed by J.Bromley reflected the structure of their hierarchy, on one side, and their historical dynamics, on the other. An evolutionary change in the individual components of an ethnic system that did not lead to a break-up of the system as a whole was conceptualised as an 'ethno-evolutionary' process. During its existence each ethnos underwent ethno-evolutionary changes almost on a continuous basis. Ethnic processes, which resulted in the destruction of ethnic systems, were termed 'ethno-transformatory' processes.

J. Bromley identified the enormous influence of technological progress on the traditional everyday culture of peoples (ethnoses) as the characteristic ethnographic feature of the present epoch. He argued that the ethnic features of modern peoples were gradually shifting from the sphere of material culture to that of non-material culture. The professional forms of the latter have become part of modern peoples' daily life and as a result have acquired an important ethnic role in industrially advanced countries.

Bromley paid special attention to the dynamics of modern ethnic systems, in particular to the interactions between socioclass and ethnic phenomena. Recognised as one of the pioneers in crossing disciplinary boundaries in Soviet ethnography, Bromley always insisted on broad ethnographic research into the ethnocultural aspects of Soviet peoples' modern way of life, their traditional everyday-life components, and the family as the basic unit of intergeneration transmission. Browley's own ethnographic study in this field focused on marriage and family in Serbia and Croatia.

J. Bromley was regarded as a prominent organiser of science in the Soviet Union. He was the Director of the Institute of Ethnography (from 1966) and the Chairman of the Scientific Council on the National Problems of the Academy of Sciences of the USSR (from 1969).

Education

Diploma of the Department of History, Moscow State University (Soviet equivalent of MA), 1950

Kandidat Nauk (Soviet equivalent of Ph.D.), Institute of Slavic Studies, Soviet Academy of Sciences, Moscow, 1956

Doktor Nauk (Soviet equivalent of Habilitation Doctor), Institute of Slavic Studies, Soviet Academy of Sciences, Moscow, 1963

Fieldwork

Zadar, Croatia, 1959, 1960–2 (1–3 months per year)

Key Publications

(1973) Ethnos I Enthnographia (Ethnos and Ethnography), Moscow: Nauka.

(1983) Ocherki Teorii Etnosa (Essays in Ethnos Theory), Moscow: Nauka.

(1984) Theoretical Ethnography, Moscow: Nauka.

(1987) Etnosotsyalnye Protsessy: Teoriya, Istoriya, Sovremennost (Ethnosocial Processes: Theory, History, Modernity), Moscow: Nauka.

TATIANA UVAROVA

Bruner, Edward M.

b. 28 September 1924, New York City, USA

Edward M. Bruner has worked on an unusually diverse range of topics. His interests have passed through a number of overlapping phases through which run a number of continuous threads. Initially in 1952 his doctoral fieldwork was among the Mandan-Hidatsa Indians, and his main interest was in acculturation, cultural transmission, and social organisation. He was interested in how Native American culture had changed and in how individuals coped with that change. In particular he was concerned to find out the extent to which aspects of native culture such as family and kinship, and which individuals, had changed the most, and why. In 1967 Bruner carried out fieldwork in Indonesia in order to study Toba Batak social organisation, urbanisation, ethnicity, and change, once again focusing on family and kinship.

In the late 1970s, Bruner became interested in post-modernism, post-structualism, and ethnographic writing, and especially the ways in which the stories, told both by informants and anthropologists, are interpreted, exchanged, and contested. Indeed, he argues that there can never be just 'a' story or 'one' story, but rather a dialogic process of many historically situated particular tellings. These interests culminated in several important papers and two edited volumes, Text, Play and Story in 1984 (reissued in 1988) and The Anthropology of Experience in 1986 (with Victor Turner). His contribution there was primarily in narrative theory and the analysis of experience. Most recently he has been publishing widely on tourism, based on data gathered in a number of countries including Bali, Kenya, Ghana, and the USA. His focus here is on how and why people travel and the diverse ways in which culture is represented to tourists. Bruner deals at some length and with considerable insight with issues of authenticity, representation, and globalisation, and he is a significant and influential contributor to our understanding of tourism in the contemporary world. Always a humanistic anthropologist, Edward Bruner has contributed to the corpus of anthropology for more than five decades; his work is consistently lucid, evocative, and elegantly written.

Education

BA Ohio State University, 1948
MA Ohio State University, 1950
Ph.D. University of Chicago, 1954

Fieldwork

Navaho Reservation, New Mexico, 1948

Fort Berthold Indian Reservation, North Dakota, 1952

American Indians, Chicago, 1966

Toba Batak, Sumatra, Indonesia, 1967

Java and Sumatra, Indonesia, 1969–73 (12 months)

Bali, Kenya, Egypt, Israel, 1983–84

Java, Bali, and Sulawesi, 1986, 1987, 1991, 1992

Lincoln's New Salem Historic Site, Illinois, 1988–90

Ghana, 1994 (6 weeks)

Kenya, 1995, 1999

Yunnan, China, 1999

Key Publications

(ed.) (1984) *Text, Play and Story: The Construction and Reconstruction of Self and Society*, Proceedings of the American Ethnological Society. Reissued (1988) Chicago: Waveland Press.

with Victor W. Turner (eds) (1986) *The Anthropology of Experience*, Urbana: University of Illinois.

(ed.) (1993) Museums and Tourism. Special issue, *Museum Anthropology* 17, 3: 3–66.

with Marie-Francoise Lanfant and John Allcock (eds) (1995) *International Tourism: Identity and Change*, London: Sage.

PETER COLLINS

Buck, Peter H. (Te Rangi Hiroa)

b. c.1877, Urenui, New Zealand

d. 1951, Honolulu, Hawaii

Peter Buck was born in rural Taranaki, New Zealand, on an unrecorded date in the aftermath of the 1860s land wars. His father was William Buck, an Irish soldier-settler, and his mother was Ngarongo-ki-tua, of the local Ngati Mutunga tribe. From each parent he received a distinctive family name, a solid cultural grounding, and a respect for the traditions of the other. While attending a Maori boys' high school, Te Rangi Hiroa helped form the Young Maori Party, a movement that sought to counter the decline in

population and the social impoverishment of Maori. It also advocated using anthropological research to achieve these ends. After graduating from university, Buck spent two decades pursuing distinguished careers in medicine (ultimately becoming national director of Maori health services), politics (serving as both a Maori member of parliament and a cabinet minister), and war (rising to deputy commander of the Maori contingent at Gallipoli, Flanders, and the Somme). During this period he also pursued ethnological research on Maori issues, notably a thesis on traditional medicine, articles on technology and somatology, and important texts on demographic change, ancient society, and clothing.

In 1927, around the age of fifty, Te Rangi Hiroa became a professional anthropologist – with the Bishop Museum in Honolulu, then the major sponsor of field research in tropical Polynesia. Welcomed by the peoples of the region as a distant kinsman of great mana, he produced pathbreaking monographs on the material cultures of Aitutaki, Samoa, the Cook Islands, Kapingamarangi, and Hawaii. Each volume is testimony to Buck's vast knowledge of Polynesian languages, technologies, and aesthetics, as expressed in hundreds of pages of written description, and innumerable fine drawings of weaving styles, canoe parts, domestic implements, adze types, personal ornaments, carved weapons, tattoo patterns, clothing designs, musical instruments, string figures, building architecture, and more. Te Rangi Hiroa likewise authored monographs on the traditional cultures of Mangaia, Tongareva, Manihiki, Rakahanga, and Mangareva, all in the Cook Islands, and books on Polynesian origins, history, religion, and anthropology. From 1936 to 1951 he was director of the Bishop Museum and a professor at Yale University. Buck also was the recipient of four honorary doctorates, numerous professional awards, and – from his homeland – a knighthood. After his death in Hawaii, Te Rangi Hiroa was accorded a chiefly interment under a monumental canoe prow at Okoki, a sacred fortress and graveyard of his Taranaki ancestors.

Education

MB 1904 University of New Zealand, Otago
Ch.B.1904 University of New Zealand, Otago
MD 1910 University of New Zealand, Otago

Fieldwork

New Zealand, 1910–26 (intermittent)
Rarotonga, 1910 (6 months)
Niue, 1911 (4 months)
Aitutaki, 1926 (1 month)
Samoa, 1927 (5 months)
Cook Islands, 1929–30 (12 months)
Kapingamarangi, 1947 (3 months)
Hawaii, 1927–51 (intermittent)

Key Publications

(1925) *The Coming of the Maori*, Nelson: Stiles & Company
(1938) *Vikings of the Sunrise*, New York: Stokes & Company
(1944) *Arts and Crafts of the Cook Islands*, Honolulu: Bishop Museum.

TOM RYAN

Bulmer, Ralph Neville Hermon

b. 1928, Hereford, UK

d. 1988, Auckland, New Zealand

Ralph Bulmer's ethnographic work amongst the Kalam- (or Karam) speaking people of the New Guinea Highlands in the period 1960s–1980s set the standard for modern ethnobiological and ethnozoological research. It also led a general shift in the focus of Melanesian anthropology from sociopolitical organisation to indigenous conceptions of natural and supernatural worlds. Bulmer's innovative approach owed much to the fact that the Kalam themselves are more interested in classifying their environment than in classifying people. He was also influenced by Harold Conklin's pioneering work in ethnobotany, and Claude Lévi-Strauss's and Mary Douglas's theories of myth and symbolism. Bulmer first developed his ideas in several essays, notably 'Why is the Cassowary not a bird?'. A subsequent book, *Birds of My Kalam Country*, co-written with Saem Majnep, a young Kalam hunter, has been called the first genuinely 'dialogical' ethnographic text. The publication of two bilingual companion volumes, on animals and plants, was disrupted by Bulmer's premature death. He also contributed significantly to the institutional development of the discipline in Oceania, especially as foundation professor of anthropology at the University of Papua New Guinea (1968–74) and professor of social anthropology at the University of Auckland (1974–88).

Education

BA Cambridge, 1953
Ph.D. Australian National University, 1960

Fieldwork

Sor-Varanger, Lapland, 1950 (4 months)
Kayaka Enga, Baiyer River, Western Highlands, Papua New Guinea, 1954–9 (17 months total)
Kalam, Upper Kaironk River, Madang Province, Papua New Guinea, 1960–85 (30 months total)

Key Publications

(1967) 'Why is the Cassowary not a bird? A problem of zoological taxonomy among the Karam of the New Guinea Highlands', *Man* 2, 1: 5–25.
with Saem Majnep, Ian (1977) *Birds of My Kalam Country*, Auckland: Auckland University Press and Oxford University Press.

TOM RYAN

Bunzel, Ruth Leah

b. 18 April 1898, New York City, USA

d. 14 January 1990, New York City, USA

Raised in an acculturated Jewish household in New York City, Ruth Bunzel switched from her undergraduate major in European history to salvage ethnography after a stint as secretary to Franz Boas. Boas encouraged her to begin fieldwork among the Pueblo Indians of the American Southwest and then to enter the graduate programme in anthropology at Columbia. Bunzel was one of many women encouraged to become anthropologists by Boas and Elsie Clews Parsons. She taught sporadically at Columbia during a career devoted primarily to fieldwork and writing.

Bunzel credits Boas for her dissertation topic, a study of Pueblo pottery making based on her own apprenticeship directed towards revealing the point of view of the potters towards their work. She was adopted into the Badger clan and given a Zuni name by Flora Zuni, her most important teacher. *The Pueblo Potter* pioneered in combining the study of art with the psychology of the individual artist.

Her second season at Zuni (and other pueblos) focused on ceremonialism. In the 1932 annual report of the Bureau of American Ethnology, Bunzel reported on the origin myths, ritual poetry, and beliefs that together constituted Zuni ceremonialism. The Zunis were more resistant to providing information on ceremonialism. On this topic she worked closely with Nick Dumaka, a former governor of the pueblo. His premature death was attributed by many to his revealing of esoteric ceremonial information. In the third year of her study, Bunzel turned to learning the language, resulting in a volume of texts in 1933.

Bunzel became interested in Mexico because of its cultural relationship to the Southwest. She carried out two extensive field trips in Guatemala where virtually no problem-oriented ethnological work had been done previously. Santo Tomas Chichicastenango was a ceremonial and market center much like Zuni, although Bunzel never became as deeply involved in the life of her second field site. Her interests in Zuni creativity broadened to deal with broader issues of culture-and-personality; she compared alcoholism in Chichicastenango where interpersonal strife was considerable but drunkenness negatively valued to that in Chamula, Chiapas, Mexico, where alcohol was socially acceptable but interfered with productive cultural activities.

The next logical extension of her work was to Spain where she was studying at the outbreak of the Second World War, during which she worked for the Office of War Information in England. After the war, Bunzel returned to New York City and Columbia to collaborate with Ruth Benedict, Margaret Mead, and others in studying contemporary cultures around the world. She directed the China group.

Education

BA Barnard College, 1918
Ph.D. Columbia University, 1929

Fieldwork

Zuni, 1924–9
Mexico and Guatemala, early 1930s
Spain, late 1930s

Key Publications

(1929) *The Pueblo Potter: A Study of Creative Imagination in Primitive Art*, New York: Columbia University Press.
(1933) *Zuni Texts*, New York: B.E. Stechert & Co.
(1940) 'The role of alcoholism in two Central American cultures', *Psychiatry* 3: 361–87.
(1952) *Chichicastenango, a Guatemalan Village*, Locust Valley, NY: J.J. Augustin Publishers.

REGNA DARNELL

Butovskaya, Marina

b. 27 June 1959, Cherkassy, Ukraine, USSR

Marina Butovskaya achieved international recognition early in her career with the ethological study of non-human primates socio-ecology, as well as ethological observations of children's social behaviour.

In 1993–9 Butovskaya carried out a field study project on socialisation for aggression and peacemaking in two cultures (Russian and Kalmyk). She conducted observations of children's interactions during free play outdoors in Moscow, the Tula region, Elista, and Iki-Chinos, a small village in Kalmykia. Using ethological methods of observations and individual interviews, she came to the conclusion that, by the age of six–seven, children are already able to cope with situations of conflict without intrusion from adults and that both natural and cultural components are present in humans' post-conflict reconciliative behaviour.

During the late 1990s Butovskaya moved towards urban anthropology with an analysis of beggars' sub-culture. She combined ethological, cultural-anthropological, and sociological methods in this study to understand the nature of these phenomena in modern Russia as well as universal mechanisms of begging behaviour in humans. At the moment she is engaged in a cross-cultural project on begging behaviour in Moscow, Prague, and Bucharest, as well as another urban anthropology project, a study of strategies of movement among urban pedestrians in Moscow and other cities in the former Soviet Union.

Education

MA Moscow State University, 1982
Ph.D. Soviet Academy of Sciences, 1986
D.Sc. Russian Academy of Sciences, 1994

Fieldwork

Abkhazia, 1980–90
Moscow, 1993–6, 1998–present
Rural central Russia, 1995
Kalmykia, 1996–7

Key Publications

with Fainberg, L. (1993) *On the Origin of Human Society*, Moscow: Nauka (in Russian).
with Korotayev, A.V. and Kazankov, A.A. (2000) 'Variabilité des relations sociales chez les primates humains et non humains: à la recherche d'un paradigme général', ('Variability of social relations among human and non human primates: towards research of a general paradigm') *Primatologie* 3: 319–63.

ANDREY KOROTAYEV

C

Caplan, Lionel

b. 16 November 1931, Montreal, Quebec, Canada

Lionel Caplan came to prominence through his study of Hindu–tribal relations in east Nepal conducted in the mid-1960s. *Land and Social Change in East Nepal* broke new ground in the way it approached the encounter between a marginalised tribal population and a dominating elite. Here a high-caste Hindu group had entered tribal territory and taken control of the land. The book examined the ways in which a dominated people responded and struggled against processes of dispossession. Unlike many of its predecessors this book placed the study of conflict – particularly around land – at the center of the anthropological understanding of tribal peoples.

Caplan's career is linked to the School of African and Oriental Studies, London, where he took up a lecturer's post in 1965 and where he received a professorial title in 1987. Canadian by birth, both his parents were Jewish migrants from Eastern Europe, and he was the first in his family to attend university. Himself a non-native in Britain, there may be something of an echo of this migrant experience in his work. The central thread that holds all of Caplan's writings together is an attention to the processes of marginalisation often foregrounding the complex cultural encounters between the dominant and the dominated.

In the mid-1970s and early 1980s he conducted fieldwork in Madras City, south India, on Christian congregations. Again a study of a marginalised group, this work examined the intersections of class and religious faith, and focused on the way mainly American 'fundamentalist' Christianity had entered and taken hold in Madras. Among the poor, especially, Christianity was combined with spirit healing and possession, practices opposed by the middle classes. Here the religious message revealed complex class divisions in an urban context.

Caplan's work anticipated the concern about 'religious fundamentalism' (an edited volume, *Studies in Religious Fundamentalism*, 1987, was among the earliest on the topic). Building on contemporary concerns with how Western scholars portrayed their non-Western subjects, in 1995 he published *Warrior Gentlemen*, which examined representations of the 'Gurkhas' – a category drawn from marginalised populations in Nepal – in the military writings of British officers. In 2001 he completed a study of Anglo-Indians, a tiny, mixed-race community that had survived though four centuries of encounter between colonial and Indian communities. This much-stereotyped population confounded colonial categories by absorbing complex cultural streams within their community and culture, and enabled Caplan to address issues of post-coloniality and cultural hybridity.

Lionel Caplan's anthropology is one that is committed to ethnographic engagement and deep listening. It is characterised by a commitment to empirical dialogue that acknowledges excluded peoples' right to speak and to be heard.

Education

B.Comm. McGill University, 1952
MA School of Oriental and African Studies, London, 1963
Ph.D. School of Oriental and African Studies, London, 1966

Fieldwork

Rural east Nepal, 1964–5, 1988
Dailekh, west Nepal, 1969
Madras City, south India, 1974–5, 1981–2, 1991–2, 1996, 1999

Key Publications

(1970) *Land and Social Change in East Nepal: A Study of Hindu–Tribal Relations*, London: Routledge and University of California Press.
(1987) *Class and Culture in Urban India: Fundamentalism in a Christian community*, Oxford: Clarendon Press.
(2001) *Children of Colonialism: Anglo-Indians in a Postcolonial World*, Oxford: Berg Press.

LES BACK

Caplan, Patricia

b. 13 March 1942, Neston, Cheshire, UK

Pat Caplan's work demonstrates a commitment to both classical anthropology and to political and epistemological challenges to the discipline. Her early work on kinship on Mafia Island, Tanzania, was formed by the expectations of British anthropology in the 1960s and resulted in a book, *Choice and Constraint in a Swahili Community* (1975). She has subsequently worked on Mafia development, government policies, food, health, and fertility, and her

latest book on the area is *African Voices, African Lives* (1997).

In 1974 she began fieldwork in Madras City, south India, examining the role of women's philanthropic and social welfare organisations, which, while providing a sphere for political involvement, were implicated in upholding a deeply unequal class system, as she shows in her monograph, *Class and Gender in India* (1985). She has continued to work in Madras on issues such as changes in food consumption patterns.

As part of the London Women's Anthropology Group in the early 1970s Caplan was central to the emergence of feminist anthropology in Britain, and was involved in the production of several texts: *Women United, Women Divided* (1978), *The Cultural Construction of Sexuality* (1987,) and *Gendered Fields* (1994). This paradigm shift was linked with a critique of objectivity, positivism, and empiricism within the discipline as a whole as well as of the gendered institutional structures of the academy. In her 1988 Audrey Richards Memorial Lecture Caplan argued that the debate surrounding the literary turn in anthropology had largely ignored the reflexive contribution of women anthropologists.

Caplan has also written extensively and researched on Swahili culture (*Les Swahili entre Afrique et Arabie*, [The Swahili between Africa and Arabia] (1991), dispute settlement (*Understanding Disputes* (1995), food (*Food, Health and Identity*, 1997), risk (*Risk Revisited*, 2000), and ethics (*The Ethics of Anthropology*, 2003). Her most recent work focuses on anthropology as a moral discipline and issues such as social justice, ethics, and human rights. She is also working on local understandings of modernity on Mafia Island.

Caplan has always sought to maintain a connection between her academic work and political activism. She was a founder member and chair of Anthropologists against Ethnic Violence in the 1990s, and chair of the Association of Social Anthropologists of the UK and Commonwealth from 1997–2001. Between 1998–2000 she was seconded away from Goldsmiths College, where she has taught since 1977 and where she has held a chair since 1989, to be director of the Institute of Commonwealth Studies, School of Advanced Study, University of London.

Education

BA (Hons) School of African and Oriental Studies, London, 1963

MA School of African and Oriental Studies, London – by dissertation, 1965

Ph.D. School of African and Oriental Studies, London, 1968

Fieldwork

Mafía Island, Tanzania, 1965–7, 1976, 1985, 1994, 2002

Nepal, Far Western Hills, 1968–70

Madras City, south India, 1974–5, 1981–2, 1987–8, 1995–6, 1998–9

Lewisham, London, 1992–6 (project director)

A small town in South Wales, 1994–6 (project director)

Key Publications

(ed.) (1987) *The Cultural Construction of Sexuality*, London: Tavistock Publications.

(1997) *African Voices, African Lives: Personal Narratives from a Swahili Village*, London: Routledge.

(ed.) (1997) *Food, Health and Identity*, London and New York: Routledge Publications.

LES BACK

Cardoso de Oliveira, Roberto

b. 1928, São Paulo, Brazil

d. 21 July 2006, Brasilia, Brazil

During the early 1960s, drawing on research among the Terena, the Tapirapé, and the Tikuna, which he had initiated in 1954 at the Museu do Índio (Indian Museum at Rio de Janeiro) and at the Protection Service of the Indians (SPI), Roberto Cardoso de Oliveira developed a theory of inter-ethnic friction, which for more than two decades served as the main framework for studies carried out in Brazil, concerned with contacts between Indian and whites. Drawing inspiration from Georges Balandier's analyses of the colonial situation, Cardoso de Oliveira situated conflict and continued interaction as structural components of contact – as is suggested by the use of the term 'friction'. Recalling Fredrik Barth's earlier propositions, this notion offered an alternative to perspectives that tended to describe contact as something accidental and instantaneous, leading to a state of social disorganisation. With this notion, it became possible to approach the situation of the indigenous groups without assuming their necessary sudden or gradual disappearance, as was usual at that time.

On the institutional side, Cardoso de Oliveira was the founder of modern social anthropology in Brazilian universities. He succeeded in providing continuity for postgraduate courses associated with specific lines of research and consolidated the previous efforts of Darcy Ribeiro (1922–77), doing for anthropology what his mentor, Florestan Fernandes (1920–95), had done for sociology at the University of São Paulo. In disagreement with the weak protection policy of the Indian Protection Agency, he quit the Museu do Índio at the end of the 1950s and was appointed to the Museu Nacional by Castro Faria where he developed an efficient course for the training of anthropological researchers. In 1968 he founded a Master's programme that was the first graduate programme in social anthropology in Brazil. At the same time he participated in fieldwork in Central Brazil that he carried out in collaboration with David Maybury-Lewis (Harvard University) and with the support of the Ford Foundation. After a period as a visiting scholar at Harvard, in 1972 he returned to his role as a distinguished teacher with the instalment of a new postgraduate course at the University of Brasilia and finally, in 1986, the establishment of a doctoral programme at the University of Campinas.

During the last few years he was working on a comparative study of different national traditions and styles in anthropology.

Education

BA University of São Paulo, 1953
Ph.D. University of São Paulo, 1966

Fieldwork

Terena, South Mato Grosso, Brazil, 1955, 1957, 1958, 1960
Tapirapé, Mato Grosso, Brazil, 1957
Tukuna, Amazonas, Brazil, 1959, 1962, 1975
Tarascos, Mexico, 1973

Key Publications

(1964) *O Índio e o mundo dos brancos* (The Indian and the White Man World), São Paulo: Difusão Européia do Livro.
(1968) *Urbanização e tribalismo* (Urbanisation and Tribalism), Rio de Janeiro: Zahar Editores.
(1974) 'Indigenous peoples and socio-cultural change in the Amazon Brazil', in Charles Wagley (ed.) *Man in Amazon*, Gainesville: Florida University Press.
(1988) *Sobre o pensamento antropológico* (On Anthropological Knowledge), Rio de Janeiro: Tempo Brasileiro.

JOSÉ SERGIO LEITE LOPES

Caro Baroja, Julio

b. 13 November 1914, Madrid, Spain

d. 18 August 1995, Vera de Bidasoa, Guipúzcoa, Spain

Julio Caro Baroja is one of the most internationally renowned Spanish anthropologists. Nevertheless, various circumstances place him in a relatively distant and singular position in relation to other academic schools and tendencies, in Spain as well as abroad: his extensive and diverse work (which includes 697 titles, from material culture to the symbolic world and the construction of ideologies), his independence from university life, and his resistance to working under the political constraints imposed by Franco's dictatorship. In fact, Caro Baroja was forced many times to place himself in between folklore, history, and anthropology, to the point of blurring his most accurate professional identity. Precisely because he did not differentiate among various types of anthropologists – but rather judged them by the standards of accuracy and competence –, it can be said that Caro Baroja asserted his identity as an anthropologist as often as he, apparently, rejected it.

Caro Baroja has frequently been labelled as a historicist anthropologist, strongly influenced by the Cultural Circles of the Viennese School. During his life, however, different theoretical influences can be traced back: Viennese and North American historicism in the 1940s, English functionalism in the 1950s – after he met J. Pitt-Rivers and studied in Oxford under E. Evans-Pritchard – and, more recently, what he called 'historic structuralism', developed in his study, *The World of the Witches*, which conforms to a methodology of his own. In fact, Caro Baroja's uneasiness with the theoretical principles of the discipline is related partly to their inability to explain conflicts and social strain, as well as individual changes in social behaviour, and partly to their lack of tools to analyse the changing and dynamic reality of a complex society with a long history, such as the society in which he conducted his fieldwork – i.e. his own country, except for his short and productive fieldwork in *Western Sahara* (a monograph published in 1955). The 'other', the 'otherness', was his main concern, which is, obviously, an anthropological motivation, as it is the criticism of and discomfort in respect to one's own society – a constant force during his life. Furthermore, his refusal to understand reality in a unidirectional way constitutes one of the threads linking his vast written work, being at the core of his research on marginalised groups and his interest in those aspects that are variable and do not follow established rules, whether they took place in seventeenth-century Spain or in the Sahara desert in 1953.

The idea that assumed contradictions between historical and anthropological data can indeed be overcome is one of Caro Baroja's most outstanding contributions to anthropology; in other words, he was convinced that it is possible to get over the opposition between functionalism and diachrony. Because of this conviction, his work is highly coherent, despite his methodological fluctuations and the wide variety of case studies he selected to exemplify the issues that interested him: Basque identity, witchcraft rituals, and religious minorities, such as those of the Jews and Muslims, among others. Though developed through several voices and paths, his prolific work constitutes a single and unique project, aimed at understanding, on the one hand, 'reality' – not in a holistic way, but in the sense of the reality surrounding him – and, on the other, the knowledge related to this reality: scientific, academic, and intellectual, as well as other emic rational and pseudo-rational constructions embedded in such a 'surrounding world'. Because of this project, Caro Baroja's works on magical thought and world view, on the one hand, and his works on the ideological aspects of 'rational' discourses created to justify difference and to take action against those who are different, on the other, need to be revived and occupy their proper place in an international history of anthropology.

Education

BA University Central of Madrid, 1940
Ph.D. University Central of Madrid, 1942

Fieldwork

Basque country, Spain, 1930–5 and henceforth
Andalusia, Spain, 1949–50
Western Sahara, Nomads, 1952–3
Navarre, Spain, 1960–70

Key Publications

(1964) The World of the Witches (Las brujas y su mundo), trans. N. Glendinning, Chicago: University of Chicago Press (French trans. M.A. Sarrailh, Les Sorcières et leur monde, Paris: Gallimard. German trans. Susanne y Benno Hübner, Die Hexen und ihre Welt, Stuttgart: E. Klett Verlag, 1967).

(1965) El Carnaval (Carnival), Madrid: Taurus (French trans., Paris: Gallimard).

(1974) Ritos y mitos equívocos (Mistaken Rites and Myths), Madrid: Istmo.

(1973–91) Estudios Vascos (Basque Studies), 19 vols, San Sebastián: Txertoa.

CARMEN ORTIZ AND LUIS DÍAZ G. VIANA

Carrier, James G.

b. 1947, Washington, DC, USA

James Carrier's work has expanded from ethnographic studies in an area of the world still often used by anthropologists and others as a unchanging model of 'traditional society' to a series of major works that are concerned with transforming the anthropological study of modern life. Even in his earliest work on the island of Ponam, Carrier (working with his then-wife, Achsah) was able to show how the relationship between this peripheral part of Papua New Guinea and the country's center was essential in understanding the way Ponam people conceptualised kinship, exchange, and other important areas of their lives. In his collection on history and tradition in Melanesian anthropology he insisted that regions such as Melanesia needed to be seen as contemporary and changing.

Carrier then began to attend to Western societies, taking both gift and commodity as dynamic forms and using them to reinterpret American and British history. In his excellent edited collection on Occidentalism he generalised from such work to insist that anthropologists and others not only tend to view non-Western societies in stylised Orientalist terms, but also that this is complemented and to a degree explained by a tendency towards an equally stylised, Occidentalist view of the West. Carrier then went on to work on the place of the market within modern life. His edited collection on this topic brought out a whole series of ways in which the concept of the market may have had as least as much of an influence upon the way we think about our society, relate, and transact as does any actual market, which in turn often shows little formal resemblance to the market as an ideal. A subsequent edited collection further explores the power of the idealised idea of the market, under the term 'virtualism'. The RAI awarded him the Rivers Medal in 1997 for this work. He has now turned to fieldwork in Jamaica, where his interests in fishing, property, and political economy are being re-explored.

Taken as a whole Carrier has constantly challenged a rather stultified image and practice of anthropology steeped in primitivist illusions and allusions, and demonstrated that irrespective of whether studies take place in Melanesia, Britain or the USA there is a need to acknowledge and analyse the constituent features of modern life within which we all live today.

Education

BA University of Virginia, 1972
MA University of Virginia, 1973
Ph.D. London School of Economics, 1977

Fieldwork

Ponam Island, Manus Province, Papua New Guinea, 1978–86 (intermittent)
Montego Bay and Negril, Jamaica, 1997–present (intermittent)

Key Publications

(ed.) (1992) *History and Tradition in Melanesian Anthropology*, Berkeley: University of California Press.
(1995) *Gifts and Commodities: Exchange and Western Capitalism since 1700*, London: Routledge.

(ed.) (1995) *Occidentalism: Images of the West*, Oxford: Oxford University Press.
(ed.) (1997) *Meanings of the Market: The Free Market in Western Culture*, Oxford: Berg.

DANIEL MILLER

Carrithers, Michael

b. 11 November 1945, Colorado Springs, Colorado, USA

Michael Carrithers conducted his first fieldwork among a group of forest-dwelling Buddhist monks in Sri Lanka. Carrithers's account indicates that, contrary to his initial expectations, forest monks are a relatively recent social phenomenon and one that is neither ancient nor unchanging. His second fieldwork project among a Jain community in India led to his growing interest in the category of the person. Most recently he has turned his attention to East German Archives in a project that involves a narrative analysis of German identity. His publications indicate a keen interest in fieldwork methods and in anthropological theory. In *Why Humans Have Cultures*, an urbane, thought-provoking, and lucidly written reflection on the place of anthropology in the social sciences, Carrithers discusses some of anthropology's fundamental questions including why human cultures differ, the manner in which anthropologists classify and characterise cultures, and how relations between cultures develop. For Carrithers, culture is not so much a static and homogeneous 'thing', as a process in constant flux. Central to his analysis is narrative or story-telling, which he argues plays an active and not merely a passive role in the construction of sociality. In emphasising the importance and subtlety of social change, Carrithers draws imaginatively on disciplines outside anthropology including history and psychology, and has attempted to deepen our understanding of the social origins of human diversity.

Education

BA Wesleyan University, 1967
MA Wesleyan University, 1968
D.Phil. University of Oxford, 1978

Fieldwork

Sri Lanka, 1972–5
Kolhapur District, Maharashtra, India, 1980–6
   (intermittently)
East Germany, 1997–present (intermittently)

Key Publications

(1983) *The Forest Monks of Sri Lanka: An Anthro-*
   pological and Historical Study, Oxford: Oxford
   University Press.
(1992) *Why Humans Have Cultures: Explaining*
   Anthropology and Social Diversity, Oxford: Oxford
   University Press.

PETER COLLINS

Cátedra, María

b. 4 March 1947, Lérida, Spain

María Cátedra's works exemplify the crisis and
debates inside anthropology in Spain. On the
one hand, anthropologists from her generation
(and the following one) are professionals who
completed their graduate studies abroad. On
the other, a significant number of them have
conducted their fieldwork in the Iberian
Peninsula, living the dilemma of ignoring
previous Spanish ethnographers (mainly phi-
lologists and historians dedicated to the history
of folklore) or connecting with the prior
native ethnographic traditions. María Cátedra
has dealt with this situation paradigmatically:
she has conducted fieldwork in both Portugal
and Spain, and her areas of interest are close
enough to those of representatives of previous
academic traditions, such as marginalised rural
communities (e.g. the *Vaqueiros* in western
Asturias), culture and folk religion, rural and
urban founding myths, oral discourses, and
the invention of tradition. However, the 'how'

differs from that of previous Spanish anthropologists. Cátedra's fieldwork in Asturias
anticipated later studies on death (and suicide), analysing a rural community from the
perspective of their inhabitants' perception of
death. While drawing on symbolic anthropology, her works enrich this approach by her
own focus on the centrality of death, and its
relationship with nature (space) and time.
During the late 1980s and early 1990s, as a
pioneer in urban anthropology in Spain,
Cátedra studied the political meanings of the
saints of Ávila by using fieldwork as well as
analysing archival documents.

Education

BA University of Complutense, Madrid, 1971
Ph.D. University of Complutense, Madrid,
   1976
Ph.D. University of Pennsylvania, 1984

Fieldwork

Asturias, Spain, 1970–2, 1974–5
Ávila, Spain, 1987–91
Evora, Portugal, 2000–1

Key Publications

(1992) *This World, Other Worlds. Sickness, Suicide,*
   Death and the Afterlife among the Vaqueiros de Alzada in
   Spain, Chicago: The University of Chicago Press.
(1997) *Un santo para una ciudad. Ensayo de*
   antropología urbana (A Saint for a City: An
   Experiment in Urban Anthropology), Barcelona: Ariel Antropología.

LUIS DÍAZ G. VIANA AND
CRISTINA SÁNCHEZ-CARRETERO

Chagnon, Napoleon A.

b. 1938, Port Austin, Michigan, USA

Napoleon A. Chagnon is the world's leading
expert on the Yanomamö Indians of southern
Venezuela and adjacent areas of Brazil, a group
of tropical-forest horticulturalists who until

recently were very isolated from the outside world. As a result of his very engaging accounts of the Yanomamö, this group has become the best known of all the various isolated societies with simple technologies that anthropologists have described. He has published three books on the Yanomamö, the best known of which is his ethnography, *Yanomamö*, which has been read by more than 2 million students in introductory anthropology courses. This is one of the best accounts of a simple society ever written. In his ethnography, Chagnon has presented large amounts of demographic and life history data documenting numerous aspects of the endemic intervillage warfare of the Yanomamö. These data support Chagnon's conclusion that the main conflict driving warfare is a scarcity of potential wives for men. Potential wives are scarce because of polygyny, and because men of all ages, young and old, compete for the younger women as wives. Land or other resources are relatively abundant among the Yanomamö and are not plausible reasons for conflict. Chagnon was the first to suggest that warfare in simple societies could be motivated by a scarcity of marriageable women. This was a very novel view when Chagnon first presented it and it became controversial. Chagnon, however, has an extensive body of data to support his position. The Yanomamö typically arrange marriages by exchanging women between local patrilineal descent groups. Villages tend to consist of two intermarrying lineages and are internally peaceful when they are small and the majority of the villagers are closely related. However, as villages grow larger, and residents become more distantly related, conflicts about marriage arrangements or illicit sexual liaisons become common. As a result larger villages split into smaller villages, which are often hostile with one another. These hostilities lead to raids between villages and revenge raids in turn. Chagnon was one of the first ethnographers to use kin selection and sexual selection, theories drawn from evolutionary biology, to explain human behaviour. In addition to his many publications on the Yanomamö, Chagnon has also produced twenty-one ethnographic films, most of them in collaboration with Timothy Asch. Several of these films have won major film awards, are considered classics, and are regularly shown in introductory anthropology courses and on educational television.

In 2000, Patrick Tierney, a journalist, published *Darkness in El Dorado*, in which he accused Chagnon and other researchers of serious crimes against the Yanomamö. Investigations by the University of Michigan, the National Academy of Sciences, the American Society of Human Genetics, and the International Society of Genetic Epidemiology found no merit in Tierney's accusations. The American Anthropological Association's official inquiry found Tierney's book deeply flawed, but said it served anthropology well by raising an ethical issue. Anthropologists remain deeply divided about this issue.

Education

BA University of Michigan, 1961
MA University of Michigan, 1963
Ph.D. University of Michigan, 1966

Fieldwork

Numerous trips between 1964 and 1995 to southern Venezuela and Brazil totaling 63 months

Key Publications

(1974) *Studying the Yanomamö*, New York: Holt, Rinehart & Winston, Inc.
with Irons, W. (eds) (1979) *Evolutionary Biology and Human Social Behavior: An Anthropological Perspective*, North Scituate, MA: Duxbury Press.
(1988) 'Life histories, blood revenge, and warfare in a tribal population', *Science* 239: 985–92.
(1997 [1968]) *Yanomamö*, fifth edn, New York: Harcourt Brace College Publishers.

WILLIAM IRONS

Clark, M. Margaret

b. 9 January 1925, Amarillo, Texas, USA

d. 23 January 2003, San Rafael, California, USA

Margaret Clark initially planned a medical career, and entered medical school after her pre-med undergraduate training. There she recognised the gender, ethnic, and class disparities between patients and physicians, and after reading and meeting Margaret Mead, Clark decided to become a cultural anthropologist. Her dissertation research in a Mexican American community in San Jose produced what may have been the first American dissertation in medical anthropology, published in 1959. She then worked in public-health projects in Colorado, Arizona, and California, developing research on ageing in an urban environment in addition to her ethnomedicine focus.

Clark's research in ethnomedicine focused on the cultural and social dimensions of disease, diagnosis, and treatment. She resisted the common dichotomising of health practice into traditional/folk medicine and modern/scientific medicine, recognised syncretism in several of the systems she studied, and established several concepts now routine in medical anthropology. Her work in the anthropology of ageing was also pioneering. Her 1967 book with Barbara Anderson is an early exploration of cultural values in ageing, noting both adaptive and maladaptive applications of cultural values.

Research, teaching, and application were integrated themes throughout Clark's career. In 1975 she joined the University of California, San Francisco, where she was a co-founder of the Medical Anthropology Training Program. She also founded the Multidisciplinary Training Program in Applied Gerontology at San Francisco.

Education

BS Southern Methodist University, 1945
Ph.D. University of California, Berkeley, 1957

Fieldwork

San Jose, California, 1954–6
Rural Colorado, 1957–8
Tuba City, Arizona, 1958–9
San Francisco Bay area, California, 1960–91

Key Publications

(1959) *Health in the Mexican-American Culture: A Community Study*, Berkeley: University of California Press (second edn 1970).

Gallatin Anderson, Barbara (1967) *Culture and Aging: An Anthropological Study of Older Americans*, Springfield, IL: Charles C. Thomas.

FREDERIC W. GLEACH

Clifford, James T.

b. 1945, Bethlehem, Pennsylvania, USA

Even without any formal training in anthropology, James Clifford's influence in the theory and practice of the discipline since the early 1980s has been enormous. After the publication of the *Writing Culture* volume in 1986, this book has been taken to epitomise the whole 'movement' of 'post-modern', 'literary', or 'post-structuralist' turn in anthropology. The debates that followed mostly had two diametrically opposing views: for some, this 'turn' was just what the discipline needed to break out of the crisis and the condition where it was essentially stagnating; while for others, the practitioners (mostly included in *Writing Culture*) have been plunging the discipline (as well as the social sciences in general) into the abyss of nihilism, charlatanism, and 'intellectual navel-gazing'.

Clifford came to anthropology via his study in the archives in France and New Caledonia of the missionary Maurice Leenhardt – who completed an extremely impressive fieldwork in Melanesia between 1905 and 1926. This study resulted in the Ph.D. dissertation, later in the book, and the stage was set for the questioning of the ethnographic authority. How is it that ethnographers or anthropologists represent 'natives'? What are the bases for their assumptions? Clifford set out to analyse how it is that anthropologists construct their objects and which strategies they employ. What was once presumed to be a set of given 'facts' – anthropologist authoritatively going to the field, objectively observing (and participating), and then writing it down – seems to be a set of constructions, resulting from different strategies as well as from specific historical and cultural consequences. Just as one interprets texts, one should also look into the image of the observer in the contexts she/he studied, as well as into the limits of representation. Upon closer inspection, all truths (especially ethnography-derived ones) appear to be incomplete and partial. Since the observers (ethnographers) are just as much products of the specific historical circumstances as the observed ones ('natives'), one way to understand their relationship is through a dialogue. This dialogue is constructed through the relationship that the participants in it have towards power.

Clifford deconstructs what one would perceive as 'reality' through various forms, primarily dealing with the concept of culture. Since 'culture' is always relational, it is best understood through dialogue and polyphony. James Clifford navigates through the styles and works of various scholars (Marcel Griaule, Michel Leiris, Victor Segalen, among others), presenting their stories as examples of hybridity of ethnographic research. This navigation sometimes takes the form of travel, culminating in the series of essays and travelogues that he published in *Routes* (1997). This book also looks at the issue of the 'institutionalisation of fieldwork'. The question that remains is how does one translate concepts from one culture into another? And is this kind of translation possible at all?

Clifford has taken a route that combines and crosses over between disciplines – history, anthropology, and literature blend and merge with cultural studies, museum studies, and art. The final products seem to be a series of

artefacts that are constructed to represent whatever 'outer image' there might be. The importance of Clifford's work is in going beyond the questioning of the authenticity and reliability of ethnographic accounts. These accounts, along with representations that they produce, are by-products of specific, historically determined and culturally articulated discourses. The deconstruction of various myths (like the myth of the fieldwork) leads to the questioning of specific narratives and rhetorical strategies like in any story-telling, as well as of the historical and power bases that the ethnographers came from. While the colonial heritage of anthropology has been discussed, this deconstructing strategy still provoked many fears and insecurities. Once one accepts that any ethnography is at least a co-authored project, this provokes new questions and new doubts when it comes to authority, authenticity, and facticity.

Essentially, it all comes down to whether one is prepared to accept doubts and indeterminancies as part of an ethnographic 'reality' or not. Before the *Writing Culture* seminar and book, these were already an integral part of the heritage of anthropology (for example, the publication of Malinowski's *Diary* in 1968), but rarely debated in public. Through his innovative and often provocative texts, James Clifford has made a great contribution to changing the way we look at texts and their authors, as well as in the way we see the future of anthropology.

Education

AB Haverford College, 1967
MA Stanford University, 1968
Ph.D. Harvard University, 1977

Key Publications

(1982) *Person and Myth: Maurice Leenhardt in the Melanesian World*, Berkeley: University of California Press.
with Marcus, George (eds) (1986) *Writing Culture: The Poetics and Politics of Ethnography*, Berkeley: University of California Press.

(1988) The Predicament of Culture: Twentieth-Century Ethnography, Literature, and Art, Cambridge, MA: Harvard University Press.

(1997) Routes: Travel and Translation in the Late Twentieth Century, Cambridge, MA: Harvard University Press.

ALEKSANDAR BOSKOVIC

Cohen, Abner

b. 11 November 1921, Baghdad, Iraq

d. 17 May 2001, Oxford, UK

Abner Cohen trained under Max Gluckman, and, like others of the Manchester School, was interested in the 'micro-histories' of specific populations. After completing his Ph.D. Cohen moved in 1961 to the School of Oriental and African Studies (SOAS) in the University of London. He moved rapidly through the ranks and became professor of African Anthropology in 1972. During his period at SOAS, he also taught at the universities of Cornell (1966–7) and the State University of New York at Binghampton (1968), and spent a year at the Center for Advanced Study in Stanford in 1978.

Cohen twice carried out extended periods of fieldwork in West Africa. His first study was of Hausa migrants in a Yoruba-speaking area of Nigeria, where he revealed the importance of ethnic and religious identity as a mobilising factor in achieving economic goals. He was able to demonstrate that, far from being primordial, ethnicity is created by social and cultural processes, and assumes significance in specific contexts.

In Two-Dimensional Man (1974) he argued that humans are political and economic beings, but they are symbolist too, hence the task of anthropology is to reveal how these two dimensions engage with one another. In 1971, Cohen organised the Annual Conference of the Association of Social Anthropologists in London, and edited the ensuing volume on Urban Ethnicity, considered a landmark for the understanding of this important topic.

Cohen's next fieldwork area was Sierra Leone, where he worked among elite Creoles in the capital, Freetown. The publications that ensued demonstrated the relationship between culture and power, and the significance of what he terms the mystification of symbolism.

Cohen then turned his attention to the politics of masquerade, with a detailed observation over many years of the annual Notting Hill Carnival in London. In his monograph, he showed the interweaving of political formations and cultural forms, the significance of the Carnival's dramaturgical and performative aspects, and the ways in which such a form of cultural performance combines the instrumental and the expressive.

Ill health obliged him to retire from SOAS in 1985, and he moved to Oxford, where he became a Senior Research Associate at Queen Elizabeth House. Cohen's final fieldwork, which remains unpublished, was of a declining Nonconformist chapel in South Wales.

Education

MA University of London (external), 1958
Ph.D. University of Manchester, 1961

Fieldwork

Arab border villages in Israel, 1958–9
Hausa traders in Ibadan, Nigeria, 1962–3
Creoles in Freetown, Sierra Leone, 1969–70
London, Notting Hill carnival, 1976–90
Welsh chapels in South Wales, 1977–2001

Key Publications

(1969) Custom and Politics in Urban Africa, London: Routledge & Kegan Paul.

(1974) Two-Dimensional Man, London: Routledge & Kegan Paul.

(1981) The Politics of Elite Culture, Berkeley and Los Angeles: University of California Press

(1993) Masquerade Politics, Berkeley and Los Angeles: University of California Press

Further Reading

Parkin, David, Caplan, Lionel, and Fisher, Humphrey (eds) (1996) *The Politics of Cultural Performance*, Oxford and Providence, RI: Berghahn.

PAT CAPLAN

Cohen, Anthony P.

b. 1946, London, UK

Anthony P. Cohen's work has focused on the organisation of difference and belonging. His doctoral study in Newfoundland, Canada, examined the politics of cultural legitimation. His subsequent fieldwork in the Scottish Shetland Islands considered the ways in which members of a fishing community maintained their commitment to an egalitarian ethos while nonetheless subtly according recognition to, as well as managing, individual and segmental differences. This focus on the management of social boundaries was explored in a number of edited works as well as a seminal theoretical exploration of the symbolic construction of community. In all these works, Cohen argued passionately against the tendency of both scholars and politicians to accord recognition to difference only in the broadest of categorical brushstrokes. In particular, Cohen argued that both anthropologists and politicians had assumed the relative homogeneity of British society, ignoring the significance of local assertions of distinctiveness and communal identity. In the realm of politics, this failure to recognise subtle diversities had resulted in misguided policies. In the realm of academic scholarship, this failure had resulted in anthropologists ignoring the rich and diverse ethnographic possibilities of Britain. As an editor, ethnographic writer, and teacher, he has made a major contribution to correcting this anthropological misrepresentation and remedying the consequent gap in the ethnographic record.

Cohen's interest in the perception and organisation of difference has focused successively on the relationship between local communities and the state and/or nation; the expression of difference within local communities and the construction and expression of selfhood. Cohen argued that an insistence on communal identities should not be taken as an expression of either consensus or homogeneity. Communality could be expressed through symbols that while shared were sufficiently ambiguous to accommodate a wide range of differing interpretations. In his later work, Cohen extended this concern with the interaction between difference and communality to argue that respect must be accorded to individuals as self-conscious agents who operate within, are shaped by, but are not determined by their social and cultural circumstances. He rejected the view expressed by some anthropologists that the notion of selfhood is a Western invention, arguing instead that we need to distinguish between an ideology of individualism particular to certain societies and the general human capacity for *self-consciousness*. Subsequently, this interest in the interaction between selfhood and the desire for collective belonging has led to a focus on the dynamics of nationalist movements.

Education

BA University of Southampton, 1967
MA University of Southampton, 1968
Ph.D. University of Southampton, 1973

Fieldwork

Springdale, Newfoundland, 1968–70
Great Northern Peninsula, Newfoundland, summer 1970
Burra Isle, Shetland, April, June–September 1973, May 1974–October 1975
Whalsay, Shetland, 1976–91 (30 months)
National identity and constitutional change in three Scottish institutions, 2000–3

Key Publications

(1985) *The Symbolic Construction of Community*, London: Tavistock Publications.

(1987) *Whalsay: Symbol, Segment and Boundary in a Shetland Island Community*, Manchester: Manchester University Press.

(1994) *Self Consciousness: An Alternative Anthropology of Identity*, London and New York: Routledge.

VERED AMIT

Cohen, Erik

b. 1932, Zagreb, Yugoslavia

Cohen's long career is marked by original contributions to a wide range of fields: the study of Israeli kibbutzim and new towns, expatriate and immigrant communities, drug addition, inter-ethnic behaviour, peace in Israel, the ethnography of Thailand, festivals, religion, and food. However, his work on tourism is especially foundational. He edited special issues of *Annals of Tourism Research* on 'Sociology' (1979), 'European Studies' (1981), 'Tourist Guides' (1985), and 'Tourist Arts' (1993).

His Israeli research led to pioneer work on 'Mixed marriages' and 'Arab boys and Tourist Girls'. In 'Towards a sociology of international tourism' (1972) and 'What is a Tourist?' (1974) he laid the groundwork for the study of tourists as consumers of pleasure in search of novelty and change, and of tourism as the institutionalism of travel to *sehenswurdigkeiten*, 'things worth seeing'. His 'Nomads from affluence' (1973) was the pioneering work on long-term 'drifter tourists', whom he saw as anti-establishment youth on a self-imposed rite of passage as a 'moratorium on adulthood'.

After another pioneering work, 'The impact of tourism on the physical environment', he proposed 'A phenomenology of tourist experiences' (1979), which challenged Dean MacCannell's monolithic view of tourists as sightseers (*The Tourist: A New Theory of the Leisure Class*, 1976) by exploring tourists with varying levels of commitment to self-change and exploration of cultural 'centers outside' (cf. pilgrims). This advance was reinforced by 'Authenticity and commoditization in tourism' (1988) where he showed that authenticity is subjective, not absolute, and that market forces do not always destroy or falsify authenticity as MacCannell claimed.

His extensive ethnographic research in Thailand has focused on hill tribe tourism, beach tourism, tourist guides, and 'open-ended prostitution' of Thai Women and foreign tourists (1996), refugee and folk arts (2000) as well as tourism and language and tourist photography. Since the 1980s, he has continued to publish on Israeli settlements and ethnicity, and on the ethnography of market towns, religion and festivals, and the resurgence of Chinese-Thai ethnicity in Thailand.

Professor emeritus Cohen taught at Hebrew University, Jerusalem, from 1964–2002, chaired the Department of Sociology and Social Anthropology, 1980–3, and was dean of social sciences, 1988–92. He also taught at Manchester, Singapore, Fiji, and Bielefeld. He is continuing research in Thailand since his retirement.

Education

BA Hebrew University, Jerusalem, 1958
MA Hebrew University, Jerusalem, 1961
Ph.D. Hebrew University, Jerusalem, 1967

Fieldwork

Israel, kibbutzim and new towns, 1956–68
Mixed Jewish–Arab city of Acre, 1966, 1972
Ayacucho, Peru, 1969
Fiji, Pacific Islands tourism, 1974, 1975
Thailand, hill tribes and beach tourism, 1977–80
Bangkok, Thailand, 1981–4, 1985–7
Israel, ethnic nusic, 1983–4
Thailand, ethnic tourism, arts, festivals, 1989–present

Key Publications

(1973) 'Nomads from affluence: notes on the phenomenon of drifter tourism', *International Journal of Comparative Sociology* 14, 1–2, 89–103.

(1979) 'A phenomenology of touristic experiences', *Sociology* 13, 179–201.

(1988) 'Authenticity and commoditization in tourism', *Annals of Tourism Research* 15, 3, 371–86.

(2000) *The Commercialized Crafts of Thailand: Hills Tribes and Lowland Villages*, Honolulu: University of Hawaii Press.

NELSON H. H. GRABURN

Cohn, Bernard S.

b. 13 May 1928, Brooklyn, New York, USA

d. 25 November 2003, Chicago, Illinois, USA

Bernard Cohn was a pioneer of a genre of historical anthropology that developed in the post-Second World War, post-colonial era. He devoted his career to an exposition of the historical context of the construction of cultural knowledge, with an emphasis on the construction of knowledge in British colonial India. He was one of the first anthropologists to analyse the discipline of anthropology itself as a form of colonial knowledge.

Cohn's early work on 'The changing status of a depressed caste' was an analysis of the impact of sociopolitical changes on an 'untouchable' caste in north India during the late-colonial and early post-colonial period. He was particularly interested in colonial transformations of land ownership, and legal systems. In a 1968 article entitled 'Notes on the study and history of Indian society', which appeared in *Structure and Change in Indian Society*, Cohn shifted his attention to the ways in which the British produced knowledge about Indian society and culture in order to facilitate their rule over India. The article examines three different modes of representing Indian society and culture, based on three different interest groups: the Orientalist scholars, the Christian missionaries, and the British administrators. This work predated Said's theory of Orientalism and Foucault's work on the power–knowledge nexus, and opened up a whole new territory for anthropological inquiry.

In 1984 Cohn published 'The census, social structure and objectification in South Asia' (later reprinted in *An Anthropologist among Historians and Other Essays*), which situated the colonial anthropologist as a key player in the construction of imperial knowledge. Cohn demonstrates that through the process of producing an official census, the British transformed, created, and fixed systems of social and cultural classification for such things as religion, caste, 'race', and language in ways that continue to have lasting effects in the post-colonial era.

A second collection of Cohn's essays, entitled *Colonialism and Its Forms of Knowledge*, was published in 1996. These essays reflect Cohn's continued interest in the ways in which the British thought Indian society could be known and represented as a series of 'facts'. Cohn explores the 'investigative modalities' that the British employed to collect such facts, including historiography, enumeration, museology, and archeology. He demonstrates the subtle ways in which the British transformed and ruled over Indian society through their study of Indian languages, creating museum displays of India's 'past', and establishing styles of clothing to symbolise the identities of colonised and colonisers alike. Cohn merges anthropology with history to reveal the processes by which colonial society and culture were constructed and the legacy that such constructions hold in the post-colonial era.

Education

BA University of Wisconsin, 1949
Ph.D. Cornell University, 1954

Fieldwork

North India, on and off from 1952–90s
London, UK, on and off from 1962–90s

Key Publications

(1955) 'The changing status of a depressed caste', in McKim Marriott (ed.) *Village India: Studies in the Little Community*, Chicago: University of Chicago Press.

with Singer, Milton (eds) (1968) *Structure and Change in Indian Society*, Chicago: Aldine Press.

(1987) *An Anthropologist among Historians and Other Essays*, Delhi: Oxford University Press.

(1996) *Colonialism and Its Forms of Knowledge: The British in India*, Princeton, NJ: Princeton University Press.

CECILIA VAN HOLLEN

Collier, Jane Fishburne

b. 12 November 1940, Charleston, South Carolina, USA

Jane Fishburne Collier's work focuses on three unique areas of anthropology: law, gender, and the family. Earlier work analysed the social impact of law among the Zinacantan of Chiapas, Mexico, by looking beyond the Western definitions of law and discovering a system whereby social contexts influenced the outcome of conflict resolution. Individuals participated in legal proceedings based on the type of settlement required. She found that participants adhered to a local, non-Western code of law less concerned with punishment as it was with avoiding 'supernatural vengeance' (1973: viii). Collier's work on Zinacantan law proved a significant contribution to the ethnology of law and advanced the theory of 'law as a language'.

During the 1980s Collier focused on feminist issues in anthropology, mainly kinship and inequality. Like earlier feminist anthropologists she embarked on ethnographic research documenting the significance of marriage and kinship in perpetuating gender inequality. Her bold, theoretical work, *Marriage and Inequality in Classless Societies*, moved beyond gender to broaden the influence of

marriage and women in a classless society. Using ethnographies from Karl Llewellyn, Edward Hoebel, and Rupert Richardson, Collier examined the classless societies of the Comanche, Cheyenne, and Kiowa. She concluded that while male members boasted of brave acts, war honours, or personal achievements, their prestige and rank was a direct result of advantageous marriages. Young males were either manipulated into years of hard labour or acts of bravery with the promise of a bride. As a result, men's accomplishments were lauded while women's contributions as motivating factor were ignored. In all cases the societies were structured to perpetuate, justify, and minimise the subordination of women.

Collier's final contribution to anthropology is the study of the modernisation of the family. After a 20-year gap she revisited an Andalusian village, 'Los Olivos' (a pseudonym), to analyse the effects inclusion into modern Spanish society had on the villagers' family structures. Los Olivos of the 1960s maintained local traditions handed-down from previous generations. Their agricultural economy measured wealth and prestige by the property one owned. Children married according to family obligations and thought in terms of 'sacrifice' and 'duty'. In contrast, Los Olivos of the 1980s embraced the 'borrowed' traditions of Andalusia and Spain, and shunned the 'old-fashioned' village traditions. Their capitalistic economy measured wealth and prestige based on job performance. Children were now allowed to marry for 'love' and parents openly showed affection. However, underneath modernity and progress Collier found the elderly marginalised by their handed-down traditions and women dependent on their wage-earning husbands. In the end Collier forced anthropology to revisit modern subjectivity in the village and its impact on the family.

Education

BA *summa cum laude*, Radcliffe College, 1962
Ph.D. Tulane University, 1970

Fieldwork

Chiapas, Mexico, most summers from 1960–73

Andalusia, Spain, summer 1980

Chiapas, Mexico, 1997–9

Key Publications

(1973) *Law and Social Change in Zinacantan*, Stanford, CA: Stanford University Press.

(1988) *Marriage and Inequality in Classless Societies*, Stanford, CA: Stanford University Press

(1997) *From Duty to Desire: Remaking Families in a Spanish Village*, Princeton, NJ: Princeton University Press

CYNTHIA A. TYSICK

Collier, John, Jr

b. 1913, Sparkill, New York, USA

d. 1992, San Jose, Costa Rica

John Collier, Jr's career was based on intense practical photographic experience that he applied to anthropology. Largely self-trained in commercial and documentary still photography, Collier adapted both still and motion picture methods to provide rich contextual information, difficult to present in verbal form, about people and social settings. Although others such as Margaret Mead and Gregory Bateson also used photography as a research tool, Collier was among the first to articulate and develop the idea of visual anthropology. He participated in a number of field studies where photographs were integral to the data gathering and analytical process behind the written ethnography. Collier explored how to adapt photographs to serve as one form of data collection about a community, its material culture and surroundings, records of social interaction, and as projective devices for interviewing.

Education

Apprentice (Maynard Dixon, painter), c.1927

Brief training, California School of Fine Arts and privately from Robert and Sarah Higgins Mack, 1930s

Fieldwork

Freelance photography in California and New Mexico, 1939–40, 1955–61

Staff photographer, Farm Security Administration and Office of War Information, 1941–3

Photographer, Standard Oil of New Jersey, in Canada, Colombia, and Peru, 1944–6

Independent study with Anibal Buitron, Otavalo, Ecuador, 1946

'Stirling County' Project, Nova Scotia, for Alexander H. Leighton, 1950–2

Navaho Reservation, the Cornell University Fruitland Project with John Adair and Tom Sasaki, 1952

Cornell–San Marcos Vicos Project, Peru, with Allan Holmberg, 1954–5

Indian Relocation Study, San Francisco, with James Hirabayashi, 1962

Film documentation and analysis of schools in Southwest Alaska, 1968–9.

Film analysis of education on the Navaho Reservation and in the San Francisco Bay area, 1972–82

Key Publications

with Buitron, Anibal (1949) *The Awakening Valley*, Chicago: University of Chicago Press.

(1973) *Alaskan Eskimo Education: A Film Analysis of Cultural Confrontation in the Schools*, New York: Holt, Rinehart & Winston.

with Collier, Malcolm (1986 [1967]) *Visual Anthropology: Photography as a Research Method*, revised and expanded edn, Albuquerque: University of New Mexico Press.

Further Reading

Doty, C. Stewart (1991) *Acadian Hard Times: The Farm Security Administration in Maine's St. John Valley, 1940–1943*, Orono: University of Maine Press.

JUDITH A. RASSON

Colson, Elizabeth Florence

b. 1917, USA

Elizabeth Colson is associated with research on resettlement, migration, refugees and social change. Her initial research on the Makah Indians of Washington State (USA) sought to examine the assimilation of the Makah into North American society, a problem that was approached through interviews, participant observation, and the use of paid interpreter/ informants from a small community of ninety-six households. Her conclusions are especially interesting in light of the acknowledged limitations of the study: after seven decades of systematic attempts by the Bureau of Indian Affairs to forcibly assimilate the Makah, they had retained a strong sense of cultural identity because of the strength of their traditions and their legal status as wards of government. Cushioned in part by the continued viability of 'traditional' livelihoods and the compactness of their community, the Makah were able to compete effectively with whites and better adapt to the changes being forced upon them. While they were by and large culturally assimilated into mainstream society, they nevertheless remained a distinct social group.

As a researcher with the Rhodes–Livingstone Institute (RLI) in Northern Rhodesia (now Zambia) she undertook initial fieldwork in 1946 among the Plateau Tonga. Colson became the Director of the RLI until ill health forced her to leave. She returned in 1956 to undertake a baseline study of the valley or Gwembe Tonga, the first phase of long-term research into the effects of resettlement caused by the creation of the Kariba Dam. The central focus of this work was to understand the social and political organisation of the valley Tonga, and within that the role of ritual which provided a vital element of social cohesion. The Gwembe Tonga did not have central political institutions, and uncharacteristically they relied upon settled agriculture in the well-watered valleys that were to be flooded by the dam. The baseline study was conducted jointly with Thayer Scudder in what was to become a long professional relationship.

Colson's long-term research on the Gwembe Tonga helped to establish the basis for subsequent anthropological involvement in and analyses of large-scale, planned social change. In methodological terms the central questions concerned the time frame for the study, the choice of communities for research, the value of different research methods, and the research focus. All these issues are carefully addressed in her work. For the Gwembe Tonga the impact of resettlement was an inevitable outcome of regional politics and development planning that failed to address the social consequences of such schemes: the greater good of securing hydroelectric power for the nation outweighed the cost to those whose homes and livelihoods were destroyed. In this context, the ecological conditions and the agricultural practices of the Tonga, together with the absence of central political institutions, affected their ability to re-establish their communities and livelihoods. Colson's analysis of the impact of forced resettlement provides a classic argument about the social consequences of large-scale river basin development. The effect of resettlement consisted of: (1) a period of upheaval that may last for five years before a semblance of social routines and livelihoods are re-established; (2) this period is marked by a situation of extreme hostility towards government; (3) local leaders associated with resettlement lose their legitimacy, which results in officials taking decisions without local consent; (4) traditional religious beliefs and values are questioned resulting in greater insecurity and vulnerability; (5) there is a new, if temporary, emphasis on shared kinship ties that provides a sense of continuity; however (6) close proximity among kinsmen soon gives way to tension and is followed by growing disputes and the dispersal of kin; finally, (7) the situation results in an unwillingness to experiment with new technologies, crops, etc., which are viewed as 'untried' costly innovations. The bottom line for Colson was that 'it is folly to allow technology to determine policy'.

Education

BA University of Minnesota, 1938
MA Radcliffe College, 1941
Ph.D. Radcliffe College, 1945

Fieldwork

North America: Pomo 1939–41; Makah 1941–2; Arizona, War Relocation Camp 1942–3; Navaho 1978
Zambia: Plateau Tonga 1946–50, 1968; Gwembe Tonga 1957–7, 1960, 1962–3, 1965, 1968, 1972–3, 1978, 1981–2, 1987, 1989
Darwin, Australia, 1966.

Key Publications

(1953) *The Makah Indians: A Study of an Indian Tribe in Modern American Society*, Manchester University Press.
(1960) *The Social Organization of the Gwembe Tonga*, University of Zambia: Manchester University Press.
(1971) *The Social Consequences of Resettlement: The Impact of the Kariba Resettlement upon the Gwembe Tonga*, University of Zambia: Manchester University Press.
(1974) *Tradition and Contract: The Problem of Order* (The 1973 Lewis Henry Morgan Lectures), Chicago: Aldine.

JOHN R. CAMPBELL

Conklin, Harold C.

b. 27 April 1926, Easton, USA

Harold C. Conklin, professor emeritus at Yale University, is widely recognised as a pioneer in the study of indigenous systems of resource use, and the founder of ethnoscience, including ethnobotany and ethnoecology, in which he has played a leading role on the basis of his intensive fieldwork in the Philippines. The first contribution of Conklin was to have revealed the extraordinary scope of indigenous knowledge of the plant world (his doctoral dissertation). Another two of his best-known works are *Hanunóo Agriculture* (1957) and *Ethnographic Atlas of Ifugao* (1980). The former is one of the first comprehensive case studies of a traditional system of swidden agriculture in the upland region of southwest Mindoro, and the latter is the most comprehensive graphic representation of the traditional system of irrigated rice terraces of Ifugao in Northern Luzon. These works have established him as a rigorous scholar who has accomplished a scientific ethnography through the development of a style of meticulous description and analysis of traditional environmental systems.

Education

B.Sc. University of California, Berkeley, 1950
Ph.D. Yale University, 1955

Fieldwork

Mindoro, Philippines (Hanunóo), four trips, from 1947 to 1958
Northern Luzon, Philippines (Ifugao), six trips, from 1961 to 1973

Key Publications

(1975 [1957]) *Hanunóo Agriculture: A Report on an Integral System of Shifting Cultivation in the Philippines*, Northford, CT: Elliot's Books (1957 edition published in Rome: Food and Agriculture Organization of the United Nations).
(1980) *Ethnographic Atlas of Ifugao: A Study of Environment, Culture, and Society in Northern Luzon*, New Haven: Yale University Press.

KATSUYOSHI FUKUI

Corin, Ellen E.

b. 1944, Liège, Belgium

Ellen Corin is a leading figure in the field of cultural psychiatry, and a practising psychoanalyst. Her work represents a sustained reflection on the notions of otherness, margins, and subjectivity, beginning with her ethnography of spirit possession in Zaïre and continuing with her comparative studies (many in concert with Gilles Bibeau) of the ways in which psychiatric patients and their families use cultural idioms to give meaning to their experience of psychosis. Rather than deconstruct otherness and deny difference, as many contemporary anthropologists are wont to do, Corin is interested in how otherness is elaborated (expressed and bounded) in different cultural settings. While centered on (and decentered by) the other, Corin's work nevertheless shows an abiding concern with issues of subjectivity. For example, she coined the term 'positive withdrawal' to refer to the ability of some psychiatric patients to keep themselves out of hospital by constructing a personal protected space at the margins of the 'normal' social world. This coping strategy is especially interesting to study in India where there exist 'myth models' (like that of the ascetic) that valorise such comportment. No such models exist in mainstream Western psychiatry, but Corin sees the alternative therapies offered by community groups as embodying a potentially fruitful opening, and so has begun to research these therapies in the North American setting as a counterpoint to her on-going research in India.

Education

Ph.D. University of Leuven, 1970

Fieldwork

Bandundu and Kinshasa, Zaïre, 1966–8, 1971–7
Abitibi and Montreal, Quebec, 1985–7, 1992–
Chennai, south India, 1997–

Key Publications

(1998) 'Refiguring the person: the dynamics of affects and symbols in an African spirit possession cult', in M. Lambek and A. Strathern (eds) *Bodies and Persons*, Cambridge, UK: Cambridge University Press.
(2002) 'The 'other' of culture in psychosis', in J. Biehl, B.J. Good, and A. Kleinman (eds), *Subjectivity Transformed*, Berkeley: University of California Press.

DAVID HOWES

Crapanzano, Vincent

b. 15 April 1939, Glen Ridge, New Jersey, USA

Vincent Crapanzano is famous for his comparison of the ethnographer with Hermes, both of whom are caught in two paradoxes. They must present their own interpretation as definitive while acknowledging all interpretations are provisional; and they must make the strange familiar while preserving its strangeness. However, while Hermes was famous as a trickster, ethnographers often fail to own up to their own tricks: the rhetorical strategies they use to convince readers of the validity of their interpretations. Crapanzano's literary, anthropological, and philosophical analysis of these strategies, most forcefully laid out in his celebrated essay, 'Hermes' Dilemma', is just one moment in three decades of research that focuses on the epistemology of interpretation and the articulation of experience.

His first monograph, *The Fifth World of Forster Bennett: Portrait of a Navaho* (1972), a presentation of journal entries detailing his reactions to his encounters with Forster Bennett, a Navaho man on a reservation in Arizona, had already begun to articulate the dilemmas of the ethnographer: to participate, but never fully; to engage, but not interfere. Though not explicitly experimental, this fell far outside the bounds of traditional ethnography: at once person-centered, episodic, reflexive, and dialogic.

Tuhami, his portrait of the life-history of a Moroccan tilemaker who was married to a she-demon, was explicitly experimental: an account not so much of the tilemaker's experience as his articulation of this experience within the ethnographic encounter. It is at once a moving account of a man's life, an experiment in ethnographic form designed to shock the anthropologist as reader, and a meditation of the relation between ethnographer and informant – now seen as interlocutors enmeshed in a web of politics, history, and desire.

Crapanzano's fourth monograph, *Waiting* (1985), treats the effects of domination on the dominators, in this case the whites of South Africa under apartheid in the early 1980s. It is presented through a cacophony of perspectives as thirty-seven English- and Afrikaans-speaking men and women talk about themselves, the non-white people around them, and the future of South Africa. He examines what it is like to wait for an apocalyptic future one cannot influence, and thus wait in the grip of fear rather than hope: the solidarity caused by shared pessimism, the rise of conversion experiences within revivalist religion, and the influx of conspiracy theories to explain world events. Experimental in its presentation of a plurality of voices, it is at the same time critical of the moral implications of those voices.

This critical stance again comes to the fore in *Serving the Word*, Crapanzano's examination of the resurgence of literalism among Christian Fundamentalists and legal thinkers in the USA. In the view of literalists, who practice modes of textual interpretation that eschew figurative understandings, there are fundamental texts, plain meanings, and original intentions. Like anthropologists, these literalists must deny their own argumentative strategies in order to make their arguments convincing. Crapanzano is especially critical of the legal thinkers, whom he sees as engaged in a 'potentially dangerous' mode of interpretation that treats meaning – moral as much as semantic – as rigid, timeless, and prescriptive.

Crapanzano's latest book, *Imaginative Horizons:*

An Essay in Literary-Philosophical Anthropology (2003), may be understood as a counterpoint to *Serving the Word*, with its focus on literalism. Using montage as a key trope – exemplifying his rhetorical but insistent use of heuristic relativism to unsettle assumptions – Crapanzano takes up a variety of themes: body, hope, trauma, memory, transgression, death, and pain. Unifying these themes is a concern with, and demonstration of, the role of interpretive horizons in constraining experience and, when articulated as constraints, enabling new experiences – a process he calls the 'dialectic between openness and closure'.

Other works by Crapanzano, too numerous and diverse to summarise here, focus on topics such as spirit possession, psychoanalysis as a historically specific 'psychology' grounded in a particular ideology of language, translation, the semiotics of selfhood, and the history of anthropology. Topically, they range from 'Interlocutory collapse' in Daniel Paul Schreber's memoirs to 'Magic, illusion, and mana' in the thought of Emile Durkheim and Marcel Mauss. Respected for its erudition and breadth as much as its grace and depth, Crapanzano's work has influenced scholars across disciplines and been translated into numerous languages. He teaches anthropology and comparative literature at the Graduate Center at the City University of New York.

Education

AB Harvard University, 1960
Ph.D. Columbia University, 1970

Fieldwork

Arizona, 1966
Morocco, 1967–8, 1972
South Africa, 1980, 1981, 1984
California, 1995

Key Publications

(1973) *The Hamadsha: A Study in Moroccan Ethnopsychiatry*, Berkeley: University of California Press.

(1980) *Tuhami: Portrait of a Moroccan*, Chicago: University of Chicago Press.
(1992) *Hermes' Dilemma and Hamlet's Desire: On the Epistemology of Interpretation*, Cambridge, MA: Harvard University Press.
(2000) *Serving the Word: Literalism in America from the Pulpit to the Bench*, New York: The New Press.

PAUL KOCKELMAN

Cruikshank, Julie

b. 1945, Wingham, Ontario, Canada

Julie Cruikshank's long-term research with older aboriginal women has focused upon how oral traditions are employed today in the Yukon (along with comparative work in Alaska and Siberia). Under the tutelage of her aboriginal collaborators, Cruikshank's interests have shifted from doing oral history committed to documenting changes in social reality towards a more processually oriented and theoretically searching investigation of narrative forms as subtle and complex means for talking about, remembering, and interpreting everyday life. Underlining the critical intelligence with which contemporary storytellers tell their narratives, Cruikshank argues that stories render meaningful connections and afford order and continuity in a rapidly changing world. Hence, oral tradition is better understood as a social activity than as reified text. Meanings do not simply inhere in a story but are, instead, created in the everyday situations within which stories are told. Linking her analysis to the work of an earlier generation of communication theorists, including Harold Innis, Mikhail Bakhtin, and Walter Benjamin, Cruikshank's work establishes the enduring power of story-telling to subvert official orthodoxies and to challenge conventional ways of thinking.

Education

BA University of Toronto, 1967
MA University of British Columbia, 1969

Diploma in Polar Studies, University of Cambridge, 1980
Ph.D. University of British Columbia, 1987

Fieldwork

Yukon Territory, Canada, 1968–continuing
Alaska, USA, 1970–1
Yakutia, Republic of Sakha, 1996

Key Publications

with Sidney, Angela, Smith, Kitty, and Ned, Annie (1990) *Life Lived Like a Story: Life Stories of Three Yukon Native Elders*, Lincoln: University of Nebraska Press; Vancouver: University of British Columbia Press.
(1998) *The Social Life of Stories: Narrative and Knowledge in the Yukon Territory*, Lincoln: University of Nebraska Press; Vancouver: University of British Columbia Press.

NOEL DYCK

Csordas, Thomas J.

b. 1952, Youngstown, Ohio, USA

The work and interests of Thomas Csordas span a range of interrelated areas and subjects including anthropological theory, comparative religion, medical and psychological anthropology, cultural phenomenology and embodiment, globalisation and social change as well as language and culture. While he has worked with various groups in different settings within the USA, the main two groups on which he has focused have been those involved in charismatic healing and the Navaho. In his work with groups of charismatic healers Csordas examined topics such as healing ritual, religious language, bodily experience, and child development. In his work with the Navaho he has investigated the experience of cancer patients, therapeutic process in religious healing and language, as well as narrative among patients and healers. In addition to his mix of theoretical and ethnographic work, which has come to influence a great many anthropologists working in psychological, medical, and linguistic anthropology, Csordas has also strongly influenced the fields of psychological and medical anthropology through his five years as editor of the journal, Ethos, and through his work on the boards of the Medical Anthropology Quarterly and Culture, Medicine and Psychiatry. Among his honours within the discipline of anthropology, he was awarded the Stirling Award for Contributions in Psychological Anthropology in 1988. From 1999–2002, Csordas also served as president of the Society for the Anthropology of Religion.

Education

BA Ohio State University, 1974
Ph.D. Duke University, 1980

Fieldwork

Arizona, Massachusetts, Michigan, New Mexico, North Carolina 1973–2003

Key Publications

(1994) The Sacred Self: A Cultural Phenomenology of Charismatic Healing, Berkeley: University of California Press.

(1997) Language, Charisma and Creativity: The Ritual Life of a Religious Movement, Berkeley: University of California Press.

DREW WALKER

Cushing, Frank Hamilton

b. 22 July 1857, northeastern Pennsylvania, USA

d. 10 April 1900, Washington, DC, USA

The scion of a distinguished New England family, young Frank Hamilton Cushing roamed the woods of upper New York State, fascinated by Indian burial grounds and arrowheads as well as by the natural history of the area. He collected minerals and fossils, and taught himself the arts of stone-chipping and basket weaving. In 1874, his precocious paper on Orleans County, New York, archaeology was published in the annual report of the Smithsonian Institution when he was only 17 years of age.

Cushing entered Cornell University, where he curated an exhibit of artefacts in 1875, to study natural history but was soon recruited by Smithsonian director, Spencer Baird, to organise the Indian materials in the museum's collections for an exhibit at the Philadelphia Centennial Exposition of 1876. Three years later he was appointed to a field research position in John Wesley Powell's newly established Bureau of American Ethnology (BAE). Under the direction of James and Matilda Stevenson, Powell sent Cushing to study the Zuni, who were less than enthusiastic about outsiders, having only recently been pacified. Cushing was only 22 years old when he led a 3-month BAE collecting party to the Zunis. He quickly became frustrated with the fieldwork conventions of the day because they did not allow him, as an outsider, access to the everyday world of the Zuni. Without invitation, Cushing brashly moved into the pueblo, into a room belonging to the governor, who was doubtless hopeful that his stay would be a short one. Cushing received permission from his scientific superiors to remain behind and thereafter ignored various calls to communicate with the home office or return to write up his results.

Although Cushing's four-and-a-half-year sojourn was evaluated ambivalently both by the Zuni and by scientific colleagues back in the national capital, it set new standards for the anthropologist's aspiration to get inside the mental world of ethnographic subjects. Fieldwork had previously been much more superficial. Cushing learned to speak fluent Zuni and was initiated as a member of the tribal council and of the Bow Priesthood in 1881 (for which he obtained an Apache scalp from the Smithsonian collections). There was considerable Zuni objection to his sketching of secret ceremonies and interference with ceremonial practices. After an overt confrontation subsided,

Cushing was permitted to pursue his studies fairly freely. It is clear, however, that he overestimated the degree of his acceptance by the Zuni.

Among the general public, Cushing became a virtual cult hero and was widely believed to have become a Zuni. He orchestrated successful tours of the East Coast with a group of Zuni. Among his professional colleagues, however, Cushing's showmanlike antics were received with considerably less enthusiasm. Powell is said to have ordered him to leave a meeting of the Anthropological Society of Washington when he appeared in full Zuni regalia. His ethnographic reports were flamboyant and personal in style, contrasting sharply to the more distanced and factual reports characteristic of the period. Nonetheless, his work pioneered in its cultural relativism; he was among the first to use the term culture in its modern sense, in the plural. His presentation of Zuni culture in its own terms moved beyond established evolutionary classifications and formal typologies of artefacts to explore the meaning of a culture to its individual members.

After his return from Zuni, Cushing pursued his archaeological interests, introducing the term 'chiefdom' for a level of sociocultural complexity beyond that of the tribe or local band. In 1886, he took a leave of absence from the Bureau to lead the Hemenway Southwest Expedition during which he was accused of faking a mosaic frog. In 1889, poor health forced him to resign. The final report was never completed. Rather, Cushing chose to return to the Bureau and continue working on his accumulated Zuni materials. During an archaeological survey of shell mounds in Florida, he was again accused of forging artefacts.

Cushing suffered from poor health throughout his life and died at the young age of forty-two, choking on a fishbone while hospitalised for one of his many ailments. He was planning to excavate shell mounds in Maine at the time. Cushing's legacy remains difficult to evaluate, despite the movement of ethnographic reporting towards a more personal style. Immersion in local worlds for a lengthy period of time, speaking the Native language, remains a standard, albeit one not always adhered to.

Education

Attended Cornell University

Fieldwork

Zuni, 1879–86

Key Publications

(1883) *Zuni Fetishes*, Second Annual Report of the Bureau of American Ethnology for 1880–1,v. 3-45.

(1896) *Outlines of Zuni Creation Myths.* Thirteenth Annual Report of the Bureau of American Ethnology for 1892, 321–447.

(1901) *Zuni Folktales*, New York: G.P. Putnam's Sons.

(1941) *My Life at Zuni. Century Magazine*, reprinted, Santa Fe: Peripetetic Press.

REGNA DARNELL

Cvijic, Jovan

b. 12 October 1865, Loznica, Kingdom of Serbia

d. 16 January 1927, Belgrade, Kingdom of Yugoslavia

It is almost impossible to single out any predominant problem in Jovan Cvijic's theoretically and methodologically diverse work. His books, articles, papers, and lectures mark the very beginning of several scientific disciplines in Serbia and former Yugoslavia, and introduce interdisciplinary research in a wide range of fields, especially in human geography and ethnology. Although Cvijic achieved international recognition early in his career with a doctoral study in geomorphology, his work in ethnology and human geography made him the most cited and internationally recognised Yugoslav human scientist of the early twentieth century. His opus has served as the methodological guide and political agenda of Serbian ethnology for decades. He is rightly considered to have been the founding father of the discipline in this national context. In 1906 he founded the Department of Ethnology at the Faculty of Philosophy in Belgrade. During the next two decades, he formed the Serbian ethnological school and trained a wide number of fieldwork professionals, initiating research, theory-building, and policy-making activities. Being in the position of power for most of his career (Cvijic served twice as rector of the University of Belgrade and as President of the Serbian Academy of Sciences), he did not only introduce key concepts and methods of professional ethnology, but also founded several editions that still publish most of the ethnological production in Serbia.

Two major texts in his rich multidisciplinary bibliography are relevant to his ethnological career. In *La Peninsule balkanique* Cvijic introduced the interdisciplinary study of the Balkans, especially focusing on migration flows and the relation of culture and environment, integrating knowledge of different historical periods and areas, and various research traditions. Cvijic paid special attention to the problems of adaptation, integration, or assimilation of migrants. His work provided an excellent basis for modern demographic, sociological, and ethnological research in the migration processes.

In 'The Balkan Peninsula II' (*Sabrana dela*, vol. II), Cvijic introduced what was for the time a subtle analysis relating human geography to the cognitive competences of ethnic groups in the Balkans. He used geomorphologic and environmental data to explain the formation of regional or even ethnic traits of whole populations, ironically subsuming ethnic groups in the Balkans under the ethnically insensitive typology of four 'ethno-psychological types' (dinaric, central, eastern, and panonic).

Most of his later articles, papers, and public speeches (*Sabrana dela*, vol. III) concentrate on the realm of politics. Being highly criticised as biased, they certainly require further reading,

especially by specialists interested in political anthropology and anthropology of policy.

Education

Diploma, Great School in Belgrade, 1888
Ph.D. University of Vienna, 1892

Fieldwork

Cvijic did not conduct any stationary ethnographic research that is classifiable as anthropological fieldwork.

Key Publications

(1918) *La Peninsule balkanique. Geographie humaine* (The Balkan Peninsula: Human Geography), Paris: Armand Colin.
(1987) *Sabrana dela* (Collected Works), Beograd: SANU, Knjizevne Novine & Zavod za udzbenike.

MILOS MILENKOVIC

Czaplicka, Maria Antonina

b. 1884, Warsaw, (then) Russian Empire

d. 1921, Bristol, UK

A student of R.R. Marett, Czaplicka took interest in the peoples of Siberia under the influence of her supervisor. The result was a book based on published ethnographic sources written in Russian, Polish, and English (Jesup North Pacific Expedition). The book reflects Marett's interest in religion, and it deals mainly with shamanism, and 'Arctic Hysteria'. She departed for her fieldwork (having been awarded the Mary Ewart Travelling Fellowship from Sommerville College) to Siberia in May 1914 to lead a joint Oxford and Pennsylvania University expedition. Yenisei Province was chosen as a field site and Tungus (now called Evenki) lived there. Despite extreme living conditions, she decided also to stay for winter. She published many articles and a popular book, and gave many lectures on the topic. She wrote her part of the expedition report, but her companion, Henry Hall, never published anything and no trace of her work was found.

After coming back to England she worked as a lecturer at Oxford, London, and Bristol, not having a permanent position. During the First World War, she worked for the Foreign Office and was active in the campaign to regain Polish statehood. The problems of her personal life together with the instability of her career caused her suicide.

Her scientific profile was shaped by geographical studies (she was given a Murchison Award by the Royal Geographical Society in 1920) and anthropological concerns. The result was the anthropo-geographical idea of a relation between man and nature, and the diffusion of cultural elements in the creation of culture.

Education

Diploma, University of Oxford, 1912

Fieldwork

Northwest Siberia, May 1914–September 1915

Key Publications

(1914) *Aboriginal Siberia. A Study in Social Anthropology*, Oxford: Clarendon Press.
(1919) *The Turks of Central Asia in History and at the Present Day*, Oxford: Clarendon Press.

GRAZYNA KUBICA-HELLER

Erratum

Revised entry

Comaroff, Jean

b. Edinburgh, 1946

Jean Comaroff's research concentrates on the *medical* and *religious anthropology* of Southern Africa, as well as the *historical anthropology* of *colonialism* and *post-coloniality*, placing emphasis on the central importance of *embodiment* and ritualized practice in the processes that produce 'collective worlds.'

She has argued forcefully for an historical anthropology that breaks down dualisms such as tradition and *modernity*, and which seeks to capture, in everyday activities, the dialectic between local phenomena and large-scale forces. Her work on the Tswana peoples of *Southern Africa* puts this programme into practice, examining how both they and their colonizers attempted to comprehend and control their changing universe.

Comaroff has also emphasized the link between British colonialism in Africa and the rise of biomedicine as a science. Missionaries used metaphors of healing to describe their work. Subsequently, concern with hygiene and the control of disease became a legitimation for colonial intervention. According to Comaroff, the colonial encounter has to be understood as a dialogue which altered both sides. Many British revalued their own world in light of the experience. For example, the British authorities developed a vision of their own poor as 'savages' without civilization.

Conversely, missionary efforts to recast African personhood, production and domestic life had unexpected results. The Tswana learned to objectify their own culture (*setswana*), which they opposed to *sekgoa*, i.e. the ways of the Europeans. While the petite bourgeoisie strove to imitate white ways, another strategy consisted in trying to subject *sekgoa* to indigenous control. Thus, the Zionist movement provided a counterculture for the illiterate poor under apartheid conditions. In contrast with more orthodox churches, Zionism questioned the rationalist dualisms bequeathed by the colonial mission, seeking to reintegrate body and spirit in a millennial ideology that offered healing to the dispossessed, and provided a resistance – in highly coded form – to the legacy of colonialism.

Far from being a methodical, linear process, colonialism was riddled with internal contradictions and often met with resistance or disdain on the part of the colonized. Yet colonialism also reconstructed local worlds; whatever else they were, missionaries were also agents of commodification, wage labor and the ideologies of European civility.

Since the late 1990s, Jean and John Comaroff have turned their attention to the nature of post-colonial society, and to the impact on African polities of the global spread of neo-liberal capitalism.

Education

B.A. (University of Cape Town) 1966
Ph.D. (London School of Economics) 1974

Fieldwork

1969–70 Mafikeng district, South Africa
1974–75 Good Hope, Botswana
1999–2001 North West Province, South Africa

Key Publications

(1985) *Body of Power, Spirit of Resistance: The Culture and History of a South African People*. Chicago: The University of Chicago Press.

(1991, 1997) with John Comaroff, *Of Revelation and Revolution*. Two Volumes. Chicago: The University of Chicago Press.

(1992) with John Comaroff, *Ethnography and the Historical Imagination*. Boulder: Westview Press.

(1997) with John Comaroff, *Of Revelation and Revolution, Volume Two: The Dialectics of Modernity on a South African Frontier*. Chicago: The University of Chicago Press.

(2001) ed., with John Comaroff, *Millennial Capitalism and the Culture of Neoliberalism*. Durham: Duke University Press.

Comaroff, John L.

b. Cape Town, South Africa, 1945

John Comaroff's research has been concerned with aspects of *law, politics, kinship* and *colonialism*, stressing the dialectical relationship between the socio-cultural order and the surface forms and processes of everyday life.

Among the Tswana of *Southern Africa*, for example, the socio-cultural order is predicated upon the organisational principles of matrilateral solidarity and agnatic rivalry. Conflicts concerning property and marriage-type relations between brothers, houses and generations, are therefore predictable and shape the form and content of everyday social interactions. Disputes being embedded in the socio-cultural order, it is artificial to separate out a 'legal system' for analysis.

Comaroff rejects both purely rule-centred and purely processual approaches to law, seeking the dynamics of dispute, in the mutually constitutive relationship between rule and process. The Tswana recognise 'laws', but these are constantly negotiated. Neither norms nor individual utility have priority in determining the outcome of conflict.

Comaroff advocates a dialectical approach to history and change. The historical anthropologist has to pay attention at once to the internal contradictions of local systems and to their articulation with social, cultural, economic and political forces from outside. Jean and John Comaroff argue that history and anthropology should not be separate disciplines. *Historical anthropology* should go beyond literary traces of the past. 'Mute meanings', transacted through goods and practices, need to be taken into account.

The two-volume study *Of Revelation and Revolution* constitutes precisely such a historical anthropology of the Nonconformist *Mission* to the Southern Tswana from 1820, and the 'long conversation' between Africans and Europeans which followed. While the missionaries tried to impose their worldview, the Tswana often refashioned signifiers of the colonizing culture. Missionary efforts to convert Africans to their version of Christianity failed on a large scale. However, the Nonconformists ushered the Southern Tswana into a world shaped by *capitalist economy*. Weber's thesis of the elective affinity between Protestantism and the 'spirit' of capitalism is shown both to hold true and to be subtly amended by the historical anthropology of the colonizing mission here.

In his work on ethnic identity, Comaroff contends that ethnicity does not refer to identities with fixed content, but to relations of inequality which result from historical processes, such as the asymmetric incorporation of different social groupings into a single political economy.

He also argues that eurocentric notions of *civil society* tend to overlook African models of civic activism such as nationalist and millennial movements that arose to counter colonialism.

Since the late 1990s, John and Jean Comaroff's work has focused on postcoloniality and the effects of the global spread of neoliberal capitalism.

Education

B.A.(University of Cape Town) 1968
Ph.D. (London School of Economics) 1973

Fieldwork

1969–70 Mafikeng district, South Africa
1974–75 Good Hope, Botswana
1999–2001 North West Province, South Africa

Key Publications

(1981) with Simon Roberts, *Rules and Processes: The Cultural Logic of Dispute in an African Context*. Chicago: The University of Chicago Press.
(1991) with Jean Comaroff, *Of Revelation and Revolution, Volume One: Christianity, Colonialism, and Consciousness in South Africa*. Chicago: The University of Chicago Press.
(1992) with Jean Comaroff, *Ethnography and the Historical Imagination*. Boulder: Westview Press.
(1997) with Jean Comaroff, *Of Revelation and Revolution, Volume Two: The Dialectics of Modernity on a South African Frontier*. Chicago: The University of Chicago Press.

ANNE FRIEDERIKE MÜLLER

D

Dahl, Gudrun

b. 1948, Stockholm, Sweden

Gudrun Dahl's work has focused on nomadic pastoralism in East Africa, gender, environment, and discourses of nationality and development. She has also been interested in the politics of representation that underlie such discourses.

In her early field studies (among the Waso Borana Oromo of Northern Kenya and Beja of Sudan), she was concerned with how local social forms had changed in response to wider political and economic forces, and how these economic adaptations had introduced new patterns of stratification and impacted on gender relations. In 1987, she edited a special issue on women in pastoral production in the journal, Ethnos. This collection of essays aimed to correct the male gender bias of earlier work on pastoral societies in the region and elsewhere. These ethnographic and theoretical studies, two of which were co-published with Anders Hjort, have made a significant contribution to the comparative study of pastoral nomadism in East and Northeast Africa.

Since the mid-1980s, her interests have shifted to examining the ideological battles that are being fought between various interest groups over words and concepts. She has analysed Swedish development discourses, national environmental idioms, and the ways in which sexuality and virtue are represented among women. In this work, she has been concerned with how language serves as a tool to gain symbolic capital, blurs conflicts of interest, and legitimises action. These analyses further the type of critical reflection she had begun to undertake, with A. Hjort, in an article published in Ethnos in 1984 on the ideology and meanings of the Western concept of development. She has also written on contemporary cultural processes in museums. In these studies, she has sought to trace the silences in discourses, to show how different actors with apparently contradictory interests draw on a common set of terms to stake out moral positions that appear to be emancipatory, without necessarily taking the side of marginalised groups.

Dahl does not consider herself to be theoretically Marxist, but acknowledges the early influence of the Marxian paradigm on her work. Her work has also been influenced by the school of symbolic interactionism.

Education

BA Stockholm University, 1970
Ph.D. Stockholm University, 1979

Fieldwork

Isiolo District, Northern Kenya, 1973–4
Sudan, 1979–1980 (5 months), 1986–7 (2 months)

Key Publications

with Hjort, A. (1976) *Having Herds: Pastoral Herd Growth and Household Economy*, Stockholm Studies in Social Anthropology, 2, Stockholm: University of Stockholm, Department of Social Anthropology.

(1978) *Suffering Grass: Subsistence and Society of Waso Borana*, Stockholm Studies in Social Anthropology, 8, Stockholm: University of Stockholm, Department of Social Anthropology.

with Hjort, A. (1991) *Responsible Man: The Atmaan Beja of Northeastern Sudan*, Stockholm Studies in Social Anthropology, 27, Stockholm: University of Stockholm, Department of Social Anthropology.

(2001) *Responsibility and Partnership in Swedish Aid Discourse*, Nordiska Afrikainstitutet, Discussion Paper 9, Uppsala: Nordiska Afrikainstitutet.

ANEESA KASSAM

Dalton, George

b. 2 August 1926, Brooklyn, New York, USA

d. 29 August 1991, Chicago, Illinois, USA

George Dalton is best known for his advocacy of the ideas of Karl Polanyi in economic anthropology and development economics. His works draw attention to the social and cultural dimensions of the economy and the ways in which rational action and 'economising' is embedded in society. Throughout his career he was an advocate of recognising the role of culture in economic behaviour. After teaching at Boston University, the University of Maryland, and Bard College, in 1961 Dalton took up a joint appointment in anthropology and economics at Northwestern University.

His *Economic Systems and Society: Capitalism, Communism and the Third World* (1974) is a an attempt at global comparison of the dominant and variant forms of economy. It was published as an attempt to move economic thinking out of the rigidity of Cold War rhetoric on freedom and the economy, and to situate free-market and command economies in their national cultural contexts.

Dalton participated energetically in the formalist-substantivist debate in economic anthropology during the 1960s and 1970s, and his essays, *Economic Anthropology and Development: Essays on Tribal and Peasant Economies* (1971), are excellent markers of one side in the debate. He was a substantivist, who in his own work, and in collaboration with Paul Bohannan, supported the position of Karl Polanyi that the economy was not an autonomous sphere of human activity, but was embedded in society. In the introduction to *Markets in Africa* Dalton with Bohannan raised questions about markets as price-setting mechanisms and used the papers they assmbled in this volume to illustrate the variation in the forms of the market occuring in different African societies. The substantivists argued that maximising return was not all that social and economic life was about. Dalton maintained that principles of exchange varied from society to society and that maximising return under market principles of exchange determined by demand and supply failed to capture either what happened in many economies, or worse falsified through reductionism complex cultural forms of behaviour.

Dalton sustained economic anthropology in his editor's role in *Research in Economic Anthropology* from its beginnings in 1978 and through publication of the work of others (Polanyi's papers and John Murra's study of the Inca state). Throughout his career he opposed simplistic notions of economic determination of history and social change, whether of left (class conflict) or right (market forces), and championed the cultural dimensions of economic action.

Education

BA Indiana University
MA Columbia University
Ph.D. University of Oregon

Fieldwork

India
Liberia
Central Africa

Key Publications

(1965) *Markets in Africa* (a symposium edited with Paul Bohannan), Evanston, IL: North-western University Press.

(1971) *Economic Anthropology and Development: Essays on Tribal and Peasant Economies*, New York: Basic Books.

(1974) *Economic Systems and Society: Capitalism, Communism and the Third World*, New York: Penguin.

MICHAEL D. LEVIN

DaMatta, Roberto A.

b. 1936, Niterói, Brazil

DaMatta initially worked with two Jê-speaking groups, the Gaviões and the Apinayé, carrying out a comparative study of interethnic contact. This early research highlighted the diversity of situations that characterised the rural frontier, as well as the importance of the culture of indigenous groups in their relationship with national society. DaMatta later distinguished himself by solving the problem of the 'Apinayé anomaly' (dualism plus parallel descent), which had been identified in Curt Nimuenda-jú's (1883–1945) monographs as well as in the works of Robert Lowie, Claude Lévi-Strauss, and David Maybury Lewis. As part of the Museu/Nacional/Harvard Central Brazil Project, co-ordinated by David Maybury Lewis and Cardoso de Oliveira, a project that brought together Americanists from both institutions on equal footing, DaMatta demonstrated in his book, *A Divided World* (1982), that although the Apinayé and the Timbira are divided into moieties, they do not regulate marriage in the elementary way that had been argued by previous authors. The moieties are basic ceremonial groups and Jê and Apinayé ritual life is an important element in the making of social life. These ceremonial groups combine a physical or substantive view of their social reality with a ceremonial or social view through the manner in which personal names are transmitted between generations.

Based on his studies of indigenous groups and on his knowledge of structuralist analytical tools, DaMatta was able to make an original contribution to the study of the *panema* (omens, augury) in the 'savage mind' of Amazonian populations (1970). DaMatta's Americanist experience and his studies of Amerindian rituals inspired his interest in national rituals. He was encouraged by Victor Turner and supported by the Wenner–Gren Foundation to develop further his early articles on Carnival as a rite of passage, and the resulting publication is a comparative analysis of different Brazilian rituals, practices, and myths (1991). A classical social anthropological approach applied to strategic 'micro-' objects in national society helped to shed new light on the contrast between authoritarian hierarchy and brotherly affection, which DaMatta claimed characterises the 'Brazilian dilemma', a point of view that gained him notoriety in the Brazilian intellectual field, and in the human sciences internationally, by the fact of providing a global interpretation of Brazilian national cultural formation although supported by precise up-to-date social anthropological tools. His analyses of the 'myth of the three races, or the problem with Brazilian-style racism', even though contained within the pages of an introductory text (*Relativizando: uma introdução à antropologia social* [Making It Relative: An Introduction to Social Anthropology] (1981) or of the paradox of the strength of the weak before authoritarian domination, as in the folklore story of Pedro Malazartes (1991), are good examples of the felicitous way DaMatta combines a subtle and inquiring analysis with clear and attractive writing. This combination is also found in the successive choice of new topics, such as football ('Soccer: opium of the people or drama of social justice?', 1988), or the totemism of the popular underground lottery, the *jogo do bicho* (*Águias, burros e borboletas:*

um *estudo antropológico do jogo do bicho* [Eagles, Donkeys, and Butterflies: An Anthropological Analysis of the 'Game of Animals'] with Elena Soarez, 1999), through which he has attempted to understand the tensions, paradoxes, and creativity of Brazilian society.

Education

BA Faculdade Fluminense de Filosofia, Niterói, Brazil, 1959
MA Harvard University, USA, 1969
Ph.D. Harvard University, USA, 1971

Fieldwork

Terêna, south of Mato Grosso, 1960
Gaviões, Pará,1961, 1962
Apinayé, northern Goiás, 1962, 1966–7, 1970, 1971, 1976
Amazon region, 1974 ('Patronage systems alongside the Transamazonic road')
Rio de Janeiro ('National rituals'), 1981–6
São João Nepomuceno, Minas Gerais, 1989
São Paulo ('The urban poor of São Paulo'), 1991–3

Key Publications

(1970) 'Les Préssages Apinayé' (The Apinayé augury), in J. Pouillon and P. Maranda, *Echanges et communications: mélanges offertes à Claude Lévi-Strauss*, Paris/The Hague: Mouton & Co.
(1982) *A Divided World: Apinayé Social Structure*, Cambridge, MA: Harvard University Press.
(1991) *Carnivals, Rogues and Heroes; An Interpretation of the Brazilian Dilemma*, Notre Dame, IL: University of Notre Dame Press (*Carnavais, malandros e heróis: para uma sociologia do dilema brasileiro*, 1979).
(1993) 'Some biased remarks on interpretativism: a view from Brazil', in R. Borofsky, *Assessing Cultural Anthropology*, New York: McGraw-Hill, Inc.

JOSÉ SERGIO LEITE LOPES

D'Andrade, Roy Goodwin

b. 1931, Brooklyn, New York, USA

Roy D'Andrade has figured large in the transformation of cognitive anthropology that resulted from the mid-twentieth-century cognitive revolution in the social sciences. He was central to the development of 'ethnosemantics', a cognitive approach to the reconstruction of culture through analysis of lexical contrast sets. As the limitations of this linguistic approach emerged, he was one of the earliest cognitive anthropologists to reconceptualise culture, in terms of schema theory, as shared schemata. He used this approach to theorise about how cultural meaning systems become internalised and gain motivational force for individuals. A dedicated methodologist, D'Andrade has demonstrated the application of various formal and statistical techniques to cultural meaning reconstruction. Notably, he has employed multidimensional scaling techniques to extract cultural dimensions from interview and survey data, for description of American national character, and cross-cultural comparison of these results. He has produced a series of cogent descriptions of American beliefs and values about work, success, interpersonal behaviour, self, and mind. He has also published a range of theoretical contributions on the cultural shaping of learning, reasoning, motivation, emotion, and color perception – distinguished by their broad synthesis of literatures and approaches from several disciplines, and their astute, often conclusive, resolution of current debates. Relatedly, D'Andrade has been the foremost anthropological chronicler of his own sub-field, charting the agenda and synthesising the findings of cognitive anthropology, and translating this contribution for psychologists.

Education

BA University of Connecticut, 1957
Ph.D. Harvard University, 1962

Fieldwork

Southwestern Pueblos, USA, 1959
Chiapas, Mexico, 1961–2
Nigeria and Ghana, 1966–7
USA, 1970–present

Key Publications

with Strauss, Claudia (eds) (1992) *Human Motives and Cultural Models*, Cambridge, UK: Cambridge University Press.
(1995) *The Development of Cognitive Anthropology*, Cambridge, UK: Cambridge University Press.

NAOMI QUINN

Daniel, E. Valentine

Valentine Daniel's ethnography on the Tamils in southern India developed from an early affinity to that region. His schooling in Sri Lanka made him familiar with its diverse lifestyles, linguistic sensibilities, and political tensions. His early fieldwork among the Tamils and Sinhalese contributed to a deeper understanding of how ancient cultures define identity and personhood, how such philosophical understandings explain syncretistic values in religious practice, and, also, the importance of indigenous systems of healing.

The values by which the Tamils define their identity in a typical village, ur, presuppose a conception of the life cycle as part of a larger cosmological totality. Implicit in a villager's question 'where are you from?' is a perception that a person's individual identity is defined by the personality of the soil where she/he lives, the water she/he bathes in, and the crops grown on the soil from which she/he gains nourishment. Their compatibility with the territory and its substance is based upon how it affects their bodily substance. Such effects are manifest in the ups and downs of personal fortune, happiness, health, anxiety, afterlife. Sacred ideas of personhood and identity such as the notion of *samsara* (salvation) or *atman* (soul) lie at the heart of procreation and reproduction. They are also expressed in living arrangements. Thus, the home is not simply a dwelling place but develops and interacts as humans do; also the direction of social activities in the home takes on metaphysical significance determining guidelines for procreation, eating, and cooking.

Further, he criticised the Cartesian 'Western' gaze that separates the body and mind, illness, and disease as a division antithetical to holistic South Asian aetiology such as Siddha medicine. Tamils believe that every sexual partnership between a woman and a man is determined by their *kunams* (humours). Astrological knowledge is also necessary for an individual to maintain equilibrium in time, space, and place, since from the moment of birth a human being enters a lifelong relationship with the nine planets.

In recent decades, Daniel's fieldwork has focused on the experiences of violence and traumas accompanying refugee status. Prior to colonisation where one lived mattered more than differences of language or religion. Sinhalese and Tamils were never monolithic communities; the differences among the Estate Tamils of Trincomalee, Battilicoa, Mannar, and Vavuniya gave them plural identities. However, colonisation and English language transformed the communities of likeness to create communities of difference, mutually antagonistic enclaves destroying the mythic reality of being Sinhalese or Tamil. A linear historical discourse is not appropriate in understanding the Indian sub-continent. Thus, it is necessary to be sensitive to perceptions within immanent traditions of being in the world, and seeing in the world.

Education

BA Amherst College, 1971
MA University of Chicago, 1973
Ph.D. University of Chicago, 1979

Fieldwork

Tamil Nadu, India
Sri Lanka

Key Publications

(1984) *Fluid Signs, Being a Person the Tamil Way*, Berkeley: University of California Press.

with Knudsen, J.C. (eds) (1995) *Mistrusting Refugees*, Berkeley: University of California Press.

with Peck, J. (eds) (1995) *Culture/Contexture: Explorations in Anthropology and Literary Study*, Los Angeles: University of California Press.

(1996) *Charred Lullabies, Chapters in an Anthropology of Violence*, Princeton, NJ: Princeton University Press.

KUSUM GOPAL

Darnell, Regna

b. 10 July 1943, Cleveland, Ohio, USA

Regna Darnell exemplifies the holistic nature of American anthropology. Trained in linguistic and cultural anthropology, and in the history of anthropology, she has made significant contributions in each area. After receiving her Ph.D., Darnell taught at the University of Alberta for over twenty years before moving to the University of Western Ontario in 1990. She has worked extensively with the Native communities of Alberta and Ontario, and in other areas for specific projects.

As an undergraduate Darnell studied with Frederica de Laguna, and was one of the last students to work with A.I. Hallowell. Both helped foster her interest in the history of anthropology. In graduate school she worked most closely with Dell Hymes, George Stocking Jr, Charles Rosenberg, and Dan Ben-Amos, which further encouraged her interdisciplinary historical interests. Her Master's thesis on D.G. Brinton (later published in 1988) demonstrated the importance of individual biographies in disciplinary history, as did her later work on Edward Sapir. Her doctoral thesis, which formed the basis for *And along Came Boas*, further developed the relationship between individuals and the discipline they constitute.

In 1996 Darnell co-organised a workshop on theorising the Americanist tradition, to confront the widespread perception that Americanist anthropology is atheoretical. *Invisible Genealogies* continues this project by demonstrating ways that contemporary anthropological theory was presaged in the work of key Americanist anthropologists. From 1999–2002 Darnell chaired the Centennial Executive Commission of the American Anthropological Association, developing numerous projects to commemorate that anniversary.

In linguistic anthropology, Darnell was among the first to formally consider culturally distinct interaction patterns in Native North America. In 1982 she organised a conference, 'Native American Interaction Patterns', which was later published (in 1988) and remains an important work in the field. She has continued research in this vein, and has demonstrated (particularly in a collaborative project with Lisa Valentine on Ojibwe and Mohawk) that these distinctive interaction patterns remain even when the language spoken is English.

At the University of Alberta, Darnell developed a program in Cree language and culture, bringing Native speakers into the classroom as active teachers; that programme became the core of the School of Native Studies there. There and at Western Ontario she has also trained many Native students, along with others.

Darnell is indefatigable in her work for a wide range of professional organisations, and is widely known for her support and encouragement of students and other scholars. She was elected a Fellow of the Royal Society of Canada in 1996.

Education

BA Bryn Mawr College, 1965
MA University of Pennsylvania, 1967
Ph.D. University of Pennsylvania, 1969

Fieldwork

Plains Cree, 1969–90

Doukhobors, 1971–3
The Gambia, 1985–7
Ojibwe and Mohawk, 1990–present

Key Publications

(1990) *Edward Sapir: Linguist, Anthropologist, Humanist*, Berkeley: University of California Press.
(1998) *And along Came Boas: Continuity and Revolution in Americanist Anthropology*, Amsterdam: John Benjamins.
with Valentine, L. (eds) (1999) *Theorizing the Americanist Tradition*, Toronto: University of Toronto Press.
(2001) *Invisible Genealogies: A History of Americanist Anthropology*, Lincoln: University of Nebraska Press.

FREDERIC W. GLEACH

Das, Veena

b. 18 February 1945, India

Veena Das gained early recognition in anthropological circles for her solid structuralist analysis of Hindu rituals, *Structure and Cognition*. Although she has continued to affirm the importance of historical and textual analysis for anthropological research, in the 1990s Das shifted her focus from more traditional anthropological themes of ritual and narrative to issues of suffering and violence. On the faculty for many years at the University of Delhi in the Department of Sociology, Das moved in the later part of the 1990s to a home base in the USA, most recently at Johns Hopkins University. Her research addresses such complex issues as riot victims, organ transplants, and pharmaceutical use among the urban poor; these topics are thematically linked through the institutional production and mediation of people's experience of pain. Das's ethnographic research is informed by her linguistic and historical expertise, and her willingness to look to a variety of interdisciplinary sources for insights into contemporary behaviours, their meanings, and their futures.

Education

BA (Hons), University of Delhi, 1964
MA University of Delhi, 1966
Ph.D. University of Delhi, 1970

Fieldwork

Gujarat (archival work in Ahmadabad, Baroda, and Surat), 1967
Delhi, Amritsar, Pune, Bombay, Ferozepur, and Bhatinda (research looking at kinship and impact of partition on lives of urban families), 1970–2, continuing till 1980
West Delhi (riot victims), 1984
Various locations (network of families, physicians, and hospitals for study of organ transplants), 1995
Delhi (team project studying social networks, health, and pharmaceuticals), 1999–present

Key Publications

(1977) *Structure and Cognition: Aspects of Hindu Caste and Ritual*, Delhi: Oxford University Press.
(1995) *Critical Events: An Anthropological Perspective on Contemporary India*, Delhi and New York: Oxford University Press,

SARAH STRAUSS

Davis, John

b. 1938, London, UK

John Davis is widely known for his groundbreaking suggestion of the value of treating the entire Mediterranean area as an anthropological entity, which provoked fruitful debate and research among area specialists. It reflected his view that the traditional ethnographic literature lacked comparative and historical evidence, and left communities implausibly isolated from the macro-polity around them. In contrast, his own work in southern Italy used a century of local records to explore the structural importance of kinship and property in understanding the regional economy. Ten years later, after fieldwork 'across the sea' in

Libya, he demonstrated the various ways in which the segmentary politics of the Zuwaya tribesmen, with its fighting and trading, was incorporated within a radical 'hydrocarbon state'. He gave a timely and nuanced depiction of Libya, exploring both the perspectives of ordinary tribesmen who were the subjects of revolutionary government, and the social and cultural roots of Qaddafi's apparatus and ideology. A highly original work of political anthropology, which shows why the classic issue of stateless politics continues to have relevance in the contemporary world, the monograph is long overdue a reprint.

A subsequent influential essay drew on this fieldwork to contrast the various structural social forces producing different kinds of historical narrative, such as the genealogical model of tribal history and the teleological history of the nation-state. He developed this insight further in his inaugural address at Oxford, where he discussed the effect of different 'thoughts about the past' (such as myth and autobiography) on naming and concepts of identity. As these themes hint, Davis has often explored the amusing and profound consequences of the complex disjunctions between ideals, rules, and practice, which he later celebrated explicitly as 'social creativity'. In this vein, and returning to economic anthropology, he brilliantly analysed the ways in which, even in industrial society, exchange rarely reflects the pursuit of maximum utility, instead being always replete with symbolic intention as social actors in real relationships inventively deploy their local repertoire of finely shaded transactions.

By virtue of his sustained engagement with the intersecting anthropologies of politics, economics, and kinship, his meticulous use of quantitative data, including a pioneering use of computer analysis (which lives on in his former department at Kent), and the unfailing clarity and elegance of his writing, Davis stands in the very best traditions of British social anthropology and his writings should long remain a source of insight.

Education

BA, University College, University of Oxford, 1961

Ph.D. London School of Economics, 1968

Fieldwork

Pisticci, Italy, 1963–6

Adjabia and Kufra, Libya, 1975–9

Key Publications

(1973) *Land and Family in Pisticci*, LSE Monographs, London: The Athlone Press.

(1977) *People of the Mediterranean*, London: Routledge.

(1987) *Libyan Politics: Tribe and Revolution*, London: IB Tauris.

(1992) *Exchange*, Minneapolis: University of Minnesota Press.

MUKULIKA BANERJEE

de Heusch, Luc

b. 7 May 1927, Brussels, Belgium

Although Luc de Heusch was always fascinated by anthropology, his œuvre could certainly not be said to be limited to that discipline. During and after the Second World War, de Heusch was close to the surrealist movement in the visual and literary arts, and after that he spent much time in the company of the painters and poets of the 'CoBrA' group. He made his début in cinema in 1947–8 as an assistant of Henri Storck, and throughout his long, distinguished career as an anthropologist he produced over a dozen films. Many of those took issue with explicitly artistic phenomena (such as his films on the painters Ensor, Alechinsky, and Magritte), whereas others were more ethnographic in nature, as in the case of a documentary about a dramatic arts circle in a small Belgian village.

After refining his anthropological knowledge and his ethnographic craft as a student of

Marcel Griaule in Paris, de Heusch became a central figure in the Centre of Cultural Anthropology at the University of Brussels. Also, he headed the *Laboratoire Systèmes de pensée en Afrique noire* (Laboratory Systems of Thought in Black Africa) in Paris with Michel Cartry. A major focus of his work there was on sacrifice in Africa, published as four collaborative *Cahiers* between 1976 and 1981, and then individually by de Heusch as *Sacrifice in Africa*. This collection of essays criticises and elaborates upon the theory of sacrifice developed by Marcel Mauss and Henri Hubert, putting forward a strongly structuralist approach.

In fact de Heusch is one of the more important Africanist anthropologists who can be considered self-professed structuralists in the tradition of Claude Lévi-Strauss. Defending structuralism against charges from both 'action-oriented' critics, who blame it for suppressing the role of human agency, and against historical determinists, who regard it as being in the way of an understanding of objective historical processes, he celebrates it as an 'innocent' approach. Both *Sacrifice in Africa* and *Why Marry Her?* analyse societal phenomena through this prism. An unreconstructed and convinced structuralist, de Heusch considers the teachings of Lévi-Strauss and his antecedents as the backbone of a superior scientific method for studying myth, ritual, and kinship. Apart from the teachings of Lévi-Strauss, he found inspiration for a comparative mythology in the work of Georges Dumézil.

The Drunken King, another piece published in English, analyses a wide selection of material from sub-Saharan African oral traditions, primarily about the origins of a range of kingdoms. His material is often secondary, gathered by missionaries or administrators, and he draws intensively from two other bodies of anthropological work: Jan Vansina and Victor Turner. De Heusch makes a case to consider the region south of the Congo forest, characterised by savannah civilisations, as one 'culture area'. The author analyses these historical narratives in order to uncover the outlines of common semiological patterns underlying the culturally diverse multitude of conceptual systems that can be found in this region. The dominant ideological function of this complex, de Heusch argues, was to legitimate the fairly recent emergence of divine monarchy, but the cosmological discourse and its view of human nature preceded this political structure.

The Drunken King, as a compilation of de Heusch's work on mythology, is an example of an ambitious research project, trying to reintegrate a regional mythical complex through the systematic and detailed collection of oral traditions. In this way, like his other publications, it bears the traits of an encyclopaedic, or even 'preservationist', approach to anthropology: for de Heusch, comparative mythology is an urgent task in the face of the changes on the African continent that pose a modernising threat to its heritage of oral tradition. However, de Heusch also argues for systematic comparison with similar material from other continents. He himself makes a beginning of this exercise by indicating some ways of linking his work to the findings of Lévi-Strauss in Latin America. Moreover, de Heusch has more recently written a number of texts on Voodoo in Haiti.

Education

Ph.D. University of Brussels, 1955
Doctorate Honoris Causa, University of Strasbourg, 1992

Fieldwork

Tetela-Hamba, Belgian Congo, 1953–4; *idem* Zaïre, summer 1975
Kongo, Zaïre, summer 1974
Haiti, 1970, 1973, 1983

Key Publications

(1981) *Why Marry Her? Society and Symbolic Structures* (partly previously published as *Pourquoi l'épouser, et autres essais* (1971), trans. J. Lloyd, Cambridge, UK: Cambridge University Press; Paris: Editions de la Maison des Sciences de l'Homme.

(1984) *The Drunken King or the Origin of the State* (*Le Roi ivre ou l'origine de l'État* (1972), trans. R. Willis, Bloomington: Indiana University Press.

(1985) *Sacrifice in Africa. A Structural Approach*, trans. L. O'Brien and A. Morton, Bloomington: Indiana University Press; Manchester: Manchester University Press.

STEFAN JANSEN

De la Peña Guillermo

b. 1943, Guadalajara, Jalisco, Mexico

Guillermo De la Peña has focused upon issues of regional structure, power, and the state, exploring a diversity of topics including popular culture and identity, education and social change, politics and ritual, urban change and regional construction. His doctoral study on the Morelos Highlands dealt with the structural arrangements for the control of land and labour for agricultural production in a peasant region of Mexico. Considered as a classic analysis of the Manchester School, this study goes beyond the description of the heterogeneity and interdependence of multiple social groups shaping a regional arrangement to show that poverty and the limits of regional growth are a function of the national distribution of power and its benefits. Building upon this conclusion he sets an agenda that has inspired his work both in individual research and in the organisation of research teams and graduate education programmes.

De la Peña has written extensively on the historical roots of regional integration and regional limits reconfiguration, labour organisation and capitalist development, small-scale economy and regional structure, local arrangements, the wider society and the state, urban centers and their role in regional organisation, agency and individual participation in regional construction, the role of the state in regional construction, and the shaping of local political arrangements. He contends that since mediation between the particular

(the community) and the general (the nation) is provided by the regional dimension, regional history can be understood as a threefold current: transformations in production, transformations in the circulation of goods, and negotiations among relevant actors and between them and the state. Regional development is heavily influenced by social networks since particular arrangements among local actors depend upon regional power arrangements. Therefore, restructuring of complex networks of power relations not only transforms the productive structure, but also blurs regional limits and subjects them to a process of continuous negotiation.

De la Peña has founded and headed some of the leading institutions in anthropological research and training in Mexico at the Universidad Autónoma Metropolitana-Iztapalapa, El Colegio de Michoacán, and CIESAS-Occidente.

His most recent work, on state social policies towards indigenous populations, focuses upon the relationships and negotiations involving indigenous leaders and organisations, government agencies, different NGOs, and civil-society groups, exploring the restructuring relationships between indigenous communities and the state.

Education

BA Instituto Libre de Filosofía y Ciencias, Mexico, 1967
MA University of Manchester, 1970
Ph.D. University of Manchester, 1973

Fieldwork

Gypsy communities, Madrid, Spain, 1969–70
Morelos Highlands, Mexico, 1970–1, 1973–5
Mexico City, popular settlements, 1974, 1975
Southern Jalisco, Mexico, 1976, 1977, 1978, 1979, 1991
Popular neighbourhoods, Guadalajara, Jalisco, Mexico, 1985–8
Huichol Highlands, Tuxpan, and Manantlán Highlands, Jalisco, Mexico, 2000–

Key Publications

(1980) *A Legacy of Promises*, Manchester: Manchester University Press.

(1984) 'Ideology and practice in southern Jalisco: peasants, rancheros, and urban entrepreneurs', in R.T. Smith (ed.) *Kinship Ideology and Practice in Latin America*, Chapel Hill: University of North Carolina.

(1992) 'Populism, regional power, and political mediation: southern Jalisco, 1900–1980', in: Eric Van Young (ed.) *Mexico's Regions: Comparative History and Development*, San Diego: Center for US–Mexican Studies, UCSD.

(1995) 'La ciudadanía étnica y la construcción de 'los indios' en el México contemporáneo' (Ethnic citizenship and the construction of 'the Indians' in contemporary Mexico), *Revista Internacional de Filosofía Política*, Madrid, 6: 116–40.

FERNANDO I. SALMERÓN CASTRO

De Laguna, Frederica

b. 3 October 1906, Ann Arbor, Michigan, USA

d. 6 October 2004, Haverford, Pennsylvania, USA

After beginning graduate work at Columbia University with Franz Boas, Frederica De Laguna took his advice and pursued her archaeological interests in Europe where she found colleagues much more responsive to a female student than their American peers. She was less impressed by a brief stint in B. Malinowski's seminar, where functionalism seemed, to her, Americanist common sense. Danish archaeologist, Therkel Mathiassen, invited her to join his expedition in Greenland. She wrote a Boasian distribution study (comparing Upper Palaeolithic and Eskimo art) for her dissertation in 1933, but had already begun a rigorous programme of fieldwork in Alaska (where she was joined for one season by Danish archaeologist, Kaj Birket-Smith).

She documented the continued distinct existence of the Eyak and carried out the first archaeological survey of the Alaskan interior.

While pursuing a distinguished academic career at Bryn Mawr College, De Laguna continued fieldwork, including a brief foray among the Pima of the Southwest, and a longer hiatus in Naval intelligence during the Second World War (resigning as Lieutenant Commander). Her intensive studies of the coastal Tlingit villages of Yakutat and Angoon began after the war, with a series of student collaborators. *The Story of a Tlingit Village* (1960) developed a holistic approach to the culture history of the coastal and interior Northwest Coast, combining archaeology, ethnology, and ethnohistory. In 1954, with Catherine McClelland, she began to study the Athabascan-speaking Copper River Atna in this larger historical context. The three volumes of *Under Mount Saint Elias* (1972) provide a monumental synthesis of De Laguna's Yakutat research. She also edited Lieutenant George T. Emmons's Tlingit manuscript (1991).

After her retirement in 1975, De Laguna returned to the field in Greenland (in 1979) and Alaska (in 1978 and 1985). In 1986, she was honoured by a potlatch at Yakutat where Tlingit language and culture are being revitalised. In 1994, she attended the first Eyak potlatch in eighty-five years. Throughout her long career and continued scholarship, De Laguna remained convinced that the subdisciplines of anthropology are integrally connected and that descriptive data based on long-term ethnography form the baseline for interpretation. In recent years, her scholarship has been much praised by scholars from the former Soviet Union for its comparative relevance to their work.

In 1975 De Laguna and Margaret Mead were the first women anthropologists elected to the National Academy of Sciences. She served as president of the American Anthropological Association and held many other honours.

Education

BA Bryn Mawr College, 1927

Ph.D. Columbia University, 1933

Fieldwork

Greenland and Alaska (especially Tlingit, Eyak), 1930 to 1994
Pima, 1936

Key Publications

(1960) *The Story of a Tlingit Village: A Problem in the Relationship between Archaeological, Ethnological and Historical Methods*, Washington, DC: Bureau of American Ethnology Bulletin 172.
(1972) *Under Mount Saint Elias: The History and Culture of the Yakutat Tlingit*, 3 vols, Washington, DC: Smithsonian Contributions to Anthropology 7.
(1977) *Voyage to Greenland: A Personal Initiation into Anthropology*, New York: W.W. Norton.
(ed.) (1991) *The Tlingit Indians* by G.T. Emmons, Seattle: University of Washington Press.

REGNA DARNELL

Densmore, Frances

b. 21 May 1867, Red Wing, Minnesota, USA

d. 5 June 1957, Red Wing, Minnesota

As a child growing up in Red Wing, Minnesota, Frances Densmore was fascinated by the music often heard from a Sioux encampment near her home. She studied music at Oberlin and Harvard Conservatories, and established a career as a music teacher and popular lecturer before becoming intrigued by the work of Alice C. Fletcher on Omaha music. She wrote to Fletcher, then associated with the Bureau of American Ethnology, whose gracious and encouraging reply motivated a 10-year preparatory study of Indian music, which she heard first at the Chicago World's Fair in 1893. In 1901, Densmore began to visit local Chippewa tribes to listen to the music and attempted a transcription of a Sioux song. In 1905, accompanied by her sister, Margaret, she embarked upon her first field trip, among the Chippewa. Two years later William H. Holmes at the Bureau of American Ethnology offered her a small stipend for fieldwork funds and recording equipment. This marked the beginning of a 50-year association with the Bureau. In return for an annual stipend of $3,000 allowing her to use the title of collaborator, Densmore could choose her own field sites and projects, including not only music but also its relationship to the rest of culture; on occasion, she also collected musical instruments.

During her career, Densmore recorded more than 3,500 songs on wax cylinders, in what she considered an exercise in urgent ethnology. Most of her musical studies were issued in the bulletins and annual reports of the Bureau of American Ethnology between 1910 and 1958 – including Chippewa, Teton Sioux, Ute, Mandan and Hidatsa, Tule (Panama), Papago, Pawnee, Menominee, Yuman and Yaqui, Cheyenne and Arapaho, Alabama, Santo Domingo Pueblo, Nootka and Quileute, Choctaw, Seminole, Acoma, Isleta, Cochita and Zuni Pueblos, and Maidu. She also published a volume on Chippewa customs, the Chippewa being the group she came to know most intensively; she recorded Midewewin or Grand Medicine Society songs over a long period of time. Densmore became an associate in ethnology at the Southwest Museum in 1950 and a consultant on Indian music at the University of Florida in 1954; she was still doing fieldwork among the Seminole at the age of eighty-seven.

Densmore's honours ranged from songs, adoption and a name bestowed by various tribes among whom she worked, to an honorary doctorate, to recognition by the Minnesota Historical Society, to a congressional tribute in 1952. Densmore never married, giving the impression of a stereotypical Victorian woman. She depended greatly on the help of her schoolteacher sister, Margaret, for rapport with Indians and mitigation of her own austere manners.

Despite her absence of any formal training in anthropology, however, Densmore was careful to obtain a cross-section of musical styles, focusing especially on curing songs and often working with elderly singers. She always identified and thanked her consultants in her publications and was careful to incorporate cultural information about the meaning and performance of the music. Although her earlier interpretations of the music are highly romanticised and sound somewhat patronising today, Densmore gradually moved towards a more rigorous style of recording and reporting her findings.

Densmore transcribed and analysed her materials after returning from the field, assuming that Western music provided adequate guidance for conveying the 'general musical character' of other musical traditions. This led her to conclude that fractional tones were not an essential feature of Indian music. Her earlier books summarised musical characteristics in tables accompanied by description of the cultural function of the songs and transcriptions. She experimented with different parameters of the music ranging from nine to twenty-two, reducing them to eleven by her final book in 1957. In 1919, writing on the Teton Sioux, she included for the first time cumulative tables from all of the music she had studied until that time. She did not, however, transfer this information to maps. At the time of her death, she had transferred many of her original recordings to more permanent formats preserved in the Smithsonian Institution archives.

Frances Densmore remains a pioneer both of ethnomusicology and for the professional employment of women in anthropology. Hers was the last generation for which research skills could be acquired in the field rather than through academic credentialisation. Her extensive documentation of North American Indian music has stood the test of time and is now invaluable.

Education

Oberlin, 1884–6
Harvard Conservatories, 1886–8

Fieldwork

Musical survey of American Indian tribes, 1920–30

Key Publications

(1942) 'The study of Indian music', *Annual Report of the Smithsonian Institution for the Year Ended June 30, 1941*: 527–550.
(1945) 'The Importance of recordings of Indian songs', *American Anthropologist* 47: 637–9.
(1950) 'The words of Indian songs as unwritten literature', *Journal of American Folklore* 63: 450–8.

REGNA DARNELL

Descola, Philippe

b. 19 June 1949, Paris, France

A student of Claude Lévi-Strauss, Philippe Descola's work has focused on the interrelationship between nature and culture. The publication of his doctoral thesis (*In the Society of Nature*), which was based on his fieldwork among the Achuar Indians of Ecuador, achieved international acclaim. Descola argued that, among the Achuar, nature is treated as homologous to the system of social relations between members of society. It is only by considering this system of relations that we can make sense of the Achuar's systematic under-exploitation of the two main ecological habitats of their territory. Descola showed that the relationships of a society with its environment could not be narrowly interpreted as strictly adaptive responses.

In *Spears of Twilight*, Descola deepened his ethnographical account of Achuar society and compared ethnographic writing to the composition procedures used by novelists of the naturalistic school. However, he also argued passionately against reducing ethnology to a hermeneutics of culture and in favor of its comparative project. He maintained that ethnology must deal with the principles of the construction of reality and the interaction of social and cultural phenomena.

Descola has been a professor at the prestigious College de France in Paris since June 2000 and holds the anthropology of nature chair. He is also the new director of the Laboratoire d'Anthropologie Sociale.

Education

MA, philosophy, University of Paris-X, 1972
Licence of ethnology, University of Paris-X, 1972
Doctorat of 3° cycle in social anthropology, École des hautes études en sciences sociales, 1983

Fieldwork

Mexico, 1973
Ecuador, 1976–8, 1979, 1981, 1984, 1993, 1997

Key Publications

(1994) In the Society of Nature: A Native Ecology in Amazonia (La Nature domestique: Symbolisme et praxis dans l'écologie des Achuar, 1986), trans. Nora Scott, Cambridge, UK: Cambridge Studies in Social and Cultural Anthropology no. 93; New York: Cambridge University Press.
(1996) Spears of Twilight: Life and Death in the Amazon Jungle (Les Lances du crépuscule. Relations jivaros. Haute Amazonie, 1993), trans. Janet Lloyd, New York: New Press.

ROBERT CRÉPEAU

Deshen, Shlomo

b. 1935, Frankfurt, Germany

Shlomo Deshen was among the leaders of a young cohort of Israeli scholars who studied Jews from the Middle East through intensive anthropological fieldwork. In doing so, he moved beyond the dominant paradigm of the first generation of Israeli sociology that had stressed how immigrants dissociated themselves from their past cultures while engaged in processes of modernisation, and focused instead on the content of immigrants' cultural worlds as they were actively reworked in social settings in the new society. His monograph on elections in a new Israeli development town was the first publication in a series growing out of a project organised at Manchester University, which had a tradition of research on social change in complex urban settings. Deshen's fieldwork in this town also generated several articles showing the dynamics of abandoning, adopting, and reworking cultural and religious symbols within a fluid social field. In this vein, he later pioneered the study of hillulot – pilgrimage celebrations in honor of sainted rabbis – demonstrating how they both stem from patterns of the past and reflect integration into Israeli society.

Much of Deshen's subsequent work was carried out not in defined 'field trips' but through continuous contact with North African Jews residing in Israel, in particular those originating from southern Tunisia. He sometimes was personally involved in their cultural projects. Several studies showed the importance of literacy in their lives, analysing the efforts to publish earlier rabbinic books and manuscripts in the Israeli setting. His knowledge of rabbinic Hebrew and culture also fed into work on the history of the Jews of Morocco. He analysed rabbinical texts combining the methods of Jewish social history and the insights of anthropological research that others had carried out in Morocco since the 1960s after most Jews had left.

Deshen was also active, in collaboration with colleagues, in publishing collections that provided a broad view of Jewish life and Judaism in the Middle East, both historically and in terms of Israeli society. In the 1980s he also conducted a study on the blind. The Hebrew versions of his publications elucidated the religious cultures of Jews from the Middle East for Israelis of European background who often viewed them disparagingly. In the 1980s–1990s, when it became politically possible for Israelis to visit some North African countries, he carried out brief visits to Morocco and to Jerba, Tunisia, to gain an ethnographic sense of the original settings of the groups about which he had been writing for decades.

Education

BA Hebrew University of Jerusalem, 1960
Ph.D. Manchester University, 1968

Fieldwork

Negev, Israel, mid-1960s
Various locales in Israel thereafter

Key Publications

(1970) *Immigrant Voters in Israel: Parties and Congregations in a Local Election Campaign*, Manchester: Manchester University Press.
with Shokeid, Moshe (1974) *The Predicament of Homecoming: Cultural and Social Life of North African Immigrants*, Ithaca: Cornell University Press.
with Zenner, Walter P. (eds) (1996) *Jews among Muslims: Communities in the Precolonial Middle East*, London: Macmillan.

HARVEY E. GOLDBERG

Desjarlais, Robert

b. 1962, Holyoke, Massachusetts, USA

Robert Desjarlais's first ethnography about the Yolmo wa of Himalayan Nepal explores how Yolmo people seek and effect healing through the visual, meditative, and aesthetic practices he studied during his apprenticeship to a Yolmo shamanic healer. The book's central questions – about how embodied 'experience' varies cross-culturally or, put differently, about variation among culturally patterned ways of sensing, feeling, acting, and being in the world – thread through his work. Desjarlais's second ethnography, about everyday life in a Boston, Massachusetts, shelter for the homeless mentally ill, asks how residents experience the world of passing time and structured space,

and of calming and threatening encounters with others. This book, Desjarlais's most radical challenge to mainstream anthropology thus far, shows how the concept of 'experience' itself derives from a particular sociocultural context: the industrialised, individualised, bureaucratised, often masculinist West. What constitutes experience, he asks, when personhood and subjectivity are embedded in webs of social relations, as among the Yolmo wa, or when one lacks the geographical anchor of 'home' and the cognitive faculties marking others as 'normal'? Desjarlais's third ethnography explores how different sensory modes of being shape the living and dying of elderly Yolmo wa. Philosophically keen and politically engaged, his work makes important contributions to medical, psychological, linguistic, and phenomenological anthropology, and to explorations of mental illness, ageing, the homeless, ritual healing, Himalayan Buddhism, and South Asia.

Education

BA University of Massachusetts Amherst, 1984
MA University of California, Los Angeles, 1987
Ph.D. University of California, Los Angeles, 1990

Fieldwork

Yolmo area, Nepal, winter 1988–spring 1989, summer 1997, winter–spring 1998, autumn 2000, autumn 2001
Boston, summer 2001–summer 2002

Key Publications

(1997) *Shelter Blues: Sanity and Selfhood among the Homeless*, Philadelphia: University of Pennsylvania.
(2003) *Sensory Biographies: Lives and Deaths among Nepal's Yolmo Buddhists*, Berkeley: University of California.

SARAH S. WILLEN

Devereux, George

b. 1908, Lugoj, Hungary

d. 1985, Paris, France

A key figure in psychological anthropology and founder of ethnopsychoanalysis and ethnopsychiatry, George Devereux's career began with studies of physics at the Sorbonne (1926–7), a diploma in Malay at the École Nationale des Langues Orientales Vivantes (1931), and courses with Mauss and Lévy-Bruhl at the Institute of Ethnology. Though he read Géza Róheim during fieldwork in Indochina, he was 'converted' to Freud by Mohave informants in 1938–9. After doctoral studies under A.L. Kroeber and R.H. Lowie, and war service as a liaison officer with the French in the Far East, he began training analysis in 1946. He worked in a veterans' hospital in Topeka, Kansas, under Karl Menninger, taught ethnopsychiatry at the School of Medicine, Temple University, and practised as a psychoanalyst in New York (1959–63), before returning to a professorship in France.

Devereux's enduring contribution to anthropology rests on his demonstrations that human phenomena require the complementary use of psychological and sociological discourses – an application of Heisenberg's uncertainty principle to ethnographic research. Because interactions between observer and observed, object and instrument, are constitutive of our knowledge of all phenomena, we must make choices of method and theory, not on the basis of an objectivist principle of representing reality as it is in itself, but on the basis of a judgement as to how we might enrich rather than impoverish both our understanding of, as well as the life of, that which we seek to explain. Devereux also argues that much of the experience–distant rhetoric and theoretical model building of anthropology may be understood on an analogy with intrapsychic defense mechanisms – subterfuges for coping with the stressful effects of fieldwork and the unsettling complexity of life.

Anthropological systematising may thus be compared with other 'unscientific' ways of bringing an illusion of order to life and creating a viable existence, such as attributing causation to inanimate things or performing rituals. Whatever their different epistemological values, scientific and magical reasoning provide alternative strategies for coping with the panic all human beings experience when confronted by the unresponsiveness of matter – the sheer otherness, non-humanness, and unmanageability of many of the forces that impinge upon us. Devereux also insisted that universal patterns underpin cultural particulars, and that 'each person is a complete specimen of Man and each society a complete specimen of Society'. Devereux's empirical, clinical, and comparative essays encompass the occult, abortion, dreams in classical Greek tragedies, shamanism, schizophrenia, kinship, and personhood.

Education

Licence ès Lettres, Sorbonne, Paris, 1932
Ph.D. University of California, Berkeley, 1935

Fieldwork

Arizona (Hopi) and Colorado (Mohave), 1932
Vietnam (Sedang), 1932–5
Colorado (Mohave), 1938–9

Key Publications

(1961) *Mohave Ethnopsychiatry and Suicide: The Psychiatric Knowledge and the Psychic Disturbances of an Indian Tribe*, Washington, DC: Bureau of American Ethnology Bulletin 175.
(1967) *From Anxiety to Method in the Behavioral Sciences*, The Hague: Mouton.
(1978) *Ethnopsychoanalysis: Psychoanalysis and Anthropology as Complementary Frames of Reference*, Berkeley: University of California Press.
(1980) *Basic Problems of Ethnopsychiatry*, Chicago: University of Chicago Press.

MICHAEL JACKSON

di Leonardo, Micaela

b. 1949, San Jose, California, USA

The hallmark of Micaela di Leonardo's anthropology is historicised Marxist feminism. Her first book explored white ethnicity through the lens of Italian American experiences in California's Bay Area. She problematised beliefs about ethnic essentialism and upward mobility by analysing how ethnic experiences vary by class, time, place, gender, and generation. She has continued to explore race, ethnicity, and gender in the USA through field research in New Haven, Connecticut, where she tracks shifts in the city's politics and economy against varied residents' ability to earn a living, make the city home, and understand and articulate social processes.

Di Leonardo has edited two books and written many articles investigating how gender expressions and inequalities take form and shift in different historical moments. She has rewritten the history of anthropology through the lens of feminist theory and interrogated such cross-disciplinary ideas as women's culture, ethnic community, deindustrialisation, and identity politics. Her research on kin work demonstrated cross-class similarities in the gendered labour of connecting households and variability in whether or not women embraced or resisted that assignment.

In *Exotics at Home*, di Leonardo traces the history of North American anthropology to contextualise how anthropology has been marginalised in public culture, and when it has been successful in comprehending power and difference. She argues that in public culture anthropologists take on the exotic, often trivialised costumes of the 'others' they study. In this book di Leonardo critically reviews ethnographies portraying women of color, using those portraits as a lens for illuminating the power relations, cultural misconceptions, and theoretical bias that can undermine anthropological work. She explores the lasting popularity of Margaret Mead, the hegemony of culture of poverty and underclass theory, and the failed project of post-modernism. She offers a trenchant critique of post-modernist anthropology as a useful methodological stance that fails to honour precursive feminist arguments and that also fails to account for relations of power beyond those of ethnographer and subject. As in her other works, di Leonardo calls on anthropologists to undertake serious studies of culture and political economy that contextualise peoples' experiences and perceptions in the material world.

Finally, di Leonardo has been an engaged public intellectual, who has published widely in such journals as the *Nation* and the *Village Voice*. She has written for general audiences about such thorny issues as rape, cultural relativism, sociobiology, urban ethnography, cultural studies, and the trivialising of women anthropologists.

Micaela di Leonardo currently holds the Board of Lady Managers of the Columbian Exposition endowed chair at Northwestern University.

Education

BA University of California, Berkeley, 1972
MA University of California, Berkeley, 1973
Ph.D. University of California, Berkeley, 1981

Fieldwork

San Francisco Bay Area, California, 1976–9
New Haven, Connecticut, 1988–ongoing

Key Publications

(1984) *The Varieties of Ethnic Experience*, Ithaca: Cornell University Press.

(ed.) (1991) *Gender at the Crossroads of Knowledge*, Berkeley: University of California Press.

(1998) *Exotics at Home*, Chicago: University of Chicago Press.

with Lancaster, Roger N. (eds) (1997) *The Gender/Sexuality Reader*, London and New York: Routledge.

BRETT WILLIAMS

Diamond, Stanley

b. 4 January 1922, New York City, USA

d. 31 March 1991, New York City, USA

Stanley Diamond carved out new terrains of anthropological theory and practice in promoting meta-theoretical perspectives on the history of anthropological theory, and in his work on state formation, post-coloniality, psychological anthropology, the anthropology of education, the anthropology of pre-state societies, the anthropology of Utopia, ethnopoetics, and Western Marxism. However, beyond his theoretical and fieldwork contributions he is noted for his pragmatic engagement with public anthropology. His work anticipated much recent anthropology debate and was prognostic of the current political/moral character of the discipline. He was the foremost theorist of his generation in conceptualising the historical position and mission of anthropology in a post-colonial world; as he frequently put it: 'anthropology is the study of people in crisis by people in crisis'.

Between 1950–60, Diamond reached theoretical and political maturity through fieldwork on post-colonial West Africa, and the socialist Utopianism of Israeli kibbutzim, and at the Brandeis History of Ideas Department where he worked with Paul Radin Herbert Marcuse, Martin Buber, and Maurice Stein. In the 1960s in a series of groundbreaking essays, such as 'Job and the Trickster' (1972) and 'Plato and the definition of the primitive' (1974), Diamond crafted his theory of the primitive/civilised dichotomy, a heuristic and politically contextualised approach to the history of ethnological theory as a critique of civilisation. The 'primitive/civilised dichotomy' has been reductively misinterpreted as Luddite nostalgia. Rather, Diamond used strategies of defamiliarisation to crack open anthropology's epistemological foundations in the on-going transhistorical repression of alterity by civilisation, an approach that presaged the perspectives of new social movements from feminism to ecological activism. His genealogical reading of anthropological theory from the seventeenth century to the present posed crucial challenges to the formation of the self, experience, and knowledge in modernity. He proposed the historical necessity of a prospective 'reconstitution' of repressed primitivity as an ethical/political vehicle for the dereification and disalienation of personhood and society – the historical alternative being a structural predilection to genocide and other forms of mass destruction.

Yet, despite his Utopian and ethical trajectory, Diamond was a shrewd and ironic political critic of the contemporary world political scene and a committed practitioner of public anthropology. In multiple fora, Diamond advocated for the Biafran Revolution and against the ethnocide of the Igbo between 1967 and 1970. He was an adviser to the Biafran insurgents and clandestinely entered Biafra during the civil war. His Biafran engagement anticipated the subsequent emergence of genocide and 'state failure' as core problematics of post-coloniality. In the 1970s and 1980s, Diamond forged political alliances with, and developed academic support networks for, Central and Eastern European opposition intelligentsia, most notably the group gathered around the Yugoslavian journal, *Praxis*.

In 1966, the Graduate Faculty of the New School of Social Research invited Diamond to create a committee on anthropology, which in 1971 he inaugurated as the first North American department dedicated to critical anthropological theory, which he chaired for fourteen years. Diamond, a dynamic and charismatic teacher, designed an innovative curriculum that was both historically and politically contextualised. He grounded anthropological training in the dialectical history of ethnological theory, a depth immersion in the Boasian four-field approach and a synthetic multidisciplinarity that embraced continental philosophy, psychoanalysis, social history, and literature. It was a department where totemic Boasians such as Irving Goldman and Gene Weltfish taught side by side with new generations of critical thinkers such as anthropologist, Bob Scholte, and psychoanalyst, Joel Kovel. Diamond resisted cordoning off the 'hard sciences' of hominid evolution and archaeology from hermeneutic and political perspectives as evidenced in *Dialectical Anthropology*, the journal he founded in 1975. In the 1980s, Diamond articulated his lifelong immersion in writing poetry and ethnography by working with the ethnopoetics journal, *Alcheringa*, and by organising symposia of ethnographically informed poets such as Nathaniel Tarn, Gary Snyder, and Jerome Rothenberg. In his last decade Diamond was appointed poet in the university and distinguished professor of humanities at the New School in addition to the appointments he held as distinguished visiting professor at the Free University of Berlin, and at Bard College.

Education

BA New York University, 1942
Ph.D. Columbia University, 1951

Fieldwork

Dahomey, 1951
Israel, 1951–3
Jos Plateau, Nigeria 1953–4, 1957–9
Gwong District, Nigeria, 1963–6
Allegheny Seneca Study, 1960–3
Culture of Schools Program, Syracuse, New York, 1965
Biafra, 1966–72 (non-continuous)

Key Publications

(ed.) (1964) *Primitive Views of the World: Essays from Culture in History*, New York: Columbia University Press.
(1974) *In Search of the Primitive: A Critique of Cvilization*, New Brunswick, NJ: Transaction Publications
(1982) *Totems*, Barrytown: Open Book Publications (a book of poetry).
(1983) *Dahomy: Transition and Conflict in State Formation*, New York: Bergin & Garvey.

ALLEN FELDMAN

Dobrowolski, Kazimierz

b. 1894, Nowy Sacz, Poland

d. 1987, Cracow, Poland

Kazimierz Dobrowolski's interdisciplinary research in history (especially socioeconomic and cultural), ethnology, and sociology secured him a position of rank in the Polish and Central European academic circles. As an ethnologist, he was predominantly interested in traditional folk culture in confrontation with urban culture in various regions of southern Little Poland, and, in particular, among the Highlanders of the Polish Tatras. The latter group had formed in the feudal period as the Walachian shepherds from the Balkans, and merged with the indigenous Polish farmers. By way of comparative analysis involving various cultural relics, Dobrowolski endeavored to explain the origin of that culture and demonstrate its Balkan roots. At the same time he attached great importance to theoretical reflection: he was one of the few scholars worldwide to formulate an outline theory of traditional peasant culture. Dobrowolski was also the first among Polish ethnologists to champion the view that their discipline should not restrict itself to the legacy of the past, but also take into account contemporary sociocultural change. He placed a strong emphasis on the need for a diachronic and interdisciplinary approach to sociocultural reality. Accordingly, he described his theoretical orientation as genetic-integral.

Education

MA Jagellonian University of Kracow, 1916
Ph.D. Jagellonian University of Kracow, 1919

Fieldwork

Tatra Region in the Polish Carpathians, 1922–38, 1952–77

Key Publications

(1971) 'Peasant traditional culture', in T.

Shanin (ed.) *Peasants and Peasant Societies*, West Drayton, Middlesex: Penguin Books.

(1977) 'Studies on the theory of folk culture. The problem of cultural relics in the light of source materials of southern Little Poland', in J. Turowski and L.M. Szwengrub (eds) *Rural Socio-cultural Change in Poland*, Wroclaw: Ossolineum.

WLADYSLAW KWASNIEWICZ

Donnan, Hastings

b. 12 March 1953, Portadown, County Armagh, Northern Ireland, UK

Hastings Donnan's doctoral ethnographic field research in rural Pakistan initiated his long-standing interest in marriage, social relations, migration, and Islam, which later led to two more periods of field research in Pakistan, and have resulted in numerous publications on Pakistan in particular and Islam in general. Donnan's focus on the role of religion within ethnic and political fields in Pakistan, as well as on the intersection of social and political relations within a wider Islam, influenced his choice of a second major research locale, Northern Ireland, where he has continued to explore the interplay of religion, ethnicity, and social structure. This resulted in two influential books on social anthropology and public policy in Ireland, co-edited with Graham McFarlane of Queens University Belfast, where Donnan has taught since 1979, and where he has been the professor of social anthropology since 1997. Donnan has also played a key role in the international development of social anthropology through his involvement in the Royal Anthropological Institute, for whom he edited the journal *Man* (now *The Journal of the Royal Anthropological Institute*) from 1993–5, and in the European Association of Social Anthropologists, in which he has served on the executive committee for four years. Drawing from his field experiences, and reflecting his interests in ethnicity and religion, since 1994 Donnan has been researching and publishing on the social anthropology of social and

political relations at and across international state borders.

Education

BA Queen's University of Belfast, 1975
D.Phil. University of Sussex, 1981

Fieldwork

Northern Pakistan, 1976–8, 1982, 1986–7
Northern Ireland, 1987–90, 1997–2001

Key Publications

(1988) *Marriage among Muslims*, London: E.J. Brill.

with Wilson, Thomas M. (1999) *Borders: Frontiers of Identity, Nation and State*, Oxford: Berg.

THOMAS M. WILSON

Dore, Ronald Philip

b. 1925, Bournemouth, UK

In a career spanning a half a century, Ronald Dore has been one of the most influential and productive scholars of Japanese society. A constant theme of his work is that Japan's distinctive modernisation demonstrates the multilinear dynamics of societal evolution. He shows that the separate, though intersecting, trajectories of modern societies are conditioned by culture, as mutable patterns of meaning that give distinctive shape but not determinant form to human actions and social institutions, and history, as the timing and unpredictable events of a society's modernisation.

Although his early training was in Japanese studies and sociology, he has always employed intensive fieldwork, as reflected in his ten major monographs on Japan. His first book, *City Life in Japan*, on a small Tokyo ward in the aftermath of the Second World War, was the first urban ethnography by a foreigner. In it, Dore resisted the tendencies of the time to emphasise Japan's backwardness and portrayed instead a lively reorganisation of local society. In subsequent books he stressed the indigenous factors behind the success of the post-Second World War Japanese land reform (as against others who attributed this to the American Occupation), and he underscored the legacies of widespread pre-modern education for Japan's precocious industrialisation and state-making. Dore elaborated Thorstein Veblen's suggestion of the beneficial effects of 'late development' into a model of comparative industrial relations, contrasting the organisation-orientation of Japanese firms with the market-orientation of Western economies, and suggesting that late industrial societies might show a 'reverse convergence' towards the Japanese form. Through comparative study of Japan, Sri Lanka, Mexico, and Senegal, Dore noted the hyper-credentialism of formal education in modern societies and the 'diploma disease' that can produce chronic unemployment and frustration when job opportunities cannot keep pace with school achievement. In several comparative case studies of industrial organisation in Japan and England, he demonstrated the efficiencies (the 'flexible rigidities') of relational contracting and the value of trust in intercompany Japanese patterns. His 1990s work had a strong applied emphasis, advocating policies for economic and social justice in both Britain and Japan.

Dore has moved between research and teaching positions for five decades. His first appointment was at the School of Oriental and African Studies. He launched the Japanese studies programme at the University of British Columbia in 1956, and later was the first sociologist at the new University of Sussex Institute of Development Studies. He also taught at Harvard University and the Massachusetts Institute of Technology, held research positions at the Food and Agriculture Organization, and directed the Japan–Europe Industry Research Centre at Imperial College. From 1991, Dore has been senior research fellow at the Centre for Economic Performance, the London School of Economics.

Education

BA University of London, 1946

Fieldwork

Japan (Tokyo), 1950–1
Japan (three villages), 1955–6
Japan (watch factory), 1965
Japan and England (electrical manufacturing companies), 1967–72 (intermittent)
Sri Lanka, 1971
Japan and England (textile companies), 1979–82
Japan (energy conservation), 1980–1

Key Publications

(1958) *City Life in Japan*, Berkeley: University of California Press.
(1973) *British Factory: Japanese Factory*, London: Allen & Unwin.
(1976) *The Diploma Disease: Education, Qualification, and Development*, Berkeley: University of California Press.
(1978) *Shinohata: A Portrait of a Japanese Village*, New York: Pantheon.

WILLIAM W. KELLY

Douglas, Margaret Mary

b. 25 March 1921, San Remo, Italy

d. 16 May 2007, London, UK

With the publication of *Purity and Danger*, in 1966, Mary Douglas (née Tew) became one of very few social anthropologists who can be counted as public intellectuals, read as widely outside her discipline as within it. Following education at the Sacred Heart Convent in Roehampton (London), Mary Douglas went up to Oxford University to take a first degree in politics, philosophy, and economics. After war service in the colonial office, she joined the Oxford Institute of Social Anthropology, which was about to flower under E.E. Evans-Pritchard's (q.v.) guidance. Here, she was particularly influenced by Evans-Pritchard himself and by the Czech-Jewish refugee, Franz Baermann Steiner, whose lectures on taboo she attended. Steiner concluded that taboo was simply one instance of a universal human tendency to express a relationship to values by invoking dangers.

Douglas's fieldwork took her to the Belgian Congo where she undertook ethnographic research on the matrilineal Lele of Kasai. As was typical during a period when great stress was put on demonstrating the coherence of different facets of life, she explored all aspects of Lele life. However, she concentrated particularly on Lele marriage and cosmology, both of which had unusual features. In 1951 Douglas moved to University College London where – aside from a decade spent in American institutions, the Russell Sage Institute, Princeton and Northwestern Universities – she would be based for the next fifty years. Completion of a monograph on the Lele was soon followed by *Purity and Danger*, which developed a complex argument about the similarities and differences between primitive and modern societies: all societies, she argued, cohered through shared schemes of classification underwritten by dangers; particularly celebrated examples of the fit between classification of people and broader classification were drawn from the dietary prohibitions of Leviticus, and from Lele attitudes towards the self-sacrificing pangolin, a classificatory anomaly – a tree-dwelling reptile that produced its young singly and simply curled up rather than fleeing from hunters. *Purity and Danger* proposed that modern societies were becoming increasingly reflexive in their understandings and that such self-consciousness represented a challenge to transcendent religious values. *Natural Symbols* developed the theme of *Purity and Danger* by arguing that there was a direct correlation between the strength of group commitment and the rigidity and comprehensiveness of classificatory schemes. This theory was formalised under the rubric, 'grid and group'. The arguments of anti-ritualists, she explained, reflected increasing individualisation within certain sectors of contemporary society. 'Grid and group' was later developed by Douglas and her collaborators into 'cultural theory', which explored the predictive capabilities of four competing ideal types of society: hierarchical, competitive individualist, isolated individualist, and enclavist (this last applying to sect-like egalitarian groupings within larger societies). In a series of collaborative studies on contemporary Western European and American societies, Douglas argued that variations in religious beliefs, consumption habits, and assessments of environmental risk correlate with living under one of these forms of social arrangement. Most recently, she returned to her interest in the ethnography of ancient Israel to propose radical reanalyses of the literary form and social contexts of the Pentateuch.

Mary Douglas's work continued to wed a liberal cultural imagination, evident both in the range of her interests and a witty self-expression delighting in paradox, with rigorous sociological analysis, especially indebted to the influence of Durkheim's school filtered through the mid-twentieth-century Oxford Institute. During her career she routinely transgressed the conventions of the anthropology in which she trained, whether in her choice of topics, or in her commitment to studying Western societies, or in her refusal to be deterred by disciplinary boundaries, or in her willingness to take positions on contested moral issues on the basis of anthropological analysis. Douglas consistently maintained her commitment to the modern discipline of anthropology that took shape in the middle of the last century and explains by systematic reference to social context. Her works both promoted this vision of anthropology to non-anthropologists and maintained a strong Durkheimian position within anthropology.

Education

MA University of Oxford, 1942

B.Sc. University of Oxford, 1948

D.Phil. University of Oxford, 1953

Fieldwork

Lele, Belgian Congo/Zaïre, 1949–50, 1953, 1987

Key Publications

(1966) *Purity and Danger: An Analysis of Concepts of Pollution and Taboo*, London: Routledge & Kegan Paul.

(1970) *Natural Symbols. Explorations in Cosmology*, London: Barrie & Rockliff, Cresset Press.

(with Baron Isherwood) (1978) *The World of Goods. Towards an Anthropology of Consumption*, New York: Basic Books.

(with Wildavsky, Aaron) (1982) *Risk and Culture: An Essay on the Selection of Technical and Environmental Dangers*, Berkeley and London: University of California Press.

RICHARD FARDON

Dozier, Edward P.

b. 1916, Santa Clara Pueblo, New Mexico, USA

d. 2 May 1971, Tucson, Arizona, USA

Edward Dozier was among the first Native Americans to obtain a doctorate in anthropology and pursue a professional career in the discipline. When he moved to Los Angeles for graduate study, many Native Americans were living in the city but his work in ethnology and linguistics set him on a separate path. In the Pueblos, where outsiders, especially anthropologists, have been unwelcome at least since the invasive investigations of the nineteenth century, coinciding with the emergence of anthropology as a profession, it was, and remains, rare for a community member to embrace an external form of recording cultural knowledge.

Despite the depth of his commitment to his natal community and to the development in North America of programmes in American Indian Studies, Dozier felt that his credibility as a scientist required him to work in a community that was not his own. He worked with the peoples of northern Luzon, the Philippines, through much of his career. This fieldwork established him as a scholar independently of his insider status.

At UCLA, Dozier held Social Science Research Council and Whitney fellowships. While completing his doctorate in 1951–2, he taught at the University of Oregon and at Northwestern University from 1952–8, reaching the rank of associate professor. He returned to his native Southwest in 1958 as professor of anthropology at the University of Arizona. In 1969 he returned to the Philippines to teach as a visiting professor of anthropology, but student unrest made it impossible to teach. After a few months in Mindanao he returned to the Center for Advanced Study in the Behavioral Sciences.

Dozier was awarded numerous fellowships, including Wenner–Gren, the National Science Foundation, and the Center for Advanced Study in the Behavioral Sciences. He served on the ethics committee of the American Anthropological Association and the Council on Anthropology and Education, and was a tireless mediator between Pueblo distrust of anthropological research and the interests of his discipline. Dozier believed that anthropology should be useful to Native American communities and consequently was active in the Society for Applied Anthropology. Taking the view that there was no intrinsic conflict between the two approaches to understanding, Dozier served as a role model for many Native Americans to study anthropology and other social sciences without rejecting their communities of origin. His election as first vice-president of the American Association of Indian Affairs demonstrates Dozier's success in working on both sides of the cultural divide between anthropologists and their research subjects.

Education

Ph.D. University of California, Los Angeles, 1952

Fieldwork

Pueblos in New Mexico and Arizona, 1930s–71
Philippines, 1960s

Key Publications

(1966) *Mountain Arbiters: The Changing Life of a Philippine Hill People*, Tucson: University of Arizona Press.
(1966) *Hano: A Tewa Community in Arizona*, New York: Holt, Rinehart & Winston.
(1967) *The Kalinga of Northern Luzon, Philippines*. New York: Holt, Rinehart & Winston.

REGNA DARNELL AND FREDERIC W. GLEACH

Driessen, Henk

b. 1950, Venlo, The Netherlands

Henk Driessen's work focuses on both sides of the Straits of Gibraltar. Two phases can roughly be distinguished. In the 1970s he carried out fieldwork in southern Spanish agro-towns on issues such as household structure and gender. From the mid-1980s onwards, his interest shifted towards the borders of Spain with Morocco, to Northern Africa and Islam, and to questions of borders and borderlands in general.

Driessen's initial foray into the anthropology of masculinity was a participant observation study of hypermasculinity in southern Spanish bars. His focus shifted away from stereotypes of machismo as ideology towards behaviour and intermale competition to reveal the discrepancy between ideal and actual sexual and gendered tasks.

His central œuvre is a detailed monograph of the town of Melilla, a Spanish enclave in Northern Africa, where he portrayed both the historical and the contemporary layers of a multiethnic society tightly intervowen with its Moroccan hinterland, the Rif. He showed how rituals of border maintenance and border transgression in the realms of religion, nationalism, and ethnicity served to maintain the balance both between the different segments within Melilla society (Catholics, Jews, Hindus, and Muslims) and between Melillans and Rifis. Since the late 1990s Driessen has investigated the transborder networks of smuggling and legal and illegal migration from Morocco into Spain as part of the process of Europeanisation and the erection as well as subversion of the outer European Union border.

Hence, Driessen's work brilliantly embeds detailed fieldwork within its political and economic context, always by including a historical and comparative perspective.

Education

MA Nijmegen, The Netherlands, 1976
Ph.D. Nijmegen, The Netherlands, 1981

Fieldwork

Córdoba Province, Spain, 1974, 1977–8
Melilla, Spain, and Nador, Morocco 1984
Algeciras, Tarifa, Ceuta (Spain), Tangier (Morocco), 1992, 1993, 1997, 2000

Key Publications

(1983) 'Male sociability and rituals of masculinity in rural Andalusia', *Anthropological Quarterly* 56, 4: 125–33.
(1992) *On the Spanish–Moroccan Frontier*, New York/Oxford: Berg.

DIETER HALLER

Du Bois, Cora

b. 26 October 1903, Brooklyn, New York, USA

d. 7 April 1991, Cambridge, Massachusetts, USA

Cora Du Bois studied history as an undergraduate and medieval thought and culture as a Master's student before turning to anthropology for her doctorate. As an undergraduate she had taken an introductory anthropology course with Franz Boas and Ruth Benedict, but on Benedict's advice she rejected Boas's proposal that she study medieval European contacts in East Africa, and moved to Berkeley. Between 1929 and 1935 she did fieldwork with several California and Oregon tribes, beginning with the Wintu. Her dissertation was a library thesis, assigned by the department, on New World female adolescent rites.

In 1935 Du Bois returned to the east coast, investigating the suitability of psychiatric training for anthropologists as a National Research Coucil Fellow at Harvard and at the New York Psychoanalytic Society, where she joined Abram Kardiner's influential seminar on culture and personality. After briefly teaching at Hunter College she began her 18-month field study of Alor, using psychological tests and collecting life histories and children's drawings in addition to traditional ethnographic work. *The People of Alor*, written while she taught at Sarah Lawrence College (1939–42), was a landmark anthropological and psychological study.

Like many of her contemporaries, in 1942 Du Bois joined the war effort, serving as chief of research and analysis in the Indonesia Section of the Office of Strategic Services. She continued in a variety of government research offices until 1954, although her sympathies did not lie in administration and management.

Du Bois was rescued from government service when she was offered the Radcliffe College Zemurray Professorship, and she joined Harvard University's Departments of Anthropology and Social Relations. Surprised by the growth and fragmentation of the discipline in her 15-year absence, she nevertheless taught there until her retirement in 1969, the only tenured woman in the two departments. The position allowed her to return to fieldwork, and from 1961–72 she focused on long-term culture change in complex societies, directing interdisciplinary collaborative research in Bhubaneswar, Orissa, India. Although she ultimately became dissatisfied with the project and didn't publish the results, concluding that conventional ethnographic methods were inadequate for the study of complex societies, the programme produced nine dissertations and trained numerous American and Indian fieldworkers.

Education

BA Barnard College, 1927
MA Columbia University, 1928
Ph.D. University of California, Berkeley, 1932

Fieldwork

California and Oregon (Wintu and other Indians), 1929–35
Alor, Indonesia, 1938–9
Switzerland, India, Sri Lanka, Southeast Asia (World Health Organization), 1942–54
Orissa, India, 1961–72

Key Publications

(1935) *Wintu Ethnography*, Berkeley: University of California Publications in American Archaeology and Ethnology 36, 1.
(1937) 'Some anthropological perspectives on psycho-analysis', *Psycho-Analytic Review* 24, 3: 246–63.
(1944) *The People of Alor*, Minneapolis: University of Minnesota Press.
(1949) *Social Forces in Southeast Asia*, Minneapolis: University of Minnesota Press.

Further Reading

Seymour, Susan (1989) 'Cora Du Bois (1903–)', in Ute Gacs, Aisha Khan, Jerrie McIntyre, and Ruth Weinberg (eds) *Women Anthropologists: Selected Biographies*, Urbana and Chicago: University of Illinois Press.

FREDERIC W. GLEACH AND REGNA DARNELL

Duerr, Hans Peter

b. 1943, Mannheim, Germany

Initially, Hans Peter Duerr's work concentrated on the anthropology of knowledge. In his early work, he developed a critique of Western (modern, rational) modes of cognition and epistemology. In *Traumzeit* (1978), he demonstrated the limits of Western rational science, emphasising the rejection and suppression of experiences of liminality, which he considers to be crucial for non-Western and archaic modes of knowledge. In *Sedna* (1984), he showed how modern modes of knowledge and perceptions of life are variations of three elementary archaic types. In the process of modernisation, an archaic basic acceptance of the world has been replaced by a general rejection of the existing world and an orientation to the future associated with notions of salvation. In his later work, Duerr developed a broad critique of modern society. His voluminous work, *Der Mythos des Zivilisations prozesses* (1988–2001), is a radical critique of modern evolution theories, in particular of Norbert Elias. The myth of the civilisation process is shown to be a mechanism of the construction of otherness, serving to justify and legitimate colonisation. Based on wide-ranging material, Duerr shows how, presumably modern, notions of intimacy and privacy, as well as specific forms of affect regulation, exist in traditional societies.

Education

Ph.D. University of Heidelberg, 1971
Habilitation, University of Kassel, 1981

Fieldwork

Pueblo Indians, 1963
Cheyenne, 1981,1982

Key Publications

(1985) *Dreamtime*, Oxford: Basil Blackwell (*Traumzeit*, 1978).
(1988–2001) *Der Mythos vom Zivlisations Prozess* (The Myth of the Civilisation Process), 5 vols, Frankfurt am Main: Suhrkamp.

WERNER SCHIFFAUER

Dumont, Louis

b. 1911, Paris, France

d. 1987, Paris, France

Louis Dumont, author of *Homo Hierarchichus*, is better known as a theoretician than he is as an ethnographer. Working as a museum clerk and occasional translator of ethnographic texts, he found his 'vocation as an ethnographer' and arrived in South India in the late 1940s where he began his fieldwork, preferring to study caste, rather than a tribe. Dumont's ethnography on the Pramalai Kallars followed in the classic tradition of British social anthropology. Like many of his contemporaries, he accepted the conventional authority of colonial terms of classification by drawing upon received wisdom, focusing on the significance of Dravidian ethnicity and semiotics; kinship, rituals, prestations, marriage, and religion.

Dumont's study of the Tamil language encouraged him to further explore Dravidian kinship terminology, which he compared with cases found among Australian aboriginal peoples. Whilst analysing the linguistics of Dravidian kinship terms, he argued that it had a systematic logical character that commanded a classification according to the generative distribution of sex and age based on two relational categories, consanguineal and affinal. Dumont's fascination with affinal and consanguineal relationships remained at the core of his analysis of kinship and cross/

parallel cousin marriages. This interest also shaped his formulation of another comparison between the West and India. Within Indian kinship, affinity is transmitted from generation to generation by marriage and is regarded as permanent and durable. Thus, affinity has an equal status to the consanguineal unlike the West where affinity is subordinate to consanguinity, Thus in India affinity is inherited, as are blood relationships. Dumont interpreted kinship authority as being vested in men and transmitted from father to son, mother's brother to sister's son.

The dominant influence of Marcel Mauss is evident in Dumont's writings, in particular, Mauss's privileging of the importance of anthropology over history, his stress on the apprehension of social life as a seamless fabric, a 'total social fact', and his critical awareness of the underlying philosophy instilled by Cartesian cognition. Thus, one of the important questions that guided Dumont's research was his effort to unravel the specific complex of a particular type of society that cannot be made to coincide with any other. To him, thus, the search for the fundamental epistemology governing values was essential to understanding this difference. Dumont's objective was to study India as a whole or even Indian civilisation through the ages. His idea of India remained firmly fixed as Vedic Brahmanical India. As he noted, 'eight centuries before the birth of Christ, tradition established an absolute distinction between power and hierarchy and that has remain unchanged' (1980: 8), as since Vedic times, the Brahamical belief system integrated diverse peoples into a society where ritual power prevailed over secular power. Thus, Brahmin priests constituted the apex of society with kings below them, ensuring harmony and the status quo.

Inspired by structuralist theory, Dumont developed his thesis of the Indian caste system based on the binary opposition between purity and impurity. Influenced as he was by the writings of Emile Senart and Celeste Bouglé, he preferred the term *varna* over *jati* to describe caste and was criticised by Edmund Leach for using these 'ancient configurations'. Describing the caste system as the social morphology of Indian civilisation, Dumont argued that the important thing about this system is not the nature of the caste groups it included, or even its sub-groups, division of labour, or body politic, but the nature of the relation between the groups as determined by its binary oppositions. The caste system is a hierarchy, not to be seen just in terms of superordination and subordination, but as an encompassing, immutable system of values. In India, hierarchy involves a gradation, but it is not one of power and authority. Rather, hierarchy is the principle by which elements of the whole are ranked in relation to the whole, what Dumont defined as holism. And, the whole is founded on the necessary and hierarchical co-existence of the two opposites, purity and impurity, which governed social relations. Thus, Dumont contrasted the hierarchical holism of India with Western egalitarianism, which is governed by individualism and equality. His early critics, M.N. Srinivas and André Beteille, wrote against his 'presumptuous' generalisations, and criticised the timeless warp into which he had placed India. Unlike the West, India was not allowed to have a history. Nevertheless, several recent monographs published on caste and ethnographies on the subcontinent have not marked a distinct departure from Dumont's paradigms.

Despite the numerous critiques of Dumont, many, if not all, of the powerful assumptions left by the theoretical legacy of *Homo Hierarchichus* are still evident in contemporary ethnographic monographs on the Indian subcontinent, particularly in the manner in which it continues to provide the cognitive grid through which people enact kin relationships. During the last decade, however, the influence of gender-sensitive, historical anthropology is gradually redressing the balance.

Fieldwork

South India, July–December 1949, December 1950, May–November 1950

Key Publications

(1986) *A South Indian Subcaste: Social Organization and Religion of the Pramalai Kallar, (Une Sous Caste de L'Inde du Sud, organisation sociale et religious de Pramalai Kallar, 1957)*, Delhi and New York: Oxford University Press.

(1980) *Homo Hierarchichus: The Caste System and Its Implications, (Homo Hierarchicus 1966)*, Chicago: University of Chicago Press.

(1983) *Affinity as Value; Marriage Alliance in South India*, Chicago: University of Chicago Press.

(1985) *Homo Aequalis*, Paris, Gallimard

KUSUM GOPAL

Dwyer, Kevin

b. 16 July 1941, New York City, USA

Kevin Dwyer's earliest fieldwork involved an investigation of the cultural bases of economic activity in southern Morocco. He soon developed a critical perspective, examining the ways in which anthropologists construct and are constructed by the other. He argued that the anthropological project must be located overtly in our accounts within a context of unequal power both at the micro or inter-personal level and also within the wider context of the colonial encounter. His interests turned to the dialogical nature of the anthropologist-informant encounter and the joint production of anthropological texts. During his lengthy interviews with Faqir Mbarek, a 60-year-old Moroccan cultivator, Dwyer discovered that self and other are metamorphosed during such encounters. The contributions of each to the dialogue are integral yet are by no means equal nor symmetrical and represent one aspect of a wider and far longer confrontation between the West and the rest of the world. Dwyer proposes a dialogical approach not merely as a means of improving the quality of anthropological data but also as a moral and political imperative. His work is innovative, carefully argued, and suspicious both of the 'scientific' and naïvely interpretative approach to doing

anthropology and always seeks to foreground the interests and concerns, in short, the voice, of the other. Dwyer spent much of the 1980s and 1990s working with Amnesty and other human rights organisations in the Middle East.

Education

BS MIT, 1963
MA University of Chicago, 1966
Ph.D. Yale University, 1974

Fieldwork

Morocco, 1969–71, 1973, 1975
Morocco, Egypt, Tunisia, Algeria (in descending order of frequency), 1975–present

Key Publications

(1982) *Moroccan Dialogues: Anthropology in Question*, Baltimore, MD: The John Hopkins University Press.

(1991) *Arab Voices: The Human Rights Debate in the Middle East*, London: Routledge.

PETER COLLINS

Dyck, Noel

b. 10 June 1947, Saskatoon, Canada

After training as a historian, focusing on the relations between aboriginal peoples and the Canadian state on the prairies, Noel Dyck turned his intellectual attention to anthropology and ethnography as ways of making knowledge. Carrying out ethnographic fieldwork in the same geographical region, he sought to understand the ways that relations between aboriginal people and government, broadly construed, have been played out locally and across the country through time. At the core of his work are a number of ethnographically detailed accounts of contemporary political life. The analytical core of Dyck's work is found in the concept of tutelage. Developing insights from Robert Paine, among others, Dyck uses this concept to tease out the ways that relations between aboriginal people and government are structurally unequal and how the state has taken on the responsibility to administer (look after) aboriginal people. It is a powerful body of work that traces the shifts and nuances of this relationship through time. More recently Dyck has turned his attention to sport. Much of this work examines the relationships between parents and children, and further develops his concerns with tutelage.

Education

BA University of Saskatchewan, 1968
BA (Hons) University of Saskatchewan, 1969
MA University of Saskatchewan, 1970
Ph.D. University of Manchester, 1977

Fieldwork

Cree: Saskatchewan 1971–3, 1980s, 1992–5
Sports: BC and Quebec ongoing from early 1990s

Key Publications

(1991) *What is the Indian 'Problem'? Tutelage and Resistance in Canadian Indian Administration*, ISER, St John's, Nfld: ISER, Memorial University of Newfoundland.
(ed.) (2000) *Games, Sports and Cultures*, Oxford and New York: Berg and SUNY.

PHILIP MOORE

E

Edgerton, Robert

b. 28 November 1931, Maywood, Illinois, USA

Robert Edgerton attained international recognition during the 1960s with the publication of *The Cloak of Competence*, based on his groundbreaking research of people with mental retardation. In this work, Edgerton highlighted individual motives and the social adaptations of people with mental retardation, exposing the frailty, even cruelty, of institutionalised forms of psychological assessment that fail to consider one's individuality in cultural life contexts.

A pioneer in the sub-field of psychological anthropology, Edgerton developed innovative approaches to cross-cultural studies of abnormality, deviancy, and social marginalisation. In 1961–2, Edgerton worked with Walter Goldschmidt and other members of the UCLA Culture and Ecology Project to develop new methodology with which to study the complex relations between individuals and their cultures in four East African societies. Each society among the four that the Project members studied included farming and pastoral populations, allowing them to make comparisons among the four societies and between farmers and pastoralists.

Edgerton developed an anthropological approach referred to as psychocultural adaptation. In *The Individual in Cultural Adaptation: A Study of Four East African Societies*, Edgerton portrayed the changing lives of individuals living in particular East African societies. Based on this research, Edgerton demonstrated the variability of psychocultural adaptations across social, cultural settings. He laid the groundwork for a sustained critique within anthropology of the Western biases in cross-cultural psychological studies, identifying the differences between cross-cultural psychology and psychological anthropology.

In the 1980s, Edgerton turned to the impact of increased modernisation and urbanisation on psychocultural adaptations. Edgerton's *Sick Societies: Challenging the Myth of Primitive Harmony*, demonstrated that small communities are not necessarily therapeutic – that, in fact, people in some societies, whether urban or rural, continue cultural practices that lead to social strife.

Within the past decade, Edgerton has published critical historical studies of conflict and war in such varied places as Africa, Japan, and the USA. Edgerton also attends to historical 'absences' – the blank spaces in our histories that likewise mark social exclusion and marginality. An innovative scholar with ranging interests, Edgerton continues to have a major impact on anthropological approaches to abnormality, deviancy, and social marginality, and upon how such concepts emerge and are deployed by people around the world.

Education

BA Universtiy of California, Los Angeles, 1956

Ph.D. University of California, Los Angeles, 1960

Fieldwork

Wisconsin, USA, 1959
East Africa (Uganda, Kenya, Tanzania), 1961–2
Hawaii, USA, 1970
Kenya, 1987, 1992
California, USA, 1960–present

Key Publications

(1971) *The Individual in Cultural Adaptation: A Study of Four East African Societies*, Los Angeles: University of California Press.

(1979) *Mental Retardation*, Cambridge, MA: Harvard University Press.

(1993 [1967]) *The Cloak of Competence*, Berkeley and Los Angeles: University of California Press.

(1992) *Sick Societies: Challenging the Myth of Primitive Harmony*, New York: The Free Press.

CONERLY CASEY

Eggan, Frederick Russell

b. 12 September 1906, Seattle, Washington, USA

d. 7 May 1991, Santa Fe, New Mexico, USA

Fred Eggan came to the study of anthropology by way of psychology leavened by geography. While still undergraduates, he and Cornelius Osgood took Edward Sapir and Fay-Cooper Cole's seminar on India; Eggan produced a study of caste that supplemented his existing fascination with race and nationality. Eggan's first anthropological love, however, was for archaeology. He spent several years digging in the Midwest with Cole before expanding into Southwestern archaeology in 1929 and 1930. Within the Chicago four-square definition of anthropology, he even studied Navaho grammar with Sapir, preparing him well for the shift from archaeology to ethnology.

Eggan was initially distressed when Sapir left for Yale in 1931, to be replaced by A.R. Radcliffe-Brown. Soon, however, as Radcliffe-Brown's research assistant, his reluctance turned to enthusiasm for synthesising the best of the British and Americanist traditions; he envisioned a method that would include both Americanist historical perspective and British problem focus. By 1932, when he attended Leslie White's University of Chicago field school in Santa Fe, Eggan's commitment to sociocultural anthropology was firmly established. His dissertation on the contrast between the matrilineal social organisation of the Western Pueblos and the dual organisation of the Eastern or Rio Grande Pueblos, with a Keresan bridge between the two, exemplified the potentials of the new synthesis (1950).

After completing his doctorate during the height of the Depression, Eggan eked out a living at Chicago and continued his fieldwork, demonstrating that the kinship systems of the Choctaw, Cheyenne, and Arapaho had changed in response to ecological and historical factors (1937). Cole sent Eggan to the Philippines to restudy Tinguian social organisation; in a remarkably Americanist mode, he described change among contiguous groups from interior to coast as a process of 'cultural drift', arguing that effects of European contact interacted with historical events. Eggan served as a Philippine expert during the Second World War.

Eggan's American Anthropological Association Presidential Address on the method of 'controlled comparison' exemplifies his version of middle-range theory (1954). Cases for comparison should be related either historically or typologically for comparison to be meaningful. His Lewis Henry Morgan lectures at the University of Rochester produced a volume on American Indian kinship and social organisation in relation to culture change (1966). Eggan's collected papers appeared in 1975. Eggan continued writing and consulting work in the Southwest until his death in 1991.

Education

BA University of Chicago, 1928
MA University of Chicago, 1929
Ph.D. University of Chicago, 1933

Fieldwork

Hopi (archaeology), 1929, 1930
Western Pueblos, 1932
Cheyenne, Choctaw, Arapaho, 1933
Philippines, beginning in 1934
Continuing work in the Southwest underway
    at the time of his death

Key Publications

(ed.) (1937) *The Social Organization of North Ameri-
    can Tribes*, Chicago: University of Chicago Press.
(1950) *Social Organization of the Western Pueblos*,
    Chicago: University of Chicago Press.
(1954) 'Social anthropology and the method
    of controlled comparison', *American Anthro-
    pologist* 56: 643–761.
(1966) *The American Indian: Perspectives for the Study
    of Social Change*, Chicago: Aldine.
(1975) *Essays in Social Anthropology and Ethnology*,
    Chicago: University of Chicago Press.

REGNA DARNELL

Eickelman, Dale F.

b. 1942, Evergreen Park, Illinois, USA

Dale Eickelman's entire work has illuminated
the interplay of evolving traditions and context
within Muslim societies. Starting with his
initial research into a regional pilgrimage
center in Morocco and continuing through
his research in Oman and later interests in
Central Asia, he has moved the anthropological
study of Islam from the tribal to the spatial and
textual. A prime inheritor of the analytical
traditions of Clifford Geertz, he argues that the
geography of a Muslim society is far from
doctrinally predetermined, but is dependent,
rather, on distributions of power and prestige
that follow a distinctive cultural logic. Critical

to such self-understandings of a Muslim
society is the role that education plays. Eickelman demonstrates through the biography of a
provincial Moroccan judge that traditional
religious education not only shapes views on
piety and learning but, increasingly, offers a
pointed commentary on social and political
order. Modern mass education increases literacy and contributes to the 'objectification' of
Muslim understandings by transforming religious beliefs into a conscious, concrete system.
In the process, religious authority is broadened to the point where multiple interpreters
emerge in a kind of competitive *embarras de
richesses* – the traditional religious authorities
('*ulama*), 'lay' intellectuals, government bureaucracies, state patrons, Islamist movements,
and Sufi orders, among others. Broadly available mass communications and inexpensive
publications constitute new Islamic texts,
whose effect is, on the one hand, fragmenting
and, on the other, constitutive of new 'publics'. These may be liberal in content –
contributing to what he optimistically referred
to as the 'Islamic Reformation' – or radical –
represented by Osama Bin Laden. They are, in
any event, modern, involving a 'reintellectua-
lisation' of Islamic discourse that reaches out
to ever wider circles of Muslims and may, but
need not, support the development of civil
society. Eickelman's invocation of the 'texts',
classical and modern of the Islamic world, and
the social processes that shape them marks an
explicit departure from both essentialising analyses of Islam that purport to argue from the
nature of Islam and structuralist accounts that
predicate Islam on materialistic, principally
economic, factors. For him, rather, the analysis
of Muslim societies belongs in the cultural –
symbolic – realm at the same time as its
nuance is contingent on social, political,
economic, and historical circumstances. In so
doing, he has helped to reconfigure the
formerly rigid boundary between Islamic
studies and anthropology.

Education

AB, *cum laude* , Dartmouth College, 1964

MA McGill University, 1967
MA University of Chicago, 1968
Ph.D. University of Chicago, 1971

Fieldwork

Boujad, Morocco, October 1968–June 1970
Morocco, summer 1972, summer 1973, summer 1976, summer 1978, March–August 1992, June–August 1993, summer 1994
Hamra, Oman, May–September 1978, August 1979–January 1981
Muscat, Oman, September–December 1982
Kuwait, December 1987
Syria, March 1996, January 2000

Key Publications

(1976) *Moroccan Islam: Tradition and Society in a Pilgrimage Center*, Austin and London: University of Texas Press.
(1985) *Knowledge and Power in Morocco: The Education of a Twentieth-Century Notable*, Princeton: Princeton University Press.
with Piscatori, James (1996) *Muslim Politics*, Princeton: Princeton University Press.
with Anderson, Jon W. (eds) (2003 [1999]) *New Media and the Muslim World: The Emerging Public Sphere*, Bloomington, IN: Indiana University Press.

JAMES PISCATORI

Eidheim, Harald

b. 1925, Western Norway

Harald Eidheim's influence far exceeds his limited production. He published a string of seminal articles on the ethnic relationship between Sami (Lapps) and Norwegians in the 1960s, anticipating and influencing the subsequent, famous theory of ethnicity proposed by his colleague Fredrik Barth, but Eidheim's writings are few and often obscurely published, whether in Norwegian or in English. Since the 1950s, the bulk of his ethnographic work has focused on the Sami–Norwegian relationship, but he has also worked among Masai in Kenya, and has authored a monograph on the fragility of social cohesion in Dominica. Eidheim was instrumental in developing the currently dominant view of ethnicity, seeing it as a dynamic and shifting aspect of relationship rather than a property of a group. Some of his pioneering articles discussed the politics of cultural identity, ethnic stigma, and entrepreneurship among Sami politicians. Informed by semiotics, system theory, and symbolic interactionism, Eidheim's sophisticated analyses demonstrate the inherent duality of ethnicity, comprising aspects of both meaning and strategy. Eidheim is deeply engaged in indigenous rights issues, and has been a major influence on the politics of Sami rights in Norway. Since his retirement from the University of Oslo in 1990, Eidheim has continued his research on Sami–Norwegian issues, now working from the University of Tromsø.

Education

Mag. Art. University of Oslo, 1958

Fieldwork

Sápmi (Sami country, Northern Norway), intermittently since 1955 (about 2 years)
Grand Bay, Dominica, 1968–9
Kadjiado, Kenya, 1985

Key Publications

(1971) *Aspects of the Lappish Minority Situation*, Oslo: Universitetsforlaget.
(1999) *Samer og Nordmenn. Temaer i jus, historie og sosialantropologi* (Sami and Norwegians: Themes from Law, History, and Social Anthropology), Oslo: Cappelen Akademisk Forlag.

THOMAS HYLLAND ERIKSEN

Elkin, Adolphus Peter

b. West Maitland, New South Wales,
Australia, 1891

d. Sydney, New South Wales, Australia, 1979

Adolphus Peter Elkin was ordained in 1915 and remained an active member of the Anglican Church throughout his career. In his anthropological work he spent much time working through the complexities of religion, ritual, totemism, mythology, and social organisation in Aboriginal Australia. He also worked and published on church topics, studiously avoiding theology.

Elkin exerted considerable effect on the institutional development of anthropology in Australia. After several years of uncertainty, following the departure of the Foundation Professor of Anthropology, A.R. Radcliffe-Brown, the University of Sydney appointed Elkin as lecturer-in-charge of the anthropology programme in 1932. He was appointed professor in 1934 and formally retired in 1956. For twelve of his twenty-three years as professor at Sydney he was the sole professor of anthropology in Australia. He remained active in anthropology following his formal retirement, editing the journal, Oceania, to which he was a regular contributor, and continuing his public role as a concerned voice in Aboriginal affairs. Some of his writings nicely bridge the relationship between anthropology and public policy. Elkin brought to Aboriginal affairs in Australia a voice that was both reasoned and reverent. He had great respect for the Aboriginal people he worked with and conveyed this through his publications. While many of his ideas seem somewhat quaint today, his was an important public voice of his times.

Being in charge of the Sydney department allowed Elkin to direct much of the anthropological research in Australia. He built an active department with students and other researchers carrying out research both in Australia and in Papua New Guinea. Elkin's own two major sorties into the field in Australia were organised as expeditions that saw him moving through a region rather than stopping for a lengthy period with any single community. His research was conducted as a series of lengthy interviews with local Aboriginal elders rather than through the participant observation methods associated with ethnographic fieldwork. He made productive use of this evidence, working his notebooks systematically and thoroughly for publication. While many anthropologists would now judge his fieldwork methods unacceptable, he made use of a limited time in the field to collect a vast array of information. His theoretical contribution is slight and his work can be described broadly as the making of empirical generalisations. His accounts remain grounded in a textual analysis of interviews rather than based on knowledge of the everyday activities of those with whom he worked. Elkin does not exert a major intellectual influence on the anthropology of Aboriginal Australia today.

Education

BA Sydney University, 1915
MA Sydney University, 1922
Ph.D. University College London, 1927

Fieldwork

Kimberley, Western Australia, 1927–8
South Australia, 1930
Central Highlands, Papua New Guinea, 1946, 1949, 1956

Key Publications

(1933) 'Studies in Australian totemism', Oceania Monographs 2, Sydney.
(1938) The Australian Aborigines, Sydney: Angus & Robertson. Many reprints.
(1977 [1945]) Aboriginal Men of High Degree, second edn, St Lucia and New York: University of Queensland Press and St Martin's Press.

PHILIP MOORE

Elwin, Verrier

b. 29 August 1902, Dover, Kent, UK

d. 22 February 1964, Delhi, India

Verrier Elwin had no formal training in anthropology. He strayed into it through poetry. However, he was one of the best-known anthropologists in India, and his anthropological knowledge, controversial as it was to some, was praised by many. His description of the tribal life and culture in central, eastern or northeastern India is undoubtedly the liveliest, the most passionate, the most legendary, and, perhaps, the most romantic as well. He not only described the tribes and fought for their land and forest rights, but also lived like them, as a true participant observer, with tribal spouses. India has not seen another ethnographer, who wrote as beautifully as he did, who was as concerned with the fate of Indian tribes as he was, who could work half as hard as he did, and who was as dear, eccentric, and influential as Elwin. Grown and tutored to be a clergyman and gifted as a poet, he lived as the messiah of the tribal world.

Elwin was a prolific writer in many genres. His publications included monographs, a collection of oral traditions, a collection of songs and poems, novels, articles, commentaries, rejoinders, etc., and he often had more than twenty publications per year, the highest being sixty in 1953. The themes of his publications, including his posthumous and undated publications, comprised Christianity, Indian national movement, myths, love and sex, tribal crimes, world views, folk songs and poetry, traditional institutions, art, development, administration, democracy, etc. Of these themes he wrote more frequently on Christianity, tribal poetry, oral traditions, songs and dances, and change and development. However, he made the most significant impact on the scholars, activists, and administrators in India with his concept of Christianity as reparation; his notion of tribal development according to tribal genius; his advocacy for a restrained relationship between the tribes and plains Hindus; and his poetry inspired by the poverty, frustration, and the passion of tribes in India. He wanted the tribes to be respected and not pitied; he opposed their conversion to either Christianity or Hinduism; and he wished their songs, dances, sports, art, poetry, dormitory, customs, etc. to survive the challenges of the outside world.

Education

BA University of Oxford, 1924
D.Sc. University of Oxford, 1944

Fieldwork

Karanjia, Mandla District, 1932–5
Sarwachappar village, Mandla District, 1935–7
Patangarh village, Mandla District 1937–40, 1942–6, 1949–54
Bastar, Madhya Pradesh, 1940–2
Orissa, 1942–51
North Eastern Frontier Agency, 1954–64

Key Publications

(1939) *The Baiga*, London: John Murray.
(1943) *The Aboriginals*, Oxford Pamphlets on Indian Affairs, No. 14.
(1957) *A Philosophy for NEFA*, Shillong: Director of Information, NEFA.
(1989) *The Tribal World of Verrier Elwin: An Autobiography*, Delhi: Oxford University Press.

Further Reading

Guha, R. (1999) *Savaging the Civilized: Verrier Elwin, His Tribals, and India*, Chicago and London: The University of Chicago Press.
Takeshi, F. (1987) 'An annotated bibliography of Verrier Elwin (1902–1964)', *Journal of South Asian Languages and Cultures* 1, pp. 5–56.

TANKA SUBBA

Epstein, Arnold L.

b. 1924, Liverpool, UK

A concern to understand social process and

conflict provides the key to Epstein's work. Fieldwork in Zambia as a research officer of the Rhodes–Livingstone Institute was seminal to his intellectual development. Quite apart from his involvement in the Manchester School of Anthropology, he made substantial methodological contributions. As the focus of his research shifted, his work became more theoretically and methodologically sophistica-ted. Thus his analysis of the role of traditional courts led to the development of the case study approach; in seeking to understand urban social organisation he pioneered the use of social network analysis; finally, a concern with 'oral aggression' led him to integrate psycho-analytic theory and anthropology.

His concern with method and theory was pursued primarily in edited collections (on law and fieldwork methods). His interest in affect, however, was explored by examining conflict at the intrapsychic and social structural levels, and led to a study of social change and the significance of ethnic identity. Issues of identity and affect were subsequently explored ethnographically through research on the Tolai of New Guinea (in the context of interethnic relations, shame, death, and personhood) and biographically in terms of his own Jewish iden-tity (discussed in terms of religious obser-vance, acculturation, and relations between generations).

The attempt to place the concept of identity at the heart of analysis led him to address anthropological concerns regarding the 'sub-jective' nature of the enterprise. Firmly grounded in situational analysis, Epstein argued that anthropology should approach the issue of affect and emotion by shifting the emphasis away from role-playing to a focus on meaning to show how the 'passions' are culturally shaped and how they are utilised in social interaction. Epstein rejected the study of 'emotion terms' and categories, and argued instead for a dynamic focus on the social/behavioural expression of affective states and their link to human physiology (specifically the motivational system that is shared by all humans regardless of cultural difference). In this way, non-verbal communication, language

use, and anthropological data can be used to understand culturally specific 'display rules' regarding the circumstances in which parti-cular emotions are expressed. He argued that ethnographic data would need to be combined with an analysis of socialisation that structures experience, shapes cognition, and links culture and psychology.

Education

LL B Queen's University of Belfast, Northern
   Ireland, 1944
Ph.D. University of Manchester, 1955

Fieldwork

Zambia, 1950–6, The Copperbelt, 1950–6
New Guinea, Gazelle Peninsula, 1959–60,
   1968, 1986, 1994

Key Publications

(1953) *The Administration of Justice and the Urban
   African*, London: HMSO.
(1958) *Politics in an Urban African Community*,
   Manchester: University Press.
(1978) *Ethos and Identity*, London: Tavistock.
(1992) *In the Midst of Life: Affect and Ideation in the
   World of the Tolai*, Berkeley: University of
   California.

JOHN R. CAMPBELL

Eriksen, Thomas Hylland

b. 1962, Oslo, Norway

In his main works Eriksen addressed key questions regarding ethnicity and nationalism by drawing on a wide range of examples, mainly from Mauritius and Trinidad. He revealed the complexity and ambiguity of ethnic classification in 'multiethnic' societies, the variability in the social and cultural importance of ethnicity, and the inherent tension between ethnicity and nationalism. His detailed historical and sociological knowl-edge of a range of different societies was employed to argue that the social importance of ethnicity depends on kinship organisation as well as political circumstances, and to illustrate the expression of ethnicity through idioms of language and religion. He also revealed how ethnic identity can be superseded by other forms of belonging and politics. Eriksen has problematised the impact of nationhood, gender, class, and modern individualism in the construction of complex collective ethnic identities.

In Eriksen's research, Mauritius appears as an exemplary case of a multiethnic and peaceful country that has been able to forge a stable and democratic society. Among the determining factors of this success Eriksen has pointed out the following: its small size and uncontested boundaries; the absence of an ethnic majority; the absence of groups claiming aboriginality; the division of power between different ethnic categories; a shared language; the existence of constitutional rights for minorities; the relatively even integration into institutions of the nation-state; emergent supra-ethnic career paths; and capitalism and parlimentarianism as two institutional pillars of compromise. The case of Mauritius led Eriksen to rethink the accepted categories of ethnicity and nationalism. Nationalism, he argued, can be reconciled with a multiplicity of myths and self-defined cultural groups provided common denominators exist in the shared public fields: the Mauritian brand of nationalism is neither ethnic, federalist, nor civic in character; it is, in a certain sense, all three and multiculturalist.

Eriksen has written an acclaimed introductory textbook in social anthropology, used in many European and Scandinavian universities. The book is rich in ethnographic examples, gives classical anthropology a prominent place, focuses on the importance of comparison, and moves from simple to ever-more complex models of explanation and sociocultural contexts. Eriksen is also a very productive scholar in his Norwegian mother tongue, writing about the interfaces between biology and anthropology; the relevance of multiculturalism and multicultural co-existence in Norway;

the danger of racism, cultural fundamentalism, and ideas of cultural purity; counterculture, utopia and the good life; and the cultural dimension of development co-operation.

Education

BA University of Oslo, 1984
MA University of Oslo, 1987
Ph.D. University of Oslo, 1991

Fieldwork

Mauritius, 1986, 1991–2, 1999
Trinidad, 1989

Key Publications

(1992) *Us and Them in Modern Societies: Ethnicity and Nationalism in Trinidad, Mauritius and Beyond*, Oslo: Scandinavian University Press.
(1993) *Ethnicity and Nationalism: Anthropological Perspectives*, London: Pluto.
(1995) *Small Places, Larger Issues. An Introduction to Social and Cultural Anthropology*, London: Pluto.
(1998) *Common Denominators: Ethnicity, Nationalism and the Politics of Compromise in Mauritius*, Oxford: Berg.

EDUARDO ARCHETTI

Erlmann, Veit

b. 1951, Essen, Germany

Veit Erlmann is an anthropologist and ethnomusicologist. Drawing not least on many years of fieldwork in apartheid South Africa, his major monographs offer a rich and thought-provoking analysis of cultural strategies under the conditions of modernity, and of global cultural processes, particularly those pertaining to the 'black Atlantic'. Above all, his work highlights the crucial role of music in the dialogic relationship between Africa and the diaspora. One of the main points in *African Stars*, and one that may be generalised to a wider context, is that there can be no easy one-to-one relationship between class and (popular) cultural practices. Equally important is Erlmann's emphasis on the close interaction between musicians and industry, and the observation that it is precisely in the sphere of popular performance that the winds of change blow early and hard.

Nightsong presents a detailed ethnography and history of the competitive performance tradition of isicathamiya, the a cappella music of Zulu migrant workers made internationally famous by Ladysmith Black Mambazo in the 1970s. In Music, Modernity, and the Global Imagination, the winner of the 2000 Alan P. Merriam award in ethnomusicology, Erlmann offers examples from South Africa, the USA, and England – including the visits of the African Choir and the Zulu Choir to London in the late nineteenth century, and Paul Simon's Graceland album – to present a detailed topography of both colonial and post-colonial global processes. Music in global culture, Erlmann suggests, is a medium that mediates mediation, a conduit for social interaction and appropriation of the world in ways that are not necessarily determined by locally situated practice and collectively maintained memory.

In the late 1990s, Erlmann has begun a study of the history of sound and listening as well as an exploration of Java and Sumatra, Indonesia. The thrust behind all of Erlmann's work, a quality that grants it particular significance in times of apparently increasing essentialism and insularity, is the ever-present recognition of the mutual entanglement, interconnectedness, and interdependency of global cultures. For this alone, Erlmann deserves our undivided attention.

Education

MA Free University, Berlin, 1974
Ph.D. University of Cologne, 1978
Dr.habil. University of Cologne, 1990
Dr.habil. Free University, Berlin, 1994

Fieldwork

Cameroon, 1975–6, 1995–6
Niger, 1979

Lesotho, 1982
South Africa, 1981–6
Ghana, 1988
Ecuador, 1989

Key Publications

(1991) African Stars: Studies in Black African Performance, Chicago and London: University of Chicago Press.
(1995) Nightsong: Performance, Power, and Practice in South Africa, Chicago and London: University of Chicago Press.
(1996) 'The aesthetics of the global imagination: reflections on world music in the 1990s', Public Culture 8: 467–87.
(1999) Music, Modernity, and the Global Imagination: South Africa and the West, New York and Oxford: University of Oxford Press.

HASSE HUSS

Ervin-Tripp, Susan Moore

1927, Minneapolis, Minnesota

Susan M. Ervin-Tripp, one of the founders of the modern fields of developmental psycholinguistics and of sociolinguistics, has been an active researcher on the interface between child language development and sociocultural patterns of interaction. A key term in her approach to pragmatics is 'context', including both the linguistic contexts in which words and grammatical constructions occur and the interpersonal contexts that give meaning to language. She is an expert on both first and second language acquisition, and has researched issues of bilingualism, conversation, speech acts, gender and language, and humour. Her early fieldwork was on the Southwest Project for Comparative Psycholinguistics. Through a long career at the University of California at Berkeley she has researched a variety of immigrant communities and their children. In sabbatical years in Geneva and Paris she investigated second language acquisition by children and by migrant workers. She played a key role in several technological advances in psycho- and sociolinguistics: computer-based analysis of tape-recorded and transcribed parent–child interactions in the 1960s, and the use of videotape to record family interactions in the 1970s. Ervin-Tripp's work balances individual and social approaches to human development, language, and communication. She was instrumental in the development of the field of gender studies and has been active in academic research and applied issues in the field. She has been honoured as a Guggenheim fellow, a Cattell fellow in psychology, and a Berkeley faculty research lecturer.

Education

BA Vassar College, 1949
Ph.D. University of Michigan, 1955

Fieldwork

New Mexico (Navaho, Zuni, Hopi, Hopi-Tewa), 1954
Washington, DC, California, USA; France; Switzerland, 1953–

Key Publications

(1973) *Language Acquisition and Communicative Choice*, Stanford, CA: Stanford University Press.
with Mitchell-Kernan, C. (eds) (1977) *Child Discourse*, New York: Academic Press.

DAN I. SLOBIN

Escobar, Arturo

b. 1951, Manizales, Colombia

Born and raised in Colombia, Arturo Escobar received training in sciences and engineering before moving to the USA for graduate work, where he progressively moved towards anthropology and critical social theory. The overriding concern of Escobar's work has been the examination of dominant social orders with an eye to their transformation. Escobar is most well known for his radical deconstruction of development, where he sought to 'anthropologise' development by examining it ethnographically as a set of expert-driven discourses and practices. The resulting concept of a post-development era took him to his second important research area, social movements. Here the focus of his work has been on the defense of different world views by social movements. His ethnographic work with the black movement of the Colombian Pacific has shown how identities are crafted by activists, and how culture increasingly functions as the very language of the political. As in the case of development, Escobar's work on social movements has done much to bring this topic to anthropological attention.

Escobar's third area of work is the anthropology of nature. His ethnographic work in this regard is again focused on the Colombian Pacific, where he has investigated the political ecology framework elaborated by social movements in their encounter with transnational biodiversity networks. The work on biodiversity has served as Escobar's entry point into his fourth major area of work, the anthropology of techno-science. From an early programmatic piece on 'the anthropology of cyberculture' (1994) to his most recent work on transnational networks, Escobar's concern with techno-science has developed into ethnographic and theoretical investigations on globalisation, place-based movements, and transnational organising. In his most recent works, Escobar restates his insistence on theorising place-based cultural, ecological, and economic difference as the necessary point of departure for a radical politics of transformation. Building on contemporary Latin American critical thought, he locates difference within an overarching framework of alternative modernities and alternatives to modernity.

Education

BS Universidad del Valle, Colombia, 1975
MFS Cornell University, Ithaca, New York, 1978
Ph.D. University of California, Berkeley, 1987

Fieldwork

Bogota and Cali, Colombia. Department of National Planning. Fieldwork with rural development, food, and nutrition planning unit, 1981–2, summers 1983, 1990

Pacific Coast rainforest, Colombia, 1993–4, summers 1996, 1997, 1998, 2000

Key Publications

with Sonia Alvarez (eds) (1992) *The Making of Social Movements in Latin America: Identity, Strategy, and Democracy*, Boulder: Westview Press.

(1995) *Encountering Development: The Making and Unmaking of the Third World*. Princeton: Princeton University Press. Best Book Award, 1996 New England Council of Latin American Studies. (Also published in Spanish and Portuguese.)

with Alvarez, Sonia and Dagnino, Evelina (eds) (1998) *Cultures of Politics/Politics of Cultures: Revisioning Latin American Social Movements*, Boulder: Westview Press. (Also published in Spanish and Portuguese.)

(1999) *El final del salvaje. Naturaleza, cultura y política en la antropología contemporánea* (The Twilight of the Savage. Nature, Culture, and Politics in Contemporary Anthropology), Bogotá: ICANH/CEREC

CLAUDIA STEINER

Evans-Pritchard, Edward Evan

b. 21 September 1902, Sussex, UK

d. 1973, Oxford, UK

Blending the theoretical framework of A.R. Radcliffe-Brown (and E. Durkheim) with the detailed ethnographic empiricism of B. Malinowski, E.E. Evans-Pritchard was the most significant figure in the foundation of modern social anthropology. Following his first degree in modern history at Oxford, in 1924 he joined C.G. Seligman at the London School of Economics (LSE) and entered B. Malinowski's famous seminar there, which already included Raymond Firth and Isaac Schapera. Under Seligman's patronage, Evans-Pritchard carried out a preliminary survey of the Azande peoples in the Anglo-Egyptian Sudan, which he wrote up for his Ph.D. at the LSE in 1927. This was a prelude to his first major field study of the Azande, which produced his masterpiece, *Witchcraft, Oracles, and Magic* (1937).

In this study, Evans-Pritchard brilliantly analyses how, far from being 'irrational primitive superstitions', Zande beliefs in witchcraft, magic, and oracles constitute a mutually sustaining, logically coherent philosophy that explains the incidence of misfortune and illness, and answers the awkward 'why me?' question, sequentially, by always blaming someone else for the injuries or failures that dog life. If one explanation, such as witchcraft, is ruled out, another is quickly mobilised. This failsafe pattern of interlocking axiomatic beliefs can be seen to operate similarly in any closed ideology: Marxism, racism, linguistic philosophy, etc., and hence protect these arcane assumptions when threatened by actual events. Evans-Pritchard shows that both mystical and non-mystical causation exist side by side (and even reinforce each other), but operate at different levels. Sociologically, witchcraft accusations reflect tensions in social relations and express enmity: they also contribute to social control. This subtle analysis thus proceeds at both the level of thought, and of social relations, and is not merely, as some have claimed, a portrait of a system of personal accountability. Nor does Evans-Pritchard neglect to explore how these beliefs, in turn, are part of a wider arena of other mystical forces including ancestors, ghosts, and gods.

From the hierarchical Zande world, Evans-Pritchard now continued his Sudan research to study a very different political system, the fiercely uncentralised Nuer. His powerfully analytical monograph (*The Nuer*), published in 1940 (by which time he held a research post at Oxford), presented this Nilotic people as living without formally appointed chiefs in a 'state of ordered anarchy'. Kinship genealogies, here, were not merely historical phenomena, but represented political identities; and loyalties were based on the 'segmentary lineage system', where kinship was mobilised opportunistically, with groups fusing and segmenting according to the context. This forcefully argued analysis had a major impact on the anthropological understanding of such stateless (or 'acephalous') societies and also influenced political scientists who appropriated the Nuer 'non-state' model.

During the Second World War, Evans-Pritchard served with British forces in the Sudan, Eritrea, North Africa, and Palestine. In Libya, where he was liaison officer to the British Commander, he applied his Nuer experience of segmentary lineage organisation to analyse how the immigrant Sufi Sanusi mystical order had established itself in Cyrenaica by infiltrating the local clan system as mediators. Such was their success that, under the impress of Italian colonisation, they ended up creating what became the state of Libya, with themselves as rulers.

In his final Nuer study (*Nuer Religion*, 1956), Evans-Pritchard applied his segmentary lineage analysis to Nuer mystical concepts, presenting their spiritual powers as entities, evoked situationally, at different lineage levels as facets of a single divinity. Having now himself embraced the Catholic faith, he maintained that Nuer beliefs, ultimately, had to be understood theologically. Significantly, there was little place here for the issue of scepticism that loomed large in his analysis of Zande witchcraft.

Increasingly rejecting what he saw as the spurious scientism of Radcliffe-Brown's structural functionalism, Evans-Pritchard considered the primary business of social anthropology to be translating 'other cultures'. These were to be treated with the same serious scholarship and depth of knowledge of local language as applied in the humane studies of European peoples and their cultures. This goal brought him close to literary studies and was reflected in his enthusiastic foundation of the Oxford Library of African Literature and in his appointment of recruits like Godfrey Lienhardt.

This literary emphasis in his approach to ethnography has been simplistically interpreted by post-modernist enthusiasts to suppose (wrongly) that Evans-Pritchard foresaw and would have approved their efforts. Although he was not an empire builder, and despised academic administrators, Evans-Pritchard was the principal founder of the Association of Social Anthropologists. The immense importance and success of his years at Oxford, which his presence made the center of the subject in the Anglo-Saxon world, are reflected in the many British and foreign honours he received, and the seven festschrifts dedicated to him.

Education

MA University of Oxford, 1924
Ph.D. University of London, London School of Economics, 1927

Fieldwork

Anglo-Egyptian Sudan, Africa, 1926–39
Ethiopia, Libya, Northeast and North Africa, Syria, Middle East, 1940–4

Key Publications

(1937) *Witchcraft, Oracles, and Magic among the Azande*, Oxford: Clarendon Press.
(1940) *The Nuer: A Description of the Modes of Livelihood and Political Institutions of a Nilotic People*, Oxford: Clarendon Press.
(1949) *The Sanusi of Cyrenaica*, Oxford: Clarendon Press.
(1956) *Nuer Religion*, Oxford: Clarendon Press.

Further Reading

Burton, J.W. (1992) *An Introduction to Evans-Pritchard*, Freiburg: Univ.-Verl.
Douglas, M. (1980) *Evans-Pritchard*, London: Fontana.

I.M. LEWIS

F

Fabian, Johannes

b. 1937, Glogau, Germany

Johannes Fabian was initially trained to become a missionary. His academic studies in Germany and Austria included courses in ethnology, linguistics, and philosophy. His first ethnology teacher was his great-uncle Paul Schebesta, missionary (Societas Verbi Divini, SVD) and Africanist. Fabian left the SVD and moved to Chicago to study anthropology. In his Ph.D. research on Jamaa, a Roman Catholic charismatic movement in Katanga (former Belgian Congo, Zaïre), he successfully fused his German intellectual formation with ideas and concepts derived from American anthropology. The result was original and innovative in at least two respects: he reformulated Weber's theory of charisma by paying systematic attention to doctrinal content by way of linguistic analysis as well as to social context, and he departed from the standard ethnographic strategy of doing participant observation in only one field location. The Jamaa book carries the seeds of all his later concerns and interests, such as a critique of anthropology, in particular of the traditional division between the anthropologist and his or her subjects; a critical interpretation of religious ideas; the importance of indigenous texts; the history of anthropology and colonialism; and a discovery of contemporary, mostly urban, popular culture.

Johannes Fabian's second book, *Time and the Other*, became even more influential, not only in general anthropology but also in cultural studies, history, and philosophy. This seminal study offers a far-reaching critique of the representation of time in anthropology, in particular of the 'ethnographic present' that locates the other in a time radically different from that of the ethnographer. His profound interest in colonial history was further pursued in a book on Swahili and colonial power in the former Belgian Congo and in his most recent study on reason and madness in the exploration of Central Africa.

In several of his later publications Johannes Fabian attempts to realise his ideal of 'coevalness' between Western anthropologist and African subject by focusing in a dialogic way on popular culture and performance, on proverbial wisdom, theatre, painting, and history in Shaba. He is also the founder of a website on Language and Popular Culture in Africa (http://www.pscw.uva.nl/lpca), which contains a journal and archive devoted to the preservation and study of texts that document popular culture as well as the use of languages such as Katanga Swahili. Johannes Fabian, who teaches at the University of Amsterdam, is preparing a book on the role of Swahili in various contexts of labour.

Education

Major Seminarium of Vienna, Universities of Bonn and Munich, 1956–63

MA University of Chicago, 1965
Ph.D. University of Chicago, 1969

Fieldwork

Shaba, Zaïre, 1965–7; 1972–4; 1985 (3 months), 1986 (2 months),1987 (summer), 1988 (summer)

Key Publications

(1983) *Time and the Other: How Anthropology Makes Its Object*, New York: Columbia University Press.
(1996) *Remembering the Present: Painting and Popular History in Zaire*, Berkeley: University of California Press.
(2000) *Out of Our Minds: Reason and Madness in the Exploration of Central Africa*, Berkeley: University of California Press.

HENK DRIESSEN

Fallers, Lloyd A.

b. 29 August 1925, Nebraska City, Nebraska, USA

d. 4 July 1974, Chicago, Illinois, USA

Lloyd A. Fallers was a prominent figure in world anthropology from the early 1950s until his tragic death from cancer at the age of forty-eight. Tom, as he was usually called, was one of the small group of young American anthropologists who also studied in England and then carried out research in British-ruled Africa in the early 1950s. Although steeped in Chicago anthropology and sociology, Fallers also worked briefly with Raymond Firth, Edmund Leach, and Audrey Richards at the London School of Economics (1949). He continued to work with Richards and other British Africanists as a fellow of the nascent East African Institute for Social Research in Kampala from 1950, on and off until 1957. (He was director in 1956–7.)

Fallers's doctoral research was in the then-popular genre of 'African political systems', but his approach was influenced more by Max Weber, Talcott Parsons, and Audrey Richards than by Radcliffe-Brown's social anthropology. His first book (1956) was a study of the dynamics of rule and administration in Busoga, first as an independent entity, and later as a district under British rule in the Uganda Protectorate. He emphasised the strains that occur when different principles of social organisation and different constituencies conflict in complex societies.

He presented the predicaments of headmen and bureaucrats in the face of the conflicting expectations that arise from the principles of the corporate lineage vs the institutions of the state and bureaucracy, and the differential expectations derived from particularistic vs universalistic norms. As in all his writings, he paid attention to the individual as 'a project-pursuing actor', constrained by many forces and factors 'but yet "free" enough to "intend" and "attempt", to "succeed" or to "fail"' (1974: 148).

While continuing to publish works about political process, inequality, law, and litigation in Uganda, in the 1960s he began an extended fieldwork project in Turkey. He was not granted time to complete this work, which drew on his experience with such mentors as Edward Shils, Lloyd Warner, and Robert Redfield. In his last book (1974), he presented a short, astute, and learned statement of his thoughts about the anthropological study of complex societies and the nation-state, and about change, history, and prediction.

After a decade of research and short teaching appointments at Princeton and Berkeley, Tom Fallers returned to the University of Chicago as an associate professor in 1960. He played an important role in establishing the Committee for the Comparative Study of New Nations, serving as director from 1970.

Education

Ph.B. University of Chicago, 1946
MA University of Chicago, 1949

Ph.D. University of Chicago, 1953

Fieldwork

Uganda, 1950–2, 1954–7
Turkey, 1964, 1968

Key Publications

(1956) *Bantu Bureaucracy: A Study of Integration and Conflict in the Political Institutions of an East African People*, Cambridge, UK: W. Heffer.
(1964) *The King's Men: Leadership and Status in Buganda on the Eve of Independence*, London: Oxford University.
(1969) *Law without Precedent: Legal Ideas in Action in the Courts of Colonial Busoga*, Chicago: University of Chicago.
(1974) *The Social Anthropology of the Nation-state*, Chicago: Aldine.

HERBERT S. LEWIS

Fals Borda, Orlando

b. 1925, Barranquilla, Colombia

Orlando Fals Borda is a towering figure in Colombian social sciences. Founder of the department of sociology of the National University at Bogotá, the country's first sociological school, his pioneering research has focused on the various dimensions of the land problem in Colombia. Both his master's and his doctoral theses were very detailed and thorough studies of small mountain communities using an orthodox structural-functionalist approach. During the 1960s his research on Colombian agrarian violence, *La Violencia*, gained him some notoriety on a national scale: it was the first time anybody singled out this previously unknown chapter of the country's social history. In 1970, following the death of Camilo Torres Restrepo, a colleague and Catholic priest who had joined the guerrillas, and a turbulent period marked by a radical student movement's opposition to Fals Borda's supposedly 'pro-imperialist' policies, he resigned his tenure at the National

University. He subsequently engaged in a 12-year research effort in the Colombian Caribbean Coast countryside, which resulted in Colombian sociology's most important work: *Historia doble de la Costa*.

In a radical departure from earlier works he launched the world renowned PAR (Participatory Action Research), a fusion of subject and object of investigation, of science and activism, of academic research and people's knowledge and experience, which tends towards a dialogic, democratic, and constructive possibility for both poor and advanced societies. Most recently he has dedicated efforts to a centuries' old Colombian land problem: *ordenamiento territorial*, a proposal that seeks the restructuring of arbitrary regional boundaries linked to local political interests and imposed by ruling classes since colonial times. He resumed tenure at the National University in 1987 and remains one of the most influential voices in Colombian science and social issues.

Education

BA Dubuque University, 1947
MA University of Minnesota, 1953
Ph.D. University of Florida, 1955

Fieldwork

Saucio, Cundinamarca, Colombia, 1950
Boyacá, Colombia, 1954–5
Tolima, Colombia 1961–2
Córdoba-Sucre, Colombia, 1970–82

Key Publications

(1955) *Peasant Society in the Colombian Andes: A Sociological Study of Saucio*, Gainesville: University of Florida Press.
(1957) *El hombre y la tierra en Boyacá* (Man and Soil in Boyaca), Bogotá: Ediciones Colombianas.
(1962) *La violencia en Colombia* (Violence in Colombia), Bogotá: Universidad Nacional.
(2002) *Historia doble de la Costa* (A Two-Way

History of the Coast), 4 vols, Bogotá: Universidad Nacional.

ADOLFO GONZÁLEZ HENRIQUEZ
(WITH THE HELP OF KELLY ESCOBAR)

Fardon, Richard

b. 1952, London, UK

Richard Fardon began his career as a lecturer in social anthropology at the University of St Andrews (1980–8), from where he moved to the School of Oriental and African Studies. He was appointed professor in West African anthropology in 1996. From 2001–5 he acted as chairman of the Association of Social Anthropologist (ASA).

Fardon has made significant contributions to the anthropology of politics and religion, as well as to the theory and methodology of anthropology, historical anthropology in particular. Fardon's ethnographic work deals with middle-belt Cameroon and Nigeria (especially the Chamba), and contemporary issues of ethnicity, broadcasting, and language. His writings also deal critically with contemporary anthropological theory, especially post-modern and post-structuralised approaches, and with the history of anthropology, especially Mary Douglas, of whom he has written an intellectual biography, and Franz Steiner, whose work he has edited.

Fardon's two monographs on the Chamba present an argument for an anthropologically informed history writing, while challenging the traditional ethnographic monograph for its misleading presentation of ethnically stable and culturally uniform peoples. Fardon's work on anthropological writing focuses on localising strategies in ethnographic writing, arguing that ethnographic authorship, while individual, is enabled by and cross-referenced to regional traditions. This emphasis on localisation is also reflected in Fardon's work on African broadcast cultures and on global and local relations, and the management of the diversity of knowledge.

Education

B.Sc. University College London, 1973
Ph.D. University College London, 1980

Fieldwork

Chamba Daka, Nigeria, 1976–8, 1987, 1990
Chamba Leko, Cameroon, 1984
Pere, Cameroon, 1985
Archival research in Oxford, Paris, Frankfurt, Basel, Berlin, Dresden, Cork, and Stuttgart, 1981–2001 (intermittent)

Key Publications

(1988) *Raiders and Refugees: Trends in Chamba Political Development 1750–1950*, Washington: Smithsonian Institution Press.
(1991) *Between God, the Dead and the Wild: Chamba Interpretations of Religion and Ritual*, Edinburgh: Edinburgh University Press.

ALEXANDER HUGO SCHULENBURG

Farmer, Paul E.

b. 1959, North Adams, Massachusetts, USA

Paul Farmer, physician-anthropologist and professor at Harvard Medical School, has stretched the boundaries of medical anthropology by incorporating a sophisticated social, clinical, and epidemiological multidisciplinary analysis of health and social inequalities and by delineating the social and political aetiology of infectious disease, particularly of HIV/AIDS and tuberculosis. Farmer, who is primarily based in a rural squatter settlement in Haiti, has studied in depth the social and historical roots of the ongoing structural violence in this impoverished Caribbean country and established solid explanations that link the suffering of the poor and the ever-increasing benefits of the powerful. Farmer combines this critical approach with the sociology of knowledge of bilateral and international health institutions and shows how they reproduce the conventional wisdom that contributes to the increasing inequality gap in access to social and economic rights, including the right to health care. Farmer's scholarly work is not only informed by practice, but also goes beyond the world of academia to bring, through what he terms pragmatic solidarity, social justice to those most affected by poverty and inequality. Farmer has published extensively on these subjects; his work is translated into several languages and is recognised by multiple national and international awards, both in anthropology and in clinical and social medicine. In 1999, Farmer received the Margaret Mead Award by the American Anthropological Association and the Society for Applied Anthropology.

Education

BA Duke University, 1982
MD Harvard Medical School, 1990
Ph.D. Harvard University, 1990

Fieldwork

Haiti, 1983–present
Peru, 1995–2000

Key Publications

(1992) *AIDS and Accusation: Haiti and the Geography of Blame*, Berkeley: University of California Press.
(2002) *Pathologies of Power: Structural Violence and the Assault on Health and Human Rights*, Berkeley: University of California Press.

ARACHU CASTRO

Favret-Saada, Jeanne

b. 26 September 1934, Sfax, Tunisia

Jeanne Favret-Saada's writings based on her research in Algeria have made a fundamental contribution to the social anthropology of North Africa. In the 1960s, she critically applied for the first time in contemporary French ethnographic studies the analysis of tribal segmentarity that had been elaborated in the works of E. Evans-Pritchard and E. Gellner. In an article that has continued to influence subsequent research in the area on tribal political systems, she demonstrated the meanings of dissidence and the manipulation of violence in the early years of Algeria's independence.

In the 1970s Favret-Saada turned her attention to the still-existent practice of sorcery in the present-day rural society of western France. Her minute descriptions and explanations of the mechanisms and functions of sorcery are woven into a 'subjective' account of her experience of fieldwork. The book has served as a classic example of ethnographic research in the teaching of social anthropology. In a second book, co-authored with the novelist, J. Contreras, a day-to-day narrative of fieldwork, totally drawn from a diary kept during research, examines the nature of ethnographic data and its translation into interpretive anthropology.

Subsequent research and writing have been concerned with a probing question: what is at stake in current public debates and polemics about religion, for example, about blasphemy? Since 1999, Favret-Saada has been preparing a book on Christianity and its Jews, a study focused on the Passion Play of Oberammergau.

Education

Licence de Philosophie, Sorbonne, Paris, 1956
Agregation de Philosophie, Sorbonne, Paris,1958

Fieldwork

Algeria, 1959–64
Mayenne, France, 1968–72

Key Publications

(1980) *Deadly Words. Witchcraft in the Bocage*, (Les mots, la mort, les sorts. La sorcellerie dans le Bocage, 1977) Cambridge, UK: Cambridge University Press.

with Contreras, Josee (1981) *Corps pour corps* (Body for Body), Paris: Gallimard.

KENNETH BROWN

Feit, Harvey A.

b. 1941, Bronx, New York, USA

Harvey Feit's research with Cree hunters in northern Québec has combined detailed ethnographic investigations of ethnoecology with penetrating theoretical analyses of evolving political and administrative relations between aboriginal peoples and governments. His work on Cree hunting and conservation practices preceded the massive hydroelectric development project constructed in the 1970s upon the lands of the James Bay Cree, was reoriented by his involvement in Cree (and Inuit) negotiations with the governments of Canada and Québec, which led to the James Bay and Northern Québec Agreement (JBNQA), and has subsequently focused upon Cree resource management in a transformed environment. Feit's careful analyses of the negotiation and implementation of the JBNQA have probed the manner in which modernist and non-modernist framings of ethnicity and nationalism articulate and create new forms of colonialism and resistance. Another strand of Feit's scholarship investigates non-indigenous environmental organisations and movements, and the cultural and political effects upon aboriginal peoples of being defined as an environmental issue.

Education

BA (Hons) Queen's University, 1967
MA McGill University, 1969
Ph.D. McGill University, 1979

Fieldwork

Waswanipi, Québec, 1968–70, 1978–87, 1997–2000
Québec, Montréal, Ottawa, 1974–85

Geneva, Paris, London, Toronto, Montréal, 1984–6

Key Publications

(1988) 'Self-management and state-management: forms of knowing and managing northern wildlife', in M.R.M. Freeman and L.N. Carbyn (eds) *Traditional Knowledge and Renewable Resource Management in Northern Regions*, Edmonton: Boreal Institute for Northern Studies and International Union for the Conservation of Nature and Natural Resources.
(1989) 'James Bay Cree self-governance and land management', in E.N. Wilmsen (ed.) *We Are Here: Politics of Aboriginal Land Tenure*, Berkeley: University of California Press.

NOEL DYCK

Feld, Steven

b. 1949, Philadelphia, Pennsylvania, USA

Steven Feld's work has focused on sound as cultural system, sociolinguistics, 'world music', and musical globalisation. His long-term ethnographic work in Bosavi, Papua New Guinea, began with his now classic doctoral study, *Sound and Sentiment*, about sound communication as an understanding of life among the Kaluli people. By examining the form and performance of weeping, poetics, and song in relation to their origin myth and bird world, Feld was able to show that Kaluli sound expressions were embodiments of deep sentiments and cosmology. In line with the concern with reflexivity in ethnomusicology and anthropology in the 1980s, Feld included a new critical postscript in the second edition of this book where he adjusted his previous findings to ideas on gender and emotion, discussed his informants' reception of the book, and argued strongly for dialogical fieldwork. A good example for his colleagues, Feld has continued to develop this dialogical stance through collaborations such as a *Bosavi–English–Tok Pisin Dictionary* and also by making a number of audio recordings, cassettes, and CDs together with informants. The CD, *Voices in the Rainforest*, a soundscape documentary, which conveys natural and human sounds during a day in the Bosavi rainforest, was produced by Grateful Dead drummer, Mickey Hart. Royalties from this CD as well as other CDs of Bosavi sound go to the Bosavi People's Fund, a small NGO (http://www.bosavipeoplesfund.org). Contrary to predictable ideas about the risk that the Western music market will exploit indigenous musics, Feld suggests that the international recognition of Kaluli sound and song has been a way to document and share an important ethnoaesthetics and a local life form in a changing environment. Writing in terms of vocal knowledge, Feld has been exploring the history of voice, performance, and politics in Bosavi.

Clearly Feld's extraordinary rapport with his informants about sound comes out of his own experience as a jazz musician. From there he takes the study of music and sound worlds to a theoretical level, and generates seminal concepts such as acoustemology, a union of acoustics and epistemology, which crystallises the importance of sound to making sense of being and to memory, place, and time. Honoring his ethnographic film teacher, Jean Rouch, Feld has compiled translations and interviews about him. Feld's highly original scholarship is characterised by musical sensibility, dialogue, and rigor.

Education

BA Hofstra University, 1971
Ph.D. Indiana University, 1979

Fieldwork

Bosavi, Papua New Guinea, 1976–7, 1982, 1984, 1990, 1992, 1994–5, 1998–9

Key Publications

(1990 [1982]) *Sound and Sentiment: Birds, Weeping, Poetics, and Song in Kaluli Expression*, expanded

second edn, Philadelphia: University of Pennsylvania Press.
with Keil, Charles (1994) *Music Grooves: Essays and Dialogues*, Chicago: University of Chicago Press.
with Basso, Keith (eds) (1996) *Senses of Place*, Santa Fe: SAR Press.
with Schieffelin, Bambi B. in collaboration with Hoido: Degelo:, Ho:nowo: Degili, Kulu Fuale, Ayasilo Ha:ina, and Da:ina Ha:waba: (1998) *Bosavi–English–Tok Pisin Dictionary*, Pacific Linguistics C-153, Australian National University Press.

HELENA WULFF

Fenton, William N.

b. 1908, New Rochelle, New York, USA

William N. Fenton has spent his professional life researching, studying with, and writing about the Northern Iroquoian peoples. He began his doctoral research in 1933 on the Allegany Seneca Reservation in western New York, initially on the False Face Society, but after receiving an appointment as a United States Indian Service community worker, he moved to the Tonawanda Seneca Reservation, just east of Buffalo, New York. Here he refocused his research on the Seneca Eagle Dance.

After receiving his doctorate, Fenton taught for a short time at St Lawrence University, and, in 1938, he replaced J.N.B. Hewitt at the Bureau of American Ethnology, where he remained until 1951. Following this, he served as assistant commissioner of the New York State Museum (1954–68), and research professor of anthropology (1968–74) and distinguished professor emeritus (1974–9) at the State University of New York at Albany.

Fenton's contributions to anthropology in general and to the sub-area of Iroquois studies have been monumental. He has centered his research on understanding and explicating Iroquois ceremonialism, its role in the preservation of Iroquois culture, its symbolism, and its meaning beyond the confines of

Iroquois culture. A skilled ethnographer and ethnohistorian, he has explored the range and breadth of Iroquois culture and social organisation, medicine and curing societies, and clan systems, analysing both their conservative and adaptive features. His work has resulted in one of the most thorough reconstructions of an American Indian society. He has added significantly to an understanding of ceremonial music and ritual through his intense and detailed studies of the Eagle Dance, and the False Face and Little Water societies

Fenton has been an active participant in the development of anthropological research through his teaching and through his participation in professional societies. Over the years he has served as president of the American Folklore Society, American Society for Ethnohistory, and the American Ethnological Society, and on the boards of the American Anthropological Association, and the Museum of the American Indian. In 1979, he was singularly honoured as the 'dean of Iroquois studies' by the Conference on Iroquois Research, which he helped to found in 1945. Finally, he has been the recipient of the Cornplanter Medal for Iroquois Research (1965) and the Peter Doctor Award of the Seneca Nation (1958).

Education

BA Dartmouth College, 1931
Ph.D. Yale University, 1937

Fieldwork

Field archaeology, Great Plains (Nebraska and South Dakota), 1932
Seneca reservations, New York State; Six Nations Reserve, Canada, 1933–84

Key Publications

(1953) *The Iroquois Eagle Dance*, USGPO: Bureau of Ethnology.
(1974) *Customs of the American Indians Compared with the Customs of Primitive Times*, ed. and trans. Elizabeth L. Moore, Toronto: The Champlain Society.

(1987) *The False Faces of the Iroquois*, Norman, Oklahoma and London, UK: University of Oklahoma.
(1998) *The Great Law and the Longhouse*, Norman and London, UK: University of Oklahoma.

JACK CAMPISI

Ferguson, James

b. 1959, Los Angeles, USA

James Ferguson's *The Anti-Politics Machine*, an ethnographically based study that incorporates insights from anthropology, social history, and development practice, quickly became an influential analysis of processes of 'development'. Throughout his work, focusing on Southern Africa, Ferguson provides a critical view of the 'development' apparatus, relying on the strengths of both political economy and Foucauldian insights into discursive practice and knowledge/power.

Related to this initial interest in the politics and the practice of 'development', Ferguson later turned his attention to localised and contested meanings, and uses of the notion of modernity. In his *Expectations of Modernity*, based on ethnographic fieldwork on the Zambian Copperbelt, he deployed the concept of cultural style as a critical tool for the study of certain aspects of everyday life, and particularly for approaching urban/rural differences.

During the mid-1990s, Ferguson's cooperation with Akhil Gupta produced some thought-provoking work on the issues of place and space in relation to 'culture'. Combining an emphasis on power and inequality with a sensitivity to (de)territorialisation, they offered a critique of anthropological practice, and particularly of the often postulated boundedness of the discipline's central notion of 'culture'. As such, Gupta and Ferguson attempt to reclaim the value of ethnographic fieldwork through a critical reappraisal, both theoretically and politically, of the 'field' in fieldwork.

Education

BA University of California, Santa Barbara, 1979

MA Harvard University, 1981

Ph.D. Harvard University, 1985

Fieldwork

Lesotho, October 1982–December 1983

Zambia, October 1985–September 1986

Zambia, July–September 1989

Key Publications

(1990) The Anti-Politics Machine: 'Development', Depoliticization and Bureaucratic Power in Lesotho, Cambridge, UK: Cambridge University Press.

(1999) Expectations of Modernity: Myths and Meanings of Urban Life on the Zambian Copperbelt, Berkeley: University of California Press.

STEFAN JANSEN

Fernandes, Florestan

b. 22 July 1920, São Paulo, Brazil

d. 10 August 1995, São Paulo, Brazil

The life of Florestan Fernandes, academic, politician, and intellectual, can be characterised by his struggle against inequalities and injustices, his work being permeated by a political consciousness. Florestan Fernandes came from a poor family, son of a Portuguese immigrant washerwoman. He started work when 6 years old and was a shoeshine boy, a cabinet-maker's assistant, a barber's assistant, a tailor and bar assistant. When he was nine he interrupted his studies to work full time. Only at seventeen did he take up his studies again. At eighteen, while working as a salesman for pharmaceutical products, he entered the Faculty of Philosophy and Arts at the University of São Paulo.

After graduating in 1943, the following year (1944) he became assistant to Professor Fernando de Azevedo in the chair of Sociology

II, a position he retained until 1952. In 1947, he completed his MA at the School of Sociology and Politics. His MA dissertation in social sciences (anthropology), published in book form as Organização social dos Tupinambá in 1948, is very rich in descriptive details. His Ph.D. thesis (1951) in social sciences at the Faculty of Philosophy, Science, and Literature, which was published in 1952 as A função social da guerra na sociedade Tupinambá, is more theoretically oriented with a concern for interpretation. He explicitly adopted the 'functionalist method'. In these academic works of the early phase of his career, he spent seven years working on a historical reconstruction of sixteenth-century Tupinambá Indians, through the documents of early travellers, missionaries, and colonisers in Brazil.

A second phase of his work was centered on studies, sponsored by UNESCO, of race relations in São Paulo, studies which sought to integrate a political perspective into academic life. In 1972 he published O negro no mundo dos brancos (Blacks in the the White World). He defended a socialist revolution as the only means of attaining social equality in a capitalist society organised on the basis of economic relations of institutionalised exploitation. A later phase of his work focuses on Brazil as a national society in relation to other nations.

His work may be characterised by an emphasis on theoretical and methodological issues, and on practical concerns with education. A movement can be detected in his work from an universalistic anthropologically oriented social science, heir of the Durkheimian–French framework, to a holistic sociological approach interested in larger national processes. This change is reflected in a movement from culture to society as principal concepts of analysis. In 1953, Florestan Fernandes obtained the title of Livre Docência in the chair of sociology at the University of São Paulo on the basis of his essay, Ensaio sobre o método de interpretação funcionalista na sociologia. In 1964 he became professor in the chair of Sociology I, on the basis of his thesis, A integração do negro na sociedade de classes.

From the 1940s Florestan Fernandes allied

himself with left-wing political organisations and in 1964 he was arrested and sent to the Army prison in São Paulo. After his release, he became full professor at the University of São Paulo in 1965. In 1969 he was compulsorily retired by the military dictatorship, on political grounds, and exiled himself to Canada where he taught at the University of Toronto. He was visiting professor at Columbia University in 1965–6 and, after his exile, taught at the University of Toronto from 1969–72. He also taught at Columbia University as Latin American scholar from 1970 to 1972 when he resigned to return to Brazil, becoming professor of courses of cultural extension in the Instituto Sedes Sapientiae in São Paulo. He was later contracted as professor of the Catholic University of São Paulo in 1977 where he became full professor in 1978. In 1977 he was visiting professor at Yale. In 1986 Florestan Fernandes was elected Constituent Federal Deputy by the Labour Party (Partido dos Trabalhadores) for the period 1987–90, and in 1987 he returned to the University of São Paulo in the University Council. He was re-elected Federal Deputy for the period 1991–4 in the same political party. He died in 1995, at the age of seventy-five, as a result of a medical error.

Education

BA University of São Paulo, 1943
MA University of São Paulo, 1947
Ph.D. University of São Paulo, 1951
Livre Docência, University of São Paulo, 1953

Fieldwork

Historical bibliographical and fieldwork in São Paulo, Brazil.

Key Publications

(1948) Organização social dos Tupinambá (Social Organisation of the Tupinambá), São Paulo: Instituto Progresso Editorial.
(1970 [1952]) A Função social da guerra na sociedade Tupinambá (The Social Function of War in Tupinambá Society), São Paulo: Livraria

Pioneira Editora; Editora da Universidade de São Paulo.
(1953) Ensaio sobre o método de interpretação funcionalista na sociologia (Essay on the Functionalist Method of Interpretation in Sociology), São Paulo:USP.
(1964) A integração do negro na sociedade de classes (The Integration of Black People in a Society of Classes), São Paulo:USP.

STEPHEN G. BAINES

Fernandez, James W.

b. 1930, Chicago, Illinois, USA

James Fernandez's work covers an array of interests, ranging from religious movements and social change to narrative and rhetoric, as well as architecture and aesthetics. He has carried out field research in Africa and Europe.

Fernandez is known above all for his research on metaphor in interaction with the other tropes, such as metonyms, and for a theory of tropology. He argues that some domains of experience are inchoate and initially less meaningful, and some more familiar and meaningful. The tropes work with these differences by displacement of meaning between domains. He sees culture as a process of continual displacement. The primary inchoate subjects of our attention are the personal pronouns such as 'I', 'you', or 'we'. They gain meaning by metaphorical predication and displacement. Fernandez's theory of 'pro-nominalism' deals with the movement of pronouns in semantic space, usually from an uncertain to a more positive identity or to a better position in cultural quality space, to use Fernandez's own spatial metaphor.

Different cultures choose sign-images, that is, convincing tropes, from characteristically different domains. According to Fernandez, the cultural lexicon or repository of these sign-images is rooted in early childhood. Some metaphors are only persuasive, while others lead to actual performance.

Fernandez has been particularly interested in

the 'play of tropes' in religious movements and the 'revitalisation' that ensues. He studied various revitalisation movements in Equatorial, West, and South Africa. In his doctoral research from which his *opus magnum*, *Bwiti: An Ethnography of the Religious Imagination in Africa*, is derived, he investigated the Bwiti cult of the Fang of Gabon.

Up to 10 per cent of the Fang population follow this syncretic religion, which developed after the First World War, and is organised around cult leaders in small local branches. After colonisation, the Fang predicament has been characterised by a sense of peripherality, monetarisation, economic individualism, and alienation. By contrast, the Bwiti religion revitalises by restoring an experience of wholeness, of complementarity between men and women, and of integration of the self into an overarching cosmic order.

The metaphoric movements of the Bwiti religion are articulated along three elemental vectors: the downriver progression of legendary-historical migrations, centripetal involution to a central point in village life, such as the council house, and vertical descent and ascent (along the central pillar of the Bwiti chapel, or along a genealogical line).

By use of analogies, such as 'we are a trading team', 'we are of one clan', 'we are one heart', the Bwiti cult predicates a more concrete and manageable identity upon the inchoate personae of the membership, i.e. the individual cult follower, the man–woman dyad, the worshiping group, the Fang people, the ancestors, and various deities.

Thus, the Fang acquire a more satisfactory sense of connection with the ancestors, the cosmos, and of complementarities between the genders and generations. In general, Fernandez seeks to understand how religion, through the 'play of tropes', moves people (i.e. their personae) to greater meaning in their lives. Consensus about this meaning change is, however, a complex problem because people will often agree to interact (social consensus) without having an adequate sense of the meanings of their interaction (cultural consensus).

In his Spanish work, Fernandez has continued to be interested in revitalisation and the 'play of tropes', in popular poetry exchange, narrative art, and particularly in language revitalisation (of the Asturian language). He has studied this 'play' and domain displacement among miners and cattle-keepers as well as among intellectual language revitalisers. In the edited volume, *Beyond Metaphor*, Fernandez was concerned with the interaction of the variety of tropes.

In *Irony in Action*, Fernandez and the other contributors to the volume defined the trope of irony as the discrepancy and displacement between what is said and what is actually meant. In particular, Fernandez looked at irony in development discourse and in the anthropological enterprise itself. He distinguished between exclusive, i.e. aggressive, dehumanising irony, and inclusive irony, which implies a questioning and self-critical stance that are, or should be, hallmarks of the anthropological project.

Education

BA Amherst College, Massachusetts, 1952
Ph.D. Northwestern University, Chicago, 1962

Fieldwork

Barcelona, Madrid, Seville, Spain, 1955
Gabon, Rio Muni, Equatorial Guinea, Cameroon, 1958–60
Natal, South Africa, 1965
Asturias, Spain, 1965–6, 1971–3, 1977–81, 1984, 1989, 1991, 1993–5, 1998–2001
Dahomey, Togo, Ghana, 1966

Key Publications

(1982) *Bwiti: An Ethnography of the Religious Imagination in Africa*, Princeton: Princeton University Press.

(1986) *Persuasions and Performances: The Play of Tropes in Culture*, Bloomington: Indiana University Press.

(ed.) (1991) *Beyond Metaphor: The Theory of Tropes*

in *Anthropology*, Stanford: Stanford University Press.

with Taylor Huber, Mary (eds) (2001) *Irony in Action: Anthropological Practice and the Moral Imagination*, Chicago: The University of Chicago Press.

ANNE FRIEDERIKE MÜLLER

Fernea, Elizabeth Warnock

b. 21 October 1927, Milwaukee, Wisconsin, USA

Elizabeth Fernea played an important role in bringing the Middle East to the forefront of anthropological theory. Best known for her ethnographies of women in Iraq, Egypt, and Morocco, she has also edited important volumes on women, family, and children in the Middle East and produced pathbreaking documentary films. Fernea has contributed to the anthropology of women, the ethnography of the Middle East, and the practice of ethnographic writing.

In 1956 Fernea accompanied her husband, Robert Fernea, on his ethnographic fieldwork in rural Iraq. Years later she wrote up her observations as *Guests of the Sheik*, thereby embarking on her own remarkably productive career as ethnographer, translator, filmmaker, teacher, and eloquent spokesperson for the Middle East.

Guests of the Sheik filled two gaps in ethnographic practice: the absence of women in ethnographic descriptions, and the absence of the author in ethnographic texts. In *Guests of the Sheik* Fernea provided a rich description of the lives of Middle Eastern women that encouraged other anthropologists to study women, and other women to undertake ethnographic research. Fernea has also written about women in urban Egypt (*A View of the Nile*) and Morocco (*A Street in Marrakech*).

Guests of the Sheik pioneered a style of ethnographic writing that inserted the author's voice into the textual description just when anthropologists were beginning to question positivist modes of representation. Written as a travel narrative, Fernea's book embeds sophisticated analysis of cultural difference in an equally sophisticated narrative form.

Fernea subsequently turned to editing, translating, and filmmaking as means for disseminating knowledge about the Middle East. *Middle Eastern Muslim Women Speak* provided an important forum for ethnographic work on Middle Eastern women and did much to introduce a new generation of Middle Eastern female scholars and writers to the West. Fernea has also produced several ethnographic films focusing on women in the Middle East.

Elizabeth Fernea's influence may be greatest as a mentor. In decades of teaching, translating, and editing, Fernea has facilitated the entry of women into ethnographic research, Middle Eastern women into ethnographic texts, and literary genres into social scientific discourses. Fernea helped establish the Association for Middle East Women's Studies and has been president of the Middle Eastern Studies Association. With her husband, Robert Fernea, she has written an excellent and widely-used textbook called *The Arab World: Forty Years of Change*.

Education

BA Reed College, 1949

Fieldwork

Iraq, 1956–8

Egypt, 1962

Morocco, 1971–2

Jordan, Libya, Lebanon, Yemen, Morocco, Israel/Palestine, Egypt, Iraq, 1983–4, 1995–6

Uzbekistan, Kuwait, Abu Dhabi, Saudi Arabia, Turkey, Israel/Palestine, Iraq, Egypt, Morocco, 1993–4, 1997

Key Publications

(1965) *Guests of the Sheik: An Ethnography of an Iraqi Village*, Garden City: Anchor Books.

(1975) *A Street in Marrakech*, Garden City: Doubleday.

with Bezirgan, B. (eds) (1977) *Middle Eastern Muslim Women Speak*, Austin: University of Texas Press.

with Fernea, R. (1997) *The Arab World: Forty Years of Change*, New York: Anchor Books.

DANIEL LEFKOWITZ

Fernea, Robert A.

b. 25 January 1932, Vancouver, Washington, USA

Robert Fernea is a long-time ethnographer, teacher, and commentator on the Middle East. He has written ethnographic monographs on southern Iraq and Nubian Egypt, an important review of anthropological scholarship on the Middle East (with J. Malarkey), and an influential textbook (with E. Fernea).

Fernea's early work focused on the relationship between water and social structure. His dissertation looked at the role of irrigation in mediating social and cultural change, as traditional, tribally organised Shi'ite communities of southern Iraq were increasingly incorporated within the Iraqi nation-state. This work, subsequently published as *Shaykh and Effendi*, described hydrological engineers as prototypical agents in the transformation of authority from the older heads of traditional patrilines, called *shaykhs*, to the younger, urban, educated professionals, called *effendis*. Fernea shows that in the village of El Nahra the *effendi* engineer came to assume many of the prestigious social functions traditionally reserved for the *shaykh*, such as dispute arbitration, thereby facilitating the transfer of authority more generally to the national entity.

In subsequent work Fernea looked at the articulation of water and social structure in Nubian (southern) Egypt, where construction of the Aswan High Dam on the Nile River flooded Nubian villages and fields situated along its banks. Ethnographic research conducted in Nubia in 1961-2, just as construction was beginning on the dam, led to the publication in 1974 of *Nubians in Egypt: Peaceful People*, a richly illustrated description of Nubian

village life. Fernea also returned to 'New Nubia' in 1991-2, two decades after the dam's completion, to study the consequences of a massive resettlement project.

Fernea's 1975 review of anthropological literature on the Middle East and North Africa (with J. Malarkey) laid an important foundation for reconceptualising the relationship between ethnographer and cultural other. This review helped return the Middle East to the forefront of ethnological theory. In 1987 Robert Fernea and his wife, Elizabeth Fernea, formalised a long and fruitful collaboration by co-authoring a textbook on the Arab Middle East, called *The Arab World: Personal Encounters*. This excellent and widely used text was subsequently updated and re-released as *The Arab World: Forty Years of Change*. Fernea also edited (with W.R. Louis) a collection of essays on the Iraqi Revolution of 1958. A long-time teacher of cultural anthropology and Middle Eastern studies at the American University in Cairo, as well as at the University of Texas at Austin, Fernea has been mentor to a generation of anthropologists working in the Middle East.

Education

BA Reed College, 1954
MA and Ph.D. University of Chicago, 1959

Fieldwork

El Nahra, Iraq, 1956-8
Nubia, Egypt, 1961-2, 1991-2
Western Afghanistan, 1967
Marrakech, Morocco, 1971-2
Hail Province, Saudi Arabia, 1984

Key Publications

(1970) *Shaykh and Effendi: Changing Patterns of Authority among the El-Shabana of Southern Iraq*, Cambridge, MA: Harvard University Press.

with Malarkey, James (1975) 'Anthropology of the Middle East and North Africa: a critical assessment', *Annual Review of Anthropology* 4: 183-206.

with Fernea, E. (1997) *The Arab World: Forty Years of Change*, New York: Anchor Books.

DANIEL LEFKOWITZ

Finnegan, Ruth Hilary

b. 1933, Londonderry, Northern Ireland, UK

Ruth Finnegan's early career began with a general ethnographic survey of the Limba of northern Sierra Leone, with particular emphasis on story-telling. The regional location for exploring her interests in oral literary genres is significant. In subsequent introductory texts to the academic study of regional 'oral literature' and cross-cultural traditions of 'oral poetry', Finnegan extensively details two main reasons for finding previous contributions to this loose area of study unreliable, which she sets out to remedy in her own analyses. She eschews the idea that 'oral poetry' possesses any absolute characteristics, pertaining either to 'orality' or the 'poetic', which may be used to naturally discriminate it from other seemingly transparent categories, such as 'literacy' or 'prose'. However, further, her thought also marks an assault on evolutionist assumptions that 'oral poetry' must be a simple reflection of the nature of those 'primitive' societies that produce it: unsophisticated, archaic, immutable, deindividualised, and closer to nature. Any study of oral literature necessitates the investigation of problems surrounding the nature of communication itself. This Finnegan conceived as an active social process involving relations between experiencing subjects who are usually co-present, an approach that differed from the exegesis of reified texts that seemed to emerge, as if *sui generis*, from amidst a mythical collective conscience in 'traditional' societies.

In 1969, a move to Bletchley, later incorporated into Milton Keynes where she taught at the Open University, coincided with another phase in her research career from which two key works were to emerge, centring on urban life in the British new town. Both of these studies sought to explain how individuals in the city, through their use of expressive tools (whether it involves local amateur music-making or urban story-telling), actively create the horizons of their own experience, engender their own worlds. This is in marked contrast to much of the sociology of Western countries where politics and economics are usually granted privileged status in the understanding of society and the motivations of individuals within it.

Finnegan has continued to publish extensively on the themes of music, orality, and literacy, and the multimodality of human communication, besides an ethnographic guide on the use of oral and auditory resources. Her many honours and rewards include Hon. Editor of the anthropological journal, *Man* (latterly *Journal of the Royal Anthropological Institute*), from 1987–9 and an OBE (services to social sciences) in 2000.

Education

BA, University of Oxford, 1956
Postgraduate Diploma, University of Oxford, 1959
B.Litt. University of Oxford, 1960
D.Phil. University of Oxford, 1963

Fieldwork

Northern Sierra Leone, 1960–1 (13 months), 1963–4 (3 months)
Suva, Fiji (part time), 1977–8
Bletchley and Milton Keynes, UK, 1980, 1982–8 (part time, intermittent)

Key Publications

(1967) *Limba Stories and Story-telling*, Oxford: Clarendon Press.
(1977) *Oral Poetry: Its Nature, Significance and Social Context*, Cambridge, UK: Cambridge University Press.
(1989) *The Hidden Musicians: Music-making in an English Town*, Cambridge, UK: Cambridge University Press.
(1998) *Tales of the City: A Study of Narrative and*

Urban Life, Cambridge, UK: Cambridge University Press.

IAN JAMES

Firth, Raymond

b. 25 March 1901, Auckland, New Zealand

d. 22 February 2002, London, UK

Raymond Firth began his university studies with degrees in economics but came under the influence of Bronislaw Malinowski when he moved from New Zealand to England and the London School of Economics (LSE) for doctoral studies. This engendered a lasting interest in anthropology and in 1928 he travelled to the small Polynesian outlier, Tikopia, where he carried out a year's fieldwork. He returned to the island twice more and this provided the basis for a corpus of nine books and nearly a hundred articles on the social organisation, religious ritual, and changing patterns of life on the island. His early training in economics influenced his writings. His doctoral thesis, published as *Economics of the New Zealand Maori* (1929), was the first English-language study to incorporate the idea of the gift (after Mauss) in economic exchange. He was also aware of the effect of colonisation and the expropriation of their land on the Maori and this concern for others is reflected in his later work.

While his publications on Tikopia are also largely based on the role of economic exchange in the ceremonies of everyday life, his greatest contribution to anthropology was his superb and detailed ethnography. From his experience of the New Zealand Maori language, which is cognate with the language spoken on Tikopia, he quickly achieved fluency in his field language and later wrote the dictionary of the Tikopia language (1985). He believed that systematic and repeated observation of events would elucidate pattern and variation. To this end he kept detailed diaries, notes, household censuses, genealogies, and specimen lists, recording not only what people said to him but also to each other (*Oceania* 60: 241, 1990). This gave a richness to his ethnography that is hard to match. At a time when other ethnographers produced eye-of-God ethnographies, describing the ideal pattern of their societies, Firth humanised his informants: the reported speech and actions of individuals are the aspects of his work most valued by the descendants of his first informants. He also gave us a picture of rational informants, rather than the exotic other, with whom he shared a common humanity.

His first ethnography, *We, the Tikopia* (1936), provides the most significant account of traditional Polynesian religion available. Conversion to Christianity had occurred on most other Pacific islands a hundred years previously and few records exist of their traditional beliefs, but Firth was able to observe the Tikopia rituals called the Work of the Gods, which were still practised by half the island during his early fieldwork. Two significant books detail the twice-yearly ritual cycle. His later fieldwork records the conversion of the whole island to Christianity and Tikopia's response to the crisis caused by two serious cyclones. Other papers, monographs, and books record oral tradition, material culture, and the emotional and symbolic life of Tikopia.

In 1939 and 1940 Firth worked in what was then Malaya, studying the peasant economy of Malay fisherman. In the mid-1950s, while teaching at the London School of Economics, he initiated a study of middle-class kinship in London. During this period he gently criticised the dominant structural functionalism of British social anthropology by insisting on the importance of personal choice and flexibility of social life. In the earlier part of the twentieth century, anthropology had not been recognised as a separate discipline; Firth worked to change this perception and in 1946 was one of the founder members of the Association of Social Anthropologists. He was also associated with a distinguished group of anthropologists who trained at LSE in the years before and after the Second World War: Edward Evans-Pritchard, Meyer Fortes, Audrey

Richards, Jomo Kenyatta, and Edmund Leach. The theoretical approaches developed through the interaction of this group of people were influential in the adoption of structuralism in British anthropology and the development of post-colonial studies.

Raymond Firth was knighted in 1973. He was made a companion of the New Zealand Order of Merit in 2001. He received the Leverhulme Medal for outstanding contributions to twentieth-century anthropology in 2002.

Education

BA Auckland University College, 1921
MA Auckland University College, 1924
Ph.D. London School of Economics, 1929

Fieldwork

Tikopia, Solomon Islands, 1928–9, 1956, 1966
Malaya, 1939, 1940
London, mid-1950s

Key Publications

(1936) *We, the Tikopia: A Sociological Study of Kinship in Primitive Polynesia*, London: George Allen & Unwin.
(1940) *The Work of the Gods in Tikopia*, London: The Athlone Press.
(1967) *Tikopia Ritual and Belief*, London: George Allen & Unwin.
(1970) *Rank and Religion in Tikopia*, London: George Allen & Unwin.

JUDITH MACDONALD

Fishman, Joshua A.

b. 18 July 1926, Philadelphia, Pennsylvania, USA

Joshua Fishman is the founder of the sociology of language, a research paradigm that applies sociological methods to the study of language and society. In the 1960s and 1970s, Fishman was one of the key figures (along with Dell Hymes and John Gumperz) establishing an anthropology of language use. Fishman's approach bridges the linguistically oriented sociolinguistics (associated with William Labov) and the anthropologically oriented ethnography of speaking (associated with Dell Hymes and John Gumperz). His careful research and prolific writing helped shape modern understandings of the relationship between language and society, and his passionate commitment to the application of his work is a model for compassionate scholarship.

Fishman is perhaps best known as an editor. He has edited the influential *International Journal for the Sociology of Language* for three decades, and as editor of the *Contributions to the Sociology of Language* series he has produced more than eighty monographs, including many of the most important contributions to the field. He has also edited more than twenty volumes on bilingualism, language planning, bilingual education, language maintenance, and language and ethnicity. These collections defined the primary subject matter while providing valuable reference works for the emergent field.

Fishman's first major book, *Bilingualism in the Barrio*, was a groundbreaking study of Spanish/English bilingualism in the USA that set out three major contributions to the field of sociolinguistics. One contribution was a taxonomy of bilingual societies in terms of societal diglossia and individual bilingualism. Fishman argued that diglossia (the functional specialisation of language varieties in a speech community) and bilingualism (an individual's use of two different languages, such that each language is used for any and all linguistic functions) were independent phenomena that could both apply or not apply to a given society. Bilingualism without diglossia, Fishman argued, was characteristic of speech communities (such as immigrant minorities in the USA) experiencing dislocation and change, leading to an unstable bilingualism (and resulting, over time, in language shift). Stable bilingualism, on the other hand, characterises those speech communities in which two languages co-exist in functional differentiation. Fishman's insight led to a significant revaluation of research on multilingual societies.

Fishman's synthesis of individual (e.g. bilingualism) and societal (e.g. diglossia) levels of analysis led to a second important theoretical contribution: the notion of domains of language behaviour. In multilingual speech communities, an individual's choice of language appears complexly influenced by both local factors, such as topic, and more institutional factors, such as setting. By theorising domains as sets of patterned behaviours within institutional contexts, Fishman revealed great regularity in language-use practices. The collection of data on such patterns constitutes Fishman's third major contribution. Towards answering the question 'Who speaks What language to Whom and When?', Fishman pioneered the use of language-use surveys and was instrumental in broadening the language component of the American census, thereby generating an incredibly detailed picture of the social life of language in the USA. Fishman also pioneered the application of rigorous statistical analysis to quantitative linguistic data.

Fishman's scholarly work was profoundly influenced by his personal history – and Fishman also applied his scholarship to the many causes he championed, as his work on Yiddish demonstrates. Born into a Yiddish-speaking family at a time when the use of Yiddish was declining, Fishman devoted his life to the language. While still in high school, Fishman met Max and Uriel Weinreich, then the most prominent scholars of Yiddish in the USA. Uriel Weinreich guided Fishman through his graduate studies, encouraging him to study social psychology (which provided the rigorous quantitative training that informs his subsequent sociolinguistic work). Fishman's personal engagement with Yiddish motivated much of his scholarly work, including his interest in language maintenance, language teaching, and language and ethnicity. In 1981 he edited *Never Say Die!*, an important collection of Yiddish texts and scholarship that became a seminal resource for general Yiddish studies,

and in 1991 he wrote *Yiddish: Turning to Life*, a more technical study of Yiddish sociolinguistics. Fishman also collaborated with Shlomo Noble in the English translation of Max Weinreich's important *History of Yiddish*.

Fishman taught at Yeshiva University from 1960 until 1988. He has received numerous honors and held many distinguished positions, including fellowships at the East–West Center in Honolulu and the Institute for Advanced Study in Princeton.

Education

BS and MS University of Pennsylvania, 1948
Ph.D. Columbia University, 1953

Key Publications

(ed.) (1968) *Readings in the Sociology of Language*, The Hague: Mouton.
with Cooper, Robert L., Ma, Roxana, *et al.* (1971) *Bilingualism in the Barrio*, Bloomington: Indiana University.
(1991) *Yiddish: Turning to Life*, Amsterdam: John Benjamins.
(ed.) (1999) *Handbook of Language and Ethnic Identity*, New York: Oxford University Press.

DANIEL LEFKOWITZ

Foner, Nancy

b. 1945, New York City, USA

Nancy Foner's work has focused on three areas of research, the Caribbean, migration, and ageing. Her earliest field research, in Jamaica, examined the impact of national political and educational changes on a rural community and later, in London, she explored status changes within the Jamaican population that resulted from migration to England. This was pioneering work in the anthropology of migration that not only encompassed field research in both the sending and receiving societies, but also delineated the significance of different social locations (age, gender, race) to the process of change within a single immigrant population. Foner argued that being black was crucial to the daily lives of Jamaicans in London and that their experience of blackness abroad was different from the way they experienced it at home. In an edited volume on West Indian migration to New York (*Islands in the City*, 2001), Foner has continued to guide research on the relationship between race and immigration, exploring in particular how 'blackness' has been renegotiated in an increasingly complex multiethnic black America. Foner has also made a sustained contribution to our understanding of the relationship between gender and migration, arguing that patterns of work and the control of economic resources are important factors in enhancing women's status within the migrant family. She has been concerned in particular with how family and kinship patterns change in the process of immigration. Her concern with context is equally apparent in her work on New York City, a complex and historically rich receiving area for immigrants that she has addressed in two edited volumes (*New Immigrants in New York*, 1987; rev edn, 2001), and a pathbreaking book that compares immigration in the age of Ellis Island with immigrants in the age of JFK airport. Foner asks incisive questions about continuity and change in the US immigrant experience, including what is new about transnationalism, an important concept for understanding post-1965 immigration. Foner has also contributed to two areas in the field of ageing: the study of cross-cultural ageing and nursing home ethnography. In *Ages in Conflict*, she examined the implications of age inequalities for relations between young and old through a comparative analysis of non- industrial societies. This work includes a critical analysis of the modernisation approach for understanding age and social change, and an exploration of age inequalities among women.

Education

BA Brandeis University, 1966
MA University of Chicago, 1968

Ph.D. University of Chicago, 1971

Fieldwork

Jamaica, 1968–9
London, 1973
New York City, 1982 (Jamaican Migrants), 1989–90 (nursing home)

Key Publications

(1978) *Jamaica Farewell: Jamaican Migrants in London*, Berkeley: University of California Press.
(1984) *Ages in Conflict: A Cross-cultural Perspective on Inequality between Old and Young*, New York: Columbia University Press
(1994) *The Caregiving Dilemma: Work in an American Nursing Home*, Berkeley: University of California Press.
(2000) *From Ellis Island to JFK: New York's Two Great Waves of Immigration*, New Haven and New York: Yale University Press and Russell Sage Foundation

CAROLINE B. BRETTELL

Forde, C. Daryll

b. 16 March 1902, Tottenham, Middlesex, UK

d. 3 May 1973, London, UK

Cyril Daryll Forde is remembered for his great curiosity and intellectual independence. His breadth of interpretation and the range and intensity of his professional involvement distinguished his career. Noting his diverse academic background in geography, archaeology, and anthropology, his fieldwork in the Southwest (USA) and southeastern Nigeria, his comprehensive approach to theory and ethnography, and his long and extraordinarily successful tenure as head of department, University College London, and as administrative director of the International African Institute (IAI) does not capture the high regard and profound appreciation of his colleagues and students. His colleagues depended on and were stimulated – and at times taken aback –

by the quality of interest in their work and lives. Forde was not identified with a particular teacher, nor as member or founder of a particular school of thought, but was thought of by those who studied and worked with him as central to anthropology and by all involved academically with Africa as essential to African Studies.

His career bridged historical periods and scholarly traditions. He studied under the diffusionist, Grafton Elliot Smith, and later at Berkeley with Alfred Kroeber and Robert Lowie, was at Oxford for two years during the Second World War (seconded to the Foreign Office Research Department) and collaborated with A.R. Radcliffe-Brown.

Forde's research interests describe a trajectory from archaeology and geography to African studies. His earliest publications were archaeological. His education and his experience at Berkeley reinforced his broad and inclusive approach to anthropology and stimulated his commitment to ecological approaches in ethnography. His most widely known and read book, *Habitat, Economy and Society* (1934), is a model of ecological anthropology showing the connections between environment, technology, and social organisation. Passages in this work anticipate studies of indigenous knowledge. His attention to gendered contributions to agricultural production and distribution is quite modern, again anticipating later foci of research.

In 1935, motivated by a desire to remedy the inadequacies in the literature on indigenous economies of West Africa especially about settled agriculturalists, he initiated fieldwork among the Yakö of southeastern Nigeria. This fieldwork was the turning point in Forde's career, leading to his involvement in African Studies that absorbed him both intellectually and administratively for the rest of his life. It produced a monograph (*Marriage and Family among the Yakö*, 1941) and a series of papers later collected in *Yakö Studies*, and led to collaboration on studies of the indigenous economies of Nigeria. These studies of what he described as an exceptionally large compact agrarian community (then about 11,000 people) is a remarkably detailed record of the agricultural economy, the gendered division of labour, and details of exchange within the household. Forde's work among the Yakö is, however, probably best remembered for his contributions to the enthusiastic discussions in the literature of descent theory, in particular, of the practices and implications of double descent in Yakö. His monograph (1941) and his collected papers are a detailed ethnographic account of the ecology of a sophisticated agricultural system, of the complex dual membership of each Yakö person in his/her father's patrilineage and in her/his mother's matrilineage, and the rituals, shrines, rights of succession, and inheritance that were associated with these groups. His detailed discussions of the rules and the challenges and evasions of them is a model of ethnographic description that gives a sense of interplay of agency and structure. His work on fosterage and adoption also anticipated much future work.

His intellectual balance and integrative approach is evidenced by the contrasting evaluations of him in the memories of those who knew and worked with him as a structural functionalist (Meyer Fortes) and as a theoretical sceptic favoring the reality of data over abstract models (Mary Douglas).

Forde was appointed administrative director of the International African Institute in 1944 and remained in that post until his death in 1973. He revived the Institute including its premier journal, *Africa*, from its wartime doldrums. In addition to the journal the Institute published *Ethnographic Survey of Africa*, some forty volumes, *African Abstracts*, the *Linguistic Survey of Africa*, and the papers, under various editors, of eleven international seminars held at African universities beginning at Kampala in 1959.

Education

BA University College London, 1922
Ph.D. University College London, 1928

Commonwealth Fellow, University of California, Berkeley, 1928–9

Fieldwork

Arizona, California, 1928, 1929
Umor (Yakö), southeastern Nigeria, 1935, 1939

Key Publications

(1934) *Habitat, Economy and Society: A Geographical Introduction to Ethnology*, London: Methuen (University Paperbacks 1963)
(1941) *Marriage and Family among the Yakö of Southeastern Nigeria*, London: LSE Monographs on Social Anthropology no. 5.
with Jones, G.I. (1950) *The Ibo and Ibo-Speaking Peoples of Southeastern Nigeria*, Ethnographic Survey of Africa, Part III, London: International African Institute.
(1964) *Yakö Studies*, London: Oxford University Press for the International African Institute.

MICHAEL D. LEVIN

Fortes, Meyer

b. 23 April 1906, Britstown, Cape, South Africa

d. 27 January 1983, Cambridge, UK

Meyer Fortes's childhood was spent in rural South Africa, the eldest son of immigrant Russian Jewish parents. He grew up speaking English, Afrikaans, and Yiddish, and was later to become equally fluent in Talni, the language of the Tallensi. He carried out fieldwork in what was then the Northern Territories of the Gold Coast, accompanied by his first wife, Sonia Donen (d. 1957). From that experience, he produced an ethnographic record unsurpassed in its subtlety and precision of detail. Throughout his life, he drew on Tallensi material both to deepen his understanding of Tallensi society and as an inspiration for wider theoretical concerns. He considered fieldwork to be an 'empirical discipline'; a science in

which it was essential to distinguish between the actor and the observer's point of view.

Fortes is probably known for his study of kinship, and his work on the Tallensi family is exemplary. His model of the development cycle in domestic-family groups, originating in the Tallensi work, is most elaborately presented using material from fieldwork among the Ashanti. The model elegantly combines earlier anthropological concerns with marriage, residence, inheritance, and succession, analysing them as part of a single process and utilising quantitative data. Fortes also suggests that the model enables synchronic observation to help conceptualise diachronic processes.

Fortes's analysis of the patrilineal Tallensi, organised into opposing clans and lineages, was complemented by later fieldwork with the matrilineal, monarchical, Ashanti. Fortes's contribution to basic theory extends well beyond kinship to illuminate politics, ritual, and theories of personhood. He stressed that in all human societies the facts of parentage are balanced by forces that act upon family and individual emanating from the 'total society' or 'the politico-jural domain'. Fortes argued that kinship systems were a consequence of the universal human confrontation with facts of parentage and siblingship, understood in diverse ways in different societies but inevitably tied to social and biological reproduction. Kinship thus cannot be seen to arise from other social, ecological, economic, or even purely biological factors.

With E. Evans-Pritchard, Fortes is responsible for discovering that a genealogical framework may be used as the basis for political organisation in which, though there may be no specialised governmental institutions, large populations are organised for production, reproduction, war, and ritual. This led to subsequent discoveries elsewhere of apparently similar polities. Though in some cases such identifications may have been mistaken, the original insight has been validated by the fieldwork of succeeding generations of anthropologists. The volume, *African Political Systems* (1940), co-edited by Fortes and Evans-

Pritchard with an Introduction mainly written by Fortes, has been an immensely influential text in political anthropology. Towards the end of his life, Fortes returned to more explicitly psychological subjects that earlier were encapsulated in his analyses of kinship. He returned to visit the Tallensi in 1964, with his second wife, the psychiatrist Doris Mayer. His late essays also deal with the religious aspect of personhood. *Oedipus and Job* is a brief but powerful example of Fortes's use of the comparative method in dealing with such matters.

Meyer Fortes was William Wyse professor of social anthropology at the University of Cambridge (1951–73) and professorial fellow of Kings College, later an honorary emeritus fellow until his death. His role as a teacher was of the greatest importance. Under his chairmanship, the department of social anthropology was transformed, and growing numbers of students were profoundly affected by his teaching. Fortes's graduate students went on to hold teaching positions throughout the English-speaking world. Through his participation in the International African Institute he was also influential among Francophone anthropologists working in West Africa. Fortes's teaching style was Socratic and he encouraged a plurality of viewpoints. Though he made his opinions and his analyses clear, he was careful not to impose them on students. His profound curiosity about human behaviour led him to try always to avoid influencing the results of research. That same curiosity was not only a major force in his own career but also an inspiration to students. Meyer Fortes saw social anthropology as a subject of more than academic importance. He considered that anthropological knowledge should be used to undermine prejudice and the mystification of privilege.

Education

BA University of Cape Town, 1925
MA University of Cape Town, 1926
Ph.D. University of London, 1930

Fieldwork

Northern Territories, Gold Coast, 1934–7
Nigeria, 1941–2
Ashanti, Gold Coast, 1943–6
Northern Ghana (Tallensi region), 1964

Key Publications

(1949) *The Web of Kinship among the Tallensi*, London and New York: Published for the International African Institute, Oxford University Press.
(1959) *Oedipus and Job in West African Religion*, Cambridge, UK: Cambridge University Press.
(1970, [1969]) *Kinship and the Social Order: The Legacy of Lewis Henry Morgan*, Chicago: Aldine Pub. Co.
(1970) *Time and Social Structure and Other Essays*, London: Athlone Press; New York: Humanities Press.

SUSAN DRUCKER-BROWN

Fortune, Reo

b. 1903, New Zealand

d. 1979, England

Reo Fortune was one of a cluster of brilliant young anthropologists that emerged in the 1920s and included Margaret Mead, Gregory Bateson, and Ruth Benedict. A New Zealander, son of a reneged Anglican priest, Fortune trained in psychology. Drawn to the work of ethnologist and psychologist, W.H.R. Rivers, he wrote a prize-winning essay on dreaming that took him, in 1926, to study with Rivers's epigone, F.C. Bartlett, in Cambridge. Fortune published his remarkable auto-interpretive study, *The Mind in Sleep*, in 1927. However, by then his attention had shifted to anthropology.

Directed by A.C. Haddon in Cambridge and with funding from A.R. Radcliffe-Brown (then simply Brown) in Sydney, Fortune began fieldwork with Dobuan speakers as well as, with wife Margaret Mead, in the Admiralty Islands. These researches became his classic ethnographies – *Sorcerers of Dobu* and *Manus Religion*. A fellowship at Columbia secured by Boas allowed Fortune to complete *Sorcerers* and work briefly with Mead on an Omaha reservation (cf. *Omaha Secret Societies*, 1932). Further Melanesian fieldwork followed before the two anthropologists separated in 1933. Fortune published one further monograph, *Arapesh*.

Sorcerers partly reinterprets the kula system made famous by Bronislaw Malinowski. However, unlike Trobriand culture, Dobuan life was electrified by the fear of sorcery. Fortune traced this functionally to an extreme emphasis on matrilineal ties and a residence rule whereby partners spent each alternate year with their hated affines. A wonderfully sharp picture of Dobu life emerges with its brittle marriages and omnipresent suspicion. *Manus Religion* is idiosyncratic in approach. Above the lintels of Manus houses were the Sir Ghosts, skulls of the recently departed, supervising in moral judgement. The living were under constant threat from the dead to confess guilty secrets or suffer dire consequences. In showing the everyday playing out of social structures, Fortune perfected a mode of event analysis presaging the work of Gluckman and others.

Fortune was a fine analyst – his 'Note' on cross-cousin marriage foreshadowed structuralism – but he was also a romantic. Mead tells of his youthful ambition to create a new Blakean mythology. In Melanesia, a rumour spread that he was leading an uprising: certainly, he was angrily resistant to colonial intrusion in the anthropologist's business. Later, as a Cambridge don, he became famously eccentric. Fortune was an *aficionado* of mathematics seminars. In one of these he formulated a still unsolved conjecture regarding certain prime numbers known as 'fortunate numbers'.

Education

MA Victoria University College, New Zealand, 1925
Dip.Anth. University of Cambridge, 1927
Ph.D. Columbia University, 1931

Fieldwork

D'Entrecasteaux Islands, Admiralty Islands, 1927–9
Omaha reservation, Nebraska, 1930
Sepik River 1931–3

Key Publications

(1932) *Sorcerers of Dobu*, London: Routledge.
(1934) 'A note on some forms of kinship structure', *Oceania* 4: 1–9.
(1935) *Manus Religion*, Philadelphia: American Philosophical Society.

Further Reading

Gray, Geoffrey (1999) '"Being honest to my science": Reo Fortune and J.H.P. Murray, 1927–30', *The Australian Journal of Anthropology* 10: 56–76.
Mead, M. (1973) *Blackberry Winter*. London: Angus & Robertson.

HUON WARDLE

Foster, George M.

b. 9 October 1913, Sioux Falls, South Dakota, USA

d. 18 May 2006, Berkeley, California, USA

George Foster began his college education at Harvard, planning to follow his father as an engineer. He transferred to Northwestern after a year, but soon realised he did not have an engineer's mind. A friend recommended an introductory course with Melville Herskovits, and there Foster found his profession, and his wife: linguistic anthropologist Mary LeCron was also a student on the course. He began graduate studies at Berkeley immediately after graduating, and studied with Alfred Kroeber and Robert Lowie. Kroeber sent him to salvage memory culture with some elderly Yuki Indians for his first fieldwork.

In 1938 Foster and LeCron were married, and they spent the following ten months in Europe studying German and French; they also unintentionally became participant-observers of the *Anschluss*. In 1940 they left for fieldwork with the Sierra Popoluca in Veracruz, Mexico, where Foster focused on the peasant economy.

After receiving his doctorate Foster taught briefly at Syracuse University and UCLA before being hired by Julian Steward to teach and lead collaborative fieldwork through the National School of Anthropology in Mexico City. From 1944–6 Foster worked in the mestizoised village of Tzintzuntzan, in Michoacan; *Empire's Children* carefully worked through both the history and contemporary culture of that peasant community. The Fosters returned to Tzintzuntzan in 1958, and at least once annually from then into the 1990s. This long-term study with the Tzintzuntzaneños fuelled Foster's understandings of peasant life and contributed to numerous publications. Foster continued his interest in peasant economies and social structure; *Tzintzuntzan* focuses on the image of limited good and dyadic contracts as organising principles of peasant life, and other works emphasise interpersonal relationships and social networks. From this research Foster also developed his understanding of peasant world view, which was and remains controversial in the anthropology of peasant societies, and his characterisation of hot–cold theories of illness. The maintenance of traditional cultures in the face of technological and social change became a major theme as the Fosters observed Tzintzuntzaneños through five decades.

From 1946 until its closure in 1952 Foster directed the Smithsonian Institution's Institute of Social Anthropology (ISA) in Washington, DC. From there he visited a number of Central and South American countries, and reflecting on Herskovits's teachings on acculturation he decided to explore Spanish origins of widespread cultural elements such as the grid-plan town, humoural medicine, and fishing and pottery techniques. Working with Julio Caro Baroja, Foster spent the academic year 1949–50 doing ethnographic research in Spain. This period also spurred Foster's interest in applied anthropology and economic development issues.

The ISA also led to Foster's involvement in medical anthropology, when he and other ISA anthropologists worked with the Institute of Inter-American Affairs to evaluate US public-health programmes in Latin America. Much of the early development of medical anthropology stems from their work, and Foster's knowledge of US technical aid programmes led to a series of consulting assignments with the Agency for International Development in India, Pakistan, Nepal, the Philippines, Afghanistan, and Northern Rhodesia (now Zambia), and later consulting with the World Health Organization.

In 1953 Foster became a professor of anthropology at Berkeley, and he taught there until his retirement in 1979; he remained professionally active into the 1990s. Much of his later work centered on medical anthropology and public health, including both folk and Western medicine, in Tzintzuntzan and elsewhere. In the 1970s Foster began to develop studies of the internal logics of medical systems, and he co-authored the first comprehensive text on medical anthropology with Barbara Gallatin Anderson, published in 1978. In 1975 Foster joined with colleagues at Berkeley and at the University of California, San Francisco to establish the Medical Anthropology Training Program as part of a joint doctoral programme between the two institutions.

Foster served as president of the American Anthropological Association in 1970, during the controversies surrounding anthropological involvement in the war in Vietnam and civil rights issues. He was instrumental in its administrative reorganisation, and played an important part in the acquisition of its new offices. In addition to his contributions to medical and applied anthropology and peasant studies, Foster has written extensively on pottery techniques and the social organisation of potters.

Education

BA Northwestern University, 1935
Ph.D. University of California, Berkeley, 1941

Fieldwork

Round Valley, California (Yuki Indians), 1937
Veracruz, Mexico, 1940–1
Tzintzuntzan, Mexico, 1944–6, 1958–92
Spain, 1949–50
Northern Rhodesia (Zambia), 1962

Key Publications

(1948) *Empire's Children: The People of Tzintzuntzan*,
  Institute of Social Anthropology Publication
  6, Washington, DC: Smithsonian Institution.
(1960) *Culture and Conquest: America's Spanish
  Heritage*, Viking Fund Publications in Anthropology 27, New York: Wenner–Gren Foundation for Anthropological Research.
(1967) *Tzintzuntzan: Mexican Peasants in a Changing
  World*, Boston: Little, Brown & Co.
(1969) *Applied Anthropology*, Boston: Little,
  Brown & Co.

FREDERIC W. GLEACH AND STEPHEN O. MURRAY

Fox, James J.

b. 29 May 1940, Milwaukee, Wisconsin, USA

James J. Fox is an anthropologist who has
distinguished himself by the breadth and
depth of his knowledge of the Austronesian
world, particularly the islands of eastern
Indonesia and more recently Java and Indonesia as a whole. For almost forty years, he has
conducted and supervised research in four
principal areas: historical ecology, ritual
speech, economic development, and comparative Austronesian ethnography. *Harvest of the Palm*
was an innovative historical ethnography of
the islands of Roti and Savu that looked
primarily at transformations in a dryland
economy, but also considered ritual and
symbolic aspects of lontar palm cultivation
and its connection to the colonial past. It set
the stage for a series of studies of the relation
between social organisation and the environment against the background of trade and
shifting forms of political control. His comparative interest in ritual languages was

inspired by the work of Roman Jakobson and
began with the publication of various Rotinese
poetic texts. This led to the publication of *To
Speak in Pairs*, a collection of similarly oriented
essays by researchers interested in ritual speech
throughout Indonesia's eastern islands. There
followed a series of articles about mythology,
ritual performance, paired speech, and social
classification, and several edited volumes of
regional ethnography.

In 1975, he moved to the Australian
National University (ANU) from where began
new research on Timor and later on Java. In
the late 1980s, when he convened the
Comparative Austronesian Project to focus on
Austronesian social and historical diversity, he
began to write about common themes
throughout the region, especially ideas of
origin, ancestry, and alliance, often articulated
around the notion of 'precedence': a ceremonial order of priority that can generate systems
of rank and status. Fox himself defines
precedence as 'a recursive asymmetric relationship that may be constructed by a variety
of means using a number of different
relational categories or operators' ('Precedence
in Practice among the Atoni Pah Meto of
Timor' in Aragon, L. V. and Russel, S. (eds)
*Structuralism's Transformations: Order and Revisions in
Indonesia and Malaysia*, Tucson: Arizona State
University, 1999: 4). These systems can be
articulated through the conventions of language, kinship terminology, ritual, or spatial
practices, and require long-term fieldwork to
be described and documented. Precedence is
reflected in the design of houses and villages,
long narratives filled with ordered place
names, and rituals, which summon the
ancestors as invisible witnesses to current
events. The historical dynamics of precedence
are often controversial, generating different
perspectives on group formation and hierarchy
from different parts of the region.

At the ANU, Fox has supervised the field
research of nearly fifty doctoral students. His
vision of Austronesian diversity has influenced
the work of several generations of Australian-
trained anthropologists (many of them from
Asia, Europe, and the USA) who have studied

these processes in societies ranging from Polynesia to Malaysia.

He has also studied pilgrimage practices and narratives of origin in Java, and has been involved in applied research as a consultant to the Indonesian government and various international development agencies on policies of resource management and the environment, especially pesticide use, the effects of El Niño, rural credit, and forestry. In 1999, he was an international observer for the UN-supervised popular consultation in East Timor and was involved thereafter as a consultant on agriculture, rural development, and security as well as serving as an observer for subsequent elections. In this work, he drew on his long-term knowledge of the languages, history, and ecology of the entire island and cultural continuities that have survived despite its political division into two parts.

Fox's own research goes beyond anthropology to engage debates in the fields of linguistics, political economy, biology, geography, history, and Southeast Asian literature and oral poetics. He has defined himself as a regional scholar of international importance, who has reshaped our views of the ways in which parts of the Austronesian world are connected to each other. Committed to field research in remote villages, he has also spelled out the national and regional implications of these forms of connections, and the ways in which they are implicated in the birth of Timor Loro Sa'e, Southeast Asia's newest nation.

Education

AB Harvard University, 1962
B.Litt. University of Oxford, 1965
D.Phil. University of Oxford, 1968, Rhodes scholar

Fieldwork

Roti, 1965–6, 1973–4, intermittently since 1975
Timor, 1981–5, 1998–2002
East Java, intermittently since 1981
Jakarta, intermittently since 1975

National development projects throughout Indonesia on agriculture, rural development, resource management, climate change, from 1982 ongoing

Key Publications

(1977) Harvest of the Palm: Ecological Change in Eastern Indonesia, Cambridge, MA: Harvard University Press.
(ed.) (1988) To Speak in Pairs: Essays on the Ritual Languages of Eastern Indonesia, Cambridge and New York: Cambridge University Press.
with Sather, Clifford (eds) (1996) Origins, Ancestry and Alliance: Explorations in Austronesian Ethnography, Canberra: Department of Anthropology, Australian National University.
with Babo Soares, Dionisio (eds) (2000) Out of the Ashes: Destruction and Reconstruction of East Timor, Adelaide: Crawford House; London: C. Hurst & Co.

JANET HOSKINS

Fox, Richard Gabriel

3 March 1939, New York Ciry, USA

In early career statements that prefigured the direction of much of his work through the 1990s, Richard G. Fox contended that the analysis of a complex society such as India needed greater historical depth and more attention to extra-local structures than that provided by then-typical village or community studies. His first book was a study of a small Indian market town, showing the increasing importance of regional influences as local overlords who regulated intercaste interaction, markets, and ritual expression disappeared, and the town was integrated into a new regime of electoral politics. Entering discussions of urban classification, he proposed a new type, the 'post-colonial' city, which could be added to then-proposed pre-industrial and industrial categories.

He next produced an historical analysis of the interaction of certain powerful lineages with the state in northern India. He used his material, along with comparative data, to show how kin-based polities could develop into non-kin-based states, thereby complicating the distinction that had been made between the two. Although Fox demonstrated that Indian political structures could be compared to those of other societies, he also argued that they had unique qualities based on attributional or ideological aspects of kinship that underwrote regional and even state political structures. Here he made reference to culture, which would later become a central theme of his work.

Continuing his interest in cities, Fox entered the emerging field of urban anthropology in the 1970s, writing one of the first textbooks on the subject. A widely read review article claimed that anthropologists had been more occupied with the city as a location for study than as an object of analysis. He criticised anthropologists for focusing on exotic sub-groups instead of the urban community as a whole and its relation to the larger society.

Fox's attention to culture was amplified in a 1980s historical project. He argued that the character of agrarian protest in the Punjab region of India in the early twentieth century had been greatly influenced by British construction of a martial identity for Sikhs. The British strategy was based on their own conceptions of race, but came to influence the Sikh self-understanding. Thus, he challenged other anthropologists' portrayal of timeless Indian conceptions of the person. He also questioned holistic, deterministic theories of culture, whether idealist or materialist, contending instead that culture is continually being remade in interactions between groups, which take place against a background of social inequality.

A concern with cultural processes was continued in the late 1980s and 1990s in work focused on the vision of an ideal Indian society associated with Mohandas Gandhi. Fox showed the development of this cultural complex by Gandhi out of both Indian and Western ideas, and discussed how it was taken over or adapted by his followers, by Hindu nationalists, and, in part, by American activists. In these writings, Fox saw culture as a complex phenomenon that could be disarti-

culated into distinct ideas and practices, and then reworked, not without struggle, by individuals or groups. He viewed his work on 'Gandhian utopia' as one example of a kind of analysis he called 'culture history'. Arguing that problems with ethnography could not be solved by new strategies of ethnographic writing, he proposed that culture history could be one appropriate remedy.

In the early part of the twenty-first century, Fox is working on a study of what he calls the 'politics of authenticity' in the West. He is looking at the way in which the idea of authenticity has moved from a focus on personal sincerity to a concern with group identity, and the part the culture concept has played in this transformation.

Fox has been the editor or co-editor of many collections of articles by himself and others. Topics of these volumes have included urban India, nationalism and national cultures, strategies for coping with the 1980s culture crisis in anthropology, and anthropological comparison.

He was editor of *American Ethnologist* from 1976–9 and of *Current Anthropology* from 1993–2000. In 2000, he became president of the Wenner–Gren Foundation for Anthropological Research.

Education

AB Columbia University, 1960
MA University of Michigan, 1961
Ph.D. University of Michigan, 1965

Fieldwork

Uttar Pradesh, India, 1963–4
Archival research: India Office Library, India, 1968
Archival research: Scottish Records Office, Edinburgh, 1975
Delhi and Punjab, India, 1980, 1981
Archival research: Delhi and other locations, India, 1988

Key Publications

(1969) *From Zamindar to Ballot Box: Community*

Change in a North Indian Market Town, Ithaca, NY: Cornell University Press.

(1971) *Kin, Clan, Raja, and Rule: State–Hinterland Relations in Pre-Industrial India*, Berkeley: University of California Press.

(1985) *Lions of the Punjab: Culture in the Making*, Berkeley: University of California Press.

(1989) *Gandhian Utopia: Experiments with Culture*, Boston: Beacon Press.

MARGARET MEIBOHM

Frankenberg, Ronald J.

b. October 1929, London, UK

Trained by Max Gluckman at Manchester, Ronald Frankenberg did his early ethnographic research on a village in North Wales struggling with industrialism, which has become a classic in the field of community studies. He is however best known for his work in medical anthropology in which he has played an important role since the mid-1960s. Particularly his theoretical contributions made him one of the leading proponents in critical medical anthropology that emerged in the late 1970s. Drawing on Marxist theory Frankenberg emphasised the importance of political and economic structures and power relations in the production of sickness and the management of healing. His concern with the body since the mid-1980s led him to complement his critical approach with a more phenomenological one and to understand sickness as cultural performance. Frankenberg has published on a wide range of topics amongst which are AIDS/HIV, temporality in biomedical practice, risk and epidemiology, illness narratives, and the life cycle.

Frankenberg's importance to medical anthropology is also due to his teaching. He has trained several generations of medical anthropologists since 1985 at Keele University, England, and since 1989 at Brunel University in West London and has been one of the key figures in establishing medical anthropology at an institutional level in the UK.

Education

BA University of Cambridge, 1950
MA University of Manchester, 1952
Ph.D. University of Manchester, 1954
D.Soc.Sci Brunel University, 1999

Fieldwork

North and South Wales, UK, 1953, 1954–6
Lusaka, Zambia, 1966–8
Tarvarnelle val di Pesa, Italy, 1983–4

Key Publications

(1957) *Village on the Border*, London: Cohen & West.

(1980) 'Medical anthropology and development: a theoretical perspective', *Social Science and Medicine*, 14B: 197–207.

BERNHARD HADOLT

Franklin, Sarah

b. 9 November 1960, Cambridge, Massachusetts, USA

Sarah Franklin's work is framed by a critical engagement with anthropological approaches towards understanding the constitution of life, the 'biological', 'nature', and relatedness. She focuses on conception and procreation as mediated by 'new' reproductive and genetic technologies, most particularly assisted conception and, more recently, cloning, in her research on Dolly, the first sheep to be cloned in the UK. Her approach combines cultural studies and critical theory perspectives on the cultural with anthropological ones, especially in her analysis of public, popular, and visual culture. Regionally, her main interest has been 'British' notions of the 'biological', because of long-standing British involvement in 'tinkering' with the 'facts of life'. Three themes underlie Franklin's work: the relation (or kinship) as key; calling anthropology to account by using other disciplines (especially feminist cultural studies and post-structuralist theory) to challenge its assumptions; and a conviction that genetic and procreative technologies, and the 'science' that goes with them, are an ideal field through which to investigate power-mediated and culturally mediated constitution of life and relatedness. This latter is on the grounds that science, broadly understood, constitutes a key domain through which public culture (again broadly understood) is being (re)constituted; and a focus on New Reproductive Technologies and genetic technologies allow an investigation of relatedness in that context. One outcome of that approach is an implied shift of anthropological attention from the comparative/contrastive project between 'cultures' to a comparative/contrastive project of 'the cultural'.

Sarah Franklin was awarded a personal chair in the anthropology of science in 2001, the first such professorship in Britain.

Education

BA Smith College, 1982
MA New York University, 1986
Ph.D. University of Birmingham, 1992

Fieldwork

West Midlands, UK, 1988–9

Key Publications

(1997) Embodied Progress: A Cultural Account of Assisted Conception, London, New York: Routledge.
with Lury, C. and Stacey, J. (eds) (2000) Global Nature. Global Culture, London: Sage.

SARAH GREEN

Frazer, James George

b. 1 January 1854, Glasgow, UK

d. 8 May 1941, Cambridge, UK

The success of the several editions of The Golden Bough made J.G. Frazer the best-known exponent in English of the kind of belletristic, comparativist, and evolutionist anthropology that was widespread in Europe before the First World War. Frazer was primarily an epistemologist: taken together, the body of his anthropological work constitutes an immense effort, based on a study of mythology and ritual from all over the world and over the course of several millennia, to produce a comparative, evolutionary anatomy of the human mind. Employing mainly classical references and the comparative ethnographic information that was an incidental by-product of the nineteenth-century imperialist rush for colonies, Frazer delineated the several stages of the pre-modern 'myth-making mind'. He was regarded as a major thinker in Britain through the 1920s, and the suggestive metaphors in his work influenced writers, artists, and literary critics throughout the first half of the twentieth century. In the English-speaking world, his kind of evolutionist library anthropology was superseded by structural functionalism and the introduction of fieldwork.

Son of a pious, middle-class Free Church of Scotland family, J.G. Frazer took his first degree at the University of Glasgow. He then studied classics at Trinity College, Cambridge, where in 1878 on the strength of an excellent result in his final examinations and a dissertation on Plato, he was awarded a fellowship. Frazer then began work on an edition of the second-century AD traveller Pausanias, whose guidebook to ancient Greece remains the best surviving description of that country before it was ravaged by earthquake and conquest. At Trinity he met and befriended William Robertson Smith (1846–94), the Scottish theologian and sociologist of Semitic religion, who had been driven into 'exile' in England as a result of the controversy surrounding his advocacy of German biblical 'higher criticism'. Smith, the editor of the ninth edition of the Encyclopaedia Britannica and as such always looking for new contributors, assigned Frazer the articles on 'Taboo' and 'Totemism'. Once initiated into anthropology, Frazer never looked back. He continued as well to work on classics, but only on subjects within that field which permitted him to employ an anthropological approach.

The importance of Frazer's best-known work, *The Golden Bough*, derives from its context. It had been an article of cultural faith in the West since the Renaissance that the remarkable intellectual and artistic achievements of the Greeks and Romans were evidence that they somehow did not participate in the general barbarism of antiquity. Frazer, however, emphasised the 'primitive' elements in ancient Greece and Rome, explicitly likening them to the beliefs and behaviour of contemporary peasants and the tribal peoples whom he (and his contemporaries) called 'savages'. This dethronement of the Greeks and Romans came as a shock to his readers, who had been brought up believing that classical antiquity was somehow 'above' such backwardness and cruelty.

Frazer is perhaps most closely associated with the idea, enunciated in the second edition of *The Golden Bough*, that the human mind had evolved through three distinct stages – in the first, characterised by what he called magic, the priest commanded the gods to do his bidding; in the second, which he called religion, the priest saw the futility of his former course of action and now beseeched rather than commanded the gods; and finally, in the third, educated persons came to understand that they no longer needed priests, or indeed anything supernatural, to understand the wholly natural workings of the world; reason, in its highest form, science, would suffice. This schema, reminiscent of the positivism of the French sociologist, Auguste Comte, was criticised even by Frazer's own contemporaries as arbitrary and rigid, and today has no adherents whatever.

Frazer's covert agenda was secularist. Much of *The Golden Bough* is devoted to an analysis of the religions of the ancient eastern Mediterranean. Although the reader learns a great deal about Attis, Adonis, Osiris, and Dionysus, vegetation deities who die in the springtime and are resurrected, not a word is said about the missing member of the set, Jesus. Frazer

leaves it to the reader to conclude that the cult of Jesus is just as much a dead letter as those of the gods he does discuss.

Education

MA University of Glasgow, 1874
BA University of Cambridge, 1878

Key Publications

(1890) *The Golden Bough*, 2 vols, London: Macmillan; second edn, 3 vols, 1900; third edn, 12 vols, 1911–15; 1-vol. abridged edn, 1922.
(1898) *Pausanias's Description of Greece*, 6 vols, London: Macmillan.
(1918) *Folk-Lore in the Old Testament*, 3 vols, London: Macmillan.

Further Reading

Ackerman, R. (1987) *J.G. Frazer: His Life and Work*, Cambridge, UK: Cambridge University Press.

ROBERT ACKERMAN

Freeman, Derek J.

b. 1916, Wellington, New Zealand

d. 2001, Canberra, Australia

Derek Freeman is best known for his extended critique on Margaret Mead's representation of Samoa and the Boasian doctrine that culture alone determines behaviour. That work was one of several significant contributions to anthropological knowledge in the areas of culture theory, social organisation, and ethnographic methodology, based on fieldwork in Southeast Asia and Oceania.

A New Zealander, Freeman studied there with Ernest Beaglehole and then went to Samoa for over three years where he developed fluency in the Samoan language and received the chiefly title, *Logana-i-Taga* ('Heard at the Tree Felling'), which was a source of pride all his life. After wartime service, study of Samoa materials at archives in London led to a postgraduate thesis on Samoan social structure under Raymond Firth, more intensive fieldwork and an invitation from Meyer Fortes to write up Iban material at Cambridge. Freeman joined the Australian National University with S.F. Nadel in 1955 and held residence there for life.

The Iban in Borneo presented the interesting problem of social integration at the level of the bilateral family rather than clan or lineage. Freeman's excellent field data showed the bilek family groups resulted from options in the property system. It was a first analysis demonstrating how optative principles of group filiation (based on choice) could result in relatively permanent corporate groups and was a major influence on the theory of cognatic social systems. Study of Iban settlement and agriculture showed that rather than maintaining functional equilibrium, this kin-based society was expansionary as groups moved 'swidden by swidden' across the Borneo rainforest.

In Mead's classic portrayal, Samoa featured unrestrained sexuality and a lack of torment and aggression often associated with adolescence; therefore behaviour was defined by cultural not biological factors. Using methods drawn from K. Popper, Freeman adduced data to show female virginity was a high moral value, assault, violence, and distress were common, and many Samoans thought Mead's portrayal of their culture was very wrong. The results were highly controversial and received harsh anthropological response since these findings challenged a central doctrine of cultural anthropology as well as one of its heroic figures. In response, there were testimonials from Samoan women who said that as girls they misled Mead by recreational lying. Freeman argued that the ethnographic basis for absolute cultural determinism is invalid and theory of culture must see interaction with biology and environment as the context for human choice.

Education

BA Victoria University College, 1937
Academic Postgraduate Diploma, University of London, 1948
Ph.D. University of Cambridge, 1953

Fieldwork

Samoa, 1940–3, 1946, 1965–8, 1981, 1987
Sarawak, 1949–51, 1957–8, 1976
Northwestern Australia, 1974

Key Publications

(1955) *Iban Agriculture*, London: HMSO.
(1970) *Report on the Iban*, London: Athlone.
(1983) *Margaret Mead and Samoa: The Making and Unmaking of an Anthropological Myth*, Cambridge, MA: Harvard.
(1999) *The Fateful Hoaxing of Margaret Mead: Historical Analysis of Her Samoan Researches*, Boulder, CA: Westview.

R. CHRISTOPHER MORGAN

Fried, Morton H.

b. 21 March 1923, New York, New York, USA

d. 18 December 1987, Leonia, New Jersey, USA

Morton H. Fried was a prominent member of the cohort that entered (or re-entered) the Columbia University anthropology department as graduate students just after the Second World War. Members of this group (including S. Diamond, R. Manners, S. Mintz, E. Service, and E. Wolf) had grown up during the Depression, many were ex-GIs, and most joined the post-Boas Columbia department looking for a positivistic social science. Julian H. Steward began teaching there at the same time, and Fried was one of those students who was deeply impressed by his (and Leslie White's) materialism and neo-evolutionism. These perspectives, plus a non-doctrinaire interest in certain problems that engaged Marx and Engels, consistently informed his work.

Morton Fried studied the Chinese language during the war, and Chinese culture and history became his speciality. His dissertation fieldwork in east central China, completed just as the communists took control of the country, was guided by his interest in the evolution of political behaviour and institutions. Applying the community study method, with due concern for the significance of kinship in Chinese society, Fried set out to study 'the points at which kin-based action is superseded by non-kin and then by civil action' (1953: 231) in a complex society. In addition to kinship he wrote of a variety of non-kin forces and relationships, including class distinctions and behaviour, and rural–urban linkages.

The problem of 'the evolution of political society' concerned him throughout his career, and culminated in his book by that title (1967), long a staple of reading lists in political anthropology. He adopted the challenge of Rousseau, and of Morgan and Engels, as to how it happened that societies went from egalitarian and kin-based to stratified, with classes and rulers in states. In his view, the key to the evolution from egalitarian, through ranked, to stratified societies, was the development of differential wealth and power in agrarian economies.

Fried insisted that warfare could not have played a role before the establishment of states, and this concern was at the heart of his problem with 'the notion of tribe'.

He rejected the idea of tribes as 'the most ancient forms of human society' (1975: i), but saw them as secondary formations, as products of states and colonialism. This view has influenced some current writing about tribes and warfare.

Morton Fried taught at Columbia from 1950 until his death in 1986. He took teaching seriously and produced two collections of readings and an introductory work for students. He was an amiable and witty lecturer whose considerable learning was borne lightly.

Education

BS City College, New York, 1942
Ph.D. Columbia University, 1951

Fieldwork

Anhwei, China 1947–8
Taiwan, 1963–4, 1964–5

Key Publications

(1953) *The Fabric of Chinese Society*, New York: Praeger.
(1957) 'The classification of corporate unilineal descent groups', *Journal of the Royal Anthropological Institute* 75: 1–27.
(1967) *The Evolution of Political Society*, New York: Random House.
(1975) *The Notion of Tribe*, Menlo Park, CA: Cummings Publishing.

HERBERT S. LEWIS

Friedl, Ernestine

b. 13 August 1920, Hungary

Initially carrying out fieldwork among the Pomo in California and the Wisconsin Chippewa, Ernestine Friedl since 1955 has focused her attention on Greek society. Among the first anthropologists to conduct fieldwork in postwar Greece, Friedl commenced with a study of the central Greek village, Vasilika, whose clarity and accessibility made it an ethnographic classic. With an astute eye for the telling anecdote, Friedl delineated the distinctive values of this peasant community while also tracing out the swiftly developing urban–rural links. In subsequent fieldwork she moved to Athens, considering how practices of dowry and inheritance were adapted as sons and daughters migrated to the cities and pursued family goals in new urban contexts. Gender relations are an enduring theme in Friedl's work, both within her Greek ethnography and at a more general, comparative level. Her prescient call in 1967 for a reconceptualisation of power relations between men and women in European peasant households triggered a far-reaching debate among Europeanists, and anticipated the broader debate in feminist anthropological work. Apart from published work, Friedl influenced generations of students through her teaching at six universities, most notably at Queens College, Duke University, and Princeton University. Friedl also provided leadership at myriad levels of anthropological activity and academic administration: among many positions, she was departmental chair at Queens (1960–9) and Duke (1973–8), dean of arts and sciences at Duke (1980–5), and served as president of both the American Ethnological Society (1967) and the American Anthropological Association (1974–5).

Education

BA Hunter College, 1941
Ph.D. Columbia University, 1950

Fieldwork

Pomo Indians of California, summer 1941
Chippewa Indians of Wisconsin, summers 1942, 1943
'Vasilika', central Greece, 1955–6, May 1976
Urban Greece, summers 1964–7

Key Publications

(1962) *Vasilika: A Village in Modern Greece*, New York: Holt, Rhinehart & Winston.
(1975) *Women and Men: An Anthropologist's View*, New York: Holt, Rhinehart & Winston.

JANE K. COWAN

Friedman, Jonathan Ames

b. 1946, New York, USA

Jonathan Friedman is one of the world's foremost theoretical anthropologists. His contributions are discussed in roughly chronological order. Certain anthropologists in the 1940s and 1950s laboured to reinvent an ecological and evolutionary cultural anthropology. Marvin Harris in the 1960s synthesised their thought into a theory he termed cultural materialism. Harris's was an explicitly non-Marxist materialism. Friedman's first foray into theoretical debates – while still a student, and of Harris at that – was a critique of cultural materialism. He compared Harris's work with the structural Marxism then current in France, demonstrating that Harris couldn't explain phenomena that could be accounted for by structural Marxism, in part because cultural materialism's assumption that human structures were adapted to make optimal use of their techno-environments was questionable.

Friedman's second contribution challenged social anthropology, which had made a theoretical living imagining society as a harmoniously integrated system in equilibrium. However, Edmund Leach reported that Kachin society in Burma alternated between *gumsa*, more hierarchical, and *gumlao*, more egalitarian, forms. This offered counterfactual evidence to the social anthropological insistence upon society as one structure in equilibrium. However, Leach simply described what occurred. Friedman theorised why, by proposing a structural Marxist model that explained Burmese historical transformations. This model viewed *gumsa* and *gumlao* organisations as structural variations in a system of systems of related social structures. The theory had components that accounted for the structural variations, explained the limiting conditions on these variations, and explicated the implications of the limiting conditions for the dynamics of the various structural variations.

At the end of the 1970s Friedman began to develop a global systems theory. This work flourished and led to a third theoretical contribution, a series of articles that elucidated the present global system in terms of a 3,000-year-old civilisational cycle of expansion and contraction. This work, influenced by the historian, Braudel, emphasised related processes of capital growth and decline. Friedman has applied global systems theory since the 1990s to the contemporary period of 'globalisation'.

His work has been especially influential explaining the relationship between different forms of identity and violence in the different horizontal and vertical places of global systems. This is Friedman's fourth, and arguably most timely, contribution to theory. Currently, there are numerous globalisation theories, many of them shamelessly shilling for neo-liberal Utopia. Friedman offers another account. Here, at the same time, cycles of accumulation, and the rise of hegemony, are equally cycles of decentralisation, and the fall of hegemony, in global systems that produce and reproduce the scarce hands of wealth and elite identity as well as the abundant ones of poverty and fragmented identity.

Education

BA Columbia College, 1967
Licence, Sorbonne, 1968
Ph.D. Columbia University, 1972

Fieldwork

Madagascar, 1973
Central Africa, 1974; 1990
Hawaii, 24 months between 1979 and 1990
Sweden, 1993–4

Key Publications

(1994) *Cultural Identity and Global Processes*, London: Sage.
(1998) *System, Structure, and Contradiction*, Walnut Creek, CA: Altamira.
(ed.) (2003) *Globalization, the State, and Violence*, Walnut Creek, CA: Altamira.

STEPHEN P. REYNA

Friedrich, Paul

22 October 1927, Cambridge, Massachusetts, USA

Paul Friedrich is best known for his rigorously sustained theoretical perspective on human language, applying it to disparate regions of culture where many anthropologists fear to tread, including classical myth and poetry, intuitions, dreams, and everyday dialogue. Long-term immersion in multiple dimensions of culture, including the hallowed interiors of intellectual life as well as everyday grit, characterises Friedrich's theoretical orientation. His own work spans research in historical linguistics, comparative poetics, Greek myth, Russian music, poetry, and American philosophy. Fieldwork in Mexico between 1953 and 1970 produced technical publications on Tarascan syntax and semantics, his classic political study of agrarian revolt, and later a methodological treatment of fieldwork in the *Princes of Naranja*. As a poet he has produced what some call 'samizdat' poetry.

Friedrich earned a reputation as an early and trenchant critic of the assumption that human use of symbols is 'arbitrary', an idea that he argued has had a debilitating and pernicious effect upon general theory ('The Lexical Symbol and its Relative Non-Arbitrariness', 1975). He argued that its application to the study of language use only conceals the objectively systematic character of symbols, and inhibits examination of the subjective intuition of users. These two perspectives, objective and analytical systematicity and human intuitive subjectivity, have underpinned all of Friedrich's work on language, culture, and the imagination. While drawing upon ideas like 'psychological reality' of language, as Edward Sapir expressed it, Friedrich rejects the rigid structuralist implication of semiotics as an iron cage of limits, while acknowledging the responsive, formative social nature of symbolic interaction. Friedrich's examination of language use draws upon the individual's process of evaluating degrees of conviction and intensity. One example is what Friedrich and Attinasi eventually labeled 'dialogic breakthrough', based in part upon Friedrich's previous work on Russian pronominal usage and the emotional pregnancy and significance of shift from, say, a formal pronoun to an intimate familiar one.

Friedrich characterises his twin approach to cultural linguistics as 'analytic-scientific' on one side and 'emotional-ethical' on the other.

He argues that the best quantitative science shares with humanistic approaches emotional and ethical inspiration, not only at the level of discovery, but also at every critical margin for understanding and insight. He argues that methodological exclusion of the study of 'unique individual' events or persons stems from a 'spurious scientism'. At the same time, and unlike many of the post-modern theorists he critically anticipated, Friedrich's work affirms the analytical 'drive to know and understand' through empirical and logical values, not just ideological values. Indeed, logic, in the philosophical sense of organising permutations of categories and combinations, including natural chaos, is a distinctive stamp of Friedrich's method.

Friedrich describes language as 'the verbal process by which the individual relates ideas and emotions to sound and other material symbolism in terms of a code and in the context of a society and its culture, and their respective, interrelated histories' (1989: 302), a definition that significantly reorients the traditional focus of linguists by regarding emotion as a parallel to ideas in human communication of meaning, and by emphasising material objectivity of language in manifestations of sound and text. Friedrich's conception of meaning rests upon the accumulation of countless elements from the mechanics of sound at play in a certain tone of voice, to qualities of music, and the rules, categories, and patterns in a language community within its particular tradition of genres, heroes, and revolutions. The unruly creativity of the individual language user takes center stage in Friedrich's studies, including life histories of warring 'princes' (1986), poetic influences of lyric poets (1997), and transformations of the rules of the twentieth-century American sonnet (1986: 84–104).

The body of Friedrich's work makes a major contribution to the reformulation of linguistic relativism. He holds that the major influence of language on thought is through the more poetic dimensions of its process. His theoretical treatment in 'Polytropy' (1991) most thoroughly maps the workings of figurative speech from the most microscopic attention to the 'firstness' (drawing on C.S. Peirce) of a word like 'red', to the finely splintered layers of metonymy, to the global qualities of irony and tragedy. Seeking to meet the intuition that theory must be able to treat socially and politically relevant events of language, including all types of chauvinism, patriotism, and discrimination, Friedrich treats power, compassion, and desperation as irreducible and complementary significances in human symbolic interaction.

Education

BA Harvard College, 1951
MA Harvard University, 1951
Ph.D. Yale University, 1957

Fieldwork

Russian refugees in Germany, 1949
Mexico, Tarascan, 1955–6, 1966–8, 1970
Malayalam, Kerala, India 1958–9

Key Publications

(1979) *Language, Context and the Imagination*, Stanford, CA: Stanford University Press.
(1986) *The Language Parallax: Linguistics, Relativism and Poetic Creativity*, Austin, TA: University of Texas Press.
(1989) 'Language, ideology and political economy', *American Anthropologist* 91: 295–309.
(1997) *Music in Russian Poetry*, New York: Peter Lang.

MARY SCOGGIN

Frobenius, Leo

b. 1873, Berlin, Germany

d. 1938, Biganzolo, Italy

As a self-taught eccentric, Leo Viktor Karl August Frobenius found it hard all his life to achieve recognition in the academic world, even though his work belongs to the greatest achievements of German-language anthropology. Starting his research in anthropological museums and Africanist libraries, he came under the influence of Friedrich Ratzel (1844–1904) and Heinrich Schurtz (1863–1903). The universities of Basel and Freiburg rejected his first genial essay, 'Der Ursprung der afrikanischen Kulturen' [The Origin of African Cultures] (1898), as insolid speculation. In 1904 Frobenius's empirical phase began with the lavish 'Deutsche Innerafrikanische Expeditionen' (DIAFE) [German Expeditions to the Interior of Africa]. He became acquainted with the Congo and Kasai, western Sudan, the Maghreb, Nigeria and Cameroon, Kordofan, the Sahara and the Red Sea, until the First World War caused an interruption in his fieldwork that also altered his own concept of culture. He defined this 'break of 1914' in the booklet called *Paideuma* in 1921, in which, partly following the model of Oswald Spengler (1880–1936), he sketched out an interpretation of the life cycle of all cultures, though going beyond Spengler in dealing especially with non-literate cultures. In the course of his fieldwork expeditions of the 1920s and 1930s, instead of collecting folk stories – in which, following Johann Gottfried Herder (1744–1803), he believed he could recognise the spirits of different peoples – he increasingly recorded rock paintings, in which he saw forms of expression from an early period that already held the key to all fundamental human ideas. Starting in 1936, this unique collection of hand-drawn copies of rock paintings was displayed as 'Reichsbildergallerie' in exhibitions at home and abroad.

Frobenius's world view, which he saw as receiving confirmation on his many voyages as well as in his studies of mainly old sources, and which he presented in popular books for a wide circle of readers, belonged to the tradition of German mysticism and romanticism. Behind the world of facts was concealed a world of reality and effectiveness in which play, purposelessness, but above all fate prevailed. At the beginning of every cultural creation stands the puzzle of death, which

human society overcomes by imitating nature, through a religious mimesis first of animals (hunter-gatherers), then plants (agriculturists), and finally heavenly bodies (states). With his enthusiasm for the determination of discipline and order by culture and fate (*paideuma*), Frobenius, the academic outsider, was welcome in the circle of the abdicated Kaiser Wilhelm II in the Dutch town of Doorn. In 1925, the mythologists Walter F. Otto and Karl Reinhardt secured the transfer of Frobenius's bankrupt private institute from Munich to Frankfurt am Main, thus providing the third tendency in German anthropology (after the culture-historical and ethno-sociological schools) with a local base. In 1934, Frobenius took over the Museum of Anthropology in Frankfurt and turned his 'Research Institute for Cultural Morphology' into the intellectual focus of an exoticism that was as expressionistic as it was conservative. The German Association for Cultural Morphology and the journal, *Paideuma*, were both founded in 1938, the year of his death, and remained dedicated to his ideas until 1965, when his key follower and successor, Adolf Ellegard Jensen, died. Thereafter, Frobenius, who had already been enthusiastically received by the African intellectual *Négritude* movement in the 1930s, seemingly became important again in postcolonial Africa, and his ideas on the anthropology of art and stylistics, his notions of form, form languages, and mimesis, or his three stages in the culture drama from emotion to expression and repetition or application, are still capable of inspiring today.

Education

Autodidact without formal qualifications.

Fieldwork

Kongo-Kasai, 1904–6
West Sudan, 1907–9
Northwest Africa, 1910
Nigeria, North Cameroon, 1910–12
Kordofan, 1912

Morocco and Algeria, 1912–14
Northern Erythräa 1915
Nubian Desert, 1926
South Africa/India, 1928–30
Tripolitania, Fezzan, 1932
Libyan Desert, 1933
North Africa, 1934–5

Key Publications

(1921) *Paideuma. Umrisse einer Kultur- und Seelenlehre* (Paideuma. Outlines of a Culture and Soul Theory), Munich: C.H. Beck.

(1921–8) *Atlantis: Volksmärchen und Volksdichtungen Afrikas* (Atlantis: Folk Tales and Folk Poetry of Africa), 12 vols, Jena: Eugen Diederichs.

(1925–9) *Erlebte Erdteile* (Experienced Continents), 7 vols, Frankfurt/M.: Frankfurter Societätsdruckerei.

(1933) *Kulturgeschichte Afrikas: Prolegomena zu einer historischen Gestaltlehre* (Culture History of Africa: Prolegomena to a Historical Morphology), Zurich: Phaidon.

BERNHARD STRECK

Frykman, Jonas

b. 1942, Nässjö, Sweden

A prominent member of the 'Lund School' of European ethnology, which is rightly credited with having turned Swedish ethnology into an analytical, comparative discipline, Nils Jonas Daniel Frykman has written extensively, mostly in Swedish, on a wide variety of issues pertaining to contemporary Sweden and transitions to modernity. His early work on prostitution in peasant society, and his historical work on bodies and discipline in *Den kultiverade människan* (1979, with Orvar Löfgren), later gave way to studies of contemporary society, but Frykman retained an interest in the body and its relationship to society, which has led to a series of excellent studies, some of them pioneering, of sports, dance, gymnastics, breast-feeding, hygiene, masculine ideals, and other fields suitable for an investigation of the cultural and social significance of the body.

Highlighting the political and symbolic significance of bodies, Frykman's work argues that the social transitions of twentieth-century Sweden, whereby a semi-feudal, largely rural society was transformed into a gleaming, rationally organised, hygienic, and efficient welfare state, were largely framed as struggles over the control of citizens' bodies. The dual concern with the state's quest for control and the individual's quest for autonomy, mediated through the body as the seat of contention, gives Frykman's work an unusual coherence.

Education

BA University of Lund, 1968
Ph.D. University of Lund, 1977

Fieldwork

Blekinge, Sweden, 1967–8
Skåne, Sweden, 1968–9
Istria, Croatia, 1999–

Key Publications

with Löfgren, Orvar (1987) *Culture Builders: A Historical Anthropology of Middle-Class Life*, New Brunswick: Rutgers University Press (Swedish edition 1979).

(1998) *Ljusnande framtid: Skola, social mobilitet och kulturell identitet* (Bright Future: School, Social Mobility and Cultural Identity), Lund: Historiska Media.

THOMAS HYLLAND ERIKSEN

Fuente, Julio de la

b. 1903, Yanga, Veracruz, Mexico

d. 1970, Mexico City, Mexico

Although Julio de la Fuente was a pioneer of Mexican anthropology his early training was as a graphic artist. He later studied with George Murdock at Yale and with Robert Redfield and Sol Tax in Chicago. He saw anthropology in

Mexico as part of a wider struggle for a more just society. Combining this commitment with a devotion to research he was impatient with dogma and facile solutions to complex problems. His most intensive fieldwork was in a Zapotec village but he had a wide experience of many other indigenous regions. His monograph on the Highland Zapotec is a classic ethnography. He worked with Bronislaw Malinowski on a seminal study of Oaxaca markets that revealed the regional interdependence of communities linked by market activities. This discovery influenced development policies in Indian regions. His later published work concentrates on interethnic relations including those resulting from USA–Mexican contacts on Mexico's northern border ('*la cultura pocha*'). He was among the earliest teachers of anthropology at university both at the National Polytechnic Institute, and at the National School of Anthropology and History. He was engaged in setting up the first centers for regional development in Indigenous areas, acting as director in the Mesquital Valley and Highland Chiapas. He drew from among his students many of the administrative personnel and researchers who followed him into the expanding number of such centers. He was director of research in the National Indianist Institute (INI) for many years, and a consultant director until his death.

Education

National University of Mexico, Mexico City, 1923–6
National School of Anthropology and History (1939–40)
University of Yale, 1941
Chicago University, 1944

Fieldwork

Oaxaca market system 1939–40
Sierra de Juarez, 1937– (ongoing)
Chiapas, 1950– (ongoing)
As Director of Research in the Instituto Nacional Indigenista Julio de la Fuente was involved in ongoing fieldwork in all those

parts of Mexico where the INI maintained community development centers (Centros Coordinadores).

Key Publications

(1949) *Yalalag; una villa zapoteca serrana*, (*Yalag: A mountain Zapotec village*) Museo Nacional de Antropologia, Mexico: DF.
(1965) *Relaciones interetnicas*, Instituto Nacional Indigenista, Mexico: DF (Interethnic Relations).

SUSAN DRUCKER-BROWN

Fukui, Katsuyoshi

b. 1943, Shimane, Japan

Fukui started his fieldwork in the late 1960s in a small mountain village in Japan. He studied shifting cultivation, focusing on the indigenous knowledge of farmers.

In the early 1970s, he spent almost two years amongst the Bodi, Surmic agro-pastoralists in southwestern Ethiopia. His investigation revealed that a classification system of cattle coat colors not only played an important role in their culture, but also coat colors themselves had been diversified through people's careful selection. He also showed that the selection was based on their knowledge of coat color heredity, which had been accumulated for generations. This fieldwork also led him to consider interethnic relationships. He was interested in the ethnic warfare that characterised nomadic societies of this area and investigated this topic through the fieldwork among the Narim, the Surmic agro-pastoralists of southern Sudan, where he examined the cultural value of cattle, strategies of raiding, and levelling mechanisms of resources. In the 1990s he attended to indigenous knowledge systems that involved the use of natural resources without causing environmental degradation. His principal interest was in strategies of diversification of domesticated animals and plants. He also started field research in the northern part of Thailand, where he investigated the impact of modernisation on indigenous shifting cultivation systems. Fukui's research has focused on how culture and nature interact and co-exist, and has always evaluated the potency of the knowledge and practices of indigenous peoples.

Education

BA Kyoto University, 1967
MA Kyoto University, 1969
Ph.D. Kyoto University, 1973

Fieldwork

Tsuba-mura, Japan, 1969–71
Bodi, Ethiopia, 1973–6
Narim, Sudan, 1982–5

Key Publications

(1991) *Ninshikito Bunka: Iroto Moyono Minzokushi* (Cognition and Culture: Ethnography of Colour and Pattern), Tokyo: University of Tokyo Press.
with Markakis, J. (eds) (1994) *Ethnicity and Conflict in the Horn of Africa*, London: James Currey.

YUKIO MIYAWAKI

Fürer-Haimendorf, Christoph von

b. 27 July 1909, Vienna, Austria

d. 11 June 1995

Christoph von Fürer-Haimendorf was an Austrian ethnographer whose curiosity resulted in prolonged (albeit intermittent) fieldwork engagements mainly among the tribes of the Indian sub-continent over the course of almost seventeen years. During his education in Vienna where he also developed a passionate love for the opera, he was influenced by his teacher Hans Heine-Geldern's Vienna School critique of *kultur kreise*. Thus, Haimendorf's first publication in 1936 attempted to connect the prehistorical ritual and symbolic systems in megalithic cultures with ethnology. After Vienna, he arrived at the London School of Economics and was drawn into the authoritative tradition of Bronislaw Malinowski's seminar where other contemporaries deliberating with functionalism included Raymond Firth, Audrey Richards, and Meyer Fortes.

Following that education, he left for fieldwork in India. The outbreak of the Second World War led to a brief internment and an enforced residence in the field for almost nine years. He was given employment by the colonial government and wrote several monographs in the prevailing tradition, notably on the Chenchus, Hill Reddis, Raj Gonds, Subanisi, and Apu Tanis. The threat of a Japanese attack presented a further opportunity to investigate the tribes of the northwestern frontier provinces (now known as Arunachal Pradesh) and Nepal, and produced writings about the Nagas, Sherpas, Thakalis, and Bhotias, the latter who were Tibetan businessmen settled in Nepal.

Haimendorf was interested in furthering an understanding of the interaction and development of cultures. He became critical of colonial rule, particularly of exploitative practices such as commercialism, tribal rehabilitation, and the alienation of tribal land rights, which became visible during the 1930s and 1940s. He further noted that the large-scale conversions of tribal peoples to Christianity were catastrophic in their effect on the values that had governed tribal cultures for centuries. The eschatological concepts introduced by Christianity had resulted in severe social and mental dislocation; many of the younger tribal members broke with tradition and became abusive and intolerant of non-Christian practices. For example, these younger members illtreated and taunted older kinsfolk as 'devil worshippers' for their belief in the sacred powers of the forest or the capacity of human beings to enter the spirit world and associate with its denizens.

In 1949 he was offered a lectureship at the School of Oriental and African Studies, where he remained until his retirement. He maintained a humane concern for the well-being of tribal peoples and actively sought to protect their rights. Thus, he provided assistance in formulating the Act of 1963 to safeguard tribal rights in India by mandating a strict prohibition of land alienation to non-tribals, particularly to big business. However, the continuation of colonial policies (after Independence) had irreversibly forced the absorption of tribal peoples into Indian society. In his later writings, Haimendorf noted for example how the destruction of bamboo had seriously crippled the Chenchu lifestyle. Further, the corruption of forest officials and the connivance of minor revenue officials everywhere had resulted in widespread land transfers to big businesses such as the paper mills. Tribal resistance had been met with the burning of whole villages such as those of the Gonds and Kolams.

Questions of morality and ethics also held a fascination. He was sternly critical of the focus of philosophers on normative ethics drawn only from limited observations in their own society. Their lack of ethnographic cross-cultural knowledge prevented them from recognising the issues raised by the diversity of moral values in different cultural environments. Thus, he felt that anthropologists must attempt to explore moral values and ethics that looked beyond the ethnography of religion, kinship, or social control. Among many tribal societies, there was a lack of codification of moral proscriptions, and the use of proverbs was one way of learning about moral codes. Men and women everywhere expect to have a stable ordered moral universe but, in the absence of formal law and institutions, values were transmitted from one generation to the next and it was deemed reprehensible to flout its prescriptions. To him, morality lay in the total sympathy between cultures, in the desire to extend not only humanitarian rights but also human fulfilment, and, in a real sense, morality derived from the forms of love. Haimendorf's ethnographic writings reflect a humanitarian commitment to respect and safeguard the genius of diverse peoples.

Education

University of Vienna
London School of Economics

Fieldwork

Arunachal Pradesh, Andhra Pradesh, Orissa Nepal, The Philippines

Key Publications

(1943) *The Chenchus, Jungle Folk of the Deccan*, London: Government of India Publication.
(1976) *Return to the Naked Nagas: An Anthropologist's View of Nagaland*, London: J. Murray.
(1982) *Tribes of India: The Struggle for Survival*, Berkeley: University of California.
(1990) *Life among Indian Tribes: The Autobiography of an Anthropologist*, Delhi and New York: Oxford University Press.

KUSUM GOPAL

G

Gailey, Christine Ward

b. 1950, Fort Hood, Texas, USA

Christine Gailey, a leading Marxist-feminist theorist, conducted ethnohistoric and ethnographic research in the Tongan Islands that focused primarily on the transformation of kinship and gender relations in contexts shaped by the two-way street constituted by the formation and dissolution of class and state structures and practices. This led her to consider how resistance to those structures and practices has been, and continues to be, waged in gendered cultural arenas, where working women and men construct alternative interpretations of everyday life to those states and dominant classes attempt to impose. Gailey understands that culture in state-based societies is not continually created on a consensual basis; rather it is created spontaneously in contexts where states and ruling classes attempt to extend their control over production and reproduction, and subordinated classes and peoples resist their efforts. While states attempt to organise dominant, universalising, and homogenising cultures, subordinated groups renew traditional forms and create alternative, potentially oppositional cultures. Her view of culture as a dialectic has been well-received by archaeologists concerned with the social origins of inequality and its manifestations in the archaeological record. In the early 1990s, she expanded her research focus to consider the ideologies of kinship and motherhood as well as the roles of race, class, and gender in international adoption. Gailey's work combines theoretical insight with an appreciation of data and their relation to praxis.

Education

BA University of Michigan, 1972
MA University of Michigan, 1973
Ph.D. New School for Social Research, 1981

Fieldwork

Tongan Islands, 1986–92
New England, 1993–9, ongoing

Key Publications

(1987) *Kinship to Kinship: Gender Hierarchy and State Formation in the Tongan Islands*, Austin: University of Texas Press.
(1988) 'Evolutionary perspectives on gender hierarchy', in B. Hess and M. Ferree (eds) *Analyzing Gender*, Newbury Park: Sage Publications.

THOMAS C. PATTERSON

Galey, Jean-Claude R.

b. 1946, Paris, France

Jean-Claude Galey's scholarship stems from an anthropological tradition R.H. Lowie once defined as the French philosophical approach to sociology. A former student of C. Lévi-Strauss and L. Dumont, Galey's work has focused on contemporary South Asia, discussing local and regional configurations of the caste system taken from examples of former Princely States, which he has approached with a holistic and comparative perspective. His doctoral study on land tenure in India represented a first entry in a series of contributions devoted to the relevant relations of kingship and caste, caste and tribe, and hierarchical loyalties that are still entertained in the sub-continent as polities and dynamics of authority continually condensed, reshuffled and transformed through their interaction with the politics and exclusive logics of power introduced by the colonial and democratic ideologies. Drawing on long periods of ethnographic fieldwork, Galey's analysis has mobilised extended descriptions of kinship, hypergamy and affinity, relations of indebtedness, and social implications of ritual and ceremonial exchanges. He takes these fields of relations as different contexts and levels of a constitutive social order, preceding every individual experience, decision and practice, all being shaped by the structure, or the spirit, of social thought in which different traditions, influences, and origins do not necessarily engender creolisation.

Jean-Claude Galey has served as executive editor of French studies on South Asian culture and society (Oxford University Press) (1985–95) and as the first editor of *Social Anthropology* (Cambridge University Press) (1990–2000). He is currently a director of studies at EHESS in Paris.

Education

BA Sorbonne, 1969
MA Sorbonne, 1970
Ph.D. Paris X-Nanterre, 1973

Fieldwork

North Cameroon, 1970

Western Himalayas, India, 1974–5, 1977, 1985 (Tehri-Garhwal)
Coastal Karnataka, 1987, 1992 (Tulu Nadu)
Orissa and Rajasthan, 1999

Key Publications

(1990) *Kingship and the Kings*, New York: Harwood Acad. Publishers.
(1994) 'L'Homme en nature. Hindouisme et pensée sauvage' (Man and nature. Hinduism and the savage mind), in D. Bourg (ed.) *Les Sentiments de la nature* (Sentiments and Nature), Paris: La Découverte.

ANDRÉ ITEANU

Gamio Martínez, Manuel

b. 1883, Mexico City, Mexico

d. 1960, Mexico City, Mexico

Initially trained as an archaeologist at the National Museum of Mexico, Manuel Gamio acquired a broad grounding at Columbia University (USA) under the tutelage of Franz Boas. He returned to Mexico in 1910, and took up a position at Escuela Internacional de Arqueología y Etnología Americanas (the International School of American Archaeology and Ethnology) where he was in touch with major scholars such as Eduard Seler and G. Engerrand, as well as Boas himself. Gamio's greatest methodological contribution was the design of a vast programme of research intended to further understanding of the socioeconomic, cultural, and historical circumstances of Mexican populations that was established at the Dirección de Antropología (Office of Anthropology at the Secretary of Agriculture), both founded in 1917. This programme advocated a regional and interdisciplinary approach for an ethnography based in fieldwork and social action. The application of his strategy took shape in the research Gamio carried out at the Teotihuacan Valley, in Mexico, which used archaeological records to formulate questions about historical continuity, as well as surveying the multi-ethnic, social, and cultural composition of this region. Another of Gamio's contributions was an emphasis on the social responsibility of researchers, that is to say, a demand that anthropological research make a contribution to the solution of social problems within Mexico, particularly amongst the more disadvantaged Indigenous and rural populations. This emphasis became the defining characteristic of Mexican social anthropology.

Gamio's greatest theoretical contribution is his model of Mexican culture based on its ethnic diversity, and the effort to understand it and contribute to its transformation with the scientific tools of anthropology. Within the ideological context of the nationalism of the Mexican Revolution, this proposal formed the basis for a policy towards the Indigenous population, in which the participation of anthropologists became fundamental. One of Gamio's most original researches was undertaken in 1925 for the American Social Science Research Council and focused on the characteristics of Mexican immigrants and the social and cultural problems they faced in the USA. This study represented pioneering research on this topic, and its relevance has become all the more evident at the beginning of the third millennium. Gamio's thinking has been the axis upon which the Mexican government formulated its policy towards the indigenous population, throughout the twentieth century.

Education

MA Columbia University, 1911
Ph.D. Columbia University, 1921

Fieldwork

Teotihuacan Valley, 1917–22
Mezquital Valley, 1931–3

Key Publications

(1916) *Forjando patria* (Forging the Nation), Mexico: Editorial Porrua.
(1922) *La poblacion del Valle de Teotihuacan* (The Population of Teotihuacan Valley), Mexico: Talleres Graficos de la Nacion.
(1930) *Mexican Immigration to the United States*, Chicago: University of Chicago Press.

ANDRÉS MÉDINA

Geertz, Clifford

b. 1926, San Francisco, California, USA

d. 30 October 2006, Philadelphia, Pennsylvania, USA

In the wake of *The Interpretation of Cultures* (1973), and its sister volume of collected papers, *Local Knowledge* (1983), Clifford Geertz became celebrated for initiating an interpretive revolution across disciplines, which shifted the focus of anthropological study from structure to meaning. The result is that the prestige of sociocultural anthropology among philosophy, literary criticism, history, and politics has never been higher.

Available Light is Geertz's second retrospective memoir where he contrives to craft the fable of 'a charmed life [and] errant career' 'before the necrologists get at him' (Princeton: Princeton University Press, 2000: 10, 20). To read *Available Light* is to appreciate also the extent to which Geertz's 'interpretation of cultures' is an application of Wittgensteinian themes. Geertz describes Wittgenstein as his 'master' (2000: xi). He it was who puts into words what Geertz only inchoately sensed: the need to critique the notion of language as private; to identify those 'forms of life' by which people's understandings of the world are framed and to make thought public (a language-game and a set of practices); to recognise matters of sameness and difference as conceptually blurred and polythetic.

Demobbed (from the US Navy) in 1946, Geertz pitched up at Antioch College, Ohio, a liberal arts college, where he met his wife, Hildred. Graduate study found them both at Harvard where Clyde Kluckhohn, with the help of Talcott Parsons and Gordon Allport, was developing a social relations department, bringing anthropology together with disciplines such as psychology and sociology.

During a 10-year association, Geertz wrote a thesis on Javanese religious life (under the supervision of Cora Du Bois), then returned to Indonesia for further fieldwork in Bali and Sumatra; he shared ideas with the likes of George Homans, Barrington Moore, Evon Vogt, Pitrim Sorokin, Roman Jakobson, David Schneider, Meyer Fortes, Edward Shils, Jerome Bruner, W.V.O. Quine, and Thomas Kuhn. There followed a year at Berkeley, then ten at Chicago, Geertz directing the Committee for the Comparative Study of New Nations, and undertaking further fieldwork in Morocco. Finally, Geertz spent more than thirty years at the Princeton Institute for Advanced Study – its first and only anthropologist – founding the School of Social Science.

Fieldwork Geertz cites as the experience that, far more than the academy, 'nourish[ed his] soul, and indeed create[d] it' (*Available Light*, 2000: 19). But then '[w]hat does the ethnographer do?', Geertz asks himself; primarily '[h]e writes' (1973: 19). And Geertz has become celebrated as a writer, and as a theorist on the writing of culture –by locals and anthropologists alike. From Javanese religion, socioeconomic and ecological change, to Balinese calendars, kinship, cockfights, village life and statehood, to Moroccan city design, social identity, marabouts, monarchs, and markets, here were enacted statements of particular ways of being-in-the-world that should be read-off as texts. This was an essentially hermeneutic enterprise that turned on the 'thick description' of cultural ethos, world view, and practice. Anthropology was not an experimental science in search of comparative structural laws so much as 'faction' (1988: 141): imaginative writing about the culture of real people in real places.

Culture, Geertz elaborates, is that accumulated totality of symbol systems (religion, ideology, common sense, economics, sport...) in terms of which people both make sense of themselves and their world, and represent themselves to themselves and to others. Members of a culture use its symbols (winks, crucifixes, cats, collars, foods, foot-balls, photographs, words) as a language through which to read and interpret, to express and share, meaning. And since the imposition of meaning on life is the major end and primary condition of human existence, this reading of culture is constant; culture members are ever making interpretations of the symbol systems they have inherited. Culture is an acted symbolic document.

Thought represents an 'intentional manipulation of cultural forms' that are socially established, sustained, and legitimised, and whose enactment is public. Giving meaning to experience is not something that happens in private, in insular individual heads, but is tied to concrete social events and occasions, and expressive of a common social world and its logics. Accessing another form of life is a matter not of thinking or feeling as someone else but of 'learning to live with them' (*Available Light*, 2000: 16).

Education

BA Antioch College, 1950
Ph.D. Harvard University, 1956

Fieldwork

Pare, Java: 1952–4, 1971, 1986
Bali: 1957–8
Sefrou, Morocco, 1963–4, 1968, 1969, 1972, 1976

Key Publications

(1963) *Peddlers and Princes: Social Change and Economic Modernization in Two Indonesian Towns*, Chicago: University of Chicago Press.
(1973) *The Interpretation of Cultures*, New York: Basic.
(1983) *Local Knowledge: Further Essays in Interpretive Anthropology*, New York: Basic.
(1988) *Works and Lives: The Anthropologist as Author*, Cambridge, UK: Polity.

NIGEL RAPPORT

Gefou-Madianou, Dimitra

b. 1 December 1948, Larissa, Greece

Dimitra Gefou-Madianou has for many years researched cultural and social dimensions of the use of mind-altering substances (hashish, alcohol) among various groups in Greek society. Initially approaching the topic within a framework of medical anthropology, she became increasingly interested in how alcohol consumption is structured by notions of gender and ethnicity, and is a means of performing and sustaining collective affiliations and identities. Trained at undergraduate level in Greece and at graduate level in the USA, Gefou-Madianou was a key voice in the debate on the possibilities and limits of an indigenous anthropology by Greek anthropologists undertaking 'anthropology at home'.

Gefou-Madianou belongs to the first generation of Western-trained social anthropologists who, since the mid-1980s, returned home to introduce the discipline in Greek universities. She was a leading figure in the establishment of a separate Section of Social Anthropology at the Panteion University, Athens, in 1989; this subsequently became a Department, and currently trains both undergraduate and postgraduate students. She is also the director of the editorial group of a publication series, 'Anthropological Horizons'. By publishing both original anthropological studies and translations into Greek of major anthropological works, this series is contributing to the development of a Greek anthropological discourse.

Education

BA Peirce College, 1970
MA Columbia, 1977
Ph.D. Columbia, 1985

Fieldwork

Thessaly, Greece, 1972–3
Greater Athens (with Asia Minor refugees), 1979–83

Messogia, Attica region, Greece (with Arvanites), 1988–present

Key Publications

(ed.) (1992) *Alcohol, Gender and Culture*, London and New York: Routledge.
(2000) *Culture and Ethnography: From Ethnographic Realism to Cultural Critique*, Athens: Greek Letters (in Greek).

JANE K. COWAN

Gell, Alfred

b. 1945, London, UK

d. 1997, Cambridge, UK

Early in his anthropological career, Alfred Antony Francis Gell was strongly influenced by the writings of Claude Lévi-Strauss, filtered through the charismatic presence of Edmund Leach at Cambridge during the 1960s. His structuralist leanings remained constant over the years. What changed was the particular form of his structuralism. There is a switch from a linguistic-based model to one that places particular emphasis on agency; i.e. a shift from a preoccupation with the communication of unarticulated symbols to an interest in complex forms of intentionality. This alteration is poignantly registered through a comparison of his first monograph *Metamorphosis of the Cassowaries*, based on fieldwork among the Umeda, Papua New Guinea, and his posthumous publication, *Art and Agency*. Gell's major contribution to anthropology in this regard is his exploration of diagrammatic imagery: the nexus between what is seen and how what is seen is understood. His most important contribution in this area is undoubtedly his analysis of artworks – both 'traditional' and 'modern' – or what he came to refer to just before his death as indexes. According to Gell 'indexes' embody an intentional complexity analogous to that exhibited by persons. This is the reason that artworks have the capacity to captivate and abduct in ways resembling that of humans. Gell's highly innovative theory is thus as much a contribution to the anthropological study of persons as to the anthropology of the artefact.

Education

BA Trinity College, Cambridge, 1967
Ph.D. London School of Economics, 1972

Fieldwork

Umeda, Papua New Guinea, 1969–70
Muria Gonds, India, 1977, 1982–3

Key Publications

(1975) *Metamorphosis of the Cassowaries: Umeda Society, Language and Ritual*, London: Athlone.
(1998) *Art and Agency: An Anthropological Theory*, Oxford: Clarendon.

ERIC HIRSCH

Gellner, Ernest

b. 9 December 1925, Paris, France

d. 5 December 1995, Prague, Czech Republic

Gellner held the William Wyse Chair in Social Anthropology at Cambridge University 1984–93, was president of the Royal Anthropological Institute 1991–4, and subsequently headed the Centre for the Study of Nationalism, Central European University, Prague. A good lecturer but scintillating improviser, he was in demand to speak all over the world. A prolific writer, his output, always maturing, changing, and distinctive, showed no signs of lessening before his death. Yet, in spite of the dominating position he reached in his profession, his work remains profoundly controversial.

A rationalist philosopher who came to anthropology only after taking up a lectureship at the London School of Economics in 1949, Gellner shot to fame with an attack on the later Wittgenstein. That pugnacious volume contains characteristics of his later writing:

stubbornness, hatred of obfuscation or vagueness, a readiness to view ideas as being a reflection of their social context, a tendency to work with sharply simplified models of social behaviour, and the assumption that belief systems are presented as whole packets that, when analysed carefully, can be separated out into their component parts.

Supervised initially by Paul Stirling, Gellner conducted Ph.D. fieldwork in the Atlas Mountains. Convinced by this experience that heterodox forms of Islamic thought may be grounded in tribal or rural societies that in turn may be illuminated by the application of segmentary lineage theory, he became a resolute defender of E. Evans-Pritchard and remained attracted to the early, functional period of British social anthropology. Drawing on a wide range of ethnographic material, he later brought together his mature thinking on Islam in collected essays that included a novel analysis of why, unlike other major world religions, the Islamic world appears to retain literal belief in its faith.

Believing strongly that philosophy should be applied to the analysis of social history, he outlined his views of changing human society in his second monograph. This extraordinarily dense text contained also a theory of nationalism that he published subsequently in much more detail. In essence, he suggests that nationalism is an almost incidental consequence of modernity – that a society's dominant culture becomes so crucial because of its capacity to act as a common medium through which citizens can communicate, co-operate. and compete with each other within the framework of an actual or putative nation-state.

Whilst these are perhaps his most distinctive contributions, he wrote also quite brilliantly on technical aspects of anthropology, particularly kinship, where he pursued a rousing battle with Rodney Needham on the question of whether kinship theory was based on a biological or social model of human life (he suggested the former). He also wrote widely on the Soviet Union, on the sociology of science (in particular a ferocious attack on Freudian psychoanalysis), on post-modernism, and the occasional essay on other areas that attracted his attention, such as Turkey, Lebanon, or Southeast Asia. This wider perspective provided material for several works of synthesis in which Islam, communism, and Western secularism are juxtaposed within a longitudinal account of modern history that self-consciously sets out to ask how, when, and where the transition to the industrial world took place.

It is easy to see why Gellner did not fit easily into any anthropological school. Profoundly influenced by Popper, he worked self-consciously as a deductive theorist in a discipline that regarded itself as primarily inductive in inclination. He detested relativism. As he worked often with abstract models, it is often possible to find gaps in his theories, as Alan Macfarlane has demonstrated with reference to his historical work. He was sociable, courteous, convivial, humane, immensely loyal to his colleagues and friends, and possessed a great lust for life and thought. On the other hand, he was not a natural fieldworker, nor indeed a natural administrator. It is highly likely that his brilliance, originality, and occasionally forceful, even impatient wit also made it difficult for his immediate colleagues to judge his work dispassionately in life. Yet, he does appear to have been nearly always correct on the substantive issues upon which he chose to enter battle. When the dust settles, it is likely that history will regard him simply as one of the twentieth century's greatest thinkers.

Education

BA University of Oxford, 1947
Ph.D. University of London, 1961

Fieldwork

Atlas Mountains, Morocco, 1954–61, 1967–8
Moscow, Russia, 1988–9

Key Publications

(1969) *Saints of the Atlas*, London: Weidenfeld & Nicholson.

(1981) *Muslim Society*, Cambridge, UK: Cambridge University Press.
(1983) *Nations and Nationalism*, Oxford: Blackwells.
(1988) *Plough, Sword and Book*, London: Collins Harvill.

Further Reading

Hall, J. and Jarvie, I. (eds) (1996) *The Social Philosophy of Ernest Gellner*, Amsterdam: Rodolpi.
Macfarlane, A. (2001) *The Riddle of the Modern World*, London: Palgrave Macmillan.

DAVID SHANKLAND

Geschiere, Peter

b. 1941, Nieuwer Amstel, The Netherlands

Geschiere's work examines the dynamics of culture in interaction with the impositions of colonial and post-colonial power in West Africa. Breaking with the localist myopia then dominating most anthropology, his early work combined 'local-level politics' with transactionalism to explore the interaction between the local and the national at the crucial transition from decolonisation to the consolidation of post-colonial states. A central theme was the confrontation between a highly segmentary, ideologically egalitarian local order and the highly authoritarian order of the (post-)colonial state.

This led to questions about the transactionalist paradigm itself. Though helpful in fieldwork and writing, it ignored the overarching historical contexts of inequality and (self-)subjugation. His subsequent work took up the challenge of French Marxist anthropology (i.e. Meillassoux, Rey) on the simultaneous articulation of different modes of production. His collaboration with Wim van Binsbergen championed a fusion: extended case studies were used to reinfuse agency into Marxian teleologies, and the idea of articulation was applied anew to the relations between power and the imaginary.

Subsequent work, often co-authored with Cyprian Fisiy, examined how local ideas that emphasised the occult sources of power could spread into nation-state politics. Developing Jean-Francois Bayart's ideas on the role of the *imaginaire* in politics and Achille Mbembe's 'carnival of power in the post-colony', Geschiere unfolded the manifold ways in which local ideas about the occult were articulated within modern settings. Witchcraft represented 'the dark side of kinship'; it was ambivalent as a tool both to accumulate and to level power; and classic classifications were useless in capturing this elusive discourse. It was, in fact, its very ambiguity and poly-interpretability that held the secret of its newly articulated power. Geschiere recognised the dilemma: clearcut distinctions, the hallmark of academic analysis, have evacuated the very object of enquiry.

Geschiere's latest work relates 'witchcraft' in Africa to other esoteric discourses, including a delightful comparison between 'witch doctors and spin doctors'. Together with Jean-François Bayart and Francis Nyamnjoh he revealed recent debates about 'autochtonie' as a powerful political weapon to exclude '*allogènes*'. Working with Birgit Meyer, Geschiere interpreted the relationship between globalisation and identity as a 'dialectic of flow and closure'. At present, Geschiere's chief project is a diachronic study of the rainforest, relating the violent boom for wild rubber in 1900s Cameroon to the present-day pillage for tropical hardwood. The struggles involved between multinational logging companies and transnational ecological lobbies threaten once again to reduce the local population to a *tertius patiens*.

Education

MA, history, Free University, Amsterdam, 1967

MA, anthropology, Free University, Amsterdam, 1969

Ph.D., anthropology, Free University, Amsterdam, 1978

Fieldwork

Tunisia, 1969
Cameroon (Francophone), 1971, 1973, 1980, intermittent since
South Senegal, 1982
Cameroon (Anglophone), 1987

Key Publications

(1982) *Village Communities and the State: Changing Relations in Maka Villages of Southeast Cameroon*, London: Kegan Paul International.

with van Binsbergen, W.M.J. (1985) *Old Modes of Production and Capitalist Encroachment. Anthropological Explorations in Africa*, London: Kegan Paul International.

(1997) *The Modernity of Witchcraft. Politics and the Occult in Postcolonial Africa*, Charlottesville: University Press of Virginia.

GERD BAUMANN

Gilsenan, Michael

b. 6 February 1940, London, UK

While conducting fieldwork with Sufi brotherhoods among Cairo's urban poor, Gilsenan was already becoming uneasy with the conventional British structural-functionalist approach to ethnography and ethnographic writing. The ideal of a holistic account of a society written in the ethnographic present appeared problematic to him not only because he was working in a complex city with a rich history, but also because of his sympathy with Weberian historical sociology and emergent critiques of anthropological and Orientalist relations to colonialism.

Gilsenan's response to these dilemmas is more evident in *Recognizing Islam* than in *Saint and Sufi*. Between writing the two books, Gilsenan had carried out fieldwork in a 'feudal' area in North Lebanon. *Recognizing Islam* is thus a transitional work: the interest in Islam as diverse forms of religious practice remains, but this book has a more reflexive tone and displays a shift in focus towards culture, power, and symbolic violence, the full development of which can be seen in *Lords of the Lebanese Marches*. The latter explores the narratives that are told and retold by the eponymous Lords and their retainers to establish and reaffirm the narrators' claims to honour or to undermine the claims of their rivals. In analysing these narratives, which frequently hinge on moments of coercive and symbolic violence, Gilsenan stresses the agency of the narrator and the performance of the narrative in social practice. However, he also locates the narratives in the larger context of an economy that was being transformed by the market. The narratives increasingly drew on a new rhetoric of jobs and wages, but it became ever more difficult to conceal the contradictions. Concealment, dissimulation, and the constitution of the social self is a central theme that Gilsenan had earlier broached in *Lying, Honor and Contradiction*.

Gilsenan has created a distinctive synthesis of description, analysis, and multivocal texts that extends ethnography. He establishes the common ground that anthropological and indigenous interpretations share as forms of narrative and, without conflating them, explores the interplay of elements within and between the narratives both in social action and in his own writing. What makes his approach distinctive is not only the focus on expressive culture but also on repressive culture: what is unexpressed and what is actively silenced in contests of power.

Education

BA University of Oxford, 1963
Dip.Anth. University of Oxford, 1964
D.Phil. University of Oxford, 1967

Fieldwork

Egypt, 1964–6
Lebanon, 1971–2
Arab diaspora project, various sites in Europe and Southeast Asia, 1999–2000, 2001–2, and ongoing

Key Publications

(1973) *Saint and Sufi in Modern Egypt: An Essay in the Sociology of Religion*, Oxford: Clarendon Press.
(1976) 'Lying, honor and contradiction', in B. Kapferer (ed.) *Transaction and Meaning: Directions in the Anthropology of Exchange and Symbolic Behavior*, Philadelphia: ISHI.
(1982) *Recognizing Islam: An Anthropologist's Introduction*, London: Croom Helm.
(1996) *Lords of the Lebanese Marches: Violence and Narrative in a Lebanese Society*, London: I.B. Tauris Press.

ANDREW FINLAY

Gingrich, Andre

b. 12 September 1952, Vienna, Austria

Andre Gingrich's researches in the 1980s and the early 1990s may be characterised by focuses on social context and regional comparison of registers of cognition. With increasing interest during the 1990s in anthropology and a decline in Austria of former major social sciences such as sociology, Gingrich's explorations have also integrated reflections about anthropology's potentials in explaining recent social processes. His most recent research focuses on the role of structural change in helping to understand contemporary social phenomena, and on the scope and new inventories of anthropological comparison. Regarding the latter, Gingrich proposes the concept of a self-reflexive, controlled macro-comparison to probe questions about the human condition and the global dimensions of social interactions.

Awarded the Wittgenstein Prize for scientific research in 2000, Andre Gingrich explores the development of local identities within the frame of translocal influences. This research theme is being scrutinised in historical as well as contemporary fields, with the main regional focuses centered on the Middle East and Europe (Western/Eastern). As a working hypothesis, Gingrich suggests three strategic options for agency in the formation of local identities: seclusion from translocal influences, or alternatively integration into them, or a more or less creative appropriation and participation in the construction of such translocal influences.

Education

Doctorate, Ph.D. University of Vienna, 1979
Habilitation (Venia Docendi), University of Vienna, 1990

Fieldwork

Northeastern Sudan, 1974
Syria, 1974, 1976
Northern Yemen, 1980, 1983, 1986
Saudi Arabia, Asir, 1981–2
Eastern Anatolia, Kurdish Provinces, 1991
Central Tibet, 1997

Key Publications

Gingrich, A. and Fox, R.G. (eds) (2002) *Anthropology by Comparison*, London and New York: Routledge.
(1999) *Erkundungen. Themen der ethnologischen Forschung* (Explorations. Themes of Anthropological Research), Vienna, Cologne, and Weimar: Böhlau.

THOMAS FILLITZ

Ginsburg, Faye

b. 28 October 1952, Chicago, Illinois, USA

Faye Ginsburg's prize-winning ethnographic portrait of conflict over a local abortion clinic in the American Midwest in the early 1980s, *Contested Lives: The Abortion Debate in an American Community* (1989), inaugurated a debate about ethnographic representations of American conservatism and fundamentalism (and the role of gender in these debates), which has become increasingly central to the anthropology of American society. Ginsburg's ethnography forcefully demonstrated the value of

charting the broad world views and distinctive life histories that lay behind the concerns of the women active on the 'two sides' of the abortion issue. Her ethnography also drew attention to the importance of dominant cultural images and representations in society, and the contradictory means by which people mobilise them to represent and define themselves.

This perspective is at the heart of Ginsburg's subsequent ethnographic study of the development of indigenous media, and in particular Australian Aboriginal self-representation in film and video. Again looking behind the 'two sides' that dominate this discussion, Ginsburg documents a wide range of means by which indigenous peoples manipulate the conditions of image-making in the service of creating visual self-definitions.

Ginsburg is thus a major contributor to the study of social movements, and conflicts over both biological and visual reproduction, as well as one of the most important anthropologists of media.

Education

Ph.D. City University of New York, Graduate Center, 1986

Fieldwork

Brooklyn (Syrian Jewish community), 1978–80
South Bronx (community groups), 1980–1
Thailand (Hmong refugee camps), 1981
Fargo, North Dakota (abortion dispute activists), 1982–3, 1994, 1995
Australia (Aboriginal media), 1988–9, 1992, 1994, 1997, 2001

Key Publications

(1989) *Contested Lives: The Abortion Debate in an American Community*, Boston: Beacon Press.
with Abu-Lughod, Lila and Larkin, Brian (eds) (2002) *Media Worlds: Anthropology on*

New Terrain, Berkeley: University of California Press.

SARAH FRANKLIN

Gledhill, John

b. 14 June 1949, West Yorkshire, UK

John Gledhill's fieldwork research in the state of Michoacán, Mexico, in the late 1970s culminated in his monograph, *Casi Nada: Agrarian Reform in the Homeland of Cardenismo*. The book focused on classic economic anthropology concerns, but it also anticipated much of the more recent literature about 'rural livelihoods' that Africanists came to consider novel and groundbreaking. Since then, Gledhill carried out ethnographic research on both indigenous and non-indigenous communities in the states of Michoacán and Chiapas, with a focus on social movements, local politics, political economy, and transnational migration, and also published extensively on broader historical, comparative, and theoretical issues in anthropology. His 1994 book, *Power and Its Disguises: Anthropological Perspectives on Politics*, demonstrated his ability to go beyond local community studies to engage with wider developments in social theory and map out a broad, comparative anthropology of politics. More recent publications have focused upon the impact of neo-liberalism, transnational migration, and theories of economic globalisation. His present project is a comparative study of contemporary Latin American social movements, new visions of rurality, and alternative models of globalisation. He has been editor of *Critique of Anthropology* since 1993, and in this capacity encouraged much new and innovative thinking in the discipline.

Education

B.Litt. University of Oxford, 1973

Fieldwork

Ciénega de Chapala, Mexico, 1979, 1982

Ciénega and Los Reyes, Michoacán, 1989–92
Michoacán and Chiapas, Mexico, 2001

Key Publications

(1991) *Casi Nada: A Study of Agrarian Reform in the Homeland of Cardenismo*, Studies on Culture and Society No. 4, Albany: State University of New York.

(2000 [1994]) *Power and Its Disguises: Anthropological Perspectives on Politics*, second edn, London: Pluto Press.

RICHARD A. WILSON

Gluckman, Max

b. 26 January 1911, Johannesburg, South Africa

d. 13 April 1975, Jerusalem, Israel

As a scholar, teacher, and organiser of research, Max Gluckman made vital contributions to social, political, and legal anthropology from the 1940s to his death in 1975. His early fieldwork in South Africa during the late 1930s led to seminal articles that, while rooted in then dominant structural-functionalist concerns about pre-contact tribal societies and social equilibrium, nonetheless addressed the impact of colonisation and white settlement. In *African Political Systems* (1940), only contributions by Audrey Richards and Gluckman (in his chapter on the Zulu Kingdom) included sections on European rule and post-European changes. In 'Analysis of a social situation in modern Zululand' (1940), he developed the concept of the social situation, in this case a bridge-opening ceremony, as an observed event from which anthropologists abstract social structure, relationships, and institutions of a particular society. Moreover, by positing 'the existence of a single African-White community', Gluckman foreshadowed a major preoccupation of the Rhodes–Livingstone Institute (RLI) anthropologists as well as the later anthropology of colonialism. He noted, for example, that the Zulu desire for European material goods and the European need for Zulu labour and wealth brought these two groups together in a situation of both interdependence and conflict.

In 1941–2, Gluckman succeeded Godfrey Wilson as director of the RLI in Northern Rhodesia (Zambia) where he and fellow anthropologists developed a research programme that used dialectical method to investigate contemporary problems, conflict and conflict resolution, economics, politics, and the environment, and how global forces shaped local situations. Under Gluckman's direction, RLI anthropologists recognised the asymmetrical relationship between town and countryside. In rural areas, research focused on land tenure, labour, depopulation, and markets; in urban settings, on migration, problems of order, and formation of labour unions.

During his RLI years, Gluckman's own research took a different direction from the main thrust of the researchers whose work he supervised. His fieldwork among the Barotse of Northern Rhodesia resulted in a number of works on Lozi jurisprudence. He analysed particular cases and the strategies of different agents against the background of European law, which enabled him to explore similarities and differences between legal systems. Gluckman drew on concepts such as reasonable man and equity to underline that Lozi courts drew on both judicial decisions and formal rules of right-doing.

In 1947, Gluckman left RLI to take a position at Oxford under A.R. Radcliffe-Brown. Two years later he departed to establish the Department of Social Anthropology at Manchester University. There, he led a group of highly productive scholars that included Victor Turner, A.L. Epstein, Max Marwick, J. Van Velsen, and W. Watson. Many of these early members of what became known as Manchester School had worked at the RLI and undertaken fieldwork in British Central Africa. Early Manchester studies, especially the rural ethnographies, focused primarily on normative inconsistency and contradiction, processes

of social conflict, and the internal dynamics of small-scale societies. Gluckman, however, continued to emphasise that, in much of Southern and Central Africa, the dominant cleavage opposed two culture-groups, European and African. Gluckman and other Manchester School anthropologists studied the asymmetrical relationship between town and countryside in the Central African Copperbelt. Industrialisation, labour migration, and urbanisation had not led to detribalisation as previous studies had argued, but to strengthened tribal and kinship systems while at the same time providing cheap labour for colonial industry.

Social process, conflict, and conflict resolution remained central concepts of Manchester School anthropologists. Analytical and methodological tools developed by the group of scholars included the social field, situational analysis, the extended-case method, intercalary and interhierarchical roles, cross-cutting alliances, the dominant cleavage, redressive ritual, repetitive and changing social systems, and processual change. Exploration into the intercalary roles of village headmen and the interhierarchical position of chiefs and even district commissioners revealed the multiple dilemmas and contradictory pressures faced by these figures due to their placement between kinship and political systems within a larger colonial political hierarchy.

Throughout his career, Gluckman remained fascinated by structural contradictions as expressed in rituals of rebellion, revolution, and civil war. Rituals of rebellion paradoxically served to strengthen existing political hierarchies and social inequalities by allowing subordinate and marginalised people to give vent to their frustrations and resentments against ruling elites. Although Gluckman never moved beyond a concern with social equilibrium so characteristic of mid-twentieth-century British social anthropology, he underlined that equilibrium was seldom a simple matter; rather, it entailed a balance of contradictions and opposed groups in a dialectical process.

Education

BA University of the Witwatersrand, 1934
Ph.D. University of Oxford, 1936

Fieldwork

South Africa (Zululand), 1936–8
Northern Rhodesia (Zambia), 1940–7, Bar-
otseland, Tondo, Lamba
Israel 1963–71 (9 months total)

Key Publications

(1940) 'Analysis of a social situation in
modern Zululand', *Bantu Studies* 14: 147–74.
(1955) *The Judicial Process among the Barotse of
Northern Rhodesia*, Manchester: Manchester
University Press.
(1963) *Order and Rebellion in Tribal Africa*, Glencoe,
IL: Free Press.
(1965) *Politics, Law, and Ritual in Tribal Society*,
Oxford: Blackwell.

JOHN M. CINNAMON

Godelier, Maurice

b. 28 February 1934, Cambrai, France

Trained at l'École Normale, one of the Grandes
Écoles of the French education system, Maurice Godelier came to anthropology via philosophy. Not surprisingly, we find that Godelier's
anthropology, the discipline that was to
become the locus and the focus of his
intellectual development and scholarly contribution, is guided by themes that are also
central to philosophy: rationality, materiality,
power. Both disciplines weave a continual
dialogue throughout his work.

Godelier's interest in rationality and its
economic manifestations developed at a time
when socialism and capitalism were understood to be the best servants of economic
rationality. Reading Karl Marx, Keynes, Roy
Harrod, and Evsey Domar, and taking classes
with Charles Bettelheim and Edmond Mal-
invaud, Godelier came to the conclusion that

both approaches shared the same theoretical
premises, namely that the transformations of
the economy will eventually transform all
societies. Yet, as he proposed in his first book,
Rationalité et irrationalité en économie, understanding
rationality as purely economic is not sociologically viable when the anthropological and
historical records of non-Western societies
reveal that economic activities are embedded
in other types of social relationships (such as
the political and the religious) that are
essential for the production and reproduction
of the economy.

Not surprisingly, economic relations and
relations of power became the main foci of his
first fieldwork among the Baruya of Papua
New Guinea, with whom he has now worked
for a total of seven years. This was Godelier's
first anthropological field research: it was to
have an important impact on his work, and led
him to engage problems of a more general
theoretical interest, such as theories of power
and the role of the imaginary in social
reproduction. Particularly noteworthy was
Godelier's understanding of the roles that
representations, practice, and institutions have
in the constitution of men as the dominant
social group in Baruya society. Observing and
analysing symbolic practices, such as ritualised
homosexual exchanges between men and
young boys, allowed him to understand the
symbolic world of the Baruya construction of
personhood and its relation to the social order
centered around the production of Great Men,
a concept he introduced. In his seminal book.
La Production des Grands-Hommes, Godelier established the now-classic distinction between
Great Men and Big Men, concepts that are
central to the analysis of power in Melanesia.

Central to this distinction is the nature of
exchange: exchange of women and exchange
of goods. Revisiting Marcel Mauss, Bronislaw
Malinowski, and Claude Lévi-Strauss in the
light of the Baruya data on exchange led
Godelier to propose in his book, *L'Enigme du don*,
that beyond the Maussian dichotomy of
agonistic and non-agonistic gift exchanges,
there exist a series of goods (the sacred) that
cannot be exchanged. This observation is fun-

damental as the presence of non-exchangeable goods informs the social life of those that can be exchanged. Continuing his re-reading of Mauss's theory of the gift, Godelier added that counter-prestations, particularly in associations with the exchange of women between clans, are not meant to cancel out earlier prestations, but rather to create another set of debts that balance the initial ones and open the door for more exchange.

More recently, Godelier has returned to the classic study of kinship. It is there that his anthropology integrates fully the relationship between power and economy. Far from being at the confines of a relationship between a mode of production and a mode of reproduction, kinship (through marriage and filiation) opens the way for other dimensions of economic life and power to emerge. Relations of hierarchy, exchange, authority, and ownership are only some of the ways by which the individual experience reveals social concerns. Here again, Godelier's interest in the role of the symbolic order in the production of social reality comes to the fore: nowhere more than in kinship do we find the active role of the mental in the development of sociality.

Education

École Normale Supérieure de Saint-Cloud, 1955–9
License de Psychologie, 1955
License en Lettres Modernes, 1955
Aggrégation de Philosophie, 1958

Fieldwork

Seven years of fieldwork in Papua New Guinea with the Baruya, between 1967 and 1988.

Key Publications

(1972) *Rationality and Irrationality in Economics*, (*Rationalité et irrationalité en économie*, 1966), trans. Brian Pearce, London: NLB.
(1986) *The Making of Great Men. Male Domination and Power among the New Guinea Baruya*, (*La Production des Grands-Hommes. Pouvoir et domination*

masculine chez les Baruya de Nouvelle-Guinée, 1982), trans. Rupert Swyer, Cambridge and New York: Cambridge University Press.
(1986) *The Mental and the Material. Thought, Economy and Society*, (*L'Idéel et le matériel*, 1984), trans. Martin Thom, London and New York: Verso.
(1999) *The Enigma of the Gift*, (*L'Enigme du Don*, 1996), Chicago: Chicago University Press.

CHRISTINE JOURDAN

Good, Byron J.

b. 1944, Rantoul, Illinois, USA

A leading figure in the development of medical anthropology as a significant and relevant critique of the health sciences, clinical practice, and medical pedagogy, Byron Good has consistently returned anthropological inquiry to the impacts upon human bodies and upon the human condition itself. Eschewing any one theoretical paradigm, Good aims to show how a variety of meaning-centered theories (phenomenological, hermeneutic, narrative analysis, and aspects of critical theory) fall within a broad interpretive paradigm. Symbolic and culture theory analysis were used by Good to formulate a key medical anthropology methodology, the semantic illness network ('The heart of what's the matter', 1977).

At the core of Good's intellectual inquiry is an enduring interest in subjectivity, as evidenced by his best-known book, *Medicine, Rationality and Experience* (1994). Moral, aesthetic, and affective dimensions of subjectivity, and the changing nature of subjectivity in contemporary medical worlds of discourse and practice, continue to interest Good as his ethnographic focus has moved from Iran and Turkey, to the USA, and, most recently, to Indonesia.

An influential figure in medical anthropology through his professorships in social medicine and anthropology at Harvard University and co-editor in chief of *Culture, Medicine and Psychiatry*, Good has very successfully communicated to health (particularly mental health) service providers how culture influences the meaning and experience of illness, and how illness narratives conjoin with bodily experience to shape patient suffering.

Education

BA Goshen College, 1966
BD Harvard Divinity School, 1969
Ph.D. University of Chicago, 1977

Fieldwork

Iran, 1972–7
America 1976–present
Turkey, 1987
Indonesia, 1996–present

Key Publications

(1994) *Medicine, Rationality and Experience: An Anthropological Perspective*, Cambridge, UK: Cambridge University Press.
(1977) 'The heart of what's the matter: the semantics of illness in northern Iran', *Culture, Medicine and Psychiatry*, 1: 25–58.

MONIQUE SKIDMORE

Goodale, Jane Carter

b. 18 May 1926, Boston, Massachusetts, USA

Jane C. Goodale's work has challenged popular contemporary models of ethnographic fieldwork, social organisation, and ultimately of cross-cultural concepts of humanity. She began her postgraduate studies intending to study the social organisation of hunters and gatherers in north India. Serendipitously she ended up studying Tiwi women on Melville Island, Australia. The result was *Tiwi Wives*, a landmark book in Australian Aboriginal ethnology and in anthropology as a whole. *Tiwi Wives* challenged the previous work of C.W.M. Hart who, with Arnold Pilling, had written that Tiwi women were powerless pawns and 'chattel' in the marriage system, which was a

male status competition; and that, though the Tiwi were matrilineal, Tiwi men were patriarchal and polygynous. Goodale found instead that: the Tiwi were indeed matrilineal; that, though the marriage system was simultaneously polygynous for men, women were serially polyandrous; and that women's access to influence and power increased with age, especially for a *taramaguti*, or senior wife.

In Goodale's work we find that 'the problem of women' was not merely one of filling in a lacuna in ethnographic data. More importantly, Goodale demonstrated how, with the addition of the other half of a society, our entire anthropological understanding of a particular culture changed. Goodale also showed the limits of British social-structural models for understanding Tiwi culture, and suggested it made much more sense to analyse the Tiwi social system in terms of significant categories of relatedness of 'persons' in the Tiwi 'behavioural environment' (after Hallowell).

Goodale took these concepts with her to the Kaulong of New Britain, Papua New Guinea. There she worked in parallel fashion with Ann Chowning, who worked among the Sengseng. The results of almost three years of fieldwork over a 12-year period can be seen clearly in *The Two-Party Line* (1995), written from the letters they exchanged while in the field, and *To Sing with Pigs is Human* (1995).

In the late 1990s Goodale's focus shifted to cultural change, using a longitudinal perspective gained from almost fifty years' fieldwork among the Tiwi.

Education

BA Radcliffe College, 1948
MA Radcliffe College, 1951
Ph.D. University of Pennsylvania, 1959

Fieldwork

Northern Arizona archaeology, 1950
North Australia (Tiwi of Melville Island), 1954, 1962 (3 weeks), 1980–1 (1 month), 1986–7 (18 months), 1995 (1 month), 1996–7 (5 months), 1999 (3 months)

Papua New Guinea (Kaulong), 1962 (9 weeks), 1963–4, 1967–8, 1974 (3 months)

Key Publications

(1971) *Tiwi Wives: A Study of the Women of Melville Island, North Australia*, Seattle: University of Washington Press (second edn, Waveland Press, 1994).

with Hart, C.W.M. and Pilling, A.R. (1988) *The Tiwi of North Australia*, revised third edn, Holt, Rinehart & Winston.

(1995) *To Sing with Pigs is Human: Concepts of Person in Papua New Guinea*, Seattle: University of Washington Press.

(1995) *The Two-Party Line: Conversations in the Field*, Lanham, MD: Rowman & Littlefield.

ALICE POMPONIO

Goodenough, Ward H.

b. 30 May 1919, Cambridge, Massachusetts, USA

Ward Goodenough's first major publication, *Property, Kin, and Community on Truk*, resulted from the intensive fieldwork he carried out on the island of Romonum in the Truk (Chuuk) group of the Central Caroline Islands in 1947 as part of the US Navy's Co-ordinated Investigation of Micronesia. The orientation Goodenough brought to this fieldwork was influenced by his dissertation director, George Peter Murdock, who was interested in the comparative study of social organisation, and by other professors at Yale including Bronislaw Malinowski and the linguist George Trager, who were concerned with the descriptive analysis of particular cultures and languages. Goodenough's doctoral dissertation, and the resulting monograph, *Property, Kin, and Community on Truk*, was also influenced by his attaining fluency in Trukese, his knowledge that his findings would be used by local administrators, and his adoption as a brother by Jejiwe, one of his informants and friends on Romonum. Many of the issues that Goodenough continued to focus on in his numerous (over

200) subsequent publications were given their initial presentation in this penetrating study of Chuukese property and social organisation.

Goodenough's approach to culture, which has had a profound influence on Oceanic anthropology, on the development of cognitive anthropology, and on general anthropological theory, was given sharp formulation in a series of articles that were published in the 1950s and 1960s. In 'Componential analysis and the study of meaning' (1956), he demonstrated that a particular cultural domain, such as kinship terminology, could be rigorously analysed in such a way as to reveal the underlying criteria that accounts for the particular distribution of terms. This article, and Goodenough's other publications on componential analysis, affected numerous formal anthropological studies of cultural models. In 'Residence rules' (1955), Goodenough argued that anthropology had been weakened by a failure to distinguish between the outside analytic language used to compare different cultures and the conceptual frameworks actually employed by the people of a given society. Drawing on the linguistic distinction between phonetics and phonemics, he showed that 'etic' anthropological comparative terms like 'matrilocal', which summarise patterns about where couples live after marriage, fail to address 'emic' distinctions, the criteria people in a given society actually use to decide where to live after marriage. This article contributed to the on-going debates about point of view in cultural interpretation and helped launch a variety of studies on decision-making structures. In 'Cultural anthropology and linguistics' (1957), Goodenough elaborated his view that culture is best understood as the system of knowledge – the conscious and unconscious assumptions, categories, beliefs, and decision-making systems – that a person needs to learn in order to operate acceptably as a member of society. In 'Rethinking status and role' (1965), Goodenough suggested that an adequate understanding of social organisation requires careful analysis of the social identities (such as kinship and occupational positions) that are recognised in a given society and the particular distributions of rights and duties that characterise the relationships of individuals interacting with each other in terms of particular social identities.

During Goodenough's second period of fieldwork on Romonum in 1965, role analysis was one of the foci of his investigations. He also worked on a Trukese dictionary, subsequently published in two volumes with his co-compiler, Hiroshi Sugita, on Trukese religion, and on the changes in social organisation that had occurred since 1947. A discussion of these changes is included in the second edition of *Property, Kin, and Community on Truk*. In analysing cultural change, Goodenough combines an interest in cultural knowledge, including the ways in which individuals in the same community vary in cultural understandings, with an interest in the social-psychological dynamics of self-maintenance. He continued work on these issues through the 1990s and they are crucial to his monumental study of Trukese religion, *Under Heaven's Brow: Pre-Christian Religious Tradition in Chuuk*. Here he provides a comprehensive account of divination, sorcery, and other religious activities, and offers a theory of religion that focuses on the ways in which rituals address the emotional concerns engendered by the social life of a particular society.

Education

BA Cornell University, 1940
Ph.D. Yale University, 1949

Fieldwork

Chuuk (Truk), Micronesia, 1947
Kiribati, Gilbert Islands, 1951
Papua New Guinea, 1954
Chuuk (Truk), Micronesia, 1965

Key Publications

(1963) *Cooperation in Change: An Anthropological*

Approach to Community Development, New York: Russell Sage.
(1978 [1951]) *Property, Kin, and Community on Truk*, second revised edn, Yale University Publications in Anthropology, No. 46, New Haven: Archon.
(1981) *Culture, Language, and Society*, Menlo Park, CA: Benjamin Cummings.
(2002) *Under Heaven's Brow: Pre-Christian Religious Tradition in Chuuk*, Philadelphia: American Philosophical Society.

Further Reading

Marshall, M. and Caughey, J. (eds) (1989) *Culture, Kin, and Cognition: Essays in Honor of Ward H. Goodenough*, Washington, DC: American Anthropological Association.

JOHN L. CAUGHEY

Goody, Esther

b. 9 August 1932, Cleveland, Ohio, USA

Esther Goody studied sociology at Antioch and social anthropology at Cambridge. Her first fieldwork was conducted among the Gonja of Northern Ghana. During this period, Goody's work addressed important themes in the sociology of the family. Goody wrote that she was concerned 'to trace interrelationships between political and domestic institutions', while trying 'to understand the working of a largely "bilateral" system' (1973: 1). She interpreted Gonja kinship and society in terms of four 'idioms of relationship', one of which, for instance, was the 'complex of greeting and begging' that forms the basis of respect behaviour fundamental to a range of social relations.

Goody's second book on kinship compares modes of parenting in West Africa focusing, in particular, on 'fostering' (1982). In the same period, Goody studied small-scale textile industries and edited a volume on the topic titled *From Craft to Industry: The Ethnography of Proto-industrial Cloth Production* (1982).

From the beginning of her career Goody has emphasised the importance of communicative practice to the organisation of social relationships. Since her pioneering work on kinship, she has come to focus more directly on issues of language and communication. The edited volume, *Questions and Politeness* (1978), included both her own analysis of questions along with Penelope Brown and Stephen Levinson's paper outlining the influential rational-choice model of politeness ('Universals in language use: politeness phenomena').

More recently, Goody has turned her attention to the evolutionary issues implicated in the human use of, and capacity for, language. In the 1990s, Goody brought together scholars from various disciplines to discuss the 'interactive bias in human thinking'. The resulting 1995 volume is a groundbreaking, multifaceted exploration of language development, intelligence, and social organisation. These themes are addressed in the Radcliffe-Brown lecture that Goody gave in 1997. Here Goody links the emergence of language to the development of social rules and accountable, role-shaped behaviours such as Radcliffe-Brown described in his classic work on joking-relationships.

Goody has always pushed the boundaries of British social anthropology. Her attempt to integrate ethnography with current developments in linguistic pragmatics, ethology, and cognitive anthropology distinguishes her from the vast majority of anthropologists working in Britain and elsewhere. As early as the 1970s Goody was attempting to understand social behaviour in relation to various patterned and observable communicative genres, forms, and practices. In this respect Goody's work in the area of kinship and social organisation both anticipated and contributed to the massive turn towards language and practice that has characterised the social theory of the last twenty years.

Education

BA Antioch College, 1954

Ph.D. University of Cambridge, 1961
Sc.D. University of Cambridge, 1985

Fieldwork

Ghana (Northern Gonja), July 1956–March 1957, July–December 1957
Ghana (Eastern Gonja – Kpembe), April–September 1964
Ghana (Western Gonja – Bole), July–October 1965
Ghana (Central Gonja – Daboya), June–December 1974
Ghana (Gonja, Wa, Birifor, and Dagaba), 1990–continuing

Key Publications

(1973) *Contexts of Kinship: An Essay in the Family Sociology of the Gonja of Northern Ghana*, Cambridge, UK: Cambridge University Press.
(1982) *Social Reproduction: Fostering and Occupational Roles in West Africa*, Cambridge, UK: Cambridge University Press.
(ed.) (1995) *Social Intelligence and Interaction: Expressions and Implications of the Social Bias in Human Intelligence*, Cambridge, UK: Cambridge University Press.
(1997) 'Social intelligence and the emergence of roles and rules', *Proceedings of the British Academy 97*, London: Oxford University Press: 119–47.

JACK SIDNELL

Goody, Jack R.

b. 27 July 1919, St Albans, UK

Jack Goody became an anthropologist in the context of the Second World War and the anti-colonial revolution it spawned. He carried out fieldwork in northwest Ghana under the direction of Meyer Fortes in Cambridge and has continued to maintain a link between the two places for half a century since. With Fortes, he founded a school of West African ethnography based on meticulous documentation of kinship and marriage practices, and especially of 'the development cycle in domestic groups' (1958). Later, Esther Goody was his partner in much of this research. *Death, Property and the Ancestors* (1962) is a masterpiece of comparative sociology, concerned with how we seek to transcend death materially and spiritually. From here, Goody launched the project of global comparison for which he is best known today.

Beginning with *Production and Reproduction* (1976), he set out over the next quarter-century to compare the pre-industrial civilisations of sub-Saharan Africa and Eurasia, with the aim of identifying why Africa is so different, while questioning Western claims to be exceptional. He found that kin groups in the major societies of Eurasia frequently pass on property through both sexes, a process of 'diverging devolution' (including bilateral inheritance and women's dowry at marriage) that is virtually unknown in sub-Saharan Africa, where inheritance follows the line of one sex only. Particularly when women's property includes the means of production, land in agricultural societies, attempts will be made to control these heiresses, banning pre-marital sex and making arranged marriages for them, often within the same group and with a strong preference for monogamy. Direct inheritance by women is also associated with the isolation of the nuclear family in kinship terminology. The greater volume of production made possible by the plough or irrigation made title to landed property of supreme importance. Mesopotamia's urban revolution 5,000 years ago spread to all of Eurasia's civilisations, making possible an elaborate bureaucracy, a complex division of labour, and stratified society based on landlordism (1976: 24).

This is where the nuclear family came from. It had nothing to do with the uniqueness of the West or its Industrial Revolution. Sub-Saharan Africa apparently missed out on these developments. Goody posits low population density as an explanation, adding that tropical soils were possibly an inferior basis for intensive agriculture. He also chose to attack the lingering opposition of 'modern' and 'primitive' cultures by studying the chief activity of literate elites – writing. He believed that much of what has been taken as evidence for different mentalities should rather be seen as an effect of different means of communication. Of these the most important are speech and writing. Once again, most African cultures are predominantly oral, whereas the ruling classes of Eurasian civilisation have relied from the beginning on literate records. He published his most general assault on the habit of opposing 'us' and 'them' in *The Domestication of the Savage Mind* (1977). This was a pointed repudiation of Claude Lévi-Strauss whose penchant for lists linking 'hot' and 'cold' societies to other pairs, such as history and myth, science and magic, far from being an instance of universal reason, was itself a product of mental habits induced by the specific practice of writing.

Simply as an exercise in the comparative history of pre-industrial civilisations, Goody's contribution would be enormous. His contrast between Eurasia and Africa reminds us of the durable inequalities of our world and suggests that the reasons for them may be less tractable than we like to think. At the same time the rise of the Asian economies underlines his warning against European complacency. We would do well to take to heart the analytical focus that lends unity to Goody's compendious work. The key to understanding social forms lies in production. Civilisation or human culture is significantly a consequence of the means of communication – once writing, now an array of mechanised forms. The site of social struggles is property. And his central issue of kinship has never been more salient than now when the ageing citizens of rich countries have difficulty reproducing themselves. The anthropology of unequal society, begun by Rousseau and established by Morgan, finds in Jack Goody its most able twentieth-century exponent.

Education

BA University of Oxford, 1946
B.Litt. University of Oxford, 1952
Ph.D. University of Cambridge, 1954
D.Sc. University of Cambridge, 1969

Fieldwork

Many trips to northwest Ghana since 1950
(LoDagaa, Gonja)

Key Publications

(ed.) (1958) *The Development Cycle in Domestic
Groups*, Cambridge, UK: Cambridge Univer-
sity Press.
(1962) *Death, Property and the Ancestors: A Study of
the Mortuary Customs of the LoDagaa of West Africa*,
Stanford, CA: Stanford University Press.
(1976) *Production and Reproduction: A Comparative
Study of the Domestic Domain*, Cambridge, UK:
Cambridge University Press.
(1977) *The Domestication of the Savage Mind*,
Cambridge, UK: Cambridge University
Press.

KEITH HART

Graburn, Nelson H. H.

b. 1936, London, UK

Nelson Graburn has led the way in developing
anthropological analyses of the behaviour and
consumption practice of tourists. He suggests
that the tourist vacation is a ludic and liminal
moment in our lives, an aesthetic and
necessary counterpoint to ordinary life, a
sacred journey and time for the re-creation
of the self. This thesis – the application to
tourism of Emile Durkheim's sacred/profane
distinction, Arnold van Gennep's notion of
rites of passage, and Edmund Leach's observation that these inversions are markers of time –
developed out of extensive ethnographic
research amongst the Inuit of Arctic Canada,
the study of kinship as part of David
Schneider's research team in Chicago, and an
examination of domestic tourism in Japan.

Graburn's main ethnographic publications
chronicle a critical time in 'Eskimo' history as
the community structures changed from
subsistence seasonal migration, moving camp
to follow resources in the late 1950s, to
permanent settlement dwelling with a high
degree of dependence upon foreign economics
by the 1970s. In his account of these
communities in transition, Graburn focused
upon ethnic and tourist arts, expressions of
identity and history for a local audience and,
increasingly, for the foreign market and the
visiting tourist. The commoditisation of non-
Western arts is exemplified in Graburn's
history of Inuit soapstone sculpture, his work
as a curator at the Hearst Museum in
California, and his advocacy work for 'ethnic
arts of the Fourth World'. According to
Graburn, Fourth World 'arts of acculturation'
are the collective artistic work of native
peoples whose lands fall within the First,
Second, and Third Worlds. These arts change
according to commercial, colonial, and local
ethnic stimuli, and are often sought out of
modern nostalgia for the primitive, for the
handmade in a plastic world.

As associate editor of the journal, *Annals of
Tourism Research*, Graburn has influenced the
direction of tourism research, using this outlet
to assert that tourism is a barometer of the
dynamics of cultural change within a society.
Graburn tested this hypothesis in the 1980s
with a penetrating analysis of the social
organisation of Japanese tourism and society,
suggesting that the collective orientation of
Japanese tourism is a reflection of traditional
cultural and kinship patterns and identities
found back home. This attention to the
relationship between the different spheres of
life – work and home vs leisure and travel –
and tourist consumption links back to his
earlier work in Arctic Canada on social
organisation, changing patterns of behaviour,
and the production of culture.

Education

BA University of Cambridge, 1958
MA McGill University, 1960
Ph.D. University of Chicago, 1963

Fieldwork

Canadian Arctic, 1959, 1960, 1963–4, 1967–8, 1972, 1976, 1986 (inc. Greenland), 2000 (39 months total)
Chicago, 1961–3
Japan, 1974, 1979, 1987, 1989–90, 1992, 1993, 1994, 2000, 2002 (16 months total)

Key Publications

(1969) *Eskimos without Igloos: Social and Economic Development in Sugluk*, Boston: Little, Brown & Company.
(ed.) (1976) *Ethnic and Tourist Arts: Cultural Expressions from the Fourth World*, Berkeley: University of California Press.
(1977) 'Tourism: the sacred journey', in V. Smith (ed.) *Hosts and Guests: The Anthropology of Tourism*, Philadelphia: University of Pennsylvania Press.
(1983) *To Pray, Pay, and Play: The Cultural Structure of Japanese Domestic Tourism*, Aix-en-Provence: Centre des Hautes Études Touristiques.

JONATHAN SKINNER

Greenhouse, Carol J.

b. 1950, New Haven, Connecticut, USA

Carol Greenhouse has made signal contributions to sociocultural anthropology in five key respects. First, Greenhouse argued that legal anthropology's focus on court cases missed instances where the avoidance of conflict served to maintain social order. Legal anthropologists had held that cases were a privileged site to witness the underlying rules of social order maintained by law or law-like institutions. Her ethnography among Baptists in suburban Atlanta demonstrated how religion, specifically prayer and notions of 'inner' faith (as opposed to public demonstrations of faith), turned social conflicts into spiritual ones and the quest for vengeance and redress into a search for salvation and forgiveness. Second, Greenhouse broke ground by bringing ethnographic tools to bear on 'modern' social forms and processes, notably, the law and religion in the USA. These domains have often been treated in isolation from one another because of the conceit that American modernity is defined by secularism. Greenhouse's work significantly complicates such an assumption. Third, Greenhouse extended her research on modern social forms by turning the anthropological gaze back on ethnography, asking whether and how ethnographic practice itself is a form of democratic discourse. This line of thinking is represented in her co-authored book on law and community in the USA as well as her writings on democracy and the legacies of liberalism. Fourth, Greenhouse's project on time and temporality demonstrates how these are fundamentally political projects and not simply the given background to social processes. Examining constructions of temporality in three very different state contexts (ancient China, the Aztec empire, and the contemporary USA), Greenhouse explores the interface between law, politics, and time in order to map out the interlocking temporal and social fields within which political authority is constituted. Fifth, and finally, Greenhouse has provided exemplary service to anthropology and interdisciplinary sociolegal research. She was president of the Law and Society Association and the Association for Political and Legal Anthropology, and has held numerous other positions in anthropological and sociolegal professional organisations. She also served as editor of *American Ethnologist* (1998–2002), which has become the most cited journal in sociocultural anthropology (according to the 2001 Institute for Scientific Information Journal Citation Report), a testament to her professional integrity and intellectual generosity.

Education

AB Radcliffe College, 1971
Ph.D. Harvard University, 1976

Fieldwork

Atlanta, Georgia, USA, 1973–5, 1980
Various archives and libraries, 1983–2002

Key Publications

(1986) Praying for Justice: Faith, Order, and Community in an American Town, Ithaca: Cornell University Press.
with Yngvesson, Barbara and Engel, David M. (1994) Law and Community in Three American Towns, Ithaca: Cornell University Press.
(1996) A Moment's Notice: Time Politics across Cultures, Ithaca: Cornell University Press.
with Kheshti, Roshanak (eds) (1998) Democracy and Ethnography: Constructing Identities in Multicultural Liberal States, Albany: State University of New York Press.

BILL MAURER

Greenwood, Davydd

b. 28 September 1942, Pueblo, Colorado, USA

Davydd Greenwood is known for challenging conservative academic anthropology and advocating for an engaged scholarship that effectively addresses actual issues and conditions. His career has ranged widely, encompassing a variety of locales, topics, audiences, and methods. He has contributed to international collaborative efforts among anthropological institutions in Europe, particularly in Spain, as well as in North America and Latin America. Greenwood has made major contributions to the scholarship of political economy, nationalism and ethnicity, the anthropology of tourism, nature–culture debates, medical anthropology, anthropological history and processes of institutionalisation, and participatory action research.

Greenwood began his career doing fieldwork in Spain, especially in the Basque country, after a brief stint in Mexico. His dissertation research challenged the mechanistic application of contemporary 'formalist' and 'substantivist' approaches to economic analysis by documenting how examining both pecuniary and non-pecuniary factors is essential to understand farming practices. He proposed an analytical model based on 'a reasoned blend of economic and cultural elements' (Greenwood 1976: 18). Stressing the inherent complexity of sociocultural processes and the conceptual importance of questioning reified categories of analysis became Greenwood's scholarly hallmark.

Greenwood recognised the importance of tourism as a significant sociocultural activity rather than just a developmental economic strategy that needed to be considered in anthropological analysis. In a foundational article for the anthropology of tourism, he documented tourism's complexity and the paradox of its commoditisation of culture while embodying significant markers of local identity and history.

Greenwood has been instrumental in developing participatory action research and is among its foremost theorisers and practitioners. At Cornell University, where he has taught since 1970, he collaborated with noted sociologist, William Foote Whyte, in promoting action research, which he has applied and practiced in Spain, Sweden, the USA, and Latin America.

Greenwood's international prominence was recognised by Spain's scholarly community in 1996, when it elected him Académico Correspondiente of the Real Academia Española de Ciencias Morales y Políticas, a notable distinction for a foreign scholar. Greenwood's wife, Pilar Fernández-Cañadas, has consistently been a significant scholarly partner and collaborator.

Education

BA Grinnell College, 1964
Ph.D. University of Pittsburgh, 1970

Fieldwork

Basque Country, Salamanca, and La Mancha, Spain, 1966–present

Oaxaca, Mexico, 1966

Sayre, Pennsylvania, 1982–3

Upstate New York, 1998–present

Key Publications

(1976) *Unrewarding Wealth: Commercialization and the Collapse of Agriculture in a Spanish Basque Town*, Cambridge, UK: Cambridge University Press.

(1989) 'Culture by the pound: an anthropological perspective on tourism as cultural commoditization', in V.L. Smith (ed.) *Hosts and Guests: The Anthropology of Tourism*, second edn, Philadelphia: University of Pennsylvania Press.

with González, José Luis (and Julio Cantón Alonso, Ino Galparsoro Markide, Alex Goiricelaya Arruza, Isabel Lagarreta Nuin, and Kepa Salaberría Amesti) (1992) *Industrial Democracy as Process: Participatory Action Research in the Fragor Cooperative Group of Mondragón*, Assen-Maastricht: Van Gorcum Publishers.

with Levin, Marten (1998) *Introduction to Action Research: Social Research for Social Change*, Thousand Oaks, CA: Sage Publications, Inc.

VILMA SANTIAGO-IRIZARRY

Griaule, Marcel

b. 1898, Aisy-sur-Armaçon, France

d. 1956, Paris, France

After spending several months in Ethiopia (1928–9), Marcel Griaule organised an ethnographic expedition across French colonial Africa, the Dakar–Djibouti mission (1931–3). The aim of this expedition was to record local knowledge and material culture, especially arts, cultures, and religious beliefs. It marked the beginning of empirical field research for French ethnography. Griaule privileged fieldwork methods based on processes of documentation (collection, observation, and interrogation) and initiation (education and socialisation), as well as interdisciplinary investigation using audio-visual techniques. Besides playing a significant role in the training of early French ethnographers, Griaule also helped organise Africanist scholars with the creation of the *Société des Africanistes* and the *Journal des Africanistes*.During the Dakar–Djibouti mission, Griaule encountered the Dogon people of Badiangara (Mali) on which he conducted most of his subsequent research and publications. He wrote extensively on Dogon masking and ritual traditions, concept of the body and soul, nomenclature, and systems of classification. His work on the Dogon can be divided into two periods. First, from 1931 to 1948, he produced descriptive accounts of Dogon life (*Les Masques Dogons*), concentrating on material culture. This early description resembled museum work, assembling photographs, maps, and recordings. The beginning of the second period is marked by *Dieu d'eau*. This book sparked remarkable interest and made Griaule's work famous. It describes Dogon world view as a coherent and logical system. It is written on the basis of conversations with Ogotemmêli, a Dogon elder. These conversations offer an unparalleled understanding of African cosmology. Through the written account of thirty-two initiatory sessions, Griaule describes the philosophical system linking Dogon society and thought with the outside world. This ethnography was highly innovative to the extent that its publication tallied with the debate on rationality in anthropology; this debate was structured around the issue of the differences and similarities between European and African modes of thought. It questioned the possibility of 'translating cultures'. In subsequent years, Griaule worked closely with G. Dieterlen. Their main publication, *Le Renard pâle*, proposed a vision of Dogon people as living their own creation in the interwoven relation between everyday life and cosmic forces. The corpus of myths and cultural explanations gathered with G. Dieterlen opened the door to a new form of investigation focused on notions of self and personhood. It established the legitimacy of the cross-cultural study of modes of thought.

Griaule was an eminent field researcher, responsible for all the major ethnographic expeditions conducted in francophone Africa between the 1930s and 1950s. He also contributed to the professionalisation of French ethnography through his teaching. As such, he left a double heritage. The research he inaugurated among the Dogon has been continued by several generations of ethnologists, in particular G. Calame-Griaule, S. de Ganay, D. Zahan, and, with a more critical stance, J. Rouch and L. de Heusch. His work is at the origin of a tradition of religious ethnology that contemporary studies of systems of thought and symbolic representation perpetuated, including redefinition of personhood, fetishism, sacrifice, totemism, divination, and rituals.

Recently, anthropologists have questioned Griaule's quest for the essence of African modes of thought, his propensity to generalise very broadly about 'the Africans' on the basis of limited comparative data, his recording of empirical data by asking Dogons to stage rituals for the camera, and his interview techniques based on a single informant. However, beyond the questioning of the validity of his ethnographic description, Griaule's work has lent scientific legitimacy to oral cultures and to non-Western systems of thoughts.

Education

Preparation for entry at Polytechnique
École Nationale des Langues Orientales vivantes, 1927
École Pratique des Hautes Études, 1933
Doctorat d'État, Université de Paris, 1938

Fieldwork

Ethiopia, 1928–9
Dakar–Djibouti mission, focus on Mali (Badiangara region) and Ethiopia (Gondar region), 1931–3
Mali, 1933 onwards

Colonial French Sudan, Cameroon, Chad, and Niger, 1935–9
Colonial French Sudan, 1935
Permanent mission on the Bend of Niger, Centre National de la Recherche Scientifique, 1950–6

Key Publications

(1938) *Les Masques Dogons* (The Dogon Masks), Thèse d'État, Paris: Institut d'Ethnologie.
(1965) *Conversations with Ogotemmeli*, trans. R. Butler and A. Richards, (*Dieu d'eau, entretiens avec Ogotemmêli*, 1948), London: Oxford University Press for the International African Institute.
with Dieterlen, G. (1954) *Le Renard pâle, ethnologie des Dogons* (Pale Fox, Dogon Ethnology), Paris: Institut d'Ethnologie, Musée de l'Homme.

Further reading

Clifford, J. (1988) 'Power and dialogue in ethnography: Marcel Griaule's initiation', in J. Clifford *Predicament of Culture. Twentieth-Century Ethnography, Literature, and Art*, Cambridge and London: Harvard University Press.
de Heusch, L. (1991) 'On Griaule on trial', *Current Anthropology* 32, 4: 434–7.
Van Beek, W.E.A. (1991) 'Dogon restudied. A field evaluation of the work of Marcel Griaule', *Current Anthropology* 32, 2: 139–66.

MARIE NATHALIE LEBLANC

Grillo, Ralph David

b. 23 April 1940, Watford, Herts, UK

Ralph Grillo's career conflates various academic interests, ranging from development to language and from the nation-state to ethnicity and migration. His first monograph skilfully took into account the linked problems of ethnicity and class formation among migrant railwaymen in Kampala, Uganda. The situational variation of identity is discussed within an Eastern African setting, where kinship and ethnic ties generate alignments of solidarity and opposition intermittently contrasting with those emerging from the social stratification within the urban context. Especially notable is the analysis of migrants' networks with their rural homes, which somehow anticipate the transnational approach to migration that characterised the anthropology of migration during the 1990s.

An interest in migration also informs the second monograph that emerged from field-work undertaken in urban France (Lyon) during the mid-1970s. This is a study of the relationship between immigration and ideology in a receiving society. There are very few compelling ethnographic studies like this on the perceptions of migrants by a receiving population, how this is translated into policy and how both change according to the broader economic and ideological framework. The approach adopted in this case becomes more complex by focusing on migrants' experiences as well as their representation within crucial institutional settings (trade unions and social services). The analysis of conflicting discourses characterising the institutions dealing with immigration (housing and work) leads to a broader discussion of ideology in French society.

Building on this work on ethnic relations in France and on the study of discourses, an interest in linguistic pluralism and its connections to power relations developed. Indeed, besides co-edited works on the anthropology of development partly emerging from experience as honorary secretary of the Association of Social Anthropologists of Britain and the Commonwealth (ASA), Ralph Grillo produced a comparative study of dominant languages in France and Britain showing how linguistic practice is a site of subordination as well as contestation in which a multiplicity of voices struggles for political attention. Drawing on this intellectual trajectory in another comparative study, Grillo advances his arguments by exploring the relationships between various forms of polity and ethnic diversity in different historical configurations (from cases in pre-colonial Africa and the Ottoman Empire

to more recent debates over integration and multiculturalism in both Europe and the USA). He provides an interesting ideal-typical model distinguishing three configurations of state and society (patrimonial, modern, and post-industrial) to which three forms of identities correspond (corporate, unitary, and hybrid). His work in the 2000s focuses on transnational migration and combines the various perspectives acquired along this path.

Education

BA University of Cambridge, 1963
Ph.D. University of Cambridge, 1967

Fieldwork

Kampala, Uganda, 1964–5
Ireland, 1969
Lyon, France, 1974, 1975–6
Italy, 1997

Key Publications

(1973) *African Railwaymen: Solidarity and Opposition in an African Labour Force*, Cambridge, UK: Cambridge University Press.
(1985) *Ideologies and Institutions in Urban France: The Representation of Immigrants*, Cambridge, UK: Cambridge University Press.
(1989) *Dominant Languages*, Cambridge, UK: Cambridge University Press.
(1998) *Pluralism and the Politics of Difference: State, Culture, and Ethnicity in Comparative Perspective*, Oxford: Clarendon Press.

BRUNO RICCIO

Gross, Feliks

b. 1906, Krakow, Poland

Feliks Gross, a Polish-born scientist working in the USA since 1941, is known as one of a few heirs to Bronislaw Malinowski, with whom he closely collaborated in the early 1940s on a volume on nationality, social boundaries, and ethnicity. The joint project, interrupted by the death of the latter, was continued by Gross, whose extraordinary capacity for combining strong political activism in the federalist movement with the scientific rigor of an anthropologist resulted in a series of passionate books based on various field studies. Although Gross achieved recognition early in his career with the book, *Nomadism*, focused on the Marxist-influenced question of material conditions and lifestyle, his main field of interest became the problem of the multiethnic state as one of the key issues of a post–Second World War cultural and political order. While accepting the anthropological framework of Malinowski's functionalism and his field study methodology, Gross put his emphasis on the development and evolution of social boundaries and their cultural as well as political meaning. Understanding neighbourhood solidarity and territorial bond as historical roots of citizenship, Gross states that even communities with cultural differences can create a workable and relatively peaceful environment. His ethnographic examination of the multiple identity, social boundaries, and neighbourhood solidarity among Arapaho Indians, fishermen communities in Maine, and the Italian village of Fumone appears to be the starting point for the more general question of the contemporary multiethnic state and its dilemma between ethnic and political bonds that dominated Gross's works in the 1980s and 1990s.

He passionately argues that no state can survive a wide and antagonistic hiatus of the ethnic and political values of its citizens. The main distinction between the tribal and civic state and the idea of citizenship as the most important social bond is the key point of his late thought. The civic state is based on the political bond and its essential institution is citizenship, the tribal state ties political identity to ethnic origin and ethnic identity. While the tribal, totalitarian state's agenda dissolves ethnicity, state, and race into a single symbolic concept, the civic state's idea of nationality distinguishes ethnicity from political association and allows dual or multiple identities and social bonds to exist in a complementary rather than conflicting way. Gross argues that in a modern, pluralistic state political bonds and identity should be clearly separated from ethnic ones. He finds such a concept essential in constructing a democratic civic state.

Education

MA Jagiellonian University, Krakow, 1929
Ph.D. Jagiellonian University, Krakow, 1930

Fieldwork

Northern Maine, USA, several stays between 1952–85
Fumone, Italy, several stays between 1957–70
Wind River Reservation of Arapaho Indians, Wyoming, USA, 1945, 1951

Key Publications

(1936) *Koczownictwo* (Nomadism), Warsaw: Mianowski Press
(1973) *Values and Social Change in an Italian Village*, New York: New York University Press.
(1978) *Ethnics in a Borderland: an Inquiry into the Nature of Ethnicity*, Westport: Greenwood Press.
(1998) *The Civic and the Tribal State*, Westport: Greenwood Press.

JOANNA BATOR

Gullestad, Marianne

28 March 1946, Kristiansand, Norway

Marianne Gullestad has achieved international recognition for her studies of everyday life, morality, and social relations in modern Norway. Her doctoral study of young, working-class women in Bergen explored what many would see as the trivial small-talk and practices of young family households, and demonstrated the rich potential of doing 'anthropology at home'. Through a keen awareness of 'what is at stake', Gullestad used her observations of everyday practices as a basis from which to address theoretical issues related to morality, family relations, children, selfhood, and consumption. By spelling out the meaning of emic cultural categories (like 'peace and quiet' and 'fitting in') an analysis that focuses on central sets of oppositions is developed, and key themes in Norwegian culture are discussed. This work has formed the basis of a range of theoretical essays, which address issues such as home-centeredness, independence, self-sufficiency, love of nature, social boundaries, and egalitarian individualism.

One of Gullestad's most important theoretical contributions relates to the notion of equality as sameness in the Norwegian context. Several scholars have maintained that lifestyle differences are much larger in Norway than most Norwegians tend to believe. Gullestad has directed attention to social mechanisms by which such misconceptions are maintained. According to Gullestad, the Norwegian egalitarian tradition involves ways of under-communicating difference during social encounters. Through an emphasis on 'fitting in', individuals who are perceived as dissimilar are systematically excluded from informal social networks. This notion of equality as sameness exists along with a pronounced individualism that emphasises self-sufficiency and independence which, taken together, give egalitarian ideals a special meaning in the Norwegian, or perhaps in the Scandinavian, context.

Gullestad later developed these ideas historically through work on autobiographies, and politically through analyses of public discourse on immigration, nationalism, and racism in Norway.

Gullestad is only one among several contemporary anthropologists working with Norwegian ethnography, yet she is by far the most prominent internationally. This is due to an extensive record of international publications, through which she has made Norwegian ethnography accessible and theoretically relevant to an English-speaking and a French-speaking audience. In Norway, Gullestad takes an active part in current public debates and her books have a lucid style that attract a wide readership.

Education

Cand. Mag. University of Bergen, 1971
Mag. Art. University of Bergen, 1975
Doctor Philos. University of Bergen, 1984

Fieldwork

Bergen, inner-city neighbourhood, 1972–3
Bergen, suburban housing estate, 1978–80
Research based on nation-wide Norwegian autobiography contest, 'Write your life' (1988–9)

Key Publications

(1984) Kitchen-Table Society. A Case Study of the Family Life and Friendships of Young Working-Class Mothers in Urban Norway, Oslo: Scandinavian University Press.

(1992) The Art of Social Relations. Essays on Culture, Thought and Social Action in Modern Norway, Oslo: Scandinavian University Press.

(1996) Everyday Life Philosophers: Modernity, Morality and Autobiography in Norway, Oslo: Scandinavian University Press.

with Segalen, M. (eds) (1997) Family and Kinship in Europe, London: Pinter.

MARIANNE E. LIEN

Gulliver, P. H. (Philip H.)

b. 2 September 1921, Maldon, UK

The authorial, theoretical, and methodological contours of ethnography are often contested. Yet Gulliver's work over more than fifty years, among East African pastoralists, horticulturalists, and labourers, with Western-style labour relations, and in an Irish town and hinterland, are examplars of how an anthropologist can fuse personal fieldwork, ethnographic writing, and theoretical development. His earliest concerns, with localised social relations and material interests, and with diachronic analysis, were later augmented by work in historical anthropology. Throughout, Gulliver has focused on the dialectic between conflict and co-operation, the nature of disputing processes, and the connection between individual action and the formation of collectivities.

Gulliver interrupted his university education in 1941 to join the RAF and spent part of the Second World War stationed in Egypt. His curiosity was piqued by nearby fellahin and, also, by Sanusi in whose company he searched for downed aeroplanes. After the war, he decided to read anthropology. Although informed by Raymond Firth in 1947 that there would be no jobs, he went off to northern Kenya (Turkana) for his Ph.D. research. It was an area that had seen few Europeans and which, for Gulliver, was well away from English authority. The resulting book (1955), which compared the Turkana with Jie pastoralists, is considered a classic.

Because of these positive experiences, and because post-war England was so dreary, Gulliver signed on as a sociologist for the government of Tanganyika. Although working on topics that were designed to meet government interests, he was in fact able to pursue his own research interests. He did so among several groups in the following six years; and he developed an abiding fascination with non-judicial processes, dispute management, and mediation. His 1979 volume, which compared East African and industrial models of negotiation, is now a required text in the field of alternative dispute resolution (ADR). Meanwhile, his research among East African horticulturalists, who had neither lineages nor kinship groups, propelled him to become a leader in the analysis of cognatic kinship and social networks (action-sets, quasi-groups) (e.g. 1971). This period of intense research in East Africa and the resulting publications (1948–58) brought him the Wellcome Medal for Anthropology (1957) and the Rivers Memorial Medal for Anthropological Research (1967).

In 1958, Gulliver left Africa for the USA, taking positions at Harvard (1958–9) and Boston University (1959–62). In 1962, he returned to England – to the School of Oriental and African Studies (SOAS) at the University of London. In 1967, he became professor of

African anthropology. Three years later, largely for personal reasons, Gulliver emigrated to Canada, spending a year at the University of Calgary and, then, until his retirement in 1992, at York University, Toronto. In this new context came a new research focus. In association with Marilyn Silverman, an anthropologist at York, he began a project in a small town and rural hinterland in the Republic of Ireland. Here, as compared with East Africa, he found extensive archives and an established historiographic tradition. He also encountered important material differences. Instead of 'simple milieux' – with a small number of undifferentiated households per village and activities actualised through 'the idiom of kinship' – Gulliver encountered differences of status (lifestyle) and class (access to the means of production). Yet, in both places, political-economic and collective action were diffuse, moulded out of situational events and the intersection of, on the one hand, individual and collective lived experiences and, on the other, material interests. Both places, too, had kinship and disputes. Gulliver dived into the archives (Dublin, Kilkenny city), spoke at length with elderly residents using archival materials to stimulate memories and explore links between the past and present, and interviewed farmers, shopkeepers, labourers, and gentry. The intensity of this research fitted well with Gulliver's relaxed and thorough fieldwork style.

In 1982, Gulliver was made a Fellow of the Royal Society of Canada (FRSC) and, in 1984, he was named a distinguished research professor at York University.

Education

B.Sc. University of London, 1947
Ph.D. London School of Economics, 1952

Fieldwork

Kenya, 1948–50 (Turkana nomads)
Uganda, 1950–1 (Jie pastoralists)
Tanzania, 1952–4 (Ndendeuli and Ngoni),

1954–5 (Nyakusa), 1955–6 (plantation workers)

Arusha, 1956–8

Shona, Rhodesia, 1961

County Kilkenny, Eire, 1980–1, 1998–9, summers 1983–4, 1987, 1989, 1992, 2000

Key Publications

(1955) The Family Herds: A Study of Two Pastoral Tribes in East Africa, London: Routledge & Kegan Paul.

(1971) Neighbours and Networks: The Idiom of Kinship among the Ndendeuli, Berkeley: University of California Press.

(1979) Disputes and Negotiations: A Cross-Cultural Perspective, New York: Academic Press.

with Silverman, Marilyn (1995) Merchants and Shopkeepers: A Historical Anthropology of an Irish Market Town, Toronto: University of Toronto Press.

MARILYN SILVERMAN

Gumperz, John J.

b. 9 January 1922, Hattingen, Germany

A pioneer of the field of sociolinguistics, John Gumperz is best known as the founder of one of its most important sub-fields: interactional sociolinguistics. Within this paradigm, he developed such fundamental concepts as code-switching and contextualisation cues, through which he integrated field study of linguistic processes with sociological concerns about social networks, social identity, and fair access to institutional resources.

Trained as a linguist, Gumperz became interested in sociolinguistic problems while working on his doctoral dissertation, a study of the Swabian dialect spoken by a community of farmers in Washtenaw County, Michigan, who had descended from two groups of German immigrants originally speaking different dialects. He argued that the linguistic convergence he had observed in this community could be attributed to social formations that resulted after settlement in the USA. This

correlation between speech and social groups would form the investigative backbone of his subsequent research, and would be the primary focus of his second fieldwork: a collaborative community study in northern India. The only linguist in a team of anthropologists, sociologists, economists, and other social scientists, he broadened his interests to include fieldwork methods and the relationship between language, culture, and society.

Upon returning from this fieldwork, Gumperz was invited to establish a Hindi–Urdu programme at the University of California at Berkeley. In 1964, he became a member of Berkeley's anthropology department and a leader in the university's new Language Behavior Research Laboratory. For the next thirty years, Gumperz would combine teaching at Berkeley with numerous research projects in the USA and abroad.

Through in-depth fieldwork in Norway, northern and central India, Austria, Slovenia, and England, he collected ethnographic data that furthered his understanding of communication in relation to social boundaries and sociolinguistic structures. Gumperz's interest in developing an ethnography of communication was prompted by his desire to study the way language was used by people in different social networks, and the way these networks were produced and reproduced in communication. He was among the first scholars to note that linguistic diversity correlates with social stratification, so that highly stratified systems (such as the caste system in India) develop highly diversified communicative styles to mark the social identity of group members as well as the exclusion of non-members. More egalitarian communities (such as the one he studied with Jan-Petter Blom in Norway), on the other hand, necessitate a much smaller linguistic repertoire to mark social boundaries.

Because of his observation of bilingual and language contact situations, Gumperz abandoned the raditional focus on language systems as distinct entities, electing to investigate instead the speech repertoire of a social network, group, or culture. By grounding the notion of speech repertoire in its ethnographic context, he was able to describe multilingual phenomena such as code-switching. The study of code-switching (the juxtaposition of passages of speech belonging to two or more different grammatical systems) allowed him to gain a deeper understanding of the inferential and interpretive processes present in the communication of multilingual speakers.

Gumperz realised that code-switching is only one of several discourse strategies that provide interlocutors with contextual information about how to interpret communicative intent. His concern with context-building strategies led him to investigate the surface speech features (prosody, rhythm, lexicalisations) by which speakers signal and listeners interpret what their speech activity is, how content must be understood, and how sentences relate to each other. The proper interpretation of what he labelled contextualisation cues requires interactants to have intimate knowledge of the communicative styles and practices of particular social networks; failure to attend to the proper cues leads to communication breakdown.

His concern with the large-scale sociological effects of small-scale interactions gave his work an important applied perspective. Most notably, he collaborated with the BBC to produce *Crosstalk*, a popular documentary on the problems faced by individuals (mostly immigrants) who are unable to use the appropriate codes in institutional encounters. Moreover, he became one of the few sociolinguists to serve as an expert witness in court cases involving cross-cultural miscommunications.

Gumperz's optimism about the prospect for overcoming prejudice by raising communicative awareness has led some critics to fault him for neglecting the power technologies through which elites guard access to social advancement and institutions resist change. Though these issues do not constitute the focus of his writing, a careful reading of Gumperz's work reveals a fluid understanding of power relations, in which power resides not in opposing blocks but in myriad asymmetrical everyday encounters, which are shaped by culture-bound judgments carrying within them the seeds of ideological struggle.

Education

BA University of Cincinnati, 1947
MA University of Michigan, 1951
Ph.D. University of Michigan, 1954

Fieldwork

Southern Michigan, 1952–4
India, 1954–6, 1964, 1967
Norway, 1964
Austria, 1969–72
England, 1974–82

Key Publications

with Hymes, Dell (eds) (1964) *The Ethnography of Communication*, Washington: American Anthropological Association.
with Hymes, Dell (eds) (1972) *Directions in Sociolinguistics: The Ethnography of Communication*, New York: Holt, Rinehart & Winston.
(1982) *Discourse Strategies*, Cambridge and New York: Cambridge University Press.
with Levinson, Stephen (eds) (1996) *Rethinking Linguistic Relativity*, Cambridge and New York: Cambridge University Press.

MARCO JACQUEMET

Gupta, Akhil

b. 21 March 1959, Bilaspur, Madhya Pradesh, India

Educated as a mechanical engineer, with a doctorate in engineering–economic systems, Akhil Gupta is well known for his contributions in the field of anthropology. His *Postcolonial Developments* reflects his interest in a historically informed political economy in post-colonial contexts (particularly in India) and in discourses of development. In the bulk of his work, Gupta focuses on the functioning of state bureaucratic power on the more localised lower levels, with a special interest in the issue of corruption, thereby engaging in what has become known as ethnography of the state.

In co-operation with James Ferguson, Gupta produced two influential edited volumes on the issues of place and space in relation to 'culture'. Their *Anthropological Locations* retains the emphasis of their individual work on political dimensions of power and inequality when addressing issues of (de)territorialisation, transnationalism, and movement. This results in a critique of anthropological practice, in terms of methodology, and its theoretical and political implications. Through an analysis of the problematic assumptions of boundedness of the discipline's central notion of 'culture', Gupta and Ferguson argue for the recognition of the value of ethnographic fieldwork, which, however, requires an updated conceptualisation of the notion of the 'field'.

Education

BS Western Michigan University, 1977
SM Massachusetts Institute of Technology, 1979
Ph.D. Stanford University, 1988

Fieldwork

Western Uttar Pradesh, India, 1984–5, 1991–2
Goa, India, preliminary fieldwork, two months during 1995–6 and 1997–8

Key Publications

with Ferguson, James (eds) (1997) *Anthropological Locations: Boundaries and Grounds of a Field Science*, Berkeley: University of California Press.
(1998) *Postcolonial Developments: Agriculture in the Making of Modern India*, Durham: Duke University Press.

STEFAN JANSEN

Gurevich, Aron Iakovlevich

b. 1924, Moscow, Russia

Aron Gurevich works in the field of historical anthropology. His early studies focused on re-constructing the world view of European medieval peoples. He was interested in the processes through which cultural self-consciousness is formed and the influence of sociocultural practice on individual behavioural patterns.

He defined the interaction between man and culture as cultural mentality and succeeded in abstracting some universal components of culture that he referred to as categories on which the mentality of culture is based. According to Gurevich these categories can serve the role of a set of conceptual co-ordinates for research, without which it is impossible to understand the attitudes of earlier peoples towards basic cultural components – to God, to labour, to right, to prosperity, to death, to social and cultural phenomena of their time. In his scientific discourse, culture, personality, and social relations are conceived as an inextricable unity.

He uses two approaches: the first approach consists in revealing cultural categories and their description on a synchronic level; the second one focuses on the interaction, relation, and balance between elite culture (i.e. written culture) and folk epic tradition (oral culture). The subject of his concern became the inner complexity and dynamic unity of medieval European culture phenomenon.

Education

BA Moscow State University, 1946
Ph.D. Moscow State University, 1955

Key Publications

(1988) *Medieval Popular Culture: Problems of Belief and Perception* (*Problemy srednevekovoi narodnoi kul'tury*, 1981), trans. János M. Bak and Paul A.

Hollingsworth, Cambridge and New York: Cambridge University Press.

with Howlett, Jana (eds) (1992) *Historical* *Anthropology of the Middle Ages*, Chicago: University of Chicago Press.

GALINA KHIZRIEVA

Haddon, Alfred Cort

b. 24 May 1855, London, UK

d. 20 April 1940, Cambridge, UK

Alfred Cort Haddon is best known for two contributions to early British anthropology: his leadership of the Cambridge Anthropological Expedition to Torres Strait in 1898–9 and his efforts to institutionalise anthropology as a discipline in the UK. He also produced a substantial body of ethnographic work on the decorative arts and material culture in Torres Strait, Papua New Guinea, Ireland, and Borneo as well as books on race, physical anthropology, and the early history of anthropology.

Haddon began his career as a marine biologist in the 1880s at the Royal College of Science, Dublin, where he was professor of zoology. In 1888–9 he made his first expedition to the Torres Strait to study the marine biology of coral reefs but became more interested in the Islanders and determined to record their way of life before it disappeared under European influences. On his return he decided to further develop his interests in anthropology though there was little opportunity as no departments of anthropology then existed in the UK. During summer fieldwork expeditions around the coast of Ireland he began to collect ethnographic data on the social life of the region's peoples, resulting in an ethnography of the Aran Islands in 1893. In 1894 he began lecturing in physical anthropology in the department of anatomy at

Cambridge, the only anthropological subject then taught. He spent the next four years planning a comprehensive anthropological expedition to Torres Strait to further the work he had begun in 1888 and to generate support for the scientific legitimacy of anthropology as a discipline.

Haddon designed the 1898 expedition as a multidisciplinary project that would encompass ethnology, linguistics, sociology, ethnomusicology, physical anthropology, and psychology. He assembled a team of six scientists whose combined efforts generated methodological advances by adapting natural science models to anthropological research. The expedition members were primarily concerned with how to collect ethnographic 'facts', leading to the integration of field research with scholarly interpretation. Haddon's emphasis on direct field research provided the basis for the development of the intensive fieldwork methodology of anthropology, later refined by Bronislaw Malinowski and others. Haddon is himself credited with appropriating the term 'fieldwork' from the natural sciences for anthropology. One of the expedition members, W.H.R. Rivers, the Cambridge experimental psychologist, devised the genealogical method that became the standard for kinship studies in anthropology well into the mid-twentieth century. Other methods pioneered on the expedition were psychological field testing and the use of recording media such as cine-cameras, still cameras, magic lantern projectors, and phonographs. The expedition also generated a massive volume of information, including the six volumes of the reports, which appeared sporadically over the following thirty-five years, hundreds of field photographs, drawings, sketches, ethnographic film, sound recordings on wax cylinders, journals, diaries, maps, correspondence, and a large collection of artefacts.

In 1901, on the strength of the scientific results of the expedition and with the influence of Sir James Frazer, the University of Cambridge created a position for Haddon as lecturer in ethnology. During that year he made an extensive trip to the USA, visiting universities and museums to determine the state of American anthropology. On his return he determined to establish a school at Cambridge based in part on Franz Boas's Columbia model. By 1906 a postgraduate programme emphasising field research was established, followed in 1913 by an undergraduate programme. With his enthusiastic commitment to the anthropological project he promoted the need for more fieldworkers, for rigorous scientific training in field methods, and for original field research. In the decades following the expedition, the generation of field anthropologists trained at Cambridge by Haddon and his colleagues exported anthropology to new academic departments worldwide. Haddon also raised the profile of anthropology in the public sphere, in museum practice, and in the wider scientific community. He served as president of the Anthropological Society from 1902 to 1904 and president of the anthropological section of the British Association for the Advancement of Science in 1902 and 1905.

Education

BA University of Cambridge, 1878
Sc.D. University of Cambridge, 1897

Fieldwork

Aran Islands, 1890, 1891
Torres Strait, 1888–9
Torres Strait, Papua New Guinea, Borneo, 1898–9
Torres Strait, Papua New Guinea, 1914

Key Publications

(ed.) (1901–35) *Reports of the Cambridge Anthropological Expedition to Torres Straits*, 6 vols, Cambridge, UK: Cambridge University Press.

(1924) *The Races of Man and Their Distribution*, Cambridge, UK: Cambridge University Press.

with Hornell, J. (1936–8) *Canoes of Oceania*, 3 vols, Honolulu: Bishop Museum.

(1946) *Smoking and Tobacco Pipes in New Guinea* (published posthumously), London: Philosophical Transactions of the Royal Society, Series B.

Further Reading

Herle, A. and Rouse, S. (eds) (1998) *Cambridge and the Torres Strait: Centenary Essays on the 1898 Anthropological Expedition*, Cambridge, UK: Cambridge University Press.

Urry, J. (1993) *Before Social Anthropology: Essays on the History of British Anthropology*, Chur: Harwood Academic.

SANDRA ROUSE

Hall, Edward Twitchell

b. 16 May 1916, Webster Groves, Missouri, USA

Hall has been a prolific writer. He has produced numerous volumes and is certainly one of the best-selling anthropological writers of the twentieth century. His work finds mention in almost every American introductory textbook that overviews the discipline for undergraduates. However, for all this, his influence on the development of contemporary discipline remains quite marginal. This is, in part, the result of the intellectual path he chose to make for himself. In his autobiography (1996) Hall has provided a candid assessment of the shaping of his career.

Hall spent much of his career demonstrating that there were ideas and insights of practical value that could grow out of an anthropological perspective and that these ideas and insights could speak to significant issues extending far beyond the university and the somewhat artificial boundaries of a discipline.

Since the publication of his first book in 1959, Hall has sought to illuminate ways in which culture systematically shapes our lives while operating beneath our conscious awareness. In developing this perspective Hall regularly came back to some foundational ideas drawn from those sharing a similar focus: he has had regular recourse to insights from linguistics, architecture, psychiatry, and ethnology. His handbook on proxemics provides ample references for this (1974). While this approach has tended to essentialise the particular cultures under consideration, to make them appear more separate, distinct, and individually coherent than they are experienced and lived by those who live their lives with them, it has allowed Hall to develop some important insights about communication.

Hall is not known for his detailed analyses from extended periods of fieldwork with particular groups of people. He has used a variety of field experiences, carried out under a varying conditions, to tease out issues and problems that interested him. In choosing not to work ethnographically, from within the frame of a single culture, and to focus instead on the relations between cultures, groups and individuals from different cultures, he gives emphasis to the ways that differing assumptions shape these interactions. His vivid examples of how different cultural notions of time and space can deeply affect relationships, without being recognised by the parties involved, remain useful insights. Indeed, for this work he is seen by many as one of the founders of what is now widely recognised as intercultural communications.

Education

BA University of Denver, 1936

MA University of Arizona, 1938

Ph.D. Columbia University, 1942

Fieldwork

Navaho and Hopi, 1933–7; and in various other places on a more *ad hoc* basis throughout his career.

Key Publications

(1959) *The Silent Language*, Garden City, NY: Anchor Press/Doubleday.

(1974) *Handbook for Proxemic Research*, Special Publication of Studies in the Anthropology of Visual Communication. Washington, DC: Society for the Anthropology of Visual Communication.

(1987) *Hidden Differences: Doing business with the Japanese*, Garden City, NY: Anchor Press/ Doubleday.

(1996) *An Anthropology of Everyday Life*, New York: Doubleday & Company.

PHILIP MOORE

Hallowell, A. Irving

b. 28 December 1892, Philadelphia, Pennsylvania, USA

d. 10 October 1974, Wayne, Pennsylvania, USA

A. Irving 'Pete' Hallowell came to anthropology by a circuitous route. He moved from business to social work, with eight years of professional employment as a social worker in his native Philadelphia, before shifting towards anthropology under the aegis of Frank Speck at the University of Pennsylvania. Although his library dissertation was on the circumpolar distribution of bear ceremonialism, Hallowell remains best known for his Ojibwa ethnography. He spent most of his teaching career at the University of Pennsylvania, working alongside Speck in Algonquian studies until the latter's death in 1950.

It was 1930 before the felicitous combination of Hallowell with the Ojibwa took form. While studying Algonquian cross-cousin marriage among the Cree north of Lake Winnipeg, Hallowell met Chief Willie Berens who would facilitate his entrée into the traditional non-Christian Ojibwa communities far up the Berens River. This highly productive collaboration lasted from 1932 to 1940, during which time Hallowell made several trips to the Berens River. In this period Hallowell's interests were moving towards the cross-cultural study of psychology or personality. He traced a gradient of acculturation among Ojibwa communities depending on their degree of isolation (from northwestern Ontario to Wisconsin) and attempted to use Rorschach profiles as a culture-free research instrument.

Hallowell's more qualitative and ethnographically focused discussions of Ojibwa perception, however, have better stood the test of time. What he called 'the behavioural environment of the self' included complex cultural constructions of time and space, measurement, myths and dreams, the emergence of a sense of self, and spirits of the dead. *Culture and Experience* (1955) collects the papers that summarise this ethnographic work. Hallowell's overall ethnography of the Ojibwa of the Berens River, emphasising history and ethnohistory, was lost in manuscript and has recently been reconstructed from a draft by Jennifer Brown of the University of Winnipeg (1992). Brown and Canadian Broadcasting Corporation ethnojournalist, Maureen Matthews, have retraced Hallowell's Berens River fieldwork route and recorded the positive memories of him in contemporary Ojibwa communities.

Some of Hallowell's later work elaborated on the Ojibwa ethnography. However, he also turned to new subjects, the history of anthropology and the evolutionary framework of human cultural adaptation (1976). He wrote an exemplary history of American anthropology for a collection of early essays from the *American Anthropologist*. Elsewhere, he argued that the history of anthropology was a problem for anthropologists rather than for historians and should be studied as an anthropological

problem, using the ethnographic methods developed for fieldwork in small communities. He also explored the evolutionary foundations of human cognition, attempting to surmount the mind–body dichotomy so firmly embedded in Western thought.

Education

BA University of Pennsylvania, 1911
MA University of Pennsylvania, 1920
Ph.D. University of Pennsylvania, 1924

Fieldwork

Cree, 1930
Ojibwa, 1932–40

Key Publications

(1955) *Culture and Experience*, Philadelphia: University of Pennsylvania Press.
(1976) *Selected Writings of A. Irving Hallowell*, ed. Raymond D. Fogelson, Chicago: University of Chicago Press.
(1992) *The Ojibwa of Berens River, Manitoba*, ed. Jennifer Brown, New York: Holt, Rinehart & Winston.

REGNA DARNELL

Hamilton, Carolyn A.

b. 17 August 1958, Johannesburg, South Africa

Carolyn Hamilton describes herself as a historical anthropologist who works in five broad areas: power and politics in the early nineteenth-century Zulu kingdom; representation of the Zulu; the nature of the archive; the production of history; and, most recently, the constitution of public intellectual life in South Africa.

With degrees in both history and anthropology, the consonance between these disciplines continues to influence Hamilton's research and interests. *Terrific Majesty* is a probing investigation into the roots of Zulu nationalism and the role of an elite ruling class in the emerging Zulu state. Hamilton examines the making of the image of Shaka Zulu and how it fed into ideas of Zulu militarism and nationalism that prevailed in late twentieth-century South Africa. Hamilton works extensively with historian John Wright in this area.

As sites of research, museums and archives have posed philosophical questions for Hamilton about the mediation of history in the politics of identity. Particularly, she is concerned with museums as public spheres of local knowledge and managed collections of material culture in a global context. Both her archaeological field research at Catalhoyuk, Turkey, and her research into South African intellectual life are extensions of these interests.

In 1997 Hamilton became director, then head, of the Graduate School for the Humanities and Social Sciences at the University of the Witwatersrand. In 2001 she became Assistant Dean of Graduate Studies at the University of the Witwatersrand in Johannesburg.

Education

BA University of Natal, Pietermaritzburg, 1979
BA (Hons) University of the Witwatersrand, Johannesburg, 1980
MA University of the Witwatersrand, Johannesburg, 1986
MA Johns Hopkins University, 1988
Ph.D. Johns Hopkins University, 1993

Fieldwork

Swaziland, KwaZulu-Natal, South Africa, 1982–8 and intermittently since
Catalhoyuk, Turkey, 1996–7

Key Publications

(1998) *Terrific Majesty: The Powers of Shaka Zulu and the Limits of Historical Invention*, Boston, MA: Harvard University Press.

EVIE PLAICE

Hammond-Tooke, William David

b. 30 August 1926, Cape Town, South Africa

David Hammond-Tooke has been a prolific writer and one of the last distinguished South African anthropologists. His interests cover a wide area, from comparative ethnography, to pre-colonial social history, to witchcraft, myth, healing, and kinship. He edited *The Bantu-Speaking Peoples of Southern Africa* (1974) – a revised and updated version of the volume published in 1938 with his former teacher, I. Schapera, as the editor.

Hammond-Tooke combined his own interest in history with his considerable fieldwork experience to produce a number of books and articles. In the 1970s, he became influenced by Claude Lévi-Strauss's structuralism – and as a result wrote some quite original analyses of Zulu myths. He was interested in religion in a very general sense – Hammond-Tooke saw religious beliefs and rituals as part of the world view, deeply embedded in people's traditions and history. Therefore, his main aim was to show the underlying structure of different beliefs, and he did it with considerable success – his monograph on the Kgaga is very much cited among the scholars of anthropology of religion. On the other hand, his failure to embrace Marxism did not bring Hammond-Tooke too many friends within the South African social anthropology that was until the late 1990s very much dominated by Marxism and functionalism. Many of his ideas went against the predominant ones – for example, Hammond-Tooke argued that there were never any 'clan-based societies' or 'lineages' (hence, no 'segmentary lineage system' either) in Southern Africa. Instead, most of the societies were organised in chiefdoms, with the household as the core unit.

During the 1990s, Hammond-Tooke wrote a very readable survey of the black South African societies, where he convincingly argued against the romanticising of the pre-colonial societies while at the same time demonstrating the complexity and uniqueness of traditional cultures. He also wrote an extremely interesting history of South African anthropology (with its uneasy relationship with colonial and later apartheid government) from its glorious beginnings in 1921, until the not-quite-so-glorious 1990.

David Hammond-Tooke has been a keen observer of South African ethnographic realities and as such a big influence on the historiography of the whole region. His attempts to look for 'deep structures' of thoughts that govern people's behaviour have won him wide recognition, and it is very likely that the results of his work will be used even more in the time when disciplines like anthropology and history cross over and complement each other.

Education

BA University of Cape Town, 1946
MA University of Cape Town, 1948
Ph.D. University of Cape Town, 1952

Fieldwork

Cape Town African Township, 1948
Transkeian Bhaca, 1949
Johannesburg urban townships, 1950
Cape Nguni, 1955–8
Mpodonmise, 1960–5
Kgaga (North Sotho), 1976–9

Key Publications

(ed.) (1974) *The Bantu-Speaking Peoples of Southern Africa*, London: Routledge & Kegan Paul.
(1981) *Boundaries and Belief*, Johannesburg: Witwatersrand University Press.
(1993) *The Roots of Black South Africa*, Johannesburg: Jonathan Ball.
(1997) *Imperfect Interpreters: South Africa's Anthropologists 1920–1990*, Johannesburg: Witwatersrand University Press.

ALEKSANDAR BOSKOVIC

Handelman, Don

b. 1939, Montreal, Canada

Don Handelman displays a creative independence of thought, in both his anthropological interests and understanding. Focused sharply on the processes of interaction and the nature of ritual, he has developed a theory of play and of the logic of 'public events.' In pursuit of these theoretical interests, and with a direct eye for the comparative, he has carried out field research in a notable variety of social settings, from shamanism among the Washo, to a sheltered workshop in Jerusalem, mummery in Newfoundland, and myth and ritual in India. His work is distinguished by analytical richness and meticulous attention to the intricacies of social ordering and symbolic processes, bringing into special relief the play of uncertainty in social life. Particularly noteworthy is his distinction between (pre-modern) ritual events that serve to 'model' change, and bureaucratic (modern) ones that serve simply to 'mirror' the social order and cosmos. This distinction manifests his concern to uncover internal 'logics,' and, correlatively, his considered analytical preference to give a certain primacy to design over practice. Behind this preference rests a phenomenological surmise that these deep logics systematically reflect human experience. Handelman has collaborated fruitfully with other scholars, including his late wife, the Israeli sociologist, Lea Shamgar-Handelman.

Education

BA McGill University, 1960
MA McGill University, 1964
Ph.D. University of Manchester, 1971

Fieldwork

Quebec, 1963
Nevada, 1964
Israel, 1968, ongoing
Newfoundland, 1973–4

Sri Lanka, summer 1979

Los Angeles, Olympic Project, 1984

Andhra Pradesh, May 1992, May 1993, December 1999

Key Publications

(1990) *Models and Mirrors: Towards an Anthropology of Public Events*, Cambridge, UK: Cambridge University Press (and New York: Berghahn Books, 1998).

with Shulman, David (1997) *God inside out: Siva's Game of Dice*, New York: Oxford University Press.

T.M.S. EVENS

Handler, Richard

b. 17 May 1950, Indiana, Pennsylvania, USA

Richard Handler's significant contribution to understanding the politics of 'culture' began with his doctoral research on Québécois nationalism. Handler is concerned with the underlying assumptions and logics in nationalism, specifically with the possessive individualism informing the objectification of what is imagined to be the nation's culture. He argues that modern individualism expresses itself in metaphors that treat the nation as a person and the individual as the nation personified. This conception of the nation as bounded and discrete has echoes in anthropologists' treatment of 'culture'. These conceptual similarities between nationalist rhetoric and social science discourse affect how anthropologists write about nationalism and ethnicity. In particular, Handler cautions against applying representational methods that simply present nationalists' arguments without attempting to unbound or deconstruct the concepts used.

This interest in the objectification of culture Handler further explores in his work on Colonial Williamsburg, the reconstructed capital of the colony of Virginia. With Eric Gable,

Handler examines how this history museum interprets history and then presents this history to visitors. As with nationalists' rhetoric, issues of authenticity predominate. Handler and Gable detail how conceptions of the authentic or real Colonial Williamsburg have changed over time but also how different views of the 'real' Colonial Williamsburg are contested within the museum. By looking at the process of interpreting history, its presentation, and consumption, Handler and Gable illuminate much about the invention of history and tradition, the manufacturing of cultural beliefs, and the packaging of American history.

Handler also turns this critical look at the production of history to anthropology itself. With a specific interest in American anthropology, Handler focuses on the canon of the history of anthropology that legitimises some and excludes others according to race, class, gender, citizenship, institutional and disciplinary affiliation, and English language proficiency. Additionally, Handler is interested in anthropologists as critics of modernity and exploring the relationship between anthropology and broader intellectual trends.

Handler also explores the intersections between anthropology and literature. One aspect of this examines the ways anthropology can use literature as a source material. Handler, with Daniel Segal, show how Jane Austen's novels illustrate well kinship rules and the conventions surrounding courtship, marriage, and above all social hierarchy. Another aspect has been Handler's interest in the literary work of Ruth Benedict and Edward Sapir.

Education

BA Columbia University, 1972

MA University of Chicago, 1976

Ph.D. University of Chicago, 1979

Fieldwork

Quebec 1976, 1977–8, 1980, 1983

Colonial Williamsburg, Virginia, 1990–1

Key Publications

(1988) *Nationalism and the Politics of Culture in Quebec*, Madison: University of Wisconsin Press.

Handler, R. and Segal, D. (1990) *The Fiction of Culture: Jane Austen and the Narration of Social Realities*, Tucson: University of Arizona.

Handler, R. and Gable, E. (1997) *The New History in an Old Museum: Creating the Past at Colonial Williamsburg*, Durham: Duke University Press.

(ed.) (2000) *Excluded Ancestors, Inventible Traditions: Essays Toward a More Inclusive History of Anthropology*, Madison: University of Wisconsin Press.

JUDITH DOYLE

Hanks, William F.

b. 1952, Providence, Rhode Island, USA

William Hanks's work has focused on the relation between language and social life within a conceptual framework derived from linguistics and anthropology. Drawing from over twenty-five years of fieldwork in the Oxkutzcab region of Yucatan, Hanks has developed a novel approach to sociolinguistics that seeks to integrate the structural, contextual, and ideological aspects of communicative practice. His research in Oxkutzcab analyses both everyday language use in domestic and agricultural labour settings and highly specialised speech used in Maya shamanic practice.

William Hanks's first book, *Referential Practice*, engages in a comprehensive analysis of Maya deixis that breaks sharply from previous formalist accounts of reference and is deeply influenced by the phenomenology of Merleau-Ponty, Ingarden, and Schutz, and by Pierre Bourdieu's practice theory. Drawing from over 500 actually attested utterances in Yucatec Maya, Hanks takes issue with previous egocentric theories of deixis to demonstrate the importance of lived space, corporeality, and interpersonal relations in how contemporary Yucatec Maya speakers make reference to themselves, others, and objects in their social world. In *Language and Communicative Practices* Hanks furthers this discussion through a critical re-evaluation of many of the classic studies in language and society. Ultimately Hanks argues for a model of communicative practice that recognises the mutually constitutive, yet analytically distinguishable, relations between agency, structure, and ideology. Unlike many sociolinguistic theories that treat discourse as a phenomenon analytically distinct from practice, for Hanks, discourse *is* a form of practice.

Maya shamanism is another area of sustained fieldwork and publication for William Hanks. Beginning in 1978, he began a sixteen-year relationship with a Maya shaman and ultimately became his sole apprentice. Through demonstrating the importance of colonial missionisation to contemporary shamanic discourse, Hanks's research on Maya shamanism has diverged significantly from much Mayanist scholarship that has sought to downplay colonial influences. Hanks's research on contemporary Maya shamanism also stimulated his interest in colonialism in Yucatan. In 1996 he was awarded a Guggenheim Fellowship to further explore the colonial missionisation of the Maya by the Spanish and this research focuses on colonial intertextuality, the spatial orientation of Franciscan missionisation in Yucatan, and the discursive formation of colonial Yucatan.

From 1983–96 William Hanks served as a professor of anthropology, linguistics, and social science at the University of Chicago. From 1996–2000 he taught in the anthropology department at Northwestern University. In 2000, Hanks accepted a position in the anthropology department at the University of California at Berkeley. Hanks has also sought out numerous international collaborations and has taught as a visiting professor at several institutions outside the USA.

Education

BS Georgetown University, 1975
MA University of Chicago, 1979
Joint Ph.D. University of Chicago, 1983

Fieldwork

Oxkutzcab Region, Yucatan, 1977–91 (28 months)
Merida and Oxkutzcab, Yucatan, 1993–6 (10 months)

Key Publications

(1990) *Referential Practice: Language and Lived Space among the Maya*, Chicago: University of Chicago Press.
(1995) *Language and Communicative Practices*, Boulder: Westview Press.
(1999) *Intertexts: Writings on Language, Utterance and Context*, Denver: Rowman & Littlefield.

MICHELLE DAY

Hann, Chris

b. 1953, Cardiff, Wales, UK

Chris Hann is one of the leading anthropological investigators of socialist and post-socialist countries in Eurasia. Despite its vast population and the range of its social forms, this region was long neglected in anthropology. External knowledge was skewed by cold-war mythologies, while 'local scholars' were constrained by the ideology of Marxist-Leninism and/or the disciplinary legacy of 'national ethnography'. By the 1970s, however, the political climate in some countries softened sufficiently to allow stereotypes of 'totalitarianism' to be reassessed through fieldwork. Hann was able to demonstrate in his early village studies that the success of collectivisation in Hungary depended on a flexible symbiosis of co-operatives and the village household (1980), while the stagnation of Polish rural society derived from a failure to reconcile rural

development with socialist property relations (1985). He later extended these comparisons with a study of smallholder adaptations in the context of capitalist social engineering in Kemalist Turkey (2001).

Even before the collapse of the socialist regimes in 1989–91, Hann was subjecting the new slogans of 'civil society' and 'market economy' to theoretical and ethnographic critique. He sustained his interest in property relations with an important edited volume (1998) and led a comparative project on decollectivisation, to which he himself contributed a restudy of the Hungarian village where he had first worked a quarter of a century earlier. His studies on 'post-socialism' opened up new questions concerning the interplay between the common experience of socialist institutions, diverse historical traditions, and variation at the level of practices.

Hann's long-term interest in ethnicity derives from his fieldwork in China (Uighur) and Turkey (Lazi) as well as Poland (Lemko-Ukrainian). In exploring the possibilities for civil religion, he again exposed shortcomings in the fashionable 'market models'. A related concern has been with misuse of the concept of culture, both in the legitimation of ethnonational claims and in neo-Darwinian theorising. At the core of his work is the conviction that comparative social anthropology, driven both by intellectual curiosity and policy relevance, has much to offer in understanding contemporary social transformations.

Education

BA University of Oxford, 1974
Ph.D. University of Cambridge, 1979

Fieldwork

Hungary, 1975–7, 2001
Poland, 1978–9, 1980–1981
Turkey, 1982–3, 1992–3
Xinjiang, China, 1986, 1996

Key Publications

(1980) *Tázlár: A Village in Hungary*, Cambridge, UK: Cambridge University Press.

(1985) *A Village without Solidarity; Polish Peasants in Years of Crisis*, New Haven: Yale University Press.

(ed.) (1998) *Property Relations: Renewing the Anthropological Tradition*, Cambridge, UK: Cambridge University Press.

with Bellér-Hann, Ildikó (2001) *Turkish Region; State, Market and Social Identities on the East Black Sea Coast*, Oxford: James Currey.

RICHARD ROTTENBURG

Hannerz, Ulf

b. 9 June 1942, Malmö, Sweden

Ulf Hannerz achieved international recognition early in his career with an ethnographic study of a black 'ghetto community' in Washington, DC, during the late 1960s. In many ways, Hannerz's ethnography of 'Soulside' was well within the tradition of American inner-city studies. This was an ethnographic tradition that included both sociologists and anthropologists, and, like other work within this genre, Hannerz's study concerned a minority population, involved intensive participant observation within a tightly circumscribed neighbourhood locale, and took cognisance of potential social policy implications. Yet, unlike other contributors to this tradition, Hannerz was not a resident of the USA. He was a Swedish doctoral student who was examining a locale in the capital city of the USA with the same kind of 'exoticist' lens as American anthropologists had been accustomed to train on 'Third World' sites far from their usual places of residence. He succeeded in carrying out this research even though the neighbourhood in which he was working was swept up in the racial tensions and riots that racked American cities during the late 1960s. The study, however, succeeded in going well beyond these circumstances and also included a carefully nuanced examination of the debate

on the 'culture of poverty' that was then engaging American social scientists, a processual view of culture which prefigured much later work in anthropology, and an ethnographic portrait that did much to counter stereotypes of black inner-city life by stressing the diversity of lifestyles and practices featured in this Washington, DC, neighbourhood as well as the commonalties between its residents.

While Ulf Hannerz went onto conduct further ethnographic research elsewhere, his most influential later works were theoretical overviews of established and emerging fields rather than ethnographic monographs. *Exploring the City* provided an account of work that has contributed to the development of an urban anthropology. This and subsequent publications have featured several key elements of Hannerz's analytical approach. He easily moves across disciplinary boundaries, has a facility for integrating diverse materials such as work from a large span of historical periods; the ethnographic with more abstract theoretical inquiries.

While an interest in metropolitan life continues to feature in Hannerz's work, since the mid-1980s, he has been best known for his pioneering contributions towards the development of a macro-anthropology concerned with transnational connections. Unlike many of his contemporaries in anthropology who have tended to over-identify transnationality with migration studies, Hannerz's reflections in this area have been concerned with much broader issues of the processes and agents involved in the organisation of culture at the turn of the twenty-first century. Artists, foreign journalists, business executives, residents of a small Swedish village, 'Third World' migrants, cosmopolitans, and locals alike come into view in his efforts to analyse the increasingly global flows of culture. There are several features or concepts appearing in this stage of Hannerz's work that are worth singling out. First, he has continued to be influenced by what he has referred to as a 'distributive' model of culture, one that draws upon a long tradition of anthropological scholarship which treats cultural sharing as problematic rather than self-evident and focuses on the varying, uneven, and unequal distribution of meanings over particular populations. From this perspective has come Hannerz's view of culture as an organisation of diversity rather than of uniformity. Thus when Hannerz refers to the globalisation of culture or to the emergence of a 'global ecumene', he does not see this process as necessarily entailing cultural homogenisation. Rather, drawing upon the linguistic concept of creole languages, Hannerz argues that the world is creolising, i.e. mixing elements deriving from different sources and traditions. Finally, Hannerz has made an effort to systematise the study of global culture by directing attention to four social frameworks organising the contemporary flow of culture: the form (or way) of life, the state, the market, and social movements.

During the 1990s, Hannerz has moved back towards ethnography, investigating his interest in transnational cultures in the form of a multi-locale study of foreign correspondents.

Education

BA University of Stockholm, 1963
MA Indiana University, 1966
FL University of Stockholm, 1966
Ph.D. University of Stockholm, 1969

Fieldwork

Washington, DC, 1966–8
Cayman Islands, 1970
Kafanchan, Nigeria, 1974–5, 1980, 1983
Foreign correspondent project, various sites in Europe, USA, Israel, South Africa, Hong Kong, 1995–2000

Key Publications

(1969) *Soulside: Inquiries into Ghetto Culture and Community*, New York and London: Columbia University Press.
(1980) *Exploring the City: Inquiries Toward an Urban Anthropology*, New York: Columbia University Press.

(1992) *Cultural Complexity: Studies in the Social Organization of Meaning*, New York: Columbia University Press.
(1996) *Transnational Connections: Culture, People, Places*, London & New York: Routledge.

VERED AMIT

Harries-Jones, Peter J.C.

b. 1937, Oxford, UK

Throughout his intellectual career, Peter Harries-Jones has, in various ways and with a variety of subject matters, worked in three anthropological areas. First, he has been concerned with the methodological and epistemological bases of social science. Second, he has engaged in critical analysis: initially of the significance of networks, more recently of ecological and biological approaches. Third has been his concern with political action and social movements. Following his African experience, which led to his first book (1975), and after moving to Canada, he concentrated on an in-depth rethinking of the theoretical bases in social anthropology and this took him to a uniquely thorough examination of the neglected work of Gregory Bateson. That turned him to an exploration of ecology, environmentalism, and advocacy – the results of which are contained in his most recent book (1995). This interpretation of Bateson has now led him into the field of bio-semiotics.

Education

BA Rhodes University, South Africa, 1958
B.Litt. University of Oxford, 1962
D.Phil. University of Oxford, 1970

Fieldwork

Zambia, 1961–5
Sudan, 1969–71
Newfoundland, 1982–98 (recurrent summer visits)

Key Publications

(1975) *Freedom and Labour: Mobilization and Political Control on the Zambian Copperbelt*, Oxford: Blackwell.

(1995) *A Recursive Vision: Ecological Understanding and Gregory Bateson*, Toronto: University of Toronto Press.

P.H. GULLIVER

Harris, Marvin

b. 18 August 1927, New York, USA

d. 25 October 2001, Gainesville, Florida, USA

Marvin Harris has been one of the most important scholars of cultural anthropology over the course of decades. He supported and developed theories of the so-called cultural materialism. Social behaviour and social structures result from material conditions and circumstances, from possibilities and restrictions of habitats. In the cultural history of mankind the relationship of material structures of the habitat to the population structure, particularly in respect to population density, has always been important. The first agrarian societies after the ice age developed due to a growth in population. Agriculture was necessary because wild animals diminished through intense hunting. The balance of habitat and population can be influenced mainly through birth control and through an increase in productivity of the soil. Agriculture and domestication of animals led to an increase in the productivity of the soil to a high level – much more than hunting and gathering could provide.

Harris argued that population pressure on natural resources is the main cause of social evolution. He did not consider cultural, normative, and cognitive phenomena to be the causes of social evolution. Not only the rise, but also the subsequent development of agrarian societies over thousands of years was to be explained against the background of materialistic and economic concepts. The beginning of agriculture and the breeding of livestock was followed by a substantial increase in population. A few generations later, however, the rapid increase in population density again pressed on the carrying capacity. Hence, members of these agrarian societies were constantly forced to improve their technologies. The use of the plough, new technologies, fertiliser, cultivation of plants, and animals continuously increased the carrying capacity. Harris argued that the increase in population density was the main cause of the development of cities, states, civilisations, technologies, labour specialisation, commerce, and economic growth.

Particularly in *Cannibals and Kings* and in *Our Kind* Harris showed that the rise and decline of civilisations are the results of the boundless exploitation of natural resources. The consequences of this boundless use are salting and erosion of soils, loss of important fertile ingredients, and total loss of soils. According to Harris such consequences are responsible for the decline of the Maya culture, of old Mesopotamia, of East Mediterranean cultures, and finally of the ancient civilisation altogether. Based upon Wittfogel's hydraulic theory Harris argued that the Chinese and the Indian peoples failed to redress the balance between high population density and poor nutrition based mostly on plants. The bureaucracy, responsible for the supply of water and for controlling the canals, prevented the development of liberty, of private property, and of innovations. On the other hand, in Northern Europe, regular precipitation did not create similar problems of water supply or the necessity to construct canals. Hence, bureaucracy did not develop and grow as it did in Asia. In Europe economic liberty could grow as a precondition for entrepreneurs to found factories.

Not only did Harris wish to explain the basic structures of social evolution and of civilisations, but he also wanted to explain cultural, cognitive, and religious phenomena through materialistic concepts. So in his book *Good to Eat* he tried to explain habits of nutrition, preferences and taboos, by strictly materialistic concepts. Ecological problems were responsible for religious taboos against eating the meat of pigs and cows. In his books *Cows, Pigs, Wars and Witches* (1975 [1974]) and in *Our Kind* (1989) he argued that ecological reasons alone could account for the suppression of women, the emergence of messiahs, and even the prosecution of witches.

Harris also wrote important textbooks on cultural anthropology: *Cultural Anthropology* (1995 [1983]) provides a comprehensive overview on all important and current subjects of this discipline and the *Rise of Anthropological Theory* contains an overview of the history of cultural anthropology.

Education

BA Columbia University, 1949
Ph.D. Columbia University, 1953

Fieldwork

Islas de la Bahia, Brazil (Town and Country in Brazil), 1956
Mozambique (Portugal's African 'Wards': A First-Hand Report on Labour and Education in Mozambique), 1958
India, Ecuador, and Africa (Minorities in the New World. Six Case Studies), 1959

Key Publications

(1968) *Rise of Anthropological Theory: A History of Theories of Cultures*, New York: T.Y. Crowell Comp./HarperCollins.
(1977) *Cannibals and Kings: The Origins of Culture*, New York: Random House.
(1985) *Good to Eat: Riddles of Food and Culture*, New York: Simon & Schuster.
(1989) *Our Kind: Who We Are, Where We Came from, Where We Are Going*, New York: Harper & Row.

GEORG W. OESTERDIEKHOFF

Harrison, Faye Venetia

b. 25 November 1951, Norfolk, Virginia, USA

Faye V. Harrison, African diaspora specialist, began fieldwork in 1974 studying West Indian immigrant youth in London. In 1978, she embarked on research in urban Jamaica that spanned two decades on grassroots politics and the political economy of poverty. Concerned with local agency, Harrison focused on transnationalism, urban informal economy, the gendered division of labour, political violence, drug trafficking, gangs, and structural adjustment. She has also written on the politics of fieldwork. Harrison is most recognised for critical meta-analyses on 'race' and its tangled history in anthropology. In *Decolonizing Anthropology*, she advocated developing a transformative and 'decolonised' anthropology. A student of the late St Clair Drake, Harrison is one of the foremost critical voices in the race debate, reflected in 'Autoethnographic reflections on hierarchies in anthropology' (1995), a reflexive narrative of personal confrontations with 'elitist obstacles' that threaten 'anthropology's democratisation', and 'The persistent power of "race" in anthropology' (1995), an exhaustive, enlightened treatment of the problematic history of race debates in anthropology. Harrison acknowledges valuable contributions by St Clair Drake and W.E.B. Du Bois, and chastises anthropologists like Franz Boas for failure to cite black scholars. For Harrison, race is still significant and warrants a prominent place on the discipline's agenda. In 'Expanding the discourse on "race"' (1998), she notes the inventive nature of racism, and advocates a four-field approach. In the 2000s, Harrison marries the contested topic of 'race' to human rights and foreign policy within a global context. Past president of the Association of Black Anthropologists, Faye V. Harrison is one of anthropology's most prolific and thought-provoking scholars.

Education

BA Brown University, 1974
MA Stanford University, 1977
Ph.D. Stanford University, 1982

Fieldwork

London, 1974–5
Jamaica, 1978–9, 1984, 1988, 1992, 1996
Denmark, USA, South Africa, 2000 and on-
going

Key Publications

(1995) 'The persistent power of "race" in the
cultural and political economy of racism',
Annual Review of Anthropology 24: 47–74.
(ed.) (1997 [1991]) *Decolonizing Anthropology:
Moving further toward an Anthropology of Liberation*,
second edn, Arlington, VA: American
Anthropological Association.

IRMA MCCLAURIN

Hart, J. Keith

b. 1943, Manchester, UK

Keith Hart, widely recognised as a public
speaker and anthropological popularist, is one
of British anthropology's great mavericks.
Hart's anthropology has focused on economics
both as a realistic baseline for human activity
and as a philosophical idea. While his early
work involved street-level ethnography of
migrant entrepreneurs in Accra, Ghana, most
recently he has pursued the concept of money
at its broadest levels of meaning – scientific,
aesthetic, memorial, and Utopian.

Hart achieved fame in the 1970s by coining
the term 'informal economy'. The orthodoxy
of the time held that Third World countries
such as Ghana suffered from unemployment.
Hart demonstrated that the so-called unem-
ployed engaged in a multiplicity of economic
activities usually unrecognised and untaxable.
This informal economy plugged the gaps in
weak state institutions. Hart then took a bird's-

eye view on the same problems. He argued
that, until agriculture in West Africa became
fully capitalised, rural involution, burgeoning
cities, and ineffectual government would
continue.

Hart's thinking has increasingly taken a
philosophical direction. Against the distinction
between 'market economy' (the West) and 'gift
economy' (the Rest) frequently made by anthropologists, Hart has argued that money and
markets have always existed at varying levels of
abstraction in human societies. Furthermore,
having gone through a long period of
fetishisation in tandem with the Industrial
Revolution, money is now becoming recon-
nected with the social networks and personal
identities that formerly gave it meaning. Hart
examines the potential of this repersonalisa-
tion of money in *Money in an Unequal World*.

Education

BA University of Cambridge, 1964
Ph.D. University of Cambridge, 1969

Fieldwork

Ghana, 1965–8
Cayman Islands, 1970
South Africa, 1998–9

Key Publications

(1982) *The Political Economy of West African
Agriculture*, Cambridge, UK: Cambridge University Press.
(1999) *Money in an Unequal World*, New York:
Texere.

HUON WARDLE

Hastrup, Kirsten

b. 1948, Copenhagen, Denmark

One cornerstone in Hastrup's far-reaching
scholarly work is her studies of Icelandic
history and society. In three monographs and
many articles, covering periods from the early

medieval settlements to present times, Hastrup makes comprehensive contributions both to the ethnography of Iceland and to the understanding and conceptualisation of historical changes in Icelandic society and in general. This early interest in historical anthropology continues to feature in her work. In *A Place Apart*, Hastrup's third and unorthodox monograph on (contemporary) Iceland, she theorises about the ways in which history and discourses of the past enter into modern Icelandic identity and images of Icelandicness, and shows how history is produced locally through daily practices.

The challenges of contemporary anthropological theorising, epistemology, and ethnographic practice are recurrent themes in Hastrup's work, notably in *A Passage to Anthropology*. She pays considerable theoretical attention to the nature of fieldwork, and to the process by which individual experience in the field is transformed into anthropological knowledge, as well as to the ethical dilemmas inherent in this process. In her continued dialogue with philosophy Hastrup claims that anthropological knowledge is a product of radical interpretation (rather than clarification), adding new and unprecedented understandings to the world and thereby contributing to the opening up of new historical avenues.

The anthropological project is essentially a theoretical one, she argues, aiming at a general understanding of the complex relationship between individual moves and singular events, and the larger collectivities and histories, rather than any inherent logic of culture. On that background Hastrup also challenges the idea of a particular 'native' anthropology; since all knowledge is positioned and partial, the origin of the researcher is of less moment that his or her anthropological competence and reflexivity.

Hastrup's long term interest in theatre anthropology and performance theory culminates in a sophisticated study of Shakespeare's theatre, with an emphasis on modern players. Hastrup provides an ethnographic analysis of the players' work and self-understanding, which forms the basis for theorising about social action, language, motivation, and human agency.

From 1998–2001 Hastrup acted as a research director at the Danish Centre for Human Rights, giving her an opportunity to study human rights from an anthropological point of view and to publish four edited volumes on the challenges posed by the claim to universality and the respect for diversity.

As the initiator, author, and editor of several Danish textbooks in anthropology Hastrup has taken a leading part in consolidating and developing anthropology as an academic discipline in Denmark, and she has worked passionately to bring anthropology in creative dialogue with other academic disciplines.

Hastrup was a founding member of the European Association of Social Anthropologists, its first secretary (1989&90), and second president (1991&2).

Education

Mag.Scient. University of Copenhagen, 1973
D.Phil. University of Oxford, 1980
Dr.Scient.Soc. University of Copenhagen, 1990

Fieldwork

Iceland, 1981–2, and intermittently
Shorter field studies in India (1975) and Columbia (1988)

Key Publications

(1990) *Nature and Policy in Iceland 1400–1800. An Anthropological Analysis of History and Mentality*, Oxford: Clarendon Press.

(1995) *A Passage to Anthropology. Between Experience and Theory*, London and New York: Routledge.

(1998) *A Place Apart. An Anthropological Study of the Icelandic World*, Oxford: Clarendon Press.

(2003) *Studying Action. Anthropology in the Company of Shakespeare*, Copenhagen: Museum Tusculanum Press.

TINE TJØRNHØJ-THOMSEN

Haudricourt, André-Georges

b. 1911, Paris, France

d. 1996, Paris, France

André-Georges Haudricourt was initially trained as an agricultural engineer. During the years 1932 to 1934, he attended the courses of Marcel Mauss. Mauss then arranged a mission in the USSR that enabled Haudricourt to study the origin of crop plants within the framework of the Phytotechnic Institute (VIR), directed by Nicolas Vavilov (1933–4). Haudricourt commenced his career as a researcher at the Laboratory of Applied Botany of the Muséum National d'Histoire Naturelle and entered the Centre National de la Recherche Scientifique (CNRS) in 1939. In 1944 he changed his orientation towards linguistics. From 1948 to 1949 he was attached in Hanoi to the Ecole Française d'Extrême-Orient. Thereafter, during the years 1959 to 1973, he carried out long missions in New Caledonia and the Far East.

Defining himself as 'polyfunctionalist',' A G. Haudricourt developed his work around three principal axes: the question of the domestication of plants, the study of technical innovations and the way in which they are adapted to societies, and, in a kind of palaeontology-linguistics, the reconstitution of older languages. Studying the relations between man and crop plants by using botany, biology, and ethnology, Haudricourt founded the discipline of ethnobotany in France. Starting from his immense work on man and the plough, in which he took into account the cultivation methods, knowledge, beliefs, representations, environment, and of course the life of the groups studied, Haudricourt became one of the principal founding fathers of ethnoscience.

In the field of linguistics, his contribution has been of major significance through a study of differential phonological features. Through the process of transphonologisation or phonic differences, he was at the origin of the reconstitution of a great number of old Asiatic and East Asiatic languages like Thai, Karen, Mnong, Rhadé, Sek, Yao, and so on. In so doing, he made an immense contribution to the emergence of 'ethnolinguistics'. He also encouraged the combination of a history of agricultural techniques with a history of mentalities, and inventions like portage, transport, clothing, and cooking, while granting an important place to comparison.

What was important for Haudricourt was to understand societies as the result of a total social 'fact' and to discern their fundamental aspects by way of a kind of interdisciplinary ethnoarchaeology. He wanted to demonstrate that human sciences can be neither juxtaposed nor ordered hierarchically but must be considered as an object of study comprising the ensemble of human activities.

Education

Diplôme de l'Institut d'Agronomique de Grignon, 1931
Diplôme de phytopathologie et de génétique, Paris, 1932
Diplôme de la IV éme section de l'École Pratique des Hautes Études, Paris, 1945
Doctorat d'Etat ès Lettres, EHESS, 1972

Fieldwork

Leningrad, Russia, 1934–5
Hanoi, Indochina, 1948–9
Hangzhou, China, 1955
New Caledonia, 1959–73
Caobang, Vietnam, 1973
Tokyo, Japan, 1978

Key Publications

with Hédin, Louis (1943) L'Homme et les plantes cultivées (Man and Cultivated Plants), Paris: Métailié.
with Delamarre, Mariel Jean-Brunhes (1955) L'Homme et la charrue (Man and the Plough around the World), Paris: Gallimard.
with Hagège, Claude (1978) Problème de phonologie panchronique (The Problem of Panachronic Phonology), Paris: Selaf.
with Dibie, Pascal (1987) Les Pieds sur terre

(One's Feet Firmly on the Ground), Paris: Métailié.

PASCAL DIBIE

Hellmann, Ellen Phyllis

b. 1908, Johannesburg, South Africa

d. 1982, Johannesburg, South Africa

Ellen Hellmann studied social anthropology under Winifred Hoernlé at the University of the Witwatersrand (Wits), where she met the Kriges, Max Gluckman, and Hilda Kuper. Unable to pursue English because of a timetable clash, Hellmann eventually completed three degrees in social anthropology although she never made it her profession. *Rooiyard* was Hellmann's Master's thesis, and she went on to publish several more papers on African slum life including a chapter in Isaac Schapera's *The Bantu-Speaking Tribes of South Africa* (1937). In 1940 she was the first woman to obtain her Ph.D. from Wits, on black school dropouts.

Academically, Hellmann continued to focus on the impacts of urbanisation on black South African family life. She lectured in sociology for several years at the Jan Hofmeyr School of Social Work. However, Hellmann's most enduring contribution was her public work, especially in the area of race relations. She served as secretary and later chairperson on the Joint Council of Europeans and Bantu. As a founding member of the South African Institute of Race Relations, Hellmann's research frequently formed the basis of various commissions (including the Tomlinson Commission). During the Second World War, Hellmann ran the colored and Indian section of the Governor General's National War Fund. She helped found the South African Progressive Party, which challenged the post-war apartheid state of the National Party. Hellmann was awarded an honorary degree from Wits and the gold medal of the Royal African Society for her dedicated service as an 'authority on race relations ... in the forefront of the battle for African advancement'.

Education

BA University of the Witwatersrand, Johannesburg

MA University of the Witwatersrand, Johannesburg

Ph.D. University of the Witwatersrand, Johannesburg, 1940

Fieldwork

Doornfontein, Johannesburg

Key Publications

(1948) *Rooiyard: A Sociological Study of an Urban Native Slumyard*, Cape Town: Oxford University Press

with Lever, Henry (eds) (1979) *Conflict and Progress: Fifty Years of Race Relations in South Africa*, Johannesburg: Macmillan South Africa, fiftieth-anniversary publication of the South African Institute of Race Relations

EVIE PLAICE

Helm, June

b. 13 September 1924, Twin Falls, Idaho, USA

d. 5 February 2004, Iowa City, Iowa, USA

June Helm was still in high school when a fascination with the theory of evolution led her to resolve that she would become an ethnologist. Throughout her career, she was engaged with the history of anthropology, exploring its changing social and intellectual foundations. Because there was no money for college in her Midwestern working-class family when she graduated from high school just after Pearl Harbor, Helm entered the local university in Kansas City, transferring to the University of Chicago in 1942.

Helm's early fieldwork was constrained by the work of her archaeologist husband, Richard 'Scotty' MacNeisch. She carried out an MA study in a Mexican *mestizo* community before the couple moved to Ottawa, where she began a career-long engagement with the Dene peoples of Canada's Northwest Territories

(NWT). In 1951, she and a fellow graduate went to Jean Marie River, NWT, as volunteer teachers. Two seasons of fieldwork produced her Ph.D. research on northern hunter-gatherers. The Lynx Point people exemplified this band-level adaptation (1961).

For the next few years, Helm worked briefly in several Dene communities. In 1959, she and Nancy Lurie began an extensive study of the Dogrib, resulting in several joint publications. Helm made ten trips to the Dogrib between 1959 and 1979. Her work in the contemporary culture, history, and ethnohistory of the Mackenzie drainage took place over more than fifty years. Topics included early historic Dene maps, female infanticide, the fur trade, changing leadership patterns, kinship, socioterritorial organisation, and the relationship of prophecy and power. Her editorship of the sub-arctic volume of the Handbook of North American Indians (1981) demonstrated her leadership among students of the Canadian North.

During the 1970s, Helm assisted the Indian Brotherhood of the NWT in its land claims research and served as an expert witness. She was also a consultant on Canada's Mackenzie Valley Pipeline Inquiry that produced a moratorium of further development.

Helm taught at several Canadian universities before moving to the University of Iowa in 1960 where she established an independent department of anthropology and served as the first chair of the American Indian and Native Studies Program. Although her fieldwork ended in 1979, Helm continued to synthesise her long-term results on power and prophecy (1994) and on the ethnohistoric profile of the 'people of Denedeh' as they move towards self-determination.

Education

Ph.B. University of Chicago, 1944
MA University of Chicago, 1947
Ph.D. University of Chicago, 1958

Fieldwork

Mexico, 1945, 1946

Mackenzie River Dene (especially Slavey and Dogrib), 1951–79

Key Publications

(1961) The Lynx Point People: The Dynamics of a Northern Athabascan Band, National Museum of Canada Bulletin 176.
(ed.) (1981) Subarctic: Handbook of North American Indians, vol. 6, Washington, DC: Smithsonian Institution.
(1994) Prophecy and Power among the Dogrib Indians, Lincoln: University of Nebraska Press.
(2000) The People of Denedeh: Ethnohistory of the Indians of Canada's Northwest Territories, Ames: University of Iowa Press; Montreal: McGill-Queens University Press.

REGNA DARNELL

Hendry, Rosemary Joy

b. 1945, Birmingham, UK

Joy Hendry began her prolific research career by an extended fieldwork in a rural community, Kyushu, focusing on Japanese family and marriage. This was followed by research here, and in a seaside town south of Tokyo, on preschool child rearing practices. From 1986, she worked on an ESRC-funded project, 'Speech Levels and Hierarchy in Japanese Society', which later broadened out into a wider interest in politeness and other forms of self-presentation, such as through clothes and the use of time and space, which she saw as epitomised in the wrapping of gifts. Hence her monograph, Wrapping Culture, which was followed by an edited volume on Indirect Communication (Routledge, 2001) resulting from a conference.

That last research opened out into further projects including: (1) diplomacy as a form of international wrapping, involving co-operation from Japanese and British diplomats and foreign-office staff; and (2) gardens as a form of wrapping space, further turning her attention to the Japanese cultural constructions of nature. These together have led to the study of cultural display, in theme parks, 'living museums', and elsewhere, culminating in her latest monograph that places Japan in an international and historical context (*The Orient Strikes Back*).

Hendry's latest research interests have begun gradually to move out of Japan. This is partly to put the Japanese material in a comparative context, but also to address some recent issues of interest in an apparently 'global' discourse. This study concerns a movement against the old European model of museum display and the diversity of local responses to the problem. Hendry's career is exemplary, first, in having each field research culminate in a solid publication, and, second, in taking each step of research leading to a next step, moving from a more area-rooted local study up to a more global perspective, and from empirical to theoretical commitment.

Education

B.Sc. Kings College, University of London, 1966

B.Litt. Lady Margaret Hall, University of Oxford, 1974

D.Phil. Lady Margaret Hall, University of Oxford, 1979

Fieldwork

Texcoco, Mexico, 1972

Parts of Japan from 1975–6, 1979, 1981, 1986–7, and annually ever since

More recently, in pursuit of global influences, fieldwork covered Jakarta, Indonesia, and Shenzhen, China (1996); Kathmandu, Nepal, Uzbekistan, Aarhus, Denmark, London, and Orlando, Florida (1997); Skansen, Sweden, Williamsburg and Jamestown, Virginia; Bangkok, Thailand (1998), Machynlleth and Port Meirion, Wales (1999); Red Lake, Minnesota; Oaxaca, Mexico; Anaheim, California; Lai'e, Hawaii; Fiji, Vanuatu, New Caledonia, New Zealand, Singapore, and Malaysia (2000); Everglades, Florida (2001); Tanzania and Kenya (2002)

Key Publications

(1993) *Wrapping Culture: Politeness, Presentation and Power in Japan and Other Societies*, Oxford: Clarendon Press.

(1999) *An Anthropologist in Japan: Routledge Research Methods Series*, London and New York: Routledge.

(1999) *Other People's Worlds: An Introduction to Social and Cultural Anthropology*, New York: New York University Press.

(2000) *The Orient Strikes Back: A Global View of Cultural Display*, Oxford and New York: Berg.

TAKIE LEBRA

Herdt, Gilbert H.

b. 24 February 1949, Oakley, Kansas, USA

As a cultural anthropologist trained in the tradition of ethnographic fieldwork, Gilbert Herdt has successfully melded intellectual influences from classical psychoanalytic theory and modern psychiatry into the historical and cross-cultural study of sexuality, gender, and human development. While maintaining a beneficial scepticism and critical appraisal of psychoanalysis, Herdt has utilised his background in psychology and anthropology to illuminate developmental subjectivities within cultural settings as diverse as ritualised initiations among the Sambia of New Guinea and the social construction of modern gay and lesbian identities among adolescents in Chicago. Perhaps Herdt's academic career is best typified by an enduring interest in the formation of individual ontological realities within broader social structures and cultural contexts. Herdt's ethnographies always provide an account of identities and subjectivities, as well as historical, social, and cultural context. Thus, Herdt's work reminds all students of larger social and cultural systems to also scrutinise the meaning of respondents' subjective experiences, while critically examining the dialectical, intersubjective, and reflexive processes through which personal narratives are obtained and interpreted.

Herdt's influential work among the Sambia has forced a critical re-evaluation of contemporary theories of gender identity and sexual development. His elucidation of the applied and theoretical conceptualisations of clinical ethnography, sexual cultures, and sexual lifeways has provided exciting new approaches for the study of personal identity formation and developmental trajectories within powerfully constraining historical and cultural contexts. Finally, Herdt's work on the many diverse cultural systems with legitimised third sex and gender categories has dramatically expanded academic thought concerning gender roles and sexual identities. Perhaps, most importantly, Herdt's sensitive examination of diverse sexualities and gender roles across numerous historical and contemporary cultures has provided two important contributions. First, it has warned us about the inappropriate application, or even imposition, of Euro-American concepts and conceptualisations in other cultures, and, second, it has prompted us to re-examine the historical boundedness and cultural construction of our own notions of what it means to be male or female, gay or straight. Thus, Herdt's work is not limited to the study of micro- or macro-levels of analyses. Rather, his work is concerned with the interplay between the internal and external, the subjective and objective, and that which is secret versus that which is overt; his work illuminates the complex relationships between informants and ethnographers, personal identities and social structures, and the personal meanings of human development within specific historical and cultural contexts.

Since he began his academic career in 1979, Dr Herdt has authored eight books, edited more than a dozen anthologies, contributed numerous book chapters, and written more than forty journal articles. He has also served on more than ten international committees or agencies, eight major national or academic committees, and approximately fifteen departmental and university-wide committees at four American universities. Dr Herdt has served as an assistant professor of anthropology at Stanford University (1979–85), as an associate and full professor at the University of Chicago Committee on Human Development (1985–98), and, since 1998, as the director of the Human Sexuality Studies Program at San Francisco State University (SFSU). In 2000, he became the founding director of the Institute on Sexuality, Inequality, and Health at SFSU, and, in 2002, he founded the National Sexuality Resource Center at SFSU.

Education

BA California State University, Sacramento, 1971

MA California State University, Sacramento, 1972

MA, Ph.D. candidate in anthropology, University of Washington, 1973

Ph.D. Australian National University, Institute for Advanced Studies, 1978

Post-doctoral Certification in Psychiatry, University of California, Los Angeles, Neuropsychiatric Institute, 1979

Fieldwork

Family interviewing and TAT testing of Japanese Americans, Sacramento and San Francisco, California, 1970–1

Psychiatric wards of the Sacramento Medical Center, 1971–2

Eastern Highlands Province, Papua New Guinea, 1974–6, 1979, 1981, 1983, 1987, 1988, 1989, 1990, 1993

Hienecke Pregnancy Project, Los Angeles, California, 1978

Project on Sexual Orientation and Cultural Competence in Chicago Teenagers, Illinois, 1986–8

Reconnaissance field trip, Vitu Island, West New Britain Province, Papua New Guinea, 1988

Key Publications

(1981) *Guardian of the Flutes: Idioms of Masculinity*, New York: McGraw-Hill.

with Stoller, Robert J. (1990) *Intimate Communications: Erotics and the Study of Culture*, New York: Columbia University Press.

with Boxer, Andrew (1993) *Children of Horizons: How Gay and Lesbian Teenagers are Leading a New Way Out of the Closet*, Boston: Beacon Press.

(1997) *Same Sex, Different Cultures: Perspectives on Gay and Lesbian Lives*, New York: Westview Press.

TODD W. RAWLS

Héritier, Françoise

b. 15 November 1933, Veauche, France

Following studies in history and geography, Françoise Héritier began her training in social anthropology in Claude Lévi-Strauss's seminar in the late 1950s. Her initial field research was among the Mossi, Bobo, Dogon, Pana, Marka, and Samo in Mali and Burkina Faso. She later concentrated her research efforts on the Samo and her first published work based on material from that group would become one of the major references in kinship studies. There she analysed Samo marriage rules that, as is characteristic of Crow/Omaha systems, rely only on stated prohibitions. She found that despite their constraints the rules do leave room for certain choices within the universe of consanguineous or affinal relations. By computerising her data Françoise Héritier showed that within those 'spaces' left vacant in the statement of the rules, the actors preferentially chose marriage partners 'as close as possible to the prohibited partner'. Thus 'semi-complex systems' would create a logical link between the formulas based on preferential choices and others that limit themselves to defining the borders of incest.

This initial work would lead her to address the issue of the variable expression of incest prohibitions. Grouping phenomena to which little attention had been previously paid with her concept of 'incest of the second type', she explained these prohibitions by the reflections of people in all cultures on their own notions of the identical and the different. One, but not the sole, of these distinctions is the fundamental disjunction constituted by the difference between the sexes. An example of one of the areas covered under this concept is the rule prohibiting a man from marrying a mother and her daughter, a union that does not place consanguineously related individuals in direct relationship but which operates through the intermediary of a common partner. Thus, in each culture a choice operates between the valorisation of the sum of the identical and its avoidance.

It was along the lines of this fundamental masculine/feminine opposition that Françoise Héritier would continue her research and address highly diverse topics including kin terminologies, violence, and bioethics. One of the major arguments in her work involves what she has termed the 'differential valence of the sexes'. This means that males have universally sought to compensate for the biological inequality which dictates that only women bear children by attempting to control fecundity and feminine sexuality at the level of the symbolic order, through the exercise of political subjugation, and with physical violence as well.

Although she never ceased to recognise the influence of Lévi-Strauss on her work and would succeed him in his chair at the Collège de France, the work of Françoise Héritier is characterised by its originality and a deep commitment to the scientific approach.

Education

Licence d'Histoire et de Géographie, 1955

Fieldwork

Mali and Burkina Faso, October 1957–June 1958, October 1963–March 1964, Burkina Faso, 1964–9 (23 months)

Key Publications

(1981) *L'Exercice de la parenté* (The Exercise of Kinship), Paris: Hautes Études-Gallimard, Le Seuil.

(1994) *Les Deux Sœurs et leur mère. Anthropologie de l'inceste* (Two Sisters and Their Mother. The Anthropology of Incest), Paris: Odile Jacob.

(1996) *Masculin/féminin. La pensée de la différence* (Masculine/Feminine. The Thought of the Difference), Paris, Odile Jacob.

(1996) *De la violence* (Of the Violence), Paris: Odile Jacob.

LAURENT BARRY

Hermitte, M. Esther A. de

b. 30 March 1921, Buenos Aires, Argentina

Esther Hermitte carried out her graduate research in Chiapas, Mexico. She showed that through nahualism Indians constructed a complex supernatural hierarchy in order to resist the earthly discrimination and oppression they faced in a bicultural Indian-ladino society.

Back in Argentina Hermitte analysed the failure of poncho-weavers' co-operatives fostered by national programmes of local development in the northwestern province of Catamarca. Here patron–client relations were enacted by women and reproduced unequal access to local resources and the national market.

In the northeastern province of Chaco, Hermitte co-ordinated an interdisciplinary project on the rural and urban aboriginal populations, showing that Chaco Indians were already 'integrated' into national society, not marginal to it.

Hermitte created the Center of Social Anthropology at the Institute of Economic and Social Development (IDES, 1974), where she instructed younger generations of ethnographers in fieldwork, medical anthropology, and belief systems. IDES was vital to the reproduction of social anthropology in Argentina in the face of the harsh political persecution faced by students and intellectuals under the military rule of 1976–83, and the exclusion of social anthropology from Argentine universities until 1984.

Education

Profesorado Buenos Aires University, 1950

MA, Roy D. Albert Prize, University of Chicago, 1962

Ph.D., Bobbs Merryll Award, University of Chicago, 1964

Fieldwork

Chiapas, Mexico, 1959–61

Belén, Catamarca, Argentina, 1967–8; 1970, 1971, 1980

Chaco, Argentina, 1970

Key Publications

(1970) *Poder sobrenatural y control social* (Supernatural Power and Social Control), Mexico: Instituto Interamericano Indigenista.

(edition prepared and presented by Nicolás Iñigo Carrera and Alejandro Isla) (1996) *Estudio sobre la situación de los aborígenes de la Provincia del Chaco, y políticas para su integración a la sociedad nacional* (Study of the Situation of the Aborigines of the Province of Chaco and Policy for their Integration into National Society) Posadas (Argentina): Editorial Universitaria.

ROSANA GUBER

Herskovits, Melville J.

b. 10 September 1895, Bellefontaine, Ohio, USA

d. 25 February 1963, Evanston, Illinois, USA

Melville Herskovits, an enthusiastic and energetic scholar, helped establish the academic fields of African and African American Studies in the USA. His wife, Frances, also an anthropologist, was his collaborator and coworker throughout his career. After majoring in history and studying biology as an undergraduate, Herskovits moved to New York and began studying with Alexander Goldenweiser at the New School for Social Research. Goldenweiser introduced him to Franz Boas's seminars at Columbia, and Herskovits soon enrolled there. Boas became a major influence, and Herskovits always considered himself a staunch defender of the Boasian tradition. In New York Herskovits also came under the influence of Thorstein Veblen.

Herskovits began with a Boasian classification of African culture areas and an assumption that African American culture retained little from its African origins. In 1925 he took a teaching position at Howard University, and began studying African Americans for the National Research Council. Explicitly a study of race in America, the project determined that 'the American Negro' was a separate racial group, distinct from its Old World origins. The findings challenged then-current genetic theory, as well as Herskovits's own prior beliefs that African Americans would soon be assimilated in the USA.

In 1927 Herskovits went to Northwestern University as its sole anthropologist in a department of sociology. He felt isolated both as an anthropologist and as a Jew, but remained at Northwestern for the rest of his career. He founded the anthropology department there in 1938, and the Program in African Studies in 1948. During the Second World War Herskovits was chief consultant for African affairs for the Board of Economic Warfare, and after the war he took on many administrative duties, building African studies locally and nationally. He founded and was first president of the African Studies Association in 1957. In 1960 he prepared a major report on Africa for the US Senate Foreign Relations Committee, encouraging international relations, and in 1962 he organised the First International Congress of Africanists, in Evanston. Throughout his career he confronted an attitude that African American anthropology was less significant than work in other areas.

From the time they arrived in Evanston the Herskovitses began a series of field studies in the Caribbean, South America, and Africa, exploring the cultural connections; they quickly discovered West African traces in the New World in the form of words, folklore, music, art and religion. Herskovits believed that by studying what had survived of African cultures under the severe stress of New World conditions he could gain better understandings of the African cultures and of cultural and historical processes, as well as African American culture itself. Gunnar Myrdal, who was heading the Carnegie Foundation-funded project on African Americans, like many was sceptical of these cultural survivals, but nevertheless asked Herskovits to contribute a volume on the subject. *The Myth of the Negro Past* challenged the widespread assumption that slavery had destroyed all remnants of African culture in the New World, and although Herskovits's arguments were dismissed by many social scientists at the time, they laid a foundation for African American studies in the 1960s and 1970s.

A tireless scholar and writer, Herskovits published over a dozen significant books and countless articles, many of which are still regularly used in research and teaching. Perhaps best remembered today for his ethnographic studies and their contributions to the development of African American studies, he also wrote important and widely read books and articles on acculturation and economic anthropology, and numerous articles on African and African American art, folklore, and music, as well as theoretical topics in anthropology. He also wrote on his own Jewish culture, and like many saw certain parallels in the cases of Jews and African Americans. His monumental textbook, *Man and His Works* (1948), was widely used and later abridged. Herskovits wrote for popular audiences as well as for professional readers, and was a major figure in reshaping American ideas of Africa and African Americans in the mid-twentieth century.

Education

AB University of Chicago, 1920
AM Columbia University, 1921
Ph.D. Columbia University, 1923

Fieldwork

Harlem, Washington, DC, and West Virginia
   (African Americans), 1925–9
Surinam, 1928, 1929
Africa, 1931, 1953, 1954, 1955, 1957, 1962
Haiti, 1934
Trinidad, 1939
Brazil, 1941–2

Key Publications

(1938) *Dahomey: An Ancient West African Kingdom*,
   New York: J.J. Augustin.
(1938) *Acculturation: The Study of Culture Contact*,
   New York: J.J. Augustin.
(1942) *The Myth of the Negro Past*, New York:
   Harper & Brothers.
(1962) *The Human Factor in Changing Africa*, New
   York: Alfred A. Knopf.

Further Reading

Jackson, Walter (1986) 'Melville Herskovitz
   and the search for Afro-American culture',
   in *Malinowski, Rivers, Benedict and Others: Essays on
   Culture and Personality*, ed. George W. Stocking,
   Jr, Madison: University of Wisconsin Press.
Simpson, George E. (1973) *Melville J. Herskovits*,
   New York: Columbia University Press.

FREDERIC W. GLEACH

Herzfeld, Michael

b. 3 August 1947, London, UK

In the course of a series of innovative studies,
Michael Herzfeld has developed a distinctive
and influential approach to the analysis of
social and cultural practice. Drawing on
diverse intellectual traditions (including
semiotic theory, linguistics, narrative and
symbolic analysis, anthropological approaches
to performance and studies of nation and
nationalism) Herzfeld has repeatedly revisited
a cluster of themes focused on his central
concept of 'social poetics' and concerning
historical consciousness, nationalism, local/

state relations, cultural intimacy, and the
ambiguities of identity for those at the margins
of Europe. In a postgraduate training that
included not only periods at Cambridge and
Oxford but also a year at the University of
Athens, Herzfeld undertook doctoral fieldwork
in Rhodes that examined categories of 'inclusion' and 'exclusion'. An earlier field project
collecting folksongs on several Dodecanese
islands resulted in the publication of several
structuralist-influenced symbolic analyses, and
a subsequent consideration of the political
manipulation of folk songs' historical reso-
nances in his first book, *Ours Once More* (1982).
Out of a different fieldwork project in a Cretan
mountain village, 'Glendi', came *The Poetics of
Manhood*. Complementing the growing corpus
of feminist and anthropological work on
women in Greece and southern Europe, that
study argued for a focus on 'poetics' in its
performative sense, outlining the Glendiot
claim not to be 'a good man' but to be 'good
at being a man'.

Herzfeld's facility in modern Greek attuned
him early on to the dilemmas, often signalled
by language play or nuance, of a people
burdened by a glorious ancient past. He
recognised the broader ramifications of the
tension between classicising and vernacularis-
ing tendencies in Greek politics, culture, and
language, dubbed by linguists as diglossia,
identifying a disemia articulated in myriad
semiotic domains, from dress to architectural
styles. This immensely useful insight was
applied directly in his study of the Cretan
seaside town of Rethemnos, *A Place in History*,
where residents were compelled to conduct
their lives and pursue their projects in an
architectural space shaped by a state agenda of
historical conservation. These issues, and the
questions they raised about historical consciousness generally, have been at the heart of
Herzfeld's subsequent fieldwork in Rome and
Thailand. The mutual engagement between the
official state and popular practices also inspired Herzfeld's explorations of cultural
intimacy and of bureaucracies.

Since his fieldwork in Glendi, when he
encountered lay social analysts every bit as

adept as the anthropologist, Herzfeld has been fascinated by the distinctive perspectives of differently positioned analysts upon a local society, a theme explored in *Portrait of a Greek Imagination* (1997), his collaborative and dialogical biography of the Cretan writer and intellectual, Andreas Nenedakis. Such an interactive approach – this time with anthropological colleagues – generated Herzfeld's most recent, comprehensive summary of the discipline in *Anthropology: Theoretical Practice in Culture and Society*, produced under the auspices of UNESCO.

Herzfeld's work is firmly grounded in ethnography. He has insisted that ethnography is inevitably informed by theory, and that what is needed is a dialectic that dissolves the distinction between theory and ethnography, as well as between post-modernism and positivism. Experiences in rural cafés and Athenian lecture halls alike thus led him to formulate his provocative meta-critique of anthropological theory and practice in *Anthropology through the Looking-Glass*, recipient of the 1994 J.I. Staley Prize. Here, Herzfeld compared Greece and the discipline of anthropology as both being products of the desire of colonialist Europe to create boundaries between itself and the rest of the world.

Michael Herzfeld's influence on the discipline has occurred not only through his many publications but also, equally, through his active involvement in academic institutions. He has served as president of both the Society for the Anthropology of Europe and the Modern Greek Studies Association, and was editor of *American Ethnologist* from 1994–8. He has taught at Vassar College (1978–80), Indiana University (1980–91), and Harvard University (since 1991), as well as at a number of European universities as a visiting professor or speaker. Herzfeld has also chosen to speak out on behalf of anthropology and anthropologists in wider public settings, in the tradition of the public intellectual engaged not only in knowing the world but also in trying to change it.

Education

BA University of Cambridge, 1969
MA University of Birmingham, 1972
D.Phil. University of Oxford, 1976
D.Litt. University of Birmingham, 1989

Fieldwork

'Pefko', Rhodes, Greece, 1973–4
'Glendi', Crete, Greece, 1974–5, 1976, 1977–8, 1981
Rethemnos, Crete, Greece 1986–7, 1992–3
Rome, Italy, 1999–2000
Bangkok, Thailand, 2002– (ongoing)

Key Publications

(1985) *The Poetics of Manhood: Contest and Identity in a Cretan Mountain Village*, Princeton, NJ: Princeton University Press.

(1987) *Anthropology through the Looking-Glass: Critical Ethnography in the Margins of Europe*, Cambridge, UK: Cambridge University Press.

(1991) *A Place in History: Social and Monumental Time in a Cretan Town*, Princeton, NJ: Princeton University Press.

(2001) *Anthropology: Theoretical Practice in Culture and Society*, Oxford: Blackwell; Paris: UNESCO.

JANE K. COWAN

Hewitt, John Napoleon Brinton

b. 16 December 1859, Tuscarora Reservation, New York, USA

d. 14 October 1937

John Napoleon Brinton Hewitt was born to a mother who was part Tuscarora and Oneida Indian and a physician father who, although not American Indian by birth, was raised on the Tuscarora reservation by his adopted Tuscarora family. Although both parents were fluent in Tuscarora, Hewitt was raised speaking only English, and did not learn the Tuscarora language until he began to pick it up from schoolmates at the age of eleven.

His preparatory work for college was impeded by a bout of sunstroke and he returned to the reservation, where he worked as a farmer, a teacher, and a newspaper correspondent. In 1880 he met Erminnie Smith, a fieldworker for the Bureau of Ethnology (BAE, later called the Bureau of American Ethnology) who was studying Iroquois languages and mythology. Hewitt served as Smith's assistant for five years. After her death in 1886, Hewitt was hired by the Bureau of Ethnology to continue Smith's work on a Tuscarora–English dictionary, which was never published despite years of work. He remained in the Bureau's employ as an ethnologist for fifty-one years until his death in 1937.

Hewitt worked with the Haudenosaunee, or Iroquois, nations of New York State and southern Ontario (Cayuga, Mohawk, Onandaga, Oneida, Seneca, and Tuscarora), and became the leading authority on their culture, customs, ceremonies, and languages. He had a speaking knowledge of Mohawk, Onandaga, Seneca, and Tuscarora. A key characteristic of Hewitt's collecting skills was his careful interest in describing the subtle nuances of exact word usage and meaning within a particular culture. His work with other languages included demonstrating the relationship of Cherokee to the Iroquois language family through the comparative analysis of vocabulary and grammatical characteristics, and the collecting of some Algonquin language vocabularies, including Chippewa, Ottawa, and Delaware.

Hewitt was known for his compulsion for accuracy and completeness in collecting data. He authored over a hundred of the entries in F.W. Hodge's *Handbook of American Indians* (1907–10) and assisted with the linguistic projects of other Bureau fieldworkers. From 1894 on, Hewitt had responsibility for maintaining the Bureau's manuscript collection, responding to correspondence received at the Bureau, and editing of a number of publications.

Fieldwork

Iroquois groups of New York and Ontario, 1880–1936

Key Publications

(1893) 'Polysynthesis in the languages of the American Indians', *American Anthropologist* 6: 381–407.
(1902) 'Orenda and a definition of religion', *American Anthropologist* 4: 33–46.
(1903) 'Iroquois cosmology, first part', in *Twenty-First Annual Report of the Bureau of American Ethnology, 1901–1902*, Washington: Government Printing Office, pp. 127–339.
(1928) 'Iroquois cosmology, second part', in *Forty-Third Annual Report of the Bureau of American Ethnology, 1925–1926*, Washington: Government Printing Office, pp. 449–819.

Further Reading

Rudes, B. (1994) 'John Napoleon Brinton Hewitt: Tuscarora Linguist', *Anthropological Linguistics* 36: 466–81.
Rudes, B. and Crouse, D. (1988) *The Tuscarora Legacy of J.N.B. Hewitt: Materials for the Study of the Tuscarora Language and Culture*, Ottowa: National Museums of Canada.

LISA BIER

Hiatt, Lester R.

b. 30 December 1931, Gilgandra, New South Wales, Australia

Les Hiatt is best known through debates that emerged from his fieldwork amongst the Gidjingali of northern Arnhem Land in Australia in the late 1950s. His critique of A.R. Radcliffe-Brown's conception of Australian territorial organisation was followed by the publication in 1965 of his Ph.D. thesis, which focused on disputes over women, the texture of everyday life, and the way individuals negotiated social norms and rules to their own advantage. This approach constituted a radical shift from the taxonomical and abstract model-building approaches then prevalent in studies of kinship and local organisation.

Hiatt instead emphasised a loosely bounded community, consisting of intermarried patrilineal descent groups, within which social conflict and rule breaking were indicative not of social breakdown but of flexibility, flux, and change. By bringing into focus the dynamics of Aboriginal residential and economic life, Hiatt illuminated a variety of perspectives including the behavioural, jural, and psychic dimensions of conflict and the interplay between them.

Hiatt's writings over the succeeding thirty years manifested his deep and abiding commitment to the Aboriginal people of Australia and the Gidjingali in particular. While kinship, marriage, land, and politics remained his central interests, he also wrote on totemism, mythology, secret male cults, avoidance relationships, and conceptualisations of the emotions. Influenced by Marx and Freud, especially as mediated by the Sydney philosopher, John Anderson, his views continued to challenge the dominant anthropological models of the time. For instance, whereas functional accounts of religion had emphasised its role in maintaining the integrity of the social totality, Hiatt argued that like other institutions it constitutes an artful means for advancing material interests, in the Aboriginal case by controlling the sexuality of young men and women. Again, in opposition to functionalist accounts of mother-in-law avoidance, he drew attention to the explicitly sexual nature of the taboos and the consequent necessity to consider their role in protecting the interests of the father-in-law.

Throughout his work Hiatt has maintained a realist and pluralist position against what he sees as idealist tendencies to reduce cognitive, conative, and affective complexes to modes of thought. His most recent writings testify to an enduring interest in evolutionary biology.

In 2002 Les Hiatt's long and fruitful association with the Gidjingali was consummated in a book and multimedia CD-ROM entitled *People of the Rivermouth: The Joborr Texts of*

Frank Gurrmanamana. Gurrmanamana, approaching eighty, had dictated the texts in 1960 as a series of scenarios portraying Gidjingali culture before the arrival of Europeans.

Education

BDS University of Sydney, 1953
BA University of Sydney, 1958
Ph.D. Australian National University, 1963
FASSA, 1974–

Fieldwork

Maningrida (Arnhem Land) 1958–98 (1958, 1960, 1967, 1975, 1978, 1985, 1998)
Thambiluvil (Sri Lanka), 1970

Key Publications

(1965) *Kinship and Conflict: A Study of an Aboriginal Community in Northern Arnhem Land*, Canberra: ANU Press.
(1984) *Aboriginal Landowners: Contemporary Issues in the Determination of Traditional Aboriginal Land Ownership*, Oceania Monograph 27, Sydney: University of Sydney.
(1994) *Arguments about Aborigines: Australia and the Evolution of Social Anthropology*, Cambridge, UK: Cambridge University Press.
(2002) *People of the Rivermouth: The Joborr Texts of Frank Gurrmanamana*, Canberra: Aboriginal Studies Press & National Museum of Australia.

Further Reading

Merlan, F., Morton, J., and Rumsey, A. (eds) (1997) *Scholar and Sceptic: Australian Aboriginal Studies in Honour of L.R. Hiatt*, Canberra: Aboriginal Studies Press.

RICHARD CHENHALL

Hill, Jane H.

b. 27 October 1939, Berkeley, California, USA

Best known for her work on language change,

Mexican and southwestern Native languages, and Spanish in the USA, Jane Hill initially wanted to be an archaeologist – but the Berkeley Field School did not admit women at that time. Having developed an interest in language from studies with David French at Reed College and William Shipley and William Jacobsen at Berkeley, Hill entered the new programme in linguistics at the University of California, Los Angeles (UCLA). She had previously spent two summers in Peru with an ethnopharmacological project (led by her mother, botanist Mildred E. Mathias, and Dermot Taylor, of the UCLA Medical School), which fostered an interest in Latin America. At UCLA she worked most closely with William Bright, Harry Hoijer, and Robert Stockwell. There she also met and married her husband and professional colleague, Kenneth C. Hill.

After receiving her Ph.D. Hill began teaching at Wayne State University, where she rose to the rank of full professor and chaired the department for several years. In 1983 she moved to the University of Arizona, where she is now Regents Professor in Anthropology and Linguistics.

Hill's dissertation research on Cupeño grammar led to a comparative study with unpublished notes on Cupeño compiled in 1919–20 by Paul-Louis Faye (a student of Alfred Kroeber). The changes from then to Hill's work with a much diminished community of indigenous speakers led her to consider language attrition more generally. Seeking a larger population for the sake of valid statistical analyses, both Hill and her husband began work in Mexicano Nahuatl-speaking communities of Puebla and Tlaxcala.

During the 1970s Hill began to shift towards linguistic anthropology, focusing on the relationships of language to other aspects of culture and society. Part of the continuing development of studies building on Dell Hymes's 'ethnography of communication', Hill was particularly interested in the strategic use of language in shaping social relations. This was developed in her work on Nahuatl, and her influential work on the racist use of 'mock' Spanish. She never abandoned her interest in structural and historical linguistics, however, and is currently working with Tohono O'odham dialectology, the history of Uto-Aztecan languages, and a reference grammar of Cupeño.

Education

BA University of California, Berkeley, 1960
MA University of California, Los Angeles, 1962
Ph.D. University of California, Los Angeles, 1966

Fieldwork

California (Cupeño), summers 1962–3
Puebla and Tlaxcala, Mexico, 1974–5, summers 1976–8, 1981
Arizona (Tohono O'odham and others), 1986–7, sporadically thereafter

Key Publications

with Nolasquez, Rosinda (eds) (1973) *Mulu'Wetam: The First People, Cupeño Oral History and Language*, Banning, CA: Malki Museum Press.
with Hill, Kenneth C. (1986) *Speaking Mexicano: Dynamics of Syncretic Language in Central Mexico*, Tucson: The University of Arizona Press.
with Irvine, Judith T. (1992) *Responsibility and Evidence in Oral Discourse*, New York: Cambridge University Press.
(1993) "'*Hasta la vista*, baby!'" Anglo Spanish in the American Southwest', *Critique of Anthropology* 13, 2: 145–76.

FREDERIC W. GLEACH AND
VILMA SANTIAGO-IRIZARRY

Hoebel, E. Adamson

b. 6 November 1906, Madison, Wisconsin, USA

d. 23 July 1993, St Paul, Minnesota, USA

Adamson Hoebel was perhaps the pre-eminent figure in the anthropology of law in the twentieth century. As an undergraduate he studied sociology at the University of Wisconsin, where fellow students included John Gillin, Clyde Kluckhohn, Lauriston Sharp, and Sol Tax. His interest in law and social control dates to that period, encouraged by sociologist, Edward A. Ross. At Columbia, Franz Boas and Ruth Benedict expressed doubts and disinterest when Hoebel suggested a dissertation on a Plains Indian legal system, but Boas arranged for Columbia law professor, Karl Llewellyn, to serve as Hoebel's thesis adviser. At the time few anthropologists believed that tribal peoples had 'law', but after reading B. Malinowski's *Crime and Custom in Savage Society* Llewellyn thought that the collaboration of legal scholars and anthropologists could demonstrate its existence and open the field to study.

Llewellyn advised Hoebel on his dissertation (published in 1940) and in his early research with the Shoshone Indians, and they then collaborated on *The Cheyenne Way*. Llewellyn's 'legal realism' shared with anthropology a focus on studies within specific cultural contexts, and together Hoebel and Llewellyn developed the 'trouble case method', a focus on actual disputes in order to understand the rules and procedures of a legal system. Influenced by Malinowski and A.R. Radcliffe-Brown, they also developed a functional framework to consider how legal systems resolve disputes and maintain order. In 1944 they began work together on the Keresan Pueblos, but that was interrupted and remained incomplete at Llewellyn's death in 1962.

Hoebel worked as an instructor in sociology at New York University throughout his graduate studies, and was promoted to assistant professor after receiving his Ph.D., then to associate professor in 1941. He left New York in 1948 to head the anthropology department at the University of Utah, and in 1954 he moved to the University of Minnesota, where he chaired the department and built its faculty from four to fourteen. He remained at Minnesota until his retirement in 1972, and after his retirement he taught in the

law school there for another nine years. He was a respected teacher, and also prepared an undergraduate textbook, *Man in the Primitive World: An Introduction to Anthropology*, first published in 1949 to serve the students who flocked to the discipline after the Second World War; it eventually went through five editions, spanning three decades, and was translated into Spanish and Finnish. His writing was always clear and realistic, whether conveying ethnographic contexts or developing concepts.

The Cheyenne Way stimulated the growth of the anthropology of law as a sub-discipline, but Hoebel had further contributions to make. In *The Law of Primitive Man* he went beyond the descriptive case studies of his earlier books to attempt a cross-cultural study of 'law'. He used clearly contextualised case studies to derive 'jural postulates' – generally shared propositions concerning the nature and qualitative value of things, the foundations for law – and 'law ways', the processes of keeping order. The book has been criticised for recognising only physical sanctions, not other forms of coercion, but nevertheless remains fundamental in legal anthropology. It is particularly important for recognising that law constitutes a dynamic, changing system, despite its apparently fixed rules, authorities, and sanctions.

Although best known for his ethnographic and analytical contributions derived from fieldwork with Plains Indians, Hoebel also worked in Pakistan in the early 1960s. He had a deep commitment to human rights, and concerns with East–West relations. In 1943 Hoebel had worked as a community analyst in the Japanese American relocation camp at Granada, Colorado. Later he worked with the Center for Cultural and Technical Interchange between East and West in Honolulu, and he participated in the UNESCO East–West Cultural Conference in Calcutta in 1961. In 1956, with legal scholar, Harold Berman, Hoebel led the first Social Science Research Council Institute on law and social science. His working partnership with Llewellyn established a pattern for his career, and Hoebel collaborated with numerous other scholars, peers, and juniors over the years.

Education

BA University of Wisconsin, 1928
MA New York University, 1931
Ph.D. Columbia University, 1934

Fieldwork

Cheyenne, Comanche, and Shoshone Indians, beginning 1930s
Granada Relocation Camp, 1943
Keresan Pueblo Indians, beginning 1944
Pakistan, early 1960s

Key Publications

(1940) *The Political Organization and Law-Ways of the Comanche Indians*, American Anthropological Association, Memoir 54, Menasha, WI: American Anthropological Association.
with Llewellyn, Karl N. (1941) *The Cheyenne Way: Conflict and Case Law in Primitive Jurisprudence*, Norman: University of Oklahoma Press.
with Wallace, Ernest (1952) *The Comanches: Lords of the South Plains*, Norman: University of Oklahoma Press.
(1954) *The Law of Primitive Man: A Study in Comparative Legal Dynamics*, Cambridge, MA: Harvard University Press.

Further Reading

Pospisil, Leopold. (1973) 'E. Adamson Hoebel and the anthropology of law', *Law and Society Review* 7, 4: 537–69.

FREDERIC W. GLEACH

Hofer, Tamás

b. 1929, Budapest, Hungary

Tamás Hofer's work has primarily focused on nineteenth- and twentieth-century peasant cultures in East-Central Europe. His doctoral study examined different rural settlement forms in Hungary. During the 1950s and 1960s, as research fellow at the Ethnographic Museum in Budapest, Hofer carried out intensive fieldwork – together with Edit Fél – in Átány, a Hungarian village. In his most famous ethnography (*Proper Peasants*) based on his fieldwork in Átány – also in collaboration with Edit Fél – Hofer described the social logic of changing peasant society in the early years of Hungarian socialism. This work is characterised by a strong social historical approach on the one hand, and by social anthropological approaches (community studies) on the other. Hofer has focused on the social network in this village and at the same time on different economical strategies; his theoretical focus was on an analysis of the changing world views of peasants living in a given historical, social, and political setting.

During the 1970s he published several books and papers about folk art in Hungary. These works argued against a romantic and partly nationalist view of folk art and analysed the historical and political context of romantic ideologies and views of peasant life in Hungary and in East-Central Europe more generally. This research led him to an ethnological analysis of the historical and cultural construction of Hungarian national culture. Hofer's research interest has focused on working out the political and social functions of peasant culture within the construction of Hungarian national culture. In this context he examined the mobilisation of the image of the Hungarian folk culture – politically as well as from an aesthetic point of view, with a special focus on folk art and oral folklore.

At the same time Hofer published several papers about the theoretical problems of ethnological and anthropological research on national culture and identity, publications that drew upon the theories of Ernest Gellner, Benedict Anderson, and Eric J. Hobsbawm. He has focused on the issue of the reflexive relationship between historical processes and actual political developments in the process of nation-building. Through his studies Hofer developed a new historically oriented form of 'home-ethnography' and at the same time introduced anthropological theories and methods to Hungary and East-Central Europe. His international reputation and activity allowed him to build up contacts between different schools and directions of ethnological or anthropological research, such as the German-type *Volkskunde* and American cultural or English social anthropology.

Education

MA Lóránd Eötvös University, Budapest, 1954
Ph.D. Lóránd Eötvös University, Budapest, 1958

Fieldwork

Átány, 1954–78
Romania, Eastern Moravia, 1949–86 (realised in several 2–6 week sessions)

Key Publications

with Fél, Edit (1969) *Proper Peasants. Traditional Life in a Hungarian Village*, Viking Found Publications in Anthropology 46, Chicago: Aldine Pub. Co.

with Fél, Edit (1972) *Bäuerliche Denkweise in Wirtschaft und Haushalt: Eine ethnographische Untersuchung über das ungarische Dorf Átány* (Peasant World View in Economy and Household: Ethnographic Research in the Hungarian Village of Átány), Göttingen: Schwarz

(1978) *Ungarische Volkskunst* (Hungarian Folk Art), Berlin: Henschel Verlag

PETER NIEDERMUELLER

Hogbin, H. Ian

b. 17 December 1904, Serlby Harworth, Nottinghamshire, UK

d. 1 August 1989, Sydney, Australia

Ian Hogbin's graduation in geography and English at Sydney University in 1926 coincided with the arrival of A.R. Radcliffe Brown to take up Australia's first chair of anthropol-

ogy. Having Rockefeller funds for research in the Pacific, Radcliffe Brown was looking for fieldworkers, and persuaded a scarcely prepared Hogbin to join an expedition to Rennell Island and Ontong Java in 1927. In 1928 he went to the London School of Economics to write his doctoral dissertation under Bronislaw Malinowski, which was published in 1934. He returned to Sydney in 1931, making this his academic base for the rest of his career, while regularly visiting London on sabbatical leave.

Hogbin's later field studies were in Melanesia. In 1933 he worked in the Solomon Islands, in Guadalcanal and Malaita. In 1934 he began research on the island of Wogeo, in New Guinea. Following the outbreak of war in the Pacific, he was retained by the Solomon Islands administration, and subsequently by the Australian authorities in New Guinea as a ranking member of the armed forces. Travelling all over the island, he advised the military authorities on the rehabilitation of villagers after Japanese occupation, and on the payment of indigenous workers. Towards the end of the war he began his final field study, in Busama. By the end of this period his knowledge of Melanesia, and particularly of New Guinea, was unrivalled.

Hogbin did no fieldwork after 1948, and did not revisit Papua New Guinea until 1974, when he acted as external examiner at the new university. However, he had accumulated enough data to keep him writing until his final book, *The Leaders and the Led* (1979).

Hogbin published nine books, in addition to reports for government, and kept up a steady flow of scholarly articles, mostly in the journal, *Oceania*. Malinowski and Radcliffe Brown remained the dominant influences in his work, though his interests were ethnographic rather than theoretical. Like others of his generation, he was preoccupied with kinship structures and local organisation, developing with Camilla Wedgewood a terminology for the comparative morphology of Melanesian societies. *The Island of Menstruating Men* (1970) is remarkable as an early essay on the cultural construction of gender.

Hogbin was among the first to write on the

changes resulting from colonial government, missions, and labour recruitment. While providing advice to colonial governments, he regarded these topics as worthy of anthropological study, particularly the development of native Christianity.

Education

BA University of Sydney, 1926
Ph.D. London School of Economics, 1931

Fieldwork

Rennell Island, Ontong Java, 1927, 1928
Guadalcanal, 1927, 1933, 1945
Malaita, 1933, 1945
Wogeo, 1934, 1948, 1974
Busama 1944, 1945

Key Publications

(1934) *Law and Order in Polynesia*, London: Christophers (second edn, Hamden, CT: Shoe String Press, 1964).

(1939) *Experiments in Civilization: The Effects of European culture on a Native Community of the Solomon Islands*, London: George Routledge & Sons (reprinted, London: Routledge & Kegan Paul, 1969).

(1951) *Transformation Scene*, London: Routledge & Kegan Paul.

(1970) *The Island of Menstruating Men: Religion in Wogeo, New Guinea*, Scranton, PA: Chandler (reprinted, Prospect Heights, IL: Waveland Press, 1996).

JEREMY BECKETT

Holy, Ladislav

b. 4 April 1933, Prague, Czechoslovakia

d. 13 April 1997, St Andrews, UK

Ladislav Holy was an early advocate of a focus on individual agency and action in the study of kinship, a field which when he first began to publish was still largely dominated by notions of function and social structure. His initial fieldwork among the Berti of Darfur, undertaken while Head of the African Department at the Institute of Ethnography and Folklore of the Czechoslovak Academy of Sciences, emphasised how people's behaviour was better understood in terms of their strategic decision-making rather than as the automatic outcome of their membership in a particular kind of group or social system. This theoretical focus on process and interpretation, in part a response to Cambridge social anthropology under Meyer Fortes, with whom Holy was in regular contact, was to inform almost all his later work. As Director of the Livingstone Museum in Zambia (1968–72), Holy carried out a second period of fieldwork, this time among the Toka, in which he developed his ideas about the relationship between structure and practice. Accepting a post in Belfast in 1973 in order to avoid returning to what he saw as a worsening regime in Czechoslovakia following the Prague Spring of 1968, Holy joined John Blacking, himself a refugee from apartheid, and old friend, Milan Stuchlik, another Czech anthropologist, with whom he went on to publish a succession of widely influential theoretical and conceptual works on folk models and anthropological interpretation. In 1979 Holy was invited to form a department of social anthropology in St Andrews, a task he set about with characteristic charm and charisma, and where he continued to explore the implicit tension between comparison and cultural interpretation in books on comparative anthropology and on cousin marriage in the Middle East. In 1992 he was awarded the Rivers Memorial Medal by the Royal Anthropological Institute.

Late in his career Holy turned to the study of the society in which he had grown up, returning to Prague in the early 1990s to carry out fieldwork on the relationship between culture and political process in the Czech Republic, and on the basis of which he published a monograph and a series of articles that pioneered our understanding of the symbols and tropes of post-socialist transformation. An invitation to spend a year at the

University of Oslo in 1994 resulted in *Anthropological Perspectives on Kinship*. Much more than a textbook, Holy's last thoughts on the subject that had first fired his own imagination will inspire and instruct students of anthropology for generations to come.

Education

BA Charles University, Prague, 1956
Ph.D. Charles University, Prague, 1961

Fieldwork

Darfur, Sudan, 1961, 1965, 1977, 1978, 1980, 1986
Southern Province, Zambia, 1968–72
Czech Republic, 1992

Key Publications

with Stuchlik, Milan (1983) *Actions, Norms and Representations: Foundations of Anthropological Inquiry*, Cambridge, UK: Cambridge University Press.
(1991) *Religion and Custom in a Muslim Society: The Berti of Darfur*, Cambridge, UK: Cambridge University Press.
(1996) *The Little Czech and the Great Czech Nation: National Identity and Post-Communist Transformation of Society*, Cambridge, UK: Cambridge University Press.
(1996) *Anthropological Perspectives on Kinship*, London: Pluto Press.

HASTINGS DONNAN

Howell, Signe

b. Rjukan, Norway

Signe Howell's doctoral study provided the first complete study of the Chewong, a small community of hunter-gatherers and shifting cultivators in Peninsular Malaysia. Her findings informed our understanding of societies lacking the structural features on which anthropologists have usually focused, for among the Chewong there are no lineages, alliances, social hierarchies, or other important political institutions, and very few elaborate rituals and ceremonies. Howell's careful examination of social relations, ideas of consciousness and relativity, implicit rules, and systems of classification provided an exemplar analysis of Chewong modes of thought. A whole range of relations, between men and women, between human and supernatural beings, and between various kinds of supernatural beings were characterised by the absence of stratification. In spite of the absence of explicit and clear structures, Chewong social life was guided by the principle of separation: the correct separation of child from mother; of placenta from child; the separation between the hunter and his catch; the care taken to avoid mixing different categories of food, of not crossing between the various parts of the cosmos, all stipulate the necessity of keeping specified objects or acts apart.

Howell's interest in the analysis of ritualised actions, gender, and kinship relations continued in her research on the Lio of Flores, Indonesia. The quality of Howell's findings made it possible for her to take part in important debates on the meaning of exchange and valuables; the role of the house in differentiated and non-differentiated societies; the significance of blood and other substances in moral discourses; the importance of traditions in the comprehension of the role of nation-states in processes of modernisation; the fact that consanguinity may represent a higher ideal than affinity; that wife-givers stand for the whole; that the brother–sister relationship is the most important cross-sex relationship; and, above all, the importance of gender in the understanding of hierarchical and complementary relations in society.

Changing focus to her own society, Norway, Howell continued her inquiry on the construction of kin relations in modern societies. After Sweden, Norway is the country with the highest number of children adopted per capita from foreign countries. Howell has carried out extensive fieldwork among parents adopting foreign children. Transnational adoption not only highlights indigenous theories of pro-creation but also the direct incorporation of visibly 'foreign elements' in the kinship structure. Howell's emphasis in ethnographic details as well as theoretical engagement places her at the core of key debates in the discipline regarding kinship, ritual, gender, and cognitive structures.

Education

BA School of Oriental and African Studies, London University, 1974
M.Litt. University of Oxford, 1977
D.Phil. University of Oxford, 1980

Fieldwork

Malaysia (the Chewong), 1977–9
Flores, Eastern Indonesia (the Lio), 1984, 1986, 1989, 1993, 2000.
Norway, 1998–

Key Publications

(1982) *Chewong Myths and Legends*, Malaysia: Royal Asiatic Society.
(1984) *Society and Cosmos: Chewong of Peninsular Malaysia*, Oxford: Oxford University Press.
with Willis, Roy (eds) (1989) *Societies at Peace: An Anthropological Perspective*, London: Routledge.
(ed.) (1997) *The Ethnography of Moralities*, London: Routledge.

EDUARDO ARCHETTI

Humphrey, Caroline

b. 1943, London, UK

Behind the wide range of thematic interests in Humphrey's writings lies a long ethnographic engagement especially with Inner Asia. In addition, this range exemplifies a belief, inherited from her teacher, Edmund Leach, that the holistic approach of social anthropology makes a distinctive contribution to understanding the human condition: one that is of relevance to all the human sciences. In writings employing concepts drawn, over time, from structuralism, neo-Marxism, economics, cognitive science, phenomenology, analytical philosophy, and psychoanalytic theory, Humphrey has addressed topics as diverse as divination in Mongolia, barter in the Buddhist Himalayas, fairs in rural India, and architecture in post-socialist Russian cities.

Three areas, however, have been enduring interests: language (e.g. of magical spells, sexual hierarchy, ethnic exclusion, political ideals), aesthetics (from shamanic landscapes in Mongolia to new-rich villas in Russia), and political economy. The fieldwork Humphrey carried out in the late 1960s in Buriyatia was virtually the only detailed study by a Westerner of life on Soviet collective farms. So her first book, *Karl Marx Collective* (expanded and republished as *Marx Went away*), provides a unique insight into that extraordinary social experiment. And Humphrey has been chronicling the chaotic transformations that have taken place since the collapse of the Soviet system, with studies on changing property relations, consumption, Mafia and protection rackets, and local political regimes. She has emphasised the enduring importance of values and concepts that were created under Soviet socialism, but also the innovations by local people in conditions of intense turmoil subsequently. Her characteristic analytical move has been to start from ethnographic observations that are exceptional or inexplicable, from the point of view of some established theoretical paradigm either within or outside anthropology, and to draw on fresh theoretical resources to attempt to understand them.

The historical, linguistic, cultural, and political complexity of Inner Asia call for collaborative research, and in recent years Humphrey has launched several such research projects. For example, a comparative study of the environmental effects of economic changes in Russia, Mongolia, and China involved scholars from all those countries, the use of remote sensing imagery, and the development of databases to be made available in the countries of the study. A study of Buddhism in Inner Mongolia involves archaeologists as well as anthropologists, and participants from a number of parts of Mongolia, including the Republic. The institutional base for much of this research has been the Mongolian and Inner Asian Studies Unit (MIASU) in the University of Cambridge. The MIASU was created by Humphrey virtually alone and run initially on a shoestring, but is now an important and established institution attracting students and researchers from all over the world.

Education

BA University of Cambridge, 1965
MA University of Cambridge, 1971
MA University of Leeds, 1971
Ph.D. University of Cambridge, 1973

Fieldwork

Russia (Siberia), 1966–7, 1975, 1990, 1996, 1999
Mongolia, 1970, 1972–3, 1990, 1993
China (Inner Mongolia), 1988, 1993, 1995, 1998, 2000
Nepal, 1979–80
India, 1981–2, 1985

Key Publications

with Laidlaw, James (1994) *The Archetypal Actions of Ritual*. Oxford: Clarendon Press.
with Onon, Urgunge (1996) *Shamans and Elders*, Oxford: Clarendon Press.
(1999) *Marx Went away, but Karl Stayed behind*, Ann Arbor: University of Michigan Press.
(2002) *The Unmaking of Soviet Life*, Ithaca: Cornell University Press.

JAMES LAIDLAW

Hurston, Zora Neale

b. 15 January 1891, Notasulga, Alabama, USA

d. 28 January 1960, Saint Lucie County, Florida, USA

Zora Neale Hurston has not yet received the recognition she deserves from anthropology. It was Alice Walker, novelist, who engraved 'Genius of the South' on Hurston's headstone thirteen years after her death. Ironically, Hurston is celebrated for her plays, short stories, and novels, especially *Their Eyes Were Watching God* (1937), which has sold over 1 million copies and is frequently labelled the first black feminist novel. Although a novelist and playwright, Hurston was simultaneously working as a passionate ethnographer, under the tutelage of Franz Boas. Devoted to what St Clair Drake has called 'salvage anthropology' and what Margaret Mead termed the 'Great Rescue Operation', which entailed the preservation of disappearing cultures, Hurston blended two genres (ethnography and literature) to create a distinctive form. Her fiction shows a commitment to historical particularism, meticulous in its ethnographic detail, while her ethnographies borrow liberally from literary stylistic conventions. She often wrote both in the field.

Hurston's commitment to the study of folklore is extraordinary. According to Robert Hemmenway, her literary biographer, in 1927 there were no academic programmes in anthropology, and black collectors of Afro-American folklore were virtually non-existent. In 1931, Hurston published 'Hoodoo in America', an exhaustive compendium of spells, beliefs, and magic incantations, in the *Journal of American Folk-Lore*, edited by Ruth Benedict. Using a human ecological perspective, Hurston argued that African survivals in Gulf coast culture resulted from cultural isolation: 'The system of absentee landlords afforded scant white contact and the retention of African custom was relatively uninterrupted and easy' (*Journal of American Folk-Lore*, p. 318).

Hurston was convinced that key cultural characteristics of Afro-Americans were performance and a sense of the dramatic. This theory is discussed in her classic 1934 essay, 'Characteristics of Negro expression', published in Nancy Cunard's *Negro: An Anthology*. Hurston also wrote plays and musicals (*Polk County*, co-authored with Dorothy Waring, 1944) based on her research and presented original data

(*From Sun to Sun*, 1933) on stage. Her motivation was the desire to salvage Afro-American folk culture and prove to outsiders its persistent, dynamic, and innovative qualities. To Hurston, black language was not 'bad English', but an adaptive strategy that fitted cultural needs. Afro-Americans used metaphor and simile, double descriptives, verbal nouns, and nouns from verbs in innovative ways that remain part of the vernacular today. As Hurston noted in her essay, 'Negro cultural expression' (published in the anthology edited by Nancy Cunard), angularity and asymmetry were core features in the visual arts and dance was a 'performance filled with dynamic suggestion' (1970: 26).

In 1935, Hurston published *Mules and Men*. This folklore collection documents her unique ethnographic strategy. In it she grapples with key questions that plague contemporary anthropologists: what is the relationship between the anthropologist and her cultural consultants?; how does one negotiate the power dynamics that inhere in fieldwork?; is fieldwork a conversation among equals or a one-way monologue that privileges the anthropologist as ethnographic authority? *Mules and Men* exemplifies two emergent ethnographic trends, and situates Hurston as an innovator. It is reflexive and it establishes the validity of a *native* anthropological approach. Hurston writes, 'And now, I'm going to tell you why I decided to go to my native village first. . . . I hurried back to Eatonville because I knew that the town was full of material and that I could get it without hurt, harm or danger' (1990 [1935]:2). Acknowledging the power of familiarity and speaking in her own (emic) voice, in *Mules and Men*, Hurston defies ethnographic conventions of the 1930s.

Tell My Horse, Hurston's second ethnography, is reminiscent of Lévi-Strauss's *Triste Tropiques*. Published in 1938, it is part travelogue, part foreign affairs commentary, and part feminist analysis. The reflexive style generated mixed reviews. It is not Hurston's greatest writing and her cultural and political ethnocentrism is evident. Despite these flaws, *Tell My Horse* is rich in ethnographic and historical details. It also is

proof that Hurston's keen observations about the status of women in Haiti and Jamaica were part of the foundation for her novel, *Their Eyes Were Watching God*, written in Haiti and published in 1937.

There are many critics of Hurston who argue that she 'tampered' with her material, once plagiarised, and that her shifts from third to first person render her work less 'scientific'. She remains a controversial figure in anthropology and in literature. Those familiar with her published works and unpublished correspondence agree Hurston was single-handedly responsible for 'salvaging' the folklore, song, and dance of Southern blacks, celebrating its creativity, and affirming a people's humanity. Tragically, when she died in 1960, Hurston had published more than any other black American woman, yet was destitute, and unacknowledged by anthropology.

Education

AA Howard University, 1920
BA Barnard College, 1928
No degree, Columbia University, 1935

Fieldwork

Southern United States (Central Florida, Mississippi, New Orleans), 1927–9, 1934–5, 1938
The Bahamas, 1929–30
Jamaica, 1936
Haiti, 1937
The Honduras, 1947

Key Publications

(1990 [1935]) *Mules and Men*, New York: Perennial Library.
(1938) *Tell My Horse*, Philadelphia: J.B. Lippincott Co.
(1970 [1934]) 'Characteristics of Negro expression', in *Negro: An Anthology; Collected and Edited by Nancy Cunard*, New York: Frederick Ungar Publishing Co., pp 24–46.

IRMA MCCLAURIN

Hymes, Dell H.

b. 7 June 1927, Portland, Oregon, USA

Dell Hymes created the ethnography of speaking and helped shape the modern field of linguistic anthropology. Hymes has written and edited scores of influential articles and books on diverse topics, including Native American languages, poetics and verbal art, pidgin and creole linguistics, language and education, and the history of linguistics and anthropology. At a time when linguistics and anthropology were diverging, Hymes's brilliant scholarship, prolific writing, and inspiring teaching solidified the relationship between the two fields, and assured the continuity of the linguistic anthropology tradition inherited from Franz Boas, Edward Sapir, Clyde Kluckhohn, and Alfred Kroeber.

Hymes began his career studying anthropology, literature, linguistics, and folklore at Reed College and Indiana University. His early work focused on the descriptive linguistics of the languages of the American Northwest. Hymes's dissertation reconstructed a grammar of Kathlamet Chinook, on the basis of written texts recorded decades earlier by Franz Boas. Thus began a lifelong devotion to the study of Wasco and Chinookan languages, and to the community of the Warm Springs Indian Reservation.

Hymes is best known as founder of the ethnography of speaking. In 'Models of the interaction of language and social setting', Hymes argued that language structure encompasses the patterns and functions of speech, in addition to the rules of grammar. Discovery of the structure of use depended upon an ethnographic approach to language. Hymes formulated this methodology in terms of a mnemonic, in which each letter of the word 'speaking' stood for a component of communicative practice: Situation, Participants, Ends, Acts, Keys, Instrumentalities, Norms, and Genres. Comparative study of speaking as a social practice, Hymes argued, would lead to a deeper understanding of language, culture, and society.

Hymes's call for the ethnographic study of language came at a time when linguistics and anthropology were diverging. In the 1950s leading practitioners in both disciplines were searching for new paradigms. Noam Chomsky's generative grammar movement led linguistics away from studying language as a social phenomenon and towards analysing the intuitions of an idealised speaker. Hymes critiqued Chomsky's notion of language as a purely cognitive phenomenon by articulating the concept of communicative competence. In essays collected in his 1974 book, *Foundations in Sociolinguistics*, Hymes argued that a speaker's knowledge of language went beyond the ability to create grammatical sentences to include the ability to use utterances appropriately in social context.

Hymes's interest in the social context of language-use led to a concern with the social and moral power of languages. Hymes's scholarship stands out for its relevance to social justice, and its application to social policy. Here too he carried on the Boasian tradition, for whom the scientific study of languages was an effective bulwark against racism. In 1972 Hymes edited an enormously influential volume entitled *Reinventing Anthropology*, which passionately called for a realignment of the purposes and values of anthropological research towards social justice in the world. Hymes devoted much of his own career to applying linguistic anthropology to education, and he has written extensively on educational linguistics.

In the 1970s Hymes returned to the study of Native American languages, focusing on verbal art. Collected in the 1981 book, *In Vain I Tried to Tell You* (recently expanded as *Now I Know Only So Far*), this work looked at the narrative structure of oral performance. Hymes showed that Native American discourse contained systematic markers of narrative structure that had not been attended to previously. The referential meaning of these markers was vague, but their patterned recurrences demarcated units within the text akin to line, verse, and stanza. Careful attention to these details of linguistic structure revealed culturally specific patterns to narrative organisation. Hymes's interest in verbal art stems from an interest in literature and a lifelong friendship with literary critic, Kenneth Burke. Hymes applied Burke's theory of literature as symbolic action in his approach to language use as social action.

Hymes has taught at Harvard, Berkeley, Pennsylvania, and Virginia, among the most prominent of American anthropology departments, and his students, including Regna Darnell, Judith Irvine, Elinor Ochs, Susan Philips, Joel Sherzer, and others, are among the most prominent linguistic anthropologists of the succeeding generation. Perhaps his most remarkable achievement, though, is having been elected president of national organisations in four disciplines: anthropology, folklore, linguistics, and education.

Education

BA Reed College, 1950
MA Indiana University, 1953

Ph.D. Indiana University, 1955

Fieldwork

Warm Springs, Oregon, periodically since 1951

Key Publications

(1967) 'Models of the interaction of language and social setting', *Journal of Social Issues* 23, 2: 8–28.
(ed.) (1972) *Reinventing Anthropology*, New York: Pantheon Books.
(1974) *Foundations in Sociolinguistics: An Ethnographic Approach*, Philadelphia: University of Pennsylvania Press.
(2003) *Now I Know Only So Far: Essays in Ethnopoetics*, Lincoln: University of Nebraska Press.

DANIEL LEFKOWITZ

Imanishi, Kinji

b. 6 January 1902, Kyoto, Japan

d. 1992, Kyoto, Japan

Kinji Imanishi was an entomologist, ecologist, a founder of Japanese primatology and anthropology in Kyoto University, as well as an accomplished mountaineer and explorer. In the discipline of anthropology, he pioneered in pastoral studies among the Mongol. He led younger researchers not only to primatological studies but also to the study of hunting-gathering and pastoral societies in East Africa. His main subjects in anthropology considered the origin of the family and social evolution on the basis of the results of primatological studies. The work of many Japanese distinguished anthropologists and primatologists including Drs T. Umesao, M. Kawai, and J. Itani was developed under his influence. He is also well known in evolutionary biology and philosophy. In 1949, he formulated an approach to viewing nature on the basis of habitat segregation in nature, that is, the differentiation of ecological niches and the co-existence of different species. This approach has contributed to the present understanding of the biosphere.

Education

BA Sc. Kyoto University, 1928
D.Sc. Kyoto University, 1939

Fieldwork

Northern China (Mongolia), four trips, from 1938 to 1945
Ponape Island in Micronesia, 1941
East Africa, five trips, from 1958 to 1964

Key Publications

(2002) *A Japanese View of Nature: The World of Living Things (Seibutsu no Sekai, 1941)*, ed. and introduced by Pamela J. Asquith, London and New York: Routledge Curzon.
with Umesao, T. (eds) (1968) *Afurika Shakai no Kenkyu: Kyoto Daigaku Afurika Gakujutsu Chousa-tai Houkoku* (Studies in African Societies: Report of the Kyoto University Africa Scientific Expedition, 1962–8), Tokyo: Nishimura-Shoten.

KATSUYOSHI FUKUI

Ingold, Tim

b. 1 November 1948, Sevenoaks, UK

Trained at Cambridge, Tim Ingold carried out doctoral fieldwork in the early 1970s among Skolt Saami people in northeastern Finland, leading to a monograph on their ecological adaptation, social organisation, and ethnic politics. This was followed by further fieldwork among Finnish farmers, forestry workers, and reindeer herdsmen in eastern Lapland, focusing on the causes of rural depopulation. At the University of Manchester, where he was appointed to a lectureship in 1974, Ingold embarked on a wider comparative study of hunting, pastoralism, and ranching as alternative modes of making a living from reindeer or caribou for peoples of the circumpolar North. This gave rise, in turn, to a more general concern with the comparative anthropology of hunter-gatherer and pastoral societies, as well as with human–animal relations. Dissatisfied with the tendency to treat animals as either material or symbolic resources, Ingold has sought to extend the notion of sociality to include relationships with animals as well as between humans. Ingold's critical rethinking of the humanity–animality interface, especially as implicated in evolutionary theory, led to a major study of the ways in which the notion of evolution has been handled in anthropology, biology, and history from the late nineteenth century to the present.

Two criteria often invoked as indices of human distinctiveness are toolmaking and speech. Though a reconsideration of these criteria, Ingold became interested in the connection, in human evolution, between language and technology, and with the biological anthropologist, Kathleen Gibson, he co-edited a volume on *Tools, Language and Cognition in Human Evolution* (1993). Since then, Ingold has sought ways of bringing together the anthropologies of technology and art, leading to his current view of the centrality of skilled practice. At the same time he has continued his research and teaching in ecological anthropology and, influenced by the writings of James Gibson on perceptual systems, has been exploring ways of integrating ecological approaches in anthropology and psychology. In his recent work, linking the themes of environmental perception and skilled practice, Ingold has attempted to replace traditional models of genetic and cultural transmission, founded upon the alliance of neo-Darwinian biology and cognitive science, with a relational approach focusing on the growth of embodied skills of perception and action within social and environmental contexts of development.

Throughout his career, Ingold has sought to build bridges between social anthropology, archaeology, and biological anthropology even as the disciplinary integration of these erstwhile sub-fields of anthropology was being dismantled in Britain. He has consistently brought together influences from diverse areas – for example from ecological psychology, phenomenology, and developmental biology. In the interdisciplinary climate of contemporary scholarship his work has generated renewed interest and opportunities for collaboration and dialogue well beyond the purviews of social anthropology.

Education

BA University of Cambridge, 1970
Ph.D. University of Cambridge, 1975

Fieldwork

Skolt Saami, northeastern Finland, 1971–2
Northern Finnish farmers and forestry workers, 1979–80

Key Publications

(1980) *Hunters, Pastoralists and Ranchers: Reindeer Economies and Their Transformations*, Cambridge, UK, and New York: Cambridge University Press.

(1986) *Evolution and Social Life*, Cambridge, UK, and New York: Cambridge University Press.

(1987) *The Appropriation of Nature: Essays on Human Ecology and Social Relations*, Manchester: Manchester University Press; Iowa City: University of Iowa Press

(2000) *The Perception of the Environment: Essays on Livelihood, Dwelling and Skill*, London and New York: Routledge.

VERED AMIT

Irimoto, Takashi

b. 1947, Kobe, Japan

Takashi Irimoto, after ecological anthropological research among the Ama, traditional breath-hold abalone divers in Japan, pursued studies of northern hunter-gatherers in sub-Arctic Canada. His doctoral thesis discussing the ecology of the Chipewyan (Dene), focusing on their group structure and caribou-hunting system, presented 'human activity systems' to understand the man–nature relationships. Later his approach expanded to include the comprehension of religious aspects. Investigations into the dynamic relations between ecology and religion were undertaken among the Ladakhi in Western Tibet. This study suggested the politico-religious mechanisms of the kingdom of Ladakh to be understood in terms of the 'ecological niche' of the kingdom. Subsequently, he pursued historic-ecological research into the Ainu in Japan that depicted their cultural changes between c.AD 1300–1867, indicating that the Ainu socio-political system was closely related to both their ecology and politico-economic ties with the Matsumae feudal clan. Since 1993 he has conducted comparative studies on the cultural dynamics and identities of northern Asian peoples. Irimoto's paradigm of original oneness between nature and culture has made a unique contribution to anthropological thought. Irimoto was a recipient in 1988 of an Award in Honour of Dr Kyosuke Kindaichi.

Education

BA Kobe University, 1970
MA University of Tokyo, 1972
Ph.D. Simon Fraser University, 1979

Fieldwork

Chipewyan, Canada, 1973; 1975–6
Western Tibet, India and Pakistan, 1982–4
Ainu, Hokkaido, Japan, 1986, 1994–2001
Research on Dr Munro's Ainu materials in London, 1987

Ladakh, India, 1988–90
Koryak, Kamchatka, Russia, 1993, 1995, 1997
Mongols, Inner Mongolia, Shinkiang, China, 1995–8
Mongols, Mongolia, 1999–2000

Key Publications

(1981) *Chipewyan Ecology: Group Structure and Caribou Hunting System*, Senri Ethnological Studies, vol. 8, Suita: National Museum of Ethnology.
(1996) *Bunka no Shizenshi* (An Anthropology of Nature and Culture), Tokyo: University of Tokyo Press.

TAKAKO YAMADA

Izumi, Seiichi

b. 3 June 1915, Tokyo, Japan

d. 15 November 1970, Tokyo, Japan

Seiichi Izumi studied at Keijo Imperial University and was initiated into anthropology by Takashi Akiba, who had once studied under Malinowski. Izumi's academic career can be divided broadly into three stages.

Izumi's initial interest lay in northeastern and inner Asia. Between 1936 and 1945, he carried out field surveys on Cheju Island, Korea, among hunting and fishing peoples of Manchuria (present-day northeastern China), and also among the Mongols of Inner Mongolia.

The ten years following Second World War made up the second stage of his research. In 1952, he was assigned by UNESCO to survey Japanese immigrants in Brazil. Up to this point, his research was in the field of socio-cultural anthropology. However, in 1956, he visited Peru and encountered the ancient civilisation of the Andes. This proved to be a decisive turning point. In 1956–7, he went to Harvard to study Andean archaeology, marking the beginning of the third stage of his research.

In 1958, the University of Tokyo launched the Andes Research Programme with Izumi as the director. One of the disputed points at that time was whether the earliest development of the Andean civilisation took place on the Pacific coast or on the eastern side of the Andes. After a general survey in 1958, Izumi decided to concentrate on the site at Kotosh, near the city of Huanuco, Peru. Here his team succeeded in demonstrating that the earliest development can be traced on the eastern slope of the Andes. The excavation of the Templo de las Manos Cruzadas established the existence of temple constructions at the earliest stage of the formative era preceding the appearance of pottery making.

In 1964, the Peruvian government decorated Izumi with her highest Orden del Sol. The city of Huanuco posthumously awarded him the title of honorary citizen in 1971.

Education

BA Imperial University of Keijo, 1938

Fieldwork

Da Singgan Ling Mountains, northeastern China, July 1936

Cheju Island, Korea, 1936–7, intermittently
Sungaree River region, northeastern China, August 1937
New Guinea, January–August 1943
Inner Mongolia, July–August 1945
Brazil, 1952–3, 1955
Peru, 1958, 1960, 1963, 1966

Key Publications

with Sono, T. (eds) (1963) *Excavation at Kotosh, Peru 1960*, Tokyo: Kadokawa-Shoten.

(1966) *Saishu-to (Cheju Island)*, Tokyo: University of Tokyo Press.

with Terada, K. (eds) (1966) *Excavations at Pechiche and Garbanzal, Tumbes Valley, Peru, 1960*, Tokyo: Kadokawa-Shoten.

(1971) 'The development of the formative culture in the Ceja de Montana: a viewpoint based on the materials from the Kotosh site', in E.P. Benson (ed.) *Dumbarton Oaks Conference on Chavin*, Washington, DC: Dumbarton Oaks Research Library.

MUTSUHIKO SHIMA

J

Jackson, Michael

b. 8 January 1940, Nelson, New Zealand

After completing undergraduate studies in anthropology, psychology, and philosophy, Jackson spent several years doing welfare work (with the Aboriginal Welfare Board, Victoria, Australia, and the London County Council Welfare Office for the Homeless, UK), and community development work (with the United Nations Operation in the Congo). He then embarked on graduate studies at Auckland and Cambridge. Influenced by innovations in communications and information theory, his MA research analysed the social and psychological consequences of literacy in early nineteenth-century Maori New Zealand, and explored cross-culturally the conditions under which oral and print-based cultures come to be regarded as mutually inimical. Since the late 1990s, he has returned to these interests in his research on the ambivalent attitudes of modern Maori to biotechnology.

Although his Ph.D. fieldwork among the Kuranko of Sierra Leone involved research on literacy and schooling, his publications in the 1970s centered mainly on existential dilemmas of knowledge and control in everyday village life. Several of his essays from this period – on ritual practice, conflict resolution in domestic life, story-telling and the resolution of ethical quandaries, divination as a coping strategy, tensions between local, national, and global frames of reference – were brought together in a widely acclaimed volume in 1989.

In the early 1980s Jackson published pioneering work on embodiment, practice theory, metaphor, and narrative, and – following new fieldwork on Kuranko ethnohistory – wrote his first book to reach an audience both within and beyond the academy. Throughout his career, he has also published several volumes of poetry, as well as novels and essays, which have received international awards.

Theoretically, Jackson has drawn on American pragmatism, critical theory, and existential-phenomenological thought in his analytical work; stylistically, he has experimented with new techniques of ethnographic writing. His contributions have influenced debates on post-modernism, reflexivity, narrativity, field methods, and ethics – in anthropology and several related disciplines.

His 2002 volume is a cross-cultural study of the politics of story-telling. Drawing on his research in Sierra Leone, Australia, and New Zealand among refugees, renegades, and war veterans, this work makes a significant contribution to the anthropology of violence, intersubjectivity, and sociality.

Education

BA Victoria University of Wellington, 1961
MA University of Auckland, 1967
Ph.D. University of Cambridge, 1972

Fieldwork

Koinadugu District, Sierra Leone, 1969–70, 1972, 1979, 1985, 2002
Northern Territory, Australia, 1989, 1990, 1991
Southeast Cape York, Australia, 1993–4, 1997

Key Publications

(1977) *The Kuranko: Dimensions of Social Reality in a West African Society*, London: C. Hurst.
(1989) *Paths toward a Clearing: Radical Empiricism and Ethnographic Inquiry*, Bloomington: Indiana University Press.
(1995) *At Home in the World*, Durham: Duke University Press.
(2002) *The Politics of Storytelling: Violence, Transgression, and Intersubjectivity*, Copenhagen: Museum Tusculanum Press.

Further Reading

Cooper, R. (1998) 'Jackson, Michael', in R. Robinson and N. Wattie (eds) *The Oxford Companion to New Zealand Literature*, Oxford: Oxford University Press.

FINN SIVERT NIELSEN

Jakobson, Roman Osipovich

b. 11 September 1896, Moscow, Russia

d. 18 July 1982, Boston, Massachusetts, USA

'Russian philologist' (the words are inscribed on his tombstone) Roman Jakobson is an outstanding theorist of structural anthropology and the founder of the 'formal school'. His work focused on the problem of invariants in cultural variation. His method was to formalise the analysis of culture in order to understand the functioning of the inner structures of cultural objects.

He initiated this approach through the study of poetry by comparing metric structures of East Slavic versification systems. He focused his efforts on the formulation of Indo-European metric universals in two aspects – historical and typological. His research into such different metric phenomena as German alliterative poetry, Mordovian versification, and schemes of the modulations in Chinese regular poetry gave birth to his theory of, and investigation into, the major laws of world poetry universals. The results of these investigations were reviewed in Jakobson's famous articles, 'Linguistics and poetics' (1960) and other papers collected in *On Verse, Its Masters and Explorers* (*Selected Writings*, vol. V, 1979).

He formulated principles of phonology as well as principles operating in the correlation between phonemes and their sense in speech prosody. From his first steps in investigations of that kind he tried to clarify the structural linguistic rules that bind prosodic elements into original systems of human language and its poetics. A similar analysis was applied by Jakobson to the complex morphonology of the Gilyak language (*Notes on Gilyak*, in *Selected Writings*, vol. II, pp. 72–97). Numerous examples of such analyses can be found in his book, *Poetry of Grammar and Grammar of Poetry* (*Selected Writings*, vol. III).

He developed the term 'binary opposition' that became popular not only among linguists (phoneticians and phonologists), but also among cultural anthropologists focusing on cultural binary oppositions. Jacobson's works encouraged Claude Lévi-Strauss to undertake his own investigations on indigenous mythologies. From the 1920s on, Jakobson reasserted the 'culture-structuring' creative power of language in self-identification, both in general, and particularly in relationship to Slavic peoples.

From the time of the Prague Linguistic Circle (from 1926 till the beginning of the Second World War this was the group that regarded language as a semiotic system and included Vilém Mathesius, Roman Jakobson, René Wellek, Nikolay Trubetzkoy, Sergei Karcevskiy, and Jan Mukarovsky), Jakobson emphasised the necessity to get rid of synchronic–diachronic opposition and to turn to the study of dynamic synchrony.

He was interested in the development of semiotics as a science. He considered its methodology to be very productive in search of integrated solutions to the problems that arise from the interaction between semiotic systems of world culture.

Education

BA Lazarev Institute of Oriental Languages (Moscow), 1914
MA Moscow University, 1918
Ph.D. German University of Prague, 1930

Key Publications

with Halle, M. (1956) *Fundamentals of Language*, Hague: Mouton de Gruyter & Co.
(1959) *The Anthropology of Franz Boas — Essays on the Centennial of His Birth*, ed. American Anthropological Association, Memoir LXXX, Menasha, WI: American Anthropological Association.
(1962–88) *Roman Jakobson. Selected Writings*, 8 vols, Berlin: Mouton de Gruyter.
(1980) *Child Language, Aphasia, and Phonological Universals*, Berlin: Mouton de Gruyter (first published in German, 1941).

GALINA KHIZRIEVA

James, Allison

b. 26 September 1954, Birmingham, UK

Allison James has carried out research with children for over three decades. Beginning in the 1970s, her early work focused on questions of language and culture with subsequent research into children's friendships and social relations. James has made significant contributions to both the theoretical and methodological study of childhood and children's lives. Her 1990 co-edited book is important to single out for advancing a new paradigm for the social study of childhood that reoriented academic thinking on the subject. Two central features of the paradigm that continue to critically inform current childhood research are: (1) that children and childhood are worthy of study in their own right, and (2)

that they are competent social actors. James has also been instrumental in exploring innovative methodologies that bring children into the research process as active and knowledgeable participants.

Exploring identity issues – in children's lives, across the life course, in agricultural families, and in food cultures – has been a central feature of James's numerous publications throughout the 1990s. Her ongoing interest in examining the local diversities and cultural variables of children and childhood, in addition to the commonalities, informs her current research on children, the law, and social policy. In this work, James explores the mutual constitution of childhood by adults, policy-makers, and by children themselves. She is presently the Director of the Centre for the Social Study of Childhood in the UK.

Education

BA University of Durham, 1977
Ph.D. University of Durham, 1983

Fieldwork

England, 1977–9 (Northeast), 1988–91 (Midlands), 1995–7, 1997–2000 (Yorkshire)

Key Publications

with Prout, A. (eds) (1990) *Constructing and Reconstructing Childhood*, Basingstoke: Falmer Press (second edn, 1997).
(1993) *Childhood Identities: Self and Social Relationships in the Experience of the Child*, Edinburgh: Edinburgh University Press.

VIRGINIA CAPUTO

James, Wendy R.

b. 1940, Timperley, Cheshire, UK

Wendy James's extended engagement with the Uduk of the Sudan has provided new challenges to the practice of anthropology. In her earlier work she dealt with issues of subsistence, kinship and settlement patterns, population history and migration. Her analysis of cultural metaphors reflects the Uduk's history of devastation and survival. The past and the present become interwoven in her work, as the past experiences narrated by the Uduk and the historical archives speak of a violent past that shapes their social organisation and the institutions of the Uduk of today.

In her second monograph James continues her ethnographic narrative of the Uduk by exploring social and moral codes, ritual practice, cosmological theories, and religious notions. She explores the historical appropriation of symbolic practices from other peoples such as Bertha, Nuer, Shilluck, Meban spirits, and Jum Jum healing cults. Her argument becomes even more striking as the Uduk are once again displaced by war and many of them end up living in refugee camps in Ethiopia. It is through those historical processes of change and displacement that the Uduk express an interest in Christianity and Islam.

James's contribution to the anthropology of religion arises out of such cross-border experience of intersymbolic and intercultural socioreligious experience. She suggests that any anthropological study of religion within globalisation requires the continual study of localised traditions and social practices that mediate between the grand narratives of the world religions and the localised understandings of the peripheries. Within such uncertainties and certainties of globalisation the choices of the periphery are more limited. Therefore James's contribution to the study of religion reaffirms the need to take the periphery seriously and to illuminate from a critical perspective the interrelations between forms of knowledge and those who pursue religious knowledge.

Education

BA University of Oxford, 1962
Diploma in Anthropology, University of Oxford, 1963
B.Litt. University of Oxford, 1964
D.Phil. University of Oxford, 1970

Fieldwork

Port Sudan, 1964–5
Blue Nile Province, Sudan, 1965–9
Western Wallega Province, Ethiopia, 1974–5
Southern Sudan, 1982–3
Khartoum, 1988
Ethiopia and Kenya, 1989
Nasir, SPLA-held territory, Southern Sudan, 1991
Gambela Region, Western Ethiopia, 1992, 1993, 1994
Nairobi, Kenya, 1995
Gambela Region, Western Ethiopia, 2000

Key Publications

(1979) *Kwanim Pa: The Making of the Uduk People: An Ethnographic Study of Survival in the Sudan-Ethiopian Borderlands*, Oxford: Clarendon Press.
with Donham, D.L. (eds) (1986) *The Southern Marches of Imperial Ethiopia: Essays in Social Anthropology and History*, Cambridge: Cambridge University Press.
(1988) *The Listening Ebony: Moral Knowledge, Religion and Power among the Uduk of Sudan*, Oxford: Clarendon Press.
(1995) *The Pursuit of Certainty: Religious and Cultural Formulations*, ASA Decennial Series on 'The Uses of Knowledge: Global and Local Relations', ed. with introduction, 'Whatever happened to the Enlightenment?', London: Routledge.

MARIO I. AGUILAR

Jenkins, Richard

b. 1952, Liverpool, UK

Richard Jenkins, by his own admission, has thrived on the ambiguity of inhabiting the interstitial disciplinary spaces between social anthropology and sociology. Qualified in the former, for much of his career he has taught and researched in areas normally regarded as the domain of sociologists. It is, however, precisely this refusal to be straitjacketed that has enabled Jenkins to range freely and with ease across not only quite diverse fieldwork sites but also topic areas – from youth culture in Ireland, to unemployment in the Midlands, disability in Wales, archival research on Satanism in Northern Ireland, and, most recently, national identity in Denmark. Nonetheless, and despite the apparent heterogeneity of this body of work, three key themes emerge. First, there is Jenkins's abiding interest in issues of identity and difference and the personal and political ramifications which these raise; second, there is his commitment to the importance of bringing anthropology back home; and third his ability to put ethnographic flesh on the bones of social theory.

This hallmark appears in his first ethnographic research among young men and women in Northern Ireland. Here Jenkins explained how it is that young men, growing up on the same housing estate on the outskirts of Belfast, nonetheless fare rather differently during the passage to the labour market of adulthood, reproducing patterns of social stratification. For Jenkins the explanation lies in the complex interweaving between individual circumstances and choice-making and the local/organisational patterning of different occupations. It is this interplay that produces – and reproduces – the varied career trajectories of the lads, ordinary kids, and citizens who inhabit this working-class estate.

The mundane ordinariness of everyday life and the different ways in which people go about coping with the problems that they encounter fascinates Jenkins as he grapples with difficult issues such as the effects of youth unemployment on family life and relationships and the prejudices faced by those who are othered, be it with regard to their different ethnicity or perceived intellectual disabilities. Understanding the precise workings of such processes of classification is important, Jenkins argues, for classificatory practices have a political dimension. Central here are questions of identification and the social and interactional contexts and power relations within which people find themselves and within which their 'difference' risks becoming classed as deviance. For Jenkins, the process of

identifying such similarities and differences in and amongst ourselves is a very human act in which every one of us is embroiled and to whose understanding the theories and practices of anthropology have a valuable contribution to make.

Education

BA Queen's University of Belfast, 1976
PhD. University of Cambridge, 1981

Fieldwork

Belfast, Northern Ireland, 1976–80
West Midlands, England, 1980–3
Swansea and Port Talbot, Wales, 1985–7
Jutland, Denmark, 1993–8
Derbyshire, England, 1999–2001

Key Publications

(1983) *Lads, Citizens and Ordinary Kids*, London: Routledge & Kegan Paul.
with Hutson, S. (1989) *Taking the Strain: Families, Unemployment and the Transition to Adulthood*, Milton Keynes: Open University Press.
(1997) *Rethinking Ethnicity*, London: Sage.

ALLISON JAMES

Jenness, Diamond

b. 10 February 1886, Wellington, New Zealand

d. 1969, Ottawa, Canada

Diamond Jenness left his native New Zealand to study classics at Balliol College, Oxford. Along with Canadian folklorist Marius Barbeau and Wilson D. Wallis, he switched to anthropology, working with R.R. Marett to earn a Diploma in 1911 and an MA in 1916. He carried out fieldwork on Goodenough Island off the New Guinea coast, co-authoring a monograph with his Methodist missionary brother-in-law, A. Ballantyne, and assembling a collection for the Pitt Rivers Museum at

Oxford. He was recovering from malaria acquired in the field when Barbeau, who had returned to Canada and its National Museum, invited him to join the Canadian Arctic Expedition led by Vilhjamur Stefansson (1913–16).

Jenness accepted with alacrity and thus began a career-long specialisation in Eskimo ethnography and culture history, including such diverse topics as culture, technology, language, archaeology, and government administration. During the First World War, he served overseas but returned to Canada in 1919 as an ethnologist at the National Museum. In 1926, Jenness became chief of the Anthropological Division when Edward Sapir resigned to move to the University of Chicago. Except for government intelligence work during the Second World War, Jenness remained in this position until 1947.

In the 1920s, Jenness extended his fieldwork and interests to include Canadian Indians: the Athabascan-speaking Sarcee, Carrier, and Sekani as well as the Ojibwa of Parry Island, Ontario. A brief bout with Bering Strait archaeology, based on surface finds by local Inuit, permitted him to define the Dorset culture and its complex relationship to the later-dominant Thule culture. In addition to his specialised publications on the Eskimos (1923, 1928), Jenness also produced the first survey and overview of 'the Indians of Canada'. His book with that title has been reprinted many times since its initial appearance in 1932. By 1932, Jenness had become the spokesperson for the anthropology of the Native peoples of the Dominion.

In the 1960s, his interest in the relationship between Indians, anthropologists, and civil servants coalesced into a monumental study of Eskimo administration across national boundaries, in Greenland and Alaska as well as in Canada (Jenness 1962–8). Jenness was a persistent critic of government policy towards Indians, but his solution to liquidate the Reserve system and thereby encourage education and citizenship now seems patronising and outdated. Nonetheless, Jenness managed to keep anthropology within the purview of

the Canadian government during a period when the Bureau of American Ethnology in the USA was effectively muffled.

While he headed the Anthropological Division of the National Museum, Jenness was the only Canadian to establish a reputation outside Canada, serving as president of the American Anthropological Association (the only Canadian to do so) and the Society for American Archaeology as well as vice-president of the American Association for the Advancement of Science. He held five honorary degrees and was a Companion of the Order of Canada.

Education

BA University of Wellington, 1908
MA University of Oxford, 1916

Fieldwork

New Guinea, 1911–12
Canadian Arctic, 1913–16
Canadian Indians, 1920s

Key Publications

(1923) *The Copper Eskimos*, Ottawa: Report of the Canadian Arctic Expedition, 1913–1918, vol. 12.
(1928) *The People of the Twilight*, New York: MacMillan.
(1932) *The Indians of Canada*, Ottawa: National Museum of Canada, Bulletin 65, Anthropological Series 15.
(1962–8) *Eskimo Administration in Canada, Alaska and Greenland*, 5 vols, Arctic Institute of North America.

REGNA DARNELL AND FREDERIC W. GLEACH

Jensen, Adolf Ellegard

b. 1899, Kiel, Germany

d. 1965, Frankfurt am Main, Germany

Jensen began his academic career as a natural scientist; he took part in both world wars as an ordinary soldier, and remained a believing Protestant throughout his life. It was very probably the experience of the breakdown of 1918 that led him to Leo Frobenius (1873–1938), in whose circle of influence he rapidly became the second leader of German cultural morphology, and after 1945 director of the Frobenius Institute. After the culture historical form of anthropology of Pater Wilhelm Schmidt (1869–1954) and the ethnosociology of Richard Thurnwald (1869–1954) and Wilhelm Mühlmann (1904–88), the cultural morphology of Frobenius and Jensen was the most distinguished manifestation of 'classical' anthropology in the German-language area.

Jensen saw the main task of anthropology to be the reconstruction of world views from which all other cultural manifestations could then be interpreted. As both Johann Gottfried Herder (1744–1803) and Frobenius had taught and practised, the most suitable material appeared to him to be folk tales, upon which myth and ritual could be grasped. The foci of his empiricism were the cultures of ancient cultivators of southern Ethiopia and eastern Indonesia who would have been the first to understand the connection – constitutive of human history – between dying and becoming, as exemplified by harvested plants. However, Jensen also drew evidence for this central construction of the world view of the killed deity from the researches of Paul Wirz (1892–1955) among the Marind Anim of New Guinea, Gunnar Landtman among the Kiwai of New Guinea, Konrad Theodor Preuss (1869–1938) among the Uitoto in Columbia, and Alfred Louis Kroeber (1876–1960) and Cora A. Du Bois (1903–1991) in California.

Jensen's basic contribution to the anthropology of religion can be seen in his working out of the 'Dema deity', a founder figure, often occurring in ensembles at the time of origin ('Urzeit'), whose suffering and death brought with them cultural goods and techniques. According to Jensen, archaic cultures practise the imitation and repetition of the original killing as a religious service. Because of the sidereal equivalent of the dying and reawakening moon, he also called this old cultural layer 'lunar'. He saw the continuation of this original religion in the plant cults of the old empires, and even in the passion play of the Christian tradition. Unacceptable in modern ethical terms, this ritual killing is without blame or heroism.

Jensen's reconstruction of this archaic belief had parallels in the work of A.M. Hocart (1883–1939), Karl Kerenyi (1897–1973), and Walter F. Otto (1874–1958), and some of his ideas were continued later by René Girard, Hans Peter Duerr, Fritz W. Kramer, or Karl-Heinz Kohl.

Education

Prom. (Ph.D.), 1922
Habil., 1933

Fieldwork

South Africa, 1928–30
Libya, 1932
Ethiopia, 1934–5
Indonesia, 1937
Ethiopia, 1951, 1954–5

Key Publications

(1939) *Hainuwele. Volkserzählungen von der Molukken-Insel Ceram* (Hainuwele Folklore from the Moluccas Island Ceram), Frankfurt am Main: Klostermann

(1948) *Das religiöse Weltbild einer frühen Kultur* (The Religious World View of an Early Culture), Stuttgart: Schroeder.

(1959) *Altvölker Süd-Äthiopiens* (Archaic Peoples in South Ethiopia), Stuttgart: Kohlhammer

(1963) *Myth and Cult among Primitive People* (Mythos und Kult bei Naturvölkern. Religionswissenschaftliche Bertrachtungen, 1951), Chicago and London: Chicago University Press.

BERNHARD STRECK

K

Kaberry, Phyllis Mary

b. 1910, California, USA

d. 1977, London, UK

Phyllis Kaberry represents the best of an ethnographic tradition linked with the changing worlds of colonialism and post-colonialism and their categories of ethnic exclusion. Her concern for women and their own perception of reality, economic change, market forces, and ritual representations provides an intellectually sound and anthropologically rigid connection between her work among Australian Aborigines, her studies of Abelam conflict resolution and decision-making in Papua New Guinea, and her extensive study of the Nso Kingdom in Cameroon. Kaberry's work opened in many ways what later was to be considered the study of gender, when she asked unanswered questions about the possibility of Australian Aborigines women painting pictures or about the way in which Grasslands women in the Cameroon were adapting to the newly formed market forces.

Together with other women anthropologists of her time, such as Jean La Fontaine and Mary Douglas, Kaberry opened a pioneering world of studies about women by women anthropologists therefore proving that women could be good anthropologists in a male-dominated colonial world. She opened avenues for a further specialisation of the anthropological profession. Thus, her ethnographic studies in two different parts of the world suggested that anthropologists could be closely related to regional specialists, however anthropologists had a distinctive methodology, i.e. participant observation within extended periods of fieldwork.

Major anthropological themes taken for granted today were developed within her long experience of fieldwork. For example, she deemed impossible to prepare a new edition of her *Aboriginal Woman: Sacred and Profane* without a new period of fieldwork in order to make her book into a new monograph. Her studies of women and men in their social structure triggered a constant concern for the natural environment as the base for any human population and an ongoing concern for individuals who spoke their own texts rather than to be objectified as 'texts'.

Nevertheless, the ongoing study of gender discrimination and its perception by insiders and outsiders, by women and men alike, remained at the center of her anthropological concerns. Thus, she advocated a middle way in which neither the insider nor the outsider could overpower each others' perceptions of a social dynamic that needed to be studied in the context of wider economic and social contexts.

Education

BA University of Sidney, 1935

Ph.D. London School of Economics, 1938

Fieldwork

Eastern Kimberleys, northwestern Australia, 1934–5

Sepik River area, Maprick, Papua New Guinea, 1939–40

Kingdom of Nso, Bamenda, Northwest Province of Cameroon, 1945–6, 1947–8, 1958

Key Publications

(1939) *Aboriginal Woman: Sacred and Profane*, London: Routledge.

(1952) *Women of the Grassfields: A Study of the Economic Position of Women in Bamenda, British Cameroons*, London: HMSO.

with Forde, Daryll (eds) (1967) *West African Kingdoms in the Nineteenth Century*, London: Oxford University Press for the International African Institute.

with Chilver, E.M. (1968) *Traditional Bamenda: The Precolonial History and Ethnography of the Bamenda Grassfields*, Buea: Government Printers.

MARIO I. AGUILAR

Kapferer, Bruce

b. 1940, Sydney, Australia

Bruce Kapferer consistently evinces deep commitment to the study of social and cultural processes, micro and macro. Kapferer stresses that there are few if any stable, structural givens in social life that anthropology can take for granted in the understanding of processuality. His anthropology strives to comprehend social life as generating and changing itself through itself, in ongoing ways. His analyses depend on detailed research materials in order to theorise the ongoing interaction among ontologies, ideologies, cultural and social formations, and forms of practice. Kapferer's vision strives to weave together cultural imaginaries and cosmologies, as the formative and generative grounds of political, ritual, and social practices.

His early research in Zambia used network analysis and exchange theory to show how social transactions among factory workers created and shaped social relationships in an urban factory setting; and how these relationships changed in the context of a strike. This work demonstrated how the shaping of social forms on the micro-level had significant consequences for macro-level organisation.

Kapferer's analyses of Sinhalese rites in southern Sri Lanka are among the most compelling works of empirical ritual analysis, informed by phenomenology, that modern anthropology has produced. His understanding of the processual dynamics of ritual form has led to profound insights into the relationships between Buddhist consciousness, cosmology, and ritual organisation, into the role of comedy and illusion in ritual, and, more generally, into the crucial role of aesthetic forms for the practising into existence of ritual forms. In recent work, Kapferer shows how, by containing ontological premises of consciousness and sacrifice within itself, a Sinhalese ritual for the negation of sorcery reoriginates human consciousness through the very practices that derive from its ontology.

Kapferer argues that modern nationalism relates sacrifice to the originary power of the state. In modern states, the practices of national sacrifice are related to issues of whether ontologies of social order are conceived of as encompassing and hierarchical, as in Sri Lanka, or as individualist and egalitarian, as in Australia. In contrasting these two states, Kapferer has developed a comparative, cultural approach to modern nationalisms, and to their relationships to ideas of power, passion, and suffering. In current research, Kapferer is developing his comparative approach to studies of globalisation, freedom, and repression in Kerala, South Africa, and Sri Lanka.

Education

BA University of Sydney, 1963
Ph.D. University of Manchester, 1969

Fieldwork

Zambia, 1963–6
Sri Lanka, 1970–present
Aboriginal/settler relations, Australia, 1972
Globalisation and the state (South Africa, Kerala, Sri Lanka), 1997–present

Key Publications

(1972) *Strategy and Transaction in an African Factory*, Manchester: Manchester University Press.

(1983) *A Celebration of Demons: Exorcism and the Aesthetics of Healing in Sri Lanka*, Bloomington: Indiana University Press.

(1988) *Legends of People, Myths of State: Violence, Intolerance, and Political Culture in Sri Lanka and Australia*, Washington, DC: Smithsonian Institution Press.

(1997) *The Feast of the Sorcerer: Practices of Consciousness and Power*, Chicago: University of Chicago Press.

DON HANDELMAN

Karp, Ivan

b. 1943, Stamford, Connecticut, USA

Ivan Karp's initial contribution to the anthropology of social change came out of his 2-year fieldwork period among the Southern Iteso, an Eastern Nilotic-speaking people that live among Bantu speakers in western Kenya and eastern Uganda. Karp suggests convincingly that social change cannot be studied by looking at a single part of society's structure, but it comes out of a comparison between different actions, whereby change in one brings change to another.

Karp's later intellectual concerns include personhood and agency, African systems of thought and ethnophilosophies, cosmology, power and action, museum exhibitions and its politics/poetics, civil society, representation and social identity, philosophy and anthropology, and the possibility of critical enquiries.

Education

BA University of Vermont and University of Rochester, 1965, 1967
MA University of Virginia, 1969
Ph.D. University of Virginia, 1974

Fieldwork

Iteso, Kenya, 1969–71, 1975, 1984, 1985
Iteso and Luo, Kenya, 1990

Key Publications

(1978) *Fields of Change among the Iteso of Kenya*, London: Routledge & Kegan Paul.

with Masolo, D.A. (eds) (2000) *African Philosophy and Critical Inquiry: Studies in Philosophy and Anthropology*, Bloomington: Indiana University Press.

MARIO I. AGUILAR

Kearney, Michael

b. 1937, California, USA

Michael Kearney's main research foci are ethnicity, migration, and the theory and ethnography of transnational communities and processes. He is currently professor of anthropology at the University of California, Riverside. Professor Kearney has researched indigenous migrant communities in Oaxaca, Mexico, and California, and written extensively on the building of transnational communities under deterritorialised conditions. He has also developed an exemplary track record in practical anthropology that deals with the creation of effective transnational indigenous organisations.

Beginning his ethnographic fieldwork in the mid-1960s, in the Zapotec community of Ixtepeji, and with the Mixtec community of San Jéronimo Progreso, in the 1980s, Kearney has stayed in contact with Zapotec and Mixtec migrants through fieldwork in multiple locations: the agricultural regions of Baja California, the *colonias* of Tijuana and Ciudad Juarez, and the labour camps in the San Joaquin Valley in California.

His wife, Carole Nagengast, professor of anthropology at the University of New Mexico, is co-author of two seminal articles on transnationalism and indigenous Mexican migration – 'Anthropological perspectives on transnational communities in rural California' (1989) and 'Mixtec ethnicity: social identity, political consciousness, and political activism' (1990). These two articles highlighted indigenous migrants as agents of social change on both sides of the USA–Mexico border and provided a nuanced understanding of Mexican immigrants' ethnic diversity for scholars, policy-makers, and advocates. These articles described how migrants' 'community' of reference transcends the limits of the border and how these communities become 'deterritorialised' spaces (Kearney and Nagengast coined the term Oaxacalifornia to refer to this transnationalised space), giving rise to novel forms of organisation and political expression.

Kearney has also made major contributions to anthropology through his critical synthesis of peasant studies in *Reconceptualizing the Peasantry: Anthropology in Global Perspective* (1996). Here he assesses dramatic transformations of rural society in light of larger global changes, and reconsiders the distinction between rural and urban. Kearney analysed the ways that peasants define themselves in a rapidly changing world through political forms of representation that correspond to contemporary post-peasant identities. Moving beyond a reconsideration of peasantry, the book situated anthropology in a global context, showing how the discipline reconstructs itself and its subjects according to changing circumstances.

Education

BA University of California, Berkeley, 1963
Ph.D. University of California, Berkeley, 1968

Fieldwork

Ixtepeji, Oaxaca, 1965–7 and sporadically to the present

Ensenada, Baja California, 1969—73
San Jerónimo Progreso, Oaxaca, 1979–present
Tijuana, Baja California, 1979–present
Central Valley, California, intensely, 1980 and 1981, and sporadically to the present
San Quintin, Baja California, sporadically, 1985–90
Riverside, California, 1979–present
Los Angeles, California, sporadically, 1985–present

Key Publications

with Runsten, D. (1994) *A Survey of Oaxacan Village Networks in California Agriculture*, Davis, CA: California Institute for Rural Studies.
(1995) 'The local and global: the anthropology of globalization and transnationalism', *Annual Review of Anthropology* 24: 547–65.
(1996) *Reconceptualizing the Peasantry: Anthropology in Global Perspective*, Boulder, CO: Westview Press.

GASPAR RIVERA-SALGADO

Keesing, Roger

b. 16 April 1935, Honolulu, Hawaii

d. 7 May 1993, Toronto, Canada

Born to a family of anthropologists (his parents Mary and Felix Keesing researched social structure in the Philippines and among the Menomini Indians of Winsconsin) and raised on the Stanford campus where his father was a professor of anthropology, Roger Keesing had childhood experiences of the discipline. He developed a taste for anthropology as an intellectual discipline while sitting in the classes of his father and Gregory Bateson at Stanford, and pursued graduate studies at Harvard under the supervision of Clyde Kluckhohn and Douglas Oliver. It is at Harvard that Keesing was exposed to kinship (his dissertation, *Kwaio Kinship and Marriage*, was written in 1965) and to cognitive anthropology represented by the work of Ward Goodenough and Harold Conklin: these two streams of studies were to remain the central interpretive focus of his work in the Solomon Islands for many years, ethnographically and theoretically. His early work, both in anthropology and in linguistics, the two disciplines that illuminated his intellectual understanding, was inspired by these paradigms.

Keesing's highly theoretical engagement with anthropology was rooted in fieldwork, as he was convinced that no theory in anthropology can be divorced from ethnography. His association with the Kwaio of Malaita in the Solomon Islands, which lasted thirty years, provided him with the type of longitudinal data that allowed him to study social change in action. His attachment to the Kwaio was deep and personal, as much as professional, but with a romantic twist: he cherished their cultural persistence, their resistance to any form of central government, colonial or post-colonial, and acted as their champion, locally and abroad. His book *Custom and Confrontation: The Kwaio Struggle for Cultural Autonomy* attests to it. His concerns with offering a forum for local voices led him to publish the biography of Elota, a local Big Man, and to edit the autobiography of another one, Jonathan Fifi'i, which he also translated from the Kwaio language.

What is particularly striking in the work of Keesing is the range of his writing. On the one hand, we find very theoretically informed ethnographic writings about the Kwaio, particularly on religion, word tabooing, language, and cultural knowledge. And, on the other hand, we find highly theoretical work in different sub-fields of the discipline, at the intersection of linguistics and anthropology: from ethnoscience to the nature of culture; from Marxist anthropology to feminism and literary criticism; from theories of kinship to theories of culture; from cognitive linguistics to formal linguistics; from historical work to post-colonial critique.

In addition to his work with the Kwaio, two main themes were to dominate Keesing's anthropology. First, a profound attraction to cultural theory led him to investigate the concepts of culture, that of 'kastom', and the role of language and cognition in culture. Keesing's work is often informed by a political critique, and is sometimes rather polemical: he saw writing as the place where a true engagement of received ideas and 'established truth' should take place. Writing against what he saw as the reification of culture, he suggested that we talk about 'the cultural'. Writing on anthropology as a discipline, he debated the exoticisation of the object of study, the founding myths of anthropology, and the interpretive quest of the discipline. His introductory textbook, *Cultural Anthropology: A Contemporary Perspective*, published in 1981, was in itself a microcosm of his anthropology as well as a true programme of research. Widely used, yet considered difficult for undergraduate usage because it raised more questions than it sought to answer, it certainly contributed a new orientation of cultural anthropology.

Second, a fascination for linguistics and its formal and interpretive strengths led him to publish widely in linguistics, where his contributions are highly respected. Besides a dictionary and a grammar of Kwaio, and many articles written on the grammar of Melanesian Pidgin between 1985 and 1992, Keesing's book, *Melanesian Pidgin and the Oceanic Substrate*, was to position him at the forefront of pidgin and creole studies. Developing his argument about the influence of Oceanic languages on Melanesian pidgins, he wove together a historical account based on a precise analysis of the resemblances between Kwaio and Solomons Pijin. The argument is provocative and represents a turning point in the discipline: clearly situated at the intersection between universalist and nativist approaches to the development of pidgin and creole languages, and more sociohistorical, substrate-oriented approaches, the book has opened a new chapter in this field of study.

Education

BA Stanford University, 1956
Ph.D. Harvard University, 1965

Fieldwork

Solomon Islands (a total of 5 years between 1962 and 1990)
Queensland, Australia, 1982
Imachal Pradesh, India, 1983

Key Publications

(1975) *Kin Groups and Social Structure*, New York: Holt, Rinehart & Winston.
(1982) *Kwaio Religion*, New York: Columbia University Press.
(1988) *Melanesian Pidgin and the Oceanic Substrate*, Stanford: Stanford University Press.
(1992) *Custom and Confrontation: The Kwaio Struggle for Cultural Autonomy*, Chicago: Chicago University Press.

CHRISTINE JOURDAN

Kelly, William W.

b. 1946, Washington, DC, USA

Known for the breadth of his knowledge across disciplinary fields and a singular ability to capture in writing the essence of Japanese cultural institutions and behaviours, Kelly is internationally considered a premier anthropologist not only for his scholarship and writing (in English, Japanese, and French), but also for service in promoting Japan studies. He joined the Yale faculty in 1980, is a former chair of the Department of Anthropology, and was appointed the Sumitomo Professor of Japanese Studies in 2000. His teaching and mentorship of younger scholars helped establish Yale as a major center for anthropology and Japan studies. Kelly's early agrarian studies adumbrated a wider interest in historical anthropology among Japan scholars. Research in the Shonai plain led to his examination of post-war cultural ideology. In a series of influential publications, he detailed how the social formation of Japan's mainstream consciousness, or 'new middle-class' modernity, has been a powerful model for the organisation of work, family, and schooling since the

1960s. In the 1990s, Kelly began publishing articles, organising conferences, and editing collections on sport, body cultures, and fandom. In 1991 he provided the first comprehensive overview of Japan anthropology in a widely read *Annual Review* article. Beginning in 1996 he conducted field research on the history and present patterns of professional baseball for a book-length study of the Hanshin Tigers.

Education

BA Amherst College, 1968
Ph.D. Brandeis University, 1980

Fieldwork

Aroostock County, Maine, 1972
Yamagata Prefecture, Japan, 1975–7, 1978, 1979, 1982, 1986, 1987, 1988, 1989, 1990, 1991, 1993, 1994, 1995
Kansai region, Japan, 1996, 1997, 1998, 1999, 2000, 2001

Key Publications

(1985) *Deference and Defiance in 19th-Century Japan*, Princeton, NJ: Princeton University Press.
(1986) 'Rationalization and nostalgia: cultural dynamics of new middle class Japan', *American Ethnologist* 13, 4: 603–18.

LAURA MILLER

Kertzer, David I.

b. 20 February 1948, New York City, USA

It is a challenge to do justice to the wide range of academic interests characterising David Kertzer's career. Drawing from various disciplinary perspectives such as social history, anthropological demography, as well as politics, his research has ranged from political symbolism and ritual to the controversial history of Vatican relations with the Jews and the state. The most compelling contribution to a political and historical anthropology of

Europe is represented by Kertzer's ability to combine detailed ethnographic case studies and historical analysis with broader statistical and comparative scenarios. His first monograph, based on fieldwork in Bologna, focuses on the complex struggle between the Communist Party and the Catholic Church for the allegiance of people. He shows the social rather than ideological background to the strength of the largest Communist Party in the West. He also discusses the ambivalences that individuals had to confront when facing the antagonistic pressures provided by both the Church and the Party.

His interest in the political dimension of life is pursued with a broader scope in his study of political ritual. Connecting historical evidences far removed in time and space (from Aztec rites to the inauguration of American presidents, from Ku Klux Klan parades to 1 May rallies in Moscow, from Kennedy's funeral to the Italian politician Moro's kidnapping) he argues for the relevance of rituals in explaining the success of various political forces. He shows how politics is not only the realm of struggle for material interests but also the sphere where various world views confront each other through symbols.

His historical studies also constitute an important contribution. Besides his jointly edited volumes on European family life in early modern times, one should remember his research on institutionalised infant abandonment in nineteenth-century Italy in which the Catholic Church with its concern for family honour plays a crucial role. The Church is also the main actor in two more recent works: the prize winning book on the kidnapping of Edgardo Mortara and the critical analysis of the Vatican role in the development of the rise of modern anti-Semitism. The first concerns a 6-year-old child secretly baptised and taken from his Jewish family in 1858, whose story provided a springboard for the revolts that contributed to the fall of the Papal state. The more recent study emerges from a research within the Inquisition archives and other Vatican archives, and traces the papal historical role in the demonisation of the Jews.

Education

BA Brown University, 1969
Ph.D. Brandeis University, 1974

Fieldwork

Bologna, Italy, 1971–2
Italy (various locales), 1990–1

Key Publications

(1980) *Comrades and Christians. Religion and Political Struggle in Communist Italy*, Cambridge: Cambridge University Press.
(1988) *Ritual, Politics, and Power*, Yale: Yale University Press.
(1997) *The Kidnapping of Edgardo Mortara*, New York: Knopf.
(2001) *The Popes against the Jews: The Vatican's Role in the Rise of Modern Anti-Semitism*, New York: Knopf.

BRUNO RICCIO

Khazanov, Anatoly M.

b. 13 December 1937, Moscow, Russia

Anatoly M. Khazanov started his professional career as an archaeologist specialising in the nomadic cultures of the early iron age. In the second half of the 1960s he shifted to sociocultural anthropology. From 1966–85, his main fields of research were pastoral nomads and the origins of complex societies. His main argument that the nomads were never autarkic, and therefore in economic, cultural, and political respects were dependent on their relations with the sedentary world, is shared now by the majority of experts with regard to the emergence of complex societies, Khazanov was trying, as much as was possible under Soviet censorship, to demonstrate the fallacy of the Marxist concept of historical process.

After his emigration in 1985 from the Soviet Union, Khazanov continued to study nomadic pastoralists, paying particular attention to the deficiencies and shortcomings of their modernisation process. He argued that various modernisation projects have failed because they did not provide room for the sustained self-development of the pastoralists and denied their participation in decision-making.

Since the beginning of the 1990s, Khazanov has also become known for his contribution to the study of ethnicity and nationalism, and transitions from communist rule. He was one of the first to argue that in many countries this transition does not guarantee an emergence of liberal democratic order. He also argued that, contrary to widespread opinion, globalisation per se is unable to reduce nationalism and ethnic strife, which will remain a salient phenomenon in the foreseeable future.

In the last few years, Khazanov has turned to the anthropology of public monuments and symbols, being particularly interested in their role in defining and redefining national and ethnic identities.

Education

BA Moscow State University, 1960
MA Moscow State University, 1966
Hab.Doc. (doktor istoricheskih nauk) Academy of
    Sciences of the USSR, 1976

Fieldwork

Central Asia, especially Kazakhstan, 1960–6,
    1970, 1973–4
Daghestan, 1976, 1980, 1984
Russia, especially Moscow, 1990, 1992–3,
    1995–8, 2000
Israel, 1985–1990, 1993, 2000

Key Publications

(1975) *Sotsial'naia istoriia skifov. Osnovnye problemy razvitiia drevnikh kochevnikov evraziiskikh stepei.* (Social History of the Scythians. Main Problems of Development of the Ancient Nomads of the Eurasian Steppes), Moscow: Nauka.
(1984) *Nomads and the Outside World*, Cambridge: Cambridge University Press (second revised

edn; Madison, WI: The University of Wisconsin Press, 1994; trans. and published in Korean, Seoul: Jisik Publishers, 1990; third revised and enlarged edn in Russian, *Kochevniki i vneshnii mir*, Almaty: Daik-Press, 2000).
(1996) *After the USSR. Ethnicity, Nationalism, and Politics in the Commonwealth of Independent States*, Madison, WI: The University of Wisconsin Press.

ANDREY KOROTAYEV

Kindaichi, Kyosuke

b. 1882, Morioka, Japan

d. 1971, Tokyo, Japan

Although Kyosuke Kindaichi specialised in linguistics at the Imperial University of Tokyo, he aspired to study the Ainu language and culture after trips to Hokkaido and Sakhalin in the late 1900s. His work is somewhat characterised by sociolinguistic and ethnological approaches to the Ainu language and culture. First of all, he elucidated the phonology and grammar of the Ainu language through studies of Ainu oral traditions, a number of examples of which he had collected and transcribed, by making field trips to Hokkaido and Sakhalin, and by inviting Ainu elders and young people to his home in Tokyo. *Ainu Seiten* was the first book in which the original text of Ainu myths was printed alongside its Japanese translation. He continued to work on the transcription and translation of Ainu epics, known as *yukar*. *Ainu Jojishi* was the greatest product of his work on Ainu epics, for which he was awarded the prize of the Academy of Imperial Japan in 1932. In 1960 he compiled a full, complete work on the Ainu language into one book. His approach to the study of Ainu oral tradition has become the model for his successors, and a great amount of Ainu folklore has been transcribed along with its Japanese translation.

Second, his work also contributed to the understanding of the Ainu way of life, especially regarding their religion and world view, and to the discussion of their ethnic origin. He presented the idea that the difference between Emishi in the north of Honshu and Ainu in Hokkaido was simply regional or local and that the Ainu who remained in northern Honshu became Emishi. Moreover, through examining Ainu myths and prayers, he depicted the Ainu religion and world view, and advanced the Ainu belief in the equality between deities and human beings. All of his work was centered on the racial and linguistic genealogy of the Ainu, as is shown in the concluding chapter of *Ainu no Kenkyu*. Based on the polysynthetic nature of the Ainu language, he concluded that the Ainu language was not included in the Ural-Altaic language family and that the Ainu might not belong to Asian stock. Although his ideas on the origin of the Ainu have not been fully accepted today, his work contributed greatly to the further development of Ainu studies.

Education

BA Literature College, Imperial University of Tokyo, 1907
DL Literature College, Imperial University of Tokyo, 1935

Fieldwork

Saru River, Hokkaido, Japan, 1906
Eastern coast of Sakhalin, Russia, 1907
Hokkaido and Sakhalin, 1915
Hokkaido, Japan, 1918, 1923, 1927, 1934, 1947

Key Publications

(1923) *Ainu Seiten* (Ainu Myth), Tokyo: Sekai Bunko Kankokai.
(1925) *Ainu no Kenkyu* (A Study of the Ainu), Tokyo: Naigai Shobo.
(1931) *Ainu Jojishi: Yukar no Kenkyu* (Ainu Epics: A Study of Yukar), 2 vols, Tokyo: Toyo Bunko.

(1960) *Ainugo Kenkyu* (A Study of the Ainu Language), Tokyo: Sanseido.

TAKAKO YAMADA

Klass, Morton

b. 24 June 1927, Brooklyn, New York, USA

d. 28 April 2001, New York City, USA

Morton Klass was an original thinker, wide-ranging in his interests and proudly eclectic in his theoretical perspectives. His ethnographic interest centered on India and overseas Indian communities while his topical concerns ranged from culture change and community organisation, to the history of caste in South Asian, and the nature of religion, revitalisation, and altered states of consciousness.

Klass did graduate work at Columbia University during the heyday of neo-evolutionism and 'scientism', but his own inclinations and the lessons he learned from his Boasian teachers at Brooklyn College were stronger influences on his work, as was the historicism of Conrad Arensberg at Columbia. He departed from the conventional wisdom of the day in his first book, *East Indians in Trinidad*, by presenting the case that the descendants of indentured servants had reconstituted a simplified composite of their former culture in the New World. His approach modified the mechanical acculturation model and showed an appreciation of a people's creative agency even under the highly exploitative conditions of indentured servitude. Although a controversial thesis for both theoretical and political reasons it remains important.

His book on caste (1980) addressed the question of origins, and was intended as a contribution to the wider study of South Asian history and culture as well as a theoretical statement and exercise. Unashamedly eclectic, Klass drew upon diverse theorists, 'including Morton Fried, Fredrik Barth, Marvin Harris, and Claude Lévi-Strauss' to produce an original thesis regarding the evolution of caste as a social system.

From the 1980s his work centered on issues of belief. His interest in revitalisation and new religious movements led him to return to Trinidad in 1985 to study the Sai Baba movement and 'the politics of revitalisation'. His general book on religion, *Ordered Universes*, is a work of rethinking and synthesis. He engages in a series of arguments, as he calls them, about fundamental issues, key conceptions, and words such as supernatural, myth, shaman, and cult, in an effort to find non-judgemental definitions that can be employed for more effective, and less ethnocentric, analysis of religions.

Morton Klass taught at Barnard College and Columbia University from 1962 until his retirement in 1997 and he served as chairman of the department during the years 1965–70, 1976–8, 1986–9. He was a very popular teacher and he and his Barnard colleagues inspired many Barnard graduates to pursue graduate study in anthropology.

Education

BA Brooklyn College, 1955
Ph.D. Columbia University, 1959

Fieldwork

Trinidad, 1957–8, 1985
West Bengal, India, 1963–4

Key Publications

(1959) *East Indians in Trinidad: A Study of Cultural Persistence*, New York: Columbia University Press.

(1978) *From Field to Factory: Community Structure and Industrialization in West Bengal*, Philadelphia: ISHI.

(1980) *Caste: The Emergence of the South Asian Social System*, Philadelphia: ISHI.

(1995) *Ordered Universes: Approaches to the Anthropology of Religion*, Boulder: Westview Press.

HERBERT S. LEWIS

Klein, Alan M.

b. 1946, Munich, Germany

Although Alan Klein conducted ethnographic and ethnohistorical research on Native American issues as part of his graduate education, his subsequent fieldwork and publications have focused primarily upon the vital but problematic place of sport in society. Klein's initial foray into the anthropology of sport was a participant observation study in California of the bodybuilding sub-culture. Klein's account stripped away the facade of hyperbolic masculinity characteristic of this sport activity to reveal the gender insecurity typical of its male participants. This was followed by an ethnographic investigation of baseball in the Dominican Republic that elucidated relationships of cultural hegemony and resistance highlighted by Dominican participation in a quintessentially American game. His third fieldwork project, conducted along the Texas–Mexico border in the mid-1990s, took the form of a detailed ethnography of a combined American and Mexican baseball team whose operations served to illustrate some distinctive features of nationalism, binationalism, and transnationalism. Since 1999 Klein has investigated the globalisation of professional baseball that is transforming major-league baseball in the USA. Klein's impressive corpus of work balances careful field research with historical, political, and economic contextualisation in order to produce theoretically sophisticated accounts that blend elements of realist and critical ethnography.

Education

BA State University of New York, Buffalo, 1970
MA State University of New York, Buffalo, 1972
Ph.D. State University of New York, Buffalo, 1977

Fieldwork

Severn River, Ontario, 1972
Gold's Gyms, California, 1979–8
Dominican Republic, 1987–90
Laredo, Texas, and Mexico, 1992–4

Key Publications

(1993) *Little Big Men: Bodybuilding Subculture and Gender Construction*, Albany: State University of New York Press.

(1997) *Baseball on the Border: A Tale of the Two Laredos*, Princeton, New Jersey: Princeton University Press.

NOEL DYCK

Kleinman, Arthur

b. 11 March 1941, New York City,
   USA

Arthur Kleinman is the Esther and Sidney Rabb professor of anthropology at Harvard University and professor of psychiatry and medical anthropology at Harvard Medical School. Dr Kleinman began his career as a student of Chinese culture in 1969–70, when, having finished medical school and his medical internship, he spent fifteen months as a National Institutes of Health research fellow in Taiwan. From 1970 through 1976, he read anthropology and completed his residency training in psychiatry, both at Harvard. His initial academic work contributed to the development of the 'Asian medical systems' tradition in medical anthropology; he organised a major international conference on medicine in Chinese cultures, which led to one of the first significant interdisciplinary works on the complex medical systems of China, Hong Kong, Taiwan, and Chinese communities throughout Asia.

Several initial essays and his founding of the journal, *Culture, Medicine and Psychiatry*, suggested new theoretical directions for a comparative, anthropological study of medical systems. However, it was his first book, *Patients and*

Healers in the Context of Culture, that provided the first full statement of what was to become a central paradigm in medical anthropology. Although many saw the book as an introduction to concepts such as disease/illness, explanatory models, and professional, folk, and popular systems of health care, the book's greater contribution was to provide a general theoretical framework for the comparative study of health care systems as cultural systems. Kleinman worked explicitly within the tradition of interpretive anthropology, integrating insights from American cultural anthropology, phenomenology, symbolic studies, and medical sociology, to create an innovative approach to the study of illness, healing, and medical system, provoking theoretical debates that launched theorising in medical anthropology.

Two important moves in the early 1980s were to have signal influence on Kleinman's work. In 1980, he began research in China, examining depression and neurasthenia, particularly among persons who had suffered the effects of the Cultural Revolution. This research resulted in numerous articles on the nature of depressive illness in Chinese society and its relation to neurasthenia and somatoform disorders. It also resulted in his second major book, *Social Origins of Distress and Disease*, which provided a remarkable picture of the role of social suffering in producing what Chinese psychiatrists come to know and treat as neurasthenia or depression. This work began a serious, critical engagement with American and Chinese psychiatry, and with biological psychiatrists' claims that mental diseases are universal entities, while at the same time turning his interests increasingly towards an understanding of the moral dimensions of human suffering.

The second important move of these years was his return to Harvard in 1982, where, after spending six years in the Department of Psychiatry at the University of Washington, he took up residence in the Department of Social Medicine and the Department of Anthropology. Building institutional bridges across two Harvard faculties, he worked with colleagues,

Byron and Mary-Jo Good, to launch what was to become a leading programme in North American medical anthropology. He chaired the Department of Social Medicine, 1991–2000, and initiated a specialised programme in medical anthropology in the Department of Anthropology.

In the 1990s, Kleinman's interests turned more and more towards studies of social suffering – studies of violence and social dislocation, narrative and moral dimensions of suffering, and depression and suicide as responses to social conditions. He outlined these themes in the William James Lecture at Harvard Divinity School and the Tanner Lectures at Stanford University. His forthcoming book, *Where Our World is Taking Us: How Moral Experience is Changing in Our Times*, will be his fullest exploration of the social, cultural, and moral dimensions of human suffering. At the same time, Kleinman organised a major effort to place mental health problems on the global public health agenda. Leading an international team of scholars, including his colleagues at Harvard, Kleinman generated the 'World Mental Health Report' that has come to have great significance in increasing attention to mental health problems in low-income societies and to efforts to develop innovative solutions to these problems.

Kleinman has led numerous studies for the National Institutes of Health and the Institute of Medicine, and has received many awards, including the 2001 Franz Boas Award of the American Anthropological Association.

Education

AB Stanford University, 1962
MD Stanford University, 1967
MA Harvard University, 1974

Fieldwork

Taiwan, 1969–70, 1975, 1977–8, 1989, 1992, 1996
China, 1980, 1983, 1986, 1989, 1991, 1998, 1999, 2001
Boston, 1983–6

Hong Kong, 1995

Key Publications

(1980) *Patients and Healers in the Context of Culture*, Berkeley: University of California Press.
(1986) *Social Origins of Distress and Disease: Depression and Neurasthenia in Modern China*, New Haven: Yale University Press.
(1988) *Rethinking Psychiatry: From Cultural Category to Personal Experience*, New York: Free Press.
(1995) *Writing at the Margin: Discourse between Anthropology and Medicine*, Berkeley: University of California Press.

BYRON GOOD

Kluckhohn, Clyde

b. 11 January 1905, Le Mars, Iowa, USA

d. 29 July 1960, Santa Fe, New Mexico, USA

Clyde Kluckhohn first became acquainted with the Navaho while visiting relatives in Ramah, New Mexico, as a high school student recovering from a bout of ill health. He wrote two books about his trek to the isolated Rainbow Bridge in Utah and resolved to maintain contact with the Navaho and the Southwest. It took him some time, however, to return to this first love. After an undergraduate major in classics, Kluckhohn studied psychoanalysis and underwent training analysis in Vienna before turning to anthropology at Oxford University with R.R. Marett on a Rhodes scholarship. He taught briefly at the University of New Mexico but was unable to resist the lure of Harvard; after receiving his Ph.D., he remained there for the rest of his academic career.

In 1936, Kluckhohn returned to Ramah intending to initiate long-term ethnographic work by a team of colleagues and students. Kluckhohn himself collaborated with Lee C. Wyman to document Navaho ceremonies and their mode of transmission across generations and among ritualists. He also worked closely with psychiatrists Dorothea and Alexander

Leighton on Navaho socialisation practices. Kluckhohn was initially optimistic about cross-cultural psychiatry, but he quickly realised the difficulties of learning a cultural pattern simultaneously with undertaking psychiatric investigation of individual adaptations to that pattern. The solution to the lack of depth in most ethnographic reports, in his view, was a longitudinal method. The Ramah project was deliberately organised to incorporate field observations by many individuals coming from the greatest possible range of disciplinary backgrounds. More than fifteen researchers participated in the summer fieldwork sessions. *Children of the People* (1947), co-authored with Dorothea Leighton, summarised the team project. Also with Dorothea Leighton, he wrote *The Navaho* (1946); this book became the standard reference work on the Navaho.

Kluckhohn remained somewhat separate from the mainstream of American anthropology because his training was in British anthropology rather than with Boas or one of his students. Nonetheless, Kluckhohn drew extensively upon Boasian developments in culture and personality. His own work was more sophisticated than most because of his explicit training in psychoanalysis. The interdisciplinary approach developed in Harvard's Department of Social Relations linked Kluckhohn's anthropology to clinical psychology and the systematic sociology of Talcott Parsons, a combination not institutionalised elsewhere.

Kluckhohn defined the anthropological concept of culture in terms of 'designs for living' or 'the set of habitual and traditional ways of thinking, feeling and reacting' that are characteristic of a particular society at a particular moment in time and space (Kluckhohn and Leighton 1946: xviii). The culture patterns he sought were overt and conscious, with explicit consequences for social structure and behaviour as well as for conceptual systems. He distinguished between ideal and actual behaviour. In addition, however, some cultural patterns or configurations were covert, usually outside the consciousness of members of culture. With such a theoretical framework, Kluckhohn was able to analyse variation within

Navaho life as well as to describe broad patterns of ritual, ceremonial, personality, and social organisation.

Navajo Witchcraft (1944) interpreted a large body of ethnographic data in functionalist terms. Witchcraft was adaptive because of its culturally defined adjustment to the Navaho social environment. Such adaptation, in his view, could operate at either the cultural or the individual level, sometimes involving cultural and biological universals taking their specific forms under particular local conditions.

The Comparative Study of Values in Five Cultures began in 1947 under Rockefeller Foundation auspices. Kluckhohn assembled an interdisciplinary team of over thirty-five fieldworkers dispersed among five cultural communities in the Ramah area: Mormons, Texas homesteaders, Spanish Americans, Zuni, and Navaho. Beginning with a concept of value-orientation as an ideal pattern, Kluckhohn identified thirteen binary oppositions or value-pairs that facilitated systematic cross-cultural comparison. Clusters revolved around man to nature, man to man, and man to man plus nature sets of relations. Kluckhohn himself never published a synthesis of the project data with his emerging theoretical framework.

During the Second World War, Kluckhohn began a long series of affiliations and consultancies with the American military in capacities ranging from research on morale to intelligence to overseas administration. From 1947–54, he was director of the Russian Research Centre at Harvard. He continued to work with the Departments of Defense and State until his sudden death in 1960. Kluckhohn is remembered primarily, however, for his Navaho ethnography and for his interdisciplinary perspective.

Education

BA University of Wisconsin, 1928
Studied at University of Vienna and University of Oxford, 1931–2
Ph.D., Harvard University, 1935

Fieldwork

Ramah Navaho, 1936–47
Five cultures in Ramah area, 1947–60

Key Publications

(1944) *Navajo Witchcraft*. Papers of the Peabody Museum of Archaeology and Ethnology, Harvard University, vol 22, no. 2.
with Leighton, Dorothea (1946) *The Navaho*, Cambridge, MA: Harvard University Press.
with Leighton, Dorothea (1947) *Children of the People*, Cambridge, MA: Peabody Museum Publications in American Archaeology and Ethnology.

REGNA DARNELL AND FREDERIC W. GLEACH

Kon, Igor S.

b. 21 May, 1928, Leningrad (presently St Petersburg), Russia

Igor Kon is best known for his pioneer contribution towards the development of the anthropology of childhood in Russia. Before Kon this subject in Russia was not considered as a properly serious task of anthropology. As an author and editor of a series specifically devoted to this subject Kon employed a broad cross-disciplinary approach, using the data and methods of such disciplines as psychology, sociology, history, and cultural anthropology. He argued that the lack of interdisciplinary co-operation and the inadequacy of factual data often made such research unproductive. He carried out his own theoretico-methodological and historiographic study of childhood within the framework of a general theory of the ecology of human development.

In dealing with age categories, Kon suggested at least three reference systems: the life course of an individual, social stratification, and symbolic representations of age. Special attention was paid to the dialectics of age stratification, social change, and intergenerational transmission of culture at various stages of socioeconomic development including the

present scientific and technological revolution. Kon argued that the processes and methods of socialisation of children depended on the normative image of human inherent in each particular culture. The scholar identified two levels of this image – ideological and mass consciousness. According to these ideas he also analysed sex role socialisation and its relations with biological sex dimorphism, historically specific sex stratification systems, and cultural stereotypes of masculinity–femininity.

During the late 1980s, Kon switched the focus of his research to the anthropology of sex, serving as a pioneer in Russia in this field as well. The study of sex was a virtual taboo up to the late 1980s (during one of the first Soviet–American TV-bridges a Soviet lady addressing the American audience even claimed: 'There is no sex in the USSR'). Kon wrote the first Russian textbook in general sexology.

Education

MA (Diplom.) A. Herzen Leningrad Pedagogical University, 1947
Ph.D. (Kandidat istoricheskih nauk), A.Herzen Leningrad Pedagogical University, 1950
Ph.D. (Kandidat philolsofskih nauk), A.Herzen Leningrad Pedagogical University, 1950
Hab.Doc. (Doktor philosofskih nauk), Leningrad University, 1960

Fieldwork

Leningrad, 1970
Krim, 1970

Key Publications

(ed.) (1983–) Seria *Ethnografija detstva*. (Ethnography of Childhood), Moscow: Nauka.
(1988) *Rebijonok I Obshchestvo* (Child and Society), Moscow: Nauka.
(1995) *Sexual Revolution in Russia*, trans. James Riordan, New York: The Free Press.
(2000) 'Sexuality and politics in Russia. 1700–2000', in *Sexual Cultures in Europe. National Histories*, eds F.X. Eder, L.A. Hall, and G.M.

Hekma, Manchester: Manchester University. Press.

TATIANA UVAROVA

Kopytoff, Igor

b. 1930, Mukden, China

Igor Kopytoff is a general practitioner in cultural anthropology with an ethnographic focus on Africa. His work deals mostly with social structure, political organisation, and religion – and the process of transformation in them.

Using a historical and comparative perspective Kopytoff and Miers (1977) outline the particular feature of indigenous African slavery, arguing that it is part of a ubiquitous set of processes that enable groups to acquire more members. They show that slavery does not constitute a unitary status, slaves being found among all classes and strata; nor is it a fixed status, since in the course of their lives slaves go through a process of social transformation that involves a succession of phases and changes in status, some of which merge with other statuses.

In The African Frontier (1987), Kopytoff revises Frederic Jackson Turner's famous Frontier Thesis as a way to bring new perspective to the history and anthropology of sub-Saharan Africa. He argues that most African frontiers have been built on an internal frontier consisting of an interstitial network of areas surrounding established societies. There, settlers out of metropoles constructed new societies by following culturally valued social models more faithfully than they could ever be followed in the metropoles. Over the centuries, this repetitive social construction of a frontier setting shaped and reinforced some basic features of African political culture.

Education

BA Northwestern University, 1955
MA University of Pennsylvania, 1957
Ph.D. Northwestern University, 1960

Fieldwork

Zaïre, 1958–9
Ivory Coast, 1964
Cameroon, 1969–72

Key Publications

with Miers, S. (eds) (1977) African Slavery: Historical and Anthropological Perspectives, Madison: University of Wisconsin Press.
(ed.) (1987) The African Frontier: The Reproduction of Traditional African Societies, Bloomington and Indianapolis: Indiana University Press.

CHANTAL COLLARD

Kramer, Fritz W.

b. 1941, Bad Salzuflen, Germany

Fritz W. Kramer's first widely remarked contribution was his Verkehrte Welten of 1977. With this essay he submitted a profound analysis of early German representational strategies of foreign cultures (Winckelmann, Görres, Creuzer, Voß, Herder, Hegel, Bachofen, Bastian), of the beginnings of modern anthropology (Bronislaw Malinowski), and of the aesthetic reaction to the experience of alterity (Max Pechstein and Emil Nolde). Two basic issues to be pursued later were laid down in this programmatic essay: the epistemological dimensions of ethnographic perspectivism (to see yourself as others see you) and the aesthetic dimensions, consequences, and solutions to this perspectivism (mimesis).

In 1987 (English 1993) Kramer published The Red Fez in which he applied the theoretical insights of his first essay. If anthropology is about perspectivism then it must be enlightening to explore the ways in which colonial Europeans have been represented in Africa. If experiences and representations of other cultures are basically aesthetic practices then it must be instructive to study African art relating to Europe. Social drama, ritual art, and spirit possession are the main topics of this monograph. Being afflicted by foreign spirits appears – analogous to the case of ancestor spirits – to be less a desperate form of handling social deprivation but more a form of mimetic understanding, of coming to terms with what seems incomprehensible and beyond control. On this theoretical background Kramer presented the first thorough and comprehensive analysis of spirit possession cults in the whole of Africa.

Together with Gertraud Marx he published in 1993 an ethnographic study on the ritual organisation of time and space in the southern Nuba Mountains Dimodonko (Krongo-Nuba). On the material level *Zeitmarken* is a contribution to the eternal anthropological debate on the intertwined relations between cosmological, ritual, and political order. On the theoretical level the monograph makes two challenging contributions. The world of Dimodonko is philologically reconstructed from conversations with war refugees outside the Nuba Mountains and from recorded songs. Essentialising and homogenising culture thus appears not as an ethnographic artefact but as a presupposition for the identity politics of the war refugees from Dimodonko.

Education

Ph.D. University of Heidelberg, 1969
Habilitation, Free University Berlin, 1977

Fieldwork

Among the Krongo of the Nuba Mountains, Sudan in Dimodonko, 1975
Among Krongo war refugees in Wad Medani, Sudan, 1987
Hamburg, 1988
Art worlds, intermittent 1990–3

Key Publications

1977 *Verkehrte Welten. Zur imaginären Ethnographie des 19. Jahrhunderts* (Mirror Worlds. On the Fictive Ethnography of the Nineteenth Century), Frankfurt am Main: Syndikat.
(1993) *The Red Fez. Art and Spirit Possession in Africa* (Der rote Fes. Über Besessenheit und Kunst in Afrika,

1987), trans. Malcom Green, London and New York: Verso.
with Marx, Gertraud (1993) *Zeitmarken. Die Feste von Dimodonko.* (Time Markers. The Feasts of Dimodonko), München: Trickster.

RICHARD ROTTENBURG

Krige, Eileen Jensen

b. 1904, Pretoria, South Africa

d. 1995, Durban, South Africa

Student of Winifred Hoernlé, Isaac Schapera, and A.R. Radcliffe-Brown, and contemporary of Max Gluckman, Ellen Helman, and Hilda Kuper, Eileen Krige is one of South Africa's foremost anthropologists. With J.D. Krige, she established the Department of African Studies at the University of Natal in Durban in 1946 – assuming the chair in 1959 after her husband's death – and published one of the seminal ethnographies of the period.

Krige began her studies at the University of Witwatersrand in 1922, turning to Anthropology after completing her Master's degree in Economics in 1926. Married in 1928, the Kriges attended Malinowski's seminar at the London School of Economics in 1935, where Eileen presented material from her research among the Lovedu that earned her a Doctor of Literature from Wits in 1936. The Kriges secured an International Institute of African Languages and Cultures Fellowship to fund the Lovedu fieldwork (1936–8) that produced the *Rain Queen*. The Kriges' innovative teamwork and close intellectual collaboration is apparent in their ethnography that, following the trends of that period, was largely descriptive and structural-functionalist.

Despite problems imposed by apartheid the Kriges encouraged black students, two of whom (Harriet Ngubane and Absalom Vilakazi) produced classic ethnographies of their own. While based in Pretoria, Krige initiated some of the first urban anthropological research to be undertaken in South Africa. Curtailed by demands of family and teaching most of Krige's theoretical work on the Lovedu was completed after her retirement in 1970, when she published numerous papers on marriage institutions and family life.

Education

BA University of the Witwatersrand, 1925
MA University of the Witwatersrand, 1926
D. Lit. University of the Witwatersrand, 1936

Fieldwork

Lovedu, northeastern Transvaal, 1928, 1930, 1932, 1936–8, 1939, 1962, 1964

Key Publications

(1936) *The Social System of the Zulus*. London: Longmans
with Krige, J.D. (1943) *The Realm of a Rain Queen: A Study of the Pattern of Lovedu Society*, Oxford: Oxford University Press.

EVIE PLAICE

Kroeber, Alfred L.

b. 11 June 1876, Hoboken, New Jersey, USA

d. autumn 1960, Paris, France

Alfred Kroeber, an American of German descent, studied English at Columbia University, turning to anthropology after taking the first course in American Indian languages taught by Franz Boas at Columbia in 1896; the students met weekly at the Boas home. After a fellowship at the American Museum of Natural History, Kroeber visited the Arapaho for his first fieldwork, presenting a dissertation on their decorative symbolism in 1901.

Kroeber began his life work in 1900 when he became curator of the California Academy of Sciences in San Francisco and immediately began fieldwork with the nearby Yurok and Mohave; he would continue to return to these groups throughout his career. Phoebe Apperson Hearst subsidised his salary to curate her archaeological collections, and Kroeber quickly began to teach anthropology at the University of California, Berkeley, although teaching was supposed to be part of his longer-term mandate. He equally promptly undertook a systematic survey of the languages and cultures of the state of California, resulting in the *Handbook of California Indians* in 1925. Although Kroeber was not primarily a linguist, linguistic classification proved the most convenient way to categorise the California tribes. Kroeber, collaborating with Roland B. Dixon of Harvard, reduced the twenty-three language families of the state into several larger units (Hokan and Penutian being the most significant of these), whose similarities they first attributed to diffusion but gradually decided must reflect genetic relationship. This California work was critical in the reduction of the number of North American linguistic stocks from fifty-five to merely six by Edward Sapir in 1921; Sapir followed Hokan, Penutian, and other new linguistic stocks into culture areas outside California to propose a synthetic picture of North American culture history. In 1918, fellow Boasian Robert Lowie joined Kroeber in the academic programme at Berkeley, although archaeology and physical anthropology were added much later.

Although Kroeber remained in California throughout his professional career, his intellectual and ethnographic interests were diverse. He worked closely with Ishi, the last survivor of the Yahi tribe and so-called 'wild Indian', who lived at the museum until his death from tuberculosis in 1916. During a sabbatical in 1915–16, Kroeber underwent psychoanalysis, practising as a lay analyst for several years after his return. He kept this work separate from his anthropology and soon decided to remain full-time in the latter. The two interests did not mix well because Kroeber defined culture as 'superorganic' and avoided talking about individuals in his cultural descriptions. Kroeber studied child language and archaeological seriation to Zuni Pueblo in 1915 and spent 1924 immersed in Mexican and Peruvian archaeology.

During the 1930s, in the midst of the

Depression, Kroeber's research team collected culture element lists designed to reveal the correspondence of cultural and natural areas in North America, producing a rather dry report of the results in 1939. His own work turned increasingly to the unique 'configuration' of style characteristic of each culture. *Configurations of Culture Growth* (1944) assembled a vast compendium of information about cultural fluorescences in historically recorded cultural traditions from around the world. He did not include pre-literate societies because the time depth for such an analysis was not available rather than because he considered them less civilised. The clear cross-cultural patterns that Kroeber had hoped to find across civilisations and across domains of cultural activity remained elusive, however. In 1957, *Style and Civilization* provided a more accessible version of the configurational argument, emphasising the correlation between women's dress length and periods of political upheaval over three centuries of European records.

Kroeber collected his theoretical papers in 1952 under the title, *The Nature of Culture*. He argued that culture was the organising feature of anthropology as an autonomous discipline and felt that all of his work could be framed around its study. A further collection of his essays, which appeared posthumously, was focused around interpretive uses of history in anthropology. Kroeber emphasised the natural science side of anthropology, although acknowledging its parallel roots in the humanities and ambiguous status among the social sciences.

Kroeber retired in 1946 but continued to serve as a central guru of Boasian anthropology until his death in 1960. The best measure of his stature may be his textbook, titled simply *Anthropology*. The first edition appeared in 1923 and was critical of the codification of the Boasian programme, both for legitimacy in emerging anthropology programmes in universities and in public discourse about culture and cultural relativism. The 1948 revision was also widely used as a textbook. In retirement, Kroeber taught at a variety of American institutions and attended many conferences

devoted to delimiting the scope of anthropology as a holistic science of man[kind].

Education

AB Columbia University, 1896
MA Columbia University, 1897
Ph.D. Columbia University, 1901

Fieldwork

Arapaho, 1899
Yurok and Mohave, beginning in 1900
Zuni, 1915

Key Publications

(1923) *Anthropology*, revised 1948, New York: Harcourt.
(1944) *Configurations of Culture Growth*, Berkeley: University of California Press.
(1952) *The Nature of Culture*, Chicago: University of Chicago Press.
(1957) *Style and Civilization*, Berkeley: University of California Press.

REGNA DARNELL

Kryukov, Mikhail Vasilyevich

b. 12 June 1932, Moscow, Russia

Kryukov's major contributions to cultural anthropology belong to two fields: (1) studies of the evolution of kinship terminology and (2) the study of long-term dynamics of the Chinese ethnos. Kryukov undertook the study of the dynamics of kinship terminology among Eurasian ethnic groups having deep historical traditions of written records. However, though he seems to consider his results as having universal applicability, they appear to be most applicable to the evolution of kinship terminology in Eurasia and among the Austronesians. He has shown that among those peoples bifurcate merging systems tended to get transformed either into bifurcate collateral, or generational ones. On the other hand, the lineal kinship terminology developed either from bifurcate collateral ones (this development is most typical for Eurasia), or from generational systems. Note that these are not mere speculations, as Kryukov supported his conclusions with a wealth of diachronic data. Being a sinologist he paid special attention to the evolution of kinship terminology among the Chinese, thoroughly documenting the transition from the bifurcate merging to bifurcate collateral kinship terminology among them in the first millennium BC and its further development up to the present.

Education

BA Moscow Institute of Oriental Studies, 1954
MA Moscow Institute of International Relations, 1955
MA Peking University, China, 1962
Ph.D. (kandidat istoricheskih nauk) Institute of Ethnography, USSR Academy of Sciences, 1965
Hab.Doc. (doktor istoricheskih nauk) Institute of Ethnography, USSR Academy of Sciences, 1965

Fieldwork

China, 1956–62; 1989–1992 (among the Lolo)
Southern Pacific, 1971
Vietnam, 1980

Key Publications

(1968) *Historical Interpretation of Kinship Terminology*, Moscow: Institute of Ethnography, USSR Academy of Sciences.
(1978–93) First author of a series of monographs (6 vols) on the historical dynamics of the Chinese ethnos from the second millennium BC to the twentieth century (Moscow: Nauka; in Russian).

ANDREY KOROTAYEV

Kuper, Adam

b. 29 December 1941, Johannesburg, South Africa

Adam Kuper's work has been concentrated mainly in two fields: the comparative ethnography of the Bantu-speaking peoples of southern Africa and the history of anthropology.

Brought up in South Africa, Adam Kuper studied anthropology at the University of the Witwatersrand and visited his aunt, Hilda Kuper, when she was conducting research in Swaziland. His own early field research was with the Kgalagari of Botswana and concentrated on kinship and political relations. Kuper's other ethnographic work, in Jamaica (where he conducted applied research on behalf of the Jamaican government) and Mauritius, has achieved less recognition. Rather, his fame as an ethnographer rests on building a framework for the understanding of kinship, traditional politics, the symbolism of the house, and other aspects of culture through 'regional structural comparison' (or regional comparison, for short).

Kuper first explored the idea of regional comparison in articles published in the 1970s. His most significant work up to 1982 was brought together as *Wives for Cattle*. In that (and some subsequent publications) he argued that the analysis of comparative regional contexts is essential for the full understanding of ethnographic detail. From 1976 to 1985 he taught at Leiden University, and this approach to African ethnography struck a chord with the long-standing Leiden structuralist tradition that was based on similar premises, though in the Leiden case with an ethnographic emphasis on the East Indies. As Dutch structuralism subsided with the passing of its key practitioners, Kuper's new comparative focus breathed life into this simple but important approach. The idea, very simply, is that by seeing a kinship system, a symbolic system, or whatever in terms of its place in a regional system of systems, one gains much greater insight than one could by focusing on but a single ethnographic case. The approach demands, of course, a wide knowledge of the ethnography of a region, and in some cases of its history as well.

Kuper's other important work has been in the history of anthropology. Not content to leave history to the historians, he has added an anthropological practitioner's gaze at times when historians of the social sciences were more content to record or argue trivial details rather than examine ideas. *Anthropology and Anthropologists*, based partly on interviews with senior colleagues in British anthropology, was a youthful *tour de force*. Kuper was accused of presenting a 'Great Man' view of history, ironic for a social scientist of structuralist predisposition. Subsequent work was to lean more towards the structuralist. In *The Invention of Primitive Society* he viewed the entire history of the discipline from 1861 (when Sir Henry Maine overthrew the hypothetical eighteenth-century notion of the social contract and placed the family at the center of anthropological attention) as one of an ever-changing image of 'primitive society', which in his view should be jettisoned and rendered obsolete. Later work, including his book-length analysis of American cultural anthropology, has moved more towards an appreciation of anthropology's place within a wider context of the human sciences as a whole. In this latter case, Kuper took issue with a then-current trend in North American anthropology that saw culture as self-explanatory and completely divorced from biology, psychology, and related disciplines.

Kuper has taught at Makerere University, University College London, the University of Leiden, and Brunel University. In the last case, his teaching in the Department of Human Sciences has brought him into close contact with psychologists, sociologists, communications specialists, and others whose interests have no doubt served to broaden his anthropological perspective. At the same time, the concentration in focus within European social anthropology, coinciding with Kuper's crucial role in the founding of the European Associations of Social Anthropologists in 1989, has led to his recognition as one of European social anthropology's greatest contemporary figures.

Education

BA University of the Witwatersrand, 1961

Ph.D. University of Cambridge, 1966

Fieldwork

Botswana, 1963–5, 1966–7
Jamaica, 1972–3
Mauritius, 1983, 1984

Key Publications

(1973) *Anthropology and Anthropologists: The British School, 1922–1972*, London: Allen Lane (second edn, 1983; third edn, 1996).

(1982) *Wives for Cattle: Bridewealth and Marriage in Southern Africa*, London: Routledge & Kegan Paul

(1988) *The Invention of Primitive Society: Transformations of an Illusion*, London: Routledge.

(1999) *'Culture': The Anthropologists' Account*. Cambridge, MA: Harvard University Press.

ALAN BARNARD

Kuper, Hilda

b. 23 August 1911, Bulawayo, Zimbabwe

d. 1992, Los Angeles, California, USA

Hilda Beemer (Kuper) was part of a remarkable cohort of undergraduate students that included Max Gluckman, Eileen Jensen Krige, and Ellen Hellmann who were taught and inspired by Agnes Winifred Hoernlé and Isaac Schapera, and who were to later constitute the 'Great Tradition' in Southern African anthropology, characterised by finely nuanced ethnographic monographs. After working for the South African Institute of Race Relations on the effect of liquor legislation on African women, research which formed the basis of her Master's thesis, she proceeded to the London School of Economics where she was Bronislaw Malinowski's research assistant and student. In 1934 she commenced her work on the Swazi for which she is justly renowned. That year at an educational conference in Johannesburg she met the Swazi king, Sobhuza II, who became a lifelong friend for more than forty years and facilitated her entry into at least the local elite and nobility.

Her first two books on the Swazi form a unit. The first focuses largely on 'traditional society' and the dynamic of status and rank, and how it is expressed largely through kinship. The hand of Malinowskian functionalism is clear in this study. The second examines the colonial situation more closely; indeed it is a pioneering work in the anthropology of colonialism, and clearly shows the subtle influence of Marx and South African radical politics.

During the 1950s, she and her sociologist husband and collaborator, Leo Kuper, moved to the University of Natal where they were heavily involved in founding the oppositional Liberal Party and the Passive Resistance campaign against apartheid. During this time she wrote a vivid ethnography of the Natal Indian community. After much political harassment the Kupers moved to the University of California, Los Angeles, in 1962.

Always concerned about issues of representation, Kuper experimented with ethnographic novels, short stories, and plays, and regarded *A Witch in My Heart* (translated into both Zulu and siSwati) as her finest work.

Her final work was an anthropological *tour de force*, a biography of Sobhuza, her long-time friend and protector. Arguing that biographies were essentially a Western genre she sought to place her subject within a complex, ethnographically rich, and historically grounded perspective.

The last course Kuper taught concerned human rights and genocide, a fitting epitaph for what she felt were the crucial issues facing anthropology.

Education

BA University of the Witwatersrand, 1930
MA University of the Witwatersrand, 1934
Ph.D. University of London, London School of Economics, 1942

Fieldwork

Johannesburg, African urban location, 1931–4
Swaziland, 1934–7 and then intermittently until 1972
Natal Indian community, 1950s intermittently

Key Publications

(1947) *An African Aristocracy*, London: Oxford University Press.
(1947) *The Uniform of Colour*, Johannesburg: Witwatersrand University Press.
(1970) *A Witch in My Heart* [play with anthropological introduction], London: Oxford University Press.
(1978) *Sobhuza II*, London: Duckworth.

Further Reading

Hammond-Tooke, W.D. (1997) *Imperfect Interpreters: South Africa's Anthropologists 1920–1990*, Johannesburg: Witwatersrand University Press.

ROBERT J. GORDON

L

La Fontaine, Jean Sybil

b. 1931, Kenya

The career of Jean La Fontaine provides an example of successfully fulfilling Malinowski's challenge to bring anthropology home. Born and spending much of her early life in the context of East Africa, La Fontaine began studying the Gisu of Uganda for her doctoral thesis, publishing both a monograph and many articles based on this ethnography. During her teaching career, which included the University of Cambridge and concluded as professor of anthropology at the London School of Economics, La Fontaine consistently promoted the status of social anthropology as an academic discipline. She was and is adamant that theory and ethnography cannot be neatly separated, but define and reinforce each other. This interrelationship between the intellectual and the practical also applies to her approach to ritual, the main focus of her academic work, claiming that the practical actions of ritual observance exist on a continuum from the purely technical to the wholly symbolic. Ritual processes thus weave a relationship between social institutions and the natural world. Not least of these processes are rites of passage, particularly initiation rites, an interest in which she built upon the interests and theories of her teacher, Audrey Richards. The book in which La Fontaine overviews and discusses initiation rites is a stimulating text of continuing importance as a teaching resource.

The study of rites marking the social change from childhood to adulthood has linked La Fontaine naturally with the increasing interest in the study of childhood since the 1980s. In official retirement La Fontaine virtually began a new career, in which she rigorously and successfully applied her theoretical knowledge of social anthropology to current political issues, with particular reference to child sexual abuse. In 1985, she was commissioned by the UK government to carry out an investigation of sexual abuse 'scandals', which had been the subject of considerable, often prurient, media interest. Following this she conducted a 2-year investigation into allegations of sexual abuse, torture, and murder said to be associated with satanic rituals. In both cases, La Fontaine applied the analytical tools of anthropology to the study of social problems, although her published reports did not always please the scandal-hungry public. Using classical anthropological views of incest, witchcraft, and the social construction of reality, and writing about painful topics with cool, but humane detachment, she succeeded in furthering understanding of child sexual abuse, disproving the existence of so-called satanic abuse, and showing why many child care professionals continued to believe in satanic abuse against the evidence.

Education

MA Newnham College, University of Cambridge

Ph.D. University of Cambridge, 1957

Fieldwork

Uganda, 1953–5
Zaïre, 1962–3
England, 1985–7, 1991–3

Key Publications

(1959) *The Gisu of Uganda*, London, International African Institute.
(1985) *Initiation: Ritual Drama and Secret Knowledge across the World*, Harmondsworth: Penguin.
(1990) *The Sexual Abuse of Children*, Cambridge: Polity Press.
(1998) *Speak of the Devil: Tales of Satanic Abuse in Contemporary England*, Cambridge, UK: Cambridge University Press.

JUDITH ENNEW

Lambek, Michael

b. 1950, Montreal, Canada

Michael Lambek is one of the leading anthropological authorities on spirit possession and indigenous systems of knowledge, subjects that he has explored during more than twenty-five years of field research in Mayotte, Comoro Islands, and Madagascar. Lambek's early work in Mayotte focused on spirit possession. Breaking out of the mould of analysing spirit possession as constitutive of social schisms in society, Lambek was one of the first anthropologists to consider it as a system of discourse in the production and reproduction of culture. In this sense, Lambek's early work was a groundbreaking scholarship that set a new ethnographic and intellectual standard for subsequent texts on spirit possession. Although Lambek began fieldwork in Madagascar in 1987, he extended his research on Mayotte to include investigation of the interstices of Islam, sorcery, and spirit possession. This extraordinary long and intense period of fieldwork bore fruit in the form of Lambek's later work, which has won great academic acclaim. This later work is on the anthropology of knowledge, an exegesis on the ethnography of religious practices as well as a philosophical reflection on incommensurable non-Western epistemologies. Lambek has compiled several anthologies concerned with memory, religion, and the notion of the person, and published numerous articles on topics including gender, kinship, and taboo. He is the editor of a book series, Anthropological Horizons: Ethnography, Culture and Theory, has co-edited *Social Analysis*, and served on several other editorial boards. More recently, Lambek has used his considerable experience in Mayotte and Madagascar to think and write about history, memory, and moral practice, topics at the forefront of contemporary anthropological debate. In his most recent work Lambek analyses these issues through an ethnography of activities surrounding a major shrine in northwest Madagascar. Lambek's signal contributions to anthropological knowledge blend long-term fieldwork and social analysis with philosophical reflection and deep respect for local systems of knowledge. The result is a body of work that is both refreshingly modest and profoundly insightful.

Education

BA McGill University, 1972
MA University of Michigan, Ann Arbor, 1973
Ph.D. University of Michigan, Ann Arbor, 1977

Fieldwork

Mayotte, Comoro Islands, 1975–6, 1980, 1985, 1992, 1995, 2000, 2001
Madagascar, 1987, 1991, 1992, 1993, 1994, 1995, 1996, 1998, 2001
Botswana, 1985–6
Reunion, 2000, 2001

Key Publications

(1981) *Human Spirits: A Cultural Account of Trance in Mayotte*, New York and Cambridge: Cambridge University Press.
(1993) *Knowledge and Practice in Mayotte: Local*

Discourses of Islam, Sorcery, and Spirit Possession, Toronto: University of Toronto Press.

with Antze, Paul (eds) (1996) *Tense Past: Cultural Essays in Trauma and Memory,* New York: Routledge.

PAUL STOLLER

Lamphere, Louise

b. 4 October 1940, St. Louis, Missouri, USA

Louise Lamphere grew up a middle-class Westerner in Denver, Colorado. At Stanford she majored in sociology and wrote an honours thesis in the interdisciplinary programme, Social Thought and Institutions; she then pursued graduate studies in Harvard's Department of Social Relations. Cora Du Bois was the only tenured woman in anthropology at the time, but about half of Lamphere's graduate cohort was female.

Lamphere had been introduced to Native American anthropology in an undergraduate class with George Spindler, and participated in the joint Harvard/Cornell/Columbia field school at Ramah. She then did dissertation research in the eastern Navaho Reservation. She was attracted to values of autonomy and co-operation, where women's roles were unsubordinated to men's.

After a year teaching at the University of Rochester, Lamphere took a tenure-track position in the all-male Sociology and Anthropology Department at Brown University. The anti-war and women's movements encouraged awareness of the political dimensions of professional life and a questioning of traditional academic roles, particularly for women. In 1974, unjustly, Lamphere was denied tenure. After an internal investigation that denied discrimination while admitting that procedures were not followed, Lamphere filed a Title VII class action suit in federal court. Brown was unco-operative, but eventually settled out of court. The case placed Brown under a consent decree, transformed hiring practices, and was one of the few successful mobilisations of class action against discrimination in faculty hiring and retention.

During this period Lamphere taught at the University of New Mexico as associate professor, and conducted research on working women in Rhode Island. In 1979 she returned to Brown, maintaining an adjunct status at New Mexico; she was promoted to full professor at Brown in 1985. She then returned to New Mexico, where she became distinguished professor of anthropology in 2001.

Lamphere is perhaps best known for her work analysing gender, ethnicity, and power in American society. *Women, Culture, and Society,* co-edited with Michelle Zimbalist Rosaldo, has sold over 60,000 copies and is one of the most widely read works of feminist anthropology. Throughout her career she has retained a dedication to research in one's local communities, and has studied generational changes in working-class immigrants in the northeast, Medicaid Managed Care reform, and women's balancing of work and family in the USA and the UK. In the 1990s she returned to the Navaho context, working with women's life histories.

Education

AB Stanford University, 1962
MA Harvard University, 1966
Ph.D. Harvard University, 1968

Fieldwork

Navaho Reservation, 1960s
London, UK, 1971–2
Central Falls, Rhode Island, 1977
Albuquerque, New Mexico, 1982–3

Key Publications

Zimbalist Rosaldo, Michelle (eds) (1974) *Women, Culture, and Society,* Stanford: Stanford University Press.

(1977) *To Run after Them: The Social and Cultural Bases of Cooperation in a Navajo Community,* Tucson: University of Arizona Press.

(1987) *From Working Daughters to Working Mothers:*

Immigrant Women in a New England Industrial Community, Ithaca: Cornell University Press.

with Zavella, Patricia, Gonzales, Felipe, and Evans, Peter B. (1993) *Sunbelt Working Mothers: Reconciling Family and Factory*, Ithaca: Cornell University Press.

FREDERIC W. GLEACH AND REGNA DARNELL

Landes, Ruth Schlossberg

b. 1908, New York, USA

d. 1991, Hamilton, Canada

A pioneer in race and gender studies, Ruth Landes was a transitional figure between the culture-and-personality studies of the 1920s and 1930s and the study of power and structural dynamics of the late twentieth century. As a social worker in Harlem in the late 1920s, her fascination with the cultural expressions of a congregation of Caribbean immigrants calling themselves 'black Jews' led her to Franz Boas and the study of anthropology. She devoted her anthropological career to recording the cultural creativity of groups negotiating conditions of social change and acculturation. An experimental writer, Landes presaged late twentieth-century reflexive ethnography. A skilled fieldworker, she insisted on the importance of experience as a source of knowledge.

In *The Ojibwa Woman*, one of the first full-length studies of women's lives, Landes portrayed the agency of Ojibwa women who, under structural conditions of poverty and marginalisation, created cultural spaces of belonging through telling stories of women's lives – stories of duress, resourcefulness, resilience, and survival. Landes used life histories to show how individuals reinterpret dominant norms and negotiate identity. *The Ojibwa Woman* introduced the theoretical possibilities that gender, as a set of often contradictory sociological practices and ideological norms, offers for the illumination of cultural processes.

In Bahia in 1938, Landes pioneered urban anthropology in a study of the Afro-Brazilian spirit possession religion, Candomblé. In contrast to the 'race relations' scholarship of her contemporaries in which Candomblé was treated as an 'African survival,' Landes saw Candomblé as a dynamic process, a local discourse, and a social space for Afro-Brazilian women and for male transvestites who lacked political representation in the wider society. Her themes are the agency and cultural production of marginalised peoples and the strategic and creative possibilities of transgressive gender identities and religious revitalisation movements. In her book, *The City of Women*, rather than producing a portrait of a homogeneous and unchanging cultural 'whole' as then typified ethnography, Landes employed multivocality to reproduce contesting local discourses on 'tradition', modernity, and structural power. Now recognised as a classic of experimental ethnography, re-editions of *The City of Women* were published in English in 1994 and in Portuguese in 2002. And, the theoretical questions Landes asked about the organisation of diversity and the interplay of rules and behaviour, pattern and action, structure and agency continue to guide anthropological research.

Education

BA New York University, 1928
MA New York School of Social Work, 1929
Ph. D. Columbia University, 1935

Fieldwork

Harlem, 1928–9
Ontario (Ojibwa), 1932
Minnesota (Chippewa), 1933
Minnesota (Sioux), 1935
Kansas (Potawatomi), 1935–6
Brazil, 1938–9; 1966
Youth gangs, Los Angeles, 1945
Caribbean migration, UK, 1951–2
Culture and education, California, 1956–62
Bilingualism, South Africa, Spain, Quebec, Switzerland, 1970s

Key Publications

(1938) *The Ojibwa Woman*, New York: Columbia University Press.

(1947) *The City of Women*, New York: Macmillan.

(1965) *Culture in American Education*, New York: John Wiley & Sons, Inc.

(1970) *The Prairie Potawatomi*, Madison: University of Wisconsin Press.

Further Reading

Cole, Sally (2003) *Ruth Landes: A Life in Anthropology*, Lincoln: University of Nebraska Press.

SALLY COLE

Lawrence, Peter

b. September 1921, Duxbury, Lancashire, UK

d. December 1987, Sydney, Australia

Peter Lawrence made lasting contributions to anthropological knowledge in his ethnographic fieldwork with the Garia and the Ngaing, two language groups in southern Madang, and with the cargo movement of the area. He looked for the Total Cosmic Order that informed people's actions, examined the intellectual basis for religious thinking, and reintroduced into British anthropology attention to ideas as generative forces in society. Lawrence credited his doctoral supervisor, Reo Fortune, with alerting him to the importance of the belief content of Melanesian religions.

Lawrence, along with his colleague, Mervyn Megitt, who had worked in the Highlands, suggested that there were areal differences in emphasis on religion between the Highlands and the Seaboard societies of Papua New Guinea that Lawrence had studied. The set of distinctions proposed were 'cultural': a term out of favor with students following in the tradition of A.R. Radcliffe-Brown.

Lawrence felt keenly, but overcame, pressures to conform in his doctoral dissertation research, when he reported that the kinship system of the Garia was cognatic, not unilineal as anticipated by the works of others in Melanesia as well as in Africa. He elaborated his own vision for anthropology in *Road Belong Cargo* (1964). In this classic work he delineated the epistemological basis for belief and activity in traditional religion and in the Cargo Movement. Lawrence was the first among his peers to document, as American anthropologists occasionally but peripherally had, the role of the individual in his work. He consulted documents to show the Cargo Movement in historical perspective in relation to European contact in the Madang area. With this book, Lawrence demonstrated that historical perspective in ethnographic research and interpretation is not only possible and legitimate but also essential.

Lawrence held the position of senior lecturer at the Australian School of Pacific Administration (1957–60), the University of Western Australia (1960–3), and the University of Sydney (1964–6). He was appointed professor of anthropology at the University of Queensland in 1966, and professor of anthropology at the University of Sydney in 1971. He remained in that position until he retired in 1986. He was known amongst his colleagues and students for his fairness, unfailing civility, and dedication to facilitating and including the work of others.

Education

M.A. 1948, University of Cambridge
PhD 1951, University of Cambridge

Fieldwork

Thirty years in the southern Madang Province, Papua New Guinea
Garia, 1949–50, 1952–3
Ngaing 1953, 1956, 1958
Southern Madang District or Province 1965, 1972, 1975, 1977, annually thereafter until 1981

Key Publications

(1964) *Road Belong Cargo: A Study of the Cargo Movement in the Southern Madang District, New Guinea*, Melbourne: University of Melbourne Press.

(1965) 'The Ngaing of the Rai coast', in P. Lawrence and M.J. Meggitt (eds) *Gods, Ghosts and Men in Melanesia: Some Religions of Australian New Guinea and the New Hebrides*, Melbourne, New York: Oxford University Press.

(1967 [1964]) *Don Juan in Melanesia*, first published *Quarant* 29, April–May, republished St Lucia, Queensland: University of Queensland Press.

(1984) *The Garia: An Ethnography of a Traditional Cosmic System in Papua New Guinea*, Manchester: Manchester University Press.

DOROTHY K. BILLINGS

Layton, Robert H.

b. 1944, UK

Robert Layton's involvement in anthropology has been at both theoretical and applied levels. Although his initial fieldwork was conducted in France, it is his contribution to Australian Aboriginal ethnography, especially rock art, for which he is most noted. During the 1970s and 1980s, Layton worked as a research anthropologist for the Australian Institute of Aboriginal Studies and the Northern Land Council, engaged to conduct research in support of Aboriginal land claims in Australia, which aimed to return dispossessed Aboriginal people to their traditional lands. Layton was engaged as anthropologist for a number of significant land claims, including Uluru (Ayers Rock) in central Australia, widely regarded as a landmark case both for restoring land rights to indigenous people and in acknowledging the role indigenous people may play in management of conservation areas. Layton's research further was instrumental in securing Uluru's second inscription on the World Heritage register, in recognition of the importance of its cultural values.

Layton's extensive fieldwork throughout Australia resulted in his seminal work on Aboriginal rock art. This definitive work is wide in scope, examining and comparing rock art styles, motifs, and methods throughout Australia, and recognises the complementary discourses of archaeology and anthropology in explicating cultural traditions. In this and other work, Layton argues that contemporary ethnography might serve to refine and criticise neo-Darwinian explanations of human cultural adaptation to the environment.

Education

B.Sc. University College London, 1966
M.Phil. University College London, 1968
D.Phil. University of Sussex, 1972

Fieldwork

Franche-Comte, eastern France, 1969, 1972, 1995
Uluru, central Australia, 1977–9
Various sites in Australia, 1974–81

Key Publications

(1986) *Uluru: An Aboriginal History of Ayers Rock*, Canberra: Aboriginal Studies Press.

(1992) *Australian Rock Art: A New Synthesis*, Cambridge, UK: Cambridge University Press.

KIM FLEET

Leach, Edmund

b. 7 November 1910, Sidmouth, UK

d. 6 January 1989, Cambridge, UK

Edmund Leach came to anthropology having read mathematics and engineering. Joining Bronislaw Malinowski's seminar at the London School of Economics (LSE), he embarked in

1939 on fieldwork in northern Burma. After nine months in the settlement of Hpalang, he was called up for military service, and for the remainder of the war was involved in operations during which he travelled widely in the Kachin Hills. The experience of cultural heterogeneity and historical complexity gained from these travels was foundational to his first major book, *Political Systems of Highland Burma*. This book shattered the convention of functionalist ethnography that every society exists in stable equilibrium. Leach argued that equilibrium models belong to an 'as if' world of words and concepts in terms of which people advance their claims and counterclaims. Political reality, messy and dynamic, fluctuates between ideal systems, alternately egalitarian and hierarchical, while conforming precisely to none.

Having left the LSE in 1953 to take up a post in Cambridge, Leach undertook fieldwork in the village of Pul Eliya in Ceylon (now Sri Lanka). In the resulting monograph, *Pul Eliya* (1961), he argued that social structure stems not from the imposition of quasi-jural 'norms' of kinship, but from the choices of individuals faced with constraints of environment and technology. The argument was part of a long-running debate with his erstwhile mentor, Meyer Fortes, who continued to insist on the 'irreducible' quality of kinship. A volume of essays also published in 1961 took its title, *Rethinking Anthropology*, from a lecture in which Leach had spurned the 'butterfly collecting' of a comparative anthropology bent on classifying societies according to type in favor of a search for connections that transcend classificatory divisions. This theme of connectivity was powerfully reiterated in his 1967 series of BBC Reith Lectures, *A Runaway World?*. Other chapters in *Rethinking Anthropology* see Leach debating with Claude Lévi-Strauss on structures of kinship and alliance – the beginning of an abiding engagement with Lévi-Straussian structuralism that subsequently extended into the field of myth analysis with a series of essays in which Leach turned an anthropological eye on biblical narratives.

The range of topics on which Leach wrote extended far beyond the frontiers of anthropology. Four themes, however, stand out. The first concerns the definition of ritual, which Leach took to encompass any aspect of action that communicates information about the 'state of play' in social relationships. Thus the symbolic significance of ritual action is public and social, whatever private emotions it might arouse in individual participants. This leads to the second theme, of the relation between social and psychological states, which was central to Leach's critiques of the psychoanalytic approach to the interpretation of symbols in papers on the magical significance of hair (1958) and the biblical story of virgin birth (1966). The third theme, which owed much to Leach's encounter with the linguist Roman Jakobson, dwells on the logic of binary oppositions that underpins the communicative function of cultural symbols. This is linked to the idea that our perception of the world depends upon how the continuum of nature is cut up by verbal categories into discrete blocks. This fourth theme was developed into a theory of taboo, exemplified by two celebrated papers, one on the kinship terminology of the Trobriand Islanders (1958), the other on the relation between animal categories and terms of abuse (1964).

Leach was a paradoxical figure. He was a creature of the academic establishment, serving as provost of King's College, Cambridge (1966–79), as president of the Royal Anthropological Institute (1971–5), and as a trustee of the British Museum (1975–80). He was knighted in 1975. Yet he was also given to ridiculing not only the pretensions of the establishment that sustained him, but also the work of his anthropological colleagues. An inveterate polemicist, he thrived on demolishing prevailing orthodoxies. His writings, though idiosyncratic and disjointed, are driven by a compelling vision of the anthropological project: no mere novelistic excursion into the moods and motivations of other cultures, but a systematic inquiry into the condition of being human whose closest affiliations are with mathematics and music.

Education

BA University of Cambridge, 1932
Ph.D. London School of Economics, 1947

Fieldwork

Iraqi Kurdistan, 1938
Northern Burma, 1939–45
Sri Lanka (Ceylon), 1953–4

Key Publications

(1954) *Political Systems of Highland Burma*, London: Athlone Press.
(1961) *Pul Eliya: A Village in Ceylon*, Cambridge: Cambridge University Press.
(1961) *Rethinking Anthropology*, London: Athlone Press.
(1976) *Culture and Communication: The Logic by which Symbols Are Connected*, Cambridge, UK: Cambridge University Press.

Further Reading

Hugh-Jones, S.P. and Laidlaw, J. (2000) *The Essential Edmund Leach* (2 vols), New Haven: Yale University Press.
Tambiah, S.J. (2002) *Edmund Leach: An Anthropological Life*, Cambridge, UK: Cambridge University Press.

TIM INGOLD

Leacock, Eleanor Burke

b. 2 July 1922, Weehawken, New Jersey, USA

d. 2 April 1987, Honolulu, Hawaii, USA

Renowned as a pioneer feminist theorist, Marxist scholar, ethnographer, and ethnohistorian, Eleanor Leacock was known for her successful combination of scholarship and social activism. While her ethnohistory of the North American fur trade and her ethnography of the hunting and gathering Naskapi Indians remain classics, she also conducted research in Africa, Europe, the Pacific, and urban America, spanning such diverse topics as schooling in New York City and Zambia, and critiques ranging from Culture of Poverty studies to biological determinism.

The daughter of literary critic Kenneth Burke and Lily (Batterham) Burke, she grew up in Greenwich Village and on family forestland in northern New Jersey. Educated at Radcliffe and Barnard Colleges, in 1941 she married Richard Leacock, a documentary filmmaker and cameraman for Robert Flaherty. They had four children. Her second husband, whom she married in 1966, was James Haughton, a Harlem-based community activist.

At Columbia for her Ph.D., combining social history and social evolution, she was most influenced by Gene Weltfish and William Duncan Strong. Strong directed her attention to the boreal forests of northern Quebec and Labrador where she conducted fieldwork with the Montagnais-Naskapi (Innu) in 1950–1. An important theoretical work, *The Montagnais Hunting Territory and the Fur Trade* was based on her 1952 doctoral dissertation. Earlier ethnographers had used the supposed existence of the Family Hunting Territory (FHT) as evidence against the theory of primitive communalism. Her evidence supported the view that the FHT was a historical artefact of the fur trade, and not an indication of the primordiality of private property.

Leacock's academic career did not follow a conventional path; in later years she often spoke of the discrimination against female anthropologists of her generation. Only in 1963 did she take up her first regular appointment: at the Brooklyn Polytechnic Institute. In 1972 she became chair of the Department of Anthropology at the City College of New York, and a member of CUNY's Graduate Faculty, positions held until her death. With her close colleague, June Nash, Leacock turned the CUNY department into a formidable center for politically engaged Marxist-feminist research.

Her research followed several pathways, always anchored in her political paradigm. Her studies of the schools of New York (1958–65) took her into the city's classrooms and homes to address the ways in which poverty, race, and mental health combined to stratify students into 'streams' and limit life chances. She later adapted this methodology to examine schooling for rapidly urbanising Africans in Zambia, and deployed many of the insights gained to critique then popular theories of the Culture of Poverty.

In the 1960s and 1970s Leacock reissued two nineteenth-century anthropological works, Lewis Henry Morgan's 1877 classic, *Ancient Society*, and Engels's 1884 *Origin of the Family, Private Property and the State*. Her critical reassessments helped to spark renewed interest among scholars in these classics.

The ethnography of native North America had long suffered a lack of understanding of the complex historical pathways of the continent's societies. With Nancy Lurie she edited a groundbreaking volume on American Indian ethnohistory that traced the trajectories of key case studies from aboriginality to modern times (1971). Her volumes with Mona Etienne (*Women and Colonization*, 1980), and Helen Safa (*Women's Work*, 1986) applied a similar framework to the changing roles of Third World women under the impact of global forces. Likewise her co-edited volume, *Politics and History in Band Societies* (1982) grounded the study of hunting and gathering peoples in history, political economy, and contemporary struggles for justice. Her collected essays appeared in *Myths of Male Dominance*.

Disturbed by Derek Freeman's attacks on Margaret Mead's Samoan fieldwork and on cultural anthropology generally, Leacock travelled to Samoa to undertake research among urban youth. While not uncritical of Mead's original work, Leacock's research indicated serious flaws in Freeman's assertions and vindicated much of Mead's original findings. However a serious illness interrupted her fieldwork; Leacock was flown to a hospital in Hawaii and died there on 2 April 1987.

Within the discipline of anthropology, Eleanor Leacock championed a strand of humanistic Marxism that differed both from the more political-economic Marxism of some of her New York contemporaries, as well as from the structural Marxism espoused by colleagues in France and the UK. Her legacy to anthropology is a dual one: as a scholar for her advances in feminist theory and historical materialism, and as an activist for providing a role-model for the politically engaged anthropologist.

Education

BA Barnard College, 1942
Ph.D. Columbia University, 1952

Fieldwork

British Columbia, 1945
Switzerland and Italy, 1948–9
Quebec and Labrador, 1950–1, 1984
New York City schools, 1958–65
Zambia, 1970–1
Samoa, 1986–7

Key Publications

(1954) *The Montagnais Hunting Territory and the Fur Trade*, Washington: American Anthropological Assn.

with Lurie, Nancy (eds) (1971) *North American Indians in Historical Perspective*, New York: Basic Books.

Engels, Friederich (1972) *Origin of the Family, Private Property and the State*, with an introduction and notes by Eleanor Burke Leacock, New York: International Publishers.

(1981) *Myths of Male Dominance*, New York: Monthly Review Press.

RICHARD LEE

Lebra, Takie Sugiyama

b. 1930, Shizuoka Prefecture, Japan

Takie Lebra's career has been mostly in the Department of Anthropology at the University of Hawaii where she progressed from lecturer, appointed in 1968, to emeritus professor (in 1996). During that time she published books and many articles that helped the next generation of anthropology students to incorporate a sound understanding of Japan into their education, and undoubtedly stimulated the interest of many to choose Japan as a special focus. In recognition of this important contribution she has spent periods visiting many other universities, notably as distinguished visitor at the University of Washington (1991), Harvard University (1998), and the National University of Singapore (1999). Over the years, she has received many awards for her work, the major ones being from the US National Science Foundation (1976–8), the Japan Society for the Promotion of Science (1978–9), the US Social Science Research Council (1982, 1988–9), the Japan Foundation (1984–5), the Wenner–Gren Foundation (1989), Fulbright (1993), and John Simon Guggenheim (1995–6). The record of Lebra's extensive research experience and publications indicate some fluctuations of interest, as shown by a publication list that consists of a wide topical range including women, marriage and motherhood socialisation, communication, silence, hierarchy, the royalty, careers, ageing, adoption, moral values, and cults. Nevertheless, she has maintained a basically constant preoccupation with the relationship between culture and personal identity. This focus is presented in *Japanese Patterns of Behavior* (1976) but can be traced further back to her dissertation and immediate post-doctoral publications that resulted from research on religiously induced identity conversion and therapy. Further, similar proclivities are discernible in her gender studies, and even in the more recent, and most 'structural', research on the aristocracy (*Above the Clouds*, 1993) to the extent that 'status' as the central variable is seen primarily from the standpoint of culture and personhood. The latest book looks at the Japanese selfhood most consciously and systematically from the standpoint of comparative cultural logic. As a native anthropologist, Lebra considers it crucial to maintain her post-field communication with non-native colleagues and students, professional and otherwise, as secondary 'informants'.

Education

Teaching Certificate, Tsuda College, 1951
BA Gakushuin University, 1954
MA University of Pittsburgh, 1960
Ph.D. University of Pittsburgh, 1967

Fieldwork

Hawaii (millenarian cult), 1963-65
A resort town in central Japan that Lebra designated Shizumi, 1976–7
Osaka–Kyoto area, 1977–8
Tokyo and vicinity, 1982, 1984–5, 1989, 1993, and thereafter yearly, research on elite-career women and men in Tokyo, and since 1998, primarily in Shizumi, on elderly care

Key Publications

(1976) *Japanese Patterns of Behavior*, Honolulu: University of Hawaii Press.
(1984) *Japanese Women: Constraint and Fulfillment*, Honolulu: University of Hawaii Press.
(1993) *Above the Clouds: Status Culture of the Modern Japanese Nobility*, Berkeley: University of California Press (the 1994 Hiromi Arisawa Memorial Award).
(In press) *The Japanese Self in Cultural Logic*, Honolulu: University of Hawaii Press.

JOY HENDRY

Lee, Richard B.

b. 1937, New York, USA

Richard B. Lee's most enduring legacy will be the remarkable corpus of ethnographic work and its impetus to theory that stem from his long-term Kalahari research, and from the scholars he inspired and mentored. Lee began his Kalahari fieldwork in 1963 as part of an interdisciplinary team dedicated to developing as complete a picture as possible of the hunting and gathering way of life. Lee's early work challenged long-held assumptions that hunter-gatherer life was 'nasty, brutish and short'. Through rigorous empirical study, Lee demonstrated the security inherent in a foraging subsistence base. This work provided a critical contribution to the rise of feminist anthropology; by using his own careful measurements and comparative data from other foraging societies, Lee revealed the importance of collected foods in relation to meat in most forager diets. By exposing women's subsistence role and their political centrality in Ju/'hoansi society, Lee and his colleagues dispelled stereotypes of 'primitive patriarchy'. His ethnography offered evocative, sympathetic, and vivid portrayals of a small-scale society that captivated an anthropological readership, the media, and, hence, the wider public. As a result of this work the Ju/'hoansi are arguably the most thoroughly documented and well-understood group in Africa.

Lee's early research was influenced by cultural ecology and evolutionary studies; in the 1980s his theoretical framework shifted to Marxist political economy with an emphasis upon examining the social and economic basis of egalitarianism. With Eleanor Leacock, he published works that affirmed Marx's construct of 'primitive communism' and explored its ethnographic foundations. They argued for the existence of societies that have the capacity to reproduce themselves while limiting the accumulation of wealth and power, and they attempted to identify the structures that enabled such societies to do so.

In the 1980s Lee's early ethnography as well as the evolutionary analytic framework that informed it came under increasing criticism. Claiming that he neglected Ju/'hoansi incorporation into coercive world power structures and arguing that their egalitarianism was a product of their subservience and not a *sui generis* phenomenon, 'revisionist' scholars prompted a lively 'Kalahari debate'. Lee answered their challenge through detailed historical research and by refining theoretical models of egalitarianism. As a result of the debates in which Lee and others engaged, our knowledge of Kalahari peoples and the models

deployed in their analysis have become more sophisticated.

Lee's politically engaged anthropology is illustrated, for example, by 'The Kalahari People's Fund', which he helped to create. By 2002, Lee's research included HIV, the greatest threat to the Ju/'hoansi as they enter the new millennium.

Education

BA University of Toronto, 1959
MA University of Toronto, 1961
Ph.D. University of California, Berkeley, 1965

Fieldwork

Kalahari Desert, Botswana, 1963–2001 (multiple long- and short-term stays)
Northern Canada, 1960, 1984, 1986, 1990

Key Publications

with De Vore, I. (eds) (1968) *Man the Hunter*, Chicago: Aldine.
(1977) *The !Kung San: Men, Women and Work in a Foraging Society*, Cambridge, UK, and New York: Cambridge University Press.
(1993) *The Dobe Ju/'hoansi*, Fort Worth: Holt Rinehart & Winston [second edn of *The Dobe !Kung*].

JACQUELINE S. SOLWAY

Leiris, Michel

b. 20 April 1901, Paris, France

d. 30 September 1990, Saint-Hillaire, France

Michel Leiris was an artist, poet, writer, critic, traveller, surrealist, and ethnographer, a true 'Renaissance man' whose friends included Breton, Bataille, Giacometti, Picasso, and Métraux. He was also a great innovator in modern confessional literature, writing several autobiographies and keeping a diary from 1922 until 1989. This confessional and very personal style influenced the creation of his first major work, *L'Afrique fantôme*, based on the notes and diaries from the Dakar–Djibouti expedition. The publication of this book brought Leiris instant fame, but also condemnation of most French ethnologists/anthropologists, from Marcel Griaule to Marcel Mauss. On the other hand, Leiris's critique of colonialism brought him acclaim in anthropology in the 1980s and 1990s, with authors like James Clifford and Clifford Geertz referring to him. Always an outspoken critic, just as he opposed European colonial practices and was a member of the French resistance during the Second World War, Leiris was vocal against the war in Algiers (1960) and protested with other intellectuals against the policies of the French Communist Party in 1972. In 1935 he started working in the Musée de l'Homme, and was research director of the CNRS (National Council for Scientific Research), 1943–71.

Leiris's first contact with colonial practices came during a 1927 trip to Egypt. He was appalled by what he perceived as the brutishness of the Europeans in Africa, referring to some of them (especially within the colonial administration) as 'sinister idiots'. In January 1931, following the recommendation of G.H. Rivière (deputy director of the Ethnographic Museum, later Musée de l'Homme), Leiris had been recruited by Marcel Griaule as the secretary-archivist and researcher (for the sociology of religion and ethnology of the secret societies) of the ethnographic and linguistic Dakar–Djibouti mission. The French parliament unanimously adopted a special law about the mission, setting aside a considerable sum of money and making this project something truly of national interest.

L'Afrique fantôme stands as the monument of this expedition. At the same time, this book stands as the stark reminder of the European colonisers' practices of 'collecting' objects that they liked – frequently resorting to treachery or even theft. Obviously, after exposing all of this in great detail (apparently, it was part of

his understanding of the role of the 'secretary-archivist'), Leiris did not enjoy very much sympathy with the local ethnographic community – especially among the ones working in museums, whose interests focused on objects of 'primitive' or 'tribal' art. As a matter of fact, following the publication of the book, Griaule broke off all contacts with him.

The project that began as a kind of personal escape from the dullness of European civilisation, a search for a 'true' or authentic other, gradually evolved into a self-reflective and subjective endeavour. Leiris's participant-observation brought him back to himself, both through questioning his own dreams and attitudes, as well as apparently very ordinary moments of everyday life. Paradoxically, the more he longed to escape from the 'corrupt' Europe, the more he found himself longing for its pleasures. The issue of authenticity is well reflected in a statement like: 'I would rather be possessed than study possessed people!'

Leiris combined highly critical attitudes towards social sciences and their place in the changing world (including an essay on ethnography and colonialism) with his own interests in the ethnographies of the everyday events. In bringing a very strong personal note to all of his writings, Leiris is one of the precursors of the styles of ethnographic writing that emerged during the 1980s. The themes that he was interested in, like the uneasy relationship between 'self' and 'other', never lost their importance since his texts were published in the 1930s. Leiris's insistence on the importance of authorship and at the same time questioning of it still provide very important points for contemporary ethnographic/anthropological research.

Education

Certificate in history of religions and sociology, University of Paris, 1936

Diploma in Oriental languages, École Nationale des Langues Orientales, 1937

Diploma in religious studies, École Pratique des Hautes Études, 1938

Fieldwork

Francophone Africa, Dakar–Djibouti mission, 19 May 1931–17 February 1933
French Antilles, 26 July–12 November 1948

Key Publications

(1934) *L'Afrique fantôme* (Phantom Africa), Paris: Gallimard.
(1948) *La Langue secrete des Dogons de Sanga (Soudan français)* (The Secret Language of the Dogon of Sanga, French Sudan), Paris: Institut d'ethnologie.
(1969) *Cinq etudes de l'ethnologie* (Five Ethnological Essays), Paris: Denoël-Gonthier.
(1996) *Miroir de l'Afrique* (Mirror of Africa), Paris: Gallimard.

Further Reading

Armel, A. (1998) *Michel Leiris*, Paris: Fayard.
Clifford, J. (ed.) (1986) *Sulfur 15*, special issue dedicated to Michel Leiris, Los Angeles: UCLA.

ALEKSANDAR BOSKOVIC

Leslie, Charles M.

b. 1923, Lake Village, Arkansas, USA

Charles Leslie's research has focused upon alternative healing traditions in Asia and North America. *Now We Are Civilized* (1960) is committed to explicating the world view of Others through Zapotec beliefs and practices regarding the body, sickness, and medicine. *Asian Medical Systems* (1976) and *Paths to Asian Medical Knowledge* (1992) (with Allan Young) established Leslie as a pioneer in the fields of Asian medicine, medical pluralism, and epistemology, and document the existence of alternate epistemologies and rationalities of

sickness beliefs, pathophysiologies, and help seeking patterns that exist with biomedicine. He has incorporated a history of science perspective into medical anthropology (*MAQ* 15, 2001) in part through an analysis of revivalism of the ancient as rhetoric for cultivating modernity. He inspires subsequent generations of medical anthropologists to study these issues throughout Asia.

Much of his influence has been 'behind the scenes' as conference organiser, senior editor, and board member for major journals, and via the offices held in professional associations. This has included his analysis of peer review in the social sciences (*Soc. Sci & Med.* 31, 1990).

He was professor emeritus of anthropology and the humanities of the Center for Science and Culture at the University of Delaware (1976–91) and was awarded the Anthropology Distinguished Service Award in 1998.

Education

AB University of Chicago, 1949
MA University of Chicago, 1950
Ph.D. University of Chicago, 1959

Fieldwork

Starved Rock, Illinois (archaeology), 1948
Tama, Iowa (Fox Indians), 1949
Oriental Institute and Peabody Museum (Near Eastern pottery collections), 1949–50
Mexico, 1953–5, 1960, 1987–8
India 1962–3, 1965, 1971–2, 1974–5
Java, Hong Kong, Taiwan, Korea (traditional medicine), 1984

Key Publications

(1976) *Asian Medical Systems: A Comparative Study*, Berkeley: University of California Press.
with Young, Allan (1992) *Paths to Asian Medical Knowledge*, Berkeley: University of California Press.

MONIQUE SKIDMORE

Lévi-Strauss, Claude

b. 28 November 1908, Bruxelles, Belgium

The fact that Claude Lévi-Strauss has been called 'one of the intellectual demigods of the twentieth century' gives one a glimpse of his influence and reputation. The influence that his studies of kinship, totemism, myth, and cognitive aspects of symbols had is enormous. His distinction between nature and culture has influenced generations of social scientists since the 1950s. On the theoretical level, Lévi-Strauss was very much influenced by the works of R. Lowie and C. Nimuendajú, and wrote a major study of Marcel Mauss's *Gift* in 1950.

By his own admission, Lévi-Strauss was brought to anthropology by an accident (an early-morning Sunday telephone call in the autumn of 1934), when he was asked to join French teachers in the newly established University of São Paulo. Lévi-Strauss taught in the sociology department (1935–8), and this Brazilian experience was the determining factor in his career. During his teaching years, he spent several months doing fieldwork among various indigenous groups in the state of Mato Grosso, especially Nambikwara (work on their social organisation would form a part of his doctoral thesis). Fleeing the Vichy regime and the Second World War, Lévi-Strauss went to the USA, where he taught in the New School for Social Research (1941–5). On his way to the USA, Lévi-Strauss met another war refugee, Roman Jakobson, who proved to be instrumental in introducing him to the structural linguistics of Ferdinand de Saussure and the works of the 'Prague linguistic circle'.

Following two years as the cultural attaché in the French Embassy in Washington (1945–7), Lévi-Strauss returned to France in 1947 and in 1950 was promoted as director of the fifth section (*sciences religieuses*) at the École Pratique des Hautes Études in Paris. In 1959, he was appointed professor of social anthropology at the Collège de France, and in 1960 founded the Laboratory for Social Anthropology, which he headed until 1982. He was one of the founders of the journal, *L'Homme*, in 1961. In 1973, Lévi-Strauss was elected to the French Academy.

In his first major work, *The Elementary Structures of Kinship*, Lévi-Strauss introduced structural anthropology. Derived from the Saussurean structural linguistics, structural anthropological research focuses on the ways in which elements combine together – not on their 'intrinsic' meanings. One of the most obvious consequences of this approach is that social events (like the simple exchange of a glass of cheap white wine in the restaurants in the south of France) cannot be explained by any functionalist approach, nor can they be explained by 'letting the facts speak for themselves'. An act of exchange has meaning only in a specific social and symbolic context. This context is not something that people willingly create – it is pre-determined, part of our unconscious cognitive structures. But just as this is pre-determined, it is also shaping what we call 'culture'. For example, the prohibition of incest had an instrumental function in forcing people to look for wives outside their own communities ('exogamous' marriage pattern). By doing so, they got in contact with other communities, peoples, and forms of expression – and this is how 'culture' originally spread.

Most of the subsequent work of Lévi-Strauss is devoted to the understanding of how these underlying cognitive structures function. Being universal, they are characteristic for all human beings – and here are combined Lévi-Strauss's humanism, structuralism, and universalism. There is no 'primitive mentality' of traditional societies – traditional peoples are trying to make sense of the world just as we are, using elaborate schemes and models.

Although myth does not reveal much about the reality it seeks to describe, in its underlying structure it is a reflection of the deeply embedded unconscious models of explaining the world. Myths are ways of making 'order' out of 'chaos', representations of some fundamental structures that enable the very existence of societies. The underlying logic of myths serves to explain certain culture-specific traits or customs, but it is also the key to deeper meanings.

In his emphasis on understanding cognitive structures of pre-industrial societies, Lévi-Strauss was instrumental in elevating these societies to the same level as the contemporary highly industrialised societies. Lévi-Strauss's structuralism has dominated French anthropology for almost four decades and, coupled with his extraordinary style and the magnitude of his opus, remains a very important tool in contemporary anthropology.

Education

Agrégation in law and philosophy, University of Paris, 1931

D.Litt. University of Paris, 1948

Fieldwork

Mato Grosso, Brazil, 1935–7 (five months)

Key Publications

(1963) *Structural Anthropology* (*Anthropologie structurale*, 1958), trans. C. Jacobson and B. Grundfest Schoepf, New York: Basic Books.

(1966) *The Savage Mind* (*La Pensée sauvage*, 1962) London: Weidenfeld & Nicolson.

(1969) *The Elementary Structures of Kinship* (*Les Structures élémentaires de la parenté*, 1949), trans. J.H. Bell and J. von Sturmer, Boston: Beacon Press.

(1973–81) *Introduction to a Science of Mythology* (*Mythologiques*, 1964–71), 4 vols, trans. J. and D. Weightman, London: Jonathan Cape.

Further Reading

Hénaff, M. (2000) *Claude Lévi-Strauss et l'anthropologie structurale* (Claude Lévi-Strauss and Structural Anthropology), Paris: Havas.

Leach, E. (1970) *Claude Lévi-Strauss*, London: Fontana.

ALEKSANDAR BOSKOVIC

Lévy-Bruhl, Lucien

b. 10 April 1857, Paris, France

d. 13 March 1939, Paris, France

Lucien Lévy-Bruhl worked as professor for philosophy and had already written books on philosophy before he decided to focus on the mind and thinking of pre-industrial societies, of what he called 'primitive peoples'. Between 1910 and 1938 he wrote and published seven comprehensive and popular books on this subject. In *Les Fonctions mentales dans les sociétés inférieures* published in 1910 his theory on 'primitive' mentality was more or less completely developed. *La Mentalité primitive*, published 1922, however, can be considered as Lévy-Bruhĺs most famous book. He wrote five more books on the subject that developed and described details of his theory and applied it to specific subjects such as myths and symbols.

According to Lévy-Bruhl there exists a fundamental difference between the thinking of primitive societies and modern ones. The collective ideas of primitive societies are 'mystique' and 'pre-logical'. They are not determined by rational concepts such as geometrical space, abstract time, causality, chance, and probability. In this view of the world all phenomena as well as living creatures not only have an empirical but also a mystical dimension. Hence, each empirical phenomenon is a personification of a mystical being and is included in a system of mystical influences ('participation mystique'). For this reason the description of a phenomenon or of an occurrence is based primarily not upon the empirical relations of cause and effect ('secondary causes'), but the mystical and invisible entity. According to Lévy-Bruhl 'participation mystique' dominates the overall thinking of all dimensions in life: ideas of social relations, concepts of soul, religion, nature, universe, language, numbers, magic, disease, and death.

'Natives' have problems thinking in logical and abstract dimensions. They often think along contradictory lines: women give birth to crocodiles that at the same time are ghosts or devils; a person can exist simultaneously in two places, etc. The mystical causes are souls of ancestors, ghosts, witches, gods, and other mystical beings. They dominate and influence each occurrence and all phenomena in the empirical and visible world. Then natives do not differentiate between cognitive images and the real world, between dream and reality. In particular, Lévy-Bruhl demonstrated in *L'Âme primitive* and in *Le Surnaturel et la nature dans la mentalité primitive* (1931) (*Primitives and the Super-natural*, trans. 1935) that in these societies all phenomena are regarded as living and psychic entities. This animistic belief does not yet know of a dualism between psychic and physical entities, mind and nature, body and soul. Physical reality always has a psychic nature and psychic reality expresses itself in physical manifestation. Mountains, trees, rivers, and animals can attain personal status and sometimes can even become an object of religious reverence. In the primitive mind God, man, and nature are not strictly separated entities. Personal identity can grow, move, and procreate in a mystical way. It is not bound to and embedded in one body only. One specific personal identity can be embodied and multiplied in various bodies, beings, and biographies. Belief in transformation of human beings (and other beings and things) into animals, plants, and ghosts is widespread among primitive societies.

There are no strict concepts of causality, chance, or probability. Causality, chance, and probability are consequences and ingredients of the mechanical view of the world. They cannot emerge from or exist in an animistic conviction, because in the animistic concept each occurrence is the result of a spiritual intention. Each occurrence or phenomenon has a deeper significance. Therefore natives believe in ordeals (complete knowledge of the past) and in oracles (complete knowledge of the future). They strictly believe in predictions and fate.

Lévy-Bruhl deeply influenced the humanities (sociology, cultural anthropology, philosophy, religion studies) for some decades. His books are very comprehensive and reach a high level of scientific analysis. However, in the course of one or two generations the influence of his books has nearly vanished. Most scholars today disapprove of his theory of 'primitive mentality'. Nowadays most authors of cultural anthropology follow the concept that these societies have the same mind as modern societies. They are convinced that Lévy-Bruhl's theory exaggerates the differences between the 'savage' and modern mind. Perhaps the time will come again when cultural anthropology and the humanities will see the necessity of studying the theories of Lucien Lévy-Bruhl.

Education

Study of philosophy at the École Normale Supérieure

Key Publications

(1926) *How Natives Think* (*Les Fonctions mentales dans les sociétés inférieures*, 1910), trans. Lilian A. Clare, New York: Arno Press.

(1923) *Primitive mentality* (*La Mentalité primitive*, 1922), trans. Lilian A. Clare. New York: The Macmillan Company.

(1928) *The 'soul' of the primitive* (*L'Âme primitive*, 1927), trans. Lilian A. Clare, New York: The Macmillan Company.

(1983) *Primitive Mythology: The Mythic World of the Australian and Papuan Natives* (*La Mythologie primitive: le monde mythique des Australiens et des Papous*, 1935), trans. Brian Elliott, St Lucia: University of Queensland Press.

GEORG W. OESTERDIEKHOFF

Lewis, Herbert S.

b. 1934, Jersey City, New Jersey, USA

The common thread running through Herbert Lewis's diverse body of work is his use of historical and contemporary material in a grounded comparative framework. A 'Boasian–Weberian' Lewis uses field research and examination of primary texts in work that has regularly challenged accepted positions, as evidenced in his work in Ethiopia, among Yemenites in Israel, and his analysis of American anthropology, past and present.

Lewis's work among the Oromo [Galla] of Ethiopia is a contribution to political anthropology through a focus on the kingdom of Jimma Abba Jifar (1830–1932). Using historical and field sources Lewis presented a Weberian view of the dynamics of monarchy in an African kingdom. In Israel, Lewis's fieldwork in a Yemenite community and comparison with other relevant material revealed the continuity and development of Yemenite culture, presenting a new view of their position in society, and contributing to knowledge about ethnic integration in Israel and the general literature on ethnicity.

In the 1990s, Lewis turned his historical, comparative and critical eye on anthropology itself, arguing that the critique as set out by American anthropologists since the late 1960s is a damaging 'misrepresentation' that is empirically falsifiable. His work on Boas presents an analysis in which Boas's approach is compared to that of pragmatist contemporaries in philosophy. In essence, Lewis's work characteristically challenges anthropologists to use a historically informed route to rethink established positions, including those relevant to contemporary anthropological practice.

Education

BA Brandeis University, 1955
Ph.D. Columbia University, 1963

Fieldwork

Ethiopia, 1958–60, 1965–6
Israel, 1975–7, 1987

Key Publications

(1965) *A Galla Monarchy: Jimma, Ethiopia 1830–1932*, Madison, WI: University of Wisconsin Press.
(1998) 'The misrepresentation of anthropology and its consequences', *American Anthropologist* 100: 716–31.

SUSAN R. TRENCHER

Lewis, Ioan Myrddin

b. 30 January 1930, Glasgow, UK

Ioan Lewis is universally recognised as the leading authority on the Somali. His initial field research focused on the northern Somali of British Somalia although, after the end of the colonial regime and the attempt to constitute a Great Somalia, his interest was extended to the Somali more generally. He followed the events that led to the collapse of the central Somali state, when every clan was set to war against any other clan. Hence at this time, for many a bitterly disillusioned Somali, Ioan Lewis was looked up to as the most knowledgeable person on Somali culture. His fluency in their language gave him a deep understanding of the Somali way of life and gained him their trust. Indeed his book, *A Pastoral Democracy*, has been accepted by the Somali as the most reliable description of their social structure and is now established as a classic of social anthropology.

Ioan Lewis's research has focused on social structure and political institutions. He has shown how traditional Somali society, though lacking those judicial, administrative, and political procedures that lie at the heart of the Western conception of government, is not without government or political institutions. Somali society is patrilineal and the key to politics lies in kinship. Political affiliation is determined by agnatic descent and political units differ according to their agnatic origin. Lineages, i.e. a group descended from a known common ancestor, are the effective political units. They are not based primarily on land-holding; rather, political ascendancy provides the basis of right. For the Somali, might is right. Political status is maintained by feud and war. Such a popular saying as 'our kinsmen, right or wrong!' speaks eloquently to the potential force of kinship. Perhaps it could be said that loyalty to one's own kinship brought to the extreme might have been one of the, if not the main, factors that caused the collapse of the Somali central state.

The second basic principle of Somali political system, complementary to kinship, is a form of social contract among lineages, each of them politically equal. Equality was the ideological foundation of traditional Somali society. Its social structure was chiefless, without a central monarch. Each lineage was governed by its head, claiming equal rights and equal opportunities with any other lineage.

Common adhesion to Islam did not however spare the Somali from the dissolution of their state. Drawing on his knowledge of Somali Islam, Lewis moved on to a comparative study of Islam in tropical Africa. He thus contributed to the development of a deeper understanding of the history and the role of Islam in sub-Saharan Africa. His book on this theme has been an important contribution to the history and the role of Islam in Africa. In his analysis Lewis was intrigued by the prominent role played by women in the rituals of spirit possession, a phenomenon that he explained in terms of women's need to act as prime actors in a way denied them by their submissive status within their own family. Spirit possession led Ioan Lewis to take a global perspective regarding such other phenomena as witchcraft, cannibalism, and shamanism. Lewis argued that while normally these phenomena are considered as totally unrelated and even mutually exclusive, they should, on the contrary, be viewed as closely related expressions of a mystical power or 'charisma'. In Ecstatic Religion (1971) he maintained that those seemingly disparate phenomena, usually attributed to separate cults and even cultures, actually play a crucial role in defining the orthodox belief itself. In all his work Ioan Lewis has been inspired by comparative work on lineage organisation, history, and social anthropology.

Ioan Lewis is emeritus professor of social anthropology at the London School of Eco-nomics. He has also held visiting posts in the Universities of Helsinki, Rome, Kyoto, Addis Ababa, and Marseilles. He was the editor of *Man, the Journal of the Royal Anthropological Institute* (London) from 1964 to 1969, and he served as the director of the International African Institute (London) from 1982 to 1988.

Education

B.Sc. University of Glasgow, 1951
Dip. Soc. Anth. University of Oxford, 1952
B.Litt. University of Oxford, 1953
D.Phil. University of Oxford, 1957

Fieldwork

British Somalia, 1955–7, 1962, 1964, 1974, 1978; 1980, 1982, 1986, 1992
Central Africa, six months in period 1957–60
Malaysia, three months 1988

Key Publications

(1961) *A Pastoral Democracy; A Study of Pastoralism and Politics among the Northern Somali of the Horn of Africa*, London and New York: Published for the International African Institute by Oxford University Press (reissued in 1982, New York: NY Africana Pub.Co. for the International African Institute).

(1965) *The Modern History of Somaliland, from Nation to State*, New York: F.A. Praeger (revised edn, London and New York: Longman, 1980; revised, updated, and expanded edn, Boulder: Westview Press, 1988).

(1971) *Ecstatic Religion: An Anthropological Study of Spirit Possession and Shamanism*, Harmondsworth, England: Penguin Books (revised edn, Harmondsworth and New York: Penguin, 1978; second edn, London and New York: Routledge, 1989; third edn, London and New York: Routledge, 2003).

(1999) *Arguments with Ethnography: Comparative Approaches to History, Politics and Religion*, London and New Brunswick, NJ: Athlone Press.

BERNARDO BERNARDI

Lewis, Oscar

b. 1914, New York, USA

d. 1970, New York, USA

Oscar Lewis's career as an anthropologist was intense and productive. A well-recognised anthropologist, Lewis's work was also controversial. In the course of his career, Lewis carried out research in the USA, Mexico, India, Puerto Rico, and Cuba. Most of his projects involved larger research teams with local collaboration. Lewis developed an elaborate methodological package involving participant observation, structured interviews, psychological testing, and household analysis, including detailed inventory listings as well as budget and income data. In addition to enhancing his comparative perspective, Lewis's various fieldworks have resulted in works whose significance lie not only in what they reflect about particular moments in the history of anthropology but also in what they impart about the continuity underpinning the anthropological endeavour.

Throughout his life, Lewis maintained a sustained interest in processes of social change and the life conditions of the poor. His choice of subjects and localities mirror this commitment. A case in point is his decision to work in Cuba in 1969. Lewis had an early interest in Marxism and in socialism, and these general orientations are reflected in his academic work, both with respect to thematic interests and research sites. Lewis was also influenced by the culture and personality studies, and his family study approach, in the form of multiple autobiographies, was elaborated in order to delineate the various factors that 'make up' individuals and cultures.

Lewis's main contribution to anthropological debates centers around three rather disparate themes: restudies, life histories and the concept of the culture of poverty. In 1943 Lewis was assigned to co-ordinate a research project in Mexico under the sponsorship of the Interamerican Indian Institute, working together with the Mexican anthropologist, Manuel Gamio, on issues of rural development. There he started his research in Tepoztlán, which was a restudy of the village where Robert Redfield had worked. Lewis's findings did not concur with those of Redfield, thus raising the issues of ethnographic disagreement, drawing attention to questions of interpretation, positioning, and the construction of ethnography.

Lewis's work in Tepoztlán took him to Mexico City. He wanted to follow the peasants who had migrated to the urban centers in order to study their adaptation to city life. This research was to generate his family studies as well as lay the basis for his much discredited theory about the culture of poverty. Lewis's concern about the meaning of poverty is aptly conveyed in his many books that narrate family histories in the form of multiple autobiographies of individual family members. Of these, *The Children of Sánchez* (1961) is exceptional, both in form and content; it is a vivid rendering of life in the slums of Mexico City. These books spurred debates about the status of ethnography and the distinction between art and science. They serve as constant reminders of the many issues to which anthropology has become sensitive, such as questions of authenticity, notions of fiction and reality, social memory, and representation.

Lewis's focus on culture and personality (with the use of extensive psychological testing), on restudies (with a view to testing the validity of earlier findings), on poverty (relying on statistics and quantitative methods), and on life histories (as a way of letting the poor speak for themselves) all presuppose a view of a factual, objective, accessible reality. This positivistic bias is furthered by Lewis's reluctance to explicitly interpret his data and the lack of sensitivity to his own role in constructing the narrative cum text. Nevertheless, his texts represent rich and detailed sources of ethnography that are best evidenced by the reanalysis that the texts open for, not least with respect to gender. This is value added to any ethnography, making its overall contribution all the more significant.

The corpus of Lewis's work cannot be fully appreciated without acknowledging the substantial role played by his wife, Ruth Lewis. She collaborated with him in all phases of his work for over thirty years and also published his work on Cuba (with Susan Rigdon) posthumously.

Education

BA College of the City of New York, 1936
Ph.D. Columbia University, 1940

Fieldwork

Brocket Reserve, Alberta, Canada, 1939
Tepoztlán, Mexico, 1943
Mexico City, Mexico, 1950–2, 1956–62
Bell County, Texas, 1946
Spain, 1949
India, 1952–3
Puerto Rico and New York City, 1963–8
Cuba, 1969–70

Key Publications

(1942) *The Effects of White Contact upon the Blackfoot Culture*, Monograph of the American Ethnological Society, New York: J.J.Augustin.
(1951) *Life in a Mexican Village. Tepoztlán Restudied*, Urbana: University of Illinois Press.
(1961) *The Children of Sánchez: Autobiography of a Mexican Family*, New York: Random House.
(1970) *Anthropological Essays*, New York: Random House.

Further Reading

Rigdon, Susan (1988) *The Culture Facade. Art, Science, and Politics in the Work of Oscar Lewis*, Urbana: University of Illinois Press.

MARIT MELHUUS

Lienhardt, Godfrey

b. 1921, Bradford, UK

d. 1993, Oxford, UK

Although he began his studies at Cambridge in 1939, like many in his generation Lienhardt would serve in the military during the Second World War. After duty in East Africa, Lienhardt returned to Cambridge to resume his studies. It was around then he met E.E. Evans-Pritchard, who brought Lienhardt along with him to Oxford that same year. From 1947–50 Lienhardt worked with the Dinka, and from 1952–4 with the Anuak, both in the Southern Sudan. It was these field studies that became the foundation for his great contributions to both anthropology and the study of Africa and religion.

In his most famous work, *Divinity and Experience: The Religion of the Dinka*, Lienhardt delivered what is perhaps the most thoughtful and poetic descriptions of a religion among a non-literate people. Over the years at Oxford Lienhardt become a well-known and much liked teacher, inspiring generations of students in anthropology, religious studies, and other areas. Lienhardt was a careful writer and analyst of the kind that is seldom matched. One of his main contributions was comparison of the religions he studied to those of Europe.

The nature and tragedy of conflict in the areas he studied was not lost on Lienhardt and he never failed to address it directly. Through his years of research among the Marsh Arabs of Iraq, Lienhardt gained a unique understanding of the conflict between the North and South in the Sudan. Far from a scholarly life cloistered and removed from local voices on such subjects, Lienhardt worked to continually make long visits by people from his areas of study a common sight and voice in the Oxford community.

While eventually becoming a figure in the administration at Oxford, Lienhardt included among his close circle many from beyond the academy, including diplomats, artists, publishers, writers, and scientists.

Education

Ph.D. University of Oxford

Fieldwork

Southern Sudan, 1947–54
Iraq, 1955–60
Sudan, 1962–

Key Publications

(1961) *Divinity and Experience: The Religion of the Dinka*, Oxford: Clarendon.
(1967) *Social Anthropology*, London, New York: Oxford University Press.

DREW WALKER

Lindenbaum, Shirley

b. 1933, Melbourne, Australia

Shirley Lindenbaum's initial collaborative field research conducted among the Fore in the Eastern Highlands, Papua New Guinea, focused on the mystery of Kuru. Her close attention to kinship ties and relations of gender and generation orienting food consumption provided a key analysis of disease transmission route. Kuru was first imagined as genetic, then as a slow, virus, and is now understood to be a prion (infectious protein) spread through the eating of infected human body parts. In Bangladesh, Lindenbaum parsed health statistics on violence and population dynamics to reveal how shifting political economic relations affected the health of families and communities. In the 1990s, Shirley Lindenbaum's research interests turned to the study of HIV/AIDS in the USA and internationally. This work engaged her in various policy-related projects. Recently, she has deployed her comparative knowledge of the sociocultural structure of epidemics to analyse Mad Cow Disease. Throughout her

work, Shirley Lindenbaum has addressed the meanings and mystifications of basic human needs and desires: food and commensuality; sexuality and sexual exchanges; fear, danger, and the spread of epidemics are central themes. Widely respected as a leader in the worldwide expansion of medical anthropology, Shirley Lindenbaum's synthetic scholarship has helped to illuminate the inextricability of the social and biological causes and amelioration of illness and disease.

Education

BA University of Melbourne, 1965
MA University of Sydney, 1971

Fieldwork

Eastern Highlands, Papua New Guinea, 1961–3, 1970, 1991, 1993, 1996, 1999
Daribe region, Papua New Guinea, 1962
East Pakistan/Bangladesh, 1963–6, 1974, 1979, 1983

Key Publications

(1979) *Kuru Sorcery: Disease and Danger in the New Guinea Highlands*, Palo Alto, CA: Mayfield.
(2001) 'Kuru, prions and human affairs: thinking about epidemics', *Annual Review of Anthropology* 30: 363–85.

RAYNA RAPP

Linton, Ralph

b. 27 February 1893, Philadelphia, Pennsylvania, USA

d. 24 December 1953, New Haven, Connecticut, USA

Ralph Linton discovered archaeology while still an undergraduate at Swarthmore, digging at Mesa Verde, in coastal lowland Guatemala, and in New Jersey. His MA in anthropology from the University of Pennsylvania combined archaeology with ethnology, under the auspices of Frank Speck. Speck sent Linton to Columbia, where he spent one year in the doctoral programme before enlisting during the First World War. Already disenchanted with what he perceived as Boas's authoritarianism, Linton rebelled on his return to Columbia and transferred to Harvard.

Linton's doctoral fieldwork was carried out in the Marquesas Islands for the Bishop Museum in Honolulu. Although he collected material culture and carried out an archaeological survey, this research confirmed his movement from archaeology to ethnology. Linton apprenticed himself to a Marquesan woodcarver (a priestly occupational class), located Gauguin's grave, and described the Marquesan polyandrous family structure. He then returned to a curatorial position at the Field Museum in Chicago. Despite a nominal American Indian focus to the appointment, Linton undertook an ethnographic survey and museum collecting expedition to Madagascar in 1925, producing a monograph on the Tanala a decade later. Severe malaria acquired during this fieldwork made further work in the tropics impossible for him.

At the University of Wisconsin in 1928, Linton discovered an unexpected vocation for teaching. He developed an independent programme in anthropology, puttered in Midwestern archaeology, and encountered British functionalism through Radcliffe-Brown, then teaching at Chicago. *The Study of Man* (1936) combined both Boasian historical process and British functionalist treatment of trait complexes. Linton distinguished status, or an individual's position within a society, from role, or the dynamic aspect of status; actual and ideal behaviour also were treated as analytically separate.

In 1937, Linton succeeded Franz Boas as head of the Columbia department of anthropology. The administration ignored the departmental preference for Ruth Benedict, who was Boas's chosen successor. Benedict's passive aggression and Linton's more overt retaliation produced considerable tension within the programme, although some students managed to work with both.

Linton edited *Acculturation in Seven American Indian Tribes* (1940) and worked hard to locate summer fieldwork funding for students during the Depression. With Robert Redfield and Melville Herskovits, he produced a memorandum on acculturation for the Social Research Council that was later published in the *American Anthropologist* (1936). Charles Wagley was assigned to study acculturation in central Brazil and Carl Withers to a Midwestern American town. Acculturation studies divorced American anthropology from the study of memory cultures as they were thought to have existed in some idealised past. Increasingly, culture change was seen as intrinsic to all societies. Certainly, anthropology was not to be restricted to the study of the formerly or recently primitive.

Linton then turned to culture and personality, establishing an interdisciplinary seminar with Abraham Kardiner at the New York Psychoanalytic Institute from 1935–8. The seminar used returned anthropologists as informants for the cultures where they had done their fieldwork. Linton presented data from both the Marquesas and Tanala, although he remained sceptical about Kardiner's emphasis on socialisation as the primary determinant of what he called basic personality structure. Linton's interpretation of this collaboration appeared in *The Cultural Background of Personality* (1945).

During the Second World War, Linton established a training programme at Columbia directed towards military government and administration; this later became the School of International Affairs and several areal institutes. *The Science of Man in the World Crisis* (1945) attempted to bring the insights of anthropology to the American public. Later, however, Linton's optimism decreased. His posthumous *The Tree of Culture* (1955), published at the height of Cold War paranoia, was much less sanguine about the possibility of sustained periods of freedom from totalitarian oppression. He felt that the forces of bigotry and intolerance were already destroying a world in which anthropology could counteract racism and parochialism.

Linton was an integral figure in revising early twentieth-century Boasian historical particularism to meet the needs of a more complex world. He brought the sociological perspective of British anthropology into cultural analysis. Linton also developed anthropology's connections to the other social sciences and represented the discipline in public discourse as prepared to advise on the policy questions facing the USA after the Second World War.

Education

BA Swarthmore College, 1915
MA University of Pennsylvania, 1916
Ph.D. Harvard University, 1925

Fieldwork

Marquesas Islands, 1920
Madagascar, 1925

Key Publications

with Redfield, Robert and Herskovits, Melville (1936)'Memorandum for the study of acculturation', *American Anthropologist* 38, 149–52.
(1945) *The Cultural Background of Personality*, New York: Appleton-Century.
(1945) *The Science of Man in the World Crisis*, New York: Columbia University Press.
(1955) *The Tree of Culture*, New York: Knopf.

REGNA DARNELL

Lisón Tolosana, Carmelo

b. 1929, La Puebla de Alfindén, near Zaragoza, Spain

Since the late 1990s, Carmelo Lisón Tolosana has been emeritus professor of social anthropology at the Complutense University of Madrid and member of Spain's Royal Academy of Moral and Political Sciences. Soon after his Ph.D. thesis on village life in Belmonte de los Caballeros in rural Aragon was published in

English, it became a key reference text in anthropological and Mediterranean studies. Drawing on the concept of generational distinction put forward by Spanish philosopher Ortega y Gasset, Carmelo Lisón Tolosana's historical analysis of Belmonte marks a break in the 'colonialist' ethnography of the recent past.

Carmelo Lisón Tolosana has since largely focused his research on the cosmogony and social symbolic structures of rural communities in Spain, principally in Aragon and Galicia. Adopting a historical perspective that takes into account social change, this has involved the study of kin relations, ritual, socioeconomic arrangements, and the construction of identity amongst inhabitants of rural regions. He has remained primarily concerned with the study of the individual in community, how the individual interacts in society and produces symbolic meaning.

Carmelo Lisón Tolosana is also the author of numerous works on the subject of social anthropological studies in Spain. These focus on the evolution of anthropology in its most innovating aspects, analysing the epistemology of the social sciences. Within this area, Carmelo Lisón Tolosana has dedicated an important part of his recent research in rural communities of Spain to the theme of witchcraft and worship of the devil. His concern with identity issues has also involved a focus on the dialectics of local, regional, and national expressions of identity in Spain. He examines how individuals in groups seek to mark difference between each other in the various local, regional, and national contexts. Lisón Tolosana proposes then the term 'cultural collage' to understand how individuals adopt and reinterpret symbols in different contexts. This interest in constructions and expressions of identity has also led Carmelo Lisón Tolosana to explore the themes of ethnicity and violence as well as the idea of Europe and processes of 'Europeanisation'.

Education

Equivalent of a BA, University of Zaragoza, Spain, 1959

MA St Catherine's College, University of Oxford, 1959

D.Phil., Exeter College, University of Oxford, 1963

Ph.D. University of Complutense, Madrid, 1970

Doctor Honoris Causa, University of Bordeaux II, 2002

Fieldwork

Aragon, 1959–61
Galicia, 1963–5

Key Publications

(1966) *Belmonte de los Caballeros. A Sociological Study of a Spanish Town*, Oxford: Oxford University Press (second edn, Princeton University Press, 1983).

(1980) *Perfiles simbólico-morales de la cultura gallega* (Symbolic-Moral Profiles of Galician Culture), Madrid: Akal (second edn, 1980).

(1979) *Brujería, estructura social y simbolismo en Galicia* (Witchcraft, social structure and symbolism in Galicia), Madrid: Akal (fourth edn, 1999).

(1997) *Las máscaras de la identidad (claves antropológicas)* (The masks of identity (anthropological keys)), Barcelona: Ariel.

ZOE BRAY

Little, Kenneth

b. 19 September 1908, Liverpool, UK

d. 28 February 1991, Edinburgh, UK

Although his work is not as widely known today as it once was, Kenneth Little was a pioneer anthropologist in three areas of study: blacks in Britain, African urbanisation, and the position of women in African society. It was of great importance in its time for establishing these now-commonplace topics and encouraging research among young anthropologists. Little also contributed greatly to the ethno-graphy of Sierra Leone and to the comparative study of African social change.

In *Negroes in Britain*, Kenneth Little combined historical research with his own ethnography of the black population in Cardiff, Wales. His widely read book on the Mende began with the historical background too. The approach was more conventional in the functionalist style of the day, but contained a greater emphasis than most such works on history, colonialism, and recent changes. In it he covered traditional warfare, the 'Mende Rising' or 'House Tax War' of 1898, geography and climate, the economy of rice farming, the kinship system, the life cycle, marriage and friendship, the position of women, chieftaincy and modern government, religion and medicine, secret societies, as well as various aspects of social change occurring at the time of his ethnography.

Little's other major works were important in moving the anthropological focus in Africa on to consider the effects of rural to urban migration. He was especially interested in the replacement of traditional institutions by many varieties of voluntary associations (sports, dining, religious, and especially women's), which he described with examples from Nigeria, Ghana, and especially Sierra Leone. His work on urban women stressed the dynamic aspect of African society. He documented women's important roles in commerce, but, more importantly, he turned anthropological attention towards aspects of the status of women, with examples ranging from prostitution to matrimonial power. He concluded that the status of women in Africa was ambiguous, both through its diversity and in its complexity.

From 1950 until retirement in 1978 Little taught at Edinburgh, where he held the chair in social anthropology from 1965 to 1971 and a personal chair in African urban studies from 1971 to 1978. In later life he suffered mental illness, but even then he continued to write prolifically and engage enthusiastically in anthropological debate within his own department and far beyond.

Education

BA University of Cambridge, 1941
MA University of Cambridge, 1944
Ph.D. University of London, 1945

Fieldwork

Cardiff, Wales, 1940–1
Sierra Leone, 1944–6, 1954, 1959
Gambia, 1949
Nigeria, 1952
Sudan, 1958

Key Publications

(1947) *Negroes in Britain: A Study of Racial Relations in English Society*, London: Kegan Paul, Trench, Trubner & Co.
(1951) *The Mende of Sierra Leone: A West African People in Transition*, London: Routledge & Kegan Paul
(1965) *West African Urbanization: A Study of Voluntary Associations in Social Change*, Cambridge, UK: Cambridge University Press
(1973) *African Women in Towns: As Aspect of Africa's Social Revolution*, Cambridge, UK: Cambridge University Press.

ALAN BARNARD

Lloyd, Peter C.

b. 7 June 1927, Bournemouth, UK

Peter C. Lloyd 'left for Nigeria in 1949 a marxist and, in spirit, a communist' ('The taming of a young Turk: fieldwork in western Nigeria in the early 1950s', *Anthropological Forum* 4, 2: 79, 1977), critical of his instructors at the London School of Economics and Oxford, and 'resolved not to study kinship'! (ibid.: 86) However, as he engaged in fieldwork on the structures and internal dynamics of Yoruba kingdoms, and considered the contemporary social and political changes and events occurring around him, the Marxist approach 'failed to provide me with answers to the questions I posed' (ibid.: 89). Instead he forged an independent and eclectic approach consciously influenced by the perceptions and notions of the people he studied.

Lloyd's early research concerned the political and economic processes in both pre-colonial and colonial British Africa. He was one of those who eschewed the static and timeless approach attributed to social anthropology, and he published generalising works about social change and the growth of elites in West Africa at the same time that he worked on the reconstruction of patterns and processes in Yoruba kingdoms. His approach to both the study of African political systems and the processes and prospects for social change in 'developing countries' (as they were then called) eschewed the high-level certainties, typologies, and generalisations of both Marxism and structural-functional social science ('modernisation theory'). He stressed the openness and unpredictability of these processes, and significant role in them played by individuals, with their own perceptions, understandings, and motivations, strategies, and choices.

His interest in the human realities and social problems of change led him to write of 'classes, crises, and coups', and to the study of urban squatter settlements, including field-work in a *barriada* in Lima, Peru. He argues against the tendency to confuse sociological and ideological generalisations with reality, and calls for the attempt to see how people 'view the world within which they live, how their behaviour is governed by their image of their society.' (*Slums of Hope?: Shanty Towns of the Third World*, New York: St Martin's Press, 1979, p. 10) Contrary to the view of these shanty towns as places of misery, marginality, and hopelessness, he presents evidence of diversity, social cohesion, developing organisations, and some material gains. Seen from the perspective of the rural migrants who flock to them, these 'young towns' are built on their aspirations for improvement: for homes, work, and education for their children. Those outsiders who attempt to ameliorate conditions in these settlements must be aware of the inhabitants' own perceptions, says Lloyd.

In addition to teaching and research positions in Nigeria in the 1960s, Peter Lloyd spent most of his career at the University of Sussex.

Education

B.Sc. University of Oxford, 1953
D.Phil. University of Oxford, 1958

Fieldwork

Nigeria, 1949–73 (Yoruba)
Nigeria, 1955–6 (Itsekiri)
Lima, Peru, 1975, 1977

Key Publications

(1967) *Africa in Social Change*, Harmondsworth: Penguin.
(1971) *Political Development of Yoruba Kingdoms in the Eighteenth and Nineteenth Centuries*, London: Royal Anthropological Institute.
(1971) *Classes, Crises and Coups: Themes in the Sociology of Developing Countries*, London: MacGibbon & Kee.
(1980) *The 'Young Towns' of Lima: Aspects of Urbanization in Peru*, Cambridge, UK: Cambridge University Press.

HERBERT S. LEWIS

Lock, Margaret

b. 1936, Bromley, UK

Margaret Lock is a pioneer in medical anthropology and brings her passion to all of her work. With colleagues at McGill, Lock has built an influential programme in medical anthropology over the last twenty years.

Lock is first and foremost an ethnographer, able to deconstruct complex social phenomena such as medicalisation in everyday life. Throughout her career she has taught us to understand how medical traditions, practices, and discourses impact upon individual bodies through the mediums of culture and power. She has demonstrated how these medicalised forces are understood, embodied, and utilised.

Doctoral fieldwork marked the beginning of three decades of research in Japan. Central to Lock's work is a strong comparative approach. Initially this took the form of pluralism within East Asian medical traditions, and then between biomedical and other ethnomedical traditions in both Japan and North America. Her works on Japan link individual experience with the history of health care in Japan and with broader political, economic, and social forces.

Lock's seminal theoretical contributions include 'The mindful body' (co-authored with N. Scheper-Hughes), an approach to the ways in which the human body can be a focus for anthropology, and a theoretical history of the anthropology of the body in *Annual Reviews of Anthropology* (1993). In addition, *Biomedicine Examined* (1988, co-edited with Deborah R. Gordon) and *Knowledge, Power and Practice* (1993, co-edited with Shirley Lindenbaum) are significant texts for medical anthropology concerned with the moral economies of scientific knowledge. They focus upon political, economic, and gendered agendas within biomedical institutions, professions, and procedures.

Lock's interest in the body led her to examine life transitions such as adolescence, ageing, menopause, and dying. Feminist analysis comprises a significant facet of her theoretical repertoire. *Encounters with Aging* (1993) is her most celebrated work, deconstructing the medicalisation of menopause cross-culturally. The significance of the multi-award-winning work, a characteristic seen throughout the corpus of Lock's work, is the ability to write an ethnography of the ways in which biomedical terms, power, and hegemony permeate nationalist and gendered discourses, and the media, and intersect with the human body, individual experience, and subjectivity. The concept of local biologies is used to explain the co-production of the biological and the social at a site of primary intersection, the socialised body. Ongoing research around dying, organ transplantation, and Alzheimer's Disease investigates relationships between culture, biomedical technologies, and the body. *Twice Dead* examines the reconceptualisation of death in the medical world in order to facilitate organ procurements.

Education

B.Sc. University of Leeds, 1961
MA University of California, Berkeley, 1970
Japanese Language Diploma, Stanford Inter-University Centre, Tokyo, 1973
Ph.D. University of California, Berkeley, 1976

Fieldwork

Japan, 1973–5, 1982–2001
Montreal, Canada, 1981–5
North America, 1987–ongoing

Key Publications

with Scheper-Hughes, N. (1987) 'The mindful body: a prolegomenon to future work in medical anthropology', *Medical Anthropology Quarterley*, n.s., 1: 6–41.
(1993) *Encounters with Aging: Mythologies of Menopause in Japan and North America*, Berkeley: University of California Press.
(2001) *Twice Dead: Organ Transplants and the Reinvention of Death*, Berkeley: University of California Press.

MONIQUE SKIDMORE

Löfgren, Orvar

b. 1943, Stockholm, Sweden

Although he is a professor of European ethnology at the University of Lund, Orvar Löfgren's work falls squarely into an anthropological tradition, often even bridging the traditional American concern with symbolic meaning and the traditional British attention to social organisation. His doctoral work ('Maritime hunters in industrial society. The transformation of a Swedish fishing community 1800–1970', 1978), while largely a historical study, was inspired by methods of analysis regarding social change developed by Fredrik

Barth and his colleagues in Bergen. Most of Löfgren's later work has focused on interpretations of the meanings inherent in practices and symbols of everyday life. His most widely read book in Scandinavia, *Den kultiverade människan* (with Jonas Frykman, English edn, 1987), is a genealogical account of the growth of particular structures of symbolic meaning embedded in the apparent trivia of the quotidian. Also a scholar of Swedish nationalism, Löfgren is deeply sceptical of what he sees as reductionist accounts of nationhood, preferring to demonstrate the ambiguity and richness of national symbols. He has also devoted considerable attention to central tensions in Swedish nation-building: class differences, the urban–rural divide, and the relationship between society and the state. Beginning with his Ph.D. work, incidentally his only work involving conventional ethnography, Löfgren has retained a consistent interest in the Swedish transition to modernity, with a particular emphasis on the massive changes brought about in the twentieth century.

Löfgren is the central figure in his generation of Swedish ethnologists, which also includes Billy Ehn and Jonas Frykman, with both of whom he has collaborated extensively with. He has been instrumental in turning Swedish ethnology into an analytical, comparative discipline, and, in spite of slight differences of method, it is regarded as that branch of anthropology which deals with Sweden – and, through his emphasis on the minutiae of everyday life, his style of analysis often resembles the hermeneutics of mid-period Geertz. An excellent writer, Löfgren publishes equally prolifically in Swedish and English. His most recent book, *On Holiday*, is the fruit of an engagement with globalisation studies that lasted throughout the 1990s and involved collaboration with Ulf Hannerz; and like much of his previous work, it shows the twentieth-century democratisation of opportunities formerly restricted to the upper classes. Even more recently, Löfgren has directed a major research project on the sociocultural implications of the Öresund bridge (opened 2000) linking Denmark and south Sweden.

Education

Ph.D. University of Stockholm, 1978

Fieldwork

Halland, Sweden, 1963–70
Intermittent ethnographic work in the USA
and Sweden

Key Publications

with Ehn, Billy (1982) Kulturanalys. Ett etnologiskt
perspektiv (Culture Analysis: An Ethnological
Perspective), Lund: Liber.
with Frykman, Jonas (1987) Culture Builders: A
Historical Anthropology of Middle-Class Life (Den
kultiverade människan, 1979), New
Brunswick: Rutgers University Press.
(1999) On Holiday. A History of Vacationing,
Berkeley: University of California Press.

THOMAS HYLLAND ERIKSEN

Loizos, Peter

b. 1937, Bexleyheath, south London, UK

In 1975 Peter Loizos published The Greek Gift, a
book about politics in the largely Greek
Cypriot village of 'Kalo'. One of the most
powerful features of this book was its
filmic quality. The book traced a number of
dramatis personae through a series of situations in a newly independent state against a
backdrop of major international evenements:
large-scale interethnic conflict, violence, con-
spiracies, threatened invasions, and the complex machinations of geopolitics. Loizos
traced the links between local actors and
national politicians such that one could
perceive, if sometimes obscurely, how his
villagers were responding, anticipating, and
reacting to the complex world of modern
politics.

It was precisely because of this prescience,
in recognising that the closer one gets to
process the more questions are raised, that
there is a tension between close observation
and the fact that the anthropologist can never
fully perhaps grasp what individuals are up to,
which is where the book's attraction lies. It is
no accident that the model of the book is
implicitly that of a film script. Loizos had
worked as a BBC film producer before taking
up anthropology and he is a major theorist of
anthropological films, and went on to shoot a
number of powerful films.

By 1974 the Kalo villagers had become
refugees and Loizos followed this in 1981 with
The Heart Grown Bitter, a chronicle of his
experiences as a fieldworker and his encounter
with Greek Cypriot culture as an formal insider
with no initial knowledge of the culture. This
was a sensitive, reflexive account that gave a
vivid and accessible account of the experience
of dislocation and initial confusion.

In addition to work on film, Loizos has also
written extensively on gender and on reproduction technologies, and was professor of
social anthropology at the London School of
Economics and Political Science.

Education

BA University of Cambridge, 1959
MA University of Pennsylvania, 1961
Ph.D., University of London, 1972

Fieldwork

Western Cyprus, 1968–9 (15 months), 1970,
1972, 1973 (short visits, total 3 months),
1975 (5 months), 1985 (1 month), 2000,
2001 (short visits, total 5 weeks), 2003 (6
months, part time)

Key Publications

(1975) The Greek Gift: Politics in a Cypriot Village,
Oxford: Blackwell.
(1981) The Heart Grown Bitter: A Chronicle of Cypriot
War Refugees, Cambridge, UK, and New York:
Cambridge University Press.

PAUL SANT CASSIA

Lomnitz, Larissa Adler

b. 17 June 1933, Paris, France

Larissa Adler Lomnitz was one of the first anthropologists who used network analysis as well as concepts and methods derived from exchange theory to understand the texture and power dynamics of Latin American urban societies. Her pioneering work on the Chilean middle class demonstrates that practices of reciprocity were crucial for political affiliation, and that political loyalty was in turn related to the formation of sectors of bureaucratic patronage that gave access to scarce public resources. Similarly, her study of a low-income informal settlement in Mexico City shows rural migrant families actively engaged in the creation and reproduction of relationships of trust with kin and neighbours, but also with patrons in higher levels of society, which enable them to carve viable social niches in the hostile urban environment. However, bonds of trust mediated by kinship and ritual have also been extremely important for the upper classes. This is clear in Lomnitz's careful historical reconstruction of the adventures, enterprises, and political manœuvring of a prominent Mexican business family.

Having established the importance of horizontal and vertical informal relationships at all levels of society, Larissa Lomnitz went on to explore the ways in which these relationships are structured within different nation-states. In Mexico, she chose the National University as a vantage point to examine the complicated mixture of strategies of coercion and co-optation, radical nationalism and technocratic pragmatism, populist discourses and authoritarian practices that have characterised Mexican political culture. This was carried out through fieldwork within research institutes and teaching faculties, which allowed her to portray different sectors of the university – including those directly connected with the high echelons of politics. In addition she did a fascinating study of the 1988 presidential campaign of the Mexican 'revolutionary' party candidate, using the tools of ritual analysis.

Her latest work aims at systematically comparing forms of political culture, national integration, and democratic transition in Mexico and Chile, but she is also doing comparative research on the same themes in former socialist countries of central Europe.

Education

BA University of California, Berkeley, 1967
Ph.D. Iberoamericana University, Mexico City, 1975

Fieldwork

Santiago de Chile, 1967, 1987–8
Mexico City,1969–72, 1974–6, 1979–83

Key Publications

(1977) *Networks and Marginality: Life in a Mexican Shanty Town*, New York and London: Academic Press.
with Perez Lizaur, Marisol (1987) *A Mexican Elite Family, 1820–1980*, Princeton NJ: Princeton University Press.
(1995) *Redes sociales, cultura y poder. Ensayos de antropologia Latinoamericana* (Social Networks, Culture, and Power. Latin American Anthropological Essays), Mexico City: Facultad Latinoamericana de Ciencias Sociales and Miguel Angel Porrúa.
with Melnick, Ana (1998) *Neoliberalismo y clase media. El caso de los profesores de Chile* (Neoliberalism and Middle Class. The Case of Chilean Teachers), Santiago de Chile: Direccion de Bibliotecas, Archivos y Museos/ Centro de Investigaciones Diego Barros Arana.

GUILLERMO DE LA PEÑA

Long, Norman E.

b. 1936, London, UK

Norman Long, a scholar in the Manchester School tradition of social anthropology, is widely considered to be a pioneer in the field of development sociology. He gained international recognition with his actor-oriented approach and interface analysis. Throughout his career, and contrary to mainstream thinking, Long has argued that processes of economic and cultural change are not simply determined by overarching, 'external' forces flowing out of abstract categories such as the state or the market. Rather, Long's point is that all forms of external intervention necessarily enter the existing lifeworlds of the individuals affected. In the process, both individuals and interventions are transformed. This insight allows for a conceptualisation of social change as the emergent outcome of the interplay and mutual determination of 'internal' and 'external' factors and relationships. Long illustrated this point through a number of publications that objected against received wisdom on planned intervention, commoditisation, exchange value, the hegemony of the state, and the dichotomy between so-called expert and local knowledge. Of particular importance are his classic studies in Peru and Mexico. In the former, Long challenged enclave theories of development by demonstrating that capitalist expansion produced substantial growth in the non-enclave sector, especially in village-based trade and transport. In the latter, he convincingly showed that planned intervention is not linear in nature, and that a separation of 'policy', 'implementation', and 'outcomes' was a gross oversimplification of much more complex processes that greatly overflowed the framing of intervention situations.

Education

BA University of Leeds, 1960
MA University of Manchester, 1962
Ph.D. University of Manchester, 1967

Fieldwork

Serenje District, Zambia, 1962–4
Mantaro Valley, Peru, 1970–2
Autlán, Mexico, 1987–2001

Key Publications

(1977) *An Introduction to the Sociology of Rural Development*, London: Tavistock Publications.
(2001) *Development Sociology: Actor Perspectives*, London: Routledge.

GERARD VERSCHOOR

Lotman, Jurii Mikailovich

b. 28 February 1922, Leningrad, Russia

d. 28 October 1993, Tartu, Estonia

As a student (after the Second World War) Lotman investigated the reflections of the lifestyle of nineteenth-century Russian nobles that occurred in Russian literature. He preserved this early interest in the nineteenth century for the rest of his life. Lotman's biography of Pushkin, in which he included a historical essay on Russia and Europe of the first half of the nineteenth century and illustrated the roots of the Decemberists movement in Russia, became a classic in the Russian poetics tradition.

In the 1950s–60s he earned a secure place in the history of anthropological study as a founder of the school of Russian structuralism. He became a leader of the Tartu School (at Tartu University, Estonia, where he took up a position) and developed the structuralist ideas of N.S. Trubetskoi, R.O. Jakobson, and Lui Jelmslev, but distanced himself from their classic semiotics.

This interest arose as a result of his rejection of the vulgar sociological methodology of Soviet official science. He turned to the international development of semiotics and structuralism as opening up the multistructural character of sign systems. His cultural interests led him to semiotic research into a variety of issues and cultural phenomena. The earliest writings on the subject matter were his Tartu publications of 1964–8: 'Game as a semiotic problem in relation to the nature of art', 'Sign problem in art', and 'On the metalanguage of typological descriptions of culture'. In his writings Lotman considered structuralism as a part of semiotics. He divided a text into two parts or plans – expression (*plan virazhenia*) and content (*plan soderzhania*), the aspects (*plani*) he divided into systems of different levels – syntactic, phonetic, morphological. In poetic texts strophic and rhythmic levels also should be taken into consideration. Within the limits of one and the same system he differentiated (segmented) between similar and opposing elements. He also studied texts in two directions – syntagmatic (real sequence of elements and their interpositions) and paradigmatic (typology of elements, invariant to variable elements). In his article, 'On the delimitation of linguistic and philological concepts of structure' (1963), he reiterated that linguists usually focus on the formal aspects of expression but a specialist in poetics should consider how the elements of a plan of expression influence the content of the text as a whole.

Lotman interpreted categories of contingency and contingent event as a part of general historic and historical-cultural contexts. In his last book, *Culture and Explosion* (Moscow: Gnosis, 1992), he prefigured and substantiated ideas of the dynamic development of cultural structure and facts.

Education

MA Leningrad University, 1950
BA Leningrad University, 1951
Ph.D. Leningrad University, 1952

Key Publications

(1975) 'On the metalanguage of typological description of culture', *Semiotica* 14, 2: 97–123.
(1976) *Analysis of the Poetic Text*, ed. and trans. D. Barton Johnson, with bibliography of Lotman's Work, Ann Arbor: Ardis.
(1976) *Semiotics of Cinema*, Ann Arbor: University of Michigan Press.
(1977) *The Structure of Artistic Text*, Ann Arbor: Univ. of Michigan.

GALINA KHIZRIEVA

Lounsbury, Floyd Glenn

b. 25 April 1914, Stevens Point, Wisconsin, USA

d. 14 May 1998, Branford, Connecticut, USA

Floyd Lounsbury was an exceptionally gifted linguist whose work on Iroquoisan languages, kinship semantics, and Mayan hieroglyphics brought linguistics and anthropology together at a time when the disciplines were diverging. Lounsbury was an undergraduate mathematics student at the University of Wisconsin in 1939 when Morris Swadesh arranged for him to direct the Works Progress Administration's Oneida Language and Folklore Project in Oneida, Wisconsin. Lounsbury developed an orthography for the language and employed community members to collect and transcribe oral histories, traditional stories, and personal narratives. Returning to academia, Lounsbury wrote a dissertation on Oneida verbal morphology that has become a classic work in structural linguistics. In the 1960s Lounsbury extended structural linguistic analysis to semantic domains. His formal analyses of kinship terminology systems helped change how anthropologists viewed kinship and contributed to the establishment of componential analysis and cognitive anthropology as major theoretical frameworks. Toward the end of his career, Lounsbury applied his talents to Mayan hieroglyphs, contributing several key breakthroughs in the decipherment of the Mayan writing system. Lounsbury taught linguistic anthropology at Yale University from 1949 until his retirement in 1979. In 1969 he was elected to the National Academy of Sciences.

Education

BA University of Wisconsin, 1941
Ph.D. Yale University, 1949

Fieldwork

Oneida, Wisconsin, 1939–40

Key Publications

(1953) *Oneida Verb Morphology*, Yale University Publications in Anthropology 48.

(1964) 'The structural analysis of kinship semantics', in H. Lunt (ed.) *Proceedings of the Ninth International Congress of Linguists*, The Hague: Mouton.

DANIEL LEFKOWITZ

Low, Setha M.

b. 1948, Los Angeles, California, USA

Setha M. Low was trained as a medical anthropologist, and her earliest research dealt with issues of health care and folk medicine. Her first full-time teaching position, in the Department of Landscape Architecture at the University of Pennsylvania, had a critical impact on her, and she is known primarily for her work in two cross-cutting areas: the design professions of landscape architecture, architecture, and (urban) planning, as they intersect with anthropological interests in urban social organisation, and symbolic meaning. Low's geographical area of expertise has been Latin America from the beginning, though she has done considerable work in the USA as well. Her work has been pivotal to the institutionalisation of the study of space and place in anthropology. She created the Cultural Aspects of Design Network for the Environmental Design Research Association (EDRA) and Space and Place, an interest group based in the American Anthropological Association (AAA). These two networks have facilitated contact and cross-fertilisation of research interests between environmental design professionals and anthropologists.

In her own work, Low has focused on both domestic and public space. She has a sophisticated methodology that combines the use of history (archival materials), contemporary mapping, observation and interviewing to identify the spatialisation of culture and the culturisation of space, the structures of society and patterns of spatial practice and behaviour.

Of particular salience is Low's distinction between social production and social construction of space: production refers to the factors involved in the physical creation of the physical setting; construction refers to the phenomenological and symbolic experience of space, the transformation of space such that it carries social meaning.

Low's analyses invariably deal with the distinctiveness of the urban cultural system – in terms of social institutions, relations and structures, political economies, diversity of population, lifestyles. More significantly, her intent is to theorise the urban setting, to move from research in the city to an anthropology of the city. While she supports the necessity for culturally specific (micro-level) research, she is also determined that anthropologists must find a way to move up a level in analysis in order to fruitfully engage in policy discourse. She herself has applied her interdisciplinary expertise to urban problems, working with the national park service, town planning boards, heritage conservation, and cultural aspects of design.

Education

BA Pitzer College, 1969
MA University of California, Berkeley, 1971
Ph.D. University of California, Berkeley, 1976

Fieldwork

Costa Rica, 1972–4, 1976, 1979, 1985–6, 1989, 1992–3
Guatemala, summers 1980–7
Cuba, 1990, 1993
Spain and Italy, 1987, 1988
Dominican Republic, 1987
Venezuela, 1991
Texas, winter and summer breaks 1993–2003
New York City, 1993–2003 (continuous)
Battery Park City, New York, 2001–2

Key Publications

(1996) 'Spatializing culture: the social production and social construction of public space', *American Ethnologist* 23, 4: 861–79.

(2000) *On the Plaza: The Politics of Public Space and Culture*, Austin: University of Texas Press.

with Lawrence-Zuniga, D. (eds) (2002) *The Anthropology of Space and Place: Locating Culture*, Oxford: Blackwell Publishers.

(2003) *Behind the Gates: The New American Dream*, New York: Routledge.

DEBORAH PELLOW

Lowie, Robert H.

b. 12 June 1883, Vienna, Austria

d. 21 September 1957

Among the first generation of students of Franz Boas, Robert H. Lowie was the one who specialised in the study of social organisation and religion. Although he approached his ethnographic work from within the Boasian cultural historical paradigm, Lowie's writing also was widely admired by colleagues in British social anthropology. Like many of his contemporaries, Lowie's background was German and Jewish, his family having emigrated to New York City when he was 10 years old. After a brief career as a schoolteacher, Lowie enrolled at Columbia University intending to study science, being drawn initially to Franz Boas because of his interest in German materialism. Lowie entered the doctoral programme in anthropology despite his recurrent frustration with Boas's sink-or-swim pedagogical style and presented a library dissertation on the 'test-theme' in North American mythology in 1908. This project fell clearly within the Boasian historical paradigm for cross-cultural comparison across North America.

Already, however, Lowie was more comfortable in his work at the American Museum of Natural History than in the circle immediately around Boas. At the Museum, Clark Wissler directed Lowie's fieldwork in various Plains tribes in order to supplement his own studies of the Blackfoot. Lowie began with the Shoshone. His 1959 autobiography describes the conditions and tribulations of the necessarily superficial survey fieldwork of these early years. After Boas's resignation from the American Museum in 1905, Lowie became Wissler's second-in-command and continued annual fieldwork in the Plains culture area. Most of his fieldwork was done during these museum years. Despite forays into the Southwest and Great Basin, Lowie was able to specialise in the Plains and to return periodically to the Crow, with whom he most identified. Although not published until many years later, Lowie's *The Crow Indians* (1935) provided one of the most complete ethnographies of a single tribe from the period. This more intensive fieldwork method allowed him to become sensitive to intracultural variability and to focus on the lives of individual Crow.

Lowie moved to the University of California in 1918, where his teaching emphasised ethnographic facts as the basis of anthropological generalisation. This was the period in which the first generation of Boas's students codified the discipline in a series of textbooks exploring various parts of the shared paradigm. Lowie was the only person to contribute three books to this fluorescence of Boasian anthropology: *Culture and Ethnology* (1917), *Primitive Society* (1920), and *Primitive Religion* (1924) took up their successive subjects in a clear and logical style that made these volumes eminently suitable for teaching anthropology, at a time when the discipline was becoming increasingly well established in American universities.

During the academic portion of his career, Lowie collaborated with Curt Nimuendaju, an independent scholar attempting an ethnographic survey of the Ge-speaking tribes of Brazil, thereby also becoming more generally involved with South American ethnology.

Lowie saw no intrinsic reason to restrict anthropological method to the study of preliterate societies. His use of the word 'primitive' had no pejorative connotation at this time. Lowie's *The History of Ethnological Theory* (1937) illustrated the internationalism and breadth of his anthropology; it was descriptive and Lowie declined to present his own evaluation of the theories and their practitioners that he discussed. In his later years, in addition to the material in his autobiography, Lowie shared recollections of colleagues from his younger days and assembled for publication his correspondence with Edward Sapir, whose intellect he highly respected. Lowie even undertook ethnographic fieldwork in Germany, from where his family had emigrated. In all of his fieldwork, he was inclined to adopt the standpoint of a witness rather than a participant in the cultures he studied. During the First World War, Lowie maintained a pacifist position, although he became a passionate opponent of Nazism before and during the Second World War. Unlike Boas, however, Lowie chose not to move his personal political commitments to the public domain. His book on Germany, which appeared only in 1954, avoided the national character stereotypes common at the time and was criticised widely for failing to demonise Germany and the Germans.

Lowie was recognised within American anthropology as an effective mediator among opposing factions, both theoretical and personal. His editorship of the *American Anthropologist* from 1924–33 facilitated the national scope and representativeness of the journal. Lowie served as president of the American Anthropological Association, the American Folklore Society, and the American Ethnological Society. Three years after his death, the University of California, Berkeley, dedicated the Robert H. Lowie Museum of Anthropology to his memory.

Education

BA Columbia University, 1901
Ph.D. Columbia University, 1908

Fieldwork

Northern Shoshone, 1906
Crow 1907, 1910–16, 1931

Key Publications

(1920) *Primitive Society*, New York: Harper.

(1924) *Primitive Religion*, New York: Boni & Liveright.
(1935) *The Crow Indians*, New York: Holt, Rinehart & Winston.
(1959) *Robert H. Lowie: A Personal Memoir*, Berkeley: University of California Press.

REGNA DARNELL

Luhrmann, Tanya

b. 24 February 1959, Dayton, Ohio, USA

Persuasions of the Witch's Craft was Tanya Luhrmann's first book. Based on her dissertation, it documented the lives of modern Pagans in England, showing how ordinary middle-class, well-educated people come to be practitioners of magic, creating and perpetuating worlds of enchantment that, to outside eyes, might seem completely irrational. Critical acclaim for this work centered on Luhrmann's treatment of the nature of belief and rationality, themes that have persisted throughout her career. In her second book, *The Good Parsi* (1996), Luhrmann studied the Zoroastrian community in Bombay, India. Luhrmann explores how a prosperous community saw itself fall from grace in the aftermath of British colonial rule; what began as an interest in the nature of evil ended as a study of beliefs about the nature of the self over time.

The theme of rationality re-emerges most forcefully in Luhrmann's third book, *Of Two Minds* (2000), a study of the mind–body split in late twentieth-century psychiatric practice. By comparing 'talk therapy' of a Freudian nature with the use of psychodynamic drug therapies, Luhrmann highlights the dualistic nature of our understandings of how mental illness is constituted and treated. Her ethnographic approach permits us to see how the psychiatric medical community has shaped itself over the last century, and what the implications of their contrastive practices for the wider American and international public may be. She continues to work on the problem of irrational belief both in the religious domain and in the domain of psychiatric symptoms.

Education

BA Harvard University, 1981
M.Phil. University of Cambridge, 1982
Ph.D. University of Cambridge, 1986

Fieldwork

Bombay, India, 1987–8, 1993
San Diego, California, and elsewhere in the USA, 1989–2000 (on three projects, in psychiatry, schizophrenia, and religion)

Key Publications

(1989) *Persuasions of the Witch's Craft*, Cambridge: Harvard University Press.
(2000) *Of Two Minds: An Anthropologist Looks at American Psychiatry*, New York: Alfred A. Knopf.

SARAH STRAUSS

Lurie, Nancy Oestreich

b. 29 January 1924, Milwaukee, Wisconsin, USA

Nancy Oestreich Lurie resolved as a child of eight years that she would someday be the curator of anthropology at the Milwaukee Public Museum, a position she finally attained in 1972.

Lurie began her studies of the Wisconsin Winnebago as an undergraduate, following up on the classic work of Paul Radin. Her doctoral work, based on both fieldwork and ethnohistorical research, compared culture change among the Wisconsin and Nebraska Winnebago. Through Mitchell Redcloud, Sr, who became her adopted father, and his family, Lurie gained access to personal and ritual information culminating in her autobiography of Mountain Wolf Woman, the sister of both Redcloud and Radin's primary consultant, Crashing Thunder (1961). This work provided

a time dimension to Winnebago ethnography as well as a female perspective on the culture.

Throughout her career, Lurie has been a proponent of Sol Tax's action anthropology, although his Fox project came together shortly after her departure from Chicago to teach in her native Milwaukee. Between 1954 and its termination in 1978, Lurie served as an expert witness for seven cases before the US Indian Claims Commission (Lower Kutenai, Lower Kalispel, Quinaielt-Quileute, Sac and Fox, Winnebago, Turtle Mountain Chippewa, and Eastern Potawatomi). In 1961–2, she assisted Sol Tax in organising the American Indian Chicago Conference, intended to test action anthropology on a national scale; ninety tribes came together to express their frustration with federal policies in a Declaration of Indian Purpose that was presented to President John F. Kennedy.

In 1959, Lurie accepted the invitation of her Chicago graduate student colleague, June Helm, for fieldwork among the Dogrib, an Athabascan-speaking group in Canada's Northwest Territories. A number of joint publications resulted from their several trips.

Lurie's action anthropology commitments continued in project development and community planning among the Wisconsin Winnebago and in the Milwaukee intertribal community. She has encouraged many Native American scholars to pursue academic careers. Between 1969 and 1974, she helped the Menomini in their successful battle to repeal federal termination of their Indian status. In her museum work, Lurie has insisted that public education can increase appreciation of how anthropology contributes to understanding the nature of humankind. She has been a firm supporter of the four-field approach and of community consultation as essential to anthropological fieldwork. Culture change, gender, and the creative role of the individual in culture have been the central concepts of her applied anthropology.

Education

BA University of Wisconsin, 1945

MA University of Chicago, 1947
Ph.D. Northwestern University, 1952

Fieldwork

Winnebago, beginning in 1944
Dogrib, 1959, 1962, 1967

Key Publications

(1961) *Mountain Wolf Woman: Sister of Crashing Thunder*, Ann Arbor: University of Michigan Press.

with Helm, June (1966) *The Dogrib Hand Game*, Ottawa: National Museum of Canada Bulletin 205.

with Levine, Stuart (1970) *The American Indian Today*, Baltimore: Penguin.

The Indian Claims Commission (1978) *Annals of the American Academy of Political and Social Sciences* 436: 97–110.

REGNA DARNELL

Lutz, Catherine

b. 1952, Jersey City, New Jersey, USA

Catherine Lutz's work has focused on the specific ways that subjective experience is shaped by social and political context. Her first and very influential book, *Unnatural Emotions*, argued that emotions were powerfully shaped by the local culture. She demonstrated that Ifaluk emotion terms did not map neatly on to English terms, that they were experienced and conceptualised as responses to social triggers specific to Ifaluk culture, and that they were imbued with moral understanding. These data suggested the need for an analysis quite different from the understanding of emotion then current within American academic psychology, where emotions were understood to be universal psychobiological responses, quite independent from moral reasoning. Lutz used her analysis to reflect back on common American understandings of emotion, and she used the Ifaluk data to point out that, in Western culture, emotions were also in many

ways gendered. Emotions were associated with women, and women were thought to be more emotional than men. Lutz then developed these insights into the social moulding of emotion in a collection that demonstrated the importance of language in shaping the subjective experience of language. The volume was titled *Language and the Politics of Emotion* and it signaled Lutz's increasing focus on the way local politics become intimately embedded in seemingly private subjective experience. Her next major work, *Reading National Geographic*, was also widely read. It analysed the way the photography in a beloved American magazine revealed often unarticulated assumptions about other people and other lands, particularly in the middle period of the twentieth century. Her most recent book addresses the social costs of military institutional growth for American society, both nationally and more specifically in eastern North Carolina. Here she again looks at gender, but also at race, and she argues that military preparation and activities – a practice seemingly independent from American racial politics – in fact has been deeply involved with them, and that the distinction between civilians and soldiers has eroded over time even while it is seen as increasingly contentious.

Education

BA Swarthmore College, 1974
Ph.D. Harvard University, 1980

Fieldwork

Ethnographic research on emotion and ethnopsychology, Micronesia, 1977–8

Research on cultural patterns and gender differences in understanding the emotions, USA, 1982–8

Research on women's productivity and citation rates in sociocultural anthropology journals, 1988–90

Ethnographic and historical textual research on *National Geographic* photography, 1987–92

Research on JROTC programme for American Friends Service Committee, 1993–5

Ethnographic and historical research on twentieth-century Fayetteville, North Carolina, and its relationship to Fort Bragg, 1994–2001

Multisited ethnographic research on local democracy, North Carolina, 1997–2001

Ethnographic research on community responses to domestic violence, North Carolina, 1999–2001

Key Publications

(1988) *Unnatural Emotions: Everyday Sentiments on a Micronesian Atoll and Their Challenge to Western Theory*, Chicago: University of Chicago Press.

with Abu-Lughod, Lila (1990) *Language and the Politics of Emotion*, Cambridge, UK: Cambridge University Press.

with Collins, Jane (1993) *Reading National Geographic*, Chicago: University of Chicago Press.

(2002) *Homefront: A Military City and the American 20th Century*, Boston: Beacon.

TANYA LUHRMANN

M

MacAloon, John Joseph

b. 22 January 1947, Detroit, Michigan, USA

John MacAloon originated the anthropology of Olympic sport. *This Great Symbol* (1981) helped propel the anthropology of history in the 1980s, and is the definitive analysis of the origins of the modern Olympic Games and biography of their founder, Pierre de Coubertin. He located Coubertin's philosophy of 'internationalism' – a respect for each national culture based on the festive performance of difference – within the turn-of-the-century emergence of an imagination of global culture, which also included scholarly and popular ethnography. In 'Olympic Games and the theory of spectacle in complex society', he extended Victor Turner's ritual theory to the study of transnational, multicultural events like the Olympic Games, providing a theoretical foundation for subsequent research on large-scale global events. His concept of nested and 'ramified' performance systems distinguished the performance types (festival, ritual, game) that occur within the compass of such 'spectacles', and separated their distinct layers of meaning. He pointed out that the joyous, multicultural, spontaneous street festival during the Olympics often evokes a greater sense of shared humanity than the nationalistic displays inside the arenas. He pioneered ethnographic methods for studying global events by co-ordinating research teams of local and international scholars who worked on multiple Olympics and developed comparative perspectives. His commitment to 'action anthropology' was evident in his writing of the world press guide to the 1996 Atlanta Olympic Games opening ceremonies, and in his push – as one of two intellectuals named to the IOC 2000 Reform Commission – for a greater attention to cultural diversity, education, and research by the IOC.

Education

BA Catholic University of America, 1969
AM University of Chicago, 1974
Ph.D. University of Chicago, 1980

Fieldwork

Ethnography of the International Olympic Committee in Lausanne, Switzerland, 1975 (up to 3 months), 1979, 1982, 1984, 1986, 1990–3, 1995–2001

Fieldwork surrounding Olympic Games, Olympic rituals, and torch relays in Ancient Olympia, Greece, 1982 (up to 2 months), 1984, 1992, 1994–5, 1996–2001

Montreal, Toronto, and Calgary, Canada, 1975–6 (up to 2 months), 1979, 1983, 1986, 1989, 1993

San Juan, Puerto Rico, May–September 1982

Los Angeles, May–September 1984

Seoul and rural South Korea, March–September 1986, April–September 1988, August–September 1989

Barcelona, Spain, April–May 1991, June–September 1992, April–June 1995

Oslo and rural Norway, October–November 1992, April–May 1994, June–July 1998

Atlanta, September 1995–October 1996

Key Publications

(1981) *This Great Symbol: Pierre de Coubertin and the Origins of the Modern Olympic Games*, Chicago: The University of Chicago Press. Online at aafla.org [Amateur Athletic Foundation of Los Angeles, 2001].

(1984) 'Olympic Games and the theory of spectacle in complex society', in J.J. MacAloon (ed.) *Rite, Drama, Festival, Spectacle: Rehearsals toward a Theory of Cultural Performance*, Philadelphia: ISHI.

(1992) 'The ethnographic imperative in comparative Olympic research', *Sociology of Sport Journal* 9, 2: 104–30.

(1995) 'Humanism as political necessity? Reflections on the pathos of anthropological science in pluricultural contexts,' in J. Fernandez and M. Singer (eds) *The Conditions of Reciprocal Understanding*, Chicago: The University of Chicago, Center for International Studies.

SUSAN BROWNELL

Macfarlane, Alan

b. 1941, Shillong, India

Alan Macfarlane trained in both history and anthropology. His research and thought have contributed to both disciplines in an original way, stressing continuities in history, and investigating the conditions for the emergence of modernity in anthropology.

In his first major work, a study of witchcraft in sixteenth- and seventeenth-century Essex, he tried to correlate witchcraft prosecutions with religious, economic, and social phenomena.

Macfarlane carried out field research in Nepal, where he assessed the impact of long-term population growth on economic resources and social structures.

In the early 1970s, he began to work on a 'total historical reconstitution' of the Essex village of Earls Colne (with Sarah Harrison). This data, with other evidence, led Macfarlane to a radical rethinking of English history. Against what can be considered the historical orthodoxy since the 1950s, Macfarlane argued that there was no 'great transition' to modernity in seventeenth- and eighteenth-century England. In social, economic, and legal terms, Englishmen were individualists as far back as written records reach. There was no peasantry; people showed 'rational', market-orientated, and acquisitive economic behaviour.

The acquisitive ethic and legal security also explain the unusual marriage pattern of England, characterised by high age at marriage and a relatively high proportion of unmarried women. Economic individualism meant children were a financial burden, rather than future providers for their aged parents.

The meticulous Malthusian comparison between England and Japan, which Macfarlane undertook in *The Savage Wars of Peace*, revealed the importance of islandhood, which made it possible for both to eliminate war and famine. Material culture, such as housing, hygiene, water supply, food, and drink, also played a significant role in the eradication of diseases.

In rejecting the 'revolutionary' view of English history, Macfarlane rediscovered the thought of eighteenth- and nineteenth-century philosophers, economists, and historians such as Montesquieu, Adam Smith, Tocqueville, Maitland, and Fukuzawa, who all reflected on the emergence of liberty, wealth, and equality. According to Macfarlane, it seemed that all Europe was set on the way to modernity around 1200, but then a large part of the continent gravitated towards a model characterised by absolutism, peasantry, and a rigid, caste-like social structure. Paradoxically, it was England's traditionalism that gave it an early affinity to the modern developments of capitalism, industrialism, and democracy.

Alan Macfarlane is also interested in the use of computerised information retrieval and visual media in anthropology, often pioneering the utilisation of new technologies.

Education

BA University of Oxford, 1963
D.Phil. University of Oxford, 1967
M.Phil. London School of Economics, 1968
Ph.D. School of Oriental and African Studies, London, 1972

Fieldwork

Thak, Nepal, 1968–70, further annual visits since 1986

Key Publications

(1970) *Witchcraft in Tudor and Stuart England: A Regional and Comparative Study*, London: Routledge & Kegan Paul.
(1978) *The Origins of English Individualism: The Family, Property and Social Transition*, Oxford: Basil Blackwell.
(1997) *The Savage Wars of Peace: England, Japan and the Malthusian Trap*, Oxford: Blackwell.
(2000) *The Riddle of the Modern World: Of Liberty, Wealth and Equality*, London: Macmillan.

Further Reading

www.alanmacfarlane.com.

ANNE FRIEDERIKE MÜLLER

Mach, Zdzislaw

b. 1954, Krakow, Poland

Although Zdzislaw Mach's early works dealt mainly with the history of anthropology (MA thesis on Malinowski and Lévi-Strauss; Ph.D. on Culture and Personality Approach), his interests were always connected with empirical research, starting with the study of student theatre, which he undertook together with colleagues from the Institute of Sociology, Jagiellonian University, and the analysis of political and national symbolism in Poland. He carried out fieldwork in Lower Silesia, an area from which the autochthonous German population was expelled after the Second World War and substituted with Polish refugees from the areas allocated to the USSR. He was interested in problems of migration and its consequences for identity, creation of landscape, and local politics. His research in Chicago among Eastern European minorities dealt with similar problems although focusing mainly on ethnicity.

His theoretical stance of constructivism, perceiving culture as negotiated by social agents, can be seen in his books based on fieldwork experience. In *Symbols, Conflict and Identity* he studied relations between power and symbolic constructions of social identities, while in the more recent *Niechciane miasta* he discussed the reconstruction of identity after migration. His focus on the anthropology of Central Europe led him towards European studies, a department of which he established at the Jagiellonian University and to which he imparted a strong social scientific bias.

Education

MA Jagiellonian University, Krakow, 1978
Ph.D. Jagiellonian University, Krakow, 1984
Habilitation, Jagiellonian University, Krakow, 1990

Fieldwork

Krakow, Poland 1980 (on student theatre)
Poland, 1985–6 (on political and national symbols)
Lower Silesia, Poland 1986–7, 1992 (on migration and identity)
Chicago, USA, 1988–9 (on ethnicity)

Key Publications

(1993) *Symbols, Conflict and Identity. Essays in Political Anthropology*, Albany: State University of New York Press.
(1998) *Niechciane miasta: migracja i tozsamo's'c*

spoleczna (Unwanted Cities. Migration and Social Identity), Kraków: Universitas.

GRAZYNA KUBICA-HELLER

Madan, T.N.

b. 12 September 1933, Srinagar, Kashmir, India

Since the publication of his classic ethnographic study of family and kinship among the Pandits of rural Kashmir in the mid-1960s, Triloki Nath Madan has been among the best known of Indian social anthropologists, both in India and internationally. Apart from his numerous scholarly writings, T.N. Madan is widely acknowledged as India's foremost social science editor. From 1967 to 1991, he was editor of the prestigious *Contributions to Indian Sociology* (new series), in succession to Louis Dumont, and, from 1999, editor of the *Indian Social Science Review*. He is also general editor of the Oxford University Press (India) series of Readings in Sociology and Social Anthropology. T.N. Madan has held several important academic administrative and organisational posts, including that of co-ordinator of the UNESCO project on the medical profession in Asia (1975–7), member-secretary of the Indian Council of Social Science Research (1978–81), director of the Institute of Economic Growth, Delhi (1986–9), member of the Advisory Committee of the Fundamentalism Project of the American Academy of Social Sciences (1989–93), and chairman, Centre for the Study of Developing Societies, Delhi, from 2002. Among numerous awards and honours are his Honorary Fellowship of the Royal Anthropological Institute of Great Britain and Ireland, and his Docteur Honoris Causa (Ethnologie) of the University of Paris X (1994).

Attracted to anthropology via an early interest in history, Madan enrolled for a composite Master's course in sociology, anthropology, and economics at the University of Lucknow. He describes his anthropological career thereafter as an attempt to steer a 'middle path' between the orientations of two of his Lucknow teachers, D.N. Majumdar and D.P. Mukerji, and two subsequent mentors, Derek Freeman and Louis Dumont. Majumdar and Freeman, he says, impressed on him the importance of rigorous empirical fieldwork, while the work of Mukerji and Dumont embodied the discipline's wider ideocentric and civilisational concerns. As editor of *Contributions to Indian Sociology*, Madan organised two symposia on Dumont's work, the first (1971) being a response to the English translation of *Homo Hierarchicus*, the second (1981), a wide-ranging interdisciplinary colloquium on Dumont's interpretation of Hindu culture (subsequently published as *Way of Life: King, Householder, Renouncer* (1982). This perhaps explains why many Indian critics locate Madan's own writing squarely within the Dumont tradition of Indologically oriented sociology.

This is a one-sided judgement, which does not reflect the complex trajectory that Madan's research has taken over the years. Following his early structural-functionalist study of Kashmiri family and kinship, Madan became interested in the process of 'secularisation', the modern division between spheres of family and religion on the one hand, and work and profession on the other. Accordingly, in the late 1960s and early 1970s, he undertook fieldwork on the medical profession in North India, resulting in the co-authored *Doctors and Society: Three Asian Case Studies* (1980), among other publications. From 'secularisation' his interest gradually shifted to interpretation of the post-colonial Indian creation of a 'secular' state, to the sociology of religion (specifically Hinduism, Sikhism, and Islam), to fundamentalism(s), and thence, in the late 1990s, to exploration of the sites, instruments, practices, and ideologies of religious 'pluralism'. A reader on *Religion in India* (1991) and an edited volume on *Muslim Communities of South Asia*, the latter revised twice since its first publication in 1976, are timely reminders of the continued importance of religion in public as well as in private life, and in the constitution of community identities.

Very early in his career, Madan developed a personal distaste for the invasionary practices of contemporary Indian anthropology, as applied to the study of the tribal 'other', and resolved to focus instead on studying his 'own' society. In a series of essays on fieldwork methodology (the first published in *Encounter and Experience: Personal Accounts of Fieldwork*, co-edited with André Béteille, 1975), Madan reflected on the tensions inherent in 'living intimately with strangers', the more so if the ethnographer is also a 'native', and the challenges of achieving, through the profession of anthropology, 'critical self-awareness' in the 'mutual interpretation of cultures'. These methodological essays, along with a number of others reflecting on aspects of disciplinary history, have contributed substantially towards enhancing the self-reflexivity of Indian social anthropology.

Education

MA University of Lucknow, 1953
Ph.D. Australian National University, Canberra, 1960

Fieldwork

Rural Kashmir, 1957–8 (13 months), with frequent revisits till 1986
Ghaziabad, Uttar Pradesh, 1968 (4 months)
All-India Institute of Medical Sciences, New Delhi, 1974–5 (6 months)

Key Publications

(1965) *Family and Kinship: A Study of the Pandits of Rural Kashmir*, Bombay: Asia Publishing House.
(1987) *Non-renunciation: Themes and Interpretations of Hindu Culture*, Delhi: Oxford University Press.
(1994) *Pathways: Approaches to the Study of Society in India*, Delhi: Oxford University Press.
(1997) *Modern Myths, Locked Minds: Secularism and Fundamentalism in India*, Delhi: Oxford University Press.

PATRICIA UBEROI

Maine, Henry James Sumner

b. 15 August 1822, UK

d. 3 February 1888, Cannes, France

Henry James Sumner Maine, like J.F. McLennan and J.J. Bachofen, developed what came to be considered an anthropological interest in the history of property and the family from the study and practice of law. He was already regius professor of civil law (1847–54) at the University of Cambridge and reader in jurisprudence and civil law at the Inns of Court in London (1852), when he took up the comparative study of ancient legal institutions.

Although educated in the legal positivism and utilitarianism of Bentham and Austin, he read the works of the new German historical school, such as those by F.K. von Savigny and Rudolf von Ihering. Indo-European linguistic studies, particularly the popular lectures of F. Max Müller, also influenced him to take a historical and conservative view of the very slow, custom-bound evolution of society, which he thought could best be studied historically by examining the remains of common Indo-European culture in Europe and elsewhere, such as ancient Rome, Germany, Russia, Ireland, and India. His first book, *Ancient Law, Its Connection with the Early History of Society and Its Relation to Modern Ideas* (1861), created an instant sensation as a breakthrough in its field. On a methodological level, it represented the application of the comparative method of Indo-European linguistics to law, as it was being applied by others at the same time to mythology. In its content, it proposed a sketchy but coherent and suggestive theory of the development of Indo-European society from a primitive, war-like patriarchy based upon familial status and common property holding to the modern, more peaceful, egalitarian society based upon rights of the individual to contract and hold individual property.

Maine continued his research on ancient kinship and property holding, based on examination of current Hindu practices, when holding office as legal member of the

Governor-General's Council of India (1862–9) in Calcutta. Upon his return to England, he was appointed for life to the Council of the Secretary of State for India (1870) and became professor of jurisprudence (1871–8) at Oxford, master of Trinity Hall, the University of Cambridge (1877), and then professor of international law (1887) at Cambridge. He produced further works based upon his Hindu and comparative researches: *Village Communities in East and West* (1871), *Lectures on the Early History of Institutions* (1875), and *Dissertations on Early Law and Custom* (1883). He continued to support his patriarchal theory for Indo-European society against the matriarchal theory of primitive society expounded by L.H. Morgan and McLennan.

Maine can perhaps be seen as one of the first in a discontinuous tradition of British colonial administrator-anthropologists, who (on a rather lofty level) tried to apply their knowledge of historical traditions to reform and conserve local practices, while emphasising legal, kinship, and economic frameworks in anthropology. He also represents the reformer and the conservative in his role in bringing to bear evidence from ancient Indian and other legal history on contemporary questions of the evolving role of law and land in British representative forms of government.

Education

BA Pembroke College, University of Cambridge, 1844
Called to the Bar, 1850

Fieldwork

Bengal, India, 1862–9
Ireland, summer 1873

Key Publications

(1861) *Ancient Law, Its Connection with the Early History of Society and Its Relation to Modern Ideas*, London: J. Murray.
(1871) *Village Communities in East and West*, London: J. Murray

(1875) *Lectures on the Early History of Institutions*, London: J. Murray.
(1883) *Dissertations on Early Law and Custom*, London: J. Murray.

Further Reading

Diamond, A. (ed.) *The Victorian Achievement of Sir Henry Maine. A Centennial Reappraisal*, Cambridge, UK: Cambridge University Press.
Feaver, G. (1969) *From Status to Contract. A Biography of Sir Henry Maine 1822–1888*, London: Longmans.

JOAN LEOPOLD

Mair, Lucy

b. 28 January 1901, Banstead, Surrey, UK

d. 1 April 1986, Blackheath, London, UK

Lucy Mair was one of Bronislaw Malinowski's students, and a major figure in British social anthropology during the period up till the 1970s when it still had a distinct identity of style and subject matter. Yet she differed from most of her peers in her strong bent towards turning anthropology to practical use. Her writings on Africa spanned the whole period during which it became independent of the colonial powers.

Born into a well-connected intellectual family, Mair read classics at Cambridge, and her first employment was as secretary to the great classicist, Sir Gilbert Murray, at a time when he was involved with the League of Nations. He wrote the preface to her first book, on the protection of minorities under the League. By the time of its publication in 1928, she held a lectureship in international relations at the London School of Economics (LSE) and had begun to attend Malinowski's famous seminars. In 1931, she began fieldwork in Uganda, which led to the publication of *An African People in the Twentieth Century*. Later in her career, she was to look back with amusement on the self-confidence of this book, with its declared aim of using anthropology to transform colonial administration from an art to a science. However, she was to remain consistent in defending the principle of giving administrative responsibility to traditional rulers, then known as Indirect Rule.

With typical irony, Mair wrote that Malinowski had sent her to study social change because she was not a good enough anthropologist to do standard fieldwork. She was not in fact a natural fieldworker, but had a rare gift of linguistic clarity and concision that enabled her to marshal data and summarise arguments forcefully. Ethnographically, she was most comfortable in the male world of political and legal institutions, then a central focus of social anthropology, with land tenure and patronage among her special interests. Her principal academic home was the LSE, where she held further posts in the 1930s, and returned in 1946 as reader in colonial administration, to be promoted to a chair in applied anthropology in 1963.

A prolific writer, Mair aimed in her earlier books at a readership of colonial administrators. However, later in her career she published an introduction to social anthropology, in its day a standard text, and a stream of authoritative books, based on her lectures, which synthesised recent research on African societies and on such topics as witchcraft. Her most original contribution was *Primitive Government*, which covers stateless societies, African states, and finally the impact of modernisation. 'Primitive', for her, meant merely lacking in advanced technology – a lack that she saw as drastically limiting human potential, but not to be confused with moral inferiority. She criticised as sentimental those anthropologists who regarded pre-colonial systems of co-operation as cultural assets deserving of protection. In this book and in *New Nations* (1963) Mair foreshadowed the debates about 'civil society' and vernacular forms of association that were to come to the fore in development studies in the 1990s.

Mair challenged simplistic models of development, whether purveyed by theoretical Marxists or by practising macro-economists, and she also criticised campaigns to preserve indigenous lifestyles. She disliked all anthropological schools that gave primacy to 'culture' as opposed to social institutions. The kernel of her thought was her insight into processes of active, but culturally constrained, choice by individuals in societies experiencing change. Towards the end of her career, recognising the failure of all ambitious schemes to eliminate poverty, she recommended applied anthropologists to be content with a necessarily scaled-down role – that of anticipating shortcomings in development plans, and explaining their unintended consequences in retrospect.

Lucy Mair was more sensitive than many anthropologists of her generation to the impact of global political change on the discipline. However, she defended it staunchly against the charge of being a handmaid of colonialism, and was ever a hardy controversialist. At LSE and later at the Universities of Durham and Kent, she provided a focus over many years for anthropologists who sought, without any sacrifice of academic rigour, to anchor their interests in the real problems afflicting the peoples of the Third World who have constituted most of the discipline's subject-matter. Her influential work is commemorated by the Royal Anthropological Institute's annually awarded Lucy Mair Medal for Applied Anthropology.

Education

BA University of Cambridge, 1922
Ph.D. University of London, 1932)

Fieldwork

Uganda, 1931–2, 1938–9
Nyasaland (now Malawi), 1949, 1961
Papua New Guinea, 1968

Key Publications

(1934) *An African People in the Twentieth Century*, London: Routledge.
(1957) *Studies in Applied Anthropology*, London: Athlone Press.

(1962) *Primitive Government*, Harmondsworth: Penguin.

(1984) *Anthropology and Development*, London: Macmillan.

JONATHAN BENTHALL

Malinowski, Bronislaw Kasper

b. 7 April 1884, Krakow, (then) Austro-Hungary

d. 16 May 1942, New Haven, Connecticut, USA

Malinowski grew up in the stimulating atmosphere of modernistic Krakow, with S.I. Witkiewicz (an innovative artist and writer) as his closest friend. At the Jagiellonian University Malinowski studied philosophy and science. In his Ph.D. thesis on second positivism the concept of function (elaborated later in functionalist theory) is already to be found. In 1910 he went to London and a new period of his academic career began in connection with social anthropology at the London School of Economics, to which he remained bound for almost all the rest of his life. Just before the First World War he departed for his fieldwork in Australia and New Guinea. His research in Mailu was carried out quite traditionally. Only the Trobriands expeditions could be called an 'archetypical fieldwork', when the rules of the basic anthropological method were established: long-term residence among the people under study, competent use of the native language, observation of daily life, sensitivity to conflict and shades of opinion, consciousness of the fact that people say one thing and do another, and a consideration of each aspect within the context of the whole culture, not in isolation. All these were required to understand 'the native's point of view', the perspective of the other.

Not interested in the historical comparisons characteristic of evolutionary theory, Malinowski postulated a form of explanation based on function, to which was added an apprecia-tion of individual motives. A 'savage' was a rational and reasonable being, able to discern his long-term interests. Malinowski treated culture as an instrumental reality and emphasised its derivation from human needs, from the basic universal needs of the individual organism to the highly elaborated and often specialised needs of a complex society.

His functional analysis of magic, science, and religion can serve as a convincing example. Magic worked because it relieved anxiety about the uncontrollable elements of the future. Religion, on the other hand, helped in situations of emotional stress. However, at the same time people behaved rationally and according to their knowledge and common sense, when they knew what to do. A Trobriander knew how to build a canoe technologically, but to cope with the emotional stress of going on the sea voyage into the unknown he needed magic and ritual.

The family could serve as another example: for Malinowski it was a means enabling the domestication of sex and providing for the care and training of children. It was also the mould of personality, the locus of man's primary emotional attachments, and the nexus within which his primary social emotions were formed.

Malinowski's special position consisted in attempting to combine three different stances: ethnographical holism (focus on bounded units), empiricism, and psychologism (appreciation of individual motives). Malinowski was accused (and aware) of being indifferent to the problem of change; he was analysing the present state of a 'savage culture' of the Trobriands instead of a colonial culture in the process of change. The accusation was justified as far as functionalist theory is concerned, but at the same time he was engaged in the political issues of colonial countries. Later he formulated a theory of cultural change which postulated that an ethnographer should take into consideration three cultural realities: the 'traditional culture', the intrusive European culture, and a new syncretic one that emerged as a result.

His theorising about myth (enforcing belief, legitimising social organisation) did not prevent him from the creation of a myth (he presented himself as a prophet of a new faith: functionalism) or duplicating an old anthropological myth that society was a matter of male solidarity (kula exchange, a leading motif of his first field monograph). He also unwillingly contributed to shattering a myth of modern anthropology through his intimate diaries (published without his authority after his death), where the empathic fieldworker of his monographs was substituted by the unsympathetic scientist irritated by his informants. These contradictory images made the way for an internal critique within anthropology.

Education

Ph.D. Jagiellonian University, Krakow, 1906
D.Sc. London School of Economics, 1916

Fieldwork

Mailu, New Guinea, August 1914–March 1915
Trobriand Island, New Guinea, May 1915–May 1916, October 1917–October 1918
Oaxaco, Mexico, summers 1940 and 1941

Key Publications

(1922) *Argonauts of the Western Pacific: An Account of Native Enterprise and Adventure in the Archipelagoes of Melanesian New Guinea*, London: Routledge.
(1935) *Coral Gardens and Their Magic*, Bloomington: Indiana University Press.
(1944) *A Scientific Theory of Culture, and Other Essays*, Chapel Hill: University of North Carolina Press.
(1967) *A Diary in the Strict Sense of the Term*, London: Routledge & Kegan Paul.

Further Reading

Ellen, R. et al. (eds) (1988) *Malinowski between Two Worlds*, Cambridge, UK: Cambridge University Press.
Firth, R. (ed.) (1957) *Man and Culture: An Evaluation of the Work of Bronislaw Malinowski*, New York: Harper.

GRAZYNA KUBICA-HELLER

Malkki, Liisa

b. 16 December 1959, Helsinki, Finland

Liisa Malkki's work with the Hutu refugees of Tanzania has focused cultural anthropologists on the question of national identity and historical consciousness among the world's displaced 'nations'. Her analysis of the dilemmas facing refugees has challenged the idea of the nation-state as immutable. Malkki has found that refugees preserve their 'statehood' through camp self-governance, discouraging intermarriage, language preservation, and eschewing official citizenship. Meanwhile, refugees seeking social and economic mobility live in nearby towns, creating a divergent identity through intermarriage, naturalisation, commerce, and claims to immigrant status. As a result of these two conflicting notions of 'national identity' camp refugees view themselves as morally 'pure' and the assimilated, town refugees as corrupt.

Malkki successfully elucidates the part reconstructed history plays justifying genocide, repression, exclusion, and other acts of political violence. This 'mythico-history', facilitated by camp isolation, allows refugees to reshape their understanding of the past, creating a moral community of pure refugees with a duty to expel the interloping repressors who forced them into exile. The outcome is a perpetual cycle of violence and racism that gives moral authority to future acts of genocide. This understanding of politically and socially sanctioned violence has allowed Malkki to make a significant contribution to human rights discourse.

An extension of her work on displacement has been an ethnographic study of Hutu refugees in Montreal and their conceptualisation of the future and a study of the perceptions of Nordic Red Cross workers in Africa. These recent projects strive to understand international organisations, the concept of an international community, and the politics of humanitarian intervention.

Education

Ph.D. Harvard University, 1989

Fieldwork

Tanzania, 1985–6

Montreal, Canada, summer 1993

Finland with International Committee of the Red Cross (ICRC) medical professionals posted to Central Africa, summers 1998, 1999, 2000, and ongoing

Key Publications

(1992) 'National geographic: the rooting of peoples and the territorialization of national identity among scholars and refugees', *Cultural Anthropology* 7, 1: 24–44.

(1995) *Purity and Exile: Historical Memory and National Identity among Hutu Refugees in Tanzania*, Chicago, IL: University of Chicago Press.

CYNTHIA A. TYSICK

Mandelbaum, David G.

b. 1911, Chicago, Illinois, USA

d. 19 April 1987, Berkeley, California, USA

David Mandelbaum's life in anthropology spanned six decades, from the late Boasian era to the high post-modern. He was active as a teacher and researcher, and was an active participant in numerous scholarly organisations. His interests and publications ranged widely, and included the ethnography of the Plains Cree, social change in India, the seclusion of women in South Asia, the Jews of Cochin and the USA, segregation in the US Army, human fertility policy in India, alcoholism, the teaching of anthropology, and the writings of Edward Sapir.

Mandelbaum studied at Northwestern University with Melville Herskovits and then moved to Yale, where he worked with Edward Sapir, Leslie Spier, and Clark Wissler. As expected in those days, his dissertation was on a North American Indian group, but the following year he became the first American cultural anthropologist to do research in India. His involvement with the cultures of South Asia led him to the anthropological study of 'complex civilisations', and he participated with such figures as A.L. Kroeber, Talcott Parsons, Robert Redfield, and Milton Singer in the development of this field.

His began his research in India among the Kota and Toda ('tribal peoples') in the Nilgiri Hills, but after the war he turned to 'village India'. In his major two-volume work, *Society in India*, he offered a comprehensive overview and interpretation of continuity and change in Indian social organisation, based on, but not restricted to, life in the villages of India. He also contributed a policy-oriented study of human fertility in India, and his last book, published posthumously, dealt with the significant and complex issue of 'women's seclusion and men's honour' in North India, Pakistan, and Bangladesh.

In 1952, he published an analytical work presenting the reasons why the integration of black and white soldiers in the American military resulted in improved efficiency and performance. Drawing upon many published studies, he brought together findings about the dynamics of primary groups, accounts of men in combat conditions, and reports about the qualities of both segregated and integrated units to demonstrate why this should be.

David Mandelbaum taught at the University of Minnesota from 1938–46 (interrupted by three years' service during the Second World War), and at the University of California, Berkeley, from 1946–78 (chair, 1955–7), remaining active after his retirement until his death. Aside from serving as chair of the department of anthropology, he founded the Center for South and Southeast Asian studies (chair, 1965–8) and held national office in the American Anthropological Association and several other scholarly organisations.

Education

BA Northwestern University, 1932
Ph.D. Yale University, 1936

Fieldwork

Plains Cree, Canada and the USA, 1934–5
India, 1937–8, 1949–50, 1963–4

Key Publications

(1940) *The Plains Cree*, New York: American
Museum of Natural History.
(1952) *Soldier Groups and Negro Soldiers*, Berkeley:
University of California.
(1970) *Society in India*, 2 vols, Berkeley:
University of California.
(1988) *Women's Seclusion and Men's Honor: Sex Roles
in North India, Bangladesh, and Pakistan*, Tucson:
University of Arizona.

HERBERT S. LEWIS

Manners, Robert A.

b. 21 August 1913, New York, USA

d. 12 July 1996, Boston, Massachusetts, USA

Throughout the six decades of his life as an
anthropologist, Robert Manners was a consistent and outspoken supporter of the materialist
and 'realist' view of human life and history. His
personal sociopolitical and theoretical perspectives meshed well with those of Julian Steward,
his major professor at Columbia University
and his collaborator on two major research
projects. Manners, like Steward, emphasised a
society's 'core culture,' features consisting of
habitat, technology, and the economic and
political organisation associated with these.
From his early work in Puerto Rico in the
1940s he also insisted on the central importance of the international political and economic forces that affected the farming
communities he studied. Like Steward, Manners believed that anthropology is a science
and that scientists must search for recurrent
causes in human affairs, and he sought

causality in the economic and material concerns rather than in the symbolic, the ideal, or
the psychological.

Robert Manners was not a prolific writer but
what he published was both carefully crafted
and often purposely provocative. Aside from
his two major ethnographic contributions
(1956, 1967), the majority of his writings
were theoretical and generalising in nature,
even polemical in design. He did not mind
taking on popular and established views in
order to present his own sense of what
anthropologists should and should not be
doing. He wanted anthropology to be used for
human economic and political improvement,
and he had a firm sense of what was needed.
His values were those of the democratic left of
his youth and he was not convinced otherwise
by changing anthropological fashions, especially those that glorified resistance to 'the
West' or to 'modernity,' or that proclaimed the
central value of cultural or group identity.
Before 'world systems' and 'dependency
theory' became popular ideas, Robert Manners
argued forcefully (e.g. 1965) that the modern
world had become one, and that even the most
remote peoples were inevitably and irretrie-
vably tied into the world economy and
structure. He believed that appeals to ethnic
and cultural distinctiveness and separation are
prescriptions for continued poverty and
powerlessness.

Robert Manners served as editor-in-chief
of the *American Anthropologist* (1973–5). He
founded the department of anthropology at
Brandeis University and spent his career there,
1952 to 1979, but remaining on campus as an
active and *engagé* professor emeritus until 1996.

Education

BA Columbia University, 1935
MA Columbia University, 1939
Ph.D. Columbia University, 1950

Fieldwork

Puerto Rico, 1948–9
Kenya, 1957–8, 1961–2

Key Publications

(1956) 'Tabara: subcultures of a tobacco and mixed crop municipality', in Julian Steward (ed.) *The People of Puerto Rico*, Urbana: University of Illinois Press.

(1965) 'Remittances and the unit of analysis in anthropological analysis', *Southwestern Journal of Anthropology* 21: 179–95.

(1967) 'The Kipsigis of Kenya: cultural change in a "model" East African tribe', in Julian Steward (ed.) *Contemporary Change in Traditional Societies*, vol. 1, Urbana: University of Illinois Press.

Kaplan, David (1972) *Culture Theory*, Englewood Cliffs, NJ: Prentice-Hall.

HERBERT S. LEWIS

Marcus, George E.

b. 9 October 1946, Pittsburgh, Pennsylvania, USA

The impact and influence of George Marcus within and well beyond the field since the early 1980s can scarcely be exaggerated. Since the late 1970s Marcus has worked both as a scholar of elites and related cultural institutions around the world, and as the foremost critic and scholar of the history and changing epistemological orientations of the discipline.

To a certain extent, the hybrids and critical breadth within Marcus' career might be said to stem from the fact that in his training, first at Yale and subsequently at Cambridge and Harvard, Marcus never became a part of any clear genealogy of anthropological figures as do most in the discipline, in one way or another. For various reasons – not the least of which was his at once love for, and critical stance towards, the ethnographic enterprise itself – throughout his graduate training he pursued a variety of interests in the humanities and the arts, which were at the time often not thought of as directly related to anthropology as a social science.

While at Cambridge in the last years of the 1960s, Marcus found his excitement for the earlier work of the great figures there, although he was disappointed in what he describes as an intellectual atmosphere that seemed tired. Later, while at Harvard, he spent a great deal of time taking courses with, and learning from, figures outside of the discipline whose work and ideas he felt offered a wealth of unrecognised and undeveloped potential to the discipline. This included work with Stanley Cavell, Barrington Moore, and Daniel Bell, to name a few. Working as a teaching fellow for a course taught by David Maybury-Lewis and Nur Yalman, Marcus began forming many of his ideas in long discussions concerning the history and future horizons of theoretical trends in social and cultural anthropology. Subsequently, he joined one of Harvard's on-going fieldwork projects that allowed him to work in the Kingdom of Tonga. His interest in Tonga was in the fact that it was a monarchical society that had made what were to his mind 'interesting adaptations to a long history of colonialism and modernity'.

Becoming chair of the Department of Anthropology at Rice University in 1980, Marcus began to expand his critical horizons in dialogue with colleagues there and in other departments. During the 1982–3 academic year he was a fellow at the Institute for Advanced Study in Princeton, during which both he and Clifford Geertz were in different ways thinking about anthropology from the angle of writing and representation. This period was a formative one for Marcus's work in the years that would follow.

Between 1985–91 Marcus both founded and served as editor of the journal, *Cultural Anthropology*. It was in this role and as a co-editor of several significant volumes that Marcus brought together a great range of scholars both from inside and outside of the discipline, constituting what remains today a list of leaders within the discipline. In addition to his work as an editor during this time, Marcus published and presented a great many papers that critically encompassed and spelled out the different, and often contradictory, directions in which the field was heading.

It is since this particular period that Marcus

has expanded and refined interests in such subjects as elites and the formation of prominent cultural institutions in the USA and other countries. Throughout the 1990s and continuing into the present, he has published and introduced a great deal on a variety of interrelated subjects seeking to further chart, critique, and suggest new directions for the discipline. This work has included a number of edited volumes, an edited monographic series, and a book. Championing creative innovation, as well as ethnographic and historical rigour, Marcus has set the bar for present and future theoretical orientations within the discipline, as well as their evaluation. Open to a wide variety of sources and ideas, Marcus has continually defied attempts to mark his work as carrying out or pushing any one theoretical agenda. Being able to understand the discipline as varying series of simultaneously macro- and micro-related phenomena, Marcus remains strongly committed to preserving the critical role of the discipline, and supporting a wide variety of approaches that do so.

Education

BA Yale University, 1968
BA Queens College, Cambridge (passed the BA Tripos examination, 1968–9)
Ph.D. Harvard University, 1976

Fieldwork

Kingdom of Tonga, 1970–1985
USA, 1985–Present
Portugal, 1997–Present

Key Publications

(1983) (ed.) Elites; Ethnographic Issues, Albuquerque: University of New Mexico Press.
with Fischer, Michael M.J. (1986) Anthropology as Cultural Critique, Chicago: University of Chicago Press.
with Clifford, James (eds)(1986) Writing Culture: The Poetics and Politics of Ethnography, Berkeley: University of California Press.

(1998) Ethnography through Thick and Thin, Princeton: Princeton University Press.

DREW WALKER

Marriott, McKim

b. 1924, St Louis, Missouri, USA

McKim Marriott borrowed from social psychology and linguistics in his early community studies and fused the interests of his teachers, W.L. Warner's in social stratification and Robert Redfield's in the peasant cultures underlying civilisations. He found persons and castes ranking each other by asymmetrical transactions in food and services, and peasants connecting with Sanskritic culture by universalising and parochialising processes. However, since residents thought lateral distinctions as important as vertical ones, Marriott developed a more comprehensive analysis, aiming to employ the civilisation's own analytic categories and logics in an Indian ethnosocial science. Drawing on his and his associates' field research as well as on Indic sociological, biological, and cosmological texts, Marriott has posited core variables that South Asians have used in making distinctions between unmarking and marking (advantaged and disadvantaged), mixing and unmixing (hotter and cooler), and matching and unmatching (coherent and incoherent) people and things. Like native thinkers, he maintains, Marriott combines these variables to analyse Indian families, genders, the life course, emotions, classes, political styles, religions, architecture, etc. His models reveal both homologies among these phenomena and sources of the civilisation's overall diversity. Marriott was the first to posit more or less 'open' persons whose capacities for exchanging properties through interaction make them composite and 'dividual' (rather than individual) – a suggestion that has spread in Melanesian as well as in South Asian studies. Marriott illustrates his models with multidimensional graphs and tests them through an original game-simulation of Indian rural life called 'SAMSARA'.

Education

MS University of Chicago, 1949
Ph.D. University of Chicago, 1955

Fieldwork

Rural Uttar Pradesh, India, 1950–2, 1968–9,
   1978–9
Urban Maharashtra, India, 1955–7, 1985
Social and mental health centers, India, 1978–9

Key Publications

(1955) *Village India: Studies in the Little Community*,
   Chicago: University of Chicago Press.
(1990) *India through Hindu Categories*, New Delhi/
   London: Sage Publications.

SARAH LAMB

Martin, Emily

b. 11 July 1944, Birmingham, Alabama, USA

Emily Martin undertook doctoral research on
the cult of the dead and marriage patterns in
Taiwan, later turning to Chinese medicine and
healing rites, and establishing an early interest
in questions of gender, national culture, and
embodiment. She turned her attention to
issues of gender, body image, and reproduction in USA society in the 1980s, resulting in
The Woman in the Body, one of the most widely
cited publications in both anthropology and
gender studies. The winner of the Eileen
Basker Prize in 1988, released as a UK edition
(1989), translated into German (1989), and
now in its third edition (2001), *The Woman in
the Body* has had a major impact both within
and beyond anthropology, influencing not
only gender studies, but also science studies,
cultural studies, and scholarship on the body
and embodiment.

The relationship between cultural and
economic forces is also at the heart of *Flexible
Bodies* (1994), in which Martin once again
investigates the relationship between cultural
ideology and embodiment. Contrasting the
idealised bodies of risk-taking corporate
managers against the demonised bodies of
patients dying of AIDS, this innovative and
provocative study explores the complex relationship between dominant cultural imagery
and the underlying forces of economic change.
As in her more recent work on representations
of manic depression, and 'manic capital',
Martin's analytical trademark is her ability to
identify the economic *Zeitgeist* beneath the
cultural trend, and to track this relationship
into very intimate aspects of peoples' lives.

Martin's work on bodies, cells, immune
systems, conception narratives, health, disease,
and reproduction is thus distinguished by
three main themes: the proximity of biological
and economic form, the intimacy of hegemonic ideology, and the irrationality of capitalist
society. Her work offers an unusual combination of classical Marxist argument and startling
cultural insight. These strengths are also the
source of the most common criticism of
Martin's work – that it leaves unanswered the
precise mechanisms of determinism linking
capitalist culture and economy. What is most
appreciated about her work is the ability to
make quite vivid connections that bring into
very clear focus overdetermined points of
conjuncture that are both obvious and peculiar
– such as the connection in her recent work on
'fluid minds' between the manic elements of
stock markets and the fetishisation of manic
illness in contemporary American society.

Emily Martin has taught at the University of
California, Irvine, Yale University, the Johns
Hopkins University, Princeton University, and
New York University. She was awarded a
Guggenheim Fellowship in 1999, and has
held fellowships from the National Endow-
ment for the Humanities (1976), the Amer-
ican Council of Learned Societies (1984), the
Mellon Foundation, the Spencer Foundation,
and the Institute of Advanced Study in the
Behavioural Sciences at Princeton.

Education

BA, with High Distinction and Honours
   University of Michigan, 1962–6

Ph.D. Cornell University, 1966–71

Fieldwork

Taiwan, 1969–70, 1972, 1975
USA, 1981–5, 1989–92, summers 1996–8, 1999–2002

Key Publications

(1973) *The Cult of the Dead in a Chinese Village*, Stanford, CA: Stanford University Press.
(1981) *Chinese Ritual and Politics*, Cambridge, UK: Cambridge University Press.
(1986) *The Woman in the Body: A Cultural Analysis of Reproduction*, Boston: Beacon.
(1994) *Flexible Bodies: Tracking Immunity in American Culture from the Days of Polio to the Age of AIDS*, Boston: Beacon.

SARAH FRANKLIN

Marx, Emanuel

b. 1927, Munich, Germany

The first anthropologist to win the Israel Prize, Emanuel Marx used the strengths of the Manchester School to introduce social anthropology to Israel. Much influenced by his mentor, Emrys Peters, whose Bedouin essays he collected in a posthumous book, Marx made his earliest major contribution, *Bedouin of the Negev*, based on his doctoral thesis, by locating Bedouin and their relations with imposed military government squarely within Israeli society.

Refugees, immigrants, people on the move as nomads loom large in his nine books, all written with a deep sympathy from his boyhood experience, being a refugee from Hitler's Germany. Marx extended his interests widely from the maintenance of West Bank and Gaza Strip refugee camps to North African Jewish immigrants' encounters with bureaucrats, to advocacy in a Bedouin resettlement project.

Marx founded the department at Tel Aviv, which grew so prominently from a Manchester–Tel Aviv research project. This he effectively ran, in the field, with Max Gluckman as its charismatic and peripatetic guru. The work of Shmuel Eisenstadt, Israeli sociology's founder, after the impact of that project, reveals how very considerable Marx's influence has been on the social sciences in Israel.

Coming to social anthropology after having been adviser on Arab Affairs to the Israeli Prime Minister, he served his country in a number of capacities in the quest for peace in the Middle East. Late in life, he became director of the Israeli Academic Centre in Cairo, where he fostered Egyptian–Israeli academic exchange, hugely increased the mutual translation of the countries' literatures, and became the first Israeli social scientist to reach a very wide Egyptian audience through *Al-Ahram*.

Education

MA Hebrew University of Jerusalem, 1958
Ph.D. University of Manchester, 1963

Fieldwork

Negev, Israel, 1960–3
Development town, Israel, 1964–6
West Bank, Gaza, 1968, ongoing

Key Publications

(1967) *Bedouin of the Negev*, Manchester: Manchester University Press.
(1976) *The Social Context of Violent Behavior*, London and Boston: Routledge & Kegan Paul.

RICHARD WERBNER

Mascia-Lees, Frances E.

b. 21 May 1953, USA

Frances E. Mascia-Lees has shaped thinking in anthropology, women's studies, and cultural studies with incisive analyses and reformulations of theory focused on the operation of power and the constitution of 'difference'. She achieved national prominence with the publication of her assessment of the post-modernist theoretical turn in anthropology in the 1980s, which remains the definitive treatment of the topic. In it, she outlined the dangers for anthropologists of turning to post-modern theory to transform the social relations of power inherent in anthropological fieldwork and ethnographic representation. Throughout the 1990s, she went on to analyse cross-cultural representation in film, literature, photography, and a range of contemporary discourses, and to assess the complexities of identification across culture, 'race', and gender at multiple ethnographic sites: tourist locations in Mexico and the Caribbean, museums, consumer culture, and the academy. These investigations resulted in nuanced ethnographies characterised by representational inventiveness.

Mascia-Lees's approach to questions of power and difference in theory and culture has been innovative, interdisciplinary, unorthodox, and revealing. Literalising theory, and using ethnographic analyses of popular culture to interrogate 'high' theory, she has challenged standard assumptions, exposed hidden suppositions, and shaken disciplinary certitudes about representation, the body, the unconscious, spectatorship, subjectivity, and subjection. She used this approach to develop a theory of politically and ethically engaged cultural criticism, set forth in the groundbreaking book, *Taking a Stand in a Postfeminist World*.

Since the late 1990s, Mascia-Lees has been concerned with assessing anthropologists' use of geographical metaphors such as 'local/global' to frame research. She has turned to physics instead to begin to formulate an alternative agenda for anthropology in the twenty-first century, one which simultaneously considers space, time, relation, and the positioned observer, yet retains ethical commitments.

Since the early 1980s, Mascia-Lees has been a professor of anthropology, co-founder of a women's studies programme, and creator of curricula, emphasising writing and critical thinking. Her expert training of students was recognised in 1998 by the American Anthropological Association's (AAA) Mayfield Award for Excellence in the Undergraduate Teaching of Anthropology. In 2001, she undertook the editorship of the *American Anthropologist*, the flagship journal of the AAA. As editor-in-chief, she instituted key changes in the journal with a clear editorial vision, revitalising its appearance, content, and role in the discipline.

Education

BA State University of New York, College at New Paltz, 1976
MA State University of New York, Albany, 1979
Ph.D. State University of New York, Albany, 1983

Fieldwork

Mashpee, Massachusetts, 1979
Multiple sites in USA, 1980–present
Yucatan, Mexico, 1990
British Virgin Islands, 1991

Key Publications

with Sharpe, Patricia and Cohen, Colleen (1989) 'The postmodernist turn in anthropology: cautions from a feminist perspective', *Signs* 15, 1: 7–33.
with Sharpe, Patricia (ed.) (1992) *Tattoo, Torture, Mutilation, and Adornment: The Denaturalization of the Body in Culture and Text*, New York: SUNY Press.
with Sharpe, Patricia (1994) 'The anthropological unconscious', *American Anthropologist* 96, 3: 649–60.
with Sharpe, Patricia (2000) *Taking a Stand in a Postfeminist World: Toward an Engaged Cultural Criticism*, New York: SUNY Press.

NANCY J. BLACK

Mauss, Marcel

b. 1872, Épinal, Vosges, France

d. 1 February 1950, Paris, France

The enduring theoretical legacy of the French tradition in the writing of ethnography owes much to Marcel Mauss. His early tutelage under his uncle Emile Durkheim and the influence of neo-Kantian thought encouraged him to engage with several philosophical lines of enquiry to explore the basis of social relations. His writings, for example on the gift, sacrifice, magic, and 'Eskimo' morphology, crucially shaped later scholarly understandings of how exchange, reciprocity, alliance, and collaboration informed other categories of social phenomena.

Central to his thinking was the idea of the 'total social fact', a phenomenon that represented the foremost cognitive objective of the social sciences, encompassing every aspect of the social system and its functions. It was also fundamental to the understanding of social solidarity and collective sentiments in different cultures. The total social fact informed different institutional values and actions, be they legal, economic, religious, or political facts, they had to be 'facts at once typical and well-studied', and seek to affirm the complete human being.

Mauss did not undertake any fieldwork, utilising his proficiency as a linguist to interpret contemporary ethnographies. Thus, he strongly disagreed with Bronislaw Malinowski's 'market' interpretation of kula among the Trobrianders. Instead, he argued that the kula was part of a vast system of prestations and counter-prestations that embraced the whole social life of the Trobrianders. The forms of exchange in archaic societies were total social movements comprising moral, economic, juridical, aesthetic, religious, mythological, and sociomorphological elements. Hence, whether it was kula, potlatch, or another form of exchange, all forms of exchange comprised not only exchanges of goods, men and women, inheritances, contracts, property, ritual services, dances, and initiations but also included courtesies and ecstatic trances, states of possession for the eternal and reincarnated spirits.

For Mauss such arguments did not preclude the necessity of recognising that there were different types of gifts based on the morality of the contract. Social life involved a constant give and take, an exchange. In primitive societies simple exchanges of goods, wealth, and produce were transacted not by individuals but by groups identified with particular representatives such as chieftains. Mauss was therefore concerned with the nature of the social force that compelled a return when a gift was given. Thus, among the Maoris, *hau* contained a magical and religious spirit, which animated it and had a hold on its recipient. Among the North American Haida and the Tolgit, gift exchange was conducted through political ranks within the sub-groups where the moral obligation attached to the gift remained even after it was abandoned by the giver. The study of human behaviour was thus a science of manners and civility.

Looking at the seasonal variation of the 'Eskimo', Mauss linked social morphology to elements of anthropology and human geography. Given their migration patterns during the summer and winter months, 'Eskimo' morphology varied with the season and affected modes of collective activity, patterns of residence, and volume and density of the population.

In seeking to establish how authority was legitimated Mauss pioneered an early exegesis on personhood and the idea of individualism. In the West, the concept of the self gives jural, moral, and social significance to the individual as a mortal human being. Mauss, however, recognised that there were other cultural conceptual expressions of personhood. Thus, the idea of the individual, prevalent in Western thought, is neither universal nor immutable but is derived from a particular social context.

Mauss was interested not just in the moral development of sacrifice as a phenomenon but also its mechanisms: how a sacrifice evolved from being a gift in primitive culture to a rite. Sacrifice entails the interdependence of both sacralisation and desacralisation. Despite the multiplicity of sacrifices practised in different cultures, the same elements recurred in these performances. For Mauss, sacrifice was a religious act that, through consecration of a victim, modified the moral condition of the person who accomplished it or the objective with which he or she was concerned.

Although the legacy of Mauss's rich contributions remains fragmented, his authoritative ideas continue to influence ethnographers several decades later. His was an early attempt to study societies comparatively and holistically.

Education

University of Bordeaux
École Pratique des Hautes Études, Paris

Key Publications

(1964) *Sacrifice, Its Nature and function (Essai sur la nature et le fonction du sacrifice, 1899)*, Chicago: University of Chicago.

(1954) *The Gift: Forms and Exchange in Archaic Societies (Essai sur le don, 1925)*, Glencoe, IL: Free Press.

(1979) *Seasonal Variations of the Eskimos, a Study in Social Morphology (Essai sur les variations saisonnières des sociétés Eskimos, 1906)*, London: Routledge & Kegan Paul.

(1985 [1938]) 'A category of the human mind: the notion of person; the notion of self', in M. Carrithers, S. Collins, and S. Lukes (eds) *The Category of the Person*, Cambridge and New York: Cambridge University Press.

KUSUM GOPAL

Maybury-Lewis, David H.P.

b. 1929, Hyderabad, Pakistan

d. 2 December 2007, Cambridge, Massachusetts, USA

David Maybury-Lewis is internationally recognised for his research on South American indigenous societies and human rights advo-

cacy. He taught at Harvard University since 1960. Maybury-Lewis's primary fieldwork focused on the Xavante of Brazil. He initiated the Harvard Central Brazil Project (1962–6), team-based comparative fieldwork on indigenous social organisations that trained an influential group of American and Brazilian anthropologists. Maybury-Lewis also taught in and helped establish several postgraduate anthropology programmes in Brazil.

Maybury-Lewis's chief theoretical contributions relate to kinship and dual organisation. He and his students cleared up anomalies presented by kinship systems of Central Brazilian societies and showed that these systems were best analysed as part of an investigation of cultural categories, necessitating understanding of native theories of their own cultures. These conclusions marked a departure in kinship analysis, a central preoccupation of sociocultural anthropology. This led to a rethinking of dual organisation, previously thought to be the same thing as a society divided into intermarrying halves, or exogamous moieties. Claude Lévi-Strauss accounted for such systems in terms of elementary kinship structures, according to which dual organisation expressed reciprocity based on elementary structures of thought. Maybury-Lewis, on the other hand, departed from the establishment of a separation between exogamous moieties and dualistic systems of thought, which he considers the essence of dual organisation. He showed how binary ideologies underlie dual organisation in tribal societies and empires alike, and how their appeal lies in their ability to combine human preoccupations with human experience in a harmonious equilibrium theory.

Maybury-Lewis had long been a public anthropologist. His work with the Xavante was reported in academic ethnography and in a popular account (*The Savage and the Innocent*, 1965). Maybury-Lewis's fieldwork took place during a period in which state expansion drastically affected indigenous peoples, so in 1972 he and his wife Pia founded Cultural Survival, a pioneer indigenous rights advocacy organisation. In international venues he has testified against the negative effects of development on indigenous peoples. Maybury-Lewis also published on ethnic pluralism, arguing for a rethinking of the nation-state to accommodate pluri-ethnic models of co-existence.

This advocacy presaged debates over anthropologists' responsibilities in the 1990s, and earned Maybury-Lewis recognition as a key spokesperson on human rights. The combination of academic and public intellectual work encapsulates his contributions to anthropological practice. He has been recognised with international awards and membership in numerous learned societies.

Education

BA University of Cambridge, 1952
MA Universities of Cambridge, Oxford, and São Paulo, 1956
Diploma in Anthropology, University of Oxford, 1957
D.Phil. University of Oxford, 1960

Fieldwork

Xerente, Kraho, Brazil, 1955–6
Xavante, Brazil, 1958–9, 1982
Northeastern Brazil, 1969–70 (elites)
Sulawesi, 1973, 1974, 1975
Xerente, Brazil, 1984

Key Publications

(1967) Akwe-Shavante Society, London: Oxford University Press.
(ed.) (1979) Dialectical Societies: The Gê and Bororo of Central Brazil, Cambridge, MA: Harvard University Press.
with Almagor, Uri (eds) (1989) The Attraction of Opposites: Thought and Society in the Dualistic Mode, Ann Arbor: University of Michigan Press.
(2002) Indigenous Peoples, Ethnic Groups, and the State, Boston: Allyn & Bacon.

BRET GUSTAFSON

Mayer, Adrian C.

b. 1922, London, UK

Adrian Mayer's career is characterised by extensive fieldwork and an emphasis on empirical detail. Principally known for his research in central India, he has also published on overseas Indians (notably in Fiji), and on work conducted in Pakistan and Japan. Analytically, his work can be seen as an extension and development of his early teacher Sir Raymond Firth's concern with the relationship between what were then called social structure and social organisation.

Mayer's first book, on land tenure in Malabar, introduces a number of themes that recur throughout his work: 'applied', relevant anthropology; the revealing use of quantitative data from surveys and censuses; the influence of wider political structures; and a seamless integration of the intimate case study (the grassroots of social organisation) with the broad abstraction of general principle (the over-arching social structure). His most significant contribution is undoubtedly derived from his work in the village of 'Ramkheri' in what is now Madhya Pradesh. The comprehensive detail of intercaste commensality in Caste and Kinship in Central India (1960) later served as a major source for Dumont's Homo Hierarchicus (1966), while the focus on sub-caste endogamy in the context of village exogamy led to a conclusive break with the earlier view of India's villages as autonomous republics.

Education

BA St John's College, Annapolis, USA, 1943
PG Diploma in Anthropology, London School of Economics, 1949
Ph.D. London School of Economics, 1953

Fieldwork

Malabar, Kerala, South India, January–May 1950

Fiji (Indian community), 1950–1, 1971

Central India, 1954–5, 1956, 1960–1, 1976, 1979–80, 1983, 1991–2

Vancouver, Canada (Sikh community), 1959

Pakistan, 1964–5

Princely States, India, 1982–3, 1984–5

Japan, 1987–8

Key Publications

(1960) *Caste and Kinship in Central India: A Village and Its Region*, London: Routledge & Kegan Paul/Berkeley: University of California Press (republished Delhi: Universal Press, 1986).

(ed.) (1981) *Culture and Morality: Essays in Honour of Christoph von Fürer-Haimendorf*, Delhi: Oxford University Press.

MARCUS BANKS

Mead, Margaret

b. 16 December 1901, Philadelphia, Pennsylvania, USA

d. 15 November 1978, New York City, USA

In the public eye, Margaret Mead was the most prominent anthropologist of her generation and the first woman to attain a central position in the discipline. Her legacy, however, has been a contentious one, with her penchant for popularisation outside the academy eliciting considerable critique from colleagues within the discipline. Mead's principal professional affiliation was with the American Museum of Natural History in New York, lasting from 1926 until her retirement in 1969; only in 1954 did she receive an adjunct appointment at Columbia.

Mead's first break with the Americanist anthropological tradition was her insistence on doing fieldwork in the Pacific rather than with American Indian societies, which she considered moribund. Her single Americanist experience with the Omaha was disastrous. After a library dissertation on cultural stability in Polynesia, Mead went to Samoa in 1925 to explore the culture-specific forms of adoles-

cence in a non-Western society, a topic suggested by Franz Boas. Boas's own interests were changing at this time from historical to psychological questions; Mead and Ruth Benedict were the primary proponents of the new orientation. Mead was attracted to the non-historical, natural science side of British social anthropology and acquired a second mentor in A.R. Radcliffe-Brown. *Coming of Age in Samoa* (1928) was a best-seller, but Mead also wrote a more technical monograph on the social organisation of a Tau village.

Mead went on to study seven New Guinea and Pacific cultures in the next fourteen years, deploying the Pacific as a convenient laboratory for a typology of potential human cultural variation. Her comparative work on adolescence, sex and temperament, socialisation and adult character supplemented her fieldwork observations in any single society. Except for her initial Samoan research, Mead worked with partners or students in the field. She was successively married to Pacific ethnographers, Reo Fortune and Gregory Bateson. Mead and Bateson worked extensively in Bali, producing pioneering studies in visual anthropology in the course of studying national character and socialisation.

During the Second World War, Mead worked for the government to ensure public acceptance of food rationing, producing an optimistic interpretation of American national character in 1942. She also pioneered, with Ruth Benedict, the development of the 'culture at a distance' method of ethnographic analysis. After the war, she turned increasingly to public fora, through lectures and popular writing. From 1961 to her death in 1978, Mead wrote a regular column for *Redbook* magazine, offering her anthropological perspective of cultural relativism on a multitude of topics.

At different times in her career, Mead's position on the relative importance of culture and biology actually changed considerably. In the 1930s, she was impressed by the degree to which culture appeared to determine behaviour and personality, e.g. in sex roles. After the war, however, her interest in the inseparability of culture and biology (race) re-emerged.

Because she was convinced that the world had changed immensely since her first fieldwork in 1925, Mead briefly but systematically revisited her former field sites and encouraged restudy by a variety of collaborators. She was further concerned to document her own participation in the history of American anthropology, writing an autobiography of her early years, collecting the letters and papers of Ruth Benedict, writing a brief biography of Benedict, and publishing her own early letters from the field (1977).

In 1983, Australian social anthropologist Derek Freeman published a potentially devastating attack on Mead's Samoan fieldwork, based on his own study of political and social organisation in another part of Samoa decades later. He asserted that Mead did not actually do much of the work Boas had entrusted to her, and that her youthful informants, in the way of young women, lied to her and assumed she would know they were joking. This purported exposé was not published during Mead's lifetime so that she could respond. Freeman used his critique of Mead in Samoa as an excuse to attack Boasian anthropology from a sociobiological standpoint (although this standpoint is not clearly acknowledged in the text). Most American anthropologists, including many who had criticised Mead's ethnography as subjective and impressionistic, rallied round to defend her reputation against what they considered decontextualised polemic. Public loss of respect both for Mead and for anthropology, however, has been substantial. Nearly two decades later, the controversy shows few signs of abating.

Education

BA Barnard College, 1923
MA Columbia University, 1924
Ph.D. Columbia University, 1929

Fieldwork

Samoa, four New Guinea cultures, Bali, 1925–39
Restudies in Manus, Tambunam, Samoa, Arapesh

Key Publications

(1928) *Coming of Age in Samoa: A Psychological Study of Primitive Youth for Western Civilization*, New York: William Morrow.
(1935) *Growing up in New Guinea*, New York: William Morrow.
(1935) *Sex and Temperament in Three Primitive Societies*, New York: William Morrow.
(1977) *Letters from the Field, 1925–1975*, New York: Harper & Row.

REGNA DARNELL

Medicine, Beatrice A.

b. 1 August 1924, Standing Rock Reservation, Wakpala, South Dakota, USA

d. 19 December 2005, Bismark, North Dakota, USA

As a child growing up on the Standing Rock Reservation in Wakpala, SD, Beatrice Medicine maintained her Lakota Sihasapa tribal heritage, both in her personal life and in her personal career. Her family included both Boasian-trained ethnologist, Ella Cara Deloria, and Indian activist lawyer and academic, Vine Deloria, Jr.. Medicine was one of few Native American scholars to have pursued an academic career, teaching at Haskell Indian Institute and more than thirty colleges and universities across Canada and the USA. She retired from California State University at Northridge in 1988, only to become co-ordinator of women's studies research for Canada's Royal Commission on Aboriginal Peoples, which reported in 1996. She returned to South Dakota after her retirement to develop local leadership.

Academic specialisations in medical anthropology, women's studies, and culture change in Native North American communities grounded her anthropology in engagement with local issues, both in the USA and in Canada. Her applied anthropology included work in urban Indian centers and among aboriginal peoples in Australia and New Zealand as well as in Canada. In 1977 she was chosen as Sacred Pipe Woman in a revival of the Lakota Sun Dance. She received the Distinguished Service Award of the American Anthropological Association in 1991.

Education

BS South Dakota State University
MA Michigan State University
Ph.D. University of Wisconsin, Madison

Fieldwork

Standing Rock and Hunkpapa

Key Publications

with Albers, Patricia (eds) (1983) *The Hidden Half: Studies of Plains Indian Women*, Washington, DC: University Press of America.
(1999) 'Ella Cara Deloria: early Lakota ethnologist (newly discovered novelist)', in Regna Darnell and Lisa Valentine (eds) *Theorizing the Americanist Tradition*, Toronto: University of Toronto Press.

REGNA DARNELL

Meggitt, Mervyn J.

b. 20 August 1924, Warwick, Australia

d. 13 November 2004, New York City, New York, USA

Mervyn Meggitt began his career at the University of Sydney, first going to Central Australia in 1953. Few Aborigines were living independently by that time, so that he had to conduct his research on government-run settlements. While having to reconstruct the tribal life as it had been prior to the 1920s, he was able to observe the working of traditional institutions in the new setting, particularly the settling of disputes and ritual. *Desert People* animated the formalism of classificatory kinship with closely observed case studies and quantified analysis of practice. *Desert People* brought the ethnography of the Australian

Aborigines back into the anthropological mainstream, resetting the terms of the debate for the next generation of Aboriginalists.

Meggitt however turned for his second field study to Papua New Guinea. The New Guinea Highlands were the focus of intensive research from the 1950s to the 1970s, for Australian, British and US anthropologists. Highlanders were still being brought under the *Pax Australiana* when Meggitt began his research in 1955, and he was able to accompany patrol officers on expeditions into uncontrolled territory. He subsequently documented these encounters in his *Studies in Enga History* (1974).

Meggitt's main project was to test the African models of British structural functionalism against the society of the Mae Enga, relating their lineage system to competition for land, through a combination of quantified data and particular case studies. As in his Aboriginal study, he took conflict in its various forms as integral to Enga society.

Meggitt's work on the Enga attracted international interest and in 1965 he left Sydney for the USA. *Blood Is Their Argument* directly addressed the problem of violent conflict, using much the same approach. Warfare had been integral to Enga society prior to the arrival of the Australians and was never completely abandoned: it returned after independence, becoming so widespread that Meggitt did not return after 1982. His collaborative work with R.J. Gordon (1985) was written in the light of these developments, emphasising not only the impact of colonial and post-colonial government on Enga, but also the way in which Enga incorporated these into their local affairs.

Meggitt's work in Andalucia, begun in 1968, did not result in any publication.

Education

BA University of Sydney, 1953
MA University of Sydney, 1955
Ph.D. University of Sydney, 1960

Fieldwork

Enga Province, Papua New Guinea, 1955–7,

1960, 1961–2, 1967, 1970, 1973, 1976, 1969, 1982

Hooker Creek, Yuendumu, Phillip Creek, Central Australia, 1956–60

Western Andalucia, Spain, 1968, 1969, 1971, 1972, 1975, 1981, 1986

Key Publications

(1962) *Desert People: A Study of the Walbiri Aborigines of Central Australia*, Sydney: Angus & Robertson.

(1965) *The Lineage System of the Mae Enga of New Guinea*, Edinburgh: Oliver & Boyd; New York, Barnes & Noble.

(1977) *Blood Is Their Argument: Warfare among the Mae Enga Tribesmen of the New Guinea Highlands*, Palo Alto: Mayfield Publishing Company.

with Gordon, R.J. (1985) *Law and Order in the New Guinea Highlands: Encounters with Enga*, Hanover and London: University of New England Press.

JEREMY BECKETT

Meillassoux, Claude

b. 26 December 1925, Roubaix, France

d. 2 January 2005, Paris, France

Urged by his father, a wealthy industrialist, Meillassoux studied economics in the USA, returning to France to serve in the administration of the Marshall Plan and work for a marketing company. His encounter with the business world soon disillusioned him, and after reading Karl Marx's *Capital* in the late 1950s, he converted to left-wing political activism and Marxian anthropology. Under the guidance of George Balandier, a lone admirer of British social anthropology in a French academe dominated by structuralism, Meillassoux conducted fieldwork among the Guro of The Ivory Coast. His article on subsistence economies in *Cahiers d'etudes Africaines* (1960) is often considered the foundational text of French Marxian anthropology.

Meillassoux's doctoral thesis was an empirical investigation of the transition from subsistence-based to capitalist economy among the Guro, inspired by British kinship studies and Marxian labour theory. The monograph was notable for its use of historical material, its focus on the devastating effects of colonialism, and the central place it accorded to control of women as agents of the reproduction of the work force – themes that Meillassoux would continue to explore in his later work.

In 1962, Meillassoux did fieldwork in Bamako, capital of Mali. His second monograph, published in English and acknowledging his debt to American economic anthropology, discussed the role of voluntary associations in mediating between traditional and modern lifestyles in a context of sudden urbanisation, and argued that voluntary associations are epiphenomena of more fundamental social forces with global roots.

In 1963, Meillassoux joined the Centre National de la Recherche Scientifique (CNRS), where he initiated a long-term regional research programme exploring pre-colonial modes of production in West Africa. He published several influential articles and a third monograph, based on nearly twenty years of field experience in the region. Here, Meillassoux focused on migration, and on kinship (particularly marriage and bride-price payments) as a means of controlling reproduction in traditional subsistence economies. Taking as his point of departure a critique of Marshall Sahlins, he developed a Marxian theory of the 'domestic mode of production', whose contradictions led to the formation of a hierarchy of lineages and a concentration of political power. When capitalist economic relations encroached on this system, they exploited it as a basis for maintenance of a reserve labour-pool.

In the pre-colonial context, however, the domestic mode of production was not conductive to demographic growth. The exploiting society could not maintain the manpower reserves necessary to consolidate political centralisation. In the 1970s and 1980s, Meillassoux therefore argued that pre-colonial African political centralisation was based on an economy of war and trade that mobilised manpower reserves in the surrounding societies through the institution of slavery. In opposition to Marx, he posited that the mode of reproduction, rather than the mode of production, determined the dynamics of such societies. In opposition to Igor Kopytoff, he argued that slavery was incompatible with kinship. As the supreme alien, the slave could never become part of the 'free' community of kinfolk, and could be exploited boundlessly.

During the 1990s, Meillassoux extended Marxian class theory with a theory of the social corps: institutions such as armies, bureaucracies, trade unions, and socialist nomenklaturas, which service particular classes, but stand outside the class system and protect their own interests. He also published critical analyses of apartheid in South Africa, of the IMF and World Bank, of Western exploitation of immigrant labour, and of child labour – which attains prominence when capitalism no longer stands in need of more costly adult labour reserves.

Meillassoux has contributed significantly to anthropological studies of West African agriculture, to studies of migration, urbanisation, slavery, and marriage. His impact on economic and historical anthropology has been profound. His empirically based, materialistic approach to social structure revolutionised French anthropology.

Education

BA Institut d'Études Politiques, Paris, 1947
MA, University of Michigan, 1949
Ph.D. Sorbonne, Paris, 1962

Fieldwork

Guro, Ivory Coast, 1957–8, July 1958–January 1959
Bamako, Mali and Senegal, July 1962–July 1963
Gumbu, Mali, 1965, 1966, 1967, 1969

Key Publications

(1964) *Anthropologie économique des Gouro de Côte d'Ivoire: de l'économie de subsistance à l'agriculture commerciale* (Economic Anthropology of the Guro of the Ivory Coast: From Subsistence Economy to Commercial Capitalism), Paris: Mouton.

(1973) 'On the mode of production of the hunting band', in P. Alexandre (ed.) *French Perspectives in African Studies*, London: Oxford University Press.

(1980) *Maidens, Meal, and Money* (*Femmes, greniers et capitaux*, 1975), Cambridge, UK: Cambridge University Press.

(1991) *The Anthropology of Slavery: The Womb of Iron and Gold* (*Anthropologie de l'esclavage: le ventre de fer et d'argent*, 1986), Chicago: University of Chicago Press.

Further Reading

Schlemmer, B. (ed.) (1998) *Terrains et engagements de Claude Meillassoux* (The Fields and Engagements of Claude Meillassoux), Paris: Karthala.

FINN SIVERT NIELSEN

Meletinskii, Eleasar Moeseevich

b. 22 October 1918, Kharkov, Ukraine

Eleasar M. Meletinskii started with investigations into the dynamic evolution of epic tradition in all the diversity of its national forms – from the European novel to the Eastern romantic epics. His investigations rested on the theoretical premise that different cultures and traditions maintain themselves through the universal mythological and ritual models that occur among peoples all over the world. From the beginning of his academic career, Meletinskii successfully employed a historical-comparative method. He used this methodology in the analysis of the heroic-epic traditions of Turkish peoples. During the 1960s, Meletinskii turned to structural-semiotic analysis, giving birth to a new direction in Soviet science that can be described as structuralist folklore studies. His structural-semiotic methodology comprises two aspects of investigation – synchronic and diachronic. He was the first among Soviet scholars to start using the tools of the natural sciences in social studies.

Meletinskii drew special attention to the social and ethnocultural roots and foundations of the archaic verbal art traditions. In his investigations of numerous texts, he embraced the peoples and folklore of many continents (including the Aboriginal peoples of Australia and Oceania, North American Indians, and peoples of Siberia), comparing them in an effort to find generalisable features, starting from the comparative analysis of their earlier forms and proceeding with the analysis of their transformation in medieval literature (for example, the epic heritage of Scandinavian peoples).

He studied the legacy of universal myths and the process of its transformation into national literary traditions. His comparatively recent studies focused on mythological allusions in the literature of the twentieth century. In The Poetics of Myth, he showed that Kafka, Joyce, and Thomas Mann used archaic patterns of mythological thinking in their works in order to enhance the artistic expressiveness of their texts.

His analytical method was more paradigmatic than syntagmatic and his research into the deeply rooted mythological semantics of traditional motifs led him to studies of folklore archetypes. The result was his corrections of the classical K.G. Jung understanding of archetype. He rejected any unilateral and modernist approaches to the problem of the genesis and functions of the most archaic mental structures in human culture.

Education

BA Institute of History, Philosophy, and Literature of Moscow, 1940

MA Institute of History, Philosophy, and Literature of Moscow, 1941

Ph.D. University of Middle Asia, Tashkent, 1946

Key Publications

(1974) Soviet Structural Folkloristics, introduction

and ed. P. Maranada, vol. 1, the Hague and Paris: Mouton.

(1976) 'Primitive Sources of Verbal Art', in Semiotics and Structuralism: Readings from the Soviet Union, introduction and ed. Henryk Baran, trans. William Mandel, Henryk Baran, and A.J. Hollander, White Plains, NY: International Arts and Sciences Press.

(1994) O literaturnykh arkhetypakh (On Literary Archetypes), Moscow: Press of Russian University for Humanities (Izdatelstvo Rossiiskogo Gumanitarnogo Universiteta).

(2000) The Poetics of Myth, (Poetika Mifa, 1976), trans. Alexandre Sadetsky and Guy Lanuui, New York and London: Routledge.

GALINA KHIZRIEVA

Merlan, Francesca

b. 23 January 1949, Taos, New Mexico, USA

Francesca Merlan came to do ethnography and linguistics around Katherine in Australia's Northern Territory. A proper Boasian, she has published descriptions with texts of the Jawoyn, Mangarayi, Ngalakan, and Wardaman languages, as well as many ethnological papers. These include overviews of Aboriginal kin terms, conception beliefs, religion, gender and women's status, and mother-in-law avoidance, all classic social anthropological topics, and she has also contributed originally to topics of objectified representations of culture, cultural constructionism, entitlement and need, the regimentation of customary practice, and the like bearing on applied anthropology.

Merlan (1981) treated the social organisation of Aboriginal languages and clearly recognised the significance for socioterritorial identities of the continent-wide understanding that the ancestral Dreamings installed indigenous languages on the landscape.

Merlan and Alan Rumsey, married 1980, have taken their partnership to research in Australia, Papua New Guinea, and Bavaria. Merlan and Rumsey (1991) sought to transcend the structure vs process antinomy and address whether it is groups or individuals that exchange in the Papua New Guinea Highlands. They analysed speech as moments of social action that might constitute particular events and groups determinately or not, and they found good evidence in the marking of segmentary person, which indexes the group character of participants.

Merlan (1998) employed Taussig's notion of mimesis to understand the state's management of Aboriginal affairs in this era of self-determination. Aborigines and non-Aborigines interact and develop mutually adjusted understandings of how Aborigines, the first people of the land, were, are, and should be. The demise of classical clan-based identities and the emergence of new regional tribal ones involve continuity and transformation, resting on traditional land–language links but imitating mainstream views of how Aborigines should be organised.

Merlan taught at Tulane, Arizona State, and Sydney before taking a chair in anthropology at the Australian National University in 1995. She has edited *Oceania* and *Oceania Monographs*, and she has also done a number of important land claims.

Merlan's work steers a clear course between the excesses of post-modernism and naïve realism. Derrida, Peirce, Radcliffe-Brown, and Sapir are grist for her mill, but it's her own superb linguistic, ethnographic, and analytic skills that provide the grain and make the nourishing flour for our bread.

Education

BA San Francisco State College, 1968
MA University of New Mexico, 1970
Ph.D. University of New Mexico, 1975

Fieldwork

Katherine Region, Northern Territory, 1976–onward
Nebilyer Valley, Papua New Guinea, 1980, 1981–3
Bavaria, Germany, 1999

Key Publications

(1981) 'Land, language and social identity in Aboriginal Australia', *Mankind* 13, 2: 133–48.
with Rumsey, A. (1991) *Ku Waru: Language and Segmentary Politics in the Western Nebilyer Valley, Papua New Guinea*, Cambridge, UK: Cambridge University Press.
with Morton, J. and Rumsey, A. (eds) (1997) *Scholar and Sceptic: Australian Aboriginal Studies in Honour of L.R. Hiatt*, Canberra: Aboriginal Studies Press.
(1998) *Caging the Rainbow: Places, Politics and Aborigines in a North Australian Town*, Honolulu: University of Hawaii Press.

BRUCE RIGSBY

Merriam, Alan P.

b. 1923, Missoula, Montana, USA

Alan P. Merriam was one of the most important scholarly figures in the anthropological study of the musical arts in the twentieth century, and a founder of the modern field of ethnomusicology. Interested in music from an early age, he was influenced by his relative, the anthropologist, Professor Harry H. Turney-High, to undertake the ethnographic study of jazz at Northwestern University. While there he came under the influence of the leading American cultural anthropologist, Melville Herskovits, and documented the music of the Flathead Indians of his native Montana. His doctoral research, however, moved him closer to Herskovits's interests in the African musics of the Americas. His dissertation on the songs of the Afro-Bahian cults of Brazil represented one of the first attempts to analyse an indigenous folk music through scientifically measured correlations of the occurrence of musical intervals. His long-term ethnomusicological fieldwork, however, was in the then-Belgian Congo, later Zaïre, where he focused on the musical ethnography of the Basongye of Eastern Kasai. By the early 1950s he was already an influential figure in African musical scholarship, and one of the four founders of the Society for Ethnomusicology in 1953. He also served as the first editor of the Society's journal, Ethnomusicology. He was as well an important influence within the African Studies Association and the American Anthropological Association in advancing the study of the arts of black Africa.

Alan Merriam is best known for his landmark volume on method and theory, The Anthropology of Music (1964). In codifying both the major problems in the study of non-Western musical practice and aesthetics, and identifying approaches to their solution, the book became a bible for generations of students in ethnomusicology, and remains one of the most influential books in ethnomusicology ever written. Just as important, Professor Merriam trained several generations of young ethnomusicologists during his years at Indiana University, many of whom have distinguished themselves in departments and programmes throughout the world. In addition to his scholarly and institutional involvements, Professor Merriam was recognised as an authority on the problems of early post-colonial Africa, and served on numerous presidential and governmental task forces, and as a US delegate to diplomatic conferences in Africa. A result of this commitment was his book, Congo: Background of Conflict (1961). Although best known as an Africanist and theoretical generalist, Alan Merriam never relinquished his scholarly commitment to the study of American jazz, reflected in his many superb ethnographic publications over the years in this field.

Education

BA Montana State University, 1947
M.Mus. Northwestern University, 1948
Ph.D. Northwestern University, 1951

Fieldwork

Western Montana, summer 1950
Belgian Congo and Ruanda-Urundi, July 1951–September 1952
Republic of the Congo, July 1959–July 1960

Key Publications

(1964) The Anthropology of Music, Evanston: Northwestern University Press.
(1967) Ethnomusicology of the Flathead Indians, Chicago: Aldine Publishing.
(1974) An African World: The Basongye Village of Lupupa Ngye, Bloomington: Indiana University Press.

DAVID B. COPLAN

Merry, Sally Engle

b. 1944, Philadelphia, Pennsylvania, USA

Sally Engle Merry's scholarship consistently advances academic and popular understandings of the interrelationships between law, culture, politics, and everyday life. Her work centers on three key intellectual problems: how law and culture inform and shape each other, legal arenas as nexus in local and global political and economic processes, and how the consequences of engaging law in struggles for social transformation are complex and contradictory. Merry analyses law as a 'contact zone'. It is a complex site where dominant power is enacted and enforced, but also where subordinated individuals may resist authority through acts of creativity, and where oppositional social and political movements mount strategic campaigns to effect social change.

Based on ethnographic research in small-town New England, Merry's 1990 book explored the use of civil courts by working-class Americans. Critiquing a popular belief that litigiousness is an American cultural trait, she argued that her research subjects usually access the courts as a last resort after informal attempts to resolve disputes have failed. Judicial decisions are significant as complainants rely on the promise of equitable treatment as rights-bearing individuals before US law. Turning her attention to legal pluralism – the co-existence of diverse legal systems within polities – Merry argues that popular justice initiatives acknowledge that multiethnic, stratified societies encompass populations with diverse legal beliefs and practices. However, these alternatives co-exist in hierarchical relationships to the dominant system and are thereby constrained and limited in their capacities.

Merry's analysis of the cultural power of law in the colonisation and decolonisation of Hawaii scrutinises how, in the past and the present, law has been used by the central US government to effect colonial domination by regulating everyday domestic life, economic practices, and structures of governance. At the same time, Merry explores the anti-colonial strategies of indigenous Hawaiian activists who deploy American law to support their assertions of sovereignty against the USA.

Merry's interests in local negotiations of transnational legal processes in areas of gender, sexuality, and domestic violence focus on the regulation of violence against women within the international human rights system. Since 1990 she has been professor of anthropology and co-director of the Peace and Justice Studies Program at Wellesley College, and past-president of the Law and Society Association and the Association for Political and Legal Anthropology.

Education

BA Wellesley College, Massachusetts, 1966
MA Yale University, 1967
Ph.D. Brandeis University, 1978

Fieldwork

Boston, Massachusetts, 1974–6
Urban neighbourhoods around Boston, 1980–5
Hawaii, 1990–2000
UN and Asia/Pacific countries, 2000–3

Key Publications

(1981) *Urban Danger: Life in a Neighborhood of Strangers*, Philadelphia, PA: Temple University Press.
(1990) *Getting Justice and Getting Even: Legal*

Consciousness among Working Class Americans, Chicago, IL: University of Chicago Press.
with Milner, N. (eds) (1993) *The Possibility of Popular Justice: A Case Study of American Community Mediation*, Ann Arbor: University of Michigan Press.
(2000) *Colonizing Hawai'i: The Cultural Power of Law*, Princeton, NJ: Princeton University Press.

DARA CULHANE

Miller, Daniel

b. 1954, London, UK

Daniel Miller's work has focused broadly on consumption and material culture. Trained in archaeology and Oriental studies, Miller soon established himself as a key figure in anthropological studies of consumption, shopping, and modern economy. Miller's first contribution to a theory of consumption in capitalist societies (*Material Culture and Mass Consumption*) appeared at a time when consumption was still a neglected field in anthropology. While many scholars would see consumption merely as the trivial and alienating outcome of capitalist forces, Miller argued that the appropriation of goods is part of the process of social self-creation whereby people attempt to overcome their sense of alienation from the forces that create commodities. Theoretically inspired by Hegelian dialectics, Miller applies the concept of objectification as a means to transcend the dualism of subjects and objects. This dualism lies at the very core of perspectives that dismiss consumer culture as inauthentic and not relevant to social theory. Focusing on the ways in which social relations are continuously maintained and refashioned through the use of physical objects, Miller has placed material culture at the heart of both social theory and ethnography.

More than many scholars in the field of consumption, Miller has insisted upon an ethnographic approach. Through extended fieldwork, first in Trinidad, later in North London, he has explored the social contexts of capitalism, from marketing (Trinidad) to shopping (North London). While sociological studies have often emphasised an aesthetic dimension of shopping through a focus on narcissistic self-interest and the making of a personal identity, Miller has brought attention to an ethical dimension as he demonstrates the integral role of shopping and consumption in the maintenance of kinship, friendship, and love. Through these studies he has also focused upon the notion of thrift, and developed an original analysis that highlights corresponding elements of shopping and rituals of sacrifice.

Miller has pursued the ethnographic approach to fields that do not easily lend themselves to the traditional anthropological fieldwork, such as shopping, capitalism, and the Internet. His extensive production includes books on a wide range of topics such as Christmas, pottery, home interiors, capitalism, fashion, sexuality, cars, and 'virtualism'. He is the founding editor of *Journal of Material Culture* and was a Lewis Henry Morgan Lecturer in 1998. Highly influential in the field of anthropology, Miller has, through his focus on material culture, also served to bridge anthropology and other disciplines, such as sociology, human geography, and cultural studies.

Education

Ph.D. University of Cambridge, 1983

Fieldwork

Moluccas, Indonesia, 1975
Solomon Islands, 1976–8
Malwa, central India, 1979, 1981
London, public housing estate, 1986
Chaguanas, Trinidad, 1988–9, 1999
North London, shopping, 1994–5
London, local government audit, 2001

Key Publications

(1987) *Material Culture and Mass Consumption*, Oxford: Basil Blackwell.
(1994) *Modernity – An Ethnographic Approach:*

Dualism and Mass Consumption in Trinidad, Oxford: Berg.
with Slater, D. (eds) (2000) *The Internet*, Oxford: Berg.
(2001) *The Dialectics of Shopping*, Chicago: University of Chicago Press.

MARIANNE E. LIEN

Mintz, Sidney W.

b. 16 November 1922, Dover, New Jersey, USA

It is hard to think of anthropology in the Caribbean and not think of Sidney Mintz; moreover, his work in the field of history may also be seen as equally seminal. Mintz first went to the Caribbean in 1948 as a member of Julian Steward's 'People of Puerto Rico' project along with Eric Wolf, Robert Manners, and others. His early essays on the Caribbean as a sociocultural area helped define the region as a conceptual unit of analysis, but his work has consistently sought to bring the region into the general discourse of anthropology. His contributions to the anthropology and history of the Caribbean range widely from the macroscopic to the microscopic, and his insights stem from the combination of keen ethnography with astute history and political economy. While his family upbringing prepared him for his subsequent intellectual trajectory (something he reflects upon explicitly in later publications), it was the hemispheric vastness of the Afro-American saga and its hidden importance in world history that has driven the depth and engagement of his vision as a Caribbeanist.

As the oldest sphere of European colonialism, Mintz shows that Caribbean societies are only superficially non-Western – indeed, that the region's 'precocious modernity' (his phrase) more accurately can be seen as the most Westernised part of the so-called First World. The growth of colonial economies based on African slavery, the plantation system, and sugarcane was an integral part of the rise of European commerce, industry, and 'development'. He importantly reframed our understanding of the plantation experience as agro-industrial in character, that we should not be fooled by the rural/urban distinction or by distinctions in time, seeing the slaves as proletarians in disguise. Various works illuminate the patterns and variations of 'reconstituted' peasant formation in the region, a mode of socioeconomic organisation that has existed – even thrived – in dynamic tension with plantation domination across time and space.

His work suggests that scholars of post-colonialism may not be paying sufficient attention to the New World – especially the Caribbean, whose first colonies became thus three centuries before Africa was conquered by Europeans. As a pioneer in what has now come into vogue as historical anthropology, Mintz's work – along with Caribbean studies in general – has long had an integral historical dimension. Because of its lengthy colonial past, the role of labour coercion, and the fact that all Caribbean traditions have had to be reinvented, Mintz shows how the region is ideal for anthropological interest in cultural change, creativity, and continuity, and for studies of political economy and forms of resistance.

Mintz himself sees *Worker in the Cane* as his most important contribution; published in 1960, it has never been out of print. Narrating the life story of a sugarcane worker, his family, and their town in south-central Puerto Rico, Mintz's ethnographic work not only illuminates Caribbean society and history from the inside-out but also represents a landmark in anthropological life history studies.

Initially published in 1974, *Caribbean Transformations* represents a collection of some of Mintz's more important essays in Caribbean anthropology covering a period of more than two decades. These papers range from the culture history of a Puerto Rican plantation to the historical sociology of peasantries, villages and markets in Jamaica, and finally to the problem of nationalism in the region.

Mintz is perhaps best known to many for his *Sweetness and Power* – an important contribution to political economy and social history linking the transformation of Caribbean islands into a series of plantation economies with changing diet and increasing sugar consumption in England from the seventeenth to the nineteenth centuries. Treating capitalism as a cultural economy, the changing structure of consumption is connected with proletarianisation and related changes in global class structure.

Particularly noteworthy among Mintz's several collaborative endeavours is his *The Birth of African-American Culture*, co-authored with Richard Price – a landmark in Caribbean ethnology that advances a coherent anthropological argument concerning the origins and dynamism of Afro-American cultures.

Education

BA Brooklyn College, 1943
Ph.D. Columbia University, 1951
MA, *honoris causa*, Yale University, 1963

Fieldwork

Puerto Rico, 1948–9, 1953, 1954, 1974, 1976
Jamaica, 1952, 1954
Haiti, 1958–9, 1961
Iran, 1966–7
Spain, 1988
Hong Kong, 1996, 1999
USA, 2000

Key Publications

(1960) *Worker in the Cane: A Puerto Rican Life History*, New Haven: Yale University Press [reprinted by W.W. Norton & Company, New York, 1974].
(1974) *Caribbean Transformations*, Chicago: Aldine Press. [reprinted by Columbia University Press, New York, 1989].
(1985) *Sweetness and Power: The Place of Sugar in Modern History*, New York: Viking-Penguin.
with Price, Richard (1976) *An Anthropological Approach to the Study of Afro-American History: A Caribbean Perspective*, Philadelphia: Ishi Publications [reprinted as *The Birth of African-American*

Culture: An Anthropological Perspective, Boston: Beacon Press, 1992].

KEITH E. MCNEAL

Mitchell, James Clyde

b. 21 June 1918, Pietermaritzburg, South Africa

Clyde Mitchell pioneered several areas in social anthropology and sociology, most notably in the study of urbanisation and in the development of methodology. A vital member of the Manchester School, he was in many ways the anchor-man developing Max Gluckman's ideas in innovative ways and continuing the Manchester direction in research in the Central and Southern African region. This was so during his directorship of the Rhodes–Livingstone Institute (later Institute of African Research, University of Zambia) and later during his tenure as professor of African studies at UCRN (later University of Zimbabwe).

Never convinced of the distinctions between social anthropology and sociology he contributed to both fields, becoming increasingly interested in the rigorous study of social complexity. He insisted that social scientists should base their understanding on intensive fieldwork (of the anthropological participatory sort), its findings expanded and tested through the application of statistical and mathematical techniques. He argued that the kind of insights and understandings these different approaches afforded were simultaneously distinct (non-reducible) and complementary. His own original research demonstrates his methodological point and is perhaps best represented in The Kalela Dance (1957), a landmark study of urban ethnicity that is as fresh and relevant today as when it was written. Mitchell came to this study, which was centered in the Zambian Copperbelt town of Luanshya, after extensive anthropological fieldwork among the Yao of Malawi. This latter work involved a development of the case method in anthropology. It became the basis for his championing of the 'extended-case method' – the study of the

same persons through a succession of linked dramatic events – which was influential upon the later work of Victor Turner and Jaap Van Velsen.

In The Kalela Dance, Mitchell describes an urban 'tribal' dance showing that it was a construct of modern urban life, an invented tradition. This was so as well with the concepts of tribe or ethnic group, created forms hybridising related though different customary and linguistic traditions. His important finding was that ethnicity or ethnic categorisation was a method by which African urbanites constituted their social relations in highly fluid and volatile situations. Mitchell developed a variety of statistical and mathematical procedures to be applied to survey data in order to test ideas that were grounded in his field observations. The Kalela Dance remains one of the more important landmark studies of ethnicity prefiguring other more recent orientations and in some ways still in advance of them.

Following on the work of Godfrey Wilson (the first director of the Rhodes–Livingstone Institute), Mitchell became interested in social change as this received focus in the mining towns of Zambia. In particular, he explored the phenomenon of labour circulation, whereby migrants stayed for periods in the towns eventually to return to their rural homes. This circulation was not merely a function of the colonial political economy but was influenced by the impact of urban- and rural-centered forces as these were mediated through specific structures of social relations. He disagreed with Wilson's modernisation hypothesis that predicted a gradual drift to the dominant urban-industrial form. Mitchell insisted that the African migrants to the towns could be oriented in multiple directions simultaneously. Social change was multidirectional and not unilinear, an idea that accords well with certain arguments in post-modern anthropology but missed by some of the proponents who have surveyed his work.

Mitchell needed tools to further develop his ideas. This was one reason for his attraction to Elizabeth Bott's application of the concept of social network to London families, the importance of the idea being further foreshadowed by Philip Mayer's work among the urban Xhosa of South Africa. Encouraging his students in Southern Africa and later in England to pursue the idea, Mitchell was at the forefront in the application of the social network idea to the study of social complexity. He was in the vanguard of the application of mathematical concepts to advance insights gained from the concept.

In numerous ways Mitchell's career bridges what many might see as the transition from a functionalist and modernist social science into post-structuralist post-modernity. Always suspicious of closed- and static-system perspectives he concentrated on approaches that drew attention to the fluidity and flux of everyday life, hence the direction of his research and methodological developments.

Education

BA Natal University College, 1941
D.Phil. University of Oxford

Fieldwork

Lamba survey, Zambia (then Northern Rhodesia), 1946
Ethnographic study of Yao, Malawi (then Nyasaland), 1946–50
Sociodemographic study in urban Zambia, 1950–3
Urban attitudes, Zimbabwe (then Southern Rhodesia), 1965

Key Publications

(1956) The Yao Village: A Study of the Social Structure of a Southern Nyasaland Tribe, Manchester: Manchester University Press.
(1957) The Kalela Dance, Rhodes–Livingstone Paper no. 27, Manchester: Manchester University Press.
(ed.) (1969) Social Networks in Urban Situations, Manchester: Manchester University Press.

(1987) Cities, Society and Social Perception: A Central African Perspective, Oxford: Clarendon Press.

BRUCE KAPFERER

Miyaoka, Osahito

b. 1936, Kobe, Japan

As a linguist, Osahito Miyaoka has been working on the study of the Yup'ik language in Alaska since 1967. However, his work is not confined to the pure linguistics of the Yup'ik language, but is expanded to consider its sociolinguistic aspects. He was engaged in the joint project for the preparation of course contents for Yup'ik orthography and grammar for school education in 1967–9. Yup'ik Eskimo Grammar and Yup'ik Eskimo Orthography are the products of the joint study in this period. Subsequently, he was involved in the enforcement of bilingual education programmes as well, and in 1977–84 he took part in the training of teachers for bilingual education at Bethel, Alaska.

Also interested in their culture, Miyaoka depicted Yup'ik ethnography based on their oral traditions and ritual ceremonies in a book entitled Eskimo: Kyokuhoku no Bunkashi (Eskimo: Ethnography of Polar Culture) in 1987. Moreover, since 1988, he has organised a project with younger linguists to study the languages of the North Pacific Rim in order to clarify the genealogy and typology of those languages. This project has currently been integrated into his new project concerning the endangered languages of the Pacific Rim. Thus, Miyaoka's work, starting from the purely linguistic study of the Yup'ik language, has been expanded to solve the very sociolinguistic issues that face minor languages today.

Education

BA Osaka University of Foreign Languages, 1959
MA Kyoto University, 1963

Fieldwork

Yup'ik, Fairbanks, Alaska, 1967–9
Yup'ik, Bethel, Alaska, 1977–84
The project of languages of the North Pacific
Rim, 1988–2000

Key Publications

with Mather, Elsie (1979) *Yup'ik Eskimo Ortho-graphy*, Fairbanks: Yup'ik Language Center, University of Alaska.
with Oshima, M. (1997) *Language of the North Pacific Rim*, Kyoto: Graduate School of Letters, Kyoto University.

TAKAKO YAMADA

Moeran, Brian

b. 1944, Woking, UK

A major figure in the anthropology of Japan, Brian Moeran is best known for his work on traditional Japanese craft production, advertising, consumption, and the media. His early fieldwork focused on a village of western Japan famous for its local pottery, and this formed the basis for both a personal memoir (*Ôkubo Diary*, 1985) and an academic study of ceramics production. In this, Moeran analysed the impact on local pottery of art theories from Japan and abroad, and of the institutions that developed around the appreciation and marketing of these objects. His interest in the language of advertisements led to his later work on the advertising industry, based on fieldwork in a Tokyo advertising agency. In this, he analysed the organisation and politics of the industry, and the relations between the company, its clients, creative artists, and the media. The connecting theme in his work is the importance of going beyond surface appearances to consider the strategies of producers and dealers in the assignment of cultural value. As series editor (with Lise Skov) of the Curzon–Hawaii ConsumAsiaN series of monographs, Moeran has also played an important role in making consumption a major research field within East Asian anthropology.

Education

BA School of Oriental and African Studies, London, 1975
Ph.D. School of Oriental and African Studies, London, 1980

Fieldwork

Oita, Japan, 1977–9, 1981–2
Tokyo, Japan, 1990, 1992

Key Publications

(1996) *A Japanese Advertising Agency: An Anthropology of Media and Markets*, Richmond, UK: Curzon; Honolulu: University of Hawaii Press.
(1997) *Folk Art Potters of Japan: Beyond an Anthropology of Aesthetics*, Richmond: Curzon.

JEREMY EADES

Mooney, James

b. 10 February 1861, Richmond, Indiana, USA

d. 22 December 1921, Washington, DC, USA

James Mooney, the son of Irish Catholic immigrants, sympathised from childhood with the plight of Native Americans as culturally oppressed peoples. His political consciousness was built around the rapid disappearance of traditional Indian cultures in the face of encroaching civilisation. By the age of eighteen, he was a journalist with strong political convictions.

In 1882, three years after its founding, Mooney wrote to Major John Wesley Powell, director of the Bureau of American Ethnology, cataloguing a decade of his library research into the tribes, languages, local names, and histories of the Indians and requesting a scientific appointment to continue this work. He was rejected because of his lack of linguistic experience and limited budgets for paid staff, but Mooney refused to accept Powell's decision. Finally, in 1885, he appeared in Washington and volunteered his services without salary until the next fiscal year. Powell put him to work on the tribal synonymy, a project quite comparable to Mooney's independent scholarship. Eventually his position at the Bureau was normalised and Mooney remained employed there throughout his career.

Mooney was eager to obtain first-hand contact with the Indians. His initial Cherokee fieldwork began with collecting material culture and learning the language. Gradually, he gained access to the small remaining number of Cherokee medicine men, often playing one of them against the others to record their knowledge. The Swimmer Manuscript, traditional formulas written in the Cherokee syllabary by their current custodian, provided Mooney with a window into the vital contemporary religious practices of Cherokee traditionalists. His cultural relativism was at odds with the rationalism and evolutionary theory that organised most of the work of the Bureau. Mooney was increasingly uncomfortable in the office and preferred to spend as much of his time as possible in the field recording salvage ethnography.

Already Mooney was intrigued by the introduction of Christianity and the mutual influences of two dramatically different cultural systems. Increasingly, he focused on ethnohistorical questions, assuming that the Cherokee religious system continued to adapt to changing external conditions. Mental inferiority was not an adequate explanation.

In 1890, Mooney shifted his focus on the Western Cherokee of Oklahoma to the Plains, where the Ghost Dance religion was spreading rapidly across tribal boundaries. Despite public interpretation of the cultural revitalisation movement as a preparation for war and therefore a threat to white American civilisation, Mooney understood the pan-tribal movement as a desperate alternative to unrelenting oppression. Mooney's powerful book reflects his anger at the tragedy of Wounded Knee with its unnecessary massacre of Indian women and children. Although the volume did not appear until 1896, Powell was worried about political repercussions for the Bureau and tried to minimise the extent of Mooney's sympathy for the ghost dancers.

Mooney became increasingly convinced that particular culture histories had to be studied in detail, through fieldwork. He chose the Kiowa for a decade-long study because they were the most conservative of the Plains tribes. His work on calendar counts and heraldic symbolism made it clear that the old ways were far from gone.

In 1903, Mooney had an opportunity to speak out against the superficial survey methods of the Bureau's ethnographic research. He testified before a Smithsonian committee determined to curtail the activities of the Bureau after Powell's death in 1902. He proposed careful study of typical tribes in each culture area, citing his own work on the Cherokee for the southeastern woodlands and the Kiowa for the southern Plains. Environment would be the major factor distinguishing about thirty such types in America north of Mexico. Mooney envisioned the possibility of a comprehensive study of the Kiowa and emphasised the urgency of salvage research. The methods of natural science would prove inadequate for the study of culture because of the vision quest symbolism by which a meaningful world was constructed. A much more humane, narrative, approach to the experiences of individuals was necessary for the American public to understand the plight of the Indians.

Although much of Mooney's work remained incomplete, he was convinced that time spent in the field was more important than publication. The opportunities to understand another religious tradition have to be seized because they would not come again.

Education

Amateur anthropologist

Fieldwork

Cherokee, 1886, 1887
Plains, beginning in 1890
Kiowa, 1893–1903

Key Publications

(1891) *Sacred Formulas of the Cherokees*, Seventh
    Annual Report of the Bureau of American
    Ethnology for 1886.
(1896) *The Ghost Dance Religion and the Sioux
    Outbreak of 1890*, Fourteenth Annual Report
    of the Bureau of American Ethnology for
    1893.
(1900) *Myths of the Cherokee*, Nineteenth Annual
    Report of the Bureau of American Ethnology
    for 1897–8.
(1932) *The Swimmer Manuscript: Cherokee Sacred
    Formulas and Medicinal Prescriptions*, Bureau of
    American Ethnology Bulletin 99 (edited and
    completed by Frans M. Olbrechts).

REGNA DARNELL

Moore, Henrietta L.

b. 18 May 1957, Saunderton, UK

Henrietta Moore's authoritative contributions
to, and influential critiques of, anthropological
theory and feminist analysis followed from her
fieldwork during the 1980s in Kenya among
the Marakwet. This fieldwork focused on the
Endo experience of gender and revealed that
the vocabulary and activities of Endo women
and men make steady allusions to the physical
and conceptual positions of persons, events, and
objects through different scales of time
symbolised during the ritual processes of
births, circumcision, marriage, procreation,
and death. Gender, Moore argued, needs to be
understood as a process rather than a category,
of 'doing gender' rather than the 'being of it'.
Through 'negotiable dependence' between
women and men, men are only able to control
women so long as they are able to renegotiate
the material basis of their domination and,

thus, can recreate the symbolic value of gender
representation.

As a teacher and ethnographer, Moore has
argued for the importance of being specific
and particular over being comparative and
universal. Thus far, many anthropologists
continue to be preoccupied with cultural
differences stressing intercultural variations at
the expense of intracultural variation within
dominant Euro-American models. Thus, sexes
are constructed as immutable and binary.
Anthropology needs to recognise the potential
of multiple and contradictory subjectivities,
which can be revealed through rigorous
contextualisation of gender and gender relations. Moore has argued that feminist anthropology is more than simply the study of
women, it is a study of the interrelations
between men and women, of the role of
gender in structuring human societies, their
histories, ideologies, economic systems, and
political structures.

Current anthropological writings agree that
there can be no firm universal concept of
'woman' or 'man' that can stand as an
analytical category, nor a taken-for-grantedness
of the universal subordination of women,
male domination, or, indeed, the position of
women. While the boundary between sex and
gender remains tenuous in contemporary
feminist debates, neither sex nor gender can
be collapsed into each other. Sex is the cultural
construction of sexed bodies, while gender is
about the sexual division of labour, cosmological beliefs, and symbolic valuations.

In recent years, praxis theory and phenomenology have influenced Moore's writing. She
has proposed a notion of of bodily praxis that
treats bodies as sites where subjects are
morphologically and socially constructed.
Sex, gender, and sexuality are the product of
material and symbolic conditions mediated
through language and embodied representations. Sex and gender thus are concepts that are
both grounded in our own bodies and our
own experiences but are also a consequence of
different traditions. Inhabiting as we do a
divided, globalised, post-colonial world,
Moore has argued for knowledge production

that both gives primacy to local understandings and integrates the humanist foundations of anthropological thought.

Education

BA, University of Durham, 1979

Ph.D. University of Cambridge, 1983

Fieldwork

Turkoman, Iran, June–August 1978

Marakwet, northwest Kenya, March–July 1980, November–August 1980–1

Northern Province, Zambia (nutrition and fertility), July–September 1986

Sierra Leone, West Africa, December 1986, July 1987 (consultant sociologist on EEC Fisheries Project)

Northern Province, Zambia (fieldwork and archival research on problems of nutrition and agricultural change), August–September 1987

Northern Province, Zambia (agriculture and labour migration), July–September 1988, July–September 1995

Southern Africa (archival and field research), March–April 1992

Mauritius (factory workers, women entrepreneurs), April, June, and September 1995

Mauritius (women entrepreneurs, consultant to Export Processing Zone), April 1996

Key Publications

(1986) *Space, Text and Gender; An Anthropological Study of the Marakwet of Kenya*, Cambridge, UK: Cambridge University Press.

(1994) *A Passion for Difference: Essays in Anthropology and Gender*, Cambridge, UK: Polity Press.

(1988) *Feminism and Anthropology*, Cambridge, UK: Polity Press.

(1999) *Anthropological Theory Today*, Cambridge, UK: Polity Press.

KUSUM GOPAL

Moore, Sally Falk

b. 1924, New York City, USA

Sally Falk Moore studied law for her first degree, worked as a staff attorney at the Nuremberg Trials and then as a lawyer in New York. In the 1950s, she completed a Ph.D. dissertation on government mechanisms and property arrangements in Inca Peru. She showed that the Utopian plan of the Inca government did not correspond to actual practice. There were important local variations in administrative practice and property rights, probably dating in part from the period before the Inca conquest. E.A. Hoebel had argued that legal anthropology should be concerned with juridical postulates. By contrast, Moore concluded that there need not be a single coherent pattern of legal ideals in any given society.

Moore went on to study the workings of law among the Chagga of Tanzania. The Chagga were banana-growers, cattle-keepers, and traders in the nineteenth and early twentieth century. Kilimanjaro, the territory on which they lived, fell under German colonial rule in 1896 and became a British colony in 1916. Around that time, coffee plantations multiplied and cash cropping developed. Moore compared law and legal institutions in these different historical periods with observations she made in post-colonial Tanzania. She found that judicial activities could not be understood outside their political context. Whatever norms were invoked, the courts generally obtained their authority from the political setting (for example, the colonial administration). Thus, Moore challenged Philip H. Gulliver's distinction between political and judicial dispute settlements. She contended that judicial decisions were hardly ever based entirely on norms, although judges will think or pretend that they are.

In the early 1970s, Moore elaborated further the processual approach to legal anthropology. She wondered how the Chagga, a people committed to an ideology of communal harmony, coped with conflict. In the post-colonial context of rapid population growth and land shortage, the Chagga were in a situation of long-term competition for scarce resources with each other. As this could not be openly admitted, some socially vulnerable persons were selected for failure. Those who were rejected were represented as morally inadequate people so that the community could preserve its harmonious self-image. Only a long-term perspective on demographic and economic changes permits us to grasp the significance of these small-scale, local disputes.

Moore suggested that in society in general there was a constant competition between processes of regularisation and processes of situational adjustment. Rituals, rules, laws, and other processes of regularisation are attempts at fixing social life despite the passage of time. In processes of adjustment, people exploit the indeterminacy of situations, for example by manipulating formal rules.

The legal anthropologist studies semi-autonomous social fields, such as Chagga neighbourhoods, which create internal rules, customs, and symbols, but are simultaneously permeated by external rules and decisions.

In 1986, Moore revisited the Chagga material in *Social Facts and Fabrications*. In the nineteenth century, Chagga law was not a domain of knowledge set apart from the flow of social life, but a mix of rules that framed social relationships. In the colonial period, 'customary law' was separated out and treated like a coherent, static set of rules. In reality, the socioeconomic and political circumstances changed over time, and the law with them. As there was no public arena where changing norms could be discussed, customary law was represented as a traditional, time-honoured entity.

In the 1990s, Moore was concerned with political trials in post-colonial Africa, land law, human rights issues, and the work of development agencies.

Moore also has a long-standing interest in the history of her own field. After a 1970 survey paper on anthropology and law, and an essay on the history of the anthropology of Africa in 1994, she assessed the development of legal anthropology again in 1999. In the 1960s and 1970s, a concern with domination and class issues asserted itself alongside the earlier paradigms of law as culture and tradition. Today, legal anthropology is sensitive to the local and global political milieus in which law is imbricated. Moore's early insights into the importance of the historical, political, social, and economic background of legal activities are shared by most anthropologists studying law at the beginning of the twenty-first century.

Education

LL B Columbia Law School, 1945
Ph.D. Columbia University, 1957

Fieldwork

Kilimanjaro, Tanzania, 1968–93
Mali, Burkina Faso, Senegal, Paris, Washington, Berlin, 1991–7

Key Publications

(1958) *Power and Property in Inca Peru*, Morningside Heights, NY: Columbia University Press.
(1978) *Law as Process: An Anthropological Approach*, London: Routledge & Kegan Paul.
(1986) *Social Facts and Fabrications: 'Customary' Law on Kilimanjaro 1880–1980*, Cambridge, UK: Cambridge University Press.
(1994) *Anthropology and Africa: Changing Perspectives on a Changing Scene*, Charlottesville: The University of Virginia Press.

Further Reading

Greenhouse, Carol J. (2000) 'Le droit, le temps et l'anthropologie: le dossier ethnographique de Sally Falk Moore', *Droits et Cultures* 40: 9–73.

ANNE FRIEDERIKE MÜLLER

Morgan, Lewis Henry

b. 1818, Aurora, New York, USA

d. 17 December 1881, Rochester, New York, USA

Lewis Henry Morgan grew up in western New York State, received a BA from Union College in Schenectady, and became a lawyer in 1942. Two years later he moved to Rochester, where successful investments in railroads and Michigan iron works allowed him to retire to full-time scholarship.

Living in the heart of Seneca country, Morgan had always been fascinated by Indian cultures. He turned to ethnology through the interests of a group of young men meeting together in a club called the Grand Order of the Iroquois, with Morgan as their chief. His search for a model Iroquois constitution led Morgan to the nearby Tonawanda Reservation, where he was fortunate to establish a close collaboration with young and educated Seneca, Ely S. Parker and his sister Caroline. Through the Parker family and his own political support of the community, Morgan was adopted into the Seneca Hawk clan. He assumed that the Iroquois were dying out and assiduously devoted himself to cataloguing their traditions while they were still practised. This work ultimately led to the publication of The League of the Ho-de-no-sau-nee, or Iroquois in 1851. In the same year, Morgan married and turned his attention to the law, business interests, and raising a family.

After joining the American Association for the Advancement of Science, Morgan returned to Iroquois ethnology in 1856 and began to formulate his argument about laws of descent. During regular summer business trips to Marquette, Michigan, he realised that the Ojibwa had a similar kinship system to the Tamil of southern India. This led him to believe that the American Indians actually were from India. By 1859 he had prepared a questionnaire, which the Smithsonian Institution agreed to circulate, intended to discover how widespread this system of relationship was. Between 1859 and 1865, Morgan personally collected schedules in the field and correlated the massive descriptive results from his questionnaires. It took him an additional five years to revise the manuscript in a more palatable and accessible form for publication as Systems of Consanguinity and Affinity of the Human Family by the Smithsonian in 1871.

During the last decade of his life, Morgan revamped his kinship argument in a more popular and philosophical format, emphasising the social evolution of inventions and discoveries, government, family, and property. He saw himself as extending Charles Darwin's evolutionary argument to the study of culture. Ancient Society (1877) took for granted the progression from savagery to barbarism to civilisation from a few 'primary germs of thought' or technological advances in subsistence activities. The Iroquois were intermediate between Morgan's savagery and civilisation, although his theory inclined him to de-emphasise their agriculture as mere horticulture. Plow agriculture was the means to lift them out of the stultification of hunting.

Education would bring integration into mainstream society, i.e. civilisation. Morgan believed that savages could be educated to embrace civilisation and was a strong advocate for Indian causes, for example, supporting the Iroquois in their 1840s dispute with the Ogden land company and defending the Sioux after Custer's ignominious defeat at Little Big Horn. He served as a New York State assemblyman but lost a bid to become Abraham Lincoln's Commissioner of Indian Affairs (although Ely Parker held this position briefly under Ulysses S. Grant).

Morgan also wrote up his data on Houses and House-Life of the American Aborigines (1881), arguing that family structure and domestic architecture were integrally connected. He was a pioneer American anthropologist entirely by avocation, without formal training or professional position. In The American Beaver and His Works (1868), he compared the natural indigenous, industrious beaver to the Iroquois themselves – both providing a model for American business prosperity. The beaver embodied the moral values of civilisation.

Morgan's ideas were enthusiastically adopted in the work of John Wesley Powell's Bureau of American Ethnology, founded in 1879 to organise US government Indian researches. However, evolutionary theory of a kind was superseded rapidly in North America by the end of the nineteenth century. Ironically, therefore, Morgan's theory of social evolution has been remembered primarily through its adaptation to his argument for a materialist history by Frederick Engels, whose *Family, Private Property and The State* (1884) became part of a Soviet communist ideology quite removed from Morgan's own position.

Education

BA Union College, 1840

Fieldwork

Tonawanda Seneca, 1844–51
Ojibwa, Western Indians, 1859–62

Key Publications

(1851) *The League of the Ho-de-no-sau-nee, or Iroquois*, Rochester: Sage & Brothers.
(1868) *The American Beaver and his Works*, Philadelphia: J.B. Lippincott and Co.
(1871) *Systems of Consanguinity and Affinity of the Human Family*, Washington, DC: Smithsonian Institution.
(1877) *Ancient Society, or Researches in the Lines of Human Progress from Savagery through Barbarism to Civilization*, New York: Henry Holt & Co.

REGNA DARNELL

Morphy, Howard

b. 1947, Hampton, Middlesex, UK

Well known as an anthropologist of Australian Aboriginal art, Howard Morphy has also made significant contributions in cultural ecology, archaeology, and the history of anthropology. His doctoral fieldwork with the Yolgnu of Northeast Arnhem Land, conducted with his wife, the linguist, Frances Morphy, was the start of an on-going engagement, with projects ranging from the purely academic to the highly practical, such as advising on land rights claims and assisting Yolgnu artists to promote their work through gallery sales and to creative arts fellowships.

Morphy's first book, written to accompany Ian Dunlop's ethnographic film, *Madarrpa Funeral at Gurka'wuy*, adopts a Saussurian approach to mortuary ritual while maintaining a primary focus on the decisions and choices made by participants leading to an understanding of ritual as creative of structure. In his work on Yolgnu art he takes a similar approach, developing key ideas in relation to art as a visual system of communication. For Morphy, the key question is not 'what does [an art object] mean?' but 'how does it mean?'. The multiple coding of communication (language, visual systems) allows for dynamism, as individuals seek to express their ideas through different and, in the Yolgnu case, layered codes. For Morphy art is an integral aspect of the Yolgnu response to colonialism, in which key concepts of 'inside' and 'outside' (the system of restricted ritual knowledge) remain meaningful, while being transformed. Morphy is a staunch defender of aesthetics as a tool of cross-cultural analysis, understanding aesthetics as a human capacity to respond to form, independently of function, and thereby as a field of discourse that mediates between culture/structure on the one hand and the individual's sensible and embodied experience of being in the world on the other. From this perspective Morphy has tracked Aboriginal art out of the local community and into national and international art markets. In his authoritative and exhaustive monograph on Aboriginal art, he pays particular attention to contemporary and avant-garde art, noting the ironic situation in which Aboriginal art is valued for its influence on wider Australian art, but deemed 'inauthentic' if it strays beyond 'traditional' forms. He consequently recommends a collapse of the Australian/Aboriginal distinction by viewing Australian art as a stage in the history of Aboriginal art, thereby removing the hierarchicalising European perspective on world art history.

Education

B.Sc. University College London, 1969
M.Phil. University College London, 1972
Ph.D. The Australian National University, 1977

Fieldwork

Yolngu people, eastern Arnhem Land, Australia, 1973–6, 1998, 1999, 2000, and other shorter visits

Ngalakan and related people, Roper Valey, Australia, 1980–1; briefly in 1998 and 1999

Darwin, Australia, 1984 (responses to Aboriginal art)

Coastal Arnhem Land, Australia, 1999 and ongoing (project director for Blue Mud Bay collaborative anthropological archaeological research on resource use and social organisation)

Biographical work on Aboriginal artist, Narritjin Maymuru, 1995 and ongoing

Archival work on Baldwin Spencer (with Alison Petch and John Mulvaney), 1993–7 and ongoing

Key Publications

(1984) *Journey to the Crocodile's Nest: An Accompanying Monograph to the Film Madarrpa Funeral at Gurka'wuy*, Canberra: Australian Institute of Aboriginal Studies.

(1991) *Ancestral Connections: Art and an Aboriginal System of Knowledge*, Chicago: University of Chicago Press.

with Banks, Marcus (eds) (1997) *Rethinking Visual Anthropology*, New Haven/London: Yale University Press.

(1998) *Aboriginal Art*, London: Phaidon.

MARCUS BANKS

Mühlmann, Wilhelm Emil

b. 1904, Düsseldorf, Germany

d. 1988, Wiesbaden, Germany

Mühlmann was certainly the most important student of Richard Thurnwald (1869–1954), and he surpassed his teacher as regards his impact on German functionalism and ethnosociology (a link between anthropology and sociology), even though he could not match him in the empirical field. Like Thurnwald, Mühlmann covered an interdisciplinary spectrum of interests, though theoretically he was able to carry this through better and more strictly, and thus formulate paradigms for modern anthropology. The tension between the sociologically oriented anthropologists and the historians and morphologists determined the dynamics of post-war anthropology in West Germany. However, Mühlmann had also acquired a profile in the Nazi period, when he desired to become active in social science in the newly acquired 'colonial space' of East Europe.

By training, Mühlmann was a physical anthropologist and social Darwinian (*Sozialanthropologe*), though he came into contact early with the phenomenology of Edmund Husserl (1859–1938), the sociology of Alfred Vierkandt (1867–1953), the anthropology of Richard Thurnwald, and the psychology of Wilhelm Wundt's successor, Felix Krueger (1874–1948). After his dissertation on the Arioi in Polynesia (1931), social sifting and leadership became the leitmotifs of his ethnosociology, which, especially before 1945, were seen as being closely linked with biological selection processes (race as a 'functional variable'). Simultaneously, however, he also concerned himself with the notion of charisma as developed by Max Weber, which he adopted first in understanding the contemporary development of the German 'millennium', and then the anti-colonial movement.

At the start of the Second World War, Mühlmann put forward a combination of his elitist, anti-pacifistic, and Darwinistic 'political anthropology' (1940). In it he was already sketching the scenario for his later research, namely the 'sociology of interethnic systems', in which more highly organised and aggressive groups dominated and marginalised less developed and more peaceable peoples. In contrast to the models of regulated anarchy and segmentary societies in Western European anthropology, the ethnosociology formulated by Thurnwald and Mühlmann concentrated entirely on the state, its rise through conquest, and its maintenance through stratification and bounding, selection and eradication. History was therefore the differentiation of humanity into 'progressive and backward groups' (*Rückzugsgruppen*), the relationship between them being determined in the first instance by force, rule, and exploitation affirmatively understood.

A further strand in Mühlmann's work was oriented towards Nietzsche's 'resentment' and Max Weber's notion of the pariah, which the latter developed in his text on 'Ancient Judaism' (1921). Following this model of the 'last who shall become the first', Mühlmann analysed messianic movements all over the world, especially the Gandhian movement in India (1950). In 1961 he put forward an overall view of such 'revolutionary movements' with egalitarian programmes, the alternative projects of the poor masses against the ruling ideologies of the elites. Yet even these processes, which other schools of sociology analysed sympathetically, became reduced in Mühlmann's work to a problem of leadership. The 'redeemer' and his promises were interpreted in terms of social psychology and religious history: the 'Hitler' experience served as the foil for his 'studies in the sociology of revolution'.

Especially in his Heidelberg years (1960–70), Mühlmann's contribution was the fertile link between anthropology and sociology, exemplified above all through long-term research on Sicily. The insights he acquired into the clientelism of the Mediterranean were milestones on the way to the theory of complex societies that both disciplines were striving for. And yet again, the many-sidedness

of his interests was demonstrated in the two main works of his old age (*Die Metamorphose der Frau*, 1981, and *Pfade in die Weltliteratur* (Paths to World Literature), 1984), one in the direction of religious sociology and feminist theory, the other in the area of literary history, which in fact had always been an important source for him in the formation of sociological theory. Even though his research work in Heidelberg fell victim to student revolts and his life work attracted increasingly severe criticism, he could pride himself on having produced several important pupils, from his younger colleagues, R.J. Llaroyora, E.W. Müller, and H. Reimann, to his adversaries (and students), Christian Sigrist, Fritz W. Kramer, Georg Elwert, Ch. Giordano, and Hans Peter Duerr.

Educational qualifications:

Ph.D., 1932
Habil., venia legendi [lecture licence] University of Berlin, 1938

Fieldwork

Sicilia, 1950 etc.
Research journeys to South and East Asia (India, Thailand, Burma, Ceylon, Indonesia) during the 1960s and 1970s

Key Publications

(1940) *Krieg und Frieden. Ein Leitfaden der politischen Ethnologie* (War and Peace. A Guide to Political Anthropology), Heidelberg: Carl Winter's Universitätsbuchhandlung.
(1948) *Geschichte der Anthropologie* (History of Anthropology), Bonn: Athenäum.
(1961) *Chiliasmus und Nativismus. Studien zur Psychologie, Soziologie und historischen Kasuistik der Umsturzbewegungen* (Chiliasm and Nativism. Studies of the Psychology, Sociology and History of Overthrow Movements), Berlin: Dietrich Reimer.
(1981) *Die Metamorphose der Frau. Weiblicher Schamanismus und Dichtung* (The Metamorphosis

of Woman. Female Shamanism and Poetry),
Berlin: Dietrich Reimer.

BERNHARD STRECK

Munn, Nancy D.

b. 1931, New York City, USA

Munn has a long-term interest in problems
involving cultural forms of space and time; she
has also focused on questions of value and
such specific topics as art and exchange.
Fundamental to her concerns is the creation
of sociocultural meaning as an aspect of the
processes of everyday life. Munn's theoretical
approach is informed by structuralism and
phenomenology but not in any narrow sense.
Overall, she makes extended use of close
symbolic (or semiotic) analysis of discourse
and practice. In her early work among the
Warlpiri, she examined the graphic art in
relation to the wider culture. One of the
important contributions of this study was the
exploration of how overtly simple elements of
the design system, elaborated by men and
women in multiple social contexts, were able
to signify meanings in varied domains and at
different levels of semantic complexity. In her
later work, Munn developed a model of
symbolic process to show how people of a
Melanesian island in the kula exchange ring
sought to create essential societal value for
themselves through transformative actions
yielding extension and control of their social
space-time. This model examined actions such
as those entailed in kula, marriage, and
mortuary exchanges as well as the value-
subversive actions of witchcraft.

Education

BA University of Oklahoma, 1951
MA Indiana University, 1955
Ph.D. Australian National University, 1961

Fieldwork

Warlpiri (Walbiri), Yuendumu, Northwest
  Territory, Australia, 1956–7
Pitjantjatjara, Areyonga, (western central)
  Australia, 1964–5
Gawa Island, Papua New Guinea, 1973–4,
  1975, 1979–81

Key Publications

(1986 [1973]) *Walbiri Iconography; Graphic Representation and Cultural Symbolism in a Central
  Australian Society*, Ithaca, NY: Cornell University Press.
(1986) *The Fame of Gawa: A Symbolic Study of Value
  Transformation in a Massim (Papua New Guinea)
  Society*, Cambridge, UK: Cambridge University Press.

JUDITH A. RASSON

Murdock, George Peter

b. 11 May 1897, Meriden, Connecticut, USA

d. 29 March 1985, Devon, Pennsylvania, USA

G.P. Murdock's most influential achievements
were the reshaping and promotion of Oceanic
ethnography for over two decades following
the Second World War and his systematic
approach to cross-cultural research and consequent results. He published over 120 articles
and books spanning fifty years, including
ethnography, a wide range of theory, and the
data upon which most of these were based.
Dedicated to anthropology as a science, he
relentlessly established conditions to advance
the discipline. Although he directly engaged
some anthropologists (and many outside
anthropology), his influence was broader.
Most of his theories, methods, and results
met with opposition from area specialists and
social and cultural theorists. However, he was
often vindicated when more reliable data
became available; his questions and their

answers had the power to impact the research agenda of even his opponents.

In 1937 Murdock initiated the Cross-Cultural Survey at Yale, with C. Ford and J. Whiting, creating an archive of individual pages of ethnography coded for cultural features. To code these systematically he collaboratively devised a cataloguing system, the Outline of Cultural Materials (1938/82). In the late 1940s he founded the Human Relations Area Files (HRAF), which was directed by Ford. However, HRAF and Murdock adopted increasingly different priorities.

Murdock's approach to cross-cultural research assumed that over time the elements of a culture will become functionally or reciprocally adjusted to each other. Cultures constantly change with innovation or borrowing of cultural features through trade, war, or simple contact. Studying a single culture, we cannot isolate these adjustments because the combination of change and time required to adapt obscures which features are integrated and which are not – we can speculate about relationships, but we cannot know.

Cross-cultural analysis is statistical, since all cultures have features not yet adjusted. Murdock had to address issues relating to statistical reliability; range of coverage, statistical validity of samples, identifying related societies to avoid 'Galton's problem' (correlations due to pre-existing relationships between societies), and facilitating cumulative research. This agenda would take over thirty years.

In *Social Structure* (1949) Murdock analysed data on 250 cultures to evaluate interrelationships between aspects of kinship and social organisation. Despite criticism of data reliability and 'mechanical' methods, most of his conclusions still stand. Murdock recognised the limitations imposed on analysis by his selection of societies and continued to improve his data and methods. *Africa: Its Peoples and Their Culture History* (1959) was a regional study where Murdock applied his comparative method to describe and reconstruct historical movements of peoples and cultural features.

He was strongly criticised by Africanist scholars who argued that it contained ethnographic inaccuracies and was incomplete. These critics could not, however, demonstrate substantial weakness in Murdock's method or core arguments. Further research has confirmed most of the results of this work.

The World Ethnographic Sample (1957) aimed to resolve problems with sampling, and between 1962 and 1980 he serialised the *Ethnographic Atlas* (1967) in *Ethnology* (which he founded in 1960). The Standard Cross-Cultural Sample (1969) was the culmination of Murdock's efforts to create a sound basis for cumulative cross-cultural research. Murdock and White defined a sampling frame of 186 representative societies designed to maximise historical independence, together with tests that corrected for the remaining non-independence in making statistical inferences, overcoming most prior criticisms. Over 100 cross-cultural research studies have been based on this sample, accumulating new data and results.

In 1971 Murdock presented his enigmatic Huxley Memorial Lecture to the Royal Anthropological Institute, 'Anthropology's Mythology', with a pair of dramatic claims; neither culture nor social structure can be reified to serve as an explanation. These were, to the extent they existed at all, our characterisation of patterns of interactions between individuals, not the source of these interactions. Anthropologists had to abandon subjects of a superorganic nature and deal with individuals and their productions to explain what we call social and cultural. After a half-century in anthropology, Murdock was introducing a programme for much of the next half-century – focusing ethnography, cross-cultural research, and theory on diversity of individual experience and choice, not commonality and conformance.

Education

AB Yale University, 1919
Ph.D. Yale University, 1925

Fieldwork

Haida (Northwest Coast, North America), summer 1932

Tenino, Oregon, summers 1934–5

Truk (Micronesia) 1947–8 (he was also leading a team of over forty researchers under the Co-ordinated Investigation of Micronesian Anthropology funded by the US Navy)

Key Publications

(1949) *Social Structure*, New York: The Free Press.

(1959) *Africa: Its Peoples and Their Culture History*, New York: McGraw-Hill.

(1967) *Ethnographic Atlas*, Pittsburgh: University of Pittsburgh Press.

with White, D. (1969) 'Standard Cross-Cultural Sample', *Ethnology* 8, 4: 329–69.

Further Reading

(1988) George Peter Murdock: Retrospective Assessment, *Behavior Science Research* 22.

MICHAEL D. FISCHER AND STEPHEN M. LYON

Murphy, Robert F.

b. 3 March 1924, Rockaway Beach, New York, USA

Robert Murphy served in the US Navy during World War Two and the impact of his experiences in Western Pacific battles during the period of Japanese kamikaze attacks remained with him throughout his life. Following the war, an undergraduate course with Charles Wagley led to his interests in both anthropology and the Amazon. With his wife, Yolanda, Murphy undertook research on Brazil's Tapajos River; he eventually wrote three books on the Mundurucú people. He was also deeply influenced at Columbia by Julian Steward, and by students a few years ahead of him, including Eric Wolf, Morton Fried, and

Elman Service. Murphy's anthropology always reflected both the intellectual cast of the materialist (or Marxian) frame of reference he shared with them and the conviction that careful, committed ethnography, with the real lives of real people as its focus, gives anthropology its *raison d'être*.

Murphy spent 1953–5 as a research associate at the University of Illinois (along with Wolf) under Steward's aegis, and then joined the University of California at Berkeley. During this period he and Yolanda engaged in ethnohistorical research with Shoshone and Bannock peoples of the Great Basin, in conjunction with land claims cases, and published a short monograph. This work drew him to his Berkeley colleague, Robert Lowie, who had worked in the same region a half-century earlier, and Murphy eventually published a volume on Lowie and his legacy. Murphy also conducted research with the Tuareg, nomadic herding people of the Sahel. Uncharacteristically, he published very little on this topic, although his paper examining why Tuareg men are veiled has been anthologised as a classic. He left for Columbia in 1963, where he taught until the end of his career, and chaired the Anthropology Department from 1969–72. Murphy's final field project came as a consequence of being confined to a wheelchair when a spinal tumour rendered him first paraplegic and, finally, quadriplegic. His last book combines autobiography with his research among the severely handicapped in the USA.

A master of the *bon mot*, Murphy sometimes said that he was a materialist on Mondays, Wednesdays, and Fridays and an idealist Tuesdays, Thursdays, and Saturdays. Certainly his published work, as well as everything he had to say in any other context, indicates that he was indeed unwilling to stake a claim on one side or the other of a divide that often agitated the Columbia department in the 1960s and 1970s. *The Dialectics of Social Life*, which I consider Murphy's finest book, is very much a product of this tension. In it he explores the notion, always at the center of his thought, that human social life is marked by cultural beliefs and norms that run at a tangent, if not entirely contrary, to the actual activities people engage in. The anthropologist's task is to explore and analyse what lies behind the obvious, what sorts of underlying sociocultural 'negatives' produce the 'positive' prints we are able to observe, and why it is that so much hangs upon seemingly 'empty' gestures. He drew upon classic social theory from, among others, Simmel and Freud, the nature of anthropology as a discipline, the standard of corpus of ethnographic work, and life in the contemporary USA.

Women of the Forest (co-authored with Yolanda) remains a popular undergraduate text. It is on one hand an accessible ethnography, with vivid accounts of women's daily subsistence and social activities, slash and burn agriculture, Mundurucú mythology, and the nature of head-hunting. On the other, it provides matchless insight into the ways men's public personas are belied by their private insecurities, while women's demure public roles are offset by their domestic influence. Murphy's long-standing theoretical emphases on the importance of the labour process in shaping social organisation and the contradictory ways in which cultural meanings are undercut by practical realities are spelled out in a coherent ethnographic setting.

In his professional life Murphy was, above all else, a teacher and raconteur. Undergraduate classes were known to give him standing ovations and he held court in his office for both graduate students and junior faculty. David Schneider, who taught with Murphy at Berkeley in the 1950s and once described him as one of the two most brilliant anthropologists of his generation, remarked to me that he had never seen Murphy either at a loss for words, nor without some witty and insightful riposte.

Education

BA Columbia University, 1949
Ph.D. Columbia University, 1954

Fieldwork

Pará, Brazil, 1951–2
Idaho and Wyoming, 1954
Niger and Nigeria, 1959–60

Key Publications

(1960) Headhunter's Heritage: Social and Economic Change among the Mundurucú Indians, Berkeley: University of California Press.

(1971) The Dialectics of Social Life: Alarms and Excursion in Anthropological Theory, New York: Basic Books.

with Murphy, Yolanda (1985 [1974]) Women of the Forest, New York: Columbia University Press.

(1987) The Body Silent, New York: Norton.

GLENN PETERSEN

Myerhoff, Barbara G.

b. 1935, Cleveland, Ohio, USA

d. 1985, Los Angeles, California, USA

Barbara Myerhoff's work focused on the role of symbols and narratives in social action. Her doctoral work on the Huichol Indians of Mexico examined three dominant symbols as they were invoked in the pilgrimage to Wirikuta, a desert region mythologically identified with their original homeland. Deer signified the Huichols' past lives as nomadic hunters, maize their current existence as sedentary cultivators, and peyote the individual, spiritual and free aspects of life. In a deeply engaging text, which was nominated for a National Book Award, Myerhoff demonstrated how these dynamic and multilayered symbols seemed to fuse in the pilgrimage to Wirikuta, just as the pilgrims themselves bridged the gap between gods and humans.

In subsequent work, Myerhoff continued to analyse symbols not as static cultural forms but as triggers for social action, contributing to change as well as continuity, and indicating the power of emotion over cognition. She also turned her attention to American culture, briefly by investigating student hippies, and in more extended fashion by exploring the culture of elderly Jews in California. In her classic *Number Our Days*, Myerhoff detailed her involvement (as someone born into the Jewish faith, but far from orthodox) with people who were Holocaust survivors and migrants from Eastern Europe, who were coming to terms with their mortality as well as the meaning of their lives. She presented her informants as performing their identity in 'definitional ceremonies', events such as birthday celebrations where people fused everyday life and myth in defining their ideas and beliefs. In addition, elderly people constantly narrated themselves in journals, poems, and stories told to whoever would listen, creating order out of their memories.

Myerhoff's interest in symbols and the dialectic between change and continuity was influenced by Victor Turner. Her work was pioneering in its detailed presentation of complex individuals as bearers of culture (such as Ramón, the Huichol shaman-priest, and Shmuel, the Jewish tailor), in its exploration of anthropology's role in feminism, and in its bridging of the gap between scholarship and the wider public. Her film (directed by Lynne Littman), also called *Number Our Days*, won an Oscar for best documentary. She died of cancer shortly after working on a film of healing rituals within the Hasidic community of Fairfax, California.

Education

BA University of California, Los Angeles, 1958
MA University of Chicago, 1963
Ph.D. University of California, Los Angeles, 1968

Fieldwork

Huichol Indians, Northern Mexico, 1965, 1966
Hippies, USA, 1970, 1971
Jewish senior citizens' center, Venice, California, 1973–4, 1975–6
Jewish community in Fairfax, California, 1982–4

Key Publications

(1974) *Peyote Hunt: The Sacred Journey of the Huichol Indians*, Ithaca and London: Cornell University Press.
with Moore, Sally F. (eds) (1975) *Symbol and Politics in Communal Ideology*, Ithaca and London: Cornell University Press.
with Moore, Sally F. (eds) (1977) *Secular Ritual*, Amsterdam: Van Gorcum.
(1978) *Number Our Days*, New York: E.P. Dutton.

SIMON COLEMAN

Myers, Fred R.

b. 10 June 1948, Baltimore, Maryland, USA

Fred R. Myers is internationally regarded as a major contributor to Aboriginal studies. Based on his fieldwork among the Pintubi peoples of Australia, he has produced a body of work that has been characterised as post-positivist. Myers has been successful in engaging a native world view rather than a Eurocentric perspective, a matter of concern that he has repeatedly addressed. His book-length ethnography on the Pintubi (1986) focuses on native intersubjectivity and how the self is constructed out of sociocultural relatedness among individual members of a culture; he also examines the social construction of the emotions, kinship, and politics among the Pintubi.

Myers's later work addresses issues regarding Aboriginal art production, its inclusion in Western institutions (art museums, art galleries), and its commodification. His publications in this area focus on material culture and its sociocultural value as it circulates in transnational art markets.

Myers did his undergraduate degree at Amherst College, and his graduate work at Bryn Mawr. After receiving his doctoral degree, he began teaching at Pitzer College but was soon recruited by the anthropology department at New York University. Myers is currently chair of the department.

Education

BA Amherst College, 1970
MA Bryn Mawr College, 1972
Ph.D. Bryn Mawr College, 1976

Fieldwork

Yayayi, Northern Territory, Australia, 1973–5, 1979
New Bore, Northern Territory, Australia, 1980–1
Balgo Hills Community, Western Australia, 1982, 1983
Kiwirrkura, Western Australia, 1984
Kintore, Northern Territory, Australia, 1988
Paris, 1993
Alice Springs, Sidney, Australia, 1996

Key Publications

(1986) *Pintubi Country, Pintubi Self: Sentiment, Place, and Politics among Western Desert Aborigines*, Washington, DC: Smithsonian Institution Press.

(ed.) (2001) *The Empire of Things: Regimes of Value and Material Culture*, Santa Fe: School of American Research Press.

VILMA SANTIAGO-IRIZARRY

Nadel, Siegfried Frederick

b. 24 April 1903, Vienna, Austria

d. 14 January 1956, Canberra, Australia

S.F. Nadel was a multitalented anthropologist, who studied psychology, philosophy, music, languages, and had his own opera company before he was thirty. Nadel's keen interest in theory and methodology of social sciences was reflected especially in *The Theory of Social Structure*. Nadel came to the London School of Economics (LSE) in London in 1932, to work with Charles Seligman and Bronislaw Malinowski, after receiving a fellowship for field research from the Rockefeller Foundation and the International Institute of African Languages and Cultures. Following fieldwork in Nigeria, he was appointed government anthropologist in the Anglo-Egyptian Sudan – a post he used to conduct field research among the Nuba. Between 1942 and 1945, Nadel served in the British Military Administration in Eritrea, following which he was promoted to the rank of lieutenant-colonel and transferred to Tripolitania to assume the post of secretary for native affairs.

After the war, Nadel took up a senior lectureship at the LSE in 1946. When the Department of Anthropology was established at the University of Durham two years later, he was appointed reader and head of the department. Nadel briefly taught at Northwestern University in the USA and in 1950 was awarded the Rivers Memorial Medal of the Royal Anthropological Institute. A year later, he took up the professorship and chair of anthropology and sociology in the Research School of Pacific Studies, Australian National University in Canberra.

Nadel saw himself as a pioneer of applied anthropology, in the sense that anthropology should help the colonial administrators. He was a firm believer in the merits of 'indirect rule'. In describing traditional African societies, Nadel remained faithful to the functionalism of Malinowski, but with some additions. First of all, Nadel wrote that it is 'the duty of anthropologist to demonstrate the native society in all its complexity, fashioned as it is by a multitude of social causes and effects, in which the efforts of administration represent causes and effects among others' (1942: vi–vii). This complexity of causes and effects led him to study the interrelationship between kinship, religion, and politics. In his monograph about the Nupe, Nadel noted that he was studying the society of half a million people, with very complex social organisation, far removed from the 'small islands of the Pacific' where functionalism was born. Thus, the Nuba society was 'comparable only with the civilizations of Imperial Rome, of Byzantium, of medieval Europe' (1942: vii). The consequence of this was an attempt to use a relatively uniform methodology in the study of an incredibly varied and differentiated society – and this brought to Nadel both praise and criticism.

Nadel's insistence on the importance of

sound methodological approaches in anthropology has been a lasting influence on generations of anthropologists since the 1950s, and his monographs still stand as fine examples of fieldwork from the 'golden days' of functionalism.

Education

Ph.D. University of Vienna, 1925

Fieldwork

Nupe, Northern Nigeria, 1934–6
Nuba, Sudan, 1938–9

Key Publications

(1942) *A Black Byzantium: The Kingdom of Nupe in Nigeria*, Oxford: Oxford University Press.
(1947) *The Nuba. An Anthropological Study of the Hill Tribes in Kordofan*, Oxford: Oxford University Press.
(1957) *The Theory of Social Structure*, Glencoe, IL: The Free Press.

ALEKSANDAR BOSKOVIC

Nader, Laura

b. 30 September 1930, Winsted, Connecticut, USA

Laura Nader's work has focused on social justice, law, and the production of scientific knowledge. She is a key figure in the development of legal anthropology. Nader was a student of Clyde Kluckhohn at Harvard in the 1950s. Her doctoral fieldwork on settlement patterns in a Zapotec village in Mexico nurtured her interest in comparative law. She frequently returned to Mexico to research local forms of conflict resolution, to which she eventually compared the USA and other societies including Lebanon, successfully arguing that each system reflected wider differences in social organisation and power structure. In *Harmony Ideology*, Nader provided a rich ethnographic account of Mexican case studies to comparative studies of law showing how colonial and neo-colonial powers have contributed to indigenous and customary law.

Influenced by Antonio Gramsci and Michel Foucault, Nader has exhibited unwavering dedication to the question of power structures. In a series of publications about 'controlling processes' as central dogmas in people's everyday lives, she has examined how institutionalised behavioural norms reinforce power structures. She has questioned the authority of Western science as a privileged form of knowledge, offering important material to science and technology studies most notably with *Naked Science*, wherein she challenges the dominance of technoscience over traditional knowledges.

Nader has advocated for a socially relevant, public anthropology beginning with her influential essay on 'studying up', in which she beseeched American anthropologists to turn their gaze on powerful organisations and institutions in the USA rather than remaining ineffectively focused on the colonised and powerless. Throughout her career she has used an anthropology of everyday life to examine social problems including nuclear and alternative energies, the Cold War, taxation, academic freedom, and children's rights, and has written for both non-academic and academic audiences, and in a variety of media including film. Critical of anthropology's preoccupation with representation in the 1990s, Nader argues that anthropology ought to be used to question the controlling processes of society including academia and to contribute to public debates.

Nader has long questioned the professional standards of anthropology and rejects fragmentation in support of a generalist anthropology that can contribute to social change. In the 2000s, her work focuses on the negative impact of globalisation for the legal processes in the USA, arguing against corporate hegemony in favor of social justice.

Education

BA Wells College, 1952
Ph.D. Radcliffe College, 1961

Fieldwork

Oaxaca, Mexico, 1957–8, 1959–60, 1962, 1963, 1964, 1967
Lebanon, 1961
New England, 1965
San Francisco Bay area, 1972–6
Morocco, 1980

Key Publications

(1969) 'Up the anthropologist: perspectives gained from studying up', in D. Hymes (ed.) *Reinventing Anthropology*, New York: Pantheon Press.

(1990) *Harmony Ideology: Justice and Control in a Mountain Zapotec Village*, Stanford: Stanford University Press.

(ed.) (1996) *Naked Science: Anthropological Inquiry into Boundaries, Power, and Knowledge*, New York: Routledge.

(1997) 'Controlling processes: tracing the dynamic components of power', *Current Anthropology* 38, 5: 711–37.

SUSAN FROHLICK

Nakane, Chie

b. 30 November 1926, Tokyo, Japan

While studying history at the University of Tokyo, Chie Nakane realised that first-hand knowledge of a society was essential for a proper understanding of its history, an awareness that drew her to anthropology. During 1953–6, she was associated with the Anthropological Survey of India and conducted fieldwork among various groups in Assam and Himalayan areas. In 1956, she conducted further fieldwork among the Nayars of Kerala. Later in the same year, she went to the London School of Economics where she formally encountered the discipline of social anthropology.

Nakane's works can be divided into three major categories. The first category consists of research on India based on field studies with a particular focus on kinship and family. *Garo and Khasi* (1968) represents the results of her research among the tribal groups in Assam. With her fieldwork among the Nayars, the focus of her research shifted to joint families in the Hindu communities. The results of her research in Kerala, Gujarat, and West Bengal are included in the volume, *Kazoku no kozo* (1970).

The second category of her work comprises studies of Japanese society. *Kinship and Economic Organization in Rural Japan* (1967) combines data obtained through field research in recent and contemporary Japan with examination of historical data. In *Japanese Society* (1970), she extended her analysis beyond traditional organisations to include modern institutions in urban settings as well as to show the continuity of basic structures. She introduced contrastive concepts of frame and attribute, and pointed out that what binds individuals in Japanese organisations is the situational frame (locality or institution) in which they are involved rather than attributes of the individuals such as kinship status or job qualifications.

The third category of her works deals with Tibetan studies. After her initial fieldwork among Tibetan refugees in India during the 1970s, since 1981 she has also carried out frequent surveys in eastern Tibet as well as central Tibet. In her several articles on Tibet, she emphasises the importance of combining historical and anthropological research.

Education

BA University of Tokyo, 1950
MA University of Tokyo, 1952

Fieldwork

Tripura, Sikkim, and Assam, India, December 1953–February 1956

Kerala, India, March–June 1956
Gujarat and West Bengal, India, December 1962–January 1963
West Bengal and Tibetan refugees in North India, since 1965
Eastern and Central Tibet, since 1981

Key Publications

(1967) *Kinship and Economic Organization in Rural Japan*, London: Athlone Press.
(1968) *Garo and Khasi: A Comparative Study in Matrilineal Systems*, The Hague: Mouton.
(1970) *Japanese Society*, London: Weidenfeld & Nicolson.
(1970) *Kazoku no kozo* (Structure of Family: Social Anthropological Analysis), Tokyo: University of Tokyo Press.

MUTSUHIKO SHIMA

Narayan, Kirin

b. 18 November 1959, Bombay, India

The publication of *Storytellers, Saints, and Scoundrels*, widely used as a textbook even a decade after its initial printing, showed Kirin Narayan to be an engaging scholar as well as a story-teller herself. For that book, which highlights the power of story-telling in religious contexts, Narayan was awarded the Victor Turner Prize from the Society for Humanistic Anthropology (AAA), as well as the Elsie Clews Parsons Prize (American Folklore Society), both in 1990. Narayan has continued to demonstrate her joint training in folklore and anthropology by emphasising the importance of narrative and aesthetic sensibilities in social life and ethnographic writing. Her fieldwork in the Himalayan foothill region of Kangra, India, yielded articles on women's songs, rituals, and stories. *Mondays on the Dark Night of the Moon* (1997), a collaborative presentation of folktales from the Himalayan foothills, calls notions of author and subject into question. Narayan's work can be grouped with that of other 'experimental' anthropologists writing since the 1970s, as she has challenged fixed representations of self and other. Further, in also expressing anthropological insights in novels, she has explored the boundary between ethnography and fiction.

Education

BA Sarah Lawrence College, 1980
Ph.D. University of California, Berkeley 1987

Fieldwork

Maharashtra, India, June–July 1983, July–October 1985
Himachal Pradesh, India, September 1990–September 1991

Key Publications

(1989) *Storytellers, Saints, and Scoundrels*, Berkeley: University of California Press.
with (1997) *Mondays on the Dark Night of the Moon: Himalayan Foothill Folktales*, in collaboration with Urmila Devi Sood, New York: Oxford University Press.

SARAH STRAUSS

Nash, June C.

b. 30 May 1927, Salem, Massachusetts, USA

June Nash's four decades of highly original ethnographic research has focused on community, culture, capitalism, and globalisation across the political economies of the Americas. Nash has sought to highlight local voices and struggles, while documenting histories of work and political practice with striking descriptive richness. She has long found oppositional positioning intellectually stimulating.

In studies of Mayan agriculturalists in Chiapas, tin miners in Bolivia, workers in the GE Pittsfield plant, and the Zapatista rebels in Chiapas, Nash has actively sought the participation of local activists to shape her projects theoretically and empirically. Nash sees her transition from the structural functionalism of classical community studies to critical Marxism as compelled by her concern to find an alternative to the internalised violence she encountered in rural Mexico. In Bolivia, she elaborated a culturally inflected historical materialism for We Eat the Mines through conversations with the members of the labour movement as Trotsky was being discussed.

Nash's work on gender involved critiques of 1970s Marxism, dependency theory, and the early American feminist paradigm of universal gender subordination. Collaborating with Helen Safa and members of the thriving networks of Latin American feminist scholars of that decade, she edited major collections on gender and class. Her pathbreaking collection with Maria Patricia Fernandez-Kelly on women, men, and the international division of labour anticipated by over a decade the debates in the social sciences over the role of multinational assembly plants in their quest for ever cheaper labour from women workers throughout the world.

Nash researched the social history of corporate management and labour organising at the GE Pittsfield plant by interviewing retired workers, former managers, and whistle blowers. To understand the historical moment when workers traded job security for their compliance with the corporate view of labour relations, Nash proposed a reading of Gramsci's notion of hegemony that focused on corporate control and worker acquiescence. This contrasts with later readings of Gramsci that have stressed the internal heterogeneity of hegemonic forms of control and the complex counter-hegemonies that contest them. Nevertheless, one sees at the edge of the Pittsfield analysis the emergence of regional social movements including environmentalists and feminists who were challenging corporate interests and regional politics. At the time, however, Nash found little anthropological interest in corporate pollution.

Nash resumed field research in Chiapas in 1988 with a project on artisanal production and the world market. Shortly thereafter, she witnessed early political mobilising that grew into the 1994 Zapatista rebellion – a post-Cold War, post-Marxist movement that fascinated researchers. In Mayan Visions, Nash argues that the Zapatistas have been successful in creating a Utopian vision of community, collective resistance, and direct democracy that interweaves Mayan culture and international rights discourse to protest NAFTA's brutal marginalisation of Mexican farmers through devastating neo-liberal economic reforms. This book makes important contributions to the literature on globalisation and social movements.

Nash continues to critique anthropological post-modernism whenever its fascination with cultural fluidity and hybridity is cut off from the political and economic situations where people experience the contradictions between transnational capital and community. She has also entered the debates on essentialism, arguing that indigenous self-essentialism has been a key tactic in the Americas for making collective claims to cultural property.

To those who critique Nash's admiration of the idealised gender complementarity that Zapatistas craft for women as nurturers, Nash argues that self-essentialising has been a successful strategy for women seeking public expression in Latin America. To her credit, Nash's ethnographic research includes evidence of gender rebels in town among the Zapatista sympathisers. These women make it clear that there is an important political gap between essentialism as a subaltern discursive tactic and the rich heterogeneity of gendered realities.

While some observers dismiss the Zapatistas as marginal because of their indigenous roots, their political practice has come to play a key international role in the political imaginary of the post-Seattle global radical democracy movement. Once again, Nash's work has anticipated new directions for social research on working-class politics and social justice.

Education

BA Barnard College, 1948
MA University of Chicago, 1953
Ph.D. University of Chicago, 1960

Fieldwork

Chiapas, Mexico, 1957, 1964, 1965, 1966, summers 1987–2001
Bolivia, 1969, 1970, 1971, 1985, 1986
Pittsfield, Massachusetts, 1982, 1985–6

Key Publications

(1970) In the Eyes of the Ancestors: Belief and Behavior in a Maya Community, New Haven: Yale University Press.
(1979) We Eat the Mines and the Mines Eat Us: Dependency and Exploitation in Bolivian Tin Mines, New York: Columbia University Press.
(1989) From Tank Town to High Tech: The Clash of Community and Industrial Cycles, Albany: SUNY Press.
(2001) Mayan Visions: The Quest for Autonomy in an Age of Globalization, New York: Routledge.

KAY B. WARREN

Needham, Rodney

b. 15 May 1923

d. 4 December 2006, Oxford, UK

Rodney Needham began his career as a social anthropologist with a fieldwork study of the Penan of Borneo at the beginning of the 1950s. After receiving the degree of Doctor of Philosophy for his dissertation on this nomadic population he published a number of articles describing various aspects of their social organisation, including the indigenous system of death names. However, it was with the publication of Structure and Sentiment in 1962 that he attracted attention as an advocate for a structural approach to the study of social facts. This book, his first, was an attempt to demonstrate the superiority of a sociological method of understanding social facts over one based on individual psychology, a demonstration that tended to confirm Durkheim's dictum that whenever a social phenomenon is directly explained by a psychological phenomenon the explanation is false. Needham achieved

this end by demolishing the arguments propounded in a monograph written by George Homans and David Schneider, Marriage, Authority, and Final Causes, itself a critique of Claude Lévi-Strauss's Les Structures élémentaires de la parenté. Needham's principal objections to Homans's and Schneider's work were that they had entirely misunderstood Lévi-Strauss's argument and had pursued a psychological instead of a sociological approach in attempting to refute the main tenets of Les Structures élémentaires de la parenté. Needham's incisive appraisal of their study generated a plethora of rejoinders, and for several years he confirmed his earlier contentions by analysing the 'kinship' arrangements of a substantial number of societies, more especially their respective relationship terminologies. This corpus of work confirmed his reputation as a leading analyst of 'kinship', a term, however, that he himself later disowned. Needham's scepticism about the analytical usefulness of terms commonly used in social anthropology had been fostered by his reading of Wittgenstein, whose work exercised a strong influence over his own critical cast of mind, and he subjected to microscopic treatment some of the more recurring key words scholars resort to in describing and analysing social facts. In his Remarks and Inventions, a collection of three essays, he asserted that such terms as 'kinship', 'descent', 'marriage', and 'incest' are too culture-bound to be of analytical advantage in comparative analysis and urged they be discarded. Needham's most elaborated disquisition on the meaning of key terms, however, came in his book, Belief, Language, and Experience, which he published in 1972. In this comparative study of how the word 'belief' is used cross-culturally Needham challenged the commonly held assumption that the term corresponded to any particular faculty of thought. It was, he suggested, merely an odd-job rubric that subsumes a myriad of disparate notions. He concluded that the word 'belief', which ethnographers routinely rely on in describing indigenous modes of thought, is virtually valueless for analysis – and of little use in ethnographic description.

Needham's later work is marked as much by originality of thought as by critical insight, but whereas his earlier work focused on structural studies of institutional forms of human behaviour his later work examined social facts as products of human nature. Resorting to his novel concept of 'primary factors of experience' – universal capacities, proclivities, and constraints that comprise human nature – he argued that these determinants generate social facts that can only be properly understood after the nature of these determinants have been established. Witchcraft, a perennial anthropological favorite, offered him one of several opportunities to demonstrate what he was advocating. Explicitly eschewing conventional sociological explanations, he argued that the image of the witch results from psychic constants to which the human mind is predisposed by its very nature.

During his years at the Institute of Social Anthropology at Oxford University Rodney Needham trained a galaxy of students whose subsequent work reveals his influence. They included Robert H. Barnes; T.O. Beidelman; Clark Cunningham; Kirk Endicott; Gregory Forth; James J. Fox; Christopher Hallpike; David Hicks; David Maybury-Lewis; and Peter Rivière. Needham spent virtually all his professional life at Oxford, where he held the position of professor of social anthropology and fellow of All Souls College, from 1976–90.

Education

Diploma in Anthropology, University of Oxford, 1949
B.Litt. University of Oxford, 1950
D.Phil. University of Oxford, 1953
MA University of Oxford, 1956
D.Litt. University of Oxford, 1970

Fieldwork

Borneo (Penan), 1951–2
Sumba (Kodi, Mamboru), 1954–5
Malaya (Siwang) and Borneo, 1955

Borneo (Penan), 1958

Key Publications

(1962) *Structure and Sentiment: A Test Case in Social Anthropology*, Chicago: University of Chicago Press.
(1972) *Belief, Language, and Experience*, Oxford: Basil Blackwell.
(1974) *Remarks and Inventions: Skeptical Essays About Kinship*, London: Tavistock Publications.
(1978) *Primordial Characters*, Charlottesville: University Press of Virginia.

DAVID HICKS

Netting, Robert McCorkle

b. 1934, Racine, Wisconsin, USA

d. 1995, Tucson, Arizona, USA

Netting was concerned with the empirical study of society and culture from the social and economic base up, rather than from a purely theoretical perspective down, avoiding reductionism in the application of ecological principles to cultural systems. His research focused consistently on intensive cultivators, non-industrial agriculturalists whom he called 'smallholders', feeling that the term 'peasant' had too many negative connotations. His contributions to anthropology lay in the development of the links among farming, households, their land, and other resources like their animals. Households were an important focus as flexible units of production, and household studies have become a topic of continuing interest in anthropology. At the time of his early death from cancer he was working on sustainability, a topic of current interest at the time. In the concern with ecological relationships that was prominent in the discipline in the 1960s, Netting was instrumental in formalising cultural ecology and contributed to the development of agricultural studies. He was at the forefront of the fruition of the collaboration between anthropology and geography in the study of agricultural evolution. In selecting his field-work venues, he took a comparative view that embraced both Africa and Europe. He sought explanations for cross-cultural regularities in behaviour that transcended specific geographic locations. In his Alpine work, he forged connections between anthropology and historical demography that had long-lasting influences in subsequent studies by others.

Education

BA Yale University, 1957
MA University of Chicago, 1959
Ph.D. University of Chicago, 1963

Fieldwork

Fort Berthold Reservation, North Dakota, 1958
Jos Plateau, Nigeria, 1960–2, 1966–7, 1984, 1992, 1994
Torbel, Valais, Switzerland, 1970–1, 1974, 1977
Senegal and Ivory Coast, 1977
Portugal, 1982, 1983, 1984

Key Publications

(1968) Hill Farmers of Nigeria; Cultural Ecology of the Kofyar of the Jos Plateau, Seattle: University of Washington Press.
(1977 [1986]) Cultural Ecology, Menlo Park, CA: Cummings.
(1981) Balancing on an Alp: Ecological Change and Continuity in a Swiss Mountain Community, Cambridge, UK: Cambridge University Press.
(1993) Smallholders, Householders: Farm Families and the Ecology of Intensive, Sustainable Agriculture, Stanford: Stanford University Press.

Further Reading

(1998) Human Ecology 26, 2. Special edition devoted to the work of Netting.

JUDITH A. RASSON

Niederer, Arnold

b. 3 December 1914, St. Gall, Switzerland

d. 6 April 1998, Zurich, Switzerland

Arnold Niederer was one of the twentieth century's greatest Swiss ethnologists. His academic career started relatively late with attendance at Zurich University, where he subsequently also held a position as professor from 1964–80. Despite the importance of his focus on alpine life, regional identity, and co-operative work forms, his research soon moved away from traditional approaches in the study of material culture. He ascribed social responsibility to the cultural sciences through a focus on applied anthropology to better understand such issues as the conflicts between native Swiss and immigrants from Southern Europe during the 1960s and 1970s, or the Zurich social protests of 1980. He thus drew attention to cultural comparisons within the framework of an Ethnologia Europaea. Niederer opened up traditional Swiss ethnological research in many new directions, integrating thereby social science issues and theories into this field.

He overcame its former long-standing fixation on rural and alpine areas by integrating into his concept the modern workaday world, industrialisation, urban life, and media influence. His studies often refer to interdisciplinary interests, clearly arising from collaboration with sociologists, ethnologists, historians, etc. By highlighting findings and debates in the field of American cultural anthropology, Niederer's work has stimulated new and original studies, including for example the non-verbal dimensions of contemporary everyday communication. Niederer played a key role in the process of integrating the ethnological research carried out on a national scale in many countries into the rubric of a comparative European ethnology. His success has further strengthened the international anchorage of Swiss ethnological research.

Education

Ph.D. University of Zurich, 1956

Key Publications

(1993/1994) *Alpine Alltagskultur zwischen Beharrung*
und *Wandel* (Alpine Everyday Culture between
Intransigence and Change), Berne, Stuttgart,
Vienna: Haupt.

UELI GYR

Obayashi, Taryo

b. 1929, Tokyo, Japan

Taryo Obayashi's work has focused on the origin of the Japanese and Japanese culture by ethnological analysis of myths, based on bibliographical materials. Although he was educated at the Vienna School, he carefully avoids the dogmatic interpretation of 'culture circle', and considers both ecological and diffusional factors for distribution of cultural elements. He argues that the Japanese archipelago was inhabited by multiethnic groups. Various peoples and cultures came to the archipelago from different areas at different times, which contributed to the formation of Japanese culture. He mentions that the Japanese myth of the descent to the earth by descendants of the Sun Goddess, which describes the origin of Japanese emperors, is rooted in Inner Asia. His theory justifies the hypothesis that the emperor system of Japan was derived from conquests by Inner Asians. Obayashi reconstructs human cultural history by analysing the myths of 'Milky Way' and of 'Rainbow' from a worldwide perspective. His conclusions are: the idea of 'Milky Way' as a road, especially the road of souls, was brought by ancestors of the Amerindo language family when they first settled the American continents, and was spread widely in North and South America; the image of Rainbow Snake came to Australia from New Guinea 6,000 years ago; Rainbow was thought to be the Dragon Snake in China since the Yin period; the distribution of the idea of Rainbow Snake overlaps especially with Bantu-speaking people, and the idea spread over Africa through these people. He further points out that images of 'Milky Way' and 'Rainbow' were associated with the nature of phenomena as well as human life, and that the original feeling of fear and respect for these phenomena has been altered to more practical manners of thought. His methodology for reconstructing culture history through the analysis of huge banks of ethnological data was based on the tradition of the 'culture circle', but he has developed it to be a more controlled and precise method by the use of cluster analysis, and by the adoption of new data from interdisciplinary perspectives. Thus, his contribution to sociocultural anthropology is to demonstrate the rich data on human images in a cultural and historical context, and to position Japanese culture in this framework.

Education

BA University of Tokyo, 1952
D.Phil. University of Vienna, 1959

Key Publications

(1961) *Nihonshinwa no Kigen* (Origins of Japanese Myth), Tokyo: Kadokawa Shoten.

(1973) *Inasaku no Shinwa* (Myth of Rice Cultivation), Tokyo: Kobundo.

(1984) *Higashi-Asia no Oken Shinwa* (Myth of the Kingship in East Asia), Tokyo: Kobundo, Showa.

(1999) *Ginga no Michi, Nijino Kakehashi* (Road of Milky Way, Bridge of Rainbow), Tokyo: Shogakukan.

TAKASHI IRIMOTO

Obeyesekere, Gananath

b. 1930, Sri Lanka

With the exception of his first monograph, Professor Obeyesekere's work focuses on the central issue of anthropology: the nature of people as cultural beings. This he does through bringing together the traditional ethnographic focus of anthropology with his strong interest in history and psychoanalytic theory. In *Medusa's Hair*, he builds upon Edmund Leach's classic analysis of hair as a social symbol to advance a complex and exciting argument concerning the personal nature of hair symbolism that he explores through the use of psychoanalytical theory. Whilst analysing in detail the significance of hair symbolism for individuals, he shows how these personal symbols relate to the wider cultural context and the dynamic two-way relationship between the individual and the collective. This was followed by his magisterial study of the goddess, Pattini. This is a historical, anthropological, and psychological study of the cult of the goddess focusing on a set of rituals known as the *gammaduva*. Here he displays his remarkable skills in handling vast amounts of data whilst retaining a strong theoretical grip on the subject. The analysis ranges across past and present Sri Lanka and South India as well as touching on the psychodynamic aspects of Western religious traditions. *The Work of Culture* continues his exploration of the interface between the social and the personal. Obeyesekere builds upon Freud's work to argue that there is a 'multiple Oedipus complex' that takes various forms in different cultures. The 'Work of Culture' is thus concerned with the way in which products of the unconscious human mind become imbued with collective significance. For Obeyesekere, the analysis of culture also involves an understanding of deep personal motivations. Obeyesekere's more recent works continues to focus on the interplay between the personal and the collective, but mention should also be made of his work on Captain Cook. Here he argues, in contrast to other anthropologists such as Marshall Sahlins, that tropes have to be understood symbolically and not literally, and that many anthropologists have been over-naïve in their understandings of native utterances. Throughout his work, Obeyesekere displays a commitment to a scholarship that denies disciplinary boundaries. His work stands as a major critique of a more narrow discipline-bound anthropology and shows the strength of an anthropology that relates itself to these wider themes.

Education

BA University of Sri Lanka, 1955
MA University of Washington, 1958
Ph.D. University of Washington, 1964

Fieldwork

Sri Lanka, various periods since 1955

Key Publications

(1981) *Medusa's Hair: An Essay on Personal Symbols and Religious Experience*, Chicago: Chicago University Press.

(1984) *The Cult of the Goddess Pattini*, Chicago: Chicago University Press.

(1990) *The Work of Culture: Symbolic Transformations in Psychoanalysis and Anthropology*, Chicago: Chicago University Press.

(1992) *The Apotheosis of Captain Cook: European Mythmaking in the Pacific*, Princeton: Princeton University Press.

R.L. STIRRAT

Obrebski, Joseph

b. 1905, Teplik, (currently) Ukraine

d. 1967, Hollis, New York, USA

Joseph [(Józef)] Obrebski's first fieldwork in the Balkans was influenced by the 'critical evolutionism' of Kazimierz Moszynski, under whom he studied the ethnography of Slavs. Obtaining a grant from the Rockefeller Foundation, Obrebski departed for London where he studied with Bronislaw Malinowski and adopted a functionalist approach. His thesis on family organisation reflected in the custom of couvade was partially based on his fieldwork materials from Macedonia.

Returning to Poland, he worked for various state institutions, carrying out research in Polesie, a remote region on the eastern border of Poland (currently in Ukraine and Belarus), which resulted in a series of articles on ethnicity. He maintained that there were no 'objective' criteria of an ethnic group, only an agreement between its members and their neighbours about a boundary between them. His stress on subjective elements in the formation and persistence of ethnic groups was, at the time, very innovative.

During the Second World War he worked for the underground Warsaw and Poznan Universities, and later he was employed by Lodz University. In 1946, at the invitation of E. Evans-Pritchard, he left for Oxford and London where he lectured on peasantry in Eastern Europe. After fieldwork in Jamaica, he worked for the United Nations till 1959, dealing with non-self-governing territories. Later he taught at universities in New York. The exhibition of his Polesie photographs was organised in Amherst in 1973.

Education

MA Jagiellonian University, Krakow, 1930
Ph.D. London School of Economics, 1934
Habilitation, Warsaw University, 1946

Fieldwork

The Balkans, summers 1927 and 1928
Poretch, Macedonia, 1932–3
Polesie, (then) Poland, 1934–7
Jamaica, 1947–8.

Key Publications

(1951) 'The Sociology of Rising Nations', UNESCO International Social Science Bulletin 3, 2: 237–43.
(1974) The Changing Peasantry of Eastern Europe, Cambridge, MA: Schenkman.

GRAZYNA KUBICA-HELLER

Ochs, Elinor

b. September 1944, Baltimore, Maryland, USA

Elinor Ochs (formerly Elinor Keenan) is a linguistic anthropologist whose research focuses on the nexus of language, culture, and society in a variety of settings. Her first fieldwork was conducted in Madagascar and resulted in a series of influential papers. For instance, 'Norm makers, norm breakers' (1974) showed that, in Vakinankaratra, it was women and not men who were considered 'direct' speakers. This went against a then commonly held view that women tend to hedge and mitigate what they say more than men. Ochs went on to show, however, that even though in this case it is the men who tend to speak more 'indirectly', their speech style is nevertheless considered superior and more eloquent. Another paper from the same period drew again from the Vakinankaratra materials to argue, against Paul Grice, that notions of 'informativeness' were culturally bound and that, as a result, the implicatures generated by flouting them were specific to a community of speakers. A third paper considered the way in which members of a speech community negotiate the sense and meaning of rules for speaking even as they are employing them in the production of public oratory. These papers illustrated the extent to which studies of discourse in non-Western communities might be brought to bear on foundational issues in the social sciences.

Since her early work in Madagascar, Ochs has conducted several large-scale research projects. In the early 1970s, Ochs, along with long-time collaborator, Bambi Schieffelin, began to look at the acquisition of communicative competence among English-speaking children. This research contributed to the emerging field of 'developmental pragmatics' which argued, against the then-dominant Chomskyian view, that studies of language acquisition should consider the contexts in which language is used and the uses to which it is put. Later, when Ochs went to Samoa and Schieffelin to Papua New Guinea, developmental pragmatics was replaced by the more ethnographically oriented Language Socialisation framework that examines both 'socialisation through the use of language' and 'socialisation to use language'.

In more recent work, Ochs has again turned her attention to discourse in US speech communities having investigated language use among physicists, autistic children, and agoraphobics. Her current research, funded by the Sloan Foundation, examines discourse and culture in US working families. Ochs continues to emphasise the great importance of narrative and related speech genres in the organisation of human experience. Throughout her career Ochs has brought her keen ethnographic eye and appreciation for the great complexity of human language to bear on the analysis of real events. Her commitment to empirical study is thus matched by an outstanding ability to locate and engage the most important and pressing theoretical issues.

Education

BA George Washington University, 1966
MA (Hons) University of Cambridge, 1974
Ph.D. University of Pennsylvania, 1974

Fieldwork

Communicative competence in Vakinankaratra, Madagascar, 1969–71
Acquisition of communicative competence in Samoa, 1978–83
Physics and scientific discourse in a US university, 1990–3
Everyday lives of working families in the USA, 2000–3

Key Publications

(1988) *Culture and Language Development: Language Acquisition and Language Socialization in a Samoan Village*, Cambridge, UK: Cambridge University Press.
with Capps, Lisa (1995) *Constructing Panic: The Discourse of Agoraphobia*, Cambridge, MA: Harvard University Press.
with Capps, Lisa (2001) *Living Narrative*, Cambridge, MA: Harvard University Press.

JACK SIDNELL

Ohnuki-Tierney, Emiko

b. Kobe, Japan

Ohnuki-Tierney's interests are symbolic and historical anthropology, patriotism/nationalism, social marginalisation and power inequality, urbanites and hunter-gatherers. Her earliest extended fieldwork was conducted among Ainu from Sakhalin Island resettled on Hokkaido. A prolific researcher, she has continued her inquiries into Japanese culture as her regional speciality, extending the studies back into the historical period in order to understand 'culture through time'. She emphasises how we must historicise the culture concept itself, rather than using it as a synchronic snapshot. Methodologically, she sees it as important to create what she calls a window (a micro–macro linkage) on a specific cultural activity that can then be related to sociocultural changes on the macro-level. Her work frequently demonstrates the importance of symbols – rice, the monkey, cherry blossoms –

and their social roles in broader geopolitical contexts. Her interest has recently turned to the role of *méconnaissance* (misrecognition) in communication. This means that actors in the same social context would read a different signification into a given symbol. She finds that this process is facilitated by aesthetics, which makes all meanings of a symbol beautiful.

This happened to the kamikaze pilots, university graduates with cosmopolitan educations, who read their own meaning and their own idealism into cherry blossoms, even after the military government transformed the meaning to represent sacrifice in war. This led to their inability to recognise the advancement of the totalitarian agenda and in the end reproduced the military ideology while defying it in thought.

Ohnuki-Tierney has also pursued a range of other topics such as ethnomedicine (including views of organ transplants in Japanese and American society), and food (including research on McDonald's restaurants in Japan). Sensitive to intellectual traditions outside of American anthropology, one of her important contributions is conveying an insider's view of Japan (and Asia) to an Anglophone audience in anthropological terms. All of her books have been rewritten and published for Japanese readers.

Education

BA Tsuda College, Tokyo, 1957
ME Wayne State University, 1960
MS University of Wisconsin, 1964
Ph.D. University of Wisconsin, 1968

Fieldwork

Detroit (Chinese), 1960–1; 1963
Hokkaido (resettled Sakhalin Ainu), June 1965–May 1966, March–May 1969, September–October 1973
The Hanshinkan area, June–July, 1976, February–June, 1979, April and May 1980
Okayama, Osaka, Tokyo, Tsukuba, and Sapporo, 1980, 1984, 1987

Kanazawa, Osaka, Kobe, and Tokyo, 1988, 1990, 1991 (several months each year)
Tokyo, Osaka, and Kobe, 1993
Tokyo and Osaka, 1994
Tokyo and Kyoto, 1995, 1996, 1997, 1999 (several months each year)

Key Publications

(1974 [1984]) *The Ainu of the Northwest Coast of Southern Sakhalin*, New York: Holt, Rinehart & Winston.
(1984 [7th printing 1997]) *Illness and Culture in Contemporary Japan: An Anthropological View*, Cambridge, UK: Cambridge University Press.
(1993) *Rice as Self: Japanese Identities through Time*, Princeton: Princeton University Press.
(2002) *Kamikaze, Cherry Blossoms, and Nationalisms: The Militarization of Aesthetics in Japanese History*, Chicago: University of Chicago Press.

JUDITH A. RASSON

Ohtsuka, Ryutaro

b. 1945, Tokyo, Japan

Although Ryutaro Ohtsuka conducted human activity research on hand- and line-fishermen in Japan as part of his graduate studies, his subsequent fieldwork and publications have primarily focused on the adaptive mechanisms of the Oriomo Papuans in lowland New Guinea. More than twenty months of field investigations among Gidra-speaking people have revealed their subsistence strategy of using wild and planted sago in combination with hunting, in order to survive in lowland ecosystems in Papua. His research into changing social organisations, due to expansion of the population into ecologically different territories, reveals their cognition of environment and its importance to the long-term survival of the human population. His references to totem animals being the symbols of two different environments, monsoon forest and savannah, reveal their roles as mediators between society and the natural environment. He then applies his human ecological and sociocultural theory to the contemporary Asian and Pacific countries through various projects, e.g. the Alliance for Global Sustainability (AGS) Programme, 'Sustainable Water Supply System in Arsenic-Affected Asian Environment', and the United Nations University's Research Project, 'People, Land Management, and Environmental Change'. Thus, his contribution to sociocultural anthropology is the description and analysis of human subsistence in ecological anthropological terms, such as population, nutrition, and adaptive strategies.

Education

BA University of Tokyo, 1967
MA University of Tokyo, 1970
D.Sc. University of Tokyo, 1980

Fieldwork

Oriomo, Papua New Guinea, 1967, 1971–2, 1980–95
Nasake Island, Japan, 1968–9
Solomon Islands, 2000

Key Publications

(1983) *Oriomo Papuans: Ecology of Sago-Eaters in Lowland Papua*, Tokyo: University of Tokyo Press.
(1996) *Nettairin no Sekai: Totem no sumu Mori* (Humans and Totem Animals in a New Guinea Microcosmos), Tokyo: University of Tokyo Press.

TAKASHI IRIMOTO

Oka, Masao

b. 5 June 1898, Nagano, Japan

d. December 1992, Tokyo, Japan

Oka is regarded as a leading figure in the establishment of Japanese ethnology since the 1930s. Traditionally Japanese ethnology and anthropology focused on the origin of Japanese peoples and the formation of their culture-society. During his stay in Vienna between 1929–34, Oka developed a basic framework for the interpretation of Japanese ethnogenesis that outlined two major cultural complexes as distinguishable factors in the formation of Japan. Inspired by Oka's approach, many Japanese ethnologists, particularly in Tokyo, have been encouraged to study various rural communities in Japan including the Okinawa Islands. Oka has organised several seminal anthropological research projects, including work among the Ainu in Hokkaido and Southeast Asia. At present his followers are among the most senior scholars in Japan, and they have in turn mentored a new generation of students, now working mainly in Oceania.

Education

BA Tokyo University, 1924
Dr.Phil. University of Vienna, 1933

Fieldwork

Orok (Ulta), Sakhalin, 1937
Saru Ainu in Hokkaido, 1951
Rural communities in Izu-Ihama, Hachijou-Jima, the Inland Sea, Aomori, and Iwate, 1953, 1958–62
Eskimo in Alaska, 1960, 1962, 1964

Key Publications

(1933) 'Kulturschichten in Alt-Japan' (Cultural stratum in Old Japan), doctoral dissertation, University of Vienna.
(1969) *Ijin Sonota: Nihon-minzoku no genryu to nihon-kokka no keisei* (Strangers and Others: Origins of the Japanese People and the Formation of the State), Tokyo: Gensousha.

KATSUYOSHI FUKUI

Okely, Judith M.

b. 1941, Malta

Judith Okely is best known for her research on Traveller Gypsies of England. This ethnography examined a nomadic ethnic group often misunderstood and mistreated within Britain. Significantly, Okely stressed the social construction and maintenance of Traveller Gypsy identity rather than asserting descent from a putative ancestor. This continued emphasis on the social construction of Traveller Gypsy identity often places Okely in direct conflict with those looking for genetic links and Indian descent for all European Traveller Gypsies. Okely's interest in Traveller Gypsies extends to an examination of the relationships between nomadic or travelling cultures and sedentary cultures, especially the ways in which Traveller Gypsies challenge the rootedness of many institutions but also use to their benefit perceptions of exoticness by sedentary cultures.

Okely's experience during her doctoral fieldwork led to her interest in ethnographic theory and methodology. Dissatisfied with the general presumption that anthropological work needed to be presented in an authoritative, objective, and scientific manner, Okely argues for a more subjective and reflexive representational style. In particular, Okely insists on the need for methodological awareness of the self in fieldwork. A key contributor in the development of feminist theory and ethnography, Okely argues that anthropologists must understand their own positioning, their own autobiography, as part of the experience of fieldwork. Okely demonstrates vividly the use of autobiography in her work on Simone de Beauvoir and in her collection of essays in *Own or Other Culture*. Amongst the dimensions of experience, Okely highlights the way in which gender, age, and class are embodied.

In the 1990s, Okely also looked at rural transformation in East Anglia, England, and Normandy, France. This work concentrated on the dynamic between the aesthetic representation of landscape and the experience of it by those who live there over an extended time span. Okely also examines how these places are used in the construction of specific ideas of 'nature' and national landscapes. Moreover, this tacit knowledge of the landscape of those who work it often confronts a scientific or authoritative knowledge of the same landscape. As with all her work, Okely contextualises the lived experience in the political and social framework.

Education

Degré Supérieur, Sorbonne, Paris, 1960
Diploma in French Civilisation, Sorbonne, Paris, 1960
BA University of Oxford, 1965
Certificate in Social Anthropology, University of Cambridge, 1970
D.Phil. University of Oxford, 1977

Fieldwork

Southern England, 1970–3
Normandy, France, 1985–6, 1987, 1988, 1995
East Anglia, England, 1986, 1988–9

Key Publications

(1983) *The Traveller Gypsies*, Cambridge, UK: Cambridge University Press.
(1986) *Simone de Beauvoir – A Re-reading*, London: Virago Press.
with Callaway, H. (eds) (1992) *Anthropology and Autobiography: Participatory Experience and Embodied Knowledge*, London: Routledge.
(1996) *Own or Other Culture*, London: Routledge.

JUDITH DOYLE

Oliver, Douglas L.

b. 10 February 1913, Ruston, Louisiana, USA

Douglas Oliver is regarded by many as the American dean of Pacific anthropologists. Beginning with his first fieldwork in Bougainville, his career spans more than a half-century. Many Americans were first introduced to the Pacific Islands when they read his 1951 survey of the history and culture of that region. His contributions to Pacific studies continue down to the present day.

Oliver's scholarly publications were at first delayed by government service during and after the Second World War. When Pearl Harbor was attacked in December 1941, he was one of the few Americans with first-hand experience in the Pacific, in an area quickly occupied by Japanese forces. During his field-work in Bougainville, he travelled widely over the island. He had supplemented his ethno-graphic data with photographs and environ-mental observations that added significantly to plans for the island's eventual recapture by the Allies.

His advice to the US government in the Pacific shifted at war's end when he collabo-rated with other anthropologists to plan for the future of that part of the Micronesian islands that was to become the US Trust Territory of the Pacific Islands. Oliver led a team that conducted an economic survey of Micronesia in 1946; later he was instrumental in establishing the Co-ordinated Investigation of Micronesian Anthropology (CIMA). CIMA was to assist the US Navy in administering the Trust Territory by providing basic research on indigenous cultures.

On the basis of these years of experience, Oliver published his first major work, de-signed to expand general readers' knowledge of the Pacific. It was his second book, *A Solomon Island Society*, that had a profound impact on anthropology as a discipline. In a fine-grained ethnography of Siwai speakers on Bougain-ville, Oliver presented for the first time a detailed description of 'Big Man' leadership in Melanesia. This classic treatment became a touchstone for Pacific anthropology that still generates theoretical attention and debate.

Most of Oliver's teaching career took place at Harvard University. There in 1954 he organised a team of graduate students to study modern culture in the Society Islands. In 1962 his gaze returned to Melanesia and, with W.W. Howells and the late Albert Damon, he helped create a cross-disciplinary team to assess health in the Solomon Islands. This effort was innovative in that graduate students conducted more than a year of ethnographic research among different groups before a medical team was sent to survey medical conditions in the same populations. All his Harvard teaching trained cohorts of students who in turn produced a substantial body of island studies.

In 1969, Oliver was appointed to a Pacific Islands chair in anthropology at the University of Hawaii, Manoa; he taught there part time until 1973 when he retired from Harvard. During that period, he also served as adviser to a multinational firm developing a huge copper mine on Bougainville. This permitted him to return to the site of his first fieldwork, and to provide funds for a new group of graduate students to conduct research there. He occu-pied the Hawaii chair until 1978 when he retired from full-time teaching. 'Retirement' hardly reflects his scholarly productivity, however. Beginning in the 1980s, an ever-growing number of historians and anthropol-ogists, including some of Oliver's own stu-dents, has sought to blend the two disciplines in order to illuminate what is still a relatively little-known part of the world. Oliver's con-tribution to this effort is as distinctive as was his earlier ethnography. In 1988 he produced an encyclopedic treatment of traditional island cultures, a work that will serve as a reference for years to come. This was followed by a more conventionally historical monograph about Captain William Bligh's second voyage to Tahiti. After assisting his terminally ill wife, Margaret Macarthur, with her own mono-graph, he has most recently written an account of Polynesian society at the time of early European contact. The breadth and depth of Douglas Oliver's record as Pacific anthropolo-gist and historian serves as inspiration to all those interested in the islands.

Education

BA Harvard University, 1933–5
D.Phil. University of Vienna, 1935

Fieldwork

Bougainville Island, New Guinea, 1938–9, 1968–72
Tahiti, 1954–9

Key Publications

(1951) *The Pacific Islands*, Cambridge, MA: Harvard University Press.

(1955) *A Solomon Island Society*, Cambridge, MA: Harvard University Press.

(1988) *Oceania: The Native Cultures of Australia and the Pacific Islands*, Honolulu: University of Hawaii Press.

(2001) *Polynesia in Early Historic Times*, Honolulu: The Bess Press.

EUGENE OGAN

Olwig, Karen Fog

b. 1948, Denmark

Karen Fog Olwig's historical ethnographic research in the West Indies has focused on the emergence, adaptation, assertion, and complexity of Afro-Caribbean culture and identity in relation to the islands' emplacement in changing global economic structures. Olwig's initial study traced the development of Afro-Caribbean communities in the former Danish colony of St John's over three centuries, from plantation economy to tourism. Olwig's treatment of enduring and loosely structured family-related exchange networks constructively challenged synchronic analyses of dysfunctional 'matrifocal' families. Olwig's subsequent work focuses both theoretically and empirically on the relationship between 'culture' and 'place'. In her study of Nevis, Olwig explored the historical development of Afro-Caribbean identity in global socioeconomic contexts of slavery, colonisation, and migration. This led beyond the remote island of Nevis to Nevisian family-related networks in the West Indies, North America, and England. Through oral history and life stories, Olwig explored the institution of family land on Nevis as an imagined and concrete place of identity. Consistently asking global questions of small islands, Olwig has produced a solid body of detailed ethnography that challenges nation-states as privileged frames of reference for studying cultural identity and 'transna-tional' migration, and perceptively probes the place-centered orientations of traditional cultural theory.

Education

BA George Washington University, 1970
MA University of Minnesota, 1972
Ph.D. University of Minnesota, 1977

Fieldwork

Danish West Indian archives, 1973–4, 1981
St John, Virgin Islands, 1974–5, 1977–80, 1994
Nevis and Nevisian migration destinations: Leeds, England, and New Haven, Connecticut, USA, 1981–9
Dispersed family networks of Caribbean background, 1996–9

Key Publications

(1987) *Cultural Adaptation and Resistance on St John*, Gainesville: University of Florida Press.

(1993) *Global Culture, Island Identity: Continuity and Change in the Afro-Caribbean Community of Nevis*, Amsterdam: Harwood Academic.

SALLY ANDERSON

Opler, Morris E.

b. 16 May 1907, Buffalo, New York, USA

d. 13 May 1996, Norman, Oklahoma, USA

A central theme of much of Morris Opler's work is the importance of individuals as cultural actors, seen in the detail of his ethnographic works and in his civil-rights work. He studied with Leslie White at Buffalo, and White encouraged him to go to Chicago to study with Edward Sapir. After Sapir left for Yale in 1931 Opler continued at Chicago, working with A.R. Radcliffe-Brown. After completing his doctorate Opler had a series of short-term appointments, including the Bureau of Indian Affairs (1936–7) and Reed

College (1937–8). In 1938 he was hired by Claremont Colleges in California in a tenure-track position, which was interrupted in 1942 by the war.

During the Second World War Opler worked as a Social Science Analyst for the War Relocation Office in two Japanese American internment camps. Himself Jewish, Opler was sensitive to persecution based on ethnocultural difference. He wrote three legal briefs in defense of Japanese American civil rights, two of which were heard before the US Supreme Court, and earned the praise of the Japanese American Citizens League. After the war he worked for a year in the Foreign Morale Analysis Division of the Office of War Information before returning to academia. Opler considered his work for Japanese Americans to be the most important contribution of his career.

Prior to the war Opler had worked with Apache Indians, establishing himself as a careful ethnographer with an eye for detail and close attention to his informants' points of view. He was interested in the culture-and-personality approaches, and used individual life histories to personalise the Apache institutions of warfare, raiding, and ritual. He also collected and studied folklore as a way to gain understanding of the culture. His focus on individual agency was unusual at the time.

In 1946 Opler became assistant professor in education and anthropology at Harvard, remaining there for two years. There he developed an interest in India, working with Rudra Datt Singh. In 1948 Opler was hired by Cornell University as professor of anthropology and Asian studies to direct the Cornell India Program, an interdisciplinary project on village India that trained many anthropologists. He helped establish Cornell as a major center for South Asian studies, complementing existing programmes in East and Southeast Asia.

Opler did publish on India, but his main responsibilities with that project were administrative. Most of his publications became more ethnological than ethnographic, although he always retained a grounding in ethnographic data. Opler developed a model of cultural themes as a cross-cultural typology for characterising cultures and the relationships of individuals within them. He also wrote on topics of general interest outside of professional anthropology, including cultural and technological change, adult education, values in American culture, and the ways people come to understand world affairs; he contributed to collections on comparative religion, political institutions, and mental health, among others. Like his work during the war, much of this more public-oriented work made policy recommendations based on his anthropological insights into the issues of development and change that seemed to be dominating the mid-twentieth-century world. For Opler such work was a necessary part of a responsible life, as a citizen and as an anthropologist.

Throughout his career Opler consistently rejected monocausal explanations of cultural phenomena, and emphasised cultural themes and ideals rather than materialist concerns. This set him against his first mentor, Leslie White, and others of more cultural-materialist persuasion (notably Marvin Harris), particularly in a series of published charges and counter-charges in the mid-1960s. Some of those exchanges became rather vitriolic, adding a personal dimension to the general social unrest of the late 1960s. In 1969 Opler retired from Cornell to teach at the University of Oklahoma. The appointment carried fewer administrative duties, and the move gave him more opportunities to return to work with the Apache Indians. He remained at Oklahoma for eight years, retiring there in 1977, but even after his second retirement Opler remained very active in research and writing. Opler's younger brother, Marvin, was also an anthropologist; he also worked during the war in the internment camps, and studied mental health and psychiatry; he died before Morris, in 1981.

Education

BA University of Buffalo, 1929
MA University of Buffalo, 1930
Ph.D. University of Chicago, 1933

Fieldwork

Apache Indians, 1930s–40s, 1970s
Poston, Arizona, and Manzanar, California (Japanese American internment camp), 1943–4
Cornell India Program (director), 1948–66

Key Publications

(1941) *An Apache Life-Way: The Economic, Social and Religious Institutions of the Chiracahua Indians*, Chicago: University of Chicago Press.
with Dobyns, Henry F. (eds) (1966) *Recommendations for Future Research on the Process of Cultural Change*, Comparative Studies of Cultural Change, Department of Anthropology, Cornell University.
(1969) *Apache Odyssey: A Journey Between Two Worlds*, New York: Holt.
with Basso, Keith (eds) (1971) *Apachean Culture History and Ethnology*, Tucson: University of Arizona Press.

FREDERIC W. GLEACH AND REGNA DARNELL

Oppitz, Michael

b. 1942, Riesengebirge, Silesia

Based on intensive fieldwork in the Himalayas, Michael Oppitz has made a substantial contribution to ethnography as well as to theoretical and visual anthropology. In his first book, using a combination of ethnographic, philological, and demographic methods, he reconstructed the ethnogenetic process of the Sherpa. While working on the Sherpa, he became attracted to the structural approach of Claude Lévi-Strauss to kinship systems, to indigenous classifications, and to the study of myths. After the completion of a book on the history of structural anthropology (1974), he studied the Northern Magar of the Dhaulagiri region. In this time he produced the documentary film, *Shamans of the Blind Country*. His monograph focuses on the matrimonial system of the Magar. Emphasis is laid on the historical development of an asymmetric system of alliance and on the cosmology structured by it. In his later work, he concentrated on a comparative study of Asian shamanic drums combining technological, ethnomusicological, philological, mythological, and symbolical approaches. His studies on the pictographic script of the Naxi focused on the transition from pictures to writing. His work on the Qiang concentrates on the connections between oral and scriptural traditions.

Education

Dr. Phil. University of Cologne, 1974
Habilitation, Free University of Berlin, 1986

Fieldwork

Solu-Khumbu, Nepal (Sherpa), 1965
Dhaulagiri region, Nepal (Magar), 1976–81
Northwest Yunnan, China (Naxi), 1996, 1998
North Sichuan, China (Quiang), 1999, 2000

Key Publications

(1974) *Notwendige Beziehungen. Abriss der strukturalen Anthropologie* (Necessary Relations. An Outline of Structural Anthropology), Frankfurt: Suhrkamp Verlag.
(1991) *Onkels Tochter, keine sonst. Heiratsbündis und Denkweise in einer Lokalkultur des Himalaya* (Uncle's Daughter, Nobody Else. Alliance and Thought Systems of a Local Culture in the Himalayas), Frankfurt: Suhrkamp Verlag.

WERNER SCHIFFAUER

Ortner, Sherry

b. 19 September 1941, Brooklyn, New York, USA

As a student of Clifford Geertz, Ortner first applied his interpretive approach to her doctoral research on religious rituals amongst Sherpas in Nepal, eventually publishing a monograph in 1978, *Sherpas through Their Rituals*, and several subsequent publications from her on-going, intermittent research in Nepal.

Early in her career, Ortner made a pivotal contribution to the new field of feminist anthropology with an oft-cited article, 'Is female to male as nature is to culture?' (1974). Drawing from structuralism, feminist philosophy, and psychology, Ortner attempted to explain universal subordination of women by arguing that in all societies men are associated with culture and women with nature. Because nature is universally devalued and women cannot escape the physiology that links them with nature, Ortner posited, women will continue to be subordinated unless both ideology and social structure change simultaneously. Ortner's theory was widely regarded by many feminists keen to understand female inequalities beyond those in the West, and aroused much debate. In a more recent discussion, Ortner has reframed the issue of male dominance in terms of power relationships between social categories and institutional structures rather than in terms of categories alone.

The question of how men are able to control women became a main focus for Ortner, who pursued questions of gender and power in an important volume, Sexual Meanings: The Cultural Construction of Gender and Sexuality, co-edited with Harriet Whitehead (1981), as well as numerous articles and book chapters. In her material published in the 1990s on the gender identities of Sherpa women mountain climbers, Ortner shifts her focus somewhat from the issue of universal subordination to that of how gender, history, and culture are interwoven for particular groups of 'gender radicals'. Her work on the impact of Western discourses of masculinity and femininity for Sherpa men and women within the transnational tourist spaces of Himalayan mountaineering, published in various articles and in her book, Life and Death on Mount Everest, marks Ortner's contributions both to borderland ethnography and to the popularisation of anthropology. It also demonstrates Ortner's deft ability to combine ethnographic storytelling with theory.

In another highly influential article, emblematic of Ortner's talent at framing disciplinary debates, Ortner outlined the major trends in anthropological theory through the 1980s including symbolic anthropology, structuralism, Marxism, and post-modernism. More important, however, is how she developed practice theory, a newly emerging actor-centered approach deriving largely from Pierre Bourdieu, Anthony Giddens, and Marshall Sahlins. Her thorough explanation influenced many anthropologists interested in resolving the problems of theories that focused either too much on structure or on agency as a way of explaining social reproduction and change. Practice theory's emphasis on the everyday actions of people as social actors as meaningful was consistent both with Clifford Geertz's notion of ethnography as 'thick description', to which Ortner was a proponent, as well as Ortner's stance that power ought to be regarded within the everyday activities of social life.

In Making Gender, a useful tracing of her own work as well as larger trends within anthropology, Ortner successfully promotes a more politicised version of practice, suggesting that feminist and subaltern theories attuned to power, agency, and resistance can provide a greater understanding of how social change occurs within moments of disorder and resistance. During the 1990s, Ortner rejected the critique of ethnography put forward by a variety of scholars outside of anthropology, and stressed the importance of ethnography to the study of resistance and domination. As editor of The Fate of Culture: Geertz and Beyond (1999) Ortner offers a revised form of interpretative anthropology in which she draws our attention to the importance of both discourse and meaning. In calling for an articulation of Geertzian and Foucaultian approaches to the study of resistance, in later years Ortner attempted to reestablish 'meaning' as central to ethnographic analysis.

Most recently, Ortner has turned her own ethnographic gaze to the USA in order to examine relationships between class, capitalism, and American culture, carrying out fieldwork amongst her New Jersey high-school classmates. With this work, Ortner has made important contributions to American ethnography, notably her insights on the relationships between anthropology and the media, and on the salience of social class in American discourse and contemporary life.

Education

BA Bryn Mawr College, 1962
MA University of Chicago, 1966
Ph.D. University of Chicago, 1970

Fieldwork

Nepal, 1966–8, 1976, 1979, 1990
Newark, New Jersey, 1992–4

Key Publications

(1984) 'Theory in anthropology since the 1960s', *Comparative Studies in Society and History* 26, 1: 126–66.
(1995) 'Resistance and the problem of ethnographic refusal', *Comparative Studies in Society and History* 37, 1: 173–93.
(1996) *Making Gender: The Politics and Erotics of Culture*, Boston: Beacon Press.
(1999) *Life and Death on Mount Everest: Sherpas and Himalayan Mountaineering*, Princeton: Princeton University Press.

SUSAN FROHLICK

Overing, Joanna

b. 12 August 1938, Takoma Park, Maryland, USA

Beginning in the 1970s, Overing's writings on Amazonia have addressed livelihood and everyday life, cosmology and shamanism, personhood and consciousness, morality and aesthetics, sociality and social organisation, egalitarianism and power, and feminism and problems of translation in anthropological analysis, among other matters. Her early work on the Venezuelan Piaroa contributed significantly to the anthropological understanding of Amazonian kinship. Her later work set trends as well, making certain matters – e.g. the

cosmological notion of a predatory universe, and the Amazonian passion for convivial everyday social relations among co-residents - central to debates in Amazonianist anthropology.

Overing's writings and her demands of her peers have always made manifest a strong commitment to detailed ethnography and a firm willingness to question critically attempts at 'grand theorising' in anthropology. Her own work is nonetheless theoretically sophisticated itself, judiciously incorporating elements from a variety of anthropological, linguistic and philosophical sources. She has made particularly persuasive use of maverick philosophers such as N. Goodman and P. Feyerabend, among others. Throughout, Overing has followed her own often explicit suggestion that anthropologists should listen seriously to natives' own discourses on social life, treating them as creative, worthy accounts in their own right, rather than forcibly making them fit into Western sociological categories.

Education

BA University of Connecticut, 1960
MA University of Connecticut, 1963
Ph.D. Brandeis University, 1974

Fieldwork

Placencia, Honduras, 1965
Piaroa communities in Amazonas, Venezuela, 1968, 1977
Iquitos, Brazil, 1991
Santa Catarina, Brazil, 1994

Key Publications

(1975) *The Piaroa; A People of the Orinoco Basin: A Study in Kinship and Marriage*, Oxford: Clarendon Press.
with Passes, Alan (eds) (2000) *The Anthropology of Love and Anger: The Aesthetics of Conviviality in Native South America*, New York: Routledge.

CARLOS DAVID LONDOÑO SULKIN

P

Paine, Robert

b. 10 April 1926, Portsmouth, UK

Robert Paine is noted for incisive essays on the understanding of human social relations, for his contribution to Saami studies as an ethnographer and an advocate, and for his academic leadership in enquiries devoted to a wide range of theoretical and topical issues. He came to the attention of a general anthropological readership in the late 1960s and early 1970s with papers on the subjects of gossip, friendship, and patronage, which subsequently became standard points of reference for discussion on these topics. Paine had been a colleague of Fredrik Barth in Norway, and the thinking in these papers was inspired by a critical reading of Barth's theory of transactionalism. Paine insisted that to understand human social forms one addressed the social action that generated them, but he was also careful to describe the social context of this action and to explore the different modes of communication that obtained between human actors. According to Paine, Barth put too much weight on structural imperatives in his study of ethnicity, but neglected matters of power in his account of interpersonal relations. Paine's later study of political rhetoric, which engaged with the work of Maurice Bloch, extended such themes: for Paine, rhetoric is doing by saying, which occurs in a negotiated world. Since 1965 Paine has lived in Newfoundland, Canada, and he went on to enthusiastically apply these ideas in sociological studies of Newfoundland politics.

Robert Paine's first fieldwork yielded an extensive account of social values, neighbourhood relations, and economic development among Lapps (Saami) living in coastal areas of northern Norway. However, he is better known for his account of Saami society in the interiors of northern Norway and Sweden where the way of life, revolving around reindeer pastoralism, more closely reflected ecological relations that had once obtained more broadly amongst the indigenous population in northern Scandinavia. These studies, marked by a meticulous attention to ethnographic detail, introduced a number of subtle analytical distinctions, such as between 'herding' and 'husbandry', which advanced our understanding of pastoral societies more broadly. Paine's interest in Saami interpersonal ties, economic strategies, and information exchange clearly influenced his more general theories of human social relations.

As director of sociological research and later the Henrietta Harvey Professor of Anthropology at Memorial University in St John's, Newfoundland, Robert Paine led and encouraged a number of ethnographic projects and intellectual workshops. These especially coincided with concerns relating to the North Atlantic region, comprising East Arctic Canada, Newfoundland and Labrador, Scotland, Norway, and Iceland. Paine was a prime mover behind a highly regarded publications series, under the imprint of the Institute of Social and Economic

Research Press (Memorial University). These endeavours saw landmark accounts, authored and edited by himself or by close colleagues, of Newfoundland 'outport communities', the contemporary situation of the Inuit in the 'White Man's' arctic, and the social and economic strategies of Atlantic fishermen.

A landmark achievement of Robert Paine was to be one of the first anthropologists to systematically elaborate and illustrate the notion of anthropological advocacy. A strong believer that anthropologists must be committed to the causes and interests of the people they study, he undertook an investigation, for the Norwegian Supreme Court, that led to strong criticisms of proposals for a hydro-electric power scheme that would entail the flooding of vital areas of reindeer pasture in northern Norway. An intellectually strong workshop on the subject of advocacy later led to the publication, under Paine's editor-ship, of what continues to be a standard text on this controversial topic. Also, these concerns have dovetailed with Paine's considera-tion of the recent ethnopolitical expressions of identity among 'Fourth World' peoples, espe-cially the Saami, but also among Indian and Inuit populations in Canada. Characteristic of all his written work, Robert Paine's concise and elegant manner of expression means that his personal standpoints on these difficult matters are put trenchantly and with great clarity.

Over the past two decades Robert Paine has not only continued researching and writing on all the above-mentioned themes, but also has entered a new area of research with commen-taries on the construction of self and national identity in modern Israel.

Education

BA University of Oxford, 1950
D.Phil. University of Oxford, 1960

Fieldwork Periods and Locale

Coastal Saami in Norway, 1951–2, 1958
Saami Reindeer Pastoralists in Norway, 1953, 1962, 1963

Newfoundland Politics, 1975–81 (intermit-tent)
Israel and Zionism, 1982 (intermittent)
Project director, Identity and Modernity in the East Arctic, 1968–71

Key Publications

(1974) *Second Thoughts about Barth's 'Models'*, London: Royal Anthropological Institute.
(ed.) (1981) *Politically Speaking: Cross-Cultural Studies of Rhetoric*, Philadelphia: ISHI.
(ed.) (1986) *Anthropology and Advocacy*, St John's: ISER Press, Memorial University.
(1994) *Herds of the Tundra: A Portrait of Reindeer Pastoralism*, Washington: Smithsonian Institu-tion Press.

DAVID RICHES

Palerm, Angel

b. 11 September 1917, Ibiza, Spain

d. 10 June 1980, Mexico City, Mexico

Angel Palerm arrived in Mexico in 1939. In 1950 he was hired by the Smithsonian Institution as an associate researcher in a study of the Totonac of Veracruz conducted by Isabel Kelly. Palerm's fieldwork centered on a careful examination of the evolution of local produc-tive organisation and its implications for power hierarchies, beliefs, and symbolism. He pursued this theme in a comparative project with Nahuatl-speaking Indians in the Sierra of Puebla, which resulted in a path-breaking article ('La civilización urbana', later included in his book, *Agricultura y sociedad en Mesoamerica*), contrasting the sociocultural con-notations of swidden and irrigated agriculture. With Eric Wolf, he wrote a series of papers on the ecological history of the Texcoco region (later collected in their book, *Agricultura y civilización en Mesoamerica*). In the following years Angel Palerm would continue this line of enquiry, which adopted multilineal evolution as its theoretical banner and delved into the nature of despotism.

As these ideas did not agree with the official orthodoxy, Angel found it difficult to get a permanent position within Mexico, and in 1953 he went to Washington to work for the Panamerican Union Social Science Bureau as an editor of the *Revista interamericana de ciencias sociales* and as a publisher of Spanish versions of classical anthropological works. In addition he started a programme of grants and fellowships for Latin American graduates, and promoted technical assistance schemes that led him to a focus on applied anthropology.

Angel Palerm returned to Mexico in 1965, and devoted the remainder of his life to an intense round of writing, teaching, and public consulting, as well as to the creation of institutions that have had a revolutionary impact on Mexican anthropology: in 1967 the Graduate School of Anthropology at the Iberoamericana University and in 1973 the Centro de Investigaciones Superiores del Instituto Nacional de Antropologia e Historia. He was the fulcrum of a group of students and younger colleagues that conducted research on a variety of innovative themes. In his own writings Angel became a champion of a critical Marxist anthropology. He rebuked modernisation theory for its unilineal, ahistorical implications. In many ways, he was the forerunner in Mexico of the anthropology of globalisation and multiculturalism, because of his on-going interest in the diversified articulation between the world system and the logic of local actors and histories.

Education

BA National University of Mexico, 1949
MA National School of Anthropology and History, Mexico City, 1953
Ph.D. University of San Marcos, Lima, 1966

Fieldwork

Coast of Veracruz and Sierra of Puebla, Mexico, 1950–2
Texcoco Valley, Mexico, 1952–3, and shorter sojourns from 1966 to 1973.

Key Publications

with Kelly, Isabel (1952) *The Tajin Totonac. Part I: History, Shelter, and Technology*, Washington: Institute of Social Anthropology, Smithsonian Institution.
(1972) *Agricultura y sociedad en Mesoamerica* (Agriculture and Society in Mesoamerica), Mexico City: Secretaria de Educacion Publica.
with Wolf, Eric (1972) *Agricultura y civilización en Mesoamerica* (Agriculture and Civilisation in Mesoamerica), Mexico City: Secretaria de Educacion Publica.
(1980) *Antropologia y Marxismo* (Anthropology and Marxism), Mexico City: Nueva Imagen.

GUILLERMO DE LA PEÑA

Palmeira, Moacir

b. 1942, Maceió, Brazil

Moacir Palmeira has distinguished himself through both his original critical analysis of the Brazilian intellectual field in what concerns the agrarian question (as in *Latifundium et capitalisme; lecture critique d'un débat* -Latifundium and Capitalism; critical lecture of a debate, 1971), and his empirical research on the social transformations in the sugarcane plantation area of the Northeast ('Casa e trabalho: nota sobre as relações sociais na "plantation" tradicional' [House and work: notes on the social relations in the traditional plantation] 1976). Through these two lines of research he has, from the 1970s onwards, incisively contributed to the renewal of the Brazilian social sciences from the vantage point of social anthropology and of studies of the intellectual field, peasant societies, citizenship, and politics. As a professor at the Museu Nacional, Palmeira has exerted a decisive influence on the preparation of researchers. He is also an important reference in matters of ethics in research and applied anthropology, having acted as a consultant for CONTAG during a period characterised by the struggle for the democratisation of the military regime; he has participated in government programmes for the implementation of agrarian reform in 1986, and for the war against famine in 1993. More recently he has been carrying out research on the anthropology of politics, co-ordinating various sub-projects on rituals, representations, and the use of violence.

Education

BA Catholic University of Rio de Janeiro, 1964
Ph.D., University of Paris, 1971

Fieldwork

Alagoas, 1961
Bahia, 1962
Pernambuco plantation areas, 1969, 1970, 1972, 1975–7
Consultant of the National Federation of Workers in Agriculture (CONTAG) in Brasilia (1978–88), present at different rural areas all over the country
Pernambuco, sertão (dry hinterlands), 1988–2000

Key Publications

(1979) 'The aftermath of peasant mobilization: rural conflicts in the Brazilian northeast since 1964', in Neuma Aguiar (ed.) The Structure of Brazilian Development, New Jersey: Transaction Books.
with Herédia, Beatriz (1994) 'Le Temps de la politique' (The time of politics), Etudes Rurales, Paris, 131–2: 73–87.

JOSÉ SERGIO LEITE LOPES

Pálsson, Gísli

b. 22 December 1949, Westman Islands, Iceland

Gísli Pálsson made his reputation by adapting models developed for hunter-gatherer collectivities to fishing regimes in his native Iceland (2002 population: 288,201). Focusing on resource management policies, climate change, and forms of ownership, he explores where language and cognition encounter the market, property regimes, and the environment. With theoretical roots in cultural ecology, political economy, and cognitive science, he adds nuance to understandings of 'adaptation' in cultural processes.

Pálsson directs a project examining how and why Europeans moralise about the commodification of the body. He analyses discussions around DeCode, Iceland's publicly traded biotechnology company that uses Icelandic genes, medical records, and genealogical data to research disease causes. Pálsson circumvents national and international political controversies to conduct comparative empirical research that defines the gap between public discourse and scientific knowledge as the location of culture-making.

Social science was emerging in Iceland when Pálsson began his university studies. Part of a cohort granted funds for postgraduate studies abroad, he participated in the nation-state's modernisation of research into history, society, and culture. While much of Pálsson's work is in English, a notable amount is in Icelandic. He has contributed to Icelanders' active curiosity about their own culture with collaborative and single-authored studies concerning class differences in language use, the Icelandic sagas, novels by Nobel-winning author, Halldór Laxness, and the diaries of Canadian-born Arctic explorer, Vilhjálmur Stefánsson.

Education

BA University of Iceland, 1972
MA University of Manchester, 1974
Ph.D. University of Manchester, 1982

Fieldwork

Iceland, 1979, 1981
Republic of Cape Verde, 1984
Iceland, 1993–2003

Key Publications

(1991) *Coastal Economies, Cultural Accounts: Human Ecology and Icelandic Discourse*, Manchester: Manchester University Press.

(1995) *The Textual Life of Savants: Ethnography, Iceland, and the Linguistic Turn*, Chur: Harwood Academic Publishers.

ANNE BRYDON

Parkin, David

b. 5 November 1940, Watford, UK

Although Parkin's main contribution to social anthropology has been his long-term field-work among the non-Muslim Giriama and Swahili-speaking Muslims of East Africa, his first fieldwork was among Luo-speaking peoples of Kenya, who had migrated to towns in Uganda and Kenya in the 1950s and 1960s, adapting to the modern urban conditions of late colonialism. Parkin analysed the way in which the Luo polysegmentary lineage system adjusted and reasserted itself in these new contexts. His work was in line with the ethnographies of the Manchester School anthropologists, who sought to understand how the 'indigenous' peoples adapted their social life, customs, and religion, by adjusting their kinship, social organisation, and political institutions to the new settings of urbanisation and industrialisation brought about by colonialism and post-colonialism.

In the late 1960s, Parkin turned his ethnographic interest to the interaction between the inland non-Muslim Giriama of Kenya and the coastal Swahili-speaking Muslims of Kenya and Tanzania. He was the first anthropologist to work among the Giriama and his analyses over four decades have explored the processes through which Giriama and Swahili have interacted with each other while at the same time keeping separate identities. Giriama resisted conversion to Islam and Christianity until recently but their increasing migration to the coastal areas, previously dominated by Swahili, is changing the relationship between both peoples and the way they construct their mutual identities. Over the last decade Parkin's research has focused on how changing economic conditions in the coastal areas of Kenya and Tanzania have impacted upon the religious and social ideologies of coastal peoples, in which new notions of 'health', 'progress', 'entrepreneurship', and 'political change' play an important role. His interest throughout his work has been on changes in knowledge, practice, and how these are expressed in language.

Currently, Parkin is preparing a monograph on Islam and medicine among the Swahili-speaking peoples. He runs a project on Indian Ocean Studies and is working in collaboration with the new Centre of Migration Policy and Society at Oxford.

Education

BA (Hons) School of Oriental and African Studies, 1962

Ph.D. School of Oriental and African Studies, 1965

Fieldwork

Kampala, Uganda, 1962–4
Kenya, 1966–7, 1968–9, 1977–8
Kenya, 1984, 1985, 1988 (8 months in all)
Kenya and Zanzibar, 1991, 1992, 1993 (4 months in all)
Zanzibar and Pemba, Tanzania, 1995 (2 months)
Zanzibar and Mombasa, Kenya, 1997–8 (2 months)
Zanzibar, 2002 (2 months)

Key Publications

(1969) *Neighbours and Nationals in an African City Ward*, London/Berkeley: Routledge & Kegan Paul/California University Press.

(1972) *Palms, Wine and Witnesses: Public Spirit and Private Gain in an African Farming Community*, San Francisco/London: Chandler (new edn, Prospect Heights, IL: Waveland Press, 1994).

(1978) *The Cultural Definition of Political Response:*

Lineal Destiny among the Luo of Kenya, London/New York: Academic Press.

(1991) *Sacred Void: Spatial Images of Work and Ritual among the Giriama of Kenya*, Cambridge/New York: Cambridge University Press.

LUÍS BATALHA

Parmentier, Richard J.

b. 25 December 1948, Newark, New Jersey, USA

The conjunction of semiotics and anthropology in Parmentier's work has led him to make original contributions to both these fields. Besides his major ethnographic work on Palau, he has pursued a wide range of interests including ethnographic studies of Colonial Williamsburg, modern advertising, and medieval Europe. His deeply erudite writings also encompass many aspects of Western intellectual history.

Parmentier draws mainly from Peircean semiotics to uncover processes of semiotic mediation. Mediation processes occur within sign relations that bring together an object (or referent), a representation, and an interpretant that mutually construct and delineate each other. These sign relations are linked in chains of signs, each transforming the other signs in the chain into more and more complex relationships even while maintaining a link with the original object. This process of semiosis mediates our relationship with internal and external reality.

Parmentier has sought to use the concept of semiosis for research and understanding in anthropology, in particular in uncovering modes of semiotic patterning. One of the main issues he has tackled is the relationship of culture and history, and, within that relationship, that of diachrony and synchrony. The semiotic concepts helpful in understanding this relationship can be summed up as pertaining to the relationship between contextualised and decontextualised signs. Contextualised signs exist in experience, in history. They exist tacitly within the sediments in

decontextualised signs that are made to appear timeless, that is naturalised. This is part of a process of semiotic regimentation that is often employed to the benefit of the upper reaches of society.

In applying these semiotic notions to his ethnographical work in Palau, Parmentier challenges the notion of people 'without history' while also showing that the ways a group conceives of history itself is culture specific. Parmentier contrasts 'signs of history', that is, all sorts of markers of past events including documents, with 'signs in history', which are signs of history that become the object of strategic manipulation, frequently for political purposes. The signs of and in history in Palau include historical narratives as well as material remains, exchange valuables, and cultural practices. Sedimented contextual signs come to be decontextualised, that is, taken out of history and/or used as signs in history, through several modes of understanding specific to Palauan culture. These are the notions of paths, cornerposts, and sides, where the notion and ritual practice linking cornerposts with hierarchy works to decontextualise the historical experiences carried by the other two.

Parmentier's work mediates categories that have been kept separate not only in Palau but also in anthropology as well.

Education

AB Princeton University, 1971
MA University of Chicago, 1976
Ph.D. University of Chicago, 1981

Fieldwork

Palau (Micronesia), 1978–80

Key Publications

with Mertz, Elizabeth (eds) (1985) *Semiotic Mediation: Sociocultural and Psychological Perspectives* (contributed three chapters), Orlando, FL: Academic Press.

(1987) *The Sacred Remains: Myth, History, and Polity*

in *Belau*, Chicago: The University of Chicago Press.

(1994) *Signs in Society: Studies in Semiotic Anthropology*, Bloomington: Indiana University Press.

(1997) *The Pragmatic Semiotics of Cultures* (special issue of *Semiotica* 116, 1), Berlin: Mouton de Gruyter.

CATHERINE TIHANYI

Parry, Jonathan P.

b. 10 September 1943, London, UK

Throughout his work in India, Jonathan Parry addresses the relationship between symbolic systems and socioeconomic practice. Parry began his anthropological career at a time when many anthropologists of South Asia were critiquing the apolitical analysis of the ideology of caste presented by Louis Dumont. In his early work, *Caste and Kinship in Kangra*, Parry argued that the idiom and symbolic practices of hierarchy typically associated with relationships between castes also structure a variety of other social relationships in which power plays an important role. He suggests that opposing views of caste as either integrative or exploitative reflect different analytical perspectives on caste as ideology versus caste as practice.

In his next research site – the Hindu pilgrimage city of Benaras – Parry studied the cultural meanings and socioeconomic practices associated with death. This work reflects his on-going interest in structural and symbolic analysis, as seen in his discussion on opposing models of death in the Hindu world. And he provides a cultural analysis of the relationship between gifts and money exchanges that inverts earlier Marxist assumptions that gifts are moral and inalienable whereas money is immoral and alienable, thereby revealing the Marxist perspectives to be culturally specific. In his ethnography based on this fieldwork, *Death in Benaras*, Parry tries to bridge the gap between culture and practical reason by arguing that the social organisation of death can only be understood through an analysis of the cultural construction of death itself and vice versa. Furthermore, although he agrees with Dumont that the division of labour within the caste system is ideologically integrative, he argues that such an orientation can only exist in an ideological universe that has conceived of its opposite.

In the 1990s Parry's research shifted to the public-sector Bhilai Steel plant in Madhya Pradesh and directly addresses economic policy. Once again he demonstrates the linkages between cultural systems and political-economic systems. He suggests that public sector workplaces allow for a 'melting pot' phenomenon such that notions of primordial ties of caste, kin, and religious identity are transcended, whereas these identities tend to be reinforced in the private sector. Therefore, he suggests that recent privatisation policies in India may play a role in the intensification of religious communal conflict and in rigidifying caste identities.

Education

BA University of Cambridge, 1965
Ph.D. University of Cambridge, 1971

Fieldwork

Kangra District, Himachal Pradesh, India, 1966–8, 1974
Banaras, India, 1976–7, 1978, 1981, 1983, 1992
Bhilainagar, Madhya Pradesh, India, 1993–4, ongoing 1995–2001

Key Publications

(1979) *Caste and Kinship in Kangra*, London: Routledge & Kegan Paul
with Bloch, M. (1989) *Money and the Morality of Exchange*, Cambridge, UK: Cambridge University Press.
(1994) *Death in Benaras*, Cambridge, UK: Cambridge University Press.

CECILIA VAN HOLLEN

Parsons, Elsie Clews

b. 27 November 1874, New York, USA

d. December 1941, New York, USA

Elsie Clews Parsons, an outspoken philanthropist and feminist who came from a prosperous and socially prominent family, received a Ph.D. in sociology in 1899 before turning to anthropology as a preferable route to the amelioration of American society. Her marriage to Herbert Parsons in 1900 created a devoted family despite its unconventional gender roles. Her social position allowed her to pursue professional work as an avocation, although she held a formal teaching position only briefly, at the New School for Social Research in 1919. Parsons was widely recognised as a public intellectual, operating at the fringes of Greenwich Village, and speaking out or writing on a wide variety of social issues. Anthropology provided her with a platform for criticising then-contemporary American society based on ethnographic data from other cultures. Her positions in favor of free love, trial marriage, and pacifism (during the First World War) were frequently embarrassing to her husband, who had political aspirations.

Although Parsons did considerable personal research, and was the first woman to become president of the American Anthropological Association in 1941, she is remembered today primarily for her philanthropic support of Americanist anthropology in the days before foundation or government grants became widely available. Parsons was particularly enthusiastic in her support of women in the field and of research among the Southwestern Pueblos. She encouraged many women to enter anthropology as a profession, e.g. Ruth Bunzel, Esther Goldfrank, Gladys Reichard, and Ruth Landes. She supported, both editorially and financially, the *Journal of American Folklore* edited by Franz Boas, and underwrote the costs for many of his other projects and for on-going editorial work.

Parsons began to work in the Southwest around 1915, arranging her trips around family responsibilities (she had four children).

Boas joined her on three of these trips, the first in 1919. Parsons's methods of clandestine recording and publication of esoteric material do not meet contemporary standards of informed consent or ethical conduct. Nonetheless, in her own time she was widely judged to have excellent rapport in Pueblo communities, which were usually hostile to outsiders. Because she worked at a number of different Pueblos, Parsons was able to attempt a comparative synthesis, particularly in the two volumes of *Pueblo Indian Religion* (1930). She habitually sought out women in the field, working, for example, with Flora Zuni at Zuni Pueblo and later with Rosita Lema in Peru.

Because of her interests in the mechanisms of Spanish influence on Native North American cultures, Parsons carried out fieldwork in Oaxaca, Mexico, comparing Spanish colonialism to the more Anglicised experience of the American Southwest in *Mitla: Town of the Souls* (1936). At the time of her death, Parsons was working on materials from her fieldwork in Peguche, Peru, where Rosita Lema provided her with an example of a woman taking an innovative role in rapid culture change. Parsons's book on Peguche appeared posthumously. Her three volumes on New World black folklore in French and English in the Antilles also appeared after her death; this material was collected at Boas's request. Parsons also supported early Caribbean folklore collecting by Melville Herskovits.

Parsons was determined that the American public needed to learn about the insights of anthropology. Her *American Indian Life* (1922) assembled life history sketches by her Boasian colleagues based on their fieldwork in a wide variety of Native American cultures but was presented in a more accessible style for nonprofessional readers. Although the sketches vary considerably in ethnographic and literary quality, this was a pioneering experiment in the presentation of ethnographic data. The project also foreshadowed the life history orientation of the culture and personality school developed by Ruth Benedict, Margaret Mead, and Edward Sapir during the interwar years.

Parsons's early feminist positions now seem

ultra-conservative. On social Darwinist grounds, she argued that women were unprepared for suffrage and that voluntary childless marriages among those who could afford to raise and educate children were irresponsible. And yet, in her own day, Parsons was considered a tireless crusader for the rights of women, both personal and professional. One index of the full generation by which she preceded other women in Americanist anthropology is the absence of women as contributors to *American Indian Life*. Ruth Benedict was still a graduate student and the others who progressed in their career partly due to Parsons's backing were much younger. She remains, then, at a crossroads in the professionalisation of the discipline, helping to create an anthropology in which her own contributions would seem increasingly outdated.

Education

BA Barnard College, 1896
MA Columbia University, 1897
Ph.D. Columbia University, 1899

Fieldwork

Southwestern Pueblos, beginning in 1915
Mexico and Peru, 1930s until her death

Key Publications

(1922) *American Indian Life*, New York: B.W. Huebsch.
(1930) *Pueblo Indian Religion*, Chicago: University of Chicago Publications in Anthropology.
(1936) *Mitla: Town of the Souls*, Chicago: University of Chicago Publications in Anthropology.
(1945) *Peguche: A Study of Andean Indians*, Chicago: University of Chicago Press.

REGNA DARNELL

Paul, Benjamin David

b. 1911, New York City, USA

d. 24 May 2005, Atlanta, Georgia, USA

Benjamin Paul's research began on the shores of Lake Atitlán, Guatemala, in the Mayan village of San Pedro La Laguna, where he worked with his wife, Lois Paul, conducting a baseline study of a town that would undergo enormous change. Over the years they documented the community's transformation as it moved from a subsistence economy to coffee exporting, which was accompanied by a profound restructuring of the town's political system, technology, and religious organisation. He later witnessed its transition from a peaceful town to one torn open by the brutal civil war that brought abductions, massacres, and death squads, claiming the lives of his closest friends.

Paul's initial investigation focused on godparenthood ties and economic relations, but, after two years of training at the Boston Psychoanalytic Institute, he conducted further research on psychology and public health, including marriage patterns, midwifery, sibling rivalry, migration, sanitation, mental disorders, and warfare.

In addition to teaching at Yale University, Harvard University, and Stanford University, for years Paul led teacher training programmes in rural Guatemala, doing community organisation for the Inter-American Educational Foundation, and directing programmes in public health, medicine, and the behavioural sciences to train students in social science methodology. In his pioneering efforts to train community workers in social science and public health, he has lain the groundwork for many generations to come.

His influence extends through not only his research and publications on a broad range of topics heretofore unexplored, but also the interdisciplinary training programmes he developed at such an early date, combining anthropology, psychology, and public health in order to better understand Mayan communities and meet their health needs. His work provides an invaluable longitudinal perspective on the consequences of social change for communities during intense turmoil.

Education

BA University of Chicago, 1938

Ph.D. University of Chicago, 1943

Fieldwork

San Pedro La Laguna, Guatemala, 1940–2, 1956, 1962–9, 1974–9, 1983–1995.
Children's Medical Center, Boston, Massachusetts, 1958–62.

Key Publications

(1955) *Health, Culture, and Community: Case Studies of Public Reactions to Health Programs*, New York: Russell Sage Foundation.
(1976) 'The Maya bonesetter as sacred specialist', *Ethnology* 15: 77–81.

NICOLE SAULT

Peacock, James

b. 31 October 1937, Montgomery, Alabama, USA

James Peacock's work is broadly synthetic and interdisciplinary in nature, grounded in ethnography but always cognisant of social theory. An undergraduate psychology major, as a senior Peacock took an anthropology course with Weston LaBarre, who also took him and a friend to the American Anthropological Association meetings in Washington. There he heard Alfred Kroeber and Alan Lomax, and became convinced that anthropology would be a more interesting career. Seeking to combine his experience in psychology with anthropology, Peacock elected to enter the Department of Social Relations at Harvard. Clyde Kluckhohn, a key part of that interdisciplinary programme, died after Peacock's first year there. Peacock studied with sociologists Talcott Parsons and Robert Bellah, and anthropologists including Cora Du Bois and David Maybury Lewis. Fellow student Thomas Kirsch became a good friend, and helped Peacock choose to work in Southeast Asia.

In August 1962 Peacock married Florence Turner Fowler, a music student and singer, and the next day they left for a year in Surabaya, Indonesia. There they lived in the slums, doing fieldwork on theatre and its relationships to the economic and political chaos in which Indonesian workers lived; it was the height of the Sukarno period, and just before the massacres that became known as the 'Year of Living Dangerously'. His dissertation drawn from that work was published in 1968 as *Rites of Modernization*. In 1969 the family – including their first two daughters – returned to Southeast Asia. Peacock had become interested in Muslim movements and planned to go to Malaya, but race riots there made it impossible to get a visa. After the family returned to the USA, Peacock went on to Indonesia, where he spent eight months working in Muslim training camps. He had developed an interest in the sociocultural dimensions of religion as an undergraduate, and this remains an important aspect of his work.

After receiving his Ph.D. Peacock began teaching at Princeton, where he helped create the doctoral programme in anthropology. However, in 1967 he took an offer to teach at the University of North Carolina, Chapel Hill – an irresistible opportunity to return to his native South. There he rose through the professorial ranks, and is currently Kenan professor of anthropology, professor of comparative literature, and director of the University Center for International Studies. He also chaired the anthropology department 1975–80 and 1990–1, and the university faculty senate 1991–4. A very active member of the campus community, in 1995 Peacock received the Thomas Jefferson Award of the University of North Carolina, a recognition of faculty leadership.

Returning to the southeastern USA encouraged Peacock to also do research there, continuing a long University of North Carolina tradition of professional anthropological involvement in the local community. Beginning in the 1970s Peacock did research in the area on religious and psychiatric institutions, faith-healing, southern Protestantism, and alcoholism. Several of these were collaborative projects with colleagues in various departments, notably including Ruel Tyson, a colleague in religious studies at the University of North Carolina. Working with students and other colleagues he also helped develop a seminar on the Nike corporation, prompted by student protests, which investigated and produced widespread awareness of their corporate practices, and led to a coalition of universities who use licensing agreements to shape working conditions.

In addition to his more ethnographic work Peacock has published several works on anthropological theory and philosophy. *Consciousness and Change* (1975) draws on Durkheimian and Weberian sociology along with psychological and symbolic anthropology – particularly the work of Victor Turner – to implicate symbol-systems in processes of change. This attempt to bridge what often seems a theoretical chasm between generally synchronic studies and those focusing on diachronic historical processes was unusual at the time, but such efforts have become more common since. There and elsewhere, Peacock also sought to maintain a holistic vision in anthropology, a recognition of and focus on the commonalities of seemingly disparate sociocultural phenomena that also demands the crossing of disciplinary boundaries. A 'unifying framework' (1975: x) of culture that includes symbolic forms, social expressions, and historical processes forms the backbone of his work, explicitly developed in his theoretical works but also underlying his ethnography.

Education

BA Duke University, 1959
Ph.D. Harvard University, 1965

Fieldwork

Indonesia, 1962–3, 1969–70, 1979, 1988, 1996
Southern Appalachia, 1980–6

Key Publications

(1975) *Consciousness and Change: Symbolic Anthropology in Evolutionary Perspective*, New York: Wiley.
(1978) *Purifying the Faith: The Muhammadijah Movement in Indonesian Islam*, Menlo Park, CA: Benjamin Cummings.
(1986) *The Anthropological Lens: Harsh Light, Soft Focus*, Cambridge, UK: Cambridge University Press (revised edn, 2001).
with Tyson, Ruel W., Jr (1989) *Pilgrims of Paradox: Calvinism and Experience among the Primitive Baptists of the Blue Ridge*, Washington: Smithsonian Institution Press.

FREDERIC W. GLEACH

Pels, Peter

b. 1958, Bussum, The Netherlands

Pels' work brings the anthropology of colonialism and missionisation to bear on a critical reassessment of current anthropological practices and self-understandings. Educated in critical anthropology by the late Bob Scholte and Johannes Fabian, Pels succeeded the former as co-editor of *Critique of Anthropology*. His work on Catholic missionaries in eastern Tanzania argued that, while missions should indeed be studied as violent harbingers of commodity culture, anthropologists tended to misrepresent such colonial contact by concentrating on the idealism and ethnocentrism of the Christian message rather than on missionaries' engagement with Africans.

This entry into the anthropology of colonialism led Pels to take issue with the tendency of professional anthropologists to dismiss colonial ethnographers (such as missionaries) as 'amateurs' and portray the discipline as if it had no more ties with its colonial past. He turned this demand for more historical sophistication in anthropological self-understandings into critiques of anthropological ethics, the anthropology of magic and witchcraft, and the study of material culture. Recently, Pels's research on colonial administration proposed revisions to the anthropology of politics under globalisation, and his study on the relationship between nineteenth-century British anthropology and the rise of modern occultism provides challenging revisions to the history of anthropology.

Education

MA University of Amsterdam, 1986
MA University of Amsterdam, 1986
Ph.D. University of Amsterdam, 1993

Fieldwork

Tanzania, Netherlands, UK (fieldwork and archival research), 1988–90, 1996–7
UK and USA (archival research), 1995, 1998

Key Publications

(1999) *A Politics of Presence. Contacts between Missionaries and Waluguru in Late Colonial Tanganyika*, Chur, Reading: Harwood Academic.
(1999) 'Professions of duplexity: a prehistory of ethical codes in anthropology', *Current Anthropology* 40, 2: 101–36.

GERD BAUMANN

Peristiany, John George

b. 4 September 1911, Athens, Greece

d. 27 October 1987, Paris, France

The relatively large number of volumes edited by John Peristiany reflected his commitment to the creation of social science structures of teaching and research in both Greece and Cyprus. Similarly the efforts he dedicated to the organisation of international conferences (1959 with J. Pitt-Rivers: Burg Wartenstein; 1961, 1963, 1966: Athens; 1981: Marseilles) reflected his commitment to the promotion of comparative studies in the Mediterranean. In addition to the participation of well-known sociologists, geographers, and anthropologists Peristiany ensured these conferences always included young scholars.

Peristiany studied law in Paris and philosophy, sociology, and anthropology in Oxford, where he eventually became senior university lecturer (1946–63) under A.R. Radcliffe-Brown and E. Evans-Pritchard. During the Second World War, Peristiany held the position of professor of social anthropology in Cairo as well as responsibility for the press office of the Greek government in exile (1941–5). This was followed by lectureships at the London School of Economics (1946) under Malinowski, and in Cambridge (1947) under Meyer Fortes.

His mentors regarded Peristiany as a great Africanist for his work among the Kipsigis and the Pokots of Kenya. Hence he was asked to deliver the Frazer Memorial Lecture in 1953. However, soon after, Peristiany decided, in a move which was fairly revolutionary for the time, to shift his work to Cyprus, believing that the methods developed in 'primitive' societies could be adapted to modern ones by mixing sociology and anthropology. He was also anxious to scrutinise his own country that, for political reasons, had been deprived of serious social studies.

In 1960, under the aegis of UNESCO, he created the Social Sciences Centre of Athens, the first institution in Greece where sociology and anthropology were taught and practised. He directed this center until 1969 when the dictatorship (1967–74) forced him to leave. In 1969 he created a similar center in Cyprus. From 1978 to 1981, he served as the ambassador of Cyprus in Paris, Madrid, and Lisbon. In 1987, he had the satisfaction of inaugurating the first Greek department of anthropology at Mytilene.

His African studies emphasised the issues raised by customary law while his Mediterranean studies pointed out the values that command the behaviour of individuals and are a key to understanding the institutions of honour, shame, rivalry, and jealousy.

Education

Ph.D. University of Paris, 1932
Ph.D. University of Oxford, 1935

Fieldwork

Kipsigis, Kenya, 1936–8
Pokots, Kenya, 1947–8
Alona, Cyprus, 1954–5, at times between 1967 and 1974

Key Publications

(1964 [1939, 1954]) *The Social Institutions of the Kipsigis*, Oxon and London: George Routledge & Sons.
(ed.) (1965) *Honour and Shame, the Values of Mediterranean Societies*, London: Weidenfeld & Nicholson.
(ed.) (1976) *Mediterranean Family Structures*, London, New York, and Melbourne: Cambridge University Press.
(ed.) (1989) *Le Prix de l'alliance en Méditerranée* (The Price of Marriage in the Mediterranean), Paris: CNRS.

Further Reading

(1995) *Les Amis et les autres. Mélanges en l'honneur de John Peristiany* (Brothers and Others. Essays in Honour of John Peristiany), compiled by S. Damianakos, M.-E. Handman, J. Pitt-Rivers, and G. Ravis-Giordani, Athens: Centre National de Recherches Sociales (EKKE).

MARIE-ÉLISABETH HANDMAN

Philips, Susan U.

b. 1943, Louisville, Kentucky, USA

The first of Philips's major publications remains one of her most influential contributions, not only to anthropology, but also to the social sciences and education. In this microethnography of schooling in an Oregon Indian community, Philips introduced a number of themes that would remain central to her subsequent work. At Warm Springs, Philips showed how the teachers' management of children's opportunities to speak in a classroom validated the power of the dominant white culture, while discrediting and silencing the contrasting culture and language of Indian children. This sociolinguistic documentation of social inequality in an institution of power reflects a political stance that will also be seen in her work in Tongan and Tucson, Arizona, courts. This approach was chosen for its potential to assist in the amelioration of such injustices. While the theoretical force of Philips's work is most often cited, her contributions to methodology are also considerable. Her fieldwork illustrates the meticulous collection of empirical speech and observational data; this degree of accountability lends weight to her claims of political inequalities. She is also a strong proponent of anthropology's distinctive comparative method; her deliberate collection of data in multiple community contexts enables her to concretely document claims for ideological diversity across genders, ethnic groups, and/or social classes.

Education

BA University of California, Riverside, 1965
Ph.D. University of Pennsylvania, 1974

Fieldwork

Warm Springs Indian Reservation, Oregon, 1969–71
Tucson, Arizona, 1978–9
Tonga, 1985, 1987–8, 1990

Key Publications

(1983) *The Invisible Culture: Communication in Classroom and Community on the Warm Springs Reservation*, New York: Longman, Inc. (reprinted by Waveland Press, Inc., Prospect Heights, IL, 1993).
(1998) *Ideology in the Language of Judges: How Judges*

Practice Law, Politics, and Courtroom Control, New York: Oxford University Press.

DEBORAH HOUSE

Piddington, Ralph O'Reilly

b. 1906, Sydney, Australia

d. 1974, Auckland, New Zealand

After studying anthropology with A.R. Radcliffe-Brown in the late 1920s at the University of Sydney, Ralph Piddington undertook fieldwork in northwest Australia, resulting in several academic articles on Karadjeri cosmology and ritual. Back in Sydney in 1932, Piddington also spoke to newspapers about the 'slavery' and violence being suffered by Aborigines in the Kimberley region. The response of academia and government was swift and harsh – Piddington was effectively banned from any further fieldwork in Australia. After completing a doctorate with B. Malinowski in London, editing the papers of the Polynesianist R.W. Williamson, curating an ethnological museum at Aberdeen, and serving as a British Army psychologist, Piddington returned to Australia for the years 1944–6 to work in its Army School, training administrators for post-war New Guinea. Then came a readership at the University of Edinburgh, during which he wrote the first volume of an introductory social anthropology text. In 1950 Piddington was appointed New Zealand's first professor of anthropology, at Auckland University College, where he rapidly established a large 'four fields' department. He strongly supported the teaching of the Maori language, and amongst his students were Maori who went on to become anthropologists, linguists, and political leaders. After publishing the second volume of his introductory text, Piddington pursued field research on kinship amongst French Canadians. Only in 1966 was he finally able to return – briefly – to northern Australia and his beloved Karadjeri country.

Education

BA University of Sydney, 1928
MA University of Sydney, 1932
Ph.D. London School of Economics, 1936

Fieldwork

La Grange and Beagle Bay, Kimberley, Western Australia, 1930–1
St Jean-Baptiste and St Boniface, Manitoba, Canada, 1957, 1962

Key Publications

(1932) 'Karadjeri initiation', *Oceania* 3, 1: 46–87.
(1950) *An Introduction to Social Anthropology*, Edinburgh: Oliver & Boyd.

TOM RYAN

Pina-Cabral, João de

b. 9 May 1954, V.N. Gaia, Portugal

Social anthropologist João de Pina-Cabral's work with the Macanese of China and the peasant communities of Alto Minho, Portugal has contributed to the understanding of kinship, the relationship between power and symbolic behaviour, and the personal construction of ethnicity.

Cabral's work in Portugal is considered one of the best of contemporary European ethnographies. This is due in large part to his comparative analysis of urban bourgeoisie and rural peasantry in matters of family and religion. Cabral brings to light the peasants' struggle between their physical and spiritual lives. Through his skilful integration of the roles of anthropologist and informant, a model for other anthropologists to emulate, Cabral reveals the symbolic connection between fertility and community, and fire and home.

Cabral's analysis of the Eurasians of Macao contributed to the understanding of how elite minorities maintain their right of succession and ethnic identity. Cabral contends that as a result of Macao's marginality from mainland China and recent economic prosperity the Macanese (people of Portuguese ancestry) have been able to reconstruct themselves from a social to administrative elite. An important result of his work in Macao is the hypothesis that power is never permanent; that there is continual interplay between the ruling and the ruled in a pluralistic society.

Education

BA (Hons) University of the Witwatersrand, 1977
Ph.D. University of Oxford, 1982

Fieldwork

Paco, Alto Minho region, Portugal, 1978–9
Couto, Alto Minho region, Portugal, 1979–80
Alto Minho region, Portugal, 1982–5
Macao, China, 1990–5

Key Publications

(1986) *Sons of Adam, Daughters of Eve: The Peasant Worldview of the Alto Minho*, New York: Clarendon Press.
(2002) *Between China and Europe: Person, Culture, and Emotion in Macao*, New York: Continuum.

CYNTHIA A. TYSICK

Polanyi, Karl

b. 21 October 1886, Vienna, Austria

d. 23 April 1964, Pickering, Ontario, Canada

Karl Polanyi is best known for *The Great Transformation*. This book has been translated into eleven languages and is considered a twentieth-century classic. In *The Great Transformation*, Polanyi documents the contradictory political interventions that were necessary to install the self-regulating market economy in the nineteenth century and the subsequent protective measures to prevent social collapse. The Utopian vision of a free-market economy

could not be realised. Polanyi's analysis is grounded in a historical and comparative framework that has challenged foundational arguments in economic theory and economic history. The failure of the self-regulating market economy was due to a misconception of how economic life is organised. All economies are embedded in social institutions; nineteenth-century liberalism wrote its own obituary in its failure to understand how societies are constituted.

Polanyi emphasised the uniqueness of nineteenth-century liberalism. Markets had existed throughout history as 'accessories of economic life'; the economy was always 'submerged in social relationships'. This is as true for modern industrial society as it is for the archaic economies of Mesopotamia and Greece or for so-called primitive societies such as the Kwakiutl in British Columbia, the Maori in New Zealand, or the Trobrianders to which Polanyi refers. Why was Polanyi interested in these societies? His search for a comparative economics led him to study the social arrangements that distinguish societies, to discover 'the place of the economy in society', thereby abandoning the artificial identification of the economy with its market form.

In 1953, while at Columbia University, Karl Polanyi, Conrad Arensberg, and Harry Pearson launched the Interdisciplinary Project on the institutional aspects of economic growth. The result was the publication of *Trade and Market in the Early Empires* in 1957. Polanyi's chapter, 'The economy as an instituted process', established the substantivist school in economic anthropology; he challenged the prevailing orthodoxy in economic anthropology and its application of the principles of neo-classical economics to non-market societies unreservedly. Polanyi's influence in economic anthropology is well known; his contribution created controversy; it generated debate; it established a school of thought. His objective was greater still, to develop a theory of the human economy.

Polanyi's substantivist meaning of economics refers to livelihood. The challenge was to go from ethnographic accounts of societies to a theory of how economic life is organised. Like its rival formalist school, the focus is on production, consumption, and distribution but, unlike the formalists, substantivists see these as derivative of social organisation. Polanyi's 'patterns of integration', reciprocity, redistribution, and exchange, capture the institutional context that sets the parameters for economic activity. Societies may be dominated by a particular pattern of integration, such as reciprocity in the case of kinship societies or redistribution in the case of hierarchical centralised societies or (market) exchange in the case of modern economies. Two or more patterns of integration may co-exist. The modern mixed economy combines elements of all three.

Polanyi's concepts of administered trade, gift trade, and ports of trade were important contributions to economic history and economic anthropology, breaking the universal association of trade with money and markets. Trade is both social and economic, embedded in institutional and historical contexts. For Polanyi, there is no *sui generis* money. Money is a 'system of symbols similar to language'. His special-purpose and all-purpose money account for the different uses and meanings attached to different money forms. This is not only true for non-market society and the use of special objects to exchange status goods, but also within modern society where special-purpose money serves specific exchanges.

Polanyi's intellectual legacy took an unexpected turn at the end of the twentieth century. The political, social, and economic upheavals that drew the century to a close recognised the need for an interdisciplinary methodology inspired by Polanyi. His work is especially important for the fields of economic sociology, economic anthropology, economic history, and socioeconomics, a subset of that which has become known as heterodox economics. In 1947, Polanyi wrote that the student of social anthropology is well equipped to understand the reality of society and to resist the universal application of economic determinism to all societies. The resistance to economic determinism is more widespread as hybrid

disciplines gain recognition. Polanyi has contributed to a broader methodology for the social sciences.

Education

Doctor of jurisprudence, University of Kolozsvár, Hungary, 1909.

Key Publications

(1944) *The Great Transformation*, Boston: Beacon Press (second edn, 2001).
with Arensberg, Conrad M. and Pearson, Harry (eds) (1957) *Trade and Market in the Early Empires. Economies in History and Theory*, Glencoe, IL: Free Press.
with Rotstein, Abraham (1966) *Dahomey and the Slave Trade*, Seattle: University of Washington Press.
(1977) *The Livelihood of Man*, introduction and ed. Harry Pearson, New York: Academic Press [a book of Polanyi's essays].

MARGUERITE MENDELL

Powdermaker, Hortense

b. 24 December 1900, Philadelphia, Pennsylvania, USA

d. 16 June 1970, Berkeley, California, USA

After earning an undergraduate degree in history, Powdermaker rebelled against the business-oriented materialism and sterility of her German-Jewish family background. She worked as a labour organiser for the Amalgamated Clothing Workers before beginning a doctoral programme as a student of Bronislaw Malinowski in 1925. Although not yet thinking in terms of a teaching career, Powdermaker presented a library dissertation on leadership in what was then called 'primitive' society in 1928 and departed the following year for fieldwork in Lesu village, New Ireland, to acquire a people of her own.

On return to the USA, Powdermaker began to synthesise the American and British anthropological traditions. At Yale's Institute of Human Relations, Edward Sapir encouraged her to elaborate the psychological side of Malinowski's functionalist agenda. Her next fieldwork project applied anthropological fieldwork methods in a complex society. She chose a mixed-race community in Indianola, Mississippi, and assessed the social and psychological costs of segregation for both blacks and whites. The fieldwork was difficult, given her commitment to employ participant-observation methods in both the black and white communities; she later argued that being a woman made her less threatening to both sides. *After Freedom* (1939) painted a dismal picture of the racist structures and stereotypes that undermined American democracy. A virtually simultaneous study of the same area by Yale sociologist John Dollard forms a strong contrast in method. Both have become classics.

Powdermaker applied her conclusions to the real world when she began to write about racial problems and prejudices, targeting a high school audience. She pursued a teaching career at Queens College in New York City, also lecturing at the William Alanson White Institute of Psychiatry, and took her relationship to students very seriously. During the Second World War, she worked for an army training programme for the Pacific based at Yale.

Her next fieldwork, just after the war, took her to Hollywood to study the filmmaking community and the totalitarian controls it exercised over its personnel. Film content and meaning were greatly influenced by the power structures of the movie industry, even though few people were aware of the subliminal messages. Anthropologists had to meet the challenge to 'study up'. Powdermaker's methodology presented the stages of film production in relation to their social production, suggesting models for the study of complex societies using anthropological fieldwork techniques. *Hollywood, the Dream Factory* (1950) was the first serious study by an anthropologist of an institution of American mass communication. The results of this study were generalised

in an edited conference volume on mass communication sponsored by the Wenner–Gren Foundation.

Powdermaker's last major fieldwork was in the Copperbelt of Northern Rhodesia. Her intention to study leisure activities was modified partially when A.L. Epstein invited her to join his study of the mining town of Luanshya. *Copper Town* (1962) focuses on shifts in self-awareness as tribal life shifts to urban. The structuralism of her British training is virtually absent in this exploration of personality in culture under conditions of rapid social change; she emphasised what would now be called personal agency. Despite her lack of linguistic skills and areal background, Powdermaker's African study balances Epstein's parallel monograph, which emphasises social and political structures in the British style.

Stranger and Friend: The Way of an Anthropologist (1966) anticipates the experimental ethnographies of the 1990s. Powdermaker compares her major field experiences, emphasising the inadequacy of scientific detachment for doing anthropology. The anthropologist must develop self-awareness and learn to alternate the dual roles of stranger and friend. Powdermaker believed that her status as a woman was, if anything, an advantage in doing fieldwork. Age of the investigator and involvement with ethnographic subjects seemed to her much more powerful constraints on the experience.

After retirement from Queens in 1968, she moved to Berkeley, California, planning fieldwork in the youth culture of the period. This work was incomplete at the time of her death. Few anthropologists have done fieldwork on so many cultures. There is, however, an abiding consistency in Powdermaker's belief that an anthropological approach empowers social critique and that fieldwork itself is the hallmark of the discipline. This conviction led her to extend fieldwork methods to modern, complex, North American communities and institutions.

Education

BA Goucher College, 1921

Ph.D. London School of Economics, 1928

Fieldwork

Lesu, New Ireland, 1929–30
Indianola, Mississippi, 1932
Hollywood, 1946–7
Luanshya, Northern Rhodesia, 1953–4

Key Publications

(1939) *After Freedom: A Cultural Study in the Deep South*, New York: Viking.
(1950) *Hollywood, the Dream Factory: An Anthropologist Studies the Movie Makers*, Boston: Little Brown & Co.
(1965) *Copper Town: Changing Africa, the Human Situation on the Rhodesian Copperbelt*, New York: Harper & Row.
(1966) *Stranger and Friend: The Way of an Anthropologist*, New York: W.W. Norton.

REGNA DARNELL

Powell, John Wesley

b. 24 March 1834, Mount Morris, New York, USA

d. 23 September 1902, Brooklin, Maine, USA

John Wesley Powell is best known for leading the successful first descent of the Colorado River. After serving in the Union Army, losing one arm at the Battle of Shiloh, and becoming a self-educated college teacher of geology, Powell became a public figure in the summer of 1869 when he travelled the Grand Canyon with a team of amateur scientists.

He repeated the trip in 1871 with some federal funding and over the next decade expanded his geological and geographical expedition into a federal surveying project that lasted ten years. In 1873, he was appointed a Special Indian Commissioner and tasked with locating, identifying, and counting the American Indian tribes of the Colorado Plateau and Great Basin, in order to facilitate the creation of a reservation system. Powell

met with over 100 independent tribes in the area, and used the experience to argue for a government-sponsored programme of ethnology. The reservation system desired by Congress, he claimed, could never be successful if the government did not understand existing intertribal relations.

In 1879, Congress combined the Powell Survey with three others that were operating in the American West to create the United States Geological Survey (USGS), and transferred ethnographic and linguistic responsibilities to the Smithsonian's newly created Bureau of Ethnology, later renamed the Bureau of American Ethnology (BAE). Powell was assigned the directorship of the Bureau, and in 1881 he became the director of the USGS as well. Powell functioned as the head of both agencies until 1894, when he resigned the directorship of the USGS to dedicate his efforts to the BAE, where he remained until his death in 1902.

Although Powell saw no viable alternatives to the US government's Indian policy of isolating Indians on reservations and assimilating them into mainstream society by eradicating their languages and cultures, he believed that the languages and lifeways of the American Indian should be recorded for the sake of science. Powell's motivation was to discover what he believed were the purely scientific laws that underlay the cultures and languages of all humans. He was interested in the specifics of particular tribes only so far as the details could illuminate the laws underlying all societies. He embraced Lewis Henry Morgan's idea of an evolutionary anthropology that classified societies according to where they fell into his evolutionary stages of savagery, barbarism, and civilisation. Comprehensive knowledge of the past, of which Powell believed Indians were a part, was the springboard to a better future.

Powell's main interest was the languages of the American Indians. He contended that language was the necessary key to understanding a culture's organisation, habits, and government. Mythologies were meaningless without knowledge of the languages in which they were originally spoken. His greatest achievement was overseeing the creation of a classification system of American Indian languages. This required guiding the continuing anthropological research goals of the Bureau and the divergent research interests of the various field anthropologists, while organising the large quantities of ethnological and linguistic manuscripts already in the possession of the Bureau. He also spearheaded the compilation of bibliographical materials and a synonymy of the names of American Indian tribal groups.

As director of the BAE in its earliest years, Powell is credited with editing the Annual Reports, Bulletins, and Miscellaneous Contributions that set a standard not only for ethnographic research, writing, and illustration, but also for publication quality as well. The publications serve today not only as sources for ethnographic information, but also as revealing records of the goals and methods of the early days of American anthropology.

After his death, Powell's autopsied brain was the subject of scrutiny. The investigator, after measuring, weighing, and sketching Powell's cerebrum, reported in *American Anthropologist* his conclusion that Powell had possessed a 'superior brain'.

Education

Illinois College, Jacksonville, IL (1855, less than 2 years)
Illinois Institute, Wheaton, IL (less than 1 year)
Oberlin College, Oberlin, OH (1858, few months)

Fieldwork

First Colorado River Expedition, 1869–70
Second Colorado River Expedition, 1871–2
Great Basin, Plateau, and Southwest USA, 1873–4

Key Publications

(1891) 'Indian linguistic families of America north of Mexico', in *Seventh Annual Report of the*

Bureau of Ethnology, 1885–1886, Washington: Government Printing Office.
(1895) *The Canyons of the Colorado*, Meadville, PA: Flood and Vincent.
with Fowler, C. and Fowler, D. (1971) *Anthropology of the Numa: John Wesley Powell's manuscripts on the Numic peoples of western North America, 1868–1880*, Washington: Smithsonian Institution.

Further Reading

Hinsley, C.M. (1981) *The Smithsonian and the American Indian: Making a Moral Anthropology in Victorian America*, Washington: Smithsonian Institution.
Judd, N. (1967) *The Bureau of American Ethnology: A Partial History*, Norman: University of Oklahoma Press.
Worster, D. (2001) *A River Running West: The Life of John Wesley Powell*, New York: Oxford University Press.

LISA BIER

Price, Richard

b. 30 November 1941, New York, USA

As an undergraduate, Richard Price devoted three summers to fieldwork – one in Peru, two in Martinique. A year studying in Paris with Claude Lévi-Strauss was followed by fieldwork in Spain and Mexico, graduate work at Harvard, and a dissertation based on two years among Saramaka Maroons (descendants of runaway slaves) in Suriname. He joined the Yale faculty and, in conjunction with courses taught there, developed the first truly comparative (hemispheric) approach to the study of Maroon societies. In 1974 he accepted an invitation from Johns Hopkins to form an anthropology department. During his first year as chair, he hired Sidney Mintz, Emily Ahern (Martin), and three others, joined Hopkins historians in an interdisciplinary programme in Atlantic studies, and became co-editor (and then editor) of the JHU Press's series in Atlantic History and Culture. After three terms as department chair, Price left Hopkins to devote himself more fully to research and bought a home in the Martiniquan fishing village where he had conducted undergraduate research. From that base, he took on a series of short-term appointments (e.g. at the University of Paris, the University of Minnesota, Stanford, Princeton, the University of Florida, and the Federal University of Bahia, Brazil). In 1994 he accepted a chair in anthropology, history, and American studies at the College of William and Mary, and, together with Sally Price, has been teaching there one semester each year.

Price has shown an abiding interest in the birth of African American cultures throughout the hemisphere and has explored this theme in a number of innovative works. Among his twenty books, most of which might be characterised as 'ethnographic history', two have been particularly important in pioneering the study of history among 'people without history' through an unusual combination of oral and documentary sources. He has also explored imaginative new forms for 'writing culture', including experiments with page layouts, typefaces, modes of reflexivity (particularly in his Martinique work), and fiction. And he has long been engaged in activist anthropology on behalf of Maroons in Suriname and French Guiana.

The importance of Price's work has been recognised in a number of awards. In particular, his 1983 book, *First-Time*, was awarded the Elsie Clews Parsons Prize of the American Folklore Society. *Alabi's World* (1990) was the winner of several awards: the American Historical Association's Albert J. Beveridge Award, the Gordon K. Lewis Memorial Award for Caribbean Scholarship, and the J.I. Staley Prize in Anthropology.

Education

AB Harvard University, 1963
Ph.D. Harvard University, 1970

Fieldwork

Vicos, Peru, 1961

Martinique, 1962, 1963, 1983, 1986, 1988, 1990–
Andalusia, Spain, 1964
Zinacantan, Mexico, 1965, 1966
Suriname, 1966, 1967–8, 1975, 1976, 1978, 1979
French Guiana, 1987, 1990, 1991, 1992, 1995, 1997, 2000, 2001, 2002

Key Publications

(1973) *Maroon Societies: Rebel Slave Communities in the Americas*, New York: Doubleday/Anchor (third edn, Johns Hopkins University Press, 1996).
(1983) *First-Time: The Historical Vision of an Afro-American People*, Baltimore: Johns Hopkins University Press (second edn, University of Chicago Press, 2002).
(1990) *Alabi's World*, Baltimore: Johns Hopkins University Press.
(1998) *The Convict and the Colonel: A Story of Colonialism and Resistance in the Caribbean*, Boston: Beacon Press.

VERED AMIT

Price, Sally

b. 16 September 1943, Boston, Massachussetts, USA

Sally Price's contributions to anthropology have spanned a wide range of subjects, from art, gender, and folklore to history, ethnography, and museum studies. After initial fieldwork in Martinique, Spain, and Mexico, she undertook intensive ethnographic research among Maroons (descendants of runaway slaves), first in the rainforest of the then-Dutch colony of Suriname and, since 1986, in neighbouring French Guiana. Her early work on the Maroons focused on aesthetic constructs, art history, and the dynamics of gender in this polygynous matrilineal society, culminating in a major travelling exhibition of Maroon arts (1980–2), the first of two books on Maroon art and aesthetics, and a study of art and gender that was awarded the Alice and

Edith Hamilton Prize in Women's Studies. She then turned her attention to Western constructions of 'primitive art', exploring the world of collectors, dealers, art critics, and museum visitors in a book characterised in *Lingua Franca* (autumn 1995) as having 'rattled glass cases throughout the art world' and now published in seven languages. With Richard Price, she has written books on folk tales (based on wakes recorded in the South American rainforest), field collecting (illustrated with her sketches), and public folklore (focused on the Festival of American Folklife), as well as a novel about art forgery, a second study of Maroon art, an introduction (in French) to Maroons in French Guiana, and an analysis of Melville and Frances Herskovits's 1920s fieldwork in Suriname. With other colleagues she edited a book about Michel Leiris and another on the Caribbean as a historical, political, and cultural region. And she translated a book into French for the Presses Universitaires de France. Broadening her interest in arts of the African diaspora, she wrote (with Richard Price) a book on the American artist, Romare Bearden. In 2000, Price was elected to the Netherlands Royal Academy of Science (Koninklijke Nederlandse Akademie van Wetenschappen), becoming – together with Claude Lévi-Strauss and James Fox – one of only three non-Dutch social anthropologists in that prestigious body. She has taught at the University of Minnesota, Stanford University, Princeton University, and the Federal University of Bahia, Brazil. Price divides her time between Martinique (her base for research and writing) and the USA, where she holds a joint appointment in anthropology and American studies at the College of William and Mary.

Education

AB Harvard University, 1965
Ph.D. Johns Hopkins University, 1982

Fieldwork

Martinique, 1963, 1983
Andalusia, Spain, 1964
Zinacantan, Mexico, 1965, 1966
Suriname, 1966, 1967–8, 1975, 1976, 1978, 1979
French Guiana, 1987, 1990, 1991, 1992, 1995, 1997, 2000, 2001, 2002

Key Publications

(1984) *Co-Wives and Calabashes*, Ann Arbor: University of Michigan Press (second edn, 1993).
(1989) *Primitive Art in Civilized Places*, Chicago: University of Chicago Press (second edn, 2002).
with Price, Richard (1999) *Maroon Arts: Cultural Vitality in the African Diaspora*, Boston: Beacon Press.
with Price, Richard (2003) *The Root of Roots: Or, How Afro-American Anthropology Got Its Start*, Chicago: Prickly Paradigm Press/University of Chicago Press.

VERED AMIT

Q

Quinn, Naomi

b. 1939, Boston, Massachusetts, USA

Naomi Quinn has been interested in the intersection between culture and cognition since her earliest ethnographic research, dealing with economic decisions in Ghana. Subsequently, Quinn continued to test and develop theories in cognitive and psychological anthropology, concentrating on cultural models of marriage in the USA. On the basis of interviews with married persons, she reconstructed an idealised event sequence that emerges from reasoning on marriage. This sequence is a task solution, reconciling seemingly contradictory expectations of personal fulfilment and lastingness, through the cultural theme of hard work to achieve success. Quinn uses a connectionist model to comprehend cognition, which is pictured like a neural network that processes information in parallel. Cultural schemata are shaped by socialisation, but can evolve subsequently. Connectionist properties of these schemata account for centripetal tendencies in culture, such as thematicity and durability, and for centrifugal tendencies, i.e. social variation and changes over time. Quinn has contributed to metaphor theory, arguing against the alleged productivity of metaphors. In everyday discourse, metaphors are generally selected to clarify an issue, rather than to perform original reasoning

tasks. Another strand in Quinn's work is her interest in gender. In the 1970s, she opposed monocausal explanations of women's supposedly universal subordination. She has been concerned with married women's self-understandings, and the place of women in academic politics. Quinn advocates cross-culturally comparative, psychoanalytically informed theorising in feminist anthropology.

Education

AB Radcliffe College, 1961
MA Stanford University, 1964
Ph.D. Stanford University, 1971

Fieldwork

Biriwa, Ghana, 1966–7, 1974–6
Durham, North Carolina, 1979–80

Key Publications

with Holland, Dorothy (1987) 'Culture and cognition', in D. Holland and N. Quinn (eds), *Cultural Models in Language and Thought*, Cambridge, UK: Cambridge University Press, pp. 3–40.
with Strauss, Claudia (1997) *A Cognitive Theory of Cultural Meaning*, Cambridge, UK: Cambridge University Press.

ANNE FRIEDERIKE MÜLLER

R

Rabinow, Paul

b. 21 June 1944, Tampa, Florida, USA

Paul Rabinow is a leading anthropologist of the biosciences, a major contributor to the auto-critique of anthropology, and one of the most important interpreters of Michel Foucault. Through a series of innovative publications charting the emergence of the biotechnology sector, and the new genetics, in the 1980s and the 1990s, he has developed on Foucault's concern with life, labour, and language through ethnographic fieldwork with prominent scientists such as Cary Mullis, awarded the Nobel Prize for his contribution to developing the technique of polymerase chain reaction (PCR), and Daniel Cohen, the Director of the Centre d'Etude du Polymorphisme Humain (CEPH) – France's leading genomics center.

Rabinow's iconoclastic approach, evident from his first publication in 1977, entitled *Reflections on Fieldwork In Morocco*, is highly critical of prevailing models and assumptions within the social sciences, and has helped to shape the meaning of 'reflexivity' within anthropology, where it refers primarily to a critique of the forms of power built into anthropological methods of description. For Rabinow, an emphasis on reading culture as a form of interpretation is vital. He has increasingly become a theorist of reason, truth, and justice, and the ethics which attach to knowledge practices. *The Anthropology of Reason* (1996) explores these themes both through critiquing the history of anthropological explanation, and by investigating the contemporary biosciences.

Both *Making PCR* (1996) and *French DNA* (1999) are based on fieldwork in scientific laboratories, and investigate the production of knowledge in the context of the new genetics. Eschewing traditional models of social structure, Rabinow's analysis instead seeks to depict the vicissitudes and unpredictabilities of events and assemblages, drawing his work closely into dialogue with both science studies and continental philosophy. In his most recent work he has turned to the model of the assemblage, or event, in order to avoid 'totalising categories' such as the terms 'culture' or 'society'. Rabinow is, in this and other respects, one of anthropology's most innovative practitioners, as well as one of its most polemical ethnographers.

Paul Rabinow is currently Professor of Anthropology at the University of California, Berkeley, where he has taught since 1978. He received a Guggenheim Fellowship in 1980 and was named Chevalier de l'Ordre des Arts et des Lettres by the French government in 1998. He was a Visiting Fulbright Professor at the National Museum in Rio de Janeiro in 1987, and at the University of Iceland in 1999. He was awarded the prestigious Chaire Internationale de Recherche Blaise Pascal at the École Normale Supérieure in 2001–2.

Education

BA University of Chicago, 1965

MA University of Chicago, 1967
Ph.D. University of Chicago, 1970

Fieldwork

Morocco, 1968–9
California (biotechnology firm), 1994–5
Paris (genomics centre), 1998
Iceland (DeCode Genetics Inc.), 1999–2000

Key Publications

(1977) *Reflections on Fieldwork in Morocco*, Berkeley: University of California Press.
(1989) *French Modern: Norms and Forms of the Social Environment*, Cambridge, MA: MIT Press.
(1996) *Making PCR: A Story of Biotechnology*, Chicago: University of Chicago Press.
(1999) *French DNA: Trouble in Purgatory*, Chicago: University of Chicago Press.

SARAH FRANKLIN

Radcliffe-Brown, A.R.

b. 17 January 1881, Birmingham, UK

d. 24 October 1955, London, UK

A.R. Radcliffe-Brown was born Alfred Reginald Brown. Although his earliest publications were under the name Brown, he began to add his mother's name (at first unhyphenated) and eventually changed his name by deed poll, in Sydney, in 1926. Among his eccentricities, he dressed extravagantly, wearing a top hat inappropriately if not pretentiously, in the egalitarian milieu of 1920s Sydney. Yet always one of contrasts, his politics were of youthful anarchism followed by later adherence to socialism. This radical streak is significant, for it must be borne in mind that far from being conservative (as later portrayed) his anthropological approach – emphasising society in the present – marked a radical break from the evolutionist and diffusionist ones of his predecessors, including his teacher, W.H.R. Rivers.

Radcliffe-Brown's early interest was in natural science, and it is sometimes said that this led to his applying the biological concepts of structure and function to the analysis of society. Indeed, when he arrived at Cambridge in 1901 his intention had been to study natural science, but his tutors, thinking him unsuited to the subject, urged him to take up instead the 'moral sciences' (including philosophy, psychology, and economics). This blend of natural science ideas and social science subject matter led to an anthropology in which the systematic relations within society became the focal point. Institutions were seen as functioning within the structured systems of kinship, politics, economics, religion that are found in all societies. Radcliffe-Brown rejected both historical trajectories and individual action as primary foci, preferring instead a description of structures of relations and of the structural form (a slightly more abstract notion) they represent. His approach is apparent in his early ethnography of the Andaman Islanders and his comparative studies of the kinship and totemic systems of Australian Aboriginal societies, but it is clearest in his general essays collected and published under the title, *Structure and Function in Primitive Society*.

Radcliffe-Brown was a brilliant lecturer, frequently lecturing without notes on complex topics, which were made simple for the ease of understanding. His collected essays, most of them first presented as lectures, retain the simplicity (some would say, the oversimplification) of his lecturing style. Many are still worthy of serious reading, perhaps most famously 'The mother's brother in South Africa' (1924, in some ways flawed, but seminal and full of insight), 'The study of kinship systems' (1941, containing an important critique of conjectural history), and 'On social structure' (1940, perhaps the best known of his pronouncements on anthropological theory).

Radcliffe-Brown, along with Bronislaw Malinowski, is credited as a co-founder of the functionalist school of anthropology – and in Radcliffe-Brown's case the structural-functionalist branch of that school. However, he rejected both the label and the association with Malinowski. He preferred to see anthropology as a science, not bound by philosophical 'isms', but dedicated both to the advancement of ethnographic knowledge and to the comparative understanding of society. Radcliffe-Brown believed that through comparison, and by inductive method, anthropology would eventually define the 'natural laws' that he saw as governing society. He regarded anthropology as 'a natural science of society'. His posthumous book by that title is indicative of his approach and illustrative of his charismatic style. Based on transcriptions of his 1937 Chicago lectures, it represents, according to one of his students present, 'the essential Radcliffe-Brown'.

Radcliffe-Brown held numerous academic appointments. He founded departments of social anthropology at the Universities of Cape Town (where he spent 1920 to 1925), the University of Sydney (1926 to 1931), the University of Chicago (1931 to 1937), and the University of Oxford (1937 to 1946). He also held short-term teaching posts at other universities in England, South Africa, China, Brazil, and Egypt. Radcliffe-Brown's travels enabled anthropology to develop in his mould, for a time throughout the British Commonwealth and even in the USA, where his approach competed with Franz Boas's vision of anthropology in the 1930s and (through some of his Chicago students) long after.

Education

BA University of Cambridge, 1904
MA University of Cambridge, 1908

Fieldwork

Andaman Islands, India, 1906–8
Western Australia, 1910–11

Key Publications

(1922) *The Andaman Islanders*, Cambridge, UK: Cambridge University Press.

(1931) *The Social Organization of Australian Tribes*, Sydney: Oceania Monographs (No. 1).
(1952) *Structure and Function in Primitive Society: Essays and Addresses*, London: Cohen & West.
(1957) *A Natural Science of Society*, Glencoe, IL: The Free Press.

ALAN BARNARD

Radin, Paul

b. 2 April 1883, Lodz, Poland

d. 21 February 1959, New York City, USA

Paul Radin was pre-eminent among the first generation of students of Franz Boas, many of whom shared his German, Russian, and Jewish background. He was a man of ideas, the son of a Reform rabbi, who studied historiography at several European universities before returning to North America and a career in anthropology. Although he dabbled in linguistics and strongly espoused the learning of Native languages in fieldwork as an entrée to the mental world of individuals in an unfamiliar culture, Radin was primarily an ethnologist, a student of culture.

Radin's ethnological work broke new ground in rendering the personal world of individuals in Native American societies intelligible to outside readers. He was among the first to concentrate on the ethnology of a single group, returning to Winnebago throughout his career. He redefined history from the point of view of ethnology, resisting the generalised events of reconstructed culture history in favor of a history based in oral tradition and memory culture. Such a history, he argued, was not static but provided the fabric within which present-day American Indian lives were structured, despite intensive culture change and assimilative pressures. His *The Autobiography of a Winnebago Indian*, published in several versions, portrayed the experience of a failed visionary empowered by the peyote church to integrate traditional and modern Winnebago experience.

Pre-literate societies were, in Radin's view, no different in kind from his own civilisation. Unlike many of his contemporaries, Radin was not convinced that modern American culture represented progress. Although he had his doubts about the intellectuals of his own society, often finding them pretentious and arrogant, Radin was fully prepared to find and to enter into conversation with the intellectuals of so-called primitive societies.

Radin's contribution to the Boasian logic of cultural relativism centered on the idea of 'primitive man as philosopher'. He argued that every society had its philosophers and that they thought about similar questions regardless of cultural context. The task of the ethnologist, then, was to enter into conversations across cultural boundaries. The major difference between Winnebago philosophy and that of his own society was that the latter had a systematic quality that was rarely valued in a simpler culture. It was not necessary for the shaman to become a priest, with a systematic canon of belief and ritual, in order to be a philosopher. Each culture, regardless of its complexity, recognised a distinction between men of ideas (the philosophers) and men of action. Radin deplored the tendency of ethnology to focus on the world of the average person, with the inevitable result that cultural descriptions made the thought of other cultures seem simple and unelaborated. Only by consulting locally acknowledged experts could the ethnologist access their traditional knowledge and compare it to that of philosophers in his own society.

Radin was led by this train of thought to a critique of North American society itself. Aboriginal civilisations excelled in respect for individual persons, integration of social and political life with the experience of individuals, and concern for the subsistence needs and emotional well-being of every member of the community. These humane values had been diluted in the North American rush towards economic success and consumerism.

Although Radin's approach to religion was sceptical and rational, he intuitively understood the Winnebago manner of couching philosophical speculation in the language of story and myth, as read through the personal experience of shamans and story-tellers. He was fascinated by the ambivalence of the Winnebago trickster figure, embodying both the creative potential and the destructive greed and coarseness of a spoiled child. Radin himself has been remembered as a trickster among anthropologists, a being out of place in everyday reality, forever shifting his form and argument.

Radin made little contribution to the institutional development of American anthropology that proceeded apace during his career. Rather he was, like his Winnebago trickster philosophers, a man of ideas, impossible to pin down and impossible to dismiss. Radin held many positions during a peripatetic career. His fieldwork research was much more constant than his employment. He worked for fellow Boasian Edward Sapir in Ottawa's Division of Anthropology and for the Bureau of American Ethnology in Washington, DC. He taught at the University of California, Berkeley, Cambridge University, Fisk University, the University of Chicago (again working with Sapir), Kenyon and Black Mountain Colleges, and Brandeis University where he was Samuel Rubin professor and department head at the time of his death.

Education

BA City College of New York, 1902
Ph.D. Columbia University, 1911

Fieldwork

Ojibwa, 1913–17
Winnebago, 1908–13
Mexico, 1910s–20s
California Indians, 1920s
Italians in San Francisco, early 1930s

Key Publications

(1920) *The Autobiography of a Winnebago Indian*, University of California Publications in

American Archaeology and Ethnology 14: 381–473.

(1927) *Primitive Man as Philosopher*, New York: Dover (rev. edn, 1958).

(1933) *Method and Theory in Ethnology: An Essay in Criticism*, New York: Basic Books.

(1937) *Primitive Religion: Its Nature and Origin*, New York: Dover.

REGNA DARNELL AND FREDERIC W. GLEACH

Rapp, Rayna R.

b. 1946, New York City, USA

Rayna Rapp has been an influential pioneer on the nature/culture frontier bringing empirically grounded and theoretically sophisticated attention to gender, to reproduction, and the genetics revolution. Trained by Eric Wolf, her initial fieldwork on French peasants coincided with her entry into the US Women's Movement. At Michigan, she helped to found one of the first women's studies programmes and to expand anthropology through critical perspectives on gender. In the 1980s, Rapp started investigating women's experiences with amniocentesis and other New Reproductive Technologies, influenced by both the women's health movement and her personal experience. Her multisited ethnographic methods revealed how cultural knowledge about biomedical science is constructed, from the labs to patients. Subsequently, she began collaborative research on the production of knowledge about genetics, involving bench scientists, physicians, and support groups for people affected by genetic disease. Her new work focuses on (1) the production of disability as a cultural category through biomedical advances and an expanding social movement; and (2) bioethics as technology regulating the relationship of bodies to sociomedical institutions. In addition to its profound impact on anthropology, Rapp's work is exemplary for its generous engagement with the worlds of the people she studies.

Education

BS University of Michigan, 1968
MA University of Michigan, 1969
Ph.D. University of Michigan, 1973

Fieldwork

Provence, France, June – August 1969, 1970, 1980, June 1971–August 1972
New York City, 24 months during 1984–1990
New York City, 18 months during 1997–2000

Key Publications

(ed.) (1975) *Toward an Anthropology of Women* [under the name Rayna R. Reiter], New York: Monthly Review Press.

(1999) *Testing Women, Testing the Fetus: The Social Impact of Amniocentesis in America*, New York: Routledge.

FAYE GINSBURG

Rappaport, Roy A.

b. 25 March 1926, New York City, USA

d. 9 October 1997, Ann Arbor, Michigan, USA

At the time of his death in 1997, Roy Rappaport was Walgreen professor for the study of human understanding and director of the program on studies in religion at the University of Michigan. Rappaport's career was distinguished. He was senior scholar at the East–West Center, University of Hawaii, from 1968 to 1969, Guggenheim Fellow in 1969, American Council of Learned Societies Fellow from 1972 to 1973, chair of the Department of Anthropology at the University of Michigan from 1975 to 1980, president elect of the American Anthropological Association (AAA) from 1985 to 1987, president of the AAA from 1987 to 1989, and a member of the National Academy of Sciences from 1988 until the time of his death.

Just turning forty when he received his Ph.D. in anthropology from Columbia University, Rappaport established his prominence quickly with *Pigs for the Ancestors: Ritual in the Ecology of a New Guinea People* (1968), a monograph stemming from his doctoral research among the Maring, a tribal people living in the interior of New Guinea. Rappaport argued that the Maring were best understood through their interchanges with the environment as these interchanges were generated and regulated by local cultural practices and world view within an overarching 'ecosystem'. The argument merged then-current concerns with ecology and evolution with cybernetics and system theory. *Pigs* was immediately recognised for its empirical strengths, paradigm-setting quality, and provocative nature.

In *Pigs*, the mechanism for keeping populations and their subsistence base in balance was ritual, and in his subsequent writings Rappaport focused increasingly on the meaning and efficacy (ecological and otherwise) of ritual and its language. These later writings have appeared in journals and anthologies as well as in his 1979 collection of essays, *Ecology, Meaning, and Religion*, and in his culminating monograph, *Ritual and Religion in the Making of Humanity*, published posthumously in 1999.

The secular trend in Rappaport's work was from a strict, even reductive, materialism to an attempt to bridge materialist and semiotic, scientific and humanistic, concerns. Indeed, the hallmark of his work was ultimately its holism. In the last decade of Rappaport's life, this holism was manifested in his insistence on the need for an 'engaged anthropology' in which theoretical and applied anthropology would go hand in glove.

Rappaport's work is critical to any understanding of twentieth-century anthropology and its defining debates, and it continues to provide context for the revival of interest in ecological anthropology and new syntheses at the dawn of a new millennium.

Education

BS Cornell University, 1949
Ph.D. Columbia University, 1966

Fieldwork

Archaeological fieldwork, Society Islands, March–August 1960
Cultural fieldwork among the Maring, New Guinea, October 1962–December 1963; among the Maring, Papua New Guinea, 1981–2 (months unknown)

Key Publications

(1968) *Pigs for the Ancestors: Ritual in the Ecology of a New Guinea People*, New Haven: Yale University Press (second edn, Yale University Press, 1984).
1979 *Ecology, Meaning, and Religion*. Richmond, CA: North Atlantic Books.
1999 *Ritual and Religion in the Making of Humanity*, Cambridge, UK: Cambridge University Press.

ALETTA BIERSACK

Rapport, Nigel

b. 1956, Cardiff, Wales, UK

Nigel Rapport's work is seminal of a new tradition within British social anthropology in its passionate argument for recognition of the importance of the individual in the analysis of social life. First appearing as a theme in his doctoral work, an ethnographic study of a rural community in England, this has developed into a major intellectual strand in Rapport's thinking. Through detailed analysis of conversational encounters the main characters of the English village are revealed both as individuals and as community members sharing in community concerns. In some circumstances their individuality and difference shines forth, belying any Durkheimian sense of a shared set of cultural beliefs; on other occasions, village people appear culturally united, the differences between their world views rendered less pressing. In Rapport's hands culture is therefore not all-powerful, standing stolidly outside, above, or against the individual; rather, it is processual with the individual inextricably involved in its creation. His informants, be they in England, Newfoundland, or Israel, are portrayed as people with choices who, as collectively they get by and muddle through, reveal their individuality as farmers, policemen, house-wives, or domino players in the pub. However, more than this, Rapport's is a political concern not to do violence to the individual. This view underpins his later call for a more liberal anthropology in which the individual might become transcendent, their consciousness as embodied beings and as moral agents with rights being fully recognised by anthropologists in their writings about the 'other'.

It is through the performative aspects of language and narration that Rapport is able to show how it is that individuals express themselves as individuals and, he argues, the anthropologist cannot escape this human condition. Thus, the interpretations that anthropologists make of other cultures find a correspondence with those made by other writers of reality, such as novelists. They are, similarly, intent on explaining people's own interpretations of the worlds they inhabit. As part of the trajectory of social anthropology Rapport therefore makes a claim for its literariness. Taking the novels of E.M. Forster and using these alongside his own analysis of life in a Cumbrian village Rapport makes a series of connections across and between these different portrayals of Englishness, arguing that each can illuminate the other. The individual creativity that fiction represents mirrors the creative individual use of collective forms which anthropologists uncover in their analysis of everyday lives. For Rapport, both the novelist and the anthropologist seek out the interconnectedness that makes social and cultural life possible.

Education

BA University of Cambridge, 1978
MA University of Cambridge, 1982
Ph.D. University of Manchester, 1983

Fieldwork

Cumbrian Dales, England, 1980–1
St John's, Newfoundland, Canada, 1984–5
Kilbride, Newfoundland, Canada, 1986–7
Mitzpe Ramon, Israel, 1989
Easterneuk, Scotland, 2000–1

Key Publications

(1993) *Diverse World-View in an English Village*, Edinburgh: Edinburgh University Press.
(1994) *The Prose and the Passion. Anthropology, Literature and the Writing of E.M. Forster*, Manchester: Manchester University Press.
(1997) *Transcendent Individual. Towards a Literary and Liberal Anthropology*, London: Routledge.

ALLISON JAMES

Redfield, Robert

b. 4 December 1897, Chicago, Illinois, USA

d. 16 October 1958, Chicago, Illinois, USA

Robert Redfield graduated from the University of Chicago in 1920 after a stint as an ambulance driver for the American Friends Field Service in France during the First World War. The same year, he married Margaret Park, daughter of distinguished Chicago sociologist, Robert Park. Redfield's father pressured him to obtain a law degree and join the family firm, which he did without enthusiasm. Park was sufficiently dismayed to provide funding for an alternative project. The couple went to Mexico in 1923 where Redfield met Manuel Gamio and decided to pursue graduate studies in Chicago's joint department of anthropology and sociology. He studied urban ethnography with Park and his colleague, Ernest Burgess, observing Mexicans in Chicago for a practicum project, as well as Boasian anthropology with Edward Sapir and Fay-Cooper Cole.

Redfield's first research grant for Mexican fieldwork was directed towards the 'scientific aspects of human migration', a targeted problem for the social science research of the time. The incomplete assimilation of immigrants was defined by the sociologists as a social problem. Redfield hoped to include attitudes and forms of communication in this study of culture change. In line with the spatial analysis favored by the Chicago sociologists, Redfield mapped change by location rather than elapsed time. He further developed this synchronic approach to modernisation in *The Folk Culture of Yucatan* (1941).

Gamio proposed a study of Tepoztlan in central Mexico, but this fieldwork was cut short because of counter-revolutionary activity in the area. Establishing his family in Mexico City, Redfield commuted to Tepoztlan. The four to five months' fieldwork was long for the 1920s, despite these difficulties. The resulting book *Tepoztlán* (1930) immediately made Redfield the foremost anthropological student of peasants and acculturation.

Redfield then obtained Carnegie Foundation funding for work in several Yucatan communities, chosen to fall on a folk–urban continuum, again understood spatially rather than temporally. In 1930–1, Redfield worked personally in Chan Kom, a peasant community that had been established relatively recently. This was the village that self-consciously 'chose progress'. In this study, Redfield collaborated with Alfonso Villa Rojas.

The publication of *Chan Kom* in 1934 coincided with Redfield's attainment of tenure at the University of Chicago where he had been teaching since 1927, the year the anthropology department attained its independence from sociology. From 1934–45, Redfield served as dean of the Division of Social Sciences, working effectively with Chicago's president, Robert Hutchins. Redfield was also active in defending the civil liberties of racial and ethnic minorities in the city of Chicago. He became a director of the American Council on Race Relations and supported efforts at desegregation by the National Association for the Advancement of Colored People.

Redfield published a restudy of Chan Kom in 1950, but his major interest had shifted to Guatemala where he began to plan fieldwork during several visits between 1937 and 1941.

During a world tour in 1948 with his wife, he began to compare the 'grand traditions' of civilisations with writing to the local, folk, or 'little traditions' embedded within them. *The Primitive World and Its Transformation* (1953) attempted to circumscribe modernisation within this dichotomy, with an implicit inevitability about the march towards progress. This model was not greatly different from the folk–urban continuum in Redfield's earlier work, although he became more interested in the grand traditions of India than in the more isolated kinds of communities within which his own fieldwork had taken place. Unfortunately, Redfield died in 1958 before fully developing these ideas.

Redfield's work employed Weberian ideal types and consequently glossed over much of the conflict and inconsistency in his ethnographic data. Tepotzlan was restudied in the 1950s by Oscar Lewis, whose portrait of conflict-ridden factionalism and anxiety contrasted dramatically with Redfield's serenely functional baseline folk culture, an idealised golden age lurking in the past of every more modernised community. Redfield himself did not consider the two interpretations incompatible; rather, each anthropologist chose to emphasise different sides of the same phenomenon. He also assumed that conflict and anxiety would have increased in the period between the two studies.

Redfield's commitment to the humanistic side of anthropology is clearly reflected in his collected papers and in his administrative work at the University of Chicago. He reoriented the anthropology of his day towards the study of peasant societies more complex than those previously studied by most anthropologists and investigated how such peasant communities were related to the larger world outside their boundaries. Although his analysis remained sociological rather than psychological, the plight of the individual faced with rapid social change was implicit and ubiquitous.

Education

BA University of Chicago, 1920

JD University of Chicago, 1922
Ph.D. University of Chicago, 1928

Fieldwork

Mexico, beginning in 1923
Tepoztlan, 1926–7
Chan Kom, 1930–1
Guatemala between 1937 and1941

Key Publications

(1930) *Tepoztlán, A Mexican Village: A Study of Folk Life*, Chicago: University of Chicago Press.
with Villa Rojas, Alfonso (1934) *Chan Kom, A Maya Village*, Washington, DC: Carnegie Institution of Washington.
(1941) *The Folk Culture of Yucatan*, Chicago: University of Chicago Press.
(1953) *The Primitive World and Its Transformation*, Ithaca, NY: Cornell University Press.

REGNA DARNELL AND FREDERIC W. GLEACH

Ribeiro, Darcy

b. 22 October 1922, Montes Claros, MG, Brazil

d. 15 February 1997, Rio de Janeiro, RJ, Brazil

Anthropologist, communist, politician, public servant, institution-builder, fiction writer, and movie maker, Darcy Ribeiro was a multifaceted, influential, and prolific author. His scholarly achievements reflect a biography deeply interwoven with the contemporary history of Brazil. His lack of a proper graduate degree and his political activism have led some Brazilian scholars to dispute his anthropological credentials.

Ribeiro's main ethnological fieldwork was done in the late 1940s and early 1950s as an official of the Studies Section of the Indian Protection Service (SPI), the government office overseeing indigenous peoples. He was hired as 'naturalist' of the SPI in 1947 following the completion of his undergraduate studies under the guidance of Herbert Baldus. The researches he did among the Kadiwéu Indians of central

Brazil and the Urubu-Kaapor Indians of the Brazilian Amazon were part of a broad investigation he helped to organise at the Studies Section. It resulted in a series of functionalist-leaning articles on kinship, social organisation, art, religion, and myth of both groups, the disruptive effects of depopulation due to epidemic diseases, and two monograph studies: one on Kadiwéu myth and religion, another on Urubu-Kaapor feather-work (with his wife and inseparable associate, Berta). The Kadiwéu monograph analyses the relationship between myth and religion, and all the other aspects of Kadiwéu culture, explaining their meaning, function, and how they intertwine with the overall sociocultural pattern and contribute to its perpetuation. The field diaries of his anthropologic-linguistic-cinematographic expeditions to the Urubu-Kaapor were published forty-five years afterwards and revealed how much his later theorisation on cultural change and the formation of the Brazilian people – and the part the Indians played in it – already permeated his ethnological understanding of distinct indigenous peoples.

In the mid-1950s, Ribeiro converted the Studies Section of the SPI into the Museum of the Indian, in Rio de Janeiro, where he organised one of Brazil's first professional training courses in anthropology. During this period he collaborated with UNESCO and WIO in preparing studies and handbooks on indigenous peoples, and developed his conception that government policies towards indigenous peoples should be shaped by scientific anthropology.

Associating himself with leading educators, Ribeiro turned to years of thinking on education, which led him to create the University of Brasilia, in 1961, and to be appointed minister of education (1962–3) and later house chief-of-staff of President Goulart's left-leaning government. He remained in office until 1964, when his political rights were stripped by the military.

During his exile in various Latin American countries, he taught anthropology, assisted universities' restructuring, and wrote five of the volumes of his *Estudos de antropologia da civilização*, in which he develops – among others – the following issues: (1) the causes of uneven socioeconomic development and the situation of Latin America; (2) the classification of American peoples in 'transplanted', 'eyewitness', 'new', and 'emergent' peoples; (3) the epoch-making theory of ethnic transfiguration and step-wise integration of the Indians into national society; and (4) the social and biological constitution of the Brazilian people. The blend of evolutionism and culturalism that moulds his *Estudos* reveals the influences of Julian Steward, Leslie White, and the German ethnologist, Richard Thurnwald, whose work was influential to Ribeiro's adviser. The *Estudos* also express the cultural profile of a post-war Latin-American intellectual elite concerned with fashioning theories of cultural change and development that could reconcile the maintenance of national identities' uniqueness.

Ribeiro returned from exile in 1976 to occupy several meaningful political assignments: vice-governor of the State of Rio de Janeiro and Rio's secretary of culture and education (1983–6), and senator elect (1991–7). While congressman he edited the periodical *Carta* (Letter), and, already debilitated by the prostate cancer that caused his death in 1997, he prepared his diaries for publication and wrote the final summation of his *Estudos*: *The Brazilian People*. His work warranted him a place in the Brazilian Academy of Letters in 1993.

Education

Bachelor's degree in social sciences, Escola Livre de Sociologia e Política/Free School of Sociology and Politics, São Paulo, Brazil, 1946

Fieldwork

Kadiwéu Indians, state of Mato Grosso do Sul, central Brazil; November–December 1947, July–October and November 1948

Urubu-Kaapor Indians, state of Maranhão, Brazilian Amazon; November 1949–April 1950, August–November 1951.

Key Publications

(1950) *Religião e mitologia Kadiwéu* (Kadiwéu Religion and Myth), Rio de Janeiro: Serviço de Proteção aos Índios (Indian Protection Service), Publication n. 106.

(1968–95) *Estudos de antropologia da civilização* (Studies in the Anthropology of Civilisation), 7 vols, Rio de Janeiro: Civilização Brasileira (later vols Petrópolis: Vozes and São Paulo: Companhia das Letras).

(1974) *Uirá sai à procura de Deus: ensaios de etnologia e indigenismo* (Uirá Departs in Search of God: Essays in Ethnology and Indigenism), Rio de Janeiro: Paz e Terra.

(1996) *Diários Índios: os Urubus-Kaapor* (Indian Journals: The Urubu-Kaapor), São Paulo: Companhia das Letras.

HENYO T. BARRETTO FILHO

Richards, Audrey Isabel

b. 8 July 1889, London, UK

d. 29 June 1984, Midhurst, UK

Widely recognised as leading the way for woman ethnographers, Audrey Richards was a student of Bronislaw Malinowski at the London School of Economics in the 1920s, where she taught for two periods during the 1930s. She also lectured at the University of the Witwatersrand, South Africa (1938–40), London University (1946–50), Makerere College, Uganda (1950–6), and for many years at the University of Cambridge (1956–67) where she founded and was the first director of the Centre for African Studies.

Richards was a pioneer in many fields, her work spanning social psychology, the culture of food and nutrition, agriculture, land use, and economic organisation, studied through minute observation of daily life, as taught by Malinowski. This included recording such details as the length of time taken to complete particular tasks, and the length of working days according to season. Her research on diet and nutrition among the Bemba of Northern Rhodesia (Zambia) drew on her undergraduate background in biology and included collaboration with the nutritionist, E.M. Widdowson. The results continued to have effects on national policies over half a century after they were first published. *Land, Labour and Diet in Northern Rhodesia* also endures as a classic teaching text, providing a vibrant description of political and religious life among the Bemba. The contextualisation of diet within social structure and land use, including consideration of environmental factors, provided the foundation of nutritional anthropology.

Like many anthropologists of her time, the majority of Richards's fieldwork took place in a colonial setting. Her early career, before studying anthropology, included experience with the colonial administration as befitted someone whose childhood had largely been spent in India, where her father was employed by the colonial administration. She took an academic interest in local political systems in the context of social change, being both an astute observer of, and critical commentator on, the effects of colonial administrative practices, while being professionally involved in making policy recommendations on the basis of her research results.

Richards also contributed to the understanding of ritual, particularly in her classic work on the initiation rights of Bemba girls, *chisungu*. The detailed ethnographic account of this month-long ceremony is a valuable work of rescue ethnography. Richards claimed to have observed the increasingly rare ceremony on only one occasion, and it probably ceased to be performed in subsequent decades. Yet above and beyond the detailed description, her analysis of the ritual in terms of matrilineal society continues both to inform and to provoke debate. As one would expect given the influence of Malinowski as teacher and close colleague, *Chisungu* (published in 1956, although begun almost two decades earlier) embraces a functionalist component, but combines this with elements that prefigure structuralism, symbolism, and postmodernism. It remains a key work for undergraduate study.

As both educator and researcher, Richards

became the inspiration, role model, and often also the mentor for at least two generations of women social anthropologists, many of whom achieved professorial status at a time when female students were relatively rare. After settling in later life in the Essex village of Elmdon, she encouraged her students and former students to develop a village ethnography, which resulted in comprehensive studies of English rural kinship, and took an active part in the intellectual life of the anthropology in Cambridge almost until her death, despite failing health.

Education

MA Newnham College, Cambridge, 1928
Ph.D. London School of Economics, 1929

Fieldwork

Northern Rhodesia (now Zambia), 1930–1, 1933–4, 1957
Northern Transvaal, 1939–40
Uganda, 1950–5

Key Publications

(1932) *Hunger and Work in a Savage Tribe: A Functional Study of Nutrition among the Southern Bantu*, London: Routledge.
(1939) *Land, Labour and Diet in Northern Rhodesia: An Economic Study of the Bemba Tribe*, London: Oxford University Press for International Institute of African Languages and Cultures.
(1956) *Chisungu: A Study of Girls' Initiation Ceremonies among the Bemba of Northern Rhodesia*, London: Faber & Faber.
(1969) *The Multicultural States of East Africa*, Montreal: McGill-Queen's University Press for Centre for Developing Area Studies (Keith Collard lectures, series 3).

Further Reading

La Fontaine, J.S. (ed.) (1972) *The Interpretation of Ritual: Essays in Honour of A.I. Richards*, London: Tavistock Publications Limited.
Moore, H.L. and Vaughan, Megan (1994)

Cutting down Trees: Gender, Nutrition and Agricultural Change in the Northern Province of Zambia, 1890–1990, London: James Currey Publishers.

JUDITH ENNEW

Richards, Paul

b. 1945, Ashton-under-Lyne, UK

Paul Richards's work is driven by a conviction that anthropology is a practical tool, that the discipline's objective of throwing light on the lives of those we do not understand can be a force for good. Development aid programmes in Africa have generally been guided by universalistic scientific assumptions. Through his work on local agriculture in Nigeria and Sierra Leone, Richards demonstrated the innovative, experimental nature of indigenous practices. Local knowledge emerges from his account as 'good science', and considerably more effective than imported knowledge, both for overcoming the hardships threatened by local environmental uncertainties, and as a tool for environmental conservation.

Western misconceptions also color both academic and media representations of modern African warfare. Through his work on conflict in Sierra Leone in the 1990s, Richards exploded the myth of African 'barbarism', exposing the rationality and effectiveness of actions that are often dismissed by outsiders as 'mindless' violence perpetrated under pressure of local environmental crises. Such actions can only be understood, Richards argued, in terms of the actors' cultural resources. These include traditional knowledge of the forest and how it can be used, and an understanding of global affairs gleaned from the international media. Richards's impressive corpus of work carries an overriding message that defines anthropology's value in the contemporary world: problems are embedded in environmental and cultural conditions, and effective solutions can only emerge from a thorough understanding of those conditions.

Education

B.Sc. University of London, 1966
MA University of London, 1967
Ph.D. University of London, 1977

Fieldwork

Nigeria, Ikale, Yorusa, 1968–77
Sierra Leone, 1982–3, 1987–1996 and from 2000 (ongoing)

Key Publications

(1985) Indigenous Agricultural Revolution: Ecology and Food Production in West Africa, London: Hutchinson.
(1996) Fighting for the Rain Forest: War, Youth and Resources in Sierra Leone, Oxford and Portsmouth: The International African Institute in association with James Curry and Heinemann.

KAY MILTON

Rigsby, Bruce

b. 1937, Louisville, Kentucky, USA

Trained as both a linguist and a social anthropologist, Bruce Rigsby has conducted long-term research into aboriginal languages and cultures in Australia, Canada, and the USA. In addition to his early study of the Sahaptin language, he has assisted with the development of a new alphabet and writing system for the Nisga'a language and has studied Aboriginal and creole languages on the eastern part of the Cape York Peninsula in Australia. His linguistic skills have facilitated extensive and varied social anthropological inquiries into aboriginal cultures and social organisation. Rigsby's precise ethnographic scholarship has been enlisted in support of several applied anthropological projects pursued in conjunction with aboriginal communities. His interests in political and intellectual issues pertaining to the recognition of native title (including marine resources) have infused his continuing involvement in aboriginal land claims research as well as a more recent concern with the history of anthropological involvement in this sphere of dealings between aboriginal peoples and governments.

Education

AB University of Louisville, 1961
Ph.D. University of Oregon, 1965

Fieldwork

Sahaptin-speaking people, southern plateau of Native North America, USA, 1963–75
Gitksan people, British Columbia, Canada, 1966–continuing
Nisga'a people, British Columbia, Canada, 1966–81
Lamalama people, North Queensland, Australia, 1972–continuing

Key Publications

(1997) 'Anthropologists, Indian title and the Indian Claims Commission: the California and Great Basin cases', in D.E. Smith and J. Finlayson (eds) *Fighting over Country: Anthropological Perspectives*, Centre for Economic Policy Research Monograph 12, Canberra: Centre for Aboriginal Economic Policy Research, Australian National University.
(1998) 'A survey of property theory and tenure types', in Nicolas Peterson and Bruce Rigsby (eds) *Customary Marine Tenure in Australia*, Oceania Monograph 48, Sydney: University of Sydney.

NOEL DYCK

Rihtman-Auguštin, Dunja

b. 6 September 1926, Sušak, Croatia

d. 4 November 2002, Zagreb, Croatia

While the work of Dunja Rihtman-Auguštin has received international recognition, elements in it – which may appear unusual for an international audience – are typical in East European scholarly careers. Namely, these are the political orientation of her writing, the deep connection between her biography and scientific concerns, and the difficulty of isolating specific research periods or locales in her long and rich research experience.

Yet, practising anthropology at home in the turbulent cultural contexts of twentieth-century Croatia can turn one's whole life into a seamless body of folkloristic fieldwork. After being incarcerated in a fascist prison at the age of sixteen, and subsequently joining the Croatian liberation movement, Dunja Rihtman-Auguštin never lacked inspirations for her profound anthropological critique of radical ideologies.

She worked first as a journalist and then joined the Institute of Economy in Zagreb. There she introduced her anthropology of cultural values, proposing traditional social patterns as conceivable alternatives for a modern socialist economy. As the head of the Institute of Ethnology and Folklore Research (1972–84), she conducted various projects that eventually established a new paradigm of Croatian ethnology, one which featured an effort to legitimise contemporary folk-life as it was, not as it was expected to be, in socialist or nationalist cultural projections. In accordance with the German post-war critique of parochial ethnology, her notion of the 'ethnos as a historical process' found its place between modernist rejections of 'primitive' folklore traditions, on one side, and nineteenth-century romantic conceptions of folk as 'dancing peasants', on the other.

Unmasking the manipulative and invented nature of political rituals and myths, she also continued her relentless cultural critique of ethnocentrism during the post-socialist period of Croatian society (2001).

Education

BA University of Zagreb, 1961
Ph.D. University of Ljubljana, 1976

Key Publications

(1984) *Struktura tradicijskog mišljenja* (The Structure of Traditional Thought), Zagreb: Školska knjiga.

(2001) *Etnologija i etnomit* (Ethnology and Ethno-Myth), Zagreb: Naklada Publica.

INES PRICA

Rivers, W.H.R.

b. 12 March 1864, Luton, Kent, UK

d. 4 June 1922, Cambridge, UK

A medical doctor by training, W.H.R. Rivers was a self-taught anthropologist, who exercised enormous influence in his relatively short career. Described as one of the founders of the Cambridge school of anthropology (along with A.C. Haddon), Rivers was also referred to (by A. Kuper) as 'the dominant European anthropologist of his generation'. His studies of kinship (derived from the 'genealogical method') influenced generations of anthropologists, and he was also instrumental in the establishment of social anthropology as a scholarly discipline. His first student at Cambridge was A.R. Radcliffe-Brown.

Rivers studied medicine in London, after illness prevented him from attending Cambridge. His primary interests were neurophysiology and psychiatry, and during the 1890s he also attended lectures in Germany. After briefly lecturing at the University College London, in 1893 Rivers moved to Cambridge. In 1897 he was appointed lecturer in psychological and experimental psychology at the University of Cambridge, in 1899 lecturer in ethnology, and a year later elected fellow of Christ's College. Between 1915 and 1918 Rivers worked as a therapist with 'war trauma' patients in several military hospitals. This experience influenced his work on the interrelationship of myths, dreams, and symbolism. After the First World War, Rivers opposed British imperialism and joined the Labour Party.

Following the suggestion of several of his students, Rivers in 1898 joined the Cambridge Anthropological Expedition to the Torres Straits and New Guinea, organised by Haddon. His main interest was to test the attribution 'to savage and semi-civilised races [of] a higher degree of acuteness of sense than is found among Europeans' (*Contributions to Reports of the Cambridge Anthropological Expedition to Torres Straits, Vol. II, Physiology and Psychology*, Cambridge, 1901, p. 12). The experiments conducted by Rivers and his students showed that there was actually no significant difference in the sensory perceptions between the Torres Strait islanders and the Europeans. More importantly for anthropology, Rivers started collecting genealogies, introducing a new and important method. He used the 'genealogical method' intensively during fieldwork among the Todas in South India. By collecting family genealogies, Rivers was able to compile a detailed sociological census of the population of around 800 individuals, as well as to check the individual genealogies and establish a whole system of relationships. This also provided him with tools for analysing various systems of folk taxonomy. Rivers noted that the Todas had no exogamous clan groups – in contrast to the anthropological theory of the time. However, even though he admitted that clans did not regulate marriage, he still tried to define a system of Toda 'clans'.

Rivers's work on genealogies, along with field research he conducted during an expedition to Melanesia in 1907–8, made him increasingly dissatisfied with evolutionism. The formal break came in 1911 with his opening address to Section H of the British Association for the Advancement of Science, where he claimed that changes in human societies were a direct consequence of the mixture of peoples and cultures. Here Rivers referred to the works of young German ethnologists (Fritz Graebner, B. Ankermann) who were establishing a diffusionist model for the development of cultures. This model would provide a crucial tool for Rivers's monumental *The History of Melanesian Society*, because, as Melanesian cultures were 'complex' (as they included a mixture of elements from a variety of different cultures), their histories could not be studied using evolutionary theories. This work (which Rivers regarded as his most important) also introduced the importance of social structure. 'The basic idea which underlies the whole argument of this book is the deeply seated and intimate character of social structure. It seems at first sight impossible that a society can change this structure and yet continue to exist' (*History*, vol. 2, p. 4). This two-volume book also provides a good example of Rivers's scholarly method: while the first volume is dedicated to the observations ('ethnography') of Melanesian societies, the second one is 'purely' methodological.

Although some of his ideas on kinship (like the whole problem of 'primitive marriage') already seemed out of date in the early twentieth century, Rivers's insistence on the importance of methodology and theory, along with his place in laying the foundations of anthropological fieldwork and the institutionalisation of anthropology, make him one of the most important figures in the history of the discipline.

Education

BM University of London, 1886
MD University of London, 1888

Fieldwork

The Torres Strait Expedition, April–October 1898
Todas, South India, 1901–2 (5 months)
The Percy Slade Trust Expedition to Melanesia (Solomon Islands, Fiji), 1907–8

Key Publications

(1906) *The Todas*, London: Macmillan.
(1914) *Kinship and Social Organisation*, London: Constable.
(1914) *The History of Melanesian Society*, 2 vols, Cambridge, UK: Cambridge University Press.
(1924) *Medicine, Magic and Religion. The Fitzpatrick*

Lectures Delivered before The Royal College of Physicians of London in 1915 and 1916, London: Kegan Paul, Trench, Trubner.

ALEKSANDAR BOSKOVIC

Rivière, Peter

b. 17 January 1934, UK

A student of Rodney Needham, Rivière completed his doctorate on the social organisation of the Trio Indians of Surinam in 1965. He taught in 1967 the first course on Amazonian societies in a British university. His considerable theoretical and methodological contributions to anthropology were made while lecturing at the University of Oxford, from 1971 until 2001. Apart from being a leading member of the first generation to set new, professional standards of ethnography in Amazonia, Rivière has delineated the field of social anthropological investigation in a way that continues to influence the development of research in lowland South America.

In *Marriage among the Trio* (1969), his first major publication and first monograph entirely dedicated to Amazonian kinship systems, Rivière demonstrated that Trio social philosophy works at conceptually blurring genealogy and residence. His analysis of the rules of alliance in a society where the local group is the primary politically autonomous unit forced kinship analysts working elsewhere in the world to interrogate long-held assumptions concerning their regions. His reconsideration of marriage and kinship also enabled him to foresee some cultural implications of new reproductive technologies. He argued that the social consequences and new ideas of relatedness created by test-tube births, artificial insemination, and embryo transplantation and donorship already had parallels in the societies documented by anthropologists. While Rivière's famous Malinowski lecture on the couvade (1974) constitutes an early attempt to provide a theory of the created person in

Amazonia, *Individual and Society in Guiana* (1984), a sober comparative study outlining the structural features specific to Amazonian societies, develops new conceptual tools for the positive characterisation of individualistic societies lacking formal social groupings. This was one of the first studies to locate the analysis of individuals within dynamic regional structures.

Education

BA, Magdalene College, University of Cambridge, 1957
MA, Magdalene College, University of Cambridge, 1961
B.litt. Magdalen College, University of Oxford, 1963
D.Phil. Magdalen College, University of Oxford, 1965

Fieldwork

Among the Trio of Surinam, 1963–4, 1978
Among Brazilians in Roraima State, 1967

Key Publications

(1969) *Marriage among the Trio: A Principle of Social Organisation*, Oxford: Clarendon Press.
(1974) 'The couvade: a problem reborn', *Man* 9, 3: 423–35.
(1984) *Individual and Society in Guiana: A Comparative Study of Amerindian Social Organisation*, Cambridge, UK: Cambridge University Press.

Further Reading

Rival, L. and Whitehead, N. (2001) 'Forty years of Amazonian anthropology, the contribution of Peter Rivière', in L. Rival and N. Whitehead (eds) *Beyond the Visible and the Material: The Amerindianization of Society in the Work of Peter Rivière*, Oxford: Oxford University Press.
Rival, L. (2002) 'Peter Rivière's contributions to Amazonian and social anthropology',

Journal of the Anthropological Society of Oxford 30, 3 (Michaelmas 1999): 213–18.

LAURA RIVAL

Rodman, Margaret Critchlow

b. 19 June 1947, Easton, Maryland, USA

Margaret Rodman's appreciation of the importance of place began early in her life and work. Her long-standing research in the South Pacific began in Vanuatu in 1969. This early work focused primarily on the pacification of Melanesia. In subsequent research and writing over the past three decades, Rodman has examined customary land tenure, fisheries development, and housing and social change in Vanuatu resulting in a number of significant articles and two books.

In 1987, Rodman began fieldwork in a second site, Toronto, Canada, examining the politics of place, culture, and social relations in co-operative and non-profit housing. This research has explored the sociocultural production of urban spaces and the relationship between housing, agency, and control. In her article 'Empowering place', Rodman draws on interdisciplinary and ethnographic expertise in arguing that the concept of place, like voice and time, is a politicised social and cultural construct. Her use of multilocality and multivocality in understanding the social construction of spatial meanings has been highly influential. The article has received international recognition for its theoretical contribution to the discipline.

Since the mid-1990s, Rodman has continued her critical investigation of place and housing in various locales. Her current research and publications explore post-colonial identities; British colonial landscapes; gender, race, and power; as well as urban research in Canada.

Education

AB Goucher College, 1969

MA McMaster University, 1976

Ph.D. McMaster University, 1981

Fieldwork

Vanuatu, December 1969–January 1971, June 1978–July 1979, July–December 1982, June–December 1985, June–August 1993, 1995, June–July 2001

Toronto, summers 1987, 1988, 1989, 1991, 1993, May–December 1988

Key Publications

(1987) *Masters of Tradition: Consequences of Customary Land Tenure in Longana, Vanuatu*, Vancouver: University of British Columbia Press.

(1992) 'Empowering place: multilocality and multivocality', *American Anthropologist* 94: 640–56.

VIRGINIA CAPUTO

Róheim, Géza

b. 12 September 1891, Budapest, Hungary

d. 7 June 1953, New York, USA

Géza Róheim was an outstanding comparative folklorist, initially focusing on Hungarian beliefs, customs, and rites. Studying in Hungary and Germany he was able to combine evolutionary anthropology and the history of religion with cultural geography and modern psychology. As a student Róheim joined the Hungarian Ethnographic Society and later the Hungarian section of Folklore Fellows. In 1917 he began work in the Hungarian National Museum. His task was to establish a modern folklore archive in Hungary. Drawing on his international training, he tried to modernise anthropology in Hungary, but only with limited success. In particular his efforts to establish a chair and research institute of ethnology were unsuccessful. After the defeat of the bourgeois and then Communist revolutions he was expelled from the Hungarian

National Museum, and worked subsequently as a private scholar and later as a psychiatrist. He was a well-known member of liberal intellectual circles in Budapest.

He took an active part in the Budapest circle of Freudianism from its inception in 1915, and he published the very first psychoanalytic papers in folklore and anthropology. In 1921, he was awarded the Freud Prize for his ethnological studies. Supported by a grant from Princess Maria Bonaparte, he carried out a worldwide research trip between 1928 and 1931. His task was to prove the Freudian interpretation of Australian totemism and to check the worldwide existence of the 'Oedipus complex'. Travelling home through Chicago, New York, Hamburg, Berlin, Paris, etc., he gave a series of lectures on his fieldwork results in which he approached a general ('ontogenetical') theory of culture.

From 1931 to 1938 Róheim lived in Budapest writing on general topics of European folklore and social psychoanalysis. After the Nazi occupation of Austria he emigrated to the USA where he was affiliated with 'traditional Freudianism' circles. However, he only managed to get minor professional positions (Worcester State Hospital, then in New York), and was only able to carry out one fieldwork project (among the Navaho Indians, 1947, sponsored by the Viking Fund). After the Second World War, he re-established contacts with his Hungarian colleagues and worked again on Old Hungarian beliefs and mythology. From 1947 he was one of the leaders of the social psychoanalysts involved in the production of the yearbook, *Psychoanalysis and Social Sciences*. However, he felt unhappy and unsuccessful, and died shortly after the death of his beloved Hungarian wife, Ilona, with whom he had conducted his fieldwork trips.

The first works of Róheim reflect a general evolutionary anthropology, especially in his description of the development of primitive conceptions of souls. The Freudian approach gave him new possibilities for interpreting Hungarian folklore topics and his interpretations quite quickly gained international acceptance in psychoanalysis, although these ideas did not win a similar acceptance in the social and cultural anthropology of the day.

As the forerunner of Freudian anthropology, his studies have been published and republished (translated) all over the world. His work became in time especially influential in the French, German, Italian, Latin American, and Japanese social sciences.

His 'ontogenetical theory of culture' stressed the fact that newborn humans are incapable of surviving alone: socialisation is essential to give them the necessary mental framework. Thus the evolutionary phases of a person's development suggested by Freud could be understood in terms of the kind of cultural manifestations described by modern social anthropologists.

During his fieldwork Róheim made very careful and comprehensive notes. He was able to learn the difficult languages of the Aborigines, and the hundreds of photos he took and the many phonogram records he made were technological innovations in fieldwork methodology. However, his fieldwork diaries were never published, and his collected texts were published only much later and not in their entirety.

His research in Australia led to critiques first of the traditional British school of social anthropology generally and then evolved into more specific criticism of Bronislaw Malinowski's work. This critical stance may well have cost Róheim the international recognition within anthropology that his rich life's work truly merited.

Education

Ph.D. Peter Pázmány University, 1914

Fieldwork

Hungary (ethnography, folklore for the Hungarian National Museum and Archive of Ethnography), 1917 onwards

French Somalia, central Australia (Aranda and Luritya tribes), Normanby Island (New Guinea), Yuma Indians (California), 1928–31

Navaho Indians, New Mexico, 1947

Key Publications

(1925) *Australian Totemism*, London: Allen & Unwin.

(1950) *Psychoanalysis and Anthropology*, New York: International Universities Press.

(1954) *Hungarian and Vogul Mythology*, New York: J.J. Augustin.

(1992) *Fire in the Dragon and Other Psychoanalytic Essays on Folklore*, Princeton, New Jersey: Princeton University Press.

KINSCO VEREBÉLYI

Rosaldo, Michelle Zimbalist

b. 4 May 1944, New York City, USA

d. 11 October 1981, Northern Luzon, Philippines

Although she died at the age of thirty-seven, by 1981 Michelle Z. Rosaldo was a highly respected ethnographer and, perhaps, the most influential feminist theorist of her generation. Rosaldo's monograph about the Ilongot, an egalitarian community of headhunters and horticulturalists, is definitely among the most successful examples of what interpretive anthropology promised in the 1970s. Through an analysis of the interdependence of knowledge (*beya*) and passion (*liget*) in the social life and hearts (*rinawa*) of men and women, as well as between married men and unmarried male youth, Rosaldo examined how these relationships are central to a cultural understanding of both marrying and killing (beheading) among the Ilongot.

In 1974 Rosaldo first broke new ground when she proposed a feminist theoretical framework based on the analysis of the domestic/public dichotomy not only to challenge anthropology's male focus but also to try to explain women's subordination cross-culturally. In 1980, she further argued that such gendered dichotomies tended to reduce women's role to biological mothering, and that such a framework was a product of Victorian ideologies from the turn of the twentieth century; and, therefore, should not be imposed on societies outside historically and culturally specific contexts.

Rosaldo also contributed to linguistic and psychological anthropology. She explored metaphor and speech act theories in order to show that linguists and philosophers of language privileged speakers' intentions while ignoring the social relations that produced such speech acts. Through this intervention, Rosaldo pioneered 'practice theory'. Finally, Rosaldo criticised both the psychologism and the biologism embedded in Western notions of the self. She demonstrated that methodological individualism did not allow for the many ways human beings make sense of who they are and how they feel in the world, thus helping to establish the anthropology of emotions in the early 1980s.

Education

BA Radcliffe College, 1966
Ph.D. Harvard University, 1972

Fieldwork

Northern Luzon, Philippines, 1967–9, 1974, 1981

Key Publications

with Lamphere, Louise (eds) (1974) *Woman, Culture, and Society*, Stanford, CA: Stanford University Press.
(1980) *Knowledge and Passion: Ilongot Notions of Self and Social Life*, New York: Cambridge University Press.

ALEJANDRO LUGO

Rosaldo, Renato I.

b. 15 April 1941, Champaign, Illinois, USA

Renato Rosaldo is a noted ethnographer of the Philippines, a pioneer in historical ethnography, and an influential voice in debates over culture.

Rosaldo's ethnography, *Ilongot Headhunting*, pioneered the use of historical methods in ethnographic research. Careful analysis of oral narratives allowed Rosaldo to construct an Ilongot chronology, even in the absence of written documents. This chronology illuminated the social structural concept of *bertan*, which Ilongots use for both residentially concentrated and geographically dispersed groups of people. The diachronic perspective Rosaldo developed highlights the relationship between social structure and human agency.

Rosaldo's subsequent work addresses the relations of power and knowledge in anthropological practice. In 'Grief and a headhunter's rage' Rosaldo probes his own reactions to the death of his wife, Michelle Rosaldo, as a means of understanding and explicating Ilongot emotional responses to bereavement. And in 'From the door of his tent' Rosaldo notes parallels in the rhetorical establishment of authorial power between E. Evans-Pritchard's 1950 ethnography, *The Nuer*, and Emmanuel Le Roy Ladurie's *Montaillou*, the celebrated social history of a fifteenth-century French town. Rosaldo's work on the politics of representation eloquently argues for authors to take the ethnographic subject's life as seriously as they take their own.

In the late 1980s Rosaldo turned to professional and popular debates over culture in the USA. His widely read book, *Culture and Truth*, repositions social analysis from a search for timeless and fixed structures to an interpretation of processes that emerge from social boundaries and points of variability. In the 1990s Rosaldo engaged with the public debate in the USA over multiculturalism, and his subsequent research theorises cultural citizenship, a term that highlights the tension in Western nation-states between ideals of citizenship (equality and sameness) and deployments of culture (hierarchy and plurality).

Education

AB Harvard College, 1963
Ph.D. Harvard University, 1971

Fieldwork

Ecuador and Peru, summers 1961, 1962
Zinacantán, Chiapas, Mexico, summers 1965, 1966
Northern Luzon, Philippines, 1967–9, 1974, 1981
San José, California, summers 1990–5

Key Publications

(1980) *Ilongot Headhunting, 1883–1974: A Study in Society and History*, Stanford: Stanford University Press.
(1984) 'Grief and a headhunter's rage', in E. Bruner (ed.) *Text, Play, and Story, 1983 Proceedings of the American Ethnological Society*, Washington, DC: American Ethnological Society.
(1986) 'From the door of his tent: the fieldworker and the inquisitor', in J. Clifford and G. Marcus (eds) *Writing Culture: The Poetics and Politics of Ethnography*, Berkeley: University of California Press.
(1989) *Culture and Truth: The Remaking of Social Analysis*, Boston: Beacon Press.

DANIEL LEFKOWITZ

Roseberry, William C.

b. 25 April 1950, Little Rock, Arkansas, USA

d. 12 August 2000, New York, USA

William Roseberry's research is characterised by its broad theoretical and historical scope, and interdisciplinary nature, examining the relationship between anthropology and history, and culture and political economy. He undertook nuanced, ethnographically informed, archivally based research, focusing on Latin American (especially Venezuelan) coffee economies, household economies in colonial Mexico and early modern England, and peasant politics and state formation in nineteenth- and twentieth-century Mexico. This research highlights the multiple trajectories that capitalist development has followed (given the contingencies of local contexts in which it developed), and how peasantries and household economies emerged during this development, rather than preceding and being transformed by it. Other essays examine the intellectual and political evolution of scholarship, placing debates in a wider context and analysing the epistemologies that inform them (an analysis that underlies his keen criticisms of intellectual fashions). His rethinking of Gramsci's concept of hegemony as a political process and on-going project, in which popular culture and state formation are mutually constitutive in a single social field, has been widely influential. Towards the end of his life, however, Roseberry began to suspect that scholars had gone too far in seeing popular political activity in reference to the state, and thus he began research that emphasised the complex and tension-laden internal politics of Mexican peasant communities.

Education

BA Southern Methodist University, 1971
MA University of Connecticut, 1974
Ph.D. University of Connecticut, 1977

Fieldwork

Taos, New Mexico, 1970, 1971
Boconó, Venezuela, 1974–6
Patzcuaro, Mexico, 1995–6, 1997, 1998

Key Publications

(1983) *Coffee and Capitalism in the Venezuelan Andes*, Austin: University of Texas Press.
(1989) *Anthropologies and Histories: Essays in Culture, History and Political Economy*, New Brunswick, NJ: Rutgers University Press.

KIM CLARK

Rottenburg, Richard

b. 1953, Hermannstadt, Romania

Richard Rottenburg's initial fieldwork was carried out in the Nuba Mountains of the Sudan. His first monograph (1991) mainly covers aspects of the economy and the social organisation of Ndemwareng (one of the hill communities of the Moro-Nuba). Yet the main focus of this book is on patterns of 'accretion' or, as one would rather call it today, on patterns of syncretism. As a reaction to the Sudanese war that began at the end of his fieldwork in 1984, Rottenburg turned to the study of modern organisations. He started with ethnographic studies in organisational anthropology at home (Berlin West) and then contributed to the transformation studies relating to post-socialist countries. Later, he embarked on the analysis of the global development arena, focusing on the production of objectivity (2001). A universal code of objectivity is shown to be required, as a common ground and as a code of politeness, to negotiate which issues are to be approached by development projects, which solutions should be chosen and by which criteria this whole process can be legitimised. Rottenburg thus opens a new perspective on hegemony.

Education

MA Free University of Berlin (West), 1978
Ph.D. Free University of Berlin (West), 1987
Habilitation, European University Viadrina, Frankfurt/Oder, 1999

Fieldwork

Among the Moro of the Nuba Mountains (Sudan), 1979–1984 (40 months)
Five private and public companies in Berlin (Germany), intermittent 1989–94 (10 months)
Nine public organisations in five African countries (Lesotho, Tanzania, Ghana, Gambia, and Mozambique), 1990–7 (19 months)

The German Bank for Reconstruction and Development (KfW), 1992 (6 months)

Key Publications

(1991) *Ndemwareng. Wirtschaft und Gesellschaft in den Morobergen.* (Ndemwareng. Economy and Society in the Moro Mountains of Sudan), München: Trickster.
(2001) *Weithergeholte Fakten. Wie Entwicklung gemacht wird* (Far-Fetched Facts. How Development is Made), Stuttgart: Lucius & Lucius.

WERNER SCHIFFAUER

Rouch, Jean

b. 31 May 1917, Paris, France

d. 18 February 2004, Niger

Jean Rouch was without question among the foremost documentary filmmakers in the world. What distinguishes Rouch's films from those of other documentarians is the artful blending of structured narratives with scientifically grounded ethnography. This fusion is most beautifully honed in what Rouch called his films of 'ethno-fiction'.

After receiving his baccalaureate, Rouch was admitted to the prestigious École des Ponts et Chausées, the Grande École for civil engineering. The Second World War disrupted Rouch's studies, but, in 1940–1, he found time to take an elective course from Professor Marcel Griaule. Despite the war, Rouch managed to complete his studies. Desperate to leave occupied France, he found work in Niamey in Colonial Niger, where he built roads for Travaux Publics.

In July 1942 a lightning bolt catapulted Rouch into anthropology. Rouch received a telegram from one of his labour bosses that Dongo had killed ten labourers. Who was Dongo and why had he killed ten labourers? He called a meeting of Nigerien associates and asked for an explanation. They said that Dongo was 'the devil' of thunder and that the fate of the labourers had nothing to do with Islam. Damouré Zika, however, spoke up and said that his grandmother, Kalia, could take care of the matter. In this way a lifelong collaboration began. In the company of Kalia and Damouré Zika, Rouch witnessed his first spirit possession ceremony. The dye was cast. Rouch attended other ceremonies and began to document the phenomenon. He wrote to Marcel Griaule, who at that time held the chair in ethnology at the Sorbonne, for advice. Having received an enthusiastic reply from Griaule, Rouch continued to document local religious practices.

Between 1946 and 1947 Rouch descended the Niger River in dugout canoes. In Ayoru in what is today the Republic of Niger, Rouch shot footage of a hippopotamus hunt, but, having broken his tripod, had to hand-hold the camera. He used the same technique to film Hauka possession ceremonies – also in Ayoru. This footage became the foundation of two of Rouch's earliest films, *Au Pays des mages noires* (1947) and *La Chasse à l'hippopatame* (1950).

Rouch became a provisional researcher for Centre National de la Recherche Scientifique (CNRS) in 1947. As part of his doctoral research, he returned to Niger and Mali in 1947–8 where he compiled oral histories of the Songhay people and continued to film Songhay ritual life. At the urging of Marcel Griaule, Rouch and Roger Rosfelder, a linguist, returned to Niger and Mali once again in 1951 where they shot films on both Songhay and Dogon social and religious life. Philosophical provocations are backgrounded in Rouch's early ethnographic films. These provocations, however, became foregrounded in the films he made during the 1950s and 1960s. The provocations, in addition, also become political as Rouch confronted the incendiary issues of a French racism contoured and deepened by French colonial culture. These works of what Rouch called 'ethno-friction' include *Jaguar* (1953–67), *Les Maîtres fous* (1955), *Moi, un noir* (1957), *La Pyramide humaine* (1959), and *Chronique d'un été* (1960); they remain Jean Rouch's greatest legacy to anthropology and to the cinema.

Throughout all of these films, which were based upon significant collaboration with African friends and colleagues, Rouch used the camera to participate in the life of the filmed as well as to provoke them and the viewers into experiencing new sociocultural dimensions. Rouch's films of this important period cut to the flesh and blood of European colonialist being. The films compel us to reflect on our latent racism, our repressed sexuality, the taken-for-granted assumptions of our intellectual heritage. They also demonstrate the importance of substantive collaboration, or what Rouch called *anthroplogie partagée*, in the production of anthropological knowledge. In the end these richly textured films expose the centrality of power relations to our dreams, thoughts, and actions.

In his later films, Rouch shifted some of his focus from Niger and Ivory Coast to Mali and the incredibly beautifully and complex Sigui ceremonies of the Dogon people, a ritual that is performed every sixty years during a cycle of seven years.

Jean Rouch's greatest contribution is to have created a body of work in which the limits of the ethnographic are the limits of the imagination. In Rouch's universe ethnographers participate fully in the lives of their others. Dreams become films; films become dreams. Feeling is fused with thought and action, and viewers are awakened from their sleep. Fusing poetry and science, Rouch has shown us the path of wise ancestors and guided us into a wondrous world where we not only encounter others but also encounter ourselves.

Education

Licence (Bachelor's degree), École des Ponts et Chausées, 1941
Licence (Bachelor's degree), Sorbonne (human sciences), 1946
Ph.D. Sorbonne, 1953

Fieldwork

Niamey (Niger), 1941–2
Niger River descent (Mali, Niger, Nigeria), 1946–7

Niger and Mali, 1947–8, 1951 (Songhay and Dogon)

Mali (Dogon), 1951, 1964, 1967–74

Ghana, 1951–2, 1953–4

Ivory Coast, 1956–8

Key Publications

(1989 [1960]) *Religion and Magic among the Songhay*, second edn, Brussels: Free University Press.

(2003) *Ciné-Ethnography* 2003, ed. and trans. Steve Feld, Minneapolis: University of Minnesota Press.

(2003) 'The camera and the man', in *Ciné-Ethnography*.

(2003) 'On the vicissitudes of the self: the possessed dancer, the magician, the sorcerer, the filmmaker, and the ethnographer', in *Ciné-Ethnography*.

PAUL STOLLER

S

Sahlins, Marshall

b. 27 December 1930, Chicago, Illinois, USA

Marshall Sahlins began his studies in an evolutionary tradition, and his own work has certainly evolved as he has come to occupy a distinctive place in anthropology. He has never been afraid to rethink earlier positions, nor reluctant to expand his intellectual horizons beyond mainstream American anthropological practice.

His first book, based on library research, developed the thesis that the basic adaptation of a culture arose from the interaction of technology with a given environment. It was this interaction, Sahlins argued, that governed the degree of social stratification in selected Polynesian island groups. The book was thus set in the framework of cultural evolutionism. Though Sahlins was not content to remain within those boundaries, his next book maintained an emphasis on ecological considerations as they affected social structure.

Sahlins next moved his continuing concern with economic issues into a more theoretical context. *Stone Age Economics* (1972) marked him as a thinker whose ideas had relevance beyond the narrowly ethnographic. His concept of 'the original affluent society' and his analysis of different forms of exchange have provoked debate among non-anthropologists seeking a broader definition of economic activity.

Some observers regard Sahlins's next book as making a sharp break with the cultural evolutionism and emphasis on material factors in culture that marked his earlier work. Others might see this as the on-going development of an original thinker who no longer found the formulations of cultural materialists adequate for what he was attempting to accomplish. It is certain that during the 1970s Sahlins seemed increasingly to immerse himself in the work of a number of French scholars. His 1975 *Culture and Practical Reason* argued that symbolic relations of cultural order were more important than environmental adaptation or other materialist approaches if anthropologists were to develop deeper understanding of human life and thought.

In 1981, Sahlins produced his first major work to put forth a structural approach to Polynesian history. Here he set out his, by now, controversial notion that Captain Cook was perceived in terms of existing Hawaiian cultural symbols, as the arrival of the god, Lono, and it was this 'structure of the conjuncture' that explains subsequent events. Sahlins expanded these ideas in *Islands of History* (1987). In this collection of essays, he also went outside Hawaii to discuss other Pacific islands but, more importantly, placed the historical materials in a wide-ranging theoretical context that displayed the extent of his reading in other disciplines.

Sahlins demonstrated his ability to innovate in his next book about Hawaii. He collaborated with an outstanding archaeologist of the Pacific, Patrick Kirch, in a two-volume work combining his historical research with Kirch's archaeological study of a valley on the island of Oíahu. Here Sahlins developed much more extensively his argument that events in the early Hawaiian kingdom are to be understood in what some readers might call a dialectical relationship between Hawaiian symbolic order and the encroachment of Western capitalism. Sahlins produced a wealth of detail about matters ranging from origin myths through environmental adaptation to Christian missionary activity. The result can fairly be described as monumental, bringing together much of Sahlins's thought as it had grown over decades.

In the same year that this book appeared, the anthropologist Ganath Obeyesekere published *The Apotheosis of Captain Cook: European Mythmaking in the Pacific*. This constituted a direct attack on Sahlins's earlier work about Hawaii. Sahlins replied at book length three years later, and the echoes of this debate continue to reverberate. However, those seeking an introduction to Sahlins's thought are better advised to consult his essays collected in 2000 as *Culture in Practice*.

The title of this latest book indicates the impact its author has had on the field of anthropology and beyond. 'Practice' and 'history' came to be regarded as key concepts in the field during the 1980s. No single anthropologist has more clearly foreseen their significance nor better exemplified them in his scholarship than Marshall Sahlins.

Education

MA University of Michigan, 1952
Ph.D. Columbia University, 1954

Fieldwork

Moala, Fiji, 1954–5

Key Publications

(1958) *Social Stratification in Polynesia: A Study of Adaptive Variation in Culture*, Seattle: University of Washington Press.
(1975) *Culture and Practical Reason*, Chicago: University of Chicago Press.

(1981) *Historical Metaphors and Mythical Realities: Studies in the Early History of the Sandwich Islands Kingdom*, Ann Arbor: University of Michigan Press.
(2000) *Culture in Practice: Selected Essays*, New York: Zone Books.

EUGENE OGAN

Salisbury, Richard F.

b. 8 December 1926, Chelsea, UK

d. 19 June 1989, Montreal, Canada

Salisbury was author or co-author of twenty books, monographs, and reports, more than sixty articles, and numerous commentaries. Like most of his generation, his interests were wide-ranging. Yet a deep commitment to intellectual rigour, via empirically informed theory and theoretically guided fieldwork, underlay all his work and his international reputation. His earliest publications, on social structure and kinship, were key to the debate then raging between 'alliance' and 'descent' theorists. His work on transactional politics (Big Men, factionalism) impelled the exploration of how economic resources and political power were related. His most distinguished work, however, was in economic anthropology, as a leader of 'formalists' (as distinct from 'substantivists') who were applying formal, economic models to the ethnography of exchange.

All of Salisbury's work, especially that which addressed culture change and economic development, had applied implications. This, plus his intellectual and moral inclinations, meant that he became as well known for his applied work as for his theoretical contributions. He saw the anthropologist as a 'societal ombudsman': an impartial adviser and information source who contributed to enabling the powerless to negotiate fair outcomes. This was the view that informed his involvement with the Cree and the James Bay hydro-electric project. Indeed, he later became very concerned that legal and adversarial frameworks had begun to typify the area of Native rights. He firmly believed that decent people, using the knowledge provided by experts, could always reach a satisfactory agreement.

Salisbury's viewpoints led him to undertake a daunting number of administrative tasks. For example, he was chair of the Anthropology Department (1966–70) and dean of arts (1986–9), McGill University; co-founder and later director of the McGill Centre for Developing Studies (1975–8); president of the Canadian Sociology and Anthropology Association (1968–70), and of the American Ethnological Society (1980). Through these academic efforts, and his work as a consultant during the 1970s and later, Salisbury was instrumental in framing an organisational structure for the discipline of anthropology in Canada and Quebec, and for raising its public profile.

Salisbury was elected to the Royal Society of Canada in 1974.

Education

BA University of Cambridge, 1949
AM Harvard University, 1955
Ph.D. Australian National University, 1957

Fieldwork

Siane, Highland New Guinea, 1951–2, 1960, 1967, 1984
Boston State Mental Hospital, 1955–6
Tolai, New Britain, 1960–1, 1967, 1984
Papua New Guinea (Port Moresby, New Britain), 1967, 1971, 1984
Guyana, periodically, 1964–6
Cree, James Bay, Quebec, 1971–7, 1979, 1980–2
Northern Canada (Yukon, Northwest Territories, Labrador), 1974, 1980, 1981

Key Publications

(1962) *From Stone to Steel: Economic Consequences of Technological Change in New Guinea*, Melbourne: Melbourne University Press.
(1970) *Vunamami: Economic Transformation in a Traditional Society*, Berkeley: University of California Press.
(1972) *Development and James Bay: Social Implications of the Hydro-electric Proposals* (co-authored), Report to the James Bay Development Corporation, Montreal: McGill University Programme in the Anthropology of Development, Monograph Series #4.
(1986) *A Homeland for the Cree: Regional Development in James Bay, 1971–1981*, Montreal: McGill-Queen's Press.

MARILYN SILVERMAN

Salmond, Anne

b. 1945, Wellington, New Zealand

Although she is herself a Pakeha (European) New Zealander, (Mary) Anne Salmond was raised on the strongly Maori east coast of the North Island. In her undergraduate years at Auckland she majored in anthropology, but with an emphasis on Maori language and culture. For her Master's thesis Salmond turned to the Luangiua language of the Ontong Java people of the Solomon Islands, while in her doctoral studies at Pennsylvania she was attracted to sociolinguistics, especially as mediated by Ward Goodenough and Irving Goffman. Her published dissertation on Maori ceremonial gatherings marked a new phase in ethnographic writing about this culture. Rather than produce another community-based account of Maori social life, Salmond attended numerous formal occasions throughout the North Island, focusing on intertribal variations and emic interpretations of performance, oratory, and ritual. Soon after, she brought into print the life story and traditional teachings, respectively, of eminent elders, Amiria and Eruera Stirling, her guiding lights on all things Maori. Along the way Salmond also has written authoritative essays on Maori semantics, cosmology, knowledge, aesthetics, and kinship. In the late 1980s she moved into the area of historical anthropology, notably producing a two-volume study of early encounters between Maori and Europeans, and an account of the cultural dynamics of Captain Cook's interactions with the peoples of the South Seas.

Education

BA University of Auckland, 1966
MA University of Auckland, 1968
Ph.D. University of Pennsylvania, Philadelphia, 1972

Fieldwork

Ontong Java settlement, Honiara, Solomon Islands, 1966–7 (4 months)
New Zealand, intensively 1970–1, intermittently since then
Tahiti, Hawaii, and Tonga, intermittently 1998–2003

Key Publications

(1975) Hui: *A Study of Maori Ceremonial Gatherings*, Wellington: Reed.
(1991) *Two Worlds: First Meetings between Maori and Europeans*, Honolulu: University of Hawaii Press.

TOM RYAN

Sanjek, Roger

b. 1944, New York City, USA

Roger Sanjek's work has engaged with urban anthropology, race and ethnicity, gender, political activism, and ageing, as well as with ethnographic method, and the history of anthropology. Sanjek's extensive field research started out with fieldwork on concepts of race in a Brazilian fishing village, moved on to ethnic relations in a neighbourhood in Accra, Ghana, and back to the USA and a study of the Gray Panthers movement of elderly activists, as well as long-term fieldwork on the changing politics of Elmhurst-Corona in Queens, New York City. The book based on the latter study, *The Future of Us All* received four major awards. *Race* (co-edited with Steven Gregory, 1994) also

received an award. This volume as well as *Fieldnotes*, analysing the early stages of ethnographic writing, are widely used in university courses.

Another important aspect of Sanjek's anthropology is his careful editorial work: in the Anthropology of Contemporary Issues Series (Cornell University Press), of which he has been the general editor, more than fifty books have appeared.

An extraordinarily wide reading, a sophisticated grasp of anthropological thought and practice, and a critical view of contemporary capitalist society continue to inform Sanjek's central contributions to a socially relevant anthropology.

Education

BA Columbia College, 1966
Columbia Graduate School of Journalism, 1966
Ph.D. Columbia University, 1972

Fieldwork

Bahia, Brazil, 1965
Accra, Ghana, 1969–71, 1974
Berkeley-Oakland, California, USA, 1977–8
Philadelphia, New York City, Berkeley, Washington DC, USA, 1980–7, 1999
Elmhurst-Corona, Queens, USA, 1983–96

Key Publications

(ed.) (1990) *Fieldnotes: The Makings of Anthropology*, Ithaca: Cornell University Press.
(1998) *The Future of Us All: Race and Neighbourhood Politics in New York City*, Ithaca: Cornell University Press.

HELENA WULFF

Sansom, Basil

b. 1938, South Africa

Sansom's anthropological contribution has displayed a consistent and on-going concern with social processes and the cultural construction of meaning in social life. Throughout his career his accounts have conjoined ethnographic evidence with theoretical and analytical sophistication in ways that have demonstrated a mastery of form. In a series of early publications dealing with fieldwork carried out with the Pedi in South Africa Sansom demonstrated keen insight in the analysis of social and cultural processes within the context of complex ecological relationships. In 1974, after working in the Department of Anthropology for over ten years, Sansom left Manchester and took a Research Fellowship with the Australian Institute for Aboriginal Studies. He is best known for his ethnographic accounts of Aboriginal fringe dwellers in and around Darwin, the capital of Australia's Northern Territory. His use of the ethnography of speaking as a way into making sense of the social lives of the peripatetic Aboriginal people of the region is impressive. In focusing on the performance of cultural life, through a method he identifies as 'processual modelling', he demonstrates how the continuity in form or structure is most appropriately understood dynamically, as always being established through the social and cultural processes of organising particular activities. Since retiring from academic life in 1994, as professor of anthropology at the University of Western Australia, Sansom has continued to publish ethnographic accounts and has worked as a consultant dealing with Aboriginal native title claims.

Education

BA University of the Witwatersrand, 1959
BA (Hons) University of the Witwatersrand, 1961
Ph.D. University of Manchester, 1970

Fieldwork

Sekhukuneland, South Africa, 1960–1
Brak Oases, Fezzan, 1966–7
Village of Charoun, Lebanon, 1972
Northern Territory, Australia, 1974 to present

Key Publications

(1980) *The Camp at Wallaby Cross*, Canberra: AIAS Press.

PHILIP MOORE

Sapir, Edward

b. 26 January 1884, Lauenberg, Pomerania

d. 4 February 1939, New Haven, Connecticut, USA

Edward Sapir grew up on the Lower East Side of New York City, distinguishing himself among the city's children of immigrants by winning a city-wide Pulitzer scholarship competition that financed his education through the four years of his BA and MA. Sapir's first two degrees were in Germanics, specialising in Indo-European linguistics (although he also took several courses in music composition). A course with Franz Boas in American Indian linguistics persuaded him that fieldwork with endangered languages was an urgent priority, leading him to switch to anthropology for his doctorate. In 1905, he completed his MA and began his American Indian fieldwork. His dissertation on Takelma was published in 1909.

After brief stints at the Universities of California and Pennsylvania, Sapir became, at the age of twenty-six, director of the newly established Division of Anthropology of the Canadian government, under the Department of Mines, Geological Survey of Canada, and housed in the Victoria Memorial Museum. Between 1910 and the escalation of the First World War around 1916, Sapir orchestrated a massive programme of ethnological and linguistic survey work across the Dominion. He reserved the Northwest Coast as his own specialisation, working particularly with the Nootka. Assisted by Diamond Jenness in the Arctic and Marius Barbeau in Quebec and later the Northwest Coast, as well as various fellow Boasians whose research he sponsored, Sapir began to build a strong research programme. Most of his personal fieldwork and much of his significant writing was done during the early Ottawa years.

In addition to his fieldwork, Sapir produced two significant codifications of the Boasian programme. Adapting the linguistics of his training to the needs of ethnological research, *Time Perspective in Aboriginal American Culture* (1916) used linguistic examples from across North America to clarify how to approach the history of unwritten languages. *Language* (1921) was designed to make linguistics intelligible to an educated general public. Sapir cited American Indian as well as more familiar Indo-European languages, taking for granted the functional equivalence of all human languages. Also during these years, he synthesised the American Indian linguistic work of the last few decades, his own and that of Boasian colleagues, in a classification of only six genetic stocks for all of North America. This classification remained the frame of reference for ethnological work until well into the 1960s; although a more conservative standard of evidence has since prevailed, many of Sapir's suggestions of distant linguistic relationship remain open to further demonstration.

Wartime curtailment of funding for research and publication, more difficult because of the illness and death of his first wife, made the early 1920s increasingly frustrating. Sapir chafed under the restrictions of museum work and longed for an academic position and for colleagues who shared his interests in linguistics and in new perspectives on culture and personality. In 1925, he was called to the University of Chicago where he quickly became the spokesman for anthropology in the interdisciplinary synthesis of Chicago sociology and psychology/psychiatry. He refused the role of purveyor of the exotic, searching instead for a method of studying personality cross-culturally through a life-history method adapted from clinical psychology.

At Yale University after 1931, the Rockefeller Foundation supported Sapir's seminar, 'The impact of culture on personality'. In collaboration with interactional psychologist, Harry Stack Sullivan, he developed a culture theory in which society provided a mediating term between culture and the individual. Although his projected book on the psychology of culture was never completed, Sapir published a series of seminal papers that are included in his selected writings (1949). The synthesis of the social sciences envisioned by interdisciplinary scholars of the interwar years was largely abortive, although many of its tenets have been revived in recent years.

Sapir's death in 1939 at the relatively young age of fifty-five prevented his participation in the further development of culture and personality within anthropology. Similarly in linguistics, American structuralism developed a less processual and meaning-oriented stance under Leonard Bloomfield in the 1940s and 1950s. Linguistics in anthropology became increasingly separate from ethnology. No scholar since Sapir has achieved such a synthesis of language, and the 'psychological reality' of cultural patterns for culture members. His students in both anthropology and linguistics remembered him as both a 'genius' and a dedicated mentor.

Education

BA Columbia University, 1904
MA Columbia University, 1905
Ph.D. Columbia University, 1909

Fieldwork

Wishram Chinook, 1905
Takelma, 1906
Yana, 1907–8
Ute and Southern Paiute, during 1908–10
Nootka, 1910–11, 1914
Sarcee, Kutchin, Ingalik, early 1920s
Hupa, 1927
Navaho, beginning in 1926

Key Publications

(1916) *Time Perspective in Aboriginal American Culture: A Study in Method*, Ottawa: Department of Mines, Geological Survey of Canada, Anthropological Series 13.

(1921) *Language: An Introduction to the Study of Speech*, New York: Harcourt Brace.

(1949) *Selected Writings of Edward Sapir*, ed. David Mandelbaum, Berkeley: University of California Press.

REGNA DARNELL

Schapera, Isaac

b. 23 June 1905, Garies, Cape Colony

d. 2003, London, UK

Initially intending to study law at the University of Cape Town, Schapera switched to social anthropology and became A.R. Radcliffe-Brown's first Master's student. He completed a library-based doctorate at the London School of Economics under C.G. Seligman before returning to South Africa to teach for a year at the University of the Witwatersrand. He then subsequently returned to the University of Cape Town, where in 1935 he was appointed to the chair of social anthropology. In 1949 he took up a chair at the London School of Economics, which he held until his retirement in 1969. In South Africa he played a defining role in promoting the study of Africa by both English- and Afrikaans-language universities, editing two landmark compilations and offering numerous memoranda on research priorities. The key role he played in shaping South African social anthropology is clear from who he taught: Max Gluckman, Ellen Hellmann, Hilda Kuper, Eileen Jensen Krige, Hans Holleman, Hugh Ashton, David Hammond-Tooke are but some of the names that spring to mind. Since his retirement Schapera has been honoured by at least four Festschriften, and was awarded an honorary doctorate from the University of Botswana.

Isaac Schapera's legacy is multiple and has withstood the test of time: He wrote the first thorough and broad synthesis of what he termed the Khoisan (now Khoekhoe) people of Southern Africa. Based on a thorough survey of the literature and displaying a rare capacity to integrate findings from other languages, it forms the benchmark for subsequent syntheses. While he never did fieldwork among the San or the Nama his interest in their rights and plight was long-standing and materialised in an important research memorandum that, because of the outbreak of the Second World War, could not be implemented. A second major contribution that was derived from this literature survey is his exceptional and thorough editing of the writings of early travellers and, in particular, that of David Livingstone, which Schapera was able to contextualise on the basis of his own extended and intensive fieldwork, his third major contribution. This sensitivity to history and rich empirical data solidified in a fourth feature of his work, a theoretical stance that avowedly rejected the atemporality of the dominant theoretical paradigm of the time, functionalism as espoused by Bronislaw Malinowski. Instead, taking his cue from Radcliffe-Brown, Schapera argued as early as 1928 that rather than the segregationist and later apartheid position (that Africans could be studied in isolation in terms of traits), the focus instead should be on interaction between persons as members of groups within the 'whole structure'. In short, Europeans and Africans could not be studied in isolation or by simply listing their 'traits' but had to be seen as participants in a single social system. This was the germinal insight that later inspired Max Gluckman's powerful critique of Malinowski's theories of culture change and was fundamental later in the elaboration of what became known as 'world-systems' theory.

Schapera's intervention was based on solid empirical data that showed that blacks in South Africa did not have an adequate land base, or that the Government could control the undermining of indigenous institutions. It also raised ethical questions about who should decide what was 'good' for indigenes or natives. Schapera's extensive research on almost all aspects of sociocultural life in Bechuanaland Protectorate was undertaken mostly at the request of the colonial authorities or the chiefs. Its longevity is evidenced by the numerous reprints of his works and it is this rich body of documentation for which he is most likely to be remembered (certainly in Botswana, which has a 'Schapera Project' to build on his pioneering work).

While too much of a grounded empiricist to engage in over-imaginative theorising, Schapera's mode of careful regional comparison has been developed in important directions by some of his protégés, notably Adam Kuper who has elaborated a controlled systematic regional comparison in order to arrive at 'structural history', and John and Jean Comaroff whose Tswana work has generated much intellectual excitement with their historically grounded approach to change.

Education

MA University of Cape Town, 1925
Ph.D London School of Economics, University of London, 1929

Fieldwork

Bechuanaland Protectorate (Botswana), 1929–43 (intermittently for 45 months)

Key Publications

(1930) *The Khoisan Peoples of South Africa: Bushmen and Hottentots*, London: Routledge & Kegan Paul.
(1938) *A Handbook of Tswana Law and Custom*, London: Oxford University Press.
(1940) *Married Life in an African Tribe*, London: Faber & Faber.
(1956) *Government and Politics in Tribal Societies*, London: Watts.

Further Reading

Fortes, M. and Patterson, S. (eds) 1975 *Studies in African Social Anthropology: Essays Presented to Professor Isaac Schapera*, London, New York and San Francisco: Academic Press.
Hammond-Tooke, W.D. (1997) *Imperfect Interpreters: South Africa's Anthropologists 1920–1990*, Johannesburg: Witwatersrand University Press.

ROBERT J. GORDON

Scheper-Hughes, Nancy

b. 1944, New York City, USA

As a medical anthropologist Nancy Scheper-Hughes researched in and wrote extensively on Ireland, Brazil, and South Africa. In particular, she is concerned with the violence and 'madness' of everyday life from the existentialist, feminist, and politically engaged perspective. Her doctoral study in County Kerry, rural Ireland, was an ethnography on mental illness among bachelor farmers in rural Ireland; and in Boston, later, she undertook a study of the 'de-institutionalisation' of those with severe mental ill health. With experience in Brazil as a Peace Corps Volunteer (1964–6) she returned in 1982 and, for four other extensive periods of fieldwork throughout the decade, she studied the sugar plantation town of Bom Jesus da Mata and the shantytown of Alto do Cruzeiro. Covering a period of over twenty-five years her ethnography of poverty-stricken northeastern Brazil deals with stories of infant mortality, the 'madness of hunger', the medicalisation of social trauma, and the experience of motherhood, deprivation, and codes of morality. She has also researched AIDS, the social body, and sexual citizenship in Cuba and Brazil, and more recently the role of violence and 'truth and reconciliation' during the transition to democracy in South Africa. Since 1997 she has been involved in a multisited research study of global traffic in human organs.

Scheper-Hughes's passionate crusade for human rights and her determination to overcome the political pressures, both local and national, that frustrate her research has meant that her work has gone beyond traditional frontiers in anthropology. Her works are widely read, many times anthologised, and have been translated into Spanish, French, and Italian. Against this background her applied acumen and analytical talents have complemented her work as editor, teacher, and ethnographic writer, and made her a major contributor to critically applied medical anthropology. All this is paralleled by her commitment to writing for the public on subjects ranging from the cultural politics of international adoption to the murder of Brazilian street children, the commercialisation of human organs, and the use of living donors in human transplant surgery. Indeed, her examination of chronic political violence has encouraged her to develop a unique style of critical theory and reflexive ethnography, which has been applied to medicine, psychiatry, and the practice of anthropology. In 1999 she founded, with Prof. Lawrence Cohen, Organs Watch, a programme created to investigate human rights violations in the harvesting, sale, and distribution of human organs and tissues.

Her book awards and prizes include: the 1981 winner of the Margaret Mead Award from the Society for Applied Anthropology and the American Anthropological Association, for *Saints, Scholars and Schizophrenics*; the 2000 winner of the J.I. Staley Prize, awarded for 'imaginative works that have gone beyond traditional frontiers in anthropology and given new dimensions to our understanding of humanity', for *Death without Weeping: the Violence of Everyday Life in Brazil*; the 1995 Wellcome Medal for Anthropology Applied to Medical Problems, awarded by the Wellcome Trust and the Royal Anthropological Institute of Great Britain and Ireland; the 1994 Bryce Wood Book Award, Latin American Studies Association, for 'Outstanding Book on Latin America in the Humanities and Social Sciences'; 1993 Premio Internazionale di Studi Etnoantropologici (the Pitre Prize) for ethnography, awarded by the Centro Internazionale di Etnostoria, Palermo, Sicily; and 1993 Harry Chapin Media Award, World Hunger Year for outstanding book on hunger and poverty.

Education

Queens College, City University of New York, 1962–4 (no degree)
BA University of California, Berkeley, 1970

Ph.D. University of California, Berkeley, 1976

Fieldwork

'Ballybran', County Kerry, rural Ireland, 1974–5, shorter trips in 1980 and 1999
Alto do Cruzeiro, Bom Jesus da Mata, Pernambuco, northeast Brazil, 1964–6 and 1982–current (multiple returns)
Cape Town and rural Western Cape, South Africa, 1993–4; 1995–current (multiple shorter trips)
South Boston, USA, 1979–80
Taos and New Mexico, USA, 1980–current (several summer periods)
Havana, Cuba, 1992, 1993, 2000 (short periods)
Buenos Aires, Argentina, 2001 (short periods)
Israel, 1994, 2000, 2001 (short periods)

Key Publications

(1979) *Saints, Scholars and Schizophrenics: Mental Illness in Rural Ireland*, Berkeley: University of California Press (paperback edn with new preface, 1982; anniversary edn, expanded and updated, 2000).
(1987) (ed.) *Child Survival: Anthropological Perspectives on the Treatment and Maltreatment of Children*, Dordrecht, Holland: D. Reidel Publishing Company.
(1992) *Death without Weeping: The Violence of Everyday Life in Brazil*, Berkeley: University of California Press.
with Sargent, Carolyn (eds) (1998) *Small Wars: The Cultural Politics of Childhood*, Berkeley: University of California Press.

ALEXANDRA GREENE

Schieffelin, Bambi B.

b. 26 April 1945, Lakewood, New Jersey, USA

Bambi Schieffelin pioneered the ethnographic study of language acquisition and helped establish the sub-fields of language socialisation and language ideology. Schieffelin's groundbreaking research positioned language acquisition as a central concern to both linguistics and anthropology, and her collaborative writing is a model for scholarly cooperation.

Schieffelin's early work broadened the field of language acquisition and brought it into mainstream linguistics. Schieffelin pushed language acquisition research beyond the child's own grammatical development to look at the child's emerging ability to use language socially. By studying the language of the child/caregiver interaction (rather than the child's utterances alone), Schieffelin demonstrated that children express propositions across turns at talk even before they express full propositions within a single utterance. Such findings shifted language acquisition research from grammar to communicative competence. Conversely, Schieffelin's work on topic and left-dislocation showed that empirical data from child language research could help resolve general problems in linguistic description and theory.

Schieffelin's subsequent work merged language acquisition and cultural anthropology. Her dissertation on children and language among the Kaluli of Papua New Guinea was an early acquisition study of a non-Indo European language that introduced ethnographic methods into child language research. Published in 1990, *The Give and Take of Everyday Life* developed the acquisition of communicative competence perspective into a theory of language socialisation. Schieffelin's analysis of the Kaluli *elema* routine, for example, showed children's socialisation to (i.e. acquisition of) language to be inseparable from their socialisation through language into culturally appropriate gender roles, kinship relations, and affective behaviours.

Schieffelin also pioneered the study of language ideology. Her work on language socialisation showed that cross-cultural differences in childcare practices correspond to differences in beliefs about the nature of language. Schieffelin has also applied this paradigm to the study of literacy, showing, for example, how debates over Haitian Creole orthography reflect social power and negotiate concepts of nationhood. Schieffelin thus argues that language ideologies mediate between social structure and forms of talk.

Schieffelin's career stands as a model for collaborative research in anthropology. With Edward Schieffelin and Steven Feld she formed an innovative team of ethnographers working among the Kaluli. With Elinor Ochs and Kathryn Woolard she has written and edited work significantly advancing theory and practice in anthropology.

Education

BS Columbia University, 1967
MA Columbia University, 1977
Ph.D. Columbia University, 1979

Fieldwork

Bolivia, 1966
Kaluli, Papua New Guinea, 1967–9, 1975–7, 1984–5, 1990, 1994–5
Literacy among Sino-Vietnamese children, Philadelphia, Pennsylvania, 1981–3
Language socialisation among Haitian Kreyol speakers, New York, New York, 1988–90

Key Publications

with Ochs, E. (1983) *Acquiring Conversational Competence*, London: Routledge & Kegan Paul.
with Ochs, E. (1984) 'Language acquisition and socialization: three developmental stories and their implications', in R. Shweder and R. LeVine, (eds) *Culture Theory: Essays on Mind, Self and Emotion*, Cambridge, UK: Cambridge University Press.
(1990) *The Give and Take of Everyday Life: Language Socialization of Kaluli Children*, New York: Cambridge University Press.
with Woolard, K. and Kroskrity, P. (1998) *Language Ideologies: Practice and Theory*, New York: Oxford University Press.

DANIEL LEFKOWITZ

Schiffauer, Werner

b. 1951, Lichtenfels, Bavaria, Germany

Werner Schiffauer has worked on rural and

urban Turkey, and on different facets of Turkish labour migration to Germany. His theoretical interest has been in the interrelation of sociocultural and psychic processes. His early studies of peasants and migrants in Subay (1987 and 1991) showed how in the transition from farming to migrant industrial work the notions of personhood, individuality, subjectivity, and identity have changed. In his subsequent studies, Schiffauer focused on the Islamist movements of Turkish migrants in Germany. His study of the caliphate state of Cemaleddin Kaplan provides an implicit criticism of the structuralist analysis of symbolic systems and emphasises instead the dynamics of religious worldmaking and community building. His work is characterised by its attention to the making of evidence, a process of crucial importance in a world with competing cultural interpretations. Another aspect of Schiffauer's work is the comparative analysis of differing processes of developing pluralist civil cultures within Europe with special reference to the case of Germany. He places emphasis on processes of inclusion as well as exclusion in the face of the challenge of globalisation faced by contemporary societies.

Education

MA Berlin, 1979
Ph.D., 1987
Habilitation, Frankfurt am Main, 1991

Fieldwork

Kastamonu, Turkey, 1977, 1982–3
Eskisehir, Turkey, 1989
Germany (Turkish migrant communities), 1977–8, 1984
Germany (Islamist communities), 1987, 1993

Key Publications

(1987) *Die Bauern von Subay. Das Leben in ein türkischen Dorf* (The Peasants from Subay. Life in a Turkish Village), Stuttgart: Klett-Cotta.
(2000) *Die Gottesmänner. Türkische Islamisten Deutsch-*

land (Men of God. Turkish Islamists in Germany), Frankfurt am Main: Suhrkamp.

RICHARD ROTTENBURG

Schneider, David

b. 11 November 1918, Brooklyn, New York, USA

d. 30 October 1995, Santa Cruz, California, USA

David Schneider completed graduate training in 1949 in Harvard's Department of Social Relations, where he wrote his dissertation on kinship and social organisation on the Micronesian islands of Yap. After two years at the London School of Economics, Schneider returned to Harvard and with George Homans wrote a critique of Claude Lévi-Strauss's theory of preferential cross-cousin marriage and an article on American kinship terms based on 209 interviews. In this period Schneider also published on Yapese kinship, with its unusual combination of matrilineal and patrilineal principles, and organised an international conference on 'matrilineal kinship'. Schneider taught at Berkeley from 1956 to 1960 and then at Chicago for twenty-five years until he joined the Department of Anthropology at Santa Cruz. Early in his career Schneider achieved a reputation as a foremost American theorist of kinship, but he is ultimately best known as a critic of the field of kinship studies, as a founder of symbolic anthropology, and for his pioneering research on kinship and culture in contemporary America.

Schneider's symbolic anthropology advocated studying culture as a system of symbols and meanings. Because people apprehend the world through meaningful categories particular to their culture, social analysis must proceed from the cultural categories and premises people take for granted. As an exponent of Talcott Parsons's 'systems theory', Schneider insisted that the 'cultural system' of ideas and values be analytically distinguished from the 'social system' of actual social arrangements. It was from this perspective that in the 1960s Schneider resumed and expanded his earlier research on American kinship and wrote his famous study of American kinship as a cultural (i.e. ideological) system. Building on his earlier observation that American kin terms used in salutation and address communicate ideological principles beyond the mere designation of genealogical positions and roles, Schneider analysed salient cultural symbols (e.g. blood, love, money, sex) that American people apply in understanding kinship relationships and showed how they communicate dominant values of American culture. Schneider argued that, although the American kinship system represents biogenetic facts such as the shared 'blood' between parents and children as the bases for American cultural kinship behaviours and feelings, such facts do not actually determine them. In other words, the American kinship system symbolically constructs what is taken to be natural fact, 'naturalising' kinship norms by representing them as if they were necessary and self-evident consequences of biology.

This critique of naturalisation formed the basis for the major polemic of Schneider's later career against the field of comparative kinship studies itself. Since cross-cultural comparison of kinship depends on the a priori categories of the 'genealogical grid', it ethnocentrically projects onto other cultures the biologistic construction of kinship found in the West, ignoring the fact that many cultures actually define kinship non-biologistically in terms of nurture. Schneider liked to observe that in American culture nationality and religion are defined using the same basic ideas that are used to define kinship (e.g. distinguishing between natural-born and legally created membership), which led him to extend the critique of naturalisation into those areas. The characteristic thrust of Schneider's work was thus to undermine prior certainties, and, indeed, in both his writing and his teaching, his style was to pose increasingly difficult questions that would push arguments to their logical limits. While Schneider raised many doubts about kinship studies, he also provided

stimulus for its reinvention beginning in the 1980s. He supported emerging work on gay and lesbian kinship, the use of new reproductive technologies, and the cultural construction of kinship and gender in diverse sub-cultures and transnational settings. Schneider's bold account of the American cultural ideology of kinship has served as a primary point of departure for much subsequent work criticising his notion of shared culture as a hegemonic ideology that gives meaning to non-normative forms. While many have pointed out the limitations of Schneider's insistence on distinguishing culture from practice, thereby removing from the domain of culture the actual situations in which meanings are contested and power is manifest, the stark clarity of his formulations have undoubtedly provided a spur to further thinking in the field.

Education

BA Cornell University, 1940
MA Cornell University, 1941
Ph.D. Harvard University, 1949

Fieldwork

Yap, Micronesia, 1947–8
Mescalero Apache, 1955, 1956
American kinship project, Cambridge, Massachusetts, 1953–5, and Chicago, Illinois, 1963–6

Key Publications

(1968) *American Kinship: A Cultural Account*, Englewood Cliffs, NJ: Prentice-Hall (second edn, Chicago: University of Chicago Press, 1980).
(1972) 'Notes toward a theory of culture', in K. Basso and H. Selby (eds) *Meaning in Anthropology*, Albuquerque: University of New Mexico Press.
(1976) 'What is kinship all about?', in P. Reining (ed.) *Kinship Studies in the Morgan Centennial Year*, Washington, DC: Anthropological Society of Washington.

(1984) *A Critique of the Study of Kinship*, Ann Arbor: University of Michigan Press.

Further Reading

Bashkow, I. (1991) 'The dynamics of rapport in a colonial situation: David Schneider's fieldwork on the islands of Yap', in G. Stocking (ed.) *Colonial Situations*, Madison: University of Wisconsin Press.

Handler, R. (1995) *Schneider on Schneider*, Durham: Duke University Press.

IRA BASHKOW

Schwimmer, Éric

b. 1923, Amsterdam, The Netherlands

Taking kinship studies and a structuralist framework as his starting point in his studies on the Maori and the Orokaiva, Schwimmer gradually moved to the study of ideology and religion, and the social consequences of colonialism, specifically in countries that would seem to be in the post-colonial era. Besides his interests resulting from the consequences of colonialism, he also has been active for many years in semiotic anthropology circles.

Schwimmer's studies are not only sociopolitical, but expand to world order, artistic expression, and the problem of reconstructing the self as a collective as well as an individual enterprise. The person partly becomes the author of the definition of self, not only in a rhetorical sense, but also in the creation of praxis. The post-colonial self is shown to have notably fractal characteristics, displaying forms of binationality, as well as great ontological complexity. His more recent work is a comparative (Quebec, Maori, Basque, Indigenous people of Canada) study of biculturalism.

Education

BA Victoria University of Wellington, New Zealand, 1948

MA Victoria University of Wellington, New Zealand, 1949

MA University of British Columbia, Canada, 1965

Ph.D. University of British Columbia, Canada, 1970

Fieldwork

Whangaruru, New Zealand 1960–1

Bloods Reserve, Alberta, and The Pas, Manitoba, 1965

Minangkabau, Indonesia, 1980

New Zealand, 1988, 1997–8

Key Publications

(1973) *Exchange in the Social Structure of the Orokaiva*, London: O Hurst.

with A. Itéanu (1996) *Parle et je t'écouterai* (Speak and I Will Listen to You), Paris: Gallimard.

CHANTAL COLLARD

Sebeok, Thomas A.

b. 9 November 1920, Budapest, Hungary

d. 21 December 2001, Bloomington, Indiana, USA

After undergraduate studies at the University of Chicago in linguistics (with Leonard Bloomfield) and semiotics (with Charles Morris), Thomas A. Sebeok finished his graduate training in Oriental languages and civilisations at Princeton University. Working closely with Roman Jakobson, Sebeok wrote his dissertation on the grammatical case systems of several Finno-Ugric languages (Siberia). Repeated archival trips to Eastern Europe (Hungary, Finland, and Russia) enabled him to collect folklore texts (charms, songs, prayers, incantations, and stories) that served as the basis for many linguistic studies of Cheremis (Mari Republic); and, later, working with a native informant resident in Indiana, he published a series of pathbreaking studies of Cheremis grammar, poetic art, and religion.

Sebeok taught for his entire career – other

than numerous visiting positions around the world – at Indiana University, where he first went in 1943 to supervise the production of language instruction books for the Army Specialized Training Program. There he founded the Department of Uralic and Altaic Studies, and became chair of the Research Center for Language and Semiotic Studies. He retired from teaching in 1991 as distinguished professor emeritus of anthropology, of linguistics, of semiotics, and of Central Eurasian studies.

Sebeok's six decades of prolific scholarship can be divided into three overlapping periods, corresponding to three areas of seminal research. His early ethnographic fieldwork and writing starting in 1942 dealt with Uralic linguistics; in this early period he also did linguistic research and published articles on the Winnebago and Aymara languages. In 1962 he began studying animal communication and, more generally, non-verbal communication. And from 1976 he concentrated on semiotics, the global study of signs and symbols.

Several threads unify all these researches. First, Sebeok's writings show a commitment to the task of methodological and historical criticism. As a historian of linguistics and semiotics, Sebeok is especially known for his delineation of the 'major tradition', stretching from Galen, through Poinsot and John Locke, to Charles S. Peirce, which does not privilege human language as the model for semiotic codes. As an editor he brought to wide readership several neglected semiotic 'masters', including the biologist, Jakob von Uexkull, the mathematician, René Thom, and the philologist, Juri Lotman. And he wrote extensively on various kinds of observer bias in research, including the Clever Hans phenomenon in which animal subjects responding to subtle signalling cues appear to have language faculties. Second, Sebeok constantly articulated the idea that, from an evolutionary perspective, language is best seen as a representational

or 'modelling' system rather than as a communicative device; in fact, he asserts that the complex products of human cultures are 'tertiary modelling systems', that is, layered upon both non-verbal and verbal codes. Third, Sebeok's late writings attempt to synthesise semiotics and biology with the view that life itself is a semiotic phenomenon, or in the words of the founder of American semiotics, Charles S. Peirce, a 'perfusion of signs'.

Sebeok's distinguished service as an editor and his energetic participation as a conference organiser and lecturer are legendary. In 1960 he co-organised with Claude Lévi-Strauss a Paris conference on the structural and semantic properties of oral literature. At an interdisciplinary conference, organised by Sebeok in Bloomington in 1962, Margaret Mead introduced the phrase 'science of semiotics', In 1969 he became the editor-in-chief of the new interdisciplinary journal, *Semiotica*, a position he held until his death. In 1975 he was president of the Linguistic Society of America. He also served as the general editor of several important book series in linguistics and semiotics, including the Uralic and Altaic Series (Indiana University), Advances in Semiotics (Indiana University Press), Approaches to Semiotics (Mouton de Gruyter), and the Semiotic Web. Sebeok edited many conference volumes, some in collaboration with his wife, Jean Umiker-Sebeok, including *Style In Language* (1960), *Animal Communication* (1968), *Speaking of Apes* (1980), *Biosemiotics* (1992), and *Advances in Visual Semiotics* (1995). He also edited the monumental fourteen-volume series *Current Trends in Linguistics* (Mouton de Gruyter) and the multi-volume *Encyclopedic Dictionary of Semiotics* (Mouton de Gruyter).

A Festschrift in his honour, *Iconicity: Essays on the Nature of Culture*, appeared in 1986. His seventieth birthday was commemorated at the International Semioticians' Conference in Honour of Thomas A. Sebeok (Budapest and Vienna) in 1990. And his eightieth birthday was marked in 2000 by a symposium at the

Nordic–Baltic Summer Institute for Semiotic and Structural Studies, International Semiotics Institute.

Education

BA University of Chicago, 1941
MA Princeton University, 1943
Ph.D. Princeton University, 1945

Fieldwork

Finland, 1947

Key Publications

(1974) *Structure and Texture: Selected Essays in Cheremis Verbal Art*, The Hague: Mouton.
(1976) *Contributions to the Doctrine of Signs*, Bloomington: University of Indiana Press.
(1979) *The Sign and Its Masters*, Austin: University of Texas Press.
(2001) *Global Semiotics*, Bloomington: Indiana University Press.

Further Reading

Petrilli, Susan and Ponzio, Augusto (2001) *Thomas Sebeok and the Life of Signs:*, Cambridge, UK: Icon Books.

RICHARD J. PARMENTIER

Segal, Daniel A.

b. 22 August 1958, New York City, USA

Daniel Segal's work incorporates fine-grained analysis of cultural ideologies and rhetorical practices within the grounded constraints of political economy and social structure, and is refracted in a sequence of interrelated projects. He initially conducted ethnographic research for his Master's degree in a US medical school, analysing cultural and ideological aspects of American biomedicine. In his dissertation-related work (published in dispersed articles),

Segal develops a critical analysis of race, nationalism, and history; he shows how nations emerge as variable, contingent objectifications of social relations by examining the shifting colonial and post-colonial discourses of race in Trinidad and Tobago within individual life histories, the state politics of national representation, symbolic politics of Carnival, and local inflections of international development discourses. His post-dissertation work involves a critical genealogical study of 'Western Civ' and World History textbooks and survey courses; he shows how social evolutionary thinking continues to organise and underlie not only Western ideologies of history but also the division of academic labour in the human sciences. And in a fruitful collaborative effort, Segal and Richard Handler have analysed the writings of Jane Austen in order to demonstrate the context sensitivity and perspectival polysemy of cultural action, suggesting insights from Austen's rhetorical strategies for ethnographic representation and cross-cultural analysis.

Education

BA Cornell University, 1980
MA University of Chicago, 1983
Ph.D. University of Chicago, 1989

Fieldwork

US medical school (anonymous), 1981–2
Trinidad and Tobago, West Indies, 1983, 1984–5, 1986, 1992

Key Publications

(2000) '"Western Civ" and the staging of history in American higher education', *American Historical Review* 105, 3: 770–805.
with Handler, Richard (1990) *Jane Austen and the Fiction of Culture: An Essay on the Narration of Social Realities*, Tucson: University of Arizona Press.

KEITH E. MCNEAL

Segalen, Martine

b. 1940, Pornichet, France

Martine Segalen's work on kinship and the family combines historical, sociological, and anthropological approaches. Her doctoral thesis contributed to the discipline of historical demography, which was at its heyday in France in the 1960s. It dealt with the developments of marriage patterns in Vraiville, a community in Normandy, over a period of 250 years. Segalen reconstituted genealogies by means of oral history and archival research.

Several years later, Martine Segalen carried out comparable research in the South Bigouden region of Lower Brittany, at the extreme northwest of France. She analysed census data, other historical documents dating from 1720 onwards, and ethnographic information, partly with computerised methods, in order to make a careful reconstruction of demographic developments, marriage patterns, and property transmission practices in that region. She found that the northern part of Bigouden was separated out by social practices. People of South Bigouden predominantly intermarried within the bounds of their own symbolically demarcated region and would rather choose marriage partners from further afield than their immediate northern neighbours.

As farms were generally leased by their occupants, rather than owned, there was a high degree of geographical mobility. Inheritance was partible and bilateral. Marriage was early and often arranged by parents or other intermediaries. In order to avoid splitting the family property more than necessary, marriages often took place between affines, i.e. rather distant relatives linked by a marriage prior to their own. The wealthier the kindred, the more endogamous it was. The high incidence of regular relinking through affinal marriage demonstrated that matrimonial regularities did exist in complex societies. Exchange of marriage partners took place within kindreds in Bigouden, not between social units as in Claude Lévi-Strauss's system of generalised exchange.

Despite these matrimonial strategies, the egalitarian system of inheritance (and agricultural crises) impoverished even the better-off families in the long run. In the 1880s, fishing industries developed, absorbing an ever-growing population. Affinal relinking continued into the 1950s, but more for symbolic rather than economic reasons. In the 1980s, fishing, tourism, and agriculture were the main economic activities. Kinship and economy remain linked, with relatives providing, for example, practical aid with house building or informal information about the labour market.

A third community that Segalen researched in detail is the town of Nanterre, situated at 10 km from Paris. Nanterre used to be an agricultural village, was industrialised in the nineteenth century, and received several waves of immigration from provincial France and from abroad. In the 1980s, a historical center co-existed with large residential areas with high-rise buildings. Recently arrived Nanterrians and members of old-established families have completely different visions of the town, its space, and its history.

Martine Segalen made use of the rich corpus of information compiled by French folklorists since the nineteenth century, but often challenged their interpretations. For instance, her analysis of husband–wife relationships in the nineteenth century stressed that, within the household, the roles of husband and wife were complementary and equilibrated, while male superiority was asserted towards the exterior. Folklorists who believed that women in rural France were systematically subordinated and their authority denigrated mistook the officially stated norms for real social relations.

Segalen argued against discourses about the 'decline' of the family, voiced by nineteenth-century philanthropists and more recently by Talcott Parsons. Against Parsons, Segalen stressed that kinship networks were not fragmented by industrialisation. On the contrary, such networks helped workers who migrated to industrial towns. At the other end of the social spectrum, many capitalists relied on family alliances to forge business relationships and finance their enterprises.

To take a more recent example, co-operation between generations in France was more frequent and intense in the 1990s than probably ever before. With life expectancy having increased by thirty years since the beginning of the twentieth century, grandparents generally accompany their grandchildren actively over a long stretch of their life, providing childcare, entertainment, and financial support.

Martine Segalen also worked on a variety of other topics, including religious fraternities, hobby genealogists, and jogging, and co-edited a seminal, two-volume History of the Family.

Education

Diploma of the Institut des Sciences Politiques, Paris, 1960
Ph.D. University of Paris V, 1970
Thèse d'état, University of Paris V, 1984

Fieldwork

Vraiville, Normandy, France, 1968–72
South Bigouden country, Brittany, France, 1974–84
Nanterre, France, 1988–90

Key Publications

(1983) Love and Power in the Peasant Family (Mari et femme dans la societe paysanne, 1980), trans. S. Matthews, Chicago: University of Chicago Press.
(1986) Historical Anthropology of the Family (Sociologie de la famille, 1981), trans. J.C. Whitehouse and S. Matthews, Cambridge, UK: Cambridge University Press.
(1991) Fifteen Generations of Bretons: Kinship and Society in Lower Brittany 1720–1980 (Quinze générations de Bas-Bretons, 1985), trans. J.A. Underwood, Cambridge, UK: Cambridge University Press.
with Attias-Donfut, C. (1998) Grands-parents: la famille à travers les générations (Grandparents: The Family across the Generations), Paris: Odile Jacob.

ANNE FRIEDERIKE MÜLLER

Seligman, Charles Gabriel

b. 24 December 1873, London, UK

d. 19 September 1940, Oxford, UK

C.G. Seligman was an indefatigable fieldworker who laid the foundations of scientific ethnology in New Guinea and the Nilotic Sudan. By the early 1930s he had done exploratory fieldwork in more locations than any other British anthropologist. At the London School of Economics (LSE) he played a key role in the institutional development of anthropology in Britain.

The only child of a Jewish wine merchant, Seligman was a shy, reclusive boy who sought consolation in natural history. Butterfly collecting exemplified his lifelong passion for collection and classification. After studying medicine in London, he specialised in pathology and his earliest publications were on tropical diseases.

At his own expense, Seligman joined the epoch-making Torres Strait Expedition led by A.C. Haddon in 1898. Like most other expedition members, Seligman approached anthropology as a biological scientist. He conducted research on local medicine and assisted W.H.R. Rivers's psycho-physiological testing of the Torres Strait islanders. He also learned at first hand the techniques Rivers was developing for sociological inquiry, notably the 'genealogical method', which Seligman later used in his own ethnographic surveys.

For several more years Seligman continued pathology research in London, but the lure of anthropology was irresistible. He was an enthusiastic adherent to the 'cult' of fieldwork of which Haddon was the high priest. As Seligman would tell his first and most distinguished pupil, Bronislaw Malinowski, fieldwork is to anthropology 'what the blood of martyrs is to the Church'.

In 1904 Seligman led an expedition to eastern New Guinea (now Papua) where he surveyed the coastal peoples he classified as Papuo-Melanesians according to physical, linguistic, and cultural criteria. He assembled ethnographic material on half-a-dozen major groups and devoted a monograph to each, which together form the compendium entitled *The Melanesians of British New Guinea*, a synoptic work of vast comparative scope and lasting historical value. The book provided Seligman with the template for his similarly monumental work on the Sudan.

In 1905 Seligman married Brenda Z. Salaman who became his constant companion, co-fieldworker, and co-author. At Haddon's urging, the couple went to Ceylon (now Sri Lanka) to study remnant groups of Veddas, family-based hunters and honey-gatherers believed to be the island's aboriginal inhabitants. Vedda men were jealously protective of their womenfolk and Seligman's access to their family life was conditional upon his wife's presence. Subsequently, Brenda Seligman pursued research on kinship and marriage, and became a respected anthropologist in her own right. Her husband admitted that, increasingly, he left to her 'the social stuff'. The couple's productive partnership continued with three government-sponsored expeditions to the southern Sudan. They surveyed the archaeology, physical anthropology, material culture, social structure, and religion of several congeries of tribes, notably the Shilluk, Nuer, Dinka, Bari, Lotuko, and Nuba. Seligman's pupils, E. Evans-Pritchard and S. Nadel, consolidated and extended this pioneering fieldwork.

From 1913, following his appointment to the foundation chair in ethnology at the LSE, Seligman offered professional training to complement Haddon's at Cambridge and R.R. Marett's at Oxford, and he mentored a generation of cosmopolitan pupils. Seligman's generous support for Malinowski during his troubled sojourn in New Guinea, for instance, was practical and financial as well as moral and intellectual. Malinowski effectively took over the LSE department at the end of the 1920s and, rather to Seligman's dismay, steered it towards the social sciences and away from Seligman's more antiquarian interests in traditional branches of ethnology.

Seligman took an empirical and eclectic approach to the evolutionary and diffusionist theories of the day. His treatment of 'shell-shocked' soldiers during the First World War, together with his reading of Freud and Jung, deepened his interest in psychopathology. He held that psychoanalysis shed comparative light on folklore, mythology, and dreams. He was uncomfortable with grand theorising, however, and the revolutionary functionalism that Malinowski was busily promoting failed to engage him. Seligman preferred to deal with raw facts, with things that could be measured and neatly classified. Independently wealthy, he accumulated a unique collection of Chinese porcelain and bronze ware, and in later life extended his academic interests to Chinese civilisation. Seligman was elected to the Royal College of Physicians in 1911 and to the Royal Society in 1919. His other honours included: president, Royal Anthropological Institute (1923–5), Rivers Medallist (1925), Huxley Medallist (1932), and Frazer Lecturer (1933).

Education

BM St Thomas's Hospital, London, 1892–6
MD University of London, 1906

Fieldwork

Cape York Peninsular, Australia, 1898
Cambridge Torres Strait Expedition, 1898–99
Cooke Daniels expedition to British New Guinea, 1904
Veddas of Ceylon, 1907–8
The Anglo-Egyptian Sudan, 1909–10, 1911–12, 1921–2

Key Publications

(1910) *The Melanesians of British New Guinea*, Cambridge, UK: Cambridge University Press.
with Seligman, Brenda Z. (1911) *The Veddas*, Cambridge, UK: Cambridge University Press.
(1930) *Races of Africa*, London: Home University Library.

with Seligman, Brenda Z. (1932) *Pagan Tribes of the Nilotic Sudan*, London: Routledge.

MICHAEL YOUNG

Seremetakis, C. Nadia

b. 23 December 1955, Athens, Greece

As the first Greek national to be comprehensively trained in American cultural anthropology, Seremetakis challenged entrenched homeostatic binary inversion models of death rituals and gender relations in Anglophone Mediterranean social anthropology. Based on long-term fieldwork and unprecedented linguistic expertise, Seremetakis rejected assumptions of social totality through intricate performance analysis of mourning, the poetics of women's resistance, divination practices, embodied labour, and a feminised material culture. Her integration of the senses and material culture has methodologically influenced recent symbolic and cognitive archaeology. Seremetakis's linkage of material culture and emotions registered methodological advances in the anthropology of the body comparable to Julia Kristeva's theory of abjection. In the 1990s, Seremetakis personally translated her American publications for Greek publication, crafting a much-needed Greek technical vocabulary for core methodological concepts of cultural anthropology. From 1991 to the present Seremetakis published numerous public anthropology articles in major Greek newspapers and a book of poetry, *Journey to Eros* (1999). Her translations have won literary awards from the Greek government and Seremetakis was the subject of a 30-minute television documentary (2002).

Education

BA Queens College, 1976
MA New York University, 1979
MA New School for Social Research, 1982
Ph.D. New School for Social Research, 1988

Fieldwork

Peloponnese and Athens, Greece (death, the body, and the poetics of mourning), 1982–9
Athens and Southern Peloponnese, Greece (pain, the senses, and emotions), 1990–2
New York City, USA (AIDS and bereavement), 1992–3
Kalamata, Greece (disaster and popular memory), 1996–7
Southern Peloponnese, Greece (programming public anthropology), 1996–9

Key Publications

(1991) *The Last Word. Women, Death and Divination in Inner Mani*, Chicago: The University of Chicago Press.
(1996) *The Senses Still. Perception and Memory as Material Culture in Modernity*, Chicago: The University of Chicago Press.

ALLEN FELDMAN

Service, Elman Rogers

b. 1915, Tecumseh, Michigan, USA

d. 1996, Santa Barbara, California, USA

Elman Service played an important role in the development of anthropological theory in the USA in the 1960s and 1970s, in his later years turning to writing on the history of anthropology. He was interested in a number of topics from Latin American studies to kinship and forager lifeways. His monograph on hunters and gatherers, which illustrated the importance of economy and technology as well as social organisation in adaptation, became a standard work and was translated into a number of languages. In contrast to the 'Boasian humanistic' approach of scholars like Ruth Benedict, Service espoused a comparative scientific approach that sought explanation – cause and effect relationships among cultural phenomena. A member of the graduate student cohort that included among others Morton Fried, Eric Wolf, and Sidney Mintz, and a student of both Julian Steward and Leslie White, he developed a long-term interest in political evolution and hierarchies, the origin(s) of inequality and the state. Perhaps impelled by the general interest in modernisation in the discipline in the 1950s, he was part of the rediscovery of the study of culture change and evolution in the 1960s (neo-evolutionism). He and Marshall Sahlins reconciled the theories of Steward and White by creating the concepts of general and specific evolution, an important contribution to the discipline. Their insistence that relationships among cultures are an element of the environment along with the natural habitat also expanded cultural ecology. Although criticised subsequently for associating levels of hierarchical social structure with evolutionary progress, Service's work resonated particularly with archaeologists. His work was influential in the thought of the 'New Archaeology' promulgated by Lewis Binford and others beginning in the 1960s, who found in his writings a rich vein of ideas for developing testable hypotheses about cultural change and evolution. Service's evolutionary scheme was first applied to Mesoamerican prehistory by William T. Sanders and Barbara Price in 1968.

Education

AB University of Michigan, 1941
Ph.D. Columbia University, 1951

Fieldwork

Paraguay, 1948–9, 1951
Mexico, 1957–8
Havasupai, Grand Canyon, Arizona, date unknown

Key Publications

with Sahlins, Marshall D. (eds) (1960) *Evolution and Culture*, Ann Arbor: University of Michigan Press.
(1971 [1962]) *Primitive Social Organization; An*

Evolutionary Perspective, New York: Random House.
(1975) *Origins of the State and Civilization: The Process of Cultural Evolution*, New York: Norton.
(1979 [1966]) *The Hunters*, Englewood Cliffs, NJ: Prentice-Hall.

Further Reading

Rambo, Terry A. and Gillogly, Kathleen (eds) (1991) *Profiles in Cultural Evolution: Papers from a Conference in Honor of Elman R. Service*, Anthropological Papers No. 85, Ann Arbor, MI: Museum of Anthropology, University of Michigan.

JUDITH A. RASSON

Sharma, Ursula M.

b. 1941, London, UK

Ursula M. Sharma has researched in and written extensively on religion, women and the household, and alternative medicine. Her doctoral study in Himachal Pradesh, India, examined religion and ritual in a Himalayan village and generated one of the first full-length ethnographic studies of gender in India. As a fieldworker in India married into an Indian family she was able to combine her knowledge of the rise in feminist consciousness, which raised questions about female roles in the West, with her interest in the question of women's position in Northern India. Sharma's aim was to develop the discussion of Indian women by identifying some of the inadequacies in social science on women's role in production. Against this background her work challenges the dominant discourse in anthropology that tends to emphasise the Orientalised ritual aspects of caste in Indian society.

As a researcher committed to interdisciplinary dialogue and community issues, she was one of the first social scientists to explore complementary medicine and to set up networks of researchers in these fields, which contribute to current debates about health care and the responsibility for therapy. Her examination of the social dimensions of complementary medicine addresses questions of both principle and policy including codes of ethics and medical litigation; there is particular focus also on the varying attitudes towards complementary and orthodox medicine, which exist among patients and practitioners of both. Sharma's interest in non-biomedical healers and their sense of professional identity led to related research on visual ethnography and beauty therapy. She worked collaboratively with Paula Black to investigate the commodified nature of bodily maintenance and the extension of the leisure industry into the bodily arena; the relationships and micro-activities of the everyday world of the salon; the professional claims and rhetoric of the beauty therapist and his or her investment in the 'emotional labour' of the trade; with a particular focus on the relationship between feminism and the investigation of beauty and femininity.

As a teacher she helped to initiate, at the University of Keele, one of the first medical anthropology courses in Britain and as an editor and a theoretical and ethnographic writer her works are widely read by the general public and her peers. She has also been involved with various local groups and campaigns, mostly concerned with anti-racist, health, and feminist issues both in India and in the UK. Sharma's interest in community projects was fuelled by her feminism, her radicalism, and anti-elitism generally.

Education

BA University of London, 1963
MA University of London, 1966
Ph.D. University of London, 1969

Fieldwork

Himachal Pradesh, India, 1965–9
London, UK, 1968–70; 1981–2
UK and India, 1971–3
North India, 1982–3
North Staffordshire, UK, 1986–8

Midlands, UK, 1988–90
New Delhi, Sidhbari, India (collaborative research), 1998–9

Key Publications

(1980) *Women, Work and Property in North West India*, London: Tavistock.
(1986) *Women's Work, Class and the Urban Household*, London: Tavistock.
(1992) *Complementary Medicine Today: Practitioners and Patients*, London: Tavistock and Routledge (revised edn, 1995).
(1999) *Caste*, Milton Keynes: Open University Press.

ALEXANDRA GREENE

Sherzer, Joel F.

b. 18 March 1942, Philadelphia, Pennsylvania, USA

Joel Sherzer is a leading figure in the ethnography of speaking. His scholarship on ethnopoetics and ritual language helped solidify the position of linguistics within anthropology, and his discourse-centered approach to ethnographic fieldwork became an influential paradigm for linguistic anthropology research in the 1990s. Sherzer's work has also profoundly influenced sociolinguistics, folklore, discourse analysis, and the ethnography of speaking.

Sherzer's early work was in the comparative linguistics of North American languages. His dissertation, directed by Dell Hymes, was an areal-typological study of North American Indian languages. In subsequent work, however, Sherzer turned to the ethnography of speaking. In 1970 he began fieldwork among the Kuna of Panama, where he was one of the first to apply Dell Hymes's framework for the ethnographic study of language use. His 1983 book, *Kuna Ways of Speaking*, represents Kuna culture through a description of ritual language, which is particularly salient in Kuna social life. In describing political oratory, curing chants, and girls' puberty rites, Sherzer links formal linguistic analysis with an ethnographic description of the physical setting, social organisation, participant structure, and other components of the ritual speech practices, thereby embedding speech in social life.

Sherzer's work on ritual speech developed into an approach to verbal art that combined ethnography and ethnopoetics. The ethnographic study of verbal art looks at the context of verbal performance – including the general cultural context, from which symbols draw their meanings, and the immediate interactional context, from which speech draws its function. Attention to the pragmatic function of speech showed the relevance of verbal art to cultural anthropology, as forms of talk came to be seen as forms of social action. Sherzer showed, for example, that the oratory of Kuna chiefs became political power through verbal performance. Sherzer also showed that verbal art genres range along a continuum from rigidly memorised texts to creatively improvised performances, arguing that the study of verbal art constitutes a window on questions of structure and agency by illuminating issues of shared tradition and individual creativity.

Sherzer's ethnopoetic approach to verbal art continues the tradition of Franz Boas, Edward Sapir, and Dell Hymes through its emphasis on the collection, transcription, and publication of Native American oral literature. Applying Roman Jakobson's theory of parallelism to oral discourse, Sherzer showed that Kuna discourse is organised into lines marked by recurrent linguistic structures, such as affixes, quotative particles, syntactic and semantic parallelisms, intonation patterns, and participation structures. His work on the line merged semantic and prosodic criteria in defining poetic structure, thereby helping to resolve a debate between Dell Hymes and Dennis Tedlock over the nature of oral discourse units. This work also contributed to scholarly debates over the nature of orality and literature.

Verbal art is central to Sherzer's notion of discourse and to the discourse-centered school of ethnographic research he helped establish. Conceptualising discourse as the nexus between language and culture, Sherzer distinguishes between 'grammar', which provides a set of linguistic potentials, or resources, and 'discourse', which is the realisation of grammar in actual instances of talk. Sherzer's notion of discourse reinvigorated debates over the Sapir–Whorf hypothesis by repositioning the point of language/culture overlap from the mind to the emergent structure of social interaction. This notion of discourse also led to the establishment (with Greg Urban) of a discourse-centered approach to ethnographic research, which argues that cultural symbols and meanings cannot be separated from the forms of discourse through which they are expressed. The study of culture is therefore best accomplished through a study of discourse, and specifically one that focuses on aesthetic and creative genres of language use, where grammatical potentials are maximally realised and the play in cultural meanings is most negotiable.

Sherzer has had a profound influence on the development of linguistic anthropology through his collaborations with scholars in related fields. With folklorist Richard Bauman, Sherzer edited the volume *Explorations in the Ethnography of Speaking*, an important early collection that linked folklore to linguistic anthropology through mutual interest in textuality and performance. With sociolinguist John Baugh, Sherzer edited *Language in Use* (1984), which linked the ethnography of speaking with sociolinguistics. And with linguist Anthony Woodbury, Sherzer edited *Native American Discourse* (1987), which helped establish an ethnographic discourse analysis.

Education

BA Oberlin College, 1964
MA, Ph.D. University of Pennsylvania, 1968

Fieldwork

Panama (Kuna Indians), periodically since 1970
Bali and Indonesia, periodically during 1980s
France, periodically since 1970

Key Publications

with Bauman, R. (eds) (1974) *Explorations in the Ethnography of Speaking*, Cambridge, UK: Cambridge University Press.

(1983) *Kuna Ways of Speaking: An Ethnographic Perspective*, Austin: University of Texas Press.

(1987) 'A discourse-centered approach to language and culture', *American Anthropologist* 89, 2: 295–309.

(2002) *Speech Play and Verbal Art*, Austin: University of Texas Press.

DANIEL LEFKOWITZ

Shirokogorov, Sergey M.

b. 1 July 1887, Suzdal, Russia

d. 19 October 1939, Peking, China

Sergey M. Shirokogorov called himself 'an ethnographer of the Ethnological School', meaning that each ethnographic study needed a theoretical basis. His field ethnographic studies began among the Tungus peoples, and they remained the main object of his research throughout his academic life.

At the beginning his fieldwork was conducted according to the general standards of the Museum of Ethnography and Anthropology (Kunstkammer, St Petersburg) where Shirokogorov worked during the 1910s. He studied language, specific features of material culture, social organisation, and religion, especially shamanism.

But already by the early 1920s Shirokogorov made his pioneer contribution to the development of the theory of ethnos, one of the fundamental problems in the ethnology of the twentieth century. According to Shirokogorov's theory, ethnos is a special unit characterised by objective and subjective factors such as language, culture, and consciousness of common origin. Shirokogorov also argued that ethnoses are biological units governed by natural laws, and that the main form of interaction between them is war. Shirokogorov's research focused on the mechanisms of ethnic and ethnographic changes.

He later used a cross-disciplinary approach for the study of the main components of the Tungus' 'psychomental complex', i.e. wide and detailed description and deep analysis of the Tungus peoples' world view. Shirokogorov defined the 'psychomental complex' as mental reactions (both psychological and intellectual) to the environment that serve as a means of adaptation to changing conditions of life. Shamanism is one of the most important parts of this complex.

Shirokogorov was an active participant in the organisation of Dalnevostochniy (Far East) University in Vladivostok, where in 1921–2 he read a course in ethnography. He subsequently taught at the Universities of Shanghai and Peking as a professor of sociology and anthropology. The substantial body of his works was first published in China and the last of them also in England. Their 'return' home, to Russia, is just at its beginning.

Education

University of Paris, Department of Philology, 1907 (not finished)

Anthropology School, Paris, 1908 (not finished)

University of St Petersburg, Department of Physics and Mathematics, 1911–15 (not finished)

Fieldwork

East Siberia and Far East, the areas of the Tungus peoples, 1912–18 (periodically 2–4 months per year)

Key Publications

(1919) *Opit issledovanija osnov shamanstva u tungusov* (A Study of Tungus Shamanism), Vladivostok: Dalnevostochniy (Far East) University.

(1923) *Ethnos. Issledovanie Osnovnyh Printsipov Izmenenij Ethnicheskih i Ethnograficheskih Javlenij* (Ethnos. Research of Main Principles of Changes in Ethnic and Ethnographic Phenomena). Vladivostok: Dalnevostochniy University.

(1935) *Psychomental Complex of the Tungus*, London: Kegan Paul, Trench, Trubner & Co. Ltd.

TATIANA UVAROVA

Shokeid, Moshe

b. 1936, Tel Aviv, Israel

Moshe Shokeid's initial work on Moroccan immigrants who were resettled in rural Israel followed the then-prevalent model of seeking to understand continuities in a new situation. He showed how the immigrants used the memories of their past circumstances in the Atlas Mountains in interpreting their situation. In his early studies of the Moroccans, he noted the decline of traditional-charismatic leadership. Later, however, he discovered that religiosity had revived in a form that he called *masorti* (traditional), but not fully orthodox. This revival included the re-emergence of the older religious leadership. Shokeid continued to follow up on this village into the late 1980s.

A theme that runs through Shokeid's later work is gaining an understanding of how minorities, ethnic and other, deal with stigmatisation. The Arab Muslims in a 'mixed town', for instance, were very concerned with the defense of the honour of their women, when facing a society that seems to view such values as antiquated. Israeli immigrants in the USA are stigmatised by their home society as deserters. They often deny that they are really permanent immigrants. At the time of Shokeid's research, they were reluctant to form formal immigrant societies, something that would announce that they were indeed immigrants, not merely sojourners. Instead they expressed their nostalgia through occasional events that Shokeid referred to as 'one-night-stands'. His studies of homosexuals and bisexuals show a similar concern with how dilemmas of identity are resolved. His first study in this realm was a gay synagogue in New York City, where the members sought to resolve the problem of adherence to a religio-ethnic tradition that prohibited homosexual behaviour. Later studies dealt with a gay community center in New York and gays in Tel Aviv.

Much of Shokeid's work is in the form of extended case studies. This technique makes it possible for Shokeid to show the interaction between the individual and the social pressures that he or she faces. Shokeid's change in research subjects shows the broadening of research projects undertaken by Israeli social anthropologists over the past forty years, combined with a continuing commitment to dealing with socially relevant issues.

Education

BA Hebrew University, 1961
MA Hebrew University, 1965
Ph.D. University of Manchester, 1968

Fieldwork

Negev region and other rural locales, Israel, 1961–4, 1965–7
Iran and Nicaragua (UN Development Projects), 1963, 1968, 1969, 1972
Among Arabs in a 'mixed town', Israel, 1972–4
Study of former Atlas Mountain Jews in various localities, 1978–9
Queens, New York City (Israeli emigrants), 1982–4
Manhattan, New York (study of a gay synagogue), 1989–90
Manhattan, New York (continued study of gays in New York City), 1995, 1999

Key Publications

(1971) *The Dual Heritage: Immigrants from the Atlas Mountains in an Israeli Village*, Manchester: Manchester University Press.
with Deshen, Shlomo (1982) *Distant Relations: Ethnicity and Politics among Arabs and North African Jews*, North Scituate, MA: Bergin & Garvey.
(1988) *Children of Circumstance: Israeli Emigrants in New York*, Ithaca, NY: Cornell University Press.

(1995) *A Gay Synagogue in New York*, New York: Columbia University Press.

WALTER P. ZENNER

Sider, Gerald M.

b. 1938, The Bronx, New York, USA

Gerald Sider focuses on the critique, elaboration, and explication of key concepts such as culture and class, and their implications for peoples' everyday life struggles. Linking field research with political activism and theorising, Sider challenges anthropologists to conceptualise their commitments to those studied in ways that engenders a creative antagonism between those who 'just want to get on with it' and solve the world's problems and others who remain locked in the ethereal worlds of text, theory, and reflection. Sider is able to span both domains and sidestep a binary either/or, thereby creating a new way forward for anthropology.

Sider's work is notable for the way he picks up a concept, elaborates upon it via close ethnographic description, and ultimately stretches it beyond its normal configuration. Whether he is critiquing the notion of resistance, the everyday, or exploring the implications of hegemony for fisherfolk in Newfoundland, his underlying concern revolves around issues of power within a capitalist social formation.

In *Becoming History*, for example, the concept of hegemony is a central link between production and of culture and appropriation of labour. Here hegemony is taken up and twisted in a way that reveals the ways in which a people actively participate in their own oppression while simultaneously creating a space of resistance. In doing this Sider avoids the pitfalls of a mechanical materialism. He carefully explicates the interconnections between the production of culture, the making of class, and the historical movements of appropriation that have resulted in the Newfoundland we know today.

Lumbee Indian Histories artfully combines the sensibilities of experimental post-modernism – locating the researcher within the narrative flow – without undermining the impact of his political economic historical anthropology. Underlying his writing is a concern with making anthropology relevant, not for those in places of power, but relevant in ways that can contribute to a better world for all (exemplified by his co-editorship, with K. Dombrowski, of Nebraska Press's Fourth World Rising series). Ultimately, Sider's work is premised upon an optimism of the will that takes issue with the nihilism of late twentieth-century anthropology.

Education

BA University of Pennsylvania, 1959
MA University of Toronto, 1960
Ph.D. New School for Social Research, 1971

Fieldwork

Robeson County, North Carolina, 1966–8 (18 months), mid-1980s, 1998–ongoing (summers and intercessions)
Newfoundland, Canada, 1972–82, 1998–ongoing (summers and intercessions)
National Archives, Paris, France, famine in colonial Africa, 1994–8

Key Publications

(1993) *Lumbee Indian Histories: Race, Ethnicity and Indian Identity in the Southern United States*, New York: Cambridge University Press.
(1996) 'Cleansing history: Lawrence, Massachusetts, the strike for four loaves of bread and no roses, and the anthropology of working class consciousness', *Radical History Review* 65, March 1996 (with responses by David Montgomery, Paul Buhle, Christine Stansell, Ardis Cameron, and reply).
with Smith, Gavin (eds) (1997) *Between History and Histories: The Production of Silences and Commemorations*, Toronto: University of Toronto Press.
(2003) *Becoming History, Becoming Tomorrow: Making and breaking everyday life in rural Newfoundland,*

(second, revised edn of *Culture and Class in Anthropology and History*, 1986), Peterborough, Ont.: Broadview Press Encore Editions.

CHARLES MENZIES

Sillitoe, Paul

b. 1949, London, UK

Paul Sillitoe has published, to date, several monographs and more than a hundred articles. His work, which innovatively spans the social science/natural science divide, revolves around three main themes: tribal political economies, natural resource management, and social change and development. These research interests are linked by what he describes, in a forthcoming monograph on *Melanesia*, as 'ethnographic determinism'. The phrase is inspired by Franz Boas's studies in historical particularism. It refers to the centrality of ethnography in his work. Like Boas, Sillitoe has attempted to document carefully the cultures he has studied, to take into account historical and environmental factors, and to privilege the emic point of view. He has thus sought to leave behind an ethnographic record, in the textual, visual, and material senses, of the Melanesian culture. He also identifies with the legacy of the Cambridge Torres Straits researchers, A.C. Haddon, W.H.R. Rivers, C.G. Seligman, and F. Myers, and shares with these scholars a preoccupation with factual detail based on intensive fieldwork. His anthropological interpretations emerge from an engagement with these ethnographic materials.

In *Give and Take*, Sillitoe develops the view that exchange is a central, organising principle through which individuals (rather than corporate groups) create the bonds and relations that form part of the social order. Sillitoe claims that it is through these acts of exchange that individuals participate in the social process, whilst maintaining personal autonomy. In a highly egalitarian, acephalous society like the Wola, exchange constitutes the basis of sociability. For Sillitoe, such acts of exchange are, nonetheless, competitive, and represent a

form of what he terms 'institutionalised corporate exchange individualism'. This interpretation goes against the mainstream academic view, which sees ceremonial (or sociopolitical) exchange in Melanesia as belonging to the sphere of collective, rather than individual, strategies of social interaction.

Sillitoe's theoretical and methodological interests in indigenous knowledge and development are a logical outcome of his earlier ethnographic work in Melanesia. They emanate from a growing concern among development theorists and practitioners that, in order for projects to be truly beneficial to the people for whom they are purportedly intended, they should build on their indigenous knowledge systems. Sillitoe and his collaborators have been elaborating methods for involving local researchers in the documentation of their knowledge systems, such as in the British-funded Bangladesh Fisheries project in the late 1990s. For Sillitoe, the future of anthropology as a discipline lies in such applied work.

Education

BA University of Durham, 1971
MA University of Durham, 1973
Ph.D. University of Cambridge, 1976

Fieldwork

Finland, Norway, 1969
Papua New Guinea, 1973 (various dates to present)
Bangladesh, 1996

Key Publications

(1979) *Give and Take. Exchange in Wola Society*, Canberra: Australian University Press and New York: St Martin's Press.
(1998) *An Introduction to the Anthropology of Melanesia*, Cambridge, UK: Cambridge University Press.
(2000) *Social Change in Melanesia*, Cambridge, UK: Cambridge University Press.
with Becker, A. and Pottier, J. (eds) (2002)

Participating in Development: Approaches to Indigenous Knowledge, London: Routledge.

ANEESA KASSAM

Silverman, Marilyn

b. 30 April 1945, Montreal, Canada

Silverman started her anthropological career working in Guyana – in a bauxite mining town and, later, in an East Indian village. There, she began to develop what became her persisting interests in political economy, history, socio-economic change, and local-level politics. She pursued these in Ecuador, studying banana production and the effects of export agriculture on agrarian processes. Continuing this concern with rural society, in 1980 she began a project in a market town in the Irish Republic. This has become a long-term commitment in which, by repeated sojourns, she has logged over forty-eight months in the field. Throughout, this research has been informed by her concern for the past and with anthropological approaches to the discovery and uses of history. Thus, by doing 'historical ethnography', she has investigated changing patterns of agricultural production, economic differentiation, class formation, and hegemonic processes. This has meant intensive work in a wide variety of archives in conjunction with extensive participant observation, deliberately emphasising a locality but always in relation to global processes.

Education

BA McGill University, 1966
MA McGill University, 1967
Ph.D. McGill University, 1973

Fieldwork

Guyana, 1966, 1969–70
Ecuador (coastal), 1977, 1978
County Kilkenny, Ireland, 1980–continuing

Key Publications

(1980) *Rich People and Rice: Factional Politics in Rural Guyana*, Leiden, Netherlands: E. J. Brill.
(2001) *An Irish Working Class: Explorations in Political Economy and Hegemony, 1800–1950*, Toronto: University of Toronto Press.

P.H. GULLIVER

Silverstein, Michael

b. 1945, Brooklyn, New York, USA

Michael Silverstein's writings focus on the relations between language structure and communicative interaction.

After taking a very early interest in linguistics, Michael Silverstein enrolled at Harvard College as an undergraduate student. There he studied Romance languages and linguistics, completing the BA in 1966. He returned to Harvard as a graduate student to study with Roman Jakobson. At this time, he also came into contact with a number of anthropological linguists who were working on descriptions of Native American languages. Silverstein's dissertation, which provided the basis for an influential, two-part article in *Language*, examined contact phenomena in Chinook Jargon. Silverstein's writings since that time have exerted an unparalleled influence on the development of linguistic anthropology. His 1976 article drew upon the work of Jakobson and Charles Sanders Peirce to argue for a rethinking of the place of language in the dialectics of social life. Silverstein's theoretical insights of this period are centered around the notion of indexicality – the dynamic relations of presupposition and entailment that link particular events (e.g. events of speaking) to the sociocultural order. Later work has emphasised the importance of metapragmatic phenomena: both explicit discourse and sign functions that signal about contextualised semiotic processes. Since 1979 and the appearance of another influential paper, Silversteinian notions of 'linguistic ideology' have come to occupy a central place in linguistic anthropology. More recently, in his own writings, Silverstein has been concerned to show the implications of a radically renovated understanding of language as real-time semiosis for cultural anthropology.

Education

BA Harvard University, 1966
Ph.D. Harvard University, 1972

Fieldwork

Wishram and Wasco Chinnokan, 1966–74
Gitksan (Tsimshian), 1969
Worora (and related northern Kimberly groups), 1974–5

Key Publications

(1976) 'Shifters, linguistic categories, and cultural description', in K. Basso and H. Selby (eds) *Meaning in Anthropology*, Albuquerque: University of New Mexico Press, pp. 11–55.
(1993) 'Metapragmatic discourse and metapragmatic function', in J.A. Lucy (ed.) *Reflexive Language: Reported Speech and Metapragmatics*, Cambridge, UK: Cambridge University Press, pp. 33–58.

JACK SIDNELL

Singer, Milton B.

b. 15 July 1912, Poland

d. 5 December 1994, Chicago, Illinois, USA

Milton Singer's professional career spanned more than five decades. He shaped the direction of Southern Asian area studies in the USA and contributed to the comparative study of modernisation and to semiotic anthropology. As a faculty member (later emeritus) at the University of Chicago from 1941 until his death in 1994, he trained several generations of scholars.

Prior to beginning his long teaching and research career at the University of Chicago, Singer earned degrees in psychology and philosophy, and completed his dissertation in philosophy under the logical positivist, Rudolph Carnap. He was introduced to anthropology as an instructor in the social sciences, while participating in the University of Chicago's experimental 'Great Books' curriculum. Singer's 1953 book, *Shame and Guilt: A Psychoanalytic and a Cultural Study*, was an early outcome of the interdisciplinary scholarship that he advocated. His teaching activities also spoke to his commitment to liberal education and intercultural communication. These were enduring themes in the many articles and essays published throughout his life.

The interdisciplinary approach in his own scholarship was carried over in his efforts to institutionalise research and training programmes in area studies during the 1950s and 1960s. He participated in Chicago's Cultural Studies Project (1951–9), an initiative designed, against the backdrop of the Cold War, to chart the ways that culture interacted with economic and technological development and political modernisation, particularly in those new nations that had arisen out of older world civilisations. The project's implicit goal was to produce knowledge that would aid in the derailment of communism in recently decolonised regions. The work was led initially by Singer and Robert Redfield, with whom Singer collaborated on several essays; after Redfield's death, Singer headed the effort. The project's team of researchers sought to generate methodological and theoretical guidelines that could be incorporated into undergraduate and graduate education, and could also contribute to more equitable relations among the world's nations and more effective political and economic development in newly decolonised regions. India, then as now the world's most populous democracy, was of special interest and, in 1954, became the project's principal focus. In addition to coordinating this work, Singer himself sought training in Southern Asian regional studies at the Universities of Chicago, Pennsylvania, and California at Berkeley. In 1954, he initiated a field project in Madras, a former colonial port city, concerned with the ways that elite proponents of the 'Great Tradition' of Sanskritic Hinduism furthered regional integration and 'traditionalised' modernity. He identified 'cultural performances' (e.g. dance, recitation, drama, ritual) as basic analytic units for the study of civilisation – seeing these as sites in which participants consciously represented and evaluated societal institutions, norms, values, and roles. He conducted subsequent fieldwork in the same city (1960–1, 1964), studying how industrialists drew on and adapted traditional values and styles of action in the context of modern economic practice. On the basis of this work, he argued, contra Weber, that capitalist economic pursuits were not inconsistent with Hindu orthopraxy. He found, instead, that a distinctively Hindu industrial ethos existed, which was built upon Sanskritic precepts pertaining to action and its moral consequences. He described adaptive social and psychological strategies, termed compartmentalisation, which enabled industrialists to adhere to Hindu orthopraxy while still pursuing modern capitalist enterprises. These findings, published as separate articles and book chapters during the 1950s and 1960s, were later revised and compiled in a major monograph, *When a Great Tradition Modernizes*.

In subsequent decades, Singer drew on his earlier work on cultural performance in arguing for a semiotic approach to anthropology. This owed much to the philosophy of Charles Sanders Peirce but also relied on Weber's view of culture as a symbolically encoded system of meaning and value. Semiotic anthropology focuses on humans' production of and dependence on signs and symbols in all contexts of human action, be it language, artistic expression, clothing, architecture, myth, or ritual. In several books and articles, Singer charted the genealogy of semiotic approaches in anthropology, developed its theoretical significance, and outlined its methods. In the last two decades of his life, Singer initiated a study of the processes and dangers of nuclear proliferation, attesting to

his commitment to the liberal project of intercultural communication.

Education

BA University of Texas, Main, 1934
MA University of Texas, Main, 1936
Ph.D. University of Chicago, 1940

Fieldwork

Madras (now Chennai), India, 1954–5, 1960–1, 1964

Key Publications

(1953, 1973) *Shame and Guilt: A Psychoanalytic and a Cultural Study*, New York: W.W. Norton.
(1972) *When a Great Tradition Modernizes*, New York: Praeger.
(1984) *Man's Glassy Existence: Explorations in Semiotic Anthropology*, Bloomington: Indiana University Press.
(1991) *Semiotics of Cities, Selves, and Cultures: Explorations in Semiotic Anthropology*, Berlin: Mouton de Gruyter

MARY E. HANCOCK

Skalník, Peter Josef Karel

b. 1945, Prague, Czechoslovakia

Skalník's career reflects the political barriers faced by many intellectuals of his generation in Central and Eastern Europe; despite formidable difficulties he has made significant contributions in many branches of anthropology.

After beginning university studies in Prague, Skalník trained as an Africa specialist at Leningrad State University, graduating with distinction in 1967. He proceeded in 1968 to his doctorate in Prague with a comparative study of political systems in five Voltaic societies. Political anthropology, in particular the emergence of the state, has remained his main field, but the politics of intellectual life in communist Czechoslovakia obstructed his progress and eventually forced him into exile in 1976. After holding posts at Leiden and Cape Town he was eventually able to return to Prague, where he became a senior lecturer at Charles University in 1990. He then spent four years as ambassador in Lebanon, before resuming his academic career in 1997. He is currently devoting his considerable energies to consolidating social and cultural anthropology in Prague and at the University of Pardubice.

Peter Skalník has been a major contributor to the history of anthropology in Central and Eastern Europe as well as a pioneer of social anthropological methods in studies of rural communities in this region. Currently he is engaged in the study of diplomacy and 'political culture' in a variety of settings, both European and non-European.

Education

MA Leningrad State University 1967
Ph.D. Charles University, Prague 1968
Candidate of Science (CSc.), Charles University 1990

Fieldwork

Tuva, Soviet Central Asia, 1966
Northern Ossetia, Caucasus, 1967 and 1971
Šuňava, northern Slovakia, 1970–6, 1991–
Tusheti, Caucasus, Georgia, 1973
Nanun, northern Ghana, 1978–97 intermittently
Lesotho, Mokhotlong District, 1988
Lihir, Papua New Guinea, 1988, 1990
Gobabis area, eastern Namibia, 1989
Lebanon, 1992–6
Dolní Roveň, eastern Bohemia, 2001–
Faial, Azores, 2002–

Key Publications

with Claessen, H. (eds) (1978) The Early State, The Hague: Mouton.

(ed.) (2002) A Post-Communist Millennium: The Struggles for Sociocultural Anthropology in Central and Eastern Europe, Prague: Set Out.

CHRIS HANN

Smart, Alan

b. 1956, Glasgow, UK

Alan Smart started as a student in primatology and co-authored a paper on gibbon behaviour based on observations conducted at the Calgary Zoo in 1979. His growing interest in phenomenology, in conjunction with exposure to cultural diversity in his travels to Europe (1977–8) and Hong Kong (1979), consolidated his switch to social anthropology at the graduate level. Hong Kong and South China have since become his geographical focus in a series of critical studies in urban anthropology and economic anthropology. His work on the history and politics of housing in Hong Kong, emphasising the organisation of squatter settlements and their interaction with government intervention, is widely consulted by non-anthropologists. His joint research with Josephine Smart on the nature and impact of Hong Kong investment in post-1978 south China was one of the first anthropological studies of globalisation in China with a critical approach to culture and local/global political economy. Their publications on the cultivation and utilisation of guanxi in investment strategies, labour management, production, and business networks in the Chinese context are highly regarded. His work since the return of Hong Kong to China in 1997 has examined the constitution of a contested transborder urban region. Alan Smart's work is rich in critical ethnography and multidisciplinary depth that integrates theories and comparative material from a wide spectrum of fields ranging from geography to law.

Education

BA University of Calgary, 1980
MA University of Toronto, 1981
Ph.D. University of Toronto, 1986

Fieldwork

Hong Kong, 1982–5, 1999–2005
Hong Kong and Guangdong, PRC, 1989–2002

Key Publications

(1992) *Making Room: Squatter Clearance in Hong Kong*, Hong Kong: Hong Kong University Press/Centre of Asian Studies Monograph Series.

(1993) 'Gifts, bribes and guanxi: a reconsideration of Bourdieu's social capital', *Cultural Anthropology* 8, 3: 388–408.

JOSEPHINE SMART

Smart, Po-Ling Josephine

b. 1952, Hong Kong

Josephine Smart's work has concentrated on Chinese entrepreneurs operating in a variety of contexts and business sectors. Her doctoral research examined how the organisation of street vending in Hong Kong was influenced by its illegality and argued that involvement was due more to resistance to wage labour than to exclusion from the formal sector. She then studied Hong Kong participants in Canada's business immigration programme, finding that structural weaknesses in the programme limited its effectiveness. Since 1989, she has researched Hong Kong-run factories in China, exploring investment strategies, labour relations, and the changing social organisation of the former rural townships that have become booming centers of manufactured exports. Most recently, Smart has studied Chinese restaurants, primarily in Alberta, as a reflection of changing ethnic relations and identities expressed through the fundamental medium of food. The localisation of Chinese cuisine to suit non-Chinese tastes co-exists with trends towards more 'authentic' dishes to suit Chinese migrant and cosmopolitan tastes. She has published works addressing the anthropology of globalisation more broadly. Her work has combined attention to broad issues of political economy combined with sensitivity to the situated agency of actors in ambiguous circumstances.

Education

B.Ed. University of Calgary, 1977
B.Sc. University of Calgary, 1980
MA University of Toronto, 1981
Ph.D. University of Toronto, 1987

Fieldwork

Hong Kong, 1982–5
Toronto, Canada, 1986–8
Hong Kong and Guangdong, China, 1987–2002
Alberta, Canada, 2000–2

Key Publications

(1989) *The Political Economy of Street Hawkers in Hong Kong*, Hong Kong: Hong Kong University Press/Centre of Asian Studies Monograph Series.

(1991) 'Personal relations and divergent economies: a case study of Hong Kong investment in South China', *International Journal of Urban and Regional Research* 15, 2: 216–33.

ALAN SMART

Smith, Gavin A.

b. 1942, Braunston, UK

Gavin Smith's work is defined by a concern with historical realism and praxis – both amongst the subjects of anthropological investigation as well as intellectuals. To Smith, historical realism implies exploring the dialectical relationship between the real forces of history and the way reality is constituted through communication and practice both amongst subjects and those who study them. Praxis refers to the relationship between the material reality of everyday life and an engagement with the political world. Smith's fieldwork therefore has been guided by an interest in the relationship between the way people make a living and their forms of political expression. In Peru, Smith focused on the links between highland farmers and migrant populations in Lima to explore their implications for the organisation and execution of peasant invasions of estate lands. By studying small enterprises in southern Spain and northern Italy, Smith has explored the political and economic practices of people who pursue their livelihood under the forces of neo-liberalism. Critical of the rigidity of political economy as well as the way the concept has been appropriated and misused within the discipline, Smith has advocated the use of historical realism in anthropology. Other fieldwork in Western Europe thus attends to the relationship between the epistemological questions that guide research agendas, and how they are realised by intellectuals within the constraints of complex and changing institutional apparatuses.

Education

BA McGill University, Montreal, 1965
MA University of Sussex, Brighton, 1972
D.Phil. University of Sussex, Brighton, 1975

Fieldwork

Peru, 1972 and continuing
Spain, 1978 and continuing
Italy, 1995–6

Key Publications

(1989) *Livelihood and Resistance: Peasants and the Politics of Land in Central Peru*, Berkeley: University of California Press.
(1999) *Confronting the Present: Toward a Politically Engaged Anthropology*, London: Berg Publishers.

WINNIE LEM

Smith, M.G.

b. 18 August 1921, Kingston, Jamaica

d. 5 January 1993, Glastonbury, UK

Michael Garfield Smith was a superlative anthropologist as well as a truly remarkable man. In his youth a distinguished Jamaican poet, he went on to become a professional social anthropologist, producing more than twenty monographs. His career included full professorships at the University of California at Los Angeles, London's University College (where he succeeded his own distinguished teacher, Darryl Forde), and Yale. Interrupting his anthropological pursuits in mid-career, he also served, from 1972 to 1977, as the special adviser to the Prime Minister of Jamaica. He was the recipient of numerous awards, including the Royal Anthropological Institute's Wellcome Medal for Research, Curle Bequest Essay Prize, Amaury Talbot Book Prize, the Institute of Jamaica's Gold Musgrave Medal, two *honoris causa* doctorates, from McGill and the University of the West Indies respectively, and his own country's highest national honour, the Jamaican Order of Merit.

Smith was a polymath, with a formidable memory and charismatic intelligence (in 1939, at age seventeen, he won the university scholarship awarded annually by the Jamaican government, earning on the Oxford and Cambridge Higher Schools Certificate examinations the highest marks in the entire British Empire). Though he could be acerbic in intellectual matters and was imposingly self-possessed, his characteristic modesty and gentleness betrayed his profound and steadfast commitment to truth and forthrightness. He was notoriously demanding of his students, but equally so of himself in commitment and kindness to them. He remained dedicated to his country of birth and to bettering it. During his tenure in the Jamaican government, he eschewed party affiliation, in order to keep his administrative counsel focused uncompromisingly on the needs of the people. Having grown up a subject of a Third-World British Crown Colony, he felt critically charged to address the social problems ensuing from colonialism. This concern informed his anthropology as well as his politics. By stark contrast to highly politicised anthropology (as well as to his own poetic faculties), Smith's 'post-colonialism' took the form of value-neutral social science: he sought to determine the conditions and preconditions of conflict, polity, and power through intensive empirical research, in order to establish a sound and rationally commanding basis on which to think through the problems of governance.

A methodical and indefatigable fieldworker, Smith did extensive research in both the Caribbean and Northern Nigeria. He had a critical control of social theory from the Greeks to Lévi-Strauss, but found singular inspiration in Weber. Setting aside Weber's phenomenology, as too subjective, but embracing this master's grand empirical and comparative scheme of ideal types of institutional structures and normative orders, Smith developed his own comparative theory of society, organised around the concept of corporations. In reaction to the serious inadequacies of the anthropological and sociological functionalism in which he was trained (its irrepressible ambiguities and inability to treat of change), he forged what amounts to an original anthropological structuralism. By contrast to the more famous structuralism of Lévi-Strauss, which appeared around the same time, Smith's focused on societal rather than linguistic or mental structures, and analytically disposed sociological empiricism instead of intellectualism. He also developed a correlative theory of pluralism, which, for example, saw West Indian societies as collections of culturally and ethnically separate and distinct corporations held together largely by dominant minorities instead of normative consensus. He elaborated his anthropological ideas in, aside from his numerous articles, ethnographically informed political histories of Hausa emirates, ethnographies of Caribbean societies, and theoretical disquisitions as such. These studies, to a one, display a daunting logical rigour and conceptual incisiveness. A mature statement of his social theory may be found in his posthumous *The Study of Social Structure* (his widow, Mary F. Smith, an anthropologist in her own right and crucial collaborator in her husband's scholarly enterprise, continues to prepare for publication his unfinished manuscripts). Though it has gone underappreciated, Smith's comparative anthropology is uncommonly powerful, one which only a scholar of truly extraordinary mental gifts could have produced.

Education

BA University College, London, 1948
Ph.D. University College, London, 1951

Fieldwork

Northern Nigeria, 1949–50, 1958–9, 1972, 1977–8
Grenada and Carriacou, 1952–3, 1990
Jamaica, 1955, 1960, 1964, 1974–5

Key Publications

(1960) *Government in Zazzau, 1800–1950*, London: Oxford University Press.
(1965) *The Plural Society in the British West Indies*, Berkeley: University of California Press.
(1974) *Corporations and Society: The Social Anthropology of Collective Action*, London: George Duckworth (reprinted by Aldine, 1975).
(1998) *The Study of Social Structure*, New York: RISM.

Further Reading

Hall, Douglas (1997) *A Man Divided: Michael Garfield Smith*, Jamaica: The Press University of the West Indies.
Research Institute for the Study of Man (1994) *Testament: Life and Work of M.G. Smith, 1921–1993*, New York: Research Institute for the Study of Man.

T.M.S. EVENS

Smith, Raymond T.

b. 12 January 1925, Oldham, UK

Lewis H. Morgan famously asked how human societies based on kinship could have evolved into the class societies that dominate our world. Raymond Smith's sustained inquiries into the relationship between kinship and class in New World societies have taken the anthropology of unequal society to a new level. His project is notable for its consistent purpose and conceptual rigour. He has developed the notion of the matrifocal family and has opposed the ideological use of race, ethnicity, and poverty to explain deviance from the presumed norm of the nuclear family.

Having grown up in an industrial town near Manchester, Smith signed up as a teenager to fight in the Second World War with the Air Force. Both of these experiences help to account for his strong commitment to building a more equal society. Following a Cambridge training in anthropology, he chose to work, not on the so-called simple societies of Africa and the Pacific, but rather on the complex societies of the Caribbean. The result was *The Negro Family in British Guiana* (1956). It established the themes that have marked Smith's work ever since.

Black families have long been known to exhibit high illegitimacy rates, unstable unions, and an emphasis on the role of women. Smith drew on the structural-functionalism of his day, but he dissented from the view that the nuclear family was universal and that black family patterns were evidence of disorganisation brought about by slavery and subsequent poverty. He also rejected the attribution of family patterns to distinct cultural segments based on race, claiming rather that in Caribbean creole societies an imposed European standard unified highly unequal classes through an ideology of race. He found that lower-class black males were marginalised by their weak political and economic position. However, the nuclear family was an integral aspect of the black development cycle, just as plural unions were a feature of upper- and middle-class society.

Smith found 'the matrifocal family' to be characteristic of Caribbean creole societies, but also of kinship systems elsewhere. He did not mean by this 'female-headed households', but rather a tendency, found also for example in working-class Britain, where male domestic authority was reinforced, but sex roles and networks were strongly differentiated. It was a cultural pattern with its own force and longevity, a robust alternative to the middle-class ideal of the conjugal nuclear family. The rapid rise of the matrifocal family everywhere in recent decades reinforces his judgement in rejecting the ideological versions of science and politics that still dominate much anthropological thinking.

In his Chicago study with David Schneider, Smith found significant differences in family structure between classes within a shared cultural pattern of American kinship that still departed from the norm of the nuclear family. Their informants reported extended kin networks, each listing about 200 relatives on average. However, the emphasis differed: the middle class gave priority to the relationship between spouses; whereas the lower class (white, black, and Hispanic) emphasised relations between mother–child, siblings, and female kin generally. The authors denied any contribution of race and ethnicity to these class differences, but Smith subsequently acknowledged some distinctive features of the black experience.

In the Caribbean, Smith strongly opposed M.G. Smith's idea of 'plural society', whereby white, brown, and black segments of colonial society were held together only by coercion and had their own separate institutions. Raymond Smith held that this was unduly pessimistic and, despite the racial conflict that destroyed Guyana's experiment in social democracy, he insisted that an egalitarian non-racial politics could be built on the basis of the common legacy of creole society. 'The problem is to face up to the reality of the situation and to find a sense of belonging in the fact of living together and building something new' (1996: 109).

Raymond Smith has been an outstanding teacher and administrator of his subject. He has been actively involved in the diffusion of the social sciences to the former colonial world. His writings are full of references to a long list of collaborators in a career that has produced a unique theoretical perspective. It was forged in the New World, but launched in mid-century Britain.

Education

BA University of Cambridge, 1949
Ph.D. University of Cambridge, 1954

Fieldwork

Guyana, 1951–3, 1956–7, 1962–7, 1975–80
Jamaica, 1955, 1972–5
Ghana, 1960–1
USA, 1967–70, 1985–9
Caribbean, 1982–95

Key Publications

(1956) *The Negro Family in British Guiana: Family Structure and Social Status in the Villages*, London: Routledge.
with Schneider, David (1973) *Class Differences and Sex Roles in American Kinship and Family Structure*, Englewood Cliffs: Prentice Hall.
(1988) *Kinship and Class in the West Indies: A Genealogical Study of Jamaica and Guyana*, Cambridge, UK: Cambridge University Press.
(1996) *The Matrifocal Family: Power, Pluralism and Politics*, New York: Routledge.

KEITH HART

Smith, Robert J.

b. 27 June 1927, Essex, Missouri, USA

Robert J. Smith was among the first American scholars to begin studies of Japan following the Second World War. His training began in 1944 with the US Army Specialized Training Reserve, at the University of Minnesota and Yale University; he served in military intelligence in Japan after the war, and was discharged in 1946. He then returned to the University of Minnesota to continue his education in anthropology and Japanese studies, and entered the graduate programme at Cornell University in 1949. His dissertation research in Kurusu, a small village on Shikoku, established the foundation for five decades of work on continuity and change in rural Japanese society. Even in that early research Smith recognised the importance of historical process to anthropology, and included a discussion of post-war changes in rural Japan. His 1978 book on Kurusu continued that focus by examining changes over the twenty-five years from his first fieldwork.

Characteristic of Smith's work is its clarity and accessibility. He sought to represent the unique differences of Japanese society in ways that non-specialists could understand, and grounded his ethnographic experience in Japanese history. *Ancestor Worship*, for example, examines the relationships of contemporary families and households to the past, through the ancestors. *Japanese Society* explores the ways Japanese tradition, and the specific relationships of individuals and society, shaped Japanese development in the nineteenth and twentieth centuries. Smith also worked with Ella Wiswell to revisit her fieldnotes from the 1930s, in storage since the death of her husband, John Embree. This collaboration produced an important anthropological study of women from an early period, the only such document of Japan.

After receiving his doctorate Smith joined the faculty at Cornell, teaching courses on Japanese society to white students interested primarily in Japanese 'high' culture. In the late 1950s Japanese American and Japanese students began to turn to Japanese studies, and the focus in teaching could be expanded. Although known primarily for work on Japan, around 1970 Smith developed a course called 'The Asian-American Experience' in response to student interests in developing ethnic studies programmes. Because of the difficulties in finding commonalities of experience for such diverse groups, the course focused on the effects of white institutionalised racism.

In 1955 Smith married Kazuko Sasaki in Japan. He was appointed Goldwin Smith Professor of Anthropology at Cornell in 1974, and made emeritus professor in 1997. In 1993 he was awarded Japan's Order of the Rising Sun for his research and teaching on Japan.

Education

BA University of Minnesota, 1949
MA Cornell University, 1951
Ph.D. Cornell University, 1953

Fieldwork

Japan, 1946, 1951–2, 1955, 1958, 1962–3, 1968, 1972, 1975

Key Publications

(1974) *Ancestor Worship in Contemporary Japan*, Stanford, CA: Stanford University Press.
(1978) *Kurusu: The Price of Progress in a Japanese Village, 1951–1975*, Stanford, CA: Stanford University Press.
with Wiswell, Ella Lury (1982) *The Women of Suye Mura*, Chicago: University of Chicago Press.
(1983) *Japanese Society: Tradition, Self, and the Social Order*, Cambridge, UK: Cambridge University Press.

FREDERIC W. GLEACH

Speck, Frank G.

b. 8 November 1881, Brooklyn, New York, USA

d. 6 February 1950, Philadelphia, Pennsylvania, USA

At a time when most anthropologists considered the Indians of eastern North America to be of little anthropological interest, Frank Speck was notable for his extensive work with many of them. His interest was fostered at an early age when poor health prompted his parents to send him to live with Mrs Fidelia Fielding in her Mohegan community in Connecticut. She encouraged his interests in botany and zoology through their Native uses, and he also learned some of the Pequot-Mohegan language while there. While Speck was an undergraduate at Columbia (studying theology), his comparative linguistics professor, J. Dyneley Prince, used examples from Pequot as a dead language – and was shocked to find that Speck could speak it. Prince introduced Speck to Franz Boas, and he soon shifted his study to American Indian languages, with a determination to help salvage languages that were dying. By the time Speck graduated he and Prince had co-authored three published articles, and Speck had published others on his own.

With their encouragement Speck undertook dissertation research with the Yuchi Indians and other groups in what was then Indian Territory. He made many friends in the Native communities where he worked, and some among Boas's students; throughout his career Speck was more comfortable with many Native people than with most academics. Edward Sapir, however, became a close and lifelong friend. Speck's fieldwork included making cylinder recordings of social and ceremonial music, which Sapir's father, a cantor, subsequently transcribed.

Offered an attractive fellowship at the University of Pennsylvania Museum, Speck finished his Ph.D. there, and remained there for the rest of his life. In 1913 he was appointed acting chair of the newly formed Anthropology Department, and he became chair in 1925. He remained an active member and chair of the department until his death in 1950. In addition to building that department, Speck taught at Swarthmore College, 1923–7.

From his base in Philadelphia Speck maintained an extraordinarily active fieldwork programme focusing particularly on eastern Algonquian groups. Some of his fieldwork involved longer-term visits, but much was done in repeated short visits; he also maintained connections with the various communities by written correspondence. Teaching and administrative responsibilities demanded his presence on campus – where he was a charismatic teacher – but he returned to the field whenever possible, and often took students with him. Quiet, attentive, knowledgeable of natural history as well as Native cultures, Speck exemplified collaborative research for his many students.

In the 1930s Speck began to work more

with Iroquois groups in New York; experience with the Cherokees in the southeast provided a bridge for him to enter that rather different cultural world. With his former student, Bill Fenton, Speck began the Iroquois Conference in 1945; it is still held annually, including Native people as well as academics. At the conference in 1947 Speck was adopted by the Seneca Eagle Society.

Speck was known for his ethnographic abilities, particularly his knack for eliciting information through informal interactions. Working with groups who had been ravaged by history, he studied that history along with the contemporary cultures. He had particular interests in ethnobotany and in traditional material culture. But since his death he has become best known for his more ethnological argument concerning family hunting territories. Speck (along with his student, Loren Eiseley, John M. Cooper, and others) argued for the pre-contact existence of such territories, challenging social evolutionary models of the origins of private property. Others believed that hunting territories were a product of the post-colonial fur trade, a position firmly argued in 1954 by Eleanor Leacock that settled the question for many. More recently, as the debate has continued, the focus has also broadened to issues of how hunting territories and other institutions operate(d) in Algonquian societies.

Education

AB Columbia University, 1904
AM Columbia University, 1905
Ph.D. University of Pennsylvania, 1908

Fieldwork

Eastern USA and Canada (Mohegan, Yuchi, Penobscot, Montagnais-Naskapi, Powhatan, Delaware, Cherokee, Cayuga, and many other Native communities), 1907–50

Key Publications

(1915) *Family Hunting Territories and Social Life of Various Algonkian Bands of the Ottawa Valley*, Ottawa: Canada Department of Mines, Geological Survey Memoir 70.

(1931) *A Study of the Delaware Indian Big House Ceremony*, Harrisburg: Publications of the Pennsylvania Historical Commission 2.

(1935) *Naskapi: The Savage Hunters of the Labrador Peninsula*, Norman: University of Oklahoma Press (reprinted 1977).

(1949) *Midwinter Rites of the Cayuga Long House*, Philadelphia: University of Pennsylvania Press (reprinted 1995, University of Nebraska Press).

Further Reading

Blankenship, Roy G. (ed.) (1991) *The Life and Times of Frank G. Speck*, Philadelphia: University of Pennsylvania Department of Anthropology.

Deschênes, Jen-Guy (1981) 'La contribution de Frank G. Speck à l'anthropologie des Amérindiens du Québec, ('The contribution of Frank Speck to the anthropology of the Amerindians of Quebec') *Recherches Amérindiennes au Québec* 21, 3: 205–20.

FREDERIC W. GLEACH

Spencer, Walter Baldwin

b. 23 June 1860, Manchester, UK

d. 14 July 1929, Hoste Island, Tierra del Fuego

Edward Tylor was a referee for Spencer's appointment to Melbourne University's biology chair. Spencer, aged twenty-six, had attended Tylor's Oxford lectures and aided him when transferring the Pitt Rivers ethnographic collection to that eponymous museum. Spencer's biology teachers also were prominent Darwinian evolutionists, so following seven years of relevant intensive Australian faunal research, Spencer brought evolutionary theory to Aboriginal studies. Despite quotable passages redolent of the evolutionary paradigm, such assumptions informed Spencer's anthropology less than critics envisage, while

Tylor's ideas influenced him chiefly in artefact classification as honorary director of the National Museum of Victoria (1899–1928).

When biologist and photographer on the 1894 Horn scientific expedition to Central Australia, Spencer met Frank Gillen, Alice Springs postmaster. Their robust partnership rekindled his anthropological interest, his learning curve dynamically illustrated through Gillen's voluminous correspondence, published in 1997. Their mutual contributions proved equally important.

Gillen commented frankly on controversies and methodology, illuminating their intellectual transformation from following armchair theorists' speculation about discrete global evolutionary sequences from assumed Australian elementary structures – group marriage, classificationary relationships, totemism, conception beliefs – to contextual accounts of the single Arunta (Arrernte) society, followed in 1901 by comparative studies of societies further north.

Spencer and Gillen were unwitting and largely uncredited pioneers of modern fieldwork procedures. Undue emphasis is given to the center–periphery model subordinating them to their initial patron, James Frazer. Careful reading of Spencer's letters to Frazer and Gillen's correspondence reveals respect but growing independence. Spencer was a participant fieldworker, emphasising empirical recording, subjecting data to inductive reasoning and critical postal dialogue with Gillen. Gillen's linguistic fluency was greater than hitherto acknowledged and they meticulously cross-checked with informants. Preceding their first book (1899) their fieldwork was notable in that century for concentration upon one group.

Both men were keen photographers before Spencer's anthropological conversion. They made innovative use of movie film and wax-cylinder recording in 1901, under incredibly more difficult conditions than A.C. Haddon in Torres Strait, enhanced by documenting ritual sequences with still photographs from different perspectives. Hundreds of photographs survive their collaboration, including evocative unposed images. Beyond anthropology, therefore, their words and images provide modern indigenous people with a vibrant documented heritage.

Their two first books and related correspondence are replete with data rarely matched in quality or volume on issues of contemporary debate, to which they added complex religious material (although Spencer's substitute term was 'sacred'). It sufficed to bolster Emile Durkheim's argument for dual religious belief systems, sacred and profane. Basic to both their interpretations was the spiritual role of churingas (tywerrenge). Gillen and Spencer gradually comprehended that these sacred icons ensured spiritual bonding between individual, clan, and territorial identity. Integral to this conceptual timeless universe was the notion of Alcheringa, occasionally termed by them 'Dream Times', (known today as 'Dreaming'). It proved the inspiration diverting attention from scientific evolutionary tenets towards humanistic oral traditions and ceremonial life.

The symbolisation of person and place involving tywerrenge assisted Spencer's hazy comprehension of ceremonial gift exchange, when people travelled to ceremonies following ritually defined routes. Australia was not the static exemplar of primeval savagery, but dynamically changing through on-going historical processes involving cultural contacts.

Gillen died in 1912 while Spencer was in Darwin advising the federal government on Aboriginal administration. He observed communities on Melville Island and western Arnhem Land, publishing a major ethnography (1914) and assembling the earliest large bark painting collection. His recommendations were ignored, including granting extensive reserves to traditional groups. His strategy for mixed-race people involved stern paternalism, anticipating later assimilation policy, with children taken from Aboriginal parental care.

Spencer's empiricism, reporting what he saw even when uncomprehended, his varied recording techniques and comprehensive publication, initiated a paradigm shift in Australian social anthropology, influencing A.R. Radcliffe-Brown and probably Bronislaw Malinowski.

Yet Spencer's work revealed unresolved tensions between evolutionary dogma and cultural anthropology, exemplified by his account of totemic landscapes in *The Arunta* (1927) and its contrasting Darwinist preface.

Education

B.Sc. University of Oxford, 1884
Hon. D.Sc. University of Manchester, 1914
Hon. D.Litt. University of Melbourne, 1915

Fieldwork

Northern Territory, Australia, 1894, 1896–7, 1901–2, 1912, 1923, 1926
Lake Eyre, South Australia, August 1903
Tierra del Fuego, 1929

Key Publications

(1914) *Native Tribes of the Northern Territory of Australia*, London: Macmillan.
with Gillen, F.J. (1899) *The Native Tribes of Central Australia*, London: Macmillan.
with Gillen, F.J. (1904) *The Northern Tribes of Central Australia*, London: Macmillan.
with Gillen, F.J. (1927) *The Arunta*, 2 vols, London: Macmillan.

Further Reading

Mulvaney, D.J. and Calaby, J.H. (1985) *'So Much That is New': Baldwin Spencer 1860–1929*, Carlton: Melbourne University Press.
Mulvaney, J., Morphy, H., and Petch, A. (1997) *My Dear Spencer, The Letters of F.J. Gillen to Baldwin Spencer*, South Melbourne: Hyland House.

JOHN MULVANEY

Sperber, Dan

b. 20 June 1942, Cagnes, France

Dan Sperber is a French anthropologist and cognitive scientist who has conducted fieldwork among the Dorze of southern Ethiopia. Most of his work, however, is theoretical and focuses on the common foundations of the social and the cognitive sciences. In *Rethinking Symbolism*, he argued that the function of cultural symbolism is not to convey a meaning encoded in symbols but to elicit a cognitive response of evocation that varies with individuals and contexts. In essays collected in *On Anthropological Knowledge* and in *Explaining Culture: A Naturalistic Approach*, he contrasts interpretive accounts, which are essential to ethnography and which seek to faithfully convey a state of affairs, with the causal explanations grounded in the natural sciences that anthropological theory should aim at.

He argues in particular for an 'epidemiological' approach to cultural representations. According to this approach, a human population can be seen as inhabited by a much wider population of mental representations. The common environment of that population is furnished with the public productions (and in particular public representations) of its members, some long lasting, like buildings, other ephemeral, like utterances. There are complex causal chains where mental representations and public productions alternate. In many cases, mental representations and public productions occurring in these causal chains inherit some of the content properties of the representations and productions of which they are causal descendants. In particular, processes of imitation can be described as having the function of bringing about such content similarity between the productions of different people, whereas communication can be described as having the function of bringing about such content similarity between the representations of different people. However, neither communication nor imitation are replication mechanisms. The human ability to understand and to reproduce or adapt another person's action or utterance involves inferential processes of reconstruction as much as processes of decoding or copying. Therefore, Sperber argues, applying the Darwinian idea of natural selection to explain the relative stability and evolution of cultural traits, as suggested by the biologist, Richard Dawkins, and pursued in 'memetics', is based on a misrepresentation of the causal processes involved. However, the psychological dispositions that make possible the individual formation and social distribution of representations are, Sperber argues, domain-specific evolved mechanisms or 'modules', to be explained in straightforward Darwinian terms. Several of Sperber's more recent essays are intended as direct contribution to evolutionary psychology.

Together with the British linguist, Deirdre Wilson, Sperber has developed an approach to linguistic pragmatics known as relevance theory. In their book, *Relevance: Communication and Cognition*, they argue that human communication is not primarily a process of coding and decoding but an inferential process: the communicator provides evidence of his or her meaning and the addressee infers this meaning on the basis of the evidence, the context, and considerations of relevance. In a number of articles, Sperber explores how this view of communication as an inferential process together with the view of the human mind as richly modular gives substance to the epidemiological approach to culture.

Education

Licence ès Lettres, Sorbonne, Paris, 1962
B.Litt. University of Oxford, 1968

Fieldwork

Dorze, Ethiopia 1969–74 (18 months)

Key Publications

(1975) *Rethinking Symbolism*, Cambridge, UK: Cambridge University Press.
(1985) *On Anthropological Knowledge*, Cambridge, UK: Cambridge University Press.
with Wilson, Deirdre (1986) *Relevance: Communication and Cognition*, Oxford: Blackwell.
(1996) *Explaining Culture: A Naturalistic Approach*, Oxford: Blackwell.

LAWRENCE A. HIRSCHFELD

Spicer, Edward H.

b. 29 November 1906, Cheltenham, Pennsylvania, USA

d. 5 April 1983, Tucson, Arizona, USA

Edward H. Spicer grew up in a liberal and literate Quaker community, where he was encouraged to write poetry and learned to love language; by the age of twelve he was copying Algonquian texts, including the whole *Walum Olum*. After a brief stay at Commonwealth College in Newellano, Louisiana, Spicer fled to New Orleans and became a merchant seaman. A strike ended that career, and Spicer enrolled at the University of Delaware, planning to be a chemist. After two years he decided to transfer to Johns Hopkins for economics, but after being diagnosed (possibly wrongly) with pulmonary tuberculosis he dropped out to see more of the world, and went to Arizona. Fascinated with the region's geology and archaeology, he decided to save money to study at the University of Arizona. He volunteered on archaeological excavations with Dean Byron Cummings, and a meeting with University of Chicago graduate student, John Provinse, interested him in social anthropology. Spicer visited Chicago and decided to continue his studies there, working with A.R. Radcliffe-Brown and Robert Redfield; Fay-Cooper Cole was also helpful. Despite an extended hospitalisation, Spicer completed fieldwork at the Yaqui village of Pascua (with fellow student and new wife, Rosamond Brown Spicer) and defended his dissertation, a functionalist community study of Yaqui cultural persistence within the larger community of Tucson, published in 1940.

While completing his dissertation Spicer taught at Dillard University in New Orleans, working in the summers with Cole's archaeological project at Kincaid, Illinois. In New Orleans the Spicers interviewed young African Americans, developing knowledge of race relations later used in teaching and civil rights work. They then spent two years at the University of Arizona, working again with the Pascua Yaquis, and Spicer prepared the manuscript that was later published as *People of Pascua*. In 1941 the Spicers began fieldwork in the Mexican Yaqui village of Potam, but following American entry into the Second World War they had to leave Mexico. Spicer became a community analyst at the Poston Relocation Center for Japanese Americans before moving to Washington as the head of the Community Analysis Section of the War Relocation Authority. He thus became one of the pioneers of applied anthropology, and was active in the development of the Society for Applied Anthropology.

Shortly after arriving in Washington, Spicer concluded that he wanted to spend the rest of his life in Arizona. In late 1945 Emil Haury, chair of the University of Arizona Anthropology Department, invited Spicer to rejoin the faculty there, and in 1946 the family returned to Tucson. Spicer became associate professor at the University of Arizona, and remained there for the rest of his life except for research and occasional visiting positions. He did comparative studies of development programmes for indigenous peoples in Latin America in 1963–4, and the Spicers travelled in Europe in 1970–1 visiting such groups as the Basques, Catalans, Irish, and Welsh, European ethnic groups maintaining separate identities within the nation-states that surrounded them. The Spicers were also active in community affairs in Tucson.

Spicer did significant work in cultural and applied anthropology, archaeology, ethnohistory, and language, with a particular focus on cultural persistence through technological and social change, and interethnic conflict. *Human Problems in Technological Change* (1952), originally prepared as a casebook for administrators of overseas development and social science programmes, became a standard text for Peace Corps and Vista volunteers in the 1960s. His magisterial *Cycles of Conquest* compares Native groups from across the southwestern USA and northwestern Mexico in considering the cultural changes since colonial contact, emphasising that these changes in Indian life cannot be understood simply as responses to Euro-American policies.

Spicer was an active member of the American Anthropological Association throughout his career, and served as president in 1973–4 while receiving radiotherapy treatments for the cancer that had been diagnosed the previous year. He remained professionally active even after his retirement from teaching in 1978.

Education

BA University of Arizona, 1932
MA University of Arizona, 1933
Ph.D. University of Chicago, 1939

Fieldwork

Arizona (archaeology), 1932–4
Yaqui, Tohono O'odham (Papago), Seri and Western Apache Indians, 1936–7, 1939–40, 1946–69
New Orleans, Louisiana (African American youth), 1938–9
Kincaid, Illinois (archaeology), 1938–9
Potam, Sonora, Mexico, 1941–2
Poston, Arizona (Japanese American internment camp), 1943–6
Mexico, Peru, Ecuador, 1963–4
Western Europe, 1970–1

Key Publications

with Caywood, Louis R. (1935) *Tuzigoot: The Excavation and Repair of a Ruin on the Verde River near Clarkdale, Arizona*, Berkeley: National Park Service.
(1962) *Cycles of Conquest: The Impact of Spain, Mexico and the United States on the Indians of the Southwest*, Tucson: University of Arizona Press.
(1980) *The Yaquis: A Cultural History*, Tucson: University of Arizona Press.
(1988) *People of Pascua*, eds Kathleen M. Sands and Rosamond B. Spicer, Tucson: University of Arizona Press.

FREDERIC W. GLEACH AND STEPHEN O. MURRAY

Spindler, George Dearborn

b. 28 February 1920, Stevens Point,
   Wisconsin, USA

George Spindler is appropriately recognised as
the 'Father of Educational Anthropology'. He
is one of the most knowledgeable ethnographers in the world today. Besides having edited
over 200 case studies in anthropology, George
Spindler was the editor of the *American
Anthropologist* and played a key role in developing a number of sub-fields in anthropological
linguistics, ethnoscience, the ethnography of
law, and in educational anthropology. His
major theoretical contributions (through his
teaching of over 14,000 students over the last
fifty years and his numerous publications)
were focused on the nature of cultural
transmission and cultural adaptation. His basic
assumption has been that school plays a key
role in the enculturation/socialisation of
children, and that often schools have ignored
or failed certain children, especially children
of color. As a psychological anthropologist,
George Spindler described complex processes
of self-identity formation and adaptation. His
classic study of Menomini acculturation has
been applied to other groups (Latinos, blacks,
Native Americans, and others). His recent
discussions on cultural therapy reflect his
concern for children whose teachers miscom-
municate and have gross misperceptions about
their adjustment to school. His methodological
contributions have enriched the repertoire of
ethnographers from all disciplines and theoretical camps. George Spindler's extraordinary
background and rich field-based experiences
played an important role in the selection of the
ethnographic case studies he edited, and the
dissemination of ethnographic research findings around the world. George Spindler is a
gifted individual who has understood the
extraordinary potential of cross-cultural research in anthropology and other social
sciences, and, in addition to knowing in detail
the most current ethnographic studies, has the
practical knowledge to guide new studies and

edit them with the skills of a master and with
an incredible speed. His long-term impact in
the fields of psychology, educational anthropology, and research methodologies will last
for a very long time. His classic pieces are read
and discussed in graduate and undergraduate
seminars around the world.

Education

BS Central State Teachers College, Stevens
   Point, Wisconsin, 1940
MS University of Wisconsin, Madison, 1947
Ph.D., cultural anthropology, sociology, and
   clinical psychology, University of California,
   Los Angeles, 1952

Fieldwork

Menominee Indians of Wisconsin, June–
   September 1948, 1949, 1950, 1952, 1953,
   1954
Blood Indians, Alberta, Canada, June–
   September 1958, 1959, 1961, 1962, 1967,
   1968, 1972
Stuggart, Germany, September–May 1959,
   1960, spring 1967, 1969, 1973, 1974,
   1975, 1981, 1984, 1985
Roseville, Wisconsin, June–October 1983,
   1984, 1985, 1988

Key Publications

(ed. and contributor) (1974) *Education and
   Cultural Process: Towards an Anthropology of Education*, New York: Holt, Rinehart – Winston
   (second, revised edn, 1987 and third edn,
   1997, published in Prospect, IL: Waveland).
(ed.) (1978) *The Making of Psychological Anthropology*, Berkeley: University of California
   Press.
with Spindler, L. (eds and contributors)
   (1994) *Pathways to Cultural Anthropology: Cultural
   Therapy with Teachers and Students*, Thousand
   Oaks: Corwin Press.
(ed.) (2000) *Fifty Years of Anthropology and
   Education 1950–2000: A Spindler Anthology*, New

Jersey: Lawrence Erlbaum Associates, Publishers.

HENRY TRUEBA

Spindler, Louise Schaubel

b. 4 March 1917, Oak Park, Illinois, USA

d. 24 January 1997, Calistoga, California, USA

Louise Spindler was the inseparable companion of George Spindler, and his continuous and strong inspiration for over fifty years. The many intangible contributions of Louise would eventually appear either as collaborative manuscripts or jointly edited volumes with George; other times simply as superbly edited manuscripts authored by George alone. It is a very difficult task to separate the work of these two extraordinary anthropologists who lived and worked together for so long, and together explored new modes of inquiry and new interpretative approaches to the world of ethnography. However, the specific theoretical and methodological contributions that were exclusively or primarily produced by Louise Spindler focus around the differential adaptive strategies of females and males within the same society. The exquisite sensitivity of Louise, her most unusual intuition about lines of reasoning, and her discovery of implicit reasoning behind available explicit textual evidence, gave Louise a power and a vision that impacted George profoundly, and often invited him to redirect, reorganise, and enrich his teaching and his writings. Louise was a remarkable and astonishingly beautiful woman who had an impressive intellect and a keen ability to see clearly what others could not see at all. Therefore, her methodological contributions in the use of ethnographic methods, her innovative creation of research instruments, and her profound understanding of psychological mechanisms in male–female relationships permitted the team of George and Louise to produce classic pieces such as *Roger Harker* and *Beth Ann*. It will be very difficult in the history of anthropology to do justice to Louise's

contributions because so many of them were hidden in the day-to-day dedication and support given to the work of George. Her kind words, subtle comments, low-key responses, and invitations to revise theoretical arguments were always powerful enough to move George and their students to rethink dissertations, books, articles, and even important personal decisions in life. The unique contributions of the Spindlers and their students to critical ethnography and equity issues were often generated by direct invitation of Louise whose vision of the world was years ahead of many of her colleagues in the social sciences.

Education

BA Carroll College, Waukeshaw, Wisconsin, 1938
MA Stanford University, 1954
Ph.D., anthropology (first woman with Ph.D. from that department), Stanford University, 1956

Fieldwork

Menominee Indians of Wisconsin, June–September 1948, 1949, 1950, 1952, 1953, 1954
Blood Indians, Alberta, Canada, June–September 1958, 1959, 1961, 1962, 1967, 1968, 1972.
Stuggart, Germany, September–May 1959, 1960, spring 1967, 1969, 1973, 1974, 1975, 1981, 1984, 1985
Roseville, Wisconsin, June–October 1983, 1984, 1985, 1988

Key Publications

(1962) 'Menomini women and culture change', *American Anthropologist* 64, 1: Part 2.
with Spindler, G. (1965) 'Researching the perception of cultural alternatives: the instrumental activities inventory', in Melford E. Spiro (ed.) *Context and Meaning in Cultural Anthropology*, in honour of A.I. Hallowell, New York: Free Press.

with Spindler, G. (1970) 'Menomini witch-craft', in Deward Walker (ed.) *Systems of North American Witchcraft and Sorcery*, Moscow, ID: University of Idaho, Anthropological Monographs No. 1.

with Spindler, G. (1990) 'Male and female in four changing cultures', in D. Jordan and M. Swartz (eds) *Personality and the Cultural Construction of Society*, Tuscaloosa, AL: University of Alabama Press.

HENRY TRUEBA

Spiro, Melford

b. 1920, Cleveland, Ohio, USA

Incisive and controversial throughout his career, Melford Spiro has battled with contemporary orthodoxies, holding firm to a conception of anthropology as a science with generalising and explanatory aims. His areas of fieldwork have ranged widely but his distinctive intellectual trajectory has had a constant theme. Throughout, he has addressed the question of a human nature and systematically linked theories of psychological motivation to social and cultural forms. By the 1970s he had become a leading figure in redirecting and revitalising psychological anthropology in America and one of the founding editors of its mouthpiece, *Ethos*.

Drawing initial inspiration from his friend and teacher, A. Irving Hallowell, his early interest was caught by the interrelationship of cultural forms, personality, and emotion. With Hallowell, he contends that the human species is a single biological species and, as such, shares a set of common psychological characteristics. This led to an early break with the relativist tenor of much American cultural anthropology. Over the years this has grown more pronounced as, against the grain of intellectual fashion, he has continued to stress the importance of explanation and the role of the 'pre-cultural' to the interpretation of cultural ideas and societal norms. The term 'pre-cultural' does not here imply pre-social or any simple biological determinism. From his

work among the Ifaluk onwards, he has argued that the deep motivational structures posited by psychoanalytic theory, and developed from the universal experience of infantile dependency, provide a key interpretative frame for understanding personality and the way emotion is channelled in cultural forms.

In the 1950s he embarked on what was to become, with his return twenty-five years later, a remarkable longitudinal study of an Israeli kibbutz. The kibbutz was formed as a radical experiment in Utopian living with the founders committed to gender equality. Identifying the origins of women's subordination in marriage and the family, they sought to institutionalise new arrangements that would lead to women entering on equal terms with men in the wider society. To this end, child rearing became a collective responsibility and children were brought up in a unisexual regime. This expectation of gender identity was not fulfilled. The children, particularly the girls, came to reject this ideology and initiated a counter-revolution, returning to more conventional ideals of marriage, family, and gender role. Women continued to argue for the equivalence of the genders but not for their identity. This, Spiro has written, shook his faith in the malleability of human culture and, while once considered a landmark study, it has, not altogether surprisingly, been almost entirely ignored in post-modernist debates over gender.

His work on religion is again preoccupied with the problem of the relation of the human universal to the culturally particular. Beginning in the early 1960s in Burma, his studies of Theravada Buddhism bring to the fore the distinction between an elaborated theological doctrine and the more pragmatic concerns of ordinary believers, concerned with their immediate fate and not a distantly imaged nirvana. It was pathbreaking in its time for its focus on the way people live their lives, in their mundane complexity, as well as for the nature of the argument that delves into the deep psychological motivation of belief.

Spiro has clearly valued his theoretical contributions and one does not have to be a

Freudian to appreciate the clarity with which he takes on issues. Whether defining religion, taking on Edmund Leach in the virgin birth controversy, and later disputing B. Malinowski's theory of a matrilineal complex among the Trobriands, his essays are models of argumentation, following through from defined positions to logical conclusions. Nevertheless, many will find as much edification in his rich ethnography and the ethnographic puzzles he has teased out; whether in the expression of emotion among the Ifaluk, the relationship between scholarly and lay traditions in Buddhism, the development of gender roles in the kibbutz, or the interpretation of religious beliefs.

Education

BA University of Minnesota, 1941
Ph.D. Northwestern University, 1950

Fieldwork

Wisconsin, 1946
Micronesia (Ifaluk), 1947–8
Israel, 1950–1, 1975–
Burma, 1961–2
Thailand, 1968–75
California, 1977–

Key Publications

(1958) *Children of the Kibbutz*, Boston: Harvard University Press.
(1967) *Burmese Supernaturalism: A Study of the Explanation and Resolution of Suffering*, Englewood Cliffs, NJ: Prentice-Hall.
(1982) *Oedipus in the Trobriands: The Making of a Scientific Myth*, Chicago: University of Chicago Press.
(1987) *Culture and Human Nature*, (eds) Benjamin Kilborne and L.L. Langness, Chicago: University of Chicago Press.

Further Reading

Avruch, Kevin (1990) 'Melford Spiro and the scientific study of culture', in D.K. Jordan

and M.J. Swartz (eds) *Personality and the Cultural Construction of Society*, Tuscaloosa, AL: University of Alabama Press.

SUZETTE HEALD

Spittler, Gerd

b. 1939, Donaueschingen, Germany

Gerd Spittler is a distinguished ethnographer of Haussa and Tuareg in Niger and Nigeria of West Africa. He started his career within the anthropology of law, analysing patterns of local conflict resolution in the shadow of state-enforced formal law. From here he turned to the spread of modern state administration among the Haussa peasants of Gobir (Niger). In his two monographs on this topic (1978, 1981) he examines the interrelation between, on the one hand, an uncaptured peasantry with its defensive reactions and, on the other hand, a state administration with its structural ignorance and tendency to despotism, typical for governments in agrarian states. At the same time he investigates the embeddedness of this whole process within aspects of urbanisation and Islamisation that provide the cultural background for changing the Haussa way of life. Spittler's early interest in nomadism was strongly influenced by the drought and subsequent famine of 1984. He became intrigued by Kel Ewey Tuareg strategies to preserve their autonomy of action in the face of famine, and presented an ethnographic study (1989) that was well received beyond the community of anthropologists. Among the Haussa, Spittler became interested in aspects of work. His close reading of Chayanov encouraged him to intensify his research on work, a key issue generally neglected in anthropology (1998). Spittler's present theoretical interests and his on-going research focus on aspects of work and consumption, of local action under conditions of globalisation.

Education

Ph.D. University of Freiburg, Germany, 1966

Habilitation, University of Freiburg, Germany,
1975

Fieldwork

Among the Haussa in Niger and Nigeria,
1967–71 (18 months)
Among the Tuareg in Niger and Nigeria,
1976–2001 (52 months)

Key Publications

(1978) *Herrschaft über Bauern. Die Ausbreitung
staatlicher Herrschaft und einer islamisch-urbanen
Kultur in Gobir (Niger)* (Dominating Peasants.
The Spread of State Authority and Urban
Islamic Culture in Gobir (Niger)), Frankfurt
am Main: Campus.
(1981) *Verwaltung in einem afrikanischen Bauernstaat.
Das koloniale Französisch Westafrika 1919–1939*
(Administration in an African Peasant State.
Colonial French Africa between 1919 and
1939), Wiesbaden: Steiner.
(1989) *Handeln in einer Hungerkrise. Tuaregnomaden
und die große Dürre von 1984* (Acting under
Conditions of Famine. The Tuareg and the
Great Drought of 1984), Opladen: West-
deutscher Verlag.
(1998) *Hirtenarbeit. Die Welt der Kamelhirten und
Ziegenhirtinnen von Timia* (Pastoral Work. Ca-
melherds-Men and Goatherds-Women of
Timia), Köln: Köppe.

RICHARD ROTTENBURG

Sponsel, Leslie E.

b. 6 November 1943, Indianapolis, Indiana,
USA

Leslie E. Sponsel was trained in biological and
cultural anthropology. His publications and
research reflect a concern with this interface
through an exploration of ecology, peace
studies, religion, biodiversity conservation,
human rights, advocacy, and sacred places. In
the early 1970s Sponsel conducted fieldwork
on primate behaviour and ecology with

squirrel monkeys in the Colombian Amazon
and in Awash, Ethopia, with vervet monkeys.
Sponsel continued to study relationships
between behaviour and ecology with fieldwork from the mid-1970s to the early 1980s
that focused on human predation among
Yanomami groups in the Venezuelan Amazon.
His analysis of research findings from these
periods played a key role in the development
of an integrated approach to biological and
cultural anthropology. From 1986 to the
present Sponsel has examined connections
between religions, environments, and ecology
in southern Thailand. Sponsel's impressive
body of scholarship is matched by a commitment to social justice and ecological issues,
and exemplified through awards for teaching
excellence at the University of Hawaii.

Education

BA Indiana University, 1965
MA Cornell University, 1973
Ph.D. Cornell University, 1981

Fieldwork

Calgary Zoo, Alberta, Canada, 1971
Colombian Amazon, 1972
Awash National Park, Ethiopia, 1973
Venezuelan Amazon, 1974–81
Thailand, 1986, 1988, 1994 (summers
1986–9 and 1994–5)
Comparative field research, southern Thailand,
Kaua'i in Hawaii, Chimayo Valley in north-
ern New Mexico, Mount Shasta in northern
California, Sorte in central Venezuela, 2000

Key Publications

and Gregor, T.A. (eds) (1994) *The Anthropology of
Peace and Nonviolence*, Boulder, CO: Lynne
Rienner Publishers.
(1997) 'The master thief: gold mining and
mercury contamination in the Amazon', in
B.R. Johnston (ed.) *Life and Death Matters:
Human Rights and the Environment at the End of the*

Millennium, Thousand Oaks, CA: Alta Mira Press.

BRIAN FREER

Srinivas, M.N.

b. 16 November 1916, Mysore City, India

d. 30 November 1999, Bangalore, India

Mysore Narasimhachar Srinivas was brought up and educated in the old city of Mysore, before he went to Bombay, where he studied under India's leading sociologist, G.S. Ghurye, and completed his Ph.D. thesis on the martial caste group of Coorgs. Srinivas then went to Oxford where, supervised by A.R. Radcliffe-Brown and E.E. Evans-Pritchard, he reanalysed his Coorg material, which was later published as *Religion and Society among the Coorgs of South India*. This pioneering book, quickly acclaimed as a 'functionalist' classic, established Srinivas's scholarly reputation. In 1948, Srinivas carried out his first fieldwork in Rampura, the subject of *The Remembered Village*, which was written largely from memory after his fieldwork notes were destroyed by fire.

Srinivas returned to India permanently in 1951. In 1959, he was appointed to a new professorship of sociology at the Delhi School of Economics. In 1972, he moved to Bangalore to take a leading role in the new Institute of Social and Economic Change, from which he retired in 1979, although he remained a very active scholar and commentator on public affairs until his death. Srinivas played a key role in the institutional development of social science in independent India, but his work in Delhi had the greatest long-term impact. In the Delhi School of Economics, in collaboration with some outstanding colleagues (many of them his former students), Srinivas built a world-class department, which laid equal stress on ethnographic fieldwork and comparative, theoretical analysis, and drew no material distinction between sociology and social (or cultural) anthropology.

Srinivas's many publications were the main basis for his international academic reputation. The Coorg monograph was ahead of its time in showing that a complex society and religion were amenable to ethnographic analysis; it also introduced the concepts of 'Sanskritic' and 'non-Sanskritic' Hinduism – variants of Robert Redfield's 'great' and 'little traditions' – and 'Sanskritisation', the process whereby upwardly mobile lower castes emulate the 'Sanskritic' customs of Brahman or higher castes. Early articles on Rampura village introduced the 'dominant caste' concept, analysed 'vertical' (intercaste) and 'horizontal' (intracaste) solidarities, and explained how village unity could co-exist with social hierarchy. All these concepts and discussions have been extremely influential, and Srinivas's publications were at the core of the caste and village ethnographic literature on which the modern anthropology of India was built. The comparison between 'Sanskritisation', 'Westernisation', and secularisation, and the tendency for 'horizontal' caste solidarity to expand in the contemporary political context, were most convincingly discussed in *Social Change in Modern India*. An earlier essay, 'Caste in modern India', had provoked hostility in India in 1957 by claiming that castes were becoming more powerful and active under democracy. Later developments showed that Srinivas was indisputably right, and for forty years he was well known in India as a perceptive but controversial commentator on society and politics.

After *The Remembered Village*, Srinivas's writings were often repetitive, although there were some notable exceptions, including several autobiographical essays. All his work, including the influential earlier publications, attracted criticism and one common objection was that Srinivas (a Brahman) tended to adopt an elitist, Brahmanical perspective. This criticism is not baseless – Sanskritic Hinduism, for example, is an obviously Brahmanical category – but it has invariably been advanced with more polemical assertion than careful argument, and his writings on Coorg or Rampura are not demonstrably more elitist than other scholars' ethnographies of comparable Indian communities. A second, common criticism –

fuelled by his own disdain for theorising – was that Srinivas's theoretical approach was naïvely functionalist and empiricist. No careful reader of the Coorg monograph (as opposed to just Radcliffe-Brown's foreword) could agree with this criticism, however, and all Srinivas's best writing (often about conflict or historical change) was shaped by his understanding of social theory. Admittedly, this understanding was conservative and rather restricted; Srinivas, for example, never engaged with Marxism (very influential among Indian intellectuals in the 1960s and 1970s) and only sporadically confronted Louis Dumont's magisterial theory of caste and hierarchy during the same period. Such criticism, however, cannot detract from the sharpness of his analytical insights and the empathetic quality of his ethnography, or indeed from M.N. Srinivas's pre-eminence among the founders of modern anthropology and sociology in India.

Education

BA University of Mysore, 1936
MA University of Bombay, 1938
LL B University of Bombay, 1939
Ph.D. University of Bombay, 1944
D.Phil. University of Oxford, 1947

Fieldwork

Coorg, Karnataka, 1940–2
Rampura village, Karnataka, 1948, 1952

Key Publications

(1952) *Religion and Society among the Coorgs of South India*, Oxford: Clarendon Press.
(1966) *Social Change in Modern India*, Berkeley: University of California Press.
(1976) *The Remembered Village*, Delhi: Oxford University Press.
(2002) *Collected Essays*, Delhi: Oxford University Press.

C.J. FULLER

Stack, Carol B.

b. 1940, The Bronx, New York, USA

Stack's initial fieldwork, on kinship networks in a small black urban community, was innovative in both method and conclusions. Living in 'The Flats' as a participant-observer, Stack became accepted as a friend by several residents. Thus she was able to study their interactions with other residents more fully than standard research techniques allow. She could also question subjects in the context of daily conversation rather than in formal interviews. Far from finding the pathology and chaos previously attributed to the matriarchal black family, Stack discovered an extended family structure of kin and non-kin whose sharing of resources functioned to ensure survival under poverty conditions.

Stack's research in the Carolinas examines a little-noted phenomenon: the reverse migration back to the South of children and grandchildren of African Americans who moved north, earlier in the twentieth century, to seek better opportunities and acceptance. The study technique was largely interview-based, but *Call to Home* blended amorphous data with fine analysis to conclude that, for most in-migrants, the value of family ties and ancestral land outweighs the poverty and political disregard they face there.

Her fieldwork in Oakland focuses on African American, Latino, and Asian youth employed in a fast-food chain, and the implications of this work for their futures.

Other, shorter studies have dealt with such topics as childraising, education, gender perceptions, and family values within various minority communities. Her breadth of interests, subject-friendly methodology, and willingness to forge new directions in theory have made Stack, a white American, a pre-eminent scholar of ethnic cultures.

Education

BA University of California, Berkeley, 1961

MA University of Illinois, 1968
Ph.D. University of Illinois, 1972

Fieldwork

'Jackson Harbor', Midwest, 1968–70.
North and South Carolina, 1975–87
Oakland, California, 1993–6

Key Publications

(1974) *All Our Kin: Strategies for Survival in a Black Community*, New York: Harper & Row.
(1996) *Call to Home: African Americans Reclaim the Rural South*, New York: Basic Books.

EMILY ALWARD

Stanner, W.E.H.

b. 1905, Sydney, New South Wales, Australia

d. 8 October 1981, Canberra, Australia

William Edward Hanley (Bill) Stanner remains a most influential figure in the anthropology of Aboriginal Australia. Stanner came to anthropology as an undergraduate student at Sydney, where at age twenty he first met A.R. Radcliffe-Brown. While putting himself through university by working as a journalist, an experience he credited with honing his research and writing skills, he focused his studies on economics and anthropology. It was in anthropology that Stanner found an intellectual and professional home that helped focus his diverse intellectual interests and social commitments. He carried out field research in Africa and the Pacific, and produced significant contributions to our knowledge from this work, but it was in his Australian research that he produced some of the most interesting and important fine-grained ethnography.

Throughout his career, Stanner remained committed to a version of Radcliffe-Brown's anthropology, even while modifying it and moving in quite different directions. In parti-cular, Stanner found Radcliffe-Brown's emphasis on the concepts of structure and function unsatisfactory and was led to develop his own analyses with an emphasis on the dynamics of social and cultural processes (the third, and relatively under-developed, concept in Radcliffe-Brown's analytical scheme). Central to Stanner's anthropological work was his on-going theoretical and ethnographic elaboration of notions of transaction, the structure of operations, and value. Later in his career, on returning to Australia to take up his first tenured academic position at the Australian National University in the 1950s, Stanner was to spend much of his time working as adviser to the government and as an advocate for Aboriginal people. In the early 1960s Stanner was involved in the establishment of what is now the Australian Institute for Aboriginal and Torres Strait Islander Studies in Canberra.

In the late 1960s Stanner delivered the Boyer Lectures, broadcast on the Australian Broadcasting Corporation and subsequently published as a small volume. Here, he publicly pointed out the absence of detailed accounts of Aboriginal people in much Australian written history. His early and insightful voice on this topic inspired a generation of historians to open up this field. However, it is his detailed ethnographic analysis of the depth and significance of Aboriginal religion that remains his most important contribution to knowledge. The breadth of knowledge, insight, and sensitivity demonstrated in this monograph ensure it a reputation as one of the most striking documents on this topic. Bill Stanner remains a living force in Australian anthropology. The interpretations and insights of his accounts of Aboriginal life continue to inspire anthropologists and others interested in Aboriginal culture and society in Australia.

Education

BA University of Sydney, 1931
MA University of Sydney, 1934
Ph.D. London School of Economics, 1938

Fieldwork

Northern Territory, Australia, 1932–4, 1952, 1954, 1957, 1958–9, and then on shorter trips until 1978
East Africa, 1938–9, 1948
South Pacific, 1946–7

Key Publications

(1953) *The South Seas in Transition: A Study of Post-War Rehabilitation and Reconstruction in Three British Pacific Dependencies*, Sydney: Australasian Publishing Company.
(1963) *On Aboriginal Religion*, University of Sydney, Oceania Monograph 36.
(1968) *After the Dreaming. Black and White Australians: An Anthropologist's View*, the Boyer Lectures 1968, Sydney: Australian Broadcasting Commission.
(1979) *White Man Got No Dreaming: Essays 1938–1973*, Canberra: Australian National University Press.

PHILIP MOORE

Stavenhagen, Rodolfo

b. 1932, Frankfurt, Germany (nationalised Mexican)

Rodolfo Stavenhagen's work started with a clear concern about Latin American development problems. The essay, *Seven Misconceived Theses about Latin America* (1973), presented to the general public a comprehensive critique of standard sociological presuppositions about social issues associated with modernisation theories. It advanced the concept of internal colonialism contending that there existed in Latin American countries an organic, structural, relationship between a pole of growth or metropolitan development and an internal, backward, increasingly underdeveloped colony. The modernisation process of urban and industrial areas was sustained by the subordination and exploitation of the so-called 'backward' areas and these, instead of being an obstacle to development, were, in fact, the source for growth. Along these lines, Stavenhagen developed substantial research on agrarian societies, peasants, and ethnic groups. His theoretical standpoint anticipated some of the heated debates in sociology during the 1970s and his position on agrarian issues was very influential in the views of Mexican agriculture in the 1980s.

Currently Stavenhagen holds that the process of national integration should maintain ethnic groups' own identity in an effective form of cultural pluralism. This view was instrumental in policy development in his official government positions as well as at UNESCO. Later he turned his view to the human and collective rights of indigenous peoples, contending that the systematic violation of these rights is due primarily to ignorance of indigenous customary law, norms, and customs regulating their social life.

Stavenhagen is currently special rapporteur on the situation of the human rights and fundamental freedoms of indigenous peoples for the U.N. High Commissioner for Human Rights, vice-president of the Interamerican Institute for Human Rights, and co-ordinator of the Follow-up and Verification Commission of San Andrés Agreements.

Education

BA University of Chicago, 1951
MA Escuela Nacional de Antropología e Historia, 1958
Ph.D. University of Paris, 1965

Fieldwork

Agrarian reform and agriculture development, Mexico, 1965–8
Ethnic minorities and economic development, Mexico, 1984–8
Ethnic conflict and development, Mexico, 1988–92
Indigenous customary law and human rights, Mexico, 1984–

Key Publications

(1974) *Estructura agraria y desarrollo agrícola en México* (Agrarian Structure and Agricultural Development in Mexico), México: Fondo de Cultura Económica.

(2001) *La cuestión étnica* (The Ethnic Issue), México: El Colegio de México.

FERNANDO I. SALMERÓN CASTRO

Steward, Julian Haynes

b. 31 January 1902, Washington, DC, USA

d. 6 February 1972, Urbana, Illinois, USA

Julian Haynes Steward was a leading contributor to both the theoretical development of American anthropology and the expansion of the scope of the field, from the late 1930s through the mid-1960s. He (and Leslie White) initiated the development of 'neo-evolutionary', materialist, and 'scientistic' approaches in American anthropology in the 1940s, and he (alone) inspired the development of ecological anthropology. Steward played a major role in the growth of South American ethnography and contributed to studies in 'peasant' societies, especially in Latin America. His emphasis on studies of 'modernisation' in an increasingly interdependent world led to 'world systems' theory.

Studying with A.L. Kroeber at Berkeley in the 1920s, Steward became dissatisfied with the emphasis there on tracing cultural traits while eschewing the question of 'cause' in favor of the relativistic pursuit of histories. By the late 1930s he had begun to devote his career to the understanding of causality in culture, searching for recurrent regularities in processes of change through cross-cultural comparison.

His approach depended upon classifying cultures into 'types' based on a few features that he considered fundamental: the subsistence base (the combination of a society's habitat and natural resources, and the technology available for coping with it) and the social organisation that developed around the problems of production. This 'core', as he called it, was the basis upon which a society's 'superstructure' was erected. His writings led to the widely cited hypothetical evolutionary sequence, from family to band to tribe to chiefdom to state, and, eventually, the world. He referred to these categories as 'levels of sociocultural integration'.

Steward advocated a return to the concept of cultural evolution, but with major differences from the earlier evolutionism of Lewis Henry Morgan and the contemporaneous approach of Leslie White. Although Steward attempted to generalise about the overall development of sociopolitical and economic complexity in human history (1955), he did not expect to find universal laws. He hoped to produce hypotheses about the kinds of social and cultural changes to be expected under 'precisely stipulated conditions'. He believed that 'like causes produce like results', but recognised that as conditions vary, so may outcomes. Thus he saw 'evolution' as 'multilinear' with various trajectories potentially possible at any point. Although he hoped to achieve predictability through cross-cultural comparison, he was wary of attempts to apply anthropological knowledge under the political and economic constraints that prevailed at that time.

Steward's ideas about cultural ecology, the ways societies adapt to their environments, have had a more lasting impact than his evolutionism. Before Steward's work, American anthropologists usually ignored or denied the role of environment in culture. His insistence on the creative possibilities of the interaction between a given environment, with its resources and constraints, and the technologies, knowledge, and skills a people have to deal with these, launched hundreds of studies and opened a new direction for American anthropology.

Steward was more influential as a writer and organiser than as a teacher, except for a remarkable period from 1946–52 at Columbia University. There Steward taught, and learned from, a group of older students, many of them veterans of the Second World War. This group included Pedro Carrasco, Stanley Diamond,

Morton Fried, Robert Manners, Betty Meggers, Sidney Mintz, Robert Murphy, Elena Padilla, Elman Service, Elliott Skinner, Eric Wolf, and, at a slight remove, Marvin Harris and Marshall Sahlins.

From 1935 to 1946 Steward worked at the Bureau of American Ethnology of the Smithsonian Institution, where one of his achievements was to conceive of and edit the extraordinary seven-volume, *Handbook of South American Indians*. Another was the establishment of the Institute for Social Anthropology, which supported teaching and field research in Latin America, focusing on 'peasant' communities and economy. This project produced more than a dozen monographs dealing with land use, agriculture, and economic change in Mexico, Guatemala, Columbia, Peru, and Brazil. Steward was influential in the development of area studies after the Second World War and he organised innovative team research projects, first in Puerto Rico (1956) and then in Africa, Asia, and Latin America. In advocating the study of the regularities of process involved in cultural change and 'modernisation', Steward always emphasised the growing interdependence of the economies and cultures of the world.

Education

BA Cornell University, 1925
Ph.D. University of California, Berkeley, 1931

Fieldwork

Ethnography and archaeology, Great Basin area, 1927–35

Key Publications

(1938) *Basin-Plateau Aboriginal Sociopolitical Groups*, Washington: Smithsonian Institution.
(1950) *Area Research: Theory and Practice*, Bulletin 63, New York: Social Science Research Council.
(1955) *Theory of Culture Change: The Methodology of Multilinear Evolution*, Urbana: University of Illinois.

with Manners, Robert, Wolf, Eric, Padilla, Elena, Mintz, Sidney, and Scheele, R.L. (1956) *The People of Puerto Rico*, Urbana: University of Illinois Press.

HERBERT S. LEWIS

Stocking, George

b. 8 December 1928, Berlin, Germany
  (US citizen)

George Stocking took his Ph.D. in the programme in American civilisation at the University of Pennsylvania, with a dissertation on 'American social scientists and race theory: 1890–1915'. He taught in the Department of History at Berkeley (1960–8), moving away from the positivistic social science that had been emphasised in his graduate training towards a more traditionally historicist approach to intellectual history. By 1968, when he joined the Department of Anthropology at the University of Chicago, he had focused his scholarship on the history of anthropology, a specialisation foreshadowed in his dissertation, in which Franz Boas figured centrally. In four decades, his work has ranged over a wide array of topics, including the interplay of 'race, culture, and evolution' in nineteenth- and twentieth-century American and British anthropology (with some attention to continental Europe), the relationship between anthropological ideas and their institutional and political contexts, paradigmatic traditions in anthropology (with special attention to the Boasians in North America and the evolutionists and structural-functionalists in Great Britain), and the changing disciplinary boundaries of anthropology in various national traditions. Still writing in his seventies, at the turn of the twenty-first century Stocking has moved 'forward' chronologically to consider post-Second World War anthropology, including an essay on one of his mentors, A.I. Hallowell. Although he considers himself a historian, his disciplinary home has been anthropology, and he has playfully suggested that anthropologists are 'his people' and the

Chicago department the site of his fieldwork. He founded the influential series, *History of Anthropology*, which he edited from 1983–96 and, in 1973, *History of Anthropology Newsletter*, which he edited for more than thirty years.

In an early, programmatic essay on 'presentism' and 'historicism' (reprinted in *Race, Culture and Evolution*), Stocking argued that scholars writing the history of their own disciplines tend to be 'presentist', that is, they see the past as leading to the triumph of the contemporary theoretical orientations they favor. In contrast, he proposed a historicist approach to the history of disciplines, contextualising past scholarship in relation to the assumptions and controversies of its time. In his work that has meant, first, understanding anthropological ideas as these occurred, or presented themselves over time, in the minds of past practitioners; and, second, explicating those ideas in terms of multiple contexts, from the biographical to the institutional to the sociopolitical. Influenced over the years by his residence among anthropologists, Stocking became more sensitive to the connection between his own historiography and its present-day cultural context. However, his basic historicist inclination has paid great dividends. The 'sub-disciplinary' specialisation in the history of anthropology, which he almost single-handedly created, has become a primary locus of critical reflection in the discipline, helping anthropologists understand that anthropology itself is cultural activity, historically located, and, as such, shaped by its contemporary contexts.

Some of Stocking's most influential work can be seen as a critique of anthropologists' 'myths' about their past. In a series of essays on late nineteenth-century British and American anthropology, Stocking debunked the notion that E.B. Tylor had 'invented' the relativistic culture concept. Stocking showed that Tylor's understanding of 'culture' and 'civilisation' was in some respects closer to Victorian evolutionary visions of progress than to twentieth-century notions of cultural plurality. At the same time, Stocking provided a careful account of Boas's progress 'from physics to ethnology', tracing the interplay of positivist and idealist strands in his early work, a tension that has been central to the American anthropological tradition since Boas. Stocking also took on the myth of the lone fieldworker, particularly in reference to B. Malinowski, locating his Trobriand research in older traditions of team research in colonial scientific expeditions. In these examples and in his other work, Stocking has been concerned not only to trace the emergence of distinctive anthropological paradigms, but also to show the connections between them and preceding or competing traditions of thought.

Although Stocking has always abjured the role of theorist, his imaginative and erudite readings of major figures in anthropology have been enormously influential. Especially in American anthropology, his recuperation of Boas stimulated a new generation of 'neo-Boasian' theorising. At the same time, Stocking brought a unique style of reflexivity to the post-modern moment in anthropology, with his rigorous practice of self-reflection embodied in his retrospective commentaries on his own published work.

Education

BA Harvard University, 1949
Ph.D. University of Pennsylvania, 1960

Key Publications

(1968) *Race, Culture and Evolution: Essays in the History of Anthropology*, New York: Free Press.
(1987) *Victorian Anthropology*, New York: Free Press.
(1992) *The Ethnographer's Magic and Other Essays in the History of Anthropology*, Madison and London: University of Wisconsin Press.
(1995) *After Tylor: British Social Anthropology, 1888–1951*, Madison and London: University of Wisconsin Press.

RICHARD HANDLER

Stoler, Ann Laura

b. 1949, Brooklyn, New York, USA

Ann Stoler's work on gender, race, and colonialism has changed how anthropologists understand these very concepts. Looking primarily at Dutch colonialism in Indonesia, Stoler discovered that sexuality was at the center of colonial discourse and domination. Her studies of interracial intimacy between coloniser and colonised – e.g. between European men and native women, as well as their mixed offspring – revealed that colonial categories of class, race, and gender were significant not just in the colonies, but also in the European metropoles as well. The four main influences on Stoler's work are political economy, feminist anthropology, the historic turn, and post-structuralism, particularly the work of Michel Foucault. Colonialism has always been a focus of her research, beginning with her first monograph on capitalism, plantation labour, and protest in colonial Indonesia. Stoler's second book provided an ethnographic, feminist, and colonial reading of Foucault's History of Sexuality, and her current projects include a monograph based on her landmark 1991 article 'Carnal knowledge and imperial power', as well as a book about the production and politics of colonial knowledge, sentiment, and archives. Ann Stoler's careful, politically engaged, and passionate scholarship has already made lasting contributions to anthropology and the world beyond.

Education

BA Barnard College, 1972
MA Columbia University, 1976
Ph.D. Columbia University, 1982

Fieldwork

Indonesia, 1972–3, 1977–9, 1982–3, 1996–7, 2000
Netherlands, 1979–80, 1984, 1987–92, 2001–2
France, 1984, 1987–90, 1993, 1997–9

Key Publications

(1991) 'Carnal knowledge and imperial power: race and morality in colonial Asia', in Micaela di Leonardo (ed.) *Gender at the Crossroads of Knowledge: Feminist Anthropology in the Postmodern Era*, Berkeley: University of California Press.
(1995) *Race and the Education of Desire: Foucault's History of Sexuality and the Colonial Order of Things*, Durham: Duke University Press.

CAROLE MCGRANAHAN

Stoller, Paul

b. 1947, Washington, DC, USA

Paul Stoller, professor at West Chester University, Pennsylvania, has had an extraordinarily productive career. An ethnographer of the Songhay of Niger, West Africa, Stoller has authored a series of influential monographs. In *Sorcery's Shadow*, a key text in the turn to narrative and reflexive ethnography, documents in a compelling and candid way the conduct of ethnographic research and provides a memorable experiential account of sorcery. This work also shows the influence of Stoller's earlier training in linguistics. Subsequent books address spirit possession; *Fusion of the Worlds* (1989) offers another well-crafted ethnographic and narrative depiction that manages to encompass both the richness of Songhay aesthetic life and the dark side of its politics, while *Embodying Colonial Memories* (1995) addresses in a more theoretical vein the mimetic qualities of possession by reflecting on the pioneering ethnographic films of Jean Rouch on the amazing Hauka possession that emerged during the colonial period.

Rouch himself has served as the subject of the aptly titled *The Cinematic Griot* (1992), which in turn led Stoller to a number of significant reflections on visual anthropology. The Rouch book further attests to the importance of Stoller's role in enhancing communication between French and American anthropology.

Not only has Stoller been a vocal advocate

for, and able practitioner of, vivid, humanistic ethnographic writing, but also he was one of the first anthropologists to focus serious attention on the senses. Two volumes of essays demonstrate the difference that consideration of sensuous experience can make to anthropological understanding. The attention to embodied experience locates Stoller firmly within the phenomenological school, but unlike many members of the latter he is able to use his insights to enhance the quality and directness of his writing.

In later years Stoller has turned his attention to Songhay and other West African street vendors in New York City, producing both a novel (*Jaguar*, 1999) and an ethnographic monograph (*Money Has No Smell*, 2002) that convey new forms of transnational practice and urban life. A tireless writer, editor, reviewer, and discussant, Stoller's evocative prose and passionate advocacy for what he once called 'The reconstruction of ethnography' (1986) have had a significant and healthy impact on younger scholars and the field in general.

Education

BA University of Pittsburgh, 1969
MS Georgetown University, 1974
Ph.D. University of Texas, Austin, 1978

Fieldwork

Republic of Niger, 1976–7, 1979–80, 1981, 1982–3, 1984, 1987–8, 1990
New York City, 1992–2002

Key Publications

with Olkes, Cheryl (1987) *In Sorcery's Shadow: A Memoir of Apprenticeship among The Songhay of Niger*, Chicago: University of Chicago Press.
(1992) *The Cinematic Griot: The Ethnography of Jean Rouch*, Chicago: University of Chicago Press.
(1997) *Sensuous Scholarship*, Philadelphia: University of Pennsylvania Press.
(2002) *Money Has No Smell: Ethnography of West*

African Traders in New York City, Chicago: University of Chicago Press.

MICHAEL LAMBEK

Strathern, Marilyn

b. 6 March 1941, North Wales, UK

Marilyn Strathern is a leading theorist of kinship, gender, and exchange, as well as one of the world's most prominent scholars in the field of Melanesian anthropology. Her innovative theoretical style and prodigious publication record have established her reputation as one of the most powerful and respected voices in contemporary anthropology. Strathern has played a major role in making the discipline of anthropology more responsive to many of its own in-built habits of thought, and in linking this critical task to wider struggles against social inequality. She is also highly regarded for her institutional contributions to social anthropology as a discipline, and to the reform of higher education policy in Britain.

Marilyn Strathern took her Ph.D. in social anthropology from Cambridge in 1968, 'Women's status in the Mt Hagen area', based on 16 months' fieldwork in 1964–5. *Women in between; Female Roles in a Male World* (1972) established a concern with gender and property that has remained a central current throughout her varied and distinguished career. In 1981, Strathern published *Kinship at the Core: An Anthropology of Elmdon, a Village in Northwest Essex in the 1960s*, a major contribution to the study of class and English kinship. A hallmark of Strathern's approach has been her juxtaposition of English and Melanesian ideas, through which she has made a powerful contribution to the emergence of a more critically reflexive anthropology. In particular her ability to expose taken-for-granted conceptual logics has resulted in a consistent attention to knowledge practices, as part of quotidian social life, institutional practices, and the discipline of anthropology itself.

In *The Gender of the Gift: Problems with Women and*

Problems with Society in Melanesia (1988), the themes of gender, property, and embodiment are inseparable from questions of the intellectual technique of cross-cultural comparison, and the elucidation of sociality. Frequently concerned with social relations as a set of forms, articulations, or effects, Strathern describes herself trying to be 'an elbow, to intervene between two sets of objectifications – Melanesian and Western European ideas – in order to turn one into the other' (1988: 310). To this end, Strathern has developed a unique vocabulary of description for both the production of difference, and the ways ideas relate or connect. Always resisting the 'obviousness' of ideas such as that of 'an individual', or a 'biological relation', Strathern is systematic in her efforts to turn such concepts inside out, and explicit about the methods by which she does so (e.g. *Partial Connections*, 1991).

During the 1990s, Strathern turned her attention to three areas of contemporary public debate: reproductive and genetic technologies, the 'enterprise' and 'audit' cultures of late twentieth-century Britain, and ownership of intellectual property. The latter concern, in particular disputes over cultural and biological property, has returned to some of the earliest themes in Strathern's work, when she served as a consultant to the Papua New Guinea government in the 1970s on dispute settlement. *Property, Substance and Effect* (1999), based in part on fieldwork in Papua New Guinea in 1995, interrogates property definitions as matters of dispute over cultural form. In all three of these areas, knowledge practices are revealed as culturally specific, and political, in their effects, especially in terms of what they make visible or obscure. The accounting mentality of the audit culture, like the institutions of copyright and patenting, or the rationales governing the status of donated embryos, all involve key questions about categorisation that are tied to prioritisation, and thus to specific effects, or consequences. A trenchant, if often elliptical, social critic, Strathern's work has long been closely allied to struggles against social injustice and inequality.

Marilyn Strathern assumed her first full-time university appointment, as chair of social anthropology at the University of Manchester in 1985, where she remained until 1993, before returning to Cambridge to chair the Department of Social Anthropology. Strathern became mistress of Girton College in 1998, and was knighted in 2001. In addition to Manchester and Cambridge, Strathern has held positions at Australian National University and the University of California, Berkeley. She was the recipient of the Rivers Memorial Medal from the Royal Anthropological Institute in 1976, and was appointed a fellow of the British Academy in 1987.

Education

BA University of Cambridge, 1963
Ph.D. University of Cambridge, 1968

Fieldwork

Mt Hagen (Melpa), Western Highlands, Papua New Guinea, 1964–5, 1967, 1970–1, 1976, 1981, 1995
Pangia (Wiru) Southern Highlands, 1967
Port Moresby, 1970–4, 1981

Key Publications

(1972) *Women in between; Female Roles in a Male World: Mount Hagen, New Guinea*, London and New York: Seminar Press.
(1988) *The Gender of the Gift: Problems with Women and Problems with Society in Melanesia*, Berkeley: University of Calfornia Press.
(1992) *After Nature: English Kinship in the Late Twentieth Century*, Cambridge and New York: Cambridge University Press.
(1999) *Property, Substance and Effect: Anthropological Essays on Persons and Things*, New Brunswick, NJ: Athlone Press.

SARAH FRANKLIN

Streck, Bernhard

b. 1945, Mannheim, Germany

Streck's main interest has long been the ethnography of the Sudan and particularly of the cultures along the River Nile, on which he published a general account in 1982, before conducting an ethnographic research programme together with F.W. Kramer. The theme was the perception of the external world and of global trends among marginalised groups, who are responding to rapid change by expanding, rather than revising, their traditional understanding of the world.

A second field of interest for Streck is the history of the discipline, with a concentration on German cultural morphology and the relationship with National Socialism. While he is able to explain the relative re-evaluation of anthropology in the 1930s mainly through the colonial revivalism of the time, he sees in the anthropology of Leo Frobenius and Adolf E. Jensen a continuation of the mystical and romantic traditions, which in the interwar period tended to develop certain parallels with French surrealism.

As a third theme, since the 1970s, Streck has worked in the field of Gypsy studies, first on the fate of Gypsies in the Third Reich, then on Gypsy groups along the Nile, and, most recently, on 'service nomads' in the broader sense in the Middle East. In this current research project, the focus is on the relationship between economic complementarity and cultural dissidence, as these are encountered all over the world, in connection with ethnic belonging and specialised niche economies.

Education

Ph.D. Johann Wolfgang Goethe-Universität Frankfurt am Main, 1975
Habilitation, Johannes Gutenberg-Universität Mainz, 1991

Fieldwork

Kenya, 1972, 1973

Sudan, 1975–86

Key Publications

(1996) *Die Halab – Zigeuner am Nil* (The Halab – Gypsies on the Nile), Wuppertal: Edition Trickster im Hammer-Verlag
(2000) *Ethnologie und Nationalsozialismus* (Ethnology and National Socialism), Gehren: Dr. Reinhard Escher

WERNER SCHIFFAUER

Stuchlik, Milan

b. 1932, Vienna, Austria

d. 1980, Belfast, UK

Milan Stuchlik studied ethnology and archaeology at Charles University, Prague, where he introduced the study of social anthropology in the 1960s. Between 1956 and 1968 he was on the staff of the Naprstek Museum of Ethnology (as keeper of the South Seas and Indonesian Collections). Following his fieldwork among the Mapuche of Chile, he lectured in anthropology at Universidad de Concepción in Chile (1969–70) and at the Catholic University Temuco (1971–3). He was a lecturer in anthropology at Queen's University, Belfast, from 1975 until his premature death in 1980. In 2001 he was posthumously awarded the Order of Bernardo O'Higgins by the state of Chile.

Milan Stuchlik's work contributed significantly to the field of theory and methodology in social sciences. He also won a reputation as an inspiring lecturer. At Belfast, Stuchlik was a chief contributor to the four volumes of the Queen's University Papers in Social Anthropology, which explored and developed interpretive approaches in social anthropology. Together with Ladislav Holy, a fellow Czech-born anthropologist, Stuchlik chaired the 1980 annual conference of the Association of Social Anthropologists (ASA) and edited its accompanying volume, *The Structure of Folk Models* (1980). In their seminal *Actions, Norms and*

Representations: Foundations of Anthropological Enquiry (1983), Stuchlik and Holy argue that a qualitative difference between actors' knowledge and explanations and anthropologists' knowledge and explanations cannot be upheld. Instead, anthropologists' explanations are only acceptable if in explaining actions they do not change the meaning that these actions have for the actors themselves, that is, actors' meanings must not be replaced by those of anthropologists.

Education

Ph.D. Charles University, Prague, 1962

Fieldwork

Mapuche, Chile, 1968–9

Key Publications

(1976) *Life on a Half Share: Mechanisms of Social Recruitment among the Mapuche of Southern Chile,* New York and London: St Martins.

with Holy, Ladislav (1983) *Actions, Norms and Representations: Foundations of Anthropological Enquiry,* Cambridge, UK: Cambridge University Press.

ALEXANDER HUGO SCHULENBURG

Sturtevant, William C.

b. 26 July 1926, Morristown, New Jersey, USA

William C. Sturtevant is a leading museum anthropologist and a noted ethnographer and ethnohistorian. As an undergraduate anthropology major he participated in archaeological work at Chaco Canyon, and studied in a summer programme at UNAM in Mexico City. Among his teachers at Berkeley he particularly credited Mary Haas in linguistics and John Rowe and David Mandelbaum in anthropology. At Yale, he continued his training in linguistics with Floyd Lounsbury (who was also his dissertation adviser) and Bernard Bloch, and

was much influenced by Wendell Bennett, Ralph Linton, and Cornelius Osgood. He saw linguistic approaches as critical to cultural anthropology, and wrote extensively in the 1960s on ethnoscience.

Sturtevant initiated fieldwork with the Florida Seminole in 1950, working closely with medical practitioner, Josie Billie. His dissertation, a study of Seminole medical beliefs and practices, remains an important work in the anthropology of southeastern Indians, particularly for its contributions to ethnobotany. He was an early and active advocate of ethnohistory, emphasising that it should involve 'the conceptions of the past shared by the bearers of a particular culture' (1964: 100). His ethnohistorical research has largely focused on eastern North American Indians, and on the early colonial period in the West Indies. He has published on Native American ritual and material culture, and early Euro-American depictions of American Indians. He is also the general editor of the *Handbook of North American Indians.*

In 1956 Sturtevant joined the Bureau of American Ethnology (BAE), rising to the rank of general anthropologist. When the BAE was merged into the National Museum of Natural History in 1965 he became that institution's curator of North American ethnology. He remains there to this date. He has done extensive research in museum collections, and is a strong proponent of their importance to the discipline of anthropology. Sturtevant taught at Yale before joining the Smithsonian, as adjunct professor at Johns Hopkins University (1974–89), and was a visiting fellow at Oxford University in 1967–8 and 1986–7. He received an honorary LHD from Brown University in 1996. He is active in professional organisations, and widely recognised for his analytical skills and his breadth and depth of knowledge.

Education

BA University of California, Berkeley, 1949
Ph.D. Yale University, 1955

Fieldwork

Seminole Indians, 1950–67, 1985, 1999–2002
   (22 months)
Iroquois Indians, 1952–65 (8 months)
Burma, 1955, 1963–4 (12 months)

Key Publications

(1955) 'The Mikasuki Seminole: medical
   beliefs and practices', Ph.D. dissertation,
   Yale University.
(1964) 'Studies in ethnoscience', in A. Kimball
   Romney and Roy Goodwin D'Andrade (eds)
   *Transcultural Studies in Cognition. American Anthro-
   pologist Special Publication* 66, 3, Part 2,
   Washington: American Anthropological Association, pp. 99–131.
(1973) 'Museums as anthropological data
   banks', in Alden Redfield (ed.) *Anthropology
   beyond the University*, Southern Anthropological
   Society Proceedings 7, Athens: University of
   Georgia Press.
(1976) 'First visual images of Native America',
   in Fredi Chiappelli (ed.) *First Images of America:
   The Impact of the New World on the Old*, Berkeley:
   University of California Press.

Further Reading

Merrill, William L. and Goddard, Ives (eds)
   (2002) *Anthropology, History, and American Indians:
   Essays in Honor of William Curtis Sturtevant*,
   Smithsonian Contributions to Anthropology
   44, Washington, DC: Smithsonian Institution Press.

FREDERIC W. GLEACH AND JASON BAIRD JACKSON

Sutton, Peter

b. 4 September 1946, Melbourne, Australia

Peter Sutton came to anthropology in 1975
after linguistic fieldwork and engagement with
some remarkable people sharpened his interest
in Aboriginal culture and society. He spent two
years with Wik-speaking people at remote
Cape Keerweer and elsewhere, focused on

speaking as social action and as the main stuff
of social organisation.

From the South Australian Museum, Sutton
organised an outstanding exhibition of Aboriginal art and took it to American and
Australian venues. Sutton (1988) was its
magnificent companion with essays on the
role of form and composition on visual effect
and aesthetic response, the relationship between the structure of artistic representations
and the things and events they signify, and the
history of Aboriginal art and its study.

A contract anthropologist from 1979–84,
and 1991–onwards, Sutton has worked on
many land claims, and he has encouraged the
development of higher standards of anthropological education and practice, and a
national ethics code. In a Queensland land
claim, he persuaded the Land Tribunal to look
beyond oral tradition and consider the clai-
mants' contemporary Aboriginal tradition to
include anthropological writings, family
photographs, cassette tapes, and the like.

Sutton's early papers argued with solid
evidence against the Tindale–Birdsell dialectal
tribe model of classical Aboriginal social
organisation, and 'People with "politicks"'
(Sutton and Rigsby 1982) developed a view
differing from Sharp's widely known 'People
without politics'.

Since the 1992 Mabo Decision, Sutton has
written original papers and monographs on
Aboriginal social organisation and land tenure
as they relate to 'native title', the rights and
interests in land and waters recognisable by
Australian law that some Aboriginal groups
hold under traditional law and custom. Sutton
(1996) argued that traditional-customary
Aboriginal land tenure continues to inform
contemporary thought, feelings, and action in
remote and settled Australia, while his 1998
monograph develops a post-classical continent-
wide model where cognatic descent groups
('families of polity') have developed from
older patriclans, and language-named tribes
('new tribes') have emerged as significant
regional land-holding groups. His work,
underpinned by indigenous language fluency
and a good ear, displays wide-ranging scholar-

ship, uncompromising realism, and attention to the tensions between individual autonomy and collectivism in social life.

Education

BA (Hons) University of Sydney, 1970
MA (Hons) Macquarie University
Ph.D. University of Queensland, 1979

Fieldwork

Tasmania, 1969
Far North Queensland, 1970–onwards
Northern Territory, 1979–onwards
New South Wales, 1983
South Australia, 1983–4, 1984–5, 1989, 1995, 1996

Key Publications

with Rigsby, B. (1982) 'People with "politicks": management of land and personnel on Australia's Cape York Peninsula', in N. Williams and E. Hunn (eds) *Resource Managers: North American and Australian Hunter-Gatherers*, Boulder, CO: Westview Press.

(ed.) (1988) *Dreamings: The Art of Aboriginal Australia*, New York: The Asia Society Galleries & George Braziller; Melbourne: Viking/Penguin.

(1996) 'The robustness of Aboriginal land tenure systems: underlying and proximate customary titles', *Oceania* 67: 7–29.

(1998) *Native Title and the Descent of Rights*, Perth: National Native Title Tribunal.

BRUCE RIGSBY

Swedenburg, Ted

b. 7 December 1949, Staten Island, New York, USA

Ted Swedenburg pioneered the anthropological study of popular culture and wrote an important ethnography of Palestine. His insightful writing about ethnographic practice in contexts of political violence contributed to debates about representation, and his theoretically sophisticated work on Palestine helped revitalise Middle East ethnography in the 1990s.

Memories of Revolt innovatively applies Foucaultian theories of discourse and Gramscian notions of hegemony to ethnographic practice. Swedenburg illuminates current hegemonic struggles in Palestine by analysing stories Palestinians tell about their past. This focus on popular memory serves political, methodological, and theoretical purposes. Politically, the elicited oral history revoices a silenced Palestinian history. Methodologically, questions about the past allow interviewees to say indirectly what they find difficult to say directly. Theoretically, critical analysis of narrative speech shows how hegemony is produced and resisted through the mediation of cultural symbols.

Subsequent work has focused on popular music in the Arab Middle East. Studies of (Algerian) Rai music in France and (Israeli) pop music in Egypt show the complex interweaving of power and resistance in modern transnational flows of culture.

Education

BA American University of Beirut, 1974
MA University of Texas, Austin, 1978
Ph.D. University of Texas, Austin, 1988

Fieldwork

Palestine (Occupied Territories) and Israel, 1984–5, 1992, 1993
France, 1992
Egypt, intermittently 1994–6, 1997, 1998, 2000
Morocco, 1999

Key Publications

(1995) *Memories of Revolt: The 1936–39 Rebellion and the Struggle for a Palestinian National Past*, Minneapolis: University of Minnesota Press.

(2000) 'Saida Sultan/Danna International: transgender pop and the polysemiotics of sex, nation, and ethnicity on the Israeli–Egyptian border', in W. Armbrust (ed.) *Mass Mediations: New Approaches to Popular Culture in the* *Middle East and Beyond*, Berkeley: University of California Press.

DANIEL LEFKOWITZ

Tambiah, Stanley Jeyaraja

b. 16 January 1929, Colombo, Ceylon (now Sri Lanka)

Although S.J. Tambiah first established his reputation within social anthropology with essays on such classical anthropological topics as kinship, systems of classification, and ritual (see *Culture, Thought, and Social Action*), it was his monumental trilogy of monographs on religion, society, and polity in Thailand that gained him international renown extending beyond the discipline. This trilogy, of which *World Conqueror and World Renouncer* achieved greatest acclaim, pioneered an interdisciplinary approach that synthesised the heretofore separate fields of social anthropology, history, and Buddhist studies in order to chart processes of social reproduction and social transformation in Thai society from medieval times to the late twentieth century. Tambiah particularly focused on the key legitimising relationship linking the Buddhist *sangha* (monastic order) and kingship (or political authority, more generally). This project established a lifelong commitment to situating ethnographic research on local communities within larger analytic frameworks involving the state, world religions, and other global forces (including colonialism, international capitalism, and mass communications). Tambiah thereby questioned the conceptual dichotomy that had separated 'little traditions' from 'great traditions', and he redefined the ontological

status of fieldwork within larger research projects. At the same time, his detailed field studies of fully historicised local cultures also destabilised many assumptions about the homogenising, uni-directionality of modernisation.

Tambiah's stock in trade in these studies was the construction of social complexes known as 'totalities' in which he interrelated various analytic domains within total sociocultural formations – encompassing economic, political, and religious phenomena. His most famous totality – the 'galactic polity' – adapted a set of spatial and hierarchical relations laid out in the Buddhist cosmological design of the mandala in order to explicate the segmented, modularly replicative, and constantly shifting political relations amongst centrally located kings and peripheral clients in the pre-colonial kingdoms of Southeast Asia. One of Tambiah's major accomplishments in this regard was to develop modes of analysis that were generated from within the concerns and referential coordinates of those societies under scrutiny rather than imposing from outside Western models of sociopolitical organisation and normative behavioural expectations.

In constructing these totalities, however, Tambiah avoided presenting Thai society as a cybernetically integrated system smoothly reproducing itself without changes over time. Rather he revealed how all social formations contained tensions and contradictions that became the locus of social contestation and cultural innovation. Thus Tambiah recognised that historical transformation has always co-existed with social persistence and has shown how these twinned processes combine into distinct amalgams that brace the flows of human history.

Since the early 1980s, Tambiah increasingly has turned his attention to the analysis of ethnic violence and communal conflict in Sri Lanka, India, and Pakistan. His numerous writings on this topic, culminating in the book, *Leveling Crowds*, rebut primordialist claims that these conflicts – between Tamils and Sinhalese in Colombo, or Hindus and Sikhs in New Delhi, or Pathans and Muhajirs in Karachi – are unchanging, age-old antagonisms. Instead, through such analytic constructs as 'focalisation' and 'transvaluation', Tambiah has charted how 'traditional' forms of social difference – which tend to be more context-bound, multiply constituted, and temporally contingent – have been transformed into context-free, monovalent, and absolute forms of social difference. In charting the emergence of this new type of social dichotomisation, he plots the role of mass media and other forms of state-sponsored mass mobilisation, the introduction of certain democratic forms, particularly as associated with party politics, and spreading global capitalism.

Within this major body of work, Tambiah also revealed much about the social texture of violence itself. He showed that violent acts are not simply bestial expressions of atavistic aggression. Rather, through his concept of the 'ritualisation of violence', Tambiah highlighted how violent acts are culturally constituted within broader webs of signification. Thus Tambiah identified modes, sequences, and patterns of ethnonationalist violence that are understandable to indigenous perpetrator and victim alike. Finally, Tambiah has also explored the social psychology of the crowds that perpetrate violence, thereby enabling him to explicate processes through which individual participants merge into collectivities and how these crowds then generate the heightened psychic states that unleash the spasmodic convulsions of collective brutality.

Education

BA University of Ceylon, 1951
Ph.D. Cornell University, 1954

Fieldwork

Ceylon/Sri Lanka, 1956–9
Thailand (particularly Bangkok and the northeast), 1960–3, 1965, 1966, 1971, 1974, 1978–9

Key Publications

(1976) *World Conqueror and World Renouncer: A Study of Buddhism and Polity against a Historical Background*, Cambridge, UK: Cambridge University Press.
(1985) *Culture, Thought, and Social Action: An Anthropological Perspective*, Cambridge, MA: Harvard University Press.
(1990) *Magic, Science and Religion, and the Scope of Rationality*, Cambridge, UK: Cambridge University Press.
(1996) *Leveling Crowds: Ethnonationalist Conflicts and Collective Violence in South Asia*, Berkeley: University of California Press.

NORBERT PEABODY

Tanaka, Jiro

b. 1941, Kyoto, Japan

Jiro Tanaka started his initial field research during the late 1960s among the G/wi and G//ana of the central Kalahari San. Through this research, he depicted their subsistence economy and social structure, and showed their adaptation strategies to the harsh arid environment. This focus on indigenous strategies of adaptation to their natural environments characterises his succeeding research as well.

After finishing his fieldwork in the Kalahari, Tanaka shifted his research field to other African societies, and with his young colleagues conducted extensive comparative research on societies in various kind of environments, ranging from Mbuti Pygmies in Zaïre to East African pastoralists like the

Rendille and Pokot. He compared the adaptation strategies of these societies according to their environments.

In the early 1980s, Tanaka returned to the Kalahari. Since then, he has been investigating social changes in San society. Though he noted the devastating influence of the world economy and nation-state as the primary factors of this change, he also attended to the importance of the active role the San played in this process. Various petty enterprises such as smallstock herding and agriculture were depicted as new strategies of adaptation.

Based on careful field research and detailed ethnographic data, Tanaka's work produces vivid image of peoples who survive with ingenuity in harsh ecological as well as political environments.

Education

BA Kyoto University, 1964
MA University of Tokyo, 1970
Ph.D. Kyoto University, 1974

Central Kalahari San, Republic of Botswana, 1966–8, 1971–3, 1982, 1984, 1988, 1990

Rendille, Republic of Kenya, 1974–5
Pokot, Republic of Kenya, 1978

Key Publications

(1980) *The San: Hunter-Gatherers of the Kalahari: A Study in Ecological Anthropology*, Tokyo: University of Tokyo Press.
(1994) *Saigono Shuryou Saishuumin: Rekishino Nagareto Bushman* (The Last Hunter-Gatherers: Bushmen Viewed from Historical Perspective), Tokyo: Doubutsusha.

YUKIO MIYAWAKI

Tantaquidgeon, Gladys

b. 15 June 1899, Mohegan, Connecticut, USA

d. 1 November 2005, Mohegan, Connecticut, USA

Gladys Tantaquidgeon was born in the Mohegan homeland of Uncasville, Connecticut, where she briefly attended grammar school. Three tribal elders, Emma Baker, Lydia Fielding, and Mercy Ann Nonesuch Mathews, whom she referred to, respectfully, as 'grandmothers', provided most of her education. From 1919–29, Gladys attended the University of Pennsylvania where she received training from anthropologist, Frank G. Speck.

Her subsequent articles on the Wampanoag Tribe, and herbal medicine monograph on the Lenni Lenape (Delaware), Nanticoke, and Mohegan, offer insider-interpretations of Native American medicine and spirituality.

In 1931, Gladys joined her brother, Harold, and father, John, in co-founding Tantaquidgeon Indian Museum, the oldest Indian-owned and operated museum in America. She was recruited by the Commissioner of Indian Affairs, John Collier, to serve as a community worker on the Yankton Sioux Reservation in South Dakota in 1934, and from 1938–47 promoted Indian art for the newly formed Federal Indian Arts and Crafts Board.

Although selected to become Medicine Woman at five years of age, Tantaquidgeon was not installed in that position until 1992. She has also been honoured with membership in the Connecticut Women's Hall of Fame and the National Organization for Women's Harriet Tubman Award.

Education

Attended University of Pennsylvania, 1919–29
Honorary Ph.D. University of Connecticut, 1987
Honorary Ph.D. Yale University, 1994

Fieldwork

Interviews (at University of Pennsylvania) with Witapanoxwe, Lenni Lenape Medicine Man, 1930
Gay Head and Mashpee, Massachusetts, 1929–31
Indian River Hundred, Sussex County, Delaware, 1921–30

Key Publications

(1942) *A Study of Delaware Indian Medicine Practice and Folk Beliefs*, Harrisburg: Pennsylvania Historical Commission, (reprinted in 1972 and 1995 as *Folk Medicine of the Delaware and Related Algonkian Indians*, Harrisburg: Pennsylvania Historical Commission).

Further Reading

Fawcett, Melissa Jayne (2000) *Medicine Trail: The Life and Lessons of Gladys Tantaquidgeon*, Tucson: University of Arizona Press.

MELISSA J.F. TANTAQUIDGEON

Taussig, Michael

b. 1941, Australia

Like many of anthropology's original contributors, Taussig came indirectly to the subject after previous training. Having worked as a doctor in Colombia aiding rural Marxist guerrillas, Taussig wrote his first book in Spanish about the history of the conflict. The traces of this violence, slavery, and liberation have marked much of his future work and have been variously developed as a way of understanding the impact of colonialism in South America.

Unlike many anthropologists, Taussig's intellectual genealogy is from outside the conventional boundaries of the subject. A consistent authority is Walter Benjamin, whose interwar reflections are reworked to release the various South American histories from their 'once upon a time' narrative. If the discipline's ancestors, or current practitioners, are mentioned it is normally to criticise. Witness the attack on Sidney Mintz and Eric Wolf, ostensibly his allies in placing local phenomena in wider socioeconomic transformations, such as Taussig did in his first book in English (1980).

More constructively, this critical proclivity has addressed central topics in the anthropological canon, namely shamanism, magic, healing, ritual, and aesthetics. In each case, a fresh perspective is brought to bear by deconstructing a bundle of assumptions. By linking contemporary folk healing with the rubber barons' atrocities committed against Peruvian Amazon Indians in the late nineteenth and early twentieth centuries, shamanism is revealed to be a complex historical artefact, constantly reinventing itself. For Taussig, it is the shaman's capacity to disrupt order and defy definitions that allows for the possibility of recovery, and even redemption. In *Mimesis and Alterity*, this theme is developed by considering how a mode of imitation is an act of harnessing the power of what is portrayed. This local project is 'mimetically at one with what it attempts to represent'. In so doing Taussig revisits James Frazer's ideas on sympathetic and contagious magic, showing them to be indistinct principles: the copy contains traces of the original in precisely the same way as the part is linked to the whole. It is the Western dissociation of seeing and tactility that prevents such an understanding.

What has linked these areas is a concern with the politics of representation. Throughout *Shamanism* (1987) the reader is told that 'writing against terror' cannot be confined to the conventional organisation of ethnographic knowledge. So montage is employed, borrowed both from cinematic representation and Benjamin, juxtaposing images, events, and people. In *The Magic of the State* this took the form of a novel, creating an imaginary but real state. Indeed the desire to embrace the fantastic in the mundane as well as the banality of terror is at the heart of Taussig's contribution. Neither a rational nor an empirical explanation of capitalism and modernity is enough. Out of this blending in the artefact of writing, new forms of cultural perception are made possible. Unlike other critical assaults on anthropology, Taussig's have been more effective in addressing the inadequacies of existing anthropological paradigms and indicating fresh insights.

Education

MBBS University of Sydney, 1964
MA London School of Economics, 1967

Ph.D. London School of Economics, 1975

Fieldwork

Colombia, 1969–present
Venezuela

Key Publications

(1980) *The Devil and Commodity Fetishism in South America*, Chapel Hill: University of North Carolina Press.
(1987) *Shamanism, Colonialism, and the Wild Man*, Chicago: University of Chicago Press.
(1993) *Mimesis and Alterity*, New York: Routledge.
(1997) *The Magic of the State*, New York: Routledge.

MARK HARRIS

Tax, Sol

b. 30 October 1907, Chicago, Illinois, USA

d. 4 January 1995, Chicago, Illinois, USA

A tireless organiser, editor, and scholar, Sol Tax made innovative contributions to anthropology in many ways. He created 'action anthropology' and founded *Current Anthropology*; he did significant fieldwork in Mesoamerica and Native North America; and he was a leader in advocating self-determination for indigenous peoples.

The third of four children of Russian Jewish immigrants, Tax grew up in the progressive community of Milwaukee, Wisconsin. From an early age he believed in using political action to improve social problems. A class with Ralph Linton prompted Tax to major in anthropology, and he accompanied Beloit's Logan Museum expedition to North Africa in 1930. His undergraduate thesis demonstrated his holistic and anticipatory vision, attempting to integrate cultural and biological aspects of anthropology and exploring the relationships between pure and applied science, with special consideration of the informant/collaborator/patient. Ruth Benedict's Summer Ethnology Program at the Mescalero Indian Reservation, which he joined before entering graduate school, introduced him to working in Native North America. At Chicago, Tax worked most closely with A.R. Radcliffe-Brown and Robert Redfield.

After defending his dissertation (on Fox social organisation) Tax left for Guatemala, beginning eight years of close and productive collaboration with Robert Redfield as ethnologists for the Carnegie Institution of Washington. *Penny Capitalism*, a study in economic anthropology drawn from that research, was influential beyond the discipline. Tax became research associate at Chicago in 1940, and taught at the National School of Anthropology in Mexico, 1942–3. In 1944 he was appointed associate professor at Chicago, and professor in 1948.

Tax developed 'action anthropology' in the early 1950s, uniting the interests of the scholar in solving theoretical problems with the interests of the administrator in solving practical problems, involving one's subjects in the process as full participants. With roots tracing to his earliest work, action anthropology grew directly from 'The Fox Project', a fieldwork and community development training programme for graduate students with the Mesquakie Indians in Iowa. Tax saw ethnographic engagement as an important and necessary form of sociopolitical action, 'solving' problems and conflict through public debate; the process was modelled on consensus-building in Native societies he had worked with.

Beginning in the 1940s, as Tax published extensively and actively did fieldwork, he also became increasingly involved in international anthropological organisations. He was a key figure in the reorganisation of the American Anthropological Association in 1945–6. He edited the *American Anthropologist* (1953–5), three volumes from the 29th International Congress of Americanists, *An Appraisal of Anthropology Today* (1953) from a Wenner–Gren symposium, *Evolution after Darwin* (1960) from the Darwin Centennial, and numerous other projects, many derived from conferences he organised. He was the founding editor of *Current Anthropology* in 1958, establishing its holistic, dialogic, and international vision of the discipline, and served as its editor until 1974.

As a result of his work on behalf of indigenous peoples' rights, in 1960 President Kennedy invited Tax to organise a gathering of Native Americans to discuss the issues and problems of their communities. Convened in 1961, the American Indian Chicago Conference brought together over 500 Native people from over ninety different groups. A 'Declaration of Indian Purpose' was adopted emphasising the retention of cultural identities and self-determination, and the conference both symbolically ended federal termination policies and initiated Indian activism in the USA.

In the 1960s Tax also became involved in more general issues of social conflict, in the USA and beyond. He participated in conferences on urban conflict and the draft, and edited publications from each. He served on a UNESCO Commission (1963–5), directed the Center for the Study of Man at the Smithsonian (1968–76), and hosted the 1973 International Congress of Anthropological and Ethnological Sciences in Chicago; he also edited the ninety+ volumes of papers from that Congress. Tax retired from teaching in 1976, but remained professionally active until his death.

Education

Ph.B. University of Wisconsin, 1931
Ph.D. University of Chicago, 1935

Fieldwork

Algeria, 1930
Mescalero Apache Indians, 1931
Mesquakie (Fox) Indians, 1932–4, 1948–59
Guatemala, 1934–44
Mexico, 1942–3

Key Publications

(1952) 'Action anthropology', *América Indígena* 12: 103–6.
(ed.) (1952) *Heritage of Conquest: The Ethnology of Middle America*, New York: Cooper Square.
(1953) *Penny Capitalism: A Guatemalan Indian Economy*, Washington, DC: Smithsonian Institution Press.
Gearing, Fred, Netting, Robert McC., and Peattie, Lisa R. (eds) (1960) *Documentary History of the Fox Project, 1948–1959: A Program in Action Anthropology, Directed by Sol Tax*, Chicago: University of Chicago Department of Anthropology.

Further Reading

Rubinstein, Robert A. (ed.) (1991) *Fieldwork: The Correspondence of Robert Redfield and Sol Tax*, Boulder, CO: Westview Press.
Stocking, George W. (2000) 'Do good, young man': Sol Tax and the world mission of liberal democratic anthropology', in Richard Handler (ed.) *Excluded Ancestors, Inventible Traditions: Essays toward a More Inclusive History of Anthropology*, Madison: University of Wisconsin Press.

FREDERIC W. GLEACH

Tedlock, Barbara

b. 9 September 1942, Battle Creek, Michigan, USA

Barbara Tedlock has merged the disciplines of psychology, astronomy, performing arts, cognitive anthropology, and ethnomedicine to achieve a profound understanding of shamanism, divination, and cosmology. Her earlier work with the Zuni of New Mexico examined the agrarian and matriarchal society through legends, songs, ceremonies, and folk medicine. As a result of her later fieldwork with the Quiché-Maya of Momostenango the anthropologist became a Mayan daykeeper and seer. By undergoing formal training as a Quiché-Mayan calendar diviner she was able to provide a detailed, personal description of the cognitive and dialectic processes between diviner and client. Her work with the Mayan calendar also resulted in contributions to the understanding of Mayan cosmology and astronomy.

According to Tedlock the process of divination combines symbolism and dialogical narration to arrive at 'an inductive, intuitive and interpretative way of knowing that diagnoses, comforts, and heals' ('Divination as a way of knowing: embodiment, visualisation, narrative, and interpretation', *Folklore*, 2001, 112, 2: 194). She argues that it should not be excluded from objective scientific investigation. Instead, she calls for a deeper exploration of the ethnography of divination.

In her seminal work, *Time and the Highland Maya*, Tedlock explores the 'art of time' as it pertains to the Mayan calendar and the role of shaman-priest. It is her explanation of the latter that crosses into the field of medical anthropology. During the divination process the shaman experiences a unique 'speaking of the blood' similar to lightning passing through the body. This experience is unlike most divination processes that describe the moment as a pulsing through the body. In the revised edition of *Time and the Highland Maya* Tedlock offers a correlation between Mayan cosmology and Momostenango geography that eloquently ties modern Quiché-Mayan to the land of their fathers and gods.

Throughout Tedlock's work she argues for the validity of practising anthropology, a theory developed by Pierre Bourdieu, whereby the investigator acquires practical knowledge of an indigenous art such as divination in order to maintain a balance between objective and subjective observation. For Tedlock the voyage of self-discovery and the defining of the 'ethnographic self' are vital to cultural understanding. As a result her work on the physical transformation during divination, the anthropological and psychological interpretation of dreams, and her analysis of the *Mayan calendar* are infused with personal spirit. This allows her accounts to go beyond merely describing a culture to move one into a deeper

level of understanding through practical mastery.

Education

BA University of California, Berkeley, 1967
MA Wesley University, Connecticut, 1973
Ph.D. State University of New York, 1978

Fieldwork

Zuni Pueblo, New Mexico, 1969–70 and summers 1972, 1973, 1977, 1980, 1982, 1983, 1984, 1986, 2001, 2002
Highland Guatemala, 1975–6 and summers of 1979, 1988, 1989, 1992
Ulaanbaatar, Mongolia, July–August 1999

Key Publications

(1987) *Dreaming: Anthropological and Psychological Interpretations*, Cambridge, UK: Cambridge University Press.
(1992) *The Beautiful and the Dangerous: Encounters with the Zuni Indians*, New York: Viking.
(1992 [1982]) *Time and the Highland Maya*, Albuquerque: University of New Mexico Press.

CYNTHIA A. TYSICK

Tedlock, Dennis

b. 19 June 1939, St Joseph, Missouri, USA

Dennis Tedlock's work as an anthropologist, linguist, translator, and poet bridges the gap between ethnographer and subject. His earlier work focused on the Zuni of New Mexico; however, it is his later work with the Quiché-Maya of Guatemala for which he received world recognition. Through formal apprenticeship as diviner and keeper of the Mayan calendar, and active participation as a Mayan 'seer' Tedlock's personal engagement blurred the roles of ethnographer and informant. While somewhat unorthodox, this approach allowed him to fluently move between the objective and subjective worlds of anthropology.

Add to this his skill as a poet and the results are a scholarship infused with a fluidity that engages rather than merely informs.

Among his books are *Popol Vuh: The Mayan Book of the Dawn of Life*, winner of the PEN Translation Prize for Poetry, and *Finding the Center: Narrative Poetry of the Zuñi Indians*, nominated for the National Book Award in translation. In 1970 his work in ethnopoetics led him to found and co-edit *Alcheringa/Ethnopoetics*, the first magazine of tribal poetics, with Jerome Rothenberg.

As an ethnographer Tedlock relies on a dialogical discourse between observer and observed that promotes the informant to the role of cultural co-interpreter, whereby the anthropologist avoids observing solely through a 'Eurocentric' lens. His linguistic work on Mayan hieroglyphs employs a similar technique, relying on the informant to provide contextuality rather than engaging in static line-by-line translation. Throughout his work Tedlock acknowledges the intrinsic threads of Mayan mythology that have woven themselves into modern Mayan life, thus creating a 'living culture'.

His major contributions include his classic translation of the Mayan creation myth, *Popol Vul*, his use of oral tradition as a translation tool, and his active participation in the spiritual, political, and social world of the modern Mayan. However, it is his ability to give Mayan texts voice and context that may be his ultimate legacy.

Education

BA University of New Mexico, 1961
Ph.D. Tulane University, 1968

Fieldwork

Elton, Louisiana, spring 1963
Zuni, New Mexico, 1964–6, 1969–70, summer 1971, summer 1982, summer 1983, spring 1986
Gallup, New Mexico, summer 1972
Momostenango, Guatemala, summer 1973, summer 1975, 1976, October 1988

Ibadan, Oshogbo, Ife, and Iwo, Nigeria, summer 1978
Chichicastenango, Chinique, San Pedro Jocopilas, and Santa Catarina Ixtahuacán, Guatemala, summer 1979
São Félix do Araguaia, Mato Grosso, and Santa Izabel do Morro, Goiás, Brazil, November 1985
Rabinal, Guatemala, summer 1988, summer 1989, January 1998
Toledo District, Belize, November 1990, summer 1991
Ulaanbaatar, Mongolia, July–August 1999

Key Publications

(1972) *Finding the Center: Narrative Poetry of the Zuñi Indians*, New York: Dial Press.
(1983) *The Spoken Word and the Work of Interpretation*, Philadelphia: University of Pennsylvania Press.
(1986) *Popol Vuh: The Mayan Book of the Dawn of Life*, New York: Simon & Schuster.
(1993) *Breath on the Mirror: Mythic Voices and Visions of the Living Maya*, Albuquerque: University of New Mexico Press.

CYNTHIA A. TYSICK

Terray, Emmanuel

b. 1935, Paris, France

Having studied philosophy with Louis Althusser, Emmanuel Terray turned to anthropology after reading Claude Lévi-Strauss's *Tristes Tropiques* in the 1960s. He carried out fieldwork among the Dida of Ivory Coast, which led him to refine Lévi-Strauss's concept of generalised exchange. Terray differentiated between the beneficiary of the marriage (the future husband) and the author of the marriage (a relative of the husband), who formed a 'matrimonial triad' with the married female relative whose dowry was used to arrange the new marriage. Study of Dida society also impelled Terray to develop the concept of 'network'. Terray elaborated a fourfold categorisation of social groups (community, collection, reunion, and network) according to the criteria of common residence and common activity. Rather than an ethnic group, the Dida were a network of local communities.

In the late 1960s, Terray participated in the theoretical debates surrounding Marxist anthropology. He suggested a Marxist reading of Lewis Henry Morgan's *Ancient Society*, which he interpreted as an insightful theory of historical change. Claude Meillassoux's analysis of the Gouro provided proof to him that the categories of historical materialism could be applied to so-called primitive societies. According to Terray, however, there was not one single mode of production in 'primitive' societies, but at least two: the tribal mode of production (based on voluntary co-operation, common ownership of tools, and egalitarian redistribution of produce), and the lineage mode of production (based on exploitation of the younger villagers by the elders).

Terray then undertook a monumental historical study of the kingdom of Gyaman. The Gyaman originated from an alliance of warrior groups who founded a state at the end of the seventeenth century and came to be situated in today's Ivory Coast and Ghana. The ruling class, a federation of lineages, was identical with the state itself and expressed its superiority vis-à-vis the ruled in ideology and exterior signs. The state worked like a unit of exploitation, with the ruling class amassing riches extracted from slave labour and tributary payments.

Terray reinterpreted Clausewitz's treatise on war as a theory of rational action in situations of uncertainty. Terray assessed the contribution of Marxist theory to anthropology again in 1992, arguing that the social and economic categories should continue to be used, while metaphysical materialism, socioeconomic determinism, and the idea of communism as ultimate harmony should be abandoned.

Education

École Normale Supérieure, Paris, 1956–60
Agrégation/state examination in philosophy, 1960

Ph.D. École Pratique des Hautes Études, Paris, 1966
Thèse d'Etat/habilitation, Université Paris V, 1984

Fieldwork

Dida country, Ivory Coast, 1964–5
Gyaman kingdom, Ivory Coast and Ghana, 1967–84

Key Publications

(1969) *L'Organisation sociale des Dida de Cote-d'Ivoire: essai sur un village Dida de la region de Lakota* (The Social Organisation of the Dida of the Ivory Coast: An Essay on a Dida Village in the Lakota Region), Abidjan: Annnales de l'Université d'Abdjan, F series, vol. 1.
(1972) *Marxism and 'Primitive' Societies* (*Le Marxisme devant les sociétés 'primitives'* 1969), trans. M. Klopper, New York: Monthly Review Press.
(1995) *Une Histoire du royaume abron du Gyaman: des origines à la conquête coloniale* (A History of the Abron Kingdom of Gyaman: from Origins until the Colonial Conquest), Paris: Karthala.
(1999) *Clausewitz*, Paris: Fayard.

ANNE FRIEDERIKE MÜLLER

Thomas, Nicholas

b. 1960, Sydney, Australia

Nicholas Thomas has held appointments at the Australian National University, where he was the foundation director of the Centre for Cross-Cultural Research, at King's College, Cambridge, and at Goldsmiths College, University of London, where in 1999 he was appointed professor of anthropology.

Thomas's prolific writings have done much to develop a historical anthropology that counters the excesses of post-colonial theory by grounding the study of colonial culture in substantive historical and ethnographic research. In his writings on history and anthropology, Thomas takes anthropology to task for excluding temporal and historical processes, arguing that historical processes and their effects are integral to social systems. Ethnographic writing based on a personal knowledge and understanding of certain localities only is of limited relevance to a historical anthropology. Instead, a historical anthropology must offer a localised vision of the constitution and reconstitution of colonial power, not of communities imagined outside global relationships.

At the same time, Thomas is critical of postcolonial studies for its lack of engagement with either localities or subjects and for its attempt to combine substantive studies with a hopelessly general critique of the humanities. He also perceives a contradiction within postcolonialism between a desire to theorise and discuss colonialism and the resulting risk of assuming colonialism to constitute a single meaningful category or totality. In particular, Thomas sees a danger in imposing an order on the colonial experience that it would never have appeared to possess, had it not been made a distinct field of inquiry. Instead, Thomas's work on colonialism aims for an ethnography of colonial projects that acknowledges the effect of larger ideologies, yet notes their adaptation in practice. Thomas stresses that insights into the varied articulations of colonising and counter-colonial representations and practices can only be provided by localised theories and historically specific accounts.

Thomas's early work reflected on and resulted in monographs stemming from his fieldwork in the Marquesas Islands and on Fiji. Since the mid-1990s Thomas's work has focused on the innovation and cross-cultural exchange in settler societies, specifically with respect to Oceanic art, exploring the dynamic of dispossession and resistance, and the use of indigenous art traditions to assert the presence of native peoples and their claim to sovereignty. He has also published work on the cultural history of voyages and cultural encounters in the eighteenth- and nineteenth-century Pacific. Since 2000 he has been working on the cultural history of James Cook's voyages and their ramifications for Oceanic and European histories.

Education

BA Australian National University, 1982
Ph.D. Australian National University, 1986

Fieldwork

Marquesas Islands, 1984
Western Viti Levu, Fiji, 1988
Aotearoa, New Zealand, 1993–9 (intermittent)

Key Publications

(1991) *Entangled Objects: Exchange, Material Culture and Colonialism in the Pacific*, Cambridge, MA: Harvard University Press.
(1994) *Colonialism's Culture: Anthropology, Travel and Government*, Cambridge, UK: Polity Press.
(1996) *Out of Time: History and Evolution in Anthropological Discourse*, second edn, Ann Arbor: University of Michigan Press.
(1999) *Possessions: Indigenous Art/Colonial Culture*, London: Thames & Hudson.

ALEXANDER HUGO SCHULENBURG

Thornton, Robert J.

b. 1949, Denver, Colorado, USA

Robert Thornton's work is very much rooted in the intersection of ethnography, literature, and philosophy – the interest that was expressed in his writings on B. Malinowski during the early 1990s. This interest lead him to question the connection of anthropology and writing. In his paper on the rhetoric of ethnographic holism (originally presented at the 'Writing Culture' seminar), Thornton questions how it is that anthropologists and ethnographers construct and seek to understand 'social wholes'. What strategies are employed and how do they try to convince their readers of the 'authority' of their accounts? The issue is one of conceiving the relationship between text and social reality, and here Thornton moves beyond the 'dialectic' and 'dialogic' approaches. He suggests that the main strategy being used is one of the 'imagination of wholeness', as something that 'guarantees the facticity of "fact"'.

In looking at the role that imagination plays in the construction of anthropological works, Thornton allies himself with the so-called 'critical ethnography', or 'post-modern' or 'post-structural' anthropology. He comes close to 'cultural studies' in his interest in different aspects of culture, from space and time, to the ways of how local and general perceptions about the whole concept are shaped when it comes to culture and power. In his studies of culture, power, and traditional authority, as well as through the critique of simplifications in studies of Southern Africa, Thornton remains an important figure in contemporary Africanist anthropology.

Education

BA Stanford University, 1972
MA University of Chicago, 1974
Ph.D. University of Chicago, 1978

Fieldwork

Tanzania, 1974–6
Lowveld, South Africa, 1992–ongoing

Key Publications

(1980) *Space, Time, and Culture among the Iraqw of Tanzania*, New York: Academic Press.
(1988) 'The rhetoric of ethnographic holism', *Cultural Anthropology* 3, 3: 285–303.

ALEKSANDAR BOSKOVIC

Thurnwald, Richard

b. 1869, Vienna, Austria

d. 1954, Berlin, Germany

Richard Thurnwald can be described as the founder and leader of functionalist anthropology in Germany, even though this perspective, which he himself called 'funktionelle Soziologie',

was for historical reasons never able to achieve dominance over other tendencies in this country. By training Thurnwald was a lawyer, and he paid great attention to legal-anthropological questions throughout his life. At that time, as a consistent teetotaller, he was close to the life-reform movement, and in 1905 he founded the 'Gesellschaft für Rassenhygiene' [Society for Racial Eugenic] with the '*Sozialanthropologen*', Alfred Ploetz (1860–1940) and Ernst Rüdin (1874–1950). Ultimately he became interested in both physical and psychological anthropology, and conducted one of the first ethnopsychological tests in the field (1913). He also showed himself to be a pioneer in ethnography through his experiments with the phonograph and movie camera, continuing his interest in empirical research into his old age.

In 1926, the better-known figure of Bronislaw Malinowski (1884–1942) respectfully called Thurnwald a 'master model', and in fact Thurnwald's research in northeast New Guinea preceded Malinowski's in the Trobriand Islands. However, the classic figures of the later structural-functionalist school also accorded Thurnwald authority for his 'discovery' of reciprocity as the fundamental principle of economy, law, and social organisation in simple societies (cf. 1916). Thus his analysis of the social structure of Bánaro, a village in the Sepik region, which appeared in English in 1916 and in German in 1922, belongs among the key texts of modern anthropology, even though it is not based on particularly intensive contact with the inhabitants of the village.

Long before Malinowski too, Thurnwald saw one goal of anthropological empiricism to be the self-reflexivity of the white man with the help of the 'native's point of view'. In the interethnic field, which Thurnwald understood to have been layered and graduated from the earliest times, mutual perceptions acquired great significance, and processes of culture change and development were strongly influenced by imitation and psychological factors. Thurnwald subscribed to the so-called theory of layers, according to which the overlayering of agricultural groups by pastoralists created a precondition for the state and for 'higher' developments such as plough cultivation. On the other hand, what interested him in such complex relationships were sociopsychological processes, which, like other sociologists and social anthropologists, he called 'sifting', and which were also to be traced particularly in the newer developments of colonialism and urbanisation.

Thurnwald initially worked as an administrator in the Austro-Hungarian monarchy, then from 1901 for the Museum of Anthropology in Berlin. After research journeys to the South Seas lasting several years, he obtained an extraordinary professorship, first in Halle, then in Berlin. Despite several guest professorships at American universities (1931–2, 1935), he never acquired a chair of his own, probably because of his age. After the Second World War, his private institute became part of the newly founded Free University in West Berlin, where, together with his wife, Hilde, he devoted himself especially to the question of the integration of the refugees from the east.

Thurnwald, whose own teachers included the pan-Babylonists Friedrich Delitzsch (1850–1922) and Hugo Winckler (1863–1913), used his wide spectrum of interests, first, in founding the Zeitschrift für Völkerpsychologie und Soziologie [Journal for Comparative Psychology and Sociology] in 1925, in which Malinowski himself and later even Pitrim A. Sorokin (1889–1968) and Edward Sapir (1884–1942) participated, and which from 1932 bore the title Sociologus; and, second, in bringing his encyclopedic knowledge together in the volumes that appeared in 1931–5 under the title Die menschliche Gesellschaft in ihren ethno-soziologischen Grundlagen. Many of his publications of the 1920s and 1930s also showed him to be a 'revisionist' demanding the return of the former colonies to Germany and in general seeing a civilising challenge in the colonial 'task' ('the white man brings peace'). On the other hand, he showed himself to be one of the first anthropologists sensitive to problems of acculturation, demanding research into questions of modernisation and independent development. His ideas were partly carried further by his students, such as Herbert Baldus in Saõ Paulo, Wilhelm Emil Mühlmann in Heidelberg, Wolfram Eberhard in Berkeley, and Sigrid Westphal-Hellbusch in Berlin.

Education

Ph.D., jurisprudence, 1895
Venia legendi [lecture licence] für Ethnologie und Völkerpsychologie [comparative psychology], Halle University, 1919
Venia legendi für Völkerpsychologie, Soziologie und Ethnologie, University of Berlin, 1923

Fieldwork

Bosnia, 1897
New Guinea, 1906–9
New Guinea, 1913–15
East Africa, 1930–1
Bougainville, 1933

Key Publications

(1916) Bánaro Society. Social Organization and Kinship System of a Tribe of the Interior of New Guinea, Memoirs of the American Anthropological Association, Vol III, No. 4, Lancaster, PA.
(1931–5) Die menschliche Gesellschaft in ihren ethno-soziologischen Grundlagen (Human Society and Its Anthropological Foundations), 5 vols, Berlin/Leipzig: Walter de Gruyter.
(1932) 'The psychology of acculturation', American Anthropologist 34, 4: 557–69
(1935) Black and White in East Africa. The Fabric of a New Civilization. With a Chapter on 'Women' by Hilde Thurnwald, London: George Routledge & Sons.

BERNHARD STRECK

Tishkov, Valery A.

b. 6 November 1941, Sverdlovsk, Russia

Valery A. Tishkov started his academic career in Canadian ethnohistory with two books on pre-Confederation Canada and the first Russian version of the *History of Canada* (1982). His publications gave birth to Canadian studies within Russia. In the 1980s he studied indigenous peoples and published a general text on the contemporary Amerindian population of North America. His primary interests were in political status, historic and comprehensive claims, Indian government and movements.

Since 1990 he has focused on the ethnic factor in Russian transformation as well as on the theory and political practice of ethnicity. He has argued that ethnicity has a multifaceted role: it is the most accessible basis for political mobilisation; a means of controlling power and resources in a transforming society; and a therapy for the great trauma suffered by individuals and groups under previous regimes. Tishkov concludes that the Soviet and post-Soviet nations, as well as the current violent ethnopolitics, stem from decrepit doctrinal projects, from elitist efforts to build a state on ethnic principles and a society on exclusivist identities, and from political malfunctioning. Valery A. Tishkov brings a unique combination of conceptual sophistication and the first-hand experience of a scholar who has been a prominent participant in, as well as a close observer of, recent developments. Tishkov's anthropology is strongly policy-oriented. His appeal to intellectuals and politicians to desist from production of confrontational ethnic ideologies goes to the heart of the tragic processes that are underway and is broadly applicable in most parts of the contemporary world.

Valery A. Tishkov's theoretical challenge came also from his formula, 'Forget the nation' (2000), where he suggested a post-nationalist understanding of nationalism. He argued that the nation is a powerful metaphor that two forms of social groupings – polity and ethnic entity – are fighting to have as their exclusive property. There is no sense in defining states and ethnic groups by the category of nation. The latter is a ghost word, escalated to a level of meta-category through historical accident and the inertia of intellectual prescription.

His two fundamental encyclopedias on ethnic groups of Russia (1994) and ethnic groups and religions of the world (1998) present a comprehensive enterprise in ethnographic reference literature.

Education

BA University of Moscow, 1964
MA Moscow Pedagogical Institute, 1969
Ph.D. USSR Academy of Sciences, 1978

Fieldwork

Quebec and Ontario provinces in Canada, 1973–4, 1976
Indian reserves and indigenous communities in the USA, including Alaska and Hawaii, 1980, 1983, 1985
Canadian Arctic communities (Northern Quebec, Western Arctic), 1986, 1988
Chukotka, Western Siberia, Russia, 1969–72, 1989
North Caucasus, Russia, 1992, 1994, 1995, 1999

Key Publications

(1990) *Indigenous Peoples of North America*, Moscow: Nauka.
(1997) *Ethnicity, Nationalism and Conflict in and after the Soviet Union. The Mind Aflame*, London: Sage Publications.
(2000) *Political Anthropology*, Lewiston-Queenston-Lampeter: The Edwin Mellen Press.

ANDREY KOROTAYEV

Todorova, Mariia Nikolaeva

b. 1949, Sofia, Bulgaria

Trained as a historian, Todorova's work has had an impact on anthropology and other social sciences because it offers a framework for understanding Southeastern Europe as a historical region. She began by investigating archival materials (including parish records and Turkish censuses) on demographic and political issues, mostly for the eighteenth and nineteenth centuries, and later began to conduct social science-oriented interviews to provide an ethnographic context for historical materials related to national symbology and memories of communism. In *Imagining the Balkans* she coined the term 'Balkanism' to describe how Westerners constructed and instrumentalised an image of the Balkans; this is not an extension of Edward Said's concept of Orientalism and might even be said to be an opposing view. Perhaps one reason that her work resonates with readers is that it is based on years of research and writing on related issues. The book coined the term 'historical legacy' and synthesises a wide range of primary source material in Turkish and Slavic languages, including travellers' accounts and other archival sources. Historical synthesis is not the sole focus of the work; it also speaks to current issues in social sciences such as alterity, provides a topical and analytical assessment of the region viewed both from the inside and outside, and addresses theoretical issues pertaining to the means for analysing historical regions.

Education

BA University of Sofia, Bulgaria, 1971
MA University of Sofia, Bulgaria, 1971
PhD University of Sofia, Bulgaria, 1977

Fieldwork

Archival research in Bulgaria, Russia, England, France, and Greece, 1970–2002
Sofia and Karlovo, Bulgaria, 1998–2002

Key Publications

(1993) *Balkan Family Structure and the European Pattern: Demographic Developments in Ottoman Bulgaria*, Washington, DC: American University Press.

(1997) *Imagining the Balkans*, Oxford: Oxford University Press.

JUDITH A. RASSON

Tokarev, Sergei A.

b. 29 December 1899, Tula, Russia

d. 19 April 1985, Moscow, Russia

Tokarev was one of the key persons in twentieth-century Russian ethnography. He was already an active participant in scientific life by the early 1920s, first as a student of the Department of Ethnography of Moscow University (1922–5) and then as a graduate student in the History Institute (1926–8). He subsequently worked at his Alma Mater (1939–73) as a professor (from 1940) and as the head of the Department of Ethnography (1956–73). Apart from that Tokarev worked at the Central Museum of Ethnography (from 1929) and at the Institute of Ethnography as the head of the Department of America, Australia, and Oceania peoples (from 1943) and of the Department of European Peoples (from 1961).

During his long and productive scientific life Tokarev wrote more than 200 publications of different genres, from reviews and reports to fundamental monographs. The most significant of these works has reflected the widest spectrum of the author's investigations. So, his first handbook in Soviet ethnography is still the most influential Russian volume in this sphere not only for university students and graduates but also for specialists. It contains a huge range of information and is a rare example of efforts to resolve one of the most complicated methodological problems in ethnographic science, that is to represent the unity and diversity of the world culture using the example of a country with such a compound ethnonational structure as the USSR. In addition to a review of comparative literature, S.A. Tokarev drew on his own extensive field data and archives files concerning peoples of south and east Siberia, especially the Altaitsy, Buryaty, Hakassy, and Yakuty.

Tokarev also received recognition for his studies in foreign ethnography. He prepared a volume devoted to the population of Australia and Oceania, which appeared as part of the Soviet ethnographic series 'The Peoples of the World'. Published in the early 1950s, it is still one of the most comprehensive sources of ethnographic materials of this region. During the 1970–80s, Tokarev took part as both an author and editor in preparing a four-volume publication characterising the calendar rites and rituals of the European countries.

A whole series of subsequent publications by Tokarev were devoted to the problems of religion as a historical and cultural phenomenon. He studied the genesis, early forms, social meaning, and role of religious consciousness and practices.

Education

Diploma of the Department of History, Moscow State University (Soviet equivalent of MA), 1925

Kandidat nauk (Soviet equivalent of Ph.D.), History Institute, 1935

Doktor nauk (Soviet equivalent of Hab.Doc.), Department of History, Moscow State University, 1940

Fieldwork

Tuva, Altay, south Siberia, early 1930s

Hakassia, Sayany, south Siberia, early 1930s

Yakutia, east Siberia, 1934 (5 months)

Balkan countries, 1946 (4 months)

Trieste, Italy, 1947 (5 months)

Berlin, Leipzig, Germany, 1951–2.

Key Publications

(1958) *Etnographia narodov SSSR* (Ethnography of the Peoples of the USSR), Moscow: Vyschaya Shkola.

(1964) *Religia v Istorii Narodov Mira* (Religion in the History of the Peoples of the World), Moscow: Nauka.

(1966) *Istoria Russkoi Etnographii* (History of Russian Ethnography), Moscow: Vyschaya Shkola.

(1978) *Istoria Zarubezhnoi Etnographii* (History of Western Anthropology), Moscow: Vyschaya Shkola.

TATIANA UVAROVA

Tonkin, Elizabeth

b. 11 February 1934, Richmond, Surrey, UK

Elizabeth Tonkin's work with the Jlao Kru, a community of coastal Liberia, has contributed to our understanding of the nature of oral tradition, history, and identity. While the use of oral data as a methodology for writing African history had been accepted practice since the 1960s, Tonkin's work builds on this tradition by engaging in a theoretical discussion of oral tradition. Tonkin argues that oral history is a social practice that is shaped by each retelling. As a result a society's history becomes not an accurate representation of the past but rather an interpretation of the past based on the present audience's experiences, what Tonkin has called 'representations of pastness'.

Studying oral history through the interdisciplinary lens of anthropology, history, psychology, and literary criticism Tonkin captures the dynamic relativism of the historical 'message'. For Tonkin the transmission of oral accounts is a social action and as such must be studied in terms of its narrator, audience, place, and time. In this way the historical narrative becomes a moving representation of the people's social relationships. Theoretically oral historians may be tempted to place greater emphasis on self when performing an oral history but for Tonkin that is an important point, the teller as a reflective, self-conscious model. By serving as an example the teller provides the audience with a model to either follow or modify. Therefore, it is the society and not the individual who determines which parts of an oral history should be passed down as a 'truthful' reflection of the people's past.

Education

MA University of Oxford, 1961
D.Phil. University of Oxford, 1971

Fieldwork

Sasstown, Liberia, 1972, 1975–6
Monrovia, Liberia, 1980

Key Publications

(1992) *Narrating Our Pasts: The Social Construction of Oral History*, Cambridge, UK, and New York: Cambridge University Press.

CYNTHIA A. TYSICK

Tonkinson, Robert

b. 12 September 1938, Perth, Western Australia, Australia

Robert Tonkinson began his training in anthropology at the University of Western Australia in 1957, then completed Honours while working as a school teacher. He commenced fieldwork under the supervision of R.M. Berndt at Jigalong, Western Australia, in 1963, subsequently published as *The Jigalong Mob: Victors of the Desert Crusade* (1974). In 1969, he enrolled as a Ph.D. student at the University of British Columbia, under the supervision of K.L.O. Burridge; his research at Jigalong, and elsewhere in the Western Desert, has produced a wealth of finely grained articles on Aboriginal Australia. Research in Vanuatu began in 1966, on Efate and Ambrym Islands; a monograph, *Maat Village, Efate: A Relocated Community in the New Hebrides* (1968), was the first of many.

He taught at the University of Oregon, Eugene, during 1968–9 and 1971–80, and at the Australian National University, Canberra, during 1980–4, before taking up the chair in anthropology at the University of Western Australia. His wife, Myrna Ewart Tonkinson, has also taught at the University of Western Australia. He has a strong commitment to the development of the discipline and has supervised a large number of postgraduate students.

Education

BA (Hons) University of Western Australia, 1962
MA University of Western Australia, 1966
Ph.D. University of British Columbia, Canada, 1972

Fieldwork

Narrogin, Western Australia, 1962
Jigalong, Western Australia, 1963–95
Efate and Ambrym Islands, Vanuatu, 1966–99

Key Publications

(1974) *The Jigalong Mob: Victors of the Desert Crusade*, Menlo Park: Benjamin/Cummings.
(1978) *The Mardudjara Aborigines: Living the Dream in Australia's Desert*, New York: Holt, Rinehart & Winston (revised, second edn, 1991, *The Mardu Aborigines: Living the Dream in Australia's Desert*, Forth Worth: Holt, Rinehart & Winston.)

JOHN E. STANTON

Toren, Christina

b. 1947, Katoomba, New South Wales, Australia

For Christina Toren the key question driving her intellectual agenda is: how do we become who we are? This theme runs throughout her work, enabling her to explore mind and cognition in an anthropological context and to forge links between psychology, biology, history, and culture. For Toren, humans are the literal embodiment of history and she has set out to chart and account for this process, ethnographically. Concentrated fieldwork exclusively carried out in Fiji, over a 20-year period, has enabled Toren to develop a particular theoretical synthesis that explains how humans develop into particular kinds of people. For Toren, a person's mind is constituted over time, through intersubjective relations, in particular environments.

The roots of this theoretical synthesis lie in her early work on concepts of hierarchy in Fiji where, refining a Piagetian perspective, Toren explored young children's growing understanding of hierarchy. Using psychological techniques and participant observation she showed how, in the Fijian context, spatial relations inform peoples' social relations and, over time, come to constitute the particular cognitive patterns through which their culturally specific notions of hierarchy are realised. In this way Toren demonstrates how group processes enter into the cognition of individuals. Through this she was able to offer a culturally sensitive account of child development and it is this phenomenology of learning that characterises her unique contribution to the anthropology of childhood.

Education

B.Sc. University College, London, 1979
M.Phil. London School of Economics, 1980
Ph.D. London School of Economics, 1986

Fieldwork

Sawaieke, Gau, Fiji, 1981–3, 1990, 1993

Key Publications

(1990) *Making Sense of Hierarchy. Cognition as Social Process in Fiji*, London: The Athlone Press.
(1999) *Mind, Materiality and History. Explorations in Fijian Ethnography*, London: Routledge

ALLISON JAMES

Traweek, Sharon

17 June 1942, Inglewood, California, USA

Sharon Traweek's writing has compared US, Japanese, and European scientific communities, integrated anthropological analysis with historical scholarship, and explored gender studies, science and technology studies, and post-structural theory. Her research has contributed to the anthropology of knowledge by examining localised examples within which professional communities create and maintain cultural boundaries through craft and tacit knowledge. Traweek's graduate training prepared her to develop this unique interdisciplinary framework. Her dissertation committee at the History of Consciousness Program at the University of California at Santa Cruz included Gregory Bateson, James Clifford, Shelley Errington, Triloki Nath Pandey, Thomas Rohlen, Michelle Zimbalist Rosaldo, and Hayden White. Traweek's 1988 monograph, *Beamtimes and Lifetimes*, was an ethnographic study of Japanese and American high-energy physicists. Traweek's work revealed a congruency among the high-energy physicists' cultural constructions of time and space in everyday life, their knowledge systems, and material culture.

Education

BA University of California, Berkeley, 1964
MA San Francisco State University, 1966
Ph.D. University of California, Santa Cruz, 1982

Fieldwork

Stanford Linear Accelerator Center, Palo Alto, California
KEK (Japanese National Physics Laboratory), Tsukuba, Japan
Fermi National Accelerator Laboratory, Illinois
CERN (European Centre for Nuclear Research), Switzerland
DESY (electron synchrotron facility), Germany
Saclay Laboratory, France

Key Publications

(1988; paperback 1992) *Beamtimes and Lifetimes: The World of High Energy Physicists*, Cambridge, MA: Harvard University Press
(1993) 'An introduction to cultural, gender, and social studies of science and technology',

Journal of Culture, Medicine, and Psychiatry 17: 3–25.

BRIAN FREER

Tremblay, Marc-Adélard

b. 24 April 1922, Les Éboulements, Quebec, Canada

Marc-Adélard Tremblay has distinguished himself as a pioneer of social and cultural anthropology within Quebec and Canada. The most significant aspect of his role in the scientific community can be characterised as that of 'builder'. He was among the first Francophones from Quebec to receive training in anthropology outside the country. He worked to make the discipline better known in Quebec and Canada, showing the richness of its potential in the fields of teaching, research, and policy-making.

His research interests have principally centered on the social transformations within Acadian and Québécois societies, and on the impact of contact on the cultural identity of the Native people, the Acadians of Nova Scotia and the Francophones of Quebec. His interest in epidemiology and applied anthropology also led him to study the role of historical and sociopolitical factors in the production of social dysfunction and individual pathologies, as well as the institutions that manage social and health services.

Marc-Adélard Tremblay had been strongly influenced in the 1950s by his training at Cornell University under the leadership of Alexander H. Leighton. His theoretical orientations, methodological approaches, and research interests all bear the mark of that initial culturalist American influence. Educated in a university renowned for its teaching on quantitative and qualitative methods, he favors a positivistic, inductive, and empirical approach of social and cultural reality, based on the ethnography of tightly circumscribed communities (most often in a minority situation), as many anthropologists of his generation did, and the use of a variety of rigorous field methods to collect data (1968). Later in his career, however, he moved away from culturalist and functionalist frameworks to embrace a systemic approach.

His first ethnographic research in 1950 with the Acadian population of Stirling County led to the description of the everyday life of a village whose main occupation was forestry. For his Ph.D. thesis he then studied the socioeconomic and cultural changes in a semi-urban community of Portsmouth, particularly the factors leading to the Anglicisation of the Acadian community. One interesting result of that study was that the maintenance of the Acadian identity and the dynamism required to ensure the survival of the Acadian culture were displayed by the well-off, while the poor concentrated on the survival of their families, which often translated into a move towards acculturation. A later research in a well-integrated community provided a closer examination of the different factors in the social structure that acted as a deterrent to acculturation, such as the Acadian family, the kinship network, and the system of authority.

His research involvement with Native people is multifaceted and more difficult to follow throughout his career. One contribution, however, stands out. In 1964, along with H.B. Hawthorn of the University of British Columbia, he accepted the direction of a large multidisciplinary inquest mandated by the Canadian federal government to study all aspects of the administration of contemporary Amerindians of Canada. The resulting report, published in 1967, comprises two volumes. The second, associated more closely with Tremblay, dealt with questions of education, the structure of reserves, and Native identity. At the time of its publication, this report provided the most comprehensive synthesis of the living conditions of the Canadian Native peoples and of their aspiration for a native identity, based, as it is today, on territory, freedom of decision and action within autonomous political structures, and resources for development.

Yet Marc-Adélard Tremblay's most important research contribution has to do not with

Amerindian but with Quebec society. In 1965 he launched a vast ethnographic project on Quebec communities, which were undergoing rapid change at the time of the Quiet Revolution, beginning with those north of the St Lawrence River (Basse-Côte-Nord). That project lasted for more than ten years, involving a large number of collaborators and students, and yielded a wealth of important ethnographic data. In *L'Identité québécoise en péril*, he synthesises the various research findings to present us with a portrait of Quebec society over the course of a century.

Education

BA Laval University, 1949
MA Laval University, 1950
Ph.D. Cornell University, 1954

Fieldwork

Acadians, Nova Scotia, 1950–63
Navaho, New Mexico, 1952
Francophones, Quebec, 1949–50, 1956–7, 1959–60
Amerindians, Quebec and Canada, 1964–8
Inhabitants of Basse-Côte-Nord, Quebec, 1965–75

Key Publications

with Hughes, C., Rappoport, Robert N., and Leighton, Alexander H. (1960) *People of the Cove and Woodlot: Communities from the Viewpoint of Social Psychiatry*, New York: Basic Books.

with Hawthorn, H.B. (1967) *A Survey of Contemporary Indians of Canada: Political, Educational Needs and Policies*, 2 vols, Ottawa: Department of Indian Affairs and Northern Development.

(1968) *Initiation à la recherche dans les sciences humaines* (Initiation into Research in the Human Sciences), Montréal: Les éditions McGraw-Hill.

(1983) *L'Identité québécoise en péril* (The Québécois Identity in Peril), Québec: Les Éditions Saint-Yves.

CHANTAL COLLARD

Trouillot, Michel-Rolph

b. 1949, Haiti

Trouillot is a Haitian anthropologist, populist writer, world capital theorist, and comprehensive ethnographer who includes his formative experiences as a youth growing up under the Duvaliers' dictatorship in Haiti. Trouillot's work ranges through the whole Atlantic world, connecting global flows and patterns to the local islands and peasant islander lives. His initial research considers the historical continuity of the peasant on Dominica; how peasants are reproduced in the post-slave emancipation Caribbean. His thesis that peasants are 'part-economies' caught up in world capitalist development overturns previous ideas such as the originality of the peasantry (R. Redfield) and of peasantry as part-culture (A. Kroeber), and dispels the myth of the worldwide (pre-capitalist) proletarian peasantry.

Trouillot gained notoriety arguing that his Caribbean region is an 'open frontier' testing ground for neo-colonialism (US and French control of Haiti) and for anthropology: traditional anthropology, built upon cornerstones such as West/non-West dichotomies and the category of the ('simple') native, was challenged originally by the civilised free black Caribbean of the nineteenth century, and is challenged now by the heterogeneous, complex, and plural nature of these societies – historical 'prefabricated enclaves'. Multilevel ethnography combined with a historical methodology are Trouillot's preferred techniques with which to interrogate what he considers to be the West and its skewed and often racist production of history, capitalism, the Caribbean region, and anthropology itself.

Education

BA City University of New York, 1978
Ph.D. Johns Hopkins University, 1985

Fieldwork

Haiti, formative experiences

Dominica, 1979, 1980–1
England, 1982

Key Publications

(1988) *Peasants and Capital: Dominica in the World Economy*, London: The John Hopkins Press.

(1992) 'The Caribbean region: an open frontier in anthropological theory', *Annual Review of Anthropology* 21: 19–42.

JONATHAN SKINNER

Turnbull, Colin MacMillan (a.k.a. Lobsong Rigdol)

b. 24 November 1924, Harrow, UK

d. 28 July 1994, Kilmarnock, Virginia, USA

Colin MacMillan Turnbull remains one of the most well-known experts on the short-statured hunter-gatherers of Central Africa, sometimes called 'Pygmies' (although the term is widely considered pejorative today), research that was described in his best selling book, *The Forest People* (1961).

Born into an upper middle-class family, Turnbull rebelled against privilege and developed a deep-seated hatred for capitalism, and Western civilisation in general. He devoted himself to demonstrating that forms of culture, especially those found in Africa and South Asia, were superior to those found in the West. Turnbull's D.Phil. thesis, completed under the direction of Rodney Needham and E. Edward Evans-Pritchard at Oxford, and based on about two years of fieldwork, was a detailed ethnographic study of the independence of the Mbuti Pygmies, a group of people who had long been assumed to exist in a state of 'serfdom' under neighbouring farmer groups, such as the Bira and Lese. However, he did not complete his thesis until many years after he took up his first academic post as a curator of African culture at the American Museum of Natural History in New York City. During the 1960s he became a public

intellectual, appearing on a variety of national talk shows.

Additional fieldwork with the Mbuti was thwarted by political crises in Central Africa. He travelled instead to Uganda to study the Ik, hunter-gatherers who had been forcibly relocated into a barren region, and prevented from hunting on their traditional lands. Turnbull's book, *The Mountain People* (1973), chronicled the Ik's response to starvation, and argued that their culture had been so devastated that Ik had become cruel and inhumane. Turnbull called for a plan, never carried out, to have Ik dispersed across Uganda so that Ik society would never again reassemble. The academic community, led by Frederik Barth, called for his censure on the grounds that he had overstepped the boundaries of cultural relativism and had written a work that threatened the safety of his hosts. *The Mountain People* was a best-seller by academic standards and director Peter Brook adapted the book for the theatre.

Turnbull became increasingly isolated from the academic community. He devoted himself to advocacy for inmates on death row, and to his partner, African American anthropologist, Joseph Towles, with whom he lived in an openly gay relationship in rural Virginia. By the mid-1980s, Towles developed AIDS and Turnbull resigned from academic work to care for him. Upon Towles's death in 1988, Turnbull abandoned his name, travelled to Indiana, Samoa, and India, and in 1992 was ordained a Buddhist monk by the Dalai Lama. Turnbull returned to Virginia in 1994 where he died of AIDS under the name Labsong Rigdol.

Education

BA Magdalen College, University of Oxford, 1948
B.Litt. University of Oxford, 1957
D.Phil. University of Oxford, 1967

Fieldwork

Ituri Forest, Belgian Congo, 1954, 1957–8

Ituri Forest, Zaïre, 1970–2

Uganda, 1965–7

Key Publications

(1961) *The Forest People*, New York: Simon & Schuster.

(1973) *The Mountain People*, New York: Simon & Schuster.

(1983) *The Human Cycle*, New York: Simon & Schuster.

(1983) *The Mbuti Pygmies: Change and Adaptation*, New York: Holt, Rinehart & Winston.

ROY RICHARD GRINKER

Turner, Terence

b. 30 December 1935, Philadelphia, Pennsylvania, USA

Despite his early training in elite American institutions and his teaching positions at Chicago and Cornell universities, Turner is a maverick figure whose influence is largely the fruit of penetrating analyses criticising the static, non-dialectical, and apolitical orientation of structuralist and culturalist anthropology. Turner was at the forefront of the growing interest in symbolic anthropology during the 1960–70s within which he distinguished himself by his attention to temporality and structural hierarchies in studies of myth, ritual, and symbolic forms more generally. He looked to pragmatic approaches, as exemplified in Marx and Piaget, to comprehend how the construction of structures creates a differentiated unity that both inflects 'inward', in the development of individual orientations and values, and socioculturally, in the social reproduction of objective structures and values. Turner's ethnographic efforts have been devoted almost exclusively toward the indigenous Kayapo people of central Brazil. He has made the defense of Kayapo rights and livelihood a cornerstone of his professional efforts, and several ethnographic films on which he collaborated have brought the situation of the Kayapo to a large audience. After the mid-1980s, coinciding with the growing public activism of the Kayapo, Turner's writings noticeably departed from the grand-theory style of earlier efforts. Later writings seek to understand how the Kayapo's representation of their culture plays a part in their political struggles within a multiethnic state.

Education

BA Harvard University, 1957

MA University of California, Berkeley, 1959

Ph.D. Harvard University, 1965

Fieldwork

Pará and Mato Grosso, Brazil, 1962–6

Mato Grosso, Brazil, 1976

Papua New Guinea, 1976

Short visits to Kayapo villages in Brazil, 1989–2002

Key Publications

(1984) 'Dual opposition, hierarchy, and value: moiety structure and symbolic polarity in central Brazil and elsewhere', in J.C. Galley (ed.) *Différences, valuers, hiérchie*, Paris: Éditions de l'École des Hautes Études en Sciences Sociales, pp. 335–70.

(1995) 'Social body and embodied subject: the production of bodies, actors and society among the Kayapo', *Cultural Anthropology* 10, 2: 143–70.

WILLIAM H. FISHER

Turner, Victor Witter

b. 28 May 1920, Glasgow, UK

d. 18 December 1983, Charlottesville, Virginia, USA

The Ndembu numbered about 17,000 when Victor Turner, with his wife and intellectual comrade, Edith, arrived in 1950 as a research officer for the Rhodes–Livingstone Institute. Trained in British structural-functionalism to view society as a structure of positions, he began his genealogical surveys and household censuses. Ritual had low priority at the Institute, but he felt that he was missing something because he was constantly aware of the thudding of ritual drums outside the village. His first theoretical insight was that the structural-functionalist vision of social life was incomplete because there are aspects of society that stand outside hierarchical social structure. These disturbances in the smooth surface of everyday social life, or 'social dramas', erupt periodically in every society. They tend to play out in a sequence of four phases: (1) breach of a social norm; (2) mounting crisis and cleavage into opposing factions; (3) redressive action, frequently involving courts, laws, or public rituals; and (4) reintegration if the conflict is successfully resolved, permanent schism if it is not. Of particular significance are the public rituals and performances often found in the third phase. These rites of passage – the rituals that accompany transitions between states, such as changes of place, social position, or age – have three phases: (1) separation – detachment from a fixed point in the social structure; (2) limen (margin) – an ambiguous period of passage; (3) reincorporation – passage is consummated. The practices and symbols associated with the second, or liminal, phase form the heart of ritual and therefore constitute the heart of the social drama.

In the liminal phase of ritual, there is often an elimination of social structure in the British sense and an elaboration of symbolic and mythical structures as described by Claude Lévi-Strauss. Initiates in a puberty rite are often said to be sexless, possessing neither property, status, clothing, nor kinship position; at the same time, liminality is frequently likened to death, being in the womb, invisibility, darkness, bisexuality, the wilderness, and to an eclipse of the sun or moon. Turner utilised Claude Lévi-Strauss's dualisms to analyse symbols – e.g. life/death, male/female – but he argued that symbols are more than just bloodless abstractions; they evoke a visceral and emotional 'experience'.

Because of the absence of social structure, the passengers through a rite of passage are equals and comrades; this human bond, or communitas (Latin 'community') is often supposed to last a lifetime. Social life is a dialectical process between alternating phases of structure (societas), characterised by hierarchy, and anti-structure, characterised by communitas. The social world is a world in becoming, not a world in being; society is a process rather than a thing. This is Turner's processual view of society.

Turner extended the theory of liminality into modern industrial society with his modified notion of the 'liminoid'. Liminality is characterised by a freedom from social structure that opens up creative possibilities, a potential that also characterises performance genres in modern societies such as theatre, art, music, games, sports, and other forms of entertainment. Because liminoid performances are perceived as outside the 'real' world of work and politics, they provide moments of detached reflection on the status quo, or 'reflexivity', which can be potentially subversive and revolutionary. They thus share with liminal genres the potential to create new social forms.

Turner was a maverick explorer of the universe of ideas who felt compelled to seek out the liminal spaces between known structures. He charted paths between academic disciplines, including anthropology, religious and liturgical studies, history, folklore, drama, literary criticism, and psychology. He traced the very human capacity of symbol-making through historical and contemporary cultures as well as through the developing and industrialised worlds. In so doing, he gave us a greater appreciation of the humanity shared by us all.

Education

BA University College, London, 1949
Ph.D. University of Manchester, 1955

Fieldwork

Ndembu tribe, Mwinilunga District, Zambia (formerly Northern Rhodesia), December 1950–February 1952 and May 1953–June 1954

Gisu tribe, Uganda, autumn 1966

Multiple pilgrimage sites around Mexico City and in Mexico; Lough Derg, Croagh Patrick, and County Mayo, Ireland, 1969–72

Rio de Janeiro, Brazil, spring 1979

Key Publications

(1967) *The Forest of Symbols: Aspects of Ndembu Ritual*, Ithaca, NY: Cornell University Press.

(1969) *The Ritual Process: Structure and Anti-Structure*, Chicago: Aldine Publishing Co.

(1974) *Dramas, Fields and Metaphors: Symbolic Action in Human Society*, Ithaca, NY: Cornell University Press.

(1982) *From Ritual to Theater: The Human Seriousness of Play*, New York: PAJ Publications.

Further Reading

Ashley, K. (ed.) (1990) *Victor Turner and the Construction of Cultural Criticism: Between Literature and Anthropology*, Bloomington: Indiana University Press.

Babcock, B. and MacAloon, J. (1987) 'Victor W. Turner (1920–1983)', *Semiotica* 65, 1–2: 1–27.

SUSAN BROWNELL

Turton, David

b. 26 March 1940, London, UK

Turton's field research on the Mursi has focused on the relationships between long-term environmental change, warfare, and political identity. He has argued for the 'emergent' nature of political identity amongst the Mursi and their neighbours, seeing ethnicity as a product rather than a cause of war and migration. His study of drought responses and warfare amongst the Mursi led

to a broader interest in the study of 'natural' disasters, forced population displacement, including refugee movements, and in international humanitarian assistance. He has been editor of the journals, *Disasters* and *Man: The Journal of the Royal Anthropological Institute*, and director of the Refugee Studies Centre at the University of Oxford. He also has an interest in ethnographic film, having collaborated with Leslie Woodhead in making six documentary films for television (including *The Mursi*, *The Kwegu*, *The Migrants*, and *The Land is Bad*). He was co-founder of the Granada Centre for Visual Anthropology at the University of Manchester.

Education

Lic. Phil. Gregorian University, Rome, 1963

B.Sc. London School of Economics, 1967

Ph.D.(London School of Economics, 1973

Fieldwork

Lower Omo Valley, southwestern Ethiopia (Mursi), 1968–70, 1973–4, and frequent shorter visits between 1981 and 2002

Key Publications

with Crawford, P.I. (eds.) (1992) *Film as Ethnography*, Manchester: Manchester University Press.

(ed.) (1997) *War and Ethnicity: Global Connections and Local Violence*, New York: Rochester University Press.

KATSUYOSHI FUKUI

Tylor, Edward Burnett

b. 2 October 1832, London, UK

d. 2 January 1917, Wellington, Somerset, UK

Edward B. Tylor is considered one of the founders of social and cultural anthropology. In fact, anthropology has been referred to (by one of his contemporaries, F. Max Müller) as 'Mr Tylor's science'. Even without any formal university training (Quakers could not enter universities in nineteenth-century Britain), Tylor's travels (especially to Mexico in 1856) inspired him to write several scholarly monographs. Elected fellow of the Royal Society in 1871, Tylor was awarded an honorary doctorate from the University of Oxford in 1875. He helped establish the 'Anthropological Section' of the British Association and became its first president in 1884. In the same year, he was made reader in anthropology at Oxford, becoming the first professor of anthropology in 1896. Just about when the course of Diploma in Anthropology was established in Oxford, Tylor retired in 1909 and was knighted in 1912.

In the first sentence of *Primitive Culture*, Tylor provided a definition that would become the main reference point for the foundation of anthropology as a scholarly (he would have preferred 'scientific') discipline. The key concept of the new emergent discipline, culture, 'taken in its wide ethnographic sense is that complex whole which includes knowledge, belief, art, morals, law, custom, and any other capabilities and habits acquired by man as a member of society'. This definition of culture has become the key one, and all the scholars after Tylor had to work either with it, or around it. Culture is taken to be the primary determinant of civilisation – so in studying culture in all its aspects, one could determine the stages that 'mankind' had to pass in its long quest towards 'civilisation'. The whole project that Tylor undertook could be described as an exercise towards describing and understanding the past. By doing so, in the best tradition of evolutionary anthropology (of which he was the most prominent representative, along with his contemporary, L.H. Morgan), one could also learn about the mistakes that led to 'degeneration' of some past cultures – like in the cases of ancient Egypt and Central America, for example.

Tylor introduced several key concepts, such as animism, as well as the concept of 'survivals'. In an article published in 1866, he defined 'animism' as 'the theory which endows the phenomena of nature with personal life'. In *Primitive Culture*, this concept is used to introduce both discussions on mythology (chapters VIII–X) and on religion (chapters XI–XVIII). In the first instance, it is again taken to refer to an 'animation of nature', while in the second it means 'the belief in Spiritual Beings'. It is clear that in its second meaning animism can be characteristic of modern-day humans (both when Tylor was writing and today).

These 'survivals' were traits of ancient beliefs and social customs that have been preserved in contemporary societies, even though their original function and meaning were lost. Through exploring survivals among the 'uncivilised' peoples, Tylor hoped to show both the origin of modern concepts and customs, as well as some pointers for future development. In his attempts to explore and to formulate 'a definite theory of the Rise and Progress of Human Civilisation in early times', his evolutionist ideas seem odd by contemporary standards – although the idea that even 'primitives' had religion must have been quite revolutionary for the late nineteenth-century scientific community.

Tylor did not publish as much as many of his contemporaries. However, the fact that *Primitive Culture* was almost immediately translated into German and Russian shows the extent of his influence. He was very much aware of all the intellectual trends and currents of his time, and tried to incorporate them in his books. His last major book, *Anthropology*, although with some oversimplifications (especially when dealing with myths), is the first general textbook of an emerging discipline. It is to the credit of Tylor's impressive erudition and knowledge (he tried to incorporate all the current ethnographic data in the examples he was discussing) that his books (especially *Researches* and *Primitive Culture*) still provide an interesting read today.

Education

Doctor of Civil Laws, University of Oxford, 1875

Key Publications

(1865) *Researches into the Early History of Mankind and the Development of Civilisation*, London: J. Murray.

(1871) *Primitive Culture: Researches into the Development of Mythology, Philosophy, Religion, Language, Art and Custom*, 2 vols, London: J. Murray.

(1881) *Anthropology, an Introduction to the Study of Man and Civilisation*, London: Macmillan.

Further Reading

Marett, R.R. (1936) *Tylor*, London: Chapman & Hall.

Leopold, J. (1980) *Culture in Comparative and Evolutionary Perspective: E.B. Tylor and the Making of Primitive Culture*, Berlin: Dietrich Riemer Verlag.

ALEKSANDAR BOSKOVIC

U

Uberoi, J.P. Singh

J.P. Singh Uberoi is best known in anthropology for his reinterpretation of the findings of Bronislaw Malinowski on the Trobriand gift exchange system known as the kula. While pursuing postgraduate study at the University of Manchester, Uberoi analysed Malinowski's original data on the exchanges but focused on their implications for local political organisation. Uberoi argued that the Trobriand polity was a segmentary state, rather than a chiefdom as Malinowski had claimed; he also found that participants in the kula exchange sought individual political and economic gain rather than status within the kinship sphere. This was a significant counter-argument to Malinowski, who maintained that the kula could not be reduced to economic or political factors because it was a total exchange system connected to all spheres of collective life. For Malinowski, the kula provided evidence that self-interested economic action was not the sole or natural motive for human action.

Uberoi subsequently conducted fieldwork in Afghanistan on kinship and political organisation. He spent most of his professional career at the Delhi School of Economics in India. He published three works on the aspects of the cultural history of European modernity and one book on the religious and social organisation of Sikhism.

Key Publications

(1962) The Politics of the Kula Ring: An Analysis of the Findings of Bronislaw Malinowski, Manchester: University of Manchester Press.
(1996) Religion, Civil Society and the State: A Study of Sikhism, New Delhi: Oxford University Press.

MARY E. HANCOCK

Umesao, Tadao

b. 13 June 1920, Kyoto, Japan

Tadao Umesao is considered the most influential anthropologist of post-war Japan as well as the founder of the National Museum of Ethnology, one of the largest research institutes of anthropology in the world. He has played a vital role in shaping Japanese identity through the influential theory developed in his 1967 publication, 'An introduction to the ecological history of civilization', as well as in promoting the spread of anthropology in Japan in a variety of other ways.

He was at first educated in animal ecology and received the degree of D.Sc. at the Faculty of Science of Kyoto University in 1961. His first fieldwork as a young anthropologist was, however, carried out earlier in Mongolia from 1944 to 1945 under the direction of Dr Imanishi Kinji. Umesao had intended to study the Mongol system of animal husbandry from an ecological point of view but became interested in their nomadic way of life. He published several detailed articles on the system of milk production among the Mongols during the 1950s and in due course his interest was drawn to the interaction between animals and humans.

In 1963–4, he conducted fieldwork among the Datoga, a Nilotic people, in northern Tanzania, where he focused on their interaction with domestic animals. He carefully inventoried their cattle names and analysed their system of naming cattle. His approach to pastoral societies was very different from Euro-American anthropologists, who focused their attention primarily on the peoples instead of animals. On the other hand, Umesao's anthropological methods were derived from his earlier ecological training and relied on the careful observation and description of the substantive interrelationship between animals and humans. This approach has been adopted by the present generation of Japanese pastoral anthropologists

Another important contribution was derived from Umesao's 1955 fieldwork among the Moghols of the Hindukush Mountains in Afghanistan. The Moghols were descendants of the Mongols who had arrived in the thirteen century when the military came down from Mongolia to establish a garrison for their empire. On the basis of his work with them, Umesao presented an influential theory on the ecological history of civilisation in which he divided the Eurasian continent into three major ecological zones, Western Europe, Japan, and the Middle region including such countries as India and Afghanistan. On the basis of an analysis of historical processes in these regions, he illustrated how the first two are basically similar while demonstrating fundamental differences between China and Japan. The 1967 publication of this theory has been chosen as one of the ten most significant books of the twentieth century according to the famous Japanese monthly journal, *Bungei Shunju*.

In 1957–8 and 1961–2, Umesao joined two expeditions organised by Osaka City Univer-

sity, and carried out extensive surveys in Thailand, Kampuchea, south Vietnam, Laos, Burma, east Pakistan, India, and Pakistan. In 1967, he also carried out a short-term research project in the Basque Provinces and visited numerous countries around the world, including many regions of China.

In 1986, Umesao completely lost his eyesight. In spite of this handicap, he has produced a number of important publications and continued his vital roles in the social as well as academic worlds to this day.

Education

B.Sc. Kyoto University, 1943
D.Sc. Kyoto University, 1961

Fieldwork

Northern China (Mongolia), 1944–5
Afghanistan (Moghol), 1955
Tanzania (Datoga), 1963–4

Key Publications

(1956) *Moghol-Zoku Tankenki* (Record of an Expedition to a Moghol Tribe), Tokyo: Iwanami-Shotren.

(1966) 'Families and herds of the Datoga: an analysis of the cattle naming system', *Kyoto University African Studies* 1: 173–206.

(2003) *An Ecological View of History: Japanese Civilization in the World Context*, (Bunmei no Setai-Shikan, 1967), ed. Harumi Befu, trans. Beth Cary, Japanese Society Series, Melbourne: Trans Pacific Pr..

KATSUYOSHI FUKUI

Urban, Greg

b. 1949, Chicago, Illinois, USA

Greg Urban is among the pioneers of a discourse-centered approach to culture propounding the empirical study of discourse to access the culture it embodies. He has made substantial ethnographic and original theoretical contributions to this approach, which he has expanded into a theory of culture as a dynamic self-propelling processual entity.

His work involves a painstaking method of analysis of textual components exemplified in his study of the relationship of a 'we' discourse with group consciousness. Among the people of P.I. Ibirama (Xokleng), group consciousness is constructed without the use of such pronouns. In contrast, 'we' discourse has been important throughout the history of the USA. 'We' discourse effects a group identity, but such discourse incorporates pre-existing cultural strands of 'we' discourses that have propelled themselves into the new strand.

Urban sees culture as defined by the repeated materialisation of immaterial ideal forms, a process at play in cultural motion. Culture moves along contrasting pathways of dissemination that can be preset, as in transmission from parent to child, or new, as in the circulation of modern global culture. In addition, cultural motion is affected by a metaculture that speaks about culture. A metaculture of tradition moves culture in preset pathways, while a metaculture of newness cuts across existing pathways and accelerates the circulation of culture. Processes of replication and dissemination are conjoined in traditional culture but dissociated in modern culture, and this disjunction leads to favoring response over replication in a culture of newness. Urban already saw the contrast between replication and response at play in the differences between myth and dream narratives in P.I. Ibirama, and he uses it in his 2001 work to help describe the rapid motion of modern culture and metaculture across the world.

Urban incorporates the notion of demand into cultural dissemination and resorts to a market model to account for the global motion of modern culture. I see some unresolved issues in his 2001 book though they should not distract from the import of his theoretical contribution. Though he argues individuals are indispensable to culture's motion, their agency remains problematical in his scheme where an anthropomorphised culture is the holder of power, where the appeal, or repulsion, of the set of core cultural elements Urban sees as grounding nations is the primary motivator for in- and out-migrations, and where the political and economic coercive factors impacting producers' and consumers' access to dissemination pathways are relegated to the realm of invisibility.

Education

BA University of Chicago, 1971
MA University of Chicago, 1973
Ph.D. University of Chicago, 1978

Fieldwork

Intensive fieldwork periods in Brazil, starting in 1974 and totalling more than 4 years (principally, with Xokleng of P.I. Ibirama (Santa Catarina), Kaingang at Ivaí (Paraná), and Pataxó-Hãhãhãi (Bahía)).

Key Publications

(1991) *A Discourse-Centered Approach to Culture: Native South American Myths and Rituals*, Austin: University of Texas Press.
(1996) *Metaphysical Community: The Interplay of the Senses and the Intellect*, Austin: University of Texas Press.
with Silverstein, Michael (eds) (1996) *Natural Histories of Discourse*, Chicago: University of Chicago Press.
(2001) *Metaculture: How Culture Moves through the World*, Minneapolis: University of Minnesota Press.

Further Reading

Karttunen, Marie-Louise (2001) 'An introduction to the theory and methodology of Greg Urban', *Suomen Antropologi* 26, 4: 5–19.

CATHERINE TIHANYI

V

van der Veer, Peter

b. 22 May 1953, Groningen, The Netherlands

Peter van der Veer began his academic career in the Netherlands during the late 1970s with a study of a Hindu monastic order in Ayodhya, India, well before that locale became synonymous with the increasing tension between Hindus and Muslims in late twentieth-century India. He has since been at the forefront of international scholarship on the problem of religious ideology and practice in relation to the development and maintenance of nationalist sentiments, and was one of the first anthropologists to engage the problem of religious belief under conditions of modernity. After teaching at the Free University of Amsterdam and the University of Utrecht for several years, van der Veer then spent some time in visiting positions at the London School of Economics, the University of Pennsylvania (where he was also an associate professor), the University of Chicago, and L'École des Hautes Études en Sciences Sociales in Paris. Since 1993, he has been the director of the Research Centre for Religion and Society at the University of Amsterdam. His research programme has been characterised by an interdisciplinary approach with an extremely strong historical orientation, seeking a way past the frequently encountered assumption that true modernity can be found only within the structure of the European metropole.

Van der Veer's most recent book, *Imperial Encounters*, documents the ways in which Great Britain and India influenced each other across a variety of spheres – religion, race, gender, and science – during the period of British colonial rule on the Indian sub-continent. Van der Veer argues that such often reified oppositions as the modern and the traditional, or the secular and the religious, should rather be considered within the same frame. Taken as a whole, van der Veer's career has exemplified the value of using a range of historical and ethnographic approaches to rethink the Western ideologies that have reinforced such dichotomies of modernity. He demonstrates that anthropology can contribute to new ways of understanding the relationship between the coloniser and the colonised that insist on the mutuality of the shared colonial experience.

Education

'Kandidaats', University of Groningen, 1976
'Doctoraal', University of Groningen, 1979
Ph.D. University of Utrecht, 1986

Fieldwork

Uttar Pradesh State, India, 1977–8, 1981, 1983, 1984, 1987
Gujarat, India, 1987
Rajasthan, India, 1987
Surat, India, 1989
Netherlands (Surinamese Hindus), 1983–90

Key Publications

(1988) *Gods on Earth: The Management of Religious Experience and Identity in a North Indian Pilgrimage Centre*, London: Athlone Press (London School of Economics Monographs on Social Anthropology 59).

(1994) *Religious Nationalism: Hindus and Muslims in South Asia*, Berkeley: University of California Press.

(2001) *Imperial Encounters: Religion and Modernity in India and Britain*, Princeton: Princeton University Press.

SARAH STRAUSS

Van Esterik, Penny

b. 19 July 1944, Toronto, Ontario, Canada

From the time her career in anthropology began in the mid-1970s Penny Van Esterik has written for academic and public audiences. Publications from her initial Thailand fieldwork, conducted between 1971–4, demonstrate equal fluency with the more 'engaged' topics of nutrition and development as well as areas of traditional anthropological concern such as cognition and symbolism in Ban Chiang pottery. During the mid-1980s Van Esterik's commissioned reports on infant feeding contributed to international food policy by showing links between macro-level development issues and lived cultural practices of bureaucracy and infant nutrition. Van Esterik's food policy research culminated in an academic monograph (1989) that developed a working framework for blending advocacy and solid academic scholarship. By showing the interrelationships among social policy, economic development, and cultural practices, this synthesis of advocacy and scholarship was intended to push anthropological analysis of social problems controversies beyond an ethnographic description of opposing sides. In the late 1990s she linked her interest in Thai studies with feminist anthropology by theorising Thai gender studies as

well as its relationship with Southeast Asian gender research. The Women in Development Consortium in Thailand, directed by Van Esterik, has been noted as a successful model for forging international institutional relationships. Her contribution to food policy scholarship and advocacy continued in 2000 by integrating detailed ethnographic research with policy-oriented risk analysis.

Education

BA University of Toronto, 1970
MA University of Illinois, 1972
Ph.D. University of Illinois, 1976

Fieldwork

Bangkok and Suphanburi, Thailand, 1971–2
Bangkok, 1973–4
Bangkok, Semarang (Indonesia), Nairobi, and Bogota (short-term visits), 1980–4
Toronto, 1986–7
Bangkok, 1992 (6 months)
Lao PDR, 1994 (3 months)

Key Publications

(1989) *Beyond the Breast Bottle Controversy*, New Brunswick, New Jersey: Rutgers University Press.

(2000) *Materializing Thailand*, Oxford: Berg Press.

BRIAN FREER

van Gennep, Arnold

b. 23 April 1873, Ludwigsburg, Germany

d. 7 May 1957, Epernay, France

Arnold van Gennep's parents were both Huguenot émigrés in Germany, where he lived the first six years of his life. His university studies were atypical: instead of the Sorbonne he attended the École Pratique des Hautes Études and then the École des Langues Orientales. He was the contemporary of Marcel

Mauss, but he pursued a very different career path. He did not hold a university position except for his brief stint in the ethnography chair at the University of Neuchâtel (Switzerland) (1912–15).

Up to 1920, his scientific interests matched those of the French sociology school: totemism, exogamy, taboo, the first forms of religion, and magic. It was the publication of his doctoral thesis, *L'État actuel du problème totémique* (The Present State of the Totemic Problem), which closed this period and which Claude Lévi-Strauss considers as 'the swan song of speculations on totemism'. From 1909 on, the publication date of his principal work, *The Rites of Passage*, a transition began that was to last for the next decade during which he undertook fieldwork in Algeria, where he focused on 'native arts and industries', as well as occupying a university position in Neuchâtel.

Even though he was kept on the margin by the sociological school headed by Emile Durkheim and fairly harshly criticised by its members, he dared to raise serious objections to the views of the uncontested master whose patronage was a requisite for a university career. He reproached Durkheim for being too uncritical of his sources in *The Elementary Forms of Religious Life* (1912), of neglecting the individual in favor of the collective, and mainly of presuming that the societies labelled primitive such as that of the Australian Aborigines were simple societies in which the genesis of religion can be readily apprehended (*Mercure de France*, 16 January 1913), while in fact these are highly complex organisations.

The Rites of Passage strikingly reveals the originality of van Gennep's thought. It was he who proposed the notion, the 'schema' as he put it, that was to spontaneously become part of the practice of social anthropology, sometimes to the point of being naturalised and its author forgotten. Those rituals that exist both in solemn occasions, as well as in ordinary social actions, are made of a ceremonial sequence, composed of three stages: separation, threshold rites, and rites of aggregation, and he also calls these preliminary, liminary, and post-liminary. Van Gennep greatly emphasises physical passage as a model for rites themselves, as well as the idea of liminality that was to be taken up and developed by Victor Turner with his notion of '*communitas*'. The function of rites of passage is to make individual and society pass from one stage to another, 'from the cradle to the grave' and through calendrical time.

This heuristic tool in hand, van Gennep then devoted himself to the ethnography of France, producing numerous regional monographs (on the Dauphiné, Burgundy, Flanders, Auvergne, Hautes-Alpes) and mostly the monumental *Manuel de folklore français contemporain* (Manual of Contemporary French Folklore) (9 volumes between 1937 and 1958, but unfinished), which led Louis Dumont to say that its author was 'an institution' in himself.

Van Gennep also added two complementary notions to the schema of the rites of passage. The first pertained to the importance of the 'opening rites' and to the 'dramatic' form of rites of passage, each ritual sequence constituting a dramatic scenario.

Van Gennep's marginalisation from the French university did not however make a hermit out of him. This is particularly attested by the chronicles of ethnography and folklore he wrote for the famous periodical, *Mercure de France*, between 1905 and 1949 – except for the interruptions of the First and Second World Wars.

Van Gennep's work, rich with new ideas and new paths for research, forms a transition between Durkheim's sociological school and modern anthropology, between folklore and the ethnology of France. However, van Gennep's greatest accomplishment remains the invention of the notion of rites of passage.

Education

Diploma, École Pratique des Hautes Études, 1904

Ph.D. (Doctorat d'État), École Pratique des Hautes Études, 1920

Fieldwork

Algeria, several periods between 1910 and 1920

Various regions of France

Key Publications

(1908–14) *Religions, moeurs et légendes: essais d'ethnographie et de linguistique* (Religions, Ways, and Legends: Ethnographic and Linguistic Essays), 5 vols, Paris: Mercure de France.

(1937–58) *Manuel de folklore français contemporain* (A Manual of Contemporary French Folklore), 9 vols, Paris: Picard.

(1960) *The Rites of Passage* (*Les Rites de passage*, 1909), trans. Monika B. Vizedom and Gabrielle L. Caffee, Chicago: The University of Chicago Press; London: Routledge & Kegan Paul Ltd.

Further Reading

Belmont, Nicole (1979) *Arnold Van Gennep. The Creator of French Ethnography* (*Arnold van Gennep, le créateur de l'ethnographie française*, 1974), trans. Derek Coltman, Chicago: University of Chicago Press.

Privat, Jean-Marie (ed. and Preface) (2001) *Chroniques de folklore. Recueil de textes parus dans le Mercure de France 1905–1949* (Folklore Chronicles: Texts by Arnold van Gennep published in 'Mercure de France' between 1905–1949), Paris: Ed. du CTHS.

van Gennep, Ketty (1964) *Bibliographie des oeuvres d'Arnold van Gennep*, (Bibliography of works by Arnold van Gennep), Paris: Picard.

NICOLE BELMONT,
TRANSLATED BY CATHERINE TIHANYI

van Velsen, Jaap

b. 1921, Java, Indonesia

d. 1990, Cambridge, UK

Though Dutch by origin, Jaap van Velsen spent a very large part of his professional career living and working in Africa but maintaining strong links with British social anthropology. After studying in Utrecht, he moved to Oxford and then to Manchester, where, under Max Gluckman, he prepared for fieldwork as a research officer of the Rhodes–Livingstone Institute, based in what was then Northern Rhodesia.

His most influential contributions derive primarily from this period of research. His analysis of Tonga politics and kinship demonstrated the central importance of examining social 'irregularities' and cultural 'exceptions' for understanding the process of building and renegotiating social and political relationships. In so doing he elaborated the extended case method that was a hallmark of Manchester anthropology and wrote a seminal paper on 'situational analysis' that continues to feature widely in anthropological methods courses. In addition, his Tonga research provided a baseline for arguing the positive impact of labour migration on peasant communities through remittances and showed how migrants continued to be part of the social, economic, and political life of their areas of origin.

He subsequently held successive positions at the East African Institute of Social Research, Uganda, the University College of Rhodesia and Nyasaland in Salisbury, the University of Zambia, and finally the chair of sociology at the University of Wales in Aberystwyth where he remained until his retirement

Education

Law degree at University of Utrecht (interrupted in the 1940s due to German Occupation)

B.Litt. University of Oxford, 1950

Ph.D. University of Manchester, 1956

Fieldwork

Lakeside Tonga, Malawi, 1952–5

Kumam of northeastern Uganda, 1957–9

Urban squatters, Lusaka, Zambia, 1970s

Key Publications

(1964) *The Politics of Kinship*, Manchester: University of Manchester Press.

(1967) 'The extended case method and situational analysis', in A.L. Epstein (ed.) *The Craft of Social Anthropology*, London: Tavistock.

NORMAN LONG

Vayda, Andrew P.

b. 1931, Budapest, Hungary

Andrew Vayda established his reputation as one of the formative figures of the new ecological anthropology of the 1960s and has remained influential during its subsequent development, and later transformation into an anthropology of the environment. His early work included a series of studies of warfare in traditional societies, beginning with a monograph on the Maori in 1960, and later publications explored how conflict escalation can best be understood through a systemic analysis that integrates ecological, demographic, and social variables. In an early classic essay with Roy Rappaport (1968) he set out the defining features of an anthropological ecology that went beyond Steward's conception of cultural adaptation, and which instead advocated an approach in which all cultural behaviour displayed by a local human population might be seen as having potential adaptive consequences and ecosystemic ramifications. Although this stance placed him with the 'ecological functionalists', his work has always emphasised process and historicity in systems, and he was later to reject the holistic, cybernetic, and energetic paradigm in favor of one increasingly influenced by methodological individualism, focusing less on systems than on individual responses to environmental 'hazards' and perturbations, and on conscious potential management strategies. This shift eventually led him to develop his event analysis and progressive contextualisation: a focus increasingly emphasising the analytical priority of answering empirical questions

about how specific socioecological events have occurred, rather than invoking a priori explanations. His research in the 1990s, for example on forest fires, has involved a critique of those political ecology models that assume political determination of environment events without first exploring whether such events might find their sufficient explanations in biophysical or other factors.

Vayda's most significant writing has always appeared in papers rather than as long monographs, and his style is concise, to the point, and utterly pragmatic. Because of the range of his influential essays, some of the most important of which have been jointly authored (with Leeds, Rappaport, McCay, and Walters, for example), the publications listed cannot be taken as completely representative. Characteristically iconoclastic and combative in defending his particular 'anti-essentialist' and inductivist position, his work is not easily pigeon-holed, extending most recently to cogent critiques of the neo-Darwinians on the one hand, and of 'spiritual ecology' on the other.

Education

AB Columbia University, 1952
Ph.D. Columbia University, 1956

Fieldwork

Cook Islands, 1956–7
New Guinea, 1962–3, 1966
South Sumatra, Indonesia, 1977
East Kalimantan, Indonesia, 1979–84, 1996, 1998, 2000, 2001
Central Java (Special Region of Yogyakarta), 1990
West Timor, Indonesia, 2001, 2002

Key Publications

with Rappaport, R.A. (1968) 'Ecology, cultural and non-cultural', in J.A. Clifton (ed.) *Introduction to Cultural Anthropology: Essays in the Scope and Methods of the Science of Man*, Boston: Houghton Mifflin.

with McCay, B.J. (1975) 'New directions in

ecology and ecological anthropology', *Annual Review of Anthropology* 4: 293–406.

(1976) *War in Ecological Perspective: Persistence, Change and Adaptive Processes in Three Oceanian Societies*, New York: Plenum Press.

(1983) 'Progressive contextualism: methods for research in human ecology', *Human Ecology* 11, 3: 265–81.

R.F. ELLEN

Velho, Gilberto C.A.

b. 1945, Rio de Janeiro, Brazil

Gilberto Velho is one of the most important pioneers in the study of urban anthropology in Brazil, as well as of stigmatisation and deviance among urban middle classes. During the period of his graduate studies he spent one year at the University of Texas (Austin) and was later visiting professor at Northwestern University in 1976 and in 1990, working closely with Howard Becker in joint projects. Gilberto Velho applied symbolic interactionism approaches to various areas and empirical objects in Brazil. He has currently been focusing on different situations of sociocultural mediation in themes related to citizenship.

His activities as professor of social anthropology and supervisor at the Museu Nacional allowed him to exert considerable influence over many generations of students, some of which have produced important work in the areas of urban sociability, national identity, erudite culture, and Brazilian popular culture. His influence extends to researchers in institutions and agencies concerned with national artistic, historical, and cultural assets, as well as to those concerned with political memory in Brazil. He is the editor of one of the best local series in national and international studies in social anthropology and has participated in different editorial committees, both these activities having greatly contributed to the important position occupied by anthropology among the social sciences in Brazil. As president of the Brazilian Anthropological Association between 1982 and 1984, and of the National Association for Postgraduate Research on Social Sciences from 1994 to 1996, he has played an important role in the institutional development of social sciences in Brazil.

Education

BA Federal University of Rio de Janeiro, 1968
MA Federal University of Rio de Janeiro, 1970
Ph.D. University of São Paulo, 1975

Fieldwork

Copacabana, Rio de Janeiro, 1968–70
Portuguese immigrants, Boston area, USA, 1971
Lifestyle in a network of upper middle-class drug consumers, Rio de Janeiro, 1972–4
Permanent supervision and participation in team fieldwork on topics of urban anthropology, Rio de Janeiro, 1976–2001

Key Publications

(1976) 'Accusations, family mobility and deviant behavior', *Social Problems*, 23, 3, February.

(1989) *A utopia urbana: um estudo de antropologia social* (The Urban Utopia: A Study in Social Anthropology, fifth edn, Rio de Janeiro: Jorge Zahar.

(1998) *Nobres e anjos: um estudo de tóxicos e hierarquia* (Nobles and Angels: A Study about Drugs and Hierarchy), Rio de Janeiro: Editora da Fundação Getulio Vargas.

(2001) 'Observing the familiar', *India International Centre Quarterly*, New Delhi, 28, 1: 47–57.

JOSÉ SERGIO LEITE LOPES

Verdery, Katherine

b. 9 July 1948, Bangor, Maine, USA

Katherine Verdery has pioneered a unified anthropological approach to state, economy, and ethnicity, grounded on village-level, long-term historical data in Transylvania and ethnographic contexts there and more widely in socialist and post-socialist Romania. Her work is important in the development of theory on ethnicity and the state, and for understanding the dynamics of state socialism and the transformations following socialism's sudden demise in Eastern Europe. Verdery's post-socialist analyses challenge assumptions about the meaning of basic economic categories, notably property. Thus her work reaches over into political science and economics.

Verdery's dissertation (*Transylvanian Villagers*) was a close study of the historical development of relations between peoples differentiating themselves from each other as Romanians, Hungarians, and Saxons (Germans). This work showed how states set the conditions for different forms of economy and thus for the ordering of ethnic groups whose members assumed differing roles in them, while providing close ethnography of 'actually existing socialism' in one of its most strongly imposed forms.

Although Marxism was supposed to be hostile to nationalism, Verdery saw that the Romanian socialist state ordered and reproduced nationalist ideologies in much the same way as its predecessors. *National Ideology under Socialism*, published just after state socialism disappeared from Eastern Europe, is the classic exposition of this conundrum and is a critical tool for understanding the nationalist ideologies that became dominant in the politics of much of post-socialist Europe.

While those with little knowledge of the region before 1989 perceived a glowing future of democracy, markets, and civil society, Verdery saw the privatisation of the state and expropriation of resources by mafias as a process analogous to feudalism. Verdery's explications of the social meanings of 'real property' in the contexts of crony capitalism and politicised land restitution, and of 'investments' in the contexts of pyramid schemes, show how and why, for many people, post-socialism led to mass impoverishment and disillusionment rather than the prosperity and

freedom they thought they had been promised. She thereby also problematised the very concepts of property and democracy that planners and less sophisticated theorists had thought most settled. Verdery's work has thus been discomfiting to both socialist and post-socialist theorists, her ethnography, like Romanian society, confounding ideologies.

Education

BA Reed College, 1970
MA Stanford University, 1971
Ph.D. Stanford University, 1977

Fieldwork

Wales and Scotland, 1970
Greece, 1971
Romania, 1973–4, 1979–80, 1984–5, 1987–8, 1990, 1991, 1992, 1993–4, 1996, 1997, 2000, 2001, 2002

Key Publications

(1983) *Transylvanian Villagers: Three Centuries of Political, Economic and Ethnic Change*, Berkeley: University of California Press.
(1991) *National Ideology under Socialism: Identity and Cultural Politics in Ceausescou's Romania*, Berkeley: University of California Press.
(1996) *What Was Socialism, and What Comes Next?*, Princeton: Princeton University Press.
(1999) *The Political Lives of Dead Bodies: Reburial and Postsocialist Change*, New York: Columbia University Press.

ROBERT M. HAYDEN

Vessuri, Hebe M.C.

b. 24 April 1942, Buenos Aires, Argentina

Hebe Vessuri analysed the transition from the cattle-raising colonial *estancia* (large estate) to the modern agricultural *finca* (farm), framing her analysis around the patron–client relationships between landlords, labourers, and small landholders. Such patterns permeated most aspects of social and symbolic organisation in Santiago del Estero, Northwest Argentina. In Tucumán, she studied the transition to soybean production of independent producers in an ecologically peripheral sugarcane region. Once Tucumán was struck by state terror in 1974, Vessuri moved with her family to Venezuela, where she studied the sociotechnical *conuco* (small landholdings) features as they were adapted to an agrarian reform setting of fixed land plots.

Since 1979 Vessuri has studied the Venezuelan scientific communities, and analysed comparatively the impact of the globalisation of science on the organisation and creativity of scientific knowledge in peripheral countries. As chair and researcher of the Department for the Study of Science at the Venezuelan Institute of Scientific Research (IVIC), she is interested in looking for viable alternative national science and development in relative autonomy from the core scientific powers.

Education

Diploma in Anthropology, University of Oxford, 1963
Baccalaureat Litterae Humaniores, University of Oxford, 1964
D.Phil. University of Oxford, 1974

Fieldwork

Santiago del Estero, Argentina, 1967–70
Tucumán, Argentina, 1971–5
Valles del Tuy, Venezuela, 1976–7
Science and scientific communities (esp. chemists, agricultural engineers, and bioscientists) in Latin America, 1980–2000

Key Publications

(1971) 'Land tenure and social structure in Santiago del Estero, Argentina', Ph.D. thesis, University of Oxford.
with Texera, Yolanda and Díaz, Elena (1983) *La Ciencia Periférica. Ciencia y Sociedad en Venezuela*

(Peripheral Science: Science and Society in Venezuela), Caracas, Venezuela: Monte Avila.

ROSANA GUBER

Villa Rojas, Alfonso

b. 1897, Merida, Yucatan, Mexico

d. 1998, Mexico City, Mexico

Alfonso Villa Rojas's long life provided him with the opportunity to make valuable and varied contributions to anthropology. He carried out his main ethnographic research through intensive fieldwork among the Maya of southeast Mexico. The culture and social organisation of the Maya peasant communities that he studied were the axis of his reflections.

In Chan Kom, a peasant village of Yucatan, Villa Rojas, together with Robert Redfield, developed a meticulous research programme based on the characterisation of this culture in terms of a folk–urban continuum, particularly in the study of culture change among Mayan peasant communities. In Tusik, Quintana Roo, he studied the cult of the 'talking cross' and the military organisation of the rebel Maya, who fought against the Mexican government. His detailed cultural descriptions were the basis of the foremost ethnographies of the Maya ever written. In Oxchuc, a Tzeltal community in Chiapas Highlands, he carried out intensive research that revealed a kinship organisation based on patrilineal principles and the presence of lineages, clans, and moities (locally known as 'kalpul', a word of Nahua origin).

His theoretical contributions focused on the study of kinship in Tzeltal communities, specifically in the constitution of political groups and social control mechanisms based on dreaming experiences and witchcraft (known in Mesoamerican ethnography as nahualism). Villa Rojas's deep knowledge of the history and archaeology of the Maya allowed him to elaborate the first theoretical statements about a Mesoamerican world view among contemporary peoples in the Maya region.

Villa Rojas's name has been linked with the Indian policy of the Mexican government, in which he occupied diverse executive positions. However, above all, he is known for his orientation towards and development of applied anthropology. Finally, another outstanding contribution of Villa Rojas is his achievement of excellent ethnographic syntheses of Maya peoples, such as the Tzeltal, the Chol, the Lacandon, the Chontal from Tabasco, the Yucatan and Quintana Roo Maya, as well as other peoples, such as the Zoque and the Mazatec.

Education

BA Universidad del Sureste, Yucatan
Studies in anthropology, University of Chicago, 1933–5

Fieldwork

Chan Kom, Yucatan, February 1930–November 1931
Tusik, Quintana Roo, September–November 1935
Chiapas Highlands, February–March 1938
Oxchuc, Chiapas, May 1942–April 1943, December 1943–June 1944

Key Publications

with Redfield, Robert (1934) *Chan Kom, a Maya Village*, Washington: Carnegie Institute.
(1945) *The Maya of East Quintana Roo*, Washington: Carnegie Institute.
(1979) 'Fieldwork in the Maya Region of Mexico', in G.M. Foster (ed.) *Longterm Field Research in Social Anthropology*, New York: Academic Press
(1987) *Estudios etnológicos. Los mayas* (Ethnological Studies. The Maya), Mexico: National University of Mexico, UNAM.

ANDRÉS MÉDINA

Vincent, Joan

b. 17 November 1928, Camberley, Surrey, UK

Joan Vincent's interests in ethnographic research, the history of anthropology, and anthropological theory have been motoring forces in the development of political and applied anthropology over the last two generations, in a career which places her among the pre-eminent political and historical anthropologists working on both sides of the Atlantic. Vincent initially trained as a secondary school teacher in England, but after teaching a few years in England and a year in Rhodesia she took her undergraduate degree at the London School of Economics. Over the succeeding four years she taught college in East Africa, where she began her lifelong anthropological association with Africa and the intersections of ethnicity, culture, class, history, law, and politics. After doing a Master's degree in political science at the University of Chicago, in 1968 she completed her Ph.D. in the anthropology department at Columbia University, where she has served as teacher, mentor, and administrator ever since. Her dissertation, based on field research in Uganda and published as *African Elite*, was an ethnography of local politics that fused British ethnographic attention to social structure and political networks with an American anthropological interest in ethnicity and history. Vincent's intellectual evolution, which in the 1970s took her away from the more staid synchronic and structural categories of political ethnography, led her to revisit her data in order to write *Teso in Transformation*, which explicitly addressed the impact of capitalism on the development of class relations and power inequities in Uganda. Vincent's interests in the changing nature of world-systems and their impact on localities have been hallmarks of all of her research, teaching, and writing, and led her to a new fieldwork locale, County Fermanagh, in Northern Ireland, where for almost thirty years she has researched the historical causes of conflict and integration, in a rural district shaped by colonialism, capitalism, imperialism, and nationalism, not unlike Teso in Uganda. Among her many important contributions to political and legal anthropology worldwide has been her commitment to the comparison of ethnographic studies of local society and politics, and their interactions with wider economic forces and fields of political power. The recipient of many professional honours, including fellowships in the Institute for Advanced Study at Princeton and the National Humanities Center, and the presidency of the Association for Political and Legal Anthropology (1993–5), Vincent may perhaps be best known for generations to come for her much-praised comprehensive review of the history of political anthropology, *Anthropology and Politics*, which is also very much her personal overview of the history of the politics of anthropology.

Education

B.Sc. London School of Economics, 1957
MA University of Chicago, 1964
Ph.D. Columbia University, 1968

Fieldwork

Teso District, Uganda, 1966–7, 1970, 1991
Rakai District, Uganda, 1988
Kampala and Soroti Town, Uganda, 1991
County Fermanagh, Northern Ireland, 1973–4, 1975–6, 1982–3, 1990, and intermittent research from 1991–2001

Key Publications

(1971) *African Elite: The Big Men of a Small Town*, New York: Columbia University Press.
(1982) *Teso in Transformation: The Political Economy of Peasant and Class in Eastern Africa*, Berkeley: University of California Press.
(1986) 'System and process, 1974–1985', *Annual Review of Anthropology* 13: 331–9.
(1990) *Anthropology and Politics: Visions, Traditions*

and Trends, Tucson: University of Arizona Press.

THOMAS M. WILSON

Vogt, Evon Zartman, Jr

b. 20 August 1918, Gallup, New Mexico, USA

d. 13 May 2004, Cambridge, Massachusetts, USA

Evon Z. Vogt was a pre-eminent American anthropologist who achieved international recognition as the founder and director of the Harvard Chiapas Project in Mexico that ran from 1957 to 1980. He was an ethnographer's ethnographer who trained a generation of students in field research techniques and contributed to the theoretical and methodological development of anthropology. Of the 142 students who participated in the Chiapas field school over the years, fully sixty-four are practising anthropologists or working in closely related fields. They constitute an important group of professionals, many of whom have continued Vogt's commitment to long-term empirical research, methodological rigour, and the overall goal of improving the database of sociocultural anthropology. As a result of Vogt's efforts, by the early 1990s a significant body of work had been published on the Maya people of the Chiapas, making it one of the best-known ethnographic regions in the world.

Vogt was born and grew up in New Mexico surrounded by people from different cultural traditions, including Zunis, Navahos, Mormons, Spanish Americans, and recently arrived Texans. He later wrote that the two factors most fundamental to becoming an anthropologist, namely, exposure to people from different cultures and a feeling of being an outsider, characterised his early life. The Vogt ranch was the meeting place of a wide variety of interesting and accomplished people, including archaeologists Frederick Webb Hodge and Neil M. Judd, ethnologists Clyde and Florence Kluckhohn, Ruth Bunzel, and David Aberle, and social-literary critic Edmund

Wilson, each of whom impressed the young Evon. Vogt was trained during anthropology's classic period and he counted among his teachers and mentors Fred Eggan, Robert Redfield, Sol Tax, W. Lloyd Warner, Robert Braidwood, and Fay-Cooper Cole. While in graduate school, Vogt participated in Warner's study of social class in a Midwestern city and conducted dissertation research on Navaho veterans. Later, on the faculty at Harvard, he became an important figure in the Comparative Study of Values in Five Cultures Project, with its focus on the American Southwest.

Vogt's work in Mexico is based on an earlier tradition of the community study that was subsequently criticised by Marxists, world-systems theorists, and post-modernists. The fundamental purpose of his research was to show that social life is coherent and systematic, and to identify key organising principles of society and culture. It followed that ethnographers should conduct detailed studies of the communities or social units in which people lived their lives. Vogt and his students produced unparalleled detailed studies of contemporary Maya kinship, ritual and symbol, the cargo system, political and economic behaviour, and other features of community life. They purposely focused on only a few of the thirty-four Tzeltal and Tzotzil communities in Highland Chiapas centered around Zinacantan and Chamula. The object of the research was to gather high-quality data on individual communities and conduct controlled comparisons to reveal determinants of cultural variation and culture change. Critics of the Chiapas Project advocated macro- or regional studies in place of the fine-grained ethnography produced by Vogt and his students.

The Chiapas Project produced empirical studies of lasting value. These studies demonstrate that contemporary Mesoamerican cultures have their roots deep in the pre-Hispanic past. They provide a body of information allowing anthropologists and ethnohistorians to chart culture change and continuity. Chiapas Project data reveal processes of acculturation, adaptation, syncretism, resistance, innovation, and accommodation. For his extraordinary efforts on behalf of anthropology and the systematic understanding of cultural and social processes, Vogt was elected to the American Academy of Arts and Sciences (1960), the National Academy of Sciences (1979), the American Philosophical Society (1999), and, perhaps most telling of all accolades, a Decorated Knight Commander, Order of the Aztec Eagle, conferred by the Republic of Mexico (1978). He continued in retirement to write and address problems stimulated by his lifelong commitment to ethnographic research.

Education

AB University of Chicago, 1941
MA University of Chicago, 1946
Ph.D. University of Chicago, 1948

Fieldwork

Zuni farming village (Pescado), July–August 1942
Ramah Navaho, June 1947–March 1948
Fence Lake, New Mexico, September 1949–September 1950
Nayarit, Mexico, June–July 1954
Highlands of Chiapas, 1955–2000 (95 months in the field)

Key Publications

(1951) *Navaho Veterans: A Study of Changing Values*, Papers of the Peabody Museum of American Archaeology and Ethnology, Harvard University. Cambridge, MA: The Museum.

(1969) *Zinacantan: A Maya Community in the Highlands of Chiapas*, Cambridge, MA: Belknap Press of Harvard University.

(1976) *Tortillas for the Gods: A Symbolic Analysis of Zinacanteco Rituals*, Cambridge, MA: Harvard University Press.

(1994) *Fieldwork among the Maya: Reflections on the Harvard Chiapas Project*, Albuquerque: University of New Mexico Press

ALAN R. SANDSTROM

Wagner, Roy

b. 2 October 1938, Cleveland, Ohio, USA

Roy Wagner was a student of David Schneider, the single most important anthropological influence on his career, particularly in regards to the development of the symbolic anthropology for which he has become renowned. He conducted fieldwork among the Daribi of Papua New Guinea in the early 1960s and his dissertation was published in 1967 as *The Curse of Souw*, a portrait of clan structure and alliance among the Daribi. This was followed by *Habu* in 1972, which analysed the ritual and religious life of the Daribi.

While a lecturer at Northwestern University, he completed his book, *The Invention of Culture* (1975), his first and still most accessible and popular work of anthropological theory. In this book, Wagner argues that there are two moments to any symbolic construction – a collectivising one, which focuses on the similarities between elements in a symbolic equation, and a differentiating one, which focuses on the differences and contrasts between them. He then goes on to observe that each human culture must articulate the contrast between the domain of human action and intention, and that which lies outside of this human domain and is the object of its symbolic transformations. In different cultures, one of these domains is viewed as the realm of 'convention', that which is accepted as tacit and taken for granted, and the other is

the product of 'invention', the conscious and avowed domain of human goals and intentions. Wagner uses the intersection of these two contrasts to make a broad characterisation of the differences between Western and non-Western traditions. For example, in the West, the differentiation of individuals is taken for granted. Against this background, human action must consciously fashion the conventional collectivities of state, nation, ethnic and religious group according to avowed laws and rules. Among the Daribi, by contrast, the commonalities of kinship and relationship are taken for granted and conventional. Achieving individuality by differentiating oneself within such a relational matrix is the avowed goal of human action. In his important article, 'Analogic kinship: a Daribi example' (1977), Wagner demonstrates how this approach explains Daribi kin term usage and their practices of affinal avoidance and exchange.

All of Wagner's subsequent works developed the implications of this broad contrast. In 1978, Wagner published *Lethal Speech*, an analysis of the rich mythology of the Daribi. In that analysis he develops his concept of symbolic obviation, a process by which a series of successive metaphoric depictions of collectivising and differentiating images succeed each other in a mythical narrative in such a way as to subvert and reveal the symbolic dimensions of the opening metaphoric image. Symbolic obviation was later shown to be a general feature of any sequentially or narratively structured cultural process that attempted to make convention and invention visible as interrelated symbolic operations – for example, a ritual, or the sequence of exchanges in an alliance relationship between wife-givers and wife-takers – in his 1986 book, *Symbols That Stand for Themselves*. Chapters 3 and 4 of that book can be considered to be Wagner's most sublime moment of ethnographic analysis, for through the use of the model of symbolic obviation, he draws together his previous ethnographies of Daribi clanship and marriage, mortuary ritual, and mythology in a stunning synthesis that stands as one of the best accomplishments of a Schneiderian ethnography of the core symbol.

Wagner's second field site was among the Usen Barok of New Ireland. His ethnography of the Barok, *Asiwinarong* (1986), introduces his interpretation of the anthropological work of 'containment'. Here Wagner draws more on the idea of 'figure-ground reversal', which he introduced in *Symbols That Stand for Themselves*. The figure-ground reversal became for Wagner a general gloss on how invention and convention are always articulated in only a 'relative' and not an absolute manner. In this manner, Wagner obviated the perennial conflict between materialist and idealist versions of the human lifeworld, a point he makes to great advantage in another key work, 'Visible sociality: The Daribi community' in 1988.

Wagner's early and vital Schneiderian insight on the primacy of relationality in the human world, and his successful adaptation of phenomenological insights in the service of anthropology, have been taken up by various scholars, most notably Marilyn Strathern, who made it the lynchpin of her important analysis of Melanesian gender, *The Gender of the Gift* (1988). Among other scholars who have utilised Wagner's anthropological phenomenology of the figure-ground reversal are Jadran Mimica, James Weiner, and David Guss.

Education

BA Harvard University, 1961
Ph.D. University of Chicago, 1966

Fieldwork

Simbu Province, Papua New Guinea 1963–5, 1968–9
New Ireland, Papua New Guinea, 1979–80, 1983

Key Publications

(1967) *The Curse of Souw. Principles of Daribi Clan Definition and Alliance in New Guinea*, Chicago: University of Chicago Press.
(1975) *The Invention of Culture*, Englewood, NJ: Prentice-Hall
(1986) *Symbols That Stand for Themselves*, Chicago: University of Chicago Press.
(2001) *An Anthropology of the Subject: Holographic Worldview in New Guinea and Its Meaning and Significance for the World of Anthropology*, Berkeley: University of California Press.

JAMES WEINER

Waligórski, Andrzej

b. 1908, Krakow, (then) Austro-Hungary

d. 1974, Krakow, Poland

Waligórski's thesis, written under the supervision of Bronislaw Malinowski, was concerned with the language of propaganda in Nazi Germany. After coming back to Poland he worked for the State Institute of Peasant Culture. At the beginning of the Second World War he fought in the Polish Army, and then after its defeat managed to escape to England where he worked for the Royal Institute of International Affairs and Polish Intelligence Service. In 1946 he went to Africa to carry out fieldwork among the Luo. Later he came back to Poland and started an academic career at the Jagiellonian University. Waligórski published several articles on agricultural knowledge, patterns of wealth, spatial and family bonds, and Luo kinship terminology; British colonial politics and white settlement in Kenya (in English and French) as well as a book on cultural change. He described how the economic policy of colonialists reoriented the life of autochthonous people, created new needs, and then tracked the later development of these processes.

His teaching resulted in an important book concerned with anthropological and pre-anthropological theories that was written from a functionalist perspective. He also lectured on the anthropology of Europe at a time when this was still considered a complete novelty. Finally, Waligórski deserves credit for promoting the work of his mentor during a period when communist state authorities regarded Malinowski as an exponent of an imperialistic science.

Education

MA Jagiellonian University, Krakow, 1931
Ph.D. London School of Economics, 1938

Fieldwork

Luo in Kenia, 1946–8

Key Publications

(1969) *Spolecznóśc afrykánska w procesie przemian 1890–1949* (African Community in the Process of Change 1890–1949), Warszawa: Uniwersytet Warszawski.
(1973) *Antropologiczna koncepcja czlowieka* (The Anthropological Concept of Man), Warszawa: Panstwowe Wydawn. Naukowe.

GRAZYNA KUBICA-HELLER

Wallace, Anthony F.C.

b. 1923, Toronto, Ontario, Canada

Several key themes run through Anthony Wallace's career: (1) the relationship between culture, personality, and historical circumstance; (2) the psychology and sociology of paradigmatic innovation; (3) the injustices suffered by American Native peoples, and their responses to them. Wallace's dissertation was supervised by psychological anthropologist, A.I. Hallowell, and employed the Rorschach Test to assay the 'modal' personality characteristics of the Iroquoian Tuscarora. However, his subsequent work led to a distinctively complex bio/psycho/social approach, summarised in his 1961 overview and critique of the culture-and-personality literature. His biomedical interests sparked research on generalisable topics such as the cultural background, social milieu, and physiological correlates of 'Arctic Hysteria' (pibloktoq) among the Inuit of the polar fringe. Wallace insisted that culture should not be reified, nor should personality be seen as its microcosm; rather, culture must be thought of as the 'organisation of diversity', and the anthropological task that of unveiling the organisational processes intrinsic to social life.

His approach was influenced by general systems theory and biological psychiatry, which in combination led to Wallace's theory of the 'mazeway' – 'the entire set of cognitive maps which an individual maintains at a given time' (1961: 15).

Wallace envisioned the degree of 'organisation' within any system as the product of its complexity and its 'orderliness'. However, mazeway organisation can be threatened by external pressures such as conquest and anomic social change, or by internal disease processes such as schizophrenia. Discrepancies between complexity and order lead to stress, and stress can lead to breakdown, or in some cases to mazeway resynthesis in the radical form of prophetic visions or paranoid delusions. Wallace developed these ideas throughout the 1950s, stimulated by his work at the Eastern Pennsylvania Psychiatric Institute and by his abiding interest in Native American history.

The outcome was the concept of the 'revitalisation movement', for which Wallace is best known among anthropologists. His pivotal case study was the Iroquois 'Handsome Lake Religion' (1970), which had been inspired by an eighteenth–nineteenth century Seneca prophet whose syncretistic revelation aimed at realigning himself and his people with their changed historical circumstances under American domination. Wallace developed these ideas into a processual analysis of revitalisation movements in general.

Economies, bureaucracies, and mazeways are all 'systems', as are the ideological configurations that the historian of science, Thomas Kuhn, called 'paradigms'. In his later work, Wallace increasingly turned towards study of the latter. Here his fieldwork site lay along a stream just down the street from where he lived: once the site of a successful water-powered cotton-spinning and weaving industry. As Wallace dug into the history of this community he uncovered a wealth of resources in the form of diaries, ledgers, memoirs, and letters. The outcome was *Rockdale* (1978), a richly satisfying work unified by Kuhn's notion of 'paradigm', which he applied, not just to a set of ideas, but to a holistic analysis of an entire mode of production (though with only the smallest of nods to Marx). Wallace paid close attention to weaving technology and the dynamics implicit in its development; however, behind the technology he also saw the financial arrangements and the personal relationships among the entrepreneurial elite that made the local industry possible. Rockdale is therefore a micro-sociological study of technological organisation and innovation, the study of a 'paradigmatic community' of artisans and managers.

However, it is also an account of a culture and time in which evangelical Christianity and capitalism could comfortably walk hand in hand. And it includes both workers and masters, demonstrating how essential family labour and women's work were to the well-being of the former, and how essential kinship and affinal ties were to the financial success of the latter. Women and men of that day speak to us in their own words. The result is a compelling portrait of nineteenth-century America that garnered Wallace the Bancroft Prize, a major award in American history writing.

Wallace expanded on these themes in later works, and then returned once more to the history of Native America in the form of a study of Thomas Jefferson's Indian policy (1999). Jefferson's ethnological theories are explored in depth, as are the involvement of prominent Revolutionary-era Americans in western land speculation and the unfortunate side-effects of democratic republican expansionism. The message is appropriately tragic in tone: 'Thomas Jefferson played a major role in...a tragedy which he so elegantly mourned: the dispossession and decimation of the First Americans' (1999: viii).

Education

BA University of Pennsylvania, 1947
MA University of Pennsylvania, 1949
Ph.D. University of Pennsylvania, 1950

Fieldwork

Tuscarora (Six Nations Iroquois) Reservation, 1948–9
Six Nations Iroquois (various locales), 1951–6
Director of clinical research, Eastern Pennsylvania Psychiatric Inst., 1955–61
Social historical research in eastern and central Pennsylvania, various periods

Key Publications

(1961) *Culture and Personality*, New York: Random House.
(1970) *The Death and Rebirth of the Seneca*, New York: Alfred A. Knopf.
(1978) *Rockdale: The Growth of an American Village in the Early Industrial Revolution*, New York: Alfred A. Knopf.
(1999) *Jefferson and the Indians: The Tragic Fate of the First Americans*, Cambridge: Belknap Press of Harvard University Press.

MICHAEL G. KENNY

Wallman, Sandra

b. 1934, London, UK

Sandra Wallman's long career within anthropology is marked by contrast: the contrast between her work on development and AIDS in Africa with that of work and well-being in

London and other European cities; between race and ethnicity as it is manifested in African and European contexts; and between academic anthropology and its application. Yet running throughout what might appear to be an unusual kind of eclecticism for an anthropologist is a strong, unifying thread which arises from the comparative framework that such contrasts can inspire: Wallman is passionately committed to anthropology as an essentially practical discipline that can find appropriate and useful outlets for its findings. From her earliest work on perceptions of development to her more recent concern with AIDS and risk, Wallman has insisted that the grander theories and models of anthropology must always acknowledge people's capacities to take charge of their own lives even in the most extreme of circumstances and, thus, anthropology must take account of how, in the local context, such circumstances are experienced and made sense of. Structural explanations and theories must recognise the inherent untidiness of social systems. It is this which facilitates choice and flexibility in people's everyday lives.

Thus, for example, in her study of eight London households, Wallman challenged common-place and policy assumptions about the inevitably bleak and deterministic relationship between inner cities, disadvantage, and ethnicity. She revealed the complex ways in which people living in Battersea managed their different resources and engaged variously with ideas of ethnicity, neighbourhood, and locality to more or less 'get by' and live out a decent life within the deprivations of the inner city. Later, in an entirely different context – Kampala, Uganda – this theme was elaborated by Wallman in her study of how ordinary African women manage their own health needs and those of their children in the time of AIDS. Confronting populist portrayals of sexually transmitted diseases and risk behaviour she identified women's potential for avoiding harm, underlining the local constraints and resources that need to be considered by policy-makers with regard to planned intervention strategies.

The supposed gap between pure and applied anthropology has therefore been consistently challenged by Wallman and it was under her leadership that the Association of Social Anthropologists first opened the doors of the academy to a broader membership and rendered British social anthropology more appropriate for the changed local and policy contexts within which many social anthropologists work contemporarily.

Education

Diploma in French language and literature, Sorbonne, Paris, 1953
B.Sc. London School of Economics, 1961
Ph.D. London School of Economics, 1965

Fieldwork

Lesotho, 1963/4
Italian Alps, 1972, 1974
London, 1975–85
Zambia, 1988–93
Kampala, Uganda, 1994, 1996
Turin, 1999–2001

Key Publications

(1984) *Eight London Households*, London: Tavistock.
(1996) *Kampala Women Getting By: Wellbeing in the time of Aids*, London: James Curry.
(1998) 'New Identities and the local factor – or when is home in town a good move', in N. Rapport and A. Dawson (eds) *Migrants of Identity*, Oxford: Berg.

ALLISON JAMES

Warman Gryj, Arturo

b. 1937, Mexico City, Mexico

Interested in peasants and rural life, Arturo Warman defined the persistent relationship between peasants and the state as one of exploitation and contradiction that is the motor of change in Mexico: the Mexican

Revolution of 1910 was an expression of this contradiction. His doctoral research in Morelos showed how the expropriation of rural communities' autonomy is at the foundation of state political domination. In this sense, the state is paramount in defining the existence and the political and economic status of peasants in Mexico. Based on this and other field research in Mexico, he emphasised that peasant households in order to survive employed creative and flexible methods of allocating scarce resources and securing their existence as peasants. The unity of the modern and traditional rural production in Mexico is considered dialectical: to survive, to fertilise with chemicals, to harvest products that are too expensive for them to consume, peasants have had to become more 'traditional'; they have to plant the corn that they will eat and establish reciprocal relations for the direct, non-capitalist exchange of labour and resources.

Between 1988 and 2000 Warman was subsequently director of the Instituto Nacional Indigenista (National Institute for Indian Affairs), Procurador Agrario (Agrarian Procurer), Secretario de Agricultura (Secretary of Agriculture), Secretario de la Reforma Agraria (Secretary of Agrarian Reform), and Coordinador del Gabinete de Desarrollo Social de la Presidencia de la República (Presidential Coordinator of the Cabinet for Social Development). While defending his view of the vitality of peasants and peasant communities, he participated in a polemical reform of the Constitution regarding agrarian property. His latest work is on the twentieth-century history of peasants in Mexico.

Education

BA Escuela Nacional de Antropología e Historia, México, 1968

MA Universidad Nacional Autónoma de México, 1968

Ph.D. Universidad Iberoamericana, 1975

Fieldwork

Ejidos in Mexico, 1961–5

Puebla-Tlaxcala, Mexico, 1965–6
Irrigation Districts, Mexico, 1967–8
Texcoco, Mexico, 1969
Michoacan, Mexico, 1970
La Angostura, Chiapas, Mexico, 1971
Eastern Morelos, Mexico, 1972–3
Yucatan, Mexico, 1977–9
Guerrero, Mexico, 1980

Key Publications

(1980) 'We Come to Object' The Peasants of Morelos and the National State, (Y venimos a contradecir... Los campesinos de Morelos y el Estado Nacional, 1976), trans. Stephen K. Ault, Baltimore: John Hopkins University Press.

(2001) El campo mexicano en el siglo XX (Mexican Agriculture in the Twentieth Century), México: Fondo de Cultura Económica.

FERNANDO I. SALMERÓN CASTRO

Warner, William Lloyd

b. 26 October 1898, Redlands, California, USA

d. 23 May 1970, Chicago, Illinois, USA

During the 1930s, 1940s, 1950s, and 1960s, W. Lloyd Warner was an important figure in cultural anthropology and sociology, authoring or influencing many significant qualitative research studies on American society. Though Warner's impact on the social sciences has been intellectual, methodological, and institutional, his interdisciplinary legacy is sometimes ignored and downplayed in many historical reconstructions of mid-century America's social scientific development. Some of this stems from the fact that Warner was working in the shadows of much more famous urban sociologists who sometimes eschewed qualitative ethnographic study for the prestige of theory-building and/or the quantitative specificity of statistical research. Even still, Warner's projects have had a major effect on the trajectory of qualitative research in the USA during much of the twentieth century, an effect that should not be understated.

Warner's commitment to the classical ethnographic monograph (deemed, by many historians of the social sciences, to be the defining feature of the so-called 'Chicago School' tradition) was, at least partially, a function of his training under British social anthropologist, A.R. Radcliffe-Brown – and was even somewhat fostered by Radcliffe-Brown's colleague at Harvard University, the physical anthropologist, Earnest Hooton. Technically, Warner never actually completed his Ph.D. in anthropology at Harvard. However, under the auspices of his graduate work there, he conducted research on the Murngin, an indigenous local group in Australia. This fieldwork was later published as *A Black Civilization, A Social Study of an Australian Tribe* in 1937, his first full-length manuscript.

After completing that research project, Warner began conducting ethnographic studies in America – most famously, the Yankee City series, his longitudinal examination of class and community in Newburyport, Massachusetts, a project that eventually encompassed some twenty years of research and several additional geographical locations. Based on his Yankee City findings, Warner was famous – some might say infamous – for offering up a six-fold model of America's class structure (upper class, lower-upper class, upper-middle class, lower-middle class, upper-lower class, and lower-lower class), arguing that this six-part schema was an emic category of social analysis used by Americans themselves and not simply imposed from without by the learned social scientist. Scholars such a C. Wright Mills subsequently critiqued Warner's sextuple class model as little more than a bourgeois ideological justification for middle-class hegemony and maintenance of a structural *status quo* – dismissing his taxonomy as subjective, arbitrary, and irremediably inadequate.

These criticisms notwithstanding, Warner's work had a substantial impact on a generation of social scientists trained at America's premier sociology department (the University of Chicago). Even still, Warner was a kind of an interstitial figure, troubling the overly policed methodological and epistemological borders between sociology and social anthropology. Although known for his expert and pioneering work with small-scale suburban communities (a provincial emphasis that, for many critics, compromised his studies' generalisability), he also brought his anthropological training to bear on some of the most pressing urban issues of the day. For instance, working alongside many of his graduate students, Warner conducted some of the earliest ethnographic studies on work and 'the industrial man' ever completed in the USA, focusing his empirical eye on the everyday configurations of large-scale industrial corporations and their cultural underpinnings.

During a time period when the field of sociology was defining its methodological center as decidedly quantitative (a move begun by the likes of William Ogburn and institutionalised by the internationally renowned, University of Chicago-housed National Opinion Research Center), Warner was spearheading and advising some of the most canonical ethnographic studies on American culture. For example, he served as a mentor and adviser for the seminal study on class differences in mid-1930s Natchez, Mississippi, *Deep South*. He was also an important influence on urban ethnographers, St Clair Drake and Horace Cayton – and on their important study, *Black Metropolis*, an ethnographic look at race, class, and identity in black Chicago during the early 1940s. Moreover, Warner was a significant influence on another Harvard-trained urban ethnographer, someone also working in Chicago during the 1940s, William Foote Whyte, author of *Street Corner Society*. Besides his own varied and ambitious ethnographic œuvre, Warner's impact on the aforementioned 'Chicago School' studies solidifies his continuing centrality to any narrative account of the history of qualitative sociology in the USA. Warner died in Chicago in 1970 while still conducting research on corporate culture and its executives.

Education

AB University of California, 1925

Fieldwork

Australia, 1926–9
Newburyport, Massachusetts ('Yankee City'
  series), 1929–50
Ireland, 1931–3
Rockford, Illinois, 1946–8

Key Publications

(1952) *Structure of American Life*, Edinburgh:
  University of Edinburgh Press.
(1953) *American Life: Dream and Reality*, Chicago:
  University of Chicago Press.
(1961) *The Corporation in the Emergent American
  Society*, New York: Harper & Brothers.
(1963) *Yankee City*, New Haven: Yale University
  Press.

JOHN L. JACKSON, JR

Watanabe, Hitoshi

b. 1919, Ujiyamada, Japan

d. 1998, Tokyo, Japan

Although Hitoshi Watanabe conducted ethnographic research on the Ainu in Japan as a part
of his doctoral dissertation, his interests have
covered a much wider range of issues on
human evolution, ecological anthropology,
and ethnoarchaeology. Written from ecological and structural-functional viewpoints, his
monograph on the Ainu is highly regarded as
source material for Ainu life in the late
nineteenth century. His ideas on the importance of technology and human activities in
human–environment relationships was the
outcome of the traditional teachings of the
Tokyo School of anthropology where he had
especially received tutelage from Professor
Ken-ichi Sugiura, a specialist of the material
culture of Micronesia, and Professor Kotondo
Hasebe, a specialist of human ergology. His
findings on the relationships between technology and individual variations of human skill –
which were based on his excavations of
Neanderthal remains and stone tools at Amud
Cave in Israel, as well as from his ethnological
survey on bows and arrows among the
contemporary Oriomo Papuans – are at
the forefront of important concepts regarding
the interactions between culture and biology
in human evolutionary processes. His meticulous comparisons of ethnological data on
northern hunter-gatherers with Jomon material culture reveal a stratified social structure
and belief in the goddess, in the religion of
Jomon people in prehistoric Japan. His
ecological-functional approach in sociocultural
anthropology has provided new insights into
the study of northern hunter-gatherers.

Education

BA University of Tokyo, 1946
D.Sc. University of Tokyo, 1960

Fieldwork

Hidaka and Tokachi, Hokkaido, Japan, 1952–9
Galilee, Israel, 1960–1, 1964
Oriomo, Papua New Guinea, 1971

Key Publications

(1972) *The Ainu Ecosystem: Environment and Group
  Structure*, Seattle and London: University of
  Washington Press.
(1990) *Jomon-shiki Kaisoka Shakai* (Jomon-Type
  Stratified Society), Tokyo: Rokko Shuppan.

TAKASHI IRIMOTO

Weaver, Sally M.

b. 1940, Fort Erie, Ontario, Canada

d. 1993, Ontario, Canada

Sally Weaver's initial fieldwork (with which
she earned the first doctorate in anthropology
awarded to a woman by the University of
Toronto) examined medical acculturation

among non-conservative (i.e. Christian) Iroquois on the Six Nations Reserve. The remainder of her career was devoted to studying liberal-democratic governments' relations with and administration of aboriginal peoples. In particular, she focused upon the factors and processes that shaped policy-making in this field. Her investigation of the Canadian government's controversial 1969 White Paper on Indian policy combined detailed interviewing of senior bureaucrats and politicians with careful analysis of documentary sources to provide a comprehensive and nuanced account that won the respect of academics, administrators, and aboriginal people. Her thoroughness in explicating the diverging perspectives and purposes of a broad range of agencies and representatives involved in particular instances of policy-making rested upon an ability to conduct incisive and revealing interviews with key informants. Her work on aboriginal–government relations was in due course extended to Australia and Norway. Weaver's invariably well-grounded analyses of policy questions pertaining to indigenous peoples in all three countries made timely and significant contributions to the development of comparative anthropological studies of the 'Fourth World'.

Education

BA University of Toronto, 1963
MA University of Toronto, 1964
Ph.D. University of Toronto, 1967

Fieldwork

Six Nations Reserve, Brantford, Ontario, 1964–78
Ottawa, Canada, 1975–93
Kakadu, Northern Territory and Canberra, Australia, 1979–83
Tromso, Norway, 1984–90

Key Publications

(1972) *Medicine and Politics among the Grand River Iroquois*, Publications in Ethnology, Mono-

graphy No. 4, Ottawa: National Museum of Man.
(1981) *Making Canadian Indian Policy: The Hidden Agenda, 1968–70*, Toronto: University of Toronto Press.

NOEL DYCK

Weiner, Annette

b. 14 February 1933, Philadelphia, Pennsylvania, USA

d. 7 December 1997, New York City, USA

Annette Weiner began her academic career late, having earlier worked in business, married, and raised children. Her major fieldwork in the Trobriand Islands and her rich ethnography and brilliant analyses of that society led to major reappraisal of Trobriand culture and to reassessment of Malinowski's pioneer contributions to anthropology.

With her dissertation and first book on the classically central Trobriand Islands, Weiner became a leading figure in the anthropology of Oceania and its contributions to anthropological theory. Her most significant contributions lay in recognising the gendered and political ramifications of exchange and kinship, rethinking such classic questions as reciprocity, incest, inalienability, and hierarchy. For example, in demonstrating that women were involved in exchange, her first publications expanded the earlier picture of Trobriand culture and society provided by Malinowski. She showed that women's exchange in mortuary rituals occupied a central role in the total Trobriand system of social organisation – through which sub-clans reproduced themselves. Their gifts were significant components of the larger exchange cycle and ought not to be understood as a 'free gift', an expression of love, as Malinowski's ethnocentric view of reciprocity wrongly held.

Weiner's approach to exchange is fully articulated in the deceptively simple *The Trobrianders of Papua New Guinea*. An innovative discussion of gifts to children and sexuality is integrated with analysis of the kula as realised through different media and cycles of exchange.

Subsequently, using comparative work from Samoa and ethnography from other Pacific societies, she developed a comparative analysis that emphasised the relative importance of the brother–sister tie. This emphasis drew attention to the centrality of reproduction as a framework for understanding men and women, a framework that did not reduce women to the role of mothers, but placed reproduction in a broader cosmological framework.

A key focus in Weiner's work was attention to 'women's wealth' and its circulation, usually in the form of cloth. The failure to recognise the significance of such forms of value, she showed repeatedly, has led to an inability to recognise the full nature of exchange and the role of different actors within such a system.

Finally, the book, *Inalienable Possessions*, drew her insights about exchange and gender into a theoretical confrontation with some of the most enduring confusions about 'reciprocity' as the central question involving exchange. She challenged the simplistic 'gift'/'commodity' dichotomy and argued that exchange should be understood as having the capacity to express identity and to produce hierarchy – ranked or valued difference. It is not a class of objects that are called 'inalienable' but rather a set of social processes in which the capacity to exchange or withhold can become a marker of social strength and identity.

Weiner succeeded in rethinking what anthropologists call 'exchange' by forcing us to move beyond the simple categories of 'reciprocity' and understanding the practices of giving, receiving, and taking as part of much more complex temporalities – extending the effects of the gift, as she often said, beyond death.

Education

BA University of Pennsylvania, 1968
Ph.D. Bryn Mawr College, 1974

Fieldwork

Antigua, Guatemala, 1969, 1970
Trobriand Islands, 1971–2, 1976, 1980, 1982, 1989
Western Samoa, 1980

Key Publications

(1976) *Women of Value, Men of Renown: New Perspectives in Trobriand Exchange*, Austin and London: University of Texas Press.
(1988) *The Trobrianders of Papua New Guinea*, New York: Holt, Rinehart & Winston.
with Schneider, Jane (eds) (1989) *Cloth and Human Experience*, Washington, DC: Smithsonian Institution Press.
(1992) *Inalienable Possessions: The Paradox of Keeping-while-Giving*, Berkeley: University of California Press.

FRED MYERS

Weingrod, Alex

b. 1931, Milwaukee, Wisconsin, USA

Alex Weingrod went to Israel in 1956 to conduct research on Moroccan Jewish immigrants living in newly founded agricultural settlements. After completing his doctoral dissertation, he continued this research and became director of the Department of Settlement Research for the Jewish Agency. In this capacity, he supervised the research of other anthropologists including Moshe Shokeid and Shlomo Deshen. From 1962 to 1974, Weingrod taught at Brandeis University in the USA. He subsequently returned to Israel first as director of the Brandeis programme and then as professor in the Department of Behavioural Sciences at Ben-Gurion University in Beersheba, where he taught until his retirement in 1999. Weingrod began his career focusing on the absorption of immigrants by a larger society and culture contact. In his work on Moroccan settlements, he stressed, first of all, that these settlements were founded as 'administered communities', mandated by the

Israeli authorities and only gradually developed an autonomy of their own. Through their resistance to the demands of the counsellors and administrators, they forced changes in the relationship that they had with Israeli society, which Weingrod called 'reciprocal acculturation'. Weingrod called attention to the social gap in Israel between the established Israeli population of European origin and the newer immigrants, who at that time came mainly from the countries of North Africa and Southwestern Asia. When he returned to Israel, Weingrod became more involved in work dealing with Jerusalem. A notable study from this period is his 1991 collaboration with Michael Romann, *Living Together Separately: Arabs and Jews in Contemporary Jerusalem*. This work is based on research conducted in the 1980s, prior to the first Intifada. The work is a finely tuned description of social conflict and integration. Chapters in the book dealing with formal political structure, statistics, and spatial patterns alternate with extended case studies of particular social settings, such as neighbourhoods where Arabs and Jews live in the same vicinity or where Jews and Arabs work together, as in a bakery and a hospital. Weingrod's approach is eclectic in the sense that he is open to a variety of methodologies. He also gives equal weight to forces of integration and conflict.

Education

BA University of Chicago, 1952
MA University of Chicago, 1954
Ph.D. University of Chicago, 1959

Fieldwork

Moroccan immigrant villages in Negev, Israel, 1957–9
Research on rural settlement in Israel, 1960–2
Regional political organisation, Sardinia, Italy, 1966–7
Political economies of industrialising agrarian states, 1968–71
Local-level changes in Israeli immigrant villages, 1973–4

Contact networks of the Israeli national elite, 1974–5
Local disputes in Jerusalem, 1977–9
Arab–Jewish relationships in Jerusalem, 1981–3
Comparative study of ethnic celebrations in Israel, 1985–8
Arab–Jewish relations in Jerusalem since the first Intifada, 1989–90
Israeli Palestinians in Jerusalem, 1993–4
Mobility among Iraqi and Moroccan Immigrants in Israel, 1993–6

Key Publications

(1966) *Reluctant Pioneers*, Ithaca: Cornell University Press
(ed.) (1985) *Studies in Israeli Ethnicity: After the Ingathering*, New York and London: Gordon & Breach.
(1989) *The Saint of Beersheba*, Albany: State University of New York Press.
with Romann, M. (1991) *Living Together Separately: Arabs and Jews in Contemporary Jerusalem*, Princeton, NJ: Princeton University Press.

WALTER P. ZENNER

Werbner, Pnina

b. 1944, South Africa

During the past quarter-century, Pnina Werbner has researched Pakistani Muslims, beginning in Manchester and opening into concentric circles of widening power and scope – of ethnography (from Britain to Pakistan), of theory (from social networks to post-modern, global identity politics), and of practice (that of Sufi cults in Britain and Pakistan). Werbner's writings are deeply informed by field research through long durations, in keeping with the tenets of Manchester anthropology, an early source of intellectual nourishment. Her research concentrated then on issues of the formation of urban, ethnic community through social networks, economic entrepreneurship, and community politics. In more recent years her research has shifted towards issues of the cultural imaginary, and the spaces – local and global, public and private, serious and playful – that Pakistani immigrants open, and within and through which they shape and shift identity formations. Werbner's concerns now engage with the creation of diasporic, hybrid, political discourses, fusing civil democratic rights with Islamic piety, and with polyphonies of voice and the contesting of representations. In Werbner's theorising, these shifting discourses and identities emerge from the intersections of Islamicisation, Empire, modernism, and nationalism.

Education

BA Hebrew University, 1970
Ph.D. University of Manchester, 1979

Fieldwork

Pakistani immigrants, Manchester, 1975–8
Pakistani community politics, Manchester, 1986–7
Mosque politics and Sufism, Manchester and Pakistan, 1989–90
Sufism and Sufi cults, Britain and Pakistan, 1990–2
Pakistani women and political activism, Britain, 1994–6
Sufi followers, Britain and Pakistan, 1999–2000
Women and the changing public sphere, Botswana, 2000–1

Key Publications

(2002) Imagined Diasporas among Manchester Muslims, Oxford: James Currey and Santa Fe: School of American Research Press.
(2003) Pilgrims of Love: The Anthropology of a Global Sufi Cult, London: Hurst Publishers and Bloomington: Indiana University Press.

DON HANDELMAN

Werbner, Richard

b. 11 August 1937, Boston, Massachusets, USA

Richard Werbner received his doctoral training during a period of intensive methodological and empirical innovation in the Department of Social Anthropology at the University of Manchester. Closely supervised by the founding figures of the Manchester School, Werbner embarked on ethnographic research in the School's traditional field in South-Central Africa in 1960. Victor Turner's influence is particularly evident in his early interest in ritual, cosmology, and divination. Werbner's pioneering work on regional cults highlighted cultural flows long before multisited fieldwork became established in anthropology's methodological arsenal.

Werbner's award-winning monograph, Tears of the Dead, built on the Manchester School's commitment to long-term observation by following the trajectories of a single family in colonial and post-colonial Zimbabwe. Its approach to 'social biography' was also influenced by Paul Radin, who inspired Werbner to collect life histories during an undergraduate project in the USA.

Tears of the Dead heralded Werbner's interest in the cultural, subjective, and political dimensions of the post-colonial condition in Africa. Between 1996 and 2002, he edited three volumes of Africanist anthropology seeking to uncover the complexities of identity, social memory, and subjectivity under post-colonialism. The distinct contribution of these volumes is to offer ethnographic nuance to debates dominated by philosophers and other theorists. In 1999, Werbner commenced fresh fieldwork in Botswana with a special interest in elite formation as well as in the changing circumstances of divination.

Education

BA Brandeis University, 1959
Ph.D. University of Manchester, 1968

Fieldwork

Nebraska, USA, 1958
Zimbabwe, 1960–1, 1989
Botswana, 1964–5, 1969, 1972–3, 1974, 1977, 1978, 1985, 1999, 2000–2

Key Publications

(1989) *Ritual Passage, Sacred Journey*, Washington, DC: Smithsonian Institution Press.
(1991) *Tears of the Dead: The Social Biography of an African Family*, Edinburgh: Edinburgh University Press for the International African Institute.

HARRI ENGLUND

White, Leslie A.

b. 19 January 1900, Salida, California, USA

d. 31 March 1975, near Death Valley, California, USA

Leslie White grew up in the Midwest and was forced to re-evaluate the platitudes of his unquestioned patriotism after a stint in the US Army in 1918. At Louisiana State University and then at Columbia, he shifted from physics to history to political science, then to psychology, sociology, and philosophy, with his first two degrees being awarded in psychology. White initially encountered anthropology not at Columbia but from Alexander Goldenweiser at the New School for Social Research.

In 1924, he moved to the University of Chicago to study sociology, which then included anthropology. His initial Keresan Pueblo fieldwork, funded by Elsie Clews Parsons, led to a dissertation on Southwestern medicine societies. White was surprisingly successful in obtaining esoteric information given the hostility of the Keresan Pueblos to outsiders. Many of his methods, however, would not meet contemporary standards for research with human subjects because of the secrecy in which many inquiries were conducted and the lack of community consent to making such materials public. White later claimed that the split of Chicago's sociology and anthropology departments in 1927 resulted directly from the feeling of some sociologists that his ethnographic work was insufficiently theoretical to merit a doctorate.

White's first teaching job at the University of Buffalo brought him into contact with Lewis Henry Morgan's work on the Iroquoian Seneca of nearby Tonawanda Reservation. He soon embarked on a lifelong crusade to rehabilitate Morgan's theory of cultural evolution, editing Morgan's letters and journals, and producing a definitive edition of *Ancient Society*. A visit to Russia in 1929, coupled with the adaptation of Morgan's schema to socialist ideology by Friedrich Engels, persuaded White that socialism would necessarily prevail in the West. This prediction did little to endear him to the administration at the University of Michigan where he succeeded Julian Stewart, another evolutionary revivalist although through a Boasian intellectual genealogy, in 1930. Although White's overtly political writings were published under the pseudonym of John Steele, a fact not widely known at the time, his career progress at Michigan was stalled for long periods. His full professorship came only in 1943 and the 'acting' was removed from his long-term chairmanship of the department of anthropology only in the following year. White was equally isolated within his own profession, where the Boasian critique of evolution still held firm sway.

To the frustration of the Michigan administration, White was a remarkably effective and popular lecturer. His large course in 'culturology' or the science of culture was thoroughly materialist in its approach to 'the mind of primitive man'. The capacity for symbolic thought was at the core of progress towards consciousness of the determining effects of culture. He preferred to speak about civilisation rather than culture. The local Catholic church aggressively attacked his purported atheism and rejection of free will, although White's academic freedom was reluctantly defended by the administration on multiple occasions. Critics were often startled to learn that White was personally quiet and self-deprecating.

White avoided the label 'neo-evolution', considering his own position to revive nineteenth-century evolutionism. *The Science of Culture* (1949) exemplifies his model. *The Evolution of Culture*, appearing a decade later, was anticlimactic, with evolution tempered by functionalism. White then turned to cultural evolution defined in terms of the harnessing of more energy per capita through technological adaptation. In his view, individuals had virtually no role in the structure of culture itself. *The Concept of Cultural Systems*, published posthumously in 1975, presented these final elaborations.

White separated his ethnographic work on Pueblo religion from his theoretical work on economics and technology. Religion persisted longest under pressure towards assimilation and thus remained the core of salvage ethnography. His cultural analysis of the behaviour of nations was simply not comparable.

White's third specialisation was in the history of anthropology. All graduate students at Michigan had to take this course. He was adamant that he did not want to establish a Michigan 'school' of anthropology, criticising Franz Boas and A.R. Radcliffe-Brown for creating such unproductive structures. His vitriolic readings of the Boasian tradition were legendary (e.g. White 1966).

A quarter-century after his death, White's evolutionary model is most often employed by archaeologists because it enables them to use material remains in a powerful theoretical framework. At the height of his theoretical ascendancy, White's model may have provided a corrective to narrowness and complacency in the Boasian tradition.

Education

BA Columbia University, 1923
MA Columbia University, 1924
Ph.D. University of Chicago, 1927

Fieldwork

Southwestern Pueblos, 1925 through 1930s

Key Publications

(1949) *The Science of Culture: A Study of Man and Civilization*, New York: Farar & Strauss.
(1959) *The Evolution of Culture: The Development of Civilization to the Fall of Rome*, New York: McGraw-Hill.
(1966) *The Social Organization of Ethnological Theory*, Houston: Rice University Studies 52, 4.
(1975) *The Concept of Cultural Systems: A Key to Understanding Tribes and Nations*, New York: Columbia University Press.

REGNA DARNELL

Whiting, Beatrice Blyth

b. 14 April 1914, New York City, USA

Beatrice Blyth Whiting is known for her lifelong commitment and contribution to the cross-cultural study of culture and human development in the lives of children, women, and families. Her influence as a scholar, mentor, and teacher in psychological and sociocultural anthropology, child development, and education spans generations (see special issue of *Ethos* 29, 3, 2001).

Whiting's pioneering theoretical and methodological approach to the study of human behaviour combines comparative ethnographic field research with quantitative methods using an interdisciplinary theoretical frame in understanding the complexities of social life and culture change. She is known for her groundbreaking collaborative and cross-disciplinary research method, and her use of apprenticeship models.

Whiting is the author of numerous journal articles on topics including children's social behaviour, the cultural meanings of household routines, the impact of economic change on women's lives, aggression and identity, fatherhood, adolescence, cultural processes of social control, and child-rearing practices. Her most recent book (edited with Carolyn Pope Edwards) is titled *Ngecha: A Kenyan Community in a Time of Rapid Social Change* (University of Nebraska Press, 2004).

Whiting directed three major comparative studies of human development. She and her husband, John Whiting, headed the Six Culture project during the 1950s. The Six Culture Study was first conceptualised as the study of one hundred cultures in a world sample. The Whitings transformed it into an intensive study of child-rearing and children's behaviour in six sites in Mexico, India, Kenya, New England, Okinawa, and the Philippines. From 1966 to 1973, she was associate director of the Child Development Research Unit at the University of Nairobi (field research in fifteen communities in Kenya), and in the 1980s she directed the Harvard Comparative Adolescence Project.

Whiting has been the recipient of numerous awards and appointments. She received the AAA's Distinguished Service Award in 1982 and the Society for Psychological Anthropology's Career Contribution Award in 1989 with John Whiting. From 1978 to 1979, Whiting held a prestigious fellowship at the Center for Advanced Study in the Behavioral Sciences in Palo Alto, California, and was a distinguished scholar at the Henry A. Murray Center for the Study of Lives at Harvard University from 1980 to 1985.

Beatrice Whiting took her first position at Harvard University in 1952 and became professor of anthropology and education in 1974. She taught at the Harvard Graduate School of Education from 1969 until her retirement in 1980.

Education

Bryn Mawr College, 1935
Ph.D. Yale University, 1942

Fieldwork

Northern Paiutes of Burns Reservation, Eastern Oregon, 1934–7
Gikuyus of Ngecha sub-location, Central Province, Kenya, 1968–73

Key Publications

(1950) *Paiute Sorcery*, New York: The Viking Fund Publications in Anthropology, No. 15.

(ed) (1963) *Six Cultures: Studies of Child Rearing*, New York: John Wiley.
with Whiting, John W.M. (1975) *Children of Six Cultures: A Psycho-cultural Analysis*, Cambridge, MA: Harvard University Press.
with Edwards, Carolyn P. (1988) *Children of Different Worlds: The Formation of Social Behavior*, Cambridge, MA: Harvard University Press.

VIRGINIA CAPUTO

Whiting, John W.M.

b. 12 June 1908, Martha's Vineyard, Massachusetts, USA

d. 13 May 1999, Martha's Vineyard, Massachusetts, USA

John Whiting was responsible for introducing new standards in the research methodology of the twentieth-century 'culture and personality movement'. He was a student of George P. Murdock, his mentor and thesis adviser at Yale University, who instilled in him an interest for cross-cultural research on a worldwide basis. Whiting was very much influenced by learning theorists such as Clark Hull, Neal Miller, and Robert Sears, while at the same time he drew from psychoanalytic theory through John Dollard and, particularly, Earl Zinn, who acted as his analyst. Whiting pushed Kardiner's analytical model of the relation between culture and personality to the level of worldwide cross-cultural surveys statistically validated. In this sense he was a continuator of the Human Relations Area Files initiated by Murdock at Yale.

Whiting and Irvin L. Child, one of his lifelong collaborators, presented a model to explain the relation between individual personality and culture that ran as follows: the 'maintenance systems' (i.e. economy, family, political systems) determine the 'child training practices' (e.g. type of mother–infant contact, infant feeding and sleeping practices, mother–father interaction, etc.), these influence the 'personality variables' (e.g. anxiety, aggressiveness, fear, self-confidence, etc.), which in turn determine the 'projective systems' (i.e. music, games, religious belief, notions of illness, initiation rites, etc.). The core of Whiting's theory is that the way each society deals with its infants influences the nature of each cultural system and the nature of the personality of its individuals. Contrary to the traditional psychoanalytical Freudian view, which put primary emphasis in the relation between enculturation practices and sexual behaviour within the family, Whiting's view extends the influence of infant enculturation practices to the whole of cultural behaviour and institutions.

The main contribution of Whiting and his collaborators to the analysis of the relation between environment, culture, and the individual was the so-called 'six-cultures' project, which aimed at comparing child-rearing practices across a number of different cultures worldwide.

Education

BA Yale University, 1931
Ph.D. Yale University, 1938

Fieldwork

Fieldwork among the Kwoma of New Guinea, 1935–6
Yale Institute of Human Relations (except for the period he worked in the US Navy during the Second World War), 1938–47
State University of Iowa, 1947–9
Laboratory of Human Development at the Graduate School of Education (Harvard University), 1949–63
Department of Social Relations at the Faculty of Arts and Sciences (Harvard University), 1963–78

Key Publications

(1941) *Becoming a Kwoma: Teaching and Training in a New Guinea Tribe*, New Haven: Yale University Press.
with Child, Irvin L. (1953) *Child Training and*

Personality: A Cross-Cultural Study, New Haven: Yale University Press.
with Whiting, Beatrice B. (1974) *Children of Six Cultures*, Cambridge, MA: Harvard University Press.
(1994) *Culture and Human Development: The Selected Papers of John Whiting*, ed. Eleanor Hollenberg Chasdi, Cambridge, UK: Cambridge University Press.

LUÍS BATALHA

Whitten, Norman Earl, Jr

b. 1937, Orange, New Jersey, USA

Norman Whitten has long been interested in ethnically diverse peoples and how they reproduce and transform cultural systems at local, regional, national, and global levels. This includes considerations of culture change, and cultural endurance in national and transnational systems. He pursues these topics in the context of local-level ethnography. His research encompasses the intersection of the environment with aesthetics, cosmology, shamanic performance, and power, a topic on which he and his wife, Dorothea Scott Whitten, have collaborated to produce books, articles, book chapters, and edited works. He has an abiding interest in cultural systems of the Upper Amazon region abutting the Andes and has collected longitudinal data there for more than forty-two years. Recognising that ethnography is in a position to unite cultural anthropology and history, he has adopted a longitudinal approach. He conducted intensive fieldwork in the 1960s among Afro-Hispanic populations in western Ecuador and Colombia, and has frequently returned to the theme of the African diaspora that he pursued there in venues as distant as Maritime Canada. He has undertaken field research with Canelos Quichua and Achuar people of Amazonian Ecuador every year since 1968, and has conducted research in various Andean regions of Ecuador, as well. Whitten has taken an applied anthropology approach from time to time in his region of specialisation. He and

Dorothea Whitten established an arts programme to enable Amazonian ceramists to market their work in the USA in order to support local medical services.

Education

AB Colgate University, 1959
MA University of North Carolina, Chapel Hill, 1961
Ph.D. University of North Carolina, Chapel Hill, 1964

Fieldwork

North Carolina,1959–60 (Afro-Americans)
Ecuador, 1961, 1963, 1968 (Afro-Americans); 1968, 1982, 1984 (Andean native peoples); 1994, 2000 (Afro-Ecuadorians); 1968, 1970, 1971, 1972–3, 1974, 1975, 1976,1977, 1978, 1979, 1980, 1981, 1982, 1983, 1984, 1985, 1986,1986–7, 1988, 1989, 1990, 1991, 1992, 1993, 1994, 1995, 1996, 1997, 1998, 1999, 2000, 2001, 2002 (Achuar Jivaroans)
Colombia, 1964–5, 1983, 1984, 1985, 1986, 1987, 1988, 1989, 1990, 1991, 1992 (Salasaca Quichua); 1982, 1983, 1984, 1985, 1986, 1986–7, 1988, 1989, 1992, 1998, 1999, 2000 (Quichua-speaking peoples)
Nova Scotia, 1966, 1967 (Afro-Canadians)
Nicaragua, 1984

Key Publications

(1976) *Sacha Runa: Ethnicity and Adaptation of Ecuadorian Jungle Quichua*, Urbana: University of Illinois Press.
(1985 [1974]) *Black Frontiersmen: Afro-Hispanic Culture from Ecuador and Colombia*, Prospect Heights, IL: Waveland Press.
(1985) *Sicuanga Runa: The Other Side of Development in Amazonian Ecuador*, Urbana: University of Illinois Press.
with Whitten, Dorothea S. (1985) *From Myth to Creation: Art from Amazonian Ecuador*, Urbana: University of Illinois Press.

JUDITH A. RASSON

Whorf, Benjamin Lee

b. 24 April 1897, Winthrop, Massachusetts, USA

d. 26 July 1941, Hartford, Connecticut, USA

Benjamin Lee Whorf, who was born to an old New England family, studied chemical engineering at MIT before becoming a fire insurance investigator for the Hartford Fire Insurance Company. By 1924, a childhood interest in Mesoamerican prehistory led him to study Mayan and Aztec hieroglyphics; Whorf learned Hebrew to clarify the apparent conflict between science and religion, and was much influenced by the religious ideas of Antoine Fabre d'Olivet. Whorf's fascination with cryptography and iconography led him to correspond with Harvard archaeologists who encouraged him because they needed a linguist to help them interpret archaeological remains in Middle America. Although Whorf's research proposal on the oligosynthetic structure of these languages was somewhat mystical, he obtained a Social Science Research Council Fellowship to do first-hand fieldwork on Milpa Alta Nahuatl (Aztec) in Mexico in 1930. He linked early Mayan and Aztec hieroglyphs, and argued that Mesoamerican writing systems were at least partially phonetic (which has since been confirmed).

When Edward Sapir, the foremost linguistic student of Franz Boas, came to Yale University in 1931, Whorf immediately enrolled in his seminar on Athabascan linguistics. Although Whorf never completed a doctorate at Yale and never sought a formal academic position, he became a core member of the school of linguistics that developed around Sapir during the 1930s. Whorf worked extensively on historical linguistics, extending the Uto-Aztecan language family into a Macro-Penutian super-stock and contributing to the revision of Sapir's classification of the North America linguistic stocks.

Increasingly after 1932 when he found a speaker with whom he could work in New York City, however, Whorf's work focused on the grammatical categories of Hopi. He used his vacation time and a SSRC grant to visit the Hopi Reservation briefly in 1938. He came to think of the 'model of the universe' encoded in Hopi and other Native American languages as contrasting dramatically with the familiar conceptual categories of English (later general-ised to SAE, Standard Average European).

Whorf's only academic position was lec-turer during Sapir's sabbatical in 1937–8. In order to make this course palatable to non-linguists in the anthropology programme, he formalised ideas about the intimate relation-ship between language, thought, and reality that were implicit in the linguistic work of both Sapir and Boas. Linguistics, for Whorf, served as a handmaiden of ethnology. He was eager to make it accessible to students of the American Indian.

The most complete summary of his position came in a Festschrift for Sapir, under the title 'The relation of habitual thought and beha-viour to language'. Despite later misreadings of his position, Whorf was not a linguistic determinist; self-conscious speakers, especially through training in linguistics, developed a multilingual awareness that could transcend the habitual categories of their native lan-guages. The linguistic relativity hypothesis, later called the Whorf (or even Sapir–Whorf) hypothesis, emphasised that speakers of dif-ferent languages lived in quite distinct worlds.

Whorf's premature death from cancer, only two years after Sapir's fatal heart attack, prevented him from developing many of his ideas. Furthermore, his publications are widely scattered, many of them in technical journals intended for an audience of scientists. Only after his death were significant papers collected and made available to colleagues in linguistics and anthropology (1949, 1956). Meanwhile,

American linguistics was turning away from mentalism and the cross-linguistic study of meaning during the 1940s and 1950s. Many of the former students of Sapir turned to a Bloomfieldian structuralism that was in many ways alien to Sapir's more processual concerns with the psychological reality of phonemes, and by extension grammatical categories, for native speakers of a language. Whorf's in-tellectual descendants attempted to test his theories as though they were scientific experi-ments. The ambiguity of the results led most linguists to ignore Whorf's formulation of linguistic relativity as interesting but not amenable to formal proof. Whorf was seen as intuitive and unscientific in this period. The return to meaning that began with the so-called Chomskian revolution of the 1960s, however, has renewed interest in many of Whorf's ideas. The emphasis in what is now called cognitive science has shifted, however, from the comparison of categories unique to specific languages towards the universals of human speech capacity.

Education

Chemical engineering, Massachusetts Institute of Technology, 1918

Fieldwork

Mexico, 1930
Hopi, 1938

Key Publications

(1941) 'The relation of habitual thought and behavior to language', in *Language, Culture, and Personality: Essays in Memory of Edward Sapir*, Menasha, WI: Sapir Memorial Publication Fund, pp. 75–93.

(1946) 'The Hopi language, Toreva dialect – The Milpa Alta dialect of Aztec, with notes on the Classical and the Tepoztlan dialects', in *Linguistic Structures of Native America*, ed. Harry Hoijer, New York: Viking Fund Publications in Anthropology.

(1949) *Four Articles on Metalinguistics*, Washington, DC: Foreign Service Institute.

(1956) *Language, Thought, and Reality: Selected Writings of Benjamin Lee Whorf*, ed. and Introduction by John B. Carroll, Cambridge, MA: MIT Press.

REGNA DARNELL

Whyte, Susan

b. 4 August 1943, New York, USA

Whyte's three decades of research in East Africa started in Uganda with a study of religion and divination. This early interest in misfortune became a long-term involvement in medical anthropology. A widening in focus from symbols and cultural logic to historical change, social relations, and pragmatism has brought transformations of health systems and health practices, subjectivity, and sociality to the forefront in Whyte's work. Pharmaceuticals and disability are two of the themes through which these issues are explored and brought into the context of development and globalisation. They provide examples of the interlinking between worldwide flows of commodities and discourses, and the intimate concerns of situated subjects. Her book, *Questioning Misfortune*, based on long-term recurrent fieldwork among the Nyole in eastern Uganda, is an insightful description of the pragmatics of uncertainty and the management of misfortune. Pragmatism has inspired not only her understanding of how Nyole engage their problems, but also how anthropologists, administrators, and policy-makers define problems, put ideas into practice, reflect on consequences, and thereby learn about the constraints of the world. Much of her work has been done jointly with Michael A. Whyte. It is characterised by dedication to the application of anthropology, to interdisciplinary co-operation, and to research collaboration with people from the developing world, through which the act of engaging problems is interlocked with theoretical developments in anthropology.

Education

BA Smith College, 1965
Ph.D. University of Washington, 1973

Fieldwork

Eastern Uganda, 1969–71, 1989–2003, and ongoing
Western, Kenya, 1978–9, 1987–8
Tanzania Mental Health Programme, 1982–3

Key Publications

with Ingstad, B. (eds) (1995) *Disability and Culture*, Berkeley: University of California Press.

(1997) *Questioning Misfortune: The Pragmatics of Uncertainty in Eastern Uganda*, Cambridge, UK: Cambridge University Press.

HANNE O. MOGENSEN

Wilson, Godfrey Baldwin

b. 1908, Oxford, UK

d. 1944

Though Godfrey Wilson's anthropological output was small, his influence extended well beyond his premature death because of the research programme he established at the Rhodes–Livingstone Institute, which had been founded in 1938 as a research agency of the colonial government. Under Wilson, and successors such as Max Gluckman, the Institute took a strikingly independent left-wing approach to the effects of Western domination and the capitalistic economy on African society. Building on Wilson's *Economics of Detribalization*, Institute researchers were learning how to deal with the new towns of Africa as an anthropological field worthy of study in their own right.

Influenced by B. Malinowski, his supervisor at the London School of Economics, Wilson envisioned society in terms of functionally interlocked sociocultural institutions with a built-in tendency towards 'coherence'. However, in situations involving rapid change, 'disequilibrium' might result between them. Wilson saw that such an imbalance had emerged in the relationship between the wage and the subsistence sectors of the Rhodesian economy, exacerbated by racially based economic discrimination. Wilson's functionalist vocabulary combines uneasily with the dynamism of his analysis; nevertheless his essay on detribalisation was a pioneering study on the political economy and cultural effects of wage-migration.

He also studied the new 'detribalised' society that was emerging as different 'tribal' groups came together in one industrial locale. Wilson articulated these findings to the world-system at large, and, though his analysis was Marxist in flavour, he himself was a Christian humanist who described communism as an 'atheistic cult'. Wilson despised the racism of colonial society, and his fraternisation with ordinary Africans eventually made him unacceptable to government and mine officials who saw him as a potentially disruptive influence on increasingly tense racial and labour relations.

Wilson's approach had matured during extended fieldwork among the Nyakyusa of southwest Tanzania, where he took a keen interest in such subjects as land tenure. In research among the related Ngonde people of northern Malawi, he considered the influence of trade on the historical development of indigenous state structures. Had he lived longer, Godfrey Wilson might well have made further notable contributions to a wide range of anthropological and historical concerns.

That was left to his South African wife, Monica Wilson, a prominent anti-apartheid anthropologist and historian at the University of Cape Town, who built on their joint Nyakyusa fieldwork to produce a remarkable series of ethnographic monographs on this unusual age-stratified society.

Education

BA University of Oxford
Ph.D. London School of Economics

Fieldwork

Tanganyika and Nyasaland (now Tanzania and Malawi), 1935–8
Northern Rhodesia (now Zambia), 1938–41

Key Publications

(1939) *The Constitution of Ngonde*, Paper # 3 of the Rhodes–Livingstone Institute, Livingstone.
(1941–2) *An Essay on the Economics of Detribalization in Northern Rhodesia* (2 parts), Papers # 5 and 6 of the Rhodes–Livingstone Institute, Livingstone.
with Wilson, Monica (1945) *The Analysis of Social Change*, Cambridge, UK: Cambridge University Press.

MICHAEL G. KENNY

Wilson, Monica

b. 1908, Lovedale Mission, Eastern Cape Province, South Africa

d. 1982

Monica Wilson (née Hunter) is mainly known to anthropologists for her series of monographs on the Nyakyusa of southwestern Tanzania, an unusual age-stratified society with political institutions approximating to the idea of 'divine kingship'. However, she has an additional claim to stature because of the character of her involvement in the intellectual life of South Africa.

Wilson's work among the Nyakyusa was the result of an ethnographic partnership with her English husband, Godfrey Wilson, a student of Bronislaw Malinowski. The Wilsons found that the Nyakyusa had institutional cleavages between fathers and sons, which were ritualised through a 'coming out' ceremony signifying a transition between generations. As the son's generation matured, a village was divided into quarters where the generations were supposed to live separately from one another, due in part to a strong avoidance between fathers-in-law and daughters-in-law.

Godfrey Wilson died young, and the writing-up of their findings fell to his wife, who generated no less than four monographs based on their 1930s fieldwork. These range from *Good Company*, an account of Nyakyusa age organisation and political structure, to two books on ritual, to a 1977 book on social change. Though faulted for their relative lack of analysis, Wilson's writings contain an amazing body of material on political structure, ritual symbolism, and the sociology of witchcraft accusations.

However, that is only half the story. Monica Wilson was brought up in a South African missionary family, and was profoundly interested in the rights of native Africans. One consequence was her monograph, *Reaction to Conquest*, which combined a detailed ethnographic description of the Pondo of Cape Province with briefer investigations of urban Africans and the lives of labourers working on white-owned farms. This set the stage for later research she inspired at the University of Cape Town, such as an ethnographic study of an African township on the city's fringe.

Wilson also considered the relation between religion and social change, and reflected on the fate of her native country. The latter distinguishes her writing as co-editor and major contributor to *The Oxford History of South Africa*, where she stressed – as she always had – how much the various racial groups of South Africa are implicated in one another's lives. One sign of her success can be seen in the fact that the full edition of the book was banned from publication in South Africa itself.

Education

BA University of Cambridge, 1930
D.Phil. University of Cambridge, 1934

Fieldwork

Among the Pondo, Eastern Cape Province, 1931–3
Among the Nyakyusa, southwestern Tanzania, 1935–8

Key Publications

(1936; as Monica Hunter) *Reaction to Conquest: Effects of Contact with Europeans on the Pondo of South Africa*, London: Oxford University Press.
(1951) *Good Company: A Study of Nyakyusa Age Villages*, London: Oxford University Press.
(1959) *Communal Rituals of the Nyakyusa*, London: Oxford University Press.
with Thompson, Leonard (eds) (1969 and 1971) *The Oxford History of South Africa*, 2 vols, Oxford: Clarendon Press.

MICHAEL G. KENNY

Wilson, Richard A.

1964, USA

Most of Richard Wilson's work to date can be classified as political anthropology, and it is wide-ranging, often innovative. His 1995 monograph, based on his Ph.D. thesis, examined the emergence of a politicised ethnic identity among Q'echi' Mayas in Guatemala, whose identity processes were shaped both by Christian evangelisation and by massive violence during the insurgency. This was the first book-length study of the rise of a new Maya politics. Subsequently, Wilson edited an acclaimed volume on anthropology and human rights, where he argued for the irrelevance of the traditional universalist/relativist dichotomy by indicating how every implementation of, or struggle for, rights involves the invocation of universal principles in the context of locally embedded issues. Developing this interest ethnographically, Wilson went on to compare the work of 'truth commissions' in post-civil war Guatemala and post-apartheid South Africa, and eventually wrote a monograph on local responses to the commission's proposals in South Africa. Both his Guatemalan and his South African work are major contributions to the anthropology of law, violence, and identity politics, and also engage with the issues of multiculturalism and human rights as discussed in political philosophy. Wilson's position entails a critical view of cultural relativism and a simultaneous emphasis on the primacy of local contexts.

A prolific writer, Wilson was also founding editor of Pluto Press's book series, 'Anthropology, Culture, and Society', and is editor of the journal, *Anthropological Theory*.

Education

B.Sc. London School of Economics, 1986
Ph.D. London School of Economics, 1990

Fieldwork

Guatemala, 1987–8, 1991, 1996
South Africa, 1995, 1996–7, 1998

Key Publications

(ed.) (1997) *Human Rights, Culture and Context: Anthropological Perspectives*, London: Pluto.
(2000) *The Politics of Truth and Reconciliation in South Africa: Legitimizing the Post-Apartheid State*, Cambridge, UK: Cambridge University Press.

THOMAS HYLLAND ERIKSEN

Wissler, Clark

b. 18 September 1870, Wayne County, Indiana, USA

d. 25 August 1947, New York City, USA

Clark Wissler was trained in experimental psychology, and entered Columbia University as an assistant in the Department of Psychology and Anthropology. In his last year as a student at Columbia he took three courses in anthropology with Livingston Farrand and Franz Boas; he had also taken a few anthropology courses as an undergraduate. From 1903–9 he taught anthropology at Columbia, but his primary appointment was in the Department of Ethnology at the American Museum of Natural History. He began as an assistant in ethnology, under Boas, and when Boas resigned in 1905 Wissler became acting curator. In 1907 archaeology and ethnology

were combined in a single department and Wissler became curator of anthropology. The position brought enmity from Boas, and that, coupled with severe illness beginning in 1907, ended his teaching at Columbia. Although Wissler was never close to Boas his anthropology was generally Boasian. Wissler remained at the museum for the rest of his career, retiring in 1942.

Wissler was better able to reconcile the museum's emphasis on public education with rewarding scientific research than Boas had been; it probably helped that the museum was then actively sending out scientific expeditions to various parts of the world. Wissler's own fieldwork during this period was limited to the 1902–5 work with Plains Indians, but as curator he sponsored fieldwork in both ethnology and archaeology throughout the Americas and Hawaii. He also encouraged physical anthropology, built the museum's collections and planned exhibitions, and supervised the 'Anthropological Papers of the American Museum of Natural History' series. In the 1920s Wissler joined the National Research Council's Committee on Scientific Problems of Human Migration and their Committee on Pacific Investigations; he also served as consulting anthropologist to the Bernice P. Bishop Museum in Honolulu.

In 1924 Wissler was invited to teach at Yale University, with a research appointment in the new Institute of Psychology (reorganised in 1929 as the Institute of Human Relations). His experience in both psychology and anthropology was useful there, as were the resources of the American Museum. Wissler did fieldwork in 1925 in Australia, New Zealand, and Hawaii as part of the Bayard Dominick Expedition to Polynesia, a joint project of Yale, the American Museum, and the Bishop Museum, working with Peter Buck among others. When Edward Sapir started an independent anthropology department at Yale in 1931, Wissler was a member. At first, in order to avoid interfering with his museum duties, Wissler would take the train to New Haven on Saturday morning, lecture and meet with students during the day, and return to New

York in the evening; later in his career he would spend at least two days a week in New Haven. He had anthropology students even before 1931, and funded fieldwork for several through the museum.

Wissler's teaching at Yale, like much of his research, emphasised cultural change and acculturation, and ethnohistory. Although not remembered as a theoretician, Wissler did have his own emphases within a generally Boasian framework, and both The American Indian and Man and Culture helped to codify Boasian anthropology. Like many of his publications, these were written for a more general audience, fitting both the museum's mandate for public education and the discipline's interest in making anthropological findings accessible to others. He also published numerous more ethnographic works, including eleven monographs on his Plains Indians research. Wissler's definition of culture went beyond the descriptive to include normative, learned complexes of ideas; he sought a rigorous definition to support cross-cultural studies. He developed culture area studies as a theory for cultural change by diffusion, and proposed the concept of culture patterns as determinants of which traits would be adopted or rejected. His age-area hypothesis, suggesting that more widely distributed cultural traits have greater antiquity, was severely criticised but is still often used as an analytical starting point. Wissler also proposed a 'universal pattern of culture' as a sort of essence of humanity, seeking to link biological, psychological, and cultural dimensions of human existence. In 1940 he supervised the sealing of the 300-pound time capsule at the New York World's Fair.

Education

AB Indiana University, 1897
AM Indiana University, 1899
Ph.D. Columbia University, 1901

Fieldwork

Plains Indians (Dakota, Gros Ventre, Blackfoot), 1902–5

Australia, New Zealand, and Hawaii, 1925

Key Publications

(ed.) (1916) Societies of the Plains Indians, American Museum of Natural History, Anthropological Papers 11.
(1917) The American Indian: An Introduction to the Anthropology of the New World, New York: Douglas C. McMurtrie.
(ed.) (1921) Sun Dance of the Plains Indians, American Museum of Natural History, Anthropological Papers 16.
(1923) Man and Culture, New York: Thomas Y. Crowell.

Further Reading

Freed, Stanley A. and Freed, Ruth S. (1983) 'Clark Wissler and the development of anthropology in the United States', American Anthropologist 85: 800–25.

FREDERIC W. GLEACH AND REGNA DARNELL

Wolf, Eric Robert

b. 1 February 1923, Vienna, Austria

d. 6 March 1999, Irvington, New York, USA

Eric Wolf's first research, for his doctoral dissertation, was as part of Julian Steward's project on the island of Puerto Rico, where Wolf studied a highland coffee-growing community. However, he departed from Steward's cultural-ecological framework by insisting on the importance of a historical perspective and attention to the market, the state, and Puerto Rico's colonial status. Wolf's first professional papers, in the early 1950s, attempted to theorise state and nation formation in Europe and other contexts. He then pursued that interest in fieldwork and historical research in the Bajío region of Mexico. His studies in Middle America yielded both Sons of the Shaking Earth (1959), which traces the long succession of civilisational regimes out of which modern Mexico grew, and a number of papers analysing how peasants and local communities are embedded in processes at the level of state and nation. For example, his concept of the 'closed corporate peasant community' highlights the role of colonial structures in shaping local forms.

Wolf's approach to peasants emphasised the cultivators' relationship to groups that held liens over their production and to the state that guaranteed those liens. It thus departed both from the dominant anthropological view of peasants as 'sub-cultures' with distinct value orientations and from the 'underdevelopment' specialists' treatment of peasant societies as amorphous and mired in tradition. In *Peasants* he presented a comprehensive analysis of the commonalities and dimensions of variability among peasantries. The book describes ecological and economic systems involving peasants; sociopolitical modalities or 'domains' whereby power-holders lay claim to their production; the 'funds' of resources required for peasants to meet their many exigencies; the various social relationships, networks, and coalitions that peasants enter into; and their relations to the larger ideological and supernatural order. The political upheavals of the 1960s turned Wolf's concern with peasants towards rebellions and political movements, and in *Peasant Wars of the Twentieth Century* (1969) he compared the involvement of rural peoples in the revolutions of Mexico, Russia, China, Vietnam, Algeria, and Cuba.

During the 1960s, too, Wolf returned to a problem that had engaged him since his early years in Central Europe: ethnicity and ethnic conflict. Carrying out fieldwork in two villages on different sides of a linguistic and political frontier in the South Tyrol, he traced the way ethnic identities were created through the villages' divergent histories, despite their continuous interaction and similar ecological adaptations to the Alpine environment. His focus on the relationships of these groups to external powers was a departure from most current treatments of ethnicity in terms of cultural patterns and assimilation or separation.

In the 1970s Wolf embarked on a major project to trace the effects of European expansion on the peoples who make up the ethnographic record. He drew on Marxian concepts, using them flexibly as analytical tools. Thus, he distinguished three 'modes of production' to grasp the different ways that societies are organised for the mobilisation of social labour: the kin-ordered mode, the tributary mode, and the capitalist mode. *Europe and the People without History* follows the successive European searches for commodities and then the spread of capitalism around the world over five centuries, showing how the peoples usually treated as timeless were intimately involved in the same history as that of Europeans.

That project raised for Wolf the question of how 'culture' and ideology enter into such political-economic processes. He was critical of the culture concept for its assumptions of boundedness and coherence, and in several papers during the 1980s he challenged anthropologists to take seriously the working of power. In the 1990s he continued to grapple with the problem of the relationship between ideas and power, and in *Envisioning Power* he did so by juxtaposing the cases of the Kwakiutl Indians, the Aztecs, and Nazi Germany. He explored in each case the historical development of forms of mobilising social labour and exercising power and the cultural processes that he saw as intrinsic to that development. The cases revealed how frenzied ideologies of violence emerged as responses to societal crises.

Wolf played a key role in the development of the anthropology of complex societies after the Second World War, leading anthropology from its focus on face-to-face groups towards its engagement with wider processes of state formation and colonial and capitalist expansion.

Education

BA Queens College, New York, 1946
Ph.D. Columbia University, 1951

Fieldwork

Puerto Rico, 1948–9

Mexico, 1951, 1953, 1954
South Tyrol, Italy, 1960–1

Key Publications

(1966) *Peasants*, Englewood Cliffs, NJ: Prentice-Hall.
(1982) *Europe and the People without History*, Berkeley: University of California Press.
(1999) *Envisioning Power: Ideologies of Dominance and Crisis*, Berkeley: University of California Press.
(2001) *Pathways of Power: Building an Anthropology of the Modern World*, Berkeley: University of California Press.

SYDEL SILVERMAN

Wolf, Margery

b. 1933, Santa Rosa, California, USA

Margery Wolf's training in anthropology and the social sciences was informal. Holding no college degrees beyond the AA, she had the good fortune to work for anthropologists and psychologists at Cornell University and the Center for Advanced Study in the Behavioral Sciences (Stanford), who were excellent teachers, generous with their time. Her fieldwork in Taiwan in the 1950s–1970s (with Arthur Wolf) was the basis for *The House of Lim* and *Women and the Family in Rural Taiwan*. The field research for *Revolution Postponed* occurred in 1980–1 in the People's Republic of China.

In her research, Wolf, like her predecessors, focused on the family; unlike her predecessors, Wolf analysed the family from the perspective of women, revealing unexpected power relations and an iconoclastic explanation of the Chinese family cycle. By examining the relationship between a woman and her uterine family, the traditional description of the cycle was revealed as only a partial explanation. She found that although men had the authority to make decisions for the future of the family – economically, politically, and socially – women with adult sons had a stronger influence over the content of those decisions than did their fathers. Using fine-grained ethnography, Wolf discovered that Chinese mothers worked hard to instil loyalty and gratitude in their children, particularly their sons, at the expense of their husbands and the male lineage. The centuries-old tradition of the male lineage was strong, but women used the institution's stress points to assure the comfort of their own old age and the best possible circumstances for their children and grandchildren.

Wolf was among the first foreign anthropologists allowed to do research in rural China. She looked closely at how women fared during the revolution and the eroding social structure that followed. *Revolution Postponed* documented the limited success of the revolution for rural women and the more promising future for women in urban China.

After the Tiananmen massacre and the so-called economic reforms that removed so many of the safeguards for women, Wolf lost her enthusiasm for research in China, but not her interest in ethnography. *A Thrice Told Tale* (1992) was a response to some of the postmodernist critiques of ethnography. She used three tellings of an event (a short story, field notes, and a published article) to illustrate the dangers, the responsibilities, and the politics of doing ethnography.

Wolf's interest in ethnography has led her into a historical ethnography of a California site and the four cultural groups that have serially displaced each other there. She studies some of the issues raised in *A Thrice Told Tale*, using the contradictory and flawed data that one finds in historical records. Competing voices, field notes collected in the 1930s, the diaries of Franciscan priests, and the writings of contemporary revisionists inform her work.

Fieldwork

Taiwan, 1958–60, 1968, 1970, 1971
California, 1976–80, 1995–6
China, 1980–1

Key Publications

(1968) *The House of Lim: A Study of a Chinese Farm Family*, New York: Appleton-Century-Crofts.
(1972) *Women and the Family in Rural Taiwan*, Stanford, CA: Stanford University Press.
(1985) *Revolution Postponed: Women in Contemporary China*, Stanford, CA: Stanford University Press.
(1992) *A Thrice Told Tale: Feminism, Postmodernism and Ethnographic Responsibility*, Stanford, CA: Stanford University Press.

FLORENCE E. BABB

Woodburn, James

b. 16 April 1934, UK

James Woodburn is best known for his pioneering studies of Hadza hunter-gatherers in Tanzania and for his contributions to twentieth-century hunter-gatherer studies. A student at Cambridge in the 1950s, he was drawn to the study of small-scale hunting and gathering societies, and began ethnographic research with Hadza in 1954. His doctoral dissertation concerned Hadza social organisation, ecology, and their relations with surrounding farmer-herders.

Woodburn first taught at University College, London, then in 1965 took up an appointment at the London School of Economics where he taught until his retirement in 1999.

Woodburn is a key figure in the modern revival of hunter-gatherer studies, attending the first Man the Hunter Conference in Chicago in 1966 and contributing two papers to the volume. His 1982 Malinowski lecture made important theoretical advances to the study of egalitarian societies. Under the impact of global capitalism the very reality of societies based on egalitarian principles had been called into question. Woodburn's lecture restored their legitimacy by critically re-examining the principles of egalitarianism and by documenting their range of variation.

Of crucial importance is Woodburn's distinction between 'immediate-return' and 'de-layed-return' societies. In the former food was consumed on the spot or soon after, while in delayed-return societies food and other resources might be stored for months or years, with marked effects on social organisation and cultural notions of property.

Woodburn's other notable achievements included his ethnographic film, *Hadza* (1966), his co-chairmanship of the 1986 Conference on Hunting and Gathering Societies, and his indefatigable efforts on behalf of human rights for the Hadza and other indigenous peoples.

Education

BA University of Cambridge, 1957
Junior Research Fellow, Makerere University, 1957–60
Ph.D. University of Cambridge, 1964

Fieldwork

Tanzania, 1954–7, 1961, 1966–99, frequent

Key Publications

(1982) 'Egalitarian societies', *Man* 17, 3: 431–51.
with Ingold, Tim and Riches, David (eds) (1988) *Hunters and Gatherers*, 2 vols, Oxford: Berg Publishers.

RICHARD LEE

Worsley, Peter M.

b. 6 May 1924, Birkenhead, Cheshire, UK

Peter Worsley was trained as a British social anthropologist in its classical period following the Second World War, but, largely as a result of being a communist, he was prevented from carrying out research in the places he wanted to (Africa and New Guinea). As a result, he became a distinguished professor of sociology instead. He wrote a number of influential works of comparison, on topics ranging from cargo cults to Third World development. A consistent theme of this work has been the question of culture, always seen from an activist's perspective. In the last decade following retirement, he has produced some magisterial syntheses, returning in *Knowledges* (1997) to the concerns of his initial fieldwork among the Australian Aborigines, only now, as Hegel says, with the experience of a lifetime behind him.

Worsley went to Cambridge to read English and, at the time of Stalingrad, joined the Communist Party (which he left in 1956). As an army officer he went to Africa and India, returning to Cambridge in 1946, where he switched to anthropology. After a short period in East Africa, where he was involved in education and linguistics, Worsley returned to Britain. He met Max Gluckman, while being turned down for a Colonial Office research post. He did a Master's degree at Manchester, choosing in his dissertation to launch a materialist critique of Meyer Fortes's work on Tallensi kinship. This was later awarded the Curl Essay Prize of the Royal Anthropological Institute. He applied to join the Rhodes–Livingstone Institute, but was vetoed on security grounds. Consequently, he took up a research studentship with S.F. Nadel at the Australian National University. Here too he was refused a visa to work in the New Guinea Highlands. He ended up carrying out fieldwork among the Aborigines of Groote Eylandt, completing a dissertation on their kinship system and related topics in 1954. On returning to Britain, Worsley rejoined Gluckman in Manchester and began working on cargo cults. Gluckman advised him that he would never get a job as a social anthropologist, so he helped to build up the sociology department at Hull. From there he was appointed professor in the new Department of Sociology at Manchester. He held the post from 1964 to 1982.

The Trumpet Shall Sound (1957) was 'written in the firm belief that anthropology can be interesting to the non-specialist', at a time when the sources on Melanesian cargo cults were scattered and superficial. Worsley saw them as proto-nationalist movements against colonial, racial, and class oppression. This book created from scratch one of the classical subjects of social anthropology, bringing a new coherence to the study of cargo cults and placing them within a wide framework of historical and regional comparison. *The Three Worlds* (1984) is the successor to the hugely successful *The Third World* (1964). Its main thesis is that culture has been largely missing from political and economic theories of development. It represents an attempt to synthesise Marxism and social anthropology on a scale that takes in the entire post-war world.

Worsley's *Introducing Sociology* (1970) sold half a million copies. His active engagements as a public intellectual have been legion. However, with *Knowledges* (1997), he has returned to the roots of culture, to problems of thought and language that first engaged him as a communist army officer and turned him to anthropology after the war. Taking off from a critique of Emile Durkheim and Claude Lévi-Strauss, Worsley looks at Australian classification, Oceanic navigation, African and Western medicine, the role of intellectuals, nationalism, and the emergence of world culture. He concludes that knowledge is always plural, undermining not only contrasts between Us and Them, but also even the attribution of thought systems to whole societies. This attempt to break down the premises of Western cultural superiority in a context of uneven world development is comparable to the project of his close contemporary, Jack Goody.

Education

BA University of Cambridge, 1947
MA University of Manchester, 1951
Ph.D. Australian National University, 1954

Fieldwork

Groote Eylandt, Arnhem Land, Australia, 1951–4
Manchester and Edinburgh Universities, 1969–70

Key Publications

(1968 [1957]) *The Trumpet Shall Sound: A Study of 'Cargo' Cults in Melanesia*, London: McGibbon & Kee.

(1984) *The Three Worlds: Culture and World Development*, London: Weidenfeld & Nicholson.

(1994) 'The nation-state, colonial expansion and the contemporary world order', in T. Ingold (ed.) *Companion Encyclopaedia of Anthropology*, London: Routledge.

(1997) *Knowledges: What Different Peoples Make of the World*, London: Profile Books.

KEITH HART

Y

Yalman, Nur

b. 1931, Istanbul, Turkey

Raised in cosmopolitan circumstances in Istanbul, Nur Yalman went to Cambridge, UK, just at the time that anthropology there was stimulated by the arrival of Edmund Leach. Yalman began fieldwork at age twenty-three in Sri Lanka. His early work focused on the classical categories of kinship, intermarriage, healing rituals, hierarchies, myths, and, in the 1960s, he developed the structural analysis of binary categories and cultural logic. His was the generation that transformed North American anthropology using comparative methodology. He joined the luminous department at the University of Chicago in 1961, focusing on comparative studies of newly independent nations.

Fluent in French, German, English, and Turkish, with ability in Persian, Arabic, Sinhalese, and Italian, Yalman surveyed the development of many intellectual traditions, particularly in their relations between the Middle East and Europe. He extended this to Japan, having been an originator of the term 'Rashomon-effect' in anthropology in the 1960s. Thirty years of his intellectual energy have been given to Harvard University, particularly Middle Eastern studies and the multidisciplinary Society of Fellows. He has become a leading thinker on the tension between secularism and fundamentalism in states, particularly concerning the roles of Westernised intellectuals in addressing this tension.

Education

BA Robert College, Istanbul, 1950
BA University of Cambridge, 1953
MA University of Cambridge, 1955
Ph.D. University of Cambridge, 1958

Fieldwork

Sri Lanka, 1954–6, 1968, 1970
Iran, 1954, 1958, 1968
Turkey, 1963, 1966, 1977, 1985
India, 1989

Key Publications

(1971 [1967]) *Under The Bo Tree: Studies in Caste, Kinship and Marriage*, Berkeley: University of California Press.
(1991) 'On secularism and its critics: notes on Turkey, India, and Iran', *Contributions to Indian Sociology* [n.s.] 25, 2: 233–66, Sage Publications.

ROBERT ANDERSON

Yanagisako, Sylvia Junko

b. 1945, Honolulu, Hawaii, USA

Sylvia Yanagisako's work has focused on

bringing an anthropological analysis to the study of kinship and gender in developed, industrial, Western societies. Her first major study concerned the symbolic processes through which the ideas and meanings of kinship, gender, and ethnic identity were forged among two generations of Japanese Americans in Seattle, Washington. Gender and kinship, she theorised in a co-edited book with her colleague, Jane Collier, are not the cultural constructions of biological givens, but are mutually constituted systems of meaning that challenge those assumptions. More recently, she has been involved in a long-term ethnographic study of silk production in Italian family firms. Investigating the way sentiments, desires, and meanings of gender and kinship are crucial to the production of Italian family capitalism, Yanagisako suggests that culture and capitalism are not two separate domains but are produced together. Her latest project on the 'new silk road' explores this insight in an attempt to understand how transnational capitalism is culturally produced in the links between Italian and Chinese silk industries. Her contributions have also had institutional impacts, most conspicuously when, as chair, she steered the newly constituted Department of Cultural and Social Anthropology at Stanford through the rough period after its highly publicised split in 1997 and launched it towards concerns of the twenty-first century.

Education

BA University of Washington, 1967
MA University of Washington, 1969
Ph.D. University of Washington, 1975

Fieldwork

Muckleshoot Indian Reservation, Auburn, Washington State, 1968–9
Seattle, Washington State, 1973–5, 1976–7
Como, Italy, 1984–5, autumn 1988, 1995–6, summer 2000

Key Publications

(1985) *Transforming the Past: Tradition and Kinship among Japanese Americans*, Stanford: Stanford University Press.
(2002) *Producing Culture and Capital: Family Firms in Italy*, Princeton: Princeton University Press.

CAROL DELANEY

Young, Allan

b. 1938, Philadelphia, Pennsylvania, USA

Allan Young is a key figure in the emergence of medical anthropology as a theoretically significant sub-discipline. Young sees ethnography as capable of rigorously examining tacit assumptions made in everyday life, public policy, and in medical diagnoses, definitions, and practices. He tackles some of the most difficult questions in the field and presents his analysis in strikingly simple and articulate ways. Young has defined, in the most definitive ways to date, many of the key terms taught as basic to medical anthropology. His definitions of Illness, Sickness, Rationality, and Efficacy are powerful tools that allow critical analysis of clinical practice, laboratory and epidemiological research, psychiatric science, and medical pluralism.

His earliest ethnographic works are concerned with medical pluralism and comparative medical systems (e.g. the co-edited *Paths to Asian Medical Knowledge*, 1992). Later works concern physician–patient interactions. Much of this research focuses upon issues in psychiatric science in North America, especially the diagnosis of Post-Traumatic Stress Disorder. Like his most recent works, *The Harmony of Illusions* (1995) is a significant ethnographic and historical text which argues that traumatic memory and psychiatric science are historical practices and that the standards and procedures of psychiatric science and psychiatric reasoning are culturally and historically contingent.

Young was awarded the Wellcome Medal for Anthropological Reseach (1998) and has helped build one of the most important centers for medical anthropology training at McGill University.

Education

BA (Hons) University of Pennsylvania, 1959
MA University of Washington, 1963
Ph.D. University of Pennsylvania, 1970

Fieldwork

Ethiopia, 1966–7, 1973
Nepal, 1976, 1979

Israel, 1979, 1981
Ohio, USA, 1980–1, 1985–8
Quebec, Canada, 1993–ongoing

Key Publications

(1982) 'The anthropologies of illness and sickness', *Annual Review of Anthropology* 11: 257–85.

(1995) *The Harmony of Illusions: Inventing Posttraumatic Stress Disorder*, Princeton: Princeton University Press.

MONIQUE SKIDMORE

Z

Zonabend, Françoise

b. 1935, Paris, France

After completing a thesis in educational sociology, Françoise Zonabend worked in the Laboratoire d'Anthropologie Sociale (founded by Claude Lévi-Strauss), specialising in kinship and memory. In the 1960s and 1970s, she participated in one of the first ethnographic studies in France. With three other fieldworkers, she conducted research in the Burgundy village of Minot. She proved that preferential marriage rules existed in complex societies such as rural France, notably a system of relinking through affinal marriage.

Zonabend also studied the impact of technological change on French village communities. Minot underwent gradual socioeconomic changes since the late nineteenth century. From the 1950s, technological change profoundly altered village sociability, kinship relationships, and consumption patterns. The villagers pictured the pre-1950s past as static, while they perceived the present as rapidly mutating. The past was associated with the 'time of the community', an apparently changeless, golden age. Several layers of memory co-existed, such as community, family, and personal memory.

Technological change was even more dramatic at the La Hague peninsula in northern France, where nuclear industries were established since the 1960s. Zonabend investigated how those living near and working in these industries came to terms with the daily risk they incurred. The strategies ranged from scientific explanations, to selective blindness, rumours, and silence about one's fear.

Zonabend has also been concerned with the use of historical documents in anthropology and the constitution of anthropological archives.

Education

Ph.D. École Pratique des Hautes Études, Paris, 1967

Fieldwork

Dakar, Senegal, February–April 1962
Minot, France, 1968–75
La Hague peninsula, France, 1983–today

Key Publications

(1984) *The Enduring Memory: Time and History in a French Village* (Mémoire longue: temps et histoires au village, 1980), trans. A. Forster, Manchester: Manchester University Press.

(1993) *The Nuclear Peninsula* (La Presqu'île au nucléaire, 1989), trans. J.A. Underwood, Cambridge, UK: Cambridge University Press.

ANNE FRIEDERIKE MÜLLER

Index of interests

myth and symbolism 79, 115, 333; worldwide 175; *see also* ritual; symbols

narratives 385; Ainu epics 275; analysis 242; epics 349; in religious contexts 376; in social practice 195; in society 87; structure 255; theory of 77; violence 262; Yukon women 102; *see also* discourse; oral tradition; verbal arts
nationalism 67, 192, 225, 242, 269; Eastern Europe 275; Hungary 248; and religion 529; Russia 513; and state socialism 535; Sweden 315; Zulu 222; *see also* ethnic identity; ethnic relations; ethnicity; violence
Native North Americans: Algonkian groups 475; Apache 35, 391; Cherokee 358; Cheyenne 247; Chipewa 259; Cree 335; Crow 321; fur trade 296; government policy 266; history 297; injustices 543; Mandan-Hidatsa 77; Menominee 482; Mohave 284; Mohegan 503; Ojibwa 292; place names 73; Seminole 497; Winnebago 323, 419; Wintu 131; Yurok 284; *see also* Inuit; Iroquois; Navaho; Northwest Coast Indians (USA); Plains Indians; Pueblo; Zuni
natural disasters 484; drought 520, 523; forest fires 533; *see also* ecology; famine
Navaho 2, 100; illness and healing 102; ritual 279; veterans 539
Nepal 51, 185; colonialism 82; Hindu-tribal relations 82; shamanism 121; Yolmo 121
New Guinea: *see* Papua New Guinea
New York City: gay synagogue 463; immigrant street vendors 493; Jamaican immigrants 165; schools 297
New Zealand: *see* Maori
Newfoundland 93; everyday life 464; politics 395
Nicaragua 68
Niger 438; Haussa 484; Songhay 493; Tuareg 484
Nigeria: Chamba 151; Hausa migrants 92; Tiv 62, 63; Tuareg 484; Yakö 166; Yoruba 313
Northwest Coast Indians (USA) 32; Chinook 255; Kwakiutl 59; Makah 98; Tlinglit 116
Norway: aboriginal-government relations 548; adoption, international 251; Bergen 212; class 31; Saami 139, 395
nuclear industries 571
Nuer 146
number system, Tzetzal Mayan 47
nutritional anthropology 427

omens 109
oral cultures 217; vs written cultures 217, 261; *see also* writing systems
oral literature 161, 508; performance 255; poetics 255; poetry 162; *see also* discourse; literary criticism; narratives; poetics; verbal arts
oral tradition: comparative mythology 115; kingdoms 115; *see also* history; verbal arts
organ transplant 314; human rights violations 448; *see also* medical practices

Pacific Islands 388
Pakistan 126; Islam 550
Palau 32, 400
Palestine 499
Panama, Kuna 461
Papua New Guinea 49, 249, 456; Baktaman 33; Bánaro 512; Baruya 199; Daribi 540; Dobu 168; Fore 309; Gidra 386; Iatmul 37; Kalam 79; Kaluli 153, 448; Kaulong 201; kinship system 31; Madang 293; Mae Enga 347; Maring 422; Massim 367; Orokaiva 452; Ponam Island 86; Sambia 237; Tolai 142; Umeda 191; Usen Barok 541; Wola 465
Paraguay 34
pastoralism 107; and Aboriginal people 43; Bodi (Ethiopia) 184; East African 41; interrelations with animals 527; reindeer herding 396; Tuareg 484
patron / clients 317; *see also* factionalism; politics; political anthropology; social networks
peasants: globalization 271; modernization 424; prostitution 183; protests and rebellions 6, 173, 180, 563; and revolutions 563; and socialism 248; values 170; world view 170, 248; Zapatistas 377
Peru: Inca 361; Lima 313, 471; Quechua verbal arts and music 16
Philippines: Hanunóo 99; Ifugao (Northern Luzon) 99; Ilongot 435; Luzon 129
photography: early 477; ethnographic 97; in magazines 324; *see also* visual anthropology
pilgrimages 120, 138, 172, 370; *see also* anthropology of religion; religion
place, import of 1, 432
Plains Indians 562; Ghost dance 359; pan-tribal movement 359
plant domestication 234
plantations 13, 355, 397; *see also* agriculture; peasants; work
poetics 181, 242, 255, 263; ethnopoetics 461, 508; tropes 157; *see also* literary criticism; verbal arts
Poland: nationalistic symbolism 328; Polish Tatras 125
politeness 204; Japan 236
political anthropology 6, 20, 24, 67, 114, 149,

Index of institutions

Index of names

Abélès, Marc 1–2 see
Aberle, David F. 2, 538
Abu-Lughod, Lila 2–3
Ackerman, Robert 176
Adams, Richard N. 4–5
Agar, Michael H. 5–6
Agier, Michel 20
Aguilar, Mario I. 264, 269, 270
Aguirre-Beltran, Gonzalo 6–7
Ahern, Emily 413
Akiba, Takashi 259
Allport, Gordon 189
Althusser, Louis 508
Alward, Emily 488
Amit, Vered 94, 229, 258, 414, 415
Amselle, Jean-Loup 25
Anderson, Barbara Gallatin: *see* Gallatin Anderson, Barbara
Anderson, Benedict 248
Anderson, John 245
Anderson, Robert S. 567
Anderson, Sally 390
Angrosino, Michael V. 7–8
Ankermann, B. 430
Appadurai, Arjun 8–9
Appell, George N. 10
Apthorpe, Raymond 10–11
Archetti, Eduardo P. 11–12, 143, 252
Ardener, Edwin W. 12–13, 13
Ardener, Shirley 12, 13–14
Arensberg, Conrad Maynadier 14–15, 409
Arguedas, José María 16–17
Arizpe Schlosser, Lourdes 17–18
Arutiunov, Sergei Aleksandrovich 18
Asad, Talal 18–19
Asch, Timothy 89
Ashton, Hugh 446
Astuti, Rita 58

Attinasi 180
Augé, Marc 19–21, 25
Austin, Diane 21
Austin, John 330
Azevedo, Fernando de 156

Babb, Florence E. 565
Babcock, Barbara A. 22–23
Bachofen, Johann Jakob 330
Back, Les 83, 84
Bailey, Frederick George 23–24, 64
Baines, Stephen G. 157
Baird, Spencer 103
Baker, Emma 503
Balandier, Georges 20, 24–26, 84, 348
Baldus, Herbert 425, 512
Balikci, Asen 26
Ballantyne, Andrew 265
Ballard, Roger 28
Banerjee, Mukulika 114
Banks, Marcus 345, 365
Banton, Michael Parker 26–28
Barbeau, Marius 28–29, 265
Barley, Nigel 29–30
Barnard, Alan 30–31, 287, 313, 419
Barnes, John A. 31–32
Barnes, Robert H. 379
Barnett, Homer Garner 32–33
Barretto Filho, Henyo T. 426
Barry, Laurent 240
Barth, Fredrik 33–34, 64, 84, 139, 276, 315, 395
Bartlett, F. C. 168
Bartolomé, Leopoldo J. 34–35
Bashkow, Ira 452
Basso, Keith 35–36
Bastide, Roger 36–37
Bataille, Georges 299
Batalha, Luís 400, 555

Index of concepts

acculturation 7, 170, 481, 562; psychology 512; reciprocal 550
acoustemology 154
action anthropology, originated 505
agency 3, 270; art 191; globalization 193; individuals as self-conscious agents 93; intersection with structure and ideology 226; in kinship 250; Marxism 193; in narratives 193; *see also* individual
alienation 57
alliance 441; *see also* kinship; moieties; segmentary systems; structuralism
alterity, grammars of 41
American historicism 59, 85, 112
animism 524
anthropological film theory 316, 438
anthropological writing 62
anthropology: as colonial knowledge 95; critiqued 504; at home 191, 254; as science 478, 483, 490; *see also* knowledge, anthropological
anthropology of anthropology 66, 68, 492
anthropology of experience 77
anthropology of gender 441
anthropology of modern power 19
anthropology of reason 417
authenticity 77, 225; arts 364; politics of 173

"Balkanism" 514
behavioral environment 201
bilingualism, societal vs individual 164
binary oppositions 133; first use of concept 262; logic 295; *see also* oppositions; structuralism
"biological, the" 175
biologies, local 314
body (the): as seat of contention 183; as site of construction of sex and gender 360; socialized 314; *see also* social identity

cargo cults as proto-nationalist 566
case method 247, 356; extended 532
caste and segmentation 53

categories: cultural 450; of the person 87; vs group 27
causality, dual (internal and external) 37
childhood 263
class and religion, links 82
class, state, kinship and gender, links 187
classification systems: consanguinal / affinal 133; as image of nature 47; social categories 52, 128; *see also* intersections; kinship; oppositions; social categories; social identity
closed corporate peasant community 563
code-switching 215; multilingual speakers 216; *see also* language
cognition: brain patterns and color terms 47; maps (mazeways) 542; natural 56; Sapir-Whorf hypothesis 461, 557; schema theory 110; structures 133, 302; *see also* culture and personality; knowledge; meaning
colonial discourse and sexuality 493
colonial knowledge 53; "investigative modalities" 95
colonialism, internal 489
commodification 22
communality vs difference 93
communication: communicative competence 255; communicative intent 216; means of 205; nature of 161; *see also* language; symbolic interactionism
community 14, 40; and the nation 117; symbolic construction of 93
componential analysis 202, 319
connectionist model 416
construction: of colonial Indian society 95; of meaning 69; of truth 91
contextualization clues 215
continuum: folk-urban 424, 536; "great traditions"-"little traditions" 424
contradictions: the state and peasants 545
cross-cutting allegiances 99, 198; *see also* equilibrium; kinship; segmentary systems; social conflict

Indexes compiled by Catherine Tihanyi